NE능률 영어교과서

대한민국 고등학생 **10명** 중 **4.7명**이 보는 교과서

영어 고등 교과서 점유율 1위
(7차, 2007 개정, 2009 개정, 2015 개정)

리딩튜터

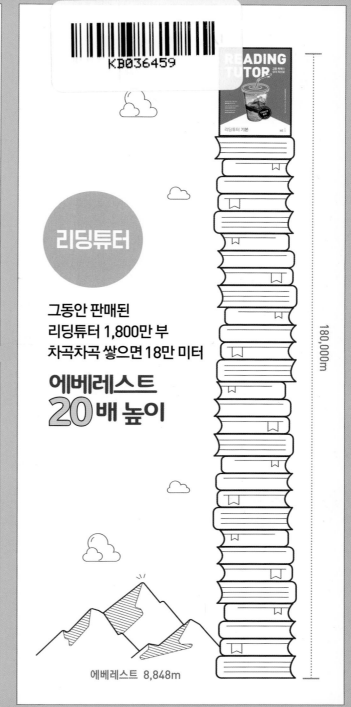

그동안 판매된
리딩튜터 1,800만 부
차곡차곡 쌓으면 18만 미터

에베레스트 20배 높이

180,000m

에베레스트 8,848m

능률보카

그동안 판매된
능률VOCA 1,100만 부

대한민국 박스오피스
천만명을 넘은 영화 단 28개

그래머존

그동안 판매된 400만 부의 그래머존을 바닥에 쭉 ~ 깔면
1000km 서울-부산 왕복가능

서울

부산

KB036459

수능만만
영어독해 20회

지은이	NE능률 영어교육연구소
선임연구원	신유승
연구원	윤인아 이현아
영문교열	Bryce Barrett Olk Thompson Curtis Robert Lan Angela Hai Yue
디자인	민유화 김연주
맥편집	김미진
영업	한기영 이경구 박인규 정철교 김남준 김남형 이우현
마케팅	박혜선 고유진 김여진

NE능률이
미래를
창조합니다.

건강한 배움의 고객가치를 제공하겠다는 꿈을 실현하기 위해
42년 동안 열심히 달려왔습니다.

앞으로도 끊임없는 연구와 노력을 통해
당연한 것을 멈추지 않고

고객, 기업, 직원 모두가 함께 성장하는 NE능률이 되겠습니다.

수능
만만

영어독해
20회

구성과 특징 ☁

**실제 수능을 100%
재현한 모의고사**

문항 유형과 문항 수, 문항 배치 및 배점 방식을 모두 최신 수능과 유사하게 구성하였습니다. 실전과 같은 환경으로 수능 독해 영역 적응력을 기르고 자신감을 가질 수 있을 것입니다.

**20회 분량의
실전 모의고사 제공**

실제 수능 독해 20회 분량에 해당하는 실전 모의고사 560문항을 엄선하여 수록하였습니다. 충분한 양의 실전 훈련을 통해 실제 수능에 철저히 대비할 수 있을 것입니다.

**최신 경향
분석 및 반영**

최신 수능 기출과 평가원 모의고사를 토대로 수능 유형에 가장 가깝게 구성하였습니다. 문항 유형뿐만 아니라, 지문의 길이와 난이도 또한 실전 수준에 맞추었기 때문에 여러분의 실력이 한 단계 더 향상될 것입니다.

**유용한
부가 자료 제공**

'어휘리스트 파일'을 www.nebooks.co.kr에서 무료로 다운받을 수 있습니다. 수능에 나올 만한 필수 어휘들을 학습할 수 있습니다.

☁ **목차**

01회 영어독해 모의고사 ·············· p. 6

02회 영어독해 모의고사 ·············· p. 16

03회 영어독해 모의고사 ·············· p. 26

04회 영어독해 모의고사 ·············· p. 36

05회 영어독해 모의고사 ·············· p. 46

06회 영어독해 모의고사 ·············· p. 56

07회 영어독해 모의고사 ·············· p. 66

08회 영어독해 모의고사 ·············· p. 76

09회 영어독해 모의고사 ·············· p. 86

10회 영어독해 모의고사 ·············· p. 96

11회 영어독해 모의고사 ·············· p. 106

12회 영어독해 모의고사 ·············· p. 116

13회 영어독해 모의고사 ·············· p. 126

14회 영어독해 모의고사 ·············· p. 136

15회 영어독해 모의고사 ·············· p. 146

16회 영어독해 모의고사 ·············· p. 156

17회 영어독해 모의고사 ·············· p. 166

18회 영어독해 모의고사 ·············· p. 176

19회 영어독해 모의고사 ·············· p. 186

20회 영어독해 모의고사 ·············· p. 196

책속의 책 ·············· 정답 및 해설

수능
만만

영어독해
모의고사

—

01회
-20회

* 3점 문항에만 점수가 표시되어 있습니다.
  점수 표시가 없는 문항은 모두 2점씩입니다.

18 다음 글의 목적으로 가장 적절한 것은?

To Whom It May Concern:

I purchased a new coffee maker from your store on Fourth Street last week. It seemed to be working fine at first, but I soon noticed that water was leaking from the back of the machine. I brought it back to the store two days later and asked the manager, a woman named Marie Dunston, to exchange it. After examining the coffee maker, she refused, claiming she did not see any damage. This is not acceptable. I have attached an image of my receipt and would like the full cost of the coffee maker to be refunded to my credit card. Once this has been done, I will gladly return the defective merchandise. Thank you in advance for taking care of this. If you have any questions, please feel free to email me.

Sincerely,
Ivan Lee

① 제품 사용 방식을 문의하려고
② 새로 출시된 제품으로 교환하려고
③ 결함 있는 제품의 환불을 요청하려고
④ 구매한 제품의 낡은 부품을 교체하려고
⑤ 본사 직원을 통한 제품 구매 방법을 알아보려고

19 다음 글에 드러난 'I'의 심경으로 가장 적절한 것은?

When I was growing up, my dad had a passion for gardening and was proud of the fact that he could grow anything in his little garden. The one exception was irises, which quickly died every time he planted them. Unfortunately, irises were my favorite flower. When I was 10 years old, I got very sick and was in bed for weeks. One morning, my father came into my room smiling. "Look what I grew in my garden," he said. It was a big bunch of irises. As soon as I saw them, I started to feel better. It didn't matter that they still had the price tag from the flower shop on them, which he had forgotten to take off. They were more beautiful than any other flowers I have seen since.

① upset   ② moved
③ relaxed   ④ apologetic
⑤ embarrassed

20 다음 글에서 필자가 주장하는 바로 가장 적절한 것은?

When my history teacher lectured us about the Iron Age, I could barely keep my eyes open. It wasn't my teacher's fault, but rather a problem with the material. As in all history classes, we began our class discussions at the dawn of humankind and covered events in chronological order. Of course, by the time we got to the 20th century, we had already reached the end of the school year and thus had no opportunity to discuss the modern issues that were affecting our lives. To me, it would seem more logical to adopt the opposite teaching approach. Why not start out with coverage of current national and world events, and then work back through time, studying the developments that made today's news stories possible? Students would undoubtedly find such a curriculum more engaging and worthwhile.

① 역사를 시대 역순으로 가르치자.
② 역사 교육의 필요성을 널리 알리자.
③ 세계사를 중심으로 역사를 가르치자.
④ 현장 학습을 통한 역사 교육을 시행하자.
⑤ 토론식 수업을 중심으로 역사 교육을 실시하자.

21 밑줄 친 create a lot of gray areas가 다음 글에서 의미하는 바로 가장 적절한 것은? [3점]

Questioning our own perceptions can lead to insights. Fiction writers sometimes make us do this by using unreliable narrators who create a lot of gray areas and force us to draw our own conclusions. These narrators are unreliable because they mislead readers, either on purpose or by accident. This may be due to their personal situations, flaws in their personalities, or psychological issues. Unreliable narrators might conceal important information from readers or even lie to them. Sometimes their unreliability is obvious from the start, and other times it is revealed as a surprise. In either case, these characters are almost always complex and interesting. More importantly, they keep readers involved in the story and motivate them to read more carefully in order to figure out what is actually going on.

① speak directly to readers as if they were close
② cause certain elements of the plot to become unclear
③ reveal their inner thoughts and motivations to readers
④ provide lots of entertaining details about themselves
⑤ make the plot more complex by adding more details

22 다음 글의 요지로 가장 적절한 것은?

There are many strategies that can help you get a good night's sleep, including avoiding caffeine and keeping a regular schedule. However, an often overlooked factor is the temperature of your room. Research shows that you have an internal thermostat which brings your body down to a set temperature while you sleep. If your body is either too hot or too cold, your system will struggle to achieve the desired temperature, often waking you up in the process. In general, it is believed that the room temperature most suitable for sleep is somewhere between 15 and 20 degrees Celsius. When the room temperatures are in this range, your body can easily raise or lower its temperature, allowing you to sleep better.

① 수면 부족은 체온에 영향을 미친다.
② 규칙적인 생활습관이 숙면을 돕는다.
③ 카페인 섭취와 수면의 질은 관련이 없다.
④ 잠을 잘 때 체내 온도 조절 장치가 활성화된다.
⑤ 숙면을 취하기 위해서는 침실 온도가 적절해야 한다.

23 다음 글의 주제로 가장 적절한 것은? [3점]

Different cultures may have their own precise definitions of "honor," but there are few human societies in which the concept does not exist at all. Some sociologists argue that our sense of honor evolved in order to encourage harmonious behavior that contributes to the cohesion and, ultimately, the survival of social groups. To me, though, there is a more self-centered explanation as to why honor exists. As mortal beings, we are constantly confronted by the fact that our lives will one day end. We only have a limited amount of time to shape the way in which others view us. After we're gone, any wealth and material objects that we have accumulated will be useless to us; we will be remembered by those still living primarily for our actions. Therefore, if we conduct our lives in an honorable fashion, we can be assured that those remembrances will be positive.

① an individualistic interpretation of honor
② the importance of being evaluated properly
③ the effects of individualism on social groups
④ the uselessness of wealth and material objects
⑤ the different concepts of honor in different cultures

24 다음 글의 제목으로 가장 적절한 것은?

When people ask about a film, "Is it like the original book?" the answer is usually, "Not really." At best, a film version can capture only a small fraction of the novel's depth. It is doubtful whether it can capture much of what lies beneath the surface. Therefore, we must accept the fact that some parts of the novel are inaccessible to film. Usually the filmmaker must limit not only the depth to which a character can be explored in detail, but also the actual number of characters included in the movie. Furthermore, in adapting a long novel to film, complex and important subplots as well as other factors often have to be eliminated because of time limitations.

① Movie Watchers vs. Book Readers
② How to Make a Great Movie from a Book
③ Difficulties of Understanding a Great Book
④ Why People Prefer Movie Versions to Books
⑤ Why Movies Are Different from Their Original Books

25 다음 도표의 내용과 일치하지 않는 것은?

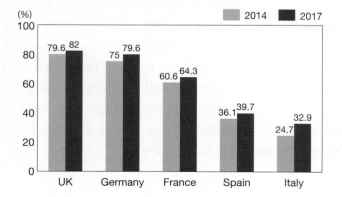

Internet Users in European Countries Using Online Shopping in 2014 and 2017

The above graph shows the percentage of internet users in various European countries who shopped online in 2014 and 2017. ① In all five countries that are shown on the graph, the percentage of online shoppers increased from 2014 to 2017. ② Of these countries, it was the UK that had the highest percentage in both years, with more than three quarters of the country's internet users shopping online. ③ In Germany, 75% of internet users shopped online in 2014, a percentage that was more than three times higher than that of Italy in the same year. ④ France had the third-highest percentage of online shoppers in 2014, but it moved up to second place in 2017, trailing only the UK. ⑤ Finally, France's increase in its percentage of online shoppers between 2014 and 2017 was roughly the same as that of Spain.

26 Clara Barton에 관한 다음 글의 내용과 일치하지 않는 것은?

Clara Barton, the organizer and founder of the American Red Cross, was born on Christmas Day 1821 in Oxford, Massachusetts. Although she was educated at home, Clara began teaching children herself at the age of fifteen in various elementary schools in Massachusetts. Prior to the Civil War, Clara's most noteworthy achievement was the establishment of a free public school in Bordentown, New Jersey. At the outbreak of the Civil War, Clara lived in Washington, D.C., where she worked at the U.S. Patent Office. Following the Baltimore Riots, upon the 6th Massachusetts Regiment arriving in Washington, it was Clara who organized a relief program for the soldiers, starting her lifelong career as a nurse and humanitarian.

① 미국 적십자사의 설립자이다.
② 당대 최고의 교육기관에서 교육을 받았다.
③ 10대 때부터 아이들을 가르쳤다.
④ 뉴저지에 무료 공립학교를 설립했다.
⑤ 남북전쟁 때 워싱턴 D.C.에서 구호 프로그램을 조직했다.

27 West Coast Tours에 관한 다음 안내문의 내용과 일치하지 <u>않는</u> 것은?

West Coast Tours — Whale Watching Trips

West Coast Tours is now offering whale watching day-trips year round! All of our trips leave from Vancouver.

If you'd like to join us, please remember that you must arrive at the West Coast Tours office in downtown Vancouver 40 minutes before departure.

Departures: 9 a.m., 12 noon and 3 p.m. daily
Duration: approximately three hours
Ticket Prices:

Regular: $80
Students: $60
Senior citizens: $60
Children 8 and under: $40

Tickets can be purchased in advance at the West Coast Tours office or in most major hotels.

① 일년 내내 참여할 수 있다.
② 참가자들은 출발 전에 해안 선착장으로 와야 한다.
③ 투어는 하루 3번 제공된다.
④ 학생 요금은 일반 요금에 비해 20달러 저렴하다.
⑤ 표는 대부분의 주요 호텔에서 구매 가능하다.

28 Apartment for Rent in Madrid에 관한 다음 안내문의 내용과 일치하는 것은?

Apartment for Rent in Madrid

Are you looking for a short-term place to stay in Madrid? We have the perfect apartment for you. It is located in the heart of the city and has two bedrooms and a balcony.

■ **Facilities and Internet**
– Our apartment is cheaper than a hotel room, and you can save even more money by cooking your own meals. The kitchen has a stove, a refrigerator, pots and pans, glasses, and dishes.
– Wi-Fi is available for a small additional fee.

■ **Check-in**
– You can check in at 2 p.m. or later. However, if you arrive after midnight, there will be a $10 late check-in fee.

■ **Note**
– We love pets, but they're not permitted in the apartment building. Sorry!

For details about rental rates and available dates, please email us at jgarcia@sbc.es.

① 아파트는 마드리드의 외곽에 위치하고 있다.
② 간단한 식기는 제공되나 취사는 불가능하다.
③ 와이파이는 무료로 사용할 수 있다.
④ 늦게 퇴실하는 경우 10달러를 내야 한다.
⑤ 아파트에는 애완동물 출입이 불가능하다.

29 다음 글의 밑줄 친 부분 중, 어법상 틀린 것은?

Long before humans or the earliest mammals were here, insects lived on earth. The oldest fossils of insects' ancestors ① found date back approximately 350 million years. The first insects most likely evolved from a primitive form of ringed worms. Since that time, they ② have evolved into probably the most successful life forms on land. ③ Because the fact that insects have a wide variety of natural predators, they have developed many means of self-defense. Producing chemicals or using a collective defense are some of the ways that insects protect ④ themselves. But the most common defense mechanism is flight. Using their wings, many insects, such as bees, mosquitoes, and butterflies, are able to leave the ground, ⑤ where many predators such as reptiles and amphibians, would otherwise eat them.

30 다음 글의 밑줄 친 부분 중, 문맥상 낱말의 쓰임이 적절하지 않은 것은?

These days, some clothing manufacturers have ① modified their size standards to such a degree that women who would once have worn a size 12 dress now fit into a size 8. This is called vanity sizing or size inflation, which is the practice of making a specific size of clothing larger over time. Many people believe the term "vanity sizing" comes from the fact that the practice is designed to ② satisfy the desire of consumers to feel thinner. An unexpected consequence of this trend was the creation of "subzero" sizes. Due to the ③ fall of fashion markets in Asia, where female consumers tend to be smaller than their Western counterparts, manufacturers found themselves faced with the need to create sizes smaller than zero, which had been the ④ smallest size available before vanity sizing. By doing so, they were able to continue to meet the needs of a ⑤ wide range of customers.

[31~34] 다음 빈칸에 들어갈 말로 가장 적절한 것을 고르시오.

31

Moral relativism is the philosophical view that morality is relative and that different people hold different moral standards. Moral relativism can be divided into ethical subjectivism and cultural relativism. Ethical subjectivism holds that morality is relative to individuals, while cultural relativism says morality is relative to culture. Both positions say there cannot be moral absolutes that hold for all people in all places at all times. Under the view of moral relativism, no given act is generally good or bad. Similarly, nobody is objectively right or wrong. According to moral relativism, there is only goodness or badness within a _____ context. That means there can never be an act that is good or bad in all situations.

① general
② specified
③ historical
④ theoretical
⑤ meaningful

32

A recent study has shown that young children from 2 to 4 years old show no preference for breakfast cereals that have been sweetened either with sugar or artificial sweeteners. However, when surveyed again years later, nearly all the children had come to prefer sweetened cereals. A second study revealed that children between 4 and 6 years old who were not exposed to advertisements for sweetened cereals still preferred unsweetened cereals upon turning 6 or 8 years old. These results show that the preference for sweetened foods _____. That means, without exposure to sweetened foods, whether in TV commercials or at home, children would avoid the primary cause of dental cavities and obesity. [3점]

① is an inherited trait

② significantly affects growth

③ is acquired rather than natural

④ indicates that obesity will occur

⑤ will later lead to health problems

33

There's a new national campaign underway _____, but its focus is a bit different than most: cutting our meat consumption. Called "Meat-Free Monday," the idea is to encourage people to go at least one day a week without eating any meat products. Some people may question what meat eating has to do with global warming, but the link exists and it's an important one. The livestock that gets processed into the meat on our plates requires a lot of land to raise, and in many parts of the world this land is created by burning enormous tracts of forest. The resulting smoke contains large amounts of carbon dioxide, the greenhouse gas most responsible for global warming. According to a UN study, as much as 18% of our worldwide greenhouse gas emissions are produced in this fashion.

① to plant new forests

② to adopt a healthier diet

③ to help slow climate change

④ to protect livestock animals

⑤ to lower air pollution in cities

34

Everyone has experienced it — we've all dropped our favorite food on the floor. And many of us act quickly to pick it back up and eat it. But is it safe to eat food dropped on the floor? One professor of agricultural science at Seoul National University performed an experiment by dropping cookies onto ceramic tiles and picking them up within five seconds. Study results showed that bacteria had already spread all over the cookies. The result is obvious. _____. One second can be enough for them to claim a new home address. We just don't realize it because bacteria aren't visible to the naked eye. Unlike a baseball, when food hits the ground, it's out. [3점]

① It's vital to eat cookies quickly

② Bacteria and viruses multiply fast

③ Bacteria can breed under any conditions

④ Sweet snacks are more vulnerable to bacteria

⑤ Viruses have existed since the beginning of the earth

35 다음 글에서 전체 흐름과 관계 <u>없는</u> 문장은?

Increasing food prices around the world are driving many into poverty, and recent reports show that a principal cause of the skyrocketing costs is the use of crops to produce biofuels. Biofuels have been promoted as a cleaner alternative to fossil fuels like coal and petroleum, and European nations and the U.S. have experienced high demand for them. ① The demand for fossil fuels has also continued to rise in most parts of the world and shows no signs of decreasing. ② However, as grains and other crops that once fed people are diverted to make biofuels, food is becoming scarcer and prices are increasing. ③ For example, one third of the corn grown in the U.S. and almost half of European vegetable oils are now consumed by biofuel manufacturers. ④ Therefore, all food products that contain corn or vegetable oils have risen in price as a result of the sudden scarcity of their ingredients. ⑤ This unforeseen drawback of biofuels is causing serious problems for many people.

36

Mayonnaise is not a very popular food, and it doesn't get as much attention as ketchup or mustard. But some animal conservationists are big fans of mayonnaise, as they are using it in their fight to protect endangered sea turtles.

(A) Because of this, the sea turtles showed signs of recovery just a few days after they were treated with mayonnaise. Once they were fully healthy, they were returned to the wild. It is possible that the mayonnaise treatment saved their lives.

(B) Conservationists discovered that mayonnaise mixed with vegetable oil was the best way to get the tar out of the sea turtles. Not only did it remove the tar from their systems, it also provided them with nourishing proteins and fats.

(C) This unusual preference began when an oil spill occurred off the coast of Israel and the coastline was covered in sticky tar. As the area is home to many sea turtles, they soon had this toxic substance inside their digestive systems.

① (A) – (C) – (B) ② (B) – (A) – (C)
③ (B) – (C) – (A) ④ (C) – (A) – (B)
⑤ (C) – (B) – (A)

37

From causing fatal forms of cancer to staining your teeth and fingers yellow, cigarettes are widely known to be unhealthy, but researchers have now found yet another way that smoking impacts health: increasing snoring.

(A) A study looking at this connection compared a group of smokers to a similar group of non-smokers and confirmed that smoking cigarettes does indeed lead to a higher incidence of snoring among subjects.

(B) Irritation leads to inflammation and swelling, which obstructs the normal process of breathing during sleep and makes it more likely that the smoker will experience snoring.

(C) It seems that cigarette smoke irritates the smoker's respiratory passageways in the nose and throat, where some cells were even shown to experience nerve damage as a result of nicotine exposure. [3점]

① (A) – (B) – (C) ② (A) – (C) – (B)
③ (B) – (C) – (A) ④ (C) – (A) – (B)
⑤ (C) – (B) – (A)

38

> Sometimes, though, there is resistance to this process.

"Positive affirmations" are short, positive statements that you can direct at negative subconscious beliefs. (①) You can use positive affirmations to undermine these beliefs and essentially replace a negative feeling with a positive one. (②) This is a way to "brainwash" yourself into changing your beliefs, but it's you that decide which beliefs you want to wash away. (③) If the belief you're trying to erase is very important in your life, or if you've held it for a long time, your subconscious will find it more comfortable to maintain the belief and will try to reject the positive affirmation. (④) However, if the issue isn't as serious, the affirmation will be easier to apply. (⑤) In such cases, you will experience a feeling of joy, and this is a sign that the affirmation is working.

39

> In response, villagers demonstrated not by protesting in the streets but by creating an organization called Blue Tongyeong 21.

The small Korean village of Dongpirang served as a military base during the Joseon Kingdom. (①) More recently, however, the village came under threat from developers who were advocating its destruction in order to rebuild the old fort. (②) This group came up with the idea to cover the tiny town with art in order to save it. (③) From all over the country, artists came to Dongpirang to participate in the movement by painting murals on buildings and decorating every available space. (④) The result was that Dongpirang took on a new identity, and with it came new value. (⑤) In the face of its newfound artistic merit, the developers had no choice but to abandon their plans. [3점]

40 다음 글의 내용을 한 문장으로 요약하고자 한다. 빈칸 (A), (B)에 들어갈 말로 가장 적절한 것은?

Everyone has their own concept of personal space. When a stranger steps inside this space, we become extremely uncomfortable. Scientists believe that this unpleasant feeling is caused by a part of the brain known as the amygdala that controls fear and processes emotional events. In an experiment, a woman who had suffered severe damage to her amygdalae was asked to walk toward another person and then stop at a comfortable distance. Whereas most people would have stopped about half a meter from the other person, the woman continued moving forward until their noses were nearly touching. The researchers believe the damage to her amygdalae prevents her from recognizing other people's emotions and judging their trustworthiness. Although there is no known way of curing the woman's condition, this research has led to a greater understanding of why we find it so unbearable to stand in close proximity to people we don't know.

*amygdala: (소뇌의) 편도체(*pl.* amygdalae)

↓

It is believed that the amygdala is responsible for the feelings of _____(A)_____ we experience when our personal space is _____(B)_____.

	(A)		(B)
①	discomfort	......	invaded
②	satisfaction	......	established
③	confusion	......	eliminated
④	aggression	......	questioned
⑤	attraction	......	expanded

According to utilitarianism, something is ethical if it maximizes total happiness while minimizing total pain. The word "total" is important, as it emphasizes that it is the happiness of everyone that matters, not the happiness of (a) individuals. There are two branches of utilitarianism: act utilitarianism and rule utilitarianism. Both of them agree on the above statement. However, they disagree on what people should do with this information. Act utilitarianism states that they should behave in whatever way will lead to the greatest amount of happiness. But rule utilitarianism argues that they should determine what type of behavior generally causes happiness and then make rules that enforce this behavior.

To understand the (b) difference, imagine a specific court case in which a judge is deciding whether to send a criminal to prison. The judge knows the man simply made a mistake and is (c) likely to commit a crime again. Setting him free will make the man happy, along with his friends and family members. Even the victim has forgiven the man, so this decision won't cause the victim any pain.

Act utilitarianism argues that the judge should let the man go, as this will (d) maximize happiness without causing additional pain. But rule utilitarianism says the judge should send the man to prison, since criminals must be punished for their crimes. The details of the situation don't matter — according to rule utilitarianism, the judge must strictly (e) follow the rules.

41 윗글의 제목으로 가장 적절한 것은?

① How to Make an Ethical Decision
② The Big Problem with Utilitarianism
③ Happiness: Humanity's Primary Goal
④ Without Rules, Nothing Can Be Good
⑤ Different Methods of Maximizing Happiness

42 밑줄 친 (a)~(e) 중에서 문맥상 낱말의 쓰임이 적절하지 않은 것은? [3점]

① (a)   ② (b)   ③ (c)   ④ (d)   ⑤ (e)

[43~45] 다음 글을 읽고, 물음에 답하시오.

(A)

One sunny afternoon during a family camping trip, my elder brother and I were out exploring the wooded campground. In a grassy clearing, we came upon an old two-story house. We peeked inside the warped windows and saw nothing but black dust and boxes of ancient-looking junk.

(B)

At the station, we came up with what we thought was a brilliant lie: that we had not broken the window or anything inside the house. In fact, we said, we had heard the same alarming noises that (a) they had, and we had actually gone into the house to try to stop a crime in progress. The true criminals must have escaped while they were arresting us. Fortunately, the owners seemed to believe us. Instead of punishing us, (b) they thanked us for our heroic action, and the police promised to let us know when they found the criminal who had destroyed these people's property.

(C)

At first, of course, we were relieved. But, over time, a rather guilty feeling crept over us — something like a weight on our chests. The feeling grew and grew. We weren't sleeping well and had no appetites. Worst of all, we couldn't bear to look our parents in the eye. After they heard the news from the police, (c) they were always remarking how courageous we had been at that campground and how sad it was that those poor people still had no justice for the criminal act (d) they had suffered. Eventually, we couldn't bear it any longer, so we confessed to what we had done. From this, I learned that honesty is the best policy.

(D)

Assuming the house to be abandoned, we did what a lot of boys our age would have done: we broke in through a window. Once inside, we started looking for other things to break. We soon learned, however, that this particular house was not abandoned after all. An old couple who owned the house were living in a mobile home not far off, and (e) they had heard the noise we were making. The authorities were called, and we were treated to our first ride in a police car.

43 주어진 글 (A)에 이어질 내용을 순서에 맞게 배열한 것으로 가장 적절한 것은?

① (B) – (D) – (C) ② (C) – (B) – (D)
③ (C) – (D) – (B) ④ (D) – (B) – (C)
⑤ (D) – (C) – (B)

44 밑줄 친 (a)~(e) 중 가리키는 대상이 나머지 넷과 다른 것은?

① (a) ② (b) ③ (c) ④ (d) ⑤ (e)

45 윗글의 'I'에 관한 내용과 일치하지 않는 것은?

① 가족 여행 중에 낡은 이층집을 발견했다.
② 용감한 행동을 한 것처럼 이야기를 꾸며냈다.
③ 소음을 듣고 집안으로 들어가게 되었다.
④ 죄책감을 느껴 자신의 잘못을 고백했다.
⑤ 야영지에서 처음으로 경찰에 체포되었다.

* 3점 문항에만 점수가 표시되어 있습니다.
  점수 표시가 없는 문항은 모두 2점씩입니다.

18 다음 글의 목적으로 가장 적절한 것은?

Dear Dr. Moore,

My name is Greg Valerio, and I'm a sophomore currently majoring in physics. I chose physics because it was my strongest subject in high school, but now I'm having second thoughts. I am struggling with my classes and feel that I would benefit from switching to computer science. I talked to my academic advisor about this and she told me that I need to get approval from you, since you're the head of that department. I know we're supposed to make these requests early in the semester and that it is almost time for midterms. So I thought I should contact you as soon as possible, before it becomes even more difficult to handle this matter. If necessary, I'd be happy to discuss my situation with you in person. Please let me know.

Sincerely yours,
Greg Valerio

① 물리학 수업 신청을 취소하려고
② 교수님과의 면담 일정을 확인하려고
③ 대학 내 학사 관리 직무에 지원하려고
④ 전공 변경이 가능한지 허락을 받으려고
⑤ 중간고사를 보러 가지 못한 이유를 설명하려고

19 다음 글에 드러난 Karen의 심경으로 가장 적절한 것은?

As Karen gradually became aware of her surroundings, she realized she wasn't sure how long she had been unconscious. She could tell that her injuries weren't serious, but her car was lying on her legs, trapping her where she was. Rising up to a sitting position, she began to push herself backwards in an attempt to pull her legs free. But hard as she pushed, she couldn't move them even a few centimeters. Switching tactics, she began to move from side to side, hoping to wriggle out, but this didn't work either. Although it seemed there was no way she was going to escape on her own, Karen did not want to accept the fact that she could do nothing but wait for help.

① calm and peaceful
② cold and indifferent
③ anxious and desperate
④ touched and sympathetic
⑤ disappointed and ashamed

20 다음 글에서 필자가 주장하는 바로 가장 적절한 것은?

Competitive sports are an important part of high school for many students, as they keep teens physically fit, teach them about teamwork, and help them learn how to work under pressure. However, if these sports are not monitored by qualified professionals, they can cause mental and physical harm. This most often occurs when the emphasis is shifted from having fun to winning, transforming a pleasurable activity into a high-pressure situation. Losing becomes failure, which causes stress and damages self-confidence. Even successful young athletes can suffer, as having a win-at-any-cost attitude can cause social problems and conflicts with their peers. High school coaches need to keep these potential dangers in mind when they're training student athletes, making sure to keep the focus on physical fitness, self-improvement, and teamwork.

① 경쟁적인 스포츠는 학생들에게 해가 된다.
② 경기에서 지는 것에 대한 두려움을 버려야 한다.
③ 고강도의 운동을 한 뒤에는 충분한 휴식이 필요하다.
④ 스포츠에 참여할 때 지나친 경쟁을 강요해선 안 된다.
⑤ 교우 관계 개선을 위해 경쟁적인 스포츠를 활용해야 한다.

21 밑줄 친 "fixing the broken window"가 다음 글에서 의미하는 바로 가장 적절한 것은? [3점]

According to the broken windows theory, a broken window that is left unrepaired will lead to more windows in the neighborhood being broken. This is because a broken window signals that nobody cares, so there will be no punishment for breaking more windows. Of course, this doesn't apply only to windows. The theory serves as a metaphor for any kind of disorder left unfixed in any sort of environment. Although it was originally used to explain unrepaired neighborhoods, it is now commonly applied to workplaces and classrooms. For example, it has been argued that in any school, there are students who will attempt to "break a window." This is often a small act of disobedience, such as changing desks without permission or checking text messages during class. This behavior may seem insignificant, but not immediately "fixing the broken window" can lead to an overall negative effect on the classroom environment.

① correcting the bad behavior of students
② helping neighbors who are less fortunate
③ asking for advice to quickly find a solution
④ improving the appearance of the classroom
⑤ forgiving small mistakes that aren't important

22 다음 글의 요지로 가장 적절한 것은?

When reading a science fiction novel, you would expect to come across many words and phrases borrowed from science itself. In certain cases, however, this process is reversed, and the field of science actually adopts the use of words that originated in the imaginations of novelists. The phrase "deep space," for example, made its first appearance in a novel called *Triplanetary* by Edward Smith, and was used to describe the vast regions of empty space between galaxies. These days, scientists use it to refer to any part of space that lies beyond our solar system. Another scientific term borrowed from a writer is "zero gravity," which was coined by Jack Binder in a short story in 1938. In this case, the meaning of the term is identical both in the story and in real life. It would seem that scientific terms are just as likely to be coined by writers as by actual scientists.

① 과학 용어의 의미가 문학에서 잘못 사용되고 있다.
② 일부 과학 용어들이 실제로는 문학에서 유래되었다.
③ 공상 과학 소설을 통해 과학을 쉽게 이해할 수 있다.
④ 모든 과학 이론들은 상상력을 통해 처음 만들어진다.
⑤ 소설가들은 새로운 과학적 발견으로부터 영감을 얻는다.

23 다음 글의 주제로 가장 적절한 것은? [3점]

Military service became a life-changing experience for more than 2 million Americans during the Vietnam War. Soldiers had to deal with tension, boredom, drugs, and widespread brutality against the Vietnamese. Even young Americans who did not fight were affected by the war, spending a major part of their late adolescence or young adulthood worrying about being drafted or trying to avoid participation in the fighting. More men stayed at home than went to Vietnam, but the war created deep divisions among an entire generation. Those who fought in the war often resented people who didn't, and those who didn't go to Vietnam sometimes viewed those who did go with scorn and pity.

① cruelty of soldiers during wartime
② problems with compulsory military service
③ the anti-war movement and the Vietnam War
④ influences of the Vietnam War on American lives
⑤ pros and cons of the wars against Asian countries

24 다음 글의 제목으로 가장 적절한 것은?

It's not uncommon to dream about winning the lottery. If you've ever had a period of financial uncertainty, then you've probably imagined how winning the lottery would solve all your money troubles. Many others have also thought this way. Unfortunately, many lottery winners actually have more financial problems after they win. Many are even forced to declare bankruptcy. There can be different reasons for this, but the main problem is that the winners don't know how to manage their newly-acquired wealth. They react to their win by buying homes and cars and other expensive things right away. Yet they fail to understand that each of these requires substantial maintenance costs after purchase. Luxury cars need expensive insurance, boats need a capable crew, and vacation homes require you to pay high property taxes. Therefore, lottery winners must manage their money carefully if they want to remain financially stable.

① The Best Investments for Lottery Winners
② Harmful Effects of Purchasing Luxury Items
③ Lottery Winners: The World's Richest People
④ Increasing Your Chances of Winning the Lottery
⑤ Why Many Lottery Winners Are in Financial Trouble

25 다음 도표의 내용과 일치하지 않는 것은?

Use of Different Media by Americans in 2020

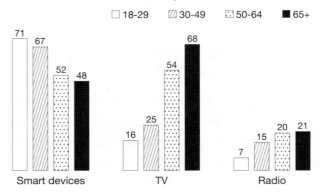

The above graph shows different forms of media and the percentage of Americans who often use them to get their news. ① The most common news source of the youngest age group is smart devices, while that of the oldest age group is the television. ② The percentage of people in the 50-to-64 age group who often get their news from the television is higher than that of the two youngest age groups combined. ③ Only seven percent of people in the youngest age group often get their news from the radio, less than one-tenth of the percentage of this same age group who often get it from smart devices. ④ The percentage of 30-to-49-year-olds who often get their news from the radio is only one percentage point higher than the percentage of 18-to-29-year-olds who often get their news from the television. ⑤ Finally, only 48 percent of the oldest age group often get their news from smart devices, four percentage points fewer than the next oldest group.

26 megamouth shark에 관한 다음 글의 내용과 일치하지 않는 것은?

Discovered in 1976, the megamouth shark resides in a habitat scientists have yet to explore in detail: the depths of the ocean. As a result, it's considered an extremely rare species, so rare that fewer than 50 specimens have ever been caught. In physical appearance the megamouth is quite distinctive, with a massive body growing up to 5.5 meters in length and a large head featuring a broad snout and rubbery lips. Its underbelly is solid white, while the color patterns on top of the animal range from brownish to black. Not surprisingly, the shark possesses a characteristically large mouth, from which its name is derived. Its teeth, on the other hand, are rather small, for instead of chewing its food, the shark simply swims through the water with mouth wide open, swallowing any jellyfish or plankton that stray into its path.

① 심해에 사는 희귀한 종이다.
② 외관상 다른 상어들과 유사한 특징을 갖는다.
③ 머리가 크고 넓은 코와 고무 같은 입술을 가졌다.
④ 커다란 입에 비해 이빨이 작다.
⑤ 먹이를 씹지 않고 삼켜 버린다.

27 Volunteer Vacations에 관한 다음 안내문의 내용과 일치하지 않는 것은?

Volunteer Vacations

Volunteer Vacations is a nonprofit organization that provides volunteer opportunities during the summer vacation.

• Our programs focus on two regions — Central America and West Africa.
• The goal of our programs is to provide small villages with modern facilities, such as schools, community centers, and hospitals. Volunteers will be expected to help in the planning and construction of these facilities.
• We have two program lengths — full summer (eight weeks) and half summer (four weeks).
• School groups are not accepted; however, individual students and families are welcome.

For more information on our current programs or to download an application form, please visit our website.

① 프로그램은 중미와 서아프리카에서 진행된다.
② 자원봉사자들은 학교, 주민센터, 병원 등을 짓는다.
③ 프로그램 기간에는 두 종류가 있다.
④ 가족 단위의 참가는 제한되어 있다.
⑤ 참가 신청서는 웹사이트에서 다운로드 가능하다.

28 Manchester Book Fair에 관한 다음 안내문의 내용과 일치하는 것은?

Come to the Manchester Book Fair

Attention book-lovers! The 4th Annual Manchester Book Fair is coming to the Manchester Civic Arena soon!

When

- November 16 to November 30
- Note: The first three days of the fair are for publishing professionals only. The public is welcome starting on the 19th.
- Open to the public from 10 a.m. to 7 p.m. every day except Sundays, when it closes one hour earlier
- Exhibitors are welcome in the arena from 9 a.m. to 9 p.m., seven days a week.

Tickets

- $5 per person
- A 20% discount is available to groups of 10 or more.

① 시 경기장에서 한 달간 개최된다.
② 박람회 첫 주는 출판 관계자들만 참여 가능하다.
③ 일반 관람객은 일요일에 8시까지 관람 가능하다.
④ 전시 참가 업체는 한 시간 일찍 행사장에 들어갈 수 있다.
⑤ 단체에는 입장권에 10% 할인이 적용된다.

29 다음 글의 밑줄 친 부분 중, 어법상 틀린 것은?

Research has found that ① learning can be divided into two categories: incidental learning and intentional learning. The former happens by chance, meaning there is no clearly defined intention to learn. For instance, a student who ② is trying to memorize the names of the 50 U.S. states may ask a friend to listen while they ③ are named. During the naming, the friend may by chance also learn the names of these 50 states. On the other hand, intentional learning happens when there's a clear purpose ④ present from the very beginning. For example, a student may sit down with a list of all the capital cities in Europe because she is taking a test. Research suggests that intentional learning ⑤ be more effective because it stays with us over time.

30 (A), (B), (C)의 각 네모 안에서 문맥에 맞는 낱말로 가장 적절한 것은?

One feature that distinguishes traditional Pueblo pottery from other types of clay art is that machinery is not used in the creative (A) process / progress . The clay is gathered, treated, and shaped by hand. Instead of using a potter's wheel to create (B) objects / objectives , the Pueblo pottery artist rolls clay into long pieces and then painstakingly coils them into layers of circles. Paints are produced from plants and minerals (C) found / founded near the Pueblo villages and applied with a handmade brush fashioned from a yucca cactus. Due to this traditional process, art collectors can be sure that every piece of Pueblo clay art is unique. It also means that Pueblo pottery makes an excellent gift.

*yucca: 【식물】 실난초, 유카과(科)

	(A)		(B)		(C)
①	process	······	objectives	······	found
②	process	······	objects	······	found
③	process	······	objects	······	founded
④	progress	······	objects	······	founded
⑤	progress	······	objectives	······	found

[31~34] 다음 빈칸에 들어갈 말로 가장 적절한 것을 고르시오.

31

It seems that just because you read something in your daily newspaper doesn't mean it's accurate. One researcher recently analyzed a variety of articles on the subject of climate change, and he found a number of errors in the reporting of units of measurement. For example, in a piece about potential changes in sea level, it was written that waters could rise 1-2 centimeters per year, though the figure should have been given in millimeters. The same mistake occurred in a different paper's article about increases in rainfall. From these findings, the researcher concluded that the mistakes were not really mistakes at all. He believes that media outlets frequently misreport figures to be larger than they actually are because these _____ help make news stories more dramatic, ensuring that they'll more easily grab the attention of readers.

① facts
② topics
③ analogies
④ exaggerations
⑤ advertisements

32

　Recent research into saliva has revealed _____. For example, doctors commonly draw blood to look for signs of disease based on the presence of particular substances, but it turns out that your saliva holds the same information. Moreover, your saliva contains DNA, which is unique in every individual. By analyzing the DNA in saliva, doctors can tell whether you are susceptible to certain diseases. Police investigators can also tell whether you were the person who drank a glass of water or licked an envelope to seal it at the scene of a crime. Dentists, too, can use information from your saliva to predict your chances of getting cavities. [3점]

① how complex and amazing DNA is
② which role saliva plays in digestion
③ how rich in information the liquid is
④ why we need to go to the dentist regularly
⑤ why DNA analysis is used in criminal investigations

33

　In most countries, attempting to escape from prison is considered to be an extremely serious crime, and prisoners who choose to do so are likely to have their original sentences significantly lengthened. Not so in Mexico, however: Mexican law is based on the underlying philosophy that all people possess _____. Thus, a prisoner caught while trying to escape from a Mexican prison is likely to go unpunished. Of course, there are some people in Mexico who oppose this policy, perceiving it as major weakness in their country's justice system. However, there are many others who wholeheartedly support it, believing that it protects the basic human rights of prisoners. [3점]

① individual moral standards
② the will to pursue legal justice
③ a natural yearning for freedom
④ a pure intention for their behavior
⑤ reason for judging right and wrong

34

　Some people are reluctant to approach others in social situations. They feel as though they are essentially asking "Do you like me?" In this kind of interaction, the other person seemingly has all the power. However, you can seize control of the encounter by starting out by asking the other person to make a small investment. Simply put, _____. It doesn't need to be anything important. Just ask the person to pass you a piece of cake or to hold your drink while you go to the bathroom. You will likely find that this causes the person to have a more positive impression of you. Contrary to what most people think, people will like you more after having done you a favor rather than the other way around.

① be kind to him or her
② leave him or her alone
③ listen to what he or she says
④ invite him or her to donate money
⑤ ask him or her to do something for you

35 다음 글에서 전체 흐름과 관계 없는 문장은?

Because breast cancer can be caused by a myriad of factors, doctors may never be able to pinpoint the exact cause of any individual case. However, it is possible to show that exposure to certain substances or conditions significantly increases a woman's risk of contracting this cancer. ① Being exposed to artificial light at night is theorized to be one such risk factor. ② The connection between this stimulus and the disease lies in melatonin, a hormone that governs our sleep-wake cycle. ③ Exposure to artificial nighttime light is known to cause decreased melatonin levels, which are often seen in breast cancer patients. ④ Since melatonin production slows down as people age, older adults tend to have lower levels. ⑤ The credibility of this theory is strengthened by the fact that women in developing countries, where artificial nighttime light is less common, have lower rates of breast cancer than women living in industrialized nations.

*melatonin: 멜라토닌(활동일 주기를 조절하는 호르몬)

[36~37] 주어진 글 다음에 이어질 글의 순서로 가장 적절한 것을 고르시오.

36

Leonardo da Vinci was both a master artist and a great inventor. He has had an influence on many fields, including mapmaking, mathematics, geology, and painting.

(A) He believed that these principles could be used in machines. In 1495, he made some sketches of a mechanical knight that could be used in battle. They showed a suit of armor with an internal mechanism that would make it move like a human body.

(B) However, Leonardo's greatest influence may have been on a field that didn't exist during his lifetime — robotics. This is because he was obsessed with human anatomy. To better understand how our muscles move our bones, he often dissected corpses.

(C) No one knows if Leonardo ever attempted to make his robot knight. However, in 2002, a robotics expert used his notes and sketches to make a working model of the knight. Some of the ideas used in it were later borrowed by NASA to design planet-exploring robots.

*dissect: 해부[절개]하다

① (A) – (B) – (C)　　② (B) – (A) – (C)
③ (B) – (C) – (A)　　④ (C) – (A) – (B)
⑤ (C) – (B) – (A)

37

From the early 19th century, events that had long been considered magical or supernatural began to be explained through logic, mathematical reasoning, and available evidence.

(A) At that time, Charles Darwin proposed a theory that broke away from the mainstream. Rather than looking to God or some other higher force to explain the natural world, he proposed a theory called natural selection.

(B) This idea was later expanded to include more than just the evolution of species. Darwin developed his theory of natural selection to proclaim that all of earth's life forms have evolved from hydrogen that was present at the birth of the universe.

(C) According to Charles Darwin, natural selection is the evolution of species over time to meet the specific needs of their environment. Thus, species are able to maintain their own survival, even when conditions in the environment change. [3점]

① (A) – (B) – (C)　　② (A) – (C) – (B)
③ (B) – (C) – (A)　　④ (C) – (A) – (B)
⑤ (C) – (B) – (A)

[38~39] 글의 흐름으로 보아, 주어진 문장이 들어가기에 가장 적절한 곳을 고르시오.

38

> The thymuses that doctors considered "enlarged" were actually of normal size.

One of the saddest and most costly mistakes in medical history occurred during the 1920s and 1930s, when attempts were made to prevent sudden infant death syndrome (SIDS). Researchers who investigated SIDS, a condition in which a baby inexplicably dies during the night, thought they had found the cause. (①) Upon examination, many of the deceased infants exhibited what was described as an enlarged thymus gland. (②) The thymus is located next to the esophagus, and it was assumed that an excessively large thymus could block airflow to the lungs if there was pressure on a sleeping child's throat. (③) So, doctors tried to shrink children's thymuses by exposing them to high doses of radiation. (④) Unfortunately, the enlarged thymus theory was based on insufficient data. (⑤) This error resulted in between 20,000 and 30,000 deaths from radiation-induced throat cancer over the next several decades.

*thymus (gland): 흉선 **esophagus: 식도

39

> The rapid growth in prison populations provides increased profits to corporations that build prisons and provide services to them.

We all know that the unhealthy links between business and politics have been a chronic problem. In the U.S., legislators and business owners are trying to strengthen this backscratching relationship by using the prison system. (①) How are they doing this? (②) Legislators are passing laws that command ever longer sentences, and as a result, prison populations are growing ever larger. (③)

As their profits grow, these corporations make large financial contributions to cooperative political candidates. (④) Once these candidates are elected into Congress, their corporate sponsors influence their legal decisions. (⑤) Unless something is done to break this immoral cycle, the U.S. prison population will continue to grow. [3점]

40 다음 글의 내용을 한 문장으로 요약하고자 한다. 빈칸 (A), (B)에 들어갈 말로 가장 적절한 것은?

> Affective forecasting, the making of predictions about one's own emotional reaction to a future event, is a skill at which humans do not generally excel. Daniel Gilbert, a member of the social psychology department at Harvard University, has shown in his new research that humans are poor affective forecasters. In fact, their predictions about how future events will make them feel often turn out to be completely inaccurate. When considering how our future emotional state will be impacted by such occurrences as elections, sporting events, movies, and big purchases, reports Gilbert, we tend to over- or underestimate the magnitude and strength of our reactions. This means that what we anticipate will fill us with joy rarely does, while what we fear will emotionally devastate us typically causes less pain than we expected.

↓

> We often fail to accurately _____(A)_____ the impact of a future event on our _____(B)_____.

	(A)		(B)
①	foretell	······	emotional state
②	explain	······	logical thinking
③	influence	······	physical power
④	conceal	······	sensitive condition
⑤	enhance	······	psychological effect

Today, people are "job-hopping" more than ever, seeking increased wages, diversity of duties, and career growth opportunities. Years ago, "job-hopping" was unheard of. In fact, many people spent their entire careers at one company and searched for new jobs only when they were (a) forced to do so. Today, it is normal for a working individual to change jobs several times in his or her lifetime.

Rapid advances in technology, such as developments in communications, computing, e-commerce, and the internet, have brought with them many new job opportunities. However, new technological developments are (b) replacing other technologies, causing some to become "extinct." Such changeover of technologies is causing even more changes among today's workers. People in today's working world are forced to stay one step (c) ahead of technological changes in order to keep their competitive edge in the job market.

While people a few decades ago used to remain (d) disloyal to their company during their entire career, people today have a more self-focused attitude toward employment. People choose jobs that offer the best compensation and benefits, good opportunities for growth, and a comfortable work environment. They seek jobs that allow them to (e) achieve their current goals instead of trying to find a company that can meet their changing needs over the years. This leads many people to choose to start their own business instead of working for others, which can be another kind of job-hopping. While technology has changed the job market, this change in attitude created new career options for modern workers.

41 윗글의 제목으로 가장 적절한 것은?

① How to Look for a New Job
② The Difficulties of Business Start-Ups
③ Making Your Own Business Decisions
④ Why Modern People Frequently Change Jobs
⑤ Alternatives to Working for a Large Corporation

42 밑줄 친 (a)~(e) 중에서 문맥상 낱말의 쓰임이 적절하지 않은 것은? [3점]

① (a)　　② (b)　　③ (c)　　④ (d)　　⑤ (e)

[43~45] 다음 글을 읽고, 물음에 답하시오.

(A)

Americans tend to keep most of their food in the refrigerator, believing it is necessary to prevent items from going bad. For this reason, they are often shocked when they learn that Europeans generally keep their eggs on the kitchen counter.

(B)

So why do Americans continue to wash and refrigerate their eggs? Unfortunately, it remains their best available option, as the U.S. government refuses to adopt the European practice of vaccinating chickens. Besides, studies have shown that eggs do last longer when they are kept cold — (a) they remain safe to eat for about 50 days in the refrigerator, as opposed to just about 21 days on the counter. On the other hand, eggs kept in the refrigerator absorb the flavors of the food around them, which negatively affects their taste. For this reason, Americans often keep (b) them separate from strong-smelling foods.

(C)

In Europe, however, food safety experts have adopted a different approach. They discourage the refrigeration of eggs and have actually made it illegal for companies to wash the eggs that they sell, which ensures that the protective cuticle remains intact. In place of washing, they created a program that makes it mandatory to vaccinate all egg-laying chickens against salmonella. (c) Their method seems to be the most effective one, as statistics show that cases of egg-related food poisoning in the UK have dropped significantly in recent years.

(D)

This difference can be traced back to the 1970s, when the American egg industry was concerned about salmonella, a type of bacteria that is a common cause of food poisoning. To get rid of salmonella, a special method of washing eggs was created, in which (d) they are cleaned with soap and hot water. Although using soap, water, and steam is effective in ridding eggs of salmonella, it removes (e) their cuticle, a thin, protective layer on the surface of the shell that not only keeps water and oxygen in but also keeps bacteria out. Therefore, eggs that have been washed must be refrigerated to prevent infection.

43 주어진 글 (A)에 이어질 내용을 순서에 맞게 배열한 것으로 가장 적절한 것은?

① (B) – (D) – (C)   ② (C) – (B) – (D)
③ (C) – (D) – (B)   ④ (D) – (B) – (C)
⑤ (D) – (C) – (B)

44 밑줄 친 (a)~(e) 중에서 가리키는 대상이 나머지 넷과 다른 것은?

① (a)   ② (b)   ③ (c)   ④ (d)   ⑤ (e)

45 윗글의 내용으로 일치하지 않는 것은?

① 냉장 보관 시 실온 보관에 비해 계란을 2배 이상 오래 보관할 수 있다.
② 유럽에서는 상업용 계란을 세척하는 것이 불법이다.
③ 미국에서는 산란계에게 백신을 접종하는 것이 의무이다.
④ 영국에서는 최근 계란과 관련한 식중독 사례가 줄어들었다.
⑤ 미국은 1970년대에 계란 세척 공법을 도입하였다.

* 3점 문항에만 점수가 표시되어 있습니다.
  점수 표시가 없는 문항은 모두 2점씩입니다.

18 다음 글의 목적으로 가장 적절한 것은?

Dear McGowan Employees,

Since last week's unfortunate accident in the company cafeteria, many of you have expressed concerns over the delay in providing emergency medical treatment to the injured individual. This was due to the McGowan Industries policy that permits only trained medical professionals to provide treatment on company property. This policy was established due to insurance requirements. However, after much discussion, we have decided to amend the policy, making it allowable for anyone who has learned medical procedures in a company first-aid class to provide appropriate treatment in an emergency. Of course, medical professionals should still be called in the case of a serious accident. As always, we appreciate the opinions expressed by our employees and hope you are satisfied with our response.

Sincerely,
The Management Team

① 업무처리 절차의 변경에 대해 안내하려고
② 의료 행위에 대한 사내 정책 변경을 알리려고
③ 응급 처치 교육에 직원들의 참석을 독려하려고
④ 부상당한 직원의 업무를 도와줄 것을 요청하려고
⑤ 사내에서 발생한 사고에 대한 보험처리를 요구하려고

19 다음 글에 드러난 Tom의 심경 변화로 가장 적절한 것은?

A few days ago, Tom was driving in a snowstorm on a country road. It was late at night, and the road conditions were really bad. Suddenly he heard a loud noise, and his heart sank as he realized he had a flat tire. Usually Tom kept a spare tire in the trunk, but he had taken it out to make more room for his luggage. There were no houses in sight, and there was no signal when Tom checked his cell phone. Just then, a pair of headlights appeared. It turned out to be a young man in a truck. Not only did the man lend Tom his spare tire, but he also helped him change it. If it hadn't been for him, the situation could have been serious.

① bored → excited
② worried → relieved
③ satisfied → confused
④ exhausted → annoyed
⑤ scared → disappointed

20 다음 글의 요지로 가장 적절한 것은?

Although nanotechnology has been around for many years, practical applications are only now being developed. These applications are expected to have an impact on a wide range of products, potentially affecting everything from clothing to batteries. Nanotechnology may lead to the development of strange new materials, since, when reduced to nanosize, familiar materials begin to develop odd properties. If aluminum foil, for example, is reduced to a small enough size — about 20 to 30 nanometers — it stops behaving as we would expect aluminum foil to behave. In fact, nanosized pieces of aluminum foil can explode. Although not all nanosize materials change their properties so dramatically, scientists are eager to work with ones that do, in the interest of creating new and useful materials.

① 나노 기술이 적용되는 분야는 정해져 있다.
② 기술을 실용화하기 전 검증 단계를 거쳐야 한다.
③ 나노 사이즈로 축소된 알루미늄 포일은 폭발할 수 있다.
④ 과학자들은 나노 사이즈 물질들의 특징을 연구해야 한다.
⑤ 나노 기술을 통해 색다르고 유용한 물질을 개발할 수 있다.

[21~22] 다음 글의 주제로 가장 적절한 것을 고르시오.

21

The British and French had been fighting for control of North America for over a hundred years by the time the American War of Independence began. So, when the American colonists declared their independence from England in 1776, the French were ready to give active support to them. The important role played by the French in the war is well represented by the 1781 Battle of the Chesapeake. American ground forces had laid siege to Yorktown, Virginia, where the top British commander and his army were stationed. British warships sailed from New York to help break the siege, but they were blocked from entering the Chesapeake Bay by French warships. The French navy succeeded in guarding the bay long enough that the British general in Yorktown was forced to surrender to the colonists.

① the French invasion of Great Britain
② France's role in America's independence
③ why British colonists emigrated to America
④ the friendship between the Americans and British
⑤ problems caused by a long battle between countries

22

Everyone enjoys Jane Austen's writing. Her novels prove how much human nature can be revealed within the limits of a controlled environment and a straightforward plot. Austen makes women her central characters. By using their wits and moral sensibilities, they bring about a desired end. This element in itself — the success of the powerless over the powerful — surely accounts for some of Austen's popularity. The greater part of her appeal, however, has to do with her ability to combine opposing qualities such as romance and humor or human connections and separations. Finally, although her novels are grounded in realism and made credible by careful observation, they are essentially fantasies that let people become lost in them. [3점]

① Jane Austen's extraordinary success
② Jane Austen's role in women's literature
③ why Jane Austen's novels are so popular
④ what everyone looks for in a good novel
⑤ the triumph of the powerless over the powerful

[23~24] 다음 글의 제목으로 가장 적절한 것을 고르시오.

23

Why do good things always happen to certain people? Is it because they carry a lucky rabbit's foot or found a four-leaf clover? Of course not. Those are just silly superstitions. In reality, luck is all about controlling things that appear to be out of your control. When you make an effort, you'll often find you have the ability to change these things for the better. What's more, luck is also a matter of perception. People who have a good attitude often believe that they are lucky. Therefore, they focus on the good things that happen to them. People with negative attitudes, on the other hand, tend to ignore the good things and focus on everything bad that occurs. This ends up making them feel as though they are unlucky.

① Don't Trust Your Perception
② Luck Is a Matter of Attitude
③ You Can't Control Everything
④ The Truth behind Superstitions
⑤ Focus on Both the Good and the Bad

24

Did you spend your staycation watching webisodes and using a sock puppet to keep an eye on your frenemies? If so, your vocabulary parallels changing trends in U.S. society, and you've already mastered some of the hundreds of new words added to the latest edition of Merriam-Webster's Collegiate Dictionary. Turn to the "W" section for a definition of webisode, "a short episode that is only viewable on a website," or look up "sock puppet" to learn about how false identities are used to deceive online communities. A staycation is defined as "spending vacation time at home," while a frenemy is someone who acts like a friend but in secret is your enemy. The adoption of words like these reflects society's increasing use of new technology. Now, as permanent parts of American vocabulary used in conversation and literature alike, these words are impossible to dismiss, so Merriam-Webster had no choice but to include them.

① Ways That New Words Are Created
② Examples of New Words in the Dictionary
③ The Popularity of New Words among Youth
④ Why New Words Are Difficult to Understand
⑤ Side Effects of Adopting New Vocabulary Words

25   다음 도표의 내용과 일치하지 <u>않는</u> 것은?

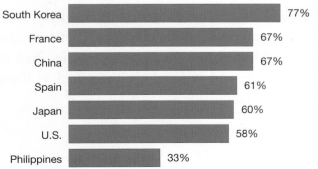

Cashless Payment Methods for Purchases

Country	Percentage
South Korea	77%
France	67%
China	67%
Spain	61%
Japan	60%
U.S.	58%
Philippines	33%

The above graph shows the percentage of people in seven different countries who said that they prefer to use cashless payment methods for their purchases. ① South Korea is the only country on the graph where more than three quarters of the people reported that they prefer cashless payments. ② In France, Spain, and Japan, between 60 and 70 percent of people reported that they would rather pay without cash. ③ The percentage in China is the same as that in France, although it is a bit lower than the percentages in Spain and Japan. ④ In the United States, more than half of the people reported that they prefer cashless payments, but this number is nearly 20 percentage points lower than that of South Korea. ⑤ Finally, the Philippines had the lowest percentage of people preferring to pay without cash, and this percentage was approximately half that of China.

26   나폴레옹에 관한 다음 글의 내용과 일치하지 <u>않는</u> 것은?

Although many believe that Napoleon died of stomach cancer, recent evidence suggests that he was poisoned to death. In his book *The Murder of Napoleon*, Sten Forshufvud argues that Napoleon was poisoned by a rival. An examination of Napoleon's body revealed an enlarged liver, which is a sign of arsenic overdose. Napoleon's family reported that during his last years, Napoleon showed symptoms of arsenic poisoning such as sleepiness, insomnia, swollen feet, and excessive weight gain. When Dr. Forshufvud chemically analyzed some of Napoleon's hair that relatives had saved, he found high traces of arsenic. The most shocking evidence of arsenic poisoning was discovered in 1840, when Napoleon's coffin was reopened. His body was well-preserved, which is an effect of arsenic.

*arsenic: 비소(독성이 강한 화학 물질)

① 사망 원인이 위암으로 알려져 있다.
② 독살되었다는 의혹이 제기되었다.
③ 시신 부검 결과 간 비대 증상이 있었다.
④ 머리카락 분석 결과 비소 잔류량이 높았다.
⑤ 비소가 시신 부패를 촉진시켰다는 증거가 발견되었다.

2021 Summer Recreation Program

Registration for our town's annual summer recreation program begins on April 15. You can sign up by calling the recreation coordinator at 593-927-2282 between the hours of 9 a.m. and 5 p.m.

Outdoor Activities
This year's outdoor activities include basketball, soccer, tennis, and badminton. All of the programs run three days a week and are open to children between the ages of 8 and 14. Please visit our website for details.

Indoor Program
The town's indoor facilities will also be available, including the swimming pool, gymnastics center, and weight room. This program gives you unlimited access to the facilities and is open to all town residents over the age of 12.

Fees
• Outdoor Activities: $25 per month for each activity
• Indoor Program: $10 per week for adults, $5 per week for children

① 전화로 등록 가능하다.
② 야외 프로그램은 주 3회 운영된다.
③ 수영이 실내 프로그램에 포함되어 있다.
④ 12세 이하 주민은 실내 체육 시설을 이용할 수 있다.
⑤ 야외 활동은 각 활동당 한 달에 $25이다.

Jungfrau Tour

The Jungfrau is one of the most popular peaks in the Alps. This one-day tour of the region is perfect for travelers on a tight schedule.

• **Type of Tour:** Unguided
• **Duration:** 8 to 10 hours
• **Physical Demand:** Moderate (includes some light hiking)

• **Route:**
This trip must begin from Interlaken. Our suggested route includes a train ride, a cable-car ride, and two short hikes. The recommended start time is 8 a.m. You can expect to be back in the city by 6 p.m. This tour is best enjoyed between the months of June and October, but it is available year round.

Tips
– If you're on a tight budget, you can pack your own lunch.
– During the winter months, check trail conditions at the tourist information center.

① 가이드가 동행한다.
② 일부 구간에 험한 등반을 포함한다.
③ 투어 출발지는 인터라켄이다.
④ 6월에서 10월 사이에만 진행된다.
⑤ 참가자는 점심 도시락을 반드시 지참해야 한다.

29 다음 글의 밑줄 친 부분 중, 어법상 틀린 것은? [3점]

Rotavirus is a virus ① that infects the stomach and bowels. It is equally common in both developed and developing countries, and is the most frequent cause of severe diarrhea among infants and children around the world. Children between the ages of six and twenty-four months have the highest risk of catching ② it, and recurring infections with different viral strains are possible. While adults also contract the virus, their symptoms are usually milder than ③ those of children. The time period from when you are infected with the virus to when symptoms start appearing is around 48 hours. Fever, vomiting, and watery diarrhea ④ are the most common symptoms. To prevent rotavirus infection, frequent hand washing is advised. ⑤ Infecting children should stay home from school or their day-care center until their diarrhea has ended.

30 다음 글의 밑줄 친 부분 중, 문맥상 낱말의 쓰임이 적절하지 않은 것은?

A website should be pleasing to the eye. To create a pleasant ① appearance that attracts users, web designers use graphic tools such as animation, flashing text and icons, scrolling images, and video clips. Still, color remains one of the most ② effective web design tools. A website is considered most ③ attractive when its color scheme is well balanced and consistent. The colors of the website must ④ complement each other well. They also need to go well with the website theme. For example, while the website of a cancer support group may use pastel or subtle colors because of its ⑤ sensible subject matter, the website of a party supply store is likely to use bright colors to create a feeling of excitement.

[31~34] 다음 빈칸에 들어갈 말로 가장 적절한 것을 고르시오.

31

When negotiating the price of a product, smart salespeople will often go back and forth until they feel the customer has reached the maximum price he or she is willing to pay. At this point, they are likely to express that they too have reached their limit. "I'd like to bring the price down further," they might say, "but my manager won't let me sell it for any cheaper than this." After allowing the customer to consider this information, they will then take a deep breath and say, "All right, how about this? I'll bring my price down by $100 if you just pay $25 more." Experienced salespeople know that customers are likely to accept such an offer of mutual _____. This is because the customer feels an obligation to respond in kind to the sacrifice that the salesperson is willing to make.

① effort
② respect
③ distrust
④ protection
⑤ concession

32

Though there are several things needed for a photographer, one of the most important things he or she must learn is to see things _____. For example, when trying to take a perfect landscape photo at a lake, the photographer might find the reflection on the water's surface more interesting. Or when creating a portrait, he or she might select an unusual background or catch the subject in a natural posture. Instead of framing the picture in the usual horizontal or vertical fashion, the photographer might take a different angle for a more dramatic effect. He or she might look beyond the subject in focus and discover an abstract work of art.

① by the book
② in perfect focus
③ in the right light
④ as they really are
⑤ from a different point of view

33

Food does more than fill our stomachs. It also satisfies feeling. So you may look for steak or pizza when you're happy. Same goes for ice cream and chocolates when you're sad. This kind of eating in response to our feelings instead of our hunger is known as "emotional eating." Some doctors estimate that 75% of overeating is caused by emotional eating. Such feelings as depression, loneliness, anger, anxiety, frustration, stress, poor self-esteem, and problems with personal relationships are all triggers which can lead to emotional eating. However, turning to food each time we face a problem can become _____ that hinders us from acquiring the skills we need to deal with life's problems. We know that we are harming ourselves by excessive overeating, but we continue anyway because we are unhappy with ourselves or the people around us. [3점]

① an especially positive trigger
② a highly self-destructive habit
③ a good way of relieving stress
④ a good reason to build self-esteem
⑤ a big financial burden on ourselves

34

The term "red herring" comes from an old hunting tradition. A herring is a fish that was often used by hunters when they trained young hunting dogs to follow a hunted animal's scent. The hunters would test the dogs by dragging the smelly fish across their path to see if it would distract them. Today, we most often use the term in discussions about literature or debates. In fiction, a red herring can be an event or a character that appears important but is really just used by the author to trick the reader. In debates, a red herring is an argument that takes the audience's focus away from the actual topic of debate. Although the definition of a red herring has changed from real to abstract, it still refers to something that diverts someone's attention by _____. [3점]

① pointing out a critical error
② suggesting a dangerous threat
③ explaining the situation in detail
④ introducing an irrelevant element
⑤ providing information that is false

35 다음 글에서 전체 흐름과 관계 <u>없는</u> 문장은?

We tend to assume that we are safest from harm when we are in our homes, but sadly this is not always the case. ① Potentially more difficult to detect and get rid of, the toxic materials from which your home is constructed can negatively affect your health. ② For example, paints produced in the U.S. prior to 1978 may contain lead, which causes learning disabilities and brain damage in children. ③ Also, the construction materials of the time were generally of low quality, so houses made from these materials are at risk of collapse. ④ But even modern lead-free paints are not entirely safe, as many give off gases known as volatile organic compounds (VOCs). ⑤ When VOCs are inhaled, they build up in the body and can lead to breathing trouble or, in some cases, problems with the immune system.

*volatile organic compound: 휘발성 유기 화합물

[36~37] 주어진 글 다음에 이어질 글의 순서로 가장 적절한 것을 고르시오.

36

In your savings account, your money grows exponentially. That is, your initial deposit earns interest, and later that interest earns its own interest, and so on as the amount of your savings increases.

(A) Consequently, whenever vital resources such as food or water become depleted, the population's exponential growth will cease, and it will either stabilize or begin to decline due to disease and starvation.

(B) However, while your money can continue to accumulate indefinitely, a population does not have this luxury. The growth of all populations, whether they're made up of humans, animals, or plants, is limited by the availability of resources in the environment.

(C) Likewise, population growth occurs in an exponential fashion, as newly born members eventually grow up, reproduce, and create more population members, who in turn reproduce and give birth to yet more.

① (A) – (C) – (B)　　② (B) – (A) – (C)
③ (B) – (C) – (A)　　④ (C) – (A) – (B)
⑤ (C) – (B) – (A)

37

Early humans thought that sickness and disease were caused by supernatural forces. But the ancient Greek physician Hippocrates had a different idea; he believed that they were caused by a person's environment.

(A) More specifically, he felt that there was "bad air" in certain places and that this was what caused people to fall ill. His ideas eventually became known as the miasma theory of disease, and they were accepted across much of the ancient world.

(B) People continued to believe that they were the cause of most diseases, such as cholera and malaria, up until the middle of the 19th century. At that time, the use of microscopes helped scientists realize that most diseases are actually caused by microscopic organisms.

(C) Although this theory wasn't exactly correct, it did help move ancient medical science in the right direction. Miasmas were thought to be poisonous substances that rose up out of things like rotting plants or corpses, making the air toxic. [3점]

*miasma: 미아즈마(나쁜 공기)

① (A) – (C) – (B)　　② (B) – (A) – (C)
③ (B) – (C) – (A)　　④ (C) – (A) – (B)
⑤ (C) – (B) – (A)

[38~39] 글의 흐름으로 보아, 주어진 문장이 들어가기에 가장 적절한 곳을 고르시오.

38

> Perhaps the most important of these is the setting in which it occurs.

Why do so many people enjoy watching horror movies when the explicit purpose of these films is to terrify us? (①) While it is true that being scared in real life is not a pleasant experience, the act of watching a horror movie is different in several important ways. (②) For most of us, movie theaters are familiar places, and we know what to expect when we go there. (③) We pay money to enter the theater and watch a particular film, and we are surrounded by like-minded people as we see the horrific scenes unfold. (④) This safe environment offsets the fright generated by the content on the screen. (⑤) As a result, there is enough terror to exhilarate us, but not enough to produce a real-life fear response.

39

> Obstacle thinking, on the other hand, focuses on the risks of undertaking new ventures.

There are two types of thought patterns that a person can adopt. One is called "opportunity thinking," and the other "obstacle thinking." Opportunity thinking means focusing on the opportunities and exciting possibilities that a situation presents. (①) It is associated with optimism. (②) Many famous leaders, artists, and inventors from history seem to have possessed this sort of thought pattern. (③) Their belief in positive future experiences encouraged them to try out new ideas and undertake new challenges. (④) This thought pattern is associated with pessimism. (⑤) It is a way of thinking that tries to avoid risks in favor of more secure actions, often with much smaller benefits. [3점]

40

다음 글의 내용을 한 문장으로 요약하고자 한다. 빈칸 (A), (B)에 들어갈 말로 가장 적절한 것은?

The timber wolf makes a vital contribution to the food chain. Like other large carnivores, it has an important role in the way populations of smaller animals are maintained. Even as a deer killer, it operates more helpfully than its rival predator, the human. While the human hunter often kills for sport and pride, regularly shooting the finest member of the deer herd, the wolf kills for food alone, picking off the weakest, the oldest, and the sickliest. Thus, humans damage the quality of the herd, but the wolf preserves the health of the herd and keeps its numbers geared to sustaining the land. The result is good for the herd, good for the wolf, and good for the browsing area.

*timber wolf: 얼룩 이리

↓

The timber wolf ___(A)___ the population of its prey by killing them ___(B)___, preserving the health of the herd.

	(A)		(B)
①	stabilizes	······	randomly
②	diminishes	······	brutally
③	balances	······	selectively
④	sustains	······	mercifully
⑤	doubles	······	distinctively

Think about how you reacted the last time you failed at something or made a mistake. It is likely that you were hard on yourself, since most people are. There is a belief that judging ourselves harshly is a positive quality. People feel that it shows they are (a) ambitious and trying to do their best. However, research suggests that this kind of self-criticism can be damaging. It makes us unhappy, (b) raises our stress levels, and causes us to stop setting challenging goals.

Rather than being self-critical, we should practice self-compassion. This involves finding ways to generously forgive our own mistakes and making an effort to protect our long-term mental and emotional health. Self-compassion might sound similar to self-esteem, but it is not. Self-esteem is related to how positively we feel about ourselves, which unfortunately means that it can cause us to become overly competitive and less able to deal with failure. This is because high self-esteem depends on being (c) successful and feeling that other people like us. Self-esteem can be (d) fragile, and the fear of losing it makes some people aggressive and unkind to the people around them.

Self-compassion, on the other hand, allows us to recognize that we are imperfect. It also makes it easier for us to pay close attention to the feelings of others. As a result, when we make mistakes or face failure, we can both (e) blame ourselves and avoid hurting the people we care about.

41 윗글의 제목으로 가장 적절한 것은?

① Become Healthier Through Self-Compassion
② Criticize Yourself Rather Than Other People
③ Raise Your Self-Esteem by Being Less Critical
④ Self-Criticism: An Essential Part of Development
⑤ Being Compassionate Can Hurt Our Loved Ones

42 밑줄 친 (a)~(e) 중에서 문맥상 낱말의 쓰임이 적절하지 않은 것은? [3점]

① (a)　　② (b)　　③ (c)　　④ (d)　　⑤ (e)

(A)

Languages are constantly evolving, which can make it difficult for modern readers to understand literature from the distant past. Fortunately, the work of two of our greatest writers, William Shakespeare and Miguel de Cervantes, is still understandable today. There have been many changes to grammar and vocabulary in the centuries since they died, but not enough to make their writing inaccessible. Interestingly, many of these changes were influenced by the authors themselves.

(B)

Unlike Shakespeare, Cervantes isn't known for his contributions to the vocabulary of his language. He, of course, wrote in Spanish and is credited with causing numerous sayings to become a common part of the language. Some of these have even been adopted by other languages, such as "the sky's the limit" and "bigger fish to fry," both of which are English translations of phrases used by Cervantes. He also contributed the adjective "quixotic" to the English language. Taken from the title of his masterpiece *Don Quixote*, it is used to mean "impractical and unrealistic."

(C)

For these reasons, Spanish is often referred to as the language of Cervantes, due to (a) his powerful and long-lasting influence nowadays. In the same way, English can be called the language of Shakespeare. (b) His native language has changed more over time than that of Cervantes, but it is still recognizable as the language (c) he wrote in more than 400 years ago. Without the influence of these two master writers of the 16th century, modern English and modern Spanish would not be the same languages they are today.

(D)

Shakespeare, for example, created many changes in the English language through (d) his unconventional use of words, such as using nouns as adjectives or verbs. Most importantly, Shakespeare is believed to have added about 1,000 new words to the English language. These include the adverbial phrase "full circle" and the color "hazel." (e) He also helped popularize the use of the prefix "un-" to mean "not."

*prefix: 접두사(단어 앞에 붙는 글자)

43 주어진 글 (A)에 이어질 내용을 순서에 맞게 배열한 것으로 가장 적절한 것은?

① (B) – (D) – (C) ② (C) – (B) – (D)
③ (C) – (D) – (B) ④ (D) – (B) – (C)
⑤ (D) – (C) – (B)

44 밑줄 친 (a)~(e) 중에서 가리키는 대상이 나머지 넷과 다른 것은?

① (a) ② (b) ③ (c) ④ (d) ⑤ (e)

45 윗글의 내용으로 일치하지 않는 것은?

① Shakespeare와 Cervantes의 작품은 오늘날까지 이해 가능하다.
② Cervantes는 스페인어로 글을 썼다.
③ Cervantes가 만든 구절은 스페인어로만 사용된다.
④ 영어는 Shakespeare의 언어라고 칭할 수 있다.
⑤ Shakespeare는 영어에 1,000여 개의 새로운 단어를 추가했다.

* 3점 문항에만 점수가 표시되어 있습니다.
 점수 표시가 없는 문항은 모두 2점씩입니다.

18 다음 글의 목적으로 가장 적절한 것은?

Dear Mr. Garland,

We've been tenants of your apartment for nearly 18 months. Our two-year lease is ending soon, and we've been discussing whether or not to renew. We really like the apartment, and the neighbors are great. Unfortunately, there are several improvements to the property that were promised in the lease but have not yet been made. Specifically, we were promised that you would replace the kitchen windows, paint the bathroom walls, and fix the broken ceiling fan. I'm afraid we won't be renewing our lease unless these improvements are made in the next two months. However, if they are, we will happily sign another two-year lease. I believe we've been excellent tenants, so I hope you will be able to do this for us.

Sincerely,
Lisa Schmitt

① 임대 계약 조건에 대한 변경을 요청하려고
② 계약 시 약속했던 조건 이행을 촉구하려고
③ 집주인의 호의에 대해 고마움을 표현하려고
④ 계약 연장을 하지 않는 이유에 대해 설명하려고
⑤ 집안 시설을 파손시킨 것에 대해 집주인에게 알리려고

19 다음 글에 드러난 Robert의 심경으로 가장 적절한 것은?

Robert was new at his company. On his first day, he kept working after everyone else went home. It was a dark winter evening. The wind was blowing strongly. Robert decided he would only stay a few minutes longer. But at that moment, a strange sound came from somewhere. He stood up and listened more carefully. It seemed to have stopped, so he tried to get back to work. But then he heard it again — the sound of slow, heavy footsteps coming closer. Robert looked out into the hallway, but no one was there. The footsteps were moving again. It sounded like they were on the roof! Suddenly, they stopped, and Robert heard a low, unnatural laugh above him. He rushed out of the office screaming and never looked back.

① relieved but bored
② panicked and terrified
③ hopeless and depressed
④ exhausted but delighted
⑤ regretful and sorrowful

20 다음 글에서 필자가 주장하는 바로 가장 적절한 것은?

Research shows that arts education is closely linked to a number of desirable outcomes in students, including academic achievement, social development, and participation in community activities. But there is another reason we should support teaching the arts in schools — personal development. Arts education encourages creativity, self-confidence, and critical thinking in students. According to a report, this is due to the fact that the arts help kids connect to the world around them and see things in new ways. There are many different kinds of arts-related activities we should be providing to young learners, from playing classical music to toddlers to taking kids to an art museum. It is important for schools to supply these kinds of experiences, as children from low-income homes tend to have little exposure to the arts.

① 저소득층 학생들의 문화 생활을 지원해야 한다.
② 다양한 예술 활동을 통해 창의성을 길러야 한다.
③ 학생 개인의 발달을 위해 예술 교육이 필요하다.
④ 예술과 다른 교과목의 통합 수업을 시행해야 한다.
⑤ 가정에서 예술을 접할 수 있는 환경을 조성해야 한다.

21 밑줄 친 the ultimate prison wall이 다음 글에서 의미하는 바로 가장 적절한 것은? [3점]

The exact location of an event horizon, which is the outer boundary of a black hole, is related to something called escape velocity. This is the speed that an object would need to reach to break free of the black hole's powerful gravitational pull. The closer an object gets to the black hole itself, the greater the speed it would have to achieve. The event horizon marks the point where an object would need to exceed the speed of light in order to escape. This is important because Einstein's theory of special relativity states that nothing can travel through space faster than the speed of light.

Therefore, unless Einstein's theory is incorrect, anything that crosses the event horizon will end up being swallowed by the black hole. For this reason, one astronomer has referred to the event horizon as the ultimate prison wall.

*escape velocity: 탈출 속도

① a method of protecting people
② a device that makes things visible
③ a line that cannot be crossed twice
④ an entrance that gradually opens up
⑤ a place for observing dangerous things

22 다음 글의 요지로 가장 적절한 것은?

Without science, the world we live in today would not be possible. It has led to cures for terrible diseases, sent humans to the moon, and allows us to communicate with one another instantly from anywhere in the world. Because of this, when the results of the latest scientific research are announced on the news, we feel obliged to blindly accept them as facts. But it's important to realize that true scientific progress is an extremely slow process that takes place over an extended period of time. Often in this process mistakes are made, only to be corrected at a later date by improved methodology. The findings you hear about on the news are just as likely to be missteps as breakthroughs. So while science is no doubt a wonderful thing, it's always wise to approach it with skepticism.

① 과학 연구의 성과들을 널리 알려야 한다.
② 과학 기술의 실용화를 적극 추진해야 한다.
③ 과학 분야에 더 많은 재정적인 지원이 필요하다.
④ 새로운 과학 연구 결과를 무조건 믿어서는 안 된다.
⑤ 장기적인 과학 인재 육성 프로그램을 실시해야 한다.

23 다음 글의 주제로 가장 적절한 것은? [3점]

It's easy to think of all insects as harmful pests; after all, we spend millions of dollars annually in efforts to get rid of them. But not all bugs are the same, and many are actually quite helpful. One essential process that would not occur without insects is pollination. Bees and other insects travel from plant to plant, allowing not only flowers to reproduce, but also the crops we depend on for food. And insects that eat plants are necessary as well, as they keep certain forms of vegetation from growing unchecked and upsetting the balance of the ecosystem. Insects have a similar effect on animals, spreading diseases that keep wildlife populations at sustainable levels. And once these animals die, there are other insects that dispose of their bodies, helping convert them into nutrients that will allow plants to grow.

① positive effects of insects
② a more effective pesticide
③ using insects to grow crops
④ how insects upset the ecosystem
⑤ different diseases spread by insects

24 다음 글의 제목으로 가장 적절한 것은?

Ecotourism is meant to provide tourists with information about the natural environment of their travel destination and to give them opportunities to help protect it. But some forms of ecotourism may not have these desired effects. In fact, many environmentalists feel that this definition is being applied to activities that can actually negatively impact the environment. Deep-sea fishing excursions are one example. Such trips are often advertised as "ecotourism" because they give tourists intimate access to the marine environment. And trip coordinators argue that the catch-and-release policy employed during deep-sea fishing trips ensures that no wildlife is harmed. However, opponents point to the fact that fishing boats use fuel that pollutes both the air and the water. Furthermore, even if fish are released after they are caught, a substantial number of them subsequently die due to stress and physical injury.

① Why Is Ecotourism Becoming Popular?
② Ecotourism Activities on the Open Ocean
③ Ecotourism: Really Good for the Environment?
④ Ecotourism and Its Effects on the Fishing Industry
⑤ How Ecotourism Is Helping to Preserve Marine Life

25 다음 도표의 내용과 일치하지 <u>않는</u> 것은?

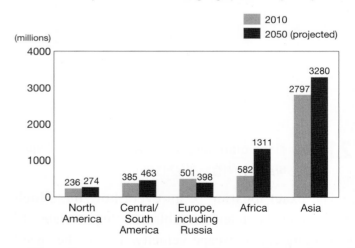

Population of Working Age(15 to 64 years)

The above graph shows the total number of working-age people in five different continents in the year 2010, as well as the projected number of working-age people in 2050. ① With the exception of Europe, all of the continents shown on the graph are projected to experience an increase in their working-age populations in 2050. ② In Central and South America, a rise of approximately 78 million people is expected. ③ Asia was home to the largest working-age population in 2010, with more than 10 times as many people as there were in North America, and this situation is projected to remain unchanged in 2050. ④ In Europe's case, its working-age population was larger than North America's in 2010, but it is expected to be smaller than North America's by 2050. ⑤ The second-largest working-age population in 2050 is expected to be found in Africa, as it was in 2010.

26 감기에 관한 다음 글의 내용과 일치하지 <u>않는</u> 것은?

People catch a cold between two and five times a year on average. Finding a cure for the common cold will be difficult. A cold can be caused by any one of two hundred different viruses. Therefore, developing a cure would literally mean finding hundreds of vaccines. Moreover, some cold viruses can change their molecular appearance. Thus, even though we may become immune to a certain cold virus this year, by next year our antibodies will probably not recognize it. Another problem is that the cold virus itself does not cause symptoms — by the time we exhibit symptoms, the viral infection is nearly over. In reality, the symptoms that we get from a cold are produced by our body's immune response, not by the virus itself.

*antibody: 항체

① 약 200종의 바이러스에 의해 발생한다.
② 완벽한 치료법을 개발하기는 어렵다.
③ 자신의 분자 형태를 변화시키는 바이러스도 있다.
④ 바이러스 감염이 시작되면 증상이 나타난다.
⑤ 증상은 신체 면역 반응과 관계가 있다.

27 Special Online Voucher에 관한 다음 안내문의 내용과 일치하는 것은?

Special Online Voucher
Hong Kong Kitchen

Weekend Dinner Buffet
– Normal price: $16 per person
– Online discount: 25% off
– You pay: $12
Click <u>HERE</u> to purchase this voucher.

Description – Save 25% off on the Hong Kong Kitchen's popular weekend buffet, served from 6 p.m. to 10 p.m. on Fridays and Saturdays. Reservations for the buffet must be made 24 hours in advance.

How to use this coupon – You must download this coupon, print it out, and bring it to the restaurant. This coupon cannot be exchanged, canceled, or refunded.

① 뷔페의 할인된 가격은 일 인당 16달러이다.
② 뷔페는 금요일부터 일요일까지 이용할 수 있다.
③ 뷔페는 당일 예약이 가능하다.
④ 쿠폰은 반드시 출력해서 가져와야 한다.
⑤ 쿠폰은 환불받을 수 있다.

28 Arkansas University Library에 관한 다음 안내문의 내용과 일치하지 <u>않는</u> 것은?

Arkansas University Library
– Student Information

Checking Out Books at the Library

- Your student ID card acts as a library card. Therefore, all students enrolled at the university are able to check out books and other materials.
- Books may be checked out for two weeks at a time. However, books can be renewed online for an additional week. A book can be renewed twice before it must be returned.
- The fine for late books is $1 per day. Students with unreturned books may not check out any other books.

Library Hours

	Main Library	Computer Lab	Study Rooms
Weekdays	7 a.m. to 11 p.m.	9 a.m. to 9 p.m.	7 a.m. to 10 p.m.
Weekends	10 a.m. to 10 p.m.	10 a.m. to 8 p.m.	10 a.m. to 10 p.m.

① 학생증으로 도서 및 자료 대출이 가능하다.
② 기본 대출 기간은 2주이다.
③ 책은 최대 6주까지 대출이 가능하다.
④ 대출 기간을 넘기면 하루에 연체료 1달러가 부과된다.
⑤ 컴퓨터실은 주중에 저녁 9시까지 개방한다.

29 다음 글의 밑줄 친 부분 중, 어법상 <u>틀린</u> 것은?

While fats have recently acquired a bad image, one should not forget how essential they are. Fats provide the body with the best means of storing energy, and they are a ① <u>far</u> more efficient energy source than either carbohydrates or proteins. They act as protection against cold and as cushioning for the internal organs, and they make the body ② <u>operate</u> more smoothly. Also, they maintain the health of skin and hair, and keep cells functioning properly. Without fats, there ③ <u>would have been</u> no way to utilize several important vitamins that require fat in order to ④ <u>be absorbed</u> into the body. Furthermore, some fats contain fatty acids that provide necessary growth factors, strengthen the immune system, and ⑤ <u>help</u> with the digestion of other foods.

*fatty acid: 지방산

30 (A), (B), (C)의 각 네모 안에서 문맥에 맞는 낱말로 가장 적절한 것은?

Newton's laws of motion can be illustrated by kicking a soccer ball. The force of the player's kick gives moving energy to the ball. This energy (A) overpowers / strengthens the tendency to resist movement, and the ball sets off into the air. But it does not travel in a straight line for long, as two forces affect its path. The first is gravity, pulling it down. This force (B) accelerates / decelerates the ball's ascent, eventually causing it to descend. Although gravity has no effect on the horizontal motion of the ball, the second force, air resistance, does. As the ball moves through the air, it must push through air molecules. This (C) increases / slows its horizontal motion. The end result of these two forces is that the ball moves in a curve.

	(A)	(B)	(C)
①	overpowers	accelerates	increases
②	overpowers	decelerates	slows
③	overpowers	decelerates	increases
④	strengthens	accelerates	slows
⑤	strengthens	decelerates	increases

31

Writers must be economical with words. Working with limited space, they rely on language that squeezes as much meaning as possible into each sentence. One linguistic tool that writers often use is the _____. Usually, this involves adding a special "noun" suffix, such as -ion, -ence, -ship, -ness, -ity, or -ment. For example, consider the following sentence: Because more and more people are migrating from rural regions to cities, many urban areas have become overdeveloped. This sentence could be economized by changing "migrating" and "overdeveloped" into nouns, expressing the same meaning in fewer words: Increasing migration from rural regions to cities has led to urban overdevelopment.

① addition of descriptive words
② elimination of unnecessary words
③ use of nouns, adjectives, and verbs
④ creation of nouns from other words
⑤ substitution of active verbs for passive ones

32

In his 1901 book, *The Psychopathology of Everyday Life*, Sigmund Freud discussed what he called "Freudian slips." According to Freud, Freudian slips are _____. Here's an example. A young woman goes for a job interview and immediately notices that the interviewer has a huge bandage on his nose. Because she needs to leave a favorable impression, she promises herself not to mention it for fear of upsetting him. At that moment, she sees a rose in a vase on his desk and decides to make a remark about the rose to break the ice. She looks at him and says, "Oh, my, what a nice nose. Where did you get it?"

*psychopathology: 정신 병리학

① verbal errors that people make regularly
② dreams that reflect the subconscious mind
③ nervousness experienced in public situations
④ psychological studies that analyze consciousness
⑤ mistakes that reveal thoughts we would prefer to keep to ourselves

33

Margaret Fuller, the 19th century writer, was respected for her great learning, but she had to endure severe headaches and eyestrain. Louisa May Alcott suffered depression and anxiety despite the fact that she, unlike the majority of 19th century American writers, could support herself with money earned from her most famous novel, *Little Women*. Another well-known female writer of that period, Harriet Beecher Stowe, suffered a similar fate. Although her novel *Uncle Tom's Cabin* was an international success, Stowe's life was haunted by mysterious sicknesses. In order to survive as female authors in a hostile environment, they needed to conquer many barriers. But, on top of that, it seems a number of the most famous 19th century female authors also had to _____. [3점]

① have various life experiences
② suffer from economic difficulties
③ wait a long time to achieve success
④ fight against discrimination against women
⑤ overcome both physical and emotional problems

34

Most people think of bacteria as something to be feared and avoided. However, there are actually bacteria living inside our digestive systems, as well as on the surface of our skin. This may sound like a disturbing problem, but the truth is that we have _____. Our bodies provide the bacteria with nutrients to consume and a place to live; in return, we receive a number of different benefits. If dangerous microbes attempt to make their home on our skin, the bacteria living there will attack and drive them away. Inside our bodies, it is bacteria that allow us to digest certain foods. They also produce vitamins and other essential compounds, and they help our immune systems develop properly and stay healthy. [3점]

① bacteria living on our skin and food
② a biological need to make bacteria go away
③ a mutualistic relationship with these bacteria
④ a method of converting bacteria into nutrients
⑤ natural defenses to stop bacteria from harming us

35 다음 글에서 전체 흐름과 관계 없는 문장은?

Desertification is an environmental issue affecting many regions around the world. It is currently occurring in more than 100 countries and threatens an estimated 900 million people, many of whom are poor and live in rural areas. ① As once-fertile soil dries up and blows away, crops die in the fields and farm animals begin to starve. ② Then, food supplies dwindle and the land falls into ruin, forcing people to leave their homes and head to the nearest cities to start new lives. ③ These migrations into cities leave the elderly in the rural areas without the support they need. ④ However, in these cities, they may be forced to live in dirty, overcrowded conditions. ⑤ If the rate of desertification is not slowed, it could result in massive droughts and famines, which would then lead to serious refugee crises as people flee the affected areas.

[36~37] 주어진 글 다음에 이어질 글의 순서로 가장 적절한 것을 고르시오.

36

Using materials that are easy to obtain, you can perform an experiment that demonstrates the principle of buoyancy, which is the upward force that causes an object in liquid to either sink or float.

(A) This occurs because the artificial sweeteners in diet soda are more concentrated than the sugar in regular soda. Consequently, the diet soda's average density is less than that of the regular soda. It experiences greater buoyancy, so it floats.

(B) To begin the experiment, acquire a can of regular soda and a can of diet soda and place them both in a sink filled with water. Now watch what happens to the two cans.

(C) Even though both are the same size and contain the same amount of liquid, you'll see the can of diet soda float, while the can of regular soda sinks.

① (A) – (B) – (C)   ② (A) – (C) – (B)
③ (B) – (A) – (C)   ④ (B) – (C) – (A)
⑤ (C) – (B) – (A)

37

Which do you think is more dangerous, being a police officer or being a logger? Based on what we are shown in movies and on the news, we're likely to conclude that the answer is being a police officer.

(A) But it can also cause us to come to incorrect conclusions, since the information that we can recall most easily isn't necessarily the information we require. This suggests that we should make our decisions more deliberately.

(B) It is a kind of mental shortcut that involves using whatever information comes to mind quickly and easily. In certain scenarios, it makes sense to do this, such as when we are in danger and need to make a decision immediately.

(C) However, this can be shown to be statistically incorrect, as loggers are actually more likely to die on the job than police officers are. One reason we make mistakes like this is because of something called the "availability heuristic." [3점]

*availability heuristic: 가용성 추단법

① (A) – (C) – (B)
② (B) – (A) – (C)
③ (B) – (C) – (A)
④ (C) – (A) – (B)
⑤ (C) – (B) – (A)

[38~39] 글의 흐름으로 보아, 주어진 문장이 들어가기에 가장 적절한 곳을 고르시오.

38

It also explains why most English speakers struggle with the vowel sounds used in French.

Studies have shown that an infant's first year is a crucial period in the acquisition of language. (①) From birth, children have the ability to distinguish between nearly all of the sounds used in the world's languages. (②) However, over the course of their first year, as they listen to the way the people around them use language to communicate, they begin to focus only on the sounds used in their native language. (③) Eventually, they begin to ignore the differences in sounds that are not part of their own language. (④) This is the reason that Japanese people of all ages tend to have trouble with the R and L sounds commonly used in English. (⑤) Due to their focus on their native language as infants, they can no longer hear any difference in these sounds. [3점]

39

Instead, coaches and players have learned how to use gaps in the rules to gain a competitive advantage.

Dr. James Frey, a professor of sports and recreation, came up with the term "normative cheating" to refer to commonly used methods of cheating in sports today. (①) This refers to strategies used to create an advantage over an opponent. (②) These strategies do not actually break the rules. (③) In baseball, for example, home teams often arrange their fields to play to their strengths and minimize the strengths of their opponents. (④) If facing a fast rival, a home team will spread water or sand between bases to slow down the runners of the other team. (⑤) And some even use psychological tricks to gain an advantage; for example, the opponent's locker room may be painted pink because this color is said to reduce strength and make people less aggressive.

40 다음 글의 내용을 한 문장으로 요약하고자 한다. 빈칸 (A), (B)에 들어갈 말로 가장 적절한 것은?

Because there are many different types of student portfolios, describing a typical portfolio is a challenge. Actually, a strong portfolio does not just show all of a student's work over a certain period of time. Instead, portfolios contain only a small portion of the student's work, and this portion of work should be carefully chosen to convey a specific idea about the student. Some portfolios, for example, seek to show how a student's skills have progressed. For these portfolios, students will need to include samples of early and later work along with a comment they've written assessing their own growth. However, to show a student's fine skills and display the best works, a portfolio should include a number of samples that clearly convey the level and range of the student's skills. Thus, before any decisions about a portfolio can be made, it is important to consider the object of the portfolio.

↓

When choosing what to _____(A)_____ in a student portfolio, its _____(B)_____ must be taken into consideration.

	(A)		(B)
①	assess	……	sample
②	examine	……	quality
③	preclude	……	objectivity
④	include	……	purpose
⑤	excuse	……	convention

[41~42] 다음 글을 읽고, 물음에 답하시오.

Although social attitudes toward the concept of property ownership may seem to be based on established laws, a new study suggests that they might actually stem from fundamental (a) intuition. In an experiment, children as young as three years old were observed in order to see how they dealt with the concept of private property before being exposed to social regulations.

Previous studies had shown that, unless presented with compelling reasons to believe otherwise, young children generally accepted the idea that the first person to (b) possess an object could be considered its rightful owner. What this new study sought to establish was whether or not "creative labor" would be considered a (c) compelling enough reason to transfer ownership of an object.

The test subjects were each given a specific type of clay animals, such as blue dogs or red cats. They then borrowed these animals from each other and made changes to them. In some cases, they (d) transformed them into something entirely new; in others, they simply made small alterations such as cutting off an ear or adding a tail. The researchers were curious to see what effect these two levels of creative labor would have.

What they found was that the children accepted that ownership of property was transferred in cases where a (e) considerate effort was made. It was clear that, when it came to ownership, transforming the animal into a completely different one was considered to be a more important act than simply adding or removing a part. The conclusion of the researchers was that, although creativity mattered, work was considered the most important factor in the transfer of ownership rights.

41 윗글의 제목으로 가장 적절한 것은?

① Teaching Kids to Share
② What Creates Ownership?
③ Creativity: The Greatest Skill
④ Making Labor Fun for Everyone
⑤ The Problem of Private Property

42 밑줄 친 (a)~(e) 중에서 문맥상 낱말의 쓰임이 적절하지 않은 것은? [3점]

① (a)　　② (b)　　③ (c)　　④ (d)　　⑤ (e)

[43~45] 다음 글을 읽고, 물음에 답하시오.

(A)

In 1934, during the dark times of the Great Depression, an unusually happy event was announced: the birth of the first known surviving quintuplets. What's more, the five infants were all girls and all identical, a statistical improbability with a chance of just 1 in 57 million. The babies were born prematurely and no one expected them to survive, but (a) they somehow held on and overcame the complications associated with their birth.

*quintuplets: 다섯 쌍둥이　**complication: 합병증

(B)

After nine years of this mistreatment, the girls' parents won a custody battle with the government to bring (b) them back home. The reunion, however, was not as happy as it should have been. The sisters faced resentment from their siblings and physical and emotional abuse at the hands of the parents who'd spent so much time trying to get them back. All five left home at the age of 18, renouncing their family, and went on to live unfulfilled and rather tragic lives, having no one to support (c) them but themselves.

(C)

That assumption was proved false when Quintland was quickly transformed into a tourist attraction. Three million visitors came from across the country to watch in fascination as the five identical girls played behind a one-way screen. And the exploitation didn't end there. The sisters became a money-making opportunity for everyone who came in contact with them, and (d) they were even featured in an exhibit at the Chicago World's Fair.

(D)

Unfortunately, their parents were unprepared to provide for five new children in addition to the six (e) they already had. So the government stepped in and removed the children from the parents' custody, taking them to a hospital facility designed specially for them and nicknamed Quintland. Here, under the care of Dr. Allan Dafoe, their delivering physician, it was assumed they'd lead a healthier childhood than at home.

43 주어진 글 (A)에 이어질 내용을 순서에 맞게 배열한 것으로 가장 적절한 것은?

① (B) – (D) – (C)　　② (C) – (B) – (D)
③ (C) – (D) – (B)　　④ (D) – (B) – (C)
⑤ (D) – (C) – (B)

44 밑줄 친 (a)~(e) 중에서 가리키는 대상이 나머지 넷과 다른 것은?

① (a)　　② (b)　　③ (c)　　④ (d)　　⑤ (e)

45 윗글의 다섯 쌍둥이에 관한 내용과 일치하지 않는 것은?

① 모두 일란성 여아들이었다.
② 조산에 따른 합병증을 이겨냈다.
③ 시카고 세계 박람회에 전시되었다.
④ 부모와 여섯 명의 형제자매들이 있었다.
⑤ Quintland라는 병원 시설에서 태어났다.

* 3점 문항에만 점수가 표시되어 있습니다.
  점수 표시가 없는 문항은 모두 2점씩입니다.

18 다음 글의 목적으로 가장 적절한 것은?

Dear Ms. Patel,

My company recently received the shipment of electronics we ordered on July 19. The delivery arrived on time, and all of the items were received. However, upon inspection of the items, we found that all 25 of the GL3100 smartphones included in the shipment are defective. In every case, the screen does not display properly. Because of this error on your part, I expect you to arrange for the delivery of 25 new devices to replace the current ones. Please contact me at your earliest convenience. All of our dealings with your company have been satisfactory in the past, so I hope we can continue to have a beneficial business relationship.

Sincerely yours,
Hanna Park

① 스마트폰 수리 비용을 문의하려고
② 기존 주문 내역에 수량을 추가하려고
③ 결함 있는 물품에 대한 교환을 요청하려고
④ 배송 일정이 연기된 이유에 대해 설명하려고
⑤ 주문한 물품을 모두 수령하였음을 알려주려고

19 다음 글에 드러난 Erica의 심경으로 가장 적절한 것은?

Erica couldn't believe she was really at Oxford, the school of her dreams. She had been preparing to move all summer, but none of it had felt real until she heard the airplane engines roaring. Now she was wandering the campus, staring at ancient buildings. For the first time in her life, she didn't have any friends around her. For a moment, the stone arches around her looked enormous and cold. Would the other students welcome her into their groups? Thinking about the hardships she was likely to encounter, she felt dizzy. She closed her eyes and imagined herself laughing, surrounded by new friends. When she opened them, the arches seemed to invite her to step into her new life.

① anxious and excited
② annoyed and nervous
③ humbled and touched
④ thankful and relieved
⑤ confused and frustrated

20 다음 글에서 필자가 주장하는 바로 가장 적절한 것은?

I would like to express my concern about the severe parking problem that students face at Riverdale Community College. There are several reasons why I am concerned about this problem. First of all, students miss essential instructional time while having to drive around the crowded parking lots looking for a parking space. As a result, they don't know what is going on in class, and they show up late for quizzes and tests. Another reason I am concerned is that some students become so frustrated over the limited parking that they fight over parking spaces. Other students park their cars illegally in fire zones. To resolve this problem, I suggest you build a parking garage or provide free shuttle buses from distant lots.

① 학생들은 강의에 더 성실하게 임해야 한다.
② 교내 운전자들의 질서 의식을 고취해야 한다.
③ 효율적인 교내 공간 활용을 위한 시스템이 필요하다.
④ 건전한 학내 문화를 위한 프로그램을 마련해야 한다.
⑤ 교내 주차 문제를 해결하기 위한 대책을 마련해야 한다.

21 다음 글의 요지로 가장 적절한 것은?

In Los Angeles in the late 1970s, it was discovered that a 13-year-old girl had spent her entire life locked in a small room by her father. He only entered the room to feed or beat her, and never spoke to the girl. After she was rescued by the authorities and placed in a hospital, the doctors realized that she had acquired almost no language skills at all. With proper care and treatment, her physical and mental condition improved greatly over the next few months. However, although she was soon able to understand many things that were said to her, she had severe difficulty communicating with others. She learned some words, but her progress was slow and she couldn't put together grammatically correct sentences. Even after receiving speech therapy for a number of years, she was never able to achieve a normal level of language ability.

① 언어 학습이 가능한 결정적 시기가 있다.
② 아동 학대는 정서 발달에 부정적인 영향을 미친다.
③ 언어 습득과 두뇌 발달 사이에는 밀접한 관계가 있다.
④ 부모와의 긍정적 관계가 아동의 학습 능력 향상에 기여한다.
⑤ 유년기의 다양한 경험은 지능을 향상시키는 데 도움이 된다.

[22~23] 다음 글의 주제로 가장 적절한 것을 고르시오.

22

For quite some time now, computer scientists have been seeking to develop some form of artificial intelligence, also known as AI. Initially, these efforts took a primarily logic-based approach, focusing on the formal reasoning and problem solving capabilities of computers. While this approach does have its advantages, ultimately it is inhibited by its limitations. These types of systems can only be successful in extremely narrow fields of knowledge, as it would be impossible to translate the entire range of human reasoning into computer code. They are also unable to make connections that are not based solely on logic. This ability is vital to any meaningful "intelligence." Furthermore, they function on a series of "if-then" decisions; but in real world situations, it is not always possible to recognize the factors necessary to make such a decision.

① the differences between computers and AIs
② how the first artificial intelligence was made
③ logical methods for solving abstract problems
④ why computers are not as intelligent as humans
⑤ the problems with logic-based artificial intelligence

23

In a meritocracy, individuals advance based on personal abilities and achievements rather than wealth or status. The primary benefit of meritocracies is that they give people from low-status groups hope that they may be able to improve their position in society's hierarchy. People living in a meritocracy generally believe that their society is fair and just, and that anyone who works hard enough can succeed. However, many people argue that this is mostly a myth. Even in modern meritocracies, large groups of people still face significant disadvantages due to their race, ethnicity, or gender. Unfortunately, this kind of myth can be used to protect existing economic inequalities and to prevent progressive social movements from forming. In the end, the same privileged groups retain control of a society's wealth and power. [3점]

*meritocracy: 실력[능력]주의 (사회, 국가)

① a fair method of distributing wealth
② how people can raise their social status
③ a political system that protects the weak
④ the unpleasant truth behind a social system
⑤ why meritocracies have become more common

24 다음 글의 제목으로 가장 적절한 것은?

Ancient Egyptian wall paintings show pictures of soldiers marching to war with dogs by their side. Similarly, Persian historians describe how dogs were used by the military to warn soldiers of approaching Greek invaders. Thousands of years later, during Napoleon's invasion of Europe, a dog named Moustache showed outstanding courage when an enemy soldier tried to steal the French flag. Moustache bit the soldier so hard that he ran away. During World War I, a British dog called Stubby was awarded a medal for capturing a German spy. And in World War II, at least ten thousand dogs served in the U.S. Army. They worked as guards, delivered messages, and were essential to search and rescue efforts.

① The Use of Animals as Spies
② War Pictures of Ancient Times
③ A Dog's Death in a Fierce Battle
④ The History of War and Civilization
⑤ Dogs' Contributions during Wartime

25 다음 도표의 내용과 일치하지 <u>않는</u> 것은?

Electricity Generation in Two Canadian Provinces by Source

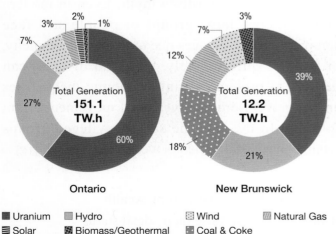

■ Uranium   ■ Hydro   ▨ Wind   ▨ Natural Gas
▤ Solar   ▨ Biomass/Geothermal   ▨ Coal & Coke

The above graphs show the amount of electricity generated in 2018 by the Canadian provinces of Ontario and New Brunswick, with the total amounts broken down by source. ① Ontario generated a total of 151.1 terawatt hours of electricity, which is an amount more than ten times greater than that generated by New Brunswick. ② The majority of Ontario's electricity came from uranium, which generated more than twice as much electricity as the number two source, which was hydro. ③ The third highest percentage of that province's electricity was generated by wind, which accounted for seven percent of its total electricity generation. ④ In New Brunswick, uranium and hydro were also the two greatest generators of electricity, but natural gas rather than wind contributed the third highest percentage. ⑤ The percentage of New Brunswick's electricity that was generated by coal and coke in 2018 was nearly as much as the percentages generated by wind and natural gas combined.

26 cuttlefish에 관한 다음 글의 내용과 일치하지 <u>않는</u> 것은?

Cuttlefish are interesting little animals. They have a smaller appearance than squid and belong to the same family as octopuses. Even though they are not thought to be the most developed of sea creatures, they are extremely intelligent. According to research, cuttlefish learn quickly, and many scientists believe that they gain much of their knowledge by watching other cuttlefish. When you look at them, it is difficult to tell who is doing the observing, you or the cuttlefish, particularly as the eyes of a cuttlefish are structurally very similar to human eyes. Cuttlefish are also very mobile and quick, possessing a small jet just below the tentacles that can shoot out water to help them move. Their most fascinating characteristic is their ability to change their body color and pattern in an instant to protect themselves. So they are sometimes referred to as the "chameleons of the sea."

*tentacle: 촉수

① 문어와 같은 과(科)에 속한다.
② 지능이 높은 해양 생물이다.
③ 눈의 구조가 인간과 유사하다.
④ 물을 내뿜으며 빠르게 움직인다.
⑤ 먹이를 유인하려고 몸의 색깔과 무늬를 바꾼다.

27 Cook Thai Food in Thailand에 관한 다음 안내문의
내용과 일치하지 <u>않는</u> 것은?

Learn to Cook Thai Food in Thailand!

Bangkok's best cooking school is now offering one-day cooking classes for foreign visitors.

Price: $30 (USD) for a four-hour class
Dishes: Six traditional Thai dishes will be taught in each class.
Convenience:
– Our modern kitchens are fully air-conditioned.
– We'll pick you up and drop you off at your hotel.
Languages: We have classes in English and Chinese.

We offer beginner, advanced, vegetarian, and private classes. All of our classes include a visit to a traditional Thai market to purchase ingredients. Please visit our website to see a full schedule of classes and reserve a place in one.

① 4시간 동안의 수업에서 6가지 요리를 배울 수 있다.
② 교통편은 요리 학교 측에서 제공한다.
③ 영어와 중국어로 요리 수업이 진행된다.
④ 채식 요리 수업을 선택할 수 있다.
⑤ 별도로 신청하면 태국 전통 시장을 방문할 수 있다.

28 Lee County Community Center Workshops에
관한 다음 안내문의 내용과 일치하는 것은?

Lee County Community Center
Fall Classes and Workshops

Category: crafts
Class: Leather Workshop
Length: 4 hours
Ages: 15 and up
Maximum class size: 18

In this workshop you will make your own unique leather pencil case. All of the materials you need are included in the cost of the class — you can even choose the color of the leather! You will learn how to cut leather, stitch it by hand, and even emboss it with your initials.

The workshop will be held on the first Saturday of each month and costs $150 per participant. You can register online at the community center's website, www.leecomm unity.org.

① 강좌당 최소 수강 인원은 18명이다.
② 수업료 외에 재료비는 별도이다.
③ 가죽의 색상은 선택할 수 없다.
④ 매달 첫 번째 토요일에 진행된다.
⑤ 커뮤니티 센터에 방문하면 등록할 수 있다.

29 다음 글의 밑줄 친 부분 중, 어법상 틀린 것은? [3점]

The penguins that inhabit the Antarctic must withstand months of sunless skies and temperatures that ① stay below freezing for the entire year. Surprisingly, though, these birds may be in more danger of overheating than ② of freezing to death. Their bodies have evolved over thousands of years in order to protect them against the frigid Antarctic weather. A penguin's feathers, for instance, form an amazingly waterproof shield around the animal's body, and beneath ③ that, a thick layer of blubber insulates it from the cold. So, just like a human ④ wearing a fluffy down coat on a hot August day, the penguin is at risk of heat exhaustion when temperatures rise. However, the species has evolved to deal with this problem as well. A penguin's bare feet are responsible for releasing heat, enabling the rest of the animal's body ⑤ remain at a constant temperature.

*blubber: 해양 동물의 지방

30 (A), (B), (C)의 각 네모 안에서 문맥에 맞는 낱말로 가장 적절한 것은?

Our senses adapt to many different conditions each day. One of the most common of these situations occurs when walking into a dark room from a bright area. For example, walking into a dark theater often makes it difficult to (A) deceive / perceive anything but darkness. However, as your eyes adjust to the darkness, you begin to see well. This change is caused by iodopsin, a chemical found in the rods and cones of the eye, which is produced in greater amounts to increase the eyes' (B) intensity / sensitivity to light. This same reaction happens in reverse when you leave the dark theater and walk out into a brightly lit room. In this situation, your eyes have (C) excess / little iodopsin, which makes the rods and cones too sensitive to light. They must bring their levels of iodopsin back down before you can see normally again.

*iodopsin: 【생화학】 요돕신 **rod: 간상체 ***cone: 추상체

	(A)		(B)		(C)
①	deceive	......	intensity	......	excess
②	deceive	......	sensitivity	......	little
③	perceive	......	intensity	......	excess
④	perceive	......	sensitivity	......	excess
⑤	perceive	......	sensitivity	......	little

[31~34] 다음 빈칸에 들어갈 말로 가장 적절한 것을 고르시오.

31

The Black Plague struck Europe in a series of outbreaks in the 13th and 14th centuries, killing more than one third of the continent's population. The epidemics brought about tremendous changes in European society, some of which were _____. Reform in the medical profession, which had mostly failed to relieve the suffering, is one example. During the plague, many doctors died or simply ran away. As a consequence, most universities lacked medical professors. People rushed into these vacancies with new ideas. In addition, ordinary people began acquiring medical texts and taking charge of their own health. Gradually, more of these texts began to appear in languages other than Latin, making medical knowledge more accessible to everyone.

① harmful
② inevitable
③ beneficial
④ reasonable
⑤ insignificant

32

More than a century ago, Henry David Thoreau went to jail to protest the Mexican War. Many people followed Thoreau's example and openly broke the law to _____.
For example, when convicted of breaking the law, the great Indian leader Gandhi served his prison sentence and went on hunger strikes instead of paying a small fine. He did this to draw attention to his cause — the independence of India from Great Britain. When highly respected people are thrown into jail for their beliefs, it often makes people reconsider the justness of the situation. When Martin Luther King Jr. went to jail to protest for racial equality, he helped many Americans realize that segregation was wrong. His example helped abolish laws that kept segregation alive.

① settle the hunger strike
② resist the colonization of India
③ raise money for political activity
④ bring public attention to injustice
⑤ justify wars that maintain security

33

Seeking to defeat the British by _____ _____, Napoleon issued the Berlin Decrees in 1806. These decrees allowed him to create an impenetrable blockade around the British isles, preventing both the import and export of any products. The initial effect was a damaging one, inflicting a great deal of hardship on the people of Britain and causing some businesses to collapse. However, by 1811, it had become clear that the strategy initiated by the Berlin Decrees had backfired on Napoleon. The economy of France was actually suffering more, deprived of its access to several key British goods. Facing revolts from both his own countrymen and his European neighbors, Napoleon was eventually forced to abandon the strategy; soon after, his armies were defeated by the British on the battlefield. [3점]

① using military force
② destroying their economy
③ executing political strategies
④ encouraging the public revolt
⑤ absorbing their cultural difference

34

If a buzzard is placed in an eight foot square cage without a ceiling, it will be trapped. This is because a buzzard only flies after running about ten feet first. Without space to run, it will not know how to fly out of its cage. Likewise, if a bumblebee is dropped into a glass, it will never be able to get out. Instead of realizing that there is an exit above it, it will keep trying to find a way out through the sides of the glass. It will persist in its futile attempts at escape until it dies. If you think about it, some people are just like buzzards and bees. They expend all of their energy uselessly struggling with their problems, never realizing that _____.
[3점]

① they should make greater efforts
② they are not as smart as they think
③ the answer is right there above them
④ they have reached the limits of their abilities
⑤ it is impossible to identify the core of their problems

35 다음 글에서 전체 흐름과 관계 <u>없는</u> 문장은?

The spotted hyenas of Africa are social animals. While living in clans of up to 90 individuals, they frequently hunt, migrate, and spend time in smaller packs. ① When packs from different clans meet, a battle for dominance may ensue. ② Of course, the larger pack is more likely to win the battle and the hyenas are aware of this fact. ③ Therefore, when confronted by an unknown pack, they immediately calculate their odds of success by counting the members of the opposing pack, using both their excellent night vision and high aural ability. ④ Furthermore, hyenas can break down nutrients from the skin and bones of animals they kill thanks to their powerful jaws and digestive tract. ⑤ If the opposing pack is larger than their own, they will attempt to retreat rather than attack.

[36~37] 주어진 글 다음에 이어질 글의 순서로 가장 적절한 것을 고르시오.

36

Many people mistakenly believe that sign language is just a loose collection of pantomime-like gestures.

(A) One indication of the great diversity in sign languages is the fact that at international conferences, it is necessary to provide sign language interpreters so that all deaf people can understand. Interestingly, a deaf signer who acquires a second sign language as an adult will actually sign with a foreign accent!

(B) There is also another misconception that there exists universal sign language. However, this is also not true. Deaf people in different countries use very different sign languages, so they need to learn new sign languages in order to communicate when they travel abroad.

(C) But in truth, sign languages are highly structured linguistic systems with all the grammatical complexity of spoken languages. Just as spoken languages have specific rules for forming words and sentences, sign languages have rules for individual signs and signed sentences.

① (A) – (B) – (C)   ② (A) – (C) – (B)
③ (B) – (C) – (A)   ④ (C) – (A) – (B)
⑤ (C) – (B) – (A)

37

In 1991, new thermometers were invented that were a vast improvement over old-fashioned mercury thermometers.

(A) It works by measuring the levels of energy being emitted by the eardrum into the ear canal. The sicker we are and the higher our body temperature, the more energy our eardrum gives off.

(B) The company that introduced these modern thermometers wanted to save time for busy hospital nurses. U.S. nurses take about a billion temperature readings each year, so the minutes wasted waiting for the mercury to rise in outdated thermometers added up to significant time loss.

(C) To free up this time, the company utilized technology developed by NASA to measure star temperatures. They came up with a heat sensor that, when placed just inside a patient's ear, can register body temperature in a matter of seconds. [3점]

① (A) – (B) – (C)   ② (B) – (A) – (C)
③ (B) – (C) – (A)   ④ (C) – (A) – (B)
⑤ (C) – (B) – (A)

38

On the other hand, a single-celled amoeba, though it is unable to do anything remarkable such as transmitting electrical impulses, is quite comfortable living apart from other cells.

There are many different types of cells, and they all have different purposes. (①) A long time ago, very simple cells lived individually. (②) As life evolved, however, more effective cells appeared, and these joined together to form advanced organisms. (③) Today, for example, one of the furthest evolved and specialized cells on earth is the human brain cell. (④) But even though brain cells have the amazing ability to send and receive the electrical signals that make our bodies function, they quickly die if removed from the brain. (⑤) As a general rule, then, simple cells are better able to survive on their own, while advanced cells can carry out intricate tasks.

39

The opposite personality type is "self-centered," which is low in all four of these traits.

In the past, psychologists identified the five main personality traits of humans: extroversion, conscientiousness, agreeableness, openness, and neuroticism. More recent research suggests that these traits often group together, creating four primary personality types. (①) The "average" personality type has medium levels of all five traits. (②) The "role model" personality type is high in extroversion, conscientiousness, agreeableness, and openness, so these people are the most pleasant to be around. (③) Finally, there is the "reserved" personality type, which is low in both openness and neuroticism. (④) The "average" personality type is the most common, but few people can be clearly placed into a single group. (⑤) Instead, most people combine aspects of all four types, with some being stronger than others. [3점]

40 다음 글의 내용을 한 문장으로 요약하고자 한다. 빈칸 (A), (B)에 들어갈 말로 가장 적절한 것은?

Personality traits such as a continual desire for perfection or the need to always be in control could be signs of obsessive-compulsive personality disorder (OCPD). People suffering from this condition rarely view themselves as dysfunctional, instead believing that the manner in which they function is proper. Every aspect of their daily lives is likely to be influenced by the strict standards they hold themselves to. Therefore, they tend to spend an excessive amount of time and energy on meaningless details, often to the point that they lose sight of their actual goals. A person with OCPD might end up spending hours on a small task, such as sending an email or proofreading a document, gripped by the need to absolutely ensure there are no mistakes. Ultimately, they end up harming their own efforts to be efficient.

↓

People suffering from OCPD are so obsessed with being ____(A)____ that they end up spending too much time on ____(B)____.

	(A)		(B)
①	competent	······	schoolwork
②	perfect	······	details
③	rigid	······	introductions
④	attractive	······	preparation
⑤	intelligent	······	exams

You might think that the number zero has always existed, but it is actually a relatively recent addition to our numerical system. In fact, it wasn't used in Europe until the 12th century. Its origins, however, began much (a) later than that. About 4,000 years ago, people used a blank space to represent the idea of zero. Then, around the third century BC, the ancient Babylonians created a symbol made up of two small triangular shapes. Although this wasn't a true zero, it was used in the same way that we now use zeros to show the (b) difference between 10 and 100.

It wasn't until the seventh century AD that zero began to be used as an actual number. An Indian mathematician named Brahmagupta started using a number with no value, which was called *sunya*. This concept eventually spread to China and then to the Middle East, where it became part of the Arabic numeral system we use today. This is when the number zero first took on its (c) familiar round form. The great Persian mathematician Muhammad ibn Musa al-Khwarizmi soon began using zero as a part of his mathematical calculations.

In the 1100s, the concept of zero finally (d) reached Europe, where it was popularized by the Italian mathematician Fibonacci. Later, zero played an important role in the work of Rene Descartes, and it was used by Sir Isaac Newton and Gottfried Leibniz in their efforts to invent calculus. Today, zero has become an indispensable part of our mathematical system, and it is used by everyone from physicists to computer programmers to (e) advance new ideas.

41 윗글의 제목으로 가장 적절한 것은?

① How Zero Got Its Round Shape
② Zero: From the Past to the Present
③ A Recent Mathematical Breakthrough
④ Controversy over the Smallest Number
⑤ Different Cultures Using Zero Differently

42 밑줄 친 (a)~(e) 중에서 문맥상 낱말의 쓰임이 적절하지 않은 것은? [3점]

① (a)　　② (b)　　③ (c)　　④ (d)　　⑤ (e)

[43~45] 다음 글을 읽고, 물음에 답하시오.

(A)

Before the construction of the Sydney Opera House, the Australian city had no proper facilities for musical performances. The Town Hall was used for orchestral concerts, and there was nowhere adequate to stage a full-scale opera. When Sir Eugene Goosens was appointed to the position of Chief Conductor of the Sydney Symphony Orchestra, he decided to make it his mission to create a performance space suitable for both classical concerts and operas.

(B)

This was not a new concept for the people of Sydney. For years and years, the government had been making promises to construct such a building as part of its reconstruction and redevelopment programs. However, despite the best efforts of Goosens, seven years passed with no action being taken. Finally, in 1954, the state government decided to stop dragging its feet and get involved with the project.

(C)

In January of 1957, Danish architect Jorn Utzon was announced as the winner of the competition. Two years later, construction began. There were a number of delays and budget problems, many of which were unfairly blamed on Utzon himself. Eventually, the government rejected his design ideas and cut off his funding. Unable to pay his workers to continue their work, Utzon had no choice but to resign in 1966. Seven years later, the Sydney Opera House was opened to the public in a grand ceremony headed by Queen Elizabeth II. Utzon, however, was not invited.

(D)

The premier at the time, a man by the name of Joseph Cahill, was highly motivated to get the project started, and quickly set about establishing a committee to organize it. Next, an international competition was announced to choose the best design for a performing arts complex in the city of Sydney. Participants were instructed to choose whichever approach to the design they felt best, and told that they need not worry about the potential costs of construction. In the end, more than 200 designs from all around the world were submitted.

43 주어진 글 (A)에 이어질 내용을 순서에 맞게 배열한 것으로 가장 적절한 것은?

① (B) – (C) – (D) ② (B) – (D) – (C)
③ (C) – (D) – (B) ④ (D) – (B) – (C)
⑤ (D) – (C) – (B)

44 윗글의 제목으로 가장 적절한 것은?

① Sydney, Australia's Musical Heritage
② One City, Two Different Opera Houses
③ How Sydney Finally Got Its Opera House
④ Jorn Utzon: Australia's Greatest Architect
⑤ The Unique Design of the Sydney Opera House

45 윗글의 Sydney Opera House에 관한 내용과 일치하지 않는 것은?

① 건립 이전에는 시(市) 청사를 공연장으로 사용했다.
② 1954년에 정부가 건립 시행 계획에 착수했다.
③ 최종 디자인이 결정된 2년 후 건설이 시작되었다.
④ 건축 담당자가 공개 행사를 이끌었다.
⑤ 세계적인 공모전을 통해 디자인을 선정했다.

* 3점 문항에만 점수가 표시되어 있습니다.
  점수 표시가 없는 문항은 모두 2점씩입니다.

18 다음 글의 목적으로 가장 적절한 것은?

To Whom It May Concern,

I am a small-business owner who frequently receives deliveries from your courier service. Last week, you delivered a package to my business. It took four days to arrive, despite the fact that the sender was promised overnight delivery. I understand that delays sometimes happen, but the package was delivered without apology or explanation. Even worse, your driver simply left it at the front door without getting a signature, as required. Your company has a good reputation, but there are many other couriers who offer the same services at competitive prices. I may feel the need to switch to one of them if you cannot assure that this type of thing will not happen again. I am awaiting your response.

Emily Greenstone
Fireside Consulting

① 배송비 할인에 대해 문의하려고
② 물품이 잘못 배송되었음을 알리려고
③ 택배 당일 배송 서비스를 예약하려고
④ 택배 회사의 무성의한 서비스에 대해 항의하려고
⑤ 배송 서비스 이용을 중단하는 이유에 대해 설명하려고

19 다음 글의 상황에 나타난 분위기로 가장 적절한 것은?

Lily Daniels was walking to the train station just as she did every morning when she noticed that something was wrong. Out of the corner of her eye, she saw smoke coming out of Mr. Johnson's house! Mr. Johnson was an elderly man in a wheelchair who lived alone. Worried, Lily dropped her bag and ran across the street. There was more smoke and the front door was too hot to touch. Looking in a window, Lily saw huge flames trapping Mr. Johnson in the kitchen. The flames were blocking the door! Quickly, she dialed 911. The operator told her to wait outside for the firefighters to arrive. But the fire was spreading fast and the man did not have much time.

① lively and festive
② tense and urgent
③ calm and peaceful
④ exciting and thrilling
⑤ gloomy and frustrating

20 다음 글에서 필자가 주장하는 바로 가장 적절한 것은?

Every year, thousands of patients die while awaiting organ transplants because there are too few people who agree to donate their organs. For this reason, there have been numerous proposals for instituting a system which encourages potential organ donors with cash payments or tax credits. This is a concept that I simply cannot support. Under no circumstances should we offer financial incentives to organ donors. The benefits of donating an organ should come from the satisfaction of saving a human life, and nothing more. To be blunt, even thinking of putting a price tag on a person's organs disgusts me. Our shortage of organ donors is an issue that must be addressed, but in a proper and ethical way.

① 장기 기증자의 건강 상태를 반드시 확인해야 한다.
② 장기 기증자를 위한 더 많은 혜택이 제공되어야 한다.
③ 생명을 살릴 수 있는 장기 기증을 적극 홍보해야 한다.
④ 장기 기증자에게 금전적인 대가를 제공해서는 안 된다.
⑤ 장기 기증을 대체할 수 있는 의학 기술이 개발되어야 한다.

21 밑줄 친 be more like fireworks exploding이 다음 글에서 의미하는 바로 가장 적절한 것은? [3점]

It's well known that people can't live without oxygen, but it's less known that too much oxygen is also dangerous. Our bodies fuel our daily activities by digesting the food we eat, which is a process that requires oxygen. Air, however, is made mostly of nitrogen. In fact, nitrogen accounts for 72% of the air, and the body uses it to slow down the digestive process. This results in a slow, controlled burn comparable to a candle burning, providing us with a steady supply of energy throughout the day. If we breathed in pure oxygen, this process would <u>be more like fireworks exploding</u>. This doesn't mean we would actually explode, but it would create interactions between chemicals in our bodies. This

could cause damage to many parts of the body, such as our eyes and lungs, and would even be dangerous to our DNA.

① cause uncontrollable chemical reactions
② produce high levels of nitrogen in the body
③ make our lungs quickly expand with oxygen
④ create a burst of energy to get rid of oxygen
⑤ defend our bodies against dangerous chemicals

22 다음 글의 요지로 가장 적절한 것은?

Computer word processing programs have spell checkers and even thesauruses to find synonyms and antonyms for highlighted words. The programs can also show recommended spellings for misspelled words. I like having a computer program that performs these functions. However, these programs do not teach a student about spelling or word meanings. A person could type in a word, get a synonym, and not have the slightest idea what either meant. Relying on this mindless way of spelling and finding synonyms, students will become completely unfamiliar with the meanings of the words they use. In fact, one of the most common misuses is to include a word that is spelled correctly but used incorrectly in the sentence.

*thesaurus: 유의어 사전

① 워드 프로그램의 활용법에 대한 교육이 필요하다.
② 워드 프로그램의 기능을 통해 철자 학습을 할 수 있다.
③ 워드 프로그램 덕분에 정확한 어휘의 사용이 가능해졌다.
④ 맞춤법 검사 기능이 포함된 워드 프로그램을 이용해야 한다.
⑤ 워드 프로그램의 기능이 학생들의 어휘력 향상에 방해가 될 수도 있다.

23 다음 글의 주제로 가장 적절한 것은? [3점]

Hydrogen gas is the primary component needed for star formation. By studying galaxies and other star-forming regions throughout the universe, though, astronomers have found that there is less and less hydrogen available to create new stars. Part of the problem is that the majority of hydrogen originally present in the universe is effectively "locked up" in stars currently in existence. When stars explode at the end of their life cycle, some of their hydrogen is released back into space, but this does not happen often enough to maintain a constant amount of available hydrogen. In addition, as the universe expands, it is getting harder and harder for galaxies to draw in hydrogen from open space through natural gravitational force. These findings support the current theory that cosmological evolution will lead to an increasingly dark and cold universe.

① the cause of the expansion of the universe
② the number of existing stars in the universe
③ the primary components that make up galaxies
④ the difficulty of predicting the life cycles of stars
⑤ the decrease in hydrogen available to form new stars

24 다음 글의 제목으로 가장 적절한 것은?

Many descriptive words may pop into your mind when you think of the skin of a frog, but chances are "miracle" and "drug" aren't among them. You'll be surprised to learn, then, that scientists recently developed a compound that mimics molecules found in frog skin and can be used to combat bacteria. A pressing need for this class of drug currently exists, as bacteria continue to develop resistance to every traditional type of antibiotic. While most antibiotics work by destroying proteins within the bacteria, thus killing them, the frog-skin-inspired compound functions very differently, simply poking thousands of holes in the bacteria until they die. Once confronted with this new method of direct attack, it's unlikely bacteria will be able to develop a resistance to it.

① Super Bacteria: A Major Threat
② A New Virus Spreads among Frogs
③ Fighting Bacteria by Copying Frog Skin
④ Are Frogs Now an Endangered Species?
⑤ How Bacteria Develop Antibiotic Resistance

25 다음 도표의 내용과 일치하지 <u>않는</u> 것은?

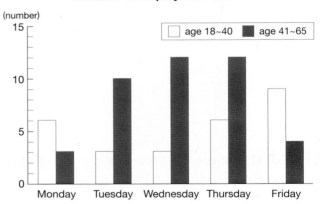

Number of Employees Absent

The above graph shows the number of employees from two age groups who were absent due to illness during a particular week. ① It can be noted immediately that younger employees were absent in higher numbers before and after the weekend. ② It was during the middle of the week that more employees from the older age group were absent. ③ On Wednesday, there were three times as many absences from the older age group as from the younger. ④ There was a total of 41 absences for the five-day period among people in the 41 to 65 age group. ⑤ Among the 18 to 40 age group, there was a much smaller total of just 27 absences.

26 woodpecker finch에 관한 다음 글의 내용과 일치하지 <u>않는</u> 것은?

Although many people believe that birds are unintelligent, this is not true. Their brains are about 10 times larger than those of similar-sized reptiles. Moreover, not only are birds capable of complex social behavior, they can also use tools. One of the best-known examples of this can be observed in the woodpecker finch of the Galapagos Islands. The woodpecker finch isn't actually a woodpecker. True woodpeckers use their long tongues to remove insects from the holes they make in trees. The woodpecker finch, however, hasn't evolved this sort of tongue. When it finds an insect in a hole, it flies off to find a sharp object, such as a cactus spine or a wood splinter. It then uses this object to catch its prey. If a suitable object isn't available, it will break off a small twig and remove its leaves. In this case, it is not just using a tool — it is actually manufacturing one.

*wood splinter: 나무 가시

① 갈라파고스 제도에 서식한다.
② 긴 혀가 발달했다.
③ 먹이를 발견하면 뾰족한 물체를 찾는다.
④ 작은 잔가지의 잎을 제거한다.
⑤ 도구를 사용할 뿐만 아니라 만들기도 한다.

27 crowned lemur에 관한 다음 글의 내용과 일치하는 것은?

Compared to its lemur relatives, the crowned lemur grows to an average size. Males tend to be a dark, reddish-brown color, while females are lighter and grayer. Both sexes, however, feature an orange pattern on their head, which gives the crowned lemur its name. It is generally active during the day, but it also has an activity period of about two hours during the night. Most of its time is spent high in forest trees, but it also frequently climbs down to the ground to look for food and move around. Crowned lemurs tend to live in small, mixed-sex groups composed of adults and offspring, which sometimes grow to have as many as 15 members. Their natural habitat is the northern forests of the African island nation of Madagascar.

① 여우원숭이 동족에 비해 크기가 작다.
② 등에 왕관 모양의 주황색 무늬가 있다.
③ 낮보다는 주로 밤에 활동하는 편이다.
④ 나무 위에서 활동하고 땅으로 내려오지 않는다.
⑤ 암수가 섞인 작은 무리를 이루어 생활한다.

28 The 15th Annual Burlington Photo Contest에 관한 다음 안내문의 내용과 일치하지 <u>않는</u> 것은?

The 15th Annual Burlington Photo Contest

This year's theme is "autumn." All Burlington residents are invited to participate!

Submissions – Photos must be submitted in a digital format. A maximum of five photos may be submitted. Both color and black-and-white photos are accepted.

Deadline – All entries must be received by October 2.

Prizes – One gold prize and two silver prizes will be awarded. The gold prize winner will receive a new camera, and the silver prize winners will each receive a $50 gift certificate.

Awards Ceremony – The Awards Ceremony will be held at 6 p.m. on Saturday, November 20 at Town Hall.

---

① 한 사람이 최대 5장의 사진을 응모할 수 있다.
② 흑백 사진 출력물만 응모 가능하다.
③ 금상은 한 명, 은상은 두 명에게 수여된다.
④ 은상 수상자는 50달러 상당의 상품권을 받는다.
⑤ 시상식은 11월에 열린다.

29 다음 글의 밑줄 친 부분 중, 어법상 틀린 것은?

Not all racism is ① as obvious as saying hateful things about an entire race or using bad language to refer to certain people ② while being polite to them in person. While such behavior is rightly considered to be socially unacceptable, institutional racism, ③ which is more systematic or structural, is harder to deal with. Institutional racism in hiring is not always a conscious decision. Some people simply hire applicants who are similar to themselves, or they advertise the job within a social network that is not racially diverse. Because of this, when the majority of people doing the hiring ④ are white, the people who are hired tend to be white as well. Therefore, the role of employment equity programs is to get companies and government departments to expand their networks, to ensure all communities hear about job opportunities, and ⑤ give applicants a fair chance.

30 (A), (B), (C)의 각 네모 안에서 문맥에 맞는 낱말로 가장 적절한 것은?

There are four principal forces that act upon an airplane during flight. Weight is one of them, and it is the result of the mass of the plane being pulled (A) from / towards the ground by gravity. The opposite of weight is lift, which is created by the plane's wings and is the force that holds the craft up in the air. The plane's propeller, or jet engines if it is a jet, produces the force of thrust, and this is responsible for creating the airplane's forward motion. Drag is the force acting against thrust, caused by (B) resistance / registration as the plane moves through the air at high speeds. To remain aloft, the plane must maintain (C) greater / weaker lift and thrust in comparison to its weight and drag.

	(A)	(B)	(C)
①	from	resistance	greater
②	from	registration	weaker
③	towards	resistance	greater
④	towards	registration	greater
⑤	towards	resistance	weaker

[31~34] 다음 빈칸에 들어갈 말로 가장 적절한 것을 고르시오.

31

Chimpanzees, like humans, prefer to use their right hands. This came as a surprise to a group of Spanish scientists who recently published a study about the trait. During their research, the researchers watched more than 100 chimpanzees in rescue centers in both Spain and Zambia. To find out which hand the chimpanzees favored, scientists gave them food placed deep inside tubes. Then, they watched the primates remove the food and recorded which hand they used. In a significant majority of cases, the chimpanzees preferred to use their right hands. Before this, scientists had assumed that only humans had this trait, since they believed that the difference was caused by unique aspects of the human brain, such as the ability to perform difficult tasks using both hands in different ways. According to the researchers, this tells us that chimpanzees and humans have _____ characteristics that determine how their brains function.

① linguistic ② discrete
③ shared ④ substantial
⑤ artificial

32

Like a computer, the human mind is equipped with two basic types of memory: working memory for judging information in the present moment and long-term memory for storing it over extended periods. Contrary to popular belief, our brains don't record everything that happens to us. There is no reason for people to remember everything, so the human memory works as a filter that enables us to forget most of the information that we receive during a given day. Most of what we perceive stays briefly in our working memory, which is similar to a computer's RAM, and then gets deleted. Working memory enables us to perform simple calculations in our heads or retain phone numbers long enough to dial them. Like RAM, it lets us analyze and invent things, while _____.

① dialing the telephone
② leaving no lasting record
③ working on our computer
④ recording everything in detail
⑤ saving the information for later

33

Words that sound the same but have different meanings are called homonyms. Some homonyms — two, to, and too, for example — are very familiar, but others are not as well-known even though they are frequently used. For example, "team" and "teem." You probably know what a team is, but do you know "teem — to be full of or to swarm"? The human brain likes _____, so learning homonyms in pairs or groups makes it easier to remember them. You could note that the word "teem" means a bigger amount than its homonym "team." Or you could create sentences that highlight the different meanings of homonyms. Memorize the sentences, and the meanings of both words will follow. [3점]

① specific patterns and rules
② the integration of five senses
③ the appropriate use of images
④ connected pieces of information
⑤ unfamiliar stimulus by an external factor

34

Colors are important to us because, in addition to making things look more appealing, they also change our behavior. People seem to have powerful emotional responses to color all around the world. However, these responses are based on culture. For example, black is the color of mourning in Europe and the United States. White represents death in Chinese culture, but purple does so in Brazil. Yellow is the color of jealousy in France, whereas green is typically associated with jealousy in North America. In this way, _____, so marketers need to take into account the attitudes and preferences of their target customers when planning the design of any promotional material. Otherwise, they won't be able to share their ideas effectively, and they'll lose valuable customers. [3점]

① color preferences are universal
② colors describe personalities of people
③ Western colors are different to Eastern ones
④ the effects of color differ among different cultures
⑤ colors are interpreted differently according to mood

35 다음 글에서 전체 흐름과 관계 <u>없는</u> 문장은?

Fluoride, a mineral that occurs naturally in many foods and water, is known to have positive effects on dental health. ① As teeth develop, fluoride can help strengthen the enamel to form a hard, cavity-resistant outer coating. ② Once teeth are fully grown, it can combine with saliva to protect enamel from sugar and harmful bacteria. ③ It is no surprise, then, that in order to improve dental health, fluoride has been added to public water supplies in many areas. ④ However, one study has shown that the dental health of people in areas with fluoridated water is essentially identical to that of people living in other areas. ⑤ For similar reasons, fluoride is often added to commercial toothpastes.

*fluoride: 불소 **fluoridate: (수돗물에) 불소를 넣다

[36~37] 주어진 글 다음에 이어질 글의 순서로 가장 적절한 것을 고르시오.

36

> Viruses and harmful bacteria can get into our intestines through the food we eat. Fortunately, they are prevented from entering other parts of the body by special cells that line the inside of the intestines and act as a barrier.

(A) This information doesn't just change the way that astronauts should be treated after they return from a mission. It will also have a big impact on future efforts to travel to other planets or set up colonies on the Moon.

(B) However, a study has shown that these cells can be significantly weakened by low-gravity environments. This presents a serious problem for astronauts who work or travel in space. Once they return to Earth, they are dangerously vulnerable to foodborne viruses and bacteria.

(C) This is because the cells remain in this weakened state for up to two weeks after the astronauts have left space. To make matters worse,

spending time in low-gravity environments also weakens the human immune system. [3점]

*foodborne: 식품기인성의

① (A) – (C) – (B)　　　② (B) – (A) – (C)
③ (B) – (C) – (A)　　　④ (C) – (A) – (B)
⑤ (C) – (B) – (A)

37

> They might sound like science fiction, but cyborg insects are becoming a reality, as the United States' Defense Advanced Research Projects Agency (DARPA) works toward this goal.

(A) Then, in adulthood, its movements can be controlled remotely by GPS or ultrasonic signals from DARPA. If they were equipped with sensors, these bugs could be sent to scout out dangerous or inaccessible areas and send back information.

(B) For years, DARPA has been developing ways to control insects remotely, using an interface that would convert living insects, such as roaches, beetles, and moths, into surveillance devices. At last, DARPA has found a method that works.

(C) This process involves scientists placing a tiny mechanical system inside the body of an insect when it is still in the earliest stages of life. As it grows, the insect incorporates these mechanical parts into its body.

① (A) – (B) – (C)　　　② (A) – (C) – (B)
③ (B) – (A) – (C)　　　④ (B) – (C) – (A)
⑤ (C) – (A) – (B)

38

> To minimize their risk of brain damage, climbers should take extra precautions.

Recent research has shown that most mountaineers who reach high altitudes return from their expeditions with some degree of brain damage. (①) In a study, MRI machines were used to examine the brains of 35 mountaineers. (②) Thirty-four of them were found to have lost brain cells after being exposed to low-oxygen environments for a prolonged period of time. (③) This included climbers who had never experienced severe mountain sickness yet still suffered brain damage. (④) These findings also indicate that brain damage may occur even in the absence of ongoing exposure to high-altitude environments. (⑤) These include descending as soon as they notice any symptoms of altitude sickness and always taking time to adjust to the conditions before climbing higher. [3점]

39

> This encourages tourists to use far more water than local people.

The problem of droughts is serious and global. (①) Tourists in Africa will take a long shower without realizing that their showers cause local shortages. (②) There are villages in Africa with just a single tap, when each hotel has taps and showers in every room. (③) It has been calculated that an average tourist in Spain uses 880 liters of water a day, compared with 250 liters by a local. (④) An 18-hole golf course in a dry country can consume as much water per day as 10,000 people. (⑤) In the Caribbean, hundreds of thousands of people go without piped water because the springs are piped to tourist hotels.

40 다음 글의 내용을 한 문장으로 요약하고자 한다. 빈칸 (A), (B)에 들어갈 말로 가장 적절한 것은?

> Some people like to defend the rights of whales and other endangered sea mammals by pointing out how similar they are to humans. They say cetaceans form close-knit family groups and are all highly intelligent creatures who can communicate with each other as humans do. Those who compare sea mammals to human beings are well-meaning, but, as naturalist Robert Finch points out, their arguments are misguided. From scientists' observations, cetaceans are remarkably intelligent. But it's arrogant and self-centered to argue that these animals should be protected because they're so much like us. This suggests that certain animals are important only if they reflect human beings and their values. In fact, whales and other sea mammals have a right to exist not because they are like us, but because they are unique.
>
> *cetacean: 고래류의 포유동물

> Whales and other sea animals must be protected not because of their _____(A)_____ to human beings but because of their own _____(B)_____.

	(A)		(B)
①	intimacy	······	favor
②	capacity	······	intelligence
③	usefulness	······	influence
④	popularity	······	circumstance
⑤	similarity	······	significance

Wolves are large predators that are found in parts of Asia, Europe, and North America. They are perhaps the most social carnivores in the animal kingdom, partly due to their evolutionary development and partly due to their unique survival needs. They live in packs, which are large groups of closely related animals that defend their territory, hunt for prey, and care for their young (a) collectively. Wolf packs have a (b) strict hierarchy in which every member has a clear place that is determined by a dominant male and female. They are called the breeding pair, and they lead the pack on hunts, often being the first to eat when prey has been killed. In most situations, they are the only wolves in the pack to mate and produce offspring, but other pack members will sometimes (c) breed during times of little danger and abundant food.

Wolf pups are usually born in spring. From an early age, there are certain pups that show signs of dominance during play and others that do not. As the pups reach adolescence, some of them will make the choice to leave the pack's territory in order to search for a mate. These young wolves famously communicate through long, loud howls in the hopes of (d) threatening a mate that has also left its pack. When two of them do meet up, the new breeding pair will seek out their own (e) territory with the intention of beginning a pack of their own.

41 윗글의 제목으로 가장 적절한 것은?

① Unusual Wolf Mating Rituals
② The Social Structure of Wolves
③ The Wolf: Nature's Best Hunter
④ How Evolution Has Changed Wolves
⑤ A Plan to Protect Endangered Wolves

42 밑줄 친 (a)~(e) 중에서 문맥상 낱말의 쓰임이 적절하지 않은 것은? [3점]

① (a)　　② (b)　　③ (c)　　④ (d)　　⑤ (e)

[43~45] 다음 글을 읽고, 물음에 답하시오.

(A)

Around 1550, the Kingdom of Portugal became involved in (a) the slave trading industry. Merchants began to purchase black Africans from other black Africans, who had forced them into slavery. These slaves would then be taken across the Atlantic Ocean to the Portuguese colony of Brazil, where they were put to work on sugar plantations. The trading of slaves was (b) a huge business, involving hundreds of ships transporting thousands of slaves from Africa to Brazil.

(B)

Hundreds of years later, in 1822, Brazil declared its independence from Portugal, and a proposal was made to end slave trading and emancipate all slaves. However, the Brazilian slave trade did not end; instead it grew larger during the 19th century. During this same period in Britain, an influential group known as the Clapham Sect existed, which held (c) the political view that slaves must be liberated and slave trading abolished.

(C)

It is believed that approximately 40% of the people captured by slave traders in inland regions died before reaching the coast, where the remaining 60% were sold to the Portuguese. And during the long ocean journeys to Brazil, another 15% perished. Upon reaching South America, 10 to 12% died before they arrived at the plantations where they were to work. All told, less than half of the Africans forced into slavery during this time survived long enough to labor on Brazilian plantations. Of course, those who did survive lived terrible lives, suffering physical violence and long hours of work.

(D)

This group campaigned for the British government to use its power to stop (d) the traffic of slaves to Brazil. For the British, it was more than just a moral issue. Brazilian slavery had an adverse effect on the trade of a number of British products, and this was part of the reason the British government eventually got involved, pressuring Brazil to end (e) this practice. Over the next several decades, the Brazilian government slowly began the process of doing so. Finally, slavery was legally ended by the Golden Law of 1888, making Brazil the last nation in the Western Hemisphere to abolish slavery.

43 주어진 글 (A)에 이어질 내용을 순서에 맞게 배열한 것으로 가장 적절한 것은?

① (B) – (D) – (C) ② (C) – (B) – (D)
③ (C) – (D) – (B) ④ (D) – (B) – (C)
⑤ (D) – (C) – (B)

44 밑줄 친 (a)~(e) 중에서 가리키는 대상이 나머지 넷과 다른 것은?

① (a) ② (b) ③ (c) ④ (d) ⑤ (e)

45 윗글의 Brazilian slave trade에 관한 내용과 일치하지 않는 것은?

① 흑인 노예들은 브라질의 사탕수수 농장으로 보내졌다.
② 브라질의 독립으로 노예 매매가 일시 중단되었다.
③ 브라질에 도착하기 전 대개 반 이상의 노예가 사망했다.
④ 영국 물품의 거래에 악영향을 끼쳤다.
⑤ 1800년대 후반이 되어서야 완전히 폐지되었다.

* 3점 문항에만 점수가 표시되어 있습니다.
  점수 표시가 없는 문항은 모두 2점씩입니다.

18 다음 글의 목적으로 가장 적절한 것은?

To the Editors:

I am writing as an American citizen who was recently hospitalized for an extended period. This experience served to remind me that the United States remains the only industrialized nation in the world that does not provide its citizens with healthcare. Instead, this important task is left to for-profit insurance companies, resulting in high costs that approximately 45 million Americans are unable to afford. Although some companies provide their employees with health coverage, there are many businesses that are unable to do so. Clearly, something must be done. The federal government needs to take steps towards implementing a single-payer system in which the government would pay for all healthcare costs. This would help ensure that all American citizens have health insurance, regardless of their income or employment status.

Sincerely,
Anthony Mallet

① 새로운 의료보험 제도를 안내하려고
② 의료보험료 지불 방식에 대해 문의하려고
③ 건강보험을 제공하는 기업들을 추천하려고
④ 정부가 지불하는 의료보험 제도 구축을 촉구하려고
⑤ 과도한 이익을 추구하는 보험사들의 횡포를 고발하려고

19 다음 글에 드러난 'I'의 심경 변화로 가장 적절한 것은?

On the day of the call, my heart was pounding. I had thought about doing it 100 times before, but I had always stopped myself. How would she react? Would she be angry? When she answered, I quickly identified myself. "My name is Mark Perez. I was a friend of your son." After a long pause she said in a trembling voice, "Then you must know he isn't here. He died in the war two years ago." I explained that I did know, because I was there. "I just wanted you to know that he wasn't alone in the end. I held his hand while he died." I could hear her start to cry, and I almost hung up. But then she said, "Thank you so much for letting me know." Afterward, it felt as if a heavy weight had been lifted from my shoulders.

① bored → excited
② anxious → envious
③ nervous → relieved
④ delighted → confused
⑤ frustrated → comforted

20 다음 글에서 필자가 주장하는 바로 가장 적절한 것은?

Once, I was invited to give a talk on job security to students at the University of Hawaii. I told students that within a few years, many of them would lose their jobs or be forced to work for less money, with less and less security. Traveling the world with my work, I have witnessed the combined power of cheap labor and innovations from technology. I began to realize that workers in Asia, Europe, and South America were really competing with workers in America. I knew the big companies would soon have to make cuts, both in the numbers of people and in the salaries they paid their workers, just to be able to compete globally.

① 여행을 통해 사고의 폭을 넓혀야 한다.
② 국가 간의 경쟁이 점점 치열해질 것이다.
③ 미래에 직업 안정성은 매우 낮아질 것이다.
④ 학생들은 다양한 직업을 경험할 기회를 가져야 한다.
⑤ 값싼 노동력 확보를 위해 기업들은 해외로 진출해야 한다.

21 다음 글의 요지로 가장 적절한 것은?

Imagine that someone has upset you, but then apologized. It is painful, but you decide that you should forgive the person who hurt you. However, the pain won't simply disappear. You carry it with you in your memory, and you think of it sometimes — even when there's no reason to. You must let go of the pain. Carrying emotional pain feels like being hurt again every day. Only you can let go of it. Ask yourself this question: If you had to walk one hundred miles and had the option of carrying a heavy cement block or carrying nothing at all, which would you choose? Of course, you would choose to carry nothing. The same is true of pain.

① 긍정적인 사고방식을 가져야 한다.
② 마음의 상처는 하루빨리 잊어야 한다.
③ 남에게 상처를 주는 말을 삼가야 한다.
④ 자신의 잘못을 인정할 줄 알아야 한다.
⑤ 타인의 잘못을 용서할 줄 알아야 한다.

[22~23] 다음 글의 주제로 가장 적절한 것을 고르시오.

22

These days, it's common for companies to purchase ad space in video games. Video game manufacturers charge companies to have their logos show up on billboards or other objects that appear in the game's virtual universe. New information suggests, however, that advertisers should know what kinds of video games they are paying to be a part of. In one study, game players were exposed to two different games that included real-world advertisements. One game featured typical violent content, such as characters shooting guns and blood splattered on walls, while the other game did not. Afterwards, the players were asked questions about the brands they had seen in the game. Those who had played the violent game had much more negative views of the brands; this difference was especially evident among female players.

① effective ways of reducing advertising costs
② the bad influence of violent games on children
③ adverse effects of advertising in violent games
④ the pros and cons of playing shooter video games
⑤ the growing number of female players in the game industry

23

Robotic fish have been developed by scientists in the interest of locating ocean pollution. These robotic fish are large and can swim through the water just like real fish. They feature chemical sensors capable of detecting sources of pollution, and can send the data back to researchers via wireless technology. They have the ability to track down toxic chemicals that have already dissolved into the seawater, as well as pollutants on the ocean's surface, such as oil slicks. They also automatically return to their handlers when their batteries begin to run low. The robotic fish were created by scientists at Essex University in England. They designed them to resemble real fish and mimic their efficient swimming motions. Although they are expensive to build, officials believe they are worth the cost. [3점]

① scientists in England who are making robotic fish
② a species that can mimic the actions of other fish
③ strategies to prevent the spread of water pollution
④ mechanical fish that look for pollution in the ocean
⑤ the dangers of dumping toxic chemicals into the ocean

24 다음 글의 제목으로 가장 적절한 것은?

Narcissism is the condition of being in love with an idealized image of oneself. Narcissists force this image on others to escape the reality of who they are — wounded, imperfect people who are struggling to belong. Narcissism can be identified by some telltale signs, such as dominating conversations. Narcissists love to talk about themselves and will quickly change the subject in order to do so. They also spend a lot of time trying to impress others with external achievements, such as expensive things they have purchased. Narcissists don't mind causing negative reactions in others. They desire any kind of attention, even bad attention, and they see their ability to create it as a kind of power. Finally, narcissists hate criticism and will react poorly or even aggressively to it.

① Is There a Cure for Narcissism?
② How to Easily Spot a Narcissist
③ The Mental Origins of Narcissism
④ The Best Way to Avoid Narcissists
⑤ Narcissism: A Misunderstood Illness

25 다음 도표의 내용과 일치하지 <u>않는</u> 것은?

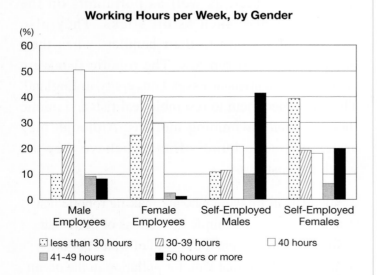

Working Hours per Week, by Gender

☒ less than 30 hours   ▨ 30-39 hours   ☐ 40 hours
▦ 41-49 hours   ■ 50 hours or more

The above bar graph illustrates distributions of normal hours worked per week for both regular employees and the self-employed, broken down by gender. ① More self-employed males than self-employed females work over 50 hours per week. ② Furthermore, there are about twice as many self-employed men working over 50 hours as self-employed women working those hours. ③ A different pattern can be seen among employees, however, with slightly more female employees working over 50 hours per week than male employees. ④ Regardless of whether they are employees or self-employed, females are likelier than males to work under 30 hours a week. ⑤ Finally, for all those who work 40 hours per week or more, males show a higher participation rate than females among both employees and the self-employed.

26 다음 글의 내용과 일치하지 <u>않는</u> 것은?

Is it common for your hair to get thicker when you're pregnant? Hair does get thicker when you are pregnant, but not because you are growing more hair. You are just losing it more slowly than you usually do. Normally, 85 to 95 percent of the hair on your head is growing while the other 5 to 15 percent is in a resting stage. After the resting period, this hair falls out and is replaced by newly growing hair. The average woman loses about 100 hairs a day. During pregnancy, however, higher levels of estrogen make the growing stage longer, and you lose fewer hairs. Also, changes in hair thickness are usually more noticeable in pregnant women with longer hair.

*estrogen: 에스트로겐(여성호르몬)

① 임신 중에는 머리카락이 더 빨리 자란다.
② 대개 전체 머리카락 중 85~95퍼센트 정도가 자란다.
③ 휴식기가 끝난 머리카락은 빠지고 새 머리카락이 난다.
④ 여성의 머리카락은 하루에 평균 100개씩 빠진다.
⑤ 임신 중에는 머리카락이 덜 빠진다.

27 The Tour de France에 관한 다음 글의 내용과 일치하는 것은?

The Tour de France, the famous cycling competition, was first organized in 1903 to increase sales for the magazine *L'Auto*. Since then, it has been held every year, having been suspended only during the two world wars. It consists of 21 to 23 days of cycling around France with only two days of rest. Cyclists travel a total distance of roughly 3,500 kilometers, which includes routes in Paris, the Alps, and the French countryside. As one can imagine, this competition is hard on the athletes. But in spite of the combination of extreme mental and physical fatigue and the high velocities at which the cyclists travel, deaths of racers at the Tour de France are rare. In fact, the three deaths that have occurred at the Tour de France since 2000 involved spectators. The race is one of Europe's most popular sporting events, with millions of fans lining the route each year.

① 자전거 판매량을 늘리기 위해 조직되었다.
② 1903년 이후로 매년 개최되었다.
③ 대회 기간 동안에는 휴식일이 허용되지 않는다.
④ 자전거 선수들이 사망하는 사고는 드물다.
⑤ 2000년 이후 세 명의 선수가 대회 중 사망했다.

28 The Silverman Art Competition에 관한 다음 안내문의 내용과 일치하지 않는 것은?

The Silverman Art Competition

The Silverman Foundation is proud to present the Silverman Junior Art Competition.

Rules: The entry fee is $5 for middle school and elementary school students. Each child may submit up to three works of art. There is also a special entry offer available to schools — 10 works of art for $10. Entries must be received by July 15. Please note that this date has been extended from the previous deadline of July 1.

Selection of Winners: A panel of artists will judge the entries. The results will be released on August 22.

Prizes
• First Prize (1) – $5,000 and a tablet computer
• Second Prize (1) – $1,000 and a digital camera

For more information on competition rules and requirements, please email the foundation at SJAC@silvermanf.org.

① 개인당 참가비는 5달러이다.
② 학교 단위로 참가할 경우 10개의 작품을 출품할 수 있다.
③ 작품 제출 기한이 앞당겨졌다.
④ 수상자는 8월 22일에 발표된다.
⑤ 일등상 수상자는 상금과 태블릿 컴퓨터를 받게 된다.

29 다음 글의 밑줄 친 부분 중, 어법상 틀린 것은? [3점]

The aim of "win-win" negotiating is to resolve situations ① <u>where</u> two parties are in conflict over what they want from each other. When ② <u>used</u> successfully, this type of negotiation leaves both parties with the sense that they've "won" something following the close of talks. Negotiations are easiest when one party wants exactly what ③ <u>the other</u> is willing to trade. Of course, this ideal scenario does not always exist, and sometimes one party must give up something they'd rather not. When this happens, it is only fair for the giving party ④ <u>trying</u> to negotiate some kind of compensation for doing so. If, at the end, both parties feel ⑤ <u>confident</u> that they have gained something from the exchange, the negotiation can be considered win-win.

30 다음 글의 밑줄 친 부분 중, 문맥상 낱말의 쓰임이 적절하지 않은 것은?

Although each edition of a newspaper contains many different and ① <u>varied</u> articles, each newspaper article is traditionally structured in much the same way. They are shaped like an ② <u>upside-down</u> pyramid in the way the information is presented. They start with the ③ <u>least</u> important points first. The opening paragraph of a news story is called the "lead" and is a summary of the whole article. If you do not have time to read the whole story, you will get the main points by reading the lead. Each paragraph after the lead is of ④ <u>decreasing</u> importance, so when faced with a shortage of page space, the editor can start removing paragraphs from the bottom of the article without ⑤ <u>affecting</u> the main content of the story.

[31~34] 다음 빈칸에 들어갈 말로 가장 적절한 것을 고르시오.

31

A country's legal system is created through the democratic participation of its citizens. Or is it? Many people assume that the law treats citizens equally and that it serves society's best interests. And if we simply read the constitution, this would appear to be the case. But focusing on the written law may be _____. It may seem that the legal system is fair and just, but to find out whether this is really true, we need to examine the law in action and how legal authorities actually operate. When we do this, it becomes apparent that in reality, legal authorities operate unjustly, favoring the rich and powerful over the poor and weak.

① trivial
② intensive
③ necessary
④ misleading
⑤ ambiguous

32

Skiing is an exciting and popular sport, but there are plenty of accidents that can happen. If you go skiing at Wachusett Mountain near Boston, you might be asked to recite the seven points of the Skiing Responsibility Code. If you name all seven points of the code, you will be given a pair of new skis or a free season pass. These rewards are offered as part of a new promotion to make people memorize the Skiing Responsibility Code. At New Hampshire's Waterville Valley Resort, or at Bromley Resort in Vermont, wearing a helmet will get you a $5 discount on your lift ticket. These resorts are definitely doing everything they can to _____.

① attract new customers
② make a considerable profit
③ promote safety on the slopes
④ improve their work environment
⑤ encourage skiers to rent equipment

33

Leonardo da Vinci discovered that sound travels in waves when he noticed the similarity between the sound of a bell and the wave made by a stone hitting water. In a similar moment of genius, the organic chemist F. A. Kekule realized that benzene molecules were ring-shaped after dreaming of a snake biting its own tail. And when the great inventor Samuel Morse noticed how teams of horses were exchanged during a relay race, he figured out how to make telegraphic signals strong enough to travel across the ocean: by giving them periodic boosts of power. From the above examples, it's clear that the skill to _____ enables geniuses to see things others miss. [3점]

*benzene: 【화학】 벤젠

① work well with others
② meet commercial needs
③ communicate with animals
④ connect the seemingly unconnected
⑤ focus on the difference between objects

34

It's commonly thought that ecology and social improvement can't work together beneficially. So many people believe that in order to look after the environment, _____. However, there are a variety of ways to expand the economy while still making responsible choices in regard to the environment. For example, when states such as California make laws that require the use of low-emissions vehicles, they are creating new markets for car manufacturers. In addition, oil companies can create new business by researching and developing alternative fuels. Meanwhile, their employees can be retrained to work with the new, environmentally-friendly technologies. In this way, a balance between conservation and sustainable development will be achieved. [3점]

① countries around the world have to collaborate
② the seriousness of pollution should be recognized
③ we need to slow down the rate of economic growth
④ more budget for the environment should be secured
⑤ it is necessary for the government to legislate more eco-friendly laws

35 다음 글에서 전체 흐름과 관계 없는 문장은?

Though genetically modified foods are now big business, this is an industry with very high set-up costs. ① The process of designing and testing genetically modified plants is long and expensive, so companies usually obtain patents for their plants to ensure they make a profit in the long-term. ② There is concern that these patents will cause the cost of plant seeds to rise, making them unaffordable to small farmers from developing countries, and thereby widening the gap between the rich and poor. ③ The economic gap between white-collar and blue-collar workers is getting worse, so each government is struggling to solve the problem. ④ Also, there is some evidence that some genetically modified crops have been implanted with a gene that prevents them from reproducing after a single season. ⑤ This makes their customers purchase new seeds every year, which keeps farmers from poor countries in constant poverty since they cannot afford this kind of ongoing investment.

36

Everyone agrees that it is wrong to discriminate against people based on their appearances. Our society is one that believes in equality, and we all like to think that we judge others fairly.

(A) For example, many Americans have a significant bias against overweight people, viewing them as being weak-willed, disorganized, and unattractive. These people often encounter discrimination in the job market and are the subject of cruel jokes.

(B) Sociological research, however, tells a different story. Although we might not want to admit it, we often use people's appearance to make unfair assumptions about their character. These assumptions then influence how we treat them.

(C) This kind of discrimination is damaging to everyone involved. Along with being hurtful, it can prevent us from forming rewarding relationships with intelligent, interesting people. In the end, everyone benefits when we treat the people around us fairly and equally.

① (A) – (B) – (C) ② (A) – (C) – (B)
③ (B) – (A) – (C) ④ (B) – (C) – (A)
⑤ (C) – (B) – (A)

37

The platypus is one of the strangest creatures on Earth. It resembles a hybrid of a beaver and a duck, and it lays eggs even though it is a mammal.

(A) It is unclear why platypus fur has this quality. The scientists think that releasing light at longer wavelengths may make it harder for ultraviolet-sensitive predators to see the platypus. However, biofluorescence may simply be an ability that was useful in the past but is no longer needed today.

(B) It occurs when a living creature absorbs short wavelengths of light and then releases them as longer wavelengths of light. This is different from bioluminescence, which occurs when a creature is able to create light with its own body.

(C) A team of scientists recently found another unusual feature of the platypus. When exposed to ultraviolet light, platypus fur has a bluish-green glow. This is apparently caused by a phenomenon that is known as biofluorescence.
[3점]

*biofluorescence: 생체 형광 **bioluminescence: 생체 발광

① (A) – (C) – (B) ② (B) – (A) – (C)
③ (B) – (C) – (A) ④ (C) – (A) – (B)
⑤ (C) – (B) – (A)

38

> Using this information, the researchers developed a theory about mass communication and suggested that it functions as a two-step process.

While analyzing the decision-making process of voters during an election period, researchers examined the effect of media messages on voting choices. (①) Initially, they predicted that they would find evidence that the media has a strong effect on voters' choices. (②) However, their research instead revealed the powerful impact that opinions shared among personal contacts have on voting behavior. (③) It starts with "opinion leaders," or individuals who closely follow the media, receiving mass-media messages. (④) They then pass along these messages to others, coloring them with their own interpretations. (⑤) In fact, these opinion leaders have been proved to have a much greater influence over voters than direct media exposure does. [3점]

39

> However, for now, classroom technology is too expensive for most schools to afford.

In some educational institutions, students may have the option to enroll in "digital" sections of courses like English, history, or science. (①) Educational authorities also encourage teachers to integrate technology into their classrooms, through the use of tools like PowerPoint, streaming video, and online research databases. (②) Naturally, old-fashioned textbooks still have a place in our educational institutions, though some believe they'll eventually be replaced by digital versions that can be accessed online. (③) These newer texts would indeed be advantageous, since they would save students from carrying around heavy paper books. (④) This is especially true for schools in poor districts that lack the resources for even traditional classroom supplies. (⑤) Work must be done to close the digital divide that separates the wealthy and the poor.

40

다음 글의 내용을 한 문장으로 요약하고자 한다. 빈칸 (A), (B)에 들어갈 말로 가장 적절한 것은?

> After the French Revolution, the people of France didn't want anything to remind them of the royal family. As a result, the French decided to change the designs on their playing cards. Before the revolution, French playing cards were the same as those used today. Each deck was made up of four suits, each with three cards displaying a king, queen, and jack. After the revolution, these royal figures were removed from the cards. The queen was replaced by symbols of freedom, the king became nature, and the jack became virtue. However, these new cards were only produced for a short period of time before a return to the traditional designs. Royalty was popular again just a few years later when Napoleon declared himself emperor of France, making kings and queens the preferred characters on French playing cards.

↓

> Right after the French Revolution, playing cards in France were _____(A)_____ changed to eliminate any reference to ____(B)____.

	(A)		(B)
①	suddenly	......	liberty
②	gradually	......	equality
③	permanently	......	colonialism
④	temporarily	......	royalty
⑤	unconsciously	......	struggle

When two people meet, the most natural thing for them to do is to engage in conversation. Yet, as we've all experienced, some people like to dominate conversations by constantly talking about themselves. Although you may find this kind of behavior annoying, research has shown that there may be a good reason behind it. According to a Harvard University study, the act of sharing information about yourself may actually stimulate the _____ regions of your brain.

Humans are social creatures; therefore, we naturally feel the need to communicate and crave social contact. One form that this contact takes is the sharing of our ideas and experiences. In previous studies, it has been estimated that 30 to 40% of our speech is devoted to doing just that. This can also explain the popularity of social networking sites such as Twitter and Facebook, where users are constantly sharing information about themselves with others. It has been shown that approximately 80% of "status updates" on this type of site are used to share a person's immediate experiences.

In order to learn more about what drives this kind of behavior, the Harvard researchers used an MRI scanner to analyze people's brain activity while they spoke. The test subjects were asked first to share their own opinions on a subject, and then to judge the opinions of others. While offering their own opinions, the subjects showed activity in the same regions of the brain that are usually stimulated when we receive basic rewards, such as food or money. These regions were also active when they discussed their own personality traits.

41 윗글의 제목으로 가장 적절한 것은?

① Listen Before You Talk
② The Science of Self-Disclosure
③ The Secrets of Good Conversations
④ Communication Can Harm Your Mental Health
⑤ Do Social Networking Sites Make Us Self-Centered?

42 윗글의 빈칸에 들어갈 말로 가장 적절한 것은? [3점]

① fear
② logic
③ anxiety
④ pleasure
⑤ language

[43~45] 다음 글을 읽고, 물음에 답하시오.

(A)

Käthe Kollwitz was a 20th-century German artist who is best known for her drawings, prints, and sculptures. She drew a large number of self-portraits, and she also designed posters in order to bring awareness to a variety of important social issues. Much of her work carries a dark theme, addressing such issues as the artist's personal relationship with death and the suffering of women who are living in poverty.

(B)

Overwhelmed with grief at the loss of her son, Kollwitz decided to focus her pain and sorrow into the creation of a meaningful work of art. (a) She began designing a memorial monument for the war cemetery in Belgium where (b) her son was buried. The project, entitled *The Grieving Parents*, took her nearly twenty years to complete. Kollwitz finally finished the monument in 1932, and it was erected in the cemetery later that same year.

(C)

This appearance of darkness likely had its source in the tragedy that defined the later years of Kollwitz's own life. (c) Her son, Peter Kollwitz, volunteered to enlist in the German military at the start of World War I. Kollwitz's husband opposed this decision, but Kollwitz herself supported her son and encouraged him to fight bravely for their homeland. In 1914, just three weeks after he had enlisted in the army, Peter was killed on the battlefield.

(D)

The work consists of two figures kneeling side by side, one male and the other female. Kollwitz gave the female figure her own face. She is wrapped in a shawl, bent over, and staring sadly at the ground, while the man, who resembles Kollwitz's husband, looks straight ahead with an expression of extreme grief on his face. Dr. Iris Berndt, director of the Käthe Kollwitz Museum, has praised Kollwitz for her contributions to the art world. "(d) She is an outstanding German artist, particularly as a woman in a male dominated world," (e) she said.

43 주어진 글 (A)에 이어질 내용을 순서에 맞게 배열한 것으로 가장 적절한 것은?

① (B) – (D) – (C)   ② (C) – (B) – (D)
③ (C) – (D) – (B)   ④ (D) – (B) – (C)
⑤ (D) – (C) – (B)

44 밑줄 친 (a)~(e) 중에서 가리키는 대상이 나머지 넷과 다른 것은?

① (a)   ② (b)   ③ (c)   ④ (d)   ⑤ (e)

45 윗글의 Käthe Kollwitz에 관한 내용과 일치하지 않는 것은?

① 많은 자화상을 그렸다.
② 대부분의 작품에서 어두운 주제를 다뤘다.
③ 참전자 묘지에 세울 기념비를 디자인했다.
④ 조국을 위해 싸우겠다는 아들의 결심에 반대했다.
⑤ 남편과 닮은 조각상의 얼굴에 슬픔을 표현했다.

* 3점 문항에만 점수가 표시되어 있습니다.
  점수 표시가 없는 문항은 모두 2점씩입니다.

18 다음 글의 목적으로 가장 적절한 것은?

Dear Professor Grayson,

　Along with all of my colleagues here at Greenview University, I am looking forward to hearing you speak at our annual symposium this November. I just wanted to go over some of the details, as the symposium is rapidly approaching. As we previously discussed, you'll be giving the keynote lecture and then leading a workshop. There's no need to prepare additional material for the workshop — it will basically be a question-and-answer session based on your lecture. Both sessions are expected to last approximately one hour. I'd also like to remind you that the school will be arranging your accommodations and meals. If anything seems unclear, please call me at (516) 812-8664.

Sincerely,
Charles O'Neill
Dean of Humanities

① 심포지엄에 교수를 초대하려고
② 교육 행사의 일정을 조정하려고
③ 워크숍 진행 방식에 대해 문의하려고
④ 심포지엄에 관한 정보를 상기시키려고
⑤ 워크숍 자료를 보내줄 것을 요청하려고

19 다음 글에 드러난 Michael의 심경 변화로 가장 적절한 것은?

　Michael was lying in bed, but he was wide awake. Although he was home alone, he could hear something in the hallway, like the sound of someone slowly walking back and forth. After a few minutes, he cautiously got up, walked over to his bedroom door, and put his ear against it. At first he heard nothing. But then the creaking of floorboards began again as someone — or something — came closer and closer to his room. He briefly thought about hiding under the bed, but he knew that would be foolish. Instead, he took a deep breath and threw the door open. There in the hallway, standing right in front of him, was the family dog. Michael had forgotten to put her out in the yard for the night.

① calm → thrilled
② thankful → angry
③ ashamed → excited
④ frightened → relieved
⑤ surprised → depressed

20 다음 글의 요지로 가장 적절한 것은?

The music business is experiencing a recession, with record sales reaching all-time lows over the past few years. Finding the cause of this has naturally become a major concern for record companies. Some blame slowing economies, but that can hardly explain why one industry is losing out so much more than others. Music today is more of a commercial product to be used up and thrown away. People are not prepared to pay as much for a "disposable" product as they are for a "reusable" one. A lot of modern music has a short but intense lifespan. Hit songs are broadcast so repeatedly that we need not buy the record. And when it stops being played, no one remembers it.

① 대중음악의 수준이 점점 낮아지고 있다.
② 시대에 따라 선호되는 음악의 장르가 다르다.
③ 현대인들의 소비 성향은 실용적이고 합리적이다.
④ 불경기가 음반 시장의 불황에 크게 영향을 미친다.
⑤ 일회성 음악의 만연으로 음반 시장이 침체되고 있다.

21 다음 글의 주제로 가장 적절한 것은? [3점]

The holiday of *Cinco de Mayo*, most enthusiastically observed in the United States, is commonly believed to celebrate Mexico's achievement of independence. However, this is not the case. *Cinco de Mayo* actually commemorates the Battle of Puebla, which occurred on May 5, 1862, fifty-two years after Mexico declared its independence. The day is remembered because Mexican forces won an unlikely victory against invading French forces. Americans may be confused because, since 1863, many Mexican-Americans have chosen to celebrate their Hispanic heritage on *Cinco de Mayo*. Americans from other backgrounds didn't know the history of the day and made the assumption that it must have something to do with Mexican independence, an error that has persisted to the present day.

① why *Cinco de Mayo* is celebrated in the U.S.
② why 1863 was an important year for Mexico
③ how Americans misunderstand *Cinco de Mayo*
④ the significance of *Cinco de Mayo* to Mexicans
⑤ the process of Mexican independence in the 1800s

[22~23] 다음 글의 제목으로 가장 적절한 것을 고르시오.

22

Many parts of the world continue to suffer from severe water shortages, which can lead to famine and disaster. Yet we know that water is simply the combination of two hydrogen molecules and a single oxygen molecule. If this chemical formula is so easy, why don't we artificially create water by combining these molecules? Unfortunately, the answer is that manufacturing water in large quantities would be enormously dangerous. To create water, a sudden burst of energy is required to cause the electrons of each molecule to link up and combine together. While a small spark in a controlled laboratory is enough to create a small amount of water, creating water on a large scale presents a major hazard. Unless scientists can come up with a less volatile method, creating enough water to satisfy the world's thirst will remain only a theoretical possibility.

① Generating Energy with Water
② Droughts: A Dangerous Threat
③ The Many Uses of Water Molecules
④ The Risk of Creating Water Artificially
⑤ Can Hydrogen and Oxygen Be Combined?

23

A diploma from a decent American university was once regarded as the key to a good job in Korea. But those days are almost gone. Now, a growing number of students who studied overseas have come home to find the job market is tight and foreign experience no longer opens doors like it used to. After Park, a graduate from a well-known American university, repeatedly failed to get the job she wanted, she realized her expectations were hard to satisfy. "I can't believe that my whole experience in the U.S. hasn't helped me that much. I am still trying to find a job that fits well with my skills and knowledge," she said.

① How to Prepare for Job Interviews
② Help with Studying English Abroad
③ Graduates and Their Dream Careers
④ Studying Abroad No Longer Guarantees a Job
⑤ Korean Students Flock to American Universities

24 다음 도표의 내용과 일치하지 않는 것은?

Participation in Selected Leisure Activities

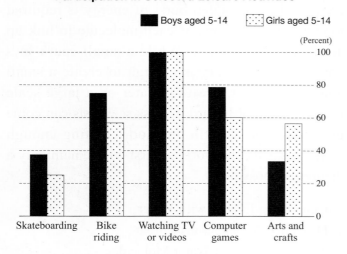

■ Boys aged 5-14   ⋯ Girls aged 5-14

The above chart represents the leisure activities in which Australian children aged 5-14 participate.

① One hundred percent of both the boys and the girls surveyed reported watching television or videos in their free time. ② Playing computer games was the next most popular activity, enjoyed by about four fifths of the boys and three fifths of the girls. ③ As for the category of arts and crafts, more than half of the girls reported engaging in this type of activity, as opposed to just more than a third of the boys. ④ Bike riding was popular with the majority of both genders, although more so with girls than boys. ⑤ Finally, the least popular activity for the girls was skateboarding, although more boys participated in it than in arts and crafts activities.

25 고대 로마의 신발에 관한 다음 글의 내용과 일치하지 않는 것은?

Several types of footwear were worn during ancient times in Rome, one of which was the *baxa*. This sandal was made from palm leaves, vegetable leaves, twigs, and fibers. Mainly worn by actors and philosophers, *baxa* shoes were simple and cheap, which meant commoners also used them. At the time, it was thought unsuitable for men to go out in sandals, so most men did not wear them in public. However, when at home, Romans mainly wore sandals made from leather. There was little difference between shoes worn by females and males, though some women's shoes had precious stones or pearls on them. Also, sandals were often colored to mark the owner's social status.

① *baxa*는 나뭇가지나 잎으로 만들어진 샌들이었다.
② 대개 남자들은 실외에서는 샌들을 신지 않았다.
③ 고대 로마인들은 집에서 주로 가죽 샌들을 신었다.
④ 남녀의 신발 생김새는 매우 달랐다.
⑤ 신분에 따라 샌들의 색깔이 달라지기도 했다.

26 malleefowl에 관한 다음 글의 내용과 일치하는 것은?

The malleefowl is sometimes referred to as the "thermometer bird." Rather than incubating their eggs with body heat by sitting on them, these birds build large mounds and lay their eggs inside. The male begins building the mound at the approach of breeding season. However, the female won't lay her eggs until it has ascertained that the temperature of the mound is exactly 33°C. To check the temperature, the male bird inserts his beak into the mound, using it as an astonishingly accurate thermometer. The male spends 11 months a year performing the important task of checking and maintaining the temperature of the mound. In the summer, he'll shield the eggs with a cool layer of sand; in the autumn, he'll uncover them to feel the warmth of the midday sun.

① 흙더미에 알을 낳은 후 체온으로 부화시킨다.
② 산란기가 다가오면 암컷은 흙더미를 만들기 시작한다.
③ 수컷은 다리를 사용해서 흙더미의 온도를 측정한다.
④ 수컷은 거의 일 년 내내 흙더미 온도를 유지시키는 일을 한다.
⑤ 가을에는 모래층으로 알을 덮어 따뜻하게 보호한다.

27 The Fresno Film Festival "Golden Ticket" Pass에 관한 다음 안내문의 내용과 일치하지 <u>않는</u> 것은?

The Fresno Film Festival "Golden Ticket" Pass

Are you a big fan of the festival? Then you should consider buying one of our new Golden Ticket passes! The benefits of this special pass include:

- admission to 10 movies of your choice
- admission for you and a guest to the opening ceremony party on August 11
- a free "I Love FFF" T-shirt
- a free large drink at each movie you attend

This is a limited offer. Only 100 Golden Tickets will be printed, and they must be purchased by August 3. Only one ticket may be purchased per person.

For more information, please visit our website www.fresnoff.org.

① 10편의 영화를 선택하여 관람할 수 있다.
② 본인 포함 2인의 개회식 초대권이 포함되어 있다.
③ 티셔츠와 음료가 무료로 제공된다.
④ 100장 한정으로 판매된다.
⑤ 8월 11일까지 구매할 수 있다.

28 다음 글의 밑줄 친 부분 중, 어법상 틀린 것은? [3점]

In 1965, a great business idea struck the entrepreneur Lionel Burleigh. He decided to launch a newspaper called the *Commonwealth Sentinel*, which was ① to be aimed at the many immigrants in London ② who came from British Commonwealth countries. He spent all of his time ③ organize the newspaper's contents and selling advertising space. However, on the morning that the first issue was scheduled to be published, he awoke to find 50,000 copies of his newspaper ④ waiting for him on the street outside his hotel. Burleigh had been so busy sorting out the details of his newspaper's launch ⑤ that he'd completely overlooked organizing any distribution. His newspaper business started on February 6 and ended on the 7th, the next day.

29 다음 글의 밑줄 친 부분 중, 문맥상 낱말의 쓰임이 적절하지 않은 것은?

The oranges of Seville, Spain, are known for their intense taste and are found in a wide range of products, from marmalade to chocolate. Surprisingly, these oranges can also be used to ① generate electricity. The city of Seville has recently introduced a plan to power a large water purification plant with electricity from the oranges. The key to this unusual project is methane. This gas is ② released by oranges as they ferment, and it can be used to drive generators that produce electricity. The city will collect unwanted oranges from the streets and ③ extract their juice. This is what will be used to produce the biogas; the rest of the fruit will become fertilizer for gardens or farms. The project is expected to ④ waste about 1,500 kWh of electricity. This is approximately the amount of electricity that is ⑤ consumed by 150 homes, and it is enough to make the water treatment plant self-sufficient.

[30~34] 다음 빈칸에 들어갈 말로 가장 적절한 것을 고르시오.

30

In Chicago, there was an elderly woman who needed to have her sink repaired. Unfortunately, a dishonest plumber took advantage of her, persuading the woman to sign a contract agreeing to pay him $50,000 for the work. When she went to the bank to withdraw $25,000 to give him as a down payment, a teller became suspicious. After asking the woman what she needed such a large sum of money for, the teller contacted the police. The plumber was quickly arrested and charged with fraud. This case offers a clear illustration of the legal limits of a contract. For one thing, it shows that the mere existence of an agreement does not guarantee the _____ of the agreement. What's more, this makes it clear that obtaining another person's consent does not necessarily create a legal agreement. In the absence of mutual benefit, a contract cannot be considered valid.

① clarity   ② length
③ results   ④ fairness
⑤ contents

31

Antonio Salieri's jealousy of his fellow composer Wolfgang Amadeus Mozart is a popular topic in contemporary books and movies. Some of these even include the accusation that Salieri poisoned Mozart. However, the possibility that he was a murderer is considered highly unlikely by musical historians. Salieri had no motive to kill Mozart, as his respected standing in Vienna's musical society provided him with all the power and influence he needed. Salieri served as court composer and conductor, as well as director of the Italian opera, and Emperor Joseph II was said to have been fond of him. Furthermore, Salieri had no personal issues with Mozart and even conducted his compositions from time to time. It is said that Salieri confessed on

his deathbed that he had killed Mozart, but there's
_____ that this is true.

① clear proof   ② no evidence
③ a reliable story   ④ no doubt at all
⑤ a high likelihood

32

We all have a natural rhythm in our bodies that is created by the beating of our heart. According to one expert in Japan, Kiyoko Yokoyama, listening to music that has its basis in this beat can _____. Yokoyama has already designed a program that can analyze a person's heartbeat and, using a complex algorithm, convert the timing, fluctuations and variations of that beat into chill-out music. In his studies, he has noticed that people exposed to the music generated by their heartbeat experience higher levels of relaxation than people who hear no music. Yokoyama is hopeful that his discovery can lead to practical applications, such as the formulation of stress- and fatigue-reducing programs for workers in high-stress environments.

*algorithm: 【수학·컴퓨터】 연산(법), 알고리즘

① interrupt deep rest
② improve overall health
③ decrease feelings of stress
④ break one's concentration
⑤ maximize one's creativity

33

On television shows and in advertisements, everyone seems to be stylish, in shape, and attractive. More importantly, they all seem to be happy. Unfortunately, this is an effective way of brainwashing people into trying to look and act in ways that satisfy certain social standards. The truth is that we are all different, but many people come to believe that they cannot be happy if they _____. Because of this, they grow up thinking that there is something wrong with who they are. They end up getting plastic surgery or simply feeling bad about themselves all the time. The bottom line is that comparing yourself to the people you see on TV will inevitably damage your self-esteem. Instead of worrying about who you think you should be, you should focus on accepting who you are. [3점]

① don't watch television
② fail to earn a lot of money
③ worry about how they look
④ are the same as everyone else
⑤ don't meet society's expectation

34

A lot of people think an empty stomach causes hunger. But it is not true. In fact, it's a small area inside the brain called the hypothalamus that really tells us when we are hungry. In studying the behavior of rats, scientists discovered that when a certain part of the brain was stimulated, rats kept on eating even though their stomachs were full. They further found that when a different part of the brain was stimulated, the rats would not eat at all even though they hadn't eaten for several days. These experiments indicate that, contrary to popular belief, _____. [3점]

*hypothalamus: 시상하부

① you will be defined by what you eat
② food is one of the most basic human needs
③ eating quickly is not that bad for your health
④ regular eating is the key to a balanced lifestyle
⑤ hunger is controlled by the brain, not by the stomach

35 다음 글에서 전체 흐름과 관계 <u>없는</u> 문장은?

Many plants depend on the help of animals to transfer pollen from their stamens to other plants' ova. Such plants have flowers that use either color or scent to attract pollinating animals. ① In an exchange that benefits both parties, nectar from the flower provides nutrition for the pollinator, usually an insect or a bird. ② When the creature proceeds to another flower for more nectar, it inadvertently carries pollen there, thus accomplishing the plant's aim of pollination. ③ There are also some plants that have both sexes in the same flower, allowing them to self-pollinate. ④ Over time, some animals even develop unique physical features, such as specially shaped beaks, to extract nectar as efficiently as possible from certain flowers. ⑤ The flowers, in turn, may develop in shapes that only allow certain animal species to get nectar from them.

*stamen: 【식물】(꽃의) 수술 **ovum: 【생물】난세포, 난자(*pl.* ova)

36 주어진 글 다음에 이어질 글의 순서로 가장 적절한 것은? [3점]

A "quarter-life crisis" is an event that sometimes occurs when people are in their early 20s to early 30s, after all of the difficult changes associated with entering adulthood have taken place.

(A) Many of these recent graduates spend this period of life traveling around, trying out different jobs, and trying to figure out just exactly what they want to do in the future.

(B) It generally occurs just after graduation from college, when young people have an average debt of about $10,000 in student loans and still lack job experience.

(C) Yet this kind of experimentation is not always the best thing for people in their 20s and 30s. If such an unstable lifestyle continues past the age of 30, it can eventually lead to a serious personal crisis.

① (A) – (B) – (C)   ② (A) – (C) – (B)
③ (B) – (A) – (C)   ④ (B) – (C) – (A)
⑤ (C) – (A) – (B)

[37~39] 글의 흐름으로 보아, 주어진 문장이 들어가기에 가장 적절한 곳을 고르시오.

37

Drawing an arrow back on a bowstring causes the bow to store up positional energy.

Archery involves much more than just pointing an arrow and letting it fly. With the technology behind shooting a bow, you can aim directly at a target and hit your mark. The process seems simple: you draw an arrow back on the bowstring while focusing on your target, and then let go of it. However, the release and subsequent flight of an arrow are influenced by a variety of forces. (①) This energy can be utilized to propel the arrow forward. (②) As the arrow is released, the positional energy is converted into kinetic energy. (③) The farther you draw the bowstring back, the faster the arrow will fly. (④) This is because you are creating greater force, which leads to more converted energy. (⑤) For this reason, the effectiveness of the bow depends on the power and skill of the person using it.

38

A fundamental trait of the blues, however, is that it makes people feel better.

American writer Washington Irving, author of "The Legend of Sleepy Hollow," created the term "the blues," meaning sadness. (①) The musical genre that took its name from this term evolved from African-American folk songs, which were sung in the fields and around slave quarters on southern plantations. (②) They were songs of pain and suffering, injustice, and longing for a better life. (③) Listening to the blues will drive the blues away; it is music that has the power to heal sadness. (④) Thus, "the blues" isn't really the correct term, for the music is moving but not melancholy. (⑤) It is, in fact, music born of hope, not despair.

39

Yet it is essential to keep in mind that these triggers don't have the same effect on everyone.

Rosacea is a common inflammatory skin condition affecting the face. (①) In its initial stages, a general redness will overwhelm the face, making it appear as if the person is permanently blushing. (②) Later on, pimples and noticeable red lines will begin to develop as the condition progresses. (③) A number of behavioral and environmental factors have been fingered as causes of rosacea, including the consumption of spicy foods and alcohol and prolonged exposure to sun, rain, or wind. (④) Therefore, to determine which specific factor is causing your rosacea, you should keep a diary of everything you eat and what the weather is like for a few weeks. (⑤) This will help you match periods of rosacea severity to a single trigger. [3점]

*rosacea: 【병리】 주사(얼굴에 생기는 만성 피지선 염증)

40

다음 글의 내용을 한 문장으로 요약하고자 한다. 빈칸 (A), (B)에 들어갈 말로 가장 적절한 것은?

Gelada monkeys living in Ethiopia have been observed allowing wolves to move freely around their territory and even through their groups. It seems the monkeys are confident that they will not be attacked by the wolves, and they show no signs of being nervous. However, when similar predators, such as feral dogs, are spotted nearby, the monkeys will run away in fear. As for the wolves, they seem to now prey on rodents rather than monkeys. This actually may be the reason behind this unlikely interspecies relationship. The wolves are about twice as successful in hunting rodents when there are monkeys nearby. This may be because the rodents relax in the presence of gelada monkeys, allowing the wolves to sneak up on them.

*feral: 야생의

↓

Gelada monkeys and wolves have been observed   (A)   in the same area, most likely because the presence of the monkeys   (B)   the wolves' efforts to capture other prey.

	(A)		(B)
①	confronting	······	explains
②	confronting	······	decreases
③	coexisting	······	aids
④	coexisting	······	obstructs
⑤	presenting	······	copies

At the end of the 19th century, a new wave of immigration caused a massive population explosion in the United States. Few immigrants found life in America easy during this period. Many of those who (a) lacked professional skills and did not speak English found themselves living in slum conditions in the large, messy cities of the Northeast, exploited by their employers, and trapped at the poverty level.

Among the responses to these problems, there were two groups which had ideas about how to assimilate these immigrants. A conservative group called the Daughters of the American Revolution approached immigrants with the expectation that newcomers should completely (b) adopt American customs and culture in order to improve their lives. Consequently, they supported laws that required immigrants to take oaths of loyalty and to pass English language tests. They also (c) banned the use of any language other than English in school.

Another conception of assimilation came from the experience of reformers such as Jane Addams. In 1889, Addams founded a volunteer organization in Chicago called Hull House. Her notion of dealing with assimilation was to attempt to improve conditions in the city's (d) poor immigrant neighborhoods and provide local government services, including medical care, legal assistance, and adult education. A fundamental aspect of the "settlement house" philosophy was to (e) disregard the cultural heritage of the new arrivals. Many workers, including Jane Addams herself, feared that attempts to "Americanize" the immigrants would deprive the United States of a cultural diversity.

41 윗글의 제목으로 가장 적절한 것은?

① New Immigration Restriction Laws
② Population Problems Caused by Immigrants
③ Reasons Why People Immigrated to the U.S.
④ Difficulties That Immigrants Faced in the U.S.
⑤ Two Different Ways of Assimilating Immigrants to the U.S.

42 밑줄 친 (a)~(e) 중에서 문맥상 낱말의 쓰임이 적절하지 않은 것은? [3점]

① (a)　　② (b)　　③ (c)　　④ (d)　　⑤ (e)

[43~45] 다음 글을 읽고, 물음에 답하시오.

(A)

That day during the summer of 1953, when some colleagues invited me to attend a meeting hosted by a professor from the medical school, was just like any other day; I had no idea of the changes it would bring into my life. (a) They had extended an invitation, which I had accepted without even asking about the meeting's topic. Therefore, when I entered the conference room and saw five somber couples sitting around a table, I could only guess at who these people were and how they were connected.

(B)

Upon hearing these families' stories, my initial reaction was one of shock, though that emotion quickly gave way to profound professional embarrassment. The conduct of my medical colleagues was shameful, and I could hardly believe that so many of my peers had behaved so disgracefully toward people who wanted nothing more than to help their children. In the end, their request was a simple one; (b) they wanted us to establish a weekly clinic to meet the medical needs of developmentally disabled children, a request I agreed to immediately without a second thought.

(C)

It turned out that what (c) they had in common was a shared problem. They were all the parents of developmentally disabled children who were unable to find the proper care and facilities to treat their children's medical needs. One by one, these parents recounted their stories, detailing all manner of mistreatment and humiliation at the hands of medical professionals who had avoided these families and turned them away. With nowhere left to turn, (d) they had come to us.

(D)

Little did I know that granting that request would mark a turning point in my life, starting what was essentially a new career dedicated to the needs of those with developmental disabilities. Soon, I would be heading the world's first medical facility devoted entirely to the needs of developmentally disabled children, all because of those five couples and an unexpected meeting with (e) them, which caused me to become not only a passionate advocate, but also a more emotionally fulfilled human being.

43 주어진 글 (A)에 이어질 내용을 순서에 맞게 배열한 것으로 가장 적절한 것은?

① (B) – (D) – (C)　　② (C) – (B) – (D)
③ (C) – (D) – (B)　　④ (D) – (B) – (C)
⑤ (D) – (C) – (B)

44 밑줄 친 (a)~(e) 중에서 가리키는 대상이 나머지 넷과 다른 것은?

① (a)　② (b)　③ (c)　④ (d)　⑤ (e)

45 윗글의 'I'에 관한 내용과 일치하는 것은?

① 1953년에 의학 학회를 주최했다.
② 모임에서 다섯 명의 발달 장애 아동들을 만났다.
③ 과거 환자 가족들을 냉대했던 자신의 행동을 부끄러워했다.
④ 주간 병원 설립 제안을 받아들이는 것을 망설였다.
⑤ 발달 장애 아동들을 위한 의료 시설을 설립할 예정이다.

* 3점 문항에만 점수가 표시되어 있습니다.
  점수 표시가 없는 문항은 모두 2점씩입니다.

18 다음 글의 목적으로 가장 적절한 것은?

To all residents in Montville

All house fires are dangerous, but those that occur at night, when people are sleeping, tend to cause the most deaths. Some people believe that the smell of smoke would wake them up, but this is often not the case. Smoke and poisonous gases produced by fires actually numb people's senses and push them into a deeper sleep. That is why safety experts say that every home should have a smoke detector. Even if you are under the numbing influence of smoke and gases, the sound made by the alarm will wake you up. Therefore, it is necessary that all houses in our town are equipped with a smoke alarm on each level, even in the basement. The best place to put them is near or on the ceiling, as smoke and hot air rise. With several functioning smoke alarms in each house, our town can be more safe from fire.

City Fire Department

① 화재 시 행동 요령을 알려주려고
② 연기 흡입의 영향에 대해 설명하려고
③ 가정 내 연기 탐지기의 설치를 촉구하려고
④ 기존에 널리 알려진 화재 예방법들을 비판하려고
⑤ 화재가 가정에 일으킬 수 있는 손해에 대해 경고하려고

19 다음 글의 상황에 나타난 분위기로 가장 적절한 것은?

The sky was getting dark, and the wind whipped the palm trees. "We need more sandbags!" my father yelled from the front yard. A storm was coming our way, and we intended to protect our house. My sister ran across the yard holding empty bags. My father and mother were already shoveling sand frantically. I tore my eyes away from them and went back to hammering a board over a window. "How many windows are left?" my younger brother called. "Four! We need to go faster!" I felt a raindrop touch my arm. Another drop fell onto my hand and then my nose. It was raining already, and the sky was covered with dark clouds.

① lonely
② urgent
③ hopeful
④ peaceful
⑤ depressing

20 다음 글에서 필자가 주장하는 바로 가장 적절한 것은?

It's been said that cloning is the next logical step in reproductive technology. Identical twins are natural clones, so it is possible to regard cloning as a technological version of a natural process. Why shouldn't infertile couples be allowed to produce clones of themselves? Why shouldn't a couple who have lost a child be able to substitute their loved individual with a clone? And why not clone people who have made great contributions to science, music, art, or literature so that we might benefit from their special talent? Finally, if we stop scientists from experimenting with cloning, we could be preventing them from making important medical breakthroughs in the future, such as the discovery of a cure for a deadly disease.

*infertile: 불임의

① 복제는 불임 부부에게 희망을 가져다준다.
② 복제 연구에 대한 국가적 지원이 필요하다.
③ 복제는 여러 가지 혜택을 가져다줄 수 있다.
④ 복제는 여러 가지 윤리적 문제를 야기할 수 있다.
⑤ 복제는 국가의 철저한 통제하에 이루어져야 한다.

21 밑줄 친 the student fails the test가 다음 글에서 의미하는 바로 가장 적절한 것은? [3점]

In computer science, the acronym GIGO, which stands for "garbage in, garbage out," is often used in reference to projects involving artificial intelligence (AI). This is because AI relies on large amounts of data, which it analyzes and uses to learn how to perform its functions better. For this reason, data collection, preparation, cleaning, and labeling are extremely important in AI projects. If AI is fed bad data, or data that has not been appropriately labeled, it will cause the program or application to produce inaccurate results. For example, if you are trying to teach an AI program to find images of airplanes in photos posted online, you have to provide it with thousands of images of airplanes to analyze. If some of these pictures are incorrectly labeled, perhaps identifying other objects as airplanes, then it will be the teacher's fault when the student fails the test.

① there are too many photos to analyze
② he or she won't decide how much data to use
③ the AI program misidentifies objects in the photos
④ the AI program suddenly stops running altogether
⑤ learning to use the AI program is difficult for students

22 다음 글의 요지로 가장 적절한 것은?

Most of us have had the experience of staying silent after someone has insulted or annoyed us. We do this because we believe it is easier than confronting the other person. In reality, however, it is not easier. It allows us to temporarily avoid an uncomfortable situation, but there are consequences for silencing ourselves. We end up feeling bad for a long time, knowing that we have taken away our own power and allowed someone else to behave badly. What we should do instead is to find a way to confront others constructively. Learning how to do this gives us a useful tool. We can stand up for ourselves and speak our mind without causing other people to become angry or aggressive.

① 침묵으로 인해 갈등 상황이 악화될 수 있다.
② 화가 나도 불쾌한 감정은 드러내지 않아야 한다.
③ 갈등의 근본적인 원인을 찾아 해결하는 것이 중요하다.
④ 다른 사람에게 맞서기 전에 먼저 생각을 정리해야 한다.
⑤ 갈등을 피하기 위해 자신의 감정을 억누르는 것은 좋지 않다.

23 다음 글의 주제로 가장 적절한 것은? [3점]

Biometrics is the science of identifying individuals based on physical or behavioral characteristics. Many private institutions and government agencies are turning to biometric identification systems, such as fingerprinting and voice and face recognition, as a means of identifying people. However, despite their increasing popularity, there are rising concerns about biometric technologies. One such concern is that the data collected by biometric scanners can be accumulated and used without your noticing. In fact, it has been reported that some governments, including the U.S. government, have collected information by using biometric technology and shared it with other countries. Furthermore, there is also the possibility that biometric information could be stolen and used for the purpose of identity theft.

① new forms of biometric technology
② the effectiveness of biometric technology
③ the dangers of using biometric technology
④ the significant characteristics of biometrics
⑤ governments' leaking of personal information

24 다음 글의 제목으로 가장 적절한 것은?

Believe it or not, being forced to retire or getting laid off can be a positive experience. It makes you re-evaluate where your career's going. But your first interview after being laid off will be scary, so role-play it first with a friend, until you feel more comfortable and confident. The new company will probably ask your old one for references and, while they're unlikely to be bad, it's best to tell your interviewers what happened. Paint things in a positive light by explaining why your position was no longer required and how much you are looking forward to a fresh challenge. Don't bad-mouth your old boss, because you will look disloyal, but do emphasize all that you learned from the experience. They will value your honesty.

① Show Your True Value in Your Résumé
② Adjusting to a New Working Environment
③ Marketing Yourself: How to Find a Good Job
④ How to Approach Interviews after Losing Your Jobs
⑤ The Best Way to Build Strong Relationships with Coworkers

25 다음 도표의 내용과 일치하지 <u>않는</u> 것은?

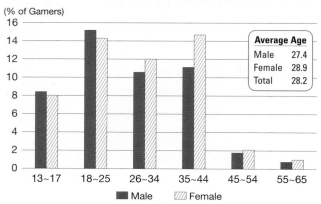

Mobile Phone Gamers by Age and Gender

Average Age	
Male	27.4
Female	28.9
Total	28.2

The above graph shows a breakdown of mobile phone game players by age group and gender. ① The average age of game players is 28.2, with female gamers an average of one and half years younger than their male counterparts. ② Among males, the largest percentage of game players is found in the 18 to 25 year old group. ③ Women aged 35 to 44, on the other hand, make up the largest percentage of female mobile phone gamers. ④ In fact, in all of the groups from the age of 26 and up, the percentage of female game players is higher than that of males. ⑤ Conversely, the percentage of males exceeds the percentage of females in the two younger age groups.

26 카멜레온에 관한 다음 글의 내용과 일치하지 <u>않는</u> 것은?

Several factors contribute to the color changes of the chameleon. The chameleon is equipped with several cell layers beneath its transparent skin. These layers are the source of the chameleon's ability to change its color. Some of the layers contain pigments, while others just reflect light to create new colors. Usually, a color change can occur in 20 seconds. The chameleon will most often change between three colors: green, brown, and gray, which often match the background colors of their habitat. So many people believe that chameleons change color to match their environment. But this is not true. In reality, light, temperature, and emotional state commonly bring about a chameleon's change in color.

*pigment: 색소

① 피부가 투명하다.
② 피부 아래 세포층의 색소로 인해 피부색이 변한다.
③ 피부색이 주로 녹색, 갈색, 회색으로 변한다.
④ 주변 환경에 맞추어 피부색을 변화시킨다.
⑤ 온도에 따라 피부색이 변하기도 한다.

27 aerogel에 관한 다음 글의 내용과 일치하는 것은?

Aerogel is the lightest, lowest-density solid known to exist. The substance resembles styrofoam, though it is a transparent blue color rather than white. Made up mostly of air, aerogel has the capacity to withstand applied force of up to 4,000 times its own weight. Unsurprisingly, then, one of its primary uses is as a lightweight building material. Since its discovery, it has been used for a number of purposes, at first as a paint additive, and now primarily as thermal insulation. It is also utilized by the space industry, in temperature-resistant windows, and as a shock-absorbing material in safety equipment. Before it can be widely used, however, a reduction in its production cost is required.

① 무겁고 밀도가 높은 고체이다.
② 파란색을 띠고 있는 반투명 물질이다.
③ 처음에는 건축용 단열재로 사용되었다.
④ 안전 장비의 완충재로 사용되기도 한다.
⑤ 생산 비용이 저렴하여 널리 활용된다.

28 Help Us Name the University's New Supercomputer에 관한 다음 안내문의 내용과 일치하지 <u>않는</u> 것은?

Help Us Name the University's New Supercomputer!

This powerful new computer will help professors and researchers do their jobs better. But we want our students to name it!

- Please choose the name of a historical figure.
- Email your idea, along with your name and student ID number, to tech@usm.edu.
- All entries must be received by November 17.
- The university's president will choose a name from the top 10 entries.
- The winner will receive a $200 gift certificate from the campus bookstore.

We will also be having a presentation contest. Participants should prepare a 15-minute presentation with "supercomputers" as the theme. The winner of this contest will win a $150 gift certificate. Please see the university's website for more details!

① 역사적인 인물의 이름을 사용해야 한다.
② 응모 기한은 11월 17일까지이다.
③ 대학 총장이 10개의 후보 중 최종 이름을 선정한다.
④ 작명 대회 수상자는 200달러 상당의 상품권을 받게 된다.
⑤ 작명 대회 수상자는 선정된 이름을 설명하는 발표를 준비해야 한다.

29 다음 글의 밑줄 친 부분 중, 어법상 틀린 것은?

According to Russian experts, stray dogs in Moscow are becoming ① much smarter. They display surprising skills, such as the ability to recognize their stop ② while riding the subway. These dogs actually commute from the suburbs ③ where they live to the city center, where there is more food to scavenge. They even know enough to get on the first or last subway car, which are usually less crowded. Once they get downtown, they display more impressively intelligent behavior. The dogs creep up on people carrying food and bark suddenly, frightening their victims and causing the food to fall to the ground. The food is then snatched up by the dogs. Not only ④ this behavior is intelligent, it also shows great intuition, as the dogs are able to determine who is likely to be ⑤ startled enough to drop their snack.

30 (A), (B), (C)의 각 네모 안에서 문맥에 맞는 낱말로 가장 적절한 것은?

Telecommunications technology has given rise to a new class of worker: telecommuters. Telecommuters work at home on their computers instead of in an office and send their work to the office by means of the internet. Many companies are (A) expiring / experimenting with telecommuting because employees who work from home can end up saving them money on office space, utilities, and parking. In addition, telecommuters can work more efficiently at home because they are not (B) attracted / distracted by other people. On the other hand, telecommuting does have some disadvantages. If telecommuters don't have sufficient self-discipline, their work efficiency may go down. Furthermore, without the companionship of coworkers and the encouragement of supervisors, they may feel (C) isolated / united .

	(A)		(B)		(C)
①	expiring	......	attracted	......	united
②	expiring	......	distracted	......	isolated
③	experimenting	......	attracted	......	united
④	experimenting	......	distracted	......	isolated
⑤	experimenting	......	distracted	......	united

[31~34] 다음 빈칸에 들어갈 말로 가장 적절한 것을 고르시오.

31

It is commonly believed that more can be achieved when people work in a group. But something called "social loafing" sometimes occurs in these situations, causing people to work less hard in a group than they would alone. The primary cause of this phenomenon is a lack of _____. People working alone can be reasonably sure that they will be judged by their performance. But in a group, people are less worried about the consequences of performing poorly, so they tend to put forth less effort. If they don't care about the others, they may stop pulling their weight and affect the performance of the entire group. Because of this, several people working alone can sometimes be more productive than a team.

① confidence
② networking
③ anonymity
④ accountability
⑤ communication

32

People are sometimes unable to reach their goals simply because they purposefully stop themselves, creating obstacles where there previously were none. They do this in the interest of maintaining their self-esteem and protecting the image that they wish to project to others. Success, of course, would seem to be the logical path toward achieving this; yet by _____, some people are able to keep both their self-esteem and external image unharmed. The obstacles they create for themselves are ready-made excuses for why they were not able to succeed, despite their best effort. They can then tell themselves, as well as others, that the failure was out of their control and not their fault. However, by doing this, a person makes it impossible to ever reach the goals he or she truly desires.

① living in fear
② ensuring failure
③ helping others excel
④ hiding their handicaps
⑤ avoiding disappointment

33

People providing full-time care for ill, elderly, or disabled family members sometimes suffer from exhaustion on a physical, mental, and emotional level. This is known as caregiver stress syndrome. It occurs when caregivers neglect their own well-being because all of their time and energy are being focused on the other person. Since caregiving situations tend to be long-term, this exhaustion grows worse and worse over time, eventually leading to burnout. To avoid caregiver stress syndrome, the first step is to take breaks occasionally. No one can handle such a heavy burden on their own, so caregivers need to find someone else to step in and take over once in a while. Seeking out local agencies and services is another way to ease the burden, as they can perform a variety of duties, such as meal delivery and transportation. The bottom line is that caregivers must remind themselves that _____ is as important as the care they are providing. [3점]

① spending quality time with others
② their ability to sympathize with the ill
③ the care that they are receiving from others
④ their own emotional and physical well-being
⑤ the compensation they receive for their work

34

I can see why genetic engineering seems attractive, but too little is known about its potential effects on health and the environment. For example, some scientists worry that GM foods could create new allergens or diseases. Not only the welfare of humans but also that of animals could be harmed. Pigs and cows that are genetically altered have been found to suffer from disease and other health problems. And in regard to the environment, growing GM crops on a large scale may have implications for biodiversity and the balance of nature. I think it's also important to remember that we're already producing more than enough food to feed the world and that it's the global economy that creates food shortages and hunger. Thus, I think it's clear that _____. [3점]

*GM(= genetically modified): 유전자가 조작된
**allergen: 알레르겐(알레르기를 일으키는 물질)

① GM food is not the answer
② GM food should not be banned by law
③ a balanced diet is important for everyone
④ excessive food production is meaningless
⑤ GM food is safe for human consumption

35 다음 글에서 전체 흐름과 관계 <u>없는</u> 문장은?

Foreign travelers visiting certain parts of India have been surprised to see groups of cows wandering freely in odd places. ① The animals might be moving through markets, interrupting the flow of business, or walking on the shoulder of a highway, causing a major traffic jam. ② Travelers don't understand how Indians put up with such a nuisance, but the people of India don't see cows in this way at all. ③ Indeed, for many practitioners of the Hindu faith, the cow is a sacred animal and its presence is considered positive. ④ Although the number of Hindus is decreasing steadily, they still make up more than 80% of India's population. ⑤ Since Hindus treat cows like members of the family, they never eat beef, just as Westerners would never eat the meat of household pets like cats and dogs.

[36~37] 주어진 글 다음에 이어질 글의 순서로 가장 적절한 것을 고르시오.

36

Montréal-Mirabel International Airport opened in 1975 during a time of great economic growth in Montréal.

(A) However, Mirabel never ended up becoming the global airport that had been envisioned and in fact never received more than 3 million passengers a year. Because of its poor location so far outside the city and inadequate transportation compared to Montréal's other, older airport, which still continued to function, airlines and passengers opted not to use Mirabel.

(B) The prevailing optimism and ambition of this period led the municipal government to expand the city's existing airport into a 21st-century air-traffic hub. It was expected to handle 50 million passengers annually, so the construction of six runways and six terminals was planned to handle the increase in travelers.

(C) Eventually, passenger flights to Mirabel were discontinued altogether, and now the airport is used exclusively for cargo flights. There has been talk of transforming it into a public park or shopping center, but it is generally agreed that such a project would simply be too costly and difficult. [3점]

① (A) – (B) – (C) ② (A) – (C) – (B)
③ (B) – (A) – (C) ④ (B) – (C) – (A)
⑤ (C) – (B) – (A)

37

Flaws in a software program or computer system are called "bugs," and the process of fixing them is known as "debugging." The very first computer bug was recorded in 1947.

(A) The situation began when a computer scientist named Grace Hopper noticed a problem with her hardware. Opening up the computer, she was surprised to find that an actual bug was causing the problem — a small moth had gotten trapped inside the machinery.

(B) However, this isn't where the term "bug" originally comes from. It was actually used 100 years earlier by the famous inventor Thomas Edison. In a letter, he described a technical problem with his telephone design as a "bug."

(C) Hopper and her colleagues were aware of his usage, so they found the incident with the moth amusing. Hopper actually taped the dead insect to a page in her diary and wrote that she had discovered the bug in her machine.

① (A) – (B) – (C) ② (A) – (C) – (B)
③ (B) – (C) – (A) ④ (C) – (A) – (B)
⑤ (C) – (B) – (A)

38

> Proud of this participation, Athenians were prepared to die for their city-state.

The victory of the small Greek city of Athens over the mighty Persian Empire in 490 B.C. is one of the most famous events in history. King Darius of Persia never thought his powerful army would lose the war. (①) So what was the secret of the Athenians' remarkable victory? (②) It was the love that they had for their city. (③) Whereas Persia was ruled over by just one man, Athens was a democracy in which all citizens helped to rule. (④) The Persian army, on the other hand, was sent into combat by the king's command. (⑤) Consequently, the Athenians won the Battle of Marathon, which ended the Persian invasion.

39

> Such characteristics are not needed for eating but are extremely helpful in pronouncing sounds such as /f/, /v/, and /θ/.

Many scholars have studied how the development of language is linked to the evolutionary progress of the human species. (①) One particular evolutionary step may have led to the development of a human vocal tract. (②) It seems that the human body was made for producing language. (③) For example, our flexible tongues can be used to create a wide variety of sounds. (④) Our upright teeth, not at an outward angle like those of apes, are roughly even in height. (⑤) Finally, our lips have more sophisticated muscles than those of apes, and their flexibility helps with sounds like /p/, /b/, and /w/. [3점]

*vocal tract: 성도(성대에서 입술 또는 콧구멍에 이르는 통로)

40 다음 글의 내용을 한 문장으로 요약하고자 한다. 빈칸 (A), (B)에 들어갈 말로 가장 적절한 것은?

Most people think that it's fine to "work like a beaver." However, what they don't know is that although beavers may work hard, they don't actually get much done. It's true that a beaver can chew through a tree very quickly, often in less than ten minutes. But then what? Often, the beaver fails to make use of the tree. One expert says that beavers waste one out of every five trees they cut. For one thing, they do not choose their trees wisely. One time, a bunch of beavers cut down a tree that was more than one hundred feet tall. They then found that they were unable to move it, and a good tree went to waste.

↓

> Beavers may be _____(A)_____ animals, but they aren't always the most _____(B)_____ ones.

	(A)		(B)
①	intelligent	·····	organized
②	hardworking	·····	efficient
③	absurd	·····	cooperative
④	competent	·····	solitary
⑤	diligent	·····	inferior

One of the primary targets of the Russian revolutionaries who came to power in 1917 was the royal family. To implement their vision of a communist state, they felt they needed to execute Czar Nicholas II, his wife, his son, and his four daughters so that no one could rise later to challenge their (a) authority. However, not long after the royal family was reported dead, rumors surfaced that various family members had escaped and survived. Seeing an opportunity, many people came forward claiming to be a royal (b) descendant, hoping to inherit the czar's wealth.

The most famous of these was "Anna Anderson," who told authorities that she was Princess Anastasia, Czar Nicholas's youngest daughter. Her claim was helped by the fact that she physically resembled certain members of the family and knew about their life at court. Though some people accepted Anna's story, wanting to believe that the royal bloodline had not entirely (c) appeared, most didn't, and in 1927 a former acquaintance of Anna announced that her real name wasn't Anna at all, but Franziska Schanzkowska. Yet, no one could disprove Anna's story with certainty, and she enjoyed some small measure of celebrity during her legal attempts to acquire the royal (d) inheritance. The courts ultimately ruled against her, but even on her deathbed in 1984, she continued to insist that her story was true.

But years later, the remains of the executed royal family were finally found, and after running a series of (e) genetic tests, experts confirmed that Czar Nicholas's entire family had been killed in 1918 and that Anna was indeed fake.

*czar: 황제

41 윗글의 제목으로 가장 적절한 것은?

① Czar Nicholas II's Hidden Treasure
② The Genetic Traits of the Russian Royal Family
③ An Unexpected Hero of the Russian Revolution
④ The Last Royal Family's Attempts to Restore Prestige
⑤ Did Princess Anastasia Survive the Russian Revolution?

42 밑줄 친 (a)~(e) 중에서 문맥상 낱말의 쓰임이 적절하지 않은 것은? [3점]

① (a)　　② (b)　　③ (c)　　④ (d)　　⑤ (e)

[43~45] 다음 글을 읽고, 물음에 답하시오.

(A)

When the tomb of Egypt's King Tutankhamen was uncovered by Howard Carter in 1922, its catalog of splendid artifacts nearly defied comprehension. There was an entire room attached to the ancient king's burial chamber that was dedicated to housing jewels, precious metals, and other treasures. It took Carter 10 years to fully categorize all the incredible artifacts he had found. Needless to say, Carter's discovery led to increased archaeological interest and activity in the Valley of the Kings.

*the Valley of the Kings: 왕가의 계곡(고대 이집트 제18, 19 왕조의 왕가 매장지)

(B)

Herihor, a top official during the rule of Ramses XI, has been named as a likely candidate to have carried out large-scale "recycling" of this kind. After the death of Ramses, Herihor took the Egyptian throne for himself. He also intervened with the priests to put himself in charge of all reburials in the Valley of the Kings, a position that would have allowed him to carry out the massive theft of past kings' treasures. The tomb of Herihor remains hidden, but when it is found, experts expect to discover perhaps the largest collection of ancient Egyptian artifacts in the world.

(C)

However, as the tombs of other kings were unearthed in this region, their discoverers met with a very different scene: treasure chambers that were almost completely empty. Of course, the work of tomb robbers over the centuries would have explained the absence of a certain quantity of the more valuable artifacts, but these chambers were so totally depleted that there had to have been some other factor at work. Archaeologists were confronted with the mysterious question: What happened to the wealth of the Egyptian pharaohs?

*pharaoh: 파라오(고대 이집트 왕의 칭호)

(D)

In order to explain this strange phenomenon, some scholars have suggested that the treasures buried with past kings were removed during ancient times. They could have been "recycled" by the priests charged with laying to rest pharaohs of later eras. There is some evidence that some pharaohs authorized this reuse of funeral artifacts in order to give themselves the most luxurious and extraordinary burial possible.

43 주어진 글 (A)에 이어질 내용을 순서에 맞게 배열한 것으로 가장 적절한 것은?

① (B) – (D) – (C)   ② (C) – (B) – (D)
③ (C) – (D) – (B)   ④ (D) – (B) – (C)
⑤ (D) – (C) – (B)

44 윗글의 제목으로 가장 적절한 것은?

① Burial Practices in Ancient Egypt
② A New Discovery in the Valley of the Kings
③ Ancient Egyptians' Beliefs about the Afterlife
④ The Mystery of the Pharaoh's Missing Treasures
⑤ The Empty Chamber: Uncovering the Tomb of Herihor

45 윗글의 내용으로 적절하지 않은 것은?

① Tutankhamen의 무덤에 엄청난 유물들이 매장되어 있었다.
② Herihor의 무덤은 아직 발견되지 않았다.
③ 도굴꾼들에 의해 이집트 왕들의 유물이 모두 사라졌다.
④ 이집트 왕들의 매장을 주도하는 사제들이 있었다.
⑤ 후대의 파라오들은 이전 왕들의 장례 유물들을 재사용했다.

* 3점 문항에만 점수가 표시되어 있습니다.
  점수 표시가 없는 문항은 모두 2점씩입니다.

18 다음 글의 목적으로 가장 적절한 것은?

These days, ambitious professionals lead such busy lives that they have almost no free time outside of their set schedules. So when it comes time to get married, many young couples are turning to wedding planners to take care of all the details. A recent survey shows that the number of people using this type of service has more than doubled in the past three years alone. With such a high demand for wedding planners, you may want to break into the business. Don't be afraid if you don't know how to start, though. All the information you need to begin an exciting career in this industry can be found in *Practical Guide for Wedding Planning*, recently released by Greystone Publishing. There are no special qualifications required to be a great wedding planner. Just drop by the bookstore today. You can find everything you need to know in this book!

① 새로 출간된 책을 홍보하려고
② 신규 웨딩 플래너들을 모집하려고
③ 새로운 웨딩 플래닝 서비스를 안내하려고
④ 웨딩 플래닝이 확산되는 추세를 설명하려고
⑤ 웨딩 플래닝 서비스에 대한 개선을 건의하려고

19 다음 글에 드러난 Kristen의 심경으로 가장 적절한 것은?

Kristen West lived alone on her farm with a herd of cows. One day, after nearly a week of rain, a nearby river flooded West's farm. Desperately trying to get her cows to safety, she slipped and hit her head on a rock. West was knocked unconscious until Daisy, her favorite cow, woke her up by licking her face. By then the water had risen to dangerous levels, making it impossible for West to walk. Instead, she wrapped her arms around Daisy's neck and let the cow drag her through the fast-moving water. Eventually they reached the top of a hill, which was now a tiny island in a sea of raging water. They were trapped there until a rescue helicopter arrived, lowered a rope to West, and lifted her up to safety. West later went back for Daisy, but she was gone. She cried for the loss of her old friend, knowing she wouldn't have survived without her.

① calm and indifferent
② amused and thrilled
③ relieved but sorrowful
④ exhausted but delighted
⑤ embarrassed but satisfied

20 다음 글에서 필자가 주장하는 바로 가장 적절한 것은?

I realize that society needs rules in order to function properly. But we've reached a point where there are too many rules. Of course, we need some rules, but let's not go so far that people become overwhelmed and can no longer keep track of them all. I hope that someday we can do away with certain rules. From joining a health club to starting a business, the amount of rules involved can really put people off from trying to do anything new. Hopefully, rule-makers will realize this and start to make fewer and simpler rules. In the meantime, let's do what we can to make following rules a little easier.

① 제정된 규칙은 반드시 지켜져야 한다.
② 각 문화에 따라 규칙은 달라져야 한다.
③ 시대의 변화에 따라 규칙은 개정될 필요가 있다.
④ 규칙을 너무 많이 만들지 말고 간소화해야 한다.
⑤ 규칙을 제정할 때 다양한 집단의 의견을 수렴해야 한다.

21 다음 글의 요지로 가장 적절한 것은?

While investing in the stock market is serious business, it's never too early to start teaching your kids some of the concepts behind it. As they get older, they can start investing small amounts and learning the financial skills they'll need later in life. In today's world, a solid understanding of finance and the economy is an important part of a child's education. So why should they wait until college to start learning the fundamentals of the stock market? You might think your children wouldn't have any interest, but don't underestimate the natural curiosity of the young. The economy and your investments have a direct impact on their lives — you might be surprised on how eager they are to fully understand it.

① 주식 거래 시에는 전문가의 조언이 필요하다.
② 저축을 통해 올바른 경제 습관을 기를 수 있다.
③ 과도한 교육은 자녀에게 부정적인 영향을 끼친다.
④ 부모의 경제 관념이 자녀의 삶에 영향을 크게 미친다.
⑤ 아이들에게 어려서부터 경제 교육을 하는 것이 중요하다.

[22~23] 다음 글의 주제로 가장 적절한 것을 고르시오.

22

Thanks to today's advanced weather satellites, forecasters can observe large weather systems, such as typhoons and hurricanes. Normally, these satellites use two different kinds of sensors. The first is called an imager. Like a camera, it uses reflected light to create images of the Earth. Because the planet's different surfaces reflect the sun's light in different ways, they can be recognized and distinguished in the images. Water, for instance, reflects little light and therefore shows up black. The second type of sensor found on weather satellites is called an infrared sounder. It uses the infrared spectrum to sense the temperature of objects. Because temperature is directly related to the amount of energy emission, a sounder can measure the amount of energy being radiated from various surfaces of the Earth. This information can be used to make more accurate weather predictions and also to measure the effects of greenhouse gases on the atmosphere.

① uses of different types of satellites
② detecting equipment on weather satellites
③ effects of greenhouse gases on the atmosphere
④ difficulties in predicting large weather systems
⑤ the invention and development of weather satellites

23

The Rotten Tomatoes website, which provides ratings of the latest movies, has partially changed its format in order to become more "fan" oriented. Along with providing links to professional reviews, the site allows viewers to post their own ratings and comments. However, they will no longer be able to do this before the movie has been released in theaters. This is to ensure that the posts are fair and genuine. These audience reviews generate a score that appears beside something called a "Tomatometer" score. This is based on the percentage of reviews by professional critics that were positive. If 60% or more of the reviews are positive, the film is rated "fresh" and receives a red tomato icon. Otherwise, it is rated "rotten" and receives a splattered green tomato icon. Audience review scores do not affect this rating system. [3점]

① an alteration to an online review system
② how a popular website deceives its users
③ reasons audiences express dissatisfaction
④ why movies receive mostly positive reviews
⑤ a problem caused by professional movie critics

24 다음 글의 제목으로 가장 적절한 것은?

There are some people who enjoy the taste of coffee but want to avoid caffeine for health or personal reasons. For many of them, the solution to this problem is drinking decaffeinated coffee. Decaffeinated coffee is made from coffee beans from which at least 97% of the caffeine has been removed. Despite this, it may still have some potentially serious effects on the health of drinkers. The main problem is the method that is employed to remove the caffeine. The beans are soaked in a variety of chemicals, some of which are also included in paint thinner or nail polish remover. These chemicals have been approved by food safety agencies, but they should still be considered a health risk. Another issue is the beans themselves, since the beans that are used to make decaffeinated

coffee contain more fat than those used for regular coffee. This could lead to higher cholesterol levels and serious heart issues.

*thinner: (페인트 등의) 희석제

① Some Coffee Beans Are Better Than Others
② The Health Dangers and Benefits of Caffeine
③ Decaf or Regular: There's Very Little Difference
④ The Downside of Drinking Decaffeinated Coffee
⑤ The Secrets to Making a Perfect Decaffeinated Coffee

25 다음 도표의 내용과 일치하지 않는 것은?

pH Level of the Mouth from Consumption of Sugars/Honey

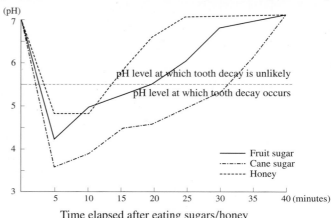

Time elapsed after eating sugars/honey

The above graph shows how eating sweet foods lowers the pH level of the mouth, which increases the likelihood of tooth decay. Tooth decay is likely to occur when pH levels drop below 5.5. ① The graph compares the effects of fruit sugar, cane sugar, and honey, showing that cane sugar lowers the pH level the most and keeps it below 5.5 for the longest time. ② Just five minutes after eating cane sugar, your mouth's pH level drops down to about pH 3.5. ③ After that, it begins to rise back up, but doesn't exceed pH 5.5 for about 25 minutes. ④ Fruit sugar, on the other hand, keeps the pH level beneath the point where tooth decay is likely to occur for about 25 minutes. ⑤ Honey is the least damaging of the three substances, dropping pH levels to about 4.75, but returning them above pH 5.5 in less than 15 minutes.

26 얼룩말에 관한 다음 글의 내용과 일치하지 <u>않는</u> 것은?

The zebra is distinguished by its striking pattern of alternating black and white stripes. In size, a zebra is larger than a donkey but smaller than a horse. It has a heavy head, stout body, stiff mane, and short tail. There are three living zebra species. Most zebras live in open plains and grasslands, while mountain zebras favor rocky hillsides. The plains zebras usually mix with other grazing animals like wildebeest and antelopes. They can run as fast as 40 miles per hour. Some experts believe that the stripes evolved as a way for herds of zebras to identify one another and form social bonds, rather than for disguise or insect protection.

*wildebeest: 누(영양의 일종)   **antelope: 영양

① 당나귀와 말의 중간 정도의 크기이다.
② 머리가 무겁고 꼬리가 짧은 편이다.
③ 대부분은 평야와 목초지에 서식한다.
④ 산얼룩말은 시속 40마일로 달릴 수 있다.
⑤ 줄무늬가 사회적 유대를 위해 진화한 것이라는 견해도 있다.

27 Paul Erdos에 관한 다음 글의 내용과 일치하는 것은?

Renowned for his brilliant solutions to perplexing mathematical equations in the field of numbers theory, Hungarian-born mathematician Paul Erdos is considered to have been more of a problem solver than a developer of theories. At the tender age of three, he already discovered negative numbers on his own and developed the ability to multiply three-digit numbers in his head. When he was just 20, he discovered a proof for Chebyshev's theorem. Completely devoting his life to mathematics, which he viewed as a sort of social activity, he was a prolific publisher of papers, writing or co-authoring about 1,500 mathematical articles over the course of his lifetime. Erdos passed away in 1996 while attempting to formulate a solution to yet another mathematical problem.

*theorem: 【수학】 정리(定理)

① 문제 해결자라기보다는 이론 개발자로 더 유명하다.
② 세 살 때 체비쇼프 정리의 증명을 이해했다.
③ 수학을 일종의 사회 활동이라고 생각했다.
④ 논문을 공동 저술하지 않는 것으로 유명했다.
⑤ 죽기 전에는 병세의 악화로 연구 활동을 중단했다.

28 San Diego Readers Club에 관한 다음 안내문의 내용과 일치하지 <u>않는</u> 것은?

San Diego Readers Club

The Readers Club is a community service designed for adults who want to improve their English reading skills. It is open to all local residents 17 and over, and there is no cost to participate.

When: Wednesday evenings from 7 to 8 p.m.
Where: San Diego Public Library, Main Branch, Meeting Room C
What: Reading classic novels in a group setting

The club meets all year, except on public holidays. However, there will be no meetings in the month of August this year, due to scheduled renovations in the library.

You can sign up online on the city's official website or in person at the library. For more information, call the library's main desk at 619-431-1815.

① 17세 이상 지역 주민은 누구나 참여 가능하다.
② 매주 수요일 저녁에 한 시간 동안 진행된다.
③ 모임 장소는 공공 도서관의 회의실이다.
④ 올해는 8월까지 모임이 열리지 않는다.
⑤ 온라인 등록과 방문 등록 모두 가능하다.

29 다음 글의 밑줄 친 부분 중, 어법상 틀린 것은? [3점]

Facial expressions are the most obvious sign of someone's emotional state. We can understand a lot about a person's emotions by observing ① whether that person is laughing, crying, smiling, or frowning. Interestingly, many facial expressions are inborn. Children who are born deaf and blind ② using the same facial expressions to express the same emotions as those who are born without such disabilities. It was Charles Darwin ③ who first advanced the theory that most animals share a common pattern of muscular facial movements. For example, dogs, tigers, and humans all show their teeth when ④ displaying rage. Darwin's idea that expressing our feelings ⑤ is rooted in evolution laid the groundwork for many modern analyses of emotional expression.

30 (A), (B), (C)의 각 네모 안에서 문맥에 맞는 낱말로 가장 적절한 것은?

People realized hundreds of years ago that crocodiles cry while they eat. The (A) physiological / psychological reason for this, however, has just recently been discovered. In 2007, some researchers noted that not only do reptiles such as crocodiles produce tears while eating, but these tears also seem to "froth and bubble" from the reptiles' eyes. This gave the researchers an important clue. Crocodiles make many breathy sounds as they eat, and this causes air to move quickly through the sinuses. The air (B) stimulates / simulates the eye to produce more tears than usual. Some of the air leaves the head through the eyes and causes the tears to bubble. Some other researchers have suggested that the tears are squeezed out of the tear ducts when crocodiles bite down hard. Still other experts believe that tears which have (C) accumulated / accelerated below the eye fall when the crocodile moves its jaw while eating. However, the exact cause is still up for debate.

*sinus: 부비강(코 안쪽으로 이어지는 두개골 속의 구멍)

	(A)	(B)	(C)
①	physiological	stimulates	accumulated
②	physiological	stimulates	accelerated
③	physiological	simulates	accelerated
④	psychological	stimulates	accumulated
⑤	psychological	simulates	accelerated

[31~35] 다음 빈칸에 들어갈 말로 가장 적절한 것을 고르시오.

31

The goal of time management is to use a set of principles, skills, and tools to get the maximum value out of your time, thereby improving the quality of your life. Time management, however, is not simply about doing as much as you can in the shortest period of time. Instead, it focuses more on ensuring that you are working on the _____ things. People with good time management skills realize that there will always be more work than can be accomplished in a single day. Rather than try to do it all, they carefully choose what they will spend their time on. Generally, they concentrate on a small number of important projects instead of spending their time on a large number of trivial things. By doing so, they are able to become more efficient workers, accomplishing more in less time.

① right
② simple
③ newest
④ demanding
⑤ insignificant

32

A lot of people feel guilty every time they have a hamburger. However, what is in a hamburger is not that bad. Don't forget that red meat is a good source of iron and that cheeseburgers contain calcium. French fries, which most people think are unhealthy, are rich in vitamin C. Nowadays, fast food restaurants pay great attention to nutrition. They use fewer additives and cook with vegetable oil. And some hamburger buns are being made from whole wheat, instead of flour. Also, most places offer salad bars, which give people the chance to balance fast food with vegetables. So, don't think you need to _____.

① eat healthy food
② become a vegetarian
③ feel guilty for being fat
④ avoid fast food completely
⑤ live on cheeseburgers and fries

33

For many years, the De Beers Corporation of South Africa has been in control of the world's supply of diamonds. It was started in 1888 by Cecil Rhodes, a British businessman who had previously run a company which rented equipment to diamond miners. After starting his new diamond mining business, Rhodes realized he was facing a serious financial dilemma. With the South African diamond rush in full swing, diamond prices were plummeting as supply began to outpace demand. He decided that the only way he could increase the value of his product and ensure a profit was to decrease the number of _____.
Production was reduced in the De Beers mines, and soon his company had a tightly controlled monopoly over the diamond market. [3점]

① diamonds available to make them rare
② ads to reduce the demand for diamonds
③ mines by selling parts of his business
④ people working for him to lower his costs
⑤ products he sold by getting rid of other gems

34

FOMO stands for the "fear of missing out." It refers to feelings of anxiety about information, events, and experiences we might not know about. As a result of this anxiety, we feel the need to stay aware of what others are doing at all times. Modern technology has made FOMO worse, but it is actually an ancient problem. Early humans needed to constantly be conscious of their surroundings in order to survive. Not knowing about a food source or nearby predator could be fatal. Later, when people started forming towns and cities, they began to rely on others _____.
At first, they got this information through gossip and rumors, and later through television and newspapers. Today, the internet has intensified FOMO by making more information available than ever before.

① to learn about new kinds of technology
② to stay informed about important events
③ to keep them safe from dangerous things
④ to help them share thoughts and opinions
⑤ to know what town or city to move to next

35

People love to read about the personal lives of celebrities. The unfaithfulness, the break-ups, the law-breaking, and other intimate facts attract the attention of millions. Gossip magazines keep readers informed of the latest happenings in the personal lives of well-known people. Some of the news is factual, though much is just rumors with no proof. These magazines are very popular, but they don't really ever tell us anything useful. So why do people read them? It's because they make people feel important, as though they were a part of stars' secret lives. _____. These magazines also allow them to temporarily leave their ordinary lives behind and become a part of Hollywood. These magazines feed off the human urge to gossip. [3점]

① People tend to avoid gossip
② Rumors usually turn out to be true
③ These magazines help people become popular
④ These magazines reveal many important secrets
⑤ People feel involved when they read these magazines

36 다음 글에서 전체 흐름과 관계 없는 문장은?

A new development in medicine may give hope to millions of cancer patients around the world. The treatment, which will be ready for large-scale testing soon, utilizes an unlikely partnership to target cancerous tumors. ① First, the patient is injected with a strain of bacteria that thrives in low-oxygen environments, such as the insides of solid tumors. ② Once the bacteria have established themselves in the tumor or tumors, the patient receives an injection of a cell-destroying drug in an inactive state. ③ The drug can only be activated when it comes in contact with an enzyme contained within the bacteria. ④ These bacteria find it difficult to survive in parts of the body with higher levels of oxygen. ⑤ In other words, the drug becomes active when it reaches the bacteria-infested tumor, destroying the cancerous growth while leaving the healthy cells that surround it unharmed.

[37~38] 주어진 글 다음에 이어질 글의 순서로 가장 적절한 것을 고르시오.

37

Anti-war sentiment is not a modern phenomenon; wars have been opposed as long as they have been fought.

(A) Some of them, known as "conscientious objectors," argued that participating in the violence of war went against their religious beliefs. Others saw it as contrary to the cause of international socialism, which encouraged the working classes of all nations to unite and create a better world.

(B) World War I was no exception. Despite the intense nationalism in Europe in 1914, there were thousands of citizens across the continent unwilling to fight for their countries.

(C) Despite these noble reasons for refusing to fight, the objectors were in the minority and were scorned by their fellow citizens, and even given lengthy prison sentences. However, looking back now on the tragic and senseless loss of life that occurred during World War I, it is difficult not to side with the objectors.

① (A) – (C) – (B)   ② (B) – (A) – (C)
③ (B) – (C) – (A)   ④ (C) – (A) – (B)
⑤ (C) – (B) – (A)

38

Professional photographers have always been competing against nature. They take pictures even in the most extreme weather conditions, although heat, humidity, dust, and cold can harm photographic materials and equipment in many ways.

(A) Armed with these devices, professional photographers have been able to avoid the worst consequences of extreme weather conditions and capture the perfect image.

(B) To avoid catastrophe, photographers have devised numerous ways to protect their equipment, from sophisticated cases to simple plastic bags and picnic coolers.

(C) The harm caused by such weather conditions is sometimes immediately noticeable, such as when the shutter breaks. Often though, the harm is impossible to detect until after the film is developed or the effects of camera corrosion begin to show. [3점]

① (A) – (B) – (C)
② (A) – (C) – (B)
③ (B) – (C) – (A)
④ (C) – (A) – (B)
⑤ (C) – (B) – (A)

39 글의 흐름으로 보아, 주어진 문장이 들어가기에 가장 적절한 곳은? [3점]

However, farmers were hit especially hard.

The Great Depression of the United States was the worst and longest economic crisis in the modern industrial world. (①) At its worst point, more than 16 million people were unemployed, and over 85,000 businesses had failed. (②) Millions of Americans lost their jobs, their savings, and even their homes. (③) A severe drought coupled with the economic crisis ruined small farms throughout the Great Plains. (④) Productive farmland turned to dust, and crop prices dropped by 50%. (⑤) Prices dropped so low that many farmers went bankrupt and lost their jobs. With the start of World War II, crop prices began to rise, and the nation simultaneously saw a return to a stable job market.

*the Great Plains: (로키산맥 동부의) 대평원

40 다음 글의 내용을 한 문장으로 요약하고자 한다. 빈칸 (A), (B)에 들어갈 말로 가장 적절한 것은?

In this weak economy, college graduates may have a hard time obtaining a job. However, companies have begun to provide more and more different types of internships. Accordingly, the internship placement service industry has exploded in recent years, helping people find internships that fit their needs. According to internship service companies, they have the resources to help their clients land difficult-to-get positions because of their numerous connections with all kinds of employers. Nonetheless, college advisors caution parents who are considering relying on an internship service company to get their child an internship. That's because it will deprive their child of the opportunity to develop the job-seeking skills they'll need once they enter the working world.

↓

Internship service companies can help students find an internship to start a _____(A)_____, but they may prevent students from learning _____(B)_____ skills.

	(A)		(B)
①	job	......	academic
②	journey	......	technical
③	business	......	fundamental
④	career	......	valuable
⑤	venture	......	secondary

[41~42] 다음 글을 읽고, 물음에 답하시오.

Too much water is currently used to make our lifestyles possible. Most of this water — almost 90% — is used to make food and energy. In fact, it takes 1.5 tons of water to make a computer and 6 tons to make a single pair of jeans.

Unfortunately, we simply do not have enough water to continue this way. Within 20 years, we will need more water than we have, and industry and agriculture will have serious problems. The two main factors (a) contributing to this terrible situation are climate change and population growth. By 2031, one-third of the world's people will not have (b) access to nearly as much water as they need.

There is good news, though. With determination, people can save water. One of the most important things we can do is find better ways to manage our water systems. Since water is not (c) limited, we should replace our older household items with newer, more efficient ones. Modern toilets, washing machines, and irrigation systems can reduce the amount of water that houses use by as much as 70% in some places.

However, it is also important to protect the quality of the water that we already have. Sadly, with weather changing in (d) unpredictable ways, large floods are occurring more frequently. These floods can overwhelm our water systems, and they can also easily introduce diseases into the water, leading to serious health concerns. Although these challenges will not resolve themselves, by managing our water wisely, we can change our situation. We should (e) adapt our water infrastructure to the changing climate so that we can protect our future.

41 윗글의 제목으로 가장 적절한 것은?

① The Future of Our Water Supply
② The Dangers of Serious Flooding
③ Purifying Water: A Complex Process
④ Population Growth: A Threat to the Water Supply
⑤ A Lesson Learned from an Environmental Challenge

42 밑줄 친 (a)~(e) 중에서 문맥상 낱말의 쓰임이 적절하지 않은 것은? [3점]

① (a)　　② (b)　　③ (c)　　④ (d)　　⑤ (e)

[43~45] 다음 글을 읽고, 물음에 답하시오.

(A)

Nearly 1,500 years after the ancient Greeks held their final Olympic Games, their 19th-century descendants attempted to bring back the tradition. Unfortunately, their efforts went unnoticed by much of the world. As it turned out, it would take Pierre de Coubertin, a French baron, to get the Olympic tradition rolling again.

(B)

In the late 1800s, Pierre de Coubertin became dedicated to the notion that education in his country should be reformed to more closely resemble that of ancient Greece. Not only should his countrymen be trained as great scholars, but also as great sportsmen, for to Coubertin, challenging the limits of one's body was just as important as challenging one's mind. To this end, he proposed the idea of a modern Olympic Games to the USFSA (Union of French Athletic Sports Societies) in 1892.

(C)

Excited by his success, Coubertin further lobbied to have France be the host for the very first modern Olympics. However, the committee felt it would be an appropriate salute to the past to allow Greece to put on the founding games in 1896. As a compromise, France was selected as the location for the second event, to be held four years later in 1900, and thus the modern Olympic Games were born. As in ancient Greece, they would be held every four years, but unlike those original games, these would take place in a different location each time they occurred.

(D)

This initial attempt was rejected, but the determined Coubertin refused to give up. Two years later, he presented the idea again, this time to a committee of international delegates. His decision to frame the concept of a modern Olympic Games as a way to improve relations between countries in an increasingly violent world won the support of the committee. Several countries — Belgium, Italy, Russia, Spain, England, Sweden, the U.S., Greece, and even Coubertin's home country of France — committed to the idea.

43 주어진 글 (A)에 이어질 내용을 순서에 맞게 배열한 것으로 가장 적절한 것은?

① (B) – (C) – (D) ② (B) – (D) – (C)
③ (C) – (D) – (B) ④ (D) – (B) – (C)
⑤ (D) – (C) – (B)

44 윗글의 제목으로 가장 적절한 것은?

① The Greek Culture Trend in France
② Ways to Challenge the Body's Limits
③ Studying the Ancient Olympic Games
④ Olympics: A Solution for World Conflicts
⑤ Reinventing an Ancient Olympic Tradition

45 윗글의 Pierre de Coubertin에 관한 내용과 일치하지 않는 것은?

① 올림픽 게임의 재개를 위해 노력한 최초의 인물이었다.
② 고대 그리스처럼 체육 교육을 중시했다.
③ 근대 올림픽 게임 재개를 프랑스 체육 협회 연합에 제안했다.
④ 프랑스가 첫 근대 올림픽 게임의 개최국이 되도록 노력했다.
⑤ 근대 올림픽 게임이 국제 관계의 증진에 도움이 된다고 믿었다.

* 3점 문항에만 점수가 표시되어 있습니다.
  점수 표시가 없는 문항은 모두 2점씩입니다.

18 다음 글의 목적으로 가장 적절한 것은?

To the Board of Directors,

  On behalf of all the employees at Lee Technologies, I would like to share our concern about the recent downturn in the economy, which has led to a significant increase in inflation. As you know, a high rate of inflation means that money loses its value; essentially, one dollar could buy a loaf of bread yesterday, but today it cannot. This has limited our ability to sustain a reasonable quality of life at our current pay level; therefore, we are seeking a pay increase that would allow our salaries to keep pace with the rise of inflation. Lee Technologies has recorded profits for the last three quarters, so the company has the means to meet this reasonable request. If possible, we would like to meet with you to further discuss this issue.

Sincerely,
Morgan Newman

① 경영진에게 월급 인상을 요청하려고
② 수익증대를 위한 방안을 제안하려고
③ 회사 매출 실적에 대한 내용을 공유하려고
④ 복리후생 증진을 위한 더 많은 혜택을 요구하려고
⑤ 경기 침체에 따른 회사 경영 방식 변경을 알리려고

19 다음 글에 드러난 Rick의 심경으로 가장 적절한 것은?

  One night, as a thunderstorm was raging outside Rick Simon's house, he heard his smoke alarm beep. Lightning flashed outside the windows, and Rick suddenly worried that his wooden house had caught fire. He left his second-floor bedroom to check for smoke. Fortunately, the stairway was clear, and the first floor also seemed safe. Then he opened the basement door. Flames leaped out of the basement, and soon there were flames everywhere. He ran to his bedroom to call the fire department, but the phone was dead. He turned to run down the stairs, but they were already covered in flames. Rick was trapped. His house was in the woods, and no one could see it from the road. If he shouted for help, no one would hear. Both escaping and being rescued were impossible.

① hesitant
② furious
③ relieved
④ hopeless
⑤ melancholy

20 다음 글에서 필자가 주장하는 바로 가장 적절한 것은?

When my wife spent three weeks in the hospital as part of her cancer treatment, I experienced the gloominess and depression of the hospital waiting room. Being unable to eat, read, or watch TV, I felt as if I had ceased to exist. All around me, I saw people in the same state, sick with worry over their loved ones. How hard would it be to provide a better environment for people in our situation? After all, while our loved ones are locked away in examination and operating facilities, we in the waiting room should not be forgotten. Hospitals should start by brightening the atmosphere of the waiting room with warm colors and cheerful pictures. Volunteers could also be enlisted to spend time with these waiting people, assuring them that their loved ones will be okay.

① 병원 대기실의 분위기 개선이 필요하다.
② 병원 대기실에 텔레비전을 설치해야 한다.
③ 병원 대기실에서 음식을 먹어서는 안 된다.
④ 병원 대기실의 실내 공기를 환기시켜야 한다.
⑤ 병원 대기실에 외부인의 출입을 막아야 한다.

21 다음 글의 요지로 가장 적절한 것은?

Certain simple noises in the workplace can seem to be oddly amplified, distracting and annoying employees attempting to focus on their work. Despite what you may think, this is not an illusion created in the minds of stressed-out, overly sensitive workers. The fact is that many offices contain a large number of hard surfaces that easily reflect sound, such as bare walls and tiled floors. The best way to cut down on this type of ambient noise without spending a lot of money is to simply buy some potted plants. Arranged properly, a few plants can break up and deflect sound waves that would otherwise be reflected off the wall and back into the room. According to a study, plants can reduce the noise level in an office by up to five decibels.

① 직장 내에 실내 정원을 가꾸어야 한다.
② 소음이 업무를 방해하는 주요 원인이다.
③ 식물을 키우면 스트레스 해소에 도움이 된다.
④ 화분을 배치하면 사무실 내의 소음을 줄일 수 있다.
⑤ 사무실 내의 소음을 줄이기 위한 규제가 마련되어야 한다.

[22~23] 다음 글의 주제로 가장 적절한 것을 고르시오.

22

The completion of the Transcontinental Railroad allowed the U.S. to populate the frontier and establish its influence on the continent. Before the railroad, there were only two ways of reaching the west coast, by wagon or ship. Both methods took several months and were quite expensive. Because of these drawbacks, the land west of Missouri was not sufficiently populated. However, President Lincoln knew that the survival of the country depended on westward expansion so he authorized the Union Pacific and Central Pacific railroads to take on the task. In 1869, the railroad was complete, and now a safe, fast way was available to migrate west. Millions of Americans ventured west and developed many of the territories in the area. The U.S. began to prosper because it could take advantage of raw materials in remote areas to feed its growing economy. The railroad allowed the U.S. to become an economic and political force in the world.

① the development of transportation in the U.S.
② synergy between the newly connected states
③ the enormous impact of the Transcontinental Railroad on the U.S. economy
④ President Lincoln's political reasons for developing the Transcontinental Railroad
⑤ how the Transcontinental Railroad slowed the development of the western states

23

CCUS stands for "carbon capture, utilization, and storage." It is technology that plays an essential role in helping the oil and gas industry reduce CO_2 emissions while continuing to meet global energy demands. CCUS reduces emissions and helps remove CO_2 from the atmosphere, so it is an important part of reaching net-zero emissions goals. The first step of CCUS involves capturing the CO_2 that is released through industrial processes or the burning of fuel. This CO_2 is then transported to sites where it can be stored safely. This is useful in reducing emissions from airplanes and industrial plants that can't easily be converted to clean energy. It is believed that CCUS projects have the potential to lead the way to reducing global CO_2 emissions by almost 20%. They are also cost-efficient, and are projected to lower the cost of fighting climate change by approximately 70%. [3점]

*net-zero emission: 순 배출 제로
(온실가스나 탄소 등의 물질을 배출하는 만큼 제거하여 존재하는 총량을 0으로 유지하는 것)

① a process that lessens the impact of CO_2 pollution
② a method of finding oil and gas in rock formations
③ the reason industrial processes release harmful gases
④ a new industry that promotes the use of clean energy
⑤ modern techniques that are ineffective in reducing CO_2 emissions

24 다음 글의 제목으로 가장 적절한 것은?

While it is often helpful to think of humans as simply another successful type of mammal, a vital distinction remains. When a pride of lions enjoys an excess of food, they are likely to eat all they can and then spend the remainder of the day sleeping in order to conserve energy. On the contrary, humans do not spend their leisure time sleeping. Our big brains cause us to be restless, which makes us engage in play. Humans speak, write love songs, build churches, or do a lot of other things that we consider worthwhile. Human beings' non-survival activities take the form of art, philosophy, science, and even government, which over time have led to the foundation of society and culture.

① Humans: Just Another Type of Animal
② What Distinguishes Humans from Animals
③ Protecting Animals from Human Destruction
④ The History of the Human Brain's Development
⑤ Art: The Distinction between Humans and Animals

25 다음 도표의 내용과 일치하지 <u>않는</u> 것은?

Markets for U.S. Exports of Scrap Paper and Plastic

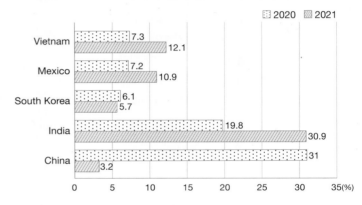

The above graph shows five major countries to which the U.S. exported scrap paper and plastic in January of 2020 and 2021. ① In 2020, the greatest amount of scrap paper and plastic was exported to China, but it was India that took in the greatest amount in 2021. ② In terms of percentage, 2021 exports to India were just one tenth of a percentage point lower than 2020 exports to China. ③ In 2020, the smallest percentage of exports went to South Korea, which was only about one percentage point less than exports to Mexico and Vietnam. ④ Exports to China showed the greatest drop between the two years, with the 2021 percentage being only about one tenth of the 2020 percentage. ⑤ India, on the other hand, saw the greatest rise, with its percentage of 2021 exports being only half of a percentage point lower than those of the other four countries combined.

26 water retention에 관한 다음 글의 내용과 일치하지 않는 것은?

"Water retention" is a condition in which water leaks from a person's blood and into their tissues, most commonly in the vicinity of the legs or feet, where it then proceeds to accumulate. In normal circumstances, this fluid is naturally drained via a series of tubes, but when it is not, the tissues become swollen. Possibly due to estrogen levels, water retention is a more common occurrence in women than in men. The factors that may lead to water retention include the consumption of salt, high temperatures, nutritional deficiencies, and the side effects of some prescription medicine. However, in some cases, water retention may be a symptom of a more serious illness, such as a disease affecting the heart, liver, or lungs.

① 수분이 혈액에서 조직으로 새어 들어가는 것이다.
② 주로 손이나 팔 부근에서 일어나는 증상이다.
③ 남성보다 여성에게서 더 많이 발생한다.
④ 약물 부작용으로 인해 일어나기도 한다.
⑤ 심장 관련 질환의 징후로 나타날 수도 있다.

27 아테네에 관한 다음 글의 내용과 일치하는 것은?

The city state of Athens, located in the region of Attica, is seen as the birthplace of modern democracy. At that time, Athens was ruled by kings. Over time, they were replaced by a series of powerful rulers, called tyrants. These men cared little for the people. In 594 BC, a famous statesman named Solon replaced the tyrants and he established a new set of rules. But, in 510 BC, the respected Athenian Cleisthenes introduced reforms to Solon's principles. He changed the division of tribes into a territorial division. He then divided Attica into districts and those districts into smaller areas each containing a representative. He also replaced Solon's Council of 400, which represented four tribes with 100 members from each tribe, with the Council of 500, which represented ten tribes with 50 members from each. His changes weakened the power of the aristocracy and made the distribution of wealth more equal, thus opening the door to democracy.

① 독재자들에 의한 통치에서 왕정으로 전환했다.
② Solon은 가장 강력한 권력을 지닌 독재자였다.
③ Attica 지역은 기원전 510년에 부족 중심으로 분할되었다.
④ Cleisthenes는 위원회를 구성하는 대표자의 수를 늘렸다.
⑤ Cleisthenes의 개혁 후 경제적 불평등이 더 커졌다.

28 Halloween at the Zoo에 관한 다음 안내문의 내용과 일치하지 않는 것은?

Halloween at the Zoo

The Bridgeport Zoo is pleased to announce its third annual Halloween party. Children of all ages are welcome, but kids under the age of 16 must be accompanied by a parent.

Time & Date
From 5 p.m. to 10 p.m. on October 31

Tickets
- $20 for zoo members
- $25 for non-members

Tickets include two free drinks and admission to all events and animal exhibits.

Details
- Local restaurants will be selling food at stands throughout the zoo. Most will accept credit cards, but some will not.
- The zoo has ATMs located inside the information center.
- The event will be held regardless of the weather. In the case of rain, all performances will be moved indoors.

① 16세 미만 어린이는 부모 동반 시 입장 가능하다.
② 회원의 입장료는 비회원보다 5달러 더 저렴하다.
③ 동물 전시관에 입장하려면 추가 금액을 지불해야 한다.
④ 일부 가판에서는 신용카드를 사용할 수 없다.
⑤ 우천 시에는 실내에서 진행된다.

29 다음 글의 밑줄 친 부분 중, 어법상 틀린 것은? [3점]

The planets of our solar system can be divided into two very distinct groups in terms of size, mass, and composition. Mercury, Venus, and Mars resemble Earth in ① being made up almost completely of rocky materials and iron. These four planets are known as "terrestrial planets." These terrestrial planets are separated from ② those farther from the Sun by a large gap containing an asteroid field. After this gap ③ comes the giant planets — Jupiter, Saturn, Uranus, and Neptune. All of these are significantly larger than Earth. Pluto, once considered the farthest planet from the Sun, is significantly different, ④ consisting mainly of methane and ice. In fact, Pluto was recently demoted from planet status and ⑤ is now considered a "dwarf planet."

*asteroid: 소행성 **dwarf planet: 왜소행성(행성과 소행성의 중간단계인 천체)

30 (A), (B), (C)의 각 네모 안에서 문맥에 맞는 낱말로 가장 적절한 것은?

Today, the term "a white elephant" refers to something that you own even though there is no practical use for it. Because the white elephant is connected with Buddha, people in Southeast Asia regard the animal as holy. Thus, white elephants are (A) despised / valued too much to allow them to do hard work. In this society, white elephants could only be obtained as a present from a king or emperor, so owning a white elephant was a privilege. However, the elephant was (B) advantageous / burdensome to the recipient of the gift since the owner had to keep and maintain the king's gift well. It used many resources while offering very few (C) benefits / disadvantages. Despite that, the owner could not help but keep it because disposing of the animal would be an insult to the king.

	(A)	(B)	(C)
①	despised	advantageous	benefits
②	despised	burdensome	disadvantages
③	valued	burdensome	disadvantages
④	valued	burdensome	benefits
⑤	valued	advantageous	benefits

[31~34] 다음 빈칸에 들어갈 말로 가장 적절한 것을 고르시오.

31

Hoarding things, regardless of what they are, is a pointless form of _____. Some people want to keep these things simply because they exist, not because they have any functional use. Cheap jewelry has some inherent use when you are actually wearing it, but people who hoard it are just throwing away their money. Soon they have countless hundreds of useless cheap jewelry that they have to sort and save. And then they have to spend more money on jewelry cases to put it all in. After that, they begin spending extravagant amounts of money to buy more and more in order to increase their collections. But there is no end to this hoarding, so the hobby just continues to get out of hand. All of that time and money could be put to a much better purpose.

① materialism
② self-display
③ practicalism
④ achievement
⑤ entertainment

32

Cajun food is a hot, spicy, delicious style of cooking which attracts many hungry tourists to its home in Louisiana. But although Louisiana is famous for being the home of Cajun cooking, this style of cuisine actually represents the blending of many cultures which has taken place during the history of Louisiana. Over the years, Louisiana has had strong influences from many cultures, including Native American, Spanish, French, Acadian, African, Italian, and more. Cajun food has evolved over the centuries as each ethnic group added its own individual touches to the local flavor. Today's Cajun cooking is so much more than simply adding hot sauce — it's _____.

*Acadian: 아카디아 지방(캐나다 남동부에 위치한 주)의

① a traditional American cuisine
② delicious without being too spicy
③ everywhere so you can eat it anywhere
④ the most popular local food among visitors
⑤ the mixing of the flavors of many cultures into one

33

Scientists generally believe that, in order to survive in the frigid conditions of the Arctic, ancient humans must have developed the ability to create form-fitting, weather-tight clothing. This clothing was probably made by stitching together pieces of animal skin with sinew. Therefore, the technological breakthrough that eventually allowed humans to begin _____ was most likely the invention of a pointed tool called the awl. Over time, the awl was developed into the "eyed needle" that is still used for stitching and sewing today. Although archaeological evidence tells that approximately 15,000 years passed between the first use of needles and the eventual migration of humans into the Arctic, it is safe to say that without the former event, the latter might never have occurred. [3점]

*sinew: 힘줄

① cooking their food
② making portable tents
③ hunting large animals
④ using written language
⑤ colonizing cold regions

34

The Forer effect, which is also called the Barnum effect, refers to the tendency of people to believe that general statements apply specifically to them. The best-known example of this is horoscopes. Even though they are written for millions of people, we feel as though they accurately describe us. This phenomenon was originally identified by a psychologist named Bertram Forer. In 1948, he conducted an experiment in which students took a personality test. They were told that each of them would be given a personal assessment based on the results. In reality, the students were all given _____ such as "You have a great need for other people to like and admire you." The students were then asked to evaluate their assessments on a scale from zero to five, with five being the most accurate. Despite the fact that the assessments had no connection to the test, they received an average rating of 4.26. [3점]

*horoscope: 별점

① the recommended answers to the test questions
② different tests that allowed for precise assessments
③ accurate results that described their personalities
④ the same personality description with general statements
⑤ personal advice based on the findings of their test results

35 다음 글에서 전체 흐름과 관계 없는 문장은?

The opera is often seen as a pastime reserved for older adults; however, there is a big push to get younger people interested in the art form. According to the Metropolitan Opera, the average age of opera audiences is rising, a trend that many opera companies around the world are facing. ① To get young audiences interested in opera, some opera companies are offering student discounts on tickets. ② In fact, to expose younger people to this art form, Opera Carolina in the U.S. even offers a happy hour when people aged 21 to 40 can get special discounts. ③ Some companies are even modernizing classical operas to reflect modern times. ④ Revised plays are rarely as popular as the original, even though they often feature reduced ticket prices. ⑤ While the music and the story remain the same, the background is placed in a setting that is more familiar with young audiences.

[36~37] 주어진 글 다음에 이어질 글의 순서로 가장 적절한 것을 고르시오.

36

There are many dangerous animals that people fear, including sharks, snakes, and spiders. It's no surprise that these animals are often portrayed as evil creatures in books and movies.

(A) However, in spite of our perception of them, these organisms are by no means the most deadly life forms on our planet. In fact, some of the world's most dangerous animals are ones that in our eyes are small, fragile, and defenseless.

(B) And the next time you're swimming in the ocean, don't bother worrying about sharks. Instead, keep an eye out for the Australian box jellyfish, whose tentacles contain enough poison to kill several people.

(C) The poison dart frog is one such example. Found in tropical forests, this tiny amphibian is as cute and brightly colored as a child's toy. If you ever see one, leave it alone. It produces a toxin powerful enough to kill 10 humans.

*amphibian: 양서 동물

① (A) – (B) – (C)　　　② (A) – (C) – (B)
③ (B) – (C) – (A)　　　④ (C) – (A) – (B)
⑤ (C) – (B) – (A)

37

X-ray technology greatly benefits the field of medicine, allowing doctors a glimpse inside their patients' bodies. However, frequent exposure to X-rays can result in serious health problems.

(A) This damage stemmed from the fact that X-rays are a type of ionizing radiation. This means that when an X-ray hits an atom, it can knock off electrons and create an ion; an electrically-charged atom. And an ion's electrical charge can destroy the DNA of a cell.

(B) DNA destruction, in turn, causes one of two things: the death of the cell or the mutation of the DNA. Widespread cell death leads to diseases, while mutated DNA can result in cancer. These risks are why doctors use X-rays less frequently today.

(C) This truth was learned in the early days of the technology, when doctors, unaware of the consequences, exposed both their patients and themselves to X-rays for lengthy periods. Soon, many people began experiencing the harmful effects of radiation sickness. [3점]

① (A) – (C) – (B)　　　② (B) – (A) – (C)
③ (B) – (C) – (A)　　　④ (C) – (A) – (B)
⑤ (C) – (B) – (A)

38

> Generally, children outgrow food neophobia as they grow older.

Neophobia is defined as the fear of new things. It can be a complicated phobia to diagnose and understand, given that human beings are generally creatures of routine. (①) This is especially true of young children, who often demonstrate behavior that can be interpreted as signs of neophobia. (②) To them, nearly everything is new; therefore, resisting change can simply be a natural response to feelings of being overwhelmed. (③) One common expression of this often occurs at the dinner table. (④) Young children can be notoriously picky eaters, refusing to touch all but a handful of familiar foods. (⑤) In some cases, however, it becomes a serious problem that they must deal with for the rest of their life.

*neophobia: 신기혐오증

39

> Enticed by such descriptions, thousands of explorers have tried and failed to locate El Dorado and claim its wealth as their own.

The legend of El Dorado was born sometime in the 1500s. It originated from stories about a gold-covered city that were recorded by European explorers in South America. (①) Apparently located in the north of the continent, the mythical city was said to overflow with jewels and other treasures. (②) Of these adventurers, one of the most well-known was an Englishman named Percy Harrison Fawcett. (③) His 1925 expedition wandered into the depths of the Amazon Jungle and was never seen again. (④) Everyone else who has attempted to uncover the location of El Dorado has either died or returned discouraged. (⑤) Indeed, modern treasure hunters may be better off buying a lottery ticket than risking their lives trying to find the legendary city. [3점]

40 다음 글의 내용을 한 문장으로 요약하고자 한다. 빈칸 (A), (B)에 들어갈 말로 가장 적절한 것은?

Is running really good for your health? A recent medical study done on marathon runners suggests that it may not be. The study showed that runners were much more likely to catch infectious diseases such as colds and flu during heavy training periods and just after a marathon. What's more, long-distance runners who ran more than 60 miles a week reported twice as many illnesses as those who ran less than 20 miles per week. And of the marathon runners who did not get sick before a race, 12.9 percent became sick during the week after the race. This compares to only 2.2 percent of similarly conditioned runners who did not take part in that particular race.

↓

_____(A)_____ running can significantly _____(B)_____ a person's immunity against infectious diseases.

(A)		(B)
① Occasional	......	transform
② Moderate	......	weaken
③ Excessive	......	diminish
④ Insufficient	......	impair
⑤ Long-distance	......	improve

People are always looking for ways to escape from the stress of real life. By reading novels, attending plays, or watching movies, people escape into imaginary worlds and picture themselves living in (a) real stories that they identify with. Virtual reality technology is another recent addition to the list of escape methods. However, virtual reality is in many ways different to other escape methods.

Whereas in fiction we (b) imagine and empathize, in cyberspace we actually step into the other world. In other escape methods such as plays, novels, and cinema, we passively follow a storyline predetermined by the author. In virtual reality, however, we (c) actively take part in the story, creating it for ourselves.

In a virtual reality, we are able to choose a desired identity and control what happens. But what happens if that virtual world is better than the real world? People could become addicted to virtual reality technology and spend most of their time using it. They may even begin to (d) neglect their responsibilities in the real world.

Before we know it, virtual reality could become a big part of our daily lives, just as television has been for decades. People will open doors to fascinating places and spend hours there. In fact, some of us may never wish to return to the daily chaos of the real world. Perhaps virtual reality may someday be made (e) illegal just like drugs.

41 윗글의 제목으로 가장 적절한 것은?

① The Latest Entertainment Facility
② Fiction: A Door to Another World
③ Escaping the Hardships of Daily Life
④ Virtual Reality: Lost in Another World
⑤ Internet Addiction: Kids Are in Danger!

42 밑줄 친 (a)~(e) 중에서 문맥상 낱말의 쓰임이 적절하지 않은 것은? [3점]

① (a)   ② (b)   ③ (c)   ④ (d)   ⑤ (e)

[43~45] 다음 글을 읽고, 물음에 답하시오.

(A)

Charles Darwin's 1859 publication of *On the Origin of Species*, which detailed his theory of evolution, shook up the scientific world. Immediately, scientists began to search for some kind of fossil evidence of extinct human ancestors. They wanted to learn exactly how human beings had evolved over the previous thousands of years. In 1910, a researcher named (a) Charles Dawson uncovered something he believed to represent such a "missing link."

(B)

(b) His discovery came to be called the Piltdown man and included pieces of what appeared to be a human skull and teeth. (c) He had dug them up in an area known as Piltdown in Sussex, England. Excited, (d) he took the bones and teeth to the famous scientist Arthur Smith Woodward, who announced that the fragments had indeed belonged to an early human. News of the Piltdown man spread around the world, but little by little the truth was revealed.

(C)

Once the truth was known, one question arose: Who was behind the fraud? To this day we can't be sure, but current thinking points to a man named Martin Hinton, who was volunteering in a natural history museum at the time of the discovery. (e) His position gave him the tools and the knowledge to pull off such a trick. Moreover, bones resembling those among the Piltdown fossils were found in his belongings. Sources say Hinton may have been trying to embarrass his boss, whom he was having a dispute about money with around that time.

(D)

First of all, further discoveries in the field began to cast doubt on the authenticity of the Piltdown man, showing that its existence didn't fit the story of human evolution. And secondly, in the 1950s, new tests proved the Piltdown skull was no more than 600 years old and that the teeth were those of an ape. Someone had arranged the bones and colored the teeth to make them appear as if they belonged to an ancient human. Scientists worldwide had been fooled.

43 주어진 글 (A)에 이어질 내용을 순서에 맞게 배열한 것으로 가장 적절한 것은?

① (B) – (C) – (D) ② (B) – (D) – (C)
③ (C) – (B) – (D) ④ (C) – (D) – (B)
⑤ (D) – (B) – (C)

44 밑줄 친 (a)~(e) 중에서 가리키는 대상이 나머지 넷과 다른 것은?

① (a) ② (b) ③ (c) ④ (d) ⑤ (e)

45 윗글에 관한 내용으로 적절한 것은?

① Charles Darwin은 1910년 진화론 관련 저서를 발표했다.
② Arthur Smith Woodward는 필트다운에서 인류 조상의 것으로 판명된 화석을 발견했다.
③ 필트다운인의 발견은 초기 인류 연구에 큰 도움을 주었다.
④ Martin Hinton은 자연사 박물관의 관장이었다.
⑤ 필트다운인의 두개골은 겨우 600년밖에 되지 않은 것이었다.

* 3점 문항에만 점수가 표시되어 있습니다.
  점수 표시가 없는 문항은 모두 2점씩입니다.

18 다음 글의 목적으로 가장 적절한 것은?

Dear Principal Johnson,

As a parent of two students at Lakeside High, I have a suggestion regarding the security situation at your school. By installing surveillance cameras, you could provide teachers with a useful tool. First of all, cameras serve as an excellent deterrent against wrongdoing. This means that students would be less likely to break the rules. And if students did break school rules, there would be a video history of it that would allow teachers to see the act. Also, since cameras do reduce the level of crime at a school, parents would not have to worry about safety. For these reasons, I hope you take my suggestion into consideration.

Sincerely,
Charlotte Vanderbilt

① 학생들의 교칙 준수를 당부하려고
② 교내 범죄 증가에 대해 항의하려고
③ 교내 보안 카메라 설치를 제안하려고
④ 교사용 수업 지원 프로그램을 홍보하려고
⑤ 영상 매체를 통한 학습 효과를 설명하려고

19 다음 글의 상황에 나타난 분위기로 가장 적절한 것은?

It was late, just after 2 a.m., when I woke up to hear the baby crying. I went to his room, lifted him from his crib, and carried him to the kitchen to prepare a warm bottle of milk. Suddenly, a cold draft of air surrounded me, and I felt a terrible presence in the room. I looked around wildly, but nothing seemed to be out of the ordinary. Then, just as quickly as it had come, the coldness was gone. I stood still for a few moments and then convinced myself I had imagined it. I went upstairs and put the baby, now sleeping soundly, back into his crib. But when I returned to the kitchen to turn off the light, I saw that the door to the back porch was standing wide open.

① calm and peaceful
② lively and vigorous
③ sad and depressing
④ scary and frightening
⑤ annoying and irritating

20 다음 글의 요지로 가장 적절한 것은?

Recently, there have been many claims made regarding probiotics. It has been said that drinks containing probiotics can stop a sick baby from crying. It has also been reported that consuming probiotics during pregnancy can prevent the development of asthma in newborns. In response, the American Academy of Pediatrics released a report that seeks to clarify what is fact and what is fiction when it comes to probiotics. The conclusion that is reached is that probiotics don't yet qualify as a wonder cure. Although they are not considered to be harmful, there has been little research done on the effectiveness of using probiotics as a supplement in foods such as yogurt and granola. And there is even less proof that probiotics are effective in reducing the risk of asthma or eczema in babies when taken by mothers who are pregnant or nursing a child.

*eczema: 습진

① 활생균 연구에 더 많은 투자가 필요하다.
② 사람에 따라 활생균의 효과가 다를 수 있다.
③ 활생균이 함유된 식품 개발은 미약한 수준이다.
④ 음식 보충물로서의 활생균의 효과는 불분명하다.
⑤ 충분한 활생균 섭취는 임산부와 아기에게 중요하다.

21 밑줄 친 a social outcast가 다음 글에서 의미하는 바로 가장 적절한 것은? [3점]

Some people get cosmetic surgery for themselves. Others, however, have it done to their dogs, paying to have part of their ears or tail cut off. This brutal practice dates back to ancient Rome, where people believed it prevented rabies. It was also done to prevent injuries to dogs that were used for hunting or fighting. There were even places where it was a way of avoiding taxes—a removed tail showed that a dog was used for work and therefore not taxable as a pet. These days, however, it is done simply to give certain breeds a more desirable appearance. In other words, dogs are undergoing unnecessary and painful surgical procedures because some people view them as fashion accessories. The removal of a dog's tail is especially cruel, as it is a vital part of how dogs communicate with one another. A tailless dog will likely be misunderstood by other dogs, possibly causing it to become a social outcast.

*rabies: 광견병

① a dog that has an unusually long tail
② a dog that isn't accepted by other dogs
③ a dog that is used for hunting or fighting
④ a dog that is aggressive to other dogs it meets
⑤ a dog that spends lots of time with its owner

22 다음 글에서 필자가 주장하는 바로 가장 적절한 것은?

Do your grades fail to improve even when you try your best? Do you know what causes this fruitless result? Few people know that the brain needs at least 10 minutes of rest each hour. Thus, when students study for hours without taking breaks, it actually results in a memory loss. Without breaks, the brain stores information into intermediate memory, which only lasts temporarily. Consequently, students remember the information while studying but fail to store it in long-term memory. The next day during an exam, all that students remember is that yesterday they knew the answer and today they don't! So, remember this: take at least a 10-minute break each hour, and your memory and recall will improve dramatically.

① 과목별로 학습 방법을 달리 해야 한다.
② 암기 위주의 학습은 효과적이지 못하다.
③ 반복 학습이 장기 기억에 가장 효과적이다.
④ 두뇌에 저장된 정보는 쉽게 지워지지 않는다.
⑤ 효과적인 학습을 위해 적절한 휴식을 취해야 한다.

23 다음 글의 주제로 가장 적절한 것은? [3점]

At first glance, the emergency center at Baptist Hospital in Miami looks more like a fancy hotel than a hospital. From the beautifully landscaped gardens to the nicely decorated lobby, there is no sign of pain or blood. For centuries, the word hospital recalled images of suffering and death. But as the Baptist Hospital emergency center and many other new hospital facilities around the U.S. prove, this image is changing fast. The 1980s revolution in health care, driven by new tools, attitudes, and cures that prolong life, is matched by a similar revolution in architecture. Plain white hospital interiors have now been replaced by pastel-colored walls and elegantly designed rooms.

*Baptist: 침례 교회의

① new functions of hospitals
② innovation in the hotel industry
③ changes in the construction of hotels
④ changes in the appearance of hospitals
⑤ the rapid growth of medical technology

24 다음 글의 제목으로 가장 적절한 것은?

When rap music first appeared in the mid 1970s, few people thought it would last. Music critics said it wasn't real music, record companies felt it was too black-oriented to cross over to a white audience, and parents dismissed it as the latest fad. By January 1992, rappers had reached as high as number three on the official top 200 album list. During the next decade, rap music turned into a powerful and controversial force in American popular culture. From its humble street beginnings in Harlem and the South Bronx, rap moved into the mainstream media through CDs, as well as radio, music videos, talk shows, concerts, rappers as actors, movie soundtracks, and advertising.

① The Origins of Hip Hop
② The Growth of Rap Music
③ Various Styles of Rap Music
④ Why Rap Music is So Popular
⑤ The Best-Selling Rappers in History

25 다음 도표의 내용과 일치하지 <u>않는</u> 것은?

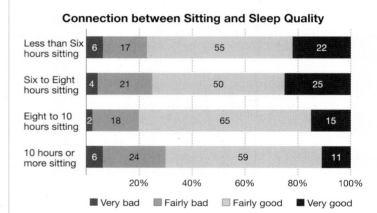

Connection between Sitting and Sleep Quality

The above graph shows the connection between the number of hours people spend sitting each day and the overall quality of their sleep. ① People who spent six to eight hours sitting each day were most likely to report the overall quality of their sleep as "very good," with three quarters of the group doing so. ② However, the percentage of respondents who reported having "fairly good" sleep was the highest in the group that sat for eight to 10 hours each day. ③ In contrast, people who sat for 10 hours or more each day were most likely to report "very bad" or "fairly bad" sleep quality. ④ The group that sat for the fewest hours each day and the group that sat for the most hours each day had the same percentage of people reporting "very bad" sleep. ⑤ However, the people who sat the least were twice as likely to report "very good" overall sleep quality as those who sat the most were.

26 Tristan da Cunha에 관한 다음 글의 내용과 일치하지 않는 것은?

Visiting Tristan da Cunha is like visiting another world, another life, and another time. The population is just under 300, with only seven surnames among the islanders: Hagan, Rogers, Glass, Lavarello, Swain, Green, and Repetto. Many live in the capital city, Edinburgh, which feels centuries old despite having all modern conveniences. Although the native language is English, it is an unusual, old-fashioned version. Tristan da Cunha is self-sufficient with a strong economy and low income tax. Unemployment is almost unknown, and there is no serious crime. In addition to fishing, a main source of the island's income is the sale of postage stamps, which are prized by collectors all over the world.

① 주민들의 성씨가 7개 밖에 없다.
② 에든버러에는 현대적인 편의 시설이 부족하다.
③ 영어를 모국어로 사용한다.
④ 범죄와 실업이 거의 존재하지 않는다.
⑤ 어업과 우표 판매가 주요한 수입원이다.

27 금성과 지구에 관한 다음 글의 내용과 일치하는 것은?

Venus and Earth have often been called "twin planets" because both planets share some similarities. They are similar in size and color. The diameters of the two planets are roughly only 650 km in difference, with Earth being a little larger than the other. They both also appear to be blue in color; water makes Earth appear blue, while the upper clouds of Venus' atmosphere make it look like a white-blue planet. They are both terrestrial planets, meaning they are "solid", but their atmospheres are very different. The atmosphere of Venus is 90 times denser than that of Earth, which means Venus has the densest atmosphere of the terrestrial planets in the solar system. At first sight, the two planets seem very much alike, but when looked at in more detail, there are more differences than similarities.

① 두 행성의 색상은 매우 다르다.
② 금성의 직경은 지구의 직경보다 조금 더 길다.
③ 지구는 구성 성분인 물 때문에 푸르게 보인다.
④ 금성은 육지를 가지고 있지 않다.
⑤ 지구의 대기는 태양계의 육지 행성 중 가장 밀도가 높다.

28 Springville Summer Art Camp에 관한 다음 안내문의 내용과 일치하지 않는 것은?

Springville Summer Art Camp

The Springville Community Center is now offering an art camp for elementary school students.

Rates and Times
Full day: 9:00 – 15:00, $200
Half day: 9:00 – 12:00, $100
Price covers class time, art supplies, aprons, and lunch.

Refund Policy
Cancellations before the first day of camp are eligible for a full refund. Cancellations after the first day are eligible for a 50 percent refund.

Availability and Registration
June 18 – 22 available spots: Full Day 0
                                              Half Day 7
June 25 – 29 available spots: Full Day 0
                                              Half Day 19
Fill out the form below with the student's name and age. For more information, please call (415) 773-9244.

① 참여 대상은 초등학생이다.
② 수업은 9시에 시작한다.
③ 수업료에 재료 비용이 포함되어 있다.
④ 캠프 시작 전에는 반액 환불이 가능하다.
⑤ 현재는 반일 수업만 신청 가능하다.

29 다음 글의 밑줄 친 부분 중, 어법상 <u>틀린</u> 것은?

The Declaration of Independence is one of ① <u>the most influential documents</u> in American history. Under the rule of King George III of Britain, the American colonists ② <u>fought</u> for their rights. They had raised objections against unfair taxation, the presence of English soldiers on American soil, and the lack of local authority in the House of Representatives, but eventually they turned to revolution. The declaration, which was drafted by Thomas Jefferson, ③ <u>announcing</u> their claim of independence to the world as well as ④ <u>to the king</u>. The formal separation from Great Britain ⑤ <u>was completed</u> with the adoption of the declaration on July 4, 1776. That day is now celebrated as Independence Day in the United States.

*the House of Representatives: (미국의) 하원

30 다음 글의 밑줄 친 부분 중, 문맥상 낱말의 쓰임이 적절하지 <u>않은</u> 것은?

A bank run is a situation in which a large number of a bank's customers panic and withdraw their money from the institution at the ① <u>same</u> time. There is generally a series of gradual events that lead up to such an occurrence, beginning with an economic ② <u>downturn</u> that makes people worry about the safety of their money. If they feel their bank is in danger of failing, they begin to transfer their money to another bank that they consider to be ③ <u>safer</u>. When other bank customers see what is happening, they begin to ④ <u>demand</u> their money back as well. However, as banks invest the money deposited by account holders, they do not have enough cash on hand if everyone ⑤ <u>withholds</u> their money at once, which can cause the bank to become insolvent.

[31~34] 다음 빈칸에 들어갈 말로 가장 적절한 것을 고르시오.

31

Young children who stubbornly refuse to eat certain vegetables often show an emotional reaction of disgust. Though this disgust may seem crazy to parents who want to give their children healthy food, scientists interested in attitudes toward cleanliness have a rational explanation. Their argument is that people have developed disgust as a _____ measure against objects that are unfamiliar and possibly harmful. A recent study has demonstrated that disgust prevents people not only from eating dangerous substances but also from entering potentially dangerous situations. For example, participants in the study reported crowded railcars to be more disgusting than empty ones and lice more disgusting than bees. Consequently, parents should not be surprised when their children are defensive about eating unknown foods or entering strange places.

*lice: 이(louse의 복수)

① creative
② reactive
③ detective
④ protective
⑤ competitive

32

It is a well-known fact that people sleep less as they get older. Research now suggests that this change in our sleeping patterns may actually be _____. In the distant past, sleeping humans were vulnerable to predators that hunted at night, so the entire group benefited if one person was awake at all times. According to the "poorly sleeping grandparent hypothesis," older individuals eventually began to play this role. This may explain why early humans tended to sleep in mixed-age groups. The researchers tested their hypothesis on a group of hunter-gatherers in Tanzania. During more than 220 hours, they observed a total of only 18 minutes during which all of the adults were sound asleep. For the rest of the time, about a third of the group was either awake or sleeping lightly.

① a personal preference
② a dangerous reaction
③ a recent phenomenon
④ an evolutionary adaptation
⑤ a temporary transformation

33

As strange as it might sound, the majority of scientific hypotheses _____! Take this simple hypothesis as an example: "Any two objects dropped from the same height will hit the ground at the same time." If this were a false hypothesis, it would be quite easy to show that it was incorrect. However, if it were true, how could you know this for certain? Since it describes the behavior of "any two objects," you would have to test every combination of objects in existence, a clearly impossible task. Through extensive testing, you could gain a great deal of confidence in the hypothesis, but you could never be sure that it was an absolute truth. There would always be a chance that the next pair of objects that you tested would behave in a manner inconsistent with the hypothesis. [3점]

① involve simple facts
② are completely false
③ cannot be proven correct
④ were not accepted in the past
⑤ describe supernatural phenomena

34

Doctors in the West are finally learning what traditional healers have always known — that _____. Until recently in Western countries, physicians have been consulted to heal the body, psychiatrists the mind, and priests the soul. However, the Western medical world is now paying more attention to holistic medicine, which believes that people's state of mind can affect the wellness of their body and vice versa. The recognition for holistic medicine is spreading so much that the World Health Organization has even changed its recommendations. It now states that in some cases, doctors might have greater success if they consider using traditional therapies alongside prescription drugs. [3점]

*holistic medicine: 전인적 의학

① the body and mind are inseparable
② medicine is the best way to heal the body
③ our bodies don't actually need any medicine
④ medical treatment can cause mental problems
⑤ physical disease is different from mental disease

35 다음 글에서 전체 흐름과 관계 <u>없는</u> 것은?

It has often been said that one man's trash is another man's treasure. This is an apt way to describe the project of a man named Robert Bezeau. It started in 2012, when he was in charge of a recycling program in Panama. After collecting thousands of plastic bottles, he decided to do something useful with them. ① Together with a team of local people, he wrapped the bottles in wire to create "bricks." ② These bricks were then used to make a building. ③ In fact, they had so many bricks that they made a whole village, including a four-story castle that people could spend the night in. ④ Consequently, people adapted to the environment of the plastic building because of their survival skills. ⑤ Bezeau hopes his village will make people realize how much plastic waste exists and think of other innovative ways to use it.

[36~37] 주어진 글 다음에 이어질 글의 순서로 가장 적절한 것을 고르시오.

36

Human beings are born with certain natural taste preferences. For example, we enjoy things that taste sweet, but we dislike foods that taste bitter.

(A) Children, for example, commonly avoid certain vegetables due to their bitter taste. But if they are fed these vegetables regularly, they will grow used to their taste and may even begin to enjoy them. Flavor preferences, however, are different.

(B) While taste is detected by taste buds, flavors are detected mostly by our sense of smell. The flavors we enjoy most are influenced by what we experience at an early age. This begins while we are still fetuses, based on the foods that our pregnant mothers eat.

(C) This is because sweetness is a sign that a food contains sugars, which give us beneficial calories. Bitterness, on the other hand, indicates the presence of a toxic compound. These preferences change as we grow older, and they can also be affected by experience. [3점]

*taste bud: 미뢰(미각 세포의 집합체) **fetus: 태아

① (A) – (C) – (B)   ② (B) – (A) – (C)
③ (B) – (C) – (A)   ④ (C) – (A) – (B)
⑤ (C) – (B) – (A)

37

Brightening our homes, producing oxygen, and purifying the air we breathe, houseplants perform many favors for us. Yet, in spite of all of this, we often forget to take care of them by watering them regularly.

(A) Such messages are possible because the devices emit electric waves and collect data about moisture levels, comparing them with optimal levels. This information is then sent to a local network, and a message is transmitted.

(B) This sensing device conveys information about the current state of the plant by sending messages to a mobile phone or over the internet. It can send reminders, thank you messages from the plant, and even warnings about over- or under-watering.

(C) Thankfully, there may now be a solution for forgetful plant owners — a sensor that can be placed in the soil of houseplants that are often in need of watering.

① (A) – (C) – (B)   ② (B) – (A) – (C)
③ (B) – (C) – (A)   ④ (C) – (A) – (B)
⑤ (C) – (B) – (A)

38

In other words, he recognized that the two processes, though they occurred in separate parts of the body, were somehow linked in the nervous system.

The Russian psychologist and physician Ivan Pavlov is perhaps best known for an experiment in which he conditioned dogs to salivate at the sound of a bell. (①) Earlier in his career, Pavlov had noted that the stomach would not begin digestion without salivation happening first. (②) In the experiment, he repeatedly exposed research dogs to a stimulus like a ringing bell when feeding them. (③) This eventually caused them to salivate when stimulated by the bell, even if there was no food present. (④) He also showed that this type of conditioned reflex dies out if the stimulus proves "wrong" too often. (⑤) For instance, if, over and over, the bell rang without food appearing, the dogs would stop salivating at the sound.

39

In a desperate attempt to keep more of its citizens from leaving, the city has invested in various attractions like hotels and ski resorts, hoping to draw tourist revenue.

Yubari, Hokkaido, once the site of a prosperous coal industry, now finds itself lacking the money it needs to function. (①) Over the years, the city's debts have grown enormously, to an amount 13 times greater than its annual budget. (②) Yet, during that time, Yubari quietly concealed its debts by taking out loans, compounding its financial problems. (③) Worse, the cost of everyday expenses rose so high that residents simply could not afford to live there. (④) The population consequently dropped from 120,000 in 1960 to just 10,000. (⑤) However, such attempts have been undermined by the city's poor image, and it seems doubtful the government will be able to recover from its financial disaster. [3점]

40 다음 글의 내용을 한 문장으로 요약하고자 한다. 빈칸 (A), (B)에 들어갈 말로 가장 적절한 것은?

Reliable knowledge of early American civilizations is limited to archaeological records. This is because most of the original artifacts were destroyed by European conquerors. Nevertheless, we have evidence of impressive achievements in architecture, healing, astronomy, mathematics, and engineering. Such achievements command respect for these cultures as well as regret for the loss of their knowledge. In agriculture, these civilizations greatly enriched the food of today's planet to include white potatoes, corn, beans, tomatoes, and chocolate. However, we have lost the secrets of the Mayan astronomers and the Incan builders as well as many medicinal practices. Perhaps the greatest casualty has been the Native American attitude toward life and the universe, since these people seldom warred with nature, choosing instead to adapt to it.

↓

It's _____ (A) _____ that the _____ (B) _____ of Native American civilizations was destroyed.

(A)	(B)
① a big shame	agricultural technology
② a great pity	rich heritage
③ a curious thing	historic architecture
④ a great honor	glorious culture
⑤ a deep sorrow	ancient religion

Robert Capa spent his early years in Paris working mainly on local photo stories. It was not until 1936, when his boss sent him to take photos of the Spanish Civil War, that his work was printed in top magazines and newspapers across Europe. The picture that brought him widespread international repute was his photo of a Loyalist soldier falling to his death. That picture became a powerful symbol of war used extensively by the media. In 1939, shortly after the Spanish Civil War ended, Capa worked briefly in New York. However, he quickly returned to Europe when World War II broke out and stayed there taking pictures for six years. His photographs of British soldiers landing in Normandy became some of the most memorable war photographs in history. It was for these pictures that Capa received the Medal of Freedom Citation.

Capa's job as a war photographer was often highly dangerous, but despite the risks he always said: "If your pictures aren't good enough, you aren't close enough." However, on 25 May 1954, while working on an assignment in Asia, Capa stepped on a land mine and was killed instantly. Today Robert Capa is considered one of the finest war photographers ever. He was an outstanding photojournalist who used his camera to record the horrors of war. Not surprisingly, Capa hated war and hated being unable to change it. In an interview he expressed how difficult it was to stand aside, unable to do anything except record the sufferings of others.

*Loyalist: (스페인 내란 때의) 국왕 지지자, 반(反) 프랑코 장군파

41 윗글의 제목으로 가장 적절한 것은?

① The Tragic Life of Robert Capa
② What It Takes to Be a War Photographer
③ How One Photojournalist Changed History
④ The Difficulties of Being a War Photographer
⑤ Robert Capa: How He Documented and Hated Wars

42 윗글의 내용을 한 문장으로 요약하고자 한다. 빈칸 (A), (B)에 들어갈 말로 가장 적절한 것은? [3점]

Although he was famous for being a ___(A)___ war photographer, he felt ___(B)___ when he recorded such suffering because he was unable to help the victims.

	(A)		(B)
①	talented	······	helpful
②	remarkable	······	helpless
③	successful	······	proud
④	shabby	······	desperate
⑤	notorious	······	hopeful

[43~45] 다음 글을 읽고, 물음에 답하시오.

(A)

In the year 1820, it looked as if the inhabitants of Lima, Peru, were getting ready to revolt against their Spanish rulers. In order to safeguard (a) the city's fabulous wealth, the Spanish representative in charge of the city decided to ship it to Spain's colony in Mexico. The jewels, gold statues, and other treasures — with a value of around $60 million — were loaded into 11 ships and sent on their way.

(B)

Once they had gained control of the ship, Thompson and his crew immediately sailed to the Cocos Islands, located in the Indian Ocean. Here, it was believed, he and his men divided the treasure and buried it. Their plan was to wait until the Spanish had given up searching for them and then return to the Cocos to retrieve (b) the jewels. However, that never happened, as the Mary Dear was captured soon after and most of Thompson's men were tried and hanged on (c) piracy charges.

(C)

Thompson and his first mate faced a similar fate, so to save their lives they agreed to show the Spanish the location of (d) the stolen treasure. They accompanied the authorities back to the Cocos Islands but then managed to escape into the jungle. Neither Thompson, his shipmate nor the treasure was ever seen again, and more than 300 expeditions to find the treasures of Lima have failed. It's now believed that Thompson actually buried it on an unknown island near Central America.

(D)

Unfortunately, the commander of the fleet that was charged with transporting (e) Lima's riches was poorly chosen. Captain William Thompson, whose vessel was the Mary Dear, was in fact a ruthless pirate, and he was not about to waste an opportunity like this. As soon as the ships were at sea, he killed the Peruvian guards that were on the Mary Dear and dumped their bodies into the water.

43 주어진 글 (A)에 이어질 내용을 순서에 맞게 배열한 것으로 가장 적절한 것은?

① (B) – (D) – (C)   ② (C) – (B) – (D)
③ (C) – (D) – (B)   ④ (D) – (B) – (C)
⑤ (D) – (C) – (B)

44 밑줄 친 (a)~(e) 중에서 가리키는 대상이 나머지 넷과 다른 것은?

① (a)   ② (b)   ③ (c)   ④ (d)   ⑤ (e)

45 윗글의 Captain William Thompson에 관한 내용과 일치하지 않는 것은?

① 코코스 섬에서 계획 실행에 실패하였다.
② 함께 도망쳤던 항해사는 정글에서 발견되었다.
③ 실종 이후 보물을 찾기 위해 탐사대가 파견되었다.
④ 리마의 보물을 운반하는 배 중 하나를 소유하고 있었다.
⑤ 배에 타고 있던 페루인 병사들을 사살하였다.

* 3점 문항에만 점수가 표시되어 있습니다.
  점수 표시가 없는 문항은 모두 2점씩입니다.

18 다음 글의 목적으로 가장 적절한 것은?

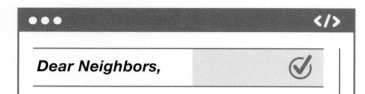

Dear Neighbors,

    In these times of economic crisis, many people are looking for ways to become financially stable. Therefore, as a service to the local community, the university is providing a great opportunity to all of our neighbors to attend a free investing seminar. It will be held in the Eldridge Hall auditorium on Thursday, November 12, at 7 p.m. Professor Paul Wesley, a renowned expert on the subject of personal investing, will be hosting the event, which will include everything from basic investing fundamentals to making the most of your current investments. If you plan on joining us, please let us know by calling the main office at 812-0921 at least 24 hours in advance.

Sincerely,
Marsha Diaz
MSU School of Economics

① 강의 일정 변경을 공지하려고
② 새로 부임한 교수를 소개하려고
③ 대학에 기부할 후원자를 모집하려고
④ 지역 재정 문제의 원인을 설명하려고
⑤ 금융 세미나에 주민들을 초대하려고

19 다음 글에 드러난 Tara의 심경으로 가장 적절한 것은?

    Walking into her kitchen, Tara was surprised to smell cigarette smoke. She immediately called the building manager, who explained that the smoke was probably coming from the apartment downstairs. The man who had just moved in was a smoker. The manager suggested she buy an air filter to get rid of the smell. Although Tara followed his advice, the filter couldn't erase the strong smell of cigarette smoke coming through the vent. Tired of the situation, Tara went downstairs and knocked on her neighbor's door. As soon as he opened it, a huge cloud of smoke drifted into the hallway, causing Tara to cough uncontrollably. "Stop it," the man said. "You're going to make me sick." Tara couldn't believe what she heard. "Actually," she replied, "you're the one making me sick!"

① pleased and grateful
② irritated and upset
③ shocked but accepting
④ amused and hopeful
⑤ confused but satisfied

20 다음 글에서 필자가 주장하는 바로 가장 적절한 것은?

Why do some women stay in physically abusive relationships for so long? The simple answer is that they usually have no place to go and are trying to protect their kids. In the U.S., there are 1,200 shelters for battered women, but only 5% of these facilities accept women with children. Usually, victims make an effort to get away from partners who are violent. But, with a lack of money, no place to go, and the inability to support themselves, most are forced to return and are socialized to extend forgiveness to their typically apologetic mates. Domestic violence is a serious violent crime and shouldn't be treated differently from other crimes. We need to prosecute the offenders and provide support services for the victims.

① 아동 학대를 보다 강력히 처벌해야 한다.
② 학대당한 여성들을 위한 보호소를 늘려야 한다.
③ 가정 폭력 피해 여성들을 위한 대책이 필요하다.
④ 직장 여성들을 위한 육아 지원책을 마련해야 한다.
⑤ 여성들의 사회 진출을 지원하는 정책을 마련해야 한다.

21 다음 글의 요지로 가장 적절한 것은?

People take prescription drugs and over-the-counter medication to deal with a variety of medical conditions. While these substances can be very helpful, they sometimes cause a situation known as "drug mugging." This is when drugs or medicines provide their intended effect but also end up stealing vital nutrients from the body. Acid blockers, for example, are commonly taken to reduce painful heartburn. They may provide relief, but at the same time they can lower your body's level of a number of nutrients, including calcium, iron, vitamin D, and B12. As a result, your immune system can be weakened and your energy level may drop. Drug mugging is believed to be caused by interactions between drugs, medications, and foods on a molecular level, so it is difficult to identify or predict. The best way to avoid this situation is by letting your doctor or pharmacist know exactly what drugs and other medications you are taking and how often you are taking them.

*acid blocker: 산 차단제

① 약을 장기간 복용하면 효과가 떨어진다.
② 영양제 섭취를 통해 면역력을 키울 수 있다.
③ 여러 종류의 영양제를 같이 섭취해서는 안 된다.
④ 부족한 영양분 보충을 위해 약을 처방 받아야 한다.
⑤ 약물 복용으로 인해 체내 영양소가 빠져 나갈 수 있다.

22 다음 글의 제목으로 가장 적절한 것은?

Lucid dreaming is a learned skill. You are lucid dreaming when you realize that you are dreaming and can control what happens in your dream while you are still asleep. MILD (Mnemonic Induction of Lucid Dreams) is one successful technique for lucid dreaming. MILD begins with telling yourself when you go to bed that you'll remember you are dreaming. Repeatedly tell yourself, "Next time I'm dreaming, I will remember I'm dreaming." Then, you should try to remember a recent dream and tell yourself that you are dreaming. You then think of what you would like to do during your next dream. For example, if you want to fly in your next dream, imagine yourself flying. Repeat these steps until you fall asleep.

*mnemonic: 기억의, 기억을 돕는

① New Attempt to Analyze Dreams
② Various Ways to Avoid Nightmares
③ The Scientific Interpretation of Dreams
④ How to Sleep Soundly Without Dreaming
⑤ Lucid Dreaming: A Way to Control Dreams

23

Fireworks have been used for hundreds of years by cultures all over the world to enhance festive moods. But while it may be fun to watch the colorful explosions, the process releases a variety of toxic materials that can then come into contact with spectators. For instance, the green colors you see in fireworks displays are produced by barium, which is known to be poisonous and radioactive, while copper compounds containing the cancer-causing agent dioxin create blue colors. Other toxic substances like lithium, cadmium, and lead are also commonly used in fireworks. In addition to their negative effects on human health, these materials lead to the creation of acid rain, which harms the environment. As awareness of this problem grows, some experts are urging cities to replace their fireworks displays with laser light shows.

① harmful effects of fireworks
② alternatives to fireworks displays
③ the history of fireworks production
④ the scientific principles of fireworks
⑤ colors of different chemicals in fireworks

24

Dyslexia is a learning difficulty that prevents people from easily breaking down words into their components, which makes it more difficult for them to read, write, and spell properly. The exact symptoms differ based on age. In young children, they can include a delay in speech, an inability to remember the spelling of words, and trouble following directions. These symptoms can lead to feelings of frustration and a lack of self-confidence. As a result, children with dyslexia often become disruptive in class and express a dislike for school in general. Although they may be labeled unintelligent or lazy, these children actually have a simple problem with the way their brains translate the information they receive. There is no cure for dyslexia, but there are treatments that can minimize the impact it has on learning. [3점]

① how dyslexia can be identified
② the best treatments for dyslexia
③ problems that dyslexia can cause
④ why dyslexia only affects young kids
⑤ conditions often mistaken for dyslexia

25 다음 도표의 내용과 일치하지 <u>않는</u> 것은?

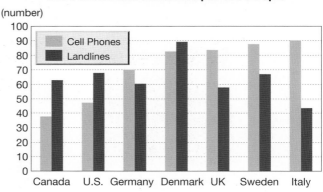

Cell Phones and Landlines per 100 People

The above graph shows the number of cell phones and landlines per 100 users in seven selected countries. ① In Sweden, there are more cell phones than landlines, but in Denmark landlines outnumber cell phones. ② Cell phones are most popular in Italy, where they outnumber landlines by more than two to one. ③ In the U.S., however, the number of landlines exceeds the number of cell phones, with twice as many people using landlines as compared to cell phones. ④ There is a similar situation in Canada, where there are fewer than 40 cell phones per 100 people. ⑤ Landlines are most common in Denmark, where they are used by almost 90 out of every 100 people.

26 Alcatraz에 관한 다음 글의 내용과 일치하지 <u>않는</u> 것은?

Alcatraz is a rocky island in San Francisco Bay; thus it's called "The Rock." Most of the space on the island is taken up by what was once a military fortress. In 1934 it was turned into a federal prison for dangerous criminals. Each cell in Alcatraz was less than 2 meters wide, 3 meters long, and about 1.8 meters high. Prisoners lived in complete darkness, not knowing whether it was night or day. They sometimes tried to escape but nobody ever succeeded. Although a few prisoners managed to reach the water, nobody ever survived the one kilometer swim to the shore. Although the prison was closed in 1963 for economic reasons, tourists can now visit the old jail cells.

① 현재 군사 요새로 사용되고 있다.
② 1934년에 흉악범들을 수용하는 교도소로 바뀌었다.
③ 교도소의 감방은 빛이 들어오지 않았다.
④ 어떤 죄수도 탈옥에 성공하지 못했다.
⑤ 교도소는 1963년에 경제적인 이유로 폐쇄되었다.

27 Voyager program에 관한 다음 글의 내용과 일치하는 것은?

Of all the space probes launched by the world's astronomical organizations, the Voyager program may have recorded the longest list of achievements. This program consists of two probes, Voyager 1 and Voyager 2, launched separately by NASA in 1977. The first and only official mission of the probes was to perform a flyby of Jupiter and Saturn. They completed this mission in 1980, sending important data and stunning photographs back to Earth. After the probes finished their mission, Voyager 2 went on to gather data on Uranus and Neptune, while Voyager 1 kept speeding toward the edge of the solar system to take a long-distance photo of Earth and the planets that surround it. Now, Voyager 1 is believed to be about 11 billion miles away from the Sun and is currently the farthest manmade object from Earth, a record that is not likely to be broken anytime soon.

① NASA는 Voyager 1, 2호를 동시에 발사하였다.
② Voyager 1, 2호는 발사 3년 후에 첫 임무를 시작했다.
③ Voyager 2호는 토성으로의 접근 비행에 실패했다.
④ Voyager 1호는 천왕성과 해왕성에 관한 자료를 모았다.
⑤ Voyager 1호는 현재에도 우주 탐사선으로 역할을 수행하고 있다.

28 Afternoon Paris Tour에 관한 다음 안내문의 내용과 일치하지 <u>않는</u> 것은?

Afternoon Paris Tour

An option for guests with little time to view the most famous attractions in the city in one day.

Attractions: Eiffel Tower, Notre Dame Cathedral, the Louvre (outdoors only)

Time: Tuesdays and Thursdays at 14:30. Other dates may be available on occasion, but individual prices may vary.

Duration: Approximately 4.5 hours

Cancellations: Full refund available 72 hours prior to start of tour

Additional Information:
→ There is a maximum of eight people in each group.
→ This is a walking tour; therefore, participants do not need to pay for transportation.

① 화요일과 목요일 외에는 비용이 달라질 수 있다.
② 소요 시간은 약 4시간 30분이다.
③ 출발 72시간 전에 취소하면 전액 환불이 가능하다.
④ 각 그룹에는 한 번에 최대 8명까지 참여할 수 있다.
⑤ 대중교통 탑승에 드는 비용을 따로 준비해야 한다.

29 다음 글의 밑줄 친 부분 중, 어법상 틀린 것은? [3점]

Research shows that scientists interested in the field of aerodynamics — the study of the forces ① involved when objects move through the air — can learn a thing or two from honeybees and bumblebees. The unique flapping motion that these insects use when they are in flight ② carries aerodynamics into new and unconventional realms. These two types of bees employ a flight system quite different from ③ those of most other small flying insects. Whereas other insects generally move their wings in large arcs, honeybees and bumblebees move theirs in much shorter arcs while ④ flapping them more rapidly. This special motion gives the bees a ⑤ by far wider power range than other insects.

*aerodynamics: 공기역학

30 다음 글의 밑줄 친 부분 중, 문맥상 낱말의 쓰임이 적절하지 않은 것은?

Trajan's Market, believed to be the world's oldest shopping mall, was built by and named after the Roman emperor who ruled from 98 AD until 117 AD. Trajan helped ① expand the Roman Empire and had many structures built throughout the city, including the market, which is now considered an ② impressive example of ancient architecture. Made of concrete and brick, it has vaulted ceilings, arched hallways, and three levels that are ③ disconnected by stairs. The shops within the market sold food from all across the vast empire, but later, during the Middle Ages, the structure was ④ converted into a fortress. At that time, a large tower, called the Torre delle Milizie, was also ⑤ added on. Today, much of the market is still standing, and it has become a popular destination for tourists.

[31~34] 다음 빈칸에 들어갈 말로 가장 적절한 것을 고르시오.

31

To most people's surprise, there are more than 500 active volcanoes in the world, and ten or more of them are erupting every day. Their eruptions add substantially to the pollution of the atmosphere. However, pollution caused by volcanoes is part of nature's way of bringing about _____ among the earth's organisms and elements, such as land and water. The most dramatic volcanic eruption occurred in June 1991 in the Philippines at Mt. Pinatubo. Vast amounts of sulfuric acid gas were blown into the atmosphere. The immediate effect was a measurable cooling of the earth so great that the warming of the earth from the greenhouse effect was actually slowed down.

*sulfuric acid: 황산

① balance
② misfortune
③ breakdown
④ disharmony
⑤ independence

32

For various reasons, people are often unable or unwilling to relate their true emotions. People often say something pleasant to avoid expressing their real emotion when they are angry with someone's behavior. In some situations, individuals cannot really figure out what they are feeling. For example, a son might actually be afraid of his father but claim that he loves him. Even when we are aware of our emotions, we sometimes underplay them, saying we are "a little nervous" about something when in fact we are terrified of it. Or we may deny the emotion completely if it is negative. So, often what people say _____.

① does not concern others
② tends to reflect the truth
③ does a lot of harm to others
④ may be helpful in every sense
⑤ does not mirror what they are feeling

33

In an experiment, a researcher pretended to be a student who had gotten lost on a college campus. She approached a professor and asked him how to get to a certain building. While the professor was giving directions, two other researchers carrying a large door walked between the pair. As they did so, the original "lost student" was replaced by a different woman of a similar age. Despite this, the professor continued to give directions as if nothing had happened. According to the researchers, this was an example of something called "change blindness." As long as both the original and replacement person _____, chances were that the professor would not notice the change. This is because he was focusing on giving directions. When a person is concentrating on one thing, his or her brain is likely to ignore other incoming information. [3점]

① focused on the professor
② asked different questions
③ fit the same basic category
④ were part of the experiment
⑤ knew where they were going

34

Some people associate migration mainly with birds. Birds do travel vast distances, but _____. For example, caribou spend warmer months grazing on the grassy slopes of northern Canada, but when the weather turns cold, these animals travel south until spring. Their tracks are so well-trodden that they are clearly visible from the air. Another example is the Alaska fur seal. These seals breed only in the Pribilof Islands in the Bering Sea. The young are born in June and by September are strong enough to go south with their mothers on a journey of over 3,000 miles. Together they swim down the Pacific coast of North America as far as the warm waters of southern California. [3점]

*caribou: 삼림순록 **hibernate: 겨울잠을 자다

① mammals also migrate
② not as far as mammals do
③ they also look after their young
④ they usually settle down in one place
⑤ they cannot hibernate the way mammals do

35 다음 글에서 전체 흐름과 관계 없는 문장은?

Cooking is an important skill that children should learn because it teaches them a great deal. Most people never really think about what goes into cooking a meal, but there is a lot. And, if you get your children interested in cooking, they easily pick up on these things. ① One of the most important things children can learn from cooking is organizational skills. ② When children are going to cook a meal, even a simple one, they have to plan their project, make sure they have all the ingredients, follow a recipe, and then execute it. ③ In addition, when children make their own food, they get a feeling of accomplishment at the end, which instills self-esteem. ④ Self-esteem that is too high can be just as problematic as low self-esteem. ⑤ Plus, learning to cook at a young age will teach children independent decision-making since they can control what is going into their food.

[36~37] 주어진 글 다음에 이어질 글의 순서로 가장 적절한 것을 고르시오.

36

It is often said that being both passionate about and skilled at something is the key to happiness. It is therefore no surprise that many people share the simple dream of getting paid to do what they love.

(A) People who love to pay attention to the latest fashion trends can also turn their passion into a living. Some may become personal stylists for clients who want advice on fashion choices, while others may choose to become designers.

(B) For example, people who have a passion for fitness can make a career of sharing their skills with others by teaching weight lifting, yoga, or mountain biking classes. Or, if they prefer, they can coach sports teams.

(C) Although it is commonly believed that it is almost impossible to achieve such a dream, this is not true. There are actually many passions that can be turned into profitable careers.

① (A) – (C) – (B)　　　② (B) – (A) – (C)
③ (B) – (C) – (A)　　　④ (C) – (A) – (B)
⑤ (C) – (B) – (A)

37

In 1697, a French lawyer wrote a letter asking for a relative's death certificate. Since the letter was confidential, the lawyer "letter locked" it. This is an ancient folding technique that was used to secure letters before there were envelopes.

(A) This was because the letter was too fragile to unfold. To avoid damaging it, the researchers examined it with an X-ray machine. This revealed a detailed image of the writing inside, but it couldn't be read because the words were folded together.

(B) The letter never reached its destination. Instead, it ended up in a postmaster's trunk, where it stayed until modern researchers discovered it. Although they wanted to read the 300-year-old letter, they didn't want to open it.

(C) To solve this problem, they created an algorithm that can decode folded words. It took them almost five years, and they had to test it several times. Finally, however, they managed to read the contents of the "locked" letter. [3점]

① (A) – (C) – (B)　　　② (B) – (A) – (C)
③ (B) – (C) – (A)　　　④ (C) – (A) – (B)
⑤ (C) – (B) – (A)

38

A life event like a pregnancy is less stressful to someone who is longing to have a child.

Stress often results from major changes in our lives, which psychologists call life events. (①) These may be negative events, such as the loss of a job or the death of a loved one. (②) They can also be positive events, such as getting married, receiving a promotion, or having a baby. (③) In other words, changes for better or for worse can impose stressful burdens on us. (④) The way we evaluate a life event also has much to do with how stressful it becomes for us. (⑤) Similarly, whether or not you find your work stressful depends a lot on whether or not you like your work in the first place.

39

However, if you let other people copy that music, then you are technically breaking copyright law.

Music file sharing takes place on websites and in communities all across the internet. Did you know that it is illegal to share files when you do not have the copyright holder's permission? (①) When you pay for a music streaming service, you also buy the rights to listen to it at home on your computer or outside on your phone. (②) Of course, many people use file sharing programs to swap music tracks. (③) But this activity is almost always illegal in the eyes of the law. (④) Unless the artist has actually approved this process, it is illegal to share music. (⑤) The same goes for videos, television shows, and movies. [3점]

40 다음 글의 내용을 한 문장으로 요약하고자 한다. 빈칸 (A), (B)에 들어갈 말로 가장 적절한 것은?

In a famous fable by Aesop, a hungry fox leaps in the air, trying to grab some ripe grapes hanging from a vine. After trying and failing several times, he announces that the grapes probably taste sour and walks away. In other words, the fox tries to hide his failure by pretending he didn't really want to succeed in the first place. This is known as a "rationalization." Rationalizations occur when we make up reasons to explain things that seem wrong or unacceptable. They protect us on an unconscious level from the cognitive disagreement that is caused by conflicts in our beliefs. Like the fox, we may rationalize that something we can't get isn't worth having anyway. Or when we make decisions that have negative consequences, we might hide behind the rationalization that things aren't really as bad as they seem.

↓

People use rationalizations to deal with the _____(A)_____ of unsatisfactory situations by creating false explanations that make them seem less _____(B)_____.

	(A)		(B)
①	hardship	......	positive
②	discomfort	......	negative
③	delight	......	important
④	anxiety	......	dangerous
⑤	pleasantness	......	valuable

A professor at the University of Chicago, Enrico Fermi was known for presenting his students with questions that seemed impossible to answer. When they protested, he would then prove to them that they already possessed the knowledge and tools needed to find the solution. This type of query eventually became known as a "Fermi question."

Fermi questions generally require answerers to quickly come up with a rough estimate of a quantity that would be impossible to measure through direct physical means. An example might be to ask how many drops of water are contained in a certain lake. To answer the question, you would first have to estimate the average size of a drop and then determine the volume of the lake based on its size and depth. The goal, of course, would not be to come up with an exact number. A Fermi question is solved by _____ rather than calculating a specific answer.

Because of this, when it comes to Fermi questions, the process used to find the solution is more important than the actual answer. There is no exact answer, only an acceptable range. The goal of these questions is to move students away from the habit of memorizing answers and encourage them to develop logical thought processes. This is an invaluable skill for anyone interested in science. But as far as most students are concerned, the best thing about Fermi questions is that they can be enjoyable to solve.

41 윗글의 제목으로 가장 적절한 것은?

① The Problem with Logic
② Answering the Impossible
③ Fermi: A Mysterious Professor
④ Improving Students' Memory Skills
⑤ The World's Most Difficult Question

42 윗글의 빈칸에 들어갈 말로 가장 적절한 것은? [3점]

① memorizing key formulas
② ignoring the actual question
③ proving assumptions are false
④ making reasonable assumptions
⑤ finding the right information source

[43~45] 다음 글을 읽고, 물음에 답하시오.

(A)

Before the arrival of the European conquerors, indigenous people living in what today is known as Colombia held gold in high esteem. Similar to our own culture, they used it to represent the power, both sociopolitical and ideological, of their leaders. Yet, the role of gold in ancient Colombia spilled over into another realm of society: the spiritual.

(B)

Furthermore, gold's spiritual properties gave it a special place in the burial rituals observed by ancient Colombians. In the religious views of this culture, the existence of death was necessary in order for new life to be born, and gold was an essential element in the transformation between death and life. Shamans presided over these rituals as well, and the dead — if they had been important people — were dressed in earrings, nose rings, and a mask and breastplate, all of which featured gold decoration.

(C)

Unfortunately, the spiritual importance the Colombians placed on gold was not respected by the Spaniards, who arrived in the 1500s and conquered this civilization and many others. They sought gold only for its monetary value and the social status it provided, so they outlawed shamans and gold-based rituals in Colombia and stole as much gold as they could find to ship back to Spain. They didn't find it all, however, and examples of ancient Colombian gold artifacts uncovered by modern archaeologists are on display in Bogotá's Museo del Oro.

(D)

In this realm, gold was seen as possessing certain mystical properties that, if used correctly, could realize tasks such as transforming one object into another, harnessing the power of the sun, and even generating life itself. Shamans, spiritual leaders who were thought to exist in both human and spirit worlds simultaneously, were responsible for caring for and using the sacred gold. During rituals in which they attempted to communicate with the dead, shamans would typically wear masks and other ornaments made out of gold.

43 주어진 글 (A)에 이어질 내용을 순서에 맞게 배열한 것으로 가장 적절한 것은?

① (B) – (D) – (C)　　② (C) – (B) – (D)
③ (C) – (D) – (B)　　④ (D) – (B) – (C)
⑤ (D) – (C) – (B)

44 윗글의 제목으로 가장 적절한 것은?

① A Deeper Value of Gold
② Colombia's Trade in Gold
③ The History of Gold Mining
④ Religion in Ancient Colombia
⑤ Gold's Role in Modern Society

45 윗글의 고대 콜롬비아인들에 관한 내용과 일치하지 않는 것은?

① 금을 권력의 상징으로 여겼다.
② 금을 삶과 죽음의 전환에 필수적인 요소로 보았다.
③ 모든 죽은 이들을 금으로 화려하게 장식했다.
④ 스페인 정복자들에 의해 많은 양의 금을 빼앗겼다.
⑤ 샤먼이라는 종교 지도자들이 금을 관리하고 사용했다.

* 3점 문항에만 점수가 표시되어 있습니다.
  점수 표시가 없는 문항은 모두 2점씩입니다.

18 다음 글의 목적으로 가장 적절한 것은?

Starting next Monday, the 4th of June, Caldwell Bridge will be temporarily closed. Due to increasing levels of traffic over the last few years, the Stark County Roads Department has decided that the bridge needs to undergo significant renovation. The work will involve widening the existing road across the bridge to include two extra lanes. The additional lanes should greatly reduce traffic and travel times across the bridge in the long term. It is expected to take the construction team six weeks to complete the work. While the work is carried out on the bridge, motorists will not be able to use it to get to and from Caldwell Harbor. Instead, they will have to take a detour along the Barton Highway. The Stark County Roads Department apologizes for any inconvenience that this may cause.

① 다리의 철거를 요청하려고
② 공사 중 실수에 대해 사과하려고
③ 도시의 교통 문제의 원인을 설명하려고
④ 운전자들에게 도로 보수에 대해 알리려고
⑤ 변경된 도로 교통 정책에 대해 공지하려고

19 다음 글에 드러난 Mr. Mitchell의 심경으로 가장 적절한 것은?

Mr. Mitchell collected antiques. For him, it was more than a hobby — when friends admired his carefully decorated house, he glowed with pride. One sunny afternoon, he was following an old couple through a house full of moving boxes. Usually these moving-away sales only had cheap modern junk, but every once in a while, Mr. Mitchell got lucky. He looked around an old-fashioned kitchen, but nothing in it was truly more than 30 years old. The living room was no better. Then, in the study, he stopped. His eyes widened, and his heart began to pound. For a moment, he thought he might be dreaming. His mouth began to curve into a smile. Standing in front of him was an antique craftsman oak bookcase, the very style he had seen in pictures and wished to add to his collection!

① proud but nervous
② thrilled and pleased
③ curious but worried
④ hurt and disappointed
⑤ relieved and grateful

20 다음 글의 요지로 가장 적절한 것은?

Unfortunately, in today's society many people hold the notion that strangers must be feared. This idea is not only regrettable, but also wrong. The idea stems from media reports, which frequently document the crimes of psychopathic killers, kidnappers, child snatchers, and other criminals. But the truth is that more victims are hurt by people they know than by strangers. Women are more likely to be attacked by their husbands and boyfriends than by strangers. Social workers and doctors frequently find that when the elderly are neglected and abused, the perpetrators are relatives, not paid care-workers. And when children are mistreated, the abuser is more often a parent, a step-parent, or a relative.

① 낯선 사람을 경계해야 한다.
② 언론 보도를 전적으로 믿어서는 안 된다.
③ 이웃간의 협조가 범죄 예방의 첫걸음이다.
④ 가정 폭력을 예방하는 제도적 뒷받침이 필요하다.
⑤ 낯선 사람보다 지인이 폭력 가해자인 경우가 많다.

21 밑줄 친 "loss of vocal culture"가 다음 글에서 의미하는 바로 가장 적절한 것은? [3점]

Regent honeyeaters are rare Australian songbirds, with a shrinking population of only a few hundred birds. They often imitate the songs of other birds, but scientists were never sure why. Some believed that mimicry was a skill males used to impress females during mating season, but a new theory is more troubling. A study showed that their mimicry could be due to a "loss of vocal culture." Because their population has become so small, young male birds may not be learning the proper mating calls. When the young first hatch, their fathers remain silent to avoid drawing attention to the nest. So it isn't until later that young males learn mating songs from adult males. But since there are few male regent honeyeaters left, they may be learning the songs of other species instead. This is a problem because female regent honeyeaters won't respond to these songs, making it less likely that the young males will find a partner.

① a single song being sung over and over again
② females singing songs that males used to sing
③ mating songs not being passed on to young males
④ the inability to sing songs loudly enough to be heard
⑤ a sharp decline in the quality of the mimicked songs

22 다음 글에서 필자가 주장하는 바로 가장 적절한 것은?

In many ways, the internet has made shopping easier and more convenient. However, it has also made it harder to choose what to purchase. This is because there are so many options to choose from. To narrow down the possibilities, people often turn to online reviews and ratings posted by other consumers. But this information isn't particularly reliable. Studies have shown that the ratings products receive online are only loosely connected to their objective quality. This is due to several factors, including the presence of fake reviews and the fact that people tend to write reviews only when they have strong feelings — either positive or negative — about a product. What shoppers need to pay attention to is the products themselves rather than the opinions of others that they find online.

① 상품에 대한 사용 후기를 상세히 써야 한다.
② 온라인 후기에 지나치게 의존하지 않아야 한다.
③ 안전한 구매를 위해 상품을 직접 보고 사야 한다.
④ 온라인 쇼핑을 할 때 상품의 가격을 비교해야 한다.
⑤ 온라인에서 높은 평가를 받은 상품을 구매해야 한다.

23 다음 글의 제목으로 가장 적절한 것은?

Although many Western health professionals once considered acupuncture to be ineffective, it has recently been found to have some scientific basis. Acupuncture is based on the belief that energy, which the Chinese call Qi, circulates along the body. When the flow of Qi is blocked, an imbalance is created, resulting in pain or disease. Acupuncturists stimulate specific points in the body to restore the proper balance and flow of Qi. Research results show that acupuncture can influence the release of naturally produced, morphine-like substances called endorphins. Acupuncture can also provide at least temporary pain relief by holding back the transmission of pain impulses through the nerves. Patients who receive acupuncture treatment say they feel calmer.

① The Role of Endorphins in Health
② Various Kinds of Alternative Medicines
③ Acupuncture: Gaining Scientific Approval
④ Alternative Medicine vs. Conventional Medicine
⑤ Why Western Doctors Are Skeptical about Acupuncture

24 다음 글의 주제로 가장 적절한 것은? [3점]

When Europeans colonized the Caribbean during the 17th and 18th centuries, they brought hundreds of thousands of Africans to the islands as slave laborers. France's Saint-Domingue, modern-day Haiti, was by far the most profitable of these slave-trading colonies. Its massive coffee and sugar plantations generated huge amounts of money. Yet, all of this wealth remained in the hands of the French plantation owners. Meanwhile, the black slaves, who outnumbered them ten to one, lived miserable lives. They didn't receive any pay for their hard work and were cruelly beaten for disobeying orders. Their growing anger at this unfair treatment resulted in the Haitian Revolution in 1791. The 15-year uprising ended with the declaration of a free and independent Haiti led by the former slave class. This made Haiti the first Latin American nation to gain independence from Europe, and the world's first black-led nation since the start of colonization.

① the terrible lives of slaves in the Caribbean
② the huge profits made from a French colony
③ which crops grew best in Caribbean colonies
④ how Haitian slaves got fair compensation for their labor
⑤ how Haiti went from a French colony to an independent nation

25 다음 도표의 내용과 일치하지 <u>않는</u> 것은?

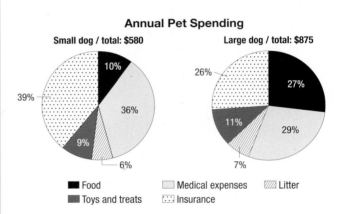

Annual Pet Spending

The above graphs show how much owners of large and small dogs spend on their pets annually, with the spending broken down by category. ① Overall, owners of large dogs spend an average of $295 per year more on their pets than the owners of small dogs do. ② Small-dog owners spend 10% of their budget on food, while large-dog owners spend over a third of their budget on it. ③ Insurance is the largest expense for small-dog owners, taking up nearly 40% of their budget, while litter is their smallest expense. ④ Litter is also the smallest expense of large-dog owners, but their biggest expense is medical costs. ⑤ For owners of both types of dogs, toys and treats are the second smallest expense, with large-dog owners spending two percentage points more on them than small-dog owners.

26 Laurent Clerc에 관한 다음 글의 내용과 일치하지 <u>않는</u> 것은?

Laurent Clerc was born in a small village near Lyons, France in 1785. When he was one year old he fell into a fire, losing both his hearing and his sense of smell. At the age of 12, Laurent entered the Royal Institution for the Deaf in Paris and excelled in his studies. After he graduated, the school asked him to become an assistant teacher. He did so and became very dedicated. Meanwhile, in America, Thomas Hopkins Gallaudet was upset to learn that there were no schools for the deaf in America. One day, Thomas visited the Royal Institution for the Deaf in Paris, where he met Laurent, and asked him to teach in America. Laurent agreed, and together they founded America's first school for the deaf.

① 프랑스에서 태어났다.
② 청각 장애를 가지고 태어났다.
③ 자신이 졸업한 농아학교에서 보조교사로 일했다.
④ 파리의 농아학교에서 토마스를 만났다.
⑤ 토마스와 함께 미국 최초의 농아학교를 설립했다.

27 인형에 관한 다음 글의 내용과 일치하는 것은?

Since the times before recorded history, humans have made dolls and used them for various purposes. The earliest of these were probably created from simple materials such as clay or wood and most likely served either as religious items or playthings for children. Although no dolls from this era exist today, archaeologists have recovered a doll fragment which is assumed to have originated from the ancient Babylonian period. There have also been dolls extracted from Egyptian graves thousands of years old. Made of flat pieces of wood, they had patterns painted on them and featured strings of beads to represent hair. Historians have also learned that young girls in ancient Greece and Rome would play with dolls, sacrificing them to goddesses when they passed into adulthood.

① 역사 기록 이전에는 인형이 존재하지 않았다.
② 초기의 인형은 단순한 재료로 만들어졌으리라 추정된다.
③ 바빌론 시대의 인형과 관련한 흔적은 전혀 남아 있지 않다.
④ 고대 이집트의 인형들은 나뭇가지로 머리카락을 만들었다.
⑤ 고대 그리스와 로마의 인형은 신을 본떠서 만들어졌다.

28 Northville Teen Fashion Show에 관한 다음 안내문의 내용과 일치하지 <u>않는</u> 것은?

Northville Teen Fashion Show

The Northville Youth Center presents its first-ever Teen Fashion Show. The event will be hosted by local clothing store owner Ashley Charles and will feature the work of three young fashion designers.

When: Saturday, May 11 from 6 p.m. to 8 p.m.
Where: Jewel Hotel, third floor banquet hall
Ticket price: $35 per person
Tickets include: admission to the fashion show and a post-show buffet

There are only 100 tickets available. They will go on sale one week before the show and can be purchased on the youth center's website www.northvilleyouth.org.

① 3명의 디자이너의 작품들을 선보인다.
② 행사는 2시간 동안 진행된다.
③ 저녁식사를 제공한다.
④ 입장권을 한정 판매 한다.
⑤ 입장권은 5월 4일까지 구매 가능하다.

29 다음 글의 밑줄 친 부분 중, 어법상 틀린 것은?

Your body uses sugar in two ways. In cells, sugar is ① either used to fuel activity or stored as fat. The fat is later broken down when your body needs to produce energy for activities such as exercise. As well as acting as fuel, sugar stimulates the brain to produce "happy hormones," which make you ② feel more cheerful. This is one reason why sweet foods like cookies and candy ③ are such popular snacks. Remember, however, that sugary foods need to be treated with caution. Too much sugar can lead to tooth decay and ④ increasing your risk of developing heart disease. Therefore, you should try ⑤ to keep the amount of sugar you consume to a minimum.

30 다음 글의 밑줄 친 부분 중, 문맥상 낱말의 쓰임이 적절하지 않은 것은?

Louis Pasteur was a 19th-century French chemist who studied food spoilage. While other scientists ① claimed that food spoilage was caused by natural chemical changes, Pasteur believed that tiny organisms in the air caused food to spoil. He ② proved his theory by heating broth to kill organisms in it and then sealing the broth. The broth did not spoil while sealed, but it spoiled when it was reopened and ③ exposed to the air. Pasteur applied the same principles to prevent wine, vinegar, and beer from spoiling. His methods were so ④ effective that England started shipping beer to its colonies in Africa and India. Later, he used the same technique to preserve milk. Today, many milk products are labeled "pasteurized" in honor of the man who ⑤ revised methods of preventing food spoilage.

[31~34] 다음 빈칸에 들어갈 말로 가장 적절한 것을 고르시오.

31

All spiders produce silk, but they produce it for different reasons. Although people first think of spiders using their silk to spin webs and hunt, spiders have a number of different _____ for it, just as humans use building materials in different ways. A large number of spiders use their silk to help them get out of danger. As they move around, they leave a line of silk thread behind them, which can serve the same function as a safety line does for a mountain climber. A spider in danger can easily escape along this thread. Many other spiders use their silk to build a cocoon for their young. This thick structure serves as a nursery for the spider's eggs. Of course, many spiders do use their silk to build webs, but each species builds them differently. Spider webs vary from cobwebs without organization to long silk tubes to massive silk sheets.

① colors
② methods
③ applications
④ explanations
⑤ organizations

32

The world's major religions have influenced people's _____. Hinduism teaches that people will be reborn again and again until they finally are released from time. Hindus believe time goes round and round in a cyclical pattern. To them, there is no sense of urgency in the wheel of time. Buddhism has a similar belief. It emphasizes the impermanence of life. To Buddhists, there is another life beyond the present life. There are other religions, however, that tend to think time runs in a straight line. According to Christianity, God created time in the beginning, and there will be an end in the future. Similarly, Muslims believe that time is limited. So, they think if we stray too far, we might not be able to make it back.

① attitude toward time
② belief in various gods
③ sense of right and wrong
④ understanding of life after death
⑤ ideas about the earth's beginning

33

A recent study has shown that the documentation of our struggles and adversities in a personal journal may actually _____. The researchers divided hospital patients into two groups — the first were instructed to write the details of all the unpleasant experiences they were dealing with on a daily basis, while the second were requested to simply keep a written record of everyday events. After several months of continuously maintaining this behavior, the subjects in the first group showed significantly more improvement in their overall health than those in the second group. The conclusion drawn by the researchers is that writing about trauma allows us to better accept these disturbing events, thereby lowering our stress levels and improving our health. [3점]

① have a positive impact on our physical well-being
② become a standard treatment for hospital patients
③ help patients talk about their traumatic life events
④ be able to help doctors find cures for serious diseases
⑤ be more common among ill people than those who are well

34

From time to time, inventors may accidentally stumble upon something beneficial that they hadn't actually been seeking. This type of occurrence is known as "serendipity." Some inventors who make discoveries in this manner admit the results were accidental; others attempt to cover it up. But the fact is that _____. The microwave oven, for example, was invented when a scientist discovered that the radar waves he was working with had melted a candy bar in his pocket. Due to occurrences such as this, researchers tend to keep an open mind toward accidental events. Accordingly, serendipitous discoveries generally occur within a scientist's chosen field of specialization. [3점]

① scientists will never admit it when their discoveries are serendipitous
② it is wrong to assume that accidental discoveries only occur in science
③ scientists use serendipity as a way of testing the results of experiments
④ scientific discoveries can only be made under systematic circumstances
⑤ serendipity is a major component of scientific discoveries and inventions

35 다음 글에서 전체 흐름과 관계 없는 문장은?

If you leaped up from bed after lying down for a while, you would probably experience light-headedness. This is a consequence of gravity draining oxygen-rich blood from your head down to the rest of your body. In some cases, the resulting dizziness is so severe that you might lose consciousness. ① However, not all animals suffer from this phenomenon — the giraffe, for example, is a species with a neck as long as seven feet. ② Surprisingly, the giraffe has the same number of bones in its neck as humans. ③ While feeding, it routinely shifts its head from the grass on the ground to as high as 17 feet to access tree leaves. ④ But despite this dramatic change in head height, the giraffe does not become light-headed. ⑤ It has evolved a high-powered circulation system that counteracts gravity and keeps blood pumping to the head regardless of changes in elevation.

[36~37] 주어진 글 다음에 이어질 글의 순서로 가장 적절한 것을 고르시오.

36

The curse of William Penn was used to explain why none of Philadelphia's professional sports teams managed to win a championship from 1987 to 2008.

(A) That year, a tower much taller than the statue was erected, and the city's teams suddenly stopped winning. People tried to put an end to the curse by adorning the statue with sports jerseys and hats, but nothing worked.

(B) Years later, however, someone came up with a great idea. An even taller building was being built in the city. When it was finished, a tiny statue of William Penn was placed on top of it.

That year, Philadelphia won the World Series, ending the curse.

(C) It was a statue of William Penn that had been placed atop City Hall in 1894 that served as the basis of the curse. The statue represented the highest point in Philadelphia, and there was a general agreement that no one would build anything taller. This agreement lasted until 1987. [3점]

① (A) – (B) – (C) ② (B) – (A) – (C)
③ (B) – (C) – (A) ④ (C) – (A) – (B)
⑤ (C) – (B) – (A)

37

In 1914, during World War I, soldiers needed cotton bandages, but the U.S. didn't have enough cotton. Kimberly-Clark created cellucotton, a substitute for cotton, which was very successful.

(A) They made advertisements that encouraged women to use the product when removing their makeup. But the people at Kimberly-Clark were surprised by the mail they received about another use for their new product.

(B) When the war was over in 1918, the company had a large amount of the new material leftover. So inventors at Kimberly-Clark came up with a new use for their product: Kleenex Kerchiefs.

(C) Many women wrote that their husbands were blowing their noses in the tissues. The men preferred the tissues to handkerchiefs. Unlike handkerchiefs, they were disposable and men liked this.

① (A) – (B) – (C) ② (A) – (C) – (B)
③ (B) – (A) – (C) ④ (B) – (C) – (A)
⑤ (C) – (B) – (A)

38

| Unfortunately, this has not been the case. |

Recently, a disturbing practice has developed among book publishers. (①) They have hired contemporary authors to write sequels to the novels of long-dead authors. (②) The sequels are written based on the original work and the original characters, so they make the readers expect the same high quality and interest. (③) For example, one author wrote a sequel to Margaret Mitchell's *Gone with the Wind* that was not considered to be nearly as good as the original. (④) It's clear that these sequels are written solely to get an author's or a literary work's fans to spend money. (⑤) Since these imitations can never equal the original, however, readers cannot help but be disappointed. [3점]

*sequel: 속편

39

| Banks are reluctant to give them loans because they are protecting their own interests. |

There are several current economic conditions that discourage the creation and success of small businesses in the U.S. (①) One is the difficulties prospective entrepreneurs face when trying to secure funds. (②) When they lend to someone who has not yet demonstrated the ability to turn a business idea into a source of capital, there is the chance that the loan will not be repaid. (③) In addition, the federal tax code provides far greater tax benefits to large corporations than it does to small businesses. (④) Reduced consumer spending as a result of the recent recession is another obstacle small businesses face. (⑤) Yet it should not be ignored that the majority of the American workforce is employed by small businesses. If the U.S. wants to maintain its economic dominance in the world, it must make it easier for this sector of the economy to thrive.

40 다음 글의 내용을 한 문장으로 요약하고자 한다. 빈칸 (A), (B)에 들어갈 말로 가장 적절한 것은?

People often claim that the patent system hinders scientific advancement by prohibiting competition. However, the law of intellectual property rests on the assumption that, without exclusive rights, no one would be willing to invest time and money in research and development. Patenting allows inventors to protect their intellectual property without secrecy. A patent grants the right to ban others from making, using, or selling the invention without the patent holder's permission. To get a patent, an inventor must fully disclose his or her invention. The patent system promotes more disclosure than would occur if secrecy was the only way to exclude competitors. Patents also promote the sharing of technology by protecting the profit incentives of innovative inventors.

↓

The patent system ____(A)____ individuals' intellectual property while at the same time enabling us to ____(B)____ knowledge.

	(A)		(B)
①	protects	······	share
②	releases	······	disclose
③	secures	······	conceal
④	acknowledges	······	standardize
⑤	incorporates	······	secrete

When the police capture a person who is suspected of committing a crime, he or she is often questioned by a detective. Meanwhile, other police officers sit quietly in the next room, listening carefully and watching everything through a one-way mirror. You might think that these mirrors are simply reflective on one side and clear on the other, but the truth is more (a) complicated than that.

A one-way mirror is actually a piece of glass that has a very thin layer of reflective material on one side of it. This is known as a "half-silvered surface," as the layer contains only half the number of reflective molecules that would be found in a normal mirror. This means it (b) reflects half of the light that hits it and allows the other half to pass through. As a result, the one-way mirror is partly (c) transparent and partly reflective.

But if this is the case, why doesn't the suspect "partly" see the police officers watching from the other room? The answer to this question is fairly simple. The police officers are in a room that is dark, while the suspect is in a room that is brightly lit. The result of this is similar to being in a (d) dark room at night. People who are on the street can easily see what's going on inside the room through the windows, but it is difficult for you to see anything that is happening (e) outside.

41 윗글의 제목으로 가장 적절한 것은?

① Do Mirrors Really Reflect Light?
② One-Way Mirrors Don't Really Exist
③ The Development of Modern Mirrors
④ One-Way Mirrors: How Do They Work
⑤ The Difference between Mirrors and Glass

42 밑줄 친 (a)~(e) 중에서 문맥상 낱말의 쓰임이 적절하지 않은 것은? [3점]

① (a) ② (b) ③ (c) ④ (d) ⑤ (e)

(A)

Prior to 1990, almost every image that humans had ever captured of outer space was taken by a ground-based telescope. And, no matter how advanced those telescopes were, they were always plagued by the same problem: the Earth's atmosphere. All of the dust particles, water molecules, and gases present in our atmosphere distort the light given off by objects far away in space, thus distorting our view of them as well.

(B)

This technology was the internet, and via the worldwide web, pictures snapped by Hubble were transmitted to eager viewers around the globe. For the first time in history, people could sit in the comfort of their homes while peering deeper into the recesses of the universe than ever before. Though Hubble is already considered outdated and work on a new generation of space telescopes is underway, it will always be remembered for ushering in a new age of interest in space and exploration of the unknown.

(C)

For decades, astronomers had a solution in mind. To achieve a view of space that would be _____, they would simply place a telescope outside of the atmosphere — in orbit around our planet. This was the Hubble Space Telescope, named after the astronomer Edwin Hubble, whose theories about the light output of distant stars would finally be able to be tested once the telescope was launched. Work on the project began in 1975 and lasted 15 years, as scientists carefully assembled each of the device's 400,000 parts.

(D)

In 1990, NASA carried out a successful insertion of the Hubble Telescope into Earth's orbit. Immediately, astronomers began receiving images of the universe they had never enjoyed before, both in terms of clarity of detail and distance. Hubble also meant that the general public's understanding of space would reach new heights, for reasons beyond the fact that the telescope possessed greater resolution and sensitivity than any of its predecessors. A very different technology was also taking off at this time, one that made access to Hubble's images easier than anyone could have imagined.

43 주어진 글 (A)에 이어질 내용을 순서에 맞게 배열한 것으로 가장 적절한 것은?

① (B) – (C) – (D) 　② (C) – (B) – (D)
③ (C) – (D) – (B) 　④ (D) – (B) – (C)
⑤ (D) – (C) – (B)

44 윗글의 제목으로 가장 적절한 것은?

① NASA's Earliest Telescopes
② The Science behind Telescopes
③ Edwin Hubble and His Theory of Stars
④ A Revolution in Telescopic Technology
⑤ A Replacement for the Hubble Telescope

45 윗글의 빈칸에 들어갈 말로 가장 적절한 것은?

① unhindered
② inadvisable
③ unmatched
④ inadequate
⑤ improbable

* 3점 문항에만 점수가 표시되어 있습니다.
  점수 표시가 없는 문항은 모두 2점씩입니다.

18 다음 글의 목적으로 가장 적절한 것은?

Dear City Council Members,

　Last week I was at the Garland Avenue playground with my daughter. Children were playing loudly in groups while their parents sat on benches quietly looking on. Just then, a bell began to ring, and a man selling ice cream pushed his cart into the middle of the playground. Isn't it enough that we're surrounded by advertisements selling things whenever we walk down the street? Shouldn't the playground be a safe haven, free of vendors and salespeople? I have made this complaint several times in the past, but I have yet to receive any kind of response. In my opinion, immediate action is needed to keep our playgrounds free of this kind of nuisance.

Sincerely,
Darren Jones

① 놀이터 추가 설치를 건의하려고
② 놀이터 소음 공해에 대해 항의하려고
③ 놀이터에 안전 장치 설치를 제안하려고
④ 잡상인의 놀이터 출입 금지를 촉구하려고
⑤ 과도한 어린이 대상 광고의 중단을 요청하려고

19 다음 글에서 필자가 주장하는 바로 가장 적절한 것은?

　Nutritional experts agree that the best way to deal with eating disorders in young people is to prevent them from happening in the first place. In other words, catch the problem before it even begins. Parents can do this by creating a healthy home environment that fosters a child's self-image, while discouraging unrealistic messages about the body that are often promoted by the media. Parents must teach their children to be comfortable with their own bodies. They should never be critical of others' appearances, nor allow their children to tease anyone about their looks. Rather, they should encourage them to treat others as they themselves would like to be treated.

① 균형 잡힌 식사는 몸매 유지에 도움이 된다.
② 아이들의 성장을 위해 계획적인 식단을 짜야 한다.
③ 날씬함에 집착하는 미에 대한 인식을 바꿔야 한다.
④ 지나친 다이어트는 아이들의 성장에 해로울 수 있다.
⑤ 섭식 장애를 예방하기 위해 부모가 올바른 교육을 해야 한다.

20 밑줄 친 <u>manmade eyespots are just as effective as the ones created by Mother Nature</u>가 다음 글에서 의미하는 바로 가장 적절한 것은? [3점]

A group of researchers has offered some unusual advice for farmers in Botswana. They recommend painting fake eyes on the rear ends of cattle in order to prevent attacks by big cats, such as lions, leopards, and cheetahs. The researchers got their idea from insects and birds that have evolved "eyespots," natural patterns that resemble eyes. These eyespots scare off approaching predators by making them think they are being watched. The scientists tested their theory on 14 cattle herds that had been attacked by big cats in the past. The cattle were divided into three groups: the first had eyes painted on them, the second had simple crosses painted on them, and the third group was left alone. Over a period of four years, none of the cattle in the first group were killed, as compared to four from the second group and 15 from the unmarked cattle. Apparently, <u>manmade eyespots are just as effective as the ones created by Mother Nature.</u>

① some cattle have evolved natural eyespots
② cattle are the natural prey of African big cats
③ the researchers' theory was proved to be wrong
④ painted crosses are more effective than painted eyes
⑤ painted eyes fool predators the same way natural eyespots do

21 다음 글의 요지로 가장 적절한 것은?

Newspapers believe they publish objective truth, providing readers with nothing but the facts. However, things are not always so simple. A reporter gathers the facts, but, space being necessarily restricted, he or she has to select what's important and what isn't. Then, the reporter or the editor must decide which of these facts will serve as the article's introduction and therefore take on greater significance than the others. Next, another editor has to say whether the article will appear on the front page, where it has much attention, or if it will be buried on page 20, where it has little. Thus, the pure facts are subject to a series of judgments in interpretation. It is fair to say, then, that newspapers don't simply deliver the news — they interpret it.

① 판단력은 기자에게 꼭 필요한 역량이다.
② 신문 기사 편집 과정의 간소화가 필요하다.
③ 신문은 오직 객관적인 사실만을 게재해야 한다.
④ 독자들은 신문을 비판적인 사고로 읽어야 한다.
⑤ 신문의 객관성은 편집 과정에서 달라질 수 있다.

22 다음 글의 주제로 가장 적절한 것은? [3점]

Animals have been observed licking clay as part of their everyday diet. Large animals such as horses, cows, and elephants roll in it to obtain relief from external wounds and sores. Amazon parrots gather along riverbanks to eat clay as a defense against a poison found in the seeds they eat. And veterinarians use it on pets for various injuries and infections. Some people even develop a longing to eat clay when they're ill because it's strongly believed that the clay alleviates diarrhea and improves digestion. Moreover, specially formulated clay baths have been shown to literally draw pollutants out of people's bodies like a magnet, eliminating years of toxic accumulation in just one bath.

① how clay works to get rid of poison
② strange habits common to wild animals
③ a new and effective way to treat diseases
④ the pros and cons of using clay to heal wounds
⑤ the role of clay in recovery and everyday health

23

Obesity in America is on the increase. In fact, statistics indicate that over 60 percent of all Americans are now overweight. Although few disagree that obesity is a health concern, there is clear evidence of what has become known as "size acceptance." Many movie theaters have begun installing wider seats, and airlines are facing pressure to allow overweight people to occupy two seats without having to pay extra. Specialty clothing stores that sell only large sizes can be found in practically every shopping mall. "Size-friendly" resorts and hotels are even replacing plastic beach chairs with stronger wooden ones. Considering that such accommodations convey the message that being obese is okay, some health experts find this trend worrisome.

① Discovery of a Fat Gene
② U.S. Trend: Accepting Obesity
③ New Developments in Treating Obesity
④ Stop Discrimination Against Obese People
⑤ Growing Concerns for the Problem of Obesity

24

During World War II, America was fighting Japan in the Pacific region. The Americans were reading secret Japanese military messages, but they couldn't fully understand them. The messages mentioned a location known as "AF," which the American military forces suspected might be Midway Island. However, they weren't sure, so they came up with a clever idea. They sent a fake message that claimed Midway was suffering from a water shortage. A short time later, the Japanese military sent a message that read "AF is short of water." This strategic lie allowed the Americans to better understand Japanese military messages and eventually helped them win the war. Although people generally agree that dishonesty is bad, it can sometimes be used in beneficial ways.

① A Fake Island Fooled Japan
② A Truthful Military Message
③ How Dishonesty Lost a Battle
④ Lying: A Useful Weapon in War
⑤ The Dangers of Bad Translations

25 다음 도표의 내용과 일치하지 <u>않는</u> 것은?

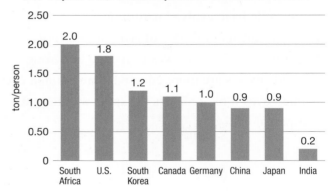

Per Capita Coal Consumption in Various Countries

Worldwide, a large amount of coal is burned each year. ① South Africa consumes the most coal per capita of any nation studied, more than twice as much as China. ② The amount of coal used by the average person in the U.S. is the second most in the world, and it is larger than the amount of coal used per capita in South Korea and Canada combined. ③ The average German consumes more coal than the average person in China, but less than the average Canadian. ④ On the other hand, China and Japan consume the same amount of coal per capita. ⑤ All of these countries, except India, consume more than 0.5 tons of coal per capita.

26 다음 글의 내용과 일치하지 <u>않는</u> 것은?

The Incas once ruled a great empire that covered a large part of South America. The empire was more than 500 years old when Spanish explorers arrived in the 16th century. The Incas were an advanced people. They were skillful engineers who paved their roads and built strong bridges. Even though they did not know about the wheel, the Incas were able to move huge stone blocks — some as heavy as ten tons — up the sides of mountains to build walls. These walls have stood firm through great storms and earthquakes that destroyed many modern buildings. The Incas were great artists, too. Today, Incan pottery is prized for its wonderful designs. And since both gold and silver were in great supply, the Incas created splendid objects from these precious metals.

① 16세기에 스페인 탐험가들이 잉카 제국에 도착했다.
② 잉카인들은 도로를 닦는 기술을 가지고 있었다.
③ 잉카인들이 세운 장벽은 폭풍우로 인해 대부분 파괴되었다.
④ 잉카 제국의 도자기는 예술적 가치가 뛰어나다.
⑤ 잉카 제국에는 금과 은이 풍부했다.

27 McCoy Tyner에 관한 다음 글의 내용과 일치하는 것은?

McCoy Tyner, born in Philadelphia in 1938, has had a long and successful career as a jazz pianist. After beginning to study piano at age 13, it didn't take him long to decide that playing music was what he wanted to do with his life. His first big break came when he joined band leader Benny Golson's group, Jazztet, as its first-ever pianist. Not even a year later, however, Tyner was given the chance to play with a group led by the famous saxophonist John Coltrane. Coltrane hired him because he was familiar with and appreciated the compositions Tyner had previously written. This relationship lasted until 1965, when Coltrane's style began to change and Tyner refused to conform. Instead, he started his own group and later established himself as one of the most celebrated solo pianists in jazz.

① 재즈 피아니스트로서의 경력은 길지 않았다.
② 13세에 피아니스트로 데뷔했다.
③ Jazztet이라는 그룹에서 1년이 넘게 활동했다.
④ 자신이 직접 작곡을 하지는 않았다.
⑤ 1965년 이후 자신의 그룹을 만들었다.

28 2021 Beautiful World Photography Contest에 관한 다음 안내문의 내용과 일치하지 <u>않는</u> 것은?

2021 Beautiful World Photography Contest For Amateur Photographers

Submit your best work for the chance to win great prizes — even a brand-new camera! We are looking for unique scenes of nature from around the world. All photos must be submitted by November 1, 2021.

Categories
Enter your photograph in one of three categories: animals, landscapes, or underwater.

Judging
- One grand-prize winner will be selected by three world-famous photographers.
- A special-prize winner will be selected from each category. These winners will be chosen by an online people's vote that will be held from November 2 to 16.

Prizes
- The grand-prize winner will receive $5,000 and a brand-new camera provided by our sponsors.
- Special-prize winners will receive $2,500.

① 제출 기한은 11월 1일까지이다.
② 세 개의 출품 분야가 있다.
③ 유명 사진작가들이 대상 수상자를 결정한다.
④ 특별상 수상자는 현장 투표로 선정된다.
⑤ 대상 수상자의 상품에는 카메라가 포함된다.

29 다음 글의 밑줄 친 부분 중, 어법상 틀린 것은?

① Entering the Louvre museum, you will encounter a large sign written in a variety of languages that ② inform all visitors that running, using a cell phone, making loud noises, and taking photographs with a flash ③ are all strictly prohibited. As encouraged as I was by this official-looking sign, I was sorely disappointed on my recent trip to the famous museum to find that these rules are neither followed nor ④ enforced. I was hoping to get a good look at da Vinci's masterpiece, the *Mona Lisa*; unfortunately it was surrounded by a noisy crowd of people who showed absolutely no respect for the great painting. Ringing cell phones filled my ears, and I was temporarily blinded by the flashes of cameras — and all the while, the museum guards stood idly by, as if nothing ⑤ were wrong.

30 (A), (B), (C)의 각 네모 안에서 문맥에 맞는 낱말로 가장 적절한 것은?

The historical beginnings of corporal punishment are not clear, but it is known that it was used in many ancient civilizations. In those times, it was often done in an exceedingly cruel manner and in full view of the general public. This was to (A) deter / defer others from committing the same crime. In the 18th century, philosophers and legal reformers began to question the use of corporal punishment, arguing that reformation, rather than retribution, should be the goal of the criminal justice system. Because of this, by the 19th century, the use of corporal punishment in Europe and North America had sharply (B) declined / descended. In Britain, the horrible deaths suffered by some criminals who were executed turned public opinion against corporal punishment. Eventually, this led to the (C) introduction / reduction of strict laws regulating the use of corporal punishment in many countries.

	(A)	(B)	(C)
①	deter	descended	introduction
②	deter	declined	reduction
③	deter	declined	introduction
④	defer	descended	reduction
⑤	defer	declined	reduction

[31~34] 다음 빈칸에 들어갈 말로 가장 적절한 것을 고르시오.

31

There was once a young woman whose educational prowess allowed her to bypass both middle school and high school, going straight to college from elementary school. By the time she had reached the age of 15, she had already graduated from a prestigious university, and by 18 she had obtained a doctorate degree. These achievements are both impressive and intriguing. Just what made her so smart? It is impossible to determine whether she was born a genius or not; however, we do know that her father sternly discouraged her from child's play. Instead, he diligently ensured that intellectual pursuits were the primary focus of her life. If she insisted on playing a game, he'd make sure it was something mentally challenging, such as chess. In fact, her situation is not unique — history tells us of many geniuses who were immersed in stimulating environments by _____ parents, including Einstein and Picasso.

① affluent
② cautious
③ sensitive
④ generous
⑤ ambitious

32

Despite the fact that many of the world's ancient religions developed thousands of miles away from one another, they developed creation myths that _____. For example, the Christians, the Chinese, and the Babylonians all believe that the first humans were created by a god from an earthy substance. The book of Genesis in the Bible describes the moment when God created Adam, forming him from the dust of the ground. In Chinese mythology, a god shaped the first humans from a lump of mud. Around the same time, the Babylonians also believed that God created humans from earth. It is fascinating to wonder how such similar stories could have developed despite the geographical obstructions separating these cultures. [3점]

*Genesis: 창세기

① believe in multiple gods
② share the same basic elements
③ describe an actual historic event
④ explain how the earth was formed
⑤ are still meaningful in today's modern world

33

It has long been believed that early humans divided their tasks by gender while searching for food — men hunted and women gathered. The discovery of a 9,000-year-old female hunter in South America, however, shows that this wasn't always the case. Archaeologists found the body buried with tools for killing and cutting up large animals, suggesting it was the grave of a hunter. Analysis of the bones revealed that the hunter had likely been a woman. This led to further research on the subject, which found that many ancient bodies buried with hunting tools were female. This information led the researchers to conclude that our assumptions about the gender roles of early humans were mistakenly based on modern attitudes. In fact, it seems that women played a significant role in _____ in prehistoric times.

① the hunting of big animals
② the division of gender roles
③ the burial of renowned hunters
④ the distribution of social tasks
⑤ the manufacture of hunting tools

34

To find out how the prison system affects people's behavior, a group of psychologists conducted an experiment. They carefully selected 24 male college students as subjects and randomly assigned half of them to play the role of guards and half to play prisoners in a fake prison. The experiment was supposed to last for two weeks. However, in just two days, the roles began to control the students' behavior. Even before a week had passed, half of the prisoners had to be released early due to extreme anxiety and depression. The guards had started to abuse the prisoners, and the experiment was stopped after only six days. This experiment shows _____. [3점]

① how mental patterns affect physical health
② how easily our behavior can be changed by social roles
③ that an environment will affect one's career development
④ that prisoners would behave better if they were treated more kindly
⑤ how much a practical learning environment contributes to students' achievement

35 다음 글에서 전체 흐름과 관계 없는 문장은?

Though art programs may not be part of the main school curriculum, they offer students many benefits. According to a study by the group Americans For the Arts (AFA), art programs can help improve learning skills in many areas. The study showed that art is helpful in developing skills in language, decision making, and critical thinking. ① Many artists earn large salaries producing commercial art for ads or product packaging. ② The same study found that young students who engage in art also learn how to work better in teams and can appreciate new ideas from different cultures. ③ Furthermore, when these students are encouraged to think freely and express themselves, they develop a feeling of self-confidence. ④ Perhaps the biggest benefit of art classes is that they improve creativity. ⑤ This sense of creativity allows students not only to express themselves in various ways, but to think and live creatively and find new solutions to common problems.

[36~37] 주어진 글 다음에 이어질 글의 순서로 가장 적절한 것을 고르시오.

36

The unfortunate paradox of tourism is that the very act of visiting a place to admire it endangers its continued existence.

(A) Over the last two decades, tourist numbers in Antarctica have skyrocketed, approaching 50,000 per summer season. With these curious adventurers come more pollution produced by cruise ships, more litter and other waste, and more destructive footsteps on the fragile frozen landscape.

(B) Antarctica is a perfect example of this paradox in action. It is a land of extreme cold, massive ice sheets, and towering mountains. Yet the frozen continent is also home to one of the world's most delicate ecosystems, a natural balance that has never had to withstand the pressures of human presence — until now.

(C) The bigger problem is that, unlike in other popular tourist destinations, there is no single governing body in Antarctica with the power to regulate visitation. The result is that Antarctica's future as an unspoiled and unique natural environment is uncertain.

① (A) – (C) – (B) ② (B) – (A) – (C)
③ (B) – (C) – (A) ④ (C) – (A) – (B)
⑤ (C) – (B) – (A)

37

Since ancient times, people have desired curly hair. From simple beginnings, continuous innovations eventually led to the modern perm.

(A) Other inventions followed, until the modern perm process was created by a man named Arnold Willat. He began constructing permanent wave machines in the 1920s, finally perfecting the process in the 1930s.

(B) Perms can be traced back to ancient Egypt, when women would put mud in their hair and wrap it around wooden sticks. Later, the invention of the blow dryer allowed people to create curls more easily. But once their hair got wet, the curls would be gone.

(C) Karl Nessler was the first to come up with an invention to create longer-lasting curls. In 1906, he constructed a device that heated perm rods with electricity. A mixture of water and cow urine was then used to hold the curls in place. The device, however, failed to gain popularity. [3점]

① (A) – (C) – (B) ② (B) – (A) – (C)
③ (B) – (C) – (A) ④ (C) – (A) – (B)
⑤ (C) – (B) – (A)

38

However, it is wrong to believe that bottled water is either better regulated or safer than tap water.

Bottled water is all the rage these days. You can find it in offices, on airplanes, and in stores everywhere. The labels on the bottles often show mountain streams, convincing consumers of the water's purity. (①) Because of this, people see it as a healthier alternative to tap water. (②) A nonprofit group recently tested more than 100 brands of bottled water. (③) It found that a third of them contained levels of either bacterial or chemical contaminants that exceeded state or industry standards. (④) Moreover, one fourth of bottled water brands actually get their water from public sources rather than mountain streams. (⑤) They simply purify it, bottle it, and sell it at ridiculously high prices. [3점]

39

Students are then asked to recall what they've written and replace the missing words.

In recent years, universities have begun to address the serious problem of student plagiarism by using special computer programs. (①) This software presents students with sentences taken directly from the papers they have submitted as their own. (②) However, every fifth word in these sentences has been removed and replaced with blanks. (③) After the test has been taken, the program analyzes the results, assuming students should be able to accurately complete sentences they have written themselves. (④) The number of errors in the test and the amount of time required to complete it are then used to determine if the student actually wrote

the paper or not. (⑤) According to the software company, the program is nearly 100 percent accurate and has yet to make any false accusations of plagiarism.

*plagiarism: 표절, 도용

40 다음 글의 내용을 한 문장으로 요약하고자 한다. 빈칸 (A), (B)에 들어갈 말로 가장 적절한 것은?

When passengers experience health emergencies aboard commercial aircraft, they are sometimes unable to receive the medical attention they require until they arrive at an airport. To address this problem, a British company has developed a special remote diagnostic system that can be installed in airplanes. When passengers complain of illness, monitors are placed on their bodies, allowing the system to transmit vital data to doctors at a hospital. Based on this data, the medical professionals can make a diagnosis, and then inform flight attendants what steps need to be taken to ensure the passenger's well-being. If the situation proves to be life-threatening, an emergency landing can be made, with ambulances waiting by the runway to rush the passenger to the nearest hospital.

↓

Remote diagnostic technology allows doctors _____(A)_____ to help ill passengers _____(B)_____ .

	(A)		(B)
①	in hospitals	.....	in airports
②	on airplanes	.....	in other locations
③	from airlines	.....	after they land
④	on the ground	.....	on flights
⑤	with special training	.....	in other countries

Kyle was born with arms that ended at the elbow and no legs. His parents didn't know what to expect, as they'd never seen anyone like Kyle, so they decided to take things a day at a time. And they very quickly stopped thinking of Kyle as (a) <u>disabled</u> because he did everything like any baby would, crawling around and playing with his toys.

Kyle's parents went on to have three more children, all daughters. Kyle played with them like any big brother. When Kyle started school, he did really well, learning new things and making friends. He began working out, (b) <u>failing</u> in building up his arms and torso and joining his school wrestling team. He was even spotlighted as a standout on the wrestling team when he graduated from high school.

When Kyle is asked if he's ever (c) <u>frustrated</u> about his disability, he answers, "Everybody has struggles. My struggles are just more apparent." Such an attitude makes people believe that they can do exactly what Kyle's done. Although his achievements seem to be (d) <u>unique</u>, he's even more impressive precisely because he's just a normal guy. When people see what Kyle has done, it makes them realize that we all have the same kind of potential inside us. We probably just need to be (e) <u>reminded</u> every once in a while by an example such as Kyle's.

41 윗글의 제목으로 가장 적절한 것은?

① The Difficulties of Having a Disabled Child
② Coaching a Sports Team for Special Children
③ Being Disabled Doesn't Make People Different
④ Kindness to Others Can Improve Difficult Lives
⑤ A Boy Who Refused to Give Up after an Accident

42 밑줄 친 (a)~(e) 중에서 문맥상 낱말의 쓰임이 적절하지 않은 것은? [3점]

① (a) ② (b) ③ (c) ④ (d) ⑤ (e)

[43~45] 다음 글을 읽고, 물음에 답하시오.

(A)

Back in the mid-90s, Catherine's career as a Wall Street stockbroker was soaring. With a six-figure income, she lived in luxury and took trips to exotic locations like Fiji and Granada whenever she felt like getting away from the city. For her hard work, she received awards and recognition from her colleagues and her boss, Olivia, and since she was at the top of her field, (a) <u>she</u> regularly appeared on a national television news program to give investment advice.

(B)

After that, Bernadette and Catherine worked hard to build a portfolio to suit her needs, and for a while, things seemed to be going fine. However, the market dropped sharply in 1995, causing investors like Bernadette to panic. Catherine tried to explain that dips in the market were natural, and that she should just have patience, but her reassurances had no effect. Having lost nearly all of her savings in the stock market drop, Bernadette was upset and convinced Catherine's employers to fire (b) her.

(C)

Catherine heard rumors before she received official word, and she walked around in a daze, unable to believe what was about to happen. Eventually, (c) she was called into Olivia's office. "Catherine," she said, "being a stockbroker is not your destiny." She explained to her that although the situation was beyond her control, (d) she shouldn't have invested all of Bernadette's money into such a narrow range of stocks. Catherine knew her fabulous life as a stockbroker was over, but she also realized that she had learned a valuable lesson that would help her in the future.

(D)

She couldn't have known then, back when everything was going perfectly, what lay ahead in her future. Her downfall began when she met Bernadette at a business dinner in New York City. She was an elderly woman, thin and bony with white hair that always looked perfectly done. They discussed (e) her financial options at the dinner, and then the next week she transferred nearly all of her savings into an account she opened with Catherine.

43 주어진 글 (A)에 이어질 내용을 순서에 맞게 배열한 것으로 가장 적절한 것은?

① (B) – (C) – (D) ② (B) – (D) – (C)
③ (C) – (B) – (D) ④ (D) – (B) – (C)
⑤ (D) – (C) – (B)

44 밑줄 친 (a)~(e) 중에서 가리키는 대상이 나머지 넷과 다른 것은?

① (a) ② (b) ③ (c) ④ (d) ⑤ (e)

45 윗글의 Catherine에 관한 내용과 일치하지 않는 것은?

① 1990년대 중반에 최고의 주식 중개인이었다.
② 텔레비전에 출연하여 투자 조언을 하기도 하였다.
③ 주식 시장의 하락으로 Bernadette에게 거액의 빚을 졌다.
④ 잘못된 투자로 직장을 관두게 되었다.
⑤ Bernadette의 주식 투자 상담과 설계를 맡았다.

* 3점 문항에만 점수가 표시되어 있습니다.
  점수 표시가 없는 문항은 모두 2점씩입니다.

18 다음 글의 목적으로 가장 적절한 것은?

Dear Mr. Kwon,

According to our records, the June edition of *Parenting Monthly* is the last issue of your 12-month subscription. I sincerely hope that you have enjoyed reading our magazine over the last year. More importantly, I hope that you will continue to do so in the future. So, in order to encourage you to continue to read *Parenting Monthly*, I'd like to offer you, as a current customer, a 15% discount on your subscription for the next 12 months. This generous offer is only available until the last day of your current agreement, so be sure to act quickly. In order to take advantage of this opportunity, please call one of our friendly customer assistance agents at 555-090-780.

Sincerely,
Wendy Johnson

① 새로운 잡지 이름 공모전을 알리려고
② 잡지 가격 인하 이벤트를 홍보하려고
③ 구독자에게 잡지 구독료를 청구하려고
④ 구독자에게 잡지 구독 연장을 권유하려고
⑤ 육아 잡지에 실릴 기사 작성을 부탁하려고

19 다음 글에서 필자가 주장하는 바로 가장 적절한 것은?

In Riverside Park, there are concrete ramps installed to give the disabled access to all of the terrace levels. But recently these ramps have been invaded by skateboarders. The combination of fast-moving skateboarders and slower people in wheelchairs makes for a dangerous situation. Clearly, these two users do not belong in the same space and need to be separated. But this is not just for them in that the safety of other park users, such as walkers and people pushing baby carriages, is also threatened. To protect all park users, as well as the skateboarders, a separate area ought to be set up just for skateboarding. There, skateboarders would have more challenging ramps, designed especially for them.

① 깨끗한 공원 환경 조성이 필요하다.
② 시내 레저 문화를 활성화해야 한다.
③ 공원 내 응급 시설을 만들어야 한다.
④ 스케이트보드 전용 공간을 만들어야 한다.
⑤ 공원 내에 장애인을 위한 시설을 확충해야 한다.

20 다음 글의 요지로 가장 적절한 것은?

Many people in today's contemporary society are at war against aging. They fear getting even the slightest wrinkle and, to counter this natural process, they buy pricy creams and cosmetics and even undergo plastic surgery. Unfortunately, in their quest to maintain a youthful appearance, people seem to have forgotten something really important — that there is true beauty in the deep wrinkles of the aged. The wrinkles on a grandmother's face attest to the ready smile that has been so much a part of her for so long. Her bright eyes, kind expression, and appreciation for life reveal a beauty far greater than any plastic surgery, wrinkle cream, or other cosmetic product could ever provide.

① 성형 수술에는 여러 부작용이 따를 수 있다.
② 꾸준히 관리하면 노년에도 건강을 유지할 수 있다.
③ 나이 드는 것에 대한 긍정적인 마음가짐이 필요하다.
④ 동안(童顔) 열풍이 사회의 새로운 트렌드가 되고 있다.
⑤ 젊어 보이려는 사람들의 증가로 화장품 산업이 성장하고 있다.

21 밑줄 친 they have already "had their turn"이 다음 글에서 의미하는 바로 가장 적절한 것은? [3점]

Ageism is a serious social issue that occurs when people are discriminated against because of their age. This can be a big problem for the elderly, who must deal with negative stereotypes about how they're supposed to act. For example, older individuals are sometimes expected to give up their jobs or other benefits to younger people. This is due to the stereotype that the elderly have gotten everything they need out of life and should be content to step aside for the next generation. But the truth is that we should all be free to do what we want, regardless of race, sex, or age. The elderly should not be treated as if they have already "had their turn." They should be treated just like everyone else — as unique individuals.

① they have missed their chance to succeed
② they are ready to stop living an active life
③ they have a clearly defined role in society
④ they are discriminating against young people
⑤ they have made positive changes to the world

22 다음 글의 제목으로 가장 적절한 것은?

In recent years, stores selling products in bulk have become popular. For example, you may be able to purchase a case of 20 boxes of cereal at a discount of 30 cents per box at a bulk store. Shoppers pay store membership fees, sometimes as much as $100 per year, because they believe buying in bulk is a way to save money. But is it? While you may save 30 cents per box on 20 boxes of cereal, you have to ask yourself: Would you want to buy all that cereal if it were not offered in bulk? And will you be able to consume it all before it goes bad? In many cases, the answer to these questions is "no." This means that bulk shopping in effect costs more, since you are buying more goods than you otherwise would.

① The Illusion of Bulk Bargains
② How to Save Money Buying in Bulk
③ Ways Not to Be Deceived by Bulk Stores
④ Bulk Stores: A Reasonable Option for Shoppers
⑤ The Relationship between Bulk Shopping and Food Waste

[23~24] 다음 글의 주제로 가장 적절한 것을 고르시오.

23

For most women, pregnancy seems to be a time of expectant joy, but a significant minority suffers moderate to severe depression. These women are more likely to overlook health care before the birth of their child. They may miss medical appointments, and some may turn to alcohol or cigarettes to tackle depression, but these can damage an unborn child. Untreated depression during pregnancy has been linked to higher rates of miscarriage, stillbirths, premature deliveries, and low-birth-weight babies. Babies born smaller because of a bad pregnancy face a bigger risk of high blood pressure and heart disease as adults. Finally, depression after a birth robs a woman of the joy of having a new baby and can seriously impair her ability to nurse and care for the infant. [3점]

① the joy of pregnancy
② the importance of post-delivery care
③ diseases that threaten pregnant women
④ the dangers of depression during pregnancy
⑤ things that you need to be aware of during pregnancy

24

The muscles of our feet are designed to constantly be pushing against the ground as we walk. Wearing shoes, however, replaces the uneven ground with a flat, firm, comfortable surface, meaning our foot muscles don't have to work nearly as hard. This might sound like the perfect situation, but it ends up making our feet weaker and prone to injury. To prevent this, some people prefer shoes with thin, flexible bottoms. Research shows that wearing them allows people's feet to move as if they were walking barefoot. As a result, their feet are stronger and healthier. For this reason, these shoes are the best option unless you're in a situation where walking in bare feet is acceptable.

① how the first shoes were made
② the healthiest shoes for our feet
③ what causes our bare feet to hurt
④ the problems with not wearing shoes
⑤ the difficulty of designing comfortable shoes

25 다음 도표의 내용과 일치하지 않는 것은?

Work-Life Balance When Working Remotely

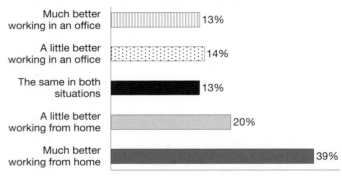

Much better working in an office	13%
A little better working in an office	14%
The same in both situations	13%
A little better working from home	20%
Much better working from home	39%

The above chart shows the responses of nearly 4,000 people who were asked whether their work-life balance was better when they worked in the office or when they worked from home. ① The largest percentage of people reported that the balance was much better when they worked from home. ② This percentage was more than double that of the next most common response, which was that the balance was a little better when they worked from home. ③ Only 13 percent of the people responded that their work-life balance was much better when they worked in the office. ④ Their answer was tied for the least common response with that of people who said the balance was the same whether they worked in the office or from home. ⑤ The percentage of people who said the balance was a little better when they worked in the office was only a single percentage point higher than the percentages of the two lowest categories.

26 다음 글의 내용과 일치하지 <u>않는</u> 것은?

Most people store food in the refrigerator to maintain its freshness. However, too many people wait too long before they put hot food in the refrigerator. Although one may save electricity by waiting until the food cools down, this can cause bacteria to breed more easily. Bacteria in food can cause people to develop various illnesses. Bacteria generally reproduce most easily at 35 degrees Celsius and reproduce more slowly at temperatures below 10 degrees Celsius. Since refrigerators are usually set at 4 degrees Celsius, food stored in refrigerators is likely to grow fewer bacteria than food left at room temperature. Thus, it is best to put food in the refrigerator while it is still hot.

① 많은 사람들은 뜨거운 음식을 식힌 후 냉장고에 넣는다.
② 음식을 식혀서 냉장고에 넣으면 전력 소모를 줄일 수 있다.
③ 음식을 식히는 과정에서 박테리아가 번식할 수 있다.
④ 박테리아는 섭씨 10도에서 가장 쉽게 번식한다.
⑤ 음식이 뜨거울 때 냉장고에 넣는 것이 좋다.

27 Southern Annular Mode에 관한 다음 글의 내용과 일치하는 것은?

The Southern Hemisphere undergoes a periodic natural fluctuation in climate called the Southern Annular Mode (SAM). During incidents of strong SAM activity, which can last decades, if not centuries, areas surrounding Antarctica experience relatively low atmospheric pressure. This in turn contributes to warmer, drier climate patterns in the Southern Hemisphere. The region of southern South America known as Patagonia is particularly affected by this. One dramatic effect of such a climatic shift is the increased prevalence of wildfire. This has been confirmed by tree-ring analysis of Patagonian forests. Now, atmospheric scientists say Patagonia is entering a new phase of strong SAM activity, which they predict will be intensified by the effects of human-induced global warming. The result is a Patagonia that will be increasingly prone to devastating wildfires for at least the next few decades.

*fluctuation: 변동

① 주기적으로 발생하며, 수 세기 동안 지속된다.
② 대기압을 높여 기후를 더 온난하고 건조하게 만든다.
③ 일부 지역의 기후를 변화시켜 잦은 산불을 일으킨다.
④ 근본적으로 지구 온난화의 결과로 나타나는 현상이다.
⑤ 전문가들은 이 현상이 점차 약화될 것으로 예상하고 있다.

28 School Poster Contest에 관한 다음 안내문의 내용과 일치하지 <u>않는</u> 것은?

School Poster Contest

The school's annual poster contest will take place this month. This year's theme is "Energy Conservation."

Guidelines
- Only original artwork will be accepted — no photographs or printed images.
- Each poster must be drawn on a 28 x 43 cm piece of paper.
- The poster may be arranged either horizontally or vertically.

Submissions
- All posters must be received by the end of the day on May 25.
- Multiple entries are allowed, but permission must be received from Ms. Kim.

Prizes
- The five best entries will be chosen by the contest's judges.
- Each winner will receive a $100 gift certificate from Mack's Art Supply Shop.

① 반드시 작품의 원본을 제출해야 한다.
② 작품은 가로 형태로 그려야 한다.
③ 여러 점의 작품을 제출하려면 승인을 받아야 한다.
④ 총 5점의 수상작이 선정된다.
⑤ 각 수상자들에게 상품권이 지급된다.

29 다음 글의 밑줄 친 부분 중, 어법상 틀린 것은?

Cholera is a sickness brought on by a bacterium in the intestines. ① Of those who contract it, around 5% experience a severe reaction, including vomiting, diarrhea, dehydration, and sometimes shock. Contaminated water is the primary means ② which it is spread, a situation that was all too prevalent during the cholera epidemics of the 1800s. Doctors of the time, ③ suspecting the link, promoted the creation of more sanitary sewer systems. It led to a sharp decline in incidents of cholera, and for several decades the disease seemed to ④ have vanished. Then, in Indonesia in 1961, it reappeared as a new strain and spread through much of the world. It has yet ⑤ to be stopped, killing thousands of people every year and sickening many more.

30 다음 글의 밑줄 친 부분 중, 문맥상 낱말의 쓰임이 적절하지 않은 것은?

Off-Broadway theater developed in 1950s New York City as a result of ① dissatisfaction with conditions on Broadway. Its founders believed that Broadway was overly concerned with producing safe, ② commercially successful hit plays rather than dramas with artistic quality. Off-Broadway producers assisted playwrights, directors, and performers who could not find work. Their shows were original and creative, and the ticket prices were ③ low. Audiences were delighted with these affordable tickets for artistic shows, and Off-Broadway theater ④ declined. However, by the 1960s, costs had begun to rise, and by the 1970s, Off-Broadway theater was ⑤ encountering many of the same difficulties as Broadway. With its decline, an experimental movement called Off-Off-Broadway theater developed.

[31~34] 다음 빈칸에 들어갈 말로 가장 적절한 것을 고르시오.

31

Poverty exists in society as a function of the extraordinary political pressure to maintain the status quo. The vested interests of the privileged classes mean that any attempts to _____ wealth throughout society will face obstacles. Individuals can only be relatively rich if others are relatively poor, and because those with the money also have the power, their interests will always take precedence over those of the poor. The middle classes perceive poor people to be suffering because they lack the character to save and work hard, but it's the poor who absorb the cost of change. There may be no premeditated strategy to keep the poor in poverty, but the reality of modern economic systems leaves people with no power to change their circumstances.

① donate
② estimate
③ surrender
④ accumulate
⑤ redistribute

32

In 1982, an African-American man named Tom Bradley, who was the mayor of Los Angeles, was running for governor of California. The night before the election, he was seven percentage points ahead of his rival, a white man named George Deukmejian. Despite this large lead, Bradley lost the election. Experts believe the reason was race — many white voters said they would vote for Bradley, but once they were alone in the voting booth, they did not. This phenomenon, in which people falsely claim to support _____, is now known as the Bradley effect. It is likely caused by a desire to appear politically correct and to avoid being accused of racist behavior. As a result, significant numbers of voters lie to the people who are taking polls.

① every politician
② voter restrictions
③ the results of polls
④ a minority candidate
⑤ the election process

33

People often find that physical attractiveness greatly influences _____. For instance, physically attractive people are viewed more positively than less attractive people. Psychologists refer to this phenomenon as the halo effect. In a study conducted by Bersheid and Walster, subjects were shown pictures of men and women of varying degrees of physical attractiveness. When asked to guess their personality traits, subjects rated the physically attractive people to be more sensitive, kind, interesting, strong, modest, sociable, intelligent, witty, honest, happy, and successful than people who were physically less attractive. With the result of this study, it is indicated that people often form various first impressions of others based on physical appearances alone. [3점]

*halo effect: 후광 효과

① the relationships in our social lives
② the personality one forms during life
③ one's positive attitude toward oneself
④ one's social or academic achievements
⑤ the early impressions that others form of us

34

Alternative histories describe worlds in which _____. In other words, alternative history is a type of science fiction which resembles historical fiction. Stories describe a world that is identical to ours until some imaginary historical event happens. At this point, the world becomes a fantasy world with an alternative history. Alternative histories might describe worlds in which the Roman Empire never fell. They may write about some technology being introduced much earlier in history than actually happened. For example: What if computers had been invented in Victorian times? Many readers find these stories interesting because they stimulate the imagination and examine the phenomenon of cause and effect in history. [3점]

① history repeats itself
② technology has been improved
③ history has taken another course
④ something terrible has happened
⑤ a war has been won by the other side

35 다음 글에서 전체 흐름과 관계 없는 문장은?

Suppose you are shopping at a department store and see a bottle of perfume that costs $50. Your initial thought may be that the department store charges too much for a tiny amount of alcohol and oils mixed with water. ① However, you should consider that this price reflects not only the cost of the raw materials, but also a wide variety of additional expenses. ② For one thing, the department store is paying the salary of the salesperson behind the counter. ③ And the manufacturer may have spent more on the fancy bottle than on the fragrance itself. ④ Accordingly, the government has been considering imposing higher taxes on luxury items, reflecting public opinion. ⑤ Also, think about how much the company spends on advertising and transporting the product.

[36~37] 주어진 글 다음에 이어질 글의 순서로 가장 적절한 것을 고르시오.

36

Imagine a teenage boy and girl whose parents forbid them to date each other. Will the boy and girl obey their parents' orders?

(A) According to one psychological perspective, they most certainly will not; rather, the prohibition will only increase the couple's desire to be together. This is known as the Romeo and Juliet effect, named after Shakespeare's tragic story of illicit love.

(B) For example, laws that prohibit certain types of political speech often drive more people to participate in what has been made illegal. According to this theory, then, whenever an authority puts limitations on individual freedoms, there will be a powerful urge to challenge those limitations.

(C) Despite the fact that the effect takes its name from two of literature's most famous lovers, it is not confined to romantic relationships. In fact, we can observe the Romeo and Juliet effect at work in many other aspects of society.

*illicit: 사회 통념에 어긋나는

① (A) – (B) – (C)   ② (A) – (C) – (B)
③ (B) – (A) – (C)   ④ (B) – (C) – (A)
⑤ (C) – (A) – (B)

37

These days, many people who have lost their jobs due to the financial crisis are leaving the job market and returning to school.

(A) However, simply going back to school and earning a new degree doesn't ensure that these people will then be able to find jobs. Returning to school is a risk, involving a significant investment of time, money, and effort.

(B) To meet the needs of these new students, some universities are offering specialized classes. A number of government programs have been designed to support both the schools offering these courses and the students enrolling in them.

(C) Therefore, before choosing a subject to study, it is important to do some serious research. Potential returning students should learn all they can about the industry they want to get involved in and its employment prospects for the future. [3점]

① (A) – (B) – (C)   ② (A) – (C) – (B)
③ (B) – (A) – (C)   ④ (B) – (C) – (A)
⑤ (C) – (A) – (B)

38

> To adapt to this new environment, humans began walking upright.

When a single species gradually develops into two distinct species, it is known as divergent evolution. (①) This generally occurs when a specific population inhabits a different environment from the rest of the species; over time it changes to meet the unique demands of its habitat. (②) For an example of how divergent evolution works, consider the stark differences in the feet of monkeys and humans. (③) Although humans and monkeys were once a single species, humans began to live on the ground while monkeys continued to spend most of their time swinging from trees. (④) Over time, the human foot changed to allow for better speed and balance when walking or running. (⑤) Despite sharing a common ancestor with monkeys, the habitat in which humans lived required them to develop different physical traits. [3점]

*divergent evolution: 분지진화 **stark: (차이가) 극명한

39

> Although owls lack mystical powers, they are powerful hunters whose skill surpasses that of other birds of prey.

For thousands of years, people believed that owls were more like gods than animals. (①) Even in modern times they have been used to signify wisdom, magic, and power, but the truth is that owls are no more divine than other birds. (②) The large, round heads and huge, forward-facing eyes that were supposed to signify divine intelligence are simply natural adaptations developed to help them catch small animals. (③) Their acute senses ensure that owls rarely fail to notice a potential meal. (④) Moreover, their ability to fly silently means that their prey never realizes they are to be attacked until it's too late. (⑤)

40 다음 글의 내용을 한 문장으로 요약하고자 한다. 빈칸 (A), (B)에 들어갈 말로 가장 적절한 것은?

Detective stories first became popular in the mid-nineteenth century, which was a time of great scientific progress. Among the most popular detective storywriters was Sir Arthur Conan Doyle. He shared a fascination for the logical approach used by scientists in their experiments. The character of Sherlock Holmes, for example, illustrates Conan Doyle's admiration for the scientific mind. In each case that Holmes investigates, he uses the most insubstantial evidence to track down his opponent. With his amazing powers of observation and ingenious reasoning, Holmes figures out the criminal's identity from such unremarkable details as the type of cigar ashes left at the crime scene or the kind of ink used in a handwritten letter.

↓

Writer Conan Doyle captured the _____(A)_____ spirit of the times by equipping the detective hero Sherlock Holmes with outstanding powers of _____(B)_____.

	(A)		(B)
①	literary	.....	scientific judgment
②	scientific	.....	logical reasoning
③	adventurous	.....	clever observation
④	pragmatic	.....	analytical skills
⑤	theoretical	.....	experiential knowledge

[41~42] 다음 글을 읽고, 물음에 답하시오.

Jamaica has a unique language that is spoken only on the island nation and by Jamaicans living elsewhere in the world. Different from Jamaican English, a dialect of English spoken on the island, this language emerged from the island's particular historical context, beginning with the arrival of European invaders.

During that era, English, a language completely foreign to the natives of Jamaica, was being used by the conquerors to facilitate communication between Jamaicans and Europeans. The need to communicate effectively fueled _____ that combined elements of English, other European languages, and Caribbean languages. Eventually, it produced what is known by linguists as Jamaican Creole. The term "creole" refers to a language that derives from the fusion of two or more languages, though in Jamaica the spoken creole is known by a local term with a similar meaning, "patois", a word of French origin.

Over time, and with the decolonization of Jamaica, Jamaican Creole came to represent national identity and earned a position of prominence. Though at times misunderstood as a form of broken English — since English remains the official and formal language of Jamaica — Jamaican Creole is much more than a divergent branch of English. Rather, it is a language in its own right, one with its own authors, singers, speakers, and poets.

41 윗글의 빈칸에 들어갈 말로 가장 적절한 것은?

① the alteration of English
② the formation of a language
③ loss of European political control
④ resentment among speakers of Jamaican Creole
⑤ the expectation that Jamaicans would learn English

42 윗글의 내용과 일치하는 것은?

① 자메이카는 다른 나라의 지배를 받은 적이 없다.
② 자메이카 원주민들은 예로부터 크리올이라는 고유의 언어를 사용했다.
③ 유럽과의 경제교류로 영어와 불어가 자메이카로 전해졌다.
④ patois는 자메이카 크리올의 구어체를 일컫는다.
⑤ 자메이카 크리올은 현재 자메이카의 공용어로 사용되고 있다.

[43~45] 다음 글을 읽고, 물음에 답하시오.

(A)

One day, the famous composer Mozart heard a knock upon his door. It was a well-dressed stranger who said he had been sent by an important person to speak with Mozart. Mozart asked who this important person was, but the man refused to answer. All he would say was that the person had lost a loved one and wanted Mozart to compose a requiem in honor of the deceased. Intrigued by the mysterious request, Mozart negotiated a price and agreed to deliver the completed piece in one month.

*requiem: 레퀴엠, 망자를 위한 곡

(B)

Although his health did not improve, Mozart quickly returned to the work. When a month had passed, the mysterious stranger reappeared at his door as promised. Shamefully, Mozart had to admit that (a) he had not finished the piece. He asked for one month more, explaining that his passion for the composition had caused it to become more complex than expected. Much to Mozart's astonishment, rather than complaining, the stranger granted the extension and said he would double the price paid for the requiem.

(C)

Soon after the stranger had departed, Mozart was thrust into a creative rage. Grabbing a pen and paper, (b) he began to feverishly compose, and continued to do so for several days and nights. Unfortunately, his health was poor and he soon collapsed from exhaustion. Forced to take a much needed break from his work, (c) he remarked to his wife that he feared the requiem he was writing would end up being played at his own funeral.

(D)

In his failing health, Mozart began to suspect that the man was either an angel or a devil, and that his presence signaled Mozart's impending death. (d) He resumed his work with even greater passion, convinced that this was to be his final and greatest composition. When the stranger knocked on Mozart's door one month later, (e) he was informed that the great composer had died. The requiem, which was unfinished, turned out to have been commissioned by a local count with a love for music.

43 주어진 글 (A)에 이어질 내용을 순서에 맞게 배열한 것으로 가장 적절한 것은?

① (B) – (C) – (D)   ② (B) – (D) – (C)
③ (C) – (B) – (D)   ④ (C) – (D) – (B)
⑤ (D) – (B) – (C)

44 윗글의 제목으로 가장 적절한 것은?

① A Composer's Final Requiem
② The Mystery of Mozart's Death
③ A Cruel Trick Played on Mozart
④ The Greatest Requiem Ever Written
⑤ The Source of Mozart's Great Passion

45 밑줄 친 (a)~(e) 중에서 가리키는 대상이 나머지 넷과 다른 것은? [3점]

① (a)   ② (b)   ③ (c)   ④ (d)   ⑤ (e)

* 3점 문항에만 점수가 표시되어 있습니다.
  점수 표시가 없는 문항은 모두 2점씩입니다.

18 다음 글의 목적으로 가장 적절한 것은?

To Whom It May Concern,

I am writing this letter at the request of Michelle Williams. Michelle was a student in several of my science classes at Malibu High School. She was a hard worker in the classroom and a pleasure to speak with after class. The level of her work in my classes was well above average, and she was a role model for her classmates, who often turned to her for assistance. I am therefore happy to recommend her for admission to your university. I am sure Michelle will succeed in whatever academic path she chooses to pursue in the future. If you have any questions or require more details, you are welcome to call me at 221-8824.

Sincerely,
Jonathan Ito

① 신규 과학 교사 자리에 지원하려고
② 대학교에 학생을 입학생으로 추천하려고
③ 학생의 과학경시대회 참가를 신청하려고
④ 대학에 입학 관련 서류 발송을 요청하려고
⑤ 학생의 진학 관련 문제에 대해 조언을 얻으려고

19 다음 글의 요지로 가장 적절한 것은?

Creativity is a trait that is almost universally viewed as positive. At the same time, only a slim minority of creative ideas proposed in the workplace are actually put into action. Why is this the case? By definition, a creative idea is novel — it represents a perspective that is beyond the norm and it may suggest a course of action that has never been conceived of or attempted before. And most businesspeople become anxious when confronted with new and untested courses of action, as they would rather be safe than sorry. So, they tend to treat creative ideas as absurd and unworthy of consideration. This is extremely unfortunate, because by doing so they pass up clear opportunities to both improve their business and benefit their customers. Creativity is the true road to progress — the sooner we recognize this, the better off we will be.

① 창의력을 포용하는 기업 풍토가 마련될 필요가 있다.
② 철저한 사전 검증이 아이디어의 성공 여부를 결정한다.
③ 근무환경은 창의적인 아이디어의 발상에 영향을 끼친다.
④ 사업에서 창의적인 아이디어가 꼭 이윤으로 이어지진 않는다.
⑤ 창의력은 모두가 생각하는 것만큼 긍정적이지 않을 수도 있다.

20 다음 글에서 필자가 주장하는 바로 가장 적절한 것은?

Some people think that life is a difficult journey and wish that it would just pass by quickly. I understand them in some ways, but what they don't realize is that the difficult moments we go through are exactly what make the journey worth taking. Likewise, all of the trials that come our way serve to make us better people. In other words, by dealing with our own problems, we become more understanding of others and more confident in ourselves. Therefore, we should look beyond our difficulties to the many benefits that may come later. Life is so much more precious when we find meaning in the problems we face.

① 여행은 인간을 성숙하게 만든다.
② 성공에는 많은 노력이 뒤따른다.
③ 역경을 발전의 기회로 삼아야 한다.
④ 다른 사람의 의견에 귀 기울여야 한다.
⑤ 목표를 성취하려면 구체적인 계획이 필요하다.

21 다음 글의 주제로 가장 적절한 것은? [3점]

Following the September 11th terrorist attacks in the United States, the Transportation Security Administration (TSA) was established to ensure the safety of American air travel. The TSA is tasked with screening passengers and their luggage prior to boarding in order to identify any dangerous persons or objects. In recent years, however, it has become obvious that the TSA itself poses big problems to people traveling to the U.S. Some of the agency's complicated screening rules, such as those requiring passengers to remove their shoes and disallowing liquids in carry-on bags, inconvenience and annoy travelers. In addition, more recent policies raise far more serious concerns. For one thing, the use of full-body security scanners, which emit dangerous levels of radiation, puts people's health at risk. Meanwhile, "enhanced security pat-downs" infringe on personal privacy and raise human rights issues. The TSA should start considering more than just tighter security.

① the need for stricter TSA rules
② what the main task of the TSA is
③ fears of another terror attack in the U.S.
④ negative effects of TSA's strong security policy
⑤ the process of passenger screening in American airports

[22~23] 다음 글의 제목으로 가장 적절한 것을 고르시오.

22

Crossbred dogs, nicknamed "designer dogs," are quickly becoming a hot trend in the U.S. The designer dog that people most want to breed is the Labradoodle, which is a cross between a Labrador and a poodle. This mix combines the intelligence and delicate frame of a poodle with the lovability and loyalty of a Labrador. Many experts believe that crossbred dogs are healthier because they have a more varied genetic background than purebreds. Pet owners look for animals that combine the best qualities of two breeds, like a pug's friendliness and a beagle's loyalty. It is no surprise then that these designer dogs have won the hearts of pet lovers and critics alike.

① How to Breed Healthy Pets
② How to Choose the Perfect Dog
③ Why It Is Difficult to Train Pets
④ Why Designer Dogs Are Gaining Popularity
⑤ Why Designer Dogs Are Healthier than Other Dogs

23

In 2016, a tiny piece of space junk hit the International Space Station (ISS). It was only a few thousandths of a millimeter in diameter, but it caused serious damage to a window. If a larger piece of space junk ever hits the ISS, it could destroy the entire station, killing everyone aboard. Unfortunately, there are more than 100 million pieces of space junk in orbit around Earth, and about 34,000 of these are larger than 10 centimeters. If this number continues to grow, it could soon be too dangerous for astronauts to orbit Earth or travel into space. That is why we need to find a solution to the space junk problem today — doing so will allow us to continue exploring the universe tomorrow.

① Safety Upgrades for the ISS
② The Dangers of Becoming an Astronaut
③ Solutions for Dealing with Junk in Space
④ Accidents Caused by Sending Astronauts into Orbit
⑤ Space Junk: A Growing Threat to Space Exploration

24 다음 도표의 내용과 일치하지 않는 것은?

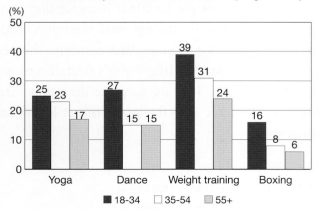

The Most Popular Fitness Classes by Age Group

(%)

Yoga: 25, 23, 17
Dance: 27, 15, 15
Weight training: 39, 31, 24
Boxing: 16, 8, 6

■ 18-34   □ 35-54   ▨ 55+

This graph shows the participation rates of various age groups in a number of different fitness class activities. ① The youngest age group, ranging from 18 to 34 years of age, had the highest participation rate in all the activities included on the chart. ② The over-55 age group had a participation rate of less than 20% in all the activities, with weight training being the most common activity and boxing the least common. ③ More than 30% of 35- to 54-year-olds took part in weight training classes, which was approximately twice the percentage that took part in dance classes. ④ Boxing was the least common activity for all three age groups, but the percentage of 18- to 34-year-olds participating was twice as high as the percentage of 35- to 54-year-olds. ⑤ Finally, a quarter of the youngest age group took part in yoga classes, 14 percentage points fewer than took part in weight training.

25 다음 글의 내용과 일치하지 않는 것은?

Unlike photographers here on Earth, astronauts can take photographs from viewpoints never experienced by anyone else. However, the fairly simple job of taking a photograph on Earth is much more troublesome in space. Lack of gravity does make it easy to deal with heavy camera equipment, but it also makes it difficult to stand still. On a more basic level, the spacesuits and other accessories worn by astronauts are very awkward when trying to actually click the button to take a picture. Other technical issues also make space photography tricky. For example, photos may be blurred by dirt on windows, and there is the possibility of damaging film due to exposure to even a small amount of radiation.

① 우주에서의 사진 촬영은 지구에서보다 어렵다.
② 우주에서 무거운 카메라 장비를 다루기는 쉽지 않다.
③ 우주복은 우주에서의 사진 촬영에 방해가 된다.
④ 우주에서 찍은 사진은 먼지로 인해 흐릿하게 나올 수 있다.
⑤ 우주에서는 방사능으로 인해 필름이 손상될 수 있다.

26 Ireland에 관한 다음 글의 내용과 일치하는 것은?

Sometimes, natural disasters can greatly affect the history of places far away from where they occur. In 1845, for example, there were between eight and ten million people living in Ireland. Nearly half of them depended on a single crop: the potato. During the summer of that year, a disease began affecting the country's potato plants and spread quickly throughout the country. By the following year, 75% of Ireland's potato crop had been lost, and people began dying of starvation. Over the next six years, one million people perished, while another million emigrated. Many of these refugees settled and built Irish communities in East Coast cities in the U.S. There, they provided a surplus of cheap labor across multiple industries, dramatically boosting American economic growth for the next several decades. Thus, the Irish Potato Famine indirectly had a meaningful impact on 19th-century American history.

① 1845년에 이미 인구가 1,000만 명을 넘어섰다.
② 식량으로서 감자에 대한 의존도가 높았다.
③ 급격한 기후 변화로 인해 심한 기근을 겪었다.
④ 1840년대 중반에 많은 사람이 질병으로 인해 사망했다.
⑤ 미국의 요청으로 많은 인력을 수출했다.

27 Enjoy a Pizza, Feed the Hungry에 관한 다음 안내문의 내용과 일치하지 <u>않는</u> 것은?

Enjoy a Pizza, Feed the Hungry

Gino's Pizzeria will be holding a fundraiser this weekend to support the Lincoln County Food Bank!

When: Friday, September 22 to Sunday, September 24
Where: Gino's Pizzeria, 247 Water Street, Newton, Vermont
How to take part:
1) Download a special fundraiser coupon from our website — www.ginospzz.net.
2) Order any pizza, either in the restaurant or to be delivered.
3) Present the coupon when you pay — you'll get a 10% discount, and we'll donate five dollars to the food bank.

Note: Only one coupon can be used per table or household. A minimum order of $15 is required.

① 총 3일 동안 진행되는 행사이다.
② 배달주문 시에도 쿠폰을 사용할 수 있다.
③ 쿠폰을 제시하면 5달러를 할인받는다.
④ 한 가구당 한 장의 쿠폰만 쓸 수 있다.
⑤ 쿠폰을 사용하려면 최소 15달러 이상 주문해야 한다.

28 다음 글의 밑줄 친 부분 중, 어법상 틀린 것은? [3점]

Reconstructing the skeletons of extinct animals from their fossil bones ① is a challenging and exacting science. Fossil bones almost never survive unbroken. When found, the bones of a single animal may ② be scattered far and wide. Furthermore, bone fragments of several animals may come to rest in the same riverbed or sandbar, and careful efforts must be taken not to mismatch ③ them. Accordingly, paleontologists must spend years ④ studying the skeletons of living animals, documenting their forms and functions, and comparing structural details of related creatures before attempting to assemble a museum display. A collection of fossils, however fascinating, ⑤ revealing its true worth only when assembled by a dedicated expert.

*paleontologist: 고생물학자

29 (A), (B), (C)의 각 네모 안에서 문맥에 맞는 낱말로 가장 적절한 것은?

When talking about international relations, we have to (A) distinguish / alternate between hard power and soft power. Hard power refers to the use of military or economic strength to force other nations to behave a certain way. Soft power, in contrast, requires the powerful nation to adopt the desired behaviors first and act as an example for others to follow. Therefore, soft power has the ability to change the (B) preferences / prevalence of others to conform to your desire. These same principles hold true in the business world. The most effective executives, for instance, are not those who force employees to act a certain way. Rather, leading by example brings about the greatest success. Through the use of soft power, executives (C) encourage / dissuade employees to make the company's goals their own, and in the process convince them to do what needs to be done voluntarily.

	(A)		(B)		(C)
①	alternate	......	preferences	......	encourage
②	alternate	......	prevalence	......	encourage
③	distinguish	......	preferences	......	encourage
④	distinguish	......	preferences	......	dissuade
⑤	distinguish	......	prevalence	......	dissuade

[30~34] 다음 빈칸에 들어갈 말로 가장 적절한 것을 고르시오.

30

One should not confuse the so-called science of astrology with the authentic science of astronomy. In fact, astrology has been a thorn in the side of scientific thinking for many generations. Disguised as true science, with piles of academic-looking books and complex charts of planetary positions, astrology claims it can explain individual personality. It has held firm in its insistence, but no scientific study has ever been able to prove this assertion. Indeed, attempts to do so have proven just how empty that assertion is. The claim that being born under a particular sign makes somebody "creative" or "goal-oriented" can't really be tested, since the presence of such qualities is largely a matter of _____.

① confidence   ② persistence
③ faithfulness   ④ responsibility
⑤ interpretation

31

The job of lexicographers, which is to write and edit dictionaries, may sound simple, but it is more complicated than it seems. This is because creating a dictionary is _____. The process starts with a person known as a definer, who writes the definition. Next, an editor ensures that all the related entries are properly referenced, and then a pronunciation specialist checks the word's phonetic spelling. After that, someone traces the word's origins, and someone else enters everything into the system. Finally, a copy editor and a proofreader review the entry to make sure no errors are left. As dictionaries contain hundreds of thousands of words, it requires a great deal of time and effort to put them together.

① a high-tech job
② an outdated goal
③ a useless attempt
④ a valuable tradition
⑤ a collaborative task

32

One of the few people in history to have his name become an English verb, Thomas Bowdler has become known as the man who bowdlerized many of Shakespeare's works. To bowdlerize means _____. Bowdler was an English doctor but is famous for his collaboration with his sister Harriet on *The Family Shakespeare*. In 1807, the siblings edited a ten-volume edition of Shakespeare by deleting words and expressions that were considered unsuitable to be read aloud in front of women and children. Although some people criticized him for contaminating Shakespeare's work, others also recognized his contribution to attracting a wider audience to Shakespeare. And finally, in 1936, Bowdler's work led to the creation of the term bowdlerize.

① to devote one's life to a determined goal
② to translate someone's words as one likes
③ to force others to follow his or her beliefs
④ to be an enthusiastic reader of a certain writer
⑤ to delete sections of work considered inappropriate

33

It's sometimes difficult to _____. When a new acquaintance says, "It's been great meeting you. Stay in touch," would that person be surprised or annoyed if you contacted him or her again? There are a lot of ritual exchanges in social contacts that don't mean what they actually appear to mean. For example, "How are you?" is rarely a question about someone's health. Many social signals like this, however, may be misleading: Using a person's first name or giving him or her a warm hug on leaving may only be an expression of a social habit rather than a heartfelt gesture. Misunderstanding these signals can often lead to disappointment or embarrassment for both sides. [3점]

① keep in contact with someone over time
② greet someone who you meet in business
③ make friends when you first meet someone
④ express your feelings to a new acquaintance
⑤ distinguish between sincere wishes and mere ritual

34

When speaking casually, people often use *up* to mean *north* and *down* to mean *south*. However, it is important to know that geographically speaking, *up* is away from the center of the earth into space, and *down* is away from space to the center of the earth. It is also important to understand *up* and *down* correctly in reference to river flow. Rivers flow downhill from elevated sources to lower mouths, where they eventually enter the sea. The problem is that some people incorrectly equate *up* with *north*; they think that all rivers originate in the north and flow down the map toward the south. They may think, for example, that the Nile River flows from the Mediterranean Sea in the north into Africa in the south. Of course, _____. [3점]

① they are right
② the opposite is true
③ it meets the sea in the end
④ the mouth of the river is wide
⑤ it has an elevated source in the north

35 다음 글에서 전체 흐름과 관계 없는 문장은?

The term "mid-century modern" refers to a design style that was popularized in the West between the mid-1930s and the mid-1960s. It was primarily seen in architecture and interior products such as furniture. ① Scandinavian design was a major influence, and unifying features included an emphasis on simplicity and flowing, organic lines. ② Mid-century modern architecture can be considered a continuation of the vision of Frank Lloyd Wright in which large windows and open floor plans dominated. ③ This helped create the illusion that the outdoor world was being incorporated with the indoor. ④ Later, Wright designed innovative examples of many different building types, including offices, schools, hotels, and museums. ⑤ Furniture design also centered around simplicity of form, as well as function; for example, the typical mid-century modern chair featured only a simple frame and cushion.

[36~37] 주어진 글 다음에 이어질 글의 순서로 가장 적절한 것을 고르시오.

36

Many people believe that some glaciers may melt completely in a few years, but according to one scientific report, the situation may not be so bad in reality.

(A) Although the glaciers that cover the Himalayan mountains are melting, the pace is slower than scientists originally thought. To find out how quickly the glaciers were melting, a group of researchers compared the size of all glaciers larger than 100 square kilometers over time.

(B) The likely reason for the difference between the projections and the actual numbers is that the projections were based only on observations of a few hundred glaciers at a low altitude.

However, the new measurements from NASA satellites, which photographed the entire earth, show that the Himalayas will still have ice in 2035.

(C) Through this process, they found that the Himalayan and Karakoram mountain ranges are losing much less ice than previously thought. Surprisingly, the glaciers are only losing 4 billion tons each year, which is much less than the 50 billion tons they were expected to lose.

① (A) – (B) – (C)   ② (A) – (C) – (B)
③ (B) – (A) – (C)   ④ (B) – (C) – (A)
⑤ (C) – (A) – (B)

37

Every year, medical imaging exposes at least four million Americans under age 65 to high levels of radiation, according to a recent study.

(A) The study goes on to suggest that this exposure would likely be the cause of cancer for thousands of people. According to the research, even low levels of radiation from medical imaging increases a person's risk of cancer.

(B) The primary reason is a shift in medical culture. Rather than examining patients, doctors habitually use imaging instead. Informed patients need to ask their doctors if each medical imaging test is truly necessary.

(C) Part of the problem is that many doctors have had CT and PET scanners installed in their offices, using them frequently to increase their profits. But money is not the only cause of the rising number of medical imaging tests. [3점]

① (A) – (B) – (C)   ② (A) – (C) – (B)
③ (B) – (A) – (C)   ④ (B) – (C) – (A)
⑤ (C) – (A) – (B)

38

> Neither of these results is a nice round measurement; nature simply is more complex than that.

It is common knowledge that a year is composed of 365 days and a day is made up of 24 hours. (①) Yet, in actuality, both of these measurements are approximations. (②) The determining factors for the exact lengths of years and days are related to the Earth's movement as it orbits the Sun — how long it takes to complete an orbit and how long it takes to rotate on its own axis. (③) But timekeepers have come up with ingenious methods for adjusting our time systems to remain in line with the true lengths of years and days. (④) That is why every fourth year is a "leap year," to which an extra day is added. (⑤) Similarly, "leap seconds" are added when needed to provide for an even finer means of temporal correction. [3점]

*leap year: 윤년 **leap second: 윤초

39

> Yet the unhealthy consequences of eating disorders can be just as severe.

For many people, food is their worst enemy. They worry so much about getting fat that they severely limit what they eat, or they eat freely and then immediately make themselves throw up. (①) Doctors who treat such people say that they have an eating disorder. (②) Eating disorders are not as common as obesity. (③) For example, not eating enough can lead to fainting spells, organ damage, weak bones, and even heart attacks. (④) And throwing up repeatedly can severely damage the stomach, cause chemical imbalances in the body,

and corrode the teeth. (⑤) If you think you might have an eating disorder, you should seek counseling right away.

*fainting spell: 졸도

40

다음 글의 내용을 한 문장으로 요약하고자 한다. 빈칸 (A), (B)에 들어갈 말로 가장 적절한 것은?

> It can be certainly said that tourism is attractive to developing countries. It brings in desperately needed money and provides valuable employment. It, however, also involves risks in some ways. Let's take a country like Thailand with its beautiful, quiet beaches. Deciding to develop beach resorts involves building large hotels nearby. Before long, those romantic deserted beaches are overlooked by huge skyscrapers full of noisy tourists. As a result, the richer visitors move on to quieter places, and then the tourist trade has to provide for less wealthy tourists who usually want cheap food and loud music. So ironically, tourists can spoil the very environment that they've come to discover.

↓

> Tourism can bring enormous ____(A)____ to developing countries, but it can also be a ____(B)____.

	(A)		(B)
①	uncertainty	......	costly business
②	burden	......	small business
③	benefits	......	serious threat
④	prosperity	......	political means
⑤	revenue	......	selective demand

[41~42] 다음 글을 읽고, 물음에 답하시오.

In the past, it was believed that providing children with affection served no real developmental purpose. Instead, it was looked upon as sentimental behavior that could be neglected without any serious consequences. In the 1960s, however, an American psychologist named Harry Harlow conducted a series of experiments to (a) disprove this. By demonstrating the powerful effect that a deprivation of affection could have on young rhesus monkeys, he showed the important role that love and caring have on child development.

The most famous of these experiments involved giving infant monkeys the choice of two artificial mothers after (b) removing them from their natural mother's care. The first was made from soft cloth; however, it did not provide the infants with any food. The second artificial mother was made of wire, but had a baby bottle attached to it which provided milk. Observations showed that the infant monkeys chose to spend the (c) majority of their time with the cloth mothers rather than with the ones made of wire. Harlow concluded that this meant affectionate (d) physical contact was more important to the infants than being fed.

Thanks to Harlow's work, psychologists now recognize that affection is a necessary component of healthy childhood development. In additional experiments, he went on to show that a (e) sufficiency of affection could cause severe psychological and emotional trauma. This work has played an important role in how orphanages, schools, and child care providers deal with young children.

*rhesus monkey: 붉은털원숭이

41 윗글의 제목으로 가장 적절한 것은?

① Affection Makes a Big Difference
② How Do Infants Learn to Find Food?
③ Artificial Rearing: Beneficial or Damaging?
④ The Need for Healthy Childhood Development
⑤ Similarities between Human and Monkey Mothers

42 밑줄 친 (a)~(e) 중에서 문맥상 낱말의 쓰임이 적절하지 않은 것은? [3점]

① (a)　　② (b)　　③ (c)　　④ (d)　　⑤ (e)

[43~45] 다음 글을 읽고, 물음에 답하시오.

(A)

Generally, the artifacts that are held in a museum's collection have come from archaeological excavations sponsored by either a government or a research institution. Yet, in some cases, museums accept ancient items as gifts from private collectors, or even purchase them from art dealers. Occasionally, although the museum may not know it, artifacts acquired in this way are stolen goods that have been smuggled out of their place of origin to be sold to the highest bidder.

(B)

Obviously, in order to fulfill their mission of sharing and preserving humanity's history, museums must in some cases display artifacts with unknown origins so as to present a complete timeline, as was the case in the Metropolitan Museum of Art exhibition. Moreover, if they avoid such objects, there is a risk that important historical artifacts will remain in private hands, where neither scholars nor the general public has access to the secrets they contain.

(C)

If museum curators limited their exhibitions to objects with documented origins, their representations of history would be incomplete. The Metropolitan Museum of Art in New York, for example, recently included a number of items with unknown origins in an exhibition on the ancient cultures of Bactria, a region in modern-day Afghanistan. Particularly in parts of the world such as this one, a region with a turbulent history and the site of an ongoing war, proof of artifacts' origins is not always possible to obtain.

*Bactria: 박트리아(고대 그리스인들이 중앙 아시아에 세운 왕국)

(D)

To discourage this, many museums have strict policies governing the acquisition of new relics. Not all curators agree with such policies, however. Of course, no curator wants to add stolen items to a museum's holdings, but sometimes proof of an artifact's origin is not available simply because it has been lost over the years as it has passed through many different hands. In other words, the fact that a centuries-old paper trail cannot be found does not necessarily mean an object was acquired illegally.

43 주어진 글 (A)에 이어질 내용을 순서에 맞게 배열한 것으로 가장 적절한 것은?

① (B) – (C) – (D)
② (B) – (D) – (C)
③ (C) – (B) – (D)
④ (D) – (B) – (C)
⑤ (D) – (C) – (B)

44 윗글의 제목으로 가장 적절한 것은?

① Stricter Museum Policies Required
② Museums' Need for Undocumented Items
③ Museum Curators No Longer Responsible
④ An Increase in the Acquisition of Stolen Artifacts
⑤ How Museum Curators Can Stop the Traffic of Stolen Artifacts

45 윗글에 관한 내용으로 적절하지 않은 것은?

① 보통 박물관에 전시된 유물들은 정부의 후원을 받는다.
② 박물관은 예술품 판매상으로부터 고대의 물건들을 구입하기도 한다.
③ 메트로폴리탄 미술관은 출처가 알려지지 않은 유물들을 전시하지 않는다.
④ 박트리아는 격정적인 역사를 지닌 곳이었다.
⑤ 많은 박물관에 새로운 유물의 획득을 관리하는 정책이 있다.

* 3점 문항에만 점수가 표시되어 있습니다.
  점수 표시가 없는 문항은 모두 2점씩입니다.

18 다음 글의 목적으로 가장 적절한 것은?

Dear Ms. Marcia Lund,

Thank you for partnering with the Children's Cancer Charity. We appreciate your support over the last five years. The Children's Cancer Charity is working to provide treatment to children around the world. In order to meet our goals, we rely on the generosity of our supporters in each region of the globe. Without your selfless support, we would not be able to serve children in your community effectively. We hope that you will take part in our annual Hope for Our Kids fundraiser this year. Our goal for your region is $10,000, and as always we appreciate any amount you are willing to contribute.

Thank you in advance for your support.

Deanna Elmer,
Regional Director

① 현재 기부금 모금 상황을 알리려고
② 자선단체의 기념행사에 초대하려고
③ 지난 후원에 대한 고마움을 전하려고
④ 연례 기부 프로그램 참여를 장려하려고
⑤ 새로운 자선단체의 설립 목적을 설명하려고

19 다음 글에 드러난 Lindsay의 심경으로 가장 적절한 것은?

Lindsay hadn't caught a single fish that morning. In fact, he had not even felt more than a couple of bites. He couldn't remember having such an unproductive morning on the boat. Feeling annoyed, he tried to cast his fishing line out one more time. He reached back with the fishing pole and swung wildly. But as he did so, the hook got caught in a fold of his T-shirt. It slashed through the fabric and ripped his shirt clean off, hurling it into the water. Lindsay was so surprised that the pole slipped out of his hands and flew overboard. He could only watch as it sunk into the dark and murky water. Now Lindsay would have to make his way back to the harbor with no fish, no fishing pole, and no shirt either.

*hurl: (거칠게) 던지다

① lonely and bored
② calm and relaxed
③ joyful and excited
④ upset and frustrated
⑤ nervous and worried

20 다음 글에서 필자가 주장하는 바로 가장 적절한 것은?

Although companies often push their employees to get involved in a variety of self-improvement activities, the average worker finds it difficult to put aside even 10 minutes a day for such pursuits. A recent survey shows that although most Koreans believe self-improvement to be extremely important, just five percent dedicate more than 10 minutes a day to learning a new skill. To deal with this situation, employers need to make an effort to assist their workers in finding the time needed to do so. Assuring that workers are able to take part in self-improvement classes not only raises employee morale, but serves as an investment in the company's future as well, potentially increasing the skills and abilities of its future workforce.

① 회사의 미래는 직원들의 기술과 역량에 달려있다.
② 대부분의 직장인에게 과도한 업무가 부여되고 있다.
③ 직원들의 사기를 높이기 위한 다양한 대책이 필요하다.
④ 회사는 직원들의 자기 계발 시간을 보장해 주어야 한다.
⑤ 직원들은 자기 계발을 위한 노력을 게을리해서는 안 된다.

21 밑줄 친 reboot our planet이 다음 글에서 의미하는 바로 가장 적절한 것은? [3점]

A group of researchers has proposed that human beings should build a "lunar ark" in case our planet is destroyed. The ark would not be a spacecraft — instead, it would be a structure built deep beneath the surface of the moon. The researchers believe it should be filled with frozen genetic material from every living species on our planet. They made this proposal because they fear the earth is currently facing serious threats from a number of sources, including nuclear weapons, asteroids, pandemics, and climate-related dangers. By protecting the world's biodiversity in a place where it cannot be harmed, we would be insuring ourselves against a terrible disaster. If the earth were to be destroyed, the surviving humans could potentially find a way to use the contents of the ark to reboot our planet in the future.

*asteroid: 소행성

① change the way that people think
② bring the earth's species back to life
③ prevent a disaster from taking place
④ travel through space to a new planet
⑤ build underground homes on the moon

22 다음 글의 요지로 가장 적절한 것은?

We love to hear stories of people who have been positively transformed by disaster. Whether the person has survived a plane crash, a hurricane, or cancer, their stories seem to testify to a proven psychological truth: Humans can flourish under even the most difficult circumstances. The life-changing effects of crises are now the province of disaster-related psychology. Research in the field has found that roughly half the people who have struggled with adversity say that their lives have improved in some ways. Although disaster-related stress is common shortly after the incident, it seems that only a small proportion of adults become chronically troubled. Eventually, most people report that their lives have been enhanced.

① 재난을 겪은 사람들이 성공할 확률이 높다.
② 재난 이후 소수의 사람들만이 재기에 성공한다.
③ 재난을 겪은 사람에게는 주변의 도움이 절실하다.
④ 재난이 오히려 더 나은 삶을 위한 계기가 되기도 한다.
⑤ 재난을 겪은 사람에게는 심리적 안정이 매우 중요하다.

23 다음 글의 주제로 가장 적절한 것은? [3점]

Economists often advocate the benefits of free trade, but unfortunately this system does little to guarantee the welfare of the workers within it. This is especially true in poor countries, where international corporations take advantage of unfairly low labor costs to make higher profits. The concept of fair trade was developed as a reaction to this. Fair trade is realized through partnerships between suppliers in developing nations and retailers in the developed world. The retailers agree to pay fair and constant prices for goods in return for suppliers' guarantees that they will generate high-quality products, while also ensuring healthy working conditions for their employees. In this way, fair trade partnerships give small operations the sense of security they need to be able to compete with large corporations in the global marketplace.

① how free trade supports fair trade
② why two systems of trade are needed
③ what fair trade is and how it has been developed
④ the long-term problems caused by global trading
⑤ the importance of protecting the global marketplace

24 다음 글의 제목으로 가장 적절한 것은?

At first glance, a roller coaster is quite similar to a passenger train. It consists of a series of connected cars that move on tracks. But unlike a passenger train, a roller coaster has no engine or power source of its own. To get started, the coaster cars are pulled up the first hill. This initial climb builds up a reserve of potential energy; the higher up it goes, the greater the distance gravity can pull it down. You experience this same phenomenon when you ride your bike to the top of a big hill. The potential energy you build going up the hill is released as the dynamic energy of motion that takes you down the hill.

*potential energy: 위치 에너지 **dynamic energy: 동적 에너지

① Why Roller Coasters Aren't Dangerous
② What Makes Roller Coasters So Exciting
③ How Roller Coasters Work Without an Engine
④ Which Materials Roller Coasters Are Built With
⑤ How We Use Potential Energy in Our Everyday Lives

25 다음 도표의 내용과 일치하지 <u>않는</u> 것은?

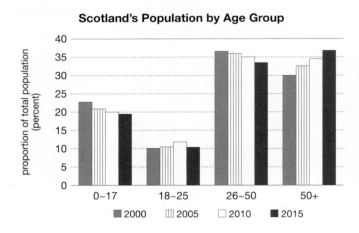

Scotland's Population by Age Group

In the graph above, four different age groups are shown as a percentage of the overall population of Scotland. ① The proportion of people aged 17 and younger dropped slightly between 2000 and 2015. ② A decline also occurred in people aged 26 to 50 during the same period. ③ Yet the largest change occurred in people over 50, with a decrease of more than 5 percentage points over 15 years. ④ The most stable segment of the population was people between the ages of 18 and 25, which experienced only a very small rise between 2000 and 2010. ⑤ However, after reaching a peak in the year 2010, the percentage of this group declined slightly in 2015.

26 monarch butterfly에 관한 다음 글의 내용과 일치하지 않는 것은?

Orange-reddish with black vein-like markings, the monarch butterfly is famous for its ability to return home after several generations. Each spring, a generation of monarchs are born and begin the journey northward from their winter home in Mexico to Canada. These butterflies, which live for only five weeks, do not complete the trip. In fact, it takes three generations to reach the insects' Canadian summer home. Then, in fall, a special generation of monarchs are born. They are able to survive eight weeks, long enough to make it all the way back to Mexico. Scientists believe the butterflies are able to accomplish this great inter-generational migration by reacting to the position of the sun.

① 여러 세대가 지나도 원래 서식지로 돌아갈 수 있다.
② 봄에 태어나는 세대는 5주 동안 산다.
③ 3세대에 걸쳐 멕시코에서 캐나다로 이동한다.
④ 가을에 태어나는 세대는 서식지 이동을 완수하지 못한다.
⑤ 태양의 위치에 반응하여 서식지 이동을 한다.

27 다음 글의 내용과 일치하는 것은?

America is named after one of the greatest frauds of all time, Amerigo Vespucci. He published an account of a voyage he had led in 1497, although this never actually took place. After reading Vespucci's writing, the King of Portugal asked him to go on two voyages led by the Portuguese explorer Coelho and write about the voyages. In his writings, Vespucci wrote that he led both voyages and never even mentioned Coelho. In 1507, a young French professor of geography named the New World "America," a variation of Amerigo. By the time people agreed that Columbus was the one who discovered the New World, it was too late. The New World had already been named America.

① Vespucci는 1497년 항해를 마치고 항해기를 출간했다.
② 포르투갈 왕은 Coelho에게 항해에 대한 기록을 부탁했다.
③ Coelho는 Vespucci가 이끄는 두 차례의 항해에 함께 했다.
④ 1507년, 프랑스 지리학자가 신세계를 아메리카로 명명했다.
⑤ 아메리카는 Vespucci에 의해 발견되었다.

28 Kona Children's Book Festival에 관한 다음 안내문의 내용과 일치하지 않는 것은?

Kona Children's Book Festival

When: Saturday, July 23, 11 a.m. to 7 p.m.
Where: the parking lot of St. Sebastian's Church

The Kona Arts Council is proud to present the annual Kona Children's Book Festival. The event lasts for one day and features many local and national authors, including National Book Prize winner Erica Kang. There will also be a book sale and fun activities for children of all ages.

Tickets:
- Tickets cost $5 in advance and $10 at the door.
- Tickets include a $5 coupon for new and used books.
- Children under 5 get in free.

Note: The coupon is not available with free tickets.

① 행사는 하루 동안 열린다.
② 국내 수상 작가가 참석한다.
③ 표를 예매하면 5달러를 할인받을 수 있다.
④ 중고 서적 구매 시에는 쿠폰을 사용할 수 없다.
⑤ 5세 미만의 아이들은 무료로 입장할 수 있다.

29 다음 글의 밑줄 친 부분 중, 어법상 틀린 것은?

Your core muscles are like a strong link in the middle of a chain that connects your upper body with your lower body. ① Whether you're kicking a ball or washing dishes, the required movements either start from your core or pass through it. ② No matter where the movement begins, it sends waves through the attached links of that metaphorical chain. This means that the strength and flexibility of your core muscles affect ③ how well your arms and legs work. The stronger your core is, the more balance and stability you will have, which affects almost everything you do. Picking up a dropped pencil, getting dressed, or even answering your phone are just ④ a few of the many typical actions you do each day ⑤ what rely on your core muscles.

30 다음 글의 밑줄 친 부분 중, 문맥상 낱말의 쓰임이 적절하지 않은 것은?

People's hands and fingers are often used to ① verify their identity. In particular, businesses that don't require high security use hand geometry readers to ② identify users. Disney theme parks, for example, use hand geometry readers to allow ticket holders into different parts of the park. Some businesses use hand geometry readers instead of timecards. To use a hand geometry reader, you place your hand on the reader, putting your fingers against several marks to ③ hinder an accurate reading. After the digital camera installed in the reader takes pictures of your hand, the reader uses this information to ④ detect the length, width, thickness, and shape of your hand or fingers. It then ⑤ translates that information into a numerical pattern to identify you.

[31~35] 다음 빈칸에 들어갈 말로 가장 적절한 것을 고르시오.

31

What is true happiness? According to a psychologist at the University of Chicago, happiness is achieved when living in a state of "flow." A flow state is one in which the person is totally _____ in an activity, whether at work or play. He developed the flow concept by studying artists. He noted that artists often became involved in their work to the point of being unaware of their surroundings, a mood more satisfying than even seeing a finished painting. Through further study, he concluded that flow requires the use of all or most of your skills. "Using too few skills," he said, "generates boredom and anxiety, which may be the biggest threats to happiness."

① satisfied   ② absorbed
③ detached   ④ frustrated
⑤ disappointed

32

Modern economies are moving more and more toward capital-intensive industry. However, the weakened rural agricultural industry, as well as local culture and sense of identity, should be _____. Even as this economic shift occurs, society will continue to have basic needs that can only be achieved through agricultural production in rural areas. We need to provide financial support to smaller agricultural programs and the people and environments that support them. At the same time, the health and animal welfare advantages of smaller-scale production and processing activities must be developed. This is a much better approach than the large-scale intensive farming and diversification schemes based solely on profit and employing cheaper outside labor.

① changed   ② removed
③ redefined   ④ protected
⑤ suppressed

33

Vegetarians can be classified according to _____. Strict vegetarians, or vegans, avoid all foods of animal origin, including dairy products and eggs. The few people who fall into this category must work hard to ensure that they get all of the essential nutrients their bodies require. Far more common are lacto-vegetarians, who eat dairy products but avoid meat. Their diet can be low in fat and cholesterol, but only if they consume skim milk and other low or nonfat products. Ovo-vegetarians add eggs to their diet, while lacto-ovo-vegetarians eat both dairy products and eggs. Pesco-vegetarians eat fish, dairy products and eggs, while semi-vegetarians eat chicken, fish, dairy products, and eggs.

① their calorie intake
② the nutrients they need
③ their dietary restrictions
④ their preference for meat
⑤ what vegetables they eat

34

During the height of ancient Rome, despite the extreme wealth of the Roman Empire, half of Roman citizens were unemployed. Because slaves were doing so much of the work, relatively few jobs existed. In fact, there was an underclass of people who lived purely on handouts of food from the state, known as the "bread" class. The state also provided free gladiator shows, known as circuses. These shows were intended to distract the bread class from their poor economic situation. As one Roman writer Juvenalis observed, the only thing keeping the unemployed masses from revolting was "bread and circuses." Now, "bread and circuses" has become a convenient general term for government policies that _____. [3점]

① give people great pleasure
② campaign for social reform
③ are grand but lack substance
④ seek short-term solutions to public unrest
⑤ provide job opportunities for the unemployed

35

The concept of a liberal arts education dates back to ancient Greece and Rome. "Liberal" comes from the Latin word *liberalis*, meaning "appropriate for free people." These ancient civilizations believed that all citizens required an education. However, they viewed vocational and technical studies as being more appropriate for slaves and people from the lowest classes of society who were not considered citizens. Only a liberal arts education was suitable for citizens, as it taught them the principles of civic duty and how to reach their full potential as human beings. It emphasized the study of grammar, rhetoric, and logic, as these were _____. Later, during medieval times, these subjects were expanded to include arithmetic, geometry, music, and astronomy, all of which were seen as necessary for the later study of philosophy and theology. Today, the primary goal of a liberal arts education remains to create well-rounded students with a general knowledge of multiple subjects. [3점]

*arithmetic: 산수 **theology: 신학

① based on ideas found in religious texts
② attractive to only a small group of scholars
③ the most essential to being a good citizen
④ easier to learn than science and mathematics
⑤ already being taught to slaves and non-citizens

36 다음 글에서 전체 흐름과 관계 없는 문장은?

In human populations of all sizes, violent and aggressive behavior increases in correlation with outdoor temperature. Environmental psychologist Craig Anderson proposed this theory in 2001, and since that time he has been able to gather evidence by comparing rates of violent crime in different cities. ① He found that temperature is the most reliable indicator of whether one population will exhibit more violent behavior than another. ② According to his research, high temperatures increase individuals' feelings of discomfort, hostility, and aggression towards others, which in turn leads to more violence. ③ Anderson's work has raised concerns among experts about how global warming could affect society at this most basic of levels. ④ One of the factors contributing to global warming is an increase in carbon dioxide production. ⑤ In addition to food and water shortages, coastal flooding, and intense storm activity, a warmer planet might also mean a higher average incidence of violent crime.

37 주어진 글 다음에 이어질 글의 순서로 가장 적절한 것은?

For years, people in the medical community have believed that redheads are more difficult to put to sleep for surgery than people with other hair colors. It sounded like a legend, but new research sheds light on the science behind this surprising fact.

(A) Just what this gene has to do with pain is unknown, but somehow the mutation that is unique to redheads is linked to increased sensitivity to pain.

(B) As a result, compared to people with blond, black, or brown hair, redheads need larger doses of medicine to prevent them from feeling pain during surgery.

(C) By definition, redheaded people have a mutation in one of the genes in the body that produces pigments, causing them to generate more red pigment and less dark pigment than others. [3점]

① (A) – (C) – (B)   ② (B) – (A) – (C)
③ (B) – (C) – (A)   ④ (C) – (A) – (B)
⑤ (C) – (B) – (A)

[38~39] 글의 흐름으로 보아, 주어진 문장이 들어가기에 가장 적절한 곳을 고르시오.

38

Some workers may feel that job-hopping provides them with a wide exposure to different work environments.

Changing jobs frequently could reflect badly on you as an employee. (①) Recruiters may see you as someone who lacks self-motivation or who becomes easily dissatisfied. (②) In addition, they may think that you lack experience since you have not stayed long at any job. (③) They may also worry that you are likely to quit too soon. (④) Furthermore, it may seem like switching jobs can be a faster way for them to get a raise. (⑤) However, these people need to weigh such advantages against the negative perception that potential employers may have about their constant job-changing habits.

39

Despite this, some of these countries have recently adopted the U.S. dollar.

After gaining independence, many nations in Latin America took great pride in establishing their own currency system. (①) The act was a visible expression of their independence from former colonial rulers. (②) The discontinuation of their currencies was done as a means of improving their economies. (③) For example, Ecuador replaced the sucre in an attempt to halt inflation, while El Salvador gave up the colón in order to make its commercial transactions with the U.S. more efficient. (④) This economic gamble, in which countries have given up their currency in the hopes of achieving greater stability, has not been universally popular. (⑤) Among those who proudly view their currency as a national symbol, adopting the dollar represents a step back to the colonial past.

[3점]

40

다음 글의 내용을 한 문장으로 요약하고자 한다. 빈칸 (A), (B)에 들어갈 말로 가장 적절한 것은?

In an experiment, a social psychologist from Harvard University repeatedly approached people waiting to use a copy machine. In the first part of the experiment, she asked the following question: "Excuse me, I have five pages. May I use the copy machine?" In response to this request, approximately 60% of the people agreed to let her use the machine. In the second part of the experiment, she changed her question slightly, saying, "Excuse me, I have five pages. May I use the copy machine because I have to make some copies?" Surprisingly, this resulted in an affirmative response 93% of the time. So what caused this change? The bottom line is that people like to have a reason to justify the decisions they make. Even though "because I have to make some copies" doesn't actually offer any new information, it was enough to initiate a positive reaction in the majority of test subjects.

↓

People are more likely to agree to a(n) _____(A)_____ if they feel they have been provided with a(n) _____(B)_____ for their decision.

	(A)		(B)
①	request	······	reason
②	command	······	excuse
③	proposal	······	solution
④	consultation	······	justification
⑤	assertion	······	alternative

The "cocktail party effect" is an interesting phenomenon that tells us a lot about how attention affects the way we process perceptual stimuli. During a conversation at a (a) <u>crowded</u> party, where there is loud music and lots of other conversations taking place, we somehow manage to tune into the voice of the one person we are talking to. All of the other noise in the room is filtered out and (b) <u>ignored</u>. This generally happens for all perceptions: some of the stimuli are filtered out for conscious analysis. This enables us to ignore the rest of the conversations at a party and (c) <u>concentrate</u> on only one person's voice. The ability to do this depends on characteristics of the speech we are focusing on, including the gender of the speaker, the intensity of the voice, and the location of the speaker. It also depends on the (d) <u>differences</u> between the speaker's voice and other sounds that are present.

The cocktail party effect relies on something called the "figure-ground" phenomenon. This is the brain's ability to separate auditory input into the components of the "figure" (the target voice) and "ground" (everything else in the background). However, an interesting point is that if somebody on the other side of the room suddenly calls out our name, we generally (e) <u>neglect</u> it right away. This suggests that some processing of other information does occur — enough to allow us to notice it in certain situations, especially if it is a familiar voice or our own name.

41 윗글의 제목으로 가장 적절한 것은?

① Auditory Processing Disorder
② Evolution of the Auditory System
③ Divided Attention vs. Focused Attention
④ Selective Attention of the Auditory System
⑤ How to Make Polite Conversation at a Cocktail Party

42 밑줄 친 (a)~(e) 중에서 문맥상 낱말의 쓰임이 적절하지 않은 것은? [3점]

① (a)　　② (b)　　③ (c)　　④ (d)　　⑤ (e)

(A)

At its peak, the Maya civilization spread across much of northern Central America and the southern portion of what is now Mexico. Its history can be divided into three main periods: the Preclassic period, which lasted from 300 BC to 250 AD, the Classic period from 250 AD to 900 AD, and the Postclassic period, which covers the time from 900 AD forward. Around 750 AD, however, the powerful Maya civilization slowly began to collapse. Although there have been many theories, historians are unsure of exactly what led to this downfall.

(B)

In addition, there are many other theories that have been proposed, including climate change, civil war, overpopulation, and disease. While none of these have as much support from archaeologists as the first two theories mentioned, they cannot be ruled out either. In the end, the collapse of the Maya civilization remains a mystery. Unless new evidence is uncovered by archaeologists in the future, it may remain unsolved forever.

(C)

Most experts now believe a peasant revolt led to the decline of the Maya civilization. There was a distinct hierarchy among the Maya people, with a small but powerful class of nobles and priests depending on slave labor to work on the farms that fed the cities. It has been theorized that these workers grew tired of the situation and ran off to live in the jungle. Without a workforce to work their fields, the priests and nobles would have been unable to hold their civilization together.

(D)

However, there are other historians who believe the collapse was caused by poor farming techniques. In an attempt to grow enough food to feed all their people, the Maya may have abused the land. This would have led to a lack of nutrients in the soil, water shortages, and erosion. Another problem could have been their "slash and burn" practices, used to clear away jungle and convert it into fields for growing crops. This might have led to a lack of food for local wildlife that the Maya hunted, causing the animals to migrate to different areas.

43 주어진 글 (A)에 이어질 내용을 순서에 맞게 배열한 것으로 가장 적절한 것은?

① (B) – (D) – (C) ② (C) – (B) – (D)
③ (C) – (D) – (B) ④ (D) – (B) – (C)
⑤ (D) – (C) – (B)

44 윗글의 제목으로 가장 적절한 것은?

① The Maya People and the Founding of Mexico
② Strange Similarities between Ancient Civilizations
③ The Maya: How Did They Get to Central America?
④ The Unexplained Collapse of the Maya Civilization
⑤ The Most Powerful Ancient Civilization in Central America

45 윗글의 마야 문명에 관한 내용과 일치하지 않는 것은?

① 크게 세 시기로 구분될 수 있다.
② 서기 750년경에 서서히 붕괴하기 시작했다.
③ 기후 변화로 인해 멸망했다는 의견이 가장 지배적이다.
④ 농업에 있어 노예의 노동력에 의존했다.
⑤ 경작지를 넓히기 위해 나무를 베어내고 숲을 불태웠다.

* 3점 문항에만 점수가 표시되어 있습니다.
  점수 표시가 없는 문항은 모두 2점씩입니다.

18 다음 글의 목적으로 가장 적절한 것은?

Dear Randal Marcus Busto,

This is Dean Heather Simmons writing to you on behalf of Minnesota State University. We have received the documents you submitted. After reviewing them, we are pleased to inform you that you have secured a spot in our student body for the fall of 2018. You can be proud of this accomplishment, as Minnesota State University has been providing students with the highest quality education for 150 years. Along with this letter, please find an admissions package with information about how to accept this offer. We ask that you respond within 28 days of receiving this letter so that we can promptly offer any unaccepted spots to prospective students on our waiting list.

Hoping to see you in the fall,
Heather Simmons

---

① 대학 합격 소식을 알리려고
② 신입생 교육 일정을 공지하려고
③ 대학 입학 관련 서류를 요청하려고
④ 입학 대기자 선정 절차를 문의하려고
⑤ 대학의 150주년 기념 행사에 초대하려고

19 다음 글에 드러난 Helena의 심경 변화로 가장 적절한 것은?

Helena's son has a medical condition that makes it difficult for him to eat solid food. In the past, she would make him special smoothies to provide him with vitamins and nutrients, but the only food he would eat was a specific brand of frozen waffles made with cinnamon and maple syrup. One day, however, she couldn't find these waffles in the local supermarket — it turned out that the company had stopped producing them. She tried other waffle brands, but he wouldn't eat them. Desperate to help her son, she got in contact with the company. They had their research-and-development team put together a recipe for making the waffles at home and sent it to the woman. Thanks to the company's kind gesture, her son now eats her homemade waffles.

① bored → joyful
② worried → grateful
③ pleased → anxious
④ frustrated → ashamed
⑤ regretful → confident

20 다음 글의 요지로 가장 적절한 것은?

For many individuals, their job is a major part of their identity. But having such a close identification with your work can cause problems. Losing your job is terrible, but if the job you've just lost is part of your self-image, you can also lose a sense of who you are. Likewise, if your self-image is tied to your job performance, a bad day at the office can make you feel worthless. For those people who identify too much with their work, I have some advice: Your job is what you do, not who you are. When I'm relaxing with my friends or family, I'm not a doctor; I'm just a normal guy. And if I gave up being a doctor to do something else, I'd still be a normal guy.

① 자신의 경력 개발에 힘써야 한다.
② 적성에 맞는 직업을 선택해야 한다.
③ 일보다는 가정 생활이 우선시되어야 한다.
④ 성공하기 위해서는 자기 관리가 필수적이다.
⑤ 자신의 일과 인격체로서의 자신을 구분해야 한다.

21 다음 글에서 필자가 주장하는 바로 가장 적절한 것은?

When my patients believe that as a doctor I have all the answers, they sometimes come across as overly dependent and passive, which is very unhelpful when I'm trying to give them the best care possible. Instead, I wish patients like these would take charge of their health and join me as active partners in their care, rather than passive recipients. A change of outlook to one that is more positive and passionate toward oneself goes a long way as part of a healthy lifestyle. My advice for patients is this: choose to be well, celebrate the small miracles of life every day, respect your body by eating well, share deep friendships with others, exercise often, and explore your creativity. Believe it or not, following these beneficial practices in your life will help you maintain your health.

① 좋은 음식을 섭취해야 한다.
② 의사의 지시를 믿고 따라야 한다.
③ 최고의 의사를 찾아가 치료를 받아야 한다.
④ 환자는 자신의 건강 관리의 주체가 되어야 한다.
⑤ 일상 생활에서 기적을 만들기 위해 노력해야 한다.

22 밑줄 친 this behavior is going the way of the dinosaurs가 다음 글에서 의미하는 바로 가장 적절한 것은? [3점]

Today's consumers make quick decisions and demand instant gratification. This is mainly due to the fact that they use their smartphones to find information and accomplish tasks in the blink of an eye. These instances of turning to their devices for immediate satisfaction are known as micro-moments. Traditionally, people purchasing products moved through three distinct stages: awareness, consideration, and decision. But thanks to micro-moments, this behavior is going the way of the dinosaurs. Instead, most consumers gather information and make decisions in dozens of short, unconnected online sessions. Because of this, modern brands need to change their marketing approach by focusing on establishing a strong internet presence. This way, consumers will be more likely to run into information about their products during their micro-moments.

① old brands are being abandoned for newer ones
② consumers are moving more slowly and carefully
③ shoppers are no longer following predictable steps
④ people prefer to buy things that are small and cheap
⑤ decisions are based on information rather than instinct

23 다음 글의 제목으로 가장 적절한 것은?

I have a very driven personality. Once I decided to commit myself to exercise, I wanted to give it the maximum effort and see some results! But I finally realized that exercising seven days a week does less for you than working out for four days does. Resting is sometimes referred to as the other half of the workout. You actually get the results of all that exercise during rest and recovery, as your body responds to the stress that it's been put under. If you are unable to sit still, try "active rest," like walking, which keeps you moving but isn't as hard on your body as a regular workout.

① Ways of Combating Stress
② Light Workouts: A Path to Fitness
③ Why We Should Exercise Regularly
④ The Right Amount of Daily Exercise
⑤ The Necessity of Resting for Efficient Exercise

24 다음 글의 주제로 가장 적절한 것은? [3점]

I think advertisers have to be more careful about the way they market things to children. Marketing to children has become such a problem that some countries have introduced laws limiting the amount of time that can be allotted to commercials for children's products during an hour of programming. For example, marketing character goods to children makes children waste money on things they don't really need. Marketers take advantage of the fact that most children are attracted to new and interesting things, such as cartoon characters. The marketing of food is also seen as a part of the growing weight problem among children. Many food companies deny any responsibility for making kids in developed nations overweight. However, in their commercials, they clearly make the fast food and sugary drinks look appealing in ways that are designed for children. Therefore, I think advertisers do share part of the blame, along with the children's parents who actually purchase the items.

① a new law limiting the length of ads
② ways to reduce unnecessary consumption
③ how to make ads more attractive to children
④ food companies' marketing strategies to kids
⑤ advertisers' responsibilities when it comes to children

25 다음 도표의 내용과 일치하지 않는 것은?

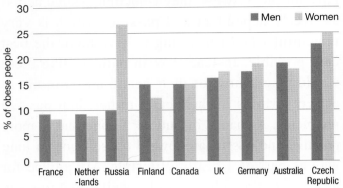

Obesity: Percentage of Population

The above graph shows the percentage of the population of nine selected countries that is obese, broken down by gender. ① France and the Netherlands have similar low levels of obesity, with less than 10% of each country's population considered obese. ② The Czech Republic, on the other hand, has the highest overall obesity rates, with more than 25% of both men and women considered obese. ③ However, it is Russian women who have the highest obesity rate of about 27%, compared to just 10% of Russian men. ④ Women have higher obesity rates than men in four of the selected countries — Russia, the UK, Germany and the Czech Republic — while men are more obese in four of the other countries. ⑤ Meanwhile, in Canada, the obesity rates of men and women are equal.

26 the Norse에 관한 다음 글의 내용과 일치하지 <u>않는</u> 것은?

Though many people believe that Christopher Columbus was the first European to make his way to the North American continent, there is enough evidence that proves that the Norse, or Vikings, reached there first. In 1961, archaeologists found a Norse settlement at the northern end of Newfoundland, Canada that was believed to have been set up about 1,000 years ago. The buildings of the settlement included homes, a workshop for metals, and a boat repair shop. Adding to this, ancient Norse tradition talks about the experiences that Norsemen from Greenland had as they explored land to the west of Greenland. The stories talk about how Norse explorers made a settlement in the new land, which researchers believe to be the one found in Canada. There is even information in the ancient stories about how early Norse settlers encountered a group of people in the new land that many scholars believe to be Native Americans.

① Columbus보다 먼저 북미 대륙에 도착했다.
② 약 천 년 전에 캐나다에 정착지를 건설했다.
③ 새 정착지에 다양한 건물을 짓고 생활했다.
④ 캐나다에 정착한 후 Greenland 서부 지역을 탐사했다.
⑤ 아메리카 원주민들로 추정되는 부족을 만났다고 전해진다.

27 백파이프에 관한 다음 글의 내용과 일치하는 것은?

It was the Romans who brought bagpipes with them when they invaded Britain. And centuries before they became part of Scottish life, the bagpipes were an English instrument, blown by Edward I's army when they confronted the Scots around the end of the 13th century. Bagpipes were once popular all over Europe, but it was in Scotland where the interest remained. Even today, when the bagpipes have become popular in some of the unlikeliest parts of the world, such as Japan, the Scottish association is as strong as ever. No matter how many other places in the world have pipes, they continue to have a distinct identity as a Scottish instrument.

① 스코틀랜드에서 처음 만들어졌다.
② 에드워드 1세가 즐겨 연주하였다.
③ 13세기 말경에 영국의 군대용 악기로 사용되었다.
④ 현재 유럽 전역에서 사랑받고 있다.
⑤ 아시아에서는 연주에 사용되는 곳을 찾을 수 없다.

28 Volunteers Needed: New City Film Festival에 관한 다음 안내문의 내용과 일치하지 <u>않는</u> 것은?

Volunteers Needed: New City Film Festival

The New City Film Festival is looking for enthusiastic volunteers who can help keep the festival running smoothly. Our festival, which has been held annually for eight years, features a wide variety of films by local directors.

When: December 11 to 17
Where: New City Art Cinema

Requirements
• Volunteers must be at least 18 years old.
• Volunteers must be available to attend two training sessions before the festival.

Duties
Volunteers are needed to help with marketing activities, provide office assistance, and work in the ticket booth.

Apply to be a volunteer by visiting the festival website at www.ncffart.org.

① 영화제는 8일간 열린다.
② 자원봉사자는 18세 이상이어야 한다.
③ 자원봉사자는 두 차례의 사전 교육에 참석해야 한다.
④ 자원봉사자는 마케팅 활동에 참여한다.
⑤ 온라인으로 자원봉사자에 지원할 수 있다.

29 다음 글의 밑줄 친 부분 중, 어법상 틀린 것은?

About the size of a hen's egg, the kiwi has bright green or golden flesh with rows of tiny black seeds. The kiwi, ① which is known for its abundance of vitamin C, is a ② modifying version of the Chinese gooseberry, native to southeastern China. In the early 20th century, Chinese gooseberry trees were imported into New Zealand for the purpose of ③ beautifying private gardens. They were selected for their pleasing appearance, not for their delicious fruit. Later, the fruit ④ was altered for size, taste, and hardiness by New Zealand fruit growers. Because the kiwi's brown furry skin resembled the body of the flightless kiwi bird, a new name ⑤ was adopted for the "new" fruit.

*Chinese gooseberry: 중국 다래 **hardiness: (식물의) 내한(耐寒)성

30 (A), (B), (C)의 각 네모 안에서 문맥에 맞는 낱말로 가장 적절한 것은?

Filling out a college application form can be tricky business, especially for students who suffer from a learning disability. In some ways, a disability can work to an applicant's advantage — university admission teams are drawn to students who have overcome personal difficulties to become academically (A) competitive / repetitive with their peers. At the same time, however, they tend to disapprove of students who seem to be using their disability as an excuse for low grades or poor test scores. For this reason, students must be very careful as to how they present this type of (B) spectacle / obstacle on college application forms. If the student fails to skillfully explain his or her disability and how it has been overcome, lower-than-average grades might be viewed as (C) predators / predictors of poor performance at the university level.

	(A)	(B)	(C)
①	competitive	spectacle	predictors
②	competitive	obstacle	predictors
③	competitive	obstacle	predators
④	repetitive	obstacle	predictors
⑤	repetitive	spectacle	predators

[31~35] 다음 빈칸에 들어갈 말로 가장 적절한 것을 고르시오.

31

Manners and morals are words that often overlap, sometimes confusingly, but here the two words are used in ways that are easier to distinguish. Manners can be considered as the standards of conduct that prevail in a group and, hence, change from group to group and year to year. Morals, on the other hand, can be thought of as the standards that determine the relations of individuals with other individuals, one on one — a child with each of its parents, a husband with his wife — as well as the relations of any person with his or her conscience. They are solutions to the age-old problems of faith, hope, charity, love, art, duty, etc. and therefore they are relatively _____.

① social
② flexible
③ constant
④ individual
⑤ changeable

32

Beneath the surface of the ocean, whale songs can be heard across vast distances. In fact, some of these songs are so loud that they penetrate the rock beneath the ocean's floor. Even more interestingly, the echoes that are created when these whale songs bounce off the rock are being used by scientists to better understand _____ of the earth's crust. The scientists are utilizing special sensors located on the bottom of the Pacific Ocean. They are usually used to detect seismic waves caused by earthquakes. However, when the sound waves of whale songs reach the ocean floor, some of their energy can similarly be converted into seismic waves. By tracking the way these seismic waves bounce off layers of rock, scientists can determine the rock's type and thickness.

*earth's crust: 지각   **seismic wave: 지진파

① the true purpose
② the time of creation
③ the slow movements
④ the geological structure
⑤ the environmental effects

33

Human beings have the ability to "self-regulate." When we are thirsty, we seek out something to drink. When we are threatened, we make the decision to either fight or flee. These kinds of reactions allow us to deal with problems and find suitable solutions. However, in some children, this self-regulation system does not develop correctly. This can lead to a number of problems, including frequent temper tantrums, impulsive behavior, and erratic sleeping and eating patterns. To avoid these kinds of difficulties and assure that children can deal with stressful situations, they should be repeatedly exposed to _____. Children have a natural alarm system that is activated when they are introduced to something new. But over time, repetition converts potential threats into something comfortable and familiar. As long as children are in an environment in which they feel safe and protected, low levels of predictable stress can create beneficial resilience.

*temper tantrum: 울화통, 짜증 **erratic: 불규칙한

① strict regulations
② educational material
③ dangerous situations
④ controllable challenges
⑤ stress-free environments

34

There is a fundamental distinction between neutral words and emotive words. Neutral words merely convey information, as in the sentence, "The train leaves in ten minutes." These words do not arouse emotions. But words like "God," "love," and "freedom" are so closely connected with our attitudes to life that they are likely to arouse emotional reactions. This categorization of words as neutral or emotive, however, _____. If a word gives you nothing but information, then it is neutral to you; if it arouses your emotions, then it is emotive to you. The word "bread" may be neutral to you, but to a compulsive eater or starving man, it may be filled with emotion. [3점]

① differs depending on our age
② reveals information about our culture
③ is heavily affected by social conditions
④ is relative to our personal experiences
⑤ determines the size of our vocabulary

35

The traditional approach to written and oral communication requires that _____ _____. In other words, we should keep in mind that every subject and verb must agree, and that the elements of a sentence must be correctly arranged in terms of their proper usage. Of course, every word must be spelled correctly and proper punctuation must be used at all times, along with the previously mentioned principles. I understand that learning all these rules and practicing them may seem like a hard task at first, but the ability to express oneself correctly is the key to effective communication. Even the most intelligent, most highly educated individual who does not use proper grammar comes across as simple-minded. [3점]

① we see the forest from the trees
② we follow an absolute set of rules
③ we speak fluently rather than correctly
④ students learn to communicate effectively
⑤ students strengthen their bond with teachers

36 다음 글에서 전체 흐름과 관계 없는 문장은?

According to astronomers, a star's mass is the deciding factor in the way it will end its lifespan. Extremely massive stars tend to end up as either black holes or neutron stars. ① As for stars with an average mass, they are most likely to shrink down to neutron stars after a gigantic explosion, known as a supernova, occurs. ② And finally, stars with a low mass generally end their lives as something called a white dwarf. ③ It is believed that some white dwarfs have a crust that is about 50 kilometers thick beneath their atmosphere. ④ White dwarfs are stars that have a mass similar to that of the Sun, but are only a little bit bigger than the Earth. ⑤ This makes them one of the densest forms of matter found in the universe.

*neutron star: 중성자성 **supernova: 초신성

37 주어진 글 다음에 이어질 글의 순서로 가장 적절한 것은?
[3점]

> The Spanish architect Gaudí came up with the concept of the Sagrada Familia, one of Barcelona's most famous cathedrals. He led its construction from 1882 until his death in 1926.

(A) Nonetheless, since tourism is a significant source of revenue, its importance cannot be overlooked by those in charge of the project. For now at least, there are no plans to halt work on the cathedral.

(B) Yet some oppose the ongoing work, since Gaudí's original plans have been lost and the reconstructed designs hardly reflect what the architect had in mind in 1926. Gaudí's creative vision has perhaps been sacrificed for the sake of tourism.

(C) The cathedral was only 15% complete at that time, and since then it still has not been finished. In fact, work continues to this day, and Gaudí's incomplete church attracts visitors from all over the world.

① (A) – (B) – (C)　　　　② (A) – (C) – (B)
③ (B) – (C) – (A)　　　　④ (C) – (A) – (B)
⑤ (C) – (B) – (A)

38

An individual's aptitude is also important, especially when trying to learn a tonal language, like Mandarin or Thai.

The simple truth is that there is no definitive answer to the question, "What are the hardest and easiest languages to learn?" It all depends on the mother tongue of the person. (①) Spanish, French, and Italian, for example, are closely related Romance languages. (②) Therefore, French will be much easier for a native Spanish speaker to learn than for someone who speaks a completely unrelated language, such as Korean. (③) After childhood, the ability to distinguish the specific tones of these languages varies greatly from person to person. (④) One English speaker may pick up Thai quickly, while another may never be able to master it. (⑤) In other words, when it comes to learning foreign languages, difficulty is relative. [3점]

*tonal language: 성조 언어 **Mandarin: 표준 중국어

39

Obviously, he chose the second option.

The residents of a low-income apartment building in America spent years living in unsanitary, horrible conditions due to a neglectful landlord who refused to make repairs. (①) Although his tenants begged him to fix their leaking pipes and hire an exterminator to get rid of the rats, he ignored their complaints. (②) Eventually, the residents reached the end of their rope and took the landlord to court. (③) After viewing the evidence, the judge ruled in favor of the residents and presented the landlord with an interesting choice. (④) As punishment, the judge gave him the option of either going to jail or moving into one of the apartments in his run-down building. (⑤) The residents were thrilled with the judge's wise ruling, knowing that living in the same conditions as them would force the landlord to change his ways.

40

다음 글의 내용을 한 문장으로 요약하고자 한다. 빈칸 (A), (B)에 들어갈 말로 가장 적절한 것은?

These days, wearing nail polish is a common way of making yourself look fashionable, but it used to have deeper meanings at different times in the past. In ancient Babylonia, warriors painted their nails before battles — men from the upper classes painted them black, while those from the lower classes painted them green. In ancient Egypt, women used henna to paint their nails. The more powerful they were, the deeper the color they used. The Chinese also used nail polish to show their social status in ancient times, with people from the upper classes wearing vibrant colors, such as red. People from the lower classes wore pale colors, and they were often forbidden from wearing any nail polish at all. If they wore the same shade as the royals, the punishment was death.

↓

In the past, the _____(A)_____ that people used on their fingernails sometimes served to show the _____(B)_____ they belonged to.

	(A)		(B)
①	color	·····	social class
②	pattern	·····	royal class
③	design	·····	ethnic group
④	style	·····	religious group
⑤	material	·····	political group

Mal Hancock's promising athletic career was cut short in high school when he had a fall that left him paralyzed from the waist down. It was a (a) challenging and heartbreaking time of life as Mal tried to adjust, both physically and mentally.

While staying in the hospital, Mal developed a keen sense of humor about the things he saw in everyday hospital life. He began to use cartoons to record his (b) observations. Soon after, the hospital employees would stop by to see what Mal had drawn, probably secretly hoping they were part of the cartoons, which were by then becoming the center of attention.

Eventually, Mal managed to sell one of his cartoons to a magazine, which later helped him to (c) abandon a career as a cartoonist. His name appears on cartoons in *The Saturday Evening Post* and *TV Guide*, as well as on the cover of his own book, *Hospital Humor*.

Mal Hancock learned that although he could not control the happenings in his life, he could control his response to those events. He (d) transformed a life-changing disaster into an opportunity to express humor about the world around him. It is an attitude that acts as a powerful force determining the (e) outcome of life's "paralyzing" events.

41 윗글의 제목으로 가장 적절한 것은?

① A Famous Hospital Patient
② Learning to Draw Cartoons
③ The Humor of Being Paralyzed
④ The End of a Great Sports Career
⑤ One Man's Success through Tragedy

42 밑줄 친 (a)~(e) 중에서 문맥상 낱말의 쓰임이 적절하지 않은 것은? [3점]

① (a)   ② (b)   ③ (c)   ④ (d)   ⑤ (e)

[43~45] 다음 글을 읽고, 물음에 답하시오.

(A)

When Rosa Parks got on a Montgomery bus to return home from work on December 1, 1955, she sat in the fifth row, which at that time was the closest to the front of a bus that black Americans could sit. As the bus filled up with passengers, people were beginning to stand in the aisles, and eventually the bus driver told Parks to give up her seat to a white passenger who was standing. But she would not.

(B)

The momentum behind the boycott was very strong. Black taxi drivers showed their support of the movement by lowering their fares to the equivalent of a bus fare. Churches raised money to purchase new shoes for Montgomery citizens who wore out theirs by walking everywhere instead of taking the bus. In response, whites who opposed the boycott fined cab drivers who lowered their fares and arrested civil rights leaders like King on more than one occasion.

(C)

These tactics failed, however, and eventually white extremists turned to violence. Black churches were bombed and people were shot at. Yet actions such as these backfired, and instead of stopping the boycott, they attracted national attention to the events in Montgomery. At last, in November of 1956, the Supreme Court ruled in favor of full racial integration, and the next month the boycott ended. It had inspired a national struggle for freedom and civil rights, and positioned Martin Luther King, Jr. as a leader of the movement.

(D)

Refusing to do what the bus driver asked got Parks into a great deal of trouble; in fact, it led to her arrest and her being sent to prison. Parks' arrest angered many in the black community, including the young minister Martin Luther King, Jr., as well as other respected local leaders and civil rights activists. Consequently, a boycott of the Montgomery bus system was organized, and word spread throughout the city. Everyone who supported the cause of Parks and King would avoid taking Montgomery buses for a year.

43 주어진 글 (A)에 이어질 내용을 순서에 맞게 배열한 것으로 가장 적절한 것은?

① (B) – (C) – (D)　　　② (B) – (D) – (C)
③ (C) – (D) – (B)　　　④ (D) – (B) – (C)
⑤ (D) – (C) – (B)

44 윗글의 제목으로 가장 적절한 것은?

① The Arrest and Trial of Rosa Parks
② The Montgomery Bus System Boycott
③ Martin Luther King, Jr.: A Civil Rights Leader
④ The End of the 1950s Civil Rights Movement
⑤ The Effects of Interracial Violence in America

45 윗글의 내용과 일치하지 않는 것은?

① 1955년 Montgomery 버스에는 인종별 자리 구분이 있었다.
② 흑인 택시기사들은 불매운동을 돕고자 택시 요금을 낮추었다.
③ 1956년 11월에 Montgomery 버스의 불매운동이 끝났다.
④ Martin Luther King, Jr.는 전국적인 시민권 투쟁의 지도자가 되었다.
⑤ Parks와 King을 지지하던 이들은 한 해 동안 버스 타는 것을 거부하기로 했다.

* 3점 문항에만 점수가 표시되어 있습니다.
  점수 표시가 없는 문항은 모두 2점씩입니다.

18 다음 글의 목적으로 가장 적절한 것은?

**Attention Employees of
United Delivery Service:**

　Due to the popularity of self-service gas stations, many of our drivers are failing to do the routine car checks that gas station attendants used to do for them. But everyone should conduct these simple safety checks on a regular basis. First, you should check the oil level with the measuring stick, as driving without sufficient oil can ruin the engine. Then check to see if the radiator needs more coolant, after making sure the engine is cool enough so as to avoid getting burned. Finally, check the air pressure of the tires. Too much or too little pressure can cause tires to wear faster. These routine checks can prevent car damage and may even help you avoid a dangerous experience on the road.

Management

*coolant: 냉각제

① 정기적인 차량 관리를 촉구하려고
② 차량 사고 시 대처법을 알려주려고
③ 교통 안전 법규 준수를 강조하려고
④ 새로운 차량 점검 서비스를 홍보하려고
⑤ 주유소 정기 회원권 구매를 제안하려고

19 다음 글에서 필자가 주장하는 바로 가장 적절한 것은?

　Although Korean universities have begun to take the positive step forward of making scholarships available to international students, nearly all of the information about these scholarships continues to be available only in Korean. These institutions must accept the fact that they have to take special measures to accommodate the needs of students who have come to Korea from another culture. Learning Korean is a necessary step, but it would be unreasonable to expect everyone to be fluent in the language before arriving. One of the driving forces behind many young people's decision to study in Korea is that there are few opportunities to learn the Korean language in their home countries. Making application forms and other documents available in other languages is one way to make a difficult process easier for these students.

① 한국어 교육 프로그램을 세계적으로 제공해야 한다.
② 한국의 대학에서 영어 교육이 더욱 활성화되어야 한다.
③ 한국의 대학들은 외국인 학생들을 더 많이 유치해야 한다.
④ 한국의 대학들은 한국어에 능숙한 외국인 학생들에게 장학금을 지급해야 한다.
⑤ 한국의 대학들은 외국인 학생들을 위해 그들의 자국어로 된 서류 양식을 제공해야 한다.

20 다음 글의 요지로 가장 적절한 것은?

A well-known quote from Confucius holds, "Victory has a thousand fathers; defeat is an orphan," referring to the fact that people are always eager to take credit for a success but are rarely willing to accept blame when something goes wrong. This behavior is not only dishonorable, misrepresenting your own work and that of your partners, but it can also come back to hurt you later in life. If you claim more credit than you actually deserve in a successful achievement, expectations for you to recreate that outcome in the future will be high, something you might not be capable of doing. Likewise, if you downplay your role in a failure, you'll be unable to learn from your mistakes and improve your performance.

① 꾸짖기보다는 칭찬을 많이 해야 한다.
② 성인의 가르침을 실천하며 살아야 한다.
③ 타인의 성공을 진심으로 축하해야 한다.
④ 타인의 성공과 실패에서 교훈을 찾아야 한다.
⑤ 결과에 대한 자신의 역할을 정확히 이해해야 한다.

[21~22] 다음 글의 주제로 가장 적절한 것을 고르시오.

21

Just like raising a dog or cat, having a computer is a serious responsibility that can end in disaster if you ignore your duties. A neglected laptop can easily be infected with a virus, causing it to experience hardware failure or a total system crash, which in turn will cause you to lose precious data. But even if you take good care of your machine, unexpected problems can still occur; therefore it is essential to create back-up copies of everything important on your computer, including documents, photos, and music files. By taking a few minutes of your time once a week, you'll be saving yourself not only a lot of grief, but possibly a large sum of money as well — it may be possible for professionals to recover data lost in a computer crash, but they'll charge you a high fee for the service.

① protecting your computer's data
② the evolution of computer viruses
③ how pets can harm your computer
④ choosing a good computer on a budget
⑤ what to do if your information is stolen

22

Scientists in Peru recently uncovered a 2,000-year-old, 35-meter-long picture of a cat that had been etched into the side of a hill. The enormous image is believed to be part of the Nazca Lines, a collection of giant drawings that were created in desert areas by the Nazca civilization between 200 BC and 600 AD. Hundreds of these drawings, which were made by shifting rocks and sand to expose the soil underneath, have been found, including images of monkeys, hummingbirds, and spiders, but scientists are still unsure of their purpose. In the past, some experts believed that they were astronomical calendars based on the movements of the stars, but this theory is no longer popular. It is possible that we will never know why they were created. [3점]

① mysterious ancient artwork found in Peru
② how people created artwork before paint and ink
③ different kinds of calendars used by ancient people
④ an ancient civilization in Peru that worshipped animals
⑤ a theory about what happened to the Nazca civilization

23 다음 글의 제목으로 가장 적절한 것은?

The true greatness of a nation is measured not by the vastness of its territory, or by the multitude of its people, or by the large amount of its imports and exports, but by the extent to which it has contributed to the life, thought, and progress of the world. Likewise, a person's greatness is not estimated by body size or wealth, and not by family connections or social position. A person's greatness is not estimated by his or her influence over the votes and empty cheers of a changing and passing crowd, but by an abiding, inspiring influence on their thoughts, upon their ways of thinking, and consequently of acting.

① How to Boost the Economy
② What Makes a Person Great
③ How to Enhance a Nation's Reputation
④ Why People Care about Their Appearance
⑤ Keys to Successful Interpersonal Relationships

24 다음 도표의 내용과 일치하지 않는 것은?

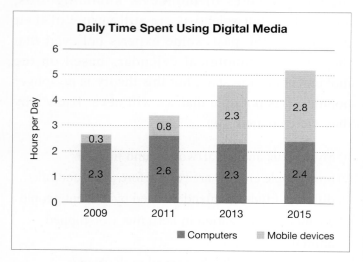

The above chart shows the amount of time adults in the U.S. spent accessing digital media per day, broken down by year and the type of device used. ① Over the years shown on the chart, daily time spent accessing digital media via mobile devices increased by 2.5 hours, while time spent accessing digital media via computers increased by only 0.1

hours. ② The biggest overall increase took place between 2011 and 2013, while the smallest overall increase took place between 2013 and 2015. ③ The average daily amount of time spent accessing digital media via computers actually increased by 0.3 hours between 2011 and 2013. ④ In 2009, the average time spent accessing digital media via computers exceeded the time spent accessing it via mobile devices by 2 hours per day. ⑤ However, the time spent accessing digital media via mobile devices increased steadily, actually surpassing the time spent accessing it via computers in 2015.

25 thermopolia에 관한 다음 글의 내용과 일치하지 않는 것은?

Takeout food has become an essential part of modern life, providing people with professionally prepared food that can be eaten in the comfort of their own homes. Surprisingly, takeout food is not a new invention. The concept actually dates back thousands of years to ancient Rome. Many Roman cities had places called *thermopolia*, which were basically street kitchens for people who didn't have kitchens in their own homes. They had both large countertops in the front and tables in the back for people to eat their food at. However, most people went to *thermopolia* to purchase takeout food, choosing from a menu that included fish, meat, cheese, and dried fruit. Archaeologists have found *thermopolia* in the ruins of many Roman cities, indicating that they were popular all across the ancient empire. It is believed that there were about 150 *thermopolia* in Pompeii, before it was destroyed by an eruption at Mount Vesuvius.

*countertop: 개수대

① 본래 집에 부엌이 없는 사람들을 위한 곳이었다.
② 뒤쪽에 음식을 먹을 수 있는 테이블이 있었다.
③ 대부분 포장된 음식을 사기 위해서 왔다.
④ 고대 로마 제국 일부 도시에서 인기가 많았다.
⑤ 화산 폭발 전 Pompeii에 150여 개가 있었다.

26 spiral galaxies에 관한 다음 글의 내용과 일치하는 것은?

Most spiral galaxies are made up of a flat disk, a bulge, and a halo. The disk is where you'd find large quantities of interstellar gas and dust, as well as the majority of the galaxy's stars. All of the material found within the disk rotates around the galaxy's center in a single direction, reaching speeds of hundreds of kilometers per second. This accounts for the impressive spiral patterns that are sometimes formed. At the center of the disk is the bulge, home to some older stars with little interstellar matter. The halo, meanwhile, surrounds the disk, and is believed to contain vast amounts of something called dark matter. Although dark matter behaves like normal matter in some ways, it cannot be seen. Astronomers can only guess at its presence based on the motion of interstellar gas and the stars.

*disk: 원반   **halo: 헤일로

① 원반은 소수의 은하계 별들을 포함한다.
② 원반 안의 물질들은 각기 다른 방향으로 회전한다.
③ 불룩한 부분에는 행성 간의 물질이 거의 없다.
④ 헤일로는 원반의 중심에 위치한다.
⑤ 헤일로 안의 암흑 물질은 육안으로도 확인이 가능하다.

27 Deluxe Coffee Tour에 관한 다음 안내문의 내용과 일치하지 <u>않는</u> 것은?

Deluxe Coffee Tour

Our region is the perfect place for growing coffee. This tour includes a visit to a local coffee plantation, where you can see how coffee beans are roasted and prepared to be shipped all around the world.

■ **Time**
There are three scheduled tours per day: 9 a.m., 1 p.m., and 5 p.m.
■ **Price:** $25 per person
■ **Details**
• Each tour is led by an expert guide.
• Both groups and individual travelers are welcome.
• The tour includes tasting five different types of coffee, all of which are available for purchase at the end of the tour.

Note: The final tour time is only available from May to September.

① 커피콩이 볶아지는 과정을 견학할 수 있다.
② 전문 가이드가 동행한다.
③ 단체 관광만 가능하다.
④ 5가지 종류의 커피를 시음할 수 있다.
⑤ 5시 관광은 가능한 시기가 정해져 있다.

28 다음 글의 밑줄 친 부분 중, 어법상 틀린 것은? [3점]

Typically, the thinkers that change the world dramatically ① are those who dare to counter the prevailing views of their times. When astronomer Nicolaus Copernicus first presented his theory of a universe ② in which the Earth orbits the Sun instead of the other way around, he was scorned by his contemporaries. Now, we recognize him to ③ have started a new era in the study of the cosmos. Similarly, Abraham Lincoln broke with his nation's precedent when he abolished slavery in America. He did this in the middle of the Civil War, which was fought over states' right ④ to permit slavery. We now remember the Emancipation Proclamation as Lincoln's greatest achievement. More than a century later, Mikhail Gorbachev channeled this spirit ⑤ what, as head of the USSR, he ended Russia's 70-year experiment in communism and promoted the spread of democracy throughout the former Soviet Union.

*Emancipation Proclamation: 노예 해방 선언
**USSR(Union of Soviet Socialist Republics): 소련

29 (A), (B), (C)의 각 네모 안에서 문맥에 맞는 낱말로 가장 적절한 것은?

Honey badgers are not easily scared. They do not need to be afraid of traditional weapons since their thick, tough skin cannot be easily pierced. Furthermore, the (A) loose / tight skin of honey badgers makes it relatively easy for a badger to move within its skin even while a predator is attacking. The badger can often move enough to harm the predator with its long claws and sharp teeth. Therefore, it is quite (B) safe / unsafe for a predator to hold a honey badger without killing it instantly. The jaws of honey badgers are quite strong, which is very useful when honey badgers eat their prey, since they can easily eat an entire animal including the bones or a turtle's shell. Another weapon used by honey badgers is a pouch in their back. Researchers have observed badgers as they turned this pouch inside out, releasing a strong odor which can cause even the largest predators to (C) attack / run away . Together, these abilities leave honey badgers with few reasons to fear predators.

	(A)		(B)		(C)
①	loose	······	safe	······	attack
②	loose	······	unsafe	······	run away
③	loose	······	safe	······	run away
④	tight	······	unsafe	······	attack
⑤	tight	······	safe	······	run away

30 다음 글의 밑줄 친 부분 중, 문맥상 낱말의 쓰임이 적절하지 않은 것은?

Much of the Arctic, including the North Pole, has been covered in a thick layer of sea ice for decades. For this reason, no one was very concerned about who ① possessed it. In recent years, however, climate change has begun to melt the ice and open up new passages for ships. Canada is now claiming that nearly half a million square miles of underwater ② territory belongs to them, joining Russia and Denmark in the fight for control of the Arctic. Whichever country owns the Arctic will also have control of its undersea natural resources. It is estimated that about 90 billion barrels of oil and trillions of cubic feet of natural gas exist in the area. Canada has ③ submitted a report outlining its case to the United Nations. It includes detailed information on the size and shape of the continental shelf along Canada's northern coastline, as ④ concealed by a number of scientific expeditions. It remains to be seen how this situation will be ⑤ resolved.

*continental shelf: 대륙붕

31

The myth that ants always put the colony before their own interests was recently disproven by research conducted on leaf-cutting ants. Using DNA fingerprinting techniques, researchers proved that the offspring of certain ants have a genetic advantage that makes them more likely to become queens. The male ants that carry this "royal" gene are careful to keep it a secret. If too many queens were coming from the same male, the other ants might destroy some of those queens. So these males are prudent to spread their offspring throughout multiple colonies. No one colony contains too many queens from the same male because these "royal" ants are _____ their fellow ants to avoid suspicion and retaliation.

① feeding
② assisting
③ breeding
④ cheating
⑤ destroying

32

It is possible that science may have finally discovered the secret to long life. Researchers studying the genetic material of birds were recently able to document a correlation between the length of certain sections of DNA and how long that bird would likely live. Our DNA contains the same sections, which are known as telomeres and are located at the ends of our chromosomes. As time passes, our cells divide, and as our cells divide, these telomeres grow shorter and shorter. At a certain point, our telomeres get so short that our cells cease to divide, and we begin to decline with age by cells' inability to divide and eventually die. Scientists are now rushing to determine whether it would be possible to extend our lifespans by _____ our telomeres.

*telomere: (염색체의) 말단소립   **chromosome: 염색체

① increasing
② shortening
③ eliminating
④ lengthening
⑤ correlating

33

"Varnishing" is a term that most artists who work with oil or acrylic paints are probably familiar with. It refers to the application of a transparent substance called varnish. The varnish, which goes directly onto the paint once it has dried, _____. It prevents the colors of the paint from fading by blocking ultraviolet rays from sunlight. But that's not all that varnish does. It also keeps pollutants in the air, such as smoke and dust, from making contact with the paint. Instead, they land on the layer of varnish, causing it to slowly become yellowy or cloudy over time. Once this occurs, the varnish can be removed and reapplied. If done properly, this can keep works of art looking fresh and vibrant for hundreds of years. [3점]

① makes the paint thicker
② removes unwanted paint
③ acts as a protective layer
④ wipes away dust and dirt
⑤ erases all of the mistakes made

34

Edgar Allan Poe is the most widely read of his contemporaries nowadays, and this is no accident, for this overly anxious and unhappy artist was strangely modern, much like our present times are. He knew what a death wish was long before Freud defined it. He was in love with violence 50 years before Hemingway was born, and he knew how to develop suspense long before the psycho-thriller was conceived. Also, he was continually concerned with inner conflict, which happens to be a major theme of present-day literature. But, unfortunately for him, he was born at a time when American cultural development was just beginning. His ideas were _____.

① filled with passion
② far in advance of his age
③ borrowed from other writers
④ too outdated to be taken seriously
⑤ widely accepted by his contemporaries

35

Upon closer examination, the phenomenon of blushing seems quite strange. Why did humans develop a process that shows people we are feeling embarrassed? Some psychologists contend that blushing evolved as a method to enforce the various social behaviors that are needed for society to function smoothly. Blushing indicates to others that we know we have made a mistake and we're suffering because of it. Furthermore, it shows that we emotionally understand how to empathize with people in certain difficult situations, a trait that humans develop around the time they begin schooling and encounter their peers in society. Psychologists have deduced from this empathy intelligence that blushing from embarrassment evolves along with consciousness of others, thus supporting the concept that _____. [3점]

*deduce: 추론하다

① people are not social by nature
② it can be consciously controlled
③ blushing is often misunderstood
④ blushing has a purely social basis
⑤ it has nothing to do with embarrassment

36 다음 글에서 전체 흐름과 관계 <u>없는</u> 문장은?

Plants, which along with soil store most of the Earth's carbon, extract their carbon from the carbon dioxide in the atmosphere. This occurs during photosynthesis, as they convert sunlight into energy. ① They later return carbon dioxide into the atmosphere during the process known as respiration. ② Trees are especially efficient at taking in carbon dioxide, meaning they remove more carbon from the atmosphere than they add. ③ Recently, a study showed how houseplants can remove some toxic gases from the air in homes. ④ When many trees grow together in one place, such as in a forest, this efficiency increases. ⑤ It is estimated that the planet's forests hold more than 75% of the carbon that exists aboveground.

*photosynthesis: 광합성

37 주어진 글 다음에 이어질 글의 순서로 가장 적절한 것은?
[3점]

If you've ever been around a newborn infant, you know that they spend most of their time sleeping. In fact, they can sleep up to 18 hours a day. But according to experts, this isn't wasted time.

(A) In their experiment, sleeping infants were videotaped while electrodes attached to their head recorded bioelectrical activity. During this time, some of the recorded brainwaves underwent changes. It is believed that this is proof that they were learning as they slept.

(B) This information can help scientists who specialize in the learning process of infants. Since they spend so much of their time asleep, it could help explain how the infants are able to adapt to their new environment so quickly.

(C) A team of university scientists has found that the brains of newborn infants continuously process information. That means that even when they are asleep, babies are learning.

① (A) – (B) – (C)   ② (B) – (A) – (C)
③ (B) – (C) – (A)   ④ (C) – (A) – (B)
⑤ (C) – (B) – (A)

[38~39] 글의 흐름으로 보아, 주어진 문장이 들어가기에 가장 적절한 곳을 고르시오.

38

Unlike the simple shapes of the letters, these traits are extremely difficult to imitate.

Using handwriting to identify people might not seem very reliable. (①) After all, with a little practice, almost anyone can learn to copy someone else's handwriting. (②) But biometric systems don't just look at how you shape each letter; instead, they analyze the act of writing. (③) They examine the pressure with which you press down on your pen while writing. (④) They also record the sequence in which you write letters, such as whether you dot your i's and cross your t's as you write them or after you finish each word. (⑤) Even if you were to trace a copy of someone's signature, the system would detect it as a fake. [3점]

39

This can be observed in the case of people who have never even seen a snake before, but have been found to fear them.

Many of us fear the same things, such as public speaking, pain, and snakes. But could there be such things as universal fears? (①) Studies suggest that human beings might be genetically inclined to fear certain animals that once posed real danger to humans through poison or disease, such as snakes and rats. (②) It is believed that their fear is really an evolutionary instinct. (③) The idea that it is indeed instinctual is supported by scientific research. (④) In an experiment, psychologist Martin Seligman tried to create a fear of certain objects in people. (⑤) He found that people begin to fear things like snakes and spiders much more easily than non-harmful things like flowers.

40 다음 글의 내용을 한 문장으로 요약하고자 한다. 빈칸 (A), (B)에 들어갈 말로 가장 적절한 것은?

The world's coldest continent, the Antarctic, has a mean annual temperature of minus seventy degrees Fahrenheit. Covered in ice and snow, the Antarctic is also the windiest continent in the world. The fiercest gusts of winds are nearly 200 miles per hour. The conditions there are extremely hostile to human inhabitation, and it is hard to imagine any form of wildlife surviving. But strangely enough, the Antarctic actually has the largest population of wildlife anywhere in the world. From microscopic sea vegetation to large birds and mammals such as penguins, whales, and seals, the Antarctic has plenty to offer for biologists' study. How these species survive in such tough conditions is a wonder of nature.

↓

Despite its ____(A)____ weather conditions, the Antarctic is ____(B)____ in a variety of wildlife.

	(A)		(B)
①	fierce	......	desperate
②	ideal	......	deficient
③	temperate	......	abundant
④	harsh	......	rich
⑤	unpredictable	......	plentiful

[41~42] 다음 글을 읽고, 물음에 답하시오.

All telescopes use curved lenses to focus the light from (a) distant objects, such as stars. Generally, the larger a telescope is, the greater its magnifying power. Two different kinds of lenses can be used. The first telescopes, made during the 16th century, were refractors. The problem with these telescopes was that their perfectly round lenses did not focus light sharply. Lenses made of a single piece of glass also bent light of different colors in (b) different ways, producing color distortions.

The problems of refractors led some telescope makers to experiment with reflectors. They used mirrors that were not perfectly round, so that light was sharply (c) unfocused. Moreover, mirrors did not produce color (d) distortions. But these early reflectors had other problems. They were made of polished metal, which did not reflect light well. Also, metal mirrors often cracked as they cooled after being cast.

For two centuries, opticians strived to perfect both of these kinds of telescopes. Finally, in 1851, two Englishmen, Varnish and Mellish, discovered a method of covering glass with a very thin sheet of silver. This made it possible to build reflecting telescopes using a large curved mirror made of silver-covered glass. These telescopes reflected much more light than earlier reflectors and did not (e) crack so easily. Today, nearly all large telescopes are built on the basic design conceived by Varnish and Mellish.

*refractor: 굴절 망원경 **optician: 광학 기계 제작자

41 윗글의 주제로 가장 적절한 것은?

① the principle of refraction
② the history of the telescope
③ changes in modern astronomy
④ how to choose the best telescope
⑤ a new kind of high-tech telescope

42 밑줄 친 (a)~(e) 중에서 문맥상 낱말의 쓰임이 적절하지 않은 것은? [3점]

① (a)　　② (b)　　③ (c)　　④ (d)　　⑤ (e)

[43~45] 다음 글을 읽고, 물음에 답하시오.

(A)

Johannes Vermeer was a celebrated Dutch painter working in the 1600s. Yet, nearly 300 years after his death, critics were still debating the breadth of his work — namely, whether or not Vermeer had painted a series of biblical scenes. Han van Meegeren, a 20th-century Dutch painter who felt contemporary critics did not fully appreciate (a) him, saw this argument as his chance to prove his talent. He set about creating a forgery of what he imagined a Vermeer biblical painting would look like, intending to pass it off as an original.

(B)

Unfortunately for van Meegeren, one of his collectors turned out to be a major figure in the German Nazi party. After the conclusion of World War II, the Dutch government arrested van Meegeren for selling the fake Vermeer — which they considered a "national treasure" — to the enemy. Faced with no other alternative, van Meegeren was forced to admit that all the paintings he had sold were not works of (b) the famous painter but rather his own forgeries.

(C)

To convince the authorities of the truth of his story and that the painting he had sold to the Nazis was not a genuine work, van Meegeren was made to demonstrate his forgery process before a group of officials. He was able to prove his innocence of the charges and was only sentenced to a year in prison for (c) his actions. However, just two months after the conclusion of his trial, he died of a heart attack.

(D)

He named his creation *The Disciples at Emmaus*, and after spending countless hours mimicking Vermeer's style and simulating the cracks and flaws one would expect to see in a 300-year-old painting, (d) his hard work paid off. Art experts accepted van Meegeren's work as the real thing. Instead of sticking to his original plan and using the fake painting to demonstrate his genius, (e) he chose to continue producing the forgeries, selling them for large sums to collectors.

43 주어진 글 (A)에 이어질 내용을 순서에 맞게 배열한 것으로 가장 적절한 것은?

① (B) – (C) – (D)　　② (B) – (D) – (C)
③ (C) – (B) – (D)　　④ (D) – (B) – (C)
⑤ (D) – (C) – (B)

44 밑줄 친 (a)~(e) 중에서 가리키는 대상이 나머지 넷과 다른 것은?

① (a)　　② (b)　　③ (c)　　④ (d)　　⑤ (e)

45 윗글의 van Meegeren에 관한 내용과 일치하지 않는 것은?

① 처음에는 자신의 실력을 증명하고자 Vermeer의 위작을 만들었다.
② 자신의 작품을 나치 당원에게 판매했다.
③ 제2차 세계대전이 끝난 후 구속되었다.
④ 자신의 결백을 증명하기 전에 사망했다.
⑤ 미술 전문가들은 그의 작품을 Vermeer의 진품으로 인정했다.

지은이

NE능률 영어교육연구소

NE능률 영어교육연구소는 혁신적이며 효율적인 영어 교재를 개발하고
영어 학습의 질을 한 단계 높이고자 노력하는 NE능률의 연구조직입니다.

수능만만 〈영어독해 20회〉

펴 낸 이	주민홍
펴 낸 곳	서울특별시 마포구 월드컵북로 396(상암동) 누리꿈스퀘어 비즈니스타워 10층
	㈜NE능률 (우편번호 03925)
펴 낸 날	2022년 1월 5일 개정판 제1쇄 발행
	2022년 9월 15일 제5쇄
전　　화	02 2014 7114
팩　　스	02 3142 0356
홈 페 이 지	www.neungyule.com
등 록 번 호	제1-68호
I S B N	979-11-253-3740-9 53740
정　　가	18,000원

NE 능률

고객센터

교재 내용 문의 : contact.nebooks.co.kr (별도의 가입 절차 없이 작성 가능)
제품 구매, 교환, 불량, 반품 문의 : 02-2014-7114
☎ 전화문의는 본사 업무시간 중에만 가능합니다.

혼자 하면 작심 3일,
함께 하면 작심 100일!

공부작당소모임

함께 공부하는 **재미**

학습 점검은 **철두철미**

다 같이 완북하는 찰떡궁합 **케미**

이번 학기 내 시험지는 전부 **동그라미!**

자신감을 키우는 진짜 스터디 그룹,

공작소에서 만나보세요.

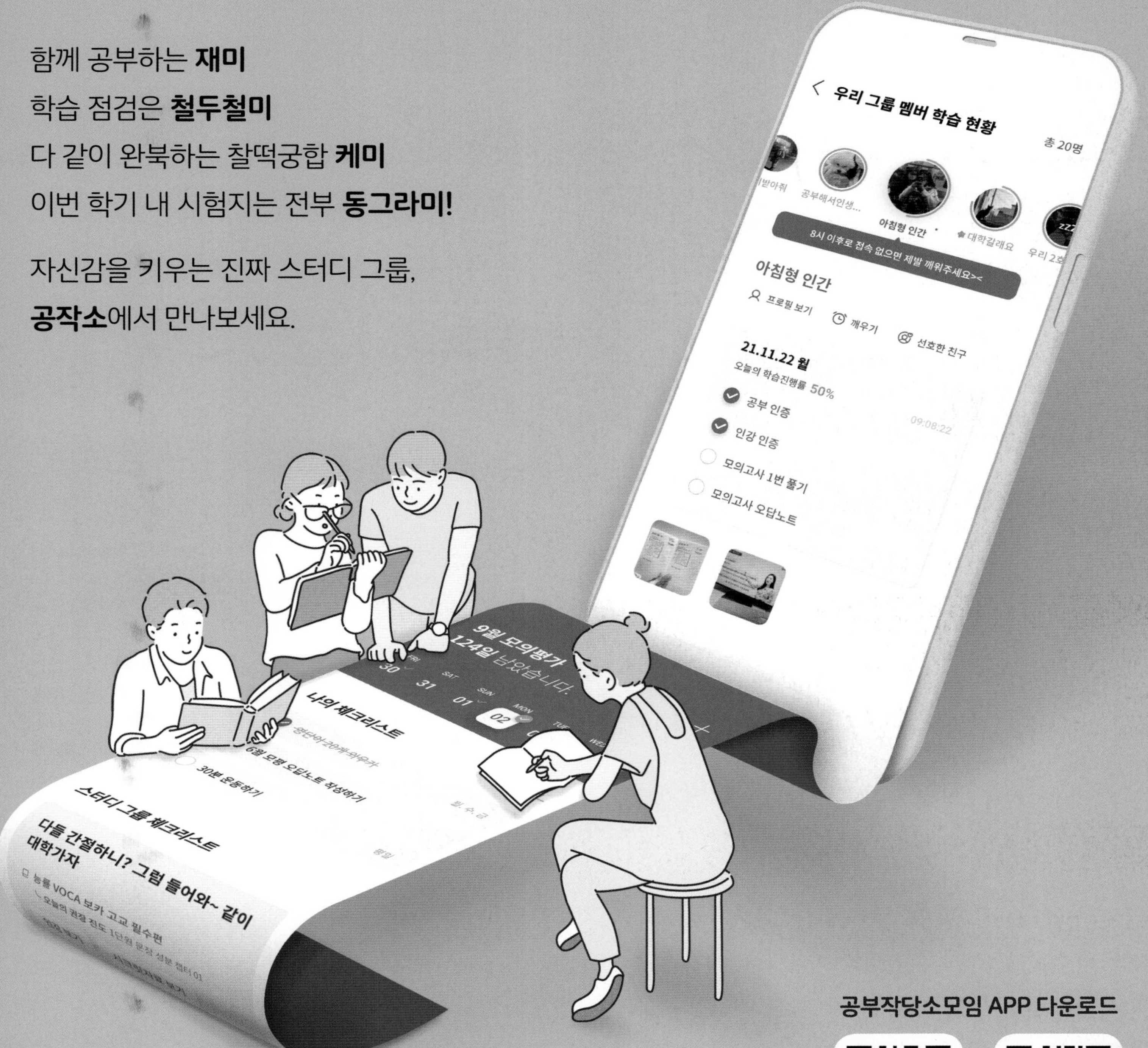

공부
공**작**소
당 **모임**

우리 그룹 멤버 학습 현황

총 20명

아침형 인간

8시 이후로 접속 없으면 제발 깨워주세요><

아침형 인간

프로필 보기   깨우기   선호한 친구

21.11.22 월
오늘의 학습진행률 50%

✓ 공부 인증
✓ 인강 인증   09:08:22
○ 모의고사 1번 풀기
○ 모의고사 오답노트

공부작당소모임 APP 다운로드

앱스토어   ▶ 구글 플레이

www.gongzakso.com

NE능률 교재 MAP

수능

아래 교재 MAP을 참고하여 본인의 현재 혹은 목표 수준에 따라 교재를 선택하세요.
NE능률 교재들과 함께 영어실력을 쑥쑥~ 올려보세요!
MP3 등 교재 부가 학습 서비스 및 자세한 교재 정보는 www.nebooks.co.kr 에서 확인하세요.

초1-2	초3	초3-4	초4-5	초5-6

초6-예비중	중1	중1-2	중2-3	중3
			첫 번째 수능 영어 기초편	첫 번째 수능 영어 유형편
				첫 번째 수능 영어 실전편

예비고-고1	고1	고1-2	고2-3, 수능 실전	수능, 학평 기출
기강잡고 독해 잡는 필수 문법	빠바 기초세우기	빠바 구문독해	빠바 유형독해	다빈출코드 영어영역 고1독해
기강잡고 기초 잡는 유형 독해	능률기본영어	The 상승 구문편	빠바 종합실전편	다빈출코드 영어영역 고2독해
The 상승 직독직해편	The 상승 문법독해편	맞수 수능듣기 실전편	The 상승 수능유형편	다빈출코드 영어영역 듣기
올클 수능 어법 start	수능만만 기본 영어듣기 20회	맞수 수능문법어법 실전편	수능만만 어법어휘 228제	다빈출코드 영어영역 어법·어휘
얇고 빠른 미니 모의고사	수능만만 기본 영어듣기 35+5회	맞수 구문독해 실전편	수능만만 영어듣기 20회	
10+2회 입문	수능만만 기본 문법·어법·어휘 150제	맞수 수능유형 실전편	수능만만 영어듣기 35회	
	수능만만 기본 영어독해 10+1회	맞수 빈칸추론	수능만만 영어독해 20회	
	맞수 수능듣기 기본편	특급 독해 유형별 모의고사	특급 듣기 실전 모의고사	
	맞수 수능문법어법 기본편	수능유형 PICK 독해 실력	특급 빈칸추론	
	맞수 구문독해 기본편	수능 구문 빅데이터 수능빈출편	특급 어법	
	맞수 수능유형 기본편	얇고 빠른 미니 모의고사	특급 수능·EBS 기출 VOCA	
	수능유형 PICK 독해 기본	10+2회 실전	올클 수능 어법 완성	
	수능유형 PICK 듣기 기본		능률 EBS 수능특강 변형 문제	
	수능 구문 빅데이터 기본편		영어(상), (하)	
	얇고 빠른 미니 모의고사		능률 EBS 수능특강 변형 문제	
	10+2회 기본		영어독해연습(상), (하)	

수능 이상/ 토플 80-89· 텝스 600-699점	수능 이상/ 토플 90-99· 텝스 700-799점	수능 이상/ 토플 100· 텝스 800점 이상		

정답 및 해설

영어독해
20회

정답 및 해설

정답 및 해설

영어독해
20회
만만한

정답 및 해설

01 영어독해 모의고사

본문 ▲ p.6

18 ③	19 ②	20 ①	21 ②	22 ⑤	23 ①
24 ⑤	25 ④	26 ②	27 ②	28 ⑤	29 ③
30 ③	31 ②	32 ③	33 ③	34 ②	35 ①
36 ⑤	37 ②	38 ③	39 ②	40 ①	41 ⑤
42 ③	43 ④	44 ③	45 ③		

18 ③ 글의 목적

관계자분께,

저는 지난주에 4번 가에 있는 귀하의 상점에서 새 커피메이커를 구입했습니다. 그것은 처음에는 잘 작동하는 것 같았지만, 저는 곧 그 기계 뒤에서 물이 새고 있는 것을 알아차렸습니다. 저는 이틀 후에 그것을 상점에 다시 가져가서 매니저인 마리 던스톤이라는 이름의 여성에게 교환해 달라고 요청했습니다. 그녀는 그 커피메이커를 살펴본 후에, 어떤 결함도 보이지 않는다고 주장하며 거절했습니다. 이것은 받아들일 수 없습니다. 저는 제 영수증 이미지를 첨부했고 이 커피메이커의 전액이 제 신용 카드로 환불되기를 바랍니다. 이것이 완료되는 대로, 저는 기꺼이 이 결함 있는 상품을 돌려보내겠습니다. 이를 처리해 주심에 미리 감사드립니다. 질문이 있다면 부담 갖지 마시고 이메일을 보내 주십시오.

진심을 담아,

이반 리 드림

어휘
concern 관련되다   purchase 구입하다   leak 새다, 새어 나오다   exchange 교환하다   examine 검사[조사]하다   refuse 거절하다   claim 주장하다   damage 손상   acceptable 받아들일 수 있는   attach 붙이다, 첨부하다   receipt 영수증   refund 환불하다   defective 결함이 있는   merchandise 물품, 상품   in advance 미리

구문해설
(3행) It **seemed to be** working fine at first, but I soon noticed [that water was leaking from the back of the machine].: 'seem to-v' 「…인 것 같다」, [ ]는 noticed의 목적절

(7행) ... and **asked** the manager, [a woman {named Marie Dunston}], **to exchange** it.: 'ask+O+to-v' 「…에게 ~해 달라고 요청하다」, the manager와 [ ]는 동격 관계, { }는 a woman을 수식하는 과거분사구

(8행) [After examining the coffee maker], she refused, [claiming {(that) she did not see any damage}].: 첫 번째 [ ]는 때를 나타내는 분사구문으로, 의미를 정확히 전달하기 위해 접속사 After를 생략하지 않음, 두 번째 [ ]는 부대상황을 나타내는 분사구문, { }는 claiming의 목적절

문제해설
자신이 구매한 새 커피메이커에 결함이 있어 환불을 요청하는 내용이므로, 글의 목적으로 ③이 가장 적절하다.

19 ② 심경

내가 자라면서, 우리 아빠는 정원 가꾸는 일을 매우 좋아하셨고 그의 작은 정원에 어떤 것이든 기를 수 있다는 사실을 자랑스러워하셨다. 한 가지 예외는 붓꽃이었는데, 그 꽃들은 아빠가 심을 때마다 빨리 죽었다. 불행히도 붓꽃은 내가 가장 좋아하는 꽃이었다. 내가 10살 때, 나는 매우 아파서 몇 주 동안 누워있었다. 어느 아침 아빠가 웃으시며 내 방에 들어

오셨다. 그는 "내가 정원에서 기른 것을 보렴."이라고 말씀하셨다. 그것은 커다란 붓꽃 한 다발이었다. 그것을 보자마자, 나는 기분이 나아지기 시작했다. 그것들에 아빠가 떼어내길 잊어버린 꽃 가게 가격표가 여전히 붙어 있다는 것은 문제가 되지 않았다. 그것들은 이후로 내가 본 다른 어떤 꽃보다 더 아름다웠다.

어휘
grow up 성장하다   have a passion for …을 매우 좋아하다   garden 정원 가꾸기를 하다; 정원   exception 예외   iris 붓꽃   every time …할 때마다   unfortunately 불행히도   bunch 다발, 송이   matter 중요하다, 문제가 되다   price tag 가격표   [문제] relaxed 편안한   apologetic 미안해하는   embarrassed 당황스러운

구문해설
(2행) ... and was proud of the fact [that he could grow anything in his little garden].: [ ]는 the fact와 동격

(11행) **It** didn't matter [that they still had the price tag from the flower shop on them, {which he had forgotten to take off}].: It은 가주어이고 [ ]가 진주어, { }는 the price tag ... them을 선행사로 하는 목적격 관계대명사절

(13행) They were **more beautiful than any other flowers** [(which/that) I *have seen* since].: '비교급+than any other+복수명사'는 비교급의 형태이나 최상급의 의미를 나타냄, [ ]는 any other flowers를 선행사로 하는 목적격 관계대명사절, have seen은 경험을 나타내는 현재완료

문제해설
'I'가 가장 좋아하지만 키우기 힘든 붓꽃을 아빠가 꽃집에서 사와서라도 자신이 기른 것인 척하며 아픈 'I'를 기쁘게 하려는 상황이므로 ② '감동한' 심경일 것이다.

20 ① 필자의 주장

역사 선생님께서 철기 시대에 대해 우리에게 강의하실 때, 나는 거의 주의를 기울일 수 없었다. 그것은 선생님의 잘못이 아니라, 오히려 그 소재의 문제였다. 모든 역사 수업에서 그러하듯, 우리는 수업 토론을 인류의 출현에서 시작하여, 연대순으로 사건들을 다루었다. 물론, 우리가 20세기에 도달했을 시기에는 이미 학년 말에 이르러 있었고, 그래서 우리의 삶에 영향을 미치고 있던 현대의 문제들은 토론해 볼 기회가 없었다. 나에게는, 그 정반대의 교수법을 채택하는 것이 더 논리적으로 보인다. 현재의 국가적 그리고 세계적인 사건들에 대한 적용 범위로 시작하여, 시간을 거슬러 올라가면서 오늘날의 뉴스거리들을 가능하게 만든 발달에 대해 배우는 것이 어떻겠는가? 학생들은 확실히 그러한 교과과정이 더욱 흥미롭고 가치 있다는 것을 알게 될 것이다.

어휘
keep one's eyes open 정신을 차리고 보다   material 재료; *소재, 자료   discussion 토의, 토론   dawn 새벽, 동틀 무렵; *시작, 시초, 발단   cover 다루다   chronological 연대순의   coverage 적용 범위   engaging 마음을 끄는, 매력적인

구문해설
(8행) ... thus had no opportunity [to discuss the modern issues {that were affecting our lives}].: [ ]는 opportunity를 수식하는 형용사적 용법의 to부정사구, { }는 the modern issues를 선행사로 하는 주격 관계대명사절

문제해설
① 시대순으로 역사를 가르치다 보면 현대의 문제들을 다룰 기회가 없어 학생들의 흥미를 떨어뜨리므로, 현재 우리에게 중요한 사건과 역사적 문제에서 시작하여 시대 역순으로 역사를 가르치자는 주장의 글이다.

21 ② 함축 의미 추론

우리 자신의 인식에 의문을 갖는 것은 통찰로 이어질 수 있다. 소설 작가들은 많은 회색 영역들을 만드는 신뢰할 수 없는 화자들을 사용함으로써 때때로 우리가 이렇게 하도록 만들고, 우리만의 결론을 내도록 한다. 이 화자들은 신뢰할 수 없는데, 왜냐하면 그들은 의도적이든 우연히든 독자들을 오도하기 때문이다. 이것은 그들의 개인적인 상황, 성격상의 결함, 또는 심리적인 문제들 때문일 수 있다. 신뢰할 수 없는 화자들은 독자들로부터 중요한 정보를 숨기거나 심지어 그들에게 거짓말을 할지도 모른다. 때로는 그들의 신뢰할 수 없는 점이 처음부터 명백하기도 하고, 어떤 때는 놀라움으로 밝혀지기도 한다. 어느 경우이건, 이러한 등장인물들은 거의 언제나 복잡하고 흥미롭다. 더 중요한 것은, 그들이 독자들을 이야기에 몰입하게 하고 실제로 무슨 일이 일어나고 있는지 알아내기 위해 더 주의 깊게 읽도록 독자들에게 동기를 부여한다.

어휘
perception 지각, 인식   insight 통찰, 통찰력   fiction 소설   unreliable 신뢰할 수 없는   conclusion 결론, 판단   mislead 오도하다   by accident 우연히   flaw 결함, 결점   conceal 감추다, 숨기다   obvious 명백한, 분명한   involved 관여하는, 몰두하는   [문제] element 요소, 성분   plot 구성, 줄거리   entertaining 재미있는

구문해설
1행 [Questioning our own perceptions] can lead to insights.: [ ]는 문장의 주어로 쓰인 동명사구

2행 Fiction writers sometimes *make* us *do* this **by using** unreliable narrators [who create a lot of gray areas] and *force* us *to draw* our own conclusions.: 문장의 동사로 쓰인 make와 force가 등위 접속사 and로 병렬 연결, 'make+O+동사원형' 「…가 ~하게 하다」, 'by v-ing' 「…함으로써」, [ ]는 unreliable narrators를 선행사로 하는 주격 관계대명사절, 'force+O+to-v' 「…가 ~하게 하다」

14행 More importantly, they *keep* readers *involved* in the story and **motivate** them to read more carefully **in order to figure out** [what is actually going on].: 문장의 동사로 쓰인 keep과 motivate가 등위 접속사 and로 병렬 연결, 'keep+O+v-ed.' 「…가 ~한 상태에 있게 하다」, 'in order to-v' 「…하기 위해서」, [ ]는 figure out의 목적어로 쓰인 의문사절

문제해설
소설 작가들은 신뢰할 수 없는 화자들을 이용하여 독자들에게 중요한 정보를 숨기거나 다르게 알려줌으로써 독자들이 자신만의 결론을 이끌어내고 이야기에 몰입하게 만든다는 내용이므로, 밑줄 친 '많은 회색 영역들을 만들다'가 의미하는 바로 가장 적절한 것은 ② '구성의 특정 요소들을 불분명하게 하다'이다.

22 ⑤ 글의 요지

카페인을 피하거나 규칙적인 스케줄을 유지하는 것을 포함하여, 당신이 숙면을 취하도록 도울 수 있는 많은 방법들이 있다. 그러나 자주 간과되는 요소는 당신 방의 온도이다. 한 연구는 당신이 잠자는 동안 당신의 몸을 정해진 온도로 낮추는 체내의 온도 조절 장치를 가지고 있음을 보여준다. 만약 당신의 몸이 너무 뜨겁거나 너무 차갑다면, 당신의 (신체) 체계는 바람직한 온도에 이르기 위해 애쓸 것이고, 그 과정에서 종종 당신을 잠에서 깨어나게 할 것이다. 일반적으로, 수면을 위한 최적의 실내 온도는 섭씨 15도에서 20도 사이라고 여겨진다. 실내 온도가 이 범위에 있을 때, 당신의 몸은 체온을 쉽게 높이거나 낮출 수 있어, 당신이 잠을 더 잘 잘 수 있게 한다.

어휘
strategy 전략; *방법   overlook 간과하다   internal 내부의; *체내의

thermostat 온도 조절 장치   room temperature 실내 온도   suitable 알맞은

구문해설
5행 Research shows [that you have an internal thermostat {which brings your body down to a set temperature **while** you sleep}].: [ ]는 shows의 목적절, { }는 an internal thermostat를 선행사로 하는 주격 관계대명사절, while은 「…하는 동안」이라는 의미의 접속사

문제해설
⑤ 실내 온도가 적정 범위에 있을 때 체내 온도 조절이 용이하여 숙면을 취할 수 있다는 내용의 글이다.

23 ① 글의 주제

각기 다른 문화들마다 '명예'에 대한 고유의 명확한 정의가 있겠지만, 그 개념이 아예 존재하지 않는 인간 사회는 거의 없다. 몇몇 사회학자들은 우리의 명예심이 화합과, 궁극적으로는 사회 집단의 생존에 기여하는 조화로운 행동을 장려하기 위해 발달했다고 주장한다. 그러나 나에게는 명예가 존재하는 이유에 관한 더 자기중심적인 설명이 있다. 죽을 운명인 존재로서 우리는 우리의 인생이 언젠가는 끝날 것이라는 사실과 끊임없이 마주한다. 우리는 다른 사람들이 우리를 바라보는 방식을 형성하는 데 오직 제한된 시간만을 가진다. 우리가 죽은 후에는 우리가 쌓아온 어떠한 부와 물질도 우리에게 쓸모없게 될 것이다. 우리는 여전히 살아 있는 사람들에게 무엇보다도 먼저 우리의 행동으로 기억될 것이다. 그러므로 만약 우리가 명예로운 방식으로 우리의 삶을 살아간다면 우리는 그 기억들이 긍정적일 것이라 확신할 수 있다.

어휘
precise 명확한, 정확한   sociologist 사회학자   evolve 진화하다; *발달하다   harmonious 조화로운   contribute 기여하다   cohesion 화합, 결합   self-centered 자기중심의   mortal 죽을 운명의   constantly 끊임없이   confront 직면하다   shape 형성하다   material 물질적인   accumulate 모으다   primarily 주로, 무엇보다도 먼저   conduct 행동하다, 처신하다   fashion 방식   assure 보장하다; *확신하다   [문제] individualistic 개인주의적인 (individualism 개인주의)   interpretation 해석, 설명   evaluate 평가하다

구문해설
2행 ..., but there are few human societies [in which the concept does **not** exist **at all**].: [ ]는 human societies를 선행사로 하는 관계대명사절(in which는 관계부사 where로 바꿀 수 있음), 'not at all' 「결코 …하지 않는」

11행 We only have a limited amount of time [to shape the way {in which others view us}].: [ ]는 a limited amount of time을 수식하는 형용사적 용법의 to부정사구, { }는 the way를 선행사로 하는 관계대명사절

문제해설
명예가 사회 집단의 유익을 위해 발달했다는 일부 사회학자들의 의견과 달리, 명예를 개인적 관점에서 설명하고 있으므로, 글의 주제로는 ① '명예에 대한 개인주의적인 해석'이 가장 적절하다.

24 ⑤ 글의 제목

사람들이 어떤 영화에 대해 "그거 원작이랑 비슷하니?"라고 물으면 대답은 보통 "별로"이다. 기껏해야 영화 버전은 소설의 깊이 중 작은 일부만을 포착할 수 있을 뿐이다. 영화가 (소설의) 표면 아래에 놓여 있는 것 중 많은 부분을 포착할 수 있는지는 의문스럽다. 그러므로, 우리는 소설의 어떤 부분은 영화로 구현할 수 없다는 사실을 받아들여야 한다. 보통 영화제작자는 등장인물이 상세히 탐색될 수 있는 깊이뿐만 아니라 영화에 포함되는 등장인물들의 실제 수도 제한해야 한다. 더구나 장편소설을

영화로 각색할 때에는, 기타 요소들뿐만 아니라 복잡하고 중요한 하부 줄거리들이 시간의 제약 때문에 종종 삭제되어야 한다.

어휘
original 원작의 at best 기껏해야 capture 포착하다 fraction 부분, 일부 beneath …밑에 surface 표면 inaccessible 접근할 수 없는 limit 제한하다(limitation 제한) explore 탐험하다; *탐구하다 adapt 적응하다; *각색하다 subplot 부차적인 줄거리 eliminate 제거하다, 삭제하다

구문해설
(4행) It is doubtful [whether it can capture much of {what lies beneath the surface}].: It은 가주어이고 [ ]가 진주어, { }는 of의 목적어로 쓰인 관계대명사절
(6행) Therefore, we must accept the fact [that some parts of the novel are inaccessible to film].: [ ]는 the fact와 동격
(7행) … the filmmaker must limit **not only** the depth [to which a character can be explored in detail], **but also** the actual number of characters …: 'not only A but also B' 「A뿐만 아니라 B도」, [ ]는 the depth를 선행사로 하는 목적격 관계대명사절

문제해설
소설을 각색한 영화는 여러 가지 제약 때문에 원작과 다를 수밖에 없다는 내용이므로 ⑤ '왜 영화는 원작과 다른가'가 제목으로 가장 적절하다.

25 ④ 도표 내용 불일치

위 도표는 2014년과 2017년에 온라인으로 쇼핑한, 다양한 유럽 국가의 인터넷 사용자 비율을 보여준다. 도표 상에 나타난 다섯 개 국가 모두에서 2014년부터 2017년까지 온라인 쇼핑객의 비율이 증가했다. 위 나라들 중에서, 두 해 모두 가장 높은 비율을 보인 것은 바로 영국이었는데, 그 나라의 인터넷 사용자 4분의 3 이상이 온라인으로 쇼핑했다. 독일에서, 2014년에 인터넷 사용자의 75퍼센트가 온라인으로 쇼핑을 했는데, 같은 해 이탈리아의 비율보다 세 배 이상으로 더 높은 비율이었다. (프랑스는 2014년에 세 번째로 높은 온라인 쇼핑객 비율을 가졌는데, 2017년에는 오직 영국에만 뒤처지면서 2위로 올라갔다.) 마지막으로, 2014년과 2017년 사이 온라인 쇼핑객 비율에 있어 프랑스의 증가는 대략 스페인의 증가와 비슷했다.

어휘
above 위의 percentage 비율 various 여러 가지의, 다양한 quarter 4분의 1 trail 지고 있다, 뒤처지다 roughly 대략, 거의

구문해설
(1행) The above graph shows the percentage of internet users in various European countries [who shopped online in 2014 and 2017].: [ ]는 internet users … countries를 선행사로 하는 주격 관계대명사절
(6행) Of these countries, **it was** the UK **that** had …, *with* more than three quarters of the country's internet users *shopping* online.: 'it is[was] … that ~' 「~하는 것은 바로 …이다[였다]」(강조구문), 'with+O+현재분사' 「…가 ~한 채로」
(10행) …, a percentage [that was more than **three times higher than** *that* of Italy in the same year].: [ ]는 a percentage를 선행사로 하는 주격 관계대명사절, '배수사+비교급+than' 「…보다 몇 배 더 ~한」, that은 a percentage를 지칭하는 대명사

문제해설
④ 프랑스의 온라인 쇼핑을 한 인터넷 이용자 비율은 2017년에도 영국, 독일 다음으로 여전히 3위이다.

26 ② 내용 불일치

미국 적십자사의 조직자이자 설립자인 클라라 바튼은 1821년 크리스마스에 매사추세츠 주의 옥스퍼드에서 태어났다. 클라라는 비록 가정에서 교육을 받았지만, 15세에 매사추세츠 주의 여러 초등학교에서 직접 아이들을 가르치기 시작했다. 남북전쟁 이전에, 클라라의 가장 주목할 만한 업적은 뉴저지 주의 보든타운에 무료 공립학교를 설립한 것이었다. 남북전쟁 발발 당시 클라라는 워싱턴 D.C.에 살았는데, 그곳에서 미국 특허청에 근무했다. 볼티모어 폭동에 이어 매사추세츠 제6연대가 워싱턴에 도착하자마자, 군인들을 위한 구호 프로그램을 조직하여 간호사와 인도주의자로서 평생의 직업을 시작한 사람이 바로 클라라였다.

어휘
founder 설립자 prior to …에 앞서 noteworthy 주목할 만한 achievement 업적 establishment 설립 outbreak 발생, 발발 patent 특허 riot 폭동, 소동 regiment 군사 연대 relief 구조, 구호 lifelong 평생의 humanitarian 인도주의자

구문해설
(4행) …, Clara began teaching children **herself** at the age …: herself는 재귀대명사의 강조용법
(11행) [Following the Baltimore Riots], **upon** the 6th Massachusetts Regiment **arriving** in Washington, *it was* Clara *who* organized …, [starting her lifelong career … humanitarian].: 두 개의 [ ]는 부대상황을 나타내는 분사구문, 'upon v-ing'는 「…하자마자」의 의미이며 the 6th Massachusetts Regiment는 동명사 arriving의 의미상 주어, 'it is[was] … who[that] ~' 「~한 사람[것]은 바로 …이다[였다]」(강조구문)

문제해설
② 클라라는 가정에서 교육을 받았다고 했다.

27 ② 내용 불일치

웨스트 코스트 투어 — 고래 견학 관광

웨스트 코스트 투어는 이제 당일 고래 견학 관광을 일 년 내내 제공하고 있습니다! 우리의 모든 관광은 밴쿠버에서 출발합니다.

우리와 함께하고 싶으시다면, 출발 40분 전에 밴쿠버 도심에 위치한 웨스트 코스트 투어 사무실에 도착해야 한다는 것을 기억하십시오.
출발: 매일 오전 9시, 정오, 오후 3시
소요 시간: 약 세 시간
티켓 요금: 일반: 80달러   학생: 60달러
          고령자: 60달러   8세 이하 어린이: 40달러
티켓은 웨스트 코스트 투어 사무실 또는 대부분의 주요 호텔에서 미리 구매하실 수 있습니다.

어휘
offer 제공하다 day-trip 당일 여행 year round 일 년 내내 departure 출발 duration 지속; *(지속하는) 기간 approximately 거의, 대략 senior citizen 노인

구문해설
(5행) If you'**d like to join** us, please remember [that you must arrive at the West Coast Tours office in downtown Vancouver 40 minutes before departure].: 'would like to-v' 「…하고 싶다」, [ ]는 remember의 목적절
(16행) Tickets can be purchased in advance **at the West Coast Tours office** or **in most major hotels**.: at the West Coast Tours office와 in most major hotels가 등위 접속사 or로 병렬 연결

② 참가자들은 출발 전에 밴쿠버 도심에 위치한 웨스트 코스트 투어 사무실로 와야 한다고 나와 있다.

28 ⑤ 내용 일치

마드리드 아파트 임대

마드리드에서 단기간 머물 장소를 찾고 있습니까? 우리에게 당신을 위한 완벽한 아파트가 있습니다. 아파트는 도시의 중심부에 위치하고 있으며 2개의 침실과 발코니가 있습니다.

■ **시설 및 인터넷**
- 우리 아파트는 호텔 방보다 저렴하고, 식사를 직접 요리함으로써 훨씬 더 많은 돈을 절약할 수 있습니다. 부엌에는 가스레인지, 냉장고, 냄비와 프라이팬, 유리잔 그리고 접시가 있습니다.
- 와이파이는 약간의 추가 요금으로 이용 가능합니다.
■ **입실**
- 오후 2시나 그 이후에 입실하실 수 있습니다. 그러나, 자정 이후에 도착하시면, 늦게 입실하는 비용으로 10달러가 부과됩니다.
■ **참고**
- 우리는 애완동물을 좋아하지만, 애완동물들은 아파트 건물 내에서 허용되지 않습니다. 죄송합니다!

임대료 및 이용 가능한 날짜에 대한 세부 사항은 jgarcia@sbc.es로 이메일을 보내주십시오.

어휘
short-term 단기의 in the heart of …의 한가운데에 stove 가스레인지 pot 냄비 available 이용 가능한 additional 추가의 fee 요금 permit 허용하다 detail 세부 사항 rental rate 임대료

구문해설
(2행) Are you looking for a short-term place [to stay in Madrid]?: [ ]는 a short-term place를 수식하는 형용사적 용법의 to부정사구
(8행) ..., and you can save **even** more money *by cooking* your own meals.: even은 「훨씬」이라는 의미로 비교급을 강조하는 부사. 'by v-ing' 「…함으로써」

문제해설
① 아파트는 마드리드의 중심부에 위치해 있다고 나와 있다. ② 취사도 가능하다고 나와 있다. ③ 와이파이는 추가 요금으로 이용 가능하다고 나와 있다. ④ 늦게 입실하는 경우 10달러를 내야 한다고 나와 있다.

29 ③ 어법

인간이나 최초의 포유류가 여기에 나타나기 오래전에, 지구상에는 곤충들이 살았다. (이제까지) 발견된 가장 오래된 곤충 조상의 화석은 대략 3억 5천만 년 전으로 거슬러 올라간다. 최초의 곤충들은 아마도 고리 무늬가 있는 벌레의 원시적인 형태로부터 진화했을 것이다. 그때 이후로 그들은 아마도 지상에서 가장 번성한 생물 형태로 진화해 왔다. 곤충들에게는 매우 다양한 자연계의 포식자가 있다는 사실 때문에 그들은 많은 자기 방어 수단을 발전시켜 왔다. 화학 물질을 만들어내거나 집단적 방어를 사용하는 것은 곤충들이 스스로를 보호하는 방법의 일부이다. 하지만 가장 흔한 방어 기제는 비행이다. 벌, 모기, 그리고 나비 같은 많은 곤충들은 날개를 이용하여, 그렇게 하지 않으면(지면을 떠나지 않으면) 파충류나 양서류 같은 많은 포식자에게 잡아먹힐 수도 있는 곳인 지면을 떠날 수 있다.

어휘
mammal 포유류 insect 곤충 fossil 화석 ancestor 조상, 선조 date

back (기원이) …이다. (시기가) …로 거슬러 올라가다 evolve 진화하다 primitive 원시적인 ringed 고리 무늬가 있는 predator 포식자 self-defense 자기 방어 mosquito 모기 reptile 파충류 amphibian 양서류

구문해설
(8행) ... the fact [that insects have a wide variety of natural predators], ...: [ ]는 the fact와 동격
(13행) Using their wings, many insects, ..., are able to leave the ground, where many predators such as reptiles and amphibians, would **otherwise** eat them.: otherwise는 「만약) 그렇지 않으면」이라는 의미의 부사(여기서는 '곤충들이 지면을 떠나지 않으면'의 뜻)

문제해설
③ the fact 이하는 명사구이므로 접속사 Because가 아닌 전치사 Due to나 Because of가 되어야 한다.

30 ③ 어휘

요즈음, 일부 의류 제조업체들은 예전이라면 12사이즈인 드레스를 입었을 여성들이 이제는 8사이즈가 맞을 정도로 그들의 치수 표준 규격을 변경하였다. 이는 배너티 사이징 혹은 치수 부풀리기라고 불리는데, 옷의 특정 치수를 시간이 갈수록 더 크게 만드는 기법이다. 많은 사람들은 그 기법이 더 날씬하다고 느끼고자 하는 소비자들의 욕구를 충족시키기 위하여 고안되었다는 사실로부터 '배너티 사이징'이라는 용어가 유래되었다고 생각한다. 이러한 추세의 예상치 못한 결과물 중 하나는 '0보다 작은' 치수의 형성이다. 여성 소비자들이 서구 여성들보다 더 작은 경향이 있는 아시아 패션 시장의 몰락(→ 성장)에 따라, 제조자들은 배너티 사이징 이전에 사용 가능한 가장 작은 사이즈였던 0보다 더 작은 사이즈를 만들 필요에 맞닥뜨렸다. 그렇게 함으로써, 그들은 넓은 범위의 소비자들의 욕구를 계속해서 충족시킬 수 있었다.

어휘
modify 수정하다 standard 기준; *표준 규격 degree 정도 fit into …에 꼭 들어맞다 inflation 인플레이션; *부풀리기 practice 실행, 실천; *관행 unexpected 예기치 않은 consequence 결과 subzero 0보다 작은 의류 사이즈 counterpart 상응하는 사람[것]

구문해설
(2행) ... their size standards to such a degree [that women {who would once have worn a size 12 dress} now fit into a size 8].: [ ]는 such a degree와 동격. { }는 women을 선행사로 하는 주격 관계대명사절
(7행) Many people believe [(that) the term "vanity sizing" comes from the fact {that the practice is designed to satisfy ... thinner}].: [ ]는 believe의 목적절. { }는 the fact와 동격
(14행) ... the need [to create sizes smaller than zero, {which had been the smallest size available before vanity sizing}].: [ ]는 the need를 수식하는 형용사적 용법의 to부정사구. { }는 zero를 선행사로 하는 계속적 용법의 주격 관계대명사절

문제해설
아시아 여성에 맞추어 제조자들이 0보다 더 작은 사이즈를 만들었다는 내용으로 아시아 패션 시장이 '성장'했다고 하는 것이 자연스러우므로, ③ fall(하락, 몰락)은 rise(상승, 성장) 등이 되어야 한다.

31 ② 빈칸 추론

도덕적 상대주의는 도덕성은 상대적이고 서로 다른 사람들은 서로 다른 도덕적 규범을 갖고 있다고 보는 철학적 견해이다. 도덕적 상대주의는 윤리적 주관주의와 문화적 상대주의로 나뉠 수 있다. 윤리적 주관주

의는 도덕성이 개인마다 상대적이라고 보는 반면, 문화적 상대주의는 도덕성이 문화마다 상대적이라고 주장한다. 두 관점 모두 모든 시대에 모든 장소에서 모든 사람들에게 유효한 도덕적 절대성은 있을 수 없다고 말한다. 도덕적 상대주의의 관점에서는, 어떠한 행동도 일반적으로 옳거나 그르지 않다. 마찬가지로, 어느 누구도 객관적으로 옳거나 그르지 않다. 도덕적 상대주의에 의하면, 특정한 정황 내에서의 옳고 그름이 있을 뿐이다. 그것은 모든 상황에서 옳거나 그른 행동은 있을 수 없다는 것을 의미한다.

moral 도덕의(morality 도덕)   relativism 상대주의(relative 상대적인)
philosophical 철학적인   standard 기준; *규범   ethical 윤리의, 도덕의
subjectivism 주관주의, 주관론   hold …라고 생각하다, 간주하다   absolute 절대적인; *절대적인 것   context 문맥; *정황, 환경   [문제] specified 특정한, 명시된   theoretical 이론적인

구문해설
(1행) Moral relativism is the philosophical view [that morality is relative] and [that different people hold ... standards].: 두 개의 [ ]는 모두 the philosophical view와 동격
(7행) Both positions say there cannot be moral absolutes [that hold for ... times].: [ ]는 moral absolutes를 선행사로 하는 주격 관계대명사절
(14행) That means there can never be an act [that is good or bad ... situations].: [ ]는 an act를 선행사로 하는 주격 관계대명사절

문제해설
빈칸의 뒷 문장에서 모든 상황에서 옳거나 그른 행동은 있을 수 없다고 말하고 있으므로 도덕적 상대주의에서는 ② '특정한' 정황에 기반하여 옳고 그름을 가늠해야 한다는 것을 추론할 수 있다.

32 ③ 빈칸 추론

최근의 한 연구는 2~4세 어린이들은 설탕이나 인공 감미료로 단맛을 첨가한 아침식사용 시리얼을 선호하지 않는다는 것을 보여 주었다. 그러나 몇 년 후 다시 조사했을 때에는, 거의 모든 아이들이 단맛을 첨가한 시리얼을 선호하게 되었다. 또 다른 연구 결과는 단맛을 첨가한 시리얼 광고에 노출되지 않았던 4~6세 아이들은 6~8세가 되었을 때에도 여전히 단맛이 첨가되지 않은 시리얼을 선호한다는 것을 나타냈다. 이러한 결과는 단맛을 첨가한 식품에 대한 선호가 선천적이라기보다 후천적인 것임을 보여 준다. 즉, TV 광고에서든 집에서든 단맛을 첨가한 식품에 노출되지 않으면 아이들은 충치와 비만의 주된 요인을 피할 수 있다는 것을 의미한다.

sweeten 달게 하다(sweetener 감미료)   artificial 인공적인   expose 드러내다. 노출시키다(exposure 노출)   dental 치아의   cavity 충치   obesity 비만   [문제] inherit 물려받다   trait 특징   significantly 상당히   acquired 후천적인   indicate …을 나타내다

구문해설
(2행) ... no preference for breakfast cereals [that have been sweetened **either** with sugar **or** (with) artificial sweeteners].: [ ]는 breakfast cereals를 선행사로 하는 주격 관계대명사절, 'either A or B' 「A 또는 B」
(4행) However, [when (they were) surveyed again years later], nearly all the children had **come to prefer** ...: [ ]는 때를 나타내는 부사절('주어+be동사'가 생략된 형태), 'come to-v' 「…하게 되다」

TV 광고나 집에서 인공 감미료가 첨가된 시리얼에 노출되지 않은 아이들은 그러한 시리얼을 선호하지 않았다는 연구 결과로 보아 단맛을 첨가한 식품에 대한 선호는 ③ '선천적이라기보다 후천적인 것이다'를 추론할 수 있다.

33 ③ 빈칸 추론

기후 변화를 늦추는 것을 도울 새로운 국가적 캠페인이 진행 중이지만, 그것의 초점은 대부분의 경우와 조금 다르다. 그것은 고기 소비량을 줄이는 것이다. 'Meat-Free Monday(채식하는 월요일)'라 불리는 이 아이디어는 사람들이 적어도 일주일에 하루는 어떤 육류 제품도 먹지 않고 지내도록 장려하는 것이다. 몇몇 사람들은 고기를 먹는 것이 지구 온난화와 어떤 관계가 있냐고 질문할지도 모르지만 그 연관관계는 존재하며 그것은 중요한 것이다. 우리 접시 위의 고기로 가공되는 가축은 사육하기 위한 많은 땅을 필요로 하고, 세계의 많은 지역에서 이런 땅은 엄청난 면적의 숲을 태움으로써 만들어진다. 그 결과로 생기는 연기에는 다량의 이산화탄소, 즉 지구 온난화의 최대 주범인 온실가스가 들어있다. UN의 한 연구에 따르면, 전 세계 온실가스 방출량의 18퍼센트 정도가 이런 방식으로 생성된다.

underway 진행 중인   consumption 소비량   livestock 가축
enormous 막대한, 엄청난   tract 넓이, 면적   carbon dioxide 이산화탄소
greenhouse gas 온실가스   emission 방출

구문해설
(9행) The livestock [that gets processed into the meat on our plates] requires a lot of land **to raise**, ...: [ ]는 The livestock을 선행사로 하는 주격 관계대명사절, to raise는 land를 수식하는 형용사적 용법의 to부정사
(12행) The resulting smoke contains large amounts of carbon dioxide, [the greenhouse gas (which is) most responsible for global warming].: [ ]는 carbon dioxide와 동격

가축 사육에 필요한 땅을 얻는 과정에서 지구 온난화의 주요 원인인 온실가스가 방출된다. 이러한 온실가스 방출을 줄이기 위해 고기 소비량을 줄이는 캠페인인 '채식하는 월요일'은 ③ '기후 변화를 늦추는 것을 도울' 방법임을 유추할 수 있다.

34 ② 빈칸 추론

누구나 좋아하는 음식을 바닥에 떨어뜨려 본 경험이 있다. 그리고 우리 중 대다수는 재빨리 그것을 다시 주워서 먹는다. 하지만 바닥에 떨어진 음식을 먹는 것이 안전할까? 서울대 한 농업 과학 교수는 과자를 도자기 타일 위에 떨어뜨리고 5초 안에 그것을 줍는 것을 통해 실험을 했다. 연구 결과는 세균이 이미 과자 전체에 퍼졌음을 보여 주었다. 결과는 명백하다. 세균과 바이러스는 빠르게 증식한다. 1초면 그들이 새로운 집 주소를 점유하기에 충분할 수 있다. 우리는 세균이 육안으로 보이지 않기 때문에 그것을 깨닫지 못할 뿐이다. 야구와는 달리, 음식은 땅에 닿으면 바로 아웃이다.

agricultural 농업의   ceramic 도예의; *도자기의   spread 퍼지다   claim 주장하다; *점유하다   visible 보이는   naked 벗은; *육안의   [문제] multiply 곱하다; *증식[번식]하다   breed 번식하다   vulnerable 취약한

구문해설
(6행) ... an experiment by **dropping** ... and **picking** them up ...: 전치사 by의 목적어로 동명사 dropping과 picking이 병렬 연결

(11행) ... enough **for them** [to claim a new home address].: them은 [ ]의 의미상 주어이며, Bacteria and viruses를 지칭

문제해설

빈칸 뒤에 세균이 보이지는 않지만 매우 빨리 번식할 수 있다는 내용이 있으므로, 빈칸에는 ② '세균과 바이러스는 빠르게 증식한다'가 오는 것이 적절하다.

35 ① 흐름과 무관한 문장

전 세계적인 식량 가격의 상승은 많은 사람들을 빈곤으로 몰아가고 있고, 최근의 보고서들은 그 치솟는 가격의 주요 원인이 바이오 연료를 생산하기 위한 작물의 사용임을 보여준다. 바이오 연료는 석탄이나 석유와 같은 화석 연료에 대한 더 깨끗한 대안으로 장려되어 왔고, 유럽 국가들과 미국은 바이오 연료에 대한 높은 수요를 경험해 왔다. (화석 연료에 대한 수요 또한 세계 대부분 지역에서 커지고 있고 줄어들만한 여지가 보이지 않는다.) 그러나, 한때 사람들이 먹던 곡물과 다른 작물들이 바이오 연료를 만들기 위해 전용됨에 따라, 식량은 더 부족해지고 가격은 상승하고 있다. 예를 들어, 미국에서 재배된 옥수수의 3분의 1과 유럽의 식물성 기름의 거의 절반이 현재 바이오 연료 제조업자들에 의해 소비된다. 그러므로, 옥수수나 식물성 기름을 포함하는 모든 식량 제품들은 갑작스런 원재료 부족의 결과로 가격이 상승하게 되었다. 바이오 연료의 이러한 예기치 못한 약점은 많은 사람들에게 심각한 문제를 야기시키고 있다.

어휘

poverty 빈곤 principal 주된, 주요한 skyrocket 치솟다 petroleum 석유 divert 전환하다; *전용하다 scarce 부족한(scarcity 부족) ingredient 원료, 재료 unforeseen 미리 알 수 없는, 뜻밖의 drawback 장애; *결점, 약점

구문해설

(10행) However, **as** grains and other crops [that once fed people] are diverted [to make biofuels], ...: as는 「…함에 따라」라는 의미의 접속사, 첫 번째 [ ]는 grains and other crops를 선행사로 하는 주격 관계대명사절, 두 번째 [ ]는 목적을 나타내는 부사적 용법의 to부정사구

문제해설

화석 연료의 대체재로서의 바이오 연료 생산에 따른 식량 가격 상승에 대한 내용의 글이므로, 화석 연료의 수요 증가에 관한 설명인 ①은 글의 흐름과 무관하다.

36 ⑤ 글의 순서

마요네즈는 매우 인기 있는 식품이 아니며, 케첩이나 머스터드만큼 주목 받지 않는다. 하지만 일부 동물 보호론자들은 마요네즈를 굉장히 좋아하는데, 그들이 멸종 위기에 처한 바다거북을 보호하려는 싸움에서 그것을 사용하고 있기 때문이다.
(C) 이 특이한 애호는 이스라엘 연안에서 기름 유출이 발생하여 그 해안 지대가 끈적거리는 타르로 뒤덮였을 때 시작되었다. 그 지역은 많은 바다거북들의 서식지여서, 그들은 곧 소화 기관 내에 이 독성 물질들을 지니게 되었다.
(B) 환경 보호론자들은 식물성 기름과 섞인 마요네즈가 바다거북에게서 타르를 빼내기에 가장 좋은 방법임을 알아냈다. 그것은 그들의 소화 기관에서 타르를 제거했을 뿐만 아니라, 그들에게 영양이 있는 단백질과 지방을 제공했다.
(A) 이 때문에, 바다거북은 마요네즈로 치료받은 지 단 며칠 후에 회복의 조짐을 보였다. 일단 그들이 완전히 건강해졌다면, 야생으로 돌려보내졌다. 마요네즈 치료법이 그들의 생명을 구했을 가능성이 있다.

어휘

attention 주의, 주목 conservationist 환경 보호 활동가 endangered 멸종 위기에 처한 recovery 회복 discover 발견하다; *찾다[알아내다]

remove 제거하다, 없애다 nourishing 자양[영양]이 되는 protein 단백질 unusual 특이한, 흔치 않은 preference 선호, 애호 spill 쏟아지다; *유출 coastline 해안 지대 sticky 끈적거리는 toxic 유독성의 substance 물질 digestive 소화의

구문해설

(9행) **It** is possible [that the mayonnaise treatment saved their lives].: It은 가주어이고 [ ]가 진주어

(11행) Conservationists discovered [that mayonnaise {mixed with vegetable oil} was the best way {to get the tar out of the sea turtles}].: [ ]는 discovered의 목적절, 첫 번째 { }는 mayonnaise를 수식하는 과거분사구, 두 번째 { }는 the best way를 수식하는 형용사적 용법의 to부정사구

(13행) **Not only** *did it* remove the tar from their systems, it **also provided** them **with** nourishing proteins and fats.: 'not only A (but) also B' 「A뿐만 아니라 B도」, 부정어 Not only가 문두로 나와 주어와 동사가 도치, 'provide A with B' 「A에게 B를 제공하다」

문제해설

⑤ 동물 보호론자들이 멸종 위기에 처한 바다거북을 보호하기 위해 마요네즈를 사용하고 있다는 내용의 주어진 글 다음에, 이 방법을 처음 사용하게 된 계기를 설명하는 (C)가 오고, 마요네즈가 바다거북의 소화 기관에 쌓인 타르를 제거하고 영양분을 제공한다는 (B)로 이어진 후, 이로 인해 바다거북이 회복의 조짐을 보였다는 (A)가 오는 것이 자연스럽다.

37 ② 글의 순서

치명적인 형태의 암을 일으키는 것에서부터 치아와 손가락을 노랗게 착색시키는 것까지, 담배는 건강에 해롭다고 널리 알려져 있지만, 연구자들은 이제 흡연이 건강에 영향을 미치는 또 다른 방식, 즉, 코골이의 증가를 발견해 냈다.
(A) 이 관계를 조사하던 한 연구는 한 흡연자 집단과 그와 유사한 비흡연자 집단을 비교하였고, 흡연이 실험 대상자들 사이에서 실제로 더 높은 코골이의 발생률로 이어진다는 것을 보여 주었다.
(C) 담배 연기는 흡연자의 코와 목에 있는 호흡 통로를 자극하는 것으로 보이는데, 이곳의 일부 세포들은 니코틴에 노출된 결과로 신경 손상까지도 겪는 것으로 보였다.
(B) (이러한) 자극은 염증과 부종으로 이어지고, 이는 잠을 자는 동안 호흡의 정상적인 과정을 방해하여 흡연자가 코골이를 경험할 가능성을 더 높게 만든다.

어휘

fatal 치명적인 stain 더럽히다, 착색하다 snoring 코골이 confirm 사실임을 보여주다 incidence 발생률 subject 실험 대상자 irritation 짜증; *자극 (irritate 자극하다, 염증을 일으키다) inflammation 염증 swelling 팽창; *(몸의) 부은 곳 obstruct 방해하다 respiratory 호흡의 passageway 통로 exposure 노출

구문해설

(6행) A study [looking at this connection] **compared** a group of smokers to a similar group of non-smokers and **confirmed** that smoking cigarettes *does* indeed lead to a higher incidence of snoring among subjects.: [ ]는 A study를 수식하는 현재분사구, compared와 confirmed가 문장의 동사, does는 that절의 동사 lead를 강조하는 조동사

문제해설

② 흡연과 코골이의 관계에 대해 언급한 주어진 글 다음에, 흡연자와 비흡연자로 나누어 실험해보니 흡연자의 코골이 발생률이 더 높았음을 확인했다는 내용의 (A)가 오고, 담배 연기가 호흡 통로를 자극한다는 내용의 (C)가 이어진 후, 그 자극으로 인해 호흡 곤

란을 겪게 되어 코골이의 가능성이 높아진다는 내용의 (B)가 오는 것이 자연스럽다.

38 ③ 주어진 문장의 위치

'긍정적 확언'은 부정적인 잠재의식적 신념을 겨냥할 수 있는 짧고 긍정적인 진술이다. 당신은 이러한 신념을 약화시키고 부정적인 감정을 긍정적인 것으로 근본적으로 바꾸기 위해 긍정적 확언을 이용할 수 있다. 이것은 당신의 신념을 바꾸도록 스스로를 '세뇌시키는' 하나의 방법이지만, 어떤 신념을 씻어내고자 하는지를 결정하는 것은 바로 당신 자신이다. 그렇지만, 때때로 이 과정에는 저항이 있다. 만약 당신이 없애고자 하는 신념이 당신의 삶에서 매우 중요하거나, 혹은 당신이 그 신념을 오랫동안 간직해왔다면, 당신의 잠재의식은 그 신념을 유지하는 것이 더 편안하다고 여겨 긍정적 확언을 거부하려 할 것이다. 하지만, 만약 그 사안이 그다지 심각하지 않다면, 확언은 적용되기 더 쉬울 것이다. 그런 경우에, 당신은 기쁨을 경험하게 될 것이고, 그것이 바로 확언이 작용하고 있다는 표시이다.

어휘
resistance 저항 positive 긍정적인(↔ negative 부정적인) affirmation 확언, 단언 statement 진술, 말 direct at …을 겨냥하다 subconscious 잠재의식의; 잠재의식 undermine 약화시키다 replace 대체하다 brainwash 세뇌시키다 erase 없애다, 지우다 apply 신청하다; *적용되다

구문해설
[8행] This is a way [to "brainwash" yourself into changing your beliefs], but **it's** you **that** decide [which beliefs you want to wash away].: 첫 번째 [ ]는 a way를 수식하는 형용사적 용법의 to부정사구, 'it is[was] … that ~'「~하는 것은 바로 …이다[였다]」(강조구문), 두 번째 [ ]는 decide의 목적어로 쓰인 의문사절
[12행] …, your subconscious will find **it** more comfortable [to maintain the belief] and …: it은 가목적어이고 [ ]가 진목적어
[18행] …, and this is a sign [that the affirmation is working].: [ ]는 a sign과 동격

문제해설
긍정적 확언에 대한 일반적인 설명이 이어지다가 ③ 뒤에 긍정적 확언을 거부하게 되는 경우에 대한 설명이 나오므로, 주어진 문장은 ③에 오는 것이 자연스럽다.

39 ② 주어진 문장의 위치

한국의 작은 마을인 동피랑은 조선 왕조 동안 군사 기지로서의 역할을 했다. 그러나 최근에 와서 그 마을은 오래된 요새를 재건축하기 위해 마을 철거를 주장하는 개발업자들로부터 위협에 처하게 되었다. 이에 대응하여, 마을 주민들은 거리에서 항의하는 것이 아니라 푸른 통영 21이라는 단체를 만들어서 시위를 했다. 이 단체는 그 작은 마을을 구하기 위해 그림으로 그 마을을 가득 채울 생각을 해냈다. 전국에서 모여든 예술가들이 동피랑으로 와서 건물에 벽화를 그리거나 가능한 모든 공간을 꾸밈으로써 이 운동에 참여했다. 그 결과 동피랑은 새로운 정체성을 갖게 되었고, 그와 더불어 새로운 가치도 생겨났다. 새로 발견된 예술적 가치 앞에서 개발업자들은 그들의 계획을 단념할 수밖에 없었다.

어휘
demonstrate 시위운동을 하다 protest 항의하다 advocate 주장하다 fort 요새, 기지 come up with …을 생각해 내다 mural 벽화 identity 정체성 in the face of …에 직면해서 newfound 새로 발견된 abandon 단념하다, 버리다

구문해설
[11행] …, artists came to Dongpirang [to participate in the movement by **painting** murals on buildings and **decorating** every available space].: [ ]는 결과를 나타내는 부사적 용법의 to부정사구, 전치사 by의 목적어로 동명사 painting과 decorating이 병렬 연결
[15행] …, and with it **came new value**.: 부사구 with it이 문두에 오면서 주어와 동사가 도치

문제해설
② 다음의 This group이 가리키는 단체가 주어진 문장의 Blue Tongyeong 21이므로, 주어진 문장이 ②에 오는 것이 자연스럽다.

40 ① 요약문 완성

모든 사람들은 개인 공간에 대한 자신만의 개념을 가지고 있다. 낯선 사람이 이 공간 안에 들어오면, 우리는 매우 불편해진다. 과학자들은 이 불편한 감정이 두려움을 통제하고 감정적인 일을 처리하는 편도체라고 알려져 있는 뇌의 한 부분에 의해 일어난다고 믿는다. 한 실험에서, 편도체에 심각한 손상을 입은 한 여성이 다른 사람을 향해 걸어가다가 편안한 거리에서 멈추도록 요청 받았다. 대부분의 사람들이 상대방으로부터 50cm 정도 떨어진 거리에서 멈추었을 것인 반면에, 그 여성은 서로의 코가 거의 닿을 때까지 계속해서 다가갔다. 연구원들은 그녀의 편도체의 손상이 그녀로 하여금 다른 이들의 감정을 인지하고 그들의 신뢰성을 판단하는 것을 못하게 한다고 생각한다. 비록 그 여성의 질환을 치료하는 것에 대해 알려져 있는 방법은 없지만, 이 연구는 우리가 왜 모르는 사람 가까이에 서 있는 것을 그렇게 견디기 힘들어하는지를 더 잘 이해하도록 해 주었다.

어휘
concept 개념 extremely 극도로, 극히 process 처리하다 severe 심각한 recognize 알아보다; *인식하다 trustworthiness 신뢰성 condition 상태; *질환 unbearable 참을[견딜] 수 없는 proximity 가까움, 근접 [문제] confusion 혼란, 혼동 invade 침입하다, 침략하다 aggression 공격, 침략 eliminate 제거하다

구문해설
[3행] Scientists believe [that this unpleasant feeling is caused by a part of the brain **known as the amygdala** {that controls fear and processes emotional events}].: [ ]는 believe의 목적절, known as the amygdala는 a part of the brain을 수식하는 과거분사구, { }는 a part of the brain을 선행사로 하는 주격 관계대명사절
[14행] The researchers believe [(that) the damage to her amygdalae **prevents** her **from recognizing** other people's emotions and **judging** their trustworthiness].: [ ]는 believe의 목적절, 'prevent+O+from v-ing'「…가 ~하지 못하게 하다」이며, recognizing과 judging이 등위 접속사 and로 병렬 연결
[18행] …, this research has led to a greater understanding of why we find **it** so unbearable [to stand in close proximity to people {(who/whom) we don't know}].: it은 가목적어이고 [ ]가 진목적어, { }는 people을 선행사로 하는 목적격 관계대명사절

문제해설
① 편도체는 우리의 개인적인 공간이 침범될 때 우리가 느끼는 불편함이라는 감정에 관여한다고 여겨진다.

41 ⑤ 42 ③ 장문

공리주의에 따르면, 무언가가 전체의 행복을 극대화하는 반면 전체의 고통을 최소화한다면 그것은 도덕적으로 옳다. '전체의'라는 단어가 중요한데, 중요한 것은 개인의 행복이 아니라 바로 모두의 행복임을 그 단어가 강조하기 때문이다. 공리주의에는 두 갈래가 있는데 행위 공리주의와

규칙 공리주의이다. 둘 다 위의 서술에 동의한다. 그러나, 그것들은 사람들이 이 정보로 무엇을 해야 하는가에 대해서는 의견을 달리한다. 행위 공리주의는 가장 많은 양의 행복을 가져올 어떤 방식으로든 사람들이 행동해야 한다고 말한다. 하지만 규칙 공리주의는 어떤 유형의 행동이 일반적으로 행복을 발생시키는지 사람들이 결정한 다음에 이 행동을 시행하는 규칙을 만들어야 한다고 주장한다.

그 차이를 이해하기 위해, 한 판사가 어느 범죄자를 감옥에 보낼지 결정하는 특정한 재판에 대해 상상해 보라. 판사는 그 사람이 단순히 실수했고 다시 범죄를 저지를 것 같다(→ 것 같지 않다)는 것을 알고 있다. 그를 석방하는 것이 그의 친구들과 가족들을 비롯하여 그 사람을 행복하게 할 것이다. 피해자조차 그 사람을 용서했으므로, 이 결정은 그 피해자에게 어떤 고통도 일으키지 않을 것이다.

행위 공리주의는 판사가 그를 놓아주어야 한다고 주장하는데, 이것이 추가적인 고통을 일으키지 않으면서 행복을 극대화할 것이기 때문이다. 하지만 규칙 공리주의는 범죄자들은 자신의 범죄에 대해 처벌을 받아야 하므로, 판사가 그 사람을 감옥에 보내야 한다고 말한다. 그 상황의 세부 사항들은 중요하지 않다. 규칙 공리주의에 따르면, 판사는 엄격히 그 규칙을 따라야 한다.

어휘

utilitarianism 공리주의 ethical 윤리적인; *도덕적으로 옳은 maximize 극대화하다(↔ minimize 최소화하다) emphasize 강조하다 matter 중요하다 branch 가지 statement 진술, 서술 argue 언쟁을 하다; *주장하다 determine 결정하다 enforce (법률 등을) 실시[시행]하다 judge 판사 criminal 범인, 범죄자 commit (범죄를) 저지르다 victim 피해자 punish 처벌하다 strictly 엄격히

구문해설

4행 ..., as it emphasizes [that **it is** the happiness of everyone **that** matters, not the happiness of individuals].: [ ]는 emphasizes의 목적절, 'it is ... that ~' 「~하는 것은 바로 …이다」(강조구문)

10행 Act utilitarianism states [that they should behave in **whatever** way will lead to the greatest amount of happiness].: [ ]는 states의 목적절, whatever는 「무슨 …든지」의 의미의 복합관계형용사

17행 [To understand the difference], imagine a specific court case [in which a judge is deciding **whether to send** a criminal to prison].: 첫 번째 [ ]는 목적을 나타내는 부사적 용법의 to부정사구, 두 번째 [ ]는 a specific court case를 선행사로 하는 관계대명사절, 'whether (or not) to-v'는 「…할지 (안 할지)」의 의미로, 'whether+S+should+동사원형'의 형태로 고쳐 쓸 수 있음

26행 Act utilitarianism argues [that the judge should **let** the man **go**], as this will maximize happiness without [causing additional pain].: 첫 번째 [ ]는 argues의 목적절, 'let+O+동사원형' 「…가 ~하게 하다」, 두 번째 [ ]는 전치사 without의 목적어로 쓰인 동명사구

문제해설

41 공리주의에서 행위 공리주의와 규칙 공리주의는 전체의 행복을 극대화하는 것이 도덕적으로 옳다는 점에는 동의하지만 그에 대한 접근법이 서로 다르다는 내용의 글이므로, 제목으로는 ⑤ '행복을 극대화하는 서로 다른 방법들'이 가장 적절하다.

42 어느 범죄자의 석방 여부를 결정하는 판사의 입장에서 그 범죄자가 단순 실수를 했고 뒤이어 피해자조차 그를 용서했으므로 석방을 결정하는 것이 피해자에게 어떤 고통도 일으키지 않는다는 것으로 보아 문맥상 그가 다시 범죄를 저지르지 않을 것 같다고 하는 것이 자연스러우므로, ③ likely(~할 것 같은)를 unlikely(~할 것 같지 않은) 등으로 고쳐야 한다.

43 ④ 44 ③ 45 ③ 장문

(A) 가족 캠핑 여행 중 어느 화창한 오후에, 형과 나는 나무가 우거진 야영지를 탐험하러 밖으로 나갔다. 풀로 덮인 빈터에서 우리는 우연히 낡은 이층집을 발견했다. 우리는 뒤틀린 창문 안을 들여다보았는데, 검은 먼지와 오래돼 보이는 고물 상자들밖에는 보이지 않았다.

(D) 그 집이 버려진 것이라고 생각해 우리는 우리 나이대의 많은 남자 아이들이 했을 법한 일을 했다. 우리는 창문을 통해 안으로 들어간 것이다. 안에 들어가자마자, 우리는 깨뜨릴 다른 것들을 찾기 시작했다. 그러나 우리는 곧 이 특별한 집이 결코 버려진 것이 아님을 알게 되었다. 이 집을 소유한 노부부가 멀리 떨어지지 않은 곳에 있는 이동 주택에 살고 있었고, 그들은 우리가 내고 있던 소음을 들었다. 당국은 신고를 받았고, 우리는 처음으로 경찰차를 타고 가게 되었다.

(B) 경찰서에서 우리는 우리가 기막힌 거짓말이라고 생각한 것을 떠올렸다. 우리가 창문이나 집 안의 그 어떤 것도 깨뜨리지 않았다는 것이다. 사실 우리는 그들이 들은 심상치 않은 소리를 똑같이 들었고, 진행 중인 범죄를 막기 위해 그 집에 들어가게 되었다고 말했다. 진짜 범인은 그들이 우리를 체포하는 동안 달아났음에 틀림없다. 다행히도 집주인들은 우리를 믿는 것 같았다. 우리를 처벌하는 대신에 그들은 우리의 용감한 행동에 대해 고마워했고, 경찰은 이 사람들의 소유물을 훼손한 범인을 찾으면 우리에게 알려주겠다고 약속했다.

(C) 물론, 처음에 우리는 안도했다. 하지만, 시간이 지나면서 우리 가슴의 무거운 짐 같은 죄책감이 조금씩 생겨나기 시작했다. 이 감정은 점점 더 커졌다. 우리는 제대로 자지도 못했고 입맛도 없었다. 무엇보다도 나쁜 것은 우리가 차마 부모님의 눈을 똑바로 쳐다볼 수 없다는 것이었다. 그들이 경찰로부터 그 소식을 들은 후에, 그들은 우리가 그 야영지에서 얼마나 용감했는지와 그 불쌍한 사람들이 겪은 범죄 행위에 대한 정의가 여전히 실현되지 못한 것이 얼마나 슬픈지에 대해 항상 말씀하셨다. 결국, 우리는 그것을 더 이상 견딜 수 없어 우리가 했던 일을 고백했다. 이로부터 나는 정직이 최상의 방책임을 배웠다.

어휘

explore 탐험하다 campground 야영지 clearing 빈터 come upon …을 우연히 발견하다 peek 살짝 들여다보다, 엿보다 warped 휜, 뒤틀린 brilliant 훌륭한; *재기가 뛰어난 alarming 놀라운, 심상치 않은 escape 달아나다, 탈출하다 arrest 체포하다 heroic 영웅적인; *용감한 property 재산, 소유물 guilty 죄책감이 드는, 가책을 느끼는 creep 살살 기다; *어느덧 스며들다 appetite 식욕 bear 참다, 견디다 courageous 용감한 confess 자백하다, 인정하다 assume 추정하다 authority 권한; *당국

구문해설

7행 ..., we came up with [what **we thought** was a brilliant lie]: [that we *had* not *broken* the window ... house].: 첫 번째 [ ]는 came up with의 목적어로 쓰인 관계대명사절, we thought는 삽입절, 두 번째 [ ]는 a brilliant lie와 동격, had broken은 대과거를 나타내는 과거완료

13행 The true criminals **must have escaped** while they were arresting us.: 'must have p.p.' 「…였음에 틀림없다」

24행 **Worst of all**, we *couldn't bear to look* our parents in the eye.: 'worst of all' 「무엇보다도 나쁜 것은」, 'cannot bear to-v' 「차마 …할 수 없다」

26행 ..., they were always remarking [how courageous we had been at that campground] and [how sad **it** was {that those poor people still had no justice ... suffered}].: 두 개의 [ ]는 모두 were remarking의 목적어로 쓰인 의문사절, it은 가주어이고 { }가 진주어

34행 [Assuming the house to be abandoned], we did [what **a lot of boys our age would have done**]...: 첫 번째 [ ]는 이유를 나타내는 분사

구문, 두 번째 [ ]는 did의 목적어로 쓰인 관계대명사절, a lot ... done은 주어가 조건절을 대신하는 가정법 과거완료 구문(과거 상황과 반대되는 가정을 나타냄)

43 ④ 필자가 가족 캠핑 중에 형과 함께 우연히 낡은 집을 발견하게 되는 (A)에 이어, 그 집이 버려진 집이라고 생각해 무단 침입했다가 경찰에 체포되는 (D)가 나오고, 경찰서에서 범인을 잡으러 들어간 것이라는 거짓말을 꾸며 내어 풀려나게 되는 (B)가 이어진 후, 죄책감 때문에 부모님께 사실을 털어 놓는 (C)로 이어지는 것이 자연스럽다.

44 ③ (c)는 필자의 부모를 가리키고, 나머지는 모두 이층집의 주인인 노부부를 가리킨다.

45 ③ 필자가 소음을 냈고, 이를 듣고 집안으로 들어가게 된 것은 집주인인 노부부였다.

02 영어독해 모의고사

본문 ▲ p.16

18 ④	19 ③	20 ④	21 ①	22 ②	23 ④
24 ⑤	25 ④	26 ②	27 ④	28 ④	29 ⑤
30 ②	31 ④	32 ③	33 ③	34 ⑤	35 ④
36 ②	37 ②	38 ⑤	39 ③	40 ①	41 ④
42 ④	43 ⑤	44 ③	45 ③		

18 ④ 글의 목적

무어 교수님께,

제 이름은 그렉 발레리오이며, 저는 현재 물리학을 전공하고 있는 2학년생입니다. 고등학교 때 물리학이 제게 가장 강점인 과목이었기 때문에 저는 그 과목을 선택했으나, 지금은 다시 생각하고 있습니다. 저는 수업에 어려움을 겪고 있으며 컴퓨터 공학으로 변경하는 것으로부터 도움을 받을 것으로 생각합니다. 저는 이것에 관해 지도 교수님과 이야기를 나누었고, 지도 교수님은 교수님이 해당 학과의 학과장이시기 때문에 교수님으로부터 승인을 받아야 한다고 말씀하셨습니다. 저는 우리가 이러한 부탁은 학기 초반에 드려야만 하며 중간고사가 거의 다가왔다는 것을 알고 있습니다. 그래서 이 문제를 처리하는 것이 훨씬 더 어려워지기 전에 최대한 빨리 교수님께 연락을 취해야 한다고 생각했습니다. 필요하다면, 직접 뵙고 제 상황에 대해 상의를 드리면 좋을 것 같습니다. 저에게 알려주십시오.

진심을 다해서,

그렉 발레리오 드림

sophomore 2학년생 major in …을 전공하다 physics 물리학 have second thoughts 다시 생각한 후 마음을 바꾸다 struggle with …으로 어려움을 겪다 benefit from …에서 득을 보다 academic advisor 지도 교수 approval 인정; *승인 department 부서; *학과 make a request 요청하다, 부탁하다 semester 학기 in person 직접

(2행) My name is Greg Valerio, and I'm a sophomore [currently majoring in physics].: [ ]는 a sophomore를 수식하는 현재분사구
(12행) I know [(that) we're supposed to make these requests early in the semester] and [that it is almost time for midterms].: 두 개의 [ ]는 모두 know의 목적절, 'be supposed to-v' 「…하기로 되어 있다. …해야 한다」
(15행) So I thought I should contact you as soon as possible, before it becomes even more difficult [to handle this matter].: it은 가주어이고 [ ]가 진주어, even은 「훨씬」이라는 의미로 비교급을 강조하는 부사

컴퓨터 공학으로 전공을 바꾸기를 원하는 학생이 학과장에게 승인을 부탁하는 내용이므로, ④가 글의 목적으로 가장 적절하다.

19 ③ 심경

카렌은 주변 상황을 차츰 알아차리면서, 자신이 얼마나 오랫동안 의식이 없었는지 확신할 수 없다는 사실을 깨달았다. 그녀는 자신의 부상이 심하지 않다는 것을 알 수 있었지만, 그녀의 차가 그녀의 다리를 누르고 있어 그 자리에서 꼼짝할 수 없게 했다. 일어나 앉으면서 그녀는 다리를 끌어당겨서 빼내려고 몸을 뒤로 밀기 시작했다. 하지만 아무리 세게

밀어도 그녀는 다리를 단 몇 센티미터도 움직일 수 없었다. 작전을 바꿔서, 그녀는 몸을 비꼬아 빠져나가기를 바라며 좌우로 움직이기 시작했지만, 이것 역시 소용이 없었다. 그녀가 혼자 힘으로 빠져나갈 방법은 전혀 없어 보였지만, 카렌은 도움을 기다리는 것 외에는 아무것도 할 수 없다는 사실을 받아들이고 싶지 않았다.

어휘
gradually 서서히　become aware of …을 알게 되다　surrounding 《*pl.*》 주변(의 상황), 환경　unconscious 의식이 없는　trap 가두다, 꼼짝할 수 없게 하다　backwards 뒤로　attempt 시도　tactic 《*pl.*》 전략, 작전　wriggle out (몸을 꼬아서) 빠져나오다　[문제] indifferent 무관심한　desperate 필사적인; *절망적인　sympathetic 동정 어린　ashamed 부끄러운

구문해설
3행 She could tell [that her injuries weren't serious], but her car was lying on her legs, [trapping her where she was].: 첫 번째 [ ]는 tell의 목적절, 두 번째 [ ]는 부대상황을 나타내는 분사구문
7행 But **hard as she pushed**, she couldn't move them even a few centimeters.: '형용사[부사]+as+S+V' 「비록 …하지만」(양보의 의미)
13행 ..., Karen did not want to accept the fact [that she could do nothing but wait for help].: [ ]는 the fact와 동격

문제해설
사고로 다리가 차에 깔려 꼼짝할 수 없는 데다 도와줄 사람도 전혀 없는 상황이므로 ③ '불안하고 절망적인' 심경일 것이다.

20 ④ 필자의 주장

경쟁적인 스포츠는 많은 학생들에게 고등학교의 중요한 부분인데, 그것이 청소년들을 신체적으로 건강하게 하고, 그들에게 팀워크를 가르쳐 주며, 그들이 압박감을 느끼는 상황에서 해내는 법을 배우도록 도와주기 때문이다. 하지만, 이러한 스포츠는 자격을 갖춘 전문가에 의해 관리되지 않으면 심신에 해를 끼칠 수 있다. 이것은 즐기는 것에서 이기는 것으로 강조점이 바뀔 때 가장 자주 일어나는데, 즐거운 활동을 스트레스가 많은 상황으로 변형시킨다. 패배는 실패가 되며, 이는 스트레스를 일으키고 자신감을 손상시킨다. 심지어 성공한 젊은 선수들도 시달릴 수 있는데, 무조건 이겨야 한다는 태도를 가지는 것이 사회적 문제 및 동료와의 갈등을 초래할 수 있기 때문이다. 고등학교 감독들은 학생 선수들을 훈련시킬 때 이러한 잠재적 위험들을 염두에 두어야 하며, 반드시 신체 단련, 자기 계발, 그리고 팀워크에 초점을 맞추어야 한다.

어휘
competitive 경쟁의, 경쟁적인　physically 신체[육체]적으로(physical 신체[육체]적인)　fit 건강한　pressure 압박, 압력　monitor 감시[관리]하다　qualified 자격이 있는　professional 전문가, 직업 선수　mental 정신의　emphasis 중요성, 강조　shift 바꾸다　transform 변형시키다　pleasurable 즐거운, 유쾌한　self-confidence 자신감　athlete (운동)선수　win-at-any-cost 어떤 비용을 치르더라도 성공하는 것　potential 잠재적인　self-improvement 자기 계발

구문해설
2행 ..., as they *keep* teens physically *fit*, **teach** them about teamwork, and **help** them *learn* [how to work under pressure].: keep, teach, help가 등위 접속사 and로 병렬 연결, 'keep+O+형용사' 「…을 계속 ~하게 하다」, 'help+O+(to-)v' 「…가 ~하는 것을 돕다」, [ ]는 learn의 목적어로 쓰인 의문사구
10행 Losing becomes failure, [which **causes** stress and **damages** self-confidence].: [ ]는 앞 절 전체를 선행사로 하는 계속적 용법의 주격 관계대

사절, causes와 damages가 등위 접속사 and로 병렬 연결
12행 ..., **as** [having a win-at-any-cost attitude] can cause social problems and conflicts with their peers.: as는 이유를 나타내는 접속사. [ ]는 주어 역할을 하는 동명사구

문제해설
④ 경쟁적인 스포츠에서 이기는 것을 지나치게 강조하면 오히려 아이들의 심신에 해를 끼칠 수 있으므로, 신체 단련과 협동심 증진에 초점을 맞춰 훈련해야 한다는 내용의 글이다.

21 ① 함축 의미 추론

깨진 유리창 이론에 따르면, 수리되지 않은 채 남겨진 깨진 유리창은 그 동네의 더 많은 유리창이 깨지는 것으로 이어질 것이다. 이것은 깨진 유리창이 아무도 관심을 가지지 않아서, 더 많은 유리창을 깨는 것에 대한 처벌이 없을 것이라는 암시하기 때문이다. 물론, 이것은 유리창에만 해당되지 않는다. 이 이론은 어떤 종류의 환경에서든 고쳐지지 않은 채로 남겨진 어떤 종류의 무질서에 대한 비유의 역할을 한다. 비록 그것은 원래 수리되지 않은 동네들을 설명하기 위해 사용되었지만, 지금은 보통 직장과 교실에 적용된다. 예를 들어, 어느 학교에나 '유리창을 깨려고' 시도할 학생들이 있다고 주장되어 왔다. 이것은 보통 허락 없이 책상을 바꾸거나 수업 중에 문자 메시지를 확인하는 것과 같은 사소한 반항의 행동이다. 이러한 행동은 대수롭지 않은 것처럼 보일지 모르지만, 즉각적으로 '깨진 유리창을 수리하지' 않는 것은 학급 환경에 전반적으로 부정적인 영향을 초래할 수 있다.

어휘
theory 이론　signal 신호를 보내다; *시사[암시]하다　punishment 벌, 처벌　apply 적용하다; 적용되다, 해당되다　metaphor 은유, 비유　disorder 무질서, 혼란　originally 원래, 본래　commonly 흔히, 보통　argue 주장하다　disobedience 불복종, 반항　permission 허락　insignificant 대수롭지 않은, 사소한　immediately 즉시, 즉각　overall 종합[전반]적인　[문제] correct 바로잡다, 정정하다　appearance 외관, 외양

구문해설
1행 According to the broken windows theory, a broken window [that is left unrepaired] will lead to **more windows in the neighborhood** {being broken}.: [ ]는 a broken window를 선행사로 하는 주격 관계대명사절, { }는 전치사 to의 목적어로 쓰인 동명사구이며 more windows in the neighborhood는 { }의 의미상 주어
7행 The theory serves as a metaphor for any kind of disorder [left unfixed] in any sort of environment.: [ ]는 disorder를 수식하는 과거분사구
12행 For example, it has been argued that in any school, there are students [who will attempt to "break a window"].: [ ]는 students를 선행사로 하는 주격 관계대명사절

문제해설
깨진 유리창을 수리하지 않은 채로 두면 더 큰 범죄로 이어질 수 있다는 깨진 유리창 이론을 교실에 적용하여, 사소한 반항의 행동을 그대로 방치할 경우 학급 전체에 부정적인 영향을 끼칠 수 있다는 내용이므로, 밑줄 친 '깨진 유리창을 수리하는 것'이 의미하는 바로 가장 적절한 것은 ① '학생들의 잘못된 행동을 바로잡는 것'이다.

22 ② 글의 요지

공상 과학 소설을 읽을 때, 당신은 과학 그 자체에서 차용된 많은 단어들과 문구들을 발견하리라 예상할 것이다. 그러나 어떤 경우들에 있어서 이 과정은 반대로 이루어지며, 과학 분야는 소설가들의 상상 속에서 생겨난 단어들의 사용을 실제로 받아들인다. 예를 들어, '먼 우주 공간

(심우주)'이라는 표현은 에드워드 스미스가 지은 '은하계 방위군'이라는 소설에서 처음 등장했고, 은하수 사이의 텅 비어있는 거대한 공간을 묘사하기 위해 사용되었다. 오늘날, 과학자들은 우리의 태양계 너머에 있는 우주 공간의 어떤 부분을 가리키기 위해 그것을 사용한다. 작가로부터 차용된 또 다른 과학 용어는 '무중력'으로, 이것은 1938년에 출간된 단편 소설에서 잭 바인더가 만든 것이다. 이 경우에, 그 용어의 의미는 소설에서와 실제 생활에서 모두 동일하다. 과학 용어들이 실제 과학자들에 의해 만들어지는 것만큼 소설가들에 의해서도 만들어지는 것 같아 보인다.

어휘
come across …을 우연히 마주치다, 발견하다   phrase 구(句)   borrow 빌리다; *차용하다   reverse 반대로 하다   region 지역, 영역   galaxy 은하, 은하수   solar system 태양계   gravity 중력   coin (신어 등을) 만들다   identical 동일한

구문해설
(11행) ..., scientists use it [to refer to any part of space {that lies beyond our solar system}].: [ ]는 목적을 나타내는 부사적 용법의 to부정사구, { }는 any part of space를 선행사로 하는 주격 관계대명사절
(16행) It would seem that scientific terms **are** just *as* **likely to be coined by writers** *as* **by actual scientists**.: 'be likely to-v' 「…할 것 같다」, 'as … as ~' 「~만큼 …한」

문제해설
② 과학 분야에서 사용되는 일부 과학 용어들이 실제로는 소설과 같은 문학 작품에서 차용한 것이라는 내용의 글이다.

23 ④ 글의 주제

군 복무는 베트남전 기간 동안 2백만 명 이상의 미국인에게 있어 인생을 바꿔놓은 경험이 되었다. 군인들은 긴장, 권태, 마약, 베트남인들에 대한 만연한 잔혹 행위를 대해야만 했다. 참전하지 않은 미국의 젊은이들조차 청소년기 후반과 청년기의 대부분을 징집될 것을 걱정하거나 참전을 피하느라 애쓰며 보내면서, 그 전쟁에 영향을 받았다. 베트남에 간 사람보다 고국에 머무른 사람이 더 많았지만, 전쟁은 세대 전체에 깊은 분열을 가져왔다. 참전한 사람들은 참전하지 않은 사람들에 대해 자주 분개했고, 베트남에 가지 않은 사람들은 때때로 갔던 사람들을 경멸과 동정의 시선으로 바라보았다.

어휘
military service 병역   tension 긴장   boredom 권태   widespread 널리 퍼진   brutality 잔인성; *만행   adolescence 사춘기   adulthood 성인기   draft 징집하다   division 분열   resent 분개하다   scorn 경멸, 조소   pity 동정   [문제] compulsory 강제적인; *의무적인   pros and cons 찬반양론

구문해설
(6행) ... were affected by the war, [**spending** a major part of their late adolescence or young adulthood **worrying** about being drafted or **trying** to avoid participation in the fighting].: [ ]는 부대상황을 나타내는 분사구문, 'spend+시간+v-ing' 「…하는 데 시간을 보내다」, worrying과 trying은 등위 접속사 or에 의해 병렬 연결
(14행) ... those [who **did** go (to Vietnam)] with scorn and pity.: [ ]는 those를 선행사로 하는 주격 관계대명사절, did는 동사 go를 강조하는 조동사

문제해설
베트남전 참전이 미국인들에게 미친 영향에 대해 설명한 글이므로 이 글의 주제로는 ④ '베트남전이 미국인들의 삶에 미친 영향'이 적절하다.

24 ⑤ 글의 제목

복권에 당첨되는 꿈을 꾸는 것은 드문 일이 아니다. 만약 당신이 재정적으로 불확실한 시기를 경험한 적이 있다면, 당신은 아마도 복권에 당첨되는 것이 어떻게 당신의 모든 금전 문제를 해결해 줄 것인지를 상상해 보았을 것이다. 많은 다른 사람들도 이렇게 생각해 본 적이 있다. 안타깝게도, 많은 복권 당첨자들이 실제로는 당첨된 후에 더 많은 재정적 어려움을 겪는다. 다수는 심지어 파산 신청을 하기에 이른다. 여기에는 여러 가지 이유들이 있을 수 있지만, 주된 문제는 당첨자들이 새로 얻은 자신의 부를 관리하는 법을 모른다는 것이다. 그들은 집과 차, 그리고 다른 사치품들을 즉시 구입함으로써 당첨에 반응한다. 하지만 그들은 이것들 각각이 구입 후 상당한 유지 비용을 필요로 한다는 것을 이해하지 못한다. 고급 승용차는 비싼 보험을 필요로 하고, 배에는 능력 있는 선원이 필요하며, 별장은 당신에게 높은 재산세를 내도록 요구한다. 그러므로, 복권 당첨자들은 재정적으로 안정을 유지하고 싶다면 자신의 돈을 신중하게 관리해야 한다.

어휘
lottery 복권   financial 재정의   uncertainty 불확실성   declare 선언하다   bankruptcy 파산   substantial 상당한   maintenance 유지   luxury 고급(품)의   insurance 보험   property 재산   stable 안정적인

구문해설
(1행) It's *not uncommon* [to dream about winning the lottery].: It은 가주어이고 [ ]가 진주어, not uncommon은 이중부정(긍정의 의미)
(9행) ..., but the main problem is [that the winners don't know {how to manage their newly-acquired wealth}].: [ ]는 주격보어로 쓰인 명사절, { }는 know의 목적어로 쓰인 의문사구

문제해설
복권 당첨자들이 재정적 어려움에서 벗어나기보다는 갑자기 얻게 된 부를 제대로 관리할 줄 몰라 오히려 더 큰 어려움에 처하게 된다는 내용이므로, 글의 제목으로는 ⑤ '많은 복권 당첨자들이 왜 재정적 어려움에 처하는가'가 가장 적절하다.

25 ④ 도표 내용 불일치

위 도표는 각기 다른 형태의 미디어와 뉴스를 접하기 위해 종종 이것들을 이용하는 미국인의 비율을 보여 준다. 최연소 연령대에서 가장 일반적인 뉴스의 출처는 스마트 기기인 반면에, 최고령 연령대에서 가장 일반적인 뉴스의 출처는 텔레비전이다. 보통 텔레비전에서 뉴스를 접하는 50세에서 64세 연령대 사람들의 비율은 두 최연소 연령대가 합쳐진 비율보다 높다. 최연소 연령대에서는 오직 7퍼센트의 사람들만이 라디오로 종종 뉴스를 접하는데, 이는 보통 스마트 기기로 뉴스를 접하는 이 동일한 연령대의 비율의 10분의 1도 되지 않는다. (보통 라디오에서 뉴스를 접하는 30세에서 49세 사람들의 비율은 텔레비전에서 종종 뉴스를 접하는 18세에서 29세 사람들의 비율보다 단 1퍼센트포인트 더 높다.) 마지막으로, 최고령 연령대의 48퍼센트만이 보통 스마트 기기로 뉴스를 접하는데, 이는 다음으로 나이가 많은 연령대보다 4퍼센트포인트 더 적다.

어휘
device 장치, 기구   combine 결합하다

구문해설
(6행) The percentage of people in the 50-to-64 age group [who often get their news from the television] is higher than **that** of the two youngest age groups combined.: [ ]는 people in the 50-to-64 age group을 선행사로 하는 주격 관계대명사절, that은 The percentage를 지칭하는 대명사
(13행) The percentage of 30-to-49-year-olds [who often get their

news from the radio] is only one percentage point higher than the percentage of 18-to-29-year-olds [who often get their news from the television].: 두 개의 [ ]는 각각 30-to-49-year-olds와 18-to-29-year-olds를 선행사로 하는 주격 관계대명사절

문제해설
④ 라디오에서 뉴스를 접하는 30세에서 49세 사이의 비율이 텔레비전에서 뉴스를 접하는 18세에서 29세 사이의 비율보다 1퍼센트포인트 더 낮다.

26 ② 내용 불일치

1976년에 발견된 메가마우스 상어는 과학자들이 아직 상세히 탐험하지 못한 서식지인 심해에 산다. 그 결과, 그것은 매우 희귀한 종(種)으로 여겨지며, 매우 희귀해서 지금까지 50마리 미만의 표본만이 잡혔다. 신체적인 외양 면에서 메가마우스는 상당히 독특한데, 거대한 몸은 길이 5.5 미터까지 자라며 커다란 머리는 넓은 코와 고무 같은 입술을 특징으로 한다. 그것의 하복부는 새하얀 색이며, 반면에 그 동물의 위쪽의 색 패턴은 갈색부터 검은색에 이른다. 당연히 이 상어는 특징적으로 커다란 입을 가지고 있으며, 이로부터 그 이름이 유래했다. 반면에 이 상어의 이빨은 오히려 작은 편인데, 그것의 먹이를 씹는 대신 단순히 입을 크게 벌리고 물속을 헤엄쳐, 상어가 가는 길목으로 길을 잃은 해파리나 플랑크톤을 삼켜버리기 때문이다.

어휘
reside 거주하다 specimen 견본, 표본 distinctive 독특한, 특이한 snout 코, 주둥이 rubbery 고무 같은, 탄력 있는 underbelly 하복부 solid (빛깔이) 무늬가 없는, 고른 derive 유래하다 swallow (꿀꺽) 삼키다 jellyfish 해파리 stray 길을 잃다, 빗나가다

구문해설
[1행] ..., the megamouth shark **resides** in a habitat [(that) scientists **have yet to explore** in detail] ...: [ ]는 a habitat를 선행사로 하는 목적격 관계대명사절, 'have yet to-v' 「아직 …하고 있지 않다」

문제해설
② 신체적인 외양 면에서 상당히 독특하다고 했다.

27 ④ 내용 불일치

자원봉사 방학
'자원봉사 방학'은 여름 방학 동안 자원봉사 기회를 제공하는 비영리 단체입니다.
• 우리 프로그램은 두 지역(중미와 서아프리카)에 중점을 둡니다.
• 우리 프로그램의 목표는 작은 마을들에 학교, 주민센터 및 병원과 같은 현대 시설을 제공하는 것입니다. 자원봉사자들은 이러한 시설의 구상 및 건설을 도울 것으로 예상됩니다.
• 여름 전체(8주)와 여름 절반(4주)의 두 가지 프로그램 기간이 있습니다.
• 학교 단위 단체는 받지 않습니다. 그러나, 개별 학생과 가족 단위는 환영합니다.
현재 진행 중인 프로그램에 대해 더 자세한 정보를 원하시거나 신청서를 다운로드하시려면, 저희 웹사이트를 방문해 주세요.

어휘
volunteer 자원봉사자 nonprofit 비영리적인 organization 조직, 단체 facility (pl.) 시설, 기관 community center 주민센터 construction 건설, 공사 length 길이; *시간, 기간 individual 각각의, 개인의 current 현재의 application form 신청서

구문해설
[2행] Volunteer Vacations is a nonprofit organization [that provides volunteer opportunities during the summer vacation].: [ ]는 a nonprofit organization을 선행사로 하는 주격 관계대명사절
[7행] The goal of our programs is [to **provide** small villages **with** modern facilities, *such as* schools, community centers, and hospitals].: [ ]는 주격보어로 쓰인 명사적 용법의 to부정사구, 'provide A with B' 「A에게 B를 제공하다」, 'such as' 「…와 같은」

문제해설
④ 개별 학생과 가족 단위의 참가는 환영한다고 나와 있다.

28 ④ 내용 일치

맨체스터 도서전에 오세요
책을 좋아하시는 분들께 알립니다! 제4회 연례 맨체스터 도서전이 곧 맨체스터 시 경기장에 올 것입니다!
일시
• 11월 16일부터 11월 30일
• 참고: 박람회 첫 3일간은 출판 관계자들만을 위한 것입니다. 일반 관람객은 19일부터 환영합니다.
• 일요일을 제외하고 매일 오전 10시부터 저녁 7시까지 일반 관람객에게 개장되는데, 이때(일요일)에는 한 시간 일찍 마감됩니다.
• 전시 참가 업체들은 오전 9시부터 저녁 9시까지 주 7일간 참가할 수 있습니다.
입장권
• 1인당 5달러
• 10인 이상 단체는 20퍼센트 할인을 받으실 수 있습니다.

어휘
fair 박람회 attention 알립니다, 주목하세요 annual 매년의, 연간의 civic (도)시의 arena 경기장, 공연장 publishing 출판, 발행 professional 전문직 종사자 the public 일반인 exhibitor (전시회) 출품자[출품 회사] discount 할인

구문해설
[10행] Open to the public **from** 10 a.m. **to** 7 p.m. every day except Sundays, [when it closes one hour earlier]: 'from A to B' 「A에서 B까지」, [ ]는 Sundays를 선행사로 하는 계속적 용법의 관계부사절

문제해설
① 시 경기장에서 약 2주간 개최된다고 나와 있다. ② 박람회 첫 3일간에는 출판 관계자들만 참여 가능하다고 나와 있다. ③ 일요일에는 한 시간 일찍 마감된다고 나와 있으므로, 6시까지 관람할 수 있다. ⑤ 단체에는 20퍼센트 할인이 적용된다고 나와 있다.

29 ⑤ 어법

연구에 따르면 학습은 우발적인 학습과 의도적인 학습의 두 범주로 나뉠 수 있다. 전자는 우연히 일어나는 것으로, 이는 분명하게 규정된 학습 의도가 없다는 것을 의미한다. 예를 들어, 미국 50개 주(州)의 이름을 암기하려는 학생이 친구에게 그 이름들을 대는 동안 들어달라고 부탁할 수 있다. 이름을 대는 동안, 그 친구도 우연히 이 50개 주의 이름을 학습하게 될지도 모른다. 반면, 의도적인 학습은 처음부터 분명한 목적이 있을 때 일어난다. 예를 들어, 한 학생이 시험을 봐야 하기 때문에 유럽 각국의 수도 목록을 가지고 자리에 앉을 수 있다. 연구는 의도적인 학습은 시간이 지나도 (기억에) 남기 때문에 더 효과적임을 시사한다.

어휘
divide A into B A를 B로 나누다 incidental 우연적인 intentional 의도적인(intention 의도) former 전자(의) by chance 우연히 define 정의하다; *규정하다, 분명히 밝히다 name 이름; 이름을 지어주다; *이름을 대다

capital city 수도

5행 ..., a student [who is trying to memorize the names of the 50 U.S. states] may ask a friend to listen while **they** are named.: [ ]는 a student를 선행사로 하는 주격 관계대명사절, they는 the 50 U.S. states를 지칭

문제해설
⑤ suggest, insist, request 등과 같이 제안·주장·요구 등을 나타내는 동사에 연결되는 that절에는 동사가 '(should+)동사원형'의 형태로 쓰이지만, suggest가 '암시하다, 시사하다'의 의미일 경우에는 that절에 '(should+)동사원형'을 사용하지 않으므로, be는 is가 되어야 한다.

30 ② 어휘

전통적인 푸에블로 도자기가 다른 형태의 점토 예술품과 구별되는 한 가지 특징은 창작 과정에서 기계가 사용되지 않는다는 점이다. 점토는 손으로 모아져서 반죽되고 빚어진다. 푸에블로 도공은 물건을 만들기 위해 물레를 이용하는 대신, 점토를 기다랗게 말아 아주 정성스럽게 원 모양으로 감아 올린다. 물감은 푸에블로 마을 근처에서 발견되는 식물과 광물로 만들고 유카과 선인장을 이용해 손으로 만든 붓으로 칠해진다. 이러한 전통적인 과정으로 인해 미술품 수집가들은 푸에블로 점토 작품은 하나하나가 모두 독특하다고 확신할 수 있다. 그것은 또한 푸에블로 도자기가 훌륭한 선물이 될 수 있음을 의미한다.

어휘
feature 특징   distinguish A from B A를 B와 구별하다   pottery 도자기 (potter 도공)   clay 진흙   machinery 기계류   creative 창의적인; *창작의   process 과정   progress 진보   wheel 물레   objective 목적   painstakingly 공들여, 정성스럽게   coil 감다   layer 층   apply 붙이다, 바르다   fashion A from B B의 재료를 써서 A의 모양으로 만들다   cactus 선인장

구문해설
1행 One feature [that distinguishes ... art] is [that machinery is not used ... process].: 첫 번째 [ ]는 One feature를 선행사로 하는 주격 관계대명사절, 두 번째 [ ]는 주격보어로 쓰인 명사절
8행 Paints are produced from plants and minerals [found near ... villages] and applied with a handmade brush [fashioned from ... cactus].: 첫 번째 [ ]는 plants and minerals를 수식하는 과거분사구, 두 번째 [ ]는 a handmade brush를 수식하는 과거분사구

문제해설
② (A) 창작 '과정'이므로 process가 적절하다. (B) 문맥상 '물건, 물체'를 의미하는 objects가 적절하다. (C) 물감 재료가 마을 근처에서 '발견되는' 것이므로 found가 적절하다. founded는 '설립하다'라는 의미의 동사 found의 과거형이다.

31 ④ 빈칸 추론

당신이 무언가를 일간 신문에서 읽었다는 이유만으로 그것이 정확하다는 것을 의미하지는 않는 듯하다. 한 연구자가 최근에 기후 변화라는 주제에 관한 다양한 기사들을 분석했고, 그는 측정 단위의 보도에서 수많은 오류를 발견했다. 예를 들어, 해수면의 잠재적 변화에 대한 기사에서, 그 수치는 밀리미터로 제시되었어야 했지만, 바닷물이 1년에 1~2센티미터씩 상승할 수 있다고 적혀 있었다. 그와 똑같은 실수가 강수량의 증가에 대한 다른 신문 기사에서 발생했다. 이러한 발견들로부터, 그 연구자는 그 실수들이 결코 실수가 아니었다고 결론 내렸다. 그는 언론 매체들이 빈번히 수치들을 실제로 그런 것보다 더 큰 수치로 잘못 보도한다고 생각하는데, 왜냐하면 이러한 과장들이 뉴스를 더 극적으로 만들게 하

여 그것들이 보다 쉽게 독자들의 관심을 사로잡을 수 있게 하기 때문이다.

어휘
accurate 정확한   article 기사   unit 단위   measurement 측정   piece 한 편의 글; *신문 기사   rainfall 강수량   media outlet 언론 매체   ensure 확실하게 하다   grab 사로잡다   [문제] analogy 유사, 유추   exaggeration 과장

구문해설
1행 It seems that [**just because** you read something ... newspaper] doesn't mean (that) it's accurate.: [ ]는 that절의 주어로 쓰인 명사절로, just because는 「…이라고 해서」의 의미(because는 명사절을 이끌기도 함)
8행 ..., though the figure **should have been given** in millimeters.: 'should have p.p.' 「…해야만 했는데 (하지 않았다)」
15행 ... because these exaggerations **help** *make* news stories *more dramatic*, [ensuring that they'll more easily grab the attention of readers].: 'help (to-)v' 「…하는 것을 돕다」, 'make+O+OC' 「…가 ~하도록 만들다」, [ ]는 부대상황을 나타내는 분사구문

문제해설
④ 다양한 기사들의 분석 결과 일부 기사에서 잘못된 측량 단위가 사용되었음이 밝혀졌는데, 이는 실수가 아니라 독자들에게 그 상황을 과장되게 설명하여 기사에 대해 흥미를 갖게 하려는 의도에서였을 것이라는 내용의 글이다.

32 ③ 빈칸 추론

타액에 대한 최근의 연구는 그 액체가 얼마나 풍부한 정보를 가지고 있는지를 밝혔다. 예를 들어, 의사들은 특정 물질의 존재 여부를 근거로 병의 징후를 찾기 위해 흔히 피를 뽑지만, 타액도 똑같은 정보를 가지고 있다는 것이 밝혀졌다. 게다가 타액은 DNA를 포함하고 있는데, 그것은 개개인에게 고유하다. 타액 속의 DNA를 분석함으로써, 의사들은 당신이 특정 질병에 걸리기 쉬운지의 여부를 알아낼 수 있다. 경찰 수사관들은 또한 당신이 범죄 현장에서 물 한 잔을 마셨던 사람인지, 봉투를 핥아서 봉했던 사람인지의 여부도 알 수 있다. 치과 의사들 또한 타액에서 비롯된 정보를 이용해 당신에게 충치가 생길 가능성을 예측할 수 있다.

어휘
saliva 타액, 침   reveal 드러내다, 알리다, 밝히다   presence 존재   substance 물질   turn out 결국 …임이 드러나다   contain 포함하다   analyze 분석하다   susceptible 영향받기 쉬운, 감염되기 쉬운   investigator 수사관, 조사관(investigation 수사, 조사)   lick 핥다   envelope 봉투   seal 봉하다   predict 예측하다   cavity 충치   [문제] digestion 소화   liquid 액체

구문해설
5행 ..., but **it** turns out [that your saliva holds the same information].: it은 가주어이고 [ ]가 진주어
9행 Police investigators can also tell [whether you were the person {who drank ... a crime}].: [ ]는 tell의 목적절, { }는 the person을 선행사로 하는 주격 관계대명사절

문제해설
빈칸 뒤에서 타액에 들어 있는 여러 가지 정보에 대해 예시를 통해 설명하고 있으므로, 빈칸에는 ③ '그 액체가 얼마나 풍부한 정보를 가지고 있는지'가 적절하다.

33 ③ 빈칸 추론

대부분의 국가에서, 감옥에서 탈출하려고 시도하는 것은 매우 심각한 범죄로 여겨지고, 그렇게 하기로 결정한 수감자들에게는 그들의 원심

이 상당히 길어질 수도 있다. 하지만, 멕시코에서는 그렇지 않다. 멕시코 법률은 모든 사람들이 자유에 대한 선천적인 열망을 가지고 있다는 기본 철학에 기반한다. 그러므로, 멕시코 감옥에서 탈출하려고 하다가 붙잡힌 수감자는 처벌을 받지 않을 수 있다. 물론, 멕시코에는 이러한 정책을 국가 사법 제도의 주된 약점으로 인식하여 이를 반대하는 사람들도 있다. 그러나, 그것을 전적으로 지지하는 많은 다른 사람들이 있는데, 그들은 그것이 수감자들의 기본적인 인권을 보호해 준다고 생각한다.

어휘
sentence 판결, 선고 lengthen 길게 하다 underlying 기본적인 philosophy 철학 perceive 인식하다 weakness 약점, 약함 justice 정의; *사법 wholeheartedly 진심으로, 전적으로 [문제] yearning 열망 intention 의도, 목적 reason 이성, 사고력

구문해설
(3행) ... prisoners [who choose to **do so**] are likely to *have* their original sentences significantly *lengthened*.: [ ]는 prisoners를 선행사로 하는 주격 관계대명사절, do so는 escape from prison을 의미, 사역동사 have의 목적어와 목적격보어의 관계가 수동이므로 목적격보어로 과거분사 lengthened가 쓰임

문제해설
③ 빈칸의 뒷부분에서 멕시코에서는 탈옥 시도 후 붙잡힌 수감자가 처벌을 받지 않을 수 있다고 언급하고 있으며, 이러한 법률의 의도가 수감자의 기본 인권 보호라는 차원에서 옳다고 옹호하는 이들이 있다는 것으로 미루어 볼 때 멕시코의 법률은 인간의 자유권에 대한 존중에 기반했다는 것을 추론할 수 있다.

34 ⑤ 빈칸 추론

어떤 사람들은 사회적 상황에서 다른 사람들에게 다가가는 것을 주저한다. 그들은 마치 본질적으로 "저를 좋아하세요?"라고 묻고 있는 것처럼 느낀다. 이러한 종류의 상호 작용에서, 겉으로 보기에는 상대방이 모든 힘을 갖고 있다. 그러나 당신은 상대방에게 작은 투자를 할 것을 권하는 것으로 시작함으로써 그 만남을 장악할 수 있다. 간단히 말해서, 그 혹은 그녀에게 당신을 위해 뭔가를 해달라고 부탁하라. 그것이 중요한 것일 필요는 없다. 그 사람에게 그저 당신한테 케이크 한 조각을 건네 달라거나 당신이 화장실에 가는 동안 당신의 음료를 들어달라고 요청하라. 당신은 아마 이것이 그 사람으로 하여금 당신에 대하여 더 긍정적인 인상을 갖게 한다는 것을 발견할 것이다. 대부분의 사람들이 생각하는 것과는 달리, 사람들은 아마도 반대의 방법(당신이 상대방의 부탁을 들어주는 것)보다는 오히려 당신의 부탁을 들어준 이후에 당신을 더 좋아하게 될 것이다.

어휘
be reluctant to-v …하는 것을 주저하다 essentially 근본[기본]적으로 interaction 상호 작용 seemingly 외견상으로, 겉보기에는 seize control of …을 장악하다 encounter 만남, 접촉 make an investment 투자하다 simply put 간단히 말해서 likely 아마, 필시 the other way around 반대로, 거꾸로

구문해설
(2행) They feel **as though** they **are** essentially asking "Do you like me?": as though가 이끄는 절에서 현실과 반대되는 가정의 의미가 없을 때는 현재시제를 사용
(11행) You will likely find [that this **causes** the person **to have** a more positive impression of you].: [ ]는 find의 목적절, 'cause+O+to-v' 「…가 ~하게 하다」

문제해설
빈칸 이후에 상대방에게 간단한 부탁을 하는 예시들이 언급되었으므로, 빈칸에는 ⑤

'그 혹은 그녀에게 당신을 위해 뭔가를 해달라고 부탁하라'가 적절하다.

35 ④ 흐름과 무관한 문장

유방암은 무수한 요인들에 의해서 발생할 수 있기 때문에, 의사들이 어떤 개별적인 경우의 정확한 원인을 결코 정확히 찾아낼 수 없을지도 모른다. 그러나, 특정 물질이나 환경에의 노출이 여성이 이 암에 걸릴 위험을 상당히 증가시킨다는 것을 보여주는 것은 가능하다. 야간에 인공 조명에 노출되는 것이 그러한 하나의 위험 요소라는 이론이 제시된다. 이 자극과 그 질병 사이의 관련성은 우리의 수면 각성 주기를 통제하는 호르몬인 멜라토닌에 있다. 인공 야간 조명에의 노출은 멜라토닌 수치를 감소시킨다고 알려져 있는데, 이는 유방암 환자들에게서 종종 발견된다. (멜라토닌 생성은 사람들이 나이가 들면서 둔화되기 때문에, 나이 든 성인들이 더 낮은 수치를 보이는 경향이 있다.) 이 이론의 신빙성은 인공 야간 조명이 덜 흔한 개발 도상국의 여성들이 산업 국가에 사는 여성들보다 유방암에 걸리는 비율이 더 낮다는 사실에 의해 강화된다.

어휘
breast cancer 유방암 a myriad of 무수한 factor 요인 pinpoint 정확히 찾아내다 exposure 노출(expose 노출시키다) substance 물질 contract 계약하다; *(병에) 걸리다 artificial 인공의 theorize 이론을 제시하다 connection 관련성 stimulus 자극(pl. stimuli) govern 지배[통제]하다 credibility 신뢰성, 신빙성 strengthen 강화하다 industrialize 산업화하다

구문해설
(3행) However, **it** is possible [to show {that exposure to certain substances or conditions significantly increases ... cancer}].: it은 가주어이고 [ ]가 진주어, { }는 show의 목적절
(8행) The connection between this stimulus and the disease lies in melatonin, [a hormone {that governs our sleep-wake cycle}].: [ ]는 melatonin과 동격, { }는 a hormone을 선행사로 하는 주격 관계대명사절
(16행) ... by the fact [that women in developing countries, {where artificial nighttime light is less common}, have lower rates ... nations].: [ ]는 the fact와 동격, { }는 developing countries를 선행사로 하는 계속적 용법의 관계부사절

문제해설
유방암 발병과 인공 야간 조명에 노출되는 것의 상관관계에 대한 글이므로, 나이가 들면서 멜라토닌 수치가 낮아진다는 내용의 ④는 글의 흐름과 무관하다.

36 ② 글의 순서

레오나르도 다빈치는 뛰어난 예술가이자 위대한 발명가였다. 그는 지도 제작, 수학, 지질학, 그리고 회화를 포함하여 여러 분야에 영향을 미쳤다.
(B) 하지만, 레오나르도의 가장 큰 영향력은 그의 생전에 존재하지 않던 분야인 로봇 공학에 있었을지도 모른다. 이것은 그가 인체 해부학에 사로잡혀 있었기 때문이다. 우리의 근육이 뼈를 어떻게 움직이는지 더 잘 이해하기 위해, 그는 종종 시체를 해부했다.
(A) 그는 이 원리들이 기계에 사용될 수 있다고 생각했다. 1495년에, 그는 전투에서 사용될 수 있는 기계로 작동되는 기사의 밑그림들을 그렸다. 그것들은 그 기사가 인간의 몸처럼 움직이게 만들 내부 기계 장치가 있는 갑옷 한 벌을 보여 주었다.
(C) 레오나르도가 그의 로봇 기사를 만들려고 시도했는지는 아무도 모른다. 하지만 2002년에, 한 로봇 공학 전문가가 그 기사의 작동 모형을 만들기 위해 그의 메모와 스케치들을 사용했다. 거기에 사용된 아이디어들의

일부는 이후 행성 탐사 로봇들을 설계하기 위해 나사에 의해 차용되었다.

master (기술이 뛰어난) 일류의 geology 지질학 principle 원리, 원칙 mechanical 기계로 작동되는 armor 갑옷 internal 내부의 mechanism 기계 장치 be obsessed with …에 사로잡히다, 집착하다 anatomy 해부학; (해부학적) 구조 corpse 시체 attempt 시도하다 design 밑그림을 만들다; 설계하다

구문해설
8행 They showed a suit of armor with an internal mechanism [that would **make** it **move** like a human body].: [ ]는 an internal mechanism을 선행사로 하는 주격 관계대명사절, 'make+O+동사원형「…가 ~하게 하다」
14행 [To better understand {how our muscles move our bones}], he often dissected corpses.: [ ]는 목적을 나타내는 부사적 용법의 to부정사구, { }는 understand의 목적어로 쓰인 의문사절
20행 **Some of the ideas** [used in it] **were** later borrowed by NASA [to design planet-exploring robots].: Some of 뒤에 나오는 명사가 복수형이므로 복수동사인 were가 쓰임. 첫 번째 [ ]는 the ideas를 수식하는 과거분사구, 두 번째 [ ]는 목적을 나타내는 부사적 용법의 to부정사구

문제해설
② 레오나르도 다빈치가 여러 분야에 영향을 미쳤다는 주어진 글 다음에, 가장 큰 영향을 미친 분야가 당시에는 존재하지 않았던 로봇 공학이라는 내용의 (B)가 온 뒤, 인체 해부학에 관심이 많았던 그가 기계로 작동되는 기사의 밑그림들을 그렸다는 (A)에 이어, 훗날 한 로봇 공학 전문가가 그 기사의 실제 모형을 만들고자 했으며 나사의 행성 탐사 로봇 설계에도 그 아이디어가 일부 차용되었다는 (C)로 이어지는 것이 자연스럽다.

37 ② 글의 순서

19세기 초반부터, 오랫동안 신비하거나 초자연적이라고 여겨졌던 사건들이 논리, 수학적 추론 그리고 입수 가능한 증거를 통해 설명되기 시작했다.
(A) 그 당시, 찰스 다윈은 주류에서 벗어난 이론을 제안했다. 그는 자연계를 설명하는 데 신이나 어떤 다른 높은 힘을 고려해보지 않고, 자연 선택이라고 불리는 이론을 제안했다.
(C) 찰스 다윈에 따르면, 자연 선택이란 생물종이 그들의 환경의 특정한 필요에 맞춰 시간의 흐름에 따라 진화한다는 이론이다. 따라서 좋은 환경 조건이 변화하더라도 그들의 생존을 유지할 수 있다는 것이다.
(B) 이런 생각은 나중에 종의 진화 이상의 것을 포함하는 것으로 확대되었다. 다윈은 자연 선택설을 발전시켜 지구의 모든 형태의 생명체가 우주 탄생 시 존재했던 수소로부터 진화했다고 주장했다.

supernatural 초자연적인 logic 논리 reasoning 추론, 추리 available 입수 가능한 propose 제안하다 break away from …에서 벗어나다, 이탈하다 mainstream (활동·사상의) 주류 force 힘, 세력 natural selection 자연 선택[도태] expand 확대하다 evolution 발달; *진화(evolve 진화하다) species (분류상의) 종(種) proclaim 선언하다 hydrogen 수소 maintain 유지하다 survival 생존

구문해설
1행 ..., events [that had long been considered magical or supernatural] began to be explained ...: [ ]는 events를 선행사로 하는 주격 관계대명사절
12행 ... natural selection **to proclaim** [that all of earth's life forms ... hydrogen {that was ... universe}].: to proclaim은 결과를 나타내는

부사적 용법의 to부정사, [ ]는 proclaim의 목적절, { }는 hydrogen을 선행사로 하는 주격 관계대명사절

문제해설
② 불가사의하게 여겨지던 사건들이 19세기에 과학적으로 설명되기 시작했다는 사회 상황 이후에, 찰스 다윈이 자연 선택설을 주장했다는 (A)가 오고, 자연 선택설의 내용을 설명하는 (C)에 이어, 그 이론의 확장에 대해 이야기하는 (B)로 이어지는 것이 자연스럽다.

38 ⑤ 주어진 문장의 위치

의료 역사상 가장 슬프고 혹독한 대가를 치른 실수들 가운데 하나가 1920년대와 1930년대에 일어났는데, 이때 영아돌연사증후군(SIDS)을 예방하려는 시도들이 이루어졌다. 아기가 밤중에 알 수 없는 이유로 사망하는 병인 SIDS를 조사했던 연구원들은 그들이 그 원인을 밝혀냈다고 생각했다. 조사 결과, 사망한 영아들 중 다수가 확대된 흉선이라고 설명되었던 것을 보였다. 흉선은 식도 옆에 위치해 있는데, 만일 자고 있는 아이의 목에 압력이 있으면 지나치게 큰 흉선이 폐로 가는 공기의 흐름을 막을 수 있다고 추정되었다. 따라서, 의사들은 아이들의 흉선을 많은 양의 방사선에 노출시킴으로써 줄어들게 하고자 했다. 안타깝게도, 이 확대된 흉선 이론은 불충분한 자료를 토대로 했다. 의사들이 '확대된' 것으로 여긴 흉선들이 실제로는 정상적인 크기였다. 이 실수는 그 후 수십 년간 방사선에 의해 유발된 인후암으로 2만 명에서 3만 명 사이의 사람들이 사망하는 결과를 초래했다.

enlarged 확대된 infant 유아 investigate 조사하다 condition 상태; *질환 inexplicably 이해할 수 없게 examination 조사, 검사 deceased 사망한 exhibit 전시하다; *보이다, 드러내다 excessively 지나치게 shrink 줄어들다; *줄어들게 하다 dose (약의) 복용량[투여량] radiation 방사선 insufficient 불충분한 induced 유도된, 유발된

구문해설
4행 ... occurred during the 1920s and 1930s, [when attempts were made to prevent ... (SIDS)].: [ ]는 the 1920s and 1930s를 선행사로 하는 계속적 용법의 관계부사절
6행 Researchers [who investigated **SIDS, a condition** {in which a baby inexplicably dies during the night}], thought [(that) they had found the cause].: 첫 번째 [ ]는 Researchers를 선행사로 하는 주격 관계대명사절, SIDS와 a condition은 동격, { }는 a condition을 선행사로 하는 목적격 관계대명사절, 두 번째 [ ]는 thought의 목적절
12행 ..., and **it** was assumed [that an excessively large thymus could block airflow to the lungs ... throat].: it은 가주어이고 [ ]가 진주어

문제해설
주어진 문장은 의사들이 정상적인 크기의 흉선들을 '확대된' 것으로 잘못 생각했다는 내용이며, ⑤ 뒤에서 의사들의 실수를 서술하고 있으므로 ⑤에 오는 것이 자연스럽다.

39 ③ 주어진 문장의 위치

우리 모두는 재계와 정계의 불건전한 관계가 고질적인 문제임을 알고 있다. 미국에서는 입법자들과 기업주들이 수감 제도를 이용하여 이런 식으로 서로 한 통속이 되어 이득을 취하는 관계를 강화하려고 하고 있다. 그들은 어떻게 이것을 하고 있는가? 입법자들은 더 긴 형량을 선고하는 법률들을 통과시키고 있고, 그 결과로 수감자 수가 점점 늘어나고 있다. 수감자 수의 급격한 증가는 교도소를 건설하고 교도소에 서비스를 제공하는 기업들의 수익이 늘어나게 해 준다. 그들의 수익이 증가함에 따라 이 기업들은 협조적인 정치 후보자들에게 큰 재정적 기부금을 제공한다.

이런 후보자들이 의회에 선출되면, 그들의 기업 후원자들은 그들의 법률상 결정에 영향을 미치게 된다. 이런 부도덕한 순환을 깨기 위해 조치가 취해지지 않는 한 미국의 수감자 수는 계속해서 증가할 것이다.

어휘
rapid 급격한 prison 교도소 corporation 회사, 기업(corporate 기업의) chronic 만성적인 legislator 입법자 backscratching (흔히 불법적인 일에) 서로 한 통속이 되어 돕기 command 명령하다, 요구하다 sentence 판결, 형벌 contribution 기부금, 성금 cooperative 협조적인 candidate 후보자 congress 국회, 의회 sponsor 후원자 legal 법률의 immoral 부도덕한

구문해설
11행 ..., prison populations are **growing** ever **larger**.: 'grow+비교급' 「점점 더 …해지다」
16행 **Unless** something **is** done [to break this immoral cycle], ...: 조건을 나타내는 부사절에서는 현재시제가 미래시제를 대신(unless = if ... not). [ ]는 목적을 나타내는 부사적 용법의 to부정사구

문제해설
주어진 문장은 교도소 수감자 수의 증가가 기업 수익의 증가로 이어진다는 내용이며, ③의 뒤에서 이 수익이 늘어남에 따라 생기는 결과에 대해 기술하고 있으므로 ③이 적절한 위치이다.

40 ① 요약문 완성

정서 예측, 즉 미래에 일어날 일에 대한 자기 자신의 감정적인 반응에 대해 예상하는 것은 사람들이 일반적으로 잘 하지 못하는 기술이다. 하버드 대학의 사회 심리학과 교수인 다니엘 길버트는 그의 새 연구에서 인간들이 서투른 정서 예측가들임을 보여주었다. 실제로, 미래의 사건들이 그들로 하여금 어떻게 느끼도록 만들 것인지에 대한 그들의 예상은 종종 완전히 부정확한 것으로 판명된다. 길버트에 따르면, 우리의 미래의 감정 상태가 선거, 스포츠 경기, 영화, 그리고 (중요도가) 큰 구매와 같은 사건들에 의해 어떻게 영향받을 것인가를 생각할 때, 우리는 우리의 반응들의 크기나 힘을 과대평가하거나 과소평가하는 경향이 있다. 이것은 우리가 기쁨으로 우리를 채워줄 것이라고 예상한 것이 좀처럼 그렇지 않으며, 반면에 정서적으로 우리를 황폐하게 할 거라고 두려워한 것은 대체로 우리가 예상했던 것보다 적은 고통을 야기한다는 것을 의미한다.

어휘
affective 감정의, 감정적인 forecasting 예상, 예보 excel 탁월하다, 뛰어나다 inaccurate 부정확한, 틀린 occurrence 사건 magnitude 크기 anticipate 예상하다 devastate 황폐화시키다, 파괴하다 [문제] foretell 예고하다 conceal 감추다, 숨기다 enhance 높이다, 강화하다

구문해설
9행 [When considering {how our future emotional state will be impacted by **such** occurrences **as** elections, sporting events, movies, and big purchases}], *reports Gilbert*, we tend to ...: [ ]는 때를 나타내는 분사구문, { }는 considering의 목적어로 쓰인 의문사절, 'such ... as ~' 「~와 같은 …」, reports Gilbert는 삽입절
14행 This means [that {what **we anticipate** will fill us with joy} rarely does, while {what **we fear** will emotionally devastate us} typically causes less pain than we expected].: [ ]는 means의 목적절, 두 개의 { }는 that절의 주어로 쓰인 관계대명사절, we anticipate와 we fear는 삽입절

문제해설
① 우리는 종종 미래의 사건이 미칠 영향을 정확하게 예측하지 못한다.

41 ④ 42 ④ 장문

오늘날 사람들은 더 많은 급여, 업무의 다양성, 경력 발전 기회를 찾아 과거 어느 때보다도 많이 '잦은 이직'을 하고 있다. 몇 년 전에는 '잦은 이직'이라는 말은 들을 수 없었다. 사실 많은 사람들이 한 회사에서 평생 직장 생활을 했고, 어쩔 수 없을 때에만 새 직장을 찾았다. 오늘날에는 직장인 한 사람이 평생 동안 직장을 여러 번 옮기는 것이 보통이다.

통신, 컴퓨터 기술, 전자상거래, 인터넷의 발전과 같은 기술의 급속한 진보는 새로운 취업 기회를 많이 가져다주었다. 그러나 신기술의 발전은 몇몇 기술들을 '사라지게' 만들면서, 다른 기술들을 대체하고 있다. 그러한 기술의 전환은 오늘날의 직장인들 사이에 더욱 많은 변화를 야기하고 있다. 오늘날의 직장에 있는 사람들은 구직 시장에서 자신의 경쟁력을 유지하기 위해 기술적 변화에 한 걸음 앞서 있어야만 한다.

수십 년 전 사람들은 직장 생활 내내 자신의 회사에 계속 불충실(→ 충실)했지만, 오늘날 사람들은 고용에 대해 더 자기중심적인 태도를 갖고 있다. 사람들은 최고의 보상과 복리 후생, 좋은 성장 기회, 편안한 근무 환경을 제공하는 직장을 택한다. 그들은 여러 해 동안 그들의 변화하는 요구를 충족시켜 줄 수 있는 회사를 찾으려 하는 대신, 자신의 현재 목표를 달성하게 해 주는 직업을 찾는다. 이는 많은 사람들이 다른 사람들을 위해 일하는 대신 자기 사업을 시작하는 것을 선택하도록 하는데, 이는 잦은 이직의 또 다른 종류라고 할 수 있다. 기술이 구직 시장에 변화를 가져왔다면 이런 태도의 변화는 현대 직장인들에게 새로운 진로 선택권을 만들어 주었다.

어휘
hop 깡충 깡충 뛰다; *(하나의 행동·주제에서 다른 것으로) 휙휙 바꾸다 wage 임금, 급여 diversity 다양성 be forced to-v …해야만 하다, …하지 않을 수 없다 e-commerce 전자상거래 extinct 멸종한, 사라진 changeover 전환, 변환 competitive edge 경쟁 우위 disloyal 불충한, 불충실한 compensation 보상, 급여 benefit 이익; *복리 후생 achieve 달성하다 [문제] alternative 양자택일; *대안

구문해설
1행 Today, people are "job-hopping" **more than ever**, [seeking ... opportunities].: 'more than ever' 「이전 어느 때보다도 더욱」, [ ]는 부대상황을 나타내는 분사구문
7행 Today, **it** is normal *for a working individual* [to change jobs several times ... lifetime].: it은 가주어이고 [ ]가 진주어, a working individual은 [ ]의 의미상 주어
28행 They seek jobs [that allow them to achieve their current goals] ... to find a company {that can meet ... over the years}.: [ ]는 jobs를 선행사로 하는 주격 관계대명사절, { }는 a company를 선행사로 하는 주격 관계대명사절

문제해설
41 오늘날 사람들이 직장을 자주 옮겨 다니는 이유를 서술한 글이므로 ④ '왜 현대인들은 자주 직장을 바꾸는가'가 가장 적절한 제목이다.
42 직장에 대해 자기중심적인 태도를 가지고 잦은 이직을 하는 오늘날의 사람들과 다르게 수십 년 전의 사람들은 자신의 회사에 충실했다고 하는 것이 자연스러우므로, ④ disloyal(불충한, 불충실한)을 loyal(충실한, 충성스러운) 등으로 고쳐야 한다.

43 ⑤ 44 ③ 45 ③ 장문

(A) 미국인들은 음식이 상하지 않게 하는 것이 중요하다고 생각하기 때문에 음식 대부분을 냉장고에 보관하는 경향이 있다. 이러한 이유로, 그들은 유럽 사람들이 보통 달걀을 부엌 조리대 위에 보관한다는 것을 알고 종종 충격받는다.

(D) 이 차이는 1970년대로 거슬러 올라갈 수 있는데, 그 당시 미국의 달걀 산업은 식중독의 흔한 원인이 되는 박테리아의 한 종류인, 살모넬라균을 우려했다. 살모넬라균을 없애기 위해, 달걀을 세척하는 특별한 공법이 만들어졌는데, 그 공법에서 달걀은 세제와 뜨거운 물로 세척된다. 세제, 물 그리고 증기를 사용하는 것은 달걀에서 살모넬라균을 없애는 데 효과적이지만, 그것은 물과 산소를 안에 머물게 할 뿐만 아니라 박테리아가 들어오지 못하게 하는 달걀 껍질 표면의 얇은 보호층인 각피를 제거한다. 따라서, 세척된 달걀은 감염을 막기 위해 냉장되어야 한다.

(C) 하지만, 유럽에서는 식품 안전 전문가들이 다른 방법을 채택했다. 그들은 달걀의 냉장 보관을 막고 실제로 회사들이 판매하는 달걀을 세척하는 것을 불법으로 만들었는데, 이는 보호하는 각피가 손상되지 않고 온전히 남아 있도록 만들어준다. 세척 대신에, 그들은 모든 산란계에게 살모넬라균 예방 접종을 하는 것을 의무로 하는 프로그램을 만들었다. 통계가 영국 내 달걀 관련 식중독 사례가 최근에 상당히 감소했다는 것을 보여주기 때문에, 그들의 방법이 가장 효과적인 것처럼 보인다.

(B) 그러면 미국인들은 왜 계속해서 달걀을 세척하고 냉장하는 것일까? 안타깝게도, 미국 정부가 닭에게 예방 접종하는 유럽의 관행을 채택하는 것을 거부하기 때문에 그것이 그들(미국인들)이 이용할 수 있는 최선의 선택으로 남는다. 게다가, 연구들은 달걀이 차갑게 보관될 때 정말로 더 오래간다는 것을 보여준다. 부엌 조리대에서 겨우 약 21일인 것과는 대조적으로, 그것들은 냉장고에서 약 50일 동안 먹기에 안전한 상태로 유지된다. 반면에, 냉장고에 보관되는 달걀은 주변 음식 냄새를 흡수하는데, 이는 그것들의 맛에 부정적인 영향을 준다. 이러한 이유로, 미국인들은 종종 달걀을 냄새가 강한 음식과 분리해서 보관한다.

어휘
kitchen counter 부엌 조리대 refrigerate (음식 등을) 냉장하다 (refrigeration 냉장, 냉동) adopt 입양하다; *채택하다 practice 관행 vaccinate (…에게) 예방 주사를 맞히다 as opposed to …와는 대조적으로 absorb 흡수하다 discourage 막다 illegal 불법의 cuticle 각피 intact 온전한, 전혀 다치지 않은 in place of …대신에 mandatory 의무적인 egg-laying 산란 statistics 통계 food poisoning 식중독 significantly 상당히 trace back 거슬러 오르다 get rid of 제거하다, 없애다 infection 감염

구문해설
(1행) Americans tend to keep most of their food in the refrigerator, [believing **it** is necessary {to *prevent* items *from going* bad}].: [ ]는 이유를 나타내는 분사구문. it은 가주어이고 { }가 진주어. 'prevent+O+from v-ing' 「…가 ~하지 않도록 하다」

(11행) Besides, studies have shown [that eggs **do** last longer when they are kept cold — they remain safe *to eat* for about 50 days in the refrigerator, ... the counter].: [ ]는 have shown의 목적절, do는 동사 last를 강조하는 조동사. to eat은 safe를 한정하는 부사적 용법의 to부정사

(22행) ... have actually made **it** illegal *for companies* [to wash the eggs that they sell], [which ensures that the protective cuticle remains intact].: it은 가목적어이고 첫 번째 [ ]가 진목적어. companies는 첫 번째 [ ]의 의미상 주어, 두 번째 [ ]는 앞 내용(have actually made it illegal ... they sell)을 선행사로 하는 계속적 용법의 주격 관계대명사절

(32행) ... to the 1970s, [when the American egg industry was concerned about salmonella, {a type of bacteria that is a common cause of food poisoning}].: [ ]는 the 1970s를 선행사로 하는 계속적 용법의 관계부사절. { }는 salmonella와 동격

(39행) ..., it removes their cuticle, [a thin, protective layer on the surface of the shell {that **not only** keeps water and oxygen in **but also** keeps bacteria out}].: [ ]는 their cuticle과 동격. { }는 a thin,

protective layer on the surface of the shell을 선행사로 하는 주격 관계대명사절. 'not only A but also B' 「A뿐만 아니라 B도」

문제해설
43 ⑤ 미국인들은 달걀을 냉장고에 보관하고 유럽인들은 부엌 조리대 위에 보관한다는 내용의 (A) 다음에, 이러한 차이가 생긴 이유로 살모넬라균 제거를 위한 미국의 달걀 세척 공법을 설명하는 (D)가 이어진 다음, 유럽에서는 세척 대신 산란계에게 살모넬라균 예방 접종을 하며 이러한 방식이 달걀 관련 식중독 예방에 효과적이었다는 내용의 (C)가 오며, 마지막으로 미국인들이 영국의 방법이 효과적임에도 계속해서 달걀을 세척하고 냉장보관 하는 이유와 달걀의 적절한 냉장 보관 방법에 관한 (B)가 오는 것이 자연스럽다.

44 ③ (c)는 유럽의 식품 안전 전문가를 가리키고, 나머지는 달걀을 가리킨다.

45 ③ 산란계에 백신 접종을 하는 것은 유럽이며, 미국은 이런 방식을 거부한다고 했다.

18 ②	19 ②	20 ⑤	21 ②	22 ③	23 ②
24 ②	25 ③	26 ⑤	27 ④	28 ②	29 ⑤
30 ⑤	31 ⑤	32 ⑤	33 ②	34 ④	35 ③
36 ⑤	37 ①	38 ②	39 ④	40 ③	41 ①
42 ⑤	43 ④	44 ①	45 ③		

18 ② 글의 목적

친애하는 맥고완 직원 여러분께,
　지난주 회사 구내식당에서 일어난 불운한 사고 이후로, 여러분 중 많은 분들이 부상을 당한 사람에게 응급 치료를 제공하는 데 있어서 지연이 발생한 것에 대해 우려를 표명해 왔습니다. 이것은 회사의 소유지 내에서는 훈련받은 전문 의료진들만이 치료를 제공할 수 있도록 하는 맥고완 산업의 정책 때문이었습니다. 이 정책은 보험 요건으로 인해 제정되었습니다. 그러나, 많은 논의 끝에, 우리는 이 정책을 개정하여 회사 내 응급 처치 강좌에서 의료 절차를 배운 사람이면 누구나 응급 상황에서 적절한 치료를 제공하는 것을 허용하기로 했습니다. 물론, 심각한 사고의 경우에는 전문 의료진들이 호출되어야 합니다. 언제나처럼, 우리는 직원들에 의해 표명된 의견에 감사드리며 여러분들이 우리의 대응에 만족하기를 바랍니다.
진심을 담아,
경영팀

어휘
unfortunate 불운한, 불행한　express (감정·생각 등을) 표현[전달]하다　concern 우려, 걱정　delay 지연, 지체　emergency 비상 (사태)　medical 의학의, 의료의　treatment 치료, 처치　individual 개인; *사람　policy 정책　permit 허용하다, 허락하다　professional 전문가　property 재산, 소유물　establish 설립하다, 설정하다　insurance 보험　requirement 필요조건, 요건　amend (법 등을) 개정[수정]하다　procedure 절차　first-aid 응급 처치의　appropriate 적절한　appreciate 고마워하다　management 경영, 운영

구문해설
6행 This was due to the McGowan Industries policy [that **permits** only trained medical professionals **to provide** treatment on company property].: [ ]는 the McGowan Industries policy를 선행사로 하는 주격 관계대명사절. 'permit+O+to-v'「…가 ~하는 것을 허용하다」
11행 ..., we have decided to amend the policy, [making **it** allowable *for anyone who has learned medical procedures in a company first-aid class* {to provide appropriate treatment in an emergency}].: [ ]는 부대상황을 나타내는 분사구문, it은 가목적어이고 { }가 진목적어, anyone ... class는 { }의 의미상 주어

문제해설
회사에서 발생한 사고를 계기로 사내 의료 행위에 대한 회사 정책을 개정하기로 했다는 내용이므로, ②가 글의 목적으로 가장 적절하다.

19 ② 심경 변화

　며칠 전에, 톰은 눈보라 속에서 시골길을 달리고 있었다. 늦은 밤이었고, 도로 상황이 정말 나빴다. 갑자기 그는 큰 소리를 들었고, 타이어가 펑크 났다는 것을 알았을 때 그의 가슴이 철렁했다. 보통 톰은 트렁크에 예비 타이어를 보관했지만, 짐을 넣을 더 많은 공간을 만들기 위해 그것을 빼놓았었다. 보이는 곳에 집이 한 채도 없었고, 그가 휴대전화를 확인했을 때 신호도 가지 않았다. 바로 그때, 한 쌍의 헤드라이트가 나타났다. 트럭을 탄 젊은 청년이라는 것이 드러났다. 그는 톰에게 그의 예비 타이어를 빌려주었을 뿐만 아니라, 그가 그것을 교체하는 것도 도와주었다. 그가 없었다면, 상황은 심각해졌을 수도 있었다.

어휘
snowstorm 눈보라　condition 상태　sink 가라앉다　have a flat tire 타이어가 펑크 나다　spare 여분의, 예비용의　room 공간　luggage 짐　in sight 보이는 곳에　appear 나타나다　turn out …인 것으로 드러나다[밝혀지다]　lend 빌려주다　[문제] relieved 안도하는　exhausted 진이 다 빠진　annoyed 짜증이 난　scared 겁먹은

구문해설
10행 ***Not only** did the man lend* Tom his spare tire, **but** he **also** helped him change it.: 'not only A but also B'「A뿐만 아니라 B도」, 부정어 Not only가 문두로 나와 주어와 동사가 도치
12행 **If it hadn't been for** him, the situation **could have been** serious.: 'if it had not been for'는 「…이 없었다면」의 의미를 나타내는 가정법 과거완료 구문으로, without으로 바꿔 쓸 수 있음

문제해설
눈보라 속에서 시골길을 달리다가 타이어가 펑크 나 도움을 청할 곳이 한 군데도 없어 '걱정스러워' 하다가 지나가던 젊은 남자의 도움을 받아 '안도하는' 상황이므로 ②가 가장 적절하다.

20 ⑤ 글의 요지

　비록 나노 기술이 수년간 존재했지만, 실용적인 응용은 이제서야 개발되고 있다. 이러한 응용은 잠재적으로는 의류에서 배터리에 이르기까지 모든 것에 영향을 주며, 광범위한 상품에 영향을 미칠 것으로 예상된다. 나노 사이즈로 축소되면, 친숙한 물질들도 특이한 특징을 나타내기 시작하기 때문에, 나노 기술은 색다른 새로운 물질의 개발로 이어질 수도 있다. 예를 들어, 만약 알루미늄 포일이 약 20에서 30 나노미터의 충분히 작은 크기로 축소되면, 그것은 우리가 알루미늄 포일이 반응하리라 예측한 대로 반응하기를 멈춘다. 사실, 나노 사이즈의 알루미늄 포일 조각은 폭발할 수 있다. 비록 모든 나노 사이즈 물질들이 그렇게 급격하게 특성을 변화시키는 것은 아니지만, 과학자들은 새롭고 유용한 물질들을 만들기 위해, 그렇게 변하는 물질을 가지고 작업하기를 간절히 원한다.

어휘
nanotechnology 나노 기술　practical 실용적인　application 적용, 응용　have an impact on …에 영향을 미치다　odd 기이한, 기묘한　dramatically 극적으로　be eager to-v 간절히 …하고 싶어 하다

구문해설
3행 These applications are expected to have an impact on a wide range of products, [potentially affecting everything from clothing to batteries].: [ ]는 부대상황을 나타내는 분사구문
14행 Although not all nanosize materials [change their properties so dramatically], scientists are eager to work with ones [that **do**], ...: do는 대동사로 첫 번째 [ ]를 의미, 두 번째 [ ]는 ones를 선행사로 하는 주격 관계대명사절

문제해설
⑤ 나노 기술로 물건을 나노 사이즈로 축소시켜 친숙한 물질도 특이한 특징을 나타내는 것으로 변모시킬 수 있다는 내용으로, 이 기술을 통해 새롭고 유용한 물질을 개발할 수 있다고 이야기하고 있다.

21 ② 글의 주제

미국 독립 전쟁이 발발했을 때 영국과 프랑스는 북미 지배권을 얻기 위해 100년이 넘도록 싸우고 있었다. 그래서 미국 식민지 주민들이 1776년에 영국으로부터 그들의 독립을 선언했을 때, 프랑스는 그들에게 적극적인 지원을 할 준비가 되어 있었다. 그 전쟁에서 프랑스에 의해 행해진 중요한 역할은 1781년 체서피크 전투에서 잘 나타난다. 미국 육군은 버지니아 주(州) 요크타운을 포위했는데, 그곳에는 영국 최고 사령관과 그의 군대가 주둔해 있었다. 포위망을 뚫는 것을 돕기 위해 영국 군함들이 뉴욕에서부터 항해해 왔으나, 그들은 프랑스 군함에 의해 체서피크 만(灣)으로 들어가는 것이 저지되었다. 프랑스 해군은 요크타운의 영국 장군이 식민지 주민들에게 항복할 수밖에 없게 될 만큼 충분히 오랫동안 그 만(灣)을 지키는 데 성공하였다.

어휘
independence 독립 colonist 식민지 주민 declare 선언하다 represent 나타내다 force 《pl.》 군대 siege 포위 commander 사령관 station (특히 군인을) 배치하다, 주둔시키다 warship 군함 sail 항해하다 general 장군 surrender 항복하다 [문제] invasion 침략 emigrate 이민 가다

구문해설
[7행] The important role [played by the French in the war] is well represented by the 1781 Battle of the Chesapeake.: [ ]는 The important role을 수식하는 과거분사구
[9행] American ground forces had laid siege to Yorktown, Virginia, [where the top British commander and his army were stationed].: [ ]는 Yorktown을 선행사로 하는 계속적 용법의 관계부사절
[11행] British warships sailed from New York [to help break the siege], but they **were blocked from entering** the Chesapeake Bay by French warships.: [ ]는 목적을 나타내는 부사적 용법의 to부정사구. 'be blocked from v-ing'는 'block+O+from v-ing' 「…가 ~하지 못하게 하다」의 수동태 구문

문제해설
② 1781년 체서피크 전투를 예로 들면서 프랑스가 미국의 독립 전쟁 승리에 큰 역할을 했음을 이야기하고 있다.

22 ③ 글의 주제

모두가 제인 오스틴의 작품을 즐긴다. 그녀의 소설은 제한된 환경과 간단한 줄거리의 한계 내에서 인간의 본성이 얼마나 많이 드러날 수 있는가를 보여 준다. 오스틴은 여성들을 그녀의 중심인물로 삼는다. 여성들은 자신의 재치와 정신적 감수성을 이용하여 그들이 바라는 결말을 성취한다. 강한 자에 대한 약한 자의 성공이라는 이런 요소 자체가 확실히 오스틴의 인기를 일부 설명해 준다. 하지만 그녀의 매력의 더 큰 부분은 로맨스와 유머, 사람들 사이의 교제와 이별과 같이 반대되는 특징을 결합시키는 그녀의 능력과 관련이 있다. 마지막으로, 비록 그녀의 소설들이 사실주의에 바탕을 두고 있고, 주의 깊은 관찰에 의해 있을 법하게 만들어졌을지라도, 그것들은 본질적으로 사람들을 그녀의 소설에 빠져들게 하는 공상적인 작품이다.

어휘
reveal 드러내다 straightforward 간단한, 쉬운 plot 줄거리 wit 재치 moral 도덕적인; *정신적인 sensibility 감각; *감수성 bring about 야기하다 element 요소 in itself 그 자체로 account for 설명하다 appeal 매력 combine 결합하다 opposing 대조적인 connection 연결; *교제 separation 분리; *이별 ground …에 근거를 두다 credible 믿을[신뢰할]

수 있는 essentially 본질적으로 fantasy 상상, 공상; *공상적인 작품 lost in …에 빠져, 정신이 팔린 [문제] triumph 승리

구문해설
[1행] Her novels prove [how much human nature can be revealed ... plot].: [ ]는 prove의 목적어로 쓰인 의문사절
[10행] ..., **has to do with** her ability [to combine ... separations].: 'have to do with …' 「…와 관련이 있다」, [ ]는 her ability를 수식하는 형용사적 용법의 to부정사구
[14행] ..., they are essentially fantasies [that **let** people **become** lost in them].: [ ]는 fantasies를 선행사로 하는 주격 관계대명사절, 'let+O+동사원형' 「…가 ~하게 하다」

문제해설
③ 제인 오스틴의 소설이 인기 있는 이유에 대해 몇 가지 특성을 예로 들어 설명한 글이다.

23 ② 글의 제목

왜 좋은 일은 항상 특정한 사람들에게만 일어날까? 그것은 그들이 행운의 토끼 발을 가지고 다니거나 네 잎 클로버를 찾았기 때문일까? 물론 그렇지 않다. 그것들은 단지 어리석은 미신일 뿐이다. 현실에서, 전적으로 행운은 당신의 통제를 벗어난 것처럼 보이는 것들을 통제하는 것에 관한 것이다. 당신이 노력을 하면, 대개는 당신이 이런 것들을 보다 나은 쪽으로 바꿀 수 있는 능력을 갖고 있다는 것을 알게 될 것이다. 게다가, 행운은 인식의 문제이기도 하다. 좋은 태도를 가지고 있는 사람들은 보통 자신이 운이 좋다고 믿는다. 따라서, 그들은 그들에게 일어나는 좋은 일들에 집중한다. 반면에, 부정적인 태도를 가지고 있는 사람들은 좋은 일들을 무시하고 일어나는 모든 나쁜 것들에 집중하는 경향이 있다. 이것은 결국 그들에게 마치 자신들이 운이 나쁜 것처럼 느끼도록 만든다.

어휘
superstition 미신 be out of control 통제를 벗어나다 make an effort 노력하다 for the better 보다 나은 쪽으로 attitude 태도 tend to-v …하는 경향이 있다 occur 일어나다. 발생하다 [문제] perception 지각, 자각; 인식 matter 물질; *일

구문해설
[6행] ..., you'll often find [(that) you have the ability {to change these things for the better}].: [ ]는 find의 목적절. { }는 the ability를 수식하는 형용사적 용법의 to부정사구
[14행] This **ends up** *making* them *feel* **as though** they are unlucky.: 'end up v-ing' 「결국 …하다」, 'make+O+동사원형' 「…가 ~하게 하다」, 'as though' 「마치 …인 것처럼」

문제해설
노력을 통해 상황을 더 좋은 쪽으로 바꿀 수 있으며 자신에게 닥친 일을 어떤 태도로 받아들이느냐에 따라 운이 좋은지 나쁜지에 대한 생각이 달라진다는 내용의 글이므로, 제목으로는 ② '운은 태도의 문제이다'가 적절하다.

24 ② 글의 제목

당신은 webisodes를 보고, 당신의 frenemies를 주시하기 위해 sock puppet을 사용하면서 당신의 staycation을 보냈는가? 만약 그렇다면, 당신의 어휘는 미국 사회의 변화하는 유행과 함께 하고 있는 것이며, 당신은 이미 메리엄 웹스터 대학생용 사전의 최신판에 추가된 수백 개의 새로운 단어들의 일부를 완전히 익힌 것이다. '웹사이트에서만 볼 수 있는 짧은 에피소드'라는 의미인 webisode의 정의를 찾아보기 위해 '(알파벳) W' 부분을 펼쳐보거나, 가짜 신분들이 온라인 커뮤니티를 속이기 위

해 어떻게 사용되는지에 대해 알고 싶다면 'sock puppet'을 찾아보라. staycation은 '집에서 휴가를 보내는 것'으로 정의 내려지고, frenemy는 친구처럼 행동하지만 비밀리에 당신의 적인 사람을 말한다. 이와 같은 단어의 차용은 사회의 새로운 기술의 증가하는 사용을 반영한다. 이제, 대화와 문학 둘 다에서 사용되는 미국 어휘의 영구적인 일부로서 이러한 단어들을 무시하는 것은 불가능하기 때문에, 메리엄 웹스터는 그것들을 (사전에) 포함시킬 수밖에 없었다.

어휘

parallel 필적하다 collegiate 대학생용의 definition 정의(define 정의하다) identity 신원 deceive 속이다 enemy 적 adoption 채택; *차용(adopt 차용하다) reflect 반영하다 permanent 영속적인, 영구적인 alike 비슷하게; *둘 다 dismiss 묵살하다

구문해설

[11행] A staycation is defined **as** "spending vacation time at home," while a frenemy is someone [who acts like a friend but in secret is your enemy].: as는 「…로(서)」라는 의미의 전치사, [ ]는 someone을 선행사로 하는 주격 관계대명사절

[18행] ..., so Merriam-Webster **had no choice but to include** them.: 'have no choice but to-v' 「…할 수밖에 없다」

문제해설

사회의 변화에 따라 생겨난 어휘들과 그 의미를 설명한 글로, 제목으로는 ② '사전 속 신조어들의 예'가 적절하다.

25 ③ 도표 내용 불일치

위 도표는 일곱 개의 서로 다른 국가에서 자신의 구매에 현금 없는 지불 방법을 이용하는 것을 선호한다고 말한 사람들의 비율을 보여 준다. 대한민국은 도표상에서 4분의 3 이상의 사람들이 현금 없는 지불을 선호한다고 말한 유일한 국가이다. 프랑스, 스페인, 일본에서는 60에서 70퍼센트 사이의 사람들이 현금 없이 지불하고 싶다고 말했다. (비록 중국의 비율은 스페인과 일본의 비율보다는 조금 더 낮지만, 프랑스의 그것과는 같다.) 미국에서는 절반 이상의 사람들이 현금 없는 지불을 선호한다고 말했지만, 이 숫자는 대한민국의 그것보다 거의 20퍼센트포인트 더 낮다. 마지막으로, 필리핀은 현금 없이 지불하는 것을 선호하는 사람들의 비율이 가장 낮았으며, 이 비율은 중국의 비율의 대략 절반 정도였다.

어휘

cashless 현금이 불필요한 payment 지불 method 방법 purchase 구입, 구매 prefer 선호하다 report 보고하다; *…라고 말하다

구문해설

[1행] The above graph shows the percentage of people in seven different countries [who said {that they prefer to use cashless payment methods for their purchases}].: [ ]는 people in seven different countries를 선행사로 하는 주격 관계대명사절, { }는 said의 목적절

[4행] South Korea is the only country on the graph [where more than three quarters of the people reported {that they prefer cashless payments}].: [ ]는 the only country on the graph를 선행사로 하는 관계부사절, { }는 reported의 목적절

[15행] Finally, the Philippines had the lowest percentage of people [preferring to pay without cash], ...: [ ]는 people을 수식하는 현재분사구

문제해설

③ 현금이 불필요한 지불 방법을 선호하는 사람들의 비율은 중국이 스페인과 일본보다 높다.

26 ⑤ 내용 불일치

많은 사람들은 나폴레옹이 위암으로 죽었다고 믿지만, 최근의 증거는 그가 독살당했다는 것을 시사한다. 스텐 포슈푸드는 그의 책 '나폴레옹 살해'에서 나폴레옹이 정적(政敵)에 의해 독살되었다고 주장한다. 나폴레옹의 시신을 부검한 결과는 비대해진 간을 드러냈는데, 이는 비소 과다 복용의 징후이다. 나폴레옹의 가족들은 그가 죽기 몇 년 전부터 졸음, 불면증, 발의 부종, 과도한 체중 증가와 같은 비소 중독 증상을 보였다고 말했다. 포슈푸드 박사가 친척들이 보존하고 있던 나폴레옹의 머리카락 몇 가닥을 화학적으로 분석했을 때 비소 잔류량이 많다는 것을 발견했다. 비소 중독의 가장 충격적인 증거는 1840년 나폴레옹의 관이 다시 열렸을 때 발견되었다. 그의 시신은 잘 보존되어 있었는데, 이는 비소의 영향이다.

어휘

poison 독살하다 examination 검사 reveal 드러내다 enlarged 커진 liver 간 overdose 과다 복용 symptom 증상 insomnia 불면증 swollen 부푼; *부은 excessive 과다한, 지나친 chemically 화학적으로 coffin 관 well-preserved 잘 보존된

구문해설

[14행] ... was discovered in 1840, [when Napoleon's coffin was reopened].: [ ]는 1840을 선행사로 하는 계속적 용법의 관계부사절

[15행] His body was well-preserved, [which is an effect of arsenic].: [ ]는 앞 절 전체를 선행사로 하는 계속적 용법의 주격 관계대명사절

문제해설

⑤ 마지막 문장에서 나폴레옹의 시신은 비소의 영향으로 보존 상태가 양호했다고 했다.

27 ④ 내용 불일치

2021 하계 레크리에이션 프로그램

우리 동네의 연간 하계 레크리에이션 프로그램 등록이 4월 15일에 시작됩니다. 여러분은 오전 9시에서 오후 5시 사이에 593-927-2282로 레크리에이션 책임자에게 전화해서 등록할 수 있습니다.

야외 활동

올해의 야외 활동에는 농구, 축구, 테니스, 그리고 배드민턴이 포함되어 있습니다. 모든 프로그램은 주 3회 운영되며 8세에서 14세 사이의 아이들에게 개방됩니다. 세부 내용을 위해 저희 웹사이트를 방문해 주세요.

실내 프로그램

수영장, 체조 센터, 그리고 체력 단련실을 포함하여 동네 실내 시설 또한 이용 가능할 것입니다. 이 프로그램으로 여러분은 시설을 무제한으로 이용할 수 있으며 12세 이상의 모든 동네 주민에게 개방됩니다.

요금

• 야외 활동: 각 활동당 한 달에 25달러
• 실내 프로그램: 성인은 한 주에 10달러, 아동은 한 주에 5달러

어휘

registration 등록 annual 연간의, 한 해의 sign up (강좌에) 등록하다, 신청하다 coordinator 동격으로 하는 것; *진행자, 책임자 facility 《pl.》 (생활 편의를 위한) 시설 available 이용할 수 있는 gymnastics 체조 weight room 역기실, 체력 단련실 unlimited 무한정의, 무제한의 access 접근(권); *이용할 권리 resident 거주자, 주민 fee 요금

구문해설

[16행] This program **gives** you [unlimited access to the facilities] and *is* open to all town residents over the age of 12.: [ ]는 gives의 직접목적어, 동사 gives와 is가 등위 접속사 and로 병렬 연결

문제해설
④ 실내 체육 시설은 12세 이하가 아닌 12세 이상의 주민이 이용 가능하다고 했다.

28 ③ 내용 일치

융프라우 투어

융프라우는 알프스에서 가장 인기 있는 봉우리 중 하나입니다. 이 지역의 일일 투어는 스케줄이 빡빡한 여행자에게 안성맞춤입니다.

- **투어 유형:** 가이드 없음
- **소요 시간:** 8~10시간
- **신체적인 (능력에 대한) 요구사항:** 보통 (가벼운 하이킹 포함)
- **경로:**

이 여행은 인터라켄에서 시작해야 합니다. 우리가 제안하는 경로는 열차 타기, 케이블카 타기, 그리고 두 번의 단거리 하이킹을 포함합니다. 권장 출발 시각은 오전 8시입니다. 여러분은 오후 6시까지 시내로 돌아올 것으로 예상할 수 있습니다. 이 투어는 6월과 10월 사이에 즐기는 것이 가장 좋지만, 연중 가능합니다.

팁
- 예산이 빠듯한 경우, 점심을 싸 오셔도 됩니다.
- 겨울철에는 관광 안내소에서 산길 상태를 확인하세요.

어휘
peak 절정; *(산의) 봉우리   region 지역   tight (여유가 없이) 빠듯한, 빡빡한   duration (지속하는) 기간   physical 육체[신체]의   demand 요구(사항)   moderate 보통의, 중간의   recommend 권장하다   available 이용할 수 있는   route 길, 경로   year round 일 년 내내   budget 예산, 비용   trail 산길   condition 상태

구문해설
(10행) Our **suggested** route includes a train ride, a cable-car ride, and two short hikes.: suggested는 route를 수식하는 과거분사
(14행) This tour is best enjoyed **between** the months of June **and** October, but it is available year round.: 'between A and B' 「A와 B 사이에」

문제해설
① '투어 유형'에 가이드가 없다고 나와 있다. ② 가벼운 등반을 포함한다고 나와 있다. ④ 투어는 연중 가능하다고 나와 있다. ⑤ 예산이 빠듯한 경우에 도시락을 싸 와도 된다고 나와 있다.

29 ⑤ 어법

로타바이러스는 위와 장을 감염시키는 바이러스이다. 그것은 선진국과 개발도상국 모두에서 동일하게 흔하며, 전 세계의 유아와 어린이들 사이에서 심한 설사의 가장 빈번한 원인이다. 6개월에서 24개월 사이의 아이들이 그것에 걸릴 위험이 가장 높으며, 다른 바이러스성 변종들로 인한 재발 감염이 가능하다. 성인들 또한 이 바이러스에 감염되기도 하지만, 그들의 증상은 대개 아이들의 것보다 더 약하다. 이 바이러스에 감염된 때부터 증상이 나타나기 시작하는 때까지의 시간은 약 48시간이다. 열, 구토, 묽은 설사가 가장 흔한 증상들이다. 로타바이러스 감염을 예방하기 위해서는 자주 손을 씻는 것이 권고된다. 감염된 아이들은 설사가 멈출 때까지 학교나 보육원에 가지 말고 집에 있어야 한다.

어휘
infect 감염시키다(infection 감염)   bowel 장(腸)   diarrhea 설사   infant 유아, 아기   recur 되돌아가다; *재발하다   viral 바이러스성의   strain 종족; *변종   contract 줄어들다; *(병에) 걸리다   vomiting 구토   watery 물의; *묽은

구문해설
(5행) Children between the ages of six and twenty-four months have the highest risk of [catching it], and **recurring** infections with different viral strains are possible.: [ ]는 전치사 of의 목적어로 쓰인 동명사구, recurring은 infections를 수식하는 현재분사
(9행) ..., their symptoms are usually milder than **those** of children.: those는 symptoms를 지칭
(10행) The time period **from** [when you are infected with the virus] **to** [when symptoms start showing] is around 48 hours.: 'from A to B' 「A에서 B까지」, 두 개의 [ ]는 특정 시간을 나타내는 관계부사절

문제해설
⑤ 문맥상 아이들이 바이러스에 '감염된' 것이므로 현재분사 Infecting을 과거분사 Infected로 고쳐야 한다.

30 ⑤ 어휘

웹사이트는 눈을 즐겁게 해야 한다. 이용자들을 매료시키는 보기 좋은 외관을 만들어 내기 위해, 웹디자이너들은 애니메이션, 번쩍이는 문자나 아이콘, 움직이는 이미지, 그리고 비디오 클립과 같은 그래픽 도구들을 이용한다. 그럼에도 불구하고 색상은 가장 효과적인 웹디자인 도구 중 하나이다. 웹사이트는 색상의 배합이 잘 조화되고 일관성이 있을 때 가장 매력적인 것으로 여겨진다. 웹사이트의 색상들은 서로 잘 보완해야만 한다. 그것들은 또한 웹사이트의 주제와도 잘 어울려야 한다. 예를 들어, 암 지원 단체의 웹사이트는 그것의 합리적인(→ 민감한) 주제 때문에 파스텔 계통이나 은은한 색깔을 사용할 수 있는 반면, 파티용품 상점의 웹사이트는 신나는 기분을 자아내기 위해 밝은색을 사용할 것이다.

어휘
flash 번쩍이다   scroll 상하좌우로 움직이다   still 여전히; *그럼에도 불구하고   scheme 계획; *배합, 구성   well balanced 균형이 잡힌   consistent 일관된   complement 보완하다   go well with …와 잘 어울리다   theme 주제   subtle 미묘한; *옅은, 은은한   sensible 합리적인

구문해설
(1행) [To create a pleasant appearance {that attracts users}], web designers use graphic tools **such as** ...: [ ]는 목적을 나타내는 부사적 용법의 to부정사구, { }는 a pleasant appearance를 수식하는 주격 관계대명사절, 'such as' 「…와 같은」

문제해설
⑤ 웹사이트의 색상은 주제와 잘 어울려야 한다는 내용에서 암 지원 단체가 다루는 주제가 합리적이라고 하는 것은 적절하지 않으므로, sensible(합리적인)을 sensitive(민감한) 등으로 고쳐야 한다.

31 ⑤ 빈칸 추론

제품의 가격을 협상할 때, 똑똑한 영업사원들은 종종 고객이 지불하고자 하는 최고 가격에 도달했다고 느낄 때까지 밀고 당기기를 한다. 이 시점에서 그들은 그들도 자신의 한계에 도달했다는 것을 드러낼 가능성이 있다. 그들은 "저는 가격을 더 낮추고 싶지만, 제 상사가 이보다 더 낮게 팔지 못하게 할 겁니다."라고 말할지도 모른다. 고객이 이 정보를 고려하게 한 다음에, 그리고 나서 그들은 심호흡을 한 번 하고, "좋습니다, 이건 어떠십니까? 고객님께서 25달러만 더 내신다면 제 가격을 100달러 낮춰 드리겠습니다."라고 말한다. 능숙한 영업사원들은 고객들이 상호 간의 양보에 대한 제안을 받아들일 가능성이 있다는 것을 안다. 이는 고객이 그 영업사원이 하려고 하는 희생에 같은 식으로 대응할 의무를 느끼기 때문이다.

[어휘]

negotiate 협상하다 go back and forth 왔다 갔다 하다 maximum 최고[최대]의 limit 한계 bring down …을 낮추다 experienced 경험[경력]이 있는, 능숙한 accept 받아들이다 offer 제의, 제안 mutual 상호 간의, 서로의 obligation 의무 respond in kind 같은 식으로 답변하다 sacrifice 희생 [문제] effort 노력 distrust 불신 concession 양보, 양해

[구문해설]

1행 [When (they are) negotiating the price of a product], smart salespeople ... the maximum price [(which/that) he or she is willing to pay].: 첫 번째 [ ]는 때를 나타내는 부사절('주어+be동사'가 생략된 형태), 두 번째 [ ]는 the maximum price를 선행사로 하는 목적격 관계대명사절

14행 ... the customer feels an obligation [to respond in kind to the sacrifice {that the salesperson is willing to make}].: [ ]는 an obligation을 수식하는 형용사적 용법의 to부정사구, { }는 the sacrifice를 선행사로 하는 목적격 관계대명사절

[문제해설]

⑤ 빈칸의 앞뒤 내용으로 보아 제품의 가격 협상 과정에서 영업사원과 고객이 서로 '양보'를 한다는 것이 적절하다.

32 ⑤ 빈칸 추론

사진작가에게 여러 가지가 필요하기는 하지만, 그들이 반드시 배워야 하는 가장 중요한 것 중 하나는 사물을 다른 시각에서 보는 것이다. 예를 들어, 호수에서 완벽한 풍경 사진을 찍으려고 할 때, 사진작가는 수면에 비친 영상이 더 흥미롭다는 점을 발견하게 될지도 모른다. 혹은 인물 사진을 찍을 때, 색다른 배경을 선택하거나 자연스러운 자세를 취하고 있는 피사체를 잡아낼 수도 있다. 평상시처럼 수평이나 수직의 방법으로 사진의 구도를 잡는 대신, 사진작가는 좀 더 극적인 효과를 위해서 다른 각도를 택할 수도 있다. 사진작가는 초점을 맞추고 있는 피사체 너머를 보고 한 점의 추상적인 예술 작품을 발견할 수도 있다.

[어휘]

landscape 풍경 reflection 반사, 영상 surface 표면, 수면 portrait 초상화, 인물 사진 subject 주제; *피사체 posture 자세, 태도 frame 구도를 잡다 horizontal 수평의 vertical 수직의 fashion 방법, 방식 angle 각도 abstract 추상적인 [문제] by the book 규칙대로

[구문해설]

4행 ..., [when (the photographer is) trying to take a perfect landscape photo at a lake], the photographer might find ...: [ ]는 때를 나타내는 부사절('주어+be동사'가 생략된 형태)

[문제해설]

빈칸 다음의 예들을 살펴보면, 사진작가가 작품을 위해 다양한 시각으로 사물을 보는 방법을 제시하고 있으므로 빈칸에는 ⑤가 가장 적절하다.

33 ② 빈칸 추론

음식은 우리의 배를 채우는 것 이상의 일을 한다. 그것은 감정 또한 만족시킨다. 그래서 당신은 기분이 좋을 때 스테이크나 피자를 찾게 될지 모른다. 마찬가지로 슬플 때는 아이스크림과 초콜릿을 찾을 것이다. 이렇듯 배고픔 대신 감정에 반응하여 먹는 것은 '감정적 식사'로 알려져 있다. 몇몇 의사들은 과식의 75퍼센트가 감정적 식사로 인한 것이라고 추정한다. 우울함, 외로움, 분노, 걱정, 좌절, 스트레스, 낮은 자존감, 그리고 인간 관계에서의 문제와 같은 감정들이 모두 감정적 식사로 이어질 수 있는 자극들이다. 하지만 어떤 문제에 직면할 때마다 음식에 의존하는 것은 우리가 인생의 문제에 대처하는 데 필요한 기술을 습득하는 것을 방해하

는 매우 자기 파괴적인 습관이 될 수 있다. 우리는 지나친 과식으로 인해 자신을 해치고 있음을 알지만, 자신에게나 주변 사람들에게 만족하지 못하기 때문에 결국 계속해서 과식을 한다.

[어휘]

in response to …에 응하여 estimate 추산하다 frustration 좌절, 낙담 self-esteem 자존감 trigger 방아쇠; *자극, 계기 turn to …에 의존하다 hinder 방해하다, 막다 acquire …을 습득하다 deal with …에 대처하다 [문제] self-destructive 자기 파괴적인 relieve 경감하다, 덜다

[구문해설]

8행 **Such** feelings **as** depression, ... are all triggers [which can lead to emotional eating].: 'such ... as ~' 「~와 같은 …」, [ ]는 triggers를 선행사로 하는 주격 관계대명사절

13행 ... a highly self-destructive habit [that **hinders** us **from acquiring** the skills {(which/that) we need to ... problems}].: [ ]는 a highly self-destructive habit을 선행사로 하는 주격 관계대명사절, 'hinder+O+from v-ing' 「…가 ~하는 것을 막다」, { }는 the skills를 선행사로 하는 목적격 관계대명사절

[문제해설]

빈칸 앞뒤에서 부정적인 감정이 감정적 식사로 이어질 수 있고, 이것은 우리 자신을 해칠 수 있다고 했으므로 ②가 가장 적절하다.

34 ④ 빈칸 추론

'레드헤링'이라는 용어는 오래된 사냥 전통에서 비롯되었다. 청어는 사냥꾼들이 어린 사냥개들에게 사냥할 동물의 냄새를 따라가도록 훈련을 시킬 때 종종 사용했던 생선이다. 사냥꾼들은 냄새나는 생선이 개들의 주의를 흐트러뜨리는지 알아보기 위해 그들의 길을 가로질러 냄새나는 생선을 끌고 감으로써 개들을 시험해보곤 했다. 오늘날, 우리는 그 용어를 문학에 대한 논의나 토론에서 가장 흔히 사용한다. 소설에서, 레드헤링은 중요해 보이지만 사실은 단순히 독자를 속이기 위해 작가에 의해 사용된 사건이나 등장인물일 수 있다. 토론에서, 레드헤링은 토론의 실질적인 주제로부터 청중의 주목을 흐트러뜨리는 주장이다. 비록 레드헤링의 의미가 실제적인 것에서 추상적인 것으로 바뀌었지만, 그것은 여전히 <u>무관한 요소를 도입함으로써</u> 누군가의 주의를 다른 데로 돌리는 것을 지칭한다.

[어휘]

herring 청어 drag 끌다 distract (주의를) 흐트러뜨리다 discussion 논의 literature 문학 debate 토론 fiction 소설 trick 속이다 argument 논거, 주장 divert 방향을 바꾸게 하다; *다른 데로 돌리다 [문제] critical 결정적인 irrelevant 무관한, 상관없는 element 요소

[구문해설]

2행 A herring is a fish [that was often used by hunters when they trained young hunting dogs {to follow a hunted animal's scent}].: [ ]는 a fish를 선행사로 하는 주격 관계대명사절, { }는 trained의 목적격 보어로 쓰인 to부정사구

4행 The hunters **would** test the dogs *by dragging* the smelly fish across their path [to see {if it would distract them}].: would는 「…하곤 했다」라는 뜻으로 과거의 습관을 나타냄, 'by v-ing' 「…함으로써」, [ ]는 목적을 나타내는 부사적 용법의 to부정사구, { }는 see의 목적절, if는 「…인지 아닌지」라는 의미의 명사절을 이끄는 접속사

[문제해설]

레드헤링이 과거에는 사냥개들의 주의를 흐트러뜨리기 위해 사용된 생선을 뜻했고, 오늘날에는 독자나 청중의 관심을 다른 곳으로 돌리기 위해서 사용되는 사건이나 등장인물, 주장 등을 뜻한다고 했으므로 빈칸에는 ④ '무관한 요소를 도입함'이 적절하다.

35 ③ 흐름과 무관한 문장

우리는 집안에 있을 때 위험으로부터 가장 안전하다고 생각하는 경향이 있지만, 애석하게도 이것이 항상 사실은 아니다. 당신의 집이 건축되는 데 쓰인 유독성 자재들은 어쩌면 탐지하고 제거하기 더 어려우며, 당신의 건강에 부정적으로 영향을 미칠 수 있다. 예를 들어, 1978년 이전에 미국에서 생산된 페인트는 납을 함유할지도 모르는데, 납은 아이들에게 학습 장애와 뇌 손상을 일으킨다. (또한, 당시의 건축 자재들은 일반적으로 품질이 낮아서, 이러한 자재로 만들어진 집들은 붕괴의 위험이 있다.) 하지만 납이 첨가되지 않은 최신 페인트조차도 완전히 안전하지는 않은데, 많은 것들이 휘발성 유기 화합물(VOCs)이라고 알려진 가스를 방출하기 때문이다. VOCs를 들이마시면 이것들이 몸에 축적되어 호흡 곤란이나 어떤 경우에는 면역 체계에 문제를 일으킬 수 있다.

어휘
assume 추정[추측]하다 case 실정, 사실; 경우 potentially 잠재적으로; *어쩌면 detect 발견하다, 감지하다 get rid of …을 제거하다 toxic 유독성의 construct 건설하다(construction 건설) prior to …에 앞서 lead 납 disability 장애 at risk of …의 위험에 처한 collapse 붕괴 lead-free 납이 첨가되지 않은 give off …을 방출하다 inhale 숨을 들이쉬다; *(가스·연기 등을) 들이마시다 immune system 면역 체계

구문해설
(2행) ..., but sadly this is **not always** the case.: 'not always ...' 「항상 …인 것은 아닌」(부분부정)
(3행) [(Being) Potentially more difficult to detect and get rid of], the toxic materials [from which your home is constructed] can negatively affect your health.: 첫 번째 [ ]는 부대상황을 나타내는 분사구문, 두 번째 [ ]는 the toxic materials를 선행사로 하는 목적격 관계대명사절
(6행) For example, paints [produced in the U.S. prior to 1978] may contain lead, [which causes learning disabilities and brain damage in children].: 첫 번째 [ ]는 paints를 수식하는 과거분사구, 두 번째 [ ]는 lead를 선행사로 하는 계속적 용법의 주격 관계대명사절

문제해설
집의 건축에 사용되는 자재의 화학적인 위험성에 관해 설명하는 글이므로, 과거 건축 자재의 내구성에 대해 언급한 ③은 글의 흐름과 무관하다.

36 ⑤ 글의 순서

당신의 저축 계좌에서 당신의 돈은 기하급수적으로 증가한다. 즉, 당신의 첫 입금액은 이자를 받고, 나중에 그 이자는 그것의 이자를 받으며, 당신의 예금액이 증가하면서 계속 그렇게 된다.
(C) 마찬가지로, 개체군의 증가는 새로 태어난 구성원들이 마침내 성장하고, 번식하여 더 많은 개체군의 구성원들을 만들어 내며, 그다음에 그 구성원들이 번식하여 더 많은 생명을 탄생시킴에 따라, 기하급수적인 방식으로 발생한다.
(B) 그러나 당신의 돈은 무한히 계속해서 축적될 수 있는 반면에, 개체군은 이 같은 호사를 누리지 못한다. 모든 개체군의 성장은 그들이 인간, 동물 또는 식물로 구성되어 있든지 간에, 환경 속 자원들의 이용 가능성에 의해 제한된다.
(A) 따라서, 음식이나 물과 같은 생명 유지에 필수적인 자원들이 고갈되면 언제든지 개체군의 기하급수적인 성장은 멈출 것이며, 개체군은 질병과 굶주림으로 인해 고정되거나 감소하기 시작할 것이다.

어휘
exponentially 기하급수적으로(exponential 기하급수적인) initial 처음의, 초기의 deposit 예금 interest 이자 vital 필수적인; *생명 유지에 필수적인 deplete 고갈시키다 population 인구; 집단; *개체군 cease 끝나다, 그만두다 stabilize 안정되다; *고정되다 starvation 굶주림 accumulate 모이다, 축적되다 indefinitely 무기한으로, 무한히 luxury 사치; *드문 호사 reproduce 번식하다

구문해설
(19행) ..., reproduce, and create more population members, [who in turn reproduce and give birth to **yet** more].: [ ]는 more population members를 선행사로 하는 계속적 용법의 주격 관계대명사절, yet은 비교급을 강조하는 부사

문제해설
⑤ 주어진 글에서 예금이 증가하는 원리를 설명한 후, 이와 같은 방법으로 개체군이 증가하는 방식을 보여주는 (C)가 이어지고, 이와 상반되는 내용으로 개체군 증가의 한계를 설명하는 (B)에 이어, 그 결과를 나타내는 (A)로 연결되는 것이 자연스럽다.

37 ① 글의 순서

초기 인류는 질병과 질환이 초자연적인 힘에 의해 유발된다고 생각했다. 그러나 고대 그리스 의사인 히포크라테스는 다른 생각이었는데, 그는 그것들이 사람의 환경에 의해 발생한다고 믿었다.
(A) 더 구체적으로, 그는 특정한 장소에 '나쁜 공기'가 있고 이것이 사람들을 병들게 하는 것이라고 믿었다. 그의 생각은 마침내 질병에 대한 미아즈마 이론으로 알려지게 되었고, 고대의 많은 지역에 걸쳐서 받아들여졌다.
(C) 비록 이 이론이 정확히 맞지는 않았지만, 그것은 고대 의학이 옳은 방향으로 가도록 도왔다. 미아즈마는 썩고 있는 식물이나 송장과 같은 것으로부터 올라오는 독성 물질로, 공기를 독성으로 만든다고 여겨졌다.
(B) 사람들은 19세기 중반까지 그것이 콜레라와 말라리아와 같은 대부분의 질병의 원인이라고 계속 믿었다. 그 당시, 현미경의 사용은 과학자들이 대부분의 질병은 실은 미생물에 의해 생긴다는 것을 깨닫게 도왔다.

어휘
supernatural 초자연적인 physician 의사, 내과 의사 theory 이론, 학설 cholera 콜레라 malaria 말라리아 microscope 현미경 microscopic organism 미생물 medical science 의학 substance 물질 rot 썩다 corpse 시체, 송장

구문해설
(7행) ... and that this was [what **caused** people **to fall** ill].: [ ]는 주격보어로 쓰인 관계대명사절, 'cause+O+to-v' 「…가 ~하도록 하다」
(15행) At that time, the use of microscopes **helped** scientists **realize** [that most diseases are actually caused by microscopic organisms].: help는 목적격보어로 동사원형 또는 to부정사를 취함. [ ]는 realize의 목적어로 쓰인 명사절
(20행) Miasmas were thought to be poisonous substances [that rose up out of things like rotting plants or corpses], [making the air toxic].: 첫 번째 [ ]는 poisonous substances를 선행사로 하는 주격 관계대명사절, 두 번째 [ ]는 결과를 나타내는 분사구문

문제해설
① 초기 인류와 다르게 히포크라테스는 사람의 환경에 의해 질병이 생긴다고 믿었다는 주어진 글 다음에, 더 구체적으로 '미아즈마'가 사람들을 아프게 만드는 것이라는 생각이 고대 사회에 널리 받아들여졌다는 (A)가 오고, 앞서 언급된 the miasma theory of disease를 this theory로 받아 미아즈마 이론의 내용을 상술하는 (C)가 이어진 후, 마지막으로 현미경의 사용으로 질병의 원인이 미생물이라는 것을 알게 되었다는 (B)가 오는 것이 자연스럽다.

38 ② 주어진 문장의 위치

공포영화의 명백한 목적은 우리를 무섭게 하는 것인데 왜 그렇게 많은 사람들이 공포영화를 보는 것을 즐길까? 현실에서 공포를 느끼는 것이 기분 좋은 경험이 아님이 사실이지만, 공포영화를 보는 행위는 여러 가지 중요한 면에서 다르다. 그중 가장 중요한 것은 아마도 그것이 발생하는 환경일 것이다. 우리 대부분에게 영화관은 익숙한 장소이고 우리는 그곳에 갈 때 무엇을 기대할지를 알고 있다. 우리는 극장에 들어가 특정 영화를 보기 위해 돈을 내고, 공포스러운 장면들이 펼쳐지는 것을 볼 때 비슷한 취향의 사람들에게 둘러싸여 있다. 이러한 안전한 환경이 스크린에 나타나는 내용에 의해 발생되는 공포를 상쇄한다. 그 결과, 우리를 아주 즐겁게 하기에는 충분하지만, 현실의 공포 반응을 일으킬 만큼 충분하지는 않은 공포가 생긴다.

어휘
explicit 명백한   terrify 무섭게 하다   surround 둘러싸다   like-minded 생각이 비슷한   horrific 끔찍한, 무시무시한   unfold 펼쳐지다   offset 상쇄하다   fright 공포   generate 발생시키다   content 내용   exhilarate 아주 신나게 만들다

구문해설
5행 **While** *it* is true [that being scared in real life is not a pleasant experience], the act **of** watching a horror movie is different in several important ways.: while은 「…이긴 하지만」이라는 의미의 접속사, it은 가주어이고 [ ]가 진주어, of는 the act와 watching a horror movie의 동격 관계를 나타냄
10행 We pay money [to enter the theater and (to) watch a particular film], ... as we **see** the horrific scenes **unfold**.: [ ]는 목적을 나타내는 부사적 용법의 to부정사구, 지각동사 see의 목적격보어로 동사원형인 unfold 사용

문제해설
현실의 공포와 공포영화에는 차이가 있다고 설명한 후, 영화 관람이라는 행위의 환경을 구체적으로 설명하고 있다. 구체적인 설명 전에 여러 차이점 중 가장 중요한 것이 환경이라는 말이 들어가야 하며, 주어진 문장의 it은 ② 앞의 the act of watching a horror movie를 가리키므로, 주어진 문장은 ②에 들어가는 것이 적절하다.

39 ④ 주어진 문장의 위치

사람이 취할 수 있는 두 가지 유형의 사고방식이 있다. 하나는 '기회 사고'라고 불리며, 다른 하나는 '장애 사고'라고 불린다. 기회 사고는 어떤 상황이 제시하는 기회나 흥미로운 가능성에 초점을 맞추는 것을 의미한다. 그것은 낙관주의와 관계가 있다. 역사 속의 많은 유명한 지도자들이나 예술가들 그리고 발명가들은 이러한 유형의 사고방식을 갖고 있었던 것 같다. 긍정적인 미래의 경험에 대한 그들의 믿음이 새로운 발상을 시험해 보게 하고 새로운 도전을 시작하도록 독려했다. 반면에, 장애 사고는 새로운 모험을 시작하는 것에 대한 위험에 초점을 맞춘다. 이런 사고방식은 비관주의와 관계가 있다. 이것은 더 안전한 행동을 위해 위험을 피하려고 애쓰는 사고방식으로, 흔히 훨씬 더 적은 이익을 가져오게 된다.

어휘
obstacle 장애(물), 방해(물)   risk 위험   undertake 착수하다, 시작하다   venture 모험, 투기   adopt 입양하다; *쓰다, 취하다   be associated with …와 관련되다   optimism 낙관주의, 낙관론   possess 소유하다, 가지다   try out 시험해 보다   pessimism 비관주의, 비관론   in favor of …을 위해   secure 안전한   benefit 이익

구문해설
4행 **One** is called "opportunity thinking," and **the other** (is called) "obstacle thinking.": 'one ..., the other ~」「(둘 중의) 하나는 …, 다른 하나는 ~이다」
11행 Their belief in positive future experiences **encouraged** them **to try out** new ideas and (to) **undertake** new challenges.: 'encourage+O+to-v'「…가 ~하도록 격려하다」

문제해설
주어진 문장은 장애 사고에 대한 설명을 시작하는 내용이므로 기회 사고에 대한 설명에서 장애 사고에 대한 설명으로 전환되는 부분인 ④에 들어가는 것이 적절하다.

40 ③ 요약문 완성

얼룩 이리는 먹이 사슬에 매우 중요한 기여를 한다. 다른 큰 육식동물과 마찬가지로, 그것은 작은 동물들의 개체 수가 유지되는 방식에서 중요한 역할을 한다. 사슴 사냥꾼으로서도, 그것은 경쟁 관계의 포식자인 인간보다 더 도움이 되는 방식으로 일한다. 인간 사냥꾼은 흔히 여흥과 자부심을 위해 사냥하기 때문에 사슴들의 무리 중 가장 뛰어난 것을 자주 쏴 죽이지만, 얼룩 이리는 오로지 먹이를 얻기 위해서만 죽이기 때문에, 가장 약하고 나이가 많으며 부실한 것을 골라 죽인다. 따라서 인간은 사슴 무리의 질을 훼손시키지만 얼룩 이리는 무리의 건강함을 보존하고 그 지역을 유지하는 데 적합하도록 개체 수를 유지한다. 그 결과는 사슴 무리에게도 좋고, 얼룩 이리에게도 좋고, (사슴 무리가) 풀을 뜯는 지역에도 좋다.

어휘
contribution 기여   food chain 먹이 사슬   carnivore 육식동물   rival 경쟁하는   predator 포식자   sport 스포츠; *오락, 재미   herd (동물의) 무리, 떼   sickly 건강이 나쁜, 병약한   preserve 보존하다   geared to …에 적합한   sustain 유지하다   browse 둘러보다; *(풀을) 뜯어먹다   [문제] prey 먹이   stabilize 안정시키다   diminish 줄이다   sustain 계속[지속]시키다   brutally 잔인하게   selectively 선택적으로   mercifully 자비롭게   distinctively 특징적으로, 구별하여

구문해설
2행 ..., it has an important role in the way [populations of smaller animals are maintained].: [ ]는 the way를 선행사로 하는 관계부사절(선행사 the way와 관계부사 how는 둘 중 하나를 생략)
6행 While the human hunter often kills for ..., [regularly shooting the finest member herd], the wolf kills for food alone, [picking off the weakest, ... sickliest].: 두 개의 [ ]는 각각 앞의 절을 부연 설명하는 분사구문

문제해설
③ 얼룩 이리는 먹잇감을 <u>선택적으로</u> 죽임으로써 그 개체 수의 <u>균형</u>을 맞추며, (먹잇감) 무리의 건강함을 보존한다.

41 ①   42 ⑤ 장문

당신이 지난번에 무언가에 실패하거나 실수했을 때 어떻게 반응했는지 생각해 보아라. 대부분의 사람들이 그러므로, 당신은 자신에게 엄격하게 했을 것 같다. 자신을 가혹하게 재단하는 것이 긍정적인 특성이라는 믿음이 있다. 사람들은 그것이 자신이 의욕적이고 최선을 다하고 있음을 보여준다고 느낀다. 그러나, 연구는 이러한 종류의 자기 비판이 해로울 수 있다는 것을 제시한다. 이는 우리를 불행하게 만들고, 우리의 스트레스 수준을 높이며, 우리가 도전적인 목표를 설정하는 것을 멈추게 한다.

자기 비판적이기보다, 우리는 자기 연민을 실천해야 한다. 이것은 우리 자신의 실수를 관대하게 용서하는 방법을 찾는 것과 우리의 정신적이고 정서적인 건강을 장기적으로 보호하려고 노력하는 것을 포함한다. 자

기 연민은 자존감과 비슷하게 들릴지도 모르지만, 그렇지 않다. 자존감은 우리가 우리 자신에 대해 얼마나 긍정적으로 느끼는가와 관련이 있는데, 그것은 불행히도 우리를 지나치게 경쟁적으로 만들고 실패에 덜 대처 가능하게 한다는 것을 의미한다. 이는 높은 자존감이 성공하는 것과 다른 사람들이 우리를 좋아한다고 느끼는 것에 달려 있기 때문이다. 자존감은 부서지기 쉬울 수 있으며, 그것을 잃는 것에 대한 두려움은 어떤 사람들을 그들 주변에 있는 사람들에게 공격적이고 불친절하게 만든다.

반면에, 자기 연민은 우리가 불완전하다는 것을 인식하게 해준다. 그것은 또한 우리가 다른 사람들의 감정에 세심한 주의를 기울이기 더 쉽게 만든다. 결과적으로, 우리가 실수하거나 실패에 직면할 때, 우리는 자신을 탓하고(→ 용서하고) 우리가 아끼는 사람들을 상처 주는 것도 피할 수 있다.

어휘

react 반응하다   judge 판단하다, 재단하다   harshly 엄격히, 엄하게   quality 질; *특성, 특징   ambitious 야심 있는; 의욕적인   self-criticism 자기 비판(self-critical 자기 비판적인)   damaging 손상을 주는, 해로운   raise 올리다   challenging 도전적인   self-compassion 자기 연민   involve 포함하다   generously 아낌없이; *관대하게   emotional 정서의, 감정의   self-esteem 자존감   unfortunately 불행하게도, 유감스럽게도   overly 너무, 몹시   competitive 경쟁을 하는   depend on …에 의존하다   fragile 부서지기 쉬운   aggressive 공격적인   recognize 인식하다

구문해설

2행 **It** is likely [that you were hard on yourself], *since* most people are.: It은 가주어이고 [ ]가 진주어. since는 「…때문에」라는 의미의 접속사

4행 There is a belief [that {judging ourselves harshly} is a positive quality].: a belief와 [ ]는 동격, { }는 that절의 주어로 쓰인 명사구

16행 Self-esteem is related to [how positively we feel about ourselves], [which unfortunately means {that it can cause us to become **overly competitive** and **less able** to deal with failure}].: 첫 번째 [ ]는 전치사 to의 목적어로 쓰인 의문사절, 두 번째 [ ]는 앞 절 전체를 선행사로 하는 계속적 용법의 주격 관계대명사절, { }는 동사 means의 목적어로 쓰인 명사절, become의 보어로 overly competitive와 less able이 등위 접속사 and로 병렬 연결

문제해설

41 실패하거나 실수했을 때 자기 비판적이기보다 자기 연민을 실천함으로써 자신을 용서하고 주변 사람들의 감정에 세심한 주의를 기울일 수 있다는 내용이므로 ① '자기 연민을 통해 더 건강해지자'가 제목으로 가장 적절하다.

42 ⑤ 성공하는 것과 타인이 우리를 좋아한다고 느끼는 것에 의존하는 자존감과 달리, 자기 연민은 우리가 불완전하다는 것을 인식하게 해주기 때문에 실수하거나 실패할 때 자신을 용서할 수 있다는 것이 자연스러우므로, blame(…을 탓하다)을 forgive(용서하다) 등으로 고쳐야 한다.

43 ④ 44 ① 45 ③ 장문

(A) 언어는 끊임없이 진화하는데, 이는 현대의 독자들이 먼 과거의 문학을 이해하는 것을 어렵게 만들 수 있다. 다행히도 우리의 위대한 작가들 가운데 두 사람인 윌리엄 셰익스피어와 미겔 데 세르반테스의 작품은 오늘날에도 여전히 이해할 수 있다. 그들이 죽은 후 수 세기 동안 문법과 어휘에 많은 변화가 있었지만, 그들의 글을 이해할 수 없게 만들 정도는 아니었다. 흥미롭게도, 이러한 변화 중 많은 것들이 그 작가들로부터 영향을 받았다.

(D) 예를 들어, 셰익스피어는 명사를 형용사나 동사처럼 사용하는 것과 같이 그의 색다른 단어 사용을 통해 영어에 많은 변화를 만들어 냈다. 무엇보다 중요한 점은 셰익스피어가 영어에 1,000개 정도의 새로운

단어를 추가했다고 여겨진다는 것이다. 이것들에는 부사적 관용구 'full circle(원점으로)'과 색 'hazel(엷은 갈색)'이 포함된다. 그는 또한 'not'을 의미하는 접두사 'un-'의 사용을 대중화하는 데 기여했다.

(B) 셰익스피어와 달리, 세르반테스는 그가 쓰는 언어의 어휘에 기여한 것으로 알려져 있지 않다. 물론, 그는 스페인어로 글을 썼으며 많은 구절이 그 언어의 흔한 일부가 되게 한 것으로 인정받는다. 이들 중 일부는 심지어 다른 언어들에서도 차용되어 왔는데, 예를 들어 'the sky's the limit(하지 못할 게 없다)'와 'bigger fish to fry(더 중요한 일)'는 둘 다 세르반테스에 의해 사용된 구절의 영어 번역이다. 그는 또한 영어에 형용사 'quixotic(돈키호테식의)'을 기여했다. 그의 걸작인 '돈키호테'의 제목에서 따온 것으로, 그것은 '터무니없고 비현실적인'이라는 의미를 나타내기 위해 사용된다.

(C) 이런 이유로, 그의 강력하고 지금까지 오래 지속되는 영향력 때문에 스페인어는 종종 세르반테스의 언어로 불린다. 마찬가지로, 영어는 셰익스피어의 언어라고 불릴 수 있다. 그의 모국어는 시간이 흐르면서 세르반테스의 언어보다 더 많이 변했지만, 그가 400년도 더 전에 썼던 언어로 아직도 알아볼 수 있다. 16세기의 이 두 문호의 영향이 없었다면, 현대 영어와 현대 스페인어는 오늘날과 같은 언어가 아니었을 것이다.

어휘

constantly 끊임없이   evolve (점진적으로) 발달하다, 진화하다   distant 먼, (멀리) 떨어져 있는   inaccessible 가까이하기 어려운; *〈작품 등이〉 난해한, 이해할 수 없는   influence 영향을 주다   contribution 기부; *공헌, 기여   be credited with …한 것으로 인정받다   numerous 많은   adopt 채택하다; *차용하다   translation 번역   phrase 구; *구절, 관용구   masterpiece 걸작, 명작   impractical 터무니없는, 비현실적인   be referred to as …로 불리다   recognizable 알아볼 수 있는   unconventional 관습에 얽매이지 않는; *색다른, 독특한   adverbial 부사의, 부사적인   popularize 대중화하다

구문해설

1행 Languages are constantly evolving, [which can make **it** difficult *for modern readers* {to understand literature from the distant past}].: [ ]는 앞 절 전체를 선행사로 하는 계속적 용법의 주격 관계대명사절, it은 가목적어이고 { }가 진목적어. modern readers는 { }의 의미상 주어

14행 ... and is credited with **causing** numerous sayings *to become* a common part of the language.: causing은 전치사 with의 목적어로 쓰인 동명사, 'cause+O+to-v' 「…가 ~하게 하다」

22행 [(Being) Taken from the title of his masterpiece *Don Quixote*], it is used **to mean** "impractical and unrealistic.": [ ]는 부대상황을 나타내는 분사구문. to mean은 목적을 나타내는 부사적 용법의 to부정사

32행 **Without** the influence of these two master writers of the 16th century, modern English and modern Spanish **would not be** the same languages they are today.: without을 사용한 가정법 과거 구문으로, 현재 사실과 반대되는 일을 가정

39행 Most importantly, Shakespeare is believed **to have added** about 1,000 new words to the English language.: to have added는 술어동사(is)의 시제보다 이전에 일어난 일을 나타내는 완료부정사

문제해설

43 ④ 위대한 두 작가 셰익스피어와 세르반테스가 언어의 변화에 많은 영향을 끼쳤다는 내용의 (A) 다음에, 먼저 단어를 독특하게 사용하고 여러 새로운 단어를 만들어 낸 셰익스피어를 예로 든 (D)가 나오고, 이와는 달리 세르반테스는 다른 언어에서도 차용될 정도로 유명한 구절들을 많이 썼다는 내용의 (B)가 온 뒤, 이 두 문호의 영향력을 설명하는 (C)로 이어지는 것이 자연스럽다.

44 ① (a)는 세르반테스를 가리키고, 나머지는 모두 셰익스피어를 가리킨다.

45 ③ 세르반테스가 사용한 구절들은 다른 언어들에서도 차용되었다고 했다.

18 ②	19 ②	20 ③	21 ③	22 ④	23 ①
24 ③	25 ④	26 ④	27 ④	28 ③	29 ③
30 ②	31 ④	32 ⑤	33 ⑤	34 ③	35 ③
36 ④	37 ⑤	38 ⑤	39 ③	40 ④	41 ②
42 ⑤	43 ⑤	44 ⑤	45 ⑤		

18 ② 글의 목적

가랜드 씨에게,

저희는 거의 18개월 동안 당신의 아파트 세입자로 지내왔습니다. 저희의 2년 임대 계약이 곧 끝날 것이고 저희는 연장할지 말지를 논의해 오고 있습니다. 저희는 정말로 그 아파트를 좋아하고 이웃들도 훌륭합니다. 안타깝게도, 임대 계약 시 약속되었지만 아직 행해지지 않은 몇 가지 건물 개선사항들이 있습니다. 구체적으로, 저희는 당신이 주방 창문을 교체하고, 화장실 벽을 도색하고, 고장난 천장 선풍기를 수리할 것이라고 약속받았습니다. 유감스럽게도 이 개선사항이 다음 두 달 이내에 행해지지 않는다면 저희는 임대 계약을 연장하지 않을 것입니다. 하지만 행해진다면, 저희는 기꺼이 2년 더 계약할 것입니다. 저희가 좋은 세입자였다고 생각하며, 당신이 저희를 위해 이것을 해 줄 수 있기를 바랍니다.

진심을 담아서,

리사 슈미트 드림

어휘

tenant 세입자, 임차인   lease 임대차 계약   renew 재개하다; *갱신하다, 연장하다   unfortunately 불행하게도, 유감스럽게도   improvement 향상; *개선점   property 재산, 소유물; *건물   specifically 분명히, 명확하게; *구체적으로 말하면   replace 바꾸다, 교체하다   ceiling fan 천장 선풍기   sign 서명하다; *계약하다

구문해설

(2행) We've been tenants of your apartment for nearly 18 months.: have been은 계속을 나타내는 현재완료

(4행) ..., and we've been discussing whether or not to renew.: have been discussing은 현재완료 진행형, 'whether (or not) to-v' 「…할지 (안 할지)」('whether+S+should+동사원형'의 형태로 고쳐 쓸 수 있음)

(6행) Unfortunately, there are several improvements to the property [that were promised in the lease but have not yet been made].: [ ]는 several improvements to the property를 선행사로 하는 주격 관계대명사절, 관계사절의 동사 were promised와 have not yet been made가 but으로 병렬 연결

문제해설

임대 계약 만료를 앞둔 세입자가 계약 연장에 앞서 집주인에게 이전 계약 시에 약속했던 사항을 개선해줄 것을 촉구하는 내용이므로 ②가 글의 목적으로 가장 적절하다.

19 ② 심경

로버트는 그의 회사에 새로 입사했다. 첫날에, 그는 다른 모든 사람들이 집에 돌아간 후 일을 계속했다. 어두운 겨울 저녁이었다. 바람이 세차게 불고 있었다. 로버트는 딱 몇 분만 더 있다 가기로 결심했다. 그러나 그 순간, 어딘가에서 이상한 소리가 났다. 그는 일어서서 더 귀 기울여 들었다. 소리가 멈춘 것 같아서, 그는 다시 일을 하려고 했다. 그러나 그 때 그는 그 소리를 또 들었는데 그것은 점점 더 가까워지는 느리고 무거운 발소리였다. 로버트는 복도를 내다보았지만, 그곳엔 아무도 없었다. 발소리가 다시 움직이고 있었다. 발소리는 지붕 위에서 나는 것처럼 들렸! 갑자기, 발소리는 멈추었고, 로버트는 위에서 나는 낮고 부자연스러운 웃음소리를 들었다. 그는 비명을 지르면서 사무실 밖으로 뛰쳐나갔고 절대 뒤돌아보지 않았다.

어휘

get back to (화제·일 등이) …로 돌아가다   footstep 발소리   hallway 복도   unnatural 부자연스러운   rush out of …에서 뛰어나가다   scream 비명을 지르다   [문제] panicked 겁에 질린   exhausted 기진맥진한   regretful 후회하는   sorrowful 슬픈

구문해설

(1행) On his first day, he **kept working** after everyone else went home.: 'keep v-ing' 「계속 …하다」

(4행) Robert decided [(that) he would only **stay** a few minutes **longer**].: [ ]는 decided의 목적절, 'stay+(시간)+longer' 「(…만큼) 더 오래 머무르다」

(7행) It seemed **to have stopped**, so he tried to get back to work.: to have stopped는 술어동사(seemed)의 시제보다 이전에 일어난 일을 나타내는 완료부정사

문제해설

밤늦게 혼자 회사에 남아 일을 하는 상황에서 어딘가에서 들리는 이상한 소리 때문에 비명을 지르면서 사무실 밖으로 달려나갔으므로, 로버트의 심경으로는 ② '겁에 질리고 무서워하는'이 가장 적절하다.

20 ③ 필자의 주장

연구는 예술 교육이 학업 성취, 사회적 발달, 그리고 지역 사회 활동에의 참여를 포함하여 학생들에게서 나타나는 여러 가지 바람직한 결과와 밀접하게 관련되어 있음을 보여준다. 하지만 우리가 학교에서 예술을 가르치는 것을 지지해야 하는 또 다른 이유가 있는데, 그것은 바로 개인의 발달이다. 예술 교육은 학생들에게서 창의성, 자신감, 그리고 비판적 사고를 촉진한다. 한 보고서에 따르면, 이것은 예술이 아이들을 자신을 둘러싼 세계에 연결하고 새로운 방식으로 사물을 보도록 도와준다는 사실로 인한 것이다. 유아에게 클래식 음악을 연주해 주는 것에서 아이들을 미술관에 데려가는 것까지, 우리가 어린 학습자들에게 제공해야 할 다양한 종류의 예술 관련 활동들이 많이 있다. 학교가 이런 종류의 경험들을 제공하는 것이 중요한데, 저소득 가정의 아이들은 예술에 거의 노출되지 않는 경향이 있기 때문이다.

어휘

desirable 바람직한   outcome 결과   achievement 성취, 달성   development 발달, 성장   participation 참가, 참여   support 지지하다, 지원하다   encourage 격려하다; *촉진하다   toddler 유아   supply 공급[제공]하다   exposure 노출

구문해설

(5행) But there is another reason [(why) we should support teaching the arts in schools]—personal development.: [ ]는 another reason을 선행사로 하는 관계부사절

(9행) According to a report, this is due to the fact [that the arts **help** kids **connect** to the world around them and **see** things in new ways].: the fact와 [ ]는 동격, 'help+O+(to-)v' 「…가 ~하는 것을 돕다」로, connect와 see가 등위 접속사 and로 병렬 연결

(15행) **It** is important *for schools* [to supply these kinds of experiences], ...: It은 가주어이고 [ ]가 진주어, schools는 [ ]의 의미상 주어

문제해설

③ 예술 교육은 학생들의 창의성, 자신감, 비판적 사고를 촉진하는 등 개인의 발달에 도움이 되며, 저소득 가정의 아이들은 예술에의 노출이 어려우므로 학교에서 예술을 가르쳐야 한다고 주장하는 글이다.

21 ③ 함축 의미 추론

블랙홀의 바깥 경계인 사건의 지평선의 정확한 위치는 탈출 속도라고 불리는 것과 관계있다. 이것은 물체가 블랙홀의 강력한 중력에서 벗어나기 위해 도달해야 하는 속도이다. 물체가 블랙홀 자체에 더 가까이 다가갈수록, 그것이 도달해야 하는 속도는 더 커진다. 사건의 지평선은 물체가 빠져나오기 위해 빛의 속도를 넘어서야 하는 지점을 나타낸다. 이것은 아인슈타인의 특수 상대성 이론이 어떤 것도 빛의 속도보다 더 빨리 우주를 통과할 수 없다고 서술하기 때문에 중요하다. 그러므로, 아인슈타인의 이론이 틀리지 않다면 사건의 지평선을 가로지르는 어떤 것이든 결국 블랙홀에 의해 삼켜질 것이다. 이런 이유로, 한 천문학자는 사건의 지평선을 궁극적인 감옥의 벽이라고 언급했다.

어휘

horizon 지평선 boundary 경계 object 물건, 물체 break free 떨치다, …에서 도망치다 gravitational pull 중력 achieve 달성하다 exceed 초과하다, 넘어서다 escape 탈출하다; 벗어나다, 빠져나오다 theory 이론 relativity 상대성 incorrect 부정확한, 틀린 swallow 삼키다 astronomer 천문학자 ultimate 궁극적인, 최후의 [문제] method 방법 device 장치, 기구 observe 관찰하다

구문해설

[1행] The exact location of an event horizon, [which is the outer boundary of a black hole], is related to something [called escape velocity].: 첫 번째 [ ]는 an event horizon을 선행사로 하는 계속적 용법의 주격 관계대명사절, 두 번째 [ ]는 something을 수식하는 과거분사구

[5행] **The closer** an object gets to the black hole itself, **the greater** the speed it would have to achieve.: 'the+비교급, the+비교급' 「…하면 할수록 더 ~하다」

[7행] The event horizon marks the point [where an object would need to exceed the speed of light **in order to escape**].: [ ]는 the point를 선행사로 하는 관계부사절, 'in order to-v' 「…하기 위해서」

[13행] Therefore, **unless** Einstein's theory is incorrect, anything [that crosses the event horizon] will *end up being swallowed* by the black hole.: unless는 「…하지 않는 한」이라는 의미(= if ... not), [ ]는 anything을 선행사로 하는 주격 관계대명사절, 'end up v-ing' 「결국 …하다」

문제해설

사건의 지평선은 물체가 블랙홀에서 빠져나오기 위해 빛의 속도를 넘어서야 하는 지점을 나타내는데, 특수 상대성 이론에 따르면 그 어떤 것도 빛의 속도보다 빠를 수 없으므로, 결국 사건의 지평선을 넘어서는 어떤 것이든 블랙홀에 삼켜져 두 번 다시는 빠져나올 수 없다는 내용이다. 따라서, 밑줄 친 '궁극적인 감옥의 벽'이 의미하는 바로 가장 적절한 것은 ③ '두 번은 넘을 수 없는 선'이다.

22 ④ 글의 요지

과학이 없다면, 오늘날 우리가 살고 있는 세상은 가능하지 않을 것이다. 과학은 끔찍한 질병의 치료법을 가져왔고, 인간을 달로 보냈으며, 우리가 세계의 어느 곳에서든 즉각적으로 서로 의사소통할 수 있도록 해 준다. 이 때문에, 최신 과학 연구 결과들이 뉴스에 발표되면 우리는 그것들을 사실로서 맹목적으로 받아들여야 한다는 의무감을 느낀다. 그러나 진정한 과학의 진보는 상당한 기간의 시간을 거쳐 발생하는 매우 느린 과정임을 깨닫는 것이 중요하다. 종종 이 과정에서 실수들이 발생되어, 결

국 훗날에 개선된 방법에 의해 수정된다. 당신이 뉴스에서 듣는 연구 결과는 큰 발견일 수 있는 만큼 실수일 수도 있다. 따라서 과학은 틀림없이 멋진 것이지만, 의심을 가지고 그것에 접근하는 것이 항상 현명하다.

어휘

oblige to-v 어쩔 수 없이 …하게 하다 blindly 맹목적으로 methodology 방법론 misstep 과실, 실수 breakthrough (과학 등의) 큰 발전, 새 발견 skepticism 의심, 회의

구문해설

[8행] But **it's** important [to realize {that true scientific progress … period of time}].: it은 가주어이고 [ ]가 진주어, { }는 realize의 목적절

문제해설

④ 새로운 과학 연구 결과는 수정·보완이 필요한 불완전한 것일 수도 있으니, 새로운 과학 연구 결과가 처음 발표되었을 때 그대로 믿지 말고 신중하게 접근해야 한다고 이야기하고 있다.

23 ① 글의 주제

모든 곤충들을 해로운 해충이라고 생각하기 쉽다. 결국 우리는 그것들을 없애려는 노력으로 매년 수백만 달러를 지출한다. 하지만 모든 곤충들이 같지는 않으며, 많은 것들은 실제로 상당히 도움이 된다. 곤충들이 없다면 일어나지 않는 하나의 중요한 과정은 수분이다. 벌들과 다른 곤충들은 식물과 식물들 사이를 돌아다니며, 꽃들이 번식하게 해 줄 뿐만 아니라 우리가 식량으로 의존하는 농작물 또한 번식하게 해 준다. 그리고 식물을 먹는 곤충들 또한 필수적인데, 그들은 특정 형태의 식물이 무분별하게 자라서 생태계의 균형을 뒤흔드는 것을 막기 때문이다. 곤충들은 동물들에게도 비슷한 영향을 미치는데, 야생동물의 개체 수를 지속 가능한 수준으로 유지시키는 질병을 퍼뜨린다. 그리고 이러한 동물들이 죽게 되면 그 사체를 처리하는 다른 곤충들이 있는데, 그것들은 사체들을 식물이 성장하게 해주는 영양분으로 전환하도록 도와준다.

어휘

pest 해충 pollination 수분(受粉) reproduce 재생하다, 번식하다 vegetation 초목, 식물 unchecked 억제되지 않은, 검사받지 않은 upset 속상하게 하다; *잘못되게 만들다 ecosystem 생태계 sustainable 지속할 수 있는 dispose of …을 없애다, 처리하다 convert 변하게 하다, 전환시키다 [문제] pesticide 살충제

구문해설

[4행] One essential process [that **would** not **occur without** insects] is pollination.: [ ]는 One essential process를 선행사로 하는 주격 관계대명사절, without을 사용한 가정법 과거구문으로, 현재 사실과 반대되는 일을 가정

[7행] …, allowing **not only** flowers to reproduce, **but also** the crops [(that) we depend on for food] (to reproduce).: 'not only A but also B' 「A뿐만 아니라 B도」, [ ]는 the crops를 선행사로 하는 목적격 관계대명사절

문제해설

① 곤충들이 생태계에 미치는 긍정적인 영향들에 대해 설명하고 있다.

24 ③ 글의 제목

생태 관광은 관광객들에게 그들의 여행지의 자연환경에 대한 정보를 제공하고 그것을 보호하는 데 도움이 될 기회를 제공하려는 의도이다. 그러나 일부 형태의 생태 관광은 이러한 바람직한 영향을 주지 못할지도 모른다. 사실, 많은 환경 운동가들은 이 정의가 실제로는 환경에 부정적으로 영향을 미칠 수 있는 활동들에 적용되고 있다고 생각한다. 심해 낚시

여행이 하나의 예이다. 그러한 여행은 관광객들에게 해양 환경에 친밀하게 접근할 수 있는 기회를 주기 때문에 종종 '생태 관광'이라고 광고된다. 그리고 여행 운영자들은 심해 낚시 여행 중에 시행되는, 물고기를 잡았다가 놓아주는 방침이 어떤 야생 생물도 피해를 입지 않는 것을 보장한다고 주장한다. 그러나 반대자들은 낚싯배들이 대기와 수질 모두를 오염시키는 연료를 사용한다는 사실을 지적한다. 게다가 물고기들이 잡힌 후에 풀려난다고 해도, 그것들 중 상당수는 그 후에 스트레스와 신체적인 상해로 인해 죽는다.

어휘
ecotourism 생태 관광   destination 목적지   environmentalist 환경 운동가   definition 정의, 의미   excursion 여행   intimate 친밀한   access 접근; *접촉 기회   marine 해양의   coordinator 조정자; *진행자   policy 정책, 방침   employ 고용하다; *이용하다   ensure 반드시 …하게 하다, 보장하다   opponent 반대자   substantial 상당한   subsequently 그 후에

구문해설
[1행] Ecotourism **is meant** *to provide* tourists with information ... and *to give* them opportunities [to help protect it].: 'be meant to-v' 「…하기로 되어 있다」, to provide와 to give는 등위 접속사 and에 의해 병렬 연결, [ ]는 opportunities를 수식하는 형용사적 용법의 to부정사구

[5행] In fact, many environmentalists feel [that this definition **is being applied** to activities {that can actually negatively impact the environment}].: [ ]는 feel의 목적절, is being applied는 현재진행형 수동태(be being p.p.)로 「…되고 있다」의 의미, { }는 activities를 선행사로 하는 주격 관계대명사절

[14행] However, opponents point to the fact [that fishing boats use fuel {that pollutes both the air and the water}].: [ ]는 the fact와 동격, { }는 fuel을 선행사로 하는 주격 관계대명사절

문제해설
자연환경을 접하고 보호하기 위한 취지로 만들어진 생태 관광이 실제로는 환경을 파괴한다는 사실을 심해 낚시 여행을 예로 들어 설명한 글이므로 제목으로는 ③ '생태 관광: 환경에 정말로 유익한가?'가 가장 적절하다.

25 ④ 도표 내용 불일치

위 도표는 5개 서로 다른 대륙의 2050년의 예상 노동 연령 인구수뿐만 아니라, 2010년 노동 연령 총 인구수를 보여준다. 유럽을 제외하고, 도표에 제시된 모든 대륙은 2050년에 노동 연령 인구의 증가를 겪을 것으로 예상된다. 중남미에서는 약 7,800만 명의 증가가 예상된다. 아시아는 2010년에 가장 많은 노동 연령 인구의 거주지였으며, 이는 북미 지역에 있던 것보다 10배 이상 많은 사람이었고, 이 상황은 2050년에도 변하지 않을 것으로 예상된다. (유럽의 경우, 2010년에 노동 연령 인구가 북미보다 더 많았지만, 2050년에는 북미보다 더 적을 것으로 예상된다.) 2010년에 그랬듯이, 2050년에 두 번째로 많은 노동 연령 인구는 아프리카에서 발견될 것으로 예상된다.

어휘
population 인구   project 계획하다; *예상하다, 추정하다   continent 대륙   working-age 노동 연령(의)   with the exception of …은 제외하고, … 외에는   rise 증가, 상승   unchanged 바뀌지 않은, 변함없는

구문해설
[1행] The above graph shows the total number of working-age people in five different continents in the year 2010, **as well as** the projected number of working-age people in 2050.: 'A as well as B' 「B뿐만 아니라 A도」

[5행] ..., all of the continents [shown on the graph] **are projected**

to experience an increase in their working-age populations in 2050.: [ ]는 all of the continents를 수식하는 과거분사구, 'be projected to-v' 「…할 것으로 예상되다」

[10행] ..., with more than **10 times as** many people **as** there were in North America, ...: '배수사+as … as' 「~배만큼 …한」

문제해설
④ 2050년에도 유럽의 노동 연령 인구는 북미보다 더 많을 것으로 예상된다.

26 ④ 내용 불일치

사람들은 연평균 2번에서 5번 정도 감기에 걸린다. 일반적인 감기에 대한 치료법을 발견하기는 어려울 것이다. 감기는 200가지의 다양한 바이러스 중 어떤 하나에 의해서 발생할 수 있다. 그러므로 치료법을 개발하는 것은 말 그대로 수백 가지의 백신을 찾아내는 것을 의미한다. 게다가 몇몇 감기 바이러스는 자신의 분자 형태를 바꿀 수 있다. 따라서 비록 우리가 올해 어떤 한 감기 바이러스에 면역이 된다 해도, 내년에는 우리 몸의 항체가 아마도 그것을 인지하지 못할 것이다. 또 다른 문제는 감기 바이러스 자체는 증상을 일으키지 않는다는 것이다. 우리가 증상을 보일 때쯤에는 바이러스 감염이 거의 끝난 상태이다. 사실 우리가 감기로부터 얻는 증상은 우리 몸의 면역 반응에 의해 생기는 것이지 바이러스 그 자체에 의한 것은 아니다.

어휘
on average 평균적으로   cure 치료(법)   literally 문자 그대로   vaccine 백신   molecular 분자의   immune 면역의   symptom 증상   exhibit 나타내다, 보이다   viral 바이러스(성)의   infection 감염   response 반응

구문해설
[13행] In reality, the symptoms [that we get from a cold] are produced ...: [ ]는 the symptoms를 선행사로 하는 목적격 관계대명사절

문제해설
④ 감기 바이러스 감염이 끝날 무렵에 증상이 나타난다고 했다.

27 ④ 내용 일치

특별 온라인 쿠폰
홍콩 키친
주말 저녁 뷔페
- 정상 가격: 일 인당 16달러
- 온라인 할인: 25퍼센트 할인
- 당신이 지불하는 금액: 12달러
이 쿠폰을 구입하려면 여기를 클릭하십시오.
설명 - 금요일과 토요일 저녁 6시부터 10시까지 제공되는 홍콩 키친의 주말 인기 뷔페에서 25퍼센트를 할인받아 절약하세요! 뷔페 예약은 24시간 전에 해야 합니다.
이 쿠폰을 사용하는 방법 - 이 쿠폰을 다운로드하고 출력하여 식당으로 가져와야 합니다. 이 쿠폰은 교환, 취소 또는 환불될 수 없습니다.

어휘
voucher 할인권, 쿠폰   discount 할인   purchase 구입하다   reservation 예약   in advance 미리   exchange 교환하다   cancel 취소하다   refund 환불하다

구문해설
[15행] This coupon cannot be **exchanged**, **canceled**, or **refunded**.: exchanged, canceled, refunded가 등위 접속사 or로 병렬 연결

① 할인된 가격은 일 인당 12달러라고 나와 있다. ② 금요일과 토요일에 이용할 수 있다고 나와 있다. ③ 24시간 전에 예약해야 한다고 나와 있다. ⑤ 쿠폰은 환불받을 수 없다고 나와 있다.

28 ③ 내용 불일치

아칸소 대학 도서관 – 학생 안내
도서관에서 책 대출하기
• 여러분의 학생증은 도서관 카드로서의 역할을 합니다. 따라서, 대학에 등록된 모든 학생은 책과 다른 자료를 대출할 수 있습니다.
• 책은 한 번에 2주 동안 대출될 수 있습니다. 하지만, 책(의 대출 기한)은 온라인으로 한 주 더 연장될 수 있습니다. 반납되어야 하기 전에 책은 (대출이) 두 번 연장될 수 있습니다.
• 연체된 책에 대한 벌금은 하루 당 1달러입니다. 반납되지 않은 책이 있는 학생은 다른 어떤 책도 대출할 수 없습니다.

도서관 이용 시간

	도서관 본관	컴퓨터실	학습실
주중	아침 7시부터 저녁 11시	아침 9시부터 저녁 9시	아침 7시부터 저녁 10시
주말	아침 10시부터 저녁 10시	아침 10시부터 저녁 8시	아침 10시부터 저녁 10시

어휘
information 정보; *안내 check out (도서관 등에서) 대출받다 act as …로서의 역할을 하다 enroll 등록하다 material 자료 at a time 한 번에 renew 재개하다; *갱신[연장]하다 additional 추가의 return 돌아오다; *반납하다 fine 벌금

구문해설
5행 Therefore, all students [enrolled at the university] are able to …: [ ]는 all students를 수식하는 과거분사구. 문장의 주어가 복수형인 all students이므로 동사는 are
12행 Students [with unreturned books] may not …: [ ]는 Students를 수식하는 전치사구

문제해설
③ 책은 한 번에 2주 동안 대출될 수 있고, 온라인으로 일주일씩 총 2번 연장할 수 있다고 했으므로 최대 대출 기간은 4주이다.

29 ③ 어법

지방은 최근 부정적인 이미지를 갖게 되었지만, 그것이 얼마나 필수적인지를 잊어서는 안 된다. 지방은 에너지를 저장하는 최상의 수단을 신체에 제공하며, 탄수화물이나 단백질보다 훨씬 더 효율적인 에너지원이다. 지방은 추위를 막는 보호막으로 그리고 내부 장기에 대한 완충재로 기능하며, 신체가 더 부드럽게 움직이도록 한다. 또한, 피부나 모발의 건강을 유지하며, 세포가 적절히 기능하도록 유지시켜 준다. 지방이 없다면, 체내에 흡수되기 위해서 지방을 필요로 하는 몇 가지 주요 비타민들을 이용할 방법이 없을 것이다. 더구나, 어떤 지방은 필수적인 성장 요소를 제공하고, 면역 체계를 강화하며, 다른 음식의 소화를 돕는 지방산을 포함하고 있다.

어휘
acquire 얻다, 획득하다 carbohydrate 탄수화물 protein 단백질 cushioning 완충재 internal 내부의 organ 장기, 기관 cell 세포 utilize 활용하다, 사용하다 be absorbed into …에 흡수되다 strengthen 강화하다 immune system 면역 체계 digestion 소화

구문해설
4행 … a far more efficient energy source …: far는 「훨씬」이라는 의미로 비교급을 강조하는 부사
13행 … fatty acids [that provide …, strengthen …, and help … other foods].: [ ]는 fatty acids를 선행사로 하는 주격 관계대명사절, provide, strengthen, help가 등위 접속사 and로 병렬 연결

문제해설
③ if절 대신 without이 쓰인 가정법 구문으로, 문맥상 과거에 일어난 일이 아닌 현재 사실에 반대되는 상황을 이야기하고 있으므로 가정법 과거로 써야 한다. 따라서 주절의 동사 형태는 '조동사의 과거형+동사원형'인 would be가 되어야 한다.

30 ② 어휘

뉴턴의 운동 법칙은 축구공을 차는 것으로 설명될 수 있다. 선수의 발차기의 힘은 공에 운동에너지를 제공한다. 이 에너지가 (공의) 움직임에 저항하려는 성향을 제압하고, 공은 공중으로 날아간다. 그러나 두 가지의 힘이 그 공의 경로에 영향을 미치기 때문에, 공은 직선으로 오랫동안 이동하지 않는다. 그 첫 번째 힘은 중력으로, 공을 아래로 잡아당긴다. 이 힘은 공의 상승을 늦추고, 결국 공이 하강하도록 만든다. 비록 중력은 공의 수평 움직임에 영향을 미치지 않지만, 두 번째 힘인 공기 저항은 공의 수평 움직임에 영향을 미친다. 공은 허공을 가로질러 움직이면서 공기 분자들을 밀고 나가야 한다. 이것이 공의 수평 움직임을 느리게 한다. 이 두 가지 힘들의 최종 결과는 공이 곡선으로 이동하는 것이다.

어휘
overpower 이기다, 제압하다 resist 저항하다(resistance 저항력) set off 시작하다, 출발하다 gravity 중력 accelerate 가속화하다 decelerate 속도를 줄이다 ascent 상승 descend 내려가다 horizontal 수평의, 가로의 molecule 분자

구문해설
10행 Although gravity has no effect on the horizontal motion of the ball, the second force, air resistance, does.: does는 대동사로 has effect on the horizontal motion of the ball을 의미

문제해설
② (A) 선수의 발차기의 힘이 움직임에 저항하려는 성향보다 커야 공이 공중으로 날아갈 수 있으므로, '제압하다(overpowers)'가 적절하다. (B) 공을 아래로 잡아당기는 힘인 중력에 대한 설명 부분이므로, 공의 상승을 '늦추다(decelerates)'가 적절하다. (C) 공이 수평 움직임을 할 때 공기 분자를 밀고 간다고 했으므로, 이는 수평 움직임을 '느리게 한다(slows)'고 하는 것이 적절하다.

31 ④ 빈칸 추론

작가들은 단어를 아껴 써야 한다. 제한된 공간을 가지고 작업하기 때문에, 그들은 가능한 한 많은 의미를 각 문장에 압축해 넣는 언어에 의존한다. 작가들이 자주 사용하는 한 언어학적 도구는 다른 단어로부터 명사를 만드는 것이다. 대개 이것은 -ion, -ence, -ship, -ness, -ity, 또는 -ment와 같은 특별한 '명사형' 접미사를 덧붙이는 것을 포함한다. 예를 들어, 다음 문장을 생각해 보자. '점점 더 많은 사람들이 지방에서 도시로 이주하고 있기 때문에, 많은 도시 지역들은 지나치게 발달되었다.' 이 문장은 'migrating'과 'overdeveloped'를 명사로 바꿈으로써, 같은 의미를 더 적은 수의 단어로 표현하여 경제적으로 사용될 수 있다. '지방에서 도시로의 이주 증가는 도시의 과잉 발달을 가져왔다'와 같이 말이다.

어휘
economical 경제적인; *절약하는 squeeze 압착하다, 밀어 넣다 linguistic 언어의, 언어학상의 suffix 접미사 overdevelop 지나치게 발달시키다

economize 절약하다; *경제적으로 사용하다   [문제] descriptive 묘사적인, 설명적인 elimination 제거 adjective 형용사 substitution 대체 active verb 능동형 동사 passive 수동의; *수동태의

구문해설
[2행] ..., they rely on language [that squeezes **as** much meaning **as possible** into each sentence].: [ ]는 language를 선행사로 하는 주격 관계대명사절, 'as ... as possible' 「가능한 한 …한[하게]」

문제해설
빈칸 이후에 단어를 명사화하는 방법과 그 예시가 제시되었으므로 빈칸에 들어갈 언어학적 도구는 ④ '다른 단어로부터 명사를 만드는 것'이다.

32 ⑤ 빈칸 추론

1901년 저서 '일상생활의 정신 병리학'에서, 지그문트 프로이트는 그가 '프로이트적 실언'이라고 칭한 것에 대해 논했다. 프로이트에 따르면, 프로이트적 실언은 우리가 마음속에 간직하고자 했던 생각을 발설하는 실수이다. 여기 한 예가 있다. 한 젊은 여성이 면접을 보러 가서 면접관이 코에 커다란 반창고를 붙이고 있는 것을 즉시 알아챘다. 그녀는 좋은 인상을 남겨야 하기 때문에, 그의 기분을 상하게 하는 것을 두려워하여 그것을 언급하지 않겠다고 마음먹는다. 그때, 그녀는 그의 책상 위 꽃병에 있는 장미 한 송이를 보고 분위기를 풀어보고자 그 장미에 대한 언급을 하기로 한다. 그녀는 그를 보고 말한다. "어머, 멋진 코네요. 어디서 났나요?"

어휘
slip 미끄럼; (가벼운) 실수, *실언 bandage 붕대 favorable 호의적인, 좋은 mention 언급하다 for fear of …을 두려워하여 make a remark 말하다 break the ice 딱딱한 분위기를 깨다 [문제] verbal 말의 subconscious 무의식적인 analyze 분석하다 consciousness 의식 keep to oneself 남에게 알리지 않다, 마음속에 간직하다

구문해설
[9행] ..., she promises herself **not to mention** it for fear of upsetting him.: to부정사의 부정은 'not to-v'

문제해설
⑤ 면접관의 코에 대한 언급을 피하려다가 무의식 중에 rose를 nose로 발음했다는 예를 통해 프로이트적 실언이 '우리가 마음속에 간직하고자 했던 생각을 발설하는 실수'임을 추론할 수 있다.

33 ⑤ 빈칸 추론

19세기 작가인 마가렛 풀러는 대단한 학식으로 존경받았지만, 심한 두통과 눈의 피로를 견뎌내야 했다. 루이자 메이 올콧은 대부분의 19세기 미국 작가들과는 달리, 자신의 가장 유명한 소설인 '작은 아씨들'을 통해 번 돈으로 생계를 꾸려 나갈 수 있었음에도 불구하고, 우울증과 불안감에 시달렸다. 그 시기의 또 다른 유명 여류 작가인 해리엇 비처 스토우도 비슷한 운명을 겪었다. 그녀의 소설 '톰 아저씨의 오두막집'이 세계적인 성공을 거두었음에도 불구하고, 알 수 없는 질병들이 그녀의 삶에서 떠나지 않았다. 호의적이지 않은 환경에서 여성 작가로서 살아남기 위해, 그들은 많은 장애물들을 이겨내야 했다. 하지만 무엇보다, 많은 19세기의 유명 여성 작가들은 신체적이고 정서적 문제 모두를 극복해야 했던 것 같다.

어휘
learning 학식 endure 참다, 인내하다 eyestrain 눈의 피로 depression 우울증 anxiety 걱정, 불안 majority 다수 support 부양하다 female 여성(의) fate 운명 haunt 괴롭히다, 따라다니다 hostile 적대

적인 conquer 극복하다 barrier 장벽, 장애물 [문제] achieve 성취하다 discrimination 차별 overcome 극복하다

구문해설
[6행] ..., could support herself with money [earned from **her most famous novel, Little Women**].: [ ]는 money를 수식하는 과거분사구, her most famous novel과 Little Women은 동격
[8행] [Another well-known female writer of that period], Harriet Beecher Stowe, suffered a similar fate.: [ ]는 Harriet Beecher Stowe와 동격

문제해설
⑤ 19세기 미국의 유명 여성 작가들이 겪었던 신체적 질병과 정신적인 문제들을 나열하고 있는 것을 통해 당대 여성 작가들에게 호의적이지 않았던 환경에서 살아남기 위해 이러한 질병과 문제들을 극복해야 했음을 추론할 수 있다.

34 ③ 빈칸 추론

대부분의 사람들은 박테리아를 두렵거나 피해야 할 것으로 생각한다. 하지만, 사실 우리 피부 표면뿐만 아니라 소화 기관 안에 살고 있는 박테리아가 있다. 이것은 충격적인 문제처럼 들릴지 모르지만, 사실은 우리는 이러한 박테리아와 공생 관계를 갖는다. 우리 몸은 박테리아에게 섭취할 영양분과 살 곳을 제공하고, 그 대신에 우리는 여러 가지 다양한 이익을 얻는다. 만약 위험한 세균들이 우리 피부에 집을 지으려고 한다면, 거기에 살고 있는 박테리아가 그것들을 공격해서 쫓아낼 것이다. 우리 몸 안에서 우리가 특정 음식을 소화하게 하는 것은 바로 박테리아이다. 그것들은 또한 비타민과 다른 필수적인 화합물들을 만들어 내며, 우리의 면역 체계가 제대로 발달하고 건강하게 유지되도록 돕는다.

어휘
bacteria 박테리아, 세균 avoid 피하다; 막다 digestive 소화의 surface 표면 disturbing 충격적인, 불안감을 주는 nutrient 영양분 consume 소비하다; *먹다 microbe 미생물, 세균 attempt 시도하다 attack 공격하다 essential 필수적인 compound 화합물 immune 면역(성)의 properly 제대로, 적절히 [문제] biological 생물학의 mutualistic 공생의 relationship 관계 convert 전환시키다 defense 방어

구문해설
[1행] Most people **think of** bacteria **as** something [to be feared and avoided].: 'think of A as B' 「A를 B로 여기다」, [ ]는 something을 수식하는 형용사적 용법의 to부정사구
[6행] Our bodies **provide** the bacteria **with** nutrients *to consume* and a place *to live*; ...: 'provide A with B' 「A에게 B를 제공하다」, to consume과 to live는 각각 nutrients와 a place를 수식하는 형용사적 용법의 to부정사
[11행] Inside our bodies, **it is** bacteria **that** *allow* us *to digest* certain foods.: 'it is ... that ~' 「~하는 것은 바로 …이다」(강조구문), 'allow+O+to-v' 「…가 ~하도록 해주다」

문제해설
빈칸 뒤에서 우리 몸이 박테리아에게 영양분과 살 곳을 제공하는 대신 박테리아로 인해 얻게 되는 여러 가지 이익에 대해 설명하고 있으므로, 빈칸에는 ③ '이러한 박테리아와 공생 관계'가 오는 것이 적절하다.

35 ③ 흐름과 무관한 문장

사막화는 전 세계적으로 많은 지역에 영향을 미치는 환경 문제이다. 이것은 현재 100개 이상의 국가들에서 발생하고 있으며 9억 명으로 추정되는 사람들을 위협하는데, 그들 중 다수는 가난하며 시골 지역에 산다.

한때는 비옥했던 토양이 말라붙어 날아가 버리면, 밭에 있는 농작물이 죽고 가축들이 굶어 죽기 시작한다. 그러면 식량 공급이 감소하고 토지는 폐허가 되어, 사람들은 어쩔 수 없이 고향을 떠나 새 삶을 시작하기 위해 가장 가까운 도시로 향하게 된다. (도시로의 이러한 이주는 시골 지역의 노인들이 자신들이 필요로 하는 도움을 받지 못한 채 남겨지게 한다.) 하지만 이러한 도시에서 그들은 지저분하고 혼잡한 환경에서 살아야만 하게 될지도 모른다. 만약 사막화 속도가 늦춰지지 않는다면, 그것은 대규모의 가뭄과 기근을 초래할 수 있으며, 이는 사람들이 피해 지역을 떠남에 따라 심각한 난민 위기로 이어질 것이다.

어휘
desertification 사막화 region 지역 threaten 위협하다 estimated 견적의, 추측의 rural 시골의 fertile 비옥한 crop 작물 starve 굶어 죽다 dwindle 줄어들다 ruin 파멸; *폐허 head 향하다 migration 이주 overcrowded 너무 붐비는, 초만원인 massive 대규모의 drought 가뭄 famine 기근 refugee 난민 crisis 위기(*pl.* crises) flee 달아나다

구문해설
(3행) ... threatens an estimated 900 million people, [many of whom are poor and live in rural areas].: [ ]는 an estimated 900 million people을 선행사로 하는 계속적 용법의 관계대명사절

(7행) Then, food supplies dwindle and the land falls into ruin, [**forcing** people **to leave** their homes and (**to**) **head** to the nearest cities ...].: [ ]는 결과를 나타내는 분사구문. 'force+O+to-v' 「…가 ~하게 하다」. to leave와 (to) head는 등위 접속사 and로 병렬 연결

문제해설
사막화로 인해 토지가 황폐해져 사람들이 고향을 떠나 도시로 들어가 난민이 된다는 내용이므로, 도시로의 이주 때문에 시골에 남겨지는 노인들의 상황에 대해 언급하는 ③은 글의 흐름과 무관하다.

36 ④ 글의 순서

여러분은 쉽게 구할 수 있는 재료를 사용하여 부력의 원리를 증명하는 실험을 수행할 수 있는데, 부력은 액체에 있는 물체를 가라앉거나 뜨게 만드는 상승력이다.
(B) 실험을 시작하기 위해, 일반 탄산음료 캔과 다이어트 탄산음료 캔을 구해서 그것들 모두를 물로 채워진 수조에 넣어 보라. 이제 그 두 개의 캔에 어떤 일이 일어나는지 관찰하라.
(C) 비록 둘이 같은 크기이고 같은 양의 액체를 담고 있다 하더라도, 여러분은 다이어트 탄산음료 캔은 물에 뜨는 반면 일반 탄산음료 캔은 가라앉는 것을 보게 될 것이다.
(A) 이것은 다이어트 탄산음료에 있는 인공 감미료가 일반 탄산음료에 들어있는 설탕보다 더 농축되어 있기 때문에 발생한다. 따라서, 다이어트 탄산음료의 평균 밀도는 일반 탄산음료의 그것보다 낮다. 그것은 더 큰 부력을 받게 되기 때문에 떠오르는 것이다.

어휘
demonstrate 증명하다 principle 원리, 원칙 buoyancy 부력 sink 가라앉다 float 떠오르다 sweetener 감미료 concentrated 농축된 density 밀도

구문해설
(1행) ..., you can perform an experiment [that demonstrates the principle of buoyancy], [which is the upward force {that causes an object in liquid to either sink or float}].: 첫 번째 [ ]와 { }는 각각 an experiment와 the upward force를 선행사로 하는 주격 관계대명사절. 두 번째 [ ]는 buoyancy를 선행사로 하는 계속적 용법의 주격 관계대명사절

문제해설
④ 쉽게 구할 수 있는 재료로 부력의 원리를 증명할 실험을 할 수 있다는 주어진 글 다음에 실험에 필요한 재료와 방법을 설명한 (B)가 오고, 실험 중에 관찰되는 현상을 서술한 (C)에 이어서, (C)에서 나타나는 현상을 This로 받아 이 현상의 원인을 설명한 (A)의 순서로 이어지는 것이 자연스럽다.

37 ⑤ 글의 순서

경찰관이 되는 것 또는 벌목꾼이 되는 것 중 당신은 어느 것이 더 위험하다고 생각하는가? 우리에게 영화와 뉴스에서 보여진 것에 근거하여, 우리는 그 답이 경찰관이 되는 것이라고 결론 내릴 가능성이 있다.
(C) 그러나, 이것은 통계상으로 틀렸다고 보일 수 있는데, 벌목꾼이 실제로 근무 중에 사망할 가능성이 경찰관보다 더 높기 때문이다. 우리가 이렇게 실수하는 한 가지 이유는 '가용성 추단법'이라 불리는 것 때문이다.
(B) 그것은 빠르고 쉽게 마음에 떠오르는 어떤 정보든 이용하는 것을 수반하는 일종의 정신적 지름길이다. 우리가 위험에 빠져 즉각적으로 결정을 내려야 할 때와 같이 특정한 시나리오 안에서는 이것을 하는 게 타당하다.
(A) 그러나 우리가 가장 쉽게 상기할 수 있는 정보가 반드시 우리가 필요로 하는 정보는 아니기 때문에, 그것은 우리가 잘못된 결론에 도달하게 할 수도 있다. 이는 우리가 더 신중하게 결정해야 한다는 것을 시사한다.

어휘
logger 벌목꾼 conclude 결론[판단]을 내리다 come to a conclusion 결론에 도달하다 recall 기억해 내다, 상기하다 deliberately 계획적으로; 신중하게 shortcut 지름길; 손쉬운 방법 statistically 통계상으로

구문해설
(2행) Based on [what we are shown in movies and on the news], we're likely to conclude [that the answer is {being a police officer}].: 첫 번째 [ ]는 전치사 on의 목적어로 쓰인 관계대명사절, 두 번째 [ ]는 conclude의 목적어로 쓰인 명사절. { }는 that절의 주격보어로 쓰인 동명사구

(11행) It is a kind of mental shortcut [that involves using **whatever** information comes to mind quickly and easily].: [ ]는 mental shortcut을 선행사로 하는 주격 관계대명사절. whatever는 '어떤 …이든'의 의미로, using의 목적어로 쓰인 명사절을 이끄는 복합관계형용사

문제해설
⑤ 영화나 뉴스에서 보여진 것을 바탕으로 벌목꾼보다 경찰관이 더 위험한 직업이라 결론 내릴 가능성이 높다는 주어진 글에 이어, 앞 내용을 this로 받아 이것이 통계적으로 틀렸다고 설명하며 가용성 추단법을 언급하는 (C)가 오고, 가용성 추단법의 개념을 설명한 (B)에 이어서, 그 사고방식이 가질 수 있는 문제점과 시사점을 언급하는 (A)가 오는 것이 자연스럽다.

38 ⑤ 주어진 문장의 위치

연구들은 유아의 첫해가 언어의 습득에서 매우 중요한 기간이라는 것을 보여준다. 태어날 때부터 아이들은 세계의 언어들에서 사용되는 거의 모든 소리들을 구별하는 능력을 가지고 있다. 하지만 그들이 첫해를 보내는 동안, 그들 주위의 사람들이 의사소통을 하기 위해 언어를 사용하는 방식을 들으면서, 그들은 자신의 모국어에서 사용되는 소리들에만 집중하기 시작한다. 결국, 그들은 그들 자신의 언어의 일부가 아닌 소리들의 차이점은 무시하기 시작한다. 이것이 모든 연령의 일본인들이 영어에서 흔히 사용되는 R 발음과 L 발음을 어려워하는 경향이 있는 이유다. 그것은 또한 왜 대부분의 영어 사용자들이 프랑스어에서 사용되는 모음을 어려워하는지를 설명해 준다. 유아일 때 그들의 모국어에 대한 집중 때문에, 그들은 더 이상 이 소리들에서 어떠한 차이점도 듣지 못한다.

어휘
infant 유아   crucial 중대한, 결정적인   acquisition 습득   distinguish between …을 구별하다   native language 모국어   eventually 결국   ignore 무시하다   have trouble with …로 고생하다

구문해설
5행 ..., children have the ability [to distinguish between nearly all of the sounds {used in the world's languages}].: [ ]는 the ability 를 수식하는 형용사적 용법의 to부정사구, { }는 nearly all of the sounds를 수식하는 과거분사구

8행 ..., as they listen to the way [the people around them use language to communicate], they begin to focus only on the sounds [used in their native language].: 첫 번째 [ ]는 the way를 선행사로 하는 관계부사절(선행사 the way와 관계부사 how는 둘 중 하나를 생략), 두 번째 [ ]는 the sounds를 수식하는 과거분사구

문제해설
유아가 첫해를 보내면서 모국어의 소리에만 집중하고 모국어에서 사용되지 않는 소리들은 무시하게 된다고 설명하고 있고, 그 예시로 일본 사람들의 경우가 나와 있다. 주어진 문장은 이에 이어지는 두 번째 예시에 해당하므로 ⑤에 들어가는 것이 적절하다.

39 ③ 주어진 문장의 위치

스포츠와 레크리에이션 교수인 제임스 프레이 박사는 오늘날 스포츠에서 흔히 사용되는 부정행위의 방법들을 일컫기 위해 '규범적 부정행위'라는 용어를 만들어냈다. 이는 상대방에 대해 우위를 점하기 위해 사용되는 전략을 의미한다. 이러한 전략은 실제로 규칙을 어기는 것은 아니다. 대신, 감독과 선수들은 경쟁 우위를 점하기 위해 규칙의 결함을 이용하는 법을 터득했다. 예를 들어, 야구 경기에서 홈팀은 종종 자신들의 강점에 효력을 발휘하고 상대의 강점은 최소화시키도록 경기장을 준비한다. 빠른 팀을 상대한다면 홈팀은 상대팀 주자의 속도를 늦추기 위해 베이스 사이에 물이나 모래를 뿌려 둘 것이다. 또한 몇몇은 우위를 점하기 위해 심리적 전략을 사용하기도 한다. 예를 들어, 상대편의 탈의실이 분홍색으로 칠해질 수도 있는데, 이는 이 색이 힘을 감소시키고 사람들을 덜 공격적으로 만든다고 알려져 있기 때문이다.

어휘
gap 틈; *결함   competitive 경쟁을 하는; *경쟁력 있는   advantage 이점; *우위   come up with …을 고안하다, 생각해내다   term 용어   normative 규범적인   cheating 속임수, 부정행위   refer to …을 가리키다, 언급하다   strategy 전략   opponent 상대편, 적수   arrange 배열하다; *준비하다   minimize …을 최소화하다   locker room (체육 시설 등의) 라커룸, 탈의실   aggressive 공격적인

구문해설
7행 This refers to strategies [used to create an advantage over an opponent].: [ ]는 strategies를 수식하는 과거분사구

13행 [If facing a fast rival], a home team will spread water or sand between bases [to slow down ... team].: 첫 번째 [ ]는 조건을 나타내는 분사구문으로, 의미를 명확히 나타내기 위해 접속사를 생략하지 않음. 두 번째 [ ]는 목적을 나타내는 부사적 용법의 to부정사구

문제해설
주어진 문장은 스포츠 경기에서 규칙을 어기는 것이 아니라 규칙의 결함을 이용한다는 내용이고 ③의 뒤에 이에 대한 예시가 나오므로, ③에 들어가는 것이 적절하다.

40 ④ 요약문 완성

많은 다양한 종류의 학생 포트폴리오들이 있기 때문에, 일반적인 포트폴리오를 설명하는 것은 어렵다. 사실, 강력한 포트폴리오는 단순히 특정 기간에 걸친 학생의 작업 전부를 보여주지 않는다. 대신 포트폴리오는 그 학생의 작업의 작은 부분만을 담고 있으며, 작업의 이러한 비중은 그 학생에 대한 세부적인 인상을 전달하기 위해 신중하게 선택되어야 한다. 예를 들어, 어떤 포트폴리오는 학생의 능력이 얼마나 발전했는지를 보여주고자 한다. 이러한 포트폴리오를 위해 학생들은 자신의 성장을 평가하면서 쓴 견해와 함께 초기와 후기의 작업 견본들을 포함해야 할 것이다. 하지만, 학생의 훌륭한 능력을 보여주고 최고의 작품을 보여주기 위해서는, 포트폴리오는 그 학생의 능력의 수준과 범위를 명확히 전달해 주는 많은 예시들을 포함해야 한다. 따라서, 포트폴리오에 대한 어떠한 결정이 내려지기 전에, 그 포트폴리오의 목적을 생각해 보는 것이 중요하다.

어휘
portfolio 작품집, 포트폴리오   typical 전형적인, 일반적인   challenge 도전, 어려운 일   contain 함유하다, 포함하다   portion 부분, 일부   convey 전달하다, 전하다   specific 구체적인, 명확한   progress 진전을 보이다   comment 논평, 견해   assess 가늠하다, 평가하다   range 범위   object 물건; *목표   [문제] take ... into consideration …을 고려하다   preclude 못하게[불가능하게] 하다   objectivity 객관성

구문해설
9행 Some portfolios, for example, seek to show [how a student's skills have progressed].: [ ]는 show의 목적어로 쓰인 의문사절

11행 ... include samples of early and later work **along with** a comment [(which/that) they've written {assessing their own growth}].: 'along with' 「…와 함께」, [ ]는 a comment를 선행사로 하는 목적격 관계대명사절, { }는 부대상황을 나타내는 분사구문

문제해설
④ 학생 포트폴리오에 무엇을 포함할지를 선택할 때, 그것의 목적이 고려되어야 한다.

41 ② 42 ⑤ 장문

비록 재산의 소유라는 개념에 대한 사회적 태도는 제정된 법에 기초를 두고 있는 듯하지만, 새로운 연구는 그 태도가 실제로는 근본적인 직감에서 나오는 것일 수 있다고 제안한다. 한 실험에서, 3세 정도의 아동들이 사회 규범들에 노출되기 전에 개인 소유물에 대한 개념을 어떻게 대하는지를 보기 위해 관찰되었다.

이전의 연구들은, 달리 믿을 만한 설득력 있는 이유가 제시되지 않는다면, 아동들은 일반적으로 사물을 소유한 최초의 사람이 그것의 정당한 소유자로 여겨질 수 있다는 생각을 받아들였다는 것을 보여주었다. 이 새로운 연구가 입증하고자 하는 것은 '창조적 노동'이 사물의 소유권을 이전하기에 충분히 설득력 있는 이유로 간주될 것인지 아닌지였다.

실험 대상자들에게는 파란 강아지나 빨간 고양이와 같은 특정한 유형의 점토 동물들이 각각 주어졌다. 그러고 나서 그들은 이 동물들을 서로에게서 빌려서 그것들을 변화시켰다. 일부의 경우에는 그들이 그것들을 완전히 새로운 것으로 변형시켰고, 또 다른 경우에서는 단순히 귀를 잘라내거나 꼬리를 덧붙이는 것과 같은 작은 변화를 주었다. 연구원들은 이러한 두 가지 수준의 창조적 노동이 어떤 영향을 끼칠지를 보고 싶었다.

그들이 발견한 것은 사려 깊은(→ 상당한) 노력이 가해지는 경우에 재산의 소유권이 이전된다는 것을 아이들이 받아들인다는 점이다. 소유권에 관해서 말하자면, 그 동물을 완전히 다른 것으로 바꾸는 것은 단순히 일부분을 덧붙이거나 제거하는 것보다 더 중요한 행위로 간주된다는 것이 분명했다. 연구원들의 결론은, 비록 창조성이 중요하기는 하지만, 노동이 소유권의 이전에서 가장 중요한 요소로 여겨진다는 것이었다.

어휘
attitude 태도, 사고방식   concept 개념   property 재산, 소유물   ownership 소유(권)   stem from …에서 생겨나다[유래하다]

fundamental 근본적인, 본질적인 intuition 직관력, 직감 observe 관찰하다 expose 드러내다, 노출하다 regulation (*pl.*) 규정, 규칙 previous 이전의 compelling 설득력 있는, 강력한 possess 소유하다 rightful 합법적인, 정당한 transfer 옮기다, 이동하다, 이전하다 subject 연구 대상, 피험자 transform A into B A를 B로 바꾸다[변형시키다] entirely 전적으로, 완전히 alteration 변화, 개조 considerate 사려 깊은 completely 완전히, 전적으로 conclusion 결론 creativity 창조성 matter 중요하다 factor 요소, 요인

(5행) ..., children [as young as three years old] were observed **in order to see** [how they dealt with the concept of private property before ... regulations].: 첫 번째 [ ]는 children을 수식하는 형용사구, 'in order to-v'「~하기 위해」, 두 번째 [ ]는 see의 목적어로 쓰인 의문사절

(11행) ..., young children generally accepted the idea [that the first person {to possess an object} could be considered its rightful owner].: [ ]는 the idea와 동격, { }는 the first person을 수식하는 형용사적 용법의 to부정사구

(28행) [What they found] was that the children accepted [that ownership of property was transferred in cases {where a considerable effort was made}].: 첫 번째 [ ]는 문장의 주어로 쓰인 관계대명사절, 두 번째 [ ]는 accepted의 목적절, { }는 cases를 선행사로 하는 관계부사절

41 이 글은 사물의 소유권이 발생하게 되는 창조적 노동에 관하여 이야기하고 있으므로, 글의 제목으로는 ② '무엇이 소유권을 발생하게 하는가?'이다.

42 아이들은 사물을 일부 변형하는 것이 아닌 완전히 다른 것으로 바꿈으로써 소유권의 이전을 받아들인다는 내용이므로, '상당한' 노력이 가해지는 경우에 재산의 소유권 이전을 받아들인다고 하는 것이 자연스럽다. 따라서 ⑤ considerate(사려 깊은)는 considerable(상당한) 등이 되어야 한다.

43 ⑤ 44 ⑤ 45 ⑤ 장문

(A) 1934년에 세계 대공황의 암울했던 시절 동안, 예외적으로 즐거운 사건이 보도되었다. 처음으로 알려진 살아 있는 다섯 쌍둥이의 탄생이 바로 그것이다. 더 흥미로운 것은, 그 다섯 명의 갓난아기들이 모두 여자아이들이고 일란성이라는 것이었는데, 이는 5천 7백만분의 1의 확률을 가진 통계적으로 일어날 것 같지 않은 일이었다. 그 아기들은 미숙하게 태어났으며 누구도 그들이 살아남을 것이라고 기대하지 않았지만, 그들은 어떻게 해서든 버텨냈으며 그들의 출생(조산)과 관련된 합병증을 이겨냈다.

(D) 애석하게도, 그들(다섯 쌍둥이)의 부모는 그들에게 이미 있었던 여섯 명의 아이들에 더해 다섯 명의 새로운 아이들을 양육할 준비가 되어있지 않았다. 그래서 정부가 개입하여 그 아이들에 대한 부모의 양육권을 박탈했고, 그들을 위해 특별히 만들어져 Quintland(다섯 쌍둥이랜드)라는 별명이 붙여진 병원 시설로 그들을 데려갔다. 이곳에서 그들의 분만을 담당했던 의사인 앨런 대포 박사의 보살핌 아래, 그들이 집에서보다 더 건강한 유년 시절을 보낼 것이라고 여겨졌다.

(C) 그 추측은 다섯 쌍둥이랜드가 관광 명소로 빠르게 탈바꿈하면서 잘못된 것으로 드러났다. 한쪽에서만(방문객들 쪽에서만) 볼 수 있는 화면 뒤에서 다섯 명의 일란성 쌍둥이 여자아이들이 놀고 있을 때 (흥미로운 장면에) 매료되어 지켜보기 위해 3백만 명의 방문객들이 전국에서 몰려들었다. 그리고 부당한 착취는 거기에서 끝나지 않았다. 그 자매들을 만나게 된 모든 사람들에게 돈벌이 기회가 되었고, 심지어 그들은 시카고 세계 박람회에서 전시품으로 다루어졌다.

(B) 9년 동안의 이러한 학대 후에, 그 여자아이들의 부모는 그들을 집으로 다시 데려오기 위한 정부와의 양육권 분쟁에서 이겼다. 그러나, 그

재결합은 (원래) 그래야 했던 것처럼 행복하지 않았다. 그 자매들은 그들의 형제자매들로부터의 적대감과 그들을 다시 데려오기 위해 매우 많은 시간을 소비했던 그 부모에 의한 육체적, 정신적 학대에 직면했다. 다섯 쌍둥이들은 모두 18세의 나이에 가족들과 인연을 끊고 집을 떠났고, 그들 스스로가 아니면 그들을 부양해줄 어느 누구도 없이, 계속해서 만족스럽지 않고 오히려 비극적인 삶을 살았다.

identical 동일한; *일란성의 improbability 사실일 것 같지 않은 일 prematurely (너무) 이르게 mistreatment 학대 custody 양육권 reunion 재결합; 화해 resentment 분노, 적대 sibling 형제자매 renounce 포기하다; *…와의 인연을 끊다 unfulfilled (욕구 등이) 충족되지 않은 assumption 추측, 추정 fascination 매혹, 매력 exploitation 착취, (부당한) 이용 come in contact with …와 만나다, 접촉하다 provide for …을 부양하다 step in 간섭하다; 참가하다 deliver 배달하다; *분만하다

(13행) The reunion, however, was not **as happy as** it *should have been* (happy).: 'as ... as ~'「~만큼 …한」, 'should have p.p.' 「…했어야 했는데 (하지 않았다)」(과거의 사실에 대한 반대를 나타내는 가정법 과거완료 표현)

(34행) So the government stepped in and removed ..., [taking them to a hospital facility {designed specially for them and nicknamed Quintland}].: [ ]는 부대상황을 나타내는 분사구문, { }는 a hospital facility를 수식하는 과거분사구

43 ⑤ 같은 성별의 일란성 다섯 쌍둥이의 탄생에 대한 내용인 (A) 다음에, 부모는 그들을 부양할 능력이 없어 정부에서 양육권을 빼앗아 양육을 의탁한 병원에 데려다 주었다는 (D)로 이어진 후, 기대와는 달리 아이들이 돈벌이 수단으로 전락했다는 내용의 (C)가 오고, 부모가 양육권을 되찾았지만 가족들의 냉대와 학대로 다섯 쌍둥이는 결국 집을 떠나 계속해서 불행한 삶을 살게 되었다는 (B)로 이어지는 것이 자연스럽다.

44 ⑤ (e)는 다섯 쌍둥이의 부모를 가리키는 반면, 나머지는 모두 다섯 쌍둥이를 가리킨다.

45 ⑤ Quintland는 다섯 쌍둥이를 보호할 목적으로 만들어진 병원 시설의 별칭이다.

18 ③	19 ①	20 ⑤	21 ①	22 ⑤	23 ④
24 ⑤	25 ④	26 ⑤	27 ⑤	28 ④	29 ⑤
30 ④	31 ③	32 ④	33 ③	34 ③	35 ④
36 ⑤	37 ③	38 ⑤	39 ③	40 ②	41 ②
42 ①	43 ②	44 ③	45 ④		

18 ③ 글의 목적

친애하는 파텔 씨께,
　우리 회사는 7월 19일에 주문한 전자 기기의 출하품을 최근에 받았습니다. 배송은 제때에 이루어졌으며, 모든 물품을 받았습니다. 그러나, 물품을 살펴본 결과, 출하품에 포함된 GL3100 스마트폰 25대 모두 결함이 있다는 것을 알게 되었습니다. 모든 경우에서, 화면이 제대로 표시되지 않습니다. 귀사 측의 이런 실수 때문에, 저는 귀사가 현재 스마트폰을 대체할 25대의 새로운 기기의 배송을 준비해 주시기를 요구합니다. 가능한 한 조속히 저에게 연락해 주십시오. 이전에는 귀사와의 모든 거래가 만족스러웠으므로, 우리가 계속 유익한 사업 관계를 유지할 수 있기를 바랍니다.
진심으로,
박한나 드림

어휘
shipment 수송; *수송 물품　electronic (pl.) 전자 기기　inspection 사찰, 순사; *점검　defective 결함이 있는　display 전시하다; *(화면에) 표시하다　properly 제대로, 적절히　arrange for 준비하다, 계획을 짜다　replace 대체하다　current 현재의　at your earliest convenience 가급적 빨리　dealing (pl.) 거래 관계　satisfactory 만족스러운　beneficial 유익한, 이로운

구문해설
(6행) ..., we found [that all 25 of the GL3100 smartphones {included in the shipment} are defective].: [ ]는 found의 목적절, { }는 all 25 of the GL3100 smartphones를 수식하는 과거분사구
(10행) ..., I **expect** you **to arrange** for the delivery of 25 new devices [to replace the current ones].: 'expect+O+to-v' 「…가 ~하기를 요구[기대]하다」, [ ]는 25 new devices를 수식하는 형용사적 용법의 to부정사구
(13행) All of our dealings with your company **have been** satisfactory in the past, so I hope [(that) we can continue {to have a beneficial business relationship}].: have been은 계속을 나타내는 현재완료, [ ]는 hope의 목적절, { }는 continue의 목적어로 쓰인 명사적 용법의 to부정사구

문제해설
결함이 있는 스마트폰을 새로운 기기로 교환해 달라고 요청하는 내용이므로, ③이 글의 목적으로 가장 적절하다.

19 ① 심경

　에리카는 자신이 꿈꾸던 학교인 옥스퍼드에 진짜로 있다는 사실을 믿을 수 없었다. 그녀는 여름 내내 이사할 준비를 하고 있었지만, 항공기 엔진이 질주하는 소리를 듣고서야 모든 것이 실감이 났다. 이제 그녀는 아주 오래된 건물들을 바라보면서 캠퍼스를 돌아다니고 있었다. 인생에서 처음으로, 그녀 주변에 친구가 아무도 없었다. 잠시 동안, 그녀 주위에 있던 석조 아치는 거대하고 차가워 보였다. 다른 학생들이 그녀를 자신들의 그룹으로 맞이해줄까? 마주하게 될지도 모르는 고난을 생각하자, 그녀는 현기증이 났다. 그녀는 눈을 감고 새로운 친구들에 둘러싸여 웃고 있는 자신의 모습을 상상했다. 그녀가 눈을 떴을 때, 그 (석조) 아치들은 그녀를 새로운 삶으로 들어서도록 초대하는 것처럼 보였다.

어휘
roar 으르렁거리다; *굉음을 내며 질주하다　wander 거닐다, 돌아다니다　arch 아치형 구조물　enormous 거대한　hardship 어려움, 곤란　encounter 맞닥뜨리다, 부딪히다　dizzy 어지러운　surround 둘러싸다, 에워싸다　[문제] humbled 겸손해진　touched 감동한　frustrated 좌절감을 느끼는

구문해설
(3행) ..., but none of it **had felt real** until she *heard* the airplane engines *roaring*.: 감각동사 had felt의 보어로 형용사 real이 쓰임, 지각동사 heard의 목적격보어로 현재분사 roaring이 쓰임
(4행) Now she was wandering the campus, [staring at ancient buildings].: [ ]는 동시동작을 나타내는 분사구문
(10행) [Thinking about the hardships {(that) she was likely to encounter}], she felt dizzy.: [ ]는 이유를 나타내는 분사구문, { }는 the hardships를 선행사로 하는 목적격 관계대명사절

문제해설
새로운 환경에 적응하며 겪을지 모르는 어려움을 생각하니 걱정이 되기도 하지만 꿈꾸던 학교에 입학해 새로운 삶을 시작하려 하는 상황이므로, 에리카의 심경으로는 ① '걱정되면서도 흥분한'이 적절하다.

20 ⑤ 필자의 주장

　저는 리버데일 지역 전문 대학의 학생들이 겪는 극심한 주차 문제에 대한 우려를 표명하고 싶습니다. 제가 이 문제를 걱정하는 데는 몇 가지 이유가 있습니다. 먼저, 학생들은 주차 공간을 찾아 붐비는 주차장을 돌아다녀야 하는 동안 귀중한 수업 시간을 놓쳐 버리게 됩니다. 그 결과 그들은 수업에서 무슨 일이 진행되고 있는지 모르게 되고, 쪽지시험과 시험에 늦게 나타납니다. 제가 걱정하는 또 다른 이유는 몇몇 학생들이 협소한 주차 장소에 불만을 느낀 나머지 주차 공간을 두고 싸운다는 것입니다. 다른 학생들은 방화 구역에 불법으로 차를 댑니다. 이 문제를 해결하기 위해, 저는 주차장 건물을 짓거나 멀리 떨어져 있는 지역에서 오는 무료 셔틀버스를 제공해 줄 것을 제안합니다.

어휘
concern 우려, 걱정　severe 극심한　community college 지역 전문 대학　instructional 지도의, 수업의　show up 나타나다; 출석하다　quiz (구두·필기에 의한) 간단한 시험　illegally 불법적으로　resolve 해결하다　parking garage 주차장 (건물)　lot 모두; *(특정 용도용) 지역, 부지

구문해설
(9행) Another reason [(why) I am concerned] is that some students become **so** frustrated over the limited parking **that** they fight ...: [ ]는 Another reason을 선행사로 하는 관계부사절, 'so ... that ~' 「너무 …해서 ~하다」
(13행) [To resolve this problem], I **suggest** (that) you (should) **build** a parking garage or (should) **provide** free ...: [ ]는 목적을 나타내는 부사적 용법의 to부정사구, suggest가 제안이나 주장의 의미일 때 목적어인 that절의 동사는 '(should+)동사원형' 형태로 쓰며, build와 provide가 병렬 연결

문제해설
⑤ 교내 주차 공간의 부족으로 인한 여러 문제들을 열거하며 마지막에 그에 대한 대책

마련을 제안하고 있다.

21 ① 글의 요지

1970년대 후반 로스앤젤레스에서, 한 13세의 여자아이가 자신의 아버지에 의해 작은 방에 갇혀서 평생을 살아왔다는 것이 밝혀졌다. 그는 딸에게 밥을 주거나 딸을 때리기 위해서만 그 방에 들어갔으며, 딸에게 절대로 말을 하지는 않았다. 그 여자아이가 정부 당국에 의해 구조되어 병원에 옮겨진 후, 의사들은 그 여자아이가 어떤 언어 능력도 거의 습득하지 못했음을 알게 되었다. 적절한 관리와 치료로, 그 여자아이의 신체와 정신 상태는 이후 몇 달 만에 크게 나아졌다. 그러나 그 여자아이는 자신에게 들리는 많은 것들을 곧 이해할 수 있었지만 다른 사람들과 의사소통을 하는 데에는 심각한 어려움을 겪었다. 그 여자아이는 몇몇 단어들을 배웠지만 진척이 느렸고 문법적으로 정확한 문장들을 구성하지 못했다. 심지어 수년간의 언어 치료를 받은 후에도, 그 여자아이는 결코 정상 수준의 언어 능력을 가질 수 없었다.

어휘
entire 전체의   rescue 구조하다   authority《pl.》 정부 당국   acquire 얻다, 습득하다   improve 나아지다   progress 진행, 진척   grammatically 문법적으로   achieve 달성하다, 이루다   normal 정상적인   ability 능력

구문해설
(1행) ..., it was discovered [that a 13-year-old girl *had spent* her entire life {(being) locked in a small room by her father}].: it은 가주어이고 [ ]가 진주어, had spent는 계속을 나타내는 과거완료, { }는 부대상황을 나타내는 분사구문
(6행) ..., the doctors realized [that she **had acquired** almost no language skills at all].: [ ]는 realized의 목적절, had acquired는 주절의 시제(realized)보다 더 이전에 일어난 일을 나타내는 과거완료
(12행) ..., she **had** severe **difficulty communicating** with others.: 'have difficulty v-ing' 「…하는 데 어려움을 겪다」

문제해설
① 평생 언어를 접하지 못했던 13세의 여자아이가 여러 해에 걸쳐 언어 치료를 받았지만 결코 정상 수준의 언어 능력에 도달하지 못했다는 내용이므로, 언어 학습에 결정적인 시기가 있다는 것이 글의 요지임을 알 수 있다.

22 ⑤ 글의 주제

지금까지 꽤 오랜 시간 동안, 컴퓨터 과학자들은 AI라고도 알려진 인공지능의 형태를 개발하기 위해 노력해 왔다. 처음에 이러한 노력들은 주로 컴퓨터의 형식 추론과 문제 해결 능력에 초점을 두며, 논리 기반의 접근법을 취했다. 이러한 접근법은 나름의 장점을 분명 가지고 있지만, 궁극적으로는 그것의 한계에 부딪혔다. 이러한 형태의 시스템은 인간이 가진 추론의 전체 범위를 컴퓨터 기호로 변형하는 것이 불가능하기 때문에, 극히 제한된 지식의 영역에서만 성공적일 수 있다. 그 시스템들은 또한 논리에만 기반하지 않은 관계들을 연결할 수 없다. 이러한 능력은 의미있는 '지능'에 매우 중요하다. 더욱이, 그것들은 일련의 '만약에, 그렇다면'이라는 식의 조건부 결정에 따라 작동하지만, 실제 상황에서는 그러한 결정을 하는 데 필요한 요소들을 인식하는 것이 항상 가능하지는 않다.

어휘
artificial intelligence 인공지능   logic 논리(logical 논리적인)   reasoning 추론   capability 능력   inhibit 금지하다, 억제하다   translate 통역[번역]하다; *바꾸다, 변형하다   a series of 일련의, 연속의   [문제] abstract 추상적인

구문해설
(6행) While this approach **does** have its advantages, ultimately it is inhibited by its limitations.: does는 동사 have를 강조하는 조동사
(10행) ..., **as** *it* would be impossible [to translate the entire range of human reasoning into computer code].: as는 이유를 나타내는 접속사, it은 가주어이고 [ ]가 진주어

문제해설
⑤ 논리에 기반한 인공지능을 개발하는 과정에서 나타나는 문제점들을 설명하고 있다.

23 ④ 글의 주제

능력주의 사회에서, 개인은 부나 지위보다는 개인의 능력과 업적에 근거하여 출세한다. 능력주의 사회의 주된 이점은 그것이 지위가 낮은 집단 출신의 사람들에게 사회의 계층 내에서 자신의 지위를 향상시킬 수 있을지 모른다는 희망을 준다는 점이다. 능력주의 사회에 살고 있는 사람들은 일반적으로 그들의 사회가 공평하고 공정하며, 충분히 열심히 일하는 사람이라면 누구나 성공할 수 있다고 믿는다. 하지만, 많은 사람들이 이것은 대개 근거 없는 믿음이라고 주장한다. 현대의 능력주의 사회에서조차도 많은 사람들이 여전히 자신의 인종, 민족성, 또는 성별 때문에 상당히 불리한 조건들에 직면한다. 유감스럽게도, 이러한 종류의 근거 없는 믿음은 기존의 경제적 불평등을 지켜내고 진보적인 사회 움직임이 형성되는 것을 막기 위해 사용될 수 있다. 결국, (이전과) 같은 특권을 가진 집단이 사회의 부와 권력에 대한 지배권을 계속 유지한다.

어휘
advance 나아가다; *승진하다, 출세하다   achievement 성취; 업적   status 지위, 신분   primary 주된, 주요한   improve 개선하다, 향상시키다   hierarchy 계층, 계급   fair 공평한, 공정한   just 공정한   succeed 성공[출세]하다   myth 신화; *근거 없는 믿음   significant 중요한; *상당한, 현저한   disadvantage 불리한 처지[조건]   ethnicity 민족성   existing 기존의   inequality 불평등, 불균등   progressive 진보적인   privileged 특권을 가진   retain (계속) 유지[보유]하다   [문제] distribute 분배하다   unpleasant 불편한

구문해설
(3행) The primary benefit of meritocracies is [that they give people from low-status groups hope {that they may be able to improve their position in society's hierarchy}].: [ ]는 주격보어로 쓰인 명사절, hope와 { }는 동격
(6행) People [living in a meritocracy] generally believe [that their society is fair and just, and that anyone {who works hard enough} can succeed].: 첫 번째 [ ]는 People을 수식하는 현재분사구, 두 번째 [ ]는 believe의 목적절, { }는 anyone을 선행사로 하는 주격 관계대명사절
(13행) Unfortunately, this kind of myth can be used **to protect** existing economic inequalities and **to prevent** progressive social movements *from forming*.: to protect와 to prevent는 목적을 나타내는 부사적 용법의 to부정사로 등위 접속사 and에 의해 병렬 연결, 'prevent+O+from v-ing' 「…가 ~하지 못하게 하다」

문제해설
개인의 능력과 업적에 근거하여 사회적 위치가 향상되고 성공할 수 있다는 믿음을 주는 능력주의가 실제로는 오히려 기존의 경제적 불평등을 보호하고 진보적인 사회 움직임을 막는 데 사용될 수 있다는 내용의 글이므로, 글의 주제로 가장 적절한 것은 ④ '한 사회 체계 이면에 숨겨진 불편한 진실'이다.

24 ⑤ 글의 제목

고대 이집트 벽화들은 옆에 개를 데리고 전쟁터로 행군하는 병사들의

그림을 보여준다. 이와 비슷하게, 페르시아의 역사학자들은 다가오는 그리스 침입자들을 병사들에게 경고하기 위해 군대에 의해서 개가 어떻게 이용되었는지를 기술하고 있다. 수천 년 후, 나폴레옹의 유럽 침략 기간 동안 무스타슈라는 이름의 개는 적군이 프랑스 국기를 훔치려고 했을 때 뛰어난 용기를 보여 주었다. 무스타슈가 그 병사를 아주 세게 물어서 그 병사가 도망친 것이다. 제1차 세계대전 중에는, 스터비라는 영국 개가 독일 간첩을 붙잡은 공로로 훈장을 받았다. 그리고 제2차 세계대전에서는 적어도 1만 마리의 개가 미국 군대에서 일했다. 그것들은 보초병으로 일했고, 서신을 전달했으며, 수색 및 구조 작업에 있어서 매우 중요했다.

어휘
ancient 고대의 military 군대 approach …에 다가가다 invader 침략자 (invasion 침략) outstanding 뛰어난 bite 물다 award 수여하다, 주다 essential 필수적인, 없어서는 안 될 rescue 구조, 구출 [문제] fierce 격렬한 civilization 문명 contribution 기여, 공헌 wartime 전시(戰時)

구문해설
3행 Similarly, Persian historians describe [how dogs were used by the military to **warn** soldiers **of** approaching Greek invaders].: [ ]는 describe의 목적어로 쓰인 의문사절. 'warn A of B' 「A에게 B를 경고하다」
9행 Moustache bit the soldier **so** hard **that** he ran away.: 'so … that ~' 「너무 …해서 ~하다」

문제해설
이 글은 전쟁에 동원된 개들이 큰 공헌을 한 사례들을 여러 시대에 걸쳐 다루고 있으므로, 제목으로는 ⑤ '전시 동안의 개들의 공헌'이 적절하다.

25 ④ 도표 내용 불일치

위 도표는 캐나다의 온타리오 주와 뉴브런즈윅 주에서 2018년에 생산된 전력량을 보여주며, 총량은 자원별로 분류되어 있다. 온타리오 주는 총 151.1테라와트 시의 전력을 생산했는데, 이는 뉴브런즈윅 주에서 생산된 것보다 10배 이상 더 많은 양이다. 온타리오 주의 전력 대부분은 우라늄에서 나왔는데, 이는 2위를 차지하는 자원인 수력 발전보다 두 배 이상 더 많은 전력을 생산했다. 그 주에서 세 번째로 높은 비율의 전력이 풍력에 의해 생산되었으며 이는 총 전력 생산의 7%를 차지했다. (뉴브런즈윅 주에서는 우라늄과 수력 발전이 두 가지 가장 큰 전력 발생원이었지만, 풍력보다는 천연가스가 세 번째로 높은 비율을 차지했다.) 2018년 석탄과 코크스에 의해 생산된 뉴브런즈윅 주의 전력 비율은 풍력과 천연가스를 합친 비율과 거의 비슷했다.

어휘
electricity 전기, 전력 generation 발생(generate 발생시키다, 만들어내다) province (행정 단위인) 주(州), 도(道) source 원천, 근원 uranium 우라늄 hydro 수력 발전 전력 natural gas 천연가스 break down (분석할 수 있도록) 나누어지다 account for (부분·비율을) 차지하다

구문해설
1행 The above graphs show the amount of electricity [generated in 2018 by the Canadian provinces of Ontario and New Brunswick], **with** the total amounts **broken down** by source.: [ ]는 the amount of electricity를 수식하는 과거분사구, 'with+O+과거분사' 「…가 ~된 채로」(부대상황을 나타내는 분사구문)
4행 Ontario generated a total of 151.1 terawatt hours of electricity, [which is an amount more than ten times greater than **that** generated by New Brunswick].: [ ]는 a total of 151.1 terawatt hours of electricity를 선행사로 하는 계속적 용법의 주격 관계대명사절. that은 앞에 언급된 electricity를 지칭
17행 The percentage of New Brunswick's electricity [that was

generated by coal and coke in 2018] was nearly as much as the percentages [generated by wind and natural gas combined].: 첫 번째 [ ]는 The percentage of New Brunswick's electricity를 선행사로 하는 주격 관계대명사절, 두 번째 [ ]는 the percentages를 수식하는 과거분사구

문제해설
④ 뉴브런즈윅 주에서 세 번째로 높은 비율을 차지한 것은 천연가스가 아니라 석탄과 코크스이다.

26 ⑤ 내용 불일치

갑오징어는 흥미로운 작은 동물이다. 그것은 오징어에 비해 약간 작고 문어와 같은 과(科)에 속한다. 비록 해양 생물 중 가장 발달된 생물이라고 여겨지지는 않지만, 그것들은 지능이 굉장히 높다. 연구에 따르면, 갑오징어는 빠르게 학습하는데, 많은 과학자들은 그것들이 다른 갑오징어를 관찰함으로써 많은 지식을 습득한다고 생각한다. 그것들을 보고 있으면 누가 관찰을 하고 있는 것인지, 당신인지 갑오징어인지 분간하기가 어려운데, 특히 갑오징어의 눈이 구조상 사람의 눈과 아주 비슷하기 때문이다. 갑오징어는 또한 촉수 바로 밑에 이동을 돕기 위해 물을 뿜어낼 수 있는 작은 분출구를 갖고 있어, 잘 움직이며 재빠르다. 그것들의 가장 흥미로운 특징은 자신을 보호하기 위해 순식간에 몸의 색깔과 무늬를 바꿀 수 있는 능력이다. 그래서 그것들은 이따금씩 '바다의 카멜레온'이라고 불린다.

어휘
cuttlefish 갑오징어 squid 오징어 family 가족; *(동식물 분류상의) 과(科) octopus 문어 extremely 극히 tell 말하다; *구별하다 observe 관찰하다 structurally 구조적으로 mobile 이동성의 possess 소유하다 jet 출(구) fascinating 멋진, 매혹할 만한 in an instant 순식간에 refer to A as B A를 B라고 부르다

구문해설
9행 ..., it is difficult [to tell who is ..., you or the cuttlefish], particularly ...: it은 가주어이고 [ ]가 진주어
12행 Cuttlefish are also very mobile and quick, [possessing a small jet just below the tentacles {that can shoot out water to help them move}].: [ ]는 이유를 나타내는 분사구문, { }는 a small jet를 선행사로 하는 주격 관계대명사절

문제해설
⑤ 갑오징어가 몸의 색깔과 무늬를 바꾸는 것은 자신을 보호하기 위해서이다.

27 ⑤ 내용 불일치

태국에서 태국 음식 요리하는 법을 배우세요!
방콕 최고의 요리 학교에서 현재 외국인 관광객에게 일일 요리 수업을 제공하고 있습니다.
가격: 4시간 수업에 30달러 (미화)
요리: 여섯 가지 태국 전통 요리를 각 수업에서 배울 수 있습니다.
편의:
- 우리의 현대적인 주방은 냉난방 장치가 완비되어 있습니다.
- 여러분의 호텔로 태우러 가고 데려다 드릴 것입니다.
언어: 영어와 중국어로 수업을 합니다.
우리는 초급, 고급, 채식주의자 그리고 개인 수업을 제공합니다. 우리의 모든 수업은 재료를 구입할 태국 전통 시장 방문을 포함합니다. 저희 웹사이트에 방문해서 전체 수업 일정을 확인하고 수업을 예약하세요.

어휘
traditional 전통의 modern 현대의 air-conditioned 냉난방 장치를 한

pick up …을 태우러 가다 advanced 선진의; *고급의, 상급의 private 개인의, 개인적인 purchase 구입하다 ingredient 재료 reserve 예약하다

구문해설
(10행) We'll **pick you up** and **drop you off** at your hotel.: '타동사＋부사'로 이루어진 구동사 pick up과 drop off의 목적어가 대명사이므로 모두 '타동사＋목적어＋부사'의 어순으로 쓰임
(17행) Please visit our website to see a full schedule of classes and reserve a place in **one**.: one은 class를 지칭

문제해설
⑤ 모든 수업이 태국 전통 시장 방문을 포함한다고 했다.

28 ④ 내용 일치

리 카운티 커뮤니티 센터
가을 강좌 및 워크숍
  카테고리: 공예
  강좌: 가죽 워크숍
  시간: 4시간
  연령대: 15세 이상
  최대 수강 인원: 18명
이 워크숍에서 여러분은 여러분만의 독특한 가죽 필통을 만들 것입니다. 필요한 모든 재료는 수업료에 포함되어 있습니다. 가죽 색상을 선택할 수도 있습니다! 가죽을 자르고, 손으로 꿰매고, 여러분의 이니셜로 양각하는 방법을 배울 것입니다.
워크숍은 매월 첫 번째 토요일에 열리며 참가자당 150달러의 비용이 듭니다. 커뮤니티 센터 웹사이트인 www.leecommunity.org에서 온라인으로 등록할 수 있습니다.

어휘
craft (수)공예 leather 가죽 length 시간, 기간 maximum 최고의, 최대의 material (물건의) 재료 stitch 바느질하다, 꿰매다 emboss 양각으로 새기다 initial 이름의 첫 글자 participant 참가자 register 등록하다

구문해설
(9행) All of the materials [(that) you need] are included in the cost of the class …!: [ ]는 All of the materials를 선행사로 하는 목적격 관계대명사절
(12행) You will learn [how **to cut** leather, **(to) stitch** it by hand, and even **(to) emboss** it with your initials].: [ ]는 learn의 목적어로 쓰인 의문사구, to cut, (to) stitch, (to) emboss는 모두 how에 병렬 연결

문제해설
① 강좌당 최대 수강 인원이 18명이라고 나와 있다. ② 재료비는 수업료에 포함되어 있다고 나와 있다. ③ 가죽의 색상을 선택할 수 있다고 나와 있다. ⑤ 커뮤니티 센터 웹사이트를 통해 등록할 수 있다고 나와 있다.

29 ⑤ 어법

남극에 서식하는 펭귄들은 수개월간의 태양 없는 하늘과 일 년 내내 영하 상태를 유지하는 기온을 견뎌 내야 한다. 그러나 놀랍게도 이 조류는 얼어 죽는 것보다 과열의 위험에 더 처해 있을지도 모른다. 그들의 몸은 몹시 추운 남극의 날씨에 맞서 스스로를 보호하기 위하여 수천 년 넘게 진화해 왔다. 예를 들어, 펭귄의 깃털은 그것의 몸 주위에 놀라울 정도로 방수가 되는 보호막을 형성하며, 그 밑에는 두꺼운 지방층이 그것을 추위로부터 단열시켜 준다. 그래서 마치 무더운 8월의 어느 날 솜털로 뒤덮인 코트를 입고 있는 인간처럼, 기온이 올라가면 펭귄은 열사병의 위험에 놓인다. 그러나 이 종은 이 문제도 해결하도록 진화해 왔다. 펭귄의 맨발이 열을 방출하는 역할을 담당해 이 동물의 몸의 나머지 부분이 일정한 체온을 유지하게 해준다.

어휘
inhabit 살다, 서식하다 Antarctic 남극; 남극의 withstand 견뎌 내다 below freezing 빙점 이하의, 영하의 freeze 얼다 overheat 과열되다 evolve 진화하다 frigid 몹시 추운 waterproof 방수의 shield 방패; *보호막 layer 층 insulate 단열 처리를 하다 fluffy 솜털로 뒤덮인 down (새의) 솜털 heat exhaustion 열사병 bare 벌거벗은 constant 끊임없는; *일정한

구문해설
(1행) The penguins [that inhabit the Antarctic] must withstand months of sunless skies and temperatures [that stay below freezing for the entire year].: 두 개의 [ ]는 각각 The penguins와 temperatures를 선행사로 하는 주격 관계대명사절
(15행) A penguin's bare feet **are responsible for** releasing heat, [enabling the rest of the animal's body ... temperature].: 'be responsible for' 「…에 책임이 있다」, [ ]는 결과를 나타내는 분사구문

문제해설
⑤ 동사 enable은 목적격보어로 to부정사를 취하므로 remain은 to remain으로 고쳐야 한다.

30 ④ 어휘

우리의 감각은 매일 많은 다양한 상황들에 적응한다. 이 상황들의 가장 흔한 것 중 하나는 밝은 곳에서 어두운 공간으로 걸어 들어갈 때 일어난다. 예를 들어, 어두운 극장 안으로 걸어가는 것은 종종 어둠 외에는 어떤 것도 감지하기 어렵게 한다. 하지만, 당신의 눈이 어둠에 적응함에 따라, 당신은 잘 볼 수 있게 되기 시작한다. 이러한 변화는 눈의 간상체와 추상체에서 발견되는 화학물질인 요돕신에 의해 일어나며, 이것은 빛에 대한 눈의 민감성을 증대하기 위해 더 많은 양이 생성된다. 이 동일한 반응은 당신이 어두운 극장을 떠나 밝게 불이 켜진 공간으로 걸어 들어갈 때는 반대로 일어난다. 이러한 상황에서, 당신의 눈은 과도한 요돕신을 갖고 있는데, 이는 간상체와 추상체를 빛에 매우 민감하게 만든다. 그것들은 당신이 다시 정상적으로 보기에 앞서 요돕신 수준을 낮춰야 한다.

어휘
sense 감각 adapt to …에 적응하다 deceive 속이다, 기만하다 perceive 감지하다 chemical 화학 물질 intensity 강도, 세기 sensitivity 민감성 (sensitive 민감한) reaction 반응 in reverse 반대로, 거꾸로 excess 초과한

구문해설
(4행) For example, [walking into a dark theater] often makes **it** difficult [to perceive anything but darkness].: 첫 번째 [ ]는 문장의 주어로 쓰인 동명사구, it은 가목적어이고 두 번째 [ ]가 진목적어
(8행) This change is caused by iodopsin, [a chemical found in the rods and cones of the eye], [which is produced in greater amounts {to increase the eyes' sensitivity to light}].: 첫 번째 [ ]는 iodopsin과 동격을 이루는 삽입구, 두 번째 [ ]는 iodopsin을 선행사로 하는 계속적 용법의 주격 관계대명사절, { }는 목적을 나타내는 부사적 용법의 to부정사구

문제해설
④ (A) 밝은 곳에서 어두운 극장 안으로 걸어가는 것은 눈이 적응하기 전까지는 어둠 외에 어떤 것도 감지하기 어렵게 하므로, '감지하다(perceive)'가 와야 한다. (B) 화학물질인 요돕신이 더 많이 생산되는 것은 빛에 대한 눈의 '민감성(sensitivity)'을 증가시키기 위함이다. (C) 어두운 곳에서 다시 밝은 곳으로 이동하는 상황에서, 우리의 눈은 '과도한(excess)' 요돕신을 갖는다.

31 ③ 빈칸 추론

흑사병은 13세기와 14세기에 몇 차례에 걸쳐 유럽을 덮쳐, 유럽 대륙 인구의 3분의 1 이상을 죽게 했다. 그 전염병은 유럽 사회에 엄청난 변화를 일으켰는데, 그중 일부는 <u>이로운</u> 것이었다. 환자들의 고통을 덜어주는 데 대부분 실패했던, 의료 분야의 개혁이 한 예이다. 흑사병이 창궐하던 중에 많은 의사들이 죽거나 그냥 도망쳐 버렸다. 그 결과, 대부분의 대학에 의학 교수들이 부족하게 되었다. 사람들은 새로운 생각을 가지고 이 빈자리에 뛰어들었다. 게다가 일반인들이 의학 서적을 입수하고 스스로의 건강을 챙기기 시작했다. 점차 더 많은 서적들이 라틴어 이외의 언어로 나오기 시작하여, 누구나 의학 지식에 더 쉽게 접근하게 되었다.

어휘
Black Plague 흑사병 outbreak 발발, 창궐 continent 대륙 epidemic 전염병 bring about …을 야기하다, 불러일으키다 tremendous 엄청난 reform 개혁 profession 직업, 직종 relieve (고통을) 없애[덜어] 주다 vacancy 공석 take charge of …을 책임지다 accessible 접근하기 쉬운 [문제] inevitable 피할 수 없는 insignificant 대수롭지 않은

구문해설
(2행) ... in the 13th and 14th centuries, [killing more than ... population].: [ ]는 결과를 나타내는 분사구문
(4행) The epidemics brought about tremendous changes in European society, [some of which were beneficial].: [ ]는 tremendous changes를 선행사로 하는 계속적 용법의 목적격 관계대명사절

문제해설
흑사병의 창궐을 계기로 발생한 이로운 일들의 예가 빈칸 뒤에 서술되어 있으므로 빈칸에는 ③ '이로운'이 가장 적절하다.

32 ④ 빈칸 추론

1세기보다 더 이전에, 헨리 데이비드 소로는 멕시코 전쟁에 항의하기 위해 감옥에 갔다. 많은 사람들이 소로의 본보기를 따랐고 <u>불의에 대한 대중의 관심을 불러일으키기</u> 위해 공개적으로 법을 어겼다. 일례로, 위법 판결을 받았을 때, 위대한 인도의 지도자 간디는 약간의 벌금을 내는 대신 형을 살면서 단식 투쟁에 들어갔다. 그는 영국으로부터의 인도의 독립이라는 자신의 대의에 관심을 끌기 위해 그렇게 했다. 매우 존경받는 사람들이 그들의 신념으로 인해 투옥될 때, 이는 흔히 사람들이 그 상황의 정당성에 대해 다시 생각하게 만든다. 마틴 루터 킹 2세가 인종 평등을 주장하려고 감옥에 갔을 때, 그는 많은 미국인들이 인종 차별이 잘못된 것임을 깨닫는 데 기여했다. 그의 본보기는 인종 차별을 유지시켰던 법을 폐지하는 데 도움이 되었다.

어휘
protest 항의하다; 주장하다 convict …의 유죄를 판결하다 serve 복역하다 sentence 판결, 형벌 hunger strike 단식 투쟁 fine 벌금 cause 주의, 주장; *대의 justness 올바름, 정당성(justify 정당화하다) equality 평등 segregation 분리; *인종 차별 abolish 폐지하다 [문제] resist …에 저항하다 colonization 식민지화 raise 올리다; *(기금을) 모금하다 maintain 유지하다 security 안전, 안보

구문해설
(5행) ..., [when (he was) convicted of breaking the law], the great Indian leader Gandhi served ...: [ ]는 때를 나타내는 부사절('주어+be동사'가 생략된 형태)
(14행) ..., he helped many Americans realize ...: 'help+O+(to-)v' 「…가 ～하는 것을 돕다」

문제해설
빈칸 뒤에서 간디와 마틴 루터 킹 2세가 대중들의 관심을 촉구하기 위해 감옥에 갔던 예를 들고 있으므로, 빈칸에는 ④ '불의에 대한 대중의 관심을 불러일으키다'가 적절하다.

33 ② 빈칸 추론

경제를 파괴함으로써 영국을 패배시키고자 했던 나폴레옹은 1806년에 베를린 칙령을 공포했다. 이 칙령은 그가 영국 제도 주변에 침입할 수 없는 장벽을 만들어, 어떤 제품이든 수입과 수출을 모두 금지할 수 있게 하였다. (베를린 칙령의) 초기 영향은 손해를 끼치는 것이었는데, 영국 국민들에게 큰 어려움을 가하고 일부 기업들이 붕괴하도록 했다. 그러나 1811년, 베를린 칙령에 의해 시작된 그 전략이 나폴레옹에게 역효과를 가져왔다는 것이 명백해졌다. 몇몇 주요 영국 제품들에 대한 접근이 허용되지 않아, 프랑스의 경제가 실제로 더 고통받고 있었다. 그의 자국민들과 이웃 유럽 국가들로부터의 반란에 직면한 나폴레옹은 결국 그 전략을 포기할 수밖에 없었고, 얼마 후 그의 군대는 전쟁에서 영국에 패배했다.

어휘
defeat 패배시키다 decree 법령, 포고 impenetrable 꿰뚫을 수 없는, 뚫고 들어갈 수 없는 blockade 봉쇄 initial 처음의, 최초의(initiate 착수시키다) inflict 주다, 가하다 hardship 고충 collapse 무너지다, 쓰러지다 backfire 역효과를 내다 revolt 반란 abandon 버리다, 포기하다 battlefield 전장, 전쟁터 [문제] execute 실행하다 absorb 흡수하다

구문해설
(3행) These decrees allowed him to create an impenetrable blockade around the British isles, [preventing both the import and export of any products].: 'allow+O+to-v' 「…가 ～하도록 허용하다」, [ ]는 부대상황을 나타내는 분사구문

문제해설
② 베를린 칙령이 영국과의 무역 금지를 통해 영국을 봉쇄시키려는 내용이므로 나폴레옹의 전략은 '그들(영국)의 경제를 파괴하는 것'이었음을 유추할 수 있다.

34 ③ 빈칸 추론

만약 독수리가 천장이 없는 8제곱 피트의 우리 안에 놓이면, 그것은 갇힐 것이다. 독수리는 먼저 10피트가량을 달린 후에만 날기 때문이다. 달릴 공간이 없으면, 그것은 우리 밖으로 날아가는 방법을 모를 것이다. 마찬가지로, 만약 호박벌이 유리컵 안에 떨어지면, 그것은 결코 밖으로 나갈 수 없을 것이다. 출구가 위쪽에 있다는 것을 알아차리지 못하고 그것은 컵의 측면을 통과하여 나갈 방법을 알아내려고 계속 노력할 것이다. 그것은 죽을 때까지 이 헛된 탈출 시도를 계속할 것이다. 생각해 보면, 어떤 사람들은 꼭 독수리와 호박벌 같다. 그들은 답이 바로 그들 위에 있다는 것을 결코 깨닫지 못한 채, 쓸데없이 문제와 씨름하는 데 모든 에너지를 소비한다.

어휘
buzzard 독수리 square 평방의, 제곱의 trap 함정에 빠뜨리다, 좁은 장소에 가두다 bumblebee 호박벌 persist 고집하다, 지속하다 futile 헛된 struggle 분투하다, 애쓰다

구문해설
(4행) Without space to run, it will not know [how to fly out of its cage].: to run은 space를 수식하는 형용사적 용법의 to부정사, [ ]는 know의 목적어로 쓰인 의문사구

문제해설
문제 상황에 처했을 때 해결책이 가까이에 있음을 깨닫지 못하고 쓸데없이 에너지만 소

비하는 독수리와 호박벌의 예를 들고 있으므로, 빈칸에는 ③ '답이 바로 그들 위에 있다' 가 가장 적절하다.

35 ④ 흐름과 무관한 문장

아프리카의 점박이 하이에나는 사회적인 동물이다. 최대 90마리로 이루어진 집단에서 살지만 그들은 종종 더 작은 무리를 지어 사냥하고 이동하며 시간을 보낸다. 서로 다른 집단에서 온 무리들이 만나면 지배권을 위한 싸움이 뒤따를 수도 있다. 물론 더 큰 무리가 싸움에서 이길 가능성이 더 높은데, 하이에나들은 이 사실을 알고 있다. 따라서, 모르는 무리와 마주치면, 그들은 그들의 뛰어난 야간 시력과 매우 발달한 청력을 모두 사용해서 상대 무리의 구성원의 수를 셈으로써 자신들의 성공 가능성을 즉시 계산한다. (게다가, 하이에나는 튼튼한 턱과 소화관 덕분에 자기들이 죽인 동물의 가죽과 뼈로부터 얻은 영양분을 분해할 수 있다.) 만약 상대 무리가 자기 무리보다 더 크면 그들은 공격하기보다는 후퇴하려고 할 것이다.

어휘
spotted 점무늬가 있는 clan 집단, 무리 migrate 이주하다, 이동하다 pack 무리, 떼 dominance 권세, 지배 ensue 뒤따르다 confront 직면하다 calculate 계산하다, 추산하다 odds 가능성 opposing 대항하는, 맞서는 aural 청각의 break down (물질을) 분해하다 jaw 턱 digestive tract 소화관 retreat 후퇴하다

구문해설
[10행] ..., [using **both** their excellent night vision **and** high aural ability].: [ ]는 동시동작을 나타내는 분사구문, 'both A and B' 「A와 B 둘 다」
[14행] [If the opposing pack **is** larger than their own (pack)], they will attempt to retreat *rather than* (to) attack.: [ ]는 조건을 나타내는 부사절이므로 현재시제가 미래시제를 대신함, 'A rather than B' 「B라기보다는 A」

문제해설
하이에나가 다른 무리와 세력 다툼을 할 때 어떻게 위험을 가늠하고 결정을 내리는지에 관한 글이므로, 하이에나의 소화 능력을 언급한 ④는 글의 흐름과 무관하다.

36 ⑤ 글의 순서

많은 사람들이 수화는 팬터마임과 비슷한 동작들을 대충 모아놓은 것이라고 잘못 생각한다.
(C) 그러나 사실 수화는 음성 언어의 모든 문법적 복잡성을 가진 고도로 구조화된 언어 체계이다. 음성 언어가 단어와 문장을 형성하는 데 있어 특정한 규칙을 가지고 있듯이, 수화에도 각각의 손짓과 수화로 나타내진 문장들에 대한 규칙이 있다.
(B) 또한, 세계 공용의 수화가 있을 것이라는 또 다른 오해가 존재한다. 그러나 이 또한 사실이 아니다. 여러 나라의 청각 장애인들은 서로 매우 다른 수화를 사용하기 때문에, 그들이 해외여행할 때 의사소통을 하기 위해서는 새로운 수화를 배워야 한다.
(A) 수화의 다양성을 보여주는 지표 중 하나는 국제 회의에서 모든 청각 장애인들이 이해할 수 있도록 수화 통역사를 제공해야 한다는 사실이다. 흥미롭게도, 성인이 되어서 제2의 수화를 습득하는 청각 장애인은 실제로 외국 말투가 섞인 수화를 구사할 것이다!

어휘
mistakenly 잘못하여, 실수로 sign language 수화 loose 헐거운; *정밀하지[세심하지] 않은 pantomime 팬터마임, 무언극 indication 암시; *지표 interpreter 통역사 signer 수화법을 쓰는 사람 sign 몸짓, 신호, 표시; 수화를 하다 accent 어투, 말투 misconception 오해, 잘못된 생각 structured 구조화된 linguistic 언어의 complexity 복잡성

구문해설
[4행] One indication of the great diversity in sign languages is the fact [that at international conferences, **it** is necessary {to provide sign language interpreters *so that* all deaf people *can* understand}].: [ ]는 the fact와 동격, it은 가주어이고 { }가 진주어, 'so that+S+can ...' 「~가 …할 수 있도록」

문제해설
⑤ 많은 사람들이 수화가 여러 동작을 대충 모아놓은 것이라고 착각한다는 주어진 문장 뒤에, 사실은 수화가 상당히 체계적인 언어 시스템이라고 설명한 (C)가 온 뒤, 사람들이 수화에 공용어가 존재한다고 생각한다는 또 다른 오해가 있지만 이는 사실이 아니며 국가별로 매우 다른 수화를 사용한다는 내용인 (B)가 오고, (B)에 대한 부연 설명인 (A)가 맨 마지막에 오는 것이 자연스럽다.

37 ③ 글의 순서

1991년에, 구식 수은 온도계에 비해 대단한 발전인 새로운 온도계가 발명되었다.
(B) 이 현대식 온도계를 창안한 회사는 바쁜 병원 간호사들에게 시간을 절약하게 해주고 싶었다. 미국의 간호사들은 매년 약 10억 회 정도 온도계 수치를 읽으므로, 구식 온도계의 수은이 올라가기를 기다리면서 수분(分)을 낭비하는 것은 상당한 시간적 손실을 가중시켰다.
(C) 이 시간을 없애기 위해, 그 회사는 별의 온도를 측정하려고 NASA(미국 항공 우주국)가 개발한 기술을 이용했다. 그들은 환자의 귀 바로 안에 그것을 넣으면, 몇 초 내에 신체 온도를 기록할 수 있는 열 센서를 고안해 냈다.
(A) 그것은 귀의 고막에서 외이도로 방출되는 에너지의 수준을 측정함으로써 작동한다. 우리가 더 아프고 체온이 높아질수록, 고막은 더 많은 에너지를 방출한다.

어휘
thermometer 온도계 improvement 성장 old-fashioned 구식의 mercury 수은 emit 방출하다, 내보내다 eardrum 고막 ear canal 외이도 give off 방출하다 outdated 구식인 free up …을 해방시키다; *(방해물을) 제거하다 register (온도계 등이) 온도를 가리키다

구문해설
[1행] ..., new thermometers were invented [that were a vast improvement ... mercury thermometers].: [ ]는 new thermometers를 선행사로 하는 주격 관계대명사절이며 종종 선행사와 관계대명사절이 떨어져 쓰이기도 함
[6행] **The sicker** we are and **the higher** our body temperature, **the more** energy our eardrum gives off.: 'the+비교급, the+비교급' 「…하면 할수록 더 ~하다」

문제해설
③ 새로운 온도계가 발명되었다는 주어진 문장 다음에, 한 회사가 간호사들의 온도 측정 시간을 줄일 수 있는 새 온도계를 만들게 된 배경을 설명한 (B)가 오고, 그 회사가 개발에 사용한 기술에 대해 설명하는 (C) 다음에, 새 온도계의 작동 원리를 설명하는 (A)로 이어지는 것이 적절하다.

38 ⑤ 주어진 문장의 위치

다양한 종류의 세포들이 많이 있는데, 그것들은 모두 서로 다른 목적을 가지고 있다. 오래전에는 매우 단순한 세포들이 개별적으로 살았다. 하지만 생물체가 진화함에 따라 더 효과적인 세포들이 나타났고, 이들이 합쳐져서 고등 유기체를 형성하였다. 예를 들어, 오늘날 지구상에서 가장 진화되고 분화된 세포들 중 하나는 인간의 뇌세포이다. 그런데 뇌세포는

우리의 몸을 기능하게 하는 전기적 신호들을 주고받는 놀라운 능력을 갖고 있지만, 뇌에서 분리되면 순식간에 죽는다. 반면에, 단세포인 아메바는 전기 자극을 전송하는 것과 같은 어떤 놀랄 만한 일은 할 수 없지만, 다른 세포들로부터 떨어져 사는 것을 꽤 수월하게 여긴다. 그렇다면 일반적으로, 고등 세포는 복잡한 일을 수행할 수 있는 반면, 단세포는 혼자서 생존하는 것을 더 잘 할 수 있다.

어휘
cell 세포 remarkable 놀랄 만한 transmit 전송하다 impulse 충동; *충격, 자극 individually 개별적으로 advanced 진보한; *고등의 organism 유기체 specialized 전문적인; *분화된, 특수화된 electrical 전기의 signal 신호 function 기능하다 carry out 수행하다 intricate 복잡한

구문해설
(1행) ..., a single-celled amoeba, [though it is unable to do anything remarkable **such as** transmitting electrical impulses], is quite comfortable ...: [ ]는 삽입된 부사절, 'such as'「…와 같은」
(12행) But even though brain cells have the amazing ability [to send and receive the electrical signals {that make our bodies function}], they quickly die [if (they are) removed from the brain].: 첫 번째 [ ]는 the amazing ability를 수식하는 형용사적 용법의 to부정사구, { }는 the electrical signals를 선행사로 하는 주격 관계대명사절, 두 번째 [ ]는 조건을 나타내는 부사절('주어+be동사'가 생략된 형태)

문제해설
주어진 문장에서 On the other hand(반면에)와 함께 단세포인 아메바의 특징에 대한 설명이 등장하는데, 이는 고등 세포의 예시로 언급된 뇌세포의 특징과 대조되는 내용이므로 이를 설명하는 문장 뒤인 ⑤에 오는 것이 적절하다.

39 ③ 주어진 문장의 위치

과거에 심리학자들은 인간의 다섯 가지 주요 성격 특성을 발견했는데, 이는 외향성, 성실성, 우호성, 개방성, 그리고 신경증적 경향이다. 보다 최근의 연구는 이러한 특성들이 종종 결합되어 네 가지 주된 성격 유형을 만들어 낸다는 점을 시사한다. '평균적' 성격 유형은 다섯 가지 특성 모두 중간 수준을 갖는다. '역할 모델적' 성격 유형은 외향성, 성실성, 우호성, 그리고 개방성이 높아서, 이러한 사람들은 주변에 있으면 가장 호감이 간다. 반대의 성격 유형은 '자기중심적'인데, 이는 이 네 가지 특성이 모두 낮다. 마지막으로, '내성적' 성격 유형이 있는데, 이는 개방성과 신경증적 경향 둘 다 낮다. '평균적' 성격 유형이 가장 흔하지만, 분명하게 단일 그룹에 들어갈 수 있는 사람은 거의 없다. 대신에, 대부분의 사람들은 네 가지 모든 유형의 측면들을 갖추는데, 어떤 것들이 다른 것들보다 더 강한 것이다.

어휘
trait 특성, 특징 identify 확인하다; *발견하다 extroversion 외향성 conscientiousness 성실성 neuroticism 신경증적 성질[경향] primary 주된, 주요한 average 평균의 medium 중간의 reserved 내성적인 combine 결합하다; *(두 가지 이상의 자질·특징 등을) 갖추다 aspect 측면

구문해설
(6행) More recent research suggests [that these traits often group together, {creating four primary personality types}].: [ ]는 suggests의 목적절, { }는 결과를 나타내는 분사구문
(12행) ..., so these people are the most pleasant [to be around].: [ ]는 한정을 나타내는 부사적 용법의 to부정사
(17행) Instead, most people combine aspects of all four types, **with** some **being** stronger than others.: 'with+O+현재분사'「…을 ~한 채로, …을 ~하며」(부대상황을 나타내는 분사구문)

문제해설
주어진 문장의 all four of these traits는 ③ 앞의 '역할 모델적' 성격 유형에서 높게 나온 네 가지 특성을 가리키며 '자기중심적' 성격 유형은 이 네 가지 특성이 낮다는 것으로 보아 문맥상 '역할 모델적' 성격 유형과 반대이므로, 주어진 문장은 ③에 오는 것이 적절하다.

40 ② 요약문 완성

완벽을 추구하는 끊임없는 욕구나 항상 통제권을 쥐려는 욕구와 같은 성격적 특성은 강박성 인격장애(OCPD)의 징후들일 수 있다. 이 병을 앓고 있는 사람들은 좀처럼 자신이 문제가 있다고 생각하지 않으며, 대신 그들이 행동하는 방식이 적절하다고 믿는다. 그들의 일상생활의 모든 면은 그들이 스스로를 붙잡아 놓은 엄격한 기준에 의해 영향을 받을 가능성이 있다. 따라서, 그들은 의미 없는 사소한 일들에, 종종 그들이 자신의 실제 목표를 망각할 정도로 과도한 양의 시간과 에너지를 낭비하는 경향이 있다. OCPD가 있는 사람은 실수가 없다고 전적으로 확신하려는 욕구에 사로잡혀, 이메일을 보내거나 서류를 교정 보는 것과 같은 사소한 일에 결국 몇 시간을 보낼 수 있다. 결국 그들은 효율적이기 위한 스스로의 노력에 해를 끼치고 만다.

어휘
personality 성격 trait 특성 continual 거듭되는, 반복되는; *끊임없는 perfection 완벽 be in control 장악하다 sign 징후, 조짐 condition 질환 dysfunctional 제대로 기능하지 않는, 고장 난 function 기능하다; *활동하다 excessive 지나친, 과도한 lose sight of …이 안 보이다; *…을 망각하다 proofread (책의) 교정을 보다 grip 꽉 잡다; *사로잡다 [문제] be obsessed with …에 사로잡히다[집착하다] rigid 엄격한 attractive 매력적인

구문해설
(4행) People [suffering from this condition] rarely view themselves as dysfunctional, [instead believing that the manner {in which they function} is proper].: 첫 번째 [ ]는 People을 수식하는 현재분사구, 두 번째 [ ]는 부대상황을 나타내는 분사구문, { }는 the manner를 선행사로 하는 목적격 관계대명사절
(13행) A person with OCPD might **end up spending** hours on a small task, ..., [(being) gripped by the need to absolutely ensure {(that) there are no mistakes}].: 'end up v-ing'「결국 …하다」, [ ]는 부대상황을 나타내는 분사구문, { }는 ensure의 목적절

문제해설
② 강박성 인격장애가 있는 사람들은 완벽한 것에 너무 집착해서, 결국 사소한 일들에 너무 많은 시간을 보내게 된다.

41 ② 42 ① 장문

당신은 아마 숫자 0이 언제나 존재했을 것으로 생각할 수도 있지만, 그것은 실제로 비교적 최근에 우리 수 체계에 추가된 것이다. 사실, 그것은 12세기까지는 유럽에서 사용되지 않았다. 하지만 그것의 기원은 그것보다 훨씬 나중에(→ 먼저) 시작되었다. 약 4,000년 전에, 사람들은 0의 개념을 나타내기 위해 빈 공간을 사용했다. 그런 후, 기원전 3세기경 고대 바빌로니아인들은 두 개의 작은 삼각형 모양으로 구성된 기호를 만들어 냈다. 비록 이것이 진정한 0은 아니었지만, 그것은 우리가 현재 10과 100 간의 차이점을 보여주기 위해 0을 사용하는 것과 같은 방식으로 쓰였다.

서기 7세기에 이르러서야 비로소 0이 진짜 숫자로 사용되기 시작했다. 브라마굽타라는 이름의 인도 수학자는 값이 없는 숫자를 사용하기 시작했는데, 이것은 'sunya'라고 불렸다. 이 개념은 마침내 중국으로, 그런 다

음 중동으로 퍼졌는데, 그곳에서 그것은 오늘날 우리가 사용하는 아라비아 숫자 체계의 일부가 되었다. 이때가 숫자 0이 처음으로 친숙한 둥근 형태를 갖게 된 시기이다. 페르시아의 위대한 수학자 무하마드 이븐무사 알콰리즈미는 이내 그의 수학 계산의 일부로 0을 사용하기 시작했다.

　1100년대에 0의 개념은 마침내 유럽에 이르렀고, 그곳에서 이탈리아 수학자 피보나치에 의해 대중화되었다. 후에, 0은 르네 데카르트의 연구에 중요한 역할을 했으며, 미적분학을 만들어 내기 위한 일환으로 아이작 뉴턴 경(卿)과 고트프리트 라이프니츠에 의해 사용되었다. 오늘날 0은 우리의 수학 체계의 필수적인 부분이 되었고, 새로운 아이디어를 진척시키기 위해 물리학자에서부터 컴퓨터 프로그래머에 이르기까지 모든 사람들에 의해 사용된다.

어휘
relatively 비교적　addition 추가된 것　numerical 수의, 수와 관련된　be made up of …로 구성되다　triangular 삼각형의　mathematician 수학자　numeral 숫자　calculation 계산　popularize 대중화하다, 많은 사람들에게 알리다　calculus 미적분학　indispensable 필수적인　physicist 물리학자　advance 진척시키다　[문제] breakthrough 큰 발전　controversy 논란

구문해설
6행 ..., people used a blank space [to represent the idea of zero].: [ ]는 목적을 나타내는 부사적 용법의 to부정사구
8행 ..., the ancient Babylonians created a symbol [made up of two small triangular shapes].: [ ]는 a symbol을 수식하는 과거분사구
10행 Although this wasn't a true zero, it was used in the same way [that we now use zeros {to show the difference between 10 and 100}].: [ ]는 the same way를 선행사로 하는 관계부사절. { }는 목적을 나타내는 부사적 용법의 to부정사구
17행 This concept eventually spread to China and then to the Middle East, [where it became part of the Arabic numeral system {(that/which) we use today}].: [ ]는 the Middle East를 선행사로 하는 계속적 용법의 관계부사절. { }는 the Arabic numeral system을 선행사로 하는 목적격 관계대명사절

문제해설
41 과거에는 개념조차 없었던 숫자 0이 어떻게 오늘날 우리가 사용하는 수 체계의 일부가 되었는지 설명하는 내용이므로 ② '0: 과거에서 현재까지'가 제목으로 가장 적절하다.
42 ① 오늘날 우리가 사용하는 0은 12세기가 되어서야 유럽에 들어와 널리 사용되었는데, 그전에도 0의 개념을 나타내기 위한 여러 가지 방법이 존재했으므로, 문맥상 later(나중에)는 earlier(먼저) 등이 되어야 한다.

43 ②　44 ③　45 ④ 장문

　(A) 시드니 오페라 하우스의 건설 이전에, 호주의 그 도시에는 음악 공연을 위한 알맞은 시설들이 없었다. 시(市) 청사가 오케스트라 콘서트를 위해 사용되었고, 대규모의 오페라를 무대에 올리기에 적절한 곳은 어디에도 없었다. 유진 구센스 경(卿)이 시드니 교향악단의 수석 지휘자로 임명되었을 때, 그는 클래식 콘서트와 오페라 모두에 알맞은 공연 공간을 만드는 것을 자신의 임무로 삼겠다고 결심했다.

　(B) 이것은 시드니 사람들에게 새로운 생각이 아니었다. 수년 동안, 정부는 재건과 재개발 프로그램의 일환으로 그러한 건물을 건설하겠다는 약속을 해왔다. 그러나, 구센스의 최선의 노력에도 불구하고, 아무런 조치가 취해지지 않은 채로 7년이 지났다. 마침내, 1954년에 주 정부는 늑장 부리는 것을 멈추고 그 계획을 시행하기로 결정했다.

　(D) 조셉 카힐이라는 이름의 그 당시의 수상은 그 계획을 시행하는 것에 매우 의욕이 넘쳤고, 그것을 주관하는 위원회를 설립하는 데 신속히

착수했다. 다음으로, 시드니 시의 공연 예술 복합공간을 위한 최고의 디자인을 선정하기 위해 국제적인 대회가 (열릴 것이라고) 공표되었다. 참가자들은 그들이 최고라고 생각하는 디자인을 위한 어떤 접근 방식이든지 선택하도록 지시받았으며, 건설에 따른 예상 비용에 대해 걱정할 필요가 없다고 들었다. 최종적으로, 전 세계에서 200개가 넘는 디자인이 출품되었다.

　(C) 1957년 1월에, 덴마크 건축가 요른 웃존이 그 대회의 우승자로 발표되었다. 2년 후에는 건설이 시작되었다. 수많은 (건설) 지연과 예산 문제들이 있었으며, 그중 많은 것들이 부당하게 웃존 그 자신의 책임으로 전가되었다. 결국, 정부는 그의 디자인 아이디어를 거부했고 자금 지원을 중단했다. 그의 인부들에게 작업을 계속하도록 임금을 지불할 수 없어서 웃존은 1966년에 사임할 수밖에 없었다. 7년 후, 시드니 오페라 하우스는 엘리자베스 2세 여왕의 지휘 아래 성대한 축하 행사 속에서 대중들에게 공개되었다. 하지만 웃존은 초대받지 못했다.

어휘
construction 건설, 건축　facility (*pl.*) 시설, 설비　adequate 적당한, 충분한　stage 상연[공연]하다　appoint 임명하다　mission 임무, 사명　drag one's feet 발을 질질 끌다; *꾸물거리다　architect 건축가　budget 예산　resign 사임하다　premier 수상, 국무총리　set about …을 시작하다　complex 복합 건물, (건물) 단지　submit 제출하다　[문제] heritage 유산

구문해설
8행 ..., he decided to make it his mission [to create a performance space {suitable for both classical concerts and operas}].: it은 가목적어이고 [ ]가 진목적어, { }는 a performance space를 수식하는 형용사구
16행 ..., seven years passed with no action being taken.: 'with+O+분사' 「…을 ~한 채로」(부대상황을 나타내는 분사구문)
26행 [(Being) Unable to pay his workers to continue their work], Utzon had no choice but to resign in 1966.: [ ]는 이유를 나타내는 분사구문, 'have no choice but to-v' 「…하지 않을 수 없다」

문제해설
43 ② 새로 부임한 오케스트라 지휘자가 시드니에 클래식 콘서트와 오페라 공연을 위한 공간을 만들겠다고 다짐하는 (A) 다음에, 건설을 미루던 주 정부가 마침내 그 계획을 시작하는 (B)가 오고, 그 건물의 디자인을 선정하는 대회가 열렸다는 내용의 (D) 다음에, 선정된 디자인과 실제 건물을 완성하기까지의 과정을 보여주는 (C)가 오는 것이 자연스럽다.
44 시드니에 오페라 하우스가 건설되기까지의 과정을 보여주고 있으므로 제목으로는 ③ '시드니는 어떻게 마침내 오페라 하우스를 얻게 되었나'가 적절하다.
45 ④ 건축 담당자인 웃존은 공개 행사에 초대받지 못했다.

06 영어독해 모의고사

18 ④	19 ②	20 ④	21 ①	22 ⑤	23 ⑤
24 ③	25 ③	26 ②	27 ⑤	28 ②	29 ⑤
30 ③	31 ③	32 ②	33 ④	34 ④	35 ④
36 ③	37 ④	38 ⑤	39 ③	40 ⑤	41 ②
42 ④	43 ②	44 ③	45 ②		

18 ④ 글의 목적

관계자분께,

　저는 귀사의 택배 서비스를 통해 배송을 자주 받는 중소기업의 운영 자입니다. 지난주에, 귀사는 우리 회사에 소포를 하나 배달했습니다. 보낸 사람이 당일 배송을 약속받은 사실에도 불구하고 (소포가) 도착하는 데 4일이 걸렸습니다. 때때로 지연이 발생한다는 것은 이해하지만, 사과나 설명 없이 소포가 배송되었습니다. 더욱 심각한 것은, 택배 기사가 (그가) 요청받았던 대로 서명을 받지도 않고 소포를 그냥 정문에 두고 갔습니다. 귀하의 회사는 좋은 평판을 가지고 있지만, 같은 서비스를 경쟁력 있는 가격으로 제공하는 다른 택배사가 많이 있습니다. 이런 종류의 일이 다시는 일어나지 않을 것을 귀사에서 장담할 수 없다면, 저는 그 회사 중 한 곳으로 바꿀 필요성을 느끼게 될 것입니다. 귀하의 회신을 기다리 겠습니다.

에밀리 그린스톤
파이어사이드 컨설팅

어휘
frequently 빈번히, 자주　courier service 택배 회사　package 소포 overnight delivery 당일 배송　delay 지연, 지체　apology 사과 explanation 설명　signature 서명　require 요구하다　reputation 평판 competitive 경쟁을 하는; *경쟁력 있는　switch 전환하다, 바꾸다　assure 장담하다, 확언하다　await 기다리다　response 대답, 회신

구문해설
5행 It **took** four days **to arrive**, despite the fact [that the sender was promised overnight delivery].: 'take+시간+to-v'「…하는 데 시간이 걸리다」, [ ]는 the fact와 동격
14행 ... the need [to switch to one of them] if you cannot assure [that this type of thing will not happen again].: 첫 번째 [ ]는 the need를 수식하는 형용사적 용법의 to부정사구, 두 번째 [ ]는 assure의 목적절

문제해설
당일 배송되어야 했을 소포가 사과나 설명 없이 지연 배송된 것, 택배 기사가 서명을 받지 않고 정문에 소포를 두고 간 것 등을 고객이 항의하는 내용이므로, 글의 목적으로 ④가 가장 적절하다.

19 ② 분위기

　릴리 다니엘스는 매일 아침처럼 기차역으로 걸어가다가 뭔가가 잘못 되었다는 것을 알아차렸다. 그녀는 존슨 씨의 집에서 연기가 나오는 것을 흘낏 보았다! 존슨 씨는 휠체어를 타는 혼자 사는 노인이었다. 릴리는 걱정이 되어 자신의 가방을 내려놓고 길을 건너갔다. 연기가 더 많이 났고, 현관문은 너무 뜨거워서 만질 수도 없었다. 창문 안을 들여다보았을 때 릴리는 거대한 불길이 존슨 씨를 부엌에 가둬놓은 것을 보았다. 그 불길

은 문을 가로막고 있었다! 재빨리 그녀는 911에 전화를 걸었다. 전화 교환원은 그녀에게 소방관들이 도착하기를 밖에서 기다리라고 말했다. 하지만 불이 급속히 번지고 있었고 그 노인에게는 시간이 많지 않았다.

어휘
out of the corner of one's eye 곁눈질로; *흘낏 보고　flame 불길, 화염 trap 가두다, 꼼짝할 수 없게 하다　dial 전화를 걸다　operator 전화 교환원 spread 퍼지다　[문제] tense 긴박한, 긴장된　urgent 긴급한, 다급한 frustrating 좌절감을 주는

구문해설
1행 Lily Daniels was walking to the train station just as she **did** every morning ...: did는 대동사로 walked to the train station을 의미
8행 [Looking in a window], Lily **saw** huge flames **trapping** Mr. Johnson in the kitchen.: [ ]는 때를 나타내는 분사구문, 지각동사 saw의 목적 격보어로 현재분사 사용
11행 The operator told her [to wait outside *for the firefighters* **to arrive**].: [ ]는 told의 목적격보어로 쓰인 to부정사구, to arrive는 wait의 목적어로 쓰인 명사적 용법의 to부정사, the firefighters는 to부정사의 의미상 주어

문제해설
② 길을 가다가 불과 연기로 가득한 집안에 갇혀 있는 노인을 목격한 상황이므로 '긴장되고 긴박한' 분위기임을 알 수 있다.

20 ④ 필자의 주장

　장기를 기증하는 데 동의하는 사람들이 거의 없기 때문에 매년 수천 명의 환자들이 장기 이식을 기다리다가 죽는다. 이러한 이유 때문에, 현금 지급이나 세금 공제로 잠재적인 장기 기증자들을 장려하는 제도의 도입을 위한 많은 제안들이 있어 왔다. 이것은 내가 결코 찬성할 수 없는 생각이다. 어떤 상황에서도 우리는 장기 기증자들에게 금전적인 보상을 제공해서는 안 된다. 장기 기증의 이점은 한 사람의 생명을 구한다는 만족 감에서 생겨나야 하며, 그 이상이 되어서는 안 된다. 솔직히 말하면, 사람의 장기에 가격표를 붙인다는 생각만으로도 나에게 혐오감을 느끼게 한다. 장기 기증자의 부족은 반드시 처리되어야 하는 문제이지만, 올바르고 윤리적인 방식으로 되어야 한다.

어휘
organ transplant 장기 이식　donate 기부하다, 기증하다　institute 제정하다, 세우다　donor 기증자　tax credit 세금 공제　satisfaction 만족(감)　to be blunt 사실대로 말해서, 솔직히 말해서　disgust 역겹게 하다, 넌더리나게 하다　address (문제 등을) 처리하다, 다루다　ethical 윤리적인

구문해설
4행 ..., there have been numerous proposals for **instituting** a system [which encourages ... or tax credits].: instituting은 전치사 for의 목적어로 쓰인 동명사, [ ]는 a system을 선행사로 하는 주격 관계대명사절
8행 Under no circumstances **should we** offer financial ...: 부정어 Under no circumstances가 문두로 나와 주어와 동사가 도치

문제해설
④ 장기 기증은 생명을 구하는 만족감에 의해 행해져야 하며, 어떤 상황에서도 금전적으로 보상받아서는 안 된다고 주장하는 글이다.

21 ① 함축 의미 추론

　사람은 산소 없이 살 수 없다는 것은 잘 알려져 있지만, 너무 많은 산소도 위험하다는 것은 잘 알려져 있지 않다. 우리 몸은 우리가 섭취하는 음식을 소화함으로써 우리의 일상 활동에 연료를 공급하는데, 이는 산소를 필요로 하는 과정이다. 그러나 공기는 대부분 질소로 구성되어 있다.

실제로, 질소는 공기의 72%를 차지하며, 신체는 이것을 소화 과정을 늦추는 데 사용한다. 이는 촛불을 태우는 것과 비슷하게 느리고 통제된 연소를 야기해서, 하루 종일 우리에게 안정적인 에너지 공급을 제공한다. 만약 우리가 순수한 산소를 들이마신다면, 이 과정은 폭죽이 터지는 것과 더 비슷할 것이다. 이는 우리가 실제로 폭발할 것을 의미하지 않지만, 우리 몸에서 화학 물질들 사이의 상호 작용을 일으킬 것이다. 이는 우리 눈과 폐와 같은 신체의 많은 부분에 손상을 줄 수 있으며, 우리 DNA조차도 위험할 수 있다.

어휘

oxygen 산소   fuel 연료를 공급하다   digest 소화하다(digestive 소화의)   process 과정   require 필요[요구]하다, 필요로 하다   nitrogen 질소   account for (부분·비율을) 차지하다   comparable 비슷한, 비교할 만한   steady 안정된   supply 공급   explode 폭발하다   interaction 상호 작용   chemical 화학 물질   [문제] reaction 반응   expand 확대[확장/팽창]되다   get rid of 제거하다   defend 방어하다

구문해설

(1행) It's well known [that people can't live without oxygen], but it's less known [that too much oxygen is also dangerous].: 두 개의 It[it]은 가주어이고 두 개의 [ ]가 각각의 진주어

(3행) Our bodies fuel our daily activities **by digesting** the food [(which/that) we eat], [which is a process that requires oxygen].: 'by v-ing' 「…함으로써」, 첫 번째 [ ]는 the food를 선행사로 하는 목적격 관계대명사절, 두 번째 [ ]는 앞 절 전체를 선행사로 하는 계속적 용법의 주격 관계대명사절

(8행) This results in a slow, controlled burn [comparable to *a candle* **burning**], [providing us with a steady supply of energy throughout the day].: 첫 번째 [ ]는 a slow, controlled burn을 수식하는 형용사구, burning은 전치사 to의 목적어 역할을 하는 동명사이고, a candle은 동명사 burning의 의미상 주어, 두 번째 [ ]는 결과를 나타내는 분사구문

문제해설

공기 중 질소는 우리 몸의 소화 과정을 늦추며 촛불을 태우는 것과 비슷하게 느리고 통제된 연소를 발생시킨다고 했고, 질소가 없이 순수한 산소만 있다면 이와 반대로 빠른 연소 작용이 일어난다는 내용이므로, 우리가 산소만을 들이마시면 '폭죽이 터지는 것과 더 비슷하다'가 의미하는 바로 가장 적절한 것은 ① '제어할 수 없는 화학 반응을 일으키다'가 가장 적절하다.

22 ⑤ 글의 요지

컴퓨터 워드 프로그램들은 철자 검사기와, 선택된 단어의 유의어와 반의어를 찾아 주는 유의어 사전까지도 갖추고 있다. 또한 그 프로그램들은 철자가 틀린 단어들에 대해 권장되는 철자를 보여 줄 수도 있다. 나는 이런 기능들을 수행하는 컴퓨터 프로그램을 갖고 있는 것이 만족스럽다. 하지만 이런 프로그램들이 학생에게 철자나 단어의 의미에 대해 가르쳐 주지는 않는다. 어떤 사람은 단어를 입력하여 유의어를 알아내고도, 두 단어가 무슨 뜻인지 전혀 모를 수도 있다. 철자를 검사하고 유의어를 찾는 이러한 생각 없는 방법에 의존한다면, 학생들은 그들이 사용하는 단어들의 의미에 대해 전적으로 잘 모르게 될 것이다. 사실, 가장 흔한 오용 중 하나는 철자는 정확하지만 문장 속에서는 부정확하게 쓰인 단어를 포함하는 경우이다.

어휘

spell checker【컴퓨터】문서 내의 철자법을 검사하는 프로그램   synonym 유의어   antonym 반의어   highlight 눈에 띄게 하다, 강조하다   recommend 추천하다; 권장하다   misspell 철자를 잘못 쓰다   rely on …에 의지하다   mindless 생각 없는, 어리석은   completely 완전히   unfamiliar 잘 모르는, 익숙하지 못한   misuse 오용, 악용   incorrectly 부정확하게

구문해설

(8행) A person could **type** in a word, **get** a synonym, and not **have** the slightest idea what *either* meant.: type, get, have가 등위 접속사 and로 병렬 연결, either는 부정문에서 「어느 쪽도 (… 않다)」라는 의미를 나타내는 대명사

(10행) [Relying on this mindless way of **spelling** and **finding** synonyms], students will …: [ ]는 조건을 나타내는 분사구문, 전치사 of의 목적어인 동명사 spelling과 finding이 등위 접속사 and로 병렬 연결

문제해설

⑤ 컴퓨터 워드 프로그램의 기능들이 학생들의 어휘 학습에 방해가 될 수 있음을 설명하고 있다.

23 ⑤ 글의 주제

수소 기체는 별 형성에 필요한 주요 구성 요소이다. 그러나 전 우주를 통틀어서 은하계와 다른 별 형성 영역들을 연구하는 것을 통해, 천문학자들은 새로운 별들을 만들기 위해 이용 가능한 수소가 점점 더 적어지고 있다는 것을 알아냈다. 문제의 일부는 우주에 원래 존재하는 수소의 대부분이 현존하는 별들 속에 사실상 '갇혀 있다'는 것이다. 별들이 생애 주기의 마지막에 폭발할 때 그 수소 중 일부가 우주로 다시 방출되지만, 이것은 일정량의 이용 가능한 수소를 유지할 만큼 충분히 자주 일어나지 않는다. 게다가 우주가 팽창하면서 은하계가 (우주의) 빈 공간으로부터 자연 발생적인 중력을 통해 수소를 끌어당기는 것이 점점 더 어려워지고 있다. 이러한 발견들은 우주의 진화가 점점 더 어둡고 차가운 우주를 초래할 것이라는 현재의 이론을 뒷받침한다.

어휘

hydrogen 수소   primary 주된   component 구성 요소, 성분   formation 형성(form 형성하다)   galaxy 은하계   astronomer 천문학자   majority 다수   originally 원래   present 존재하는   effectively 효과적으로; *사실상   lock up 가두다   currently 현재(current 현재의)   in existence 현존하는   explode 폭발하다   life cycle 생애 주기   constant 일정한   expand 팽창하다(expansion 확대, 팽창)   gravitational force 중력   cosmological 우주(론)의

구문해설

(4행) …, astronomers have found that there is **less and less** hydrogen [available {to create new stars}].: '비교급+and+비교급' 「점점 더 …한」, [ ]는 hydrogen을 수식하는 형용사구, { }는 목적을 나타내는 부사적 용법의 to부정사구

(6행) Part of the problem is that **the majority of hydrogen** [(which is) originally present in the universe] **is** effectively "locked up" in stars …: the majority of 뒤에 나오는 명사가 단수형이므로 단수동사인 is가 쓰임. [ ]는 hydrogen을 선행사로 하는 주격 관계대명사절

(12행) In addition, as the universe expands, **it** is getting harder and harder *for galaxies* [to draw in hydrogen … force].: it은 가주어이고 [ ]가 진주어, galaxies는 [ ]의 의미상 주어

문제해설

우주에서 별을 형성하는 주된 구성 요소인 수소가 점점 적어지고 있다는 내용이므로 ⑤ '새로운 별을 형성하기 위해 이용 가능한 수소의 감소'가 글의 주제로 적절하다.

24 ③ 글의 제목

당신이 개구리의 피부에 대해 생각을 할 때 마음속에 많은 묘사하는 말들이 떠오를지도 모르지만, 아마도 그 말들 가운데 '기적'과 '약'은 없을 것이다. 그렇다면 당신은 과학자들이 최근에 개구리 피부에서 발견된 분자들을 모방하여 박테리아를 제거하는 데 사용될 수도 있는 화합물을

개발했다는 것을 알게 되면 놀랄 것이다. 박테리아가 기존의 모든 종류의 항생제에 계속해서 저항력을 키우고 있기 때문에 현재 이러한 종류의 약에 대한 절박한 필요성이 존재한다. 대부분의 항생제들은 박테리아 내부의 단백질을 파괴함으로써 작용하여 그것들을 죽이는 반면, 개구리 피부에서 영감을 얻은 화합물은 매우 다르게 기능하여 단순히 박테리아가 죽을 때까지 박테리아에 수천 개의 구멍을 내는 것이다. 이 새로운 직접적인 공격 방식과 대면하게 되면, 박테리아는 그에 대한 저항력을 키울 수 없을 것이다.

어휘
descriptive 기술적인, 설명적인   compound 화합물, 혼합물   mimic 흉내 내다, 모방하다   molecule 분자   combat 제거하기 위해 싸우다   pressing 긴급한, 절박한   resistance 저항   antibiotic 항생제   inspired 영감을 받은   poke 찌르다   confront 직면하다, 맞서다   [문제] copy 복사하다; *모방하다   endangered 멸종 위기에 처한

구문해설
[2행] ..., but (the) **chances are** (that) "miracle" and "drug" aren't among them.: '(the) chances are (that) ...' 「아마 …일 것이다, …할 가능성이 충분하다」
[3행] You'll be surprised to learn, then, [that scientists recently developed a compound {that mimics molecules **found in frog skin** and can be used to combat bacteria}].: [ ]는 learn의 목적절, { }는 a compound를 선행사로 하는 주격 관계대명사절, found in frog skin은 molecules를 수식하는 과거분사구

문제해설
개구리 피부를 모방하여 만든 화합물로 박테리아를 없애는 방법을 설명하고 있으므로 제목으로는 ③ '개구리 피부를 모방하여 박테리아와 싸우기'가 적절하다.

25 ③ 도표 내용 불일치

위의 도표는 특정한 한 주 동안 병으로 인해 결근했던 두 연령대 직원들의 수를 나타낸다. 젊은 직원들은 주말 전후에 더 많은 수가 결근했음을 바로 알 수 있다. 높은 연령대의 더 많은 직원들이 결근한 것은 주의 중반 동안이었다. (수요일에는 젊은 연령대보다 높은 연령대의 결근이 세 배만큼 많았다.) 41세에서 65세 연령대의 사람들 가운데서는 5일 동안 총 41건의 결근이 있었다. 18세에서 40세 연령대에서는 그보다 훨씬 더 적은 총 27건의 결근뿐이었다.

어휘
employee 고용인, 종업원   absent 결석의, 결석한(absence 결석, 결근)   immediately 곧, 즉시   period 기간

구문해설
[3행] **It** can be noted immediately [that younger employees were absent ... weekend].: It은 가주어이고 [ ]가 진주어
[6행] **It was** during the middle of the week **that** more employees from ...: 'it is[was] ... that ~' 「~하는 것은 바로 …이다[였다]」(강조구문)
[8행] On Wednesday, there were **three times as** many absences from the older age group **as** from the younger.: '배수사+as ... as' 「~배만큼 …한」

문제해설
③ 수요일에 높은 연령대의 결근자 수(12명)는 젊은 연령대의 결근자 수(3명)의 네 배다.

26 ② 내용 불일치

비록 많은 사람들이 새는 영리하지 못하다고 생각하지만, 이것은 사

실이 아니다. 그들의 뇌는 비슷한 크기의 파충류들의 뇌보다 약 10배 더 크다. 게다가, 새는 복잡한 사회적 행동을 할 수 있을 뿐만 아니라, 도구도 사용할 수 있다. 이것의 가장 잘 알려진 예시 중 하나는 갈라파고스 제도의 딱따구리 핀치에게서 관찰될 수 있다. 딱따구리 핀치는 사실 딱따구리가 아니다. 진짜 딱따구리는 나무에 그들이 만드는 구멍에서 곤충을 제거하기 위해 그들의 긴 혀를 사용한다. 하지만, 딱따구리 핀치는 이런 종류의 혀가 발달되지 않았다. 그것이 구멍에서 벌레를 발견하면, 선인장 가시나 나무 가시와 같은 뾰족한 물체를 찾기 위해 날아간다. 그런 다음 먹이를 잡기 위해 이 물체를 사용한다. 만약 적절한 물체를 구할 수 없다면, 그것은 작은 잔가지를 꺾고 잎을 제거할 것이다. 이러한 경우, 그것은 단지 도구를 사용하는 것이 아니라, 실제로 도구를 만들어 내는 것이다.

어휘
unintelligent 영리하지 못한, 우둔한   reptile 파충류   be capable of …할 수 있다   complex 복잡한   social 사회의, 사회적인   behavior 행동   tongue 혀   evolve 발달하다   insect 곤충   object 물건, 물체   cactus spine 선인장 가시   suitable 적합한   available 구할[이용할] 수 있는   twig 잔가지   manufacture 제조하다; *만들어 내다

구문해설
[2행] Their brains are about **10 times larger than** *those* of similar-sized reptiles.: '배수사+비교급+than' 「…보다 몇 배 더 ~한」, those는 앞에 언급한 brains를 지칭하는 대명사
[4행] Moreover, **not only** *are birds* capable of complex social behavior, they can **also** use tools.: 'not only A (but) also B' 「A뿐만 아니라 B도」, 부정어 not only가 문두로 나와 주어와 동사가 도치됨
[5행] **One of the best-known examples** of this can be observed in the woodpecker finch of the Galapagos Islands.: 'one of the+최상급+복수명사' 「가장 …한 것들 중 하나」

문제해설
② 딱따구리 핀치는 진짜 딱따구리처럼 긴 혀가 발달되지 않았다고 했다.

27 ⑤ 내용 일치

여우원숭이 동족들과 비교했을 때, 관여우원숭이는 평균 크기로 자란다. 수컷들은 어둡고 불그스름한 갈색인 반면, 암컷들은 더 밝고 더 회색빛이다. 그런데, 두 성별 모두 머리에 주황색 무늬가 특징인데, 이것이 관여우원숭이에게 그 이름을 부여한다. 관여우원숭이는 일반적으로 낮에 활동적이지만, 밤에도 약 두 시간의 활동기를 가진다. 그것은 대부분의 시간을 삼림수의 높은 곳에서 보내지만, 먹이를 찾고 돌아다니기 위해 땅으로도 종종 내려온다. 관여우원숭이는 다 자란 원숭이들과 새끼들로 이루어진 작은 혼성 무리 속에서 사는 경향이 있는데, 그것은 때때로 커져서 15마리만큼 많은 수로 이루어지기도 한다. 그것들의 자연 서식지는 아프리카의 섬나라인 마다가스카르의 북부 삼림지대이다.

어휘
relative 친척; *동족   average 평균의   reddish 불그스름한   offspring 자식; *(동식물의) 새끼

구문해설
[1행] [(Being) Compared to its lemur relatives], the crowned lemur grows to an average size.: [ ]는 조건을 나타내는 분사구문
[11행] Crowned lemurs tend to live in small, mixed-sex groups [composed of adults and offspring], [which sometimes grow to have **as many as** 15 members].: 첫 번째 [ ]는 small, mixed-sex groups를 수식하는 과거분사구, 두 번째 [ ]는 small, mixed-sex groups를 선행사로 하는 계속적 용법의 주격 관계대명사절, 'as ... as ~' 「~만큼 …한」(동등비교)

는 'get+O+to-v'에 병렬 구조로 연결되므로 to give가 되어야 한다.

문제해설
① 여우원숭이 동족의 평균 크기로 자란다. ② 주황색 무늬는 등이 아닌 머리에 있다. ③ 주로 낮에 활동적이며 밤에는 두 시간 정도의 활동기를 갖는다. ④ 주로 나무에서 활동하지만 종종 땅으로 내려온다.

28 ② 내용 불일치

제15회 연례 벌링턴 사진 대회

이번 해의 주제는 '가을'입니다. 모든 벌링턴 주민들을 참여하도록 초대합니다!

제출 - 사진은 디지털 서식으로 제출되어야 합니다. 최대 다섯 장까지 제출 가능합니다. 컬러와 흑백 사진 모두 받습니다.

마감 기한 - 모든 출품작은 10월 2일까지 접수되어야 합니다.

상품 - 금상 한 개와 은상 두 개가 수여될 것입니다. 금상 수상자는 새 카메라를, 그리고 은상 수상자들은 각각 50달러 상당의 상품권을 받을 것입니다.

시상식 - 시상식은 11월 20일 토요일 저녁 6시에 시청에서 열릴 것입니다.

어휘
theme 주제   participate 참가하다   submission 항복; *제출(submit 제출하다)   format 구성 방식; *포맷, 서식   maximum 최고, 최대   accept 받다, 받아들이다   deadline 기한, 마감 시간   entry 들어감; *출품[응모/참가]작   award 상; 수여하다   gift certificate 상품권

구문해설
6행 **Both** color **and** black-and-white photos *are* accepted.: 'both A and B'는 'A와 B 둘 다'라는 의미이며 복수 취급하여 복수동사 are 사용

문제해설
② 컬러와 흑백 사진 모두 받는다고 했다.

29 ⑤ 어법

모든 인종 차별이, 면전에서는 예의를 갖추면서 인종 전체에 대해 혐오적인 것들을 말하거나 특정 사람들을 가리키는 데 욕설을 사용하는 것처럼 명백한 것은 아니다. 그런 행동은 마땅히 사회적으로 수용될 수 없다고 받아들여지지만, 더 체계적이고 구조적인 제도적 인종 차별은 해결하기가 더 어렵다. 고용에 있어서의 제도적 인종 차별은 항상 의식적인 결정인 것은 아니다. 어떤 사람들은 단지 자신과 비슷한 지원자들을 고용하거나, (그들은) 인종적으로 그다지 다양하지 않은 사회적 네트워크에 구인 광고를 낸다. 이 때문에, 채용을 하는 사람들의 대다수가 백인일 때, 채용되는 사람들 또한 백인일 가능성이 있는 것이다. 따라서, 고용 평등 프로그램의 역할은 회사나 정부 부처로 하여금 그들의 인적 네트워크를 확장하게 하고, 취업 기회에 대해 모든 지역사회가 접할 수 있도록 보장하며, 지원자들에게 공정한 기회를 주도록 하는 것이다.

어휘
racism 인종 차별   obvious 명백한   rightly 당연히, 마땅히   institutional 제도적인   hire 고용하다   conscious 의식적인   applicant 지원자, 신청자   diverse 다양한   majority 다수   employment 고용   equity 공평, 평등   expand 확장하다   ensure 확실히 하다

구문해설
1행 **Not all** racism is *as* obvious *as* saying ... or using ...: 'not all ...' 「모두 …인 것은 아니다」(부분부정), 'as ... as ~' 「~만큼 …한」(동등 비교)
8행 Some people simply hire applicants [who are similar to themselves], ...: [ ]는 applicants를 선행사로 하는 주격 관계대명사절

문제해설
⑤의 동사는 companies and government departments를 목적어로 하

30 ③ 어휘

비행하는 동안 비행기에 작용하는 네 가지 주요 힘들이 있다. 무게는 그중 하나이며, 이는 중력에 의해 땅으로 끌어당겨지는 비행기의 질량의 결과이다. 무게의 반대되는 힘은 상승력으로, 이것은 비행기의 날개에 의해 생겨나며 비행기를 공중에 받치고 있는 힘을 말한다. 비행기의 프로펠러, 혹은 제트기라면 제트 엔진이 추진력을 만들어내고 이것이 비행기의 앞으로 나아가는 움직임을 만드는 역할을 한다. 저항력은 비행기가 빠른 속도로 공중을 가로지를 때 저항에 의해 야기된, 추진력에 반대로 작용하는 힘이다. 공중에 떠 있기 위해서, 비행기는 그 무게와 저항력에 비해 더 큰 상승력과 추진력을 유지해야 한다.

어휘
mass 질량   gravity 중력   lift 들어 올림; *상승력   craft 항공기   propeller 추진기, 프로펠러   thrust 밀침; *추진력   drag 끌기, 당기기; *저항력   aloft 위에, 공중에   maintain 유지하다   [문제] resistance 저항, 저항력   registration 등록

구문해설
4행 The opposite of weight is lift, [which is created by the plane's wings and is the force {that holds the craft up in the air}].: [ ]는 lift를 선행사로 하는 계속적 용법의 주격 관계대명사절, { }는 the force를 선행사로 하는 주격 관계대명사절

문제해설
③ (A) 무게는 중력에 의해 비행기 기체가 땅 쪽으로 잡아당겨지는 힘이므로 '…쪽으로(towards)'라고 하는 것이 적절하다. (B) 저항력은 비행기가 공중을 가로지를 때 '저항(resistance)'에 의해 생긴 힘이라고 하는 것이 적절하다. (C) 비행기가 떠 있으려면, 무게보다 상승력이 커야 하고 저항력에 비해 추진력이 커야 하므로 '더 큰 (greater)'이 적절하다.

31 ③ 빈칸 추론

침팬지들은 인간과 같이 그들의 오른손을 사용하는 것을 선호한다. 이것은 그 특성에 관한 연구를 최근에 출간한 스페인의 과학자 집단에게 놀라운 일이었다. 연구원들은 그들이 연구하는 동안 스페인과 잠비아 두 나라의 구조센터에 있는 100마리 이상의 침팬지들을 관찰했다. 침팬지들이 어느 손을 더 선호하는지를 알아내기 위해, 과학자들은 그들에게 튜브 안쪽 깊숙이 놓여 있는 먹이를 주었다. 그리고 나서, 그들은 그 영장류들(= 침팬지들)이 먹이를 꺼내는 것을 보고, 어느 손을 사용하였는지를 기록했다. 대다수의 경우에서, 침팬지들은 그들의 오른손을 사용하는 것을 선호했다. 이전에는 과학자들이 오직 인간만이 이러한 특성을 가지고 있다고 추측했었는데, 다양한 방법으로 양손을 사용하여 어려운 일을 수행하는 능력과 같은 인간의 뇌의 독특한 면에 의해 차이점이 생겨났다고 믿었기 때문이다. 연구원들에 따르면, 이것은 우리에게 침팬지와 인간이 그들의 뇌가 기능하는 방법을 결정하는 공유된 특징을 가지고 있다는 것을 말해준다.

어휘
trait 특성   rescue 구조   primate 《pl.》 영장류   significant 중요한, 의미 있는, 커다란   assume 추정하다   unique 유일무이한, 독특한   aspect 측면   perform 행하다, 수행하다   determine 알아내다; *결정하다   function 기능하다   [문제] discrete 별개의   substantial 상당한

구문해설
8행 Then, they **watched** the primates **remove** the food and recorded [which hand they used].: 지각동사 watched의 목적격보어로 동

사원형이 쓰임. [ ]는 recorded의 목적어로 쓰인 의문사절

(13행) ..., since they believed [that the difference was caused by unique aspects of the human brain, such as the ability {to perform difficult tasks using both hands in different ways}].: [ ]는 believed의 목적절. { }는 the ability를 수식하는 형용사적 용법의 to부정사구

문제해설
③ 스페인의 과학자들이 침팬지를 연구한 결과 인간과 마찬가지로 오른손 사용을 선호한다는 것을 알아냈으므로, 뇌의 독특한 작용으로 손을 사용하는 인간처럼 침팬지도 뇌의 작용에 있어서 인간과 '공유된' 특징을 갖는다고 할 수 있다.

32 ② 빈칸 추론

컴퓨터와 마찬가지로, 인간의 정신은 두 가지 기본적인 종류의 기억을 갖고 있다. 현 순간의 정보를 판단하는 작동 기억과 오랜 기간에 걸쳐서 정보를 저장하는 장기 기억이다. 일반적인 생각과 달리, 우리의 뇌는 우리에게 일어나는 모든 일을 기록하지는 않는다. 사람들이 모든 것을 기억할 필요는 없기에 인간의 기억은 특정한 날에 받아들인 정보의 대부분을 우리가 잊어버릴 수 있도록 하는 여과 장치로 작용한다. 우리가 인지하는 것의 대부분은 컴퓨터의 램과 유사한 작동 기억에 잠깐 머물렀다가 지워져 버린다. 작동 기억은 우리가 머릿속으로 간단한 암산을 하거나 다이얼을 누를 때까지 전화번호를 기억할 수 있도록 해 준다. 램과 마찬가지로, 작동 기억은 지속적인 기록은 남기지 않으면서, 우리가 무언가를 분석하고 발명해 낼 수 있게 한다.

어휘
be equipped with …을 갖추다 judge 판단하다, 평가하다 long-term 장기적인 extended 넓은; *장기간에 걸친 contrary to …와 대조적으로 filter 여과 장치 given 정해진, 특정한 perceive 지각하다, 인식하다 briefly 간단히; *잠시 동안 delete 지우다 perform 수행하다 calculation 계산 retain 보유하다, 유지하다 [문제] lasting 오래 지속되는

구문해설
(10행) [Most of what we perceive] stays briefly in our working memory, [which is similar to a computer's RAM], and then gets deleted.: 첫 번째 [ ]는 문장의 주어로 쓰인 관계대명사절. 두 번째 [ ]는 our working memory를 선행사로 하는 계속적 용법의 주격 관계대명사절
(15행) ..., it lets us analyze and invent things, [while leaving no lasting record].: 'let+O+동사원형'「…가 ~하게 하다」. [ ]는 부대상황을 나타내는 분사구문

문제해설
② 빈칸이 있는 문장의 주어 it이 가리키는 것이 working memory이므로 이에 해당하는 특징은 지속적인 기록을 남기지 않고 잠깐 머물렀다 지워지는 것이다.

33 ④ 빈칸 추론

소리는 같게 들리지만 다른 의미를 지닌 단어들은 동음이의어라 불린다. 예를 들어, two, to 그리고 too와 같은 몇몇 동음이의어들은 매우 친숙하지만, 다른 것들은 빈번하게 사용됨에도 불구하고 그만큼 잘 알려져 있지 않다. 예를 들어 'team'과 'teem'이 있다. 당신은 아마 team이 무엇인지는 알겠지만, '가득 차다, 꽉 차다'라는 의미의 'teem'이라는 단어는 알고 있는가? 인간의 뇌는 연관된 정보들을 좋아하므로, 쌍이나 여러 개의 동음이의어를 함께 학습하는 것은 그것들을 기억하기 더 쉽게 한다. 당신은 'teem'이라는 단어가 동음이의어인 'team'보다 더 큰 양을 의미한다는 데에 주목할 수 있을 것이다. 또는 동음이의어의 다른 의미를 부각시키는 문장을 만들 수도 있다. 그 문장을 외우면, 두 단어의 의미는 (자연히) 따라올 것이다.

어휘
homonym 동음이의어 frequently 빈번하게 teem 충만하다, 가득하다 swarm 꽉 차다 note …에 주목하다 highlight 돋보이게 하다 memorize 암기하다 [문제] integration 통합 stimulus 자극(pl. stimuli) external 외부의

구문해설
(6행) You probably know [what a team is], ...: [ ]는 know의 목적어로 쓰인 의문사절

문제해설
④ 빈칸의 뒷부분에서 쌍이나 여러 개의 동음이의어를 함께 학습하면 기억하기가 쉬워진다고 했으므로 인간의 뇌가 서로 연관성이 있는 정보를 더 쉽게 처리한다는 것을 유추할 수 있다.

34 ④ 빈칸 추론

색깔은 사물을 더욱 매력적으로 보이게 할 뿐만 아니라 우리의 행동을 변화시키기도 하기 때문에 중요하다. 전 세계적으로 사람들은 색깔에 강한 정서적 반응을 보이는 것 같다. 그러나 이러한 반응은 문화에 기초한다. 예를 들어, 검은색은 유럽과 미국에서 애도의 색이다. 중국 문화에서는 흰색이 죽음을 상징하지만, 브라질에서는 보라색이 그러하다. 노란색은 프랑스에서 질투의 색인 반면, 북미에서는 녹색이 흔히 질투와 연관된다. 이렇게 색깔의 효과는 문화마다 다르므로, 마케팅 담당자들은 모든 판촉 자료의 디자인을 기획할 때 목표 고객의 태도와 선호도를 고려해야 한다. 그렇지 않으면, 그들은 자신의 생각을 효과적으로 공유할 수 없을 것이며, 소중한 고객을 잃게 될 것이다.

어휘
appealing 매력적인 mourning (죽음의) 애도 represent 대표하다; *상징하다 jealousy 질투 whereas …하는 반면 be associated with …와 연관되다 marketer 마케팅 담당자 take into account …을 고려하다 preference 선호(하는 것) promotional 판촉의 [문제] interpret 해석하다

구문해설
(7행) White represents death in Chinese culture, but purple **does so** in Brazil.: does so는 represents death를 대신함
(13행) ... their target customers [when planning the design of any promotional material].: [ ]는 때를 나타내는 분사구문

문제해설
④ 빈칸 앞에 In this way가 있으므로 빈칸에는 앞의 내용을 요약하는 내용인 '색깔의 효과는 문화마다 다르다'가 적절하다.

35 ④ 흐름과 무관한 문장

불소는 많은 식품과 물에서 자연적으로 생기는 광물질로, 치아 건강에 긍정적인 영향을 주는 것으로 알려져 있다. 치아가 자랄 때, 불소는 단단하고 충치를 방지하는 외부 막을 형성하는 법랑질을 강화하는 데 도움을 줄 수 있다. 일단 치아가 다 자라고 나면, 불소는 침과 섞여 당분과 해로운 박테리아로부터 법랑질을 보호할 수 있다. 그러므로 여러 지역에서 치아 건강을 개선하기 위해 공공 상수도에 불소를 첨가해온 것은 놀라운 일이 아니다. (그러나, 한 연구에서 불소가 첨가된 물이 있는 지역에 사는 사람들의 치아 건강이 다른 지역에 사는 사람들의 그것과 기본적으로 동일한 것으로 나타났다.) 비슷한 이유로, 불소는 종종 상업용 치약에도 첨가된다.

어휘
mineral 광물질 dental 치아의 strengthen 강화하다 enamel 법랑질 cavity 충치 resistant 저항하는; *방지하는 outer 외부의 coating (막 같

이 두른) 칠 saliva 침, 타액 essentially 근본적으로 identical 동일한, 똑같은 commercial 상업의, 시판되는

구문해설
1행 **Fluoride, a mineral** [that occurs naturally in many foods and water], is known to have positive effects on dental health.: Fluoride와 a mineral은 동격. [ ]는 a mineral을 선행사로 하는 주격 관계대명사절

7행 **It** is no surprise, then, [that *in order to improve* dental health, fluoride **has been added** to public water supplies in many areas].: It은 가주어이고 [ ]가 진주어. 'in order to-v' 「…하기 위해서」, has been added는 현재완료 수동태

10행 However, one study has shown [that the dental health of people in areas with fluoridated water is essentially identical to **that** of people {living in other areas}].: [ ]는 has shown의 목적절. to 뒤의 that은 the dental health를 지칭하는 대명사, { }는 people을 수식하는 현재분사구

문제해설
불소가 치아 건강 향상에 도움이 된다는 내용이므로, 불소가 첨가된 물이 있는 지역과 그렇지 않은 지역에 사는 사람들의 치아 건강에 차이가 없다는 내용의 ④는 글의 흐름에서 벗어난다.

36 ③ 글의 순서

바이러스와 유해 세균은 우리가 섭취하는 음식을 통해 장으로 들어올 수 있다. 다행스럽게도, 그것들은 장 속의 막을 형성하여 장벽 역할을 하는 특수 세포들에 의해 신체의 다른 부분으로 들어가는 것이 막힌다. (B) 하지만, 한 연구는 이 세포들이 저중력 환경에 의해 상당히 약해질 수 있다는 것을 보여 주었다. 이것은 우주에서 일하거나 장거리로 간 우주 비행사들에게 심각한 문제를 야기한다. 그들이 일단 지구로 돌아오면, 음식으로 인한 바이러스와 세균에 위험할 정도로 취약하다. (C) 이는 세포들이 우주 비행사가 우주를 떠난 후 2주까지 여전히 이렇게 약해진 상태이기 때문이다. 설상가상으로, 저중력 환경에서 시간을 보내는 것은 인간의 면역 체계도 약화시킨다. (A) 이 정보로 우주 비행사들이 임무에서 돌아온 뒤 처치되어야 하는 방식만이 바뀌는 것은 아니다. 그것은 또한 다른 행성으로 가거나 달에 거류지를 세우는 향후 노력에 중대한 영향을 미칠 것이다.

어휘
intestine 장 cell 세포 line (어떤 것의 안에서) 막을 형성하다 barrier 장벽 astronaut 우주 비행사 set up 건립하다 colony 식민지; *거류지 weaken 약화시키다 low-gravity 저중력인 present 수여하다; *야기하다 vulnerable 취약한, 연약한 immune system 면역 체계

구문해설
2행 Fortunately, **they** are prevented from entering other parts of the body by special cells [that line the inside of the intestines and act as a barrier].: they는 앞 문장의 Viruses and harmful bacteria를 가리킴. [ ]는 special cells를 선행사로 하는 주격 관계대명사절

6행 This information doesn't just change the way [that astronauts should be treated after they return from a mission].: [ ]는 the way를 선행사로 하는 관계부사절

문제해설
③ 우리의 장 속에 형성된 특수한 세포막 덕분에 바이러스와 유해 세균이 몸에 들어오지 못한다는 주어진 글 다음에, 이 세포가 저중력 환경에서는 약해질 수 있어서 우주 비행사들은 이에 취약한 상태가 된다는 (B)가 이어지고, 우주 비행사들의 약해진 상태를 상술하는 (C)가 온 후, 그것이 다른 행성으로 가거나 달에 거류지를 세우는 향후 계

획에 미칠 영향에 대해 언급하는 (A)가 오는 것이 자연스럽다.

37 ④ 글의 순서

공상 과학 소설처럼 들릴지도 모르나, 사이보그 곤충들은 미국 국방 고등 연구 기획청(DARPA)이 이러한 목표를 지향하여 노력하면서 현실이 되어가고 있다. (B) 수년 동안, DARPA는 바퀴벌레, 딱정벌레, 그리고 나방과 같은 살아 있는 곤충들을 감시 장치로 전환할 수 있는 회로를 이용하여 곤충들을 원거리에서 조정하는 방법들을 개발해 왔다. 마침내, DARPA는 유효한 방법을 찾아냈다. (C) 이 과정은 과학자들이 아직 태어난 지 얼마 안 된 곤충의 몸속에 작은 기계장치를 설치하는 것을 수반한다. 곤충은 성장하면서 이 기계 장치를 자신의 몸 안에 통합시킨다. (A) 그러고 나서, 성충기에 곤충의 움직임은 GPS나 DARPA로부터의 초음파 신호에 의해 원격으로 제어될 수 있다. 곤충들에게 센서가 장착된다면, 그것들은 위험하거나 접근 불가능한 지역들을 정찰하고 정보를 되돌려 보내기 위해 파견될 수 있을 것이다.

어휘
remotely 멀리; *원격 조정으로 ultrasonic 초음파의 equip 장비를 갖추다 scout 정찰하다 interface 회로 convert 전환하다 roach 바퀴벌레 moth 나방 surveillance 감시 incorporate 통합시키다

구문해설
13행 ..., [using an interface {that would **convert** living insects, such as roaches, beetles, and moths, **into** surveillance devices}].: [ ]는 부대상황을 나타내는 분사구문. { }는 an interface를 선행사로 하는 주격 관계대명사절. 'convert A into B' 「A를 B로 변하게 하다」

문제해설
④ DARPA가 사이보그 곤충 개발을 현실화시키고 있다는 내용의 주어진 문장 다음에, 그동안 개발해온 방법을 제시하면서 성공적인 방법을 찾아냈다는 (B)가 오고, 그 방법을 자세히 소개하는 (C) 다음에, 이렇게 만들어진 사이보그 곤충의 제어 방법과 그 쓰임을 설명하는 (A)가 오는 것이 자연스럽다.

38 ⑤ 주어진 문장의 위치

최근 연구는 높은 고도에 도달하는 대부분의 등반가들이 그들의 원정에서 어느 정도의 뇌 손상을 입은 채 돌아온다는 것을 보여 준다. 한 실험에서, MRI 기계가 35명의 등반가들의 뇌를 조사하는 데 사용되었다. 그중 34명의 뇌가 장시간 저산소 환경에 노출된 후 뇌세포가 줄어든 것으로 발견되었다. 이 중에는 심한 고산병을 전혀 겪지 않았지만 뇌 손상을 입은 등산가들도 포함되었다. 이 연구는 또한 고도가 높은 환경에 지속적으로 노출되지 않고도 뇌 손상이 일어날 수 있다는 것을 보여 준다. 그들의 뇌 손상 위험을 최소화하기 위해서, 등반가들은 추가적인 예방조치를 취해야 한다. 그중에는 어떤 고산병 증상을 조금이라도 알아차리면 바로 내려오는 것과 더 높이 올라가기 전에 항상 환경에 적응하는 시간을 가지는 것이 포함된다.

어휘
minimize 최소화하다 take precaution 조심하다, 예방조치를 취하다 mountaineer 등반가 altitude 고도 expedition 탐험, 원정 degree 정도 expose 드러내다; *노출시키다(exposure 노출) prolonged 장기의 mountain sickness 고산병, 산악병(= altitude sickness) indicate 나타내다, 보여 주다 absence 부재 ongoing 계속 진행 중인 descend 내려오다 symptom 증상 adjust 적응하다

(10행) This included climbers [who **had** never **experienced** severe mountain sickness yet still suffered brain damage].: [ ]는 climbers를 선행사로 하는 주격 관계대명사절, had experienced는 경험을 나타내는 과거완료

(15행) These include **descending** as soon as they notice any symptoms of altitude sickness and always **taking** time [to adjust to the conditions] before climbing higher.: 동명사 descending과 taking이 등위 접속사 and로 병렬 연결, 'as soon as'「…하자마자」, [ ]는 time을 수식하는 형용사적 용법의 to부정사구

문제해설

등반가들에게 뇌 손상이 쉽게 발생한다는 내용이 나오고 마지막에 이를 예방할 수 있는 방법들이 나와 있으므로, 손상을 최소화하기 위해 예방조치를 취해야 한다는 내용의 주어진 문장은 그 사이인 ⑤에 오는 것이 적절하다.

39 ③ 주어진 문장의 위치

가뭄 문제는 심각하고 전 세계적이다. 아프리카의 관광객들은 샤워를 하면 그 지역에 물 부족을 야기할 수 있다는 것을 인식하지 못한 채 오랫동안 샤워를 한다. 아프리카에 수도꼭지가 단 한 개뿐인 마을들이 있을 때도, 호텔에는 방마다 수도꼭지와 샤워기가 갖추어져 있다. 이는 관광객들이 지역 주민들보다 훨씬 더 많은 물을 사용하도록 조장한다. 스페인의 주민 한 사람이 하루에 250리터의 물을 사용하는 것에 비해, 스페인에 온 관광객 한 사람은 하루 평균 880리터의 물을 사용하는 것으로 추산된 바 있다. 물이 부족한 나라에서, 18홀 골프장은 하루에 만 명의 사람들이 사용하는 양만큼의 물을 소비할 수 있다. 카리브 해에서는 수원지가 수도관을 통해 관광객들의 호텔로 연결되기 때문에, 수십만 명의 사람들이 수돗물 없이 지내고 있다.

어휘

local 지역의; 지역 주민 drought 가뭄 shortage 부족, 결핍 tap 수도꼭지 calculate 계산하다, 추산하다 go without …없이 지내다 pipe 관을 설치하다, 파이프를 통해 나르다 spring (*pl.*) 샘, 수원지

구문해설

(11행) ... can consume **as much** water per day **as** 10,000 people (consume).: 'as much ... as ~'「~만큼 많은 …」

문제해설

주어진 문장의 This가 가리키는 것은 ③의 앞 문장 내용이므로, 주어진 문장은 ③에 들어가는 것이 자연스럽다.

40 ⑤ 요약문 완성

어떤 사람들은 고래와 기타 멸종 위기에 처한 해양 포유동물이 인간과 얼마나 비슷한지 언급함으로써 그들의 권리를 옹호하기를 좋아한다. 그들은 고래류 동물들이 서로 밀접하게 연결된 가족 집단을 이루며 그들은 모두 인간이 그러는 것처럼 서로 의사소통을 할 수 있는 매우 지능이 높은 동물이라고 말한다. 해양 포유동물을 인간과 비교하는 사람들은 선의에서 그렇게 하지만, 박물학자인 로버트 핀치가 지적하듯, 그들의 주장은 잘못되었다. 과학자들의 관찰에 따르면 고래류는 대단히 지능이 높다. 그러나 이 동물들이 우리와 매우 비슷하기 때문에 보호받아야 한다고 주장하는 것은 오만하고 자기 중심적인 것이다. 이는 어떤 동물이 인간과 인간의 가치관을 반영하는 경우에만 중요하다는 것을 암시한다. 사실 고래와 다른 해양 포유동물이 존재할 권리를 갖는 것은 그들이 우리와 비슷해서가 아니라 그들이 고유하기 때문이다.

어휘

defend 방어[변호]하다 whale 고래 endangered 멸종 위기에 처한 mammal 포유동물 point out …을 지적[언급]하다 close-knit (구성원들 간의 관계가) 가까운, 밀접한 intelligent 지적인; 총명한 creature 동물, 생물 well-meaning 선의의, 호의에서 비롯된 naturalist 자연주의자; *박물학자 misguided 잘못 지도된, 잘못 알고 있는 remarkably 대단히 arrogant 오만한, 거만한 reflect 반영하다, 나타내다 [문제] intimacy 친밀함 capacity 능력 similarity 유사성 significance 중요성

구문해설

(2행) ... by pointing out [how similar they are to humans].: [ ]는 pointing out의 목적어로 쓰인 의문사절

(11행) But **it**'s arrogant and self-centered [to argue {that these animals should be protected ... like us}].: it은 가주어이고 [ ]가 진주어, { }는 argue의 목적절

문제해설

⑤ 고래와 다른 해양 동물들은 인간과의 유사성 때문이 아니라 그들 자체의 중요성 때문에 보호되어야 한다.

41 ② 42 ④ 장문

늑대는 아시아, 유럽 및 북미 지역에서 발견되는 큰 포식자이다. 그들은 아마도 동물계에서 가장 사회적인 육식 동물일 것인데, 부분적으로는 그들의 진화적인 발달 때문이며 또 다른 부분적으로는 그들의 독특한 생존 요구 때문이다. 그들은 무리 지어 생활하는데, 그것은 그들의 영역을 방어하고, 먹이를 사냥하며, 그들의 새끼들을 집단으로 돌보는, 밀접한 관계를 갖는 큰 동물 집단이다. 늑대 무리들은 모든 구성원이 지배적인 수컷과 암컷에 의해 결정되는 명확한 위치에 있는 엄격한 계급을 갖는다. 그들은 번식 쌍이라고 불리고 사냥에서 무리를 이끄는데, 먹잇감이 죽었을 때 그것을 종종 가장 먼저 먹는다. 대부분의 상황에서, 그들은 무리 중에서 짝짓기를 하고 자손을 번식하는 유일한 늑대들이지만, 위험이 거의 없고 음식이 풍부한 시기에 다른 무리 구성원들은 때때로 번식을 할 것이다.

새끼 늑대들은 대개 봄에 태어난다. 어릴 때부터, 놀이를 하는 동안 지배의 징후를 보이는 어떤 새끼들과 그렇지 않은 새끼들이 있다. 새끼가 청소년기에 이르면, 그들 중 일부는 짝을 찾기 위해서 무리의 영역을 떠나기로 결정할 것이다. 이러한 어린 늑대들은, 또한 그들의 무리를 떠난 짝을 위협하기를(→ 끌어들이기를) 바라면서 길고 크게 울부짖는 소리로 소통하는 것으로 유명하다. 그들 중 두 마리가 만나게 되면, 그 새로운 번식 쌍은 그들 자신의 무리를 시작하려는 의도로 그들의 영역을 찾을 것이다.

어휘

predator 포식자 carnivore 육식 동물 evolutionary 진화의(evolution 진화, 발전) survival 생존 pack 무리, 떼 defend 방어하다 territory 영역 prey 먹이, 사냥감 collectively 집합적으로, 총괄하여 strict 엄격한 hierarchy 계급, 계층 determine 알아내다; *결정하다 dominant 우세한, 지배적인(dominance 우월, 지배) breeding 번식(breed 번식하다) mate 짝짓기를 하다; 짝 offspring 자식; *(동식물의) 새끼 abundant 풍부한 pup (여러 동물의) 새끼 adolescence 청소년기 howl (개, 늑대 등이) 길게 짖는 소리 with the intention of …할 작정으로, …할 의도로 [문제] ritual 의식 절차, 의례 endangerd 멸종 위기에 처한

구문해설

(6행) They live in packs, [which are large groups of closely related animals {that defend their territory, hunt for prey, and care for their young collectively}].: [ ]는 packs를 선행사로 하는 계속적

용법의 주격 관계대명사절, { }는 closely related animals를 선행사로 하는 주격 관계대명사절

(9행) Wolf packs have a strict hierarchy [in which every member has a clear place {that is determined by a dominant male and female}].: [ ]는 a strict hierarchy를 선행사로 하는 목적격 관계대명사절, { }는 a clear place를 선행사로 하는 주격 관계대명사절

(12행) They are called the breeding pair, and they lead the pack on hunts, [often being the first **to eat** when prey *has been killed*].: [ ]는 부대상황을 나타내는 분사구문, to eat은 the first를 수식하는 형용사적 용법의 to부정사구, has been killed는 현재완료 수동태

문제해설

41 무리 생활을 하는 늑대는 분명히 구분된 역할과 계급이 있으며 번식 쌍에 의해 지배되고, 일부 나이가 어린 늑대는 무리를 떠나 새로운 번식 쌍을 이루어 그들만의 무리를 시작한다는 내용이므로, 글의 제목으로는 ② '늑대들의 사회 구조'가 가장 적절하다.

42 ④ 무리를 떠난 늑대가 자신의 짝을 찾아 새로운 번식 쌍을 만들어 그들의 무리를 시작하고자 한다는 내용이므로 threatening(위협하는)을 attracting(끌어들이는) 등으로 고쳐야 한다.

43 ② 44 ③ 45 ② 장문

(A) 1550년경, 포르투갈 왕국은 노예 매매 산업에 관여하게 되었다. 상인들은 다른 아프리카 흑인들로부터 아프리카 흑인들을 사들이기 시작했고, 그들은 (팔려온) 아프리카 흑인들에게 노예 신분을 강요했다. 그러고 나서 이 노예들은 대서양을 건너 포르투갈의 식민지인 브라질로 보내졌고, 그곳에서 그들은 사탕수수 농장에서 일하게 되었다. 노예 매매는 아프리카에서 브라질로 수천 명의 노예들을 실어 나르는 수백 척의 배들을 포함하는 큰 산업이었다.

(C) (아프리카의) 내륙지역에서 노예 매매상에 의해 붙잡힌 사람들의 약 40퍼센트가 해안에 도착하기 전에 죽었고, 나머지 60퍼센트는 그 해안에서 포르투갈인들에게 팔린 것으로 여겨진다. 그리고 브라질로 가는 긴 해상 여정 중 또 다른 15퍼센트가 사망했다. 남아메리카에 도착하자마자, 10에서 12퍼센트가 그들이 일하게 될 농장에 도착하기 전에 사망했다. 모두 합쳐서, 이 기간 동안 노예 신분을 강요받은 아프리카인들의 절반도 안 되는 수가 브라질 농장에서 일하게 될 만큼 오래 살아남았다. 물론, 살아남은 사람들도 신체적 폭력과 긴 노동 시간으로 고통받으며 끔찍한 삶을 살았다.

(B) 수백 년 후, 1822년에 브라질은 포르투갈로부터 독립을 선언했고, 노예 매매를 중단하고 모든 노예를 해방하는 (법률) 제안이 만들어졌다. 그러나, 브라질의 노예 매매는 중단되지 않았다. 대신에 19세기 동안 더 크게 성장했다. 같은 기간 동안에 영국에는 클래펌파(派)라고 알려진 영향력 있는 단체가 있었는데, 그들은 노예들은 반드시 해방되어야 하고 노예 매매는 폐지되어야 한다는 정치적 견해를 가지고 있었다.

(D) 이 단체는 영국 정부가 브라질로 노예 수송을 중단하도록 영향력을 행사할 것을 주장했다. 영국으로서는 그것이 윤리적인 문제 이상의 것이었다. 브라질의 노예 제도는 수많은 영국 제품들의 거래에 악영향을 미치고 있었고, 이것은 영국 정부가 마침내 브라질이 이 관행을 중단하도록 압력을 가함으로써 (노예 제도 문제에) 관여하게 된 이유의 일부였다. 이후 수십 년간, 브라질 정부는 서서히 노예 제도를 중단하는 과정을 시작했다. 마침내, 노예 제도는 1888년의 황금법에 의해 끝이 났고, 이로써 브라질은 서반구에서 노예 제도를 폐지한 마지막 국가가 되었다.

어휘

slave 노예(slavery 노예 제도) merchant 상인 colony 식민지
plantation 농장, 플랜테이션 transport 수송하다 declare 선언하다
emancipate (노예 등을) 해방하다, 석방하다 liberate 해방하다 abolish 폐지하다 inland 오지의, 내륙의 perish 죽다, 멸망하다 all told 모두 합해서 traffic 교통; *수송 moral 도덕의, 윤리의 adverse effect 역효과 hemisphere (지구의) 반구

구문해설

(21행) It is believed that approximately 40% of the people [captured by slave traders in inland regions] died before reaching the coast, [where the remaining 60% were sold to the Portuguese].: 첫 번째 [ ]는 the people을 수식하는 과거분사구, 두 번째 [ ]는 the coast를 선행사로 하는 계속적 용법의 관계부사절

문제해설

43 ② 포르투갈이 아프리카의 노예들을 브라질로 보내기 시작했다는 내용의 (A) 다음에, 노예로 붙잡힌 아프리카 흑인들이 브라질로 이주하는 과정에서 많이 사망했다는 내용의 (C)로 이어진 후, 브라질의 독립 이후 노예 제도를 폐지하자는 주장에도 불구하고 19세기에 노예 매매가 더 성행했다는 내용의 (B)가 오고, 영국 정부의 압력으로 브라질이 마침내 노예 제도를 폐지하게 되었다는 내용의 (D)로 이어지는 것이 적절하다.

44 ③ (c)는 노예 제도에 반대하는 정치적 견해를 가리키는 반면에, 나머지는 모두 노예 매매(산업)를 가리킨다.

45 ② 브라질의 독립 이후에도 노예 매매는 끝나지 않았으며 19세기에 오히려 성행했다.

07 영어독해 모의고사

본문 ▲ p.66

18 ④	19 ③	20 ③	21 ②	22 ③	23 ④
24 ②	25 ③	26 ①	27 ④	28 ③	29 ④
30 ③	31 ④	32 ③	33 ④	34 ④	35 ③
36 ③	37 ⑤	38 ③	39 ④	40 ④	41 ②
42 ④	43 ②	44 ⑤	45 ④		

18 ④ 글의 목적

편집자님들께,

저는 최근에 장기간 입원해 있었던 한 미국 시민의 입장에서 이 글을 씁니다. 이 경험은 제게 미국이 자국민에게 의료보험을 제공하지 않는 세계 유일의 산업 국가로 남아있다는 사실을 상기시켜 주었습니다. 대신에, 이 중요한 과업이 영리 목적의 보험 회사들에 맡겨져 있어서, 약 4,500만 명의 미국인들이 감당할 수 없는 높은 비용을 초래했습니다. 일부 회사들은 자사의 직원들에게 건강보험을 제공하지만, 그렇게 할 수 없는 기업체들이 많습니다. 분명히, (이에 대해) 무언가가 행해져야 합니다. 연방정부는 정부가 모든 의료보험료를 지불하는 단일 보험자 제도를 시행하는 방향으로 조치를 취할 필요가 있습니다. 이것은 모든 미국 국민들이 수입이나 고용 상태에 상관없이 건강보험을 가질 수 있게 도와줄 것입니다.

진심을 담아,

앤서니 맬럿 드림

어휘 industrialized 산업화된 healthcare 건강 관리; *의료보험 for-profit 이익을 추구하는, 영리 목적의 insurance 보험 approximately 대략 health coverage 건강보험 federal government 연방정부 take steps 조치를 취하다 implement 시행하다 ensure 반드시 …하게 하다, 보장하다 regardless of …에 상관없이 employment 고용

구문해설
[5행] ... the United States remains the only industrialized nation in the world [that does not **provide** its citizens **with** healthcare].: [ ]는 the only industrialized nation in the world를 선행사로 하는 주격 관계대명사절, 'provide A with B' 「A에게 B를 제공하다」
[8행] Instead, this important task is left to for-profit insurance companies, [resulting in high costs {that approximately 45 million Americans are unable to afford}].: [ ]는 결과를 나타내는 분사구문. { }는 high costs를 선행사로 하는 목적격 관계대명사절

문제해설
④ 모든 미국 국민이 경제적 부담 없이 의료 혜택을 받을 수 있도록 정부가 지불하는 단일 의료보험 제도를 시행할 것을 촉구하는 글이다.

19 ③ 심경 변화

전화를 하던 날, 내 심장은 두근거리고 있었다. 나는 전에 이 일을 하는 것에 대해 백 번은 생각했지만, 항상 자제했었다. 그녀는 어떻게 반응할까? 그녀는 화를 낼까? 그녀가 전화를 받았을 때, 나는 재빠르게 내 신원을 밝혔다. "제 이름은 마크 페레즈입니다. 저는 당신 아들의 친구였습니다." 긴 침묵 끝에 그녀는 떨리는 목소리로 말했다. "그렇다면 당신은 그가 여기에 없다는 것을 알겠네요. 그는 2년 전에 전쟁에서 죽었어요." 내가 그곳에 있었기 때문에 나는 확실히 알고 있다고 설명했다. "저는 단지 그가 마지막에 혼자가 아니었다는 것을 당신에게 알려주고 싶었어요. 그가 죽을 때 저는 그의 손을 잡고 있었어요." 나는 그녀가 울기 시작하는 것을 들을 수 있었고, 나는 거의 전화를 끊으려던 참이었다. 하지만 그때 그녀는 "나에게 알려 줘서 정말 고마워요."라고 말했다. 그 후에, 마치 내 어깨에서 무거운 짐이 내려진 것처럼 느껴졌다.

어휘 pound 치다, 두드리다; *(가슴이) 쿵쿵 뛰다 stop oneself 자제하다 identify (신원 등을) 확인하다[알아보다] pause 멈춤 tremble 떨리다 hang up 전화를 끊다 weight 무게; *(무거운 책임감 같은) 짐, 부담 [문제] anxious 불안해하는 envious 부러워하는 relieved 안도하는 frustrated 좌절감을 느끼는 comforted 안심한

구문해설
[8행] I explained [that I **did** know, because I was there].: [ ]는 explained의 목적절, did는 동사 know를 강조하는 조동사
[11행] I could **hear** her **start** to cry, and I almost hung up.: 지각동사 hear의 목적격보어로 동사원형 start가 쓰임
[13행] Afterward, it felt **as if** a heavy weight **had been lifted** from my shoulders.: 'as if'는 「마치 …인 것처럼」으로, 과거 사실에 반대되는 일을 나타내는 가정법 과거완료 구문과 함께 쓰임

문제해설
전쟁터에서 죽은 동료의 어머니와 통화를 하기 전에는 심장이 매우 두근거렸지만, 통화를 끝낸 후 무거운 짐이 어깨에서 내려진 것처럼 느꼈다고 했으므로, 'I'의 심경 변화로 가장 적절한 것은 ③ '초조한 → 안도하는'이다.

20 ③ 필자의 주장

나는 전에 하와이 대학교에서 학생들에게 직장의 안정성에 대한 강연을 해 달라는 초청을 받았다. 나는 학생들에게, 몇 년 안에 그들 중 많은 이들이 직장을 잃거나, 더 적은 돈을 받고 안정성은 점점 줄어드는 상황에서 일할 수밖에 없게 될 거라고 말했다. 업무차 전 세계를 돌아다니면서, 나는 값싼 노동력과 기술적인 혁신이 결합되어 나타나는 힘을 목격했다. 나는 아시아, 유럽, 그리고 남미의 노동자들이 실제로 미국의 노동자들과 경쟁하고 있다는 것을 깨닫기 시작했다. 나는 대기업들이 전 세계를 상대로 경쟁할 수 있으려면, 직원들의 수와 직원들에게 지급하는 임금 두 가지 모두를 곧 삭감해야 할 것임을 알았다.

어휘 once 한번은, 전에 security 보장; *안정(성) witness 목격하다 labor 노동(력) innovation 혁신 compete 겨루다, 경쟁하다 cut 삭감 globally 전 세계적으로

구문해설
[5행] [Traveling the world with my work], I have witnessed ...: [ ]는 때를 나타내는 분사구문
[10행] I knew [(that) the big companies would soon have to make cuts, **both** in the numbers of people **and** in the salaries {(which/that) they paid their workers}, ... globally].: [ ]는 knew의 목적절, 'both A and B' 「A와 B 둘 다」, { }는 the salaries를 선행사로 하는 목적격 관계대명사절

문제해설
③ 필자는 값싼 노동력과 기술 혁신의 결합, 국제적인 경쟁 체제 등으로 인해 미래에는 직업 안정성이 낮아질 수밖에 없다고 주장하고 있다.

21 ② 글의 요지

누군가가 당신의 기분을 상하게 했지만, 그러고 나서 사과했다고 상상

해 보라. 그것은 고통스럽지만, 당신은 당신에게 상처를 준 그 사람을 용서하기로 결정한다. 하지만 그 고통은 쉽게 사라지지 않을 것이다. 당신은 그 일을 당신의 마음속에 담고 있다가, 그럴 이유가 없을 때조차 그 일에 대해 가끔 생각한다. 당신은 그 고통을 놓아 주어야 한다. 감정적인 고통을 지니고 있는 것은 날마다 다시 상처를 받는 것과 같은 느낌이다. 오로지 당신만이 그것을 놓을 수 있다. 당신 자신에게 이와 같은 질문을 해 보라. 당신이 100마일을 걸어야 하는데, 무거운 시멘트 벽돌을 가지고 가느냐 또는 아무것도 가지고 가지 않느냐를 선택할 수 있다면, 당신은 어느 쪽을 택하겠는가? 당신은 당연히 아무것도 가져가지 않는 쪽을 택할 것이다. 고통의 경우도 마찬가지이다.

어휘
apologize 사과하다　let go of …을 놓다　option 선택권　cement 시멘트

구문해설
7행 [Carrying emotional pain] feels like [being hurt again every day].: 첫 번째 [ ]는 문장의 주어로 쓰인 동명사구, 두 번째 [ ]는 전치사 like의 목적어로 쓰인 동명사구

문제해설
② 타인에 의한 마음의 상처는 고통스러운 것이기에 자기 자신을 위해 빨리 잊어야 한다는 요지의 글이다.

22　③　글의 주제

요즘에는 기업들이 비디오 게임 속의 광고 공간을 구매하는 것이 흔하다. 비디오 게임 제조사들은 게임의 가상 세계에 나오는 광고판이나 다른 물체들에 회사의 로고를 나타나게 하는 기업들에게 요금을 청구한다. 그러나 새로운 정보는, 광고주들이 어떤 종류의 비디오 게임의 일부가 되고자 비용을 지불하고 있는지를 알아야 한다고 권한다. 한 연구에서 게임 이용자들이 실제 세계의 광고들을 포함한 두 개의 서로 다른 게임에 노출되었다. 한 게임은 총을 쏘는 캐릭터들과 벽에 튄 피와 같이 전형적인 폭력적 내용을 특징으로 했고, 반면에 다른 게임은 그렇지 않았다. 나중에, 그 게임 이용자들은 그들이 게임에서 봤던 상표에 대한 질문을 받았다. 폭력적인 게임을 했던 사람들은 상표에 대해 훨씬 더 부정적인 견해를 갖고 있었다. 이러한 차이는 특히 여성 게임 이용자들 사이에서 분명했다.

어휘
purchase 구매하다　manufacturer 제조사　billboard 광고판　virtual 가상의　advertiser 광고주　expose 노출하다　feature 특징으로 삼다 violent 폭력적인　content 내용　splatter 튀다　evident 분명한　[문제] adverse effect 역효과

구문해설
2행 Video game manufacturers charge companies to **have** their logos **show up** on billboards or other objects [that appear in the game's virtual universe].: 사역동사 have의 목적격보어로 동사원형이 쓰임. [ ]는 billboards or other objects를 선행사로 하는 주격 관계대명사절
5행 New information **suggests**, however, [that advertisers **should know** {what kinds of video games they are paying to be a part of}].: [ ]는 suggests의 목적절이며, suggest와 같은 제안, 주장 등의 뜻을 가진 동사의 목적어로 쓰인 that절이 당위성을 나타낼 때 동사는 '(should+)동사원형', { }는 know의 목적어로 쓰인 의문사절
10행 **One** game featured typical violent content, such as characters [shooting guns] and blood [splattered on walls], while **the other** game did not.: 'one … the other ~' 「(둘 중의) 하나는 …, 다른 하나는 ~」, 두 개의 [ ]는 각각 characters와 blood를 수식하는 분사구

문제해설
폭력적인 게임에 나타나는 광고는 게임 이용자들에게 그 상표에 대한 부정적인 인상을 남길 수 있다는 내용이므로 글의 주제로는 ③ '폭력적인 게임에 광고하는 것의 역효과'가 적절하다.

23　④　글의 주제

로봇 물고기는 해양 오염을 찾아내기 위해 과학자들에 의해 개발되었다. 이 로봇 물고기들은 크기가 크고, 실제 물고기와 똑같이 물살을 헤치며 헤엄칠 수 있다. 그것들은 오염원을 감지할 수 있는 화학 센서를 특징으로 하고, 무선 기술을 통해 자료를 연구자들에게 전송할 수 있다. 그것들은 기름띠처럼 바다 표면에 있는 오염물질뿐만 아니라, 해수에 이미 용해된 독성 화학물질을 추적하는 능력도 있다. 그것들은 또한 배터리가 떨어져 가기 시작하면 자동으로 조작자에게 되돌아온다. 로봇 물고기는 영국 에섹스 대학 과학자들에 의해 만들어졌다. 그들은 그 물고기들을 실제 물고기와 (외관이) 유사하도록, 그리고 실제 물고기의 효율적인 헤엄 동작을 모방하도록 설계했다. 그것들은 제작하는 데 비용이 많이 들지만, 관계자들은 그것들이 비용을 들일 가치가 있다고 생각한다.

어휘
in the interest of …을 위해　locate 장소를 알아내다, 찾아내다　feature … 을 특징으로 하다　via …을 거쳐, …을 통해　wireless 무선의　track down …을 추적하다　toxic 독성의　dissolve 녹다, 용해되다　pollutant 오염물질 oil slick 기름띠　handler 사용자, 조작자　mimic 모방하다　[문제] strategy 계획, 전략　dump (쓰레기 등을) 버리다

구문해설
4행 They feature chemical sensors [(which are) **capable of** detecting sources of pollution], …: [ ]는 chemical sensors를 선행사로 하는 주격 관계대명사절. 'be capable of …' 「…할 수 있다」

문제해설
바다에서 센서로 해양 오염물질을 찾아내는 로봇 물고기에 관한 내용이므로, 글의 주제로는 ④ '바다에서 오염물질을 찾는 기계 물고기'가 적절하다.

24　②　글의 제목

나르시시즘은 자신의 이상화된 이미지와 사랑에 빠진 상태이다. 나르시시스트는 자신이 누구인지, 즉 소속감을 느끼기 위해 몸부림치는 상처받고 불완전한 사람이라는 현실을 피하기 위해 이 이미지를 다른 사람들에게 강요한다. 나르시시즘은 대화를 지배하는 것과 같은 몇 가지 숨길 수 없는 징후들에 의해 확인될 수 있다. 나르시시스트는 자신에 대해 이야기하는 것을 매우 좋아해서 그렇게 하기 위해 주제를 재빨리 바꿀 것이다. 그들은 또한 자신이 구입한 비싼 물건들과 같이 외면적으로 얻은 것들로 다른 사람들에게 깊은 인상을 주려고 노력하는 데 많은 시간을 쓴다. 나르시시스트는 타인에게 부정적인 반응을 일으키는 것을 신경 쓰지 않는다. 그들은 심지어 좋지 않은 관심이라도 어떤 종류의 관심이든 바라며, 그것을 만들어 내는 자신의 능력을 일종의 권력으로 여긴다. 마지막으로, 나르시시스트는 비판을 싫어해서 그것에 형편없이 또는 심지어 공격적으로 반응할 것이다.

어휘
condition 상태　idealized 이상화된　escape 달아나다; *피하다　reality 현실　wounded 부상을 입은; *(마음을) 상한[다친]　struggle 투쟁하다, 몸부림치다　belong 제자리에 있다; *소속감을 느끼다　identify 확인하다　telltale 숨길 수 없는, 역력한　dominate 지배하다　impress 깊은 인상을 주다 external 외부의, 외면적인　attention 주의; *관심　criticism 비판, 비난 aggressively 공격적으로　[문제] misunderstood 오해를 받는

머리카락은 덜 빠지게 된다. 또한 머리숱의 변화는 보통 머리카락이 긴 임산부들에게서 더 눈에 띈다.

어휘
thick 굵은; *머리숱이 많은 pregnant 임신한(pregnancy 임신) fall out 빠지다 replace 대체하다 noticeable 눈에 띄는

구문해설
(1행) Is **it** common *for your hair* [to get thicker when you're pregnant]?: it은 가주어이고 [ ]가 진주어, your hair는 [ ]의 의미상 주어
(2행) Hair **does** get thicker when you are pregnant, ...: does는 동사 get을 강조하는 조동사

문제해설
① 임신 중에는 머리카락이 더 천천히 빠져서 평소보다 머리숱이 많아지는 것이며, 머리카락이 더 빨리 자라는 것은 아니다.

27 ④ 내용 일치

유명한 자전거 경주 대회인 투르 드 프랑스는 1903년에 '엘 오토'라는 잡지의 판매를 늘리기 위해 처음 조직되었다. 그 후로 두 차례의 세계대전 동안에만 중단되었을 뿐, 그것은 매년 개최되어 왔다. 그것은 단 이틀간만 쉬면서 21일에서 23일 동안 프랑스 전역을 자전거로 다니는 것으로 이루어진다. 자전거 선수들은 대략 총 3,500 킬로미터의 거리를 이동하는데, 이는 파리, 알프스산맥, 그리고 프랑스 시골 지역에 있는 경로들을 포함한다. 누구나 상상할 수 있듯이, 이 대회는 선수들에게 고되다. 하지만 극도의 정신적, 신체적 피로와 자전거 선수들이 이동하는 빠른 속도에도 불구하고 투르 드 프랑스에서 경주자들의 사망은 드물다. 실제로, 2000년 이후 투르 드 프랑스에서 발생한 세 건의 사망은 관중들과 연관되었다. 경주는 유럽에서 가장 인기 있는 스포츠 경기 중 하나이며, 매년 수백만 명의 팬들이 경로를 따라 늘어서 있다.

어휘
competition 경쟁; 대회 suspend 매달다; *중단하다 consist (부분·요소로) 이루어져 있다 roughly 대략, 거의 route 길, 경로 combination 조합, 결합 extreme 극도의 mental 정신의 physical 육체의 fatigue 피로 velocity 속도 spectator 관중

구문해설
(3행) Since then, it has been held every year, [having been suspended only during the two world wars].: [ ]는 부대상황을 나타내는 분사구문
(10행) But **in spite of** the combination of extreme mental and physical fatigue and the high velocities [at which the cyclists travel], ...: 'in spite of' 「...에도 불구하고」, [ ]는 the high velocities를 선행사로 하는 목적격 관계대명사절
(14행) In fact, the three deaths [that have occurred at the Tour de France since 2000] involved spectators.: [ ]는 the three deaths를 선행사로 하는 주격 관계대명사절

문제해설
① 잡지 판매를 늘리기 위해 조직되었다. ② 두 차례의 세계대전 동안에는 일시 중단되었다. ③ 이틀간의 휴식을 포함한다. ⑤ 2000년 이후 사망한 세 명은 모두 관중이었다.

28 ③ 내용 불일치

실버맨 미술 대회
실버맨 재단은 실버맨 청소년 미술 대회를 개최하게 되어 자랑스럽습니다.
규정: 중학생과 초등학생의 참가 비용은 5달러입니다. 각각의 아동은 작

구문해설
(2행) Narcissists force this image on others [to escape the reality of {who they are}—wounded, imperfect people {who are struggling to belong}].: [ ]는 목적을 나타내는 부사적 용법의 to부정사구, 첫 번째 { }는 전치사 of의 목적어로 쓰인 의문사절, 두 번째 { }는 wounded, imperfect people을 선행사로 하는 주격 관계대명사절
(9행) They also **spend** a lot of time **trying** to impress others with external achievements, such as expensive things [(which/that) they have purchased].: 'spend+시간+v-ing' 「...하는 데 시간을 보내다」, [ ]는 expensive things를 선행사로 하는 목적격 관계대명사절
(14행) ..., and they **see** their ability [to create it] **as** a kind of power.: 'see A as B' 「A를 B로 여기다」, [ ]는 their ability를 수식하는 형용사적 용법의 to부정사구

문제해설
나르시시즘을 확인할 수 있는 몇 가지 뚜렷한 징후들을 열거한 글이므로, 글의 제목으로는 ② '나르시시스트를 쉽게 알아차리는 방법'이 가장 적절하다.

25 ③ 도표 내용 불일치

위의 막대그래프는 성별에 따라 나눈 정규 근로자들과 자영업자들 양쪽의 주당 평균 근무 시간의 분포를 보여준다. 여성 자영업자들보다 더 많은 남성 자영업자들이 주당 50시간 이상 근무한다. 게다가, 50시간 이상 근무하는 남성 자영업자가 같은 시간만큼 일하는 여성 자영업자보다 두 배가량 많다. (그러나 근로자들 사이에서는 다른 양상을 볼 수 있는데, 남성 근로자들보다 약간 더 많은 여성 근로자들이 주당 50시간 이상 일한다.) 그들이 근로자이건 혹은 자영업자이건 간에 여성들이 남성들보다 주당 30시간 미만으로 근무하는 경향이 더 있다. 마지막으로, 주당 40시간 혹은 그 이상 근무하는 모든 사람들에 대해, 근로자와 자영업자 모두에서 남성들이 여성들보다 더 높은 참여율을 보인다.

어휘
self-employed 자영업의 illustrate 설명하다; *보여주다 distribution 분배, 분포 participation 관여, 참여

구문해설
(6행) ... **twice as** many self-employed men [working over 50 hours] **as** self-employed women working those hours.: '배수사+as ... as' 「~배만큼 ...한」, [ ]는 self-employed men을 수식하는 현재분사구
(15행) Finally, for all those [who work 40 hours per week or more], males show a higher participation rate than females among **both** employees **and** the self-employed.: [ ]는 all those를 선행사로 하는 주격 관계대명사절, 'both A and B' 「A와 B 둘 다」

문제해설
③ 도표에서 주당 50시간 이상 근무하는 근로자는 자영업자들의 경우에서처럼 남성이 여성보다 더 많다.

26 ① 내용 불일치

임신 중에 머리숱이 더 많아지는 것은 흔한 일일까? 임신했을 때 머리숱은 분명 더 많아지지만, 이는 머리카락이 더 많이 나기 때문은 아니다. 다만 보통 때 그런 것보다 머리카락이 더 천천히 빠지는 것뿐이다. 일반적으로 당신 머리의 머리카락의 85~95퍼센트는 자라고 있지만 나머지 5~15퍼센트는 휴식기에 있다. 그 휴식기가 끝나면 이 머리카락들은 빠지고 새로 자라는 머리카락으로 대체된다. 보통 여성은 하루에 약 100가닥의 머리카락이 빠진다. 그러나 임신 중에는 (임신하지 않았을 때보다) 높은 에스트로겐 수치가 (머리카락의) 성장기를 더 길어지게 하고 당신의

품을 3개까지 제출할 수 있습니다. 학교들이 이용 가능한 특별 참가 신청 할인도 있는데 이는 10달러에 10개의 작품입니다. 참가작은 7월 15일까지 접수되어야 합니다. 이 날짜는 이전의 마감 기한인 7월 1일에서 연장되었음에 주목해 주세요.

수상자 선정: 예술가 위원회가 출품작들을 심사할 것입니다. 결과는 8월 22일에 발표될 것입니다.

상품
• 1등상 (1) – 5,000달러와 태블릿 컴퓨터 한 대
• 2등상 (1) – 1,000달러와 디지털 카메라 한 대
  대회 규정과 자격 요건에 대해 더 많은 정보를 원하시면, SJAC@silvermanf.org로 재단에 이메일을 보내주세요.

구문해설

(2행) The Silverman Foundation is proud [to present the Silverman Junior Art Competition].: [ ]는 감정의 원인을 나타내는 부사적 용법의 to부정사구

(9행) Please note [that this date **has been extended** from ... July 1].: [ ]는 note의 목적절, has been extended는 현재완료 수동태

문제해설

③ 이전의 마감 기한인 7월 1일에서 7월 15일로 작품 제출 기간이 연장되었다.

29 ④ 어법

'윈윈' 협상의 목적은 양측이 서로에게 원하는 것을 두고 갈등하는 상황을 해결하는 것이다. 성공적으로 사용되면, 이런 유형의 협상은 논의의 종료 이후에 양측 모두에게 뭔가를 '얻었다'는 느낌을 남긴다. 협상은 상대방이 기꺼이 거래하려고 하는 바로 그것을 다른 한쪽이 원할 때 가장 수월하다. 물론, 이런 이상적인 시나리오가 항상 존재하는 것은 아니며, 그래서 때로 한쪽은 포기하고 싶지 않은 무언가를 포기해야만 한다. 이런 일이 발생하면, 내주는 쪽이 그렇게 하는 것에 대한 어떤 종류의 보상을 협상하려고 하는 것은 당연하다. 결국 양측이 모두 교환으로부터 무언가를 얻었다고 확신한다면, 그 협상은 윈윈이라고 볼 수 있다.

어휘

aim 목적   win-win 모두에게 유리한, 윈윈의   negotiate 협상하다 (negotiation 협상)   resolve 해결하다   party 당사자   conflict 갈등, 충돌   trade 거래하다   ideal 이상적인   compensation 보상   at the end 결국   confident 자신감 있는; *확신하는   gain 얻다   exchange 교환

구문해설

(1행) The aim of "win-win" negotiating is [to resolve situations {where two parties are in conflict over **what** they want from each other}].: [ ]는 주격보어로 쓰인 명사적 용법의 to부정사구, { }는 situations를 선행사로 하는 관계부사절, what은 선행사를 포함한 관계대명사로, 전치사 over의 목적어 역할을 하는 명사절을 이끎

(3행) [When (it is) used successfully], this type of negotiation leaves both parties with the sense [that they've "won" something following the close of talks].: 첫 번째 [ ]는 때를 나타내는 부사절('주어+be동사'가 생략된 형태), 두 번째 [ ]는 the sense와 동격

(13행) If, at the end, both parties **feel confident** [that they have gained something from the exchange], the negotiation can be

considered win-win.: 감각동사 feel의 보어로 형용사인 confident가 쓰임. [ ]는 confident의 목적절(일부 형용사는 that절을 목적어로 취함)

문제해설

④ 가주어 it이 사용된 문장의 진주어 자리이므로 trying은 to부정사인 to try가 되어야 한다. the giving party는 to try의 의미상 주어

30 ③ 어휘

신문의 각 판(版)은 다수의 각기 다르고 다양한 기사를 담고 있지만, 각각의 신문 기사들은 전통적으로 거의 같은 방식으로 구성된다. 그 기사들은 정보가 제시되는 방식에 있어서 역피라미드 같은 모양을 이룬다. 그것들은 맨 먼저 가장 덜(→ 가장 많이) 중요한 요점으로부터 시작된다. 뉴스 기사의 첫 문단은 '머리글'이라고 불리며 기사 전체의 요약 내용이다. 만약 당신이 기사 전체를 읽을 시간이 없다면, 머리글을 읽고 요점을 파악할 수 있다. 머리글 뒤의 각 문단은 갈수록 중요성이 점점 낮아지므로, 지면이 부족한 상황에 직면하면, 편집자는 기사의 주요 내용에 영향을 주지 않으면서 기사의 맨 밑부분에서부터 문단을 제거하기 시작할 수 있다.

어휘

edition (신문의) 판   varied 여러 가지의, 다양한   article 기사   structure 구조; *…을 구성하다, 구조화하다   upside-down (위아래가) 뒤집힌   pyramid 피라미드   paragraph 문단   lead (신문 기사의) 머리글, 도입부   editor 편집자

구문해설

(12행) ..., so [when (being) faced with a shortage of page space], the editor can start removing paragraphs ...: [ ]는 때를 나타내는 분사구문으로, 접속사 when은 뜻을 분명히 하기 위해 생략되지 않고 함께 쓰임

문제해설

③ 기사들은 전체의 요점을 다루는 머리글로 시작하며 머리글 뒤의 문단으로 갈수록 중요성이 점차 낮아진다고 했으므로, least(가장 덜)를 most(가장 많이) 등으로 고쳐야 한다.

31 ④ 빈칸 추론

한 국가의 법 체제는 시민들의 민주적 참여를 통해 만들어진다. 실제로 그럴까? 많은 사람들이 법은 시민들을 평등하게 대우하며, 사회의 최선의 이익에 이바지한다고 생각한다. 그리고 헌법만 읽어보면 이것이 사실인 듯하게 보일 것이다. 하지만 성문법에 초점을 맞추는 것은 오해의 소지가 있다. 법 체제가 공정하고 공평한 것처럼 보이지만, 이것이 정말 사실인가를 밝혀내기 위해 우리는 실제 적용되는 법과 법률 기관이 실제로 어떻게 직무를 수행하는지를 고찰할 필요가 있다. 우리가 그렇게 하면, 실제로 법률 기관은 가난하고 약한 사람들보다 부유하고 권력 있는 사람들 편에서 불공평하게 직무를 수행한다는 것이 명백해진다.

어휘

legal 법률의, 합법적인   democratic 민주적인   participation 참여   citizen 시민   assume 사실이라고 생각하다, 추정하다   constitution 헌법   just 공정한   in action 실행되는   authority (pl.) 당국, 정부기관   apparent 명백한   favor …에게 호의를 보이다, 유리하게 작용하다   [문제] trivial 사소한   intensive 집중적인   misleading 오해하게 하는   ambiguous 애매모호한, 여러 가지로 해석할 수 있는

구문해설

(8행) ..., but [to find out {whether this is really true}], we need to examine **the law in action** and **how legal authorities actually operate**.: [ ]는 목적을 나타내는 부사적 용법의 to부정사구, { }는 find out의 목적절, 명사구(the law in action)와 의문사절(how ... operate)은 examine의

11행 ..., **it** becomes apparent [that in reality, legal authorities operate unjustly, {favoring *the rich and powerful* over *the poor and weak*}].: it은 가주어이고 [ ]가 진주어, { }는 부대상황을 나타내는 분사구문, 'the+형용사' 「…한 사람들」(복수보통명사)

문제해설
④ 빈칸의 앞부분에서는 법 체제가 평등과 최선의 이익을 위한다는 일반적인 관념이 있다고 말하고 있으며, 빈칸 뒷부분에서는 법 체제의 불공정성에 대해 언급하고 있으므로 성문법에만 기반을 두는 것은 오해를 불러일으킬 수 있다는 내용이 적절하다.

32 ③ 빈칸 추론

스키는 흥미진진하고 인기 있는 스포츠이지만, 일어날 수 있는 사고가 많다. 만약 당신이 보스턴 근처의 와추셋 산에 스키를 타러 간다면, '스키 의무 조항'의 일곱 가지 항목을 암송할 것을 요구받을 것이다. 그 조항의 일곱 개 항목을 모두 대면, 당신은 새 스키 한 벌 또는 시즌 무료 이용권을 받을 것이다. 이러한 보상들은 사람들이 '스키 의무 조항'을 외우게 하기 위한 새로운 홍보 활동의 일환으로 제공된다. 뉴햄프셔의 워터빌 계곡 리조트나 버몬트의 브롬리 리조트에서는 헬멧을 착용하면 당신이 리프트 이용권을 5달러 할인받도록 할 것이다. 이러한 리조트들은 확실히 슬로프에서의 안전을 증진시키기 위해 그들이 할 수 있는 모든 일을 하고 있다.

어휘
recite 암송하다   code 규칙, 규약   pass 입장권   reward 보상   promotion 상품 판매, 판촉   definitely 명확히; *확실히   [문제] considerable 상당한   slope 비탈, 경사지; *(스키장의) 슬로프   rent 빌리다   equipment 장비

구문해설
12행 These resorts are definitely doing everything [(that) they can (do)] [to promote safety on the slopes].: 첫 번째 [ ]는 everything을 선행사로 하는 목적격 관계대명사절, 두 번째 [ ]는 목적을 나타내는 부사적 용법의 to부정사구

문제해설
③ 스키 탈 때의 의무 조항을 외우면 선물을 제공하고 헬멧 착용자에게 할인 혜택을 주는 등 각 리조트들이 하는 행사는 모두 '슬로프에서의 안전을 증진시키기' 위한 것이다.

33 ④ 빈칸 추론

레오나르도 다빈치는 종소리와 물에 떨어지는 돌에 의해 만들어지는 파장 사이의 유사성을 알아차렸을 때, 소리는 파장을 이루며 이동한다는 것을 발견했다. 이와 비슷한 천재성의 순간에, 유기 화학자인 F. A. 케쿨레는 뱀이 자신의 꼬리를 물고 있는 꿈을 꾼 후, 벤젠 분자가 고리 모양을 하고 있다는 것을 깨달았다. 그리고 위대한 발명가인 새뮤얼 모스가 릴레이 경주 동안 말의 무리가 교대되는 방식을 알아차렸을 때, 그는 바다를 건너 전해질 수 있을 정도로 강한 전신 신호를 만들어 내는 방법을 생각해 냈다. 그것은 바로 전신 신호에 주기적인 힘의 증폭을 가하는 것이었다. 이상의 사례들을 보면, 겉보기에 무관해 보이는 것들을 연관시키는 능력이 천재들로 하여금 남들이 놓치는 것들을 보게 한다는 것이 확실하다.

어휘
similarity 유사성   genius 천재성; 천재   organic 유기체의   chemist 화학자   molecule 분자   relay race 계주   figure out …을 생각해 내다   telegraphic 전송의, 전신의   periodic 주기적인   boost 증폭, 추진   [문제] commercial 상업적인   seemingly 겉보기에

구문해설
3행 ... the sound of a bell and the wave [made by a stone {hitting water}].: [ ]는 the wave를 수식하는 과거분사구, { }는 a stone을 수식하는 현재분사구

5행 ... realized [that benzene molecules ... ring-shaped] after dreaming of a snake [biting its own tail].: 첫 번째 [ ]는 realized의 목적절, 두 번째 [ ]는 a snake를 수식하는 현재분사구

13행 ... the skill [to connect the seemingly unconnected] **enables** geniuses **to see** things others miss.: [ ]는 the skill을 수식하는 형용사적 용법의 to부정사구, 'enable+O+to-v' 「…가 ~할 수 있게 하다」

문제해설
④ 돌이 물에 떨어져서 생기는 파장, 꼬리를 물고 있는 뱀, 경주에서의 말 교대는 각각 겉보기에 관련이 없어 보이는 소리의 파장, 벤젠 분자의 구조, 전신 신호 장치를 발견하도록 천재들에게 영감을 부여했다는 내용의 글이다.

34 ③ 빈칸 추론

환경과 사회적 발전은 상호 유익하게 작용할 수 없다고 생각하는 것이 일반적이다. 그래서 많은 사람들이 환경을 보호하기 위해서 우리가 경제 성장률을 늦출 필요가 있다고 생각한다. 하지만 환경을 고려하여 책임 있는 선택을 하면서도 경제를 확대시킬 수 있는 다양한 방법들이 있다. 예를 들어, 캘리포니아와 같은 주(州)들이 배기가스 배출이 적은 차량의 이용을 요구하는 법을 제정하면, 그들은 자동차 제조업자에게 새로운 시장을 창출해 주는 것이 된다. 또한 석유회사들은 대체 연료를 연구하고 개발함으로써 새로운 사업을 창출할 수 있다. 한편, 근로자들은 새롭고 환경친화적인 기술을 갖추고 일할 수 있도록 재훈련받을 수 있다. 이런 식으로 환경 보호와 지속 가능한 발전의 균형이 이루어질 것이다.

어휘
ecology 생태   improvement 향상, 개선   beneficially 유익하게   expand 확장하다, 확대하다   in[with] regard to …을 고려하여   emission 방출; *배기가스   manufacturer 제조업자   alternative fuel 대체 연료   retrain 재훈련하다   conservation (자연환경) 보호   sustainable 지속 가능한   [문제] budget 예산   secure 확보하다   legislate 법률을 제정하다

구문해설
5행 However, there are a variety of ways [to expand the economy] [while (we are) still making responsible choices ... the environment].: 첫 번째 [ ]는 a variety of ways를 수식하는 형용사적 용법의 to부정사구, 두 번째 [ ]는 때를 나타내는 부사절('일반 주어+be동사' 생략)

문제해설
③ 앞에서 환경과 사회 발전이 상호 유익하게 작용할 수 없다고 생각하는 것이 일반적이라고 한 진술에 덧붙여 추가 설명을 하는 부분이므로, 사람들이 환경 보호를 위해서는 그에 상반되는 경제 성장을 늦추어야 한다고 생각한다는 내용이 오는 것이 자연스럽다.

35 ③ 흐름과 무관한 문장

유전자 변형 식품이 현재 대형 사업이기는 하지만, 이것은 절차비가 매우 많이 드는 산업이다. 유전자 변형 식물을 고안하고 시험하는 과정은 오래 걸리고 비용이 많이 들어서, 기업들은 보통 장기적으로 이윤을 내는 것을 보장하기 위해 자사의 식물에 대해 특허를 획득한다. 이런 특허들은 식물 종자의 가격을 오르게 하여, 개발도상국의 영세한 농부들이 그 종자들을 구입할 수 없게 만들고, 그로 인해 빈부 격차를 커지게 만든다는 우려가 있다. (사무직과 생산직 노동자들의 경제적 격차가 점점 심해져서 각 정부는 그 문제를 해결하려 노력하고 있다.) 또한, 일부 유전자 변형

작물에는 한 철이 지나면 그것들이 번식을 못하게 하는 유전자가 이식되어 있다는 몇몇 증거가 존재한다. 이는 그들의 고객들이 매년 새로운 종자를 구매하도록 만드는데, 빈민국 농부들은 이런 종류의 지속적인 투자를 할 여력이 없기 때문에 이것은 그들을 지속적인 빈곤에 처하게 한다.

구문해설

3행 The process of [**designing** and **testing** genetically modified plants] is long and expensive, so companies usually obtain patents for their plants [to ensure ... in the long-term].: 첫 번째 [ ]는 전치사 of의 목적어로 쓰인 동명사구로 designing과 testing이 and로 병렬 연결. 두 번째 [ ]는 목적을 나타내는 부사적 용법의 to부정사구

14행 Also, there is some evidence [that some genetically modified crops have been implanted with a gene {that **prevents** them **from reproducing** after a single season}].: [ ]는 some evidence와 동격. { }는 a gene을 선행사로 하는 주격 관계대명사절. 'prevent+O+from v-ing'「…가 ~하는 것을 막다」

문제해설

기업들이 유전자 변형 식품 사업의 높은 비용을 감당하기 위해 특허를 획득하거나 종자를 번식할 수 없게 하여 국가 간 빈부 격차를 증가시킨다는 내용의 글이므로, 사무직과 생산직 노동자들의 경제적 격차에 관해 언급한 ③은 글의 흐름과 무관하다.

36 ③ 글의 순서

모든 사람들은 외모를 바탕으로 하여 사람들을 차별하는 것은 잘못된 것이라고 동의한다. 우리 사회는 평등을 믿는 사회이며, 우리 모두 우리가 다른 사람들을 공정하게 판단한다고 생각하고 싶어한다.
(B) 그런데, 사회학적 연구는 다른 이야기를 한다. 비록 우리가 그것을 인정하고 싶지 않을지도 모르지만, 우리는 종종 사람들의 외모를 그들의 성격에 대한 불공평한 추측을 하는 데 이용한다. 그러고 나서 이러한 추측들은 우리가 그들을 대하는 방식에 영향을 준다.
(A) 예를 들어, 많은 미국인들이 비만인 사람들에 대하여 상당한 편견을 가지고 있어서, 그들을 의지가 약하고 체계적이지 못하며 매력이 없다고 여긴다. 이 사람들은 종종 구직 시장에서 차별에 직면하고 잔인한 농담의 대상이 된다.
(C) 이러한 종류의 차별은 관련된 모든 사람들에게 해롭다. 마음이 상하는 것과 더불어, 그것은 우리로 하여금 똑똑하고 재미있는 사람들과 보람 있는 관계를 형성하지 못하게 할 수 있다. 결국, 우리가 주변의 사람들을 공정하게 그리고 동등하게 대할 때 모두가 이득을 본다.

구문해설

1행 Everyone agrees [that **it** is wrong {to discriminate against people based on their appearances}].: [ ]는 agrees의 목적절. it은 that절의 가주어이고 { }가 진주어

13행 ..., we often use people's appearance [to make unfair assumptions about their character].: [ ]는 목적을 나타내는 to부정사구

문제해설

③ 사람들 스스로가 타인을 차별하지 않고 공정하게 판단한다고 믿는다는 내용의 주어진 글 다음에, 실제 연구에서는 이와는 반대로 외모로 불공평하게 차별한다는 내용의 (B)가 오고, 외모로 차별하는 구체적인 예를 제시한 (A)가 온 다음에, 마지막으로 이런 방식으로 사람을 차별하지 않고 공정하고 동등하게 모두를 대해야 한다는 (C)가 오는 것이 자연스럽다.

37 ⑤ 글의 순서

오리너구리는 지구상에서 가장 이상한 생물 중 하나이다. 그것은 비버와 오리를 합친 모습을 닮았으며, 포유류임에도 불구하고 알을 낳는다.
(C) 한 과학자 팀이 최근에 오리너구리의 또 다른 특이한 특징을 발견했다. 자외선에 노출되면, 오리너구리 털이 푸르스름한 녹색 빛을 낸다. 이것은 보기에 생체 형광으로 알려진 현상에 의해 일어나는 것 같다.
(B) 그것은 생명체가 짧은 파장의 빛을 흡수하고 나서 이를 더 긴 파장의 빛으로 방출할 때 발생한다. 이것은 생체 발광과는 다른데, 이는 생물이 자신의 몸으로 빛을 만들 수 있을 때 발생한다.
(A) 오리너구리 털이 왜 이런 특성을 갖는지는 분명하지 않다. 과학자들은 더 긴 파장으로 빛을 방출하는 것이 자외선에 민감한 포식자가 오리너구리를 보는 것을 더 어렵게 만들지도 모른다고 생각한다. 그러나 생체 형광은 그저 과거에는 유용했지만 오늘날에는 더 이상 필요하지 않은 능력일 수도 있다.

구문해설

6행 The scientists think [that releasing light at longer wavelengths may **make** it **harder** for ultraviolet-sensitive predators {to see the platypus}].: [ ]는 think의 목적어로 쓰인 명사절. 'make+O+형용사'「…을 ~하게 만들다」, it은 가목적어이고 { }가 진목적어, ultraviolet-sensitive predators는 { }의 의미상 주어
21행 This is apparently caused by a phenomenon [that **is known as** biofluorescence].: [ ]는 a phenomenon을 선행사로 하는 주격 관계대명사절. 'be known as'「…로 알려지다」

문제해설

⑤ 오리너구리의 독특한 특징을 설명하는 주어진 글에 이어, 오리너구리의 또 다른 특징으로 자외선에 노출되면 털에서 빛이 나는 생체 형광에 대해 설명하는 (C)가 오고, 생체 형광에 대한 부가적인 설명을 하는 (B)가 이어진 후, 오리너구리가 왜 이런 특성을 갖는지는 분명하지 않다고 마무리하는 (A)로 이어지는 것이 자연스럽다.

38 ③ 주어진 문장의 위치

선거 기간 동안 유권자들의 의사 결정 과정을 분석하면서, 연구자들은 투표 결정에 미치는 매체 메시지의 영향을 조사했다. 처음에 그들은 매체가 유권자들의 결정에 강한 영향을 미친다는 증거를 발견할 것이라고 예상했다. 그러나, 그들의 연구는 대신에 개인 간의 만남 사이에서 공유된 의견들이 투표 행위에 미치는 강력한 영향력을 밝혀냈다. 이 정보를 이용하여 연구자들은 매스컴에 대한 이론을 개발했고, 그것이 두 단계의

과정으로 작용한다고 제시했다. 그것은 '여론 주도자들', 즉 매체를 밀접하게 좇아 대중 매체의 메시지를 수신하는 개인들로 시작한다. 그러고 나서 그들은 그들 자신만의 해석으로 그 메시지들을 각색하면서 이러한 메시지를 다른 사람들에게 전달한다. 실제로, 직접적인 매체 노출이 영향을 미치는 것보다 이러한 여론 주도자들이 유권자들에게 훨씬 더 많은 영향을 미치는 것으로 입증되었다.

어휘
mass communication 매스컴, 대중 전달 매체   analyze 분석하다
decision-making 의사 결정   voter 투표자, 유권자   election 선거   color
색칠하다; *영향을 끼치다   interpretation 해석, 설명   exposure 드러냄, 노출

구문해설
[14행] They then pass along these messages to others, [coloring them with their own interpretations].: [ ]는 부대상황을 나타내는 분사구문

문제해설
주어진 문장의 this information은 ③ 앞의 내용인 개인 간에 공유된 의견들이 투표 행위에 강력한 영향을 미친다는 것을 가리키며, ③ 뒤의 내용은 주어진 문장의 a two-step process를 설명하고 있으므로 주어진 문장은 ③에 들어가는 것이 적절하다.

39 ④ 주어진 문장의 위치

일부 교육 기관에서 학생들은 영어, 역사 또는 과학과 같은 과목들의 '디지털' 과정에 등록할 수 있는 선택권을 가지고 있을지도 모른다. 교육 당국은 또한 교사들에게 파워포인트, 실시간 재생 동영상, 그리고 온라인 검색 자료와 같은 (수업) 도구들의 사용을 통해 과학 기술을 그들의 교실에 통합하도록 장려한다. 물론, 몇몇 사람들은 구식의 교과서들이 결국에는 온라인으로 접근할 수 있는 디지털 버전으로 대체될 것이라고 생각하지만, 그것들은 여전히 우리의 교육 시설에서 자리를 차지하고 있다. 이러한 더 새로운 교재들은 무거운 종이 책들을 짊어지고 다니는 것으로부터 학생들을 해방시킬 수 있기 때문에, 실제로 이로울 수 있다. 그러나, 지금으로서는 교실 내 과학 기술은 너무 비용이 많이 들어 대부분의 학교들이 감당하기 어렵다. 이것은 심지어 전통적인 학급 물품 지원조차 부족한 가난한 학군에 있는 학교들에 있어서 특히 그러하다. 부자와 가난한 사람을 가르는 디지털 (기술의) 분할을 없애기 위한 조치들이 취해져야 한다.

어휘
institution 기관, 단체, 협회   enroll 등록하다   integrate 통합하다
streaming 인터넷에서 음성이나 영상 등을 실시간으로 재생하는 기법
advantageous 이로운, 유익한   district 구역, 지구   supply 공급; *공급품
divide 분할, 분계   separate 분리하다, 떼어놓다

구문해설
[11행] ..., though some believe [(that) they'll eventually be replaced by digital versions {that can be accessed online}].: [ ]는 believe의 목적절, { }는 digital versions를 선행사로 하는 주격 관계대명사절

문제해설
과학 기술을 이용한 온라인 학습 과정의 장점을 언급하다가 ④ 이후에서 가난한 학군에 있는 학교들에서 특히 어떤 일이 사실이며 이를 해결해야 한다는 단점이 제시되므로, 역접의 접속사인 However로 시작하여 그 기술들을 대부분의 학교에서 이용하기에는 비용이 많이 든다는 내용, 즉 그 어떤 일에 해당하는 내용인 주어진 문장이 ④에 들어가는 것이 적절하다.

40 ④ 요약문 완성

프랑스 혁명 후에 프랑스 국민들은 그들에게 왕족을 떠올리게 하는

어떠한 것도 원하지 않았다. 그 결과 프랑스인들은 놀이용 카드의 디자인을 바꾸기로 결정했다. 혁명 전에 프랑스의 놀이용 카드는 오늘날 사용되는 카드와 같은 것이었다. 각 카드 한 벌은 네 가지 패로 이루어졌고 각 패에는 왕, 여왕, 잭을 나타내는 세 장의 카드가 있었다. 혁명 후에 이러한 왕족의 모습은 카드에서 사라졌다. 여왕은 자유의 상징물로 대체되었고, 왕은 자연, 그리고 잭은 도덕이 되었다. 그러나 이러한 새 카드는 기존의 디자인으로 되돌아가기 전의 짧은 기간 동안에만 생산되었다. 나폴레옹이 스스로를 프랑스의 황제로 공표하고 단 몇 년 후 왕족은 다시 일반적인 것이 되었으며, 이로 인해 왕과 왕비는 프랑스 놀이용 카드에서 선호되는 등장인물이 되었다.

어휘
revolution 혁명   remind A of B A에게 B를 생각나게 하다   royal 왕실의
(royalty 왕위, 왕족)   deck (카드 패의) 한 벌   suit 한 벌; *한 패   figure 형상;
*인물   virtue 덕, 선행   emperor 황제   [문제] eliminate 없애다, 제거하다
reference 관련, 관계   gradually 차츰   permanently 영구히
temporarily 일시적으로   unconsciously 무의식적으로   colonialism 식민주의   struggle 노력; 전투

구문해설
[5행] Before the revolution, French playing cards were **the same as** *those* [used today].: 'the same as ...' 「…와 같은」, 대명사 those는 앞에 언급된 playing cards를 대신함. [ ]는 those를 수식하는 과거분사구

문제해설
④ 프랑스 혁명 직후, 프랑스의 놀이용 카드는 왕족과의 어떤 연관도 없애기 위해 일시적으로 바뀌었다.

41 ② 42 ④ 장문

두 사람이 만나면, 그들이 하는 가장 자연스러운 일은 대화에 참여하는 것이다. 그러나, 우리 모두가 경험했듯이, 몇몇 사람들은 자기 자신에 대해 끊임없이 이야기를 하여 대화를 지배하는 것을 좋아한다. 당신은 이러한 종류의 행동이 짜증 난다고 생각할 수도 있지만, 연구는 그 이면에 적절한 이유가 있을지도 모른다는 것을 보여주었다. 하버드 대학의 한 연구에 따르면, 당신 자신에 관한 정보를 공유하는 행위가 실제로 당신의 뇌의 즐거움의 영역을 자극할 수도 있다.

인간은 사회적 동물이라서, 우리는 자연스럽게 의사소통하고자 하는 욕구를 느끼며 사회적인 접촉을 열망한다. 이러한 접촉이 띠고 있는 한 형태는 우리의 생각과 경험의 공유다. 이전의 연구들에서는 우리가 하는 말의 30에서 40퍼센트가 단지 그것을 하는 데에만 할애된다고 추정되었다. 이것은 또한 트위터와 페이스북과 같은 SNS의 인기를 설명해 주는데, SNS에서 사용자들은 다른 사람들과 자신에 대한 정보를 지속적으로 공유하고 있다. 이러한 종류의 사이트에 있는 '상태 업데이트'의 80퍼센트 정도가 개인의 즉각적인 경험을 공유하는 데 사용된다고 알려져 있다.

무엇이 이러한 종류의 행동을 유발하는지에 대하여 더 알기 위해서, 하버드 연구원들은 MRI 스캐너를 사용하여 사람들이 말하는 동안에 그들의 뇌의 움직임을 분석했다. 실험 대상자들은 우선 한 가지 주제에 관하여 그들 자신의 의견들을 공유하고 나서 다른 사람의 의견들을 판단하도록 요청받았다. 그들 자신의 의견을 말하는 동안 실험 대상자들은 우리가 음식이나 돈과 같은 기본적인 보상을 받을 때 주로 자극되는 것과 동일한 뇌의 부분들에서 활성화가 일어나는 것을 보여 주었다. 이 부분들은 그들이 그들 자신의 성격 특성을 논할 때 또한 활동적이었다.

어휘
engage in …에 관여하다, 참여하다   dominate 지배하다   constantly 끊임

없이   stimulate 자극하다   crave 갈망하다, 열망하다   contact 연락, 접촉   estimate 추정하다   devote 바치다   popularity 인기   approximately 거의   immediate 즉각적인   reward 보상   personality 성격   trait 특성, 특징   [문제] self-disclosure 자기 노출   self-centered 자기 중심의; *이기적인

구문해설
1행 ..., the most natural thing *for them* **to do** is [to engage in conversation].: to do는 the most natural thing을 수식하는 형용사적 용법의 to부정사, them은 to부정사의 의미상 주어, [ ]는 주격보어로 쓰인 명사적 용법의 to부정사구

25행 **In order to learn** more about [what drives this kind of behavior], the Harvard researchers used an MRI scanner ...: 'in order to-v'「…하기 위해서」, [ ]는 about의 목적어로 쓰인 의문사절

30행 [While (they were) offering their own opinions], the subjects showed activity in the same regions of the brain [that are usually stimulated ... food or money].: 첫 번째 [ ]는 때를 나타내는 부사절('주어 +be동사'가 생략된 형태), 두 번째 [ ]는 the same regions of the brain을 선행사로 하는 주격 관계대명사절

문제해설
41 자신의 경험을 실시간으로 SNS에 올리는 것과 같이 끊임없이 자신에 대해 이야기하려는 행동의 원인을 뇌의 움직임에 관한 하버드 대학의 연구를 바탕으로 밝히고 있으므로 제목으로 ② '자기 노출의 과학'이 적절하다.

42 ④ 자기 자신에 대해 이야기하는 동안 사람들의 뇌의 일부분은 기본적인 보상을 받을 때와 동일하게 반응한다고 했으므로, 빈칸에는 '즐거움'이라는 말이 들어가는 것이 가장 적절하다.

43 ② 44 ⑤ 45 ④ 장문

(A) 케테 콜비츠는 소묘, 판화 및 조각으로 가장 잘 알려진 20세기 독일 예술가였다. 그녀는 수많은 자화상을 그렸고, 다양한 중요 사회 문제에 대한 인식을 불러일으키기 위해 포스터도 디자인했다. 그녀의 작품 대부분이 어두운 주제를 담고 있는데, 죽음에 대한 예술가의 개인적인 관련성과 빈곤하게 살고 있는 여성들의 고통과 같은 문제를 다룬다.

(C) 이 어둠의 출현은 콜비츠 자신의 삶의 말년을 정의한 비극에 그 근원이 있었을 것이다. 그녀의 아들인 페터 콜비츠는 1차 세계대전이 시작될 때 독일군 입대를 자원했다. 콜비츠의 남편은 이 결정에 반대했지만, 콜비츠 자신은 아들을 지지했고 그가 그들의 조국을 위해 용감하게 싸울 것을 장려했다. 1914년, 군에 입대한 지 불과 3주 후에 페터는 전장에서 사망했다.

(B) 그녀의 아들을 잃은 슬픔에 휩싸여, 콜비츠는 의미 있는 예술 작품을 만드는 데 그녀의 고통과 슬픔을 집중하기로 결심했다. 그녀는 그녀의 아들이 묻힌 벨기에의 참전자 묘지를 위한 기념비를 디자인하기 시작했다. '비통한 부모'라는 제목의 그 프로젝트는 완료하는 데 거의 20년이 걸렸다. 1932년 콜비츠는 마침내 기념비를 완성했고, 그것은 같은 해 후반에 묘지에 세워졌다.

(D) 그 작품은 나란히 무릎을 꿇고 있는 두 인물로 구성되어 있는데, 하나는 남성이고 다른 하나는 여성이다. 콜비츠는 여성 인물에게 자신의 얼굴을 갖게 했다. 그녀는 숄에 싸여 몸을 구부리고 슬프게 땅을 응시하고 있는 반면, 콜비츠의 남편을 닮은 남성은 얼굴에 극심한 슬픔의 표정을 지닌 채 앞을 똑바로 쳐다본다. 케테 콜비츠 박물관의 관장인 아이리스 베른트 박사는 예술계에 대한 콜비츠의 기여에 찬사를 보냈다. "그녀는 특히나 남성이 우세한 세계에서 여성으로서 뛰어난 독일 예술가입니다."라고 그녀는 말했다.

어휘
sculpture 조각   self-portrait 자화상   awareness 의식, 관심   theme 주제   address 연설하다; *(문제·상황 등에 대해) 고심하다[다루다]   suffering 고통, 괴로움   poverty 가난, 빈곤   overwhelm (격한 감정이) 휩싸이다[압도하다]   sorrow 슬픔, 비애   creation 창조, 창작   meaningful 의미 있는, 중요한   memorial monument 기념비   cemetery 묘지   erect 건립하다   tragedy 비극   define 정의하다   volunteer 자원봉사로 하다; *(군대에) 자원 입대하다   enlist 요청하다; *입대하다   homeland 고국, 조국   battlefield 싸움터, 전장   kneel 무릎을 꿇다   stare 응시하다   resemble 닮다, 비슷하다   extreme 극도의   grief 비탄, 큰 슬픔   praise 칭찬하다   contribution 기부금; *기여, 이바지   outstanding 뛰어난, 걸출한   dominate 지배하다

구문해설
6행 Much of her work carries a dark theme, [addressing such issues as **the artist's personal relationship with death** and **the suffering of women** {who are living in poverty}].: [ ]는 부대상황을 나타내는 분사구문, 전치사 as의 목적어 역할을 하는 the artist's personal relationship with death와 the suffering of women who are living in poverty가 등위 접속사 and로 병렬 연결, { }는 women을 선행사로 하는 주격 관계대명사절

13행 She began designing a memorial monument for the war cemetery in Belgium [where her son was buried].: [ ]는 the war cemetery in Belgium을 선행사로 하는 관계부사절

32행 She **is wrapped** in a shawl, **(is) bent over**, and **(is) staring** sadly at the ground, *while* the man, [who resembles Kollwitz's husband], looks straight ahead with an expression of extreme grief on his face.: is wrapped, (is) bent over, (is) staring은 등위 접속사 and로 병렬 연결, while은 「…인 데 반하여」라는 의미의 접속사, [ ]는 the man을 선행사로 하는 계속적 용법의 주격 관계대명사절

문제해설
43 ② 케테 콜비츠에 대한 소개와 그녀의 작품이 어두운 주제를 다룬다고 하는 (A) 다음에, 이러한 어둠은 콜비츠가 겪은 비극에서 비롯되었다고 하며 전장에서 아들을 잃은 경험을 이야기하는 (C)가 오고, 아들을 잃은 슬픔을 예술 작품에 쏟았고 '비통한 부모'라는 작품을 완성했다는 (B)가 온 후에, 그 작품의 구성과 콜비츠에 대한 평가가 언급된 (D)가 마지막에 오는 것이 적절하다.

44 ⑤ (e)는 케테 콜비츠 박물관의 관장인 아이리스 베른트 박사를 가리키고, 나머지는 케테 콜비츠를 가리킨다.

45 ④ 조국을 위해 싸우겠다는 아들의 결심을 지지했다.

18 ④	19 ④	20 ⑤	21 ③	22 ④	23 ④
24 ④	25 ④	26 ④	27 ⑤	28 ③	29 ④
30 ④	31 ②	32 ③	33 ⑤	34 ⑤	35 ③
36 ③	37 ①	38 ③	39 ④	40 ③	41 ⑤
42 ⑤	43 ②	44 ①	45 ⑤		

18 ④ 글의 목적

친애하는 그레이슨 교수님께,

이곳 그린뷰 대학의 모든 동료들과 마찬가지로 저는 이번 11월에 개최되는 저희 연례 심포지엄에서 교수님이 연설하시는 것을 듣기를 고대하고 있습니다. 심포지엄이 급속도로 다가오고 있기 때문에 저는 일부 세부 사항을 검토하고 싶었습니다. 이전에 저희가 논의한 바와 같이, 교수님께서는 기조 연설을 하시고 나서 워크숍을 진행할 것입니다. 워크숍을 위한 추가 자료는 준비하실 필요가 없습니다. 워크숍은 기본적으로 교수님의 강의 내용을 토대로 한 질의응답 세션이 될 것이기 때문입니다. 두 세션 모두 약 한 시간 동안 진행될 것으로 예상됩니다. 또한, 학교 측에서 교수님의 숙소와 식사를 마련해드릴 것임을 상기시켜 드리고자 합니다. 명확하지 않은 점이 있다면, (516) 812-8664로 저에게 전화 주십시오.

진심을 담아,

찰스 오닐

인문학부 학과장

어휘
colleague 동료 look forward to …을 고대하다 symposium 심포지엄, 학술 토론회 go over …을 점검하다, 검토하다 approach 다가가다, 다가오다 previously 이전에 give a lecture 강연하다 keynote (책·연설 등의) 주안점, 기조 additional 추가의 material 자료 basically 기본적으로 arrange 마련하다 accommodation 숙소 unclear 불분명한 dean (대학의) 학과장 humanities 인문학

구문해설
3행 ..., I am looking forward to [**hearing** you **speak** at our annual symposium this November].: [ ]는 전치사 to의 목적어로 쓰인 동명사구, 지각동사 hearing의 목적격보어로 동사원형 speak이 쓰임

15행 I'd also like to remind you [that the school will be arranging your accommodations and meals].: [ ]는 remind의 직접목적어로 쓰인 명사절

문제해설
곧 다가오는 심포지엄에 앞서 일부 세부사항을 검토하고 싶다고 했으므로, ④가 이 글의 목적으로 가장 적절하다.

19 ④ 심경 변화

마이클은 침대에 누워 있었지만 완전히 깨어 있었다. 비록 그는 집에 혼자 있었지만, 복도에서 누군가 천천히 왔다 갔다 걸어 다니는 소리 같은 무언가를 들을 수 있었다. 몇 분 후에, 그는 조심스럽게 일어나서 침실 문으로 걸어가 그곳에 귀를 댔다. 처음에 그는 아무것도 듣지 못했다. 하지만 그때 누군가 혹은 무언가가 그의 방으로 점점 더 가까이 다가오는 것처럼 마룻바닥의 삐걱거리는 소리가 다시 시작되었다. 그는 잠시 침대 밑에 숨는 것을 생각했지만, 그것이 바보 같다는 것을 알았다. 대신에 그는 숨을 깊이 들이마시고 문을 열어젖혔다. 집에서 기르는 개가 복도에서 그의 바로 앞에 서 있었다. 마이클은 그날 밤 개를 마당에 내놓는 것을 잊었던 것이다.

어휘
hallway 복도 cautiously 조심스럽게 creak 삐걱거리다 briefly 간단히; *잠시 동안 foolish 어리석은; *바보 같은 [문제] thrilled 아주 신이 난 ashamed 부끄러운 relieved 안도하는

구문해설
3행 ..., like the sound of **someone** [slowly walking back and forth].: [ ]는 전치사 of의 목적어로 쓰인 동명사구이며 someone은 [ ]의 의미상 주어

9행 He briefly thought about [hiding under the bed], but he knew [(that) that would be foolish].: 첫 번째 [ ]는 전치사 about의 목적어로 쓰인 동명사구, 두 번째 [ ]는 knew의 목적절

12행 There in the hallway, [standing right in front of him], **was the family dog**.: 장소를 나타내는 There in the hallway가 문두에 오면서 주어(the family dog)와 동사(was)가 도치, [ ]는 부대상황을 나타내는 분사구문

문제해설
마이클은 복도에서 누군가 자신의 침실로 다가오는 듯한 소리를 듣고 겁먹었지만 문을 열어 보니 자신이 기르는 개라는 것을 알게되었으므로, 마이클의 심경 변화로 가장 적절한 것은 ④ '겁먹은 → 안도하는'이다.

20 ⑤ 글의 요지

음악 산업이 지난 몇 년에 걸쳐 전례 없이 저조한 음반 판매를 기록하며 불황을 겪고 있다. 이에 대한 원인을 찾는 것이 자연히 음반 회사들의 주요 관심사가 되었다. 일부는 침체된 경제를 탓하지만, 그것은 한 산업이 다른 산업들보다 훨씬 더 부진한 이유에 대해서는 거의 설명하지 못한다. 오늘날의 음악은 대부분 다 쓰고 나면 버려지는 상품이 되어 버렸다. 사람들은 '재사용하는' 제품에 대해서만큼 '일회용' 제품에 많은 돈을 낼 준비가 되어 있지 않다. 많은 현대 음악이 짧지만 강렬한 수명을 지닌다. 히트곡들은 너무 자주 방송되어서 그 음반을 살 필요가 없다. 그리고 그 음악을 더 이상 틀어 주지 않을 때쯤에는 아무도 그것을 기억하지 못한다.

어휘
recession 불경기 record 음반 all-time 전례 없는 concern 걱정; *관심사 blame 비난하다 lose out 실패하다 commercial 상업의 use up …을 다 쓰다 disposable 일회용의 reusable 다시 쓸 수 있는 intense 강렬한 lifespan 수명 broadcast 방송하다

구문해설
2행 ..., **with** record sales **reaching** all-time lows ...: 'with+O+현재분사' 「…가 ~한 채로」(부대상황을 나타내는 분사구문)

9행 People are not prepared to pay **as much** for a "disposable" product **as** they are (prepared to pay) for a "reusable" one.: 'as much ... as ~' 「~만큼 많은 …」

문제해설
⑤ 음악이 일회성으로 소비되는 상황에서 음반 시장이 유례 없는 불황을 겪고 있다는 내용의 글이다.

21 ③ 글의 주제

미국에서 가장 열광적으로 기념되는 신코 데 마요 휴일은 보통 멕시코의 독립 쟁취를 축하하기 위한 것으로 믿어진다. 그러나 이것은 사실이

아니다. 신코 데 마요는 사실 푸에블라 전투를 기념하는데 그것은 멕시코가 독립을 선언한 지 52년 후인 1862년 5월 5일에 일어났다. 그날은 멕시코 군대가 침입해오는 프랑스 군대에 맞서 예상 밖의 승리를 거두었기 때문에 기억된다. 1863년 이후로 많은 멕시코계 미국인들이 신코 데 마요에 그들의 히스패닉 유산을 기념하기로 했기 때문에 미국인들이 혼란스러워하는 것일지도 모른다. 다른 배경을 가진 미국인들은 그날의 역사를 알지 못했고 그날이 멕시코의 독립과 관련이 있음이 틀림없다고 가정했는데, 이것이 현재까지 지속되고 있는 오류이다.

어휘
enthusiastically 열광적으로 observe 관찰하다; *(축제일 등을) 축하하다 achievement 업적; *성취 independence 독립 commemorate 기념하다 declare 선언하다 unlikely 있음 직하지 않은, 예상 밖의 invade 침입하다 heritage 유산 assumption 가정 persist 지속되다 [문제] misunderstand 오해하다 significance 중요성

구문해설
1행 The holiday of *Cinco de Mayo*, [most enthusiastically observed in the United States], is commonly believed ...: [ ]는 The holiday of *Cinco de Mayo*를 부연 설명하는 과거분사구
5행 *Cinco de Mayo* actually commemorates the Battle of Puebla, [which occurred on May 5, 1862, {fifty-two years after Mexico declared its independence}].: [ ]는 the Battle of Puebla를 선행사로 하는 계속적 용법의 주격 관계대명사절, { }는 May 5, 1862와 동격
14행 ... made the assumption [that it must **have something to do with** Mexican independence], [an error {that has persisted to the present day}].: 첫 번째 [ ]는 the assumption과 동격, 'have something to do with ...' 「…와 관련이 있다」, 두 번째 [ ]는 첫 번째 [ ]의 내용과 동격, { }는 an error를 선행사로 하는 주격 관계대명사절

문제해설
푸에블라 전투에서의 승리를 기념하는 신코 데 마요를 미국인들이 멕시코의 독립을 기념하는 날로 오해하게 된 배경을 설명하고 있으므로, 이 글의 주제로는 ③ '미국인들은 신코 데 마요를 어떻게 오해하는가'가 가장 적절하다.

22 ④ 글의 제목

세계의 많은 지역들이 계속해서 심각한 물 부족을 겪고 있으며, 이것은 기근과 재난으로 이어질 수 있다. 하지만 우리는 물이 단순하게 두 개의 수소 분자와 한 개의 산소 분자의 결합물이라는 것을 안다. 만약 이 화학 공식이 그렇게 간단하다면, 우리는 왜 이 분자들을 결합시켜서 인공적으로 물을 만들어내지 않는 것일까? 안타깝게도 그 대답은 물을 대량으로 제조하는 것이 엄청나게 위험할 수 있기 때문이라는 것이다. 물을 만들기 위해서는, 각 분자의 전자들이 연결되어 함께 결합하도록 하기 위한 갑작스런 에너지의 폭발이 필요하다. 소량의 물을 생산하기에는 통제된 실험실에서의 작은 불꽃으로도 충분하지만, 대량으로 물을 만드는 것은 큰 위험을 야기한다. 과학자들이 폭발성이 덜한 방식을 고안해내지 않는 이상, 세계의 갈증을 해소하기에 충분한 물을 만드는 것은 이론적인 가능성으로만 남게 될 것이다.

어휘
shortage 부족 famine 기근 disaster 재해, 재난 combination 결합물 (combine 결합하다) hydrogen 수소 molecule 분자 oxygen 산소 formula 공식 artificially 인위적으로 manufacture 제조하다 quantity 양 enormously 엄청나게, 대단히 burst 파열, 폭발 electron 전자 link up 연결하다 spark 불꽃 scale 규모 present 주다; *야기하다 hazard 위험 volatile 휘발성의, 폭발하기 쉬운 theoretical 이론적인 [문제] generate 발생시키다 drought 가뭄

구문해설
9행 [To create water], a sudden burst of energy is required to **cause** the electrons of each molecule **to link up** and **(to) combine** together.: [ ]는 목적을 나타내는 부사적 용법의 to부정사구. 'cause+O+to-v' 「…가 ~하도록 하다」, to link up과 (to) combine이 and로 병렬 연결
15행 Unless scientists can come up with a less volatile method, [creating enough water {to satisfy the world's thirst}] will remain only a theoretical possibility.: [ ]는 주절의 주어로 쓰인 동명사구, { }는 enough를 한정하는 부사적 용법의 to부정사구

문제해설
대량의 물을 인공적으로 만들기 위해서는 커다란 에너지의 폭발이 수반되어 위험할 수 있다는 내용이므로 ④ '인공적으로 물을 만드는 것의 위험성'이 제목으로 적절하다.

23 ④ 글의 제목

괜찮은 미국 대학의 졸업장은 한때 한국에서 좋은 직업을 구하는 비결로 여겨졌다. 그러나 그런 시절은 거의 지나가 버렸다. 현재 점점 늘어나는 해외 유학생들은 고국에 돌아와서 취업 시장이 어렵다는 것과 외국 경험이 더 이상 과거에 그랬던 것처럼 (취업)문을 열어주지는 않는다는 것을 알게 된다. 미국의 유명 대학 졸업생인 박 씨는 그녀가 원하던 직업을 얻는 데 계속 실패한 뒤, 자신의 기대를 충족시키기 어렵다는 것을 깨달았다. "미국에서의 모든 경험이 저에게 그다지 도움이 되지 않았다는 게 믿겨지지 않아요. 저는 여전히 제 능력과 지식에 걸맞은 직업을 찾으려고 노력 중입니다."라고 그녀는 말했다.

어휘
diploma 졸업장 decent (수준·질이) 괜찮은, 제대로 된 once 언젠가, 한때 regard A as B A를 B로 여기다 tight 단단한; *(상황이) 어려운 graduate 졸업생 repeatedly 반복적으로 expectation 기대 fit with …에 어울리다 [문제] guarantee 보증하다 flock 모이다

구문해설
3행 Now, a growing number of students ... have come home [to find {(that) the job market is tight} and {(that) foreign experience no longer opens doors like it used to (open doors)}].: [ ]는 결과를 나타내는 부사적 용법의 to부정사구, 두 개의 { }는 find의 목적절

문제해설
④ 해외 유학 경험이 과거에 그랬던 것만큼 국내에서의 취업을 보장해 주지는 않는다는 내용이다.

24 ④ 도표 내용 불일치

위 도표는 5세에서 14세 사이의 호주 어린이들이 참여하는 여가 활동들을 보여준다. 조사된 남자아이들과 여자아이들 100퍼센트가 그들의 여가 시간에 텔레비전이나 비디오를 시청하는 것으로 보고했다. 컴퓨터 게임은 그다음으로 가장 인기 있는 활동으로, 남자아이들의 약 5분의 4와 여자아이들의 5분의 3이 즐겨 한다. 미술과 공예의 범주에 있어서, 남자아이들의 단 3분의 1 이상이 참여하는 것과는 대조적으로 여자아이들의 절반 이상이 이 같은 활동에 참여하고 있다고 보고했다. (자전거 타기는 남자아이들보다 여자아이들에게 더 인기가 있기는 했지만, 남녀 모든 아이들의 대다수에게 인기가 있었다.) 마지막으로, 더 많은 남자아이들이 미술과 공예 활동보다 스케이트보드 타기에 참여했지만, 여자아이들에게는 스케이트보드 타기가 가장 인기 없는 활동이었다.

어휘
arts and crafts 미술과 공예 represent 나타내다, 보여주다 engage in …에 참가하다 as opposed to …에 대조적으로, …와 대립하여

astonishingly 놀랍게도; *놀랄 만큼, 몹시   shield 보호하다, 가리다   uncover 폭로하다; *노출시키다

구문해설

(6행) However, the female won't lay her eggs until it has ascertained [that the temperature of the mound is exactly 33℃].: 'not ... until ~' 「~한 후에 비로소 …하다」, [ ]는 has ascertained의 목적절

(11행) The male spends 11 months a year performing the important task of [checking and maintaining the temperature of the mound].: 'spend+시간+v-ing' 「…하는 데 시간을 보내다」, [ ]는 the important task와 동격

문제해설

① 체온이 아닌 지열로 알을 부화시킨다. ② 흙더미를 만드는 것은 수컷이다. ③ 수컷은 부리를 사용해서 흙더미의 온도를 측정한다. ⑤ 여름에 시원한 모래층으로 알을 보호하고, 가을에는 알을 태양에 노출시킨다.

27 ⑤ 내용 불일치

프레스노 영화제 '골든 티켓' 입장권

당신은 이 축제의 열렬한 팬인가요? 그렇다면 우리의 새로운 골든 티켓 입장권 중 하나를 구매하는 것을 고려해 보셔야 합니다! 이 특별한 입장권의 혜택은 다음과 같습니다.
- 본인이 선택한 영화 10편에의 입장
- 당신과 동반 1인의 8월 11일에 있을 개회식에의 입장
- 무료 'I Love FFF' 티셔츠 한 장
- 참석하는 영화별 라지 사이즈 무료 음료

이것은 한정 판매입니다. 골든 티켓 100장만이 인쇄될 것이며, 그것들은 8월 3일까지 구매되어야 합니다. 일 인당 한 장만 구입하실 수 있습니다.

자세한 정보를 원하시면, 저희 웹사이트인 www.fresnoff.org를 방문해 주세요.

어휘

big fan 열혈팬   consider 고려하다   benefit 혜택, 이득   admission 입장   opening ceremony 개회식   attend 참석하다   limited 한정된   purchase 구매하다

구문해설

(3행) Then you should consider [buying one of our new Golden Ticket passes]!: [ ]는 consider의 목적어로 쓰인 동명사구

(11행) a free large drink at each movie [(that) you attend]: [ ]는 each movie를 선행사로 하는 목적격 관계대명사절

문제해설

⑤ 8월 11일은 개회식 날짜이며, 티켓은 8월 3일까지 구매해야 한다고 나와 있다.

28 ③ 어법

1965년에 기업가 라이오넬 버레이에게 대단한 사업 아이디어가 떠올랐다. 그는 영연방 국가에서 온 런던의 많은 이민자들을 대상으로 한 '영연방 파수꾼'이라는 신문을 창간하기로 결정했다. 그는 신문 내용을 구성하고 광고 지면을 팔면서 모든 시간을 보냈다. 그러나 제1호가 발행되기로 예정되어 있던 아침, 그는 잠자리에서 일어나 그의 신문 50,000부가 그가 묵고 있던 호텔 밖 길가에서 자신을 기다리고 있는 것을 발견했다. 버레이는 신문 창간의 세부 내용을 해결하느라 너무 분주했던 나머지 유통망을 조직하는 것을 완전히 간과했던 것이다. 그의 신문 사업은 2월 6일에 시작되었고 그 다음날인 7일에 끝이 났다.

구문해설

(1행) The above chart represents the leisure activities [in which Australian children aged 5-14 participate].: [ ]는 the leisure activities를 선행사로 하는 목적격 관계대명사절

(3행) [One hundred percent of both the boys and the girls surveyed] reported watching television or videos in their free time.: [ ]는 문장의 주어이고 reported가 동사, surveyed는 both the boys and the girls를 수식하는 과거분사

문제해설

④ 자전거 타기 활동은 여자아이들보다 남자아이들에게 더 인기가 많았다.

25 ④ 내용 불일치

고대 로마 시대에는 여러 종류의 신발을 신었는데 그중 하나가 '박사'였다. 이 샌들은 야자나무 잎과 채소 이파리, 나뭇가지, 그리고 섬유로 만들어졌다. 주로 배우들과 철학자들이 신던 박사는 수수하고 저렴했는데, 이는 평민들도 그것을 신었음을 의미했다. 그 당시, 남자가 샌들을 신고 밖에 나가는 것은 부적절하다고 여겨졌으므로, 대부분의 남자들은 다른 사람들 앞에서는 그것을 신지 않았다. 그러나 로마인들은 집에서는 주로 가죽으로 만든 샌들을 신었다. 몇몇 여자들의 신발에 보석이나 진주가 달려 있기는 했지만, 여자가 신는 신발과 남자가 신는 신발은 거의 차이가 없었다. 또한 샌들 주인의 사회적 지위를 표시하기 위해 샌들에 색깔을 칠하는 경우도 종종 있었다.

어휘

footwear 신발류   palm 야자수   twig 가지   fiber 섬유   philosopher 철학자   commoner 일반인, 평민   unsuitable 부적절한   precious stone 보석   pearl 진주   status 지위

구문해설

(1행) Several types of footwear were worn during ancient times in Rome, [one of which was the baxa].: [ ]는 Several types of footwear를 선행사로 하는 계속적 용법의 목적격 관계대명사절

(4행) [(Being) Mainly worn by actors and philosophers], baxa shoes were simple and cheap, [which meant ... them].: 첫 번째 [ ]는 baxa shoes를 부연 설명하는 분사구문, 두 번째 [ ]는 앞 절 전체를 선행사로 하는 계속적 용법의 주격 관계대명사절

문제해설

④ 일부 여자들의 신발에 보석이나 진주가 달려 있는 것 외에는 남녀의 신발에 거의 차이가 없다고 했다.

26 ④ 내용 일치

풀숲무덤새는 종종 '온도계 새'라고 불린다. 이 새들은 알 위에 앉아서 체온으로 알을 품기보다는, 큰 흙더미를 만들고 그 안에 알을 낳는다. 수컷은 산란기가 다가오면 흙더미를 만들기 시작한다. 하지만, 암컷은 흙더미의 온도가 정확하게 33℃인 것을 확인한 후에야 비로소 알을 낳는다. 온도를 측정하기 위해 수컷은 흙더미 안에 부리를 집어넣는데, 그것을 놀랄 만큼 정확한 온도계로 사용한다. 수컷은 흙더미의 온도를 확인하고 유지하는 중요한 임무를 수행하는 데 일 년 중 11개월을 보낸다. 여름철에는 수컷은 시원한 모래층으로 알을 보호하고, 가을철에는 한낮의 태양의 온기를 느낄 수 있게 알을 노출시킨다.

어휘

thermometer 온도계   incubate (알을) 품다   mound 흙더미   lay 놓다; *(알을) 낳다(lay-laid-laid)   breeding season 번식기, 산란기   ascertain 알아내다, 확인하다   insert 끼우다, 삽입하다   beak (새의) 부리

어휘
strike …에게 갑자기 떠오르다 entrepreneur 기업인 launch 상품을 출시[출간]하다 commonwealth 연방 sentinel 보초, 파수병 be aimed at …을 대상으로 하다 immigrant 이민자 content 내용 issue (신문 등의) 호, 판 sort out …을 해결하다 overlook 간과하다 distribution 유통

구문해설
(2행) He decided to launch a newspaper [called the *Commonwealth Sentinel*], which **was to be aimed** …: [ ]는 a newspaper를 수식하는 과거분사구, was to be aimed는 예정의 의미로 쓰인 'be+to-v' 용법
(9행) …, he awoke [to find 50,000 copies of his newspaper waiting for him … hotel].: [ ]는 결과를 나타내는 부사적 용법의 to부정사구

문제해설
③ 「…하는 데 시간을 보내다」라는 뜻의 'spend+시간+v-ing' 구문이므로 organize을 organizing으로 고쳐야 한다.

29 ④ 어휘

스페인 세비야의 오렌지는 강력한 맛으로 알려져 있으며 마멀레이드에서 초콜릿에 이르기까지 광범위한 제품들에서 발견된다. 놀랍게도, 이 오렌지들은 전기를 생산하는 데도 사용될 수 있다. 세비야 시는 최근 오렌지에서 발생한 전기로 대형 정수장에 전력을 공급할 계획을 선보였다. 이 특이한 프로젝트의 핵심은 메탄이다. 이 가스는 오렌지가 발효됨에 따라 방출되며, 전기를 생산하는 발전기를 구동하기 위해 사용될 수 있다. 그 도시는 거리에서 원치 않는 오렌지를 모아서 그것의 즙을 추출할 것이다. 이것은 바이오가스를 생산하기 위해 쓰일 것이고, 남은 과일은 정원이나 농장을 위한 비료가 될 것이다. 그 프로젝트는 약 1,500kWh의 전기를 낭비할(→ 만들어낼) 것으로 예상된다. 이것은 대략 150가구에 의해 소비되는 전력량이며, 정수장을 자급자족하게 만들 만큼 충분하다.

어휘
intense 강렬한 a wide range of 광범위한, 다양한 marmalade 마멀레이드(오렌지·레몬 등으로 만든 잼) generate 발생시키다, 만들어내다 introduce 소개하다; *도입하다 power 동력을 공급하다, 작동시키다 purification 정화, 정제 plant 시설 methane 메탄 release 놓아 주다, 날려 보내다, 방출하다 ferment 발효되다, 발효시키다 generator 발전기 extract 뽑다[얻다], 추출하다 biogas 생물[바이오] 가스 fertilizer 비료 approximately 거의, 가까이 treatment 치료; *처리 self-sufficient 자급자족하는, 스스로 충분한

구문해설
(8행) This gas is released by oranges **as** they ferment, and it can be used [to drive generators {that produce electricity}].: as는 「…함에 따라」라는 의미의 접속사, [ ]는 목적을 나타내는 부사적 용법의 to부정사구, { }는 generators를 선행사로 하는 주격 관계대명사절
(12행) This is [what will be used {to produce the biogas}]; …: [ ]는 주격보어로 쓰인 관계대명사절, { }는 목적을 나타내는 부사적 용법의 to부정사구
(16행) This is approximately the amount of electricity [that is consumed by 150 homes], and it is **enough to make** the water treatment plant self-sufficient.: [ ]는 the amount of electricity를 선행사로 하는 주격 관계대명사절, 'enough to-v' 「…하기에 충분한」

문제해설
오렌지가 발효될 때 방출되는 가스로 전기를 생산한다는 내용이므로, ④ waste(낭비하다)를 create(만들어내다) 등으로 고쳐야 한다.

30 ④ 빈칸 추론

시카고에서 자신의 싱크대를 수리받을 필요가 있었던 한 나이 든 여성이 있었다. 안타깝게도, 정직하지 못한 배관공이 그 여성을 이용하여, 그녀가 작업에 대하여 50,000달러를 지불할 것을 동의하는 계약서에 서명하도록 설득했다. 그녀가 계약금으로 그에게 지불할 25,000달러를 인출하기 위해 은행에 갔을 때, 한 은행원이 의심을 하게 되었다. 그런 큰 금액이 무엇을 위해 필요한지 그 여성에게 물어본 후에, 은행원은 경찰에 연락하였다. 배관공은 곧 체포되어 사기죄로 기소되었다. 이 사건은 계약의 법적 한계에 관한 확실한 예를 제시한다. 우선 첫째로, 그것은 계약서의 단순한 존재 자체가 그 계약서의 공정성을 보장하지는 않는다는 것을 보여준다. 게다가, 이것은 다른 사람의 동의를 얻는 것이 반드시 법적인 계약을 생성하지는 않는다는 것을 분명히 해준다. 상호 이득이 없이, 계약서는 유효하다고 간주될 수 없다.

어휘
persuade 설득하다 contract 계약(서) agree 동의하다(agreement 협정, 계약) withdraw (계좌에서 돈을) 인출하다 down payment 착수금, 계약금 suspicious 의심스러운, 수상쩍은 arrest 체포하다 charge 기소하다, 고소하다 fraud 사기(죄) illustration 삽화; *실례 mere 단순한, 단지 …에 불과한 guarantee 보장하다, 약속하다 obtain 얻다, 구하다 consent 동의 absence 결석; *없음, 결핍 mutual 상호간의, 서로의 valid 유효한 [문제] clarity 명료성 fairness 공정성 content 《*pl.*》 내용(물)

구문해설
(2행) Unfortunately, a dishonest plumber took advantage of her, [persuading the woman to sign a contract {agreeing to pay him $50,000 for the work}].: [ ]는 부대상황을 나타내는 분사구문, { }는 a contract를 수식하는 현재분사
(14행) …, this makes **it** clear [that obtaining another person's consent does *not necessarily* create a legal agreement].: it은 가목적어이고 [ ]가 진목적어, 'not necessarily' 「반드시[꼭] …는 아닌」(부분부정)

문제해설
공정하지 않은 계약 내용 때문에 배관공이 체포되고 사기죄로 기소되었다고 했으므로, 빈칸에는 ④ '공정성'이 들어가는 것이 가장 적절하다.

31 ② 빈칸 추론

안토니오 살리에리의 동료 작곡가 볼프강 아마데우스 모차르트에 대한 질투는 현대 서적과 영화에서 인기 있는 주제이다. 이 중 일부는 심지어 살리에리가 모차르트를 독살했다는 혐의를 포함한다. 그러나, 그가 살인자일 가능성은 음악 사학자들에게는 무척 희박하다고 여겨진다. 살리에리에게는 모차르트를 죽일 동기가 없었는데, 비엔나의 음악 사회에서 그의 존경받는 입지가 그가 필요로 했던 모든 권력과 영향력을 제공했기 때문이다. 살리에리는 이탈리아의 오페라 감독이었을 뿐만 아니라 궁중 작곡가이자 지휘자였으며, 조셉 2세 황제는 그를 아꼈다고 한다. 게다가, 살리에리는 모차르트와 관련하여 개인적인 문제가 없었으며, 때때로 그의 곡들을 지휘하기까지 했다. 살리에리가 임종 때 자신이 모차르트를 살해했음을 자백했다고 하지만, 이것이 사실이라는 증거는 없다.

어휘
jealousy 질투 fellow 친구; *동료 composer 작곡가 contemporary 동시대의; *현대의 accusation 혐의 (제기), 비난 poison 독살하다 murderer 살인범 motive 동기, 이유 standing 지위, 평판 court 법정, 법원; *궁중 conductor 지휘자(conduct (특정한 활동을) 하다; *지휘하다) composition *작품; 작곡 from time to time 때때로 confess 자백하다, 고백하다 deathbed 임종 [문제] proof 증거(물) reliable 신뢰할 만한

likelihood 가능성

구문해설
[3행] Some of these even include the accusation [that Salieri poisoned Mozart].: [ ]는 the accusation과 동격
[7행] Salieri had no motive [to kill Mozart], **as** his respected standing in Vienna's musical society *provided* him *with* all the power and influence [(that) he needed].: 첫 번째 [ ]는 motive를 수식하는 형용사적 용법의 to부정사구, as는 이유를 나타내는 접속사, 'provide A with B' 「A에게 B를 제공하다」, 두 번째 [ ]는 all the power and influence를 선행사로 하는 목적격 관계대명사절
[15행] **It** is said [that Salieri confessed on his deathbed {that he *had killed* Mozart}], …: It은 가주어이고 [ ]가 진주어, { }는 confessed의 목적절, had killed는 that절의 시제(confessed)보다 더 이전에 일어난 일을 나타내는 과거완료

문제해설
살리에리가 모차르트를 독살했을 가능성은 희박하다는 내용의 글이므로, 빈칸에는 ② '증거 없음'이 들어가는 것이 적절하다.

32 ③ 빈칸 추론

우리 모두는 심장 박동에 의해 생겨나는 신체의 자연적 리듬을 가지고 있다. 일본의 한 전문가인 키요코 요코야마에 따르면, 이 (심장) 박동에 기초한 음악을 듣는 것은 스트레스를 줄일 수 있다고 한다. 요코야마는 이미 사람의 심장 박동을 분석하고, 복잡한 알고리즘을 사용하여 그 (심장) 박동의 타이밍, 파동, 변동을 편안한 음악으로 전환시킬 수 있는 프로그램을 설계했다. 그의 연구에서 그는 자신의 심장 박동에 의해 생성된 음악에 노출된 사람들은 음악을 듣지 않은 사람들보다 더 높은 수준의 휴식을 경험한다는 것을 발견했다. 요코야마는 그의 발견이 스트레스가 심한 환경의 근로자들을 위한 스트레스 및 피로 경감 프로그램의 형성과 같은 실용화로 이어질 수 있기를 희망한다.

어휘
heartbeat 심장 박동 convert 전환시키다 fluctuation 변동, 오르내림; *파동 chill-out 편안한 application 적용, 응용 formulation 공식화, 체계화 fatigue 피로 [문제] concentration 집중 maximize 극대화하다

구문해설
[4행] …, listening to music [that has its basis in this beat] can decrease feelings of stress.: [ ]는 music을 선행사로 하는 주격 관계대명사절
[10행] …, he has noticed that people [exposed to the music {generated by their heartbeat}] experience …: [ ]는 people을 수식하는 과거분사구, { }는 the music을 수식하는 과거분사구

문제해설
자신의 심장 박동에 기초하여 만들어진 음악을 들을 경우 더 높은 수준의 휴식을 경험할 수 있으며 이러한 발견이 근로자들의 스트레스 및 피로 경감에 도움이 되기를 바란다고 했으므로, 빈칸에는 ③ '스트레스를 줄이다'가 들어가는 것이 적절하다.

33 ⑤ 빈칸 추론

텔레비전 프로그램과 광고에서는 모두가 멋지고 몸매가 좋으며 매력적으로 보인다. 더 중요한 것은, 그들이 모두 행복해 보인다는 것이다. 안타깝게도 이것은 사람들을 세뇌시켜 특정한 사회적 기준을 충족하는 방식으로 보이고 행동하게 만드는 효과적인 방법이다. 사실은 우리는 모두 서로 다른데, 많은 사람들이 사회의 기대를 충족시키지 않으면 행복할 수 없다고 여기게 된다. 이 때문에 사람들은 그들의 (현재) 모습에 있어 무언

가가 잘못되었다고 생각하기 시작한다. 그들은 결국 성형수술을 받거나 늘 자신에 대해 그저 나쁘게만 생각하기에 이른다. 결국 당신 자신을 당신이 텔레비전에서 보는 사람들과 비교하는 것은 분명히 당신의 자존감에 상처를 준다. 당신은 당신이 생각하기에 되어야 할 모습에 대해 걱정하는 대신에, (현재) 당신 자신의 모습을 받아들이는 것에 초점을 맞추어야 한다.

어휘
effective 효과적인 brainwash 세뇌시키다 end up v-ing 결국 …하다 plastic surgery 성형수술 the bottom line is (that) 요컨대[결국은] …이다 inevitably 필연적으로, 분명히 self-esteem 자부심, 자존감 [문제] meet 충족시키다 expectation 예상; *기대

구문해설
[13행] The bottom line is that [comparing yourself to the people {(who/whom) you see on TV}] will inevitably damage your self-esteem.: [ ]는 that절의 주어로 쓰인 동명사구, { }는 the people을 선행사로 하는 목적격 관계대명사절

문제해설
텔레비전 프로그램이나 광고에 나오는 사람들의 모습에 자신을 비교하며 스스로에 대해 불만족하고 성형수술을 받는 등의 행동은 결국 매체에 등장하는 사람들과 같이 사회가 보여주는 일정 기준을 만족시켰을 때만 안정감을 느끼는 것에서 비롯하므로, 빈칸에는 ⑤ '사회의 기대를 충족시키지 않는다'가 들어가는 것이 적절하다.

34 ⑤ 빈칸 추론

많은 사람들은 위가 비어서 배가 고파진다고 생각한다. 그러나 이것은 사실이 아니다. 사실, 우리에게 언제 배가 고픈지를 알려주는 것은 바로 시상하부라고 불리는 뇌 안의 작은 부분이다. 쥐의 행동 연구에서 과학자들은 쥐가 뇌의 특정 부위에 자극을 받으면 위가 가득 차 있는데도 계속 먹는다는 것을 밝혀냈다. 그들은 나아가 뇌의 다른 부위에 자극을 받으면, 며칠 동안 굶었더라도 쥐가 전혀 먹으려 하지 않는다는 것도 발견했다. 이러한 실험들은 일반적인 생각과 달리 배고픔은 위가 아니라 뇌에 의해 조절된다는 것을 보여 준다.

어휘
stomach 위 stimulate 자극하다 further 더 나아가 experiment 실험 indicate 나타내다 [문제] balanced 균형 잡힌

구문해설
[2행] …, it's a small area inside the brain [called the hypothalamus] **that** really tells us …: 'it is … that ~' 「~하는 것은 바로 …이다」(강조구문), [ ]는 a small area inside the brain을 수식하는 과거분사구
[9행] …, the rats **would** not eat at all even though they *hadn't eaten* for several days.: would는 「…하려고 하다」라는 의미로 주어의 의지를 나타내는 조동사, hadn't eaten은 계속을 나타내는 과거완료

문제해설
⑤ 쥐를 이용한 실험을 통해, '배고픔은 위가 아니라 뇌에 의해 조절된다'는 것을 증명했다는 내용이다.

35 ③ 흐름과 무관한 문장

많은 식물들이 자신의 수술에서 다른 식물의 난세포로 꽃가루를 옮기기 위해 동물의 도움에 의존한다. 그런 식물들에는 수분(受粉)을 해주는 동물들을 끌어들이기 위해 색이나 향기를 이용하는 꽃들이 있다. 쌍방에게 이익이 되는 교환에서, 꽃에서 나오는 꿀은 보통 곤충 또는 새인 꽃가루 매개자에게 영양분을 제공한다. 그 생물이 더 많은 꿀을 얻기 위해 다른 꽃으로 나아갈 때, 그것은 무심코 그곳으로 꽃가루를 가지고 가서,

그 식물의 목적인 수분을 완수한다. (하나의 꽃 안에 양성을 모두 지녀 자가수분을 가능하게 하는 식물들도 있다.) 시간이 지나면서, 어떤 동물들은 특정 꽃들로부터 가능한 한 효율적으로 꿀을 추출하기 위해서, 특별한 모양의 부리와 같은 독특한 신체적 특징들을 발달시키기도 한다. 결과적으로 꽃들은 특정 종의 동물만이 자신들에게서 꿀을 가져가도록 하는 형태로 변할지도 모른다.

36 ③ 글의 순서

'청년 위기(인생의 4분의 1의 시점에 오는 위기)'는 성인기에 접어드는 것과 관련된 모든 어려운 변화들 이후인, 20대 초반에서 30대 초반일 때 종종 일어나는 사건이다.
(B) 이것은 대체적으로 대학을 갓 졸업한 후에 일어나는데, 이때 젊은이들은 학자금 대출로 평균 1만 달러 정도의 빚을 지고 있으며 아직 직업 경험이 부족하다.
(A) 이러한 최근 졸업생들 중 다수는 여행을 하고 다양한 직업을 경험하며, 미래에 그들이 무엇을 하기를 원하는지를 정확하게 알아내기 위해 애쓰면서 이 시기를 보낸다.
(C) 그러나 이런 종류의 실험이 20대와 30대의 사람들에게 항상 최선인 것만은 아니다. 그러한 불안정한 삶의 방식이 30세가 지나고 나서도 계속된다면, 그것은 결국 심각한 개인적인 위기로 이어질 수 있다.

37 ① 주어진 문장의 위치

양궁은 단순히 화살을 겨눠서 그것을 날리는 것보다 훨씬 더 많은 것을 수반한다. 활을 쏘는 것 이면의 기술로, 당신은 표적을 똑바로 겨누고 목표물을 맞출 수 있다. 그 과정은 간단해 보이는데, 당신이 표적에 집중하면서 활시위에 화살을 뒤로 당기고, 그리고 나서 화살을 놓는다. 그러나, 화살의 발사와 이어지는 비행은 다양한 힘의 영향을 받는다. 활시위에 화살을 뒤로 당기는 것은 활이 위치 에너지를 저장하도록 한다. 이 에너지는 화살이 앞으로 나아가게 하는 데 이용될 수 있다. 화살이 날아갈 때, 위치 에너지는 운동 에너지로 전환된다. 당신이 활시위를 뒤로 더 멀리 당길수록, 화살은 더 빠르게 날아갈 것이다. 이는 당신이 더 큰 힘을 만들고 있기 때문인데, 그것은 전환된 에너지를 더 많이 일으킨다. 이러한 이유로, 활의 효과는 그것을 사용하는 사람의 힘과 기술에 달려 있다.

38 ③ 주어진 문장의 위치

'슬리피 할로우의 전설'의 저자인 미국 작가 워싱턴 어빙은 슬픔을 의미하는 '블루스'라는 용어를 만들었다. 이 용어에서 그 명칭을 차용한 음악 장르는 아프리카계 미국인의 민속 노래에서 발달한 것으로, 이 음악은 남부 대농장의 들판과 노예 막사 주변에서 불렸다. 그것들은 아픔과 시련, 불공평함, 그리고 더 나은 삶에 대한 갈망의 노래였다. 그러나 블루스의 근본적인 특징은 사람들의 기분을 더 나아지게 한다는 것이다. 블루스를 듣는 것은 우울함을 사라지게 할 것이다. 그것은 슬픔을 치유하는 힘을 지닌 음악인 것이다. 그러므로 '블루스'는 사실 정확한 용어가 아닌데, 이는 그 음악이 감동적이지만 우울하지는 않기 때문이다. 그것은 사실 절망이 아닌 희망에서 태어난 음악이다.

[13행] Thus, "the blues" isn't really the correct term, **for** the music is moving but not melancholy.: for는 이유를 나타내는 접속사

문제해설

주어진 문장은 블루스가 사람들의 기분을 나아지게 한다는 내용이며, ③의 뒤에서 블루스를 통해 우울함이 사라지고 치유의 힘이 생긴다고 기술하고 있으므로 ③이 적절한 위치이다.

39 ④ 주어진 문장의 위치

주사는 얼굴에 영향을 미치는 흔한 염증성 피부병이다. 초기 단계에서는 전반적인 붉은 기가 얼굴 전체를 뒤덮어 마치 그 사람이 지속적으로 얼굴을 붉히고 있는 것처럼 보이게 만든다. 나중에는 병이 진행됨에 따라 뾰루지와 눈에 띄는 붉은 선이 생기기 시작한다. 매운 음식과 술의 섭취, 그리고 태양, 비, 또는 바람에의 장시간의 노출을 포함하는 많은 행동적, 환경적 요소가 주사의 원인으로 지적되어 왔다. 그러나 이런 요인들이 모든 사람에게 똑같은 영향을 미치지는 않는다는 것을 명심하는 것이 중요하다. 그러므로 어떤 특정 요인이 당신의 주사를 일으키는 것인지 알아내기 위해서는 당신이 먹은 모든 것과 몇 주간 날씨가 어떤지에 관해 기록해 두어야 한다. 이것은 당신이 주사가 심해진 기간과 단일 요인을 연결짓는 데 도움을 줄 것이다.

어휘

trigger 방아쇠; *유인, 동기   inflammatory 선동적인; *염증성의   condition 상태; *병   initial 초기의   overwhelm 압도하다; *뒤덮다   permanently 영구적으로; *상시   blush 얼굴을 붉히다   pimple 뾰루지, 여드름   finger 만지작거리다; *…라고 지적하다   prolonged 장시간의   severity 격렬(함)

구문해설

[1행] Yet **it** is essential [to **keep in mind** that these triggers don't *have* the same *effect on* everyone].: it은 가주어이고 [ ]가 진주어, 'keep in mind …' 「…을 명심하다」, 'have an effect on …' 「…에 영향을 미치다」

문제해설

주사의 발생 단계와 여러 원인들에 대한 설명이 나오고, 이러한 요인들이 모든 사람에게 같은 영향을 미치는 것은 아니라는 주어진 문장이 ④에 전개된 뒤, 그중 어떤 요인이 주사를 일으키는 것인지 알아내는 방법에 대한 설명으로 이어지는 것이 자연스럽다.

40 ③ 요약문 완성

에티오피아에 살고 있는 겔라다 원숭이는 늑대들이 그들의 영역 주변과 심지어는 그들의 무리 속으로 자유롭게 돌아다니도록 허용하는 것이 관찰되었다. 그 원숭이들은 그들이 늑대들에게 공격을 받지 않을 것이라고 확신하는 것처럼 보이며, 그들은 긴장한 기색을 보이지 않는다. 그러나 야생개와 같이 비슷한 포식자가 근처에 발견되면, 원숭이들은 두려워 달아날 것이다. 늑대에 관해 말하자면, 그들은 지금 원숭이보다는 설치류를 먹이로 하는 것처럼 보인다. 이것이 실제로 이러한 예상 밖의 종간(種間) 관계 이면의 이유일지도 모른다. 그 늑대들은 원숭이들이 근처에 있을 때 설치류를 사냥하는 데 약 두 배 더 성공적이다. 이것은 설치류들이 겔라다 원숭이가 있는 데서 안심하기 때문일 수 있는데, 이는 늑대들이 그들(설치류들)에게 몰래 다가갈 수 있게 해준다.

어휘

observe 관찰하다   territory 영역   confident 자신감 있는, 확신하는   nervous 불안해하는   spot 발견하다, 찾다   as for …에 관해 말하자면   prey on …을 먹이로 하다   rodent 설치류   unlikely …할 것 같지 않은; *(일반적인) 예상 밖의   interspecies 종간(種間)의   in the presence of …가 있는 데서   sneak up 살금살금[몰래] 다가가다   [문제] effort 수고; *(특정 성과를 위한 조직

적인) 활동   confront 맞서다   coexist 동시에[같은 곳에] 있다, 공존하다   aid 돕다   obstruct 막다, 방해하다

구문해설

[3행] **It** seems [(that) the monkeys are confident {that they will not be attacked by the wolves}], and they show no signs of being nervous.: It은 가주어이고 [ ]가 진주어, { }는 confident의 목적절(일부 형용사는 that절을 목적어로 취함)

[13행] This may be because the rodents relax in the presence of gelada monkeys, [**allowing** the wolves **to sneak** up on them].: [ ]는 결과를 나타내는 분사구문, 'allow+O+to-v' 「…가 ~하도록 허용하다」

문제해설

③ 겔라다 원숭이들과 늑대들이 같은 지역에 공존하는 것이 관찰되었는데, 아마 원숭이들의 존재가 다른 먹이를 잡는 늑대들의 활동을 돕기 때문일 것이다.

41 ⑤ 42 ⑤ 장문

19세기 말에 새롭게 불어닥친 이민 물결은 미국에 엄청난 인구 폭발을 가져왔다. 이 기간 동안 미국에서의 삶이 수월하다고 생각한 이민자들은 거의 없었다. 전문 기술도 없고 영어도 못하던 그들 중 대부분은 크고 지저분한 동북부 도시의 빈민 지역에 살았고, 고용주들에게 착취를 당했으며, 빈민 계층에 묶여 있었다.

이런 문제에 대해 반응을 보인 이들 중에는 이 이민자들을 동화시킬 방안을 갖고 있던 두 단체가 있었다. '미국 혁명의 딸들'이라는 보수단체는 이민자들이 삶을 향상시키기 위해서는 미국의 관습과 문화를 완전히 받아들여야 한다는 기대를 가지고 이민자들에게 다가갔다. 그 결과 그들은 이민자들이 충성의 서약을 하고 영어 시험에 통과할 것을 요구하는 법을 지지했다. 그들은 또한 영어 외의 다른 언어를 학교에서 사용하는 것을 금지했다.

동화에 관한 또 하나의 개념은 제인 아담스 같은 개혁가들의 경험에서 비롯되었다. 1889년에 아담스는 시카고에 '헐 하우스'라는 자원봉사 단체를 설립했다. (이민자) 동화를 다루는 것에 대한 그녀의 생각은 도시의 가난한 이민자 거주 지역의 환경을 개선하고 의료, 법적 원조, 성인 교육 등의 지방 정부 서비스를 제공하려는 시도를 하는 것이었다. 그 '사회 복지관' 철학의 기본 방향은 새로 온 사람들의 문화유산을 무시하는(→ 존중하는) 것이었다. 제인 아담스 그녀 자신을 포함한 많은 노동자들은 이민자들을 '미국화'시키려는 시도가 미국의 문화적 다양성을 박탈할까 우려했다.

어휘

immigration 이민   massive 대량의, 엄청난   explosion 폭발적인 증가   immigrant 이민자   slum 빈민굴, 슬럼가   messy 더러운, 번잡한   exploit 착취하다   trap 움직일 수 없게 하다, 곤궁한 처지로 몰다   assimilate 동화시키다(assimilation 동화)   conservative 보수적인   revolution 혁명   adopt 채택하다, 받아들이다   custom 관습   consequently 그 결과   oath 맹세, 서약, 선서   loyalty 충성   conception 개념   attempt 시도하다; 시도   assistance 보조   fundamental 기본적인   aspect 면, 측면   settlement house 사회 복지관   philosophy 철학   disregard 무시하다   Americanize 미국화하다   deprive A of B A에게서 B를 빼앗다, 박탈하다   diversity 다양성, 포괄성   [문제] restriction 제한

구문해설

[5행] Many of those [who lacked … English] **found** themselves **living** in …, **exploited** by …, and **trapped** at … level: [ ]는 those를 선행사로 하는 주격 관계대명사절, found의 목적격보어 역할을 하는 세 개의 분사 living, exploited, trapped가 병렬 연결

[14행] … immigrants with the expectation [that newcomers should

... lives].: [ ]는 the expectation과 동격

[17행] Consequently, they supported laws [that **required** immigrants **to take** ... and **to pass** ... tests].: [ ]는 laws를 선행사로 하는 주격 관계대명사절. 'require+O+to-v' 「…가 ~할 것을 요구하다」(to take와 to pass가 and로 병렬 연결)

[26행] Her notion ... was [to attempt to improve ... education].: [ ]는 주격보어로 쓰인 명사적 용법의 to부정사구

문제해설

41 19세기 미국 이민자들의 동화 방안으로, 이민자들을 미국에 완전히 동화시켜야 한다고 주장하는 단체와 이민자 고유의 문화를 존중하고 의료, 법률, 교육을 지원하자고 주장하는 단체가 있었다는 내용의 글이므로 ⑤ '이민자들을 미국에 동화시키는 두 가지의 다른 방법'이 적절하다.

42 뒤에서 이민자들을 미국에 완전히 동화시키려는 시도가 미국의 문화적 다양성을 박탈할까 두려워했다는 내용이 나오므로, ⑤ disregard(무시하다)를 respect(존중하다) 등으로 고쳐야 한다.

43 ② 44 ① 45 ⑤ 장문

(A) 몇몇 동료들이 나를 한 의대 교수가 주최하는 모임에 참석하라고 초대했던 1953년 여름의 그날은 여느 다른 날들과 같았다. 나는 그것이 나의 인생에 가져올 변화에 대해 전혀 알지 못했다. 그들은 초대장을 보내왔고, 나는 심지어 그 모임의 주제에 대해 물어보지도 않고 그 초대를 받아들였다. 그러므로, 내가 그 회의실에 들어가 테이블 주위에 앉아 있는 다섯 쌍의 침울한 사람들을 보았을 때, 나는 이 사람들이 누구이며 그들이 어떻게 관련되어 있는지 짐작만 할 수 있을 뿐이었다.

(C) 그들이 지닌 공통점은 하나의 공유된 문제였음이 밝혀졌다. 그들은 모두 자녀들의 의학적 필요에 부응할 알맞은 치료와 시설들을 찾을 수 없던 발달 장애를 가진 아이들의 부모들이었다. 한 명씩 차례로 부모들은 자신들의 이야기를 자세히 했는데, 이들 가족들을 피하고 그들을 돌려보낸 의료 전문가들에게 받은 모든 홀대와 모욕을 상세히 설명했다. 의지할 곳이 남아있지 않아, 그들은 우리에게 온 것이었다.

(B) 이 가족들의 이야기들을 듣자마자 나의 첫 반응은 충격이었고, 그 감정은 빠르게 깊은 전문가적 당혹감으로 바뀌었다. 나의 의료계 동료들의 행동이 부끄러웠고, 동료들의 상당수가 단지 자신의 아이들을 돕기 원했던 사람들을 향해 그렇게 수치스럽게 행동했다는 것을 믿을 수 없었다. 결국, 그들의 요구는 간단한 것이었다. 그들은 우리가 발달 장애를 가진 아이들의 의학적 필요를 충족시켜줄 주간 병원을 설립해 주기를 원했는데, 나는 더 생각할 것도 없이 그 요구에 즉시 동의했다.

(D) 나는 그 요청을 받아들인 것이 내 인생의 전환점이 될 것임을 전혀 알지 못했는데, 이는 발달 장애를 가진 사람들의 요구에 헌신하는 완전히 새로운 직업을 시작하는 것이었다. 곧, 나는 발달 장애 아이들만을 위한 세계 최초의 의료 시설을 이끌게 될 것이고, 이 모든 것은 내가 열정적인 (그들의) 대변자뿐만 아니라 또한 보다 감정적으로 충만한 사람이 되게 해주었던, 그 다섯 쌍의 부부와 그들과의 예상치 못한 만남 때문이었다.

어휘

host 주최하다 extend an invitation 초대장을 보내다 somber 칙칙한; *우울한 profound 깊은 embarrassment 당혹감, 당황 disgracefully 수치스럽게, 망신스럽게 second thought 재고 facility (*pl.*) 설비, 시설 recount 자세히 말하다 mistreatment 학대; *홀대 humiliation 굴욕, 창피 turn away 돌려보내다 developmental disability 발달 장애 advocate 대변자, 옹호자 fulfilled 만족하는, 충족감을 가진

구문해설

[26행] They were all the parents of developmentally disabled children [who were unable to find the proper care ... needs].: [ ]는 the parents를 선행사로 하는 주격 관계대명사절

[35행] Little **did I** know that [granting that request] would mark a turning point in my life, ...: 부정어 Little이 문두에 나와 주어와 동사의 어순이 도치, [ ]는 that절의 주어로 쓰인 동명사구

문제해설

43 ② 아무것도 모르고 초대받은 모임에 참석하여 다섯 쌍의 부부들을 보게 되었다는 내용의 (A) 다음에, 그 부부들이 모임에 참석하게 된 이유를 설명하는 (C)가 오고, 그들의 이야기에 충격을 받아 그들의 요청을 수락하게 된 (B) 이후에, 요청 수락 후 인생의 전환점을 맞이하게 되었다는 내용의 (D)로 연결되는 것이 자연스럽다.

44 ① (a)는 필자를 모임에 초대한 동료 의사들을 가리키고, 나머지는 도움을 요청하기 위해 모임에 참석한 발달 장애 아이들의 부모 다섯 쌍을 가리킨다.

45 ① 1953년에 한 모임에 초대되어 참석하였다. ② 모임에서 발달 장애를 가진 아이들의 부모 다섯 쌍을 만났다. ③ 환자 가족들을 냉대했던 것은 다른 의료 전문가들이었다. ④ 부모들의 주간 병원 설립 요구에 바로 동의했다.

18 ③	19 ②	20 ③	21 ③	22 ⑤	23 ③
24 ④	25 ①	26 ④	27 ④	28 ⑤	29 ④
30 ④	31 ④	32 ②	33 ④	34 ①	35 ④
36 ③	37 ①	38 ④	39 ⑤	40 ②	41 ⑤
42 ③	43 ③	44 ④	45 ③		

18 ③ 글의 목적

모든 몬트빌 주민 여러분께

모든 가정집 화재는 위험하지만 사람들이 잠을 자고 있는 밤에 발생하는 것들이 가장 많은 사망자를 야기하는 경향이 있습니다. 어떤 사람들은 연기 냄새가 그들을 깨울 것이라고 생각하지만 이것은 종종 사실이 아닙니다. 화재로 인해 발생하는 연기와 유독 가스는 실제로 사람들의 감각을 마비시켜 그들을 더 깊은 수면으로 빠져들게 합니다. 그것이 안전 전문가들이 모든 가정에 연기 탐지기가 있어야 한다고 말하는 이유입니다. 비록 여러분이 감각을 마비시키는 연기와 가스의 영향 하에 놓일지라도, 경보기가 내는 소리가 여러분을 깨워줄 것입니다. 따라서, 우리 도시의 모든 집들은 각 층에 연기 탐지기가 설비되어야 합니다. 그것들을 두기에 가장 좋은 장소는 천장 근처나 천장인데, 연기와 뜨거운 공기는 상승하기 때문입니다. 각 가정에 있는 몇 개의 기능성 연기 탐지기로, 우리 도시는 화재로부터 좀 더 안전해질 수 있습니다.

시 소방국

어휘
poisonous 유독한   numb 마비시키다(numbing 감각을 마비시키는)   detector 탐지기   alarm 경보; *경보기   be equipped with …을 갖추고 있다   basement 지하실   ceiling 천장

구문해설
(2행) All house fires are dangerous, but **those** [that occur at night], [when people are sleeping], tend to cause the most deaths.: those는 house fires를 지칭, 첫 번째 [ ]는 those를 선행사로 하는 주격 관계대명사절, 두 번째 [ ]는 night을 선행사로 하는 계속적 용법의 관계부사절
(12행) ..., the sound [made by the alarm] will **wake you up**.: [ ]는 the sound를 수식하는 과거분사구, '타동사＋부사'로 이루어진 구동사 wake up의 목적어가 대명사(you)이므로 '타동사＋목적어＋부사'의 어순을 따름

문제해설
③ 야간 화재 발생 시 연기와 유독 가스가 수면 중인 사람들의 감각을 마비시켜 더 깊은 잠에 빠지게 하므로, 이러한 피해를 줄이기 위해 도시의 각 가정에 연기 탐지기를 설치할 것을 촉구하는 글이다.

19 ② 분위기

하늘이 어두워지고 있었고, 바람이 야자수를 세차게 흔들었다. "우리는 모래주머니가 더 필요해!" 아버지는 앞마당에서 소리쳤다. 폭풍이 몰려오고 있었고, 우리는 집을 보호하려고 했다. 여동생이 빈 (모래)주머니를 들고 마당을 가로질러 뛰어갔다. 아버지와 어머니는 이미 미친 듯이 모래를 삽으로 뜨고 계셨다. 나는 그들에게서 눈을 떼고 창문 위로 널빤지에 못질하는 것을 다시 시작했다. "창문은 몇 개 남았어?" 남동생이 외쳤다. "네 개! 우리는 더 서둘러야 해!" 나는 빗방울이 내 팔에 닿는 것을 느

껐다. 다른 한 방울이 내 손에 그리고 그 후에는 코에 떨어졌다. 이미 비가 내리고 있었고, 하늘은 어두운 구름으로 덮여 있었다.

어휘
whip 휘몰아치게 하다   palm tree 야자수   sandbag 모래주머니   come one's way (일이) 닥치다. 손에 들어오다   intend 의도하다. 작정하다. (…하려고) 생각하다   shovel 삽질하다. 삽으로 뜨다   frantically 미친 듯이   tear away (…에서) 억지로 떼어내다   hammer 망치로 치다. …에 못질하다   [문제] urgent 긴박한   depressing 우울한

구문해설
(10행) I **felt** a raindrop **touch** my arm.: 지각동사 felt의 목적격보어로 동사원형 touch를 사용
(12행) It was raining already, and the sky **was covered with** dark clouds.: 'be covered with' 「…으로 덮여 있다」

문제해설
폭풍이 곧 몰려올 상황에서 가족 모두가 집을 지키기 위해 다급하게 고군분투하고 있으므로, 글의 분위기는 ②가 가장 적절하다.

20 ③ 필자의 주장

복제가 생식 기술의 필연적인 다음 단계라고들 한다. 일란성 쌍둥이는 자연 복제이므로, 복제를 자연적 과정을 기술화한 것으로 여길 수 있다. 왜 불임 부부가 자신들의 복제 인간을 만들도록 허락해선 안 되는가? 왜 아이를 잃은 부부가 사랑하는 그 아이를 복제아로 대체할 수 있어서는 안 되는가? 그리고 왜 과학, 음악, 미술 또는 문학에 커다란 기여를 한 사람들을 우리가 그들의 특별한 재능으로부터 혜택을 받을 수 있도록 복제해서는 안 되는가? 마지막으로, 우리가 만약 과학자들의 복제 실험을 중지시킨다면, 그들이 치명적인 질병에 대한 치료책 발견과 같은 미래의 중요한 의학적 돌파구를 찾는 것을 막을 수도 있다.

어휘
clone 복제하다; 복제 (생물)   logical 필연[논리]적인   reproductive 생식의   identical twin 일란성 쌍생아   regard A as B A를 B로 간주하다   version (어떤 것의) 변형, …판   substitute A with B A를 B로 대체하다   contribution 기여   literature 문학   benefit from …의 혜택을 입다   breakthrough 돌파구   deadly 치명적인

구문해설
(8행) And why (should) not (we) clone people [who have made ... literature] **so that** we **might** benefit from their special talent?: [ ]는 people을 선행사로 하는 주격 관계대명사절, 'so that+S+may[might] ...' 「~가 …하도록」

문제해설
③ 복제로 인한 다양한 혜택을 강조하며 복제를 옹호하는 내용의 글이다.

21 ③ 함축 의미 추론

컴퓨터 공학에서, '쓰레기가 들어가면, 쓰레기가 나온다'를 의미하는 두문자어 GIGO는 인공 지능(AI)을 포함한 프로젝트들과 관련하여 종종 사용된다. 이는 AI가 많은 양의 데이터에 의존하기 때문인데, AI는 그것의 기능을 더 잘 수행하는 방법을 배우기 위해 이 데이터를 분석하고 사용한다. 이러한 이유로, 데이터 수집, 준비, 정리 및 분류는 AI 프로젝트에서 매우 중요하다. 만약 AI에 잘못된 데이터나 적절하게 분류되지 않은 데이터가 주어지면, 프로그램 또는 응용 프로그램이 부정확한 결과를 생성하게 할 것이다. 예를 들어, 만약 당신이 AI 프로그램에게 온라인에 게시된 사진들에서 비행기 이미지를 찾도록 가르치려 한다면, 당신은 분석할 수천 개의 비행기 이미지들을 그 프로그램에 제공해야 한다. 만약

이 사진들 중 일부가 아마 다른 물체를 비행기로 식별하면서 부정확하게 분류되었다면, 그러면 그것은 <u>학생이 시험에서 실패할 때</u> 교사의 잘못일 것이다.

acronym 두문자어 **stand for** …을 상징하다, …을 의미하다 **in reference to** …에 관하여 **artificial intelligence** 인공 지능 **rely on** 기대다, 의존하다 **analyze** 분석하다 **function** 기능 **collection** 수집 **preparation** 준비 **label** (라벨을 붙여서) 분류하다 **extremely** 극도로, 극히 **feed** 밥을 먹이다; *(충고 · 정보 등을) 주다 **appropriately** 적당하게, 알맞게 **application** 응용 프로그램 **inaccurate** 부정확한, 오류가 있는 **incorrectly** 부정확하게 **identify** 확인하다, 식별하다 [문제] **misidentify** 오인하다, 잘못 확인하다 **altogether** 완전히

구문해설

1행 In computer science, the acronym GIGO, [which stands for "garbage in, garbage out,"] is often used in reference to projects [involving artificial intelligence (AI)].: 첫 번째 [ ]는 the acronym GIGO를 선행사로 하는 계속적 용법의 주격 관계대명사절, 두 번째 [ ]는 projects를 수식하는 현재분사구

4행 This is because AI relies on large amounts of data, [which it analyzes and uses {to learn **how to perform its functions better**}].: [ ]는 large amounts of data를 선행사로 하는 계속적 용법의 목적격 관계대명사절, { }는 목적을 나타내는 부사적 용법의 to부정사구, how to perform its functions better는 learn의 목적어로 쓰인 의문사구

14행 If some of these pictures are incorrectly labeled, [perhaps identifying other objects as airplanes], then it ....: [ ]는 부대상황을 나타내는 분사구문

문제해설

AI 프로그램에 잘못된 데이터를 제공하면 프로그램이 부정확한 결과를 생성한다는 내용으로, 교사는 AI 프로그램에게 데이터(사진)를 제공하는 사람을, 학생은 AI 프로그램을 비유적으로 표현한 것이다. 따라서 밑줄 친 '학생이 시험에서 실패하다'가 의미하는 바로 가장 적절한 것은 ③ 'AI 프로그램이 사진 속 사물들을 잘못 인식하다'이다.

22 ⑤ 글의 요지

우리 대부분은 어떤 사람이 우리를 모욕하거나 짜증 나게 한 이후에 침묵을 유지해 본 경험이 있다. 우리는 그것이 상대방에게 맞서는 것보다 더 편하다고 믿기 때문에 이렇게 한다. 그러나 실제로 그것은 더 편하지 않다. 그것은 우리가 일시적으로 불편한 상황을 피하게 하지만, 스스로를 침묵하게 한 결과가 따른다. 우리가 우리의 힘을 빼앗아서 다른 사람이 나쁘게 행동하도록 했다는 걸 알기 때문에, 우리는 결국 오랫동안 기분 나쁘게 된다. 대신에 우리가 해야 할 일은 타인에게 건설적으로 맞서는 방법을 찾는 것이다. 이것을 하는 방법을 배우는 것은 우리에게 유용한 도구를 준다. 우리는 남에게 좌우되지 않고, 다른 사람들을 화나게 하거나 공격적이 되지 않으면서 심경을 토로할 수 있다.

silent 말을 안 하는, 침묵을 지키는(**silence** 침묵을 지키다) **insult** 모욕하다 **annoy** 짜증 나게 하다 **confront** 맞서다, 정면으로 부딪치다 **temporarily** 일시적으로 **consequence** 결과 **take away** 제거하다, 치우다 **constructively** 건설적으로 **stand up for oneself** 자립하다, 남에게 좌우되지 않다 **aggressive** 공격적인

구문해설

3행 We do this because we believe [(that) **it** is easier than confronting the other person].: [ ]는 believe의 목적어로 쓰인 명사절, it은 앞 문장의 staying silent를 가리킴

7행 We end up feeling bad for a long time, [knowing that we **have taken** away our own power and **(have) allowed** someone else to behave badly].: [ ]는 이유를 나타내는 분사구문, have taken과 (have) allowed가 등위 접속사 and로 병렬 연결

10행 [What we should do instead] is [to find a way {to confront others constructively}].: 첫 번째 [ ]는 주어로 쓰인 관계대명사절, 두 번째 [ ]는 주격보어로 쓰인 명사적 용법의 to부정사구, { }는 a way를 수식하는 형용사적 용법의 to부정사구

문제해설

⑤ 타인과 갈등이 생겼을 때 침묵하는 것은 우리의 마음을 불편하게 하고 상대방이 나쁜 행동을 계속하게 만들기 때문에 좋은 방법이 아니므로, 감정을 억누르기보다는 타인에게 건설적으로 맞서는 방법을 찾아야 한다는 내용의 글이다.

23 ③ 글의 주제

생체 인식은 신체적 혹은 행동적 특징에 기반하여 개인의 신원을 밝히는 과학이다. 많은 사설 기관들과 정부 기관들이 사람들의 신원을 확인하는 수단으로 지문 채취와 음성 및 얼굴 인식과 같은 생체 인식 식별 시스템에 의지하고 있다. 하지만 그것의 높아지는 인기에도 불구하고, 생체 인식 기술에 대한 우려가 증대되고 있다. 그러한 우려 중 하나는 생체 인식 스캐너에 의해 수집된 자료들이 축적되어 당신이 알지도 못한 채 사용될 수 있다는 것이다. 실제로, 미국 정부를 포함한 몇몇 정부들이 생체 인식 기술을 이용해 정보를 수집해 그것을 다른 국가들과 공유해 온 것으로 알려졌다. 그뿐만 아니라 생체 인식 정보가 도난당하거나 신원 도용의 목적으로 사용될 수 있는 가능성도 있다.

biometrics 생체 인식(**biometric** 생체 인식의) **identify** (신원 등을) 확인하다(**identification** 신원 확인, 식별) **behavioral** 행동의 **institution** 기관, 단체 **turn to** …에 의지하다 **fingerprinting** 지문 채취 **recognition** 인식 **accumulate** 모으다, 축적하다 [문제] **effectiveness** 효과성 **significant** 중요한, 의미 있는 **leak** (액체 · 기체가) 새게 하다; *(비밀을) 누설[유출]하다

구문해설

11행 In fact, **it** has been reported [that some governments, ... shared it with other countries].: it은 가주어이고 [ ]가 진주어

15행 Furthermore, there is also the possibility [that biometric information could be stolen ... theft].: [ ]는 the possibility와 동격

문제해설

생체 인식 기술의 사용으로 인해 초래될 수 있는 위험한 상황들에 관한 글이므로, 주제로는 ③ '생체 인식 기술을 사용하는 것의 위험성'이 가장 적절하다.

24 ④ 글의 제목

믿거나 말거나, 퇴직을 강요당하거나 해고되는 것은 긍정적인 경험이 될 수 있다. 그것은 당신이 당신 경력의 현주소를 재평가하게 해준다. 그러나 해고된 후의 첫 면접은 두려울 것이므로, 보다 편안함과 자신감을 느낄 때까지 친구와 먼저 역할극을 해보라. 새 회사에서는 아마 신원 조회를 위해 옛 회사에 (당신에 대해) 물을 것이며, 그쪽에서 나쁜 말을 해주지는 않을 것이므로 면접관에게 있었던 대로 얘기하는 것이 가장 좋다. 왜 당신의 직위가 더 이상 필요 없게 되었는지 그리고 당신이 새로운 도전을 얼마나 기대하고 있는지를 설명함으로써 상황을 긍정적인 관점에서 묘사하라. 신의 없어 보일 수 있으므로 옛 상사를 욕하지 말고, 그때의 경험을 통해 배운 모든 것을 반드시 강조하라. 그들은 당신의 정직성을 가치 있게 여길 것이다.

어휘

retire 퇴직하다　laid off 일시 해고된　re-evaluate 재평가하다　confident 자신감 있는　reference 신원 조회서, 신원 증명서　light 빛; *관점, 견해　bad-mouth 욕하다, 헐뜯다　disloyal 충성스럽지 못한, 신의 없는　emphasize 강조하다　value 소중하게[가치 있게] 생각하다　[문제] résumé 이력서　approach 접근하다; *(일·문제 등에) 착수하다

구문해설

⟨8행⟩ …, while they're **unlikely to be** bad, it's best [to tell your interviewers what happened].: 'be unlikely to-v' 「…할 것 같지 않다」, it 은 가주어이고 [ ]가 진주어

⟨13행⟩ …, but **do** emphasize all [that you learned from the experience].: do는 동사 emphasize를 강조하는 조동사, [ ]는 all을 선행사로 하는 목적격 관계대명사절

문제해설

퇴직이나 해고를 당했을 때, 새 직장을 구하기 위한 면접에서 어떻게 하는 것이 좋은지에 대한 글이므로 제목으로는 ④ '실직 후 면접을 보는 방법'이 적절하다.

25 ① 도표 내용 불일치

위의 그래프는 연령대와 성별에 따른 휴대전화 게임 이용자의 분류를 보여 준다. (게임 이용자들의 평균 연령은 28.2세이며, 여성 게임 이용자들은 남성 게임 이용자들보다 평균 1.5세 어리다.) 남성들 중에서는, 가장 많은 비율의 게임 이용자들이 18세에서 25세 그룹에서 발견된다. 반면에, 35세에서 44세의 여성들은 여성 휴대전화 게임 이용자들의 가장 큰 비율을 차지한다. 사실, 26세 이상의 모든 그룹에서 여성 게임 이용자들의 비율은 남성들의 비율보다 더 높다. 반대로, 나이가 더 어린 두 그룹에서는 남성들의 비율이 여성들의 비율을 넘어선다.

어휘

gender 성별　average 평균의　breakdown 분해; *분류　counterpart 상대, 대응 관계에 있는 사람[것]　make up …을 이루다[구성하다]　conversely 정반대로, 역으로　exceed 넘다, 초과하다

구문해설

⟨3행⟩ The average age of game players is 28.2, **with** female gamers an average of one and half years **younger** than their male counterparts.: 'with+O+형용사' 「…가 ~하면서[~한 채로]」

⟨7행⟩ Women [aged 35 to 44], on the other hand, make up the largest percentage …: [ ]는 Women을 수식하는 형용사구(aged는 명사 뒤에서 수식)

문제해설

① 여성 게임 이용자들이 남성 게임 이용자들보다 평균 1.5세 나이가 더 많다.

26 ④ 내용 불일치

여러 가지 요소들이 카멜레온의 색깔 변화에 기여한다. 카멜레온은 투명한 피부밑에 여러 개의 세포층이 갖춰져 있다. 이 세포층들은 카멜레온이 (몸의) 색을 바꾸는 능력의 근원이다. 일부 세포층에는 색소가 들어 있는 반면 다른 세포층은 새로운 색깔을 만들어 낼 수 있도록 빛을 반사시킨다. 보통, 색의 변화는 20초 이내에 일어날 수 있다. 카멜레온은 초록색, 갈색, 회색의 세 가지 색 사이에서 변하는 경우가 가장 흔한데, 이 색들은 흔히 서식지의 배경 색과 일치한다. 그래서 많은 사람들이 카멜레온이 주변 환경과 맞추기 위해 색을 바꾼다고 믿는다. 하지만 이것은 사실이 아니다. 실제로는 빛, 기온, 감정 상태가 일반적으로 카멜레온의 색 변화를 유발한다.

어휘

factor 요소, 요인　contribute 기여하다　be equipped with …이 갖춰져 있다　layer 층　transparent 투명한　occur 일어나다, 발생하다　habitat 서식지　emotional 감정적인　state 상태　bring about …을 유발하다

구문해설

⟨5행⟩ **Some** of the layers contain pigments, while **others** just reflect light …: 'some …, others ~' 「일부는 …, 또 다른 일부는 ~」

문제해설

④ 카멜레온의 피부색은 서식지 환경이 아닌 보통 빛, 기온, 감정 상태에 따라 달라진다고 했다.

27 ④ 내용 일치

에어로겔은 존재한다고 알려진 가장 가볍고 가장 밀도가 낮은 고체이다. 이 물질은 흰색이 아닌 투명한 파란색이지만 스티로폼과 비슷하다. 대부분 공기로 이루어진 에어로겔은 자체 무게의 4,000배까지 가해지는 힘을 견딜 수 있는 능력을 가지고 있다. 그래서 당연히, 그것의 주된 용도 중 하나는 경량 건축 자재로서이다. 발견 이후 그것은 여러 용도로 사용되어 왔는데, 처음에는 페인트 첨가제로, 그리고 현재는 주로 단열재로 사용되고 있다. 그것은 또한 우주 산업에서 내온도성이 있는 창문에, 그리고 안전 장비에서 완충재로도 활용된다. 하지만 그것이 널리 쓰일 수 있기 전에, 그것의 생산비 절감이 필요하다.

어휘

density 밀도　solid 고체　substance 물질　capacity 수용력; *능력　withstand 견디어 내다　apply 신청하다; 적용하다; *힘을 가하다　primary 주된(primarily 주로)　lightweight 가벼운, 경량의　additive 첨가제　thermal 열의　insulation 단열(재)　utilize 활용하다　resistant 저항력 있는, …에 잘 견디는　shock-absorbing 완충적인

구문해설

⟨1행⟩ Aerogel is the lightest, lowest-density solid [known to exist].: [ ]는 the lightest, lowest-density solid를 수식하는 과거분사구

⟨4행⟩ [(Being) Made up mostly of air], aerogel has the capacity [to withstand applied force of up to 4,000 times its own weight].: 첫 번째 [ ]는 부대상황을 나타내는 분사구문, 두 번째 [ ]는 the capacity를 수식하는 형용사적 용법의 to부정사구

문제해설

① 가볍고 밀도가 낮은 고체이다. ② 투명한 파란색을 띠고 있다. ③ 처음에는 페인트 첨가제로 사용되었다. ⑤ 광범위하게 사용되려면 생산비 절감이 필요하다.

28 ⑤ 내용 불일치

대학교의 새 슈퍼컴퓨터의 이름을 짓도록 도와주세요!

이 강력한 새 컴퓨터는 교수들과 연구원들이 그들의 일을 더 잘하도록 도와줄 것입니다. 그러나 우리는 우리 학생들이 그것의 이름을 지어주기 바랍니다!

• 역사적인 인물의 이름을 선택하세요.

• 이름 및 학생증 번호와 함께 당신의 아이디어를 tech@usm.edu로 이메일 보내주세요.

• 모든 응모작은 11월 17일까지 접수되어야 합니다.

• 대학 총장이 상위 10개의 응모작 중에서 이름을 선정할 것입니다.

• 수상자는 교내 서점으로부터 200달러 상품권을 받게 될 것입니다.

우리는 또한 프레젠테이션 경연 대회를 개최할 예정입니다. 참가자들은 '슈퍼컴퓨터'를 주제로 15분짜리 발표를 준비해야 합니다. 이 경연 대회의 우승자는 150달러 상품권을 받을 것입니다. 자세한 내용은 대학 웹

사이트를 참조하세요!

어휘 | name 이름 짓다, 명명하다 historical 역사적인 figure 수치; *인물 along with …에 덧붙여 entry 입장; *응모(작), 출전 gift certificate 상품권 presentation 발표, 설명, 프레젠테이션 contest 대회, 시합 participant 참가자 theme 주제, 테마

구문해설 | 3행 This powerful new computer will **help** professors and researchers **do** their jobs better.: 'help+O+(to-)v'「…가 ~하는 것을 돕다」

문제해설 | ⑤ 작명 대회 수상자가 아닌 프레젠테이션 경연 대회 참가자들이 발표를 준비해야 한다고 나와 있다.

29 ④ 어법

러시아의 전문가들에 의하면, 모스크바의 길 잃은 개들이 훨씬 더 똑똑해지고 있다. 그들은 지하철을 타고 가는 도중에 내릴 곳을 인식하는 능력과 같은 놀라운 기술들을 보여준다. 이 개들은 실제로 그들이 살고 있는 교외에서 도시 중심가로 통근하는데, 그곳에는 뒤질만한 먹이가 더 많다. 그들은 심지어 일반적으로 사람이 덜 붐비는 지하철의 첫째 칸이나 마지막 칸에 탈 만큼 충분히 알고 있다. 일단 시내에 도착하면, 그들은 더욱 인상적으로 지능적인 행동을 보여준다. 그 개들은 음식을 들고 가는 사람들에게 살며시 다가가 갑자기 짖어대고는, 그 피해자들에게 겁을 주어 음식을 땅바닥에 떨어뜨리게 만든다. 그리고 나서 그 개들은 그 음식물을 낚아챈다. 이러한 행동은 지능적일 뿐만 아니라 대단한 직관력을 보여주는 것인데, 그 개들은 간식을 떨어뜨릴 만큼 깜짝 놀랄 것 같은 사람이 누구인지 판단할 수 있기 때문이다.

어휘 | stray 길 잃은, 주인이 없는 commute 통근[통학]하다 scavenge 쓰레기 더미를 뒤지다 impressively 인상적으로, 인상 깊게 creep up on …에게 살며시 다가가다 snatch up 잡아채다 intuition 직관, 육감 determine 결정하다; *판단하다 startle 깜짝 놀라게 하다

구문해설 | 5행 These dogs actually commute from the suburbs [where they live] to the city center, [where there is more food to scavenge].: 첫 번째 [ ]는 the suburbs를 선행사로 하는 관계부사절, 두 번째 [ ]는 the city center를 선행사로 하는 계속적 용법의 관계부사절

문제해설 | ④ Not only와 같은 부정어가 문두에 오면 문장의 주어와 동사가 도치되므로, **is this behavior intelligent**로 고쳐야 한다.

30 ④ 어휘

원거리 통신 기술은 재택근무자라는 새로운 근로자 계층을 생겨나게 했다. 재택근무자들은 사무실 대신 집에서 컴퓨터로 일하며 작업한 것을 인터넷을 통해 사무실로 보낸다. 집에서 근무를 하는 직원들로 결국 회사가 사무실 공간, 공공 설비, 그리고 주차에 드는 비용을 절약할 수 있게 되기 때문에 많은 회사들이 재택근무를 시도해보고 있다. 또한 재택근무자들은 다른 사람들로 인해 주의가 산만해지지 않기 때문에 집에서 더 효율적으로 일할 수 있다. 반면에, 재택근무에도 단점은 있다. 만약 재택근무자들에게 충분한 자기 절제력이 없다면, 그들의 업무 능률은 떨어질지도 모른다. 게다가 동료들과의 교제와 관리자의 격려가 없어서 고립감을 느낄 수도 있다.

어휘 | telecommunication (원거리) 통신 give rise to …을 일으키다, 야기하다 telecommuter 재택근무자(telecommute 재택근무하다) by means of …을 통해 utility (전기, 수도, 가스 등) 공공 서비스[설비] efficiently 효율적으로 sufficient 충분한 self-discipline 자기 절제(력) companionship 교제 encouragement 격려 [문제] expire 만료되다 distract 주의를 산만하게 하다 isolated 고립된 united 연합한

구문해설 | 7행 ... employees [who work from home] can **end up saving** them money ...: [ ]는 employees를 선행사로 하는 주격 관계대명사절, 'end up v-ing'「결국 …하다」

12행 ..., telecommuting **does** have some disadvantages.: does는 동사 have를 강조하는 조동사

문제해설 | ④ (A) 재택근무자들이 집에서 근무하면 회사가 사무실 공간, 시설 및 주차 공간에 관련된 비용을 절감하는 데 도움이 되므로, 많은 회사들이 재택근무를 '시도해보고 있다(experimenting)'고 하는 것이 적절하다. (B) 재택근무자들이 집에서 더 효율적으로 일할 수 있는 것은 다른 사람으로 인해 '주의가 산만해지지(distracted)' 않기 때문이라고 하는 것이 적절하다. (C) 동료 및 상사와의 교류가 없는 환경에서 재택근무자들이 '고립된(isolated)' 감정을 느낄 수 있다고 하는 것이 적절하다.

31 ④ 빈칸 추론

흔히 사람들이 집단으로 일할 때 더 많은 것을 성취할 수 있다고 믿는다. 하지만 이러한 상황들에서 '사회적 태만'이라고 불리는 것이 때때로 발생하는데, 이것은 사람들이 혼자 일할 때보다 공동 작업을 할 때 덜 열심히 일하게 만든다. 이런 현상의 주요 원인은 책임 부족이다. 혼자서 일하는 사람들은 자신의 성과로 평가받게 될 것을 이성적으로 확신할 수 있다. 하지만 집단 속에서 사람들은 형편없는 수행의 결과에 대해 덜 걱정하고, 그래서 그들은 노력을 덜 하는 경향이 있다. 만약 그들이 다른 사람들에 대해 신경 쓰지 않는다면, 그들은 자신의 역할을 다 하지 않아서 전체 집단의 성과에 영향을 미칠지 모른다. 이 때문에 몇몇의 혼자 일하는 사람들이 한 집단보다 때로는 더 생산적일 수 있다.

어휘 | social loafing 사회적 태만 reasonably 사리에 맞게, 합리적으로 performance 실행; *성과(perform 수행하다) consequence 결과 put forth (힘을) 발휘하다 pull one's weight 자기의 역할을 다하다 affect …에 영향을 미치다 [문제] confidence 자신감 anonymity 익명성 accountability 책임

구문해설 | 7행 People [working alone] can be reasonably sure [that they will be judged by their performance].: 첫 번째 [ ]는 People을 수식하는 현재분사구, 두 번째 [ ]는 sure의 목적절(일부 형용사는 that절을 목적어로 취함)

문제해설 | ④ 집단으로 일할 때 오히려 태만해지는 원인은 '책임' 부족 때문이며 그에 대한 원인이 빈칸 뒤에 이어진다.

32 ② 빈칸 추론

사람들은 순전히 전에는 아무것도 없던 곳에 장애물을 만들어내면서 의도적으로 스스로를 멈추기 때문에 때때로 목표에 도달하지 못한다. 그들은 자존감을 유지하고 다른 사람들에게 보여주고 싶은 (자신의) 이미지를 지키기 위해서 이렇게 한다. 물론 성공이 이러한 것을 얻기 위한 합당한 경로로 보일 것이다. 그러나 실패를 확보함으로써 어떤 사람들은 자

존감과 외적인 이미지 모두를 손상시키지 않은 채로 지킬 수 있다. 그들이 스스로 만들어낸 장애물은 그들의 최선의 노력에도 불구하고 왜 성공할 수 없었는가에 대한 미리 만들어진 핑계이다. 그러면 그들은 남들에게뿐만 아니라 자기 자신에게도 실패는 그들이 어쩔 수 없는 것이었고 그들의 잘못이 아니었다고 말할 수 있다. 그러나 이렇게 함으로써 그 사람은 그가 진정으로 바라는 목표에 도달하는 것을 불가능하게 만든다.

어휘
purposefully 고의로, 일부러   obstacle 장애물   in the interest of …을 위하여   self-esteem 자존심   project 계획; 투사하다; *전하다, 표현하다   external 외부의   ready-made 이미 만들어져 나오는   excuse 변명   [문제] ensure 안전하게 하다; *확보하다   excel 능가하다

구문해설
(4행) They do this in the interest of [maintaining their self-esteem] and [protecting the image {that they wish to project to others}].: 두 개의 [ ]는 모두 전치사 of의 목적어로 쓰인 동명사구, { }는 the image를 선행사로 하는 목적격 관계대명사절
(15행) ..., a person makes it impossible [to ever reach the goals {(that) he or she truly desires}].: it은 가목적어이고 [ ]가 진목적어, { }는 the goals를 선행사로 하는 목적격 관계대명사절

문제해설
사람들이 미리 장애물을 만들어내고는 그로 인해 실패할 수밖에 없었다고 변명함으로써 자존감이 다치거나 이미지가 손상되는 것을 피하려는 경향이 있다고 말하고 있으므로, 빈칸에는 ② '실패를 확보함'이 적절하다.

33 ④ 빈칸 추론

아프거나 나이 들거나 또는 장애가 있는 가족 구성원에게 하루 종일 보살핌을 제공하는 사람들은 때때로 신체적, 정신적, 그리고 정서적 수준에서 피로에 시달린다. 이것은 간병인 스트레스 증후군으로 알려져 있다. 이것은 간병인이 자신의 모든 시간과 에너지가 다른 사람에게 집중되어 있기 때문에 자신의 행복을 소홀히 할 때 발생한다. 간병 상황은 장기적인 경향이 있기 때문에, 이 피로는 시간이 지남에 따라 점점 더 악화되어 결국 극도의 피로로 이어진다. 간병인 스트레스 증후군을 피하기 위해, 첫 번째 단계는 가끔 휴식을 취하는 것이다. 누구도 이런 무거운 짐을 혼자서 감당할 수 없으므로, 간병인은 가끔씩 돕고 나서서 일을 맡을 다른 사람을 찾을 필요가 있다. 지역 기관 및 서비스를 찾는 것은 부담을 덜어 주는 또 다른 방법인데, 그들이 식사 배달과 차량 이동과 같은 다양한 업무를 수행할 수 있기 때문이다. 요점은 간병인이 제공하는 보살핌만큼이나 그들 자신의 정서적이고 신체적인 행복이 중요하다는 것을 스스로 상기시켜야 한다는 것이다.

어휘
ill 아픈   elderly 연세가 드신   disabled 장애를 가진   suffer from …로 고통 받다   exhaustion 탈진, 기진맥진   caregiver 돌보는 사람, 간병인   neglect (돌보지 않고) 방치하다   well-being (건강과) 행복, 웰빙   burnout (신체적 또는 정신적인) 극도의 피로   occasionally 가끔   step in 돕고 나서다   take over …을 인계받다   seek out …을 찾아내다   agency 단체   bottom line 요점, 핵심   [문제] quality time 귀중한 시간   sympathize with …에 공감하다, 동정심을 갖다   compensation 보상

구문해설
(1행) People [providing full-time care for ill, elderly, or disabled family members] sometimes suffer from exhaustion on a physical, mental, and emotional level.: [ ]는 People을 수식하는 현재분사구
(8행) Since caregiving situations tend to be long-term, this

exhaustion grows *worse and worse* over time, [eventually leading to burnout].: since는 이유를 나타내는 접속사, '비교급+and+비교급' 「점점 더 …한」, [ ]는 결과를 나타내는 분사구문
(19행) ... that their own emotional and physical well-being is **as important as** the care [(that/which) they are providing].: 'as ... as ~' 「~만큼 …한」, [ ]는 the care를 선행사로 하는 목적격 관계대명사절

문제해설
간병인들이 자신의 모든 시간과 에너지를 다른 사람에게 쏟아 자신의 행복을 소홀히 할 때 간병인 스트레스 증후군이 발생한다는 내용이며, 다른 이들의 도움을 받아 휴식을 취해야 한다고 했으므로, 빈칸에는 ④ '그들 자신의 정서적이고 신체적인 행복'이 들어가는 것이 적절하다.

34 ① 빈칸 추론

나는 왜 유전 공학이 매력적인 것처럼 보이는지 이해할 수는 있지만, 건강과 환경에 대한 그것의 잠재적인 영향에 대해 알려진 것이 너무 없다. 예를 들어, 어떤 과학자들은 유전자 변형 식품이 새로운 알레르기를 일으키는 물질이나 질병을 만들어낼 수 있다고 우려한다. 인간의 복지뿐만 아니라 동물의 복지도 훼손될 수 있다. 유전적으로 변형된 돼지와 소는 질병과 다른 건강 문제로 고통을 받는다는 것이 발견된 바 있다. 그리고 환경에 있어서는 유전자 변형 농작물을 대규모로 재배하는 것은 생물의 다양성과 자연의 균형에 영향을 미칠지도 모른다. 나는 우리가 벌써 세계를 먹여 살리고도 남을 식량을 생산하고 있으며, 식량 부족과 기아를 유발하는 것은 바로 세계 경제라는 것을 기억하는 것 또한 중요하다고 생각한다. 따라서, 나는 유전자 변형 식품이 해결책이 아닌 것이 분명하다고 본다.

어휘
genetic 유전의(genetically 유전(학)적으로)   potential 잠재적인   welfare 복지   harm 해치다, 훼손하다   alter 변경하다, 바꾸다   in regard to …에 관해서는   implication (*pl.*) 영향   biodiversity 생물의 다양성   shortage 부족   [문제] ban 금지하다   excessive 지나친, 과도한   consumption 소비

구문해설
(7행) Pigs and cows [that are genetically altered] **have been found** ...: [ ]는 Pigs and cows를 선행사로 하는 주격 관계대명사절, have been found는 현재완료 수동태
(12행) ... it's also important [to remember {that we're already ... world} and {that *it's* the global economy *that* creates ... hunger}].: it은 가주어이고 [ ]가 진주어, 두 개의 { }는 모두 remember의 목적절, 'it is ... that ~' 「~하는 것은 바로 …이다」(강조구문)

문제해설
유전 공학이 미치는 영향이 알려진 바가 적고, 유전자 변형 식품이 다양한 분야에 해를 끼칠 수 있다고 언급하고 있으므로 빈칸에는 ① '유전자 변형 식품이 해결책이 아니다'가 들어가는 것이 적절하다.

35 ④ 흐름과 무관한 문장

인도의 특정 지역들을 방문하는 외국인 관광객들은 여러 무리의 소들이 뜻밖의 장소에서 자유롭게 돌아다니는 것을 보고 놀란다. 그 동물들은 시장 사이로 다니며 장사의 흐름을 방해하거나, 고속도로의 갓길로 다니며 심각한 교통 체증을 일으킬지도 모른다. 관광객들은 인도 사람들이 어떻게 그런 성가신 일을 참는지 이해하지 못하지만, 인도 사람들은 소들을 결코 이런 방식으로 보지 않는다. 사실, 힌두교 신앙을 실천하는 많은 사람들에게 소는 신성한 동물이고 그것의 존재는 긍정적으로 여겨진다. (비록 힌두교 신자들의 수가 꾸준히 감소하고 있지만, 그들은 여전

히 인도 인구의 80퍼센트 이상을 차지하고 있다.) 힌두교 신자들은 소를 가족 구성원처럼 대해서, 서구 사람들이 고양이와 개와 같은 가정용 반려 동물들의 고기를 절대 먹지 않는 것처럼 소고기를 먹지 않는다.

어휘
wander 돌아다니다   odd 이상한; *생각하지 못한, 뜻밖의   interrupt 방해하다
flow 흐름   shoulder 어깨; *(도로의) 갓길   put up with …을 참다, 견디다
nuisance 성가신 것   practitioner (종교의 가르침을) 실천하는 사람   sacred
신성한   presence 존재   steadily 꾸준히

구문해설
[1행] Foreign travelers [visiting certain parts of India] have been surprised [to **see** groups of cows **wandering** freely in odd places].: 첫 번째 [ ]는 Foreign travelers를 수식하는 현재분사구, 두 번째 [ ]는 감정의 원인을 나타내는 부사적 용법의 to부정사구, 지각동사 see의 목적격보어로 현재분사 wandering을 사용
[3행] The animals might be **moving** through markets, [interrupting the flow of business], or **walking** on the shoulder of a highway, [causing a major traffic jam].: moving과 walking이 등위 접속사 or로 병렬 연결, 두 개의 [ ]는 부대상황을 나타내는 분사구문

문제해설
소를 신성시하는 인도 사람들의 생활 방식을 설명하는 글이므로, 인도의 힌두교 신자 비율에 관한 내용인 ④는 글의 흐름과 무관하다.

36 ③ 글의 순서

몬트리올 미라벨 국제 공항은 몬트리올의 커다란 경제 성장의 시기였던 1975년에 문을 열었다.
(B) 그 시기에 만연했던 낙관론과 야심은 시 정부가 그 도시의 기존 공항을 21세기 항공 교통의 중심으로 확장하게끔 했다. 그것은 연간 5천만 명의 승객을 수용할 것으로 기대되어, 이 여행객의 증가를 감당하기 위해 6개의 활주로와 6개의 터미널의 건설이 계획되었다.
(A) 그러나 미라벨은 끝내 계획했던 세계적인 공항이 되지 못했고, 실제로는 한 해에 3백만 명 이상의 승객을 받은 적이 없었다. 여전히 운영 중인 몬트리올의 다른 더 오래된 공항에 비해 도시에서 너무 떨어진 나쁜 입지와 불충분한 교통편 때문에, 항공사와 승객들은 미라벨을 이용하지 않는 것을 선택한 것이다.
(C) 결국 미라벨로 가는 여객기들은 모두 끊어졌고, 현재 그 공항은 화물기 전용으로 사용되고 있다. 그것을 공원이나 쇼핑센터로 전환하자는 논의도 있어왔으나, 그러한 프로젝트가 단지 너무 비싸고 고될 것이라는 것이 전반적으로 합의되었다.

어휘
envision 계획하다   inadequate 불충분한   opt 선택하다   prevailing (특정 시기에) 우세한, 지배적인   optimism 낙관(론)   ambition 야망, 포부
municipal 자치 도시의   hub 중심, 중추   construction (도로 · 빌딩 · 교량 등의) 건설   runway 활주로   exclusively 독점적으로, 오직   cargo 화물

구문해설
[11행] ..., airlines and passengers opted **not to use** Mirabel.: to부정사의 부정형으로, to부정사 앞에 not을 씀
[13행] The prevailing optimism and ambition of this period **led** the municipal government **to expand** the city's existing airport ...: 'lead+O+to-v' 「…가 ~하도록 이끌다, …가 ~하게 하다」

문제해설
③ 미라벨 공항이 몬트리올의 경제적 성장기에 문을 열었다고 언급하는 주어진 글 뒤에 이 시기의 낙관론으로 인해 시 정부가 공항을 확장했다는 설명인 (B)가 오고, 이어서 그러한 낙관론과 달랐던 결과를 설명하는 (A)와 현재 미라벨 공항의 상황에 대해 설명하

는 (C)가 순서대로 이어지는 것이 적절하다.

37 ① 글의 순서

소프트웨어 프로그램이나 컴퓨터 시스템에서의 결함은 '버그'라고 불리며, 그것들을 고치는 과정은 '디버깅'으로 알려져 있다. 최초의 컴퓨터 버그는 1947년에 기록되었다.
(A) 그레이스 호퍼라는 한 컴퓨터 과학자가 그녀의 하드웨어에서 문제를 알아챘을 때 상황은 시작되었다. 컴퓨터를 열자, 그녀는 실제 벌레가 문제를 일으키고 있었다는 것을 발견하고 놀랐는데, 작은 나방이 기계 안쪽에 갇혀 있었던 것이다.
(B) 그러나 이것은 '버그'라는 용어가 원래 유래된 경우가 아니다. 그것은 실제로 100년 전에 유명한 발명가인 토머스 에디슨에 의해 사용되었다. 한 편지에서, 그는 그의 전화 설계의 기술적 문제를 '버그'라고 표현했다.
(C) 호퍼와 그녀의 동료들은 그가 사용했던 것을 알아서, 그들은 나방과 관련된 사건이 재미있다고 여겼다. 호퍼는 실제로 그 죽은 곤충을 그녀의 일기장의 한 페이지에 테이프로 붙였고 그녀의 기계에서 버그를 발견했다고 썼다.

어휘
flaw 결함   record 기록하다   notice …을 의식하다[(보거나 듣고) 알다]
moth 나방   trap 가두다   machinery 기계   term 용어   originally 원래,
본래   colleague 동료   be aware of …을 알다   incident 일, 사건
amusing 재미있는, 즐거운

구문해설
[7행] [Opening up the computer], she was surprised to find [that an actual bug was causing the problem]—a small moth had gotten trapped inside the machinery.: 첫 번째 [ ]는 부대상황을 나타내는 분사구문, 두 번째 [ ]는 find의 목적어로 쓰인 명사절
[16행] Hopper and her colleagues were aware of his usage, so they **found** the incident with the moth **amusing**.: 'find+O+OC' 「…가 ~하다는 것을 발견하다」

문제해설
① '버그'와 '디버깅'이라는 용어에 대해 설명하는 주어진 글 다음에, 그레이스 호퍼라는 컴퓨터 과학자가 하드웨어 문제로 컴퓨터를 열자 나방을 발견했다는 (A)에 이어, 원래 '버그'라는 용어는 그보다 더 먼저 토머스 에디슨이 사용했다는 (B)가 온 뒤, 호퍼와 그녀의 동료들이 토머스 에디슨이 이 용어를 사용한 것을 알아서 나방과 관련된 사건을 '버그'라고 기록했다는 (C)로 이어지는 것이 자연스럽다.

38 ④ 주어진 문장의 위치

기원전 490년에 일어난 강대한 페르시아 제국에 대한 그리스의 작은 도시 국가였던 아테네의 승리는 역사상 가장 유명한 사건 중 하나이다. 페르시아의 다리우스 왕은 그의 강력한 군대가 그 전쟁에서 패하리라고는 결코 생각하지 못했다. 그렇다면 아테네인들의 주목할 만한 승리의 비밀은 무엇이었을까? 그것은 바로 그들이 자신의 도시에 대해 지녔던 애정이었다. 페르시아는 오직 한 사람에 의해 통치되었던 반면에, 아테네는 모든 시민들이 협력해서 통치했던 민주주의 국가였다. 이러한 참여에 자부심을 가져서 아테네인들은 그들의 도시 국가를 위해 죽을 준비가 되어 있었다. 반면에 페르시아 군대는 왕의 명령에 의해 전쟁터로 보내졌다. 결과적으로 아테네인들은 마라톤 전투에서 승리하였고, 이는 페르시아의 침략을 종결시켰다.

어휘
participation 참여   city-state 도시 국가   mighty 강력한, 강대한
remarkable 주목할 만한, 놀랄 만한   whereas …인 반면에   rule 지배하다

democracy 민주주의; *민주주의 국가　citizen 시민　combat 전투
command 명령　consequently 결과적으로　invasion 침략

구문해설

14행 Consequently, the Athenians won the Battle of Marathon,
[which ended the Persian invasion].: [ ]는 앞 절 전체를 선행사로 하는 계
속적 용법의 주격 관계대명사절

문제해설

주어진 문장은 통치에 참여하는 민주 국가에 대한 자긍심으로 참전했던 아테네 사람들
의 태도에 대한 내용이다. 따라서 on the other hand라는 접속사로 이에 반대되어
왕의 명령으로 참전한 페르시아 군대의 상황을 서술하는 문장 앞인 ④에 오는 것이 적
절하다.

39 ⑤ 주어진 문장의 위치

　많은 학자들은 언어의 발달이 인간의 진화 과정과 어떻게 관련이 있
는지를 연구해 왔다. 어느 특정 진화 단계가 인간의 성도 발달을 가져왔
을지도 모른다. 인간의 몸은 언어를 발화하도록 만들어진 것 같다. 예를
들어, 유연한 혀는 다양한 소리를 내는 데 쓰일 수 있다. 영장류들의 이빨
처럼 바깥으로 뻗지 않고 곧게 선 우리의 치아는 높이도 대략 고르다. 이
런 특징들은 음식을 먹을 때는 필요하지 않지만 /f/, /v/, /θ/와 같은 소리
를 발음하는 데는 굉장히 도움이 된다. 마지막으로 우리의 입술은 영장류
의 입술보다 더 정교한 근육을 갖고 있으며, 그 유연성은 /p/, /b/, /w/와
같은 소리를 내는 데 도움이 된다.

어휘

characteristic 특징　pronounce 발음하다　evolutionary 진화의
species 종(種)　lead to …을 유발하다　flexible 유연한(flexibility 유연성)
upright 똑바로 선　outward 외부로의　angle 각도　ape 영장류, 유인원
roughly 대략　even 평평한; *고른　sophisticated 정교한, 복잡한

구문해설

6행 One particular evolutionary step may have led to the
development of a human vocal tract.: 'may have p.p.' 「…했을지도 모
른다」

11행 Our upright teeth, [(which are) not at an outward angle like
those of apes], are roughly even in height.: [ ]는 Our upright teeth
를 선행사로 하는 주격 관계대명사절, those는 teeth를 지칭

문제해설

주어진 문장의 Such characteristics는 /f/, /v/, /θ/와 같은 소리를 내는 데 필요
한 인간의 혀와 치아에 관한 특징임을 알 수 있다. 따라서 인간의 혀와 치아에 관해 설
명한 부분 다음인 ⑤에 오는 것이 자연스럽다.

40 ② 요약문 완성

　대부분의 사람들은 '비버처럼 일하는' 것이 괜찮다고 생각한다. 그러
나 그들이 잘 모르는 것은 비버가 열심히 일하기는 하지만 실제 많은 결
과물을 얻지 못한다는 것이다. 비버가 종종 10분도 안 돼 매우 빨리 나무
를 갉아버리는 것은 사실이다. 하지만 그러면 뭐하겠는가? 종종 비버는
그 나무를 잘 이용하지 못한다. 한 전문가의 말에 따르면 비버는 자신들
이 자른 나무 다섯 그루 중 한 그루를 낭비한다고 한다. 우선 비버는 나
무를 현명하게 고르지 않는다. 한 번은 비버 한 무리가 100피트가 넘는
나무를 베어 넘어뜨렸다. 그리고 나서 자신들이 그것을 옮길 수 없다는
것을 알게 되었고, 그 좋은 나무는 쓰레기가 되어 버렸다.

어휘

beaver *비버;《구어》근면한 사람　chew 씹다, 깨물어 부수다　make use of
…을 이용하다　for one thing 우선, 첫째로　bunch 다발, 묶음; *무리　[문제]

---

hardworking 근면한, 열심히 일하는　absurd 우스꽝스러운, 터무니없는
organized 계획적인, 정돈된　efficient 효율적인　solitary 혼자 하는
inferior 열등한

구문해설

2행 However, [what they don't know] is [that although beavers
may work hard, they don't actually get much done].: 첫 번째 [ ]는
문장의 주어로 쓰인 관계대명사절, 두 번째 [ ]는 주격보어로 쓰인 명사절, 'get+O+
p.p.' 「…가 ~한 상태가 되게 하다」

문제해설

② 비버는 열심히 일하는 동물이기는 하지만, 항상 가장 효율적인 동물은 아니다.

41 ⑤　42 ③ 장문

　1917년에 정권을 잡은 러시아 혁명가들의 주요 (공격) 표적 중 하나는
왕실이었다. 공산주의 국가의 비전을 실행하기 위해, 그들은 황제 니콜라
스 2세와 그의 부인, 아들 그리고 네 명의 딸들을 처형해서 어느 누구도
나중에 그들의 권위에 도전하지 못하도록 해야 할 필요가 있다고 생각했
다. 그러나 그 왕실이 사망했다고 발표된 후 얼마 지나지 않아, 여러 가족
구성원들이 탈출하여 살아남았다는 소문이 떠돌았다. 기회를 포착했기
에, 많은 사람들이 황제의 재산을 상속받을 수 있기를 희망하면서 왕실
의 후예임을 주장하며 나섰다.

　이들 중 가장 유명한 사람은 '안나 앤더슨'이었는데, 그녀는 관계 당국
에 자신이 니콜라스 황제의 막내딸인 아나스타샤 공주라고 말했다. 그녀
의 주장은 그녀가 신체적으로 왕실 구성원들 중의 몇 명과 닮았다는 사
실과, 궁전에서의 그들의 삶에 대해 알고 있다는 사실에 의해 뒷받침되
었다. 왕실의 혈통이 완전히 나타나지(→ 사라지지) 않았다고 믿기 원했
던 몇몇 사람들은 안나의 이야기를 받아들였지만 대부분은 인정하지 않
았고, 1927년에 안나와 예전에 알고 지내던 사람이 그녀의 진짜 이름은
결코 안나가 아니며, 프란치스카 샨츠코브스카임을 발표했다. 그러나 어
느 누구도 안나의 이야기가 확실하게 거짓임을 증명할 수 없었고 그녀는
왕실의 유산을 획득하기 위한 그녀의 법적인 시도 동안에 어느 정도 유
명세를 누렸다. 법원은 마침내 그녀에게 불리한 판결을 내렸지만, 그녀는
1984년 임종의 순간에도 자신의 이야기가 사실이라고 계속 주장했다.

　그러나 수년 후에, 처형된 왕실의 유해가 마침내 발견되었고, 일련의
유전자 검사를 거친 후에, 전문가들은 니콜라스 황제의 모든 가족들이
1918년에 죽임을 당했었고 안나는 확실히 가짜였음을 확인했다.

어휘

revolutionary 혁명의; *혁명가　come to power 정권을 장악하다
implement 시행하다　communist 공산주의　execute 처형하다
authority *권위; (pl.) 당국　surface (문제 등이) 표면화하다, 겉으로 드러나다
descendant 자손, 후예　inherit 물려받다, 상속하다(inheritance 유산)
court 궁정, 왕실; 법정, 법원　acquaintance 아는 사람　disprove …의 반증
을 들다, 그릇됨을 증명하다　certainty 확실성; 확신　ultimately 마침내, 결국
rule against …에게 불리한 판결을 내리다　deathbed 임종　remain (pl.)
나머지; *유해　genetic 유전의, 유전적인　confirm 확인하다, 확증하다　[문제]
trait 특징　restore 회복하다　prestige 명예

구문해설

3행 [To implement their vision of a communist state], they
felt (that) they needed to execute Czar Nicholas II, his wife, his
son, and his four daughters so that no one could rise later to
challenge their authority.: [ ]는 목적을 나타내는 부사적 용법의 to부정사구,
'so that+S+could …' 「~가 …하도록」

17행 Her claim was helped by the fact [that she physically
resembled ... at court].: [ ]는 the fact와 동격

[20행] Though some people accepted Anna's story, [wanting to believe {that the royal bloodline had not entirely disappeared}], most didn't (accept Anna's story), ...: [ ]는 부대상황을 나타내는 분사구문, { }는 believe의 목적절

문제해설

41 ⑤ 이 글은 러시아 혁명 이후 아나스타샤 공주의 사망 여부가 밝혀짐에 따라 안나라는 여성의 거짓말이 드러났다는 내용을 다루고 있다.

42 왕실의 혈통이 완전히 사라지지 않고 유지되길 바랐던 사람들이 자신이 아나스타샤 공주라고 주장하는 안나의 주장을 믿기 원했다고 하는 것이 자연스러우므로, ③ appeared(나타났다)는 disappeared(사라졌다) 등이 되어야 한다.

43 ③ 44 ④ 45 ③ 장문

(A) 이집트의 왕 투탕카멘의 무덤이 1922년에 하워드 카터에 의해 발견되었을 때, 놀라운 유물들의 목록은 거의 이해를 뛰어넘는 것이었다. 보석, 귀금속, 기타 다른 보물들을 보관했던 잘 갖추어진 방이 그 고대 왕의 묘실에 딸려 있었다. 카터는 그가 찾은 놀라운 유물들을 전부 분류하는 데 10년이 걸렸다. 말할 것도 없이, 카터의 발견은 왕가의 계곡에서의 고고학적 관심과 활동의 증가를 가져왔다.

(C) 그러나 다른 왕들의 무덤이 이 지역에서 발굴되었을 때, 그것들을 발견한 이들은 매우 다른 광경과 마주했는데, 그것은 거의 텅 비어있었던 보물방이었다. 물론 수 세기에 걸친 도굴꾼들의 작업으로 일정량의 더 값어치 있는 유물이 없어진 것을 설명할 수는 있겠지만, 이 방들은 지나치게 완전히 비어있었기 때문에 거기에 작용하는 다른 요인이 있어야 했다. 고고학자들은 불가사의한 의문에 직면하게 되었다. 이집트 파라오들의 보물에 무슨 일이 일어난 것일까?

(D) 이러한 이상한 현상을 설명하기 위해, 일부 학자들은 과거의 왕들과 함께 묻힌 보물들이 고대에 사라졌을 것으로 추정했다. 그것들은 후대의 파라오들을 매장하는 일을 담당했던 사제들에 의해 '재활용' 되었을 수 있다. 일부 파라오들이 그들 자신들을 가능한 한 가장 호화롭고 멋지게 매장되도록 하기 위해 장례 유물들의 이 같은 재사용을 허락했다는 증거가 있다.

(B) 람세스 11세 통치 시기의 고위 관리였던 헤리호르는 이 같은 종류의 대규모 '재활용'을 수행했을 만한 인물로 거론되어 왔다. 람세스의 죽음 이후, 헤리호르는 스스로 이집트 왕위에 올랐다. 그는 또한 과거 왕들의 보물들에 대한 방대한 절도를 행하도록 할 수 있는 지위인, 왕가의 계곡의 모든 재매장의 권한을 그 자신이 가지려고 사제들에게 간섭했다. 헤리호르의 무덤은 발견되지 않았지만, 그것이 발견되면 전문가들은 전 세계에서 가장 큰 규모의 고대 이집트 유물들을 발견하게 될 것이라고 예상한다.

어휘

tomb 무덤 uncover 발견하다 splendid 멋진, 굉장한 artifact 공예품; *유물 defy 반항하다; *믿기[설명하기] 불가능하다 comprehension 이해력 burial 매장(bury 묻다, 매장하다) chamber 방 dedicate 바치다 house 살 곳을 주다; *보관[소장]하다 categorize 분류하다 archaeological 고고학적인 candidate 후보자, 지원자; *…이 될 만한 사람 take the throne 왕위에 오르다 intervene 방해하다; *간섭하다 priest 사제 unearth 발굴하다, 파내다 deplete 고갈시키다 at work 작용하여 confront 직면하다, 맞서다 phenomenon 현상 lay ... to rest …을 매장하다 luxurious 호화로운 extraordinary 기이한, 이상한; *멋진, 훌륭한 [문제] practice (pl.) 풍습

구문해설

[4행] There was an entire room [attached to the ancient king's burial chamber] [that was dedicated to housing jewels, precious metals, and other treasures].: 첫 번째 [ ]는 an entire room을 수식하는 과거분사구, 두 번째 [ ]는 an entire room을 선행사로 하는 주격 관계대명사절

[16행] He also intervened with the priests [to put himself ... the Kings], a position [that would have allowed ... past kings' treasures].: 첫 번째 [ ]는 목적을 나타내는 부사적 용법의 to부정사구, 두 번째 [ ]는 a position을 선행사로 하는 주격 관계대명사절

[38행] ..., some scholars have suggested [that the treasures {buried with past kings} were removed during ancient times].: [ ]는 have suggested의 목적절, { }는 the treasures를 수식하는 과거분사구

문제해설

43 ③ 이집트 왕 투탕카멘의 무덤에서 발견된 엄청난 유물들이 많은 고고학적 활동을 활성화했다는 내용의 (A) 다음에, 이와는 달리 다른 왕들의 무덤은 텅 빈 채로 발견되었다는 내용의 (C)가 오고, 그 이유로 추측되는 유물의 재사용을 설명하는 (D) 다음에, 이를 행한 인물로 추정되는 헤리호르의 묘를 발견하면 거기에 엄청난 양의 사라진 보물들이 있을 것이라 예상된다는 내용의 (B)로 이어지는 것이 자연스럽다.

44 이집트 왕들의 사라진 유물의 행방에 관한 이야기이므로, 이 글의 제목으로는 ④ '파라오의 사라진 보물들에 관한 미스터리'가 적절하다.

45 ③ 도굴꾼들의 작업은 일부 유물의 손실에만 영향이 있을 뿐, 전체 유물의 완전한 손실에 미친 영향은 설명할 수 없다고 했다.

10 영어독해 모의고사

본문 ▲ p.96

18 ①	19 ③	20 ④	21 ⑤	22 ②	23 ①
24 ④	25 ④	26 ④	27 ⑤	28 ④	29 ②
30 ①	31 ①	32 ④	33 ①	34 ②	35 ⑤
36 ④	37 ②	38 ⑤	39 ③	40 ④	41 ①
42 ③	43 ②	44 ⑤	45 ①		

18 ① 글의 목적

요즘, 야심 있는 전문직 종사자들은 너무 바쁜 생활을 하기 때문에 자신의 고정된 일정을 벗어난 자유 시간이 거의 없습니다. 따라서 결혼할 시기가 오면, 다수의 젊은 커플들이 모든 세부사항들을 처리하기 위해 웨딩 플래너에 의지하고 있습니다. 최근의 한 조사는 이러한 유형의 서비스를 이용하는 사람들의 수가 지난 3년 동안에만 두 배 이상이 되었음을 보여 줍니다. 웨딩 플래너에 대한 이런 높은 수요로 인해, 당신은 이 사업에 진출하고 싶을지도 모릅니다. 하지만 당신이 어떻게 시작해야 할지 몰라도 두려워하지 마십시오. 최근에 그레이스톤 출판사에서 발간된 '웨딩 플래닝을 위한 실제적 지침서'에서 이 산업에서 흥미진진한 일을 시작하기 위해 당신에게 필요한 모든 정보를 찾으실 수 있습니다. 탁월한 웨딩 플래너가 되기 위해 요구되는 특별한 필요 요건은 없습니다. 오늘 서점에 들르기만 하십시오. 당신이 알아야 할 모든 것을 이 책에서 찾을 수 있습니다!

어휘
ambitious 야심 있는 professional 전문직 종사자 turn to …에 의지하다 double 두 배가 되다 break into 침입하다; *(직업·분야 등에) 진출하다 practical 실제적인 release 풀어 주다; *(대중들에게) 발표하다 publishing 출판 (사업) qualification 자격, 필요 요건

구문해설
9행 With **such a high demand** for wedding planners, you may want to break into the business.: 'such+a(n)+형용사+명사' 「그 정도로 …한 ~」
13행 All the information [(that) you need to begin an exciting career in this industry] can be found in *Practical Guide for Wedding Planning*, [recently released by Greystone Publishing].: 첫 번째 [ ]는 All the information을 선행사로 하는 목적격 관계대명사절, 두 번째 [ ]는 Practical Guide for Wedding Planning을 부연 설명하는 과거분사구

문제해설
① 웨딩 플래너의 수요가 증가하는 추세를 이야기하면서 웨딩 플래닝 사업 진출에 도움이 되는 신간 서적을 홍보하는 글이다.

19 ③ 심경

크리스틴 웨스트는 소 한 무리와 함께 그녀의 농장에서 홀로 살았다. 비가 거의 일주일이나 내린 후의 어느 날, 인근 강이 범람하여 웨스트의 농장이 물에 잠겼다. 그녀의 소들을 안전한 곳으로 데려가려고 필사적으로 애를 쓰다가, 그녀는 미끄러져서 바위에 머리를 부딪쳤다. 그녀가 가장 좋아하는 소인 데이지가 그녀의 얼굴을 핥아서 그녀를 깨울 때까지 웨스트는 (바위에) 부딪혀 의식을 잃고 있었다. 그때까지 물은 위험한 수준으로 상승하여 웨스트가 걷는 것을 불가능하게 만들었다. 대신에, 그녀는 데이지의 목에 그녀의 팔을 감싸서, 그 소가 빠르게 움직이는 물을 헤치

며 그녀를 끌고 가게 했다. 마침내 그들은 언덕 꼭대기에 도착했는데, 그곳은 이제 휘몰아치는 물바다 속의 작은 섬이었다. 구조 헬리콥터가 도착해서 웨스트에게 밧줄을 내려주어 그녀를 안전한 곳에 이르게 들어 올리기까지 그들은 그곳에 갇혀 있었다. 웨스트는 나중에 데이지를 찾으러 돌아갔지만, 그녀는 사라져버렸다. 그녀(웨스트)는 그녀(데이지) 없이 살아남지 못했을 거라는 것을 알고 있었기 때문에 자신의 오랜 친구를 잃어버린 것에 대해 울었다.

어휘
herd (짐승의) 떼 flood 물에 잠기다, 잠기게 하다 desperately 필사적으로 knock (때리거나 가격해) …한 상태가 되게 만들다 unconscious 의식을 잃은, 의식이 없는 lick 핥다 wrap (무엇의 둘레를 단단히) 두르다 drag 끌다, 끌고 가다 rage 몹시[격렬히] 화를 내다; *(폭풍 등이) 맹위를 떨치다 trap (위험한 장소·궁지에) 가두다 rescue 구조 survive 살아남다 [문제] thrilled 신이 난 exhausted 기진맥진한 sorrowful 슬픈 embarrassed 당황스러운

구문해설
7행 By then the water had risen to dangerous levels, making **it** impossible *for West* to walk.: it은 가목적어이고 to walk가 진목적어. West는 to walk의 의미상 주어
11행 Eventually they reached the top of a hill, [which was now a tiny island in a sea of raging water].: [ ]는 the top of a hill을 선행사로 하는 계속적 용법의 주격 관계대명사절
16행 She cried for the loss of her old friend, [knowing {(that) she **would**n't **have survived without** her}].: [ ]는 이유를 나타내는 분사구문, { }는 knowing의 목적절이며 without을 사용한 가정법 과거완료 구문으로 과거 사실과 반대되는 일을 가정

문제해설
크리스틴이 가장 좋아하는 소 데이지 덕분에 위험한 상황에서 벗어나 구조되었으나 다시 데이지를 찾으러 갔을 때 사라져 찾지 못해 울었다고 했으므로 ③ '안도하지만 슬픈' 심경일 것이다.

20 ④ 필자의 주장

사회가 적절하게 기능을 하기 위해서는 규칙이 필요하다는 것을 이해한다. 하지만 우리는 규칙이 너무 많은 지경에 이르렀다. 물론 어떤 규칙들은 필요하지만, 사람들이 압도되어서 더 이상 그 모든 것들을 파악하기 힘들 정도가 되지는 말아야 한다. 나는 언젠가는 특정 규칙들을 폐지할 수 있기를 바란다. 헬스클럽에 가입하는 것에서부터 사업을 시작하는 것에 이르기까지, 관련 규칙의 양은 사람들이 어떤 새로운 일이든지 시작하려는 의욕을 정말로 꺾어버릴 수도 있다. 바라건대, 규칙 제정자들이 이 사실을 깨달아 수가 더 적고 더 단순한 규칙을 만들기 시작했으면 한다. 그동안에, 우리는 규칙을 준수하는 것이 보다 용이하도록 우리가 할 수 있는 일을 하자.

어휘
function 기능을 하다 properly 적절하게 overwhelmed 압도된 keep track of …을 놓치지 않고 따라가다, 이해하다 do away with …을 폐지하다 put off …할 의욕을 꺾다 in the meantime 그 사이에, 그러는 동안에

구문해설
2행 ... reached a point [where there are too many rules].: [ ]는 a point를 선행사로 하는 관계부사절
4행 ..., but let's not go **so** far **that** people become ...: 'so ... that ~' 「너무 …해서 ~하다」

문제해설
④ 현재 규칙이 지나치게 많아 발생하는 문제를 거론하며, 규칙이 단순화되어야 한다고 주장하는 글이다.

21 ⑤ 글의 요지

주식 시장에 투자하는 것은 만만찮은 일이지만, 자녀들에게 그 이면의 여러 개념들을 가르치기 시작하는 것은 결코 이르지 않다. 아이들은 점점 자라면서 적은 액수를 투자하고 인생에서 나중에 그들이 필요로 하게 될 금융 기술들을 배우기 시작할 수 있다. 오늘날의 세계에서, 금융과 경제에 대한 확고한 이해는 자녀 교육의 중요한 부분이다. 그러므로 왜 그들이 주식 시장의 기본 원칙을 배우기 시작하는 것을 대학 때까지 기다려야 하는가? 당신은 당신의 자녀들이 아무런 흥미가 없을 것이라고 생각할지도 모르지만, 어린아이들의 타고난 호기심을 과소평가하지 마라. 경제와 당신의 투자는 자녀들의 삶에 직접적인 영향을 미친다. 당신은 자녀들이 그것을 완전히 이해하려고 얼마나 노력하는지에 깜짝 놀라게 될지도 모른다.

어휘
invest 투자하다(investment 투자)   stock market 주식 시장   solid 기초가 튼튼한, 확고한   fundamental (pl.) 기본 원칙   underestimate 과소평가하다   eager 열심인, 열망하는

구문해설
3행 As they get older, they can **start investing** small amounts and **learning** the financial skills [(which/that) they'll need later in life].: 'start v-ing' 「…하기를 시작하다」, investing과 learning이 and로 병렬 연결, [ ]는 the financial skills를 선행사로 하는 목적격 관계대명사절

문제해설
⑤ 자녀들에게 금융과 경제에 대해 조기에 교육을 하는 것이 중요하다는 내용의 글이다.

22 ② 글의 주제

오늘날의 발달한 기상 위성들 덕분에, 일기 예보관들은 태풍과 허리케인 같은 커다란 일기계를 관찰할 수 있다. 보통 이러한 위성들은 두 종류의 감지기를 사용한다. 첫 번째는 영상기라고 불린다. 카메라처럼, 그것은 반사된 빛을 사용하여 지구의 영상들을 만든다. 지구의 다양한 표면들은 각각 다른 방식으로 태양빛을 반사하기 때문에, 그것들은 영상에서 인식되고 구별될 수 있다. 예를 들어, 물은 빛을 거의 반사하지 않으며 따라서 검은색으로 나타난다. 기상 위성에서 발견되는 두 번째 종류의 감지기는 적외선 탐지기라고 불린다. 이것은 적외선 스펙트럼을 사용하여 물체의 온도를 감지한다. 온도는 에너지 방출량과 직접적으로 관련되어 있기 때문에, 탐지기는 다양한 지구의 표면으로부터 방출되고 있는 에너지의 양을 측정할 수 있다. 이 정보는 좀 더 정확한 일기 예보를 하고 온실가스가 대기에 미치는 영향을 측정하는 데에도 사용될 수 있다.

어휘
weather satellite 기상 위성   sensor 감지기   reflect 반사하다   recognize 알아보다   show up 나타나다   infrared 적외선의   emission (빛·열 등의) 방출   radiate (빛·에너지 등을) 방출하다   [문제] detect 발견하다, 탐지하다

구문해설
11행 The second type of sensor [found on weather satellites] is called an infrared sounder.: [ ]는 The second type of sensor를 수식하는 과거분사구
15행 ..., a sounder can measure the amount of energy [being radiated from various surfaces of the Earth].: [ ]는 energy를 수식하는 현재분사구

문제해설
기상 위성에 주로 사용되는 두 가지 감지기의 역할과 활용에 대한 글이므로, 주제로는

② '기상 위성의 탐지 장비'가 가장 적절하다.

23 ① 글의 주제

최신 영화들의 평가를 제공하는 로튼 토마토 웹 사이트는 좀 더 '팬' 위주로 되기 위해 구성 방식을 부분적으로 변경했다. 전문가 리뷰의 링크를 제공하는 것과 함께, 그 사이트는 관객들이 자신만의 평가와 의견을 게시할 수 있게 한다. 하지만 그들은 영화가 극장에서 개봉되기 전에 이제 이것을 할 수 없을 것이다. 이것은 게시물들이 공정하고 진실되는 것을 보장하기 위함이다. 이러한 관객 리뷰들은 '토마토미터' 점수라고 불리는 것 옆에 나타나는 점수를 만들어 낸다. 이것은 긍정적이었던 전문 평론가들의 리뷰의 비율에 근거한다. 만약 리뷰의 60퍼센트 이상이 긍정적이라면, 그 영화는 '신선한' 것으로 평가되고 빨간 토마토 아이콘을 받는다. 그렇지 않으면, 그것은 '썩은' 것으로 평가되고 (뭉개져서) 튀긴 초록색 토마토 아이콘을 받는다. 관객 리뷰 점수는 이 평가 시스템에 영향을 미치지 않는다.

어휘
rating 순위, 평가   partially 부분적으로   oriented …을 지향하는   comment 논평, 의견   release 풀어 주다; *(대중들에게) 공개[발표]하다   ensure 보장하다   genuine 진짜의; *진실한   generate 발생시키다, 만들어 내다   critic 비평가, 평론가   splatter 후드득 떨어지다; *(물·흙탕 등을) 튀기다   [문제] alteration 변화, 변경   deceive 속이다

구문해설
1행 The Rotten Tomatoes website, [which provides ratings of the latest movies], has partially changed its format **in order to become** more "fan" oriented.: [ ]는 The Rotten Tomatoes website를 선행사로 하는 계속적 용법의 주격 관계대명사절, 'in order to-v' 「…하기 위해서」
4행 **Along with** [providing links to professional reviews], the site *allows* viewers *to post* their own ratings and comments.: 'along with' 「…와 함께」, [ ]는 전치사 with의 목적어로 쓰인 동명사구, 'allow+O+to-v' 「…가 ~하도록 허용하다」
9행 These audience reviews generate a score [that appears beside something {called a "Tomatometer" score}].: [ ]는 a score를 선행사로 하는 주격 관계대명사절, { }는 something을 수식하는 과거분사구

문제해설
최신 영화의 평가를 제공하는 한 웹 사이트에서 일부 변경된 구성 방식을 설명하고 있으므로, 글의 주제로는 ① '한 온라인 리뷰 시스템의 변화'가 가장 적절하다.

24 ④ 글의 제목

커피의 맛을 즐기지만 건강이나 개인적인 이유로 카페인을 피하고 싶어하는 일부 사람들이 있다. 그들 중 많은 사람들에게, 이 문제에 대한 해결책은 디카페인 커피를 마시는 것이다. 디카페인 커피는 적어도 97%의 카페인이 제거된 커피 원두로 만들어진다. 이럼에도 불구하고, 이것은 (커피) 마시는 사람들의 건강에 여전히 잠재적으로 심각한 영향을 미칠지도 모른다. 주요 문제는 카페인을 제거하는 데 쓰이는 방법이다. 원두는 다양한 화학 물질에 담궈지는데, 그중 일부는 페인트 희석제 또는 매니큐어 제거제에도 포함되어 있다. 이러한 화학 물질은 식품 안전 기관에 의해 승인을 받았지만, 여전히 건강상의 위험으로 간주되어야 한다. 또 다른 문제는 원두 그 자체로, 디카페인 커피를 만드는 데 사용되는 원두는 일반 커피에 사용되는 것보다 더 많은 지방을 포함하기 때문이다. 이것은 더 높은 콜레스테롤 수치와 심각한 심장 문제로 이어질 수 있다.

어휘
caffeine 카페인   personal 개인의, 개인적인   solution 해법, 해결책

decaffeinated 카페인을 제거한[줄인]　potentially 가능성 있게, 잠재적으로　employ 고용하다; *쓰다[이용하다]　soak 담그다, 적시다　a variety of 여러 가지의　chemical 화학 물질　nail polish remover 매니큐어 제거제　approve 승인하다　cholesterol 콜레스테롤　[문제] downside 불리한[덜 긍정적인] 면

구문해설

10행 The beans are soaked in a variety of chemicals, [some of which are also included in paint thinner or nail polish remover].: [ ]는 a variety of chemicals를 선행사로 하는 계속적 용법의 관계대명사절

15행 Another issue is the beans themselves, **since** the beans [that are used to make decaffeinated coffee] contain more fat than *those* [used for regular coffee].: since는 「…이기 때문에」라는 의미의 접속사, 첫 번째 [ ]는 the beans를 선행사로 하는 주격 관계대명사절, those는 the beans를 지칭하는 지시대명사, 두 번째 [ ]는 those를 수식하는 과거분사구

문제해설

카페인을 제거하는 데 사용되는 화학 물질과 지방이 많이 포함된 원두로 인해 디카페인 커피가 건강상의 위험을 제기할 수 있다는 내용이므로 ④ '디카페인 커피를 마시는 것의 안 좋은 면'이 제목으로 가장 적절하다.

25 ④ 도표 내용 불일치

위의 그래프는 단 음식을 먹는 것이 입안의 pH 농도를 낮추는 방식을 보여주는데, 이는 충치의 가능성을 증가시킨다. 충치는 pH 농도가 5.5 미만으로 떨어질 때 생길 가능성이 있다. 그래프는 과당, 사탕수수당, 그리고 꿀의 영향을 비교하는데, 사탕수수당이 pH 농도를 가장 많이 낮추고 가장 오랜 시간 동안 pH 농도를 5.5 아래로 유지하는 것을 보여준다. 사탕수수당을 섭취한 후 단 5분 만에, 당신의 입안의 pH 농도는 약 pH 3.5까지 떨어진다. 그 후, 그것은 다시 오르기 시작하지만, 약 25분 동안 pH 5.5를 초과하지는 않는다. (한편, 과당은 약 25분 동안 충치가 발생할 가능성이 있는 지점 이하의 pH 농도를 유지한다.) 꿀은 세 가지 물질 가운데 가장 적게 손상을 미치는데, pH 농도를 약 4.75 정도로 떨어뜨리기는 하지만, 15분 이내에 pH 5.5 이상으로 (pH 농도를) 돌려놓는다.

어휘

consumption 소비(량); *음식 섭취(량)　tooth decay 충치　cane sugar 사탕수수당　elapse (시간이) 경과하다　likelihood 가능성, 있음 직함　exceed 초과하다　substance 물질

구문해설

13행 ... the point [where tooth decay is likely to occur] for about 25 minutes.: [ ]는 the point를 선행사로 하는 관계부사절

문제해설

④ 과당 섭취 후 20분이 지나면 pH 농도는 충치가 발생할 가능성이 적은 수준(pH 5.5 이상)으로 오른다.

26 ④ 내용 불일치

얼룩말은 검은 줄과 흰 줄이 번갈아 있는 인상적인 무늬로 식별된다. 크기 면에서 얼룩말은 당나귀보다는 크지만 말보다는 작다. 그것은 무거운 머리와 튼튼한 몸, 뻣뻣한 갈기와 짧은 꼬리를 가지고 있다. 세 종(種)의 얼룩말이 현존하고 있다. 대부분의 얼룩말은 넓게 펼쳐진 평야와 목초지에 살지만, 산얼룩말은 바위가 많은 산비탈을 좋아한다. 평야얼룩말은 보통 누 또는 영양 같은 다른 방목 동물들과 어울려 산다. 그들은 시속 40마일의 속도로 달릴 수 있다. 어떤 전문가들은 줄무늬가 위장이나 벌레들로부터의 보호를 위한 것이기보다는, 얼룩말 무리가 서로를 식별하고 사회적 유대를 형성하는 수단으로서 진화한 것이라고 믿는다.

어휘

distinguish 구별하다, 식별하다　striking 현저한, 두드러진　pattern 무늬　alternate 교차시키다, 엇갈리게 하다　stout 살찐; *튼튼한　stiff 뻣뻣한　mane 갈기　grassland 목초지　hillside 산비탈　graze 풀을 뜯어먹다　evolve 진화하다　herd 떼, 무리　identify 확인하다; *식별하다　bond 유대, 결속　disguise 위장

구문해설

11행 ... the stripes evolved as a way **for herds of zebras** [to identify one another and form social bonds], ...: [ ]는 a way를 수식하는 형용사적 용법의 to부정사구, herds of zebras는 [ ]의 의미상 주어

문제해설

④ 시속 40마일로 달릴 수 있는 것은 평야얼룩말이다.

27 ③ 내용 일치

수 이론 분야에서 복잡한 수학 방정식에 대한 명석한 해법으로 유명한, 헝가리 태생의 수학자 폴 에르되시는 이론 개발자라기보다는 문제 해결자였던 것으로 여겨진다. 세 살이라는 어린 나이에, 그는 이미 음수를 혼자서 깨쳤고, 암산으로 세 자릿수를 곱하는 능력을 발달시켰다. 그가 겨우 20세였을 때, 그는 체비쇼프 정리의 증명을 알아냈다. 그는 일종의 사회 활동으로 간주했던 수학에 자신의 일생을 전적으로 헌신했으며, 평생에 걸쳐 약 1,500편의 수학 논문을 집필하거나 공동 저술한 다작의 논문 발표자였다. 에르되시는 또 다른 수학적 문제에 대한 해법을 공식화하려 시도하던 중 1996년에 세상을 떠났다.

어휘

renowned 유명한, 명성 있는　perplexing 당황하게 하는; *복잡한　equation 방정식, 등식　tender 부드러운; *어린　negative number 음수　multiply 곱하다　three-digit 세 자리의　devote 바치다, 헌신하다　prolific 아이를 많이 낳는; *다작의　co-author 공동 저술하다　formulate 공식화하다

구문해설

5행 At the tender age of three, he already **discovered** negative numbers on his own and **developed** the ability [to multiply three-digit numbers in his head].: discovered와 developed가 and로 병렬 연결, [ ]는 the ability를 수식하는 형용사적 용법의 to부정사구

10행 [Completely devoting his life to mathematics, {which he viewed as a sort of social activity}], he was a prolific publisher of papers, ...: [ ]는 부대상황을 나타내는 분사구문, { }는 mathematics를 선행사로 하는 계속적 용법의 목적격 관계대명사절

문제해설

① 이론 개발자라기보다는 문제 해결자로 더 유명하다. ② 20세에 체비쇼프 정리의 증명을 알아냈다. ④ 평생에 걸쳐 약 1,500편의 수학 논문을 집필하고 공동 저술했다. ⑤ 죽는 순간까지 수학 문제의 해법을 공식화하려고 노력했다.

28 ④ 내용 불일치

샌디에이고 독자 클럽

해당 독자 클럽은 영어 독해 능력을 향상하고자 하는 성인을 위해 고안된 지역 사회 서비스입니다. 17세 이상의 모든 지역 주민에게 열려 있으며 참가비는 없습니다.

일시: 매주 수요일 저녁 7시부터 8시까지

장소: 샌디에이고 공공 도서관 본점, 회의실 C

내용: 그룹 단위로 고전 소설 읽기

해당 클럽은 공휴일을 제외하고 일 년 내내 모입니다. 그러나, 올해 8

월에는 예정된 도서관 보수로 인해 모임이 없습니다.

시의 공식 웹사이트에서 온라인으로 등록하거나 도서관에서 직접 등록하실 수 있습니다. 자세한 정보를 위해서는 619-431-1815로 도서관의 메인 데스크에 전화해 주십시오.

[어휘]

community 지역 사회   design 고안하다   improve 개선하다, 향상하다   local 지역의   resident 주민   participate 참가하다, 참여하다   branch 나뭇가지; *지사, 분점   classic novel 고전 소설   scheduled 예정된   renovation 수리, 수선   sign up (강좌에) 등록하다   official 공식적인, 공적인   in person 직접

[구문해설]

2행 The Readers Club is a community service [designed for adults {who want to improve their English reading skills}].: [ ]는 a community service를 수식하는 과거분사구, { }는 adults를 선행사로 하는 주격 관계대명사절

5행 ..., and there is no cost **to participate**.: to participate는 cost를 수식하는 형용사적 용법의 to부정사

[문제해설]

④ 올해 8월에만 도서관 보수로 인해 모임이 열리지 않는다고 나와 있다.

29 ② 어법

얼굴 표정은 어떤 사람의 감정 상태를 보여 주는 가장 확실한 표시다. 우리는 어떤 사람이 웃고 있는지, 울고 있는지, 미소 짓고 있는지, 혹은 찡그리고 있는지를 관찰함으로써 그 사람의 감정에 대해 많은 것을 이해할 수 있다. 흥미롭게도 많은 얼굴 표정은 선천적이다. 청각 및 시각 장애를 갖고 태어난 아이들은 그러한 장애 없이 태어난 아이들과 동일한 감정을 표현하기 위해 동일한 표정을 사용한다. 대부분의 동물들이 공통된 형태의 얼굴 근육 움직임을 공유한다는 이론을 처음으로 주장한 사람은 바로 찰스 다윈이었다. 예를 들어, 개, 호랑이, 인간 모두 분노를 나타낼 때 이를 드러낸다. 우리의 감정을 표현하는 것이 진화에 뿌리를 두고 있다는 다윈의 생각은 감정 표현에 대한 근대의 여러 분석에 토대를 제공했다.

[어휘]

obvious 분명한   state 상태   frown 찡그리다   inborn 타고난, 선천적인   disability 장애   advance (아이디어·이론을) 제기하다   muscular 근육의   display 나타내다   rage 분노   be rooted in …에 뿌리[기원]를 두고 있다   evolution 진화   groundwork 토대, 기초 작업   analysis 분석(pl. analyses)

[구문해설]

6행 Children [who are born deaf and blind] use *the same* facial expressions to express the same emotions *as* **those** [who are born without such disabilities].: 두 개의 [ ]는 각각 Children과 those를 선행사로 하는 주격 관계대명사절, those는 Children을 지칭, 'the same A as B' 「B와 같은 A」

13행 Darwin's idea [that expressing our feelings is rooted in evolution] laid the groundwork for ...: [ ]는 Darwin's idea와 동격

[문제해설]

문장의 주어는 Children who are born deaf and blind이며 동사가 없으므로 ② using은 use가 되어야 한다.

30 ① 어휘

사람들은 악어가 먹이를 먹는 동안에 운다는 것을 수백 년 전에 알았다. 하지만, 이것의 생리학적 이유는 단지 최근에서야 발견되었다. 2007

년에 몇몇 연구원들은 악어와 같은 파충류가 먹이를 먹는 동안에 눈물을 생성할 뿐 아니라, 이 눈물이 파충류의 눈에서 '거품이 생겨 부글거리는' 것처럼 보일지도 모른다는 것에 주목했다. 이것은 연구원들에게 중요한 단서를 제공했다. 악어는 먹을 때 숨소리가 섞인 소리를 많이 내는데, 이것은 공기가 부비강을 통해 빠르게 이동하게 해준다. 그 공기는 눈을 자극해서 평소보다 더 많은 눈물을 만들어낸다. 그 공기 중의 일부는 머리에서 눈으로 나가, 눈물에 거품이 일게 한다. 또 다른 연구원들은 악어가 세게 베어 물 때 눈물이 누관 밖으로 짜내어진다고 주장했다. 또 다른 전문가들은 눈 밑에 모인 눈물이 악어가 먹이를 먹는 동안 턱을 움직일 때 흐른다고 믿는다. 그러나 정확한 원인은 아직 논쟁 중이다.

[어휘]

physiological 생리학(상)의   psychological 심리(학)적인   note 주목하다   reptile 파충류   froth 거품이 생기다, 거품이 생기게 하다   bubble 거품이 일다   breathy 숨소리가 섞인   stimulate 자극하다   simulate 흉내 내다; 모의실험을 하다   squeeze out of …에서 짜내다   tear duct 누관, 눈물길   accumulate 모이다, 축적하다   accelerate 속도를 높이다   jaw 턱   be up for …이 고려되다, …이 진행 중이다

[구문해설]

4행 In 2007, some researchers noted [that ***not only* do reptiles *such as crocodiles*** produce tears while (they are) eating, **but** these tears **also** seem to "froth and bubble" ... eyes].: [ ]는 noted의 목적절, 'not only A but also B' 「A뿐만 아니라 B도」, that절에서 부정어 not only가 문두에 나와 주어와 동사가 도치

[문제해설]

① (A) 악어가 먹이를 먹을 때 눈물이 나는 원리를 악어의 몸 구조와 관련지어 이야기하고 있으므로, '생리학적인(physiological)'이라는 의미의 단어가 와야 한다. (B) 문맥상 부비강을 통해 전달된 공기가 눈을 '자극해서(stimulates)' 더 많은 눈물을 생성한다는 내용이다. (C) 눈물이 눈 밑에 '축적되었다(accumulated)'라고 하는 것이 문맥상 적절하다.

31 ① 빈칸 추론

시간 관리의 목적은 당신의 시간에서 최대의 가치를 얻기 위해 일련의 원칙과 기술, 그리고 도구들을 사용하는 것이며, 그렇게 함으로써 삶의 질을 향상시키는 것이다. 그런데 시간 관리는 단순히 최단 시간에 당신이 할 수 있는 한 최대한 많은 것을 하는 것이 아니다. 대신, 그것은 당신이 제대로 된 일을 하고 있다고 확신하는 것에 더 중점을 둔다. 훌륭한 시간 관리 능력을 갖춘 사람들은 하루 만에 이루어질 수 있는 것보다 늘 더 많은 일이 있으리라는 것을 깨닫는다. 그들은 그것을 모두 하려고 노력하기보다는 오히려 무엇에 시간을 보낼지를 신중하게 선택한다. 일반적으로 그들은 수많은 사소한 일들에 자신의 시간을 보내는 대신, 적은 수의 중요한 업무들에 집중한다. 그렇게 함으로써 그들은 더 효율적인 근로자가 될 수 있어서 더 적은 시간에 더 많이 성취한다.

[어휘]

management 경영, 운영; *관리   principle 원칙   maximum 최고의, 최대의   value 가치   thereby 그렇게 함으로써, 그것 때문에   accomplish 성취하다, 해내다   concentrate on …에 집중하다   trivial 사소한, 하찮은   efficient 능률적인, 유능한; *효율적인   [문제] demanding 힘든   insignificant 대수롭지 않은, 사소한

[구문해설]

1행 The goal of time management is [to use a set of principles, skills, and tools] [to get the maximum value out of your time], ...: 첫 번째 [ ]는 주격보어로 쓰인 명사 용법의 to부정사구. 두 번째 [ ]는 목적을 나타내는 부사적 용법의 to부정사구

(14행) By **doing so**, they are able to become more efficient workers, [accomplishing more in less time].: doing so는 앞 문장 전체를 의미. [ ]는 결과를 나타내는 분사구문

문제해설
단순히 최단 시간에 최대한의 일을 하는 것이 아닌 몇 가지 중요한 일에 집중하는 것이 시간 관리를 잘 하는 것이라는 내용이므로, 빈칸에는 ① '제대로 된'이 가장 적절하다.

32 ④ 빈칸 추론

많은 사람들이 햄버거를 먹을 때마다 가책을 느낀다. 그러나 햄버거 안에 든 것이 그렇게 나쁜 것은 아니다. 붉은색 육류는 철분의 훌륭한 공급원이고, 치즈버거는 칼슘을 함유하고 있다는 것을 기억하라. 감자튀김은 대부분의 사람들이 건강에 안 좋다고 여기는데, 비타민 C가 풍부하다. 요즘 들어 패스트푸드점들은 영양에 지대한 관심을 쏟는다. 그들은 첨가제를 더 적게 사용하고 식물성 기름으로 요리를 한다. 그리고 몇몇 햄버거 빵은 밀가루 대신 통밀로 만들어지고 있다. 또한 대다수 패스트푸드점에 샐러드바가 마련되어 있어, 사람들에게 패스트푸드와 채소의 균형을 맞출 기회를 제공한다. 그러므로 패스트푸드를 완전히 피해야 한다고는 생각하지 마라.

어휘
guilty 떳떳하지 못한, 가책을 느끼는 iron 철분 calcium 칼슘 nutrition 영양 additive 첨가제 bun 둥근 빵 whole wheat 통밀 flour 밀가루 [문제] vegetarian 채식주의자

구문해설
(1행) ... **every time** they have a hamburger.: every time은 「…할 때마다(= whenever)」라는 의미
(2행) However, [what is in a hamburger] is not that bad.: [ ]는 문장의 주어로 쓰인 관계대명사절
(5행) French fries, [which **most people think** are unhealthy], are rich in vitamin C.: [ ]는 French fries를 선행사로 하는 계속적 용법의 주격 관계대명사절. most people think는 삽입절

문제해설
사람들의 일반적인 생각과는 달리 패스트푸드가 건강에 나쁜 것만은 아니라는 내용의 글이므로, 빈칸에는 ④ '패스트푸드를 완전히 피하다'가 적절하다.

33 ① 빈칸 추론

여러 해 동안, 남아프리카의 드비어스 기업은 세계의 다이아몬드 공급을 관리해 왔다. 그 기업은 이전에 다이아몬드 광부들에게 장비를 대여하는 회사를 운영했던 영국 사업가인 세실 로즈에 의해 1888년에 시작되었다. 새로운 다이아몬드 채굴 사업을 시작한 후에, 로즈는 그가 심각한 재정상의 딜레마에 직면해 있음을 깨달았다. 남아프리카의 다이아몬드 러시가 한창이어서, 다이아몬드 가격은 공급이 수요를 넘어서기 시작하면서 곤두박질치고 있었다. 그는 그의 제품(다이아몬드)의 가치를 높이고 수익을 확보할 수 있는 유일한 방법은 희소하게 만들기 위해 구할 수 있는 다이아몬드의 수를 줄이는 것이라고 판단했다. 드비어스 광산에서의 (다이아몬드) 생산량은 감소했고, 곧 그의 회사는 다이아몬드 시장을 엄격히 통제하는 독점권을 얻었다.

어휘
equipment 장비, 설비 rush (금광 등에의) 쇄도 in full swing 한창 진행 중인 plummet 곤두박질치다 outpace 따라가 앞지르다, 능가하다 monopoly 독점, 전매 [문제] available 구할[이용할] 수 있는 gem 보석

구문해설
(10행) He decided [that the only way {he could increase the value

of his product and ensure a profit} was to decrease the number of diamonds available and (to) make them rare].: [ ]는 decided의 목적절. { }는 the only way를 선행사로 하는 관계부사절(선행사 the way와 관계부사 how는 둘 중 하나를 생략)

문제해설
① 다이아몬드의 공급이 수요를 뛰어넘어 가격이 하락하자 로즈는 다이아몬드 공급을 줄여 희소하게 만듦으로써 가격을 상승시키고 시장을 통제하게 되었다는 내용이다.

34 ② 빈칸 추론

포모 증후군은 '(기회를) 놓치는 것에 대한 두려움'을 의미한다. 그것은 우리가 모를 수도 있는 정보, 사건, 그리고 경험에 대한 불안감을 나타낸다. 이 불안의 결과로, 우리는 다른 사람들이 항상 무엇을 하고 있는지 알고 있어야 할 필요를 느낀다. 현대 기술이 포모 증후군을 더욱 악화시켰지만, 그것은 사실 아주 오래된 문제이다. 초기 인류는 생존하기 위해 끊임없이 자신의 환경을 알고 있을 필요가 있었다. 식량원이나 인근의 약탈자에 대해 알지 못하는 것은 죽음을 초래할 수 있었다. 나중에 사람들이 마을과 도시를 형성하기 시작했을 때, 그들은 중요한 사건들에 대해 알고 있기 위해서 다른 사람들에게 의존하기 시작했다. 처음에 그들은 이러한 정보를 소문과 풍문으로 얻었고, 이후에는 텔레비전과 신문을 통해서였다. 오늘날, 인터넷은 과거 어느 때보다 더 많은 정보를 구할 수 있게 만듦으로써 포모 증후군을 심화시켰다.

어휘
stand for (약어나 상징물이) …을 나타내다[의미하다] fear 공포, 두려움 miss out …을 놓치다 refer to …을 나타내다 anxiety 불안, 염려 aware 알고[의식/자각하고] 있는 ancient 고대의; *아주 오래된 constantly 끊임없이 be conscious of …을 자각하다, 알고 있다 surroundings 환경 fatal 죽음을 초래하는, 치명적인 rely on …에 의존하다 intensify 심해지다; 심화시키다 [문제] informed 잘 아는

구문해설
(1행) It refers to feelings of anxiety about information, events, and experiences [(which/that) we might not know about].: [ ]는 information, events, and experiences를 선행사로 하는 목적격 관계대명사절
(4행) ..., we feel the need [to stay aware of {what others are doing at all times}].: [ ]는 the need를 수식하는 형용사적 용법의 to부정사구, { }는 전치사 of의 목적어로 쓰인 의문사절
(9행) [**Not knowing** about a food source or nearby predator] could be fatal.: [ ]는 문장의 주어로 쓰인 동명사구이며, 동명사의 부정은 'not+v-ing'

문제해설
② 정보를 놓치면 불안감을 느끼는 포모 증후군이 초기 인류부터 시작되었으며 생존을 위해 주변 환경을 계속 의식해야 했다고 한 것으로 보아 사람들이 마을을 형성하면서부터 타인에게 의존한 목적이 '중요한 사건들에 대해 알고 있기 위해서'라는 것을 추론할 수 있다.

35 ⑤ 빈칸 추론

사람들은 유명인의 사생활에 대한 글을 읽는 것을 무척 좋아한다. (배우자에 대한) 부정, 파경, 범법 행위, 그리고 기타 사적인 사실들이 수백만 명의 관심을 끈다. 가십 잡지들은 독자들에게 유명인들의 사생활에 관한 최근 소식을 끊임없이 알려준다. 그 소식들 중 일부는 사실이지만, 많은 것들은 전혀 근거 없는 소문일 뿐이다. 이러한 잡지들은 매우 인기가 있지만 사실 우리에게 유용한 어떤 것도 말해 주지 않는다. 그러면 사

람들은 왜 그것들을 읽을까? 이는 그 잡지들이 사람들에게 자신이 스타들의 비밀스러운 삶의 일부인 양 중요한 사람이라고 느끼게 해 주기 때문이다. 사람들은 이러한 잡지를 읽을 때 그들이 관련되어 있다고 느낀다. 이 잡지들은 또한 그들이 일시적으로 그들의 평범한 삶을 뒤로 남겨두고 떠나 헐리우드의 일부가 되게 해 준다. 이 잡지들은 남 얘기를 하고 싶어 하는 인간의 욕구에서 동력을 얻는다.

어휘
celebrity 유명인사 unfaithfulness 불성실, 부정함 break-up (연인 · 부부의) 헤어짐, 파경 intimate 친밀한; *사적인 gossip 소문, 험담; 험담[남 얘기]을 하다 factual 사실에 근거한 feed off …을 먹다; *(정보원 · 동력 등을) …에서 얻다 urge 욕구, 충동 [문제] turn out …인 것으로 드러나다[밝혀지다] reveal (비밀 등을) 드러내다 involve (상황 · 사건 · 활동이 사람을) 관련[연루]시키다

구문해설
(12행) These magazines also **allow** them **to** temporarily **leave** their ordinary lives behind and **(to) become** a part of Hollywood.: 'allow+O+to-v「…가 ~하도록 허용하다」(to leave와 (to) become이 and로 병렬 연결)

문제해설
사람들이 가십 잡지를 읽는 이유는 자신들이 스타들의 삶의 일부가 된 것처럼 느끼게 해주기 때문이라고 했으므로, 빈칸에는 ⑤ '사람들은 이러한 잡지를 읽을 때 그들이 관련되어 있다고 느낀다'가 들어가는 것이 적절하다.

36 ④ 흐름과 무관한 문장

의학에서의 새로운 발달 하나가 전 세계의 수백만 명의 암 환자들에게 희망을 줄지도 모른다. 곧 대규모 실험을 할 준비가 된 이 치료법은, 암 종양을 겨냥하기 위해 예상 밖의 동반자 관계를 이용한다. 우선, 환자는 단단한 종양의 내부처럼 저산소 환경에서 번식하는 변종 박테리아를 주사 맞는다. 일단 그 박테리아가 종양 또는 종양들에 자리를 잡으면, 환자는 세포를 파괴하는 비활성 상태의 약물 주사를 맞는다. 이 약물은 박테리아 내부에 함유된 효소와 접촉할 때만 활성화될 수 있다. (이러한 박테리아는 산소 수치가 더 높은 신체 부위에서 생존하는 것이 어렵다는 것을 느낀다.) 다시 말해서, 이 약물은 박테리아가 들끓는 종양에 닿을 때 활성화되어, 그것을 둘러싸고 있는 건강한 세포들은 손상되지 않게 하면서 암 종양을 파괴한다.

어휘
cancer 암(cancerous 암의) utilize 활용[이용]하다 unlikely 있을 것 같지 않은; *예상 밖의 partnership 동반자 관계 target 겨냥하다 tumor 종양 inject 주사하다(injection 주사) strain 종족; *변종 thrive 번성하다 establish 설립하다; *확고히 하다 inactive 활동하지 않는 state 상태 activate 활성화시키다 come in contact with …와 접촉하다 enzyme 효소 infest 들끓다, 우글거리다 growth 성장; *종양 surround 둘러싸다 unharmed 손상되지 않은

구문해설
(3행) The treatment, [which will be ready for large-scale testing soon], utilizes an unlikely partnership …: [ ]는 The treatment를 선행사로 하는 계속적 용법의 주격 관계대명사절
(15행) …, the drug becomes active when it reaches the bacteria-infested tumor, [destroying the cancerous growth while leaving the healthy cells {that surround it} unharmed].: [ ]는 결과를 나타내는 분사구문, { }는 the healthy cells를 선행사로 하는 주격 관계대명사절

문제해설
저산소 환경에서 번식하는 변종 박테리아를 주사한 후 이 박테리아의 내부에 함유되어

있는 효소와 접촉해야 활성화되는 약물 주사를 투여하는 암 치료법에 관한 내용이므로, 고산소 환경에서 이 박테리아의 상태에 대해 언급하는 ④는 글의 흐름과 무관하다.

37 ② 글의 순서

반전 정서는 현대적인 현상이 아니다. 사람들이 싸워온 만큼 오랫동안 전쟁은 반대되어 왔다.
(B) 제1차 세계대전도 예외가 아니었다. 1914년 유럽의 극심한 민족주의에도 불구하고, 대륙 전역에 자국을 위해 싸우는 것을 꺼렸던 수천 명의 시민들이 있었다.
(A) 그들 중 '양심적 병역 거부자'라고 알려진 몇몇 사람들은 전쟁의 폭력에 참여하는 것이 그들의 종교적 신념을 거스른다고 주장했다. 또 다른 사람들은 그것을 국제 사회주의의 대의명분과 반대되는 것으로 여겼는데, 국제 사회주의는 모든 국가의 노동자 계급이 연합해서 더 좋은 세상을 만들도록 장려했다.
(C) 싸우는 것을 거부하는 이러한 숭고한 이유들에도 불구하고, 반대자들은 소수였고, 다른 동료 시민들에게 멸시를 받았으며 심지어는 긴 징역형까지 받았다. 그러나 지금 제1차 세계대전 동안에 발생했던 비극적이고 무의미한 인명 손실을 돌아보면, 그 반대자들의 편을 들지 않기는 어렵다.

어휘
anti-war 반전의 sentiment 정서, 감정 phenomenon 현상 oppose 반대하다 conscientious 양심적인 objector 반대자 violence 폭력 religious 종교의 cause 원인; *대의명분 socialism 사회주의 unite 연합하다 exception 예외 intense 극심한 nationalism 민족주의 continent 대륙 scorn 경멸하다, 멸시하다 fellow 같은 처지에 있는, 동료의 lengthy 긴, 오랜 sentence 형벌, 형 tragic 비극적인 senseless 무의미한 side with …의 편을 들다

구문해설
(4행) Some of them, [(being) known as "conscientious objectors,"] argued [that {participating in the violence of war} went against their religious beliefs].: 첫 번째 [ ]는 부대상황을 나타내는 분사구문, 두 번째 [ ]는 argued의 목적절, { }는 that절의 주어로 쓰인 동명사구
(7행) Others **saw** it **as** contrary to the cause of international socialism, [which *encouraged* the working classes of all nations *to unite* and (to) *create* a better world].: 'see A as B「A를 B로 여기다」, [ ]는 international socialism을 선행사로 하는 계속적 용법의 주격 관계대명사절, 'encourage+O+to-v「…가 ~하도록 장려하다」
(12행) …, there were thousands of citizens across the continent [unwilling to fight for their countries].: [ ]는 thousands of citizens … continent를 수식하는 형용사구

문제해설
② 반전 정서가 오랫동안 지속되어 온 감정이라고 설명하는 주어진 글 다음에, 제1차 세계대전에도 시민들 사이에 반전 정서가 있었다고 소개하는 (B)가 오고, 전쟁 반대자들이 반전 정서를 가지고 있었던 두 가지 이유를 설명한 (A)가 온 뒤, 전쟁 반대자들이 당대의 사람들에게는 멸시와 처벌을 받았지만 그들의 행동이 유의미했다고 평가하는 (C)가 오는 것이 자연스럽다.

38 ⑤ 글의 순서

전문 사진사들은 언제나 자연과 겨뤄 왔다. 더위, 습기, 먼지 그리고 추위가 여러 방식으로 촬영물과 장비를 망칠 수 있음에도 불구하고 그들은 가장 극한 기상 조건에서도 사진을 찍는다.
(C) 그러한 기상 조건에 의해 발생되는 피해는 셔터가 고장 나는 경우와 같이 때로는 즉시 눈에 띌 수 있다. 그러나 필름이 현상된 이후나 카메라의 부식 효과가 나타나기 시작할 때까지 감지할 수 없는 피해도 자주 있

다.

(B) 재앙을 피하기 위해, 사진사들은 정교한 케이스부터 단순한 비닐봉지와 소풍용 아이스박스까지 자신의 장비를 보호할 수많은 방법들을 고안해 냈다.

(A) 이러한 도구들로 무장하고서, 전문 사진사들은 극한 기상 조건으로 인한 최악의 결과를 피하고 완벽한 이미지를 포착할 수 있었다.

어휘
professional 전문가의 humidity 습도 dust 먼지 be armed with …으로 무장하다 device 기구, 도구(devise 고안하다) consequence 결과 capture (사진 등으로) 기록하다 catastrophe 재앙, 재난 numerous 수많은 sophisticated 세련된; *정교한 cooler 아이스박스 noticeable 눈에 잘 띄는 detect 감지하다 develop 현상하다 corrosion 부식

구문해설
7행 [(Being) Armed with these devices], professional photographers have **been able to avoid** ... and **(to) capture** the perfect image.: [ ]는 부대상황을 나타내는 분사구문, 「…을 할 수 있다」의 의미인 'be able to' 구문에서 to avoid와 (to) capture가 and로 병렬 연결
11행 [To avoid catastrophe], photographers have devised numerous ways [to protect their equipment], ...: 첫 번째 [ ]는 목적을 나타내는 부사적 용법의 to부정사구, 두 번째 [ ]는 numerous ways를 수식하는 형용사적 용법의 to부정사구

문제해설
⑤ 전문 사진사들이 극한 기상 조건에서도 사진을 찍는다는 내용인 주어진 글 다음에, 이러한 조건에 의해 발생되는 피해를 나열한 (C)가 오고, 이러한 피해를 막기 위해 사진사들이 고안한 방법이 설명된 (B)가 온 뒤, 결과적으로 완벽한 사진을 찍을 수 있게 된다는 (A)가 오는 것이 자연스럽다.

39 ③ 주어진 문장의 위치

미국의 대공황은 근대 산업 사회에서 발생한 최악이자 최장기간 지속된 경제 위기였다. 최악의 시기에는 1천 6백만 명 이상이 실직했고, 8만 5천 개 이상의 기업이 도산했다. 수백만 명의 미국인이 직장, 저축한 돈, 심지어 집까지 잃었다. 그러나, 농부들이 특히 타격을 크게 받았다. 경제 위기와 겹친 극심한 가뭄은 대평원 전역의 소규모 농가들을 붕괴시켰다. 생산성이 높았던 농지는 사라졌고, 농작물 가격이 50퍼센트까지 하락했다. (농작물의) 가격이 너무 많이 하락해서 농부들은 파산했고 직업을 잃었다. 제2차 세계대전의 발발로 인해, 농작물의 가격이 오르기 시작했고 동시에 그 나라는 안정적인 취업 시장으로의 복귀를 보였다.

어휘
the Great Depression 미국 대공황 crisis 위기 industrial 산업의 saving (pl.) 자금, 저축 severe 극심한 drought 가뭄 throughout 전체에 걸쳐, …를 통틀어 productive 생산성이 높은 farmland 농지 turn to dust 사라지다 go bankrupt 파산하다 simultaneously 동시에, 일제히 stable 안정된

구문해설
8행 A severe drought [(which **was**) **coupled with** the economic crisis] ruined ...: [ ]는 A severe drought를 선행사로 하는 주격 관계대명사절, 'be coupled with' 「…와 짝을 이루다, …와 동시에 발생하다」

문제해설
③ 뒤에 대공황으로 타격을 입은 농가들에 대한 구체적인 내용이 나오므로, 농부들의 타격이 특히 컸다는 내용의 주어진 문장의 위치로는 ③이 가장 적절하다.

40 ④ 요약문 완성

이런 취약한 경제 속에서, 대학 졸업생들은 직장을 구하는 데 힘든 시간을 보낼지도 모른다. 그러나 기업들이 점점 더 다양한 형태의 인턴직을 제공하기 시작했다. 이에 따라, 인턴십 직업 서비스 업계는 최근 몇 년 사이에 폭발적으로 증가하여, 사람들이 그들이 필요에 부합하는 인턴직을 찾을 수 있게 돕는다. 인턴십 서비스 회사에 따르면, 그들은 모든 업종의 고용주들과 수많은 연계가 되어 있기 때문에, 그들의 고객들이 구하기 어려운 자리를 얻을 수 있도록 도와줄 자원들을 가지고 있다고 한다. 그럼에도 불구하고, 대학의 지도 교수들은 자녀에게 인턴직을 구해 주기 위해 인턴십 서비스 회사에 의존하는 것을 고려하고 있는 부모들에게 주의를 준다. 왜냐하면 그것이 그들의 자녀가 직업 세계에 들어가면 필요하게 될 구직 역량을 키울 수 있는 기회를 박탈할 것이기 때문이다.

어휘
obtain 얻다, 획득하다 accordingly (상황에) 부응해서, 그에 맞춰 placement 직업 소개 explode 폭발적으로 증가하다 land (노력의 결과로서) 획득하다 deprive A of B A에게서 B를 빼앗다[박탈하다] [문제] venture 벤처 (사업), 모험 academic 학업의, 학문의 fundamental 근본[본질]적인 valuable 가치 있는; *유익한 secondary 부수적인

구문해설
8행 ..., they have the resources [to **help** their clients **land** difficult-to-get positions] ...: [ ]는 the resources를 수식하는 형용사적 용법의 to부정사구, 'help+O+(to-)v' 「…가 ~하는 것을 돕다」

문제해설
④ 인턴 서비스 회사는 학생들이 직장 생활을 시작하기 위해 인턴직을 찾도록 도와줄 수 있지만, 학생들이 가치 있는 기량을 배울 기회를 막기도 한다.

41 ① 42 ③ 장문

현재 너무 많은 물이 우리의 생활 방식을 가능하게 하기 위해 사용된다. 이 물의 대부분인 거의 90퍼센트는 음식과 에너지를 만드는 데 사용된다. 실제로, 컴퓨터 한 대를 만드는 데 1.5톤의 물이 사용되고, 청바지 한 벌을 만드는 데 6톤이 사용된다.

안타깝게도 우리는 그저 이러한 방식을 계속하기에 충분한 물을 가지고 있지 않다. 20년 안에 우리는 가지고 있는 것보다 더 많은 물을 필요로 할 것이며, 산업과 농업에서는 심각한 문제점들이 생길 것이다. 이러한 끔찍한 상황의 원인이 되는 두 가지 주요 요인은 기후 변화와 인구 증가다. 2031년에는 세계 인구의 3분의 1이 그들이 필요로 하는 만큼의 물을 거의 이용하지 못할 것이다.

그래도 좋은 소식은 있다. 의지를 가지면 사람들은 물을 절약할 수 있다. 우리가 할 수 있는 가장 중요한 일 중 하나는 우리의 상수도를 관리할 더 나은 방법들을 찾는 것이다. 물은 제한된(→ 무제한의) 것이 아니기 때문에, 우리는 옛 버전의 가정용품을 더 새롭고 더 효율적인 버전으로 대체해야 한다. 현대식 화장실, 세탁기, 그리고 관개 설비는 가정에서 사용하는 물의 양을 일부 지역에서는 70퍼센트 정도까지 줄일 수 있다.

그런데, 우리가 이미 가지고 있는 물의 질을 보존하는 것 또한 중요하다. 애석하게도, 예측할 수 없는 방식으로 변하는 날씨로 인하여, 대규모의 홍수가 더 자주 일어나고 있다. 이 홍수들은 우리의 상수도를 뒤덮을 수 있으며, 물속에 질병을 쉽게 유입시켜 심각한 건강상의 문제를 가져올 수도 있다. 이러한 어려움들이 저절로 해결되지 않을지라도, 우리의 물을 현명하게 관리함으로써 우리는 상황을 바꿀 수 있다. 우리는 미래를 보호할 수 있도록 물 기반 시설을 변화하는 기후에 적응시켜야 한다.

어휘
currently 현재, 지금 agriculture 농업 contribute 기여하다; *원인이 되다

access 접근; *접근권, 이용[입수]하는 기회 determination 투지, 의지 water system 상수도 irrigation 관개, 물을 끌어들임 reduce 줄이다 sadly 애석하게도 unpredictable 예측할 수 없는 frequently 자주, 흔히 overwhelm 압도하다 resolve 해결하다 infrastructure 기반 시설 [문제] supply 공급 purify 정화하다

9행 The two main factors [contributing to this terrible situation] **are** climate change and population growth.: [ ]는 문장의 주어인 The two main factors를 수식하는 현재분사구, 문장의 주어가 복수명사이므로 복수동사인 are가 사용됨

16행 One of the most important things [(that) we can do] is [(to) find better ways {to manage our water systems}].: 첫 번째 [ ]는 the most important things를 선행사로 하는 목적격 관계대명사절, 두 번째 [ ]는 주격보어로 쓰인 명사적 용법의 to부정사구(be동사의 주어 부분에 do가 있는 경우, 보어로 쓰인 to부정사의 to 생략 가능), { }는 better ways를 수식하는 형용사적 용법의 to부정사구

24행 However, **it** is also important [to protect the quality of the water {that we already have}].: it은 가주어이고 [ ]가 진주어, { }는 the water를 선행사로 하는 목적격 관계대명사절

문제해설

41 미래에 부족하게 될 물을 양적·질적인 측면에서 어떻게 효율적으로 보존하고 사용할지에 관한 글이므로 제목으로는 ① '물 공급의 미래'가 가장 적절하다.

42 앞에서 물이 점점 부족하게 될 것이라고 언급했으며 뒷부분에 물 사용량을 줄이는 방법이 나와 있으므로, ③ limited(제한된)를 unlimited(무제한의) 등으로 고쳐야 한다.

43 ② 44 ⑤ 45 ① 장문

(A) 고대 그리스인들이 마지막 올림픽 경기를 연지 거의 1,500년 후에, 그들의 19세기 후손들은 그 전통을 되살리려고 시도했다. 불행히도 그들의 노력은 전 세계에 많이 알려지지 않았다. 나중에 밝혀진 것처럼, 그로 인해 프랑스 남작인 피에르 드 쿠베르탱이 올림픽의 전통을 다시 시작되게 하였다.

(B) 1800년대 후반, 피에르 드 쿠베르탱은 자국의 교육이 고대 그리스의 교육과 더욱 유사하도록 개선되어야 한다는 생각에 몰두하게 되었다. 쿠베르탱에게 있어서 신체의 한계에 도전하는 것은 정신(의 한계)에 도전하는 것만큼 중요했기 때문에, 국민들은 위대한 학자로서 훈련받는 것뿐만 아니라, 위대한 운동선수로서도 훈련받아야 했다. 이 때문에, 그는 1892년에 USFSA(프랑스 체육 협회 연합)에 근대 올림픽 게임에 대한 생각을 제안했다.

(D) 이 첫 시도는 거절당했지만, 결의에 찬 쿠베르탱은 포기하지 않았다. 2년 후에 그는 그 생각을 다시, 이번에는 국제 대표단 위원회에 제안했다. 근대 올림픽 게임의 개념을 점차 난폭해져 가는 세계에서 국가 간의 관계를 향상시킬 방법의 일환으로 잡은 그의 결심은 위원회의 지지를 얻었다. 벨기에, 이탈리아, 러시아, 스페인, 영국, 스웨덴, 미국, 그리스 그리고 심지어 쿠베르탱의 고국인 프랑스까지 여러 국가들이 그 생각에 동의했다.

(C) 성공에 신이 난 쿠베르탱은 더 나아가 프랑스가 첫 근대 올림픽의 개최국이 될 수 있도록 활동을 벌였다. 그러나, 위원회는 그리스가 1896년에 그 첫 경기들을 개최할 수 있도록 하는 것이 과거에 대한 적절한 예의일 것이라고 생각했다. (그에 대한) 절충안으로, 프랑스는 4년 후인 1900년에 열릴 두 번째 올림픽 게임의 개최지로 선정되었고, 그리하여 근대 올림픽 게임이 탄생했다. 고대 그리스에서처럼 올림픽 게임은 4년마다 열리게 되었지만, 본래의 올림픽 게임과는 달리, 이 근대 올림픽 게임은

개최되는 매 시기마다 다른 장소에서 열리게 되었다.

descendant 자손, 후손 baron 남작 roll 구르다; *착수하다, 시작하다 dedicated 헌신적인 notion 생각, 개념 to this end 이 때문에 lobby 로비 활동을 하다, 영향력을 행사하다 committee 위원회 salute 경의의 표시 put on 개최하다 found …을 시작하다 compromise 타협, 절충안 determined 결연한, 단호한 delegate 대표, 사절 frame 틀에 넣다; *틀을 잡다, 만들어 내다 [문제] conflict 갈등 reinvent 재발명하다

구문해설

19행 ..., Coubertin further lobbied to **have** France **be** the host for the very first modern Olympics.: 'have+O+동사원형' 「…가 ~하게 하다」

35행 His decision [to frame the concept a modern Olympic Games as a way {to improve relations between countries in an increasingly violent world}] won the support of the committee.: [ ]는 His decision을 수식하는 형용사적 용법의 to부정사구, { }는 a way를 수식하는 형용사적 용법의 to부정사구

문제해설

43 ② 피에르 드 쿠베르탱이 고대 올림픽 게임의 재개를 위해 노력했다는 내용인 (A) 다음에, 고대 그리스 올림픽 정신의 중요성을 깨닫고 근대 올림픽 게임에 대한 생각을 프랑스 체육 협회 연합에 제안했다는 (B)가 오고, 이 제안은 거절당했지만 그 이후 국제 대표단 위원회에 제안하여 동의를 이끌어냈다는 (D) 다음에, 근대 올림픽의 첫 번째와 두 번째 개최지 선정과 고대 올림픽 게임과의 차이점을 언급한 (C)가 오는 것이 자연스럽다.

44 고대 올림픽 게임의 재개를 위해 노력한 쿠베르탱의 이야기를 담고 있으므로 제목으로는 ⑤ '고대 올림픽 전통의 재탄생'이 적절하다.

45 ① 널리 알려지는 않았으나 고대 올림픽 게임의 재개를 위해 19세기의 그리스인들이 노력했다는 내용이 (A)에 제시되었다.

18 ①	19 ④	20 ①	21 ④	22 ③	23 ①
24 ②	25 ⑤	26 ②	27 ④	28 ③	29 ③
30 ④	31 ①	32 ⑤	33 ⑤	34 ④	35 ④
36 ②	37 ④	38 ⑤	39 ②	40 ③	41 ④
42 ①	43 ②	44 ⑤	45 ⑤		

18 ① 글의 목적

이사회분들께,

리 테크놀로지의 전 직원을 대표하여, 저는 최근 경제 침체에 관한 저희의 우려를 공유하고자 하는데, 이는 물가상승률의 상당한 증가를 야기했습니다. 아시다시피 높은 물가상승률은 화폐가 그 가치를 잃는다는 것을 의미합니다. 기본적으로, 어제는 1달러로 빵 하나를 살 수 있었지만 오늘은 그럴 수 없습니다. 이것은 현재 저희 급여 수준으로 합리적인 삶의 질을 유지할 수 있는 저희의 능력을 제한시켰습니다. 따라서, 저희는 저희 급여가 물가상승률의 상승과 보조를 맞출 수 있도록 해줄 급여 인상을 원하고 있습니다. 리 테크놀로지는 지난 3분기 동안 수익을 기록했으니, 회사에는 이런 합리적인 요구를 충족시켜줄 재력이 있습니다. 가능하다면, 우리는 이 문제에 대해 더 논의하기 위해 이사회분들과 만나기를 원합니다.

진심을 담아,
모건 뉴먼 드림

어휘
downturn 침체 inflation 물가상승률 essentially 기본적으로 sustain 지탱하다; *유지하다 seek 바라다 keep pace with …와 보조를 맞추다 means 수단; *재력 request 요구

구문해설
[3행] ..., I would like to share our concern about the recent downturn in the economy, [which has led to a significant increase in inflation].: [ ]는 the recent downturn in the economy 를 선행사로 하는 계속적 용법의 주격 관계대명사절
[12행] ..., we are seeking a pay increase that would **allow** our salaries **to keep** pace with the rise of inflation.: 'allow+O+to-v' 「…가 ~하도록 하다」

문제해설
경기 침체로 물가상승률이 높아지고 있고, 이로 인해 삶의 질을 유지하기가 힘들어졌다고 말하면서 직원들의 급여를 올려줄 것을 요구하고 있으므로, 글의 목적으로는 ①이 적절하다.

19 ④ 심경

어느 날 밤, 릭 사이몬의 집 밖에서 뇌우가 맹위를 떨치고 있을 때, 그는 연기 탐지기가 삐 소리를 내는 것을 들었다. 번개가 창 밖에서 번쩍였고, 릭은 갑자기 그의 나무집에 불이 붙었을까 봐 걱정되었다. 그는 연기를 확인하려고 2층에 있는 침실을 나섰다. 다행히, 복도는 깨끗했고, 1층도 안전한 것 같았다. 그러고 나서 그는 지하실 문을 열었다. 불길이 지하실 밖으로 튀어나왔고, 곧 사방에 불길이 있었다. 그는 소방서에 전화하기 위해 침실로 달려갔지만, 전화는 먹통이었다. 그는 계단을 달려

내려가기 위해 몸을 돌렸지만, 계단은 이미 불길에 휩싸여 있었다. 릭은 갇혀 버렸다. 그의 집은 숲 속에 있었고 아무도 도로에서 그의 집을 볼 수 없었다. 그가 도와달라고 외치더라도 아무도 들을 수 없을 것이다. 탈출하는 것과 구조되는 것 모두 불가능했다.

어휘
thunderstorm 뇌우 rage 맹위를 떨치다 smoke alarm 연기 탐지기(화재 경보 장치의 하나) beep 삐 소리를 내다 flash (잠깐) 번쩍이다 catch fire 불붙다 stairway 복도 flame 불길 trap 가두다 escape 달아나다, 탈출하다 rescue 구조하다 [문제] hesitant 주저하는 furious 몹시 화가 난 melancholy 구슬픈

구문해설
[2행] ..., he **heard** his smoke alarm **beep**.: 지각동사 heard의 목적격보어로 동사원형 beep이 쓰임
[5행] He left his second-floor bedroom [to check for smoke].: [ ]는 목적을 나타내는 부사적 용법의 to부정사구
[15행] [**Both** escaping **and** *being rescued*] were impossible.: [ ]는 문장의 주어로 쓰인 동명사구, 'both A and B' 「A와 B 둘 다」, 동명사의 수동형은 'being p.p.'

문제해설
집에 불이 났는데 전화도 먹통이고 집이 숲 속에 있어 사람들이 볼 가능성이 희박해 탈출이나 구조가 어려운 상황이므로 ④ '절망적인' 심경일 것이다.

20 ① 필자의 주장

내 아내가 암 치료를 받느라 병원에서 3주를 보냈을 때, 나는 병원 대기실의 음침함과 우울함을 경험했다. 음식을 먹을 수도, 책을 읽을 수도, 텔레비전을 볼 수도 없었기에, 나는 마치 존재하기를 멈춘 듯 느껴졌다. 내 주위에서 사랑하는 이에 대한 걱정으로 마음 아파하며 나와 같은 처지에 있는 사람들을 보았다. 우리와 같은 상황의 사람들을 위해 더 나은 환경을 제공하는 것이 얼마나 어려운 일일까? 어쨌든, 우리가 사랑하는 이들이 검사실과 수술실에 격리되어 있는 동안, 대기실에 있는 우리가 잊혀져서는 안 된다. 병원들은 따뜻한 색과 기분 좋은 그림들로 대기실의 분위기를 밝게 만드는 것부터 시작해야 한다. 또한 자원봉사자들은 이처럼 기다리는 사람들과 시간을 보내는 데 동참하여, 그들이 사랑하는 이들은 좋아질 것이라고 그들을 안심시켜야 한다.

어휘
gloominess 우울함, 침울함 cease 그만두다; 중지하다 state 상태, 형편 lock away …을 가두어 넣다 facility (*pl.*) 설비, 시설 enlist (협조 · 참여를) 요청하다 assure 안심시키다

구문해설
[4행] [Being unable to eat, read, or watch TV], I felt **as if** I **had ceased** to exist.: [ ]는 이유를 나타내는 분사구문(= Because I was unable to eat, read, or watch TV), 'as if' 「마치 …인 것처럼」(이 문장에서는 과거 사실에 반대되는 가정법 과거완료 구문과 쓰임)
[14행] Volunteers could also be enlisted to spend time with these waiting people, [assuring them that their loved ones will be okay].: [ ]는 연속동작을 나타내는 분사구문

문제해설
① 병원 대기실의 분위기를 개선하여 대기실에서 기다리는 환자 가족들을 편안하게 해주어야 한다는 내용의 글이다.

21 ④ 글의 요지

직장에서의 어떤 단순한 소음은 업무에 집중하려고 애쓰는 직원들의

주의를 흐트러뜨리고 성가시게 하면서, 이상하게 크게 들릴 수 있는 것 같다. 당신이 생각할지도 모르는 것에도 불구하고, 이것은 스트레스로 지치고 지나치게 예민해진 직원들의 마음속에서 만들어진 착각이 아니다. 사실 많은 사무실들이 텅 빈 벽면과 타일로 된 바닥과 같이 소리를 쉽게 반사하는 수많은 단단한 표면을 가지고 있다. 많은 돈을 들이지 않고 이러한 종류의 주변 소음을 줄이는 가장 좋은 방법은 그저 화분에 심어져 있는 식물들을 구입하는 것이다. 적절히 배치된다면, 몇 그루의 식물들은 그렇지 않으면 벽에 반사되어 방 안으로 되돌아올 소리의 파동을 분산시켜 빗나가게 할 수 있다. 한 연구에 따르면 식물은 최대 5데시벨까지 사무실 내의 소음 수준을 줄일 수 있다고 한다.

어휘
oddly 기묘하게, 기이하게 amplify 확대하다 distract (주의를) 흐트러뜨리다 illusion 착각, 환상 stressed-out 스트레스로 지친, 스트레스가 쌓인 overly 몹시, 지나치게 reflect 반사하다 bare 벌거벗은; *텅 빈 ambient 에워싼, 주위의 deflect 빗나가게 하다

구문해설
4행 Despite [what you may think], this is not an illusion [created in the minds of stressed-out, overly sensitive workers].: 첫 번째 [ ]는 Despite의 목적어로 쓰인 관계대명사절. 두 번째 [ ]는 an illusion을 수식하는 과거분사구
8행 The best way [to cut down on this type of ambient noise without {spending a lot of money}] is [to simply buy ... plants].: 첫 번째 [ ]는 The best way를 수식하는 형용사적 용법의 to부정사구, { }는 without의 목적어로 쓰인 동명사구, 두 번째 [ ]는 주격보어로 쓰인 명사적 용법의 to부정사구

문제해설
④ 사무실 내에 화분을 적절히 배치하면 소음이 감소되는 효과를 볼 수 있다는 내용이다.

22 ③ 글의 주제

대륙횡단 철도의 완성은 미국이 국민들을 국경 지역으로 이주시키고 대륙에 대한 그 영향력을 확고히 할 수 있게 해주었다. 대륙횡단 철도 이전에는 서부 해안에 도달할 방법이 마차와 선박 두 방법 밖에 없었다. 두 가지 방법 모두 여러 달이 걸렸고 비용이 꽤 들었다. 이런 단점 때문에 미주리 주의 서부 땅에는 충분히 인구가 이주하지 않았다. 그러나 링컨 대통령은 미국의 생존은 서부로의 확장에 달려 있다는 것을 알았기 때문에 그는 유니온 퍼시픽과 센트럴 퍼시픽 철도 회사가 그 임무를 맡도록 인가했다. 1869년에 철도가 완성되었고 이제는 서부로 이주할 안전하고 빠른 방법을 이용할 수 있게 되었다. 수백 만 미국인들이 미국 서부를 개척했고 그 지역의 많은 영토를 개발했다. 미국은 성장하는 자국 경제에 동력을 공급하기 위해 먼 지역의 원자재를 활용할 수 있었기 때문에 번영하기 시작했다. 대륙횡단 철도는 미국이 세계에서 경제와 정치의 강국이 되도록 해 주었다.

어휘
completion 완성 transcontinental 대륙횡단의 populate 살다; *이주시키다 frontier 국경 continent 대륙 wagon 마차 drawback 단점 sufficiently 충분히 expansion 확장 authorize 인가하다 take on 맡다 migrate 이주하다 venture 개척하다 prosper 번영하다 remote 먼 [문제] synergy 시너지 효과, 동반 상승효과

구문해설
1행 The completion of the Transcontinental Railroad **allowed** the U.S. **to populate** the frontier and establish its influence on the continent.: 'allow+O+to-v' 「…가 ~하게 하다」

8행 However, President Lincoln knew [that the survival of the country depended on westward expansion] ...: [ ]는 knew의 목적절

문제해설
대륙횡단 철도가 완성되고 나서 인구가 미국 서부로 이동해 그 지역이 개발되었고 그로 인해 미국 경제가 발전했다는 내용이므로, 글의 주제는 ③ '미국 경제에 미친 대륙횡단 철도의 막대한 영향'이다.

23 ① 글의 주제

CCUS는 '탄소 포집, 활용 및 저장'을 의미한다. 이것은 석유와 가스 산업이 전 세계 에너지 수요를 지속적으로 충족시키면서 이산화탄소 배출을 줄이도록 돕는 데 필수적인 역할을 하는 기술이다. CCUS는 배출을 줄이고 대기 중 이산화탄소를 제거하는 데 도움이 되므로, 이는 순 배출 제로 목표를 달성하는 데 중요한 부분이다. CCUS의 첫 번째 단계는 산업 공정 또는 연료 연소를 통해 방출되는 이산화탄소를 포집하는 것을 포함한다. 이 이산화탄소는 그런 다음 안전하게 저장될 수 있는 장소로 수송된다. 이는 청정에너지로 쉽게 전환될 수 없는 비행기와 산업 공장들의 배출을 줄이는 데 유용하다. CCUS 프로젝트는 전 세계 이산화탄소 배출을 거의 20퍼센트까지 줄이는 데 앞장설 잠재력이 있다고 여겨진다. 그것들은 또한 비용 효율적이며, 기후 변화에 대처하는 데 드는 비용을 대략 70퍼센트까지 낮출 것으로 예상된다.

어휘
stand for …을 의미하다 carbon 탄소 capture 포집[포착]; 포집[포착]하다 utilization 이용, 활용 storage 저장, 보관 emission 배출 demand 수요 atmosphere 대기 reach …에 이르다[도달하다] release 놓아 주다[날려 보내다/방출하다] industrial 산업의 burning 연소 transport 수송하다 convert 전환시키다 lead the way 앞장서다, 솔선하다 cost-efficient 비용 효율적인 be projected to …할 것으로 예상되다 approximately 거의, 가까이 [문제] lessen 줄이다 formation 형성 promote 촉진하다 ineffective 효과 없는

구문해설
2행 It is technology [that plays an essential role in **helping** the oil and gas industry **reduce** CO₂ emissions {while continuing to meet global energy demands}].: [ ]는 technology를 선행사로 하는 주격 관계대명사절, 'help+O+(to-)v' 「…가 ~하는 것을 돕다」, { }는 부대상황을 나타내는 분사구문으로, 접속사 while은 뜻을 분명히 하기 위해 생략되지 않음
11행 This is useful **in reducing** emissions from airplanes and industrial plants [that can't easily be converted to clean energy].: 'in v-ing' 「…하는 데 있어서」, [ ]는 airplanes and industrial plants를 선행사로 하는 주격 관계대명사절

문제해설
이산화탄소 배출을 줄이는 CCUS 공정의 과정과 이에 따른 기대 효과를 설명하고 있으므로, 글의 주제로는 ① '이산화탄소 오염의 영향을 줄이는 과정'이 가장 적절하다.

24 ② 글의 제목

인간을 단순히 또 하나의 성공적인 포유류 형태로 보는 것이 종종 도움이 되기는 하지만, 아주 중요한 차이점이 남아있다. 한 무리의 사자들은 많은 음식을 먹을 때, 그들이 먹을 수 있을 만큼 먹고는 에너지를 보존하기 위해 하루 중 남는 시간을 잠을 자는 데 쓸 것이다. 반면 인간은 여가 시간을 잠을 자는 데 보내지 않는다. 우리의 우수한 두뇌는 우리를 부단히 활동하게 하며, 이는 우리를 놀이에 참여하게 한다. 인간은 말하고 사랑 노래를 쓰며, 교회를 짓고 우리가 가치 있다고 여기는 많은 다른 일들을 한다. 인간의 생존과 무관한 활동들은 예술, 철학, 과학, 그리고 심

지어 국가 조직의 형태를 띠는데, 이들은 시간이 지나면서 사회와 문화의 토대로 이어져 왔다.

mammal 포유류　vital 극히 중요한　distinction 구별; 차이　a pride of lions 사자 한 무리　excess 과잉, 과다　remainder 나머지　conserve 보존하다, 보호하다　leisure 여가　restless 부단히 활동하는　engage in …에 참여하다　worthwhile 가치 있는　take the form of …의 형식을 취하다　philosophy 철학　foundation 기반, 토대　[문제] destruction 파괴

구문해설
1행 While **it** is often helpful [to *think of* humans *as* simply another successful type of mammal], ...: it은 가주어이고 [ ]가 진주어, 'think of A as B' 「A를 B로 여기다」
6행 ..., humans do not **spend** their leisure time **sleeping**.: 'spend+시간+v-ing' 「…하는 데 시간을 보내다」

문제해설
다른 포유류와 달리 인간은 여가 시간을 이용하여 사회와 문화의 토대가 되는 다양한 예술, 학문, 제도 등을 발전시키는 차이점을 가지고 있다는 내용이므로, ② '무엇이 인간과 동물을 구별하나'가 제목으로 가장 적절하다.

25 ⑤ 도표 내용 불일치

위 도표는 미국이 2020년과 2021년 1월에 파지와 플라스틱을 수출한 다섯 개의 주요 국가들을 보여준다. 2020년에, 가장 많은 양의 파지와 플라스틱이 중국으로 수출되었지만, 2021년에 가장 많은 양을 차지한 것은 바로 인도였다. 비율의 측면에서, 2021년 인도로의 수출은 2020년 중국으로의 수출보다 0.1퍼센트포인트 더 낮았다. 2020년에, 가장 적었던 수출 비율은 한국이었는데, 그것은 멕시코와 베트남에 수출한 것보다 약 1퍼센트포인트만 더 적었다. 중국으로의 수출은 두 연도 사이에 가장 큰 하락을 보였는데, 2021년의 비율은 2020년 비율의 단지 약 10분의 1에 불과했다. (반면 인도는 가장 큰 상승을 보였는데, 인도의 2021년 수출 비율은 다른 네 개 국을 합친 것보다 0.5퍼센트포인트만 더 낮았다.)

export 수출하다; 수출　scrap paper 파지　in terms of ~의 면에서　drop 하락　rise 상승

구문해설
3행 In 2020, the greatest amount of scrap paper and plastic was exported to China, but **it was** India **that** took in the greatest amount in 2021.: 'it is[was] ... that ~' 「~한 것은 바로 …이다[였다]」(강조구문)
14행 India, on the other hand, saw the greatest rise, **with** its percentage of 2021 exports **being only half of a percentage point lower** than *those* of the other four countries **combined**.: 'with+O+현재분사' 「…을 ~한 채로」(부대상황을 나타내는 분사구문), those는 the percentages of 2021 exports를 지칭, combined는 the other four countries를 수식하는 과거분사

문제해설
⑤ 2021년 인도의 수출 비율(30.9%)은 다른 네 개의 주요 국가를 합친 것(31.9%)보다 1퍼센트포인트 더 낮았다.

26 ② 내용 불일치

'수분 저류'는 가장 흔하게는 다리나 발 주변에서 일어나는데, 수분이 사람의 혈액에서 조직으로 새어 들어가서 거기에(조직에) 축적되는 현상이다. 정상적인 상태에서는 이 액체가 일련의 관을 통해 자연적으로 배출되지만, 그렇지 않을 때는 조직이 부풀게 된다. 아마도 에스트로겐 수치

로 인해 수분 저류는 남성보다는 여성에게 더 흔히 일어난다. 수분 저류를 일으킬 수 있는 요인들에는 염분 섭취, 높은 체온, 영양 결핍, 그리고 일부 처방약의 부작용 등이 포함된다. 그러나 어떤 경우에 수분 저류는 심장이나 간, 폐에 영향을 미치는 질병과 같은 더욱 심각한 질병의 증상일지도 모른다.

retention 보유, 유지; *정체　leak 새다　vicinity 근처, 부근　proceed 나아가다, 이르다　accumulate 축적하다　drain 서서히 배출하다; 빠지다　swollen 부풀어 오른, 부은　occurrence 발생, 일어남　consumption 소비; *체내 섭취　deficiency 부족, 결핍　symptom 증상

구문해설
1행 "Water retention" is a condition [in which water leaks from a person's blood and into their tissues, most commonly in the vicinity of the legs or feet, {where it then proceeds to accumulate}].: [ ]는 a condition을 선행사로 하는 목적격 관계대명사절, { }는 their tissues를 선행사로 하는 계속적 용법의 관계부사절

문제해설
② 손이나 팔이 아니라 다리나 발 부근에서 주로 일어나는 증상이다.

27 ④ 내용 일치

아티카 지역에 위치한 도시국가인 아테네는 근대 민주주의의 발생지로 여겨진다. 그 당시에 아테네는 왕에 의해 통치되고 있었다. 시간이 흐르면서 그들은 독재자라 불리는 일련의 강력한 통치자들에 의해 대체되었다. 이들은 국민들을 거의 돌보지 않았다. 기원전 594년, 솔론이라는 이름의 유명한 정치인이 그 독재자들을 대신하였고 새로운 일련의 규정을 확립하였다. 그러나 기원전 510년, 존경받던 아테네인 클레이스테네스는 솔론의 원칙에 개혁안을 도입했다. 그는 부족의 분할을 영토 분할로 바꾸었다. 그리고 나서 그는 아티카를 여러 지역으로 나눈 후 그 지역을 각각의 대표를 포함하고 있는 더 작은 지역으로 나누었다. 그는 또한 각 부족당 100명의 구성원으로 4개의 부족을 대표하던 400명의 솔론의 위원회를 각 부족당 50명의 구성원으로 10개의 부족을 대표하는 500명의 위원회로 대체했다. 그가 만든 변화는 귀족정치의 힘을 약화시켰고 부의 분배를 더 평등하게 만들어 민주주의의 장을 열었다.

city state 도시국가　located 위치한　birthplace 발생지　democracy 민주주의　a series of 일련의　tyrant 폭군, 독재자　statesman 정치가　establish 확립하다, 세우다　reform 개혁　principle 원칙　division 분열, 분할　territorial 영토의　district 구역　contain 포함하다　representative 대표자(represent 대표하다)　aristocracy 귀족정치　distribution 분배

구문해설
1행 The city state of Athens, [located in the region of Attica], is seen as ...: [ ]는 삽입구로 The city state of Athens를 부연 설명하는 과거분사구
18행 ... made the distribution of wealth more equal, [thus opening the door to democracy].: [ ]는 결과를 나타내는 분사구문

문제해설
① 왕정이 독재자들에 의한 통치로 대체되었다. ② 솔론은 독재자들의 자리를 대신한 정치인이었다. ③ 기원전 **510**년에 부족 분할에서 영토 분할로 전환하였다. ⑤ 클레이스테네스의 개혁으로 더 평등한 부의 분배가 이루어졌다.

28 ③ 내용 불일치

동물원에서의 핼러윈

브리지포트 동물원은 세 번째 연례 핼러윈 파티를 공지하게 되어 기쁩니다. 모든 연령대의 아이들을 환영하지만, 16세 미만의 아동은 반드시 부모와 동행해야 합니다.

시간 및 날짜
10월 31일 오후 5시부터 밤 10시까지

입장권
• 동물원 회원은 20달러
• 비회원은 25달러
입장권은 무료 음료 2잔과 모든 행사 및 동물 전시관 입장을 포함합니다.

세부 사항
• 지역 음식점들이 동물원 곳곳의 가판대에서 음식을 판매할 것입니다. 대부분은 신용카드를 받을 것이지만, 몇몇은 받지 않을 것입니다.
• 동물원에는 안내소 안에 위치한 현금 자동 입출금기가 있습니다.
• 날씨에 상관없이 행사가 열릴 것입니다. 우천 시, 모든 공연은 실내로 옮겨질 것입니다.

어휘
announce 공지하다, 알리다 welcome 환영받는 accompany 동반하다 admission 입장 exhibit 전시(회) stand 가판대, 좌판 throughout 도처에 regardless of …에 상관없이 in case of …이 발생할 시에는 indoors 실내에서, 실내로

구문해설
2행 The Bridgeport Zoo is pleased [to announce its third annual Halloween party].: [ ]는 감정의 원인을 나타내는 부사적 용법의 to부정사구
17행 The zoo has ATMs [located inside the information center].: [ ]는 ATMs를 수식하는 과거분사구

문제해설
③ 입장권은 무료 음료 2잔과 모든 행사 및 동물 전시관의 입장을 포함한다고 했다.

29 ③ 어법

우리 태양계의 행성들은 크기, 질량, 구성 성분에 따라 아주 뚜렷하게 구별되는 두 개의 무리들로 나뉠 수 있다. 수성, 금성, 화성은 거의 전적으로 암석 물질과 철로 이루어져 있다는 점에서 지구와 닮았다. 이러한 4개의 행성들은 '지구형 행성'으로 알려져 있다. 이 지구형 행성들은 소행성대를 포함하는 넓은 간격에 의해, 태양에서 더 멀리 있는 행성들과 분리되어 있다. 이 간격 다음에는 거대 행성들인 목성, 토성, 천왕성, 해왕성이 있다. 이것들 모두는 지구보다 훨씬 더 크다. 한때는 태양에서 가장 먼 행성으로 여겨졌던 명왕성은 매우 다르며, 주로 메탄과 얼음으로 구성되어 있다. 사실 명왕성은 최근에 행성의 지위에서 강등되어, 이제는 '왜소 행성'으로 간주된다.

어휘
solar system 태양계 divide A into B A를 B로 나누다 in terms of …에 의하여, …의 측면에서 mass 질량 composition 구성 성분 Mercury 수성 Venus 금성 Mars 화성 terrestrial 육생[지상]의; *지구형의 be separated from ... …에서 분리되다 Jupiter 목성 Saturn 토성 Uranus 천왕성 Neptune 해왕성 significantly 상당히 Pluto 명왕성 methane 메탄 demote 지위를 떨어뜨리다, 강등시키다 status 지위, 신분

구문해설
6행 These terrestrial planets are separated from **those** farther from the Sun by a large gap [containing an asteroid field].: those는 planets를 지칭. [ ]는 a large gap을 수식하는 현재분사구

12행 Pluto, [once considered the farthest planet from the Sun], is significantly different, [consisting mainly of methane and ice].: 첫 번째 [ ]는 삽입구로 Pluto를 부연 설명하는 과거분사구, 두 번째 [ ]는 주절을 부연 설명하는 분사구문

문제해설
③ 장소를 나타내는 부사구 After this gap이 문두에 오면서 주어와 동사가 도치되었는데, 주어인 the giant planets가 복수이므로 동사는 단수형인 comes가 아닌 복수형 come으로 써야 한다.

30 ④ 어휘

오늘날, '흰 코끼리'라는 용어는 비록 그것에 실용적인 쓰임새가 전혀 없더라도 당신이 소유하고 있는 것을 가리킨다. 흰 코끼리는 부처와 관련이 있기 때문에, 동남아시아 사람들은 그 동물을 신성하게 여긴다. 따라서 흰 코끼리는 너무 소중하게 여겨져서 그들이 힘든 일을 하도록 하는 것이 용납되지 않는다. 이 사회에서 흰 코끼리는 왕이나 황제로부터의 선물로만 얻을 수 있어서, 흰 코끼리를 소유하는 것은 특권이었다. 그러나 그 코끼리는 선물을 받는 사람에게 부담스러웠는데, 소유자가 왕의 선물을 잘 지키고 유지해야 했기 때문이었다. 그것은 이익은 거의 주지 못하는 반면 많은 자원을 소모했다. 그럼에도 불구하고, 그 동물을 버리는 것은 왕에 대한 모욕이 될 수 있기 때문에 소유자는 그것을 가지고 있을 수밖에 없었다.

어휘
term 용어, 말 own 소유하다 practical 현실적인, 실제적인 be connected with …와 관계가 있다 regard ... as ~ …을 ~하게 여기다[간주하다] holy 신성한 despise 경멸하다 privilege 특권 burdensome 부담스러운 recipient 받는 사람, 수령인 resource 자원, 재원 dispose of …을 처리하다[없애다]

구문해설
1행 Today, the term "a white elephant" refers to something [that you own even though there is no practical use for it].: [ ]는 something을 선행사로 하는 목적격 관계대명사절
5행 Thus, white elephants are valued **too** much **to allow** them to do hard work.: 'too ... to-v' 「너무 …해서 ~할 수 없다」
15행 ..., the owner **could not help but** keep it ...: 'cannot help but+동사원형' 「…하지 않을 수 없다」

문제해설
④ (A) 흰 코끼리가 힘든 일을 하도록 용납되지 않았으므로 그들이 매우 '소중하게 여겨졌다(valued)'라고 하는 것이 적절하다. (B) 흰 코끼리가 힘든 일에 사용되지 않았다는 앞 내용과 왕의 선물을 잘 보살펴야 하는 의무가 주어졌다는 이어지는 내용으로 미루어 그 코끼리가 받는 사람에게 '부담스러운(burdensome)' 것이었다고 하는 것이 적절하다. (C) 코끼리는 노동에 사용되지 않았기 때문에 '이익(benefits)'을 거의 발생시키지 않았다고 하는 것이 적절하다.

31 ① 빈칸 추론

그것이 무엇이든 간에 물건을 비축하는 것은 물질주의의 의미 없는 한 형태일 뿐이다. 어떤 사람들은 어떤 물건이 기능적인 쓸모가 있어서가 아니라, 다만 존재하기 때문에 가지고 있길 원한다. 싸구려 장신구는 실제로 착용을 할 때 어떤 고유의 쓸모가 있지만, 그것을 비축하는 사람들은 그저 돈을 버리고 있을 뿐이다. 곧 그들은 분류하고 모아 두어야 할 쓸모 없는 싸구려 장신구들을 수없이 많이 갖게 된다. 그리고 나서 그것들 모두를 넣어 둘 보석 보관함에 더 많은 돈을 써야 한다. 그다음에는 자신의 수집품을 늘리기 위해 점점 더 많이 사느라 굉장히 많은 돈을 쓰기 시

작한다. 그러나 이러한 비축에는 끝이 없어서, 그 취미는 계속되다가 걷잡을 수 없게 되어 버린다. 그런 것에 들이는 모든 시간과 돈은 훨씬 더 나은 목적을 위해 쓰일 수도 있는데 말이다.

구문해설
[7행] Soon they have countless hundreds of useless cheap jewelry [that they have to sort and save].: [ ]는 useless cheap jewelry를 선행사로 하는 목적격 관계대명사절
[11행] ..., they begin spending extravagant amounts of money [to buy more and more **in order to increase** their collections].: [ ]는 목적을 나타내는 부사적 용법의 to부정사구, 'in order to-v'「…하기 위해서」

문제해설
실용성이 없는 물건을 수집하는 것은 시간과 돈을 낭비하는 것이라는 내용으로 미루어 볼 때 빈칸에는 ① '물질주의'가 적절하다.

32 ⑤ 빈칸 추론

케이준 음식은 많은 배고픈 관광객들을 루이지애나의 그 본고장으로 끌어들이는 맵고 향긋하며 맛있는 요리 방식이다. 그러나 루이지애나가 케이준 요리의 본고장으로 유명하기는 하지만, 이 요리 방식은 사실 루이지애나의 역사 속에서 일어난 많은 문화의 혼합을 보여준다. 오랫동안 루이지애나는 북미 원주민, 스페인, 프랑스, 아카디아, 아프리카, 이탈리아 등의 많은 문화로부터 큰 영향을 받아왔다. 케이준 음식은 그 지역 특유의 맛에 각각의 민족 집단이 자신들의 개별적인 특징을 더함으로써 수 세기에 걸쳐 발전하였다. 오늘날의 케이준 음식은 단순히 매운 소스만을 첨가하는 것 이상이다. 그것은 <u>많은 문화의 풍미가 하나로 섞인 것</u>이다.

구문해설
[1행] Cajun food is a hot, spicy, delicious style of cooking [which attracts many hungry tourists ... in Louisiana].: [ ]는 a hot ... cooking을 선행사로 하는 주격 관계대명사절

문제해설
이 글은 케이준 음식이 단순히 매운 음식이 아니라, 다양한 문화가 융합된 산물임을 강조하고 있으므로, 빈칸에는 ⑤ '많은 문화의 풍미가 하나로 섞인 것'이 적절하다.

33 ⑤ 빈칸 추론

일반적으로 과학자들은 북극의 매우 추운 환경에서 생존하기 위해 고대 인류가 몸에 딱 맞고 비바람에 견디는 의복을 만드는 능력을 개발했음에 틀림없다고 생각한다. 이러한 의복은 아마도 동물 가죽의 조각들을 힘줄을 가지고 바느질하여 만들어졌을 것이다. 따라서, 마침내 인간이 <u>추운 지방을 지배하는 것</u>을 시작하게 해준 기술적인 돌파구는 아마도 송곳이라 불리는 뾰족한 도구의 발명이었을 것이다. 시간이 흘러 송곳은 오늘날에도 여전히 꿰매고 깁는 데 사용되는 '바늘귀가 있는 바늘'로 발전했다. 비록 고고학적 증거는 바늘의 최초 사용과 인류의 북극으로의 최종적인 이주 사이에 거의 15,000년의 시간이 흘렀다는 것을 말해주지만, 이전의 사건 없이는 이후의 사건도 결코 일어나지 않았을 것이라고 해도

과언이 아니다.

구문해설
[1행] Scientists generally believe [that, in order to survive in the frigid conditions of the Arctic, ancient humans **must have developed** the ability {to create form-fitting, ... clothing}].: [ ]는 believe의 목적절, 'must have p.p.'「…였음에 틀림없다」, { }는 the ability를 수식하는 형용사적 용법의 to부정사구
[6행] Therefore, the technological breakthrough [that eventually **allowed** humans **to begin** colonizing cold regions] was most likely the invention of a pointed tool [called the awl].: 첫 번째 [ ]는 the technological breakthrough를 선행사로 하는 주격 관계대명사절, 'allow+O+to-v'「…가 ~하도록 허용하다」, 두 번째 [ ]는 a pointed tool을 수식하는 과거분사구
[10행] Over time, the awl was developed into the "eyed needle" [that is still used ... today].: [ ]는 the "eyed needle"을 선행사로 하는 주격 관계대명사절

문제해설
바느질하는 도구를 사용하게 됨으로써 추위를 막는 옷을 만들 수 있고, 북극과 같은 추운 지방에서도 살 수 있게 되었다고 이야기하고 있으므로, 빈칸에는 ⑤ '추운 지방을 지배하는 것'이 적절하다.

34 ④ 빈칸 추론

바넘 효과라고도 불리는 포러 효과는 일반적인 진술이 특별하게 자신에게 적용된다고 믿는 사람들의 경향을 나타낸다. 이것의 가장 잘 알려진 예는 별점이다. 비록 그것들은 수백만 명의 사람들을 위해 작성되었지만, 우리는 마치 그것들이 우리를 정확하게 묘사하는 것처럼 느낀다. 이 현상은 원래 버트럼 포러라는 이름의 심리학자에 의해 밝혀졌다. 1948년에, 그는 학생들이 성격 검사를 받는 실험을 수행했다. 그들은 각자가 결과에 근거한 개인 평가를 받을 것이라고 들었다. 실제로, 학생들은 모두 '당신은 다른 사람들이 당신을 좋아하고 존경하는 것에 대한 큰 욕구가 있습니다'와 같이 <u>일반적인 진술로 된 동일한 성격 묘사</u>를 받았다. 그런 다음 학생들은 그들의 평가를 0에서 5까지의 등급으로 평가하도록 요구받았는데, 5가 가장 정확한 것이었다. 그 평가들이 검사와 관련이 없었다는 사실에도 불구하고, 그것들은 평균 4.26점을 받았다.

구문해설
[1행] The Forer effect, [which is also called the Barnum effect], refers to the tendency of people [to believe {that general

statements apply specifically to them}].: 첫 번째 [ ]는 The Forer effect를 선행사로 하는 계속적 용법의 주격 관계대명사절, 두 번째 [ ]는 the tendency of people을 수식하는 형용사적 용법의 to부정사구, { }는 동사 believe의 목적어 역할을 하는 명사절

(15행) The students **were** then **asked to evaluate** their assessments on a scale from zero to five, *with* five *being* the most accurate.: 'be asked to-v'는 'ask+O+to-v' 「…에게 ~하도록 요구[요청]하다」의 수동태 구문, 'with+O+현재분사' 「…가 ~한 채로」

(17행) Despite the fact [that the assessments had no connection to the test], they received an average rating of 4.26.: the fact와 [ ]는 동격

문제해설

일반적인 진술이 자신에게 특별히 적용된다고 믿는 포러 효과에 대한 글로, 빈칸 뒤에서 사실은 일반적인 진술이지만 학생들이 개인 성격 평가라고 알고 있는 진술에 대해 비교적 정확하다고 평가했으므로, 빈칸에는 ④ '일반적인 진술로 된 동일한 성격 묘사'가 오는 것이 적절하다.

35 ④ 흐름과 무관한 문장

오페라는 노년층을 위한 취미로 종종 여겨진다. 그러나 젊은이들이 이 예술 형태에 관심을 갖게 만들려는 큰 움직임이 있다. 메트로폴리탄 오페라에 따르면 오페라 관객의 평균 연령이 상승하고 있는데, 이는 전 세계적으로 많은 오페라 극단들이 직면하고 있는 추세이다. 젊은 관객들이 오페라에 관심을 갖게 하기 위해서 일부 오페라 극단들은 티켓에 학생 할인을 제공하고 있다. 실제로 젊은이들이 이러한 예술 형태를 접하게 하기 위해, 미국의 오페라 캐롤라이나는 심지어 21세부터 40세의 사람들이 특별 할인을 받을 수 있는 해피 아워(할인 시간대)를 제공한다. 일부 극단들은 심지어 현시대를 반영하기 위해서 고전 오페라를 현대화하기도 한다. (각색된 극들은 종종 할인된 입장료를 특징으로 함에도 불구하고, 좀처럼 원작만큼 인기를 끌지 못한다.) 음악과 이야기는 그대로 유지되는 반면, 배경은 젊은 관객들에게 더 친숙한 환경으로 설정된다.

어휘

pastime 취미 push 노력, 압박 trend 경향 expose 노출시키다; *접하게[경험하게] 하다 happy hour 할인 시간대 modernize 현대화하다 reflect 반영하다 revise 수정하다; *각색하다, 개작하다

구문해설

(1행) The opera **is** often **seen as** a pastime [reserved for older adults] ...: 'see A as B' 「A를 B로 간주하다」, [ ]는 a pastime을 수식하는 과거분사구

(10행) ..., Opera Carolina in the U.S. even offers a happy hour [when people {aged 21 to 40} can get special discounts].: [ ]는 a happy hour를 선행사로 하는 관계부사절, { }는 people을 수식하는 과거분사구

문제해설

젊은 연령층의 오페라 관객 수를 늘리기 위한 노력에 관한 글이므로, 현대식으로 각색한 오페라 작품들이 인기가 없다는 내용의 ④는 글의 흐름에 맞지 않는다.

36 ② 글의 순서

상어, 뱀 그리고 거미를 포함하여 사람들이 두려워하는 많은 위험한 동물이 존재한다. 이러한 동물들이 종종 책이나 영화에서 사악한 생명체들로 묘사되는 것은 놀라운 일이 아니다. (A) 그러나, 그것들에 대한 우리의 인식에도 불구하고, 이 생물들은 결코 지구상에서 가장 치명적인 생물체는 아니다. 사실, 세상에서 가장 위험한 동물들 중 몇몇은 우리 눈에 작고 연약하며, 무방비 상태로 보이는 것들

이다.

(C) 독화살 개구리가 그 한 예이다. 열대우림에서 발견되는 이 작은 양서류는 어린아이의 장난감만큼이나 귀엽고 밝은 색을 띠고 있다. 만약 이 개구리를 본다면, 그냥 두어라. 그것은 10명의 사람을 죽이기에 충분히 강력한 독소를 만들어 낸다.

(B) 그리고 당신이 다음에 바다에서 수영을 하게 되면 상어에 대해서는 괜히 걱정할 필요가 없다. 대신에, 호주의 상자 해파리를 경계해야 하는데, 이 해파리의 촉수는 여러 사람을 죽이기에 충분한 독소를 가지고 있다.

어휘

portray (그림·글로) 그리다, 묘사하다 perception 지각; *인식 by no means 결코 …이 아닌 fragile 깨지기 쉬운; *연약한 defenseless 무방비의 jellyfish 해파리 tentacle 촉수, 더듬이 toxin 독소

구문해설

(13행) Instead, **keep an eye out for** the Australian box jellyfish, [whose tentacles contain *enough poison to kill* several people].: 'keep an eye out for' 「…을 경계하다」, [ ]는 the Australian box jellyfish를 선행사로 하는 계속적 용법의 소유격 관계대명사절, 'enough+명사+to-v' 「…하기에 충분한 ~」

문제해설

② (A)의 them은 주어진 글의 '사람들이 무서워하는 동물들'을 가리키므로, 주어진 글 바로 뒤에 오는 것이 적절하며, (A)의 마지막 부분에서 언급된 작고 연약해 보이지만 위험한 동물들의 첫 번째 예시에 대한 내용인 (C)가 오고, 추가적인 예시에 해당하는 (B)로 이어지는 것이 적절하다.

37 ④ 글의 순서

엑스레이 기술은 의사들이 환자의 몸 안을 들여다볼 수 있게 함으로써 의학 분야에 큰 혜택을 가져왔다. 그러나, 엑스레이에 자주 노출되면 심각한 건강상의 문제를 가져올 수 있다.

(C) 이러한 사실은 엑스레이 기술의 초창기에 알려졌는데, 의사들은 그 (엑스레이에 자주 노출되었을 경우의) 결과에 대해 무지했기 때문에 환자와 자신 모두를 오랜 시간 동안 엑스레이에 노출시켰다. 곧 많은 사람들이 방사선 병의 해로운 영향을 경험하기 시작했다.

(A) 이러한 피해는 엑스레이가 일종의 이온화된 방사선이라는 사실에서 기인했다. 이것은 엑스레이가 원자에 닿으면 그것이 원자에게서 전자를 나오게 하여 이온을 만드는 것을 뜻하는데, 그 이온은 전기적으로 충전된 원자이다. 그리고 이온의 전기적 충전은 세포의 DNA를 파괴할 수 있다.

(B) DNA 파괴는 이번에는 세포의 죽음 또는 DNA의 돌연변이 둘 중 하나를 일으킨다. 광범위한 세포의 죽음은 질병으로 이어지고, 한편 돌연변이를 일으킨 DNA는 결국 암을 유발할 수 있다. 이러한 위험들이 의사들이 오늘날 엑스레이를 덜 자주 사용하는 이유이다.

어휘

glimpse 흘끗 봄, 어렴풋이 감지함 exposure 노출(expose 노출시키다) stem from …에서 생기다, 유래하다 ionize 이온화하다, 이온을 발생시키다 radiation 방사선 atom 원자 knock off (쳐서) 떨어져나가게 하다 electron 전자 mutation 변화, 돌연변이(mutate 돌연변이하다) consequence 결과 lengthy 긴, 오랜

구문해설

(17행) This truth was learned in the early days of the technology, [when doctors, {(being) unaware of the consequences}, exposed **both** their patients **and** themselves to X-rays for lengthy periods].: [ ]는 the early days of the technology를 선행사로 하는 계속적 용법의 관계부사절, { }는 이유를 나타내는 분사구문, 'both A and B' 「A와 B 둘

다.」

문제해설

④ (C)의 This truth는 주어진 글의 마지막에 언급된 '엑스레이에 자주 노출되면 건강상의 심각한 문제를 일으킬 수 있다'는 사실을 가리키므로, 주어진 글 다음에 (C)가 와야 한다. 그 다음으로는 (C)의 마지막 문장의 many people began ... radiation sickness를 This damage로 받아 그 원인을 설명한 (A)가 오고, (A)의 마지막에 언급된 내용인 DNA 파괴에 대해 설명하는 (B)가 이어지는 것이 적절하다.

38 ⑤ 주어진 문장의 위치

신기혐오증은 새로운 것들에 대한 공포라고 정의된다. 일반적으로 인간이 일상적으로 생활하는 존재라는 것을 고려하면, 그것은 진단하고 이해하기에 복잡한 혐오증일 수도 있다. 이것은 특히 어린 아이들에 대하여 사실인데, 그들은 종종 신기혐오증의 징후로 해석될 수 있는 행동을 보여준다. 그들에게는 거의 모든 것이 새로운 것이어서, 변화를 거부하는 것은 압도당하는 느낌에 대한 그저 자연스러운 반응일 수 있다. 이것의 한 가지 흔한 표출은 종종 식사 자리에서 일어난다. 어린 아이들은 한 움큼의 친숙한 음식 외에는 모두 손대는 것을 거부하면서 악명 높은 편식가가 될 수 있다. 아이들은 보통 자라면서 음식 신기혐오증이 없어진다. 그러나, 어떤 경우에는 이것이 그들이 남은 일생 동안 대처해야 하는 심각한 문제가 되기도 한다.

어휘

outgrow 더 커지다; *(나이가 들면서) …을 그만두다   define 정의하다   complicated 복잡한   phobia 공포증, 혐오증   diagnose 진단하다   routine (틀에 박힌) 일상   demonstrate 입증하다; *보여주다   interpret 설명하다, 해석하다   sign 징후, 조짐   overwhelm 압도하다   notoriously 악명 높게   picky eater 식성이 까다로운 사람, 편식가   refuse 거절하다, 거부하다   a handful of 한 움큼의   deal with …을 다루다[처리하다]

구문해설

(4행) It can be a complicated phobia [to diagnose and understand], **given that** human beings are ...: [ ]는 complicated를 한정하는 부사적 용법의 to부정사구, 'given that' 「…을 고려하면」

(13행) Young children can be notoriously picky eaters, [refusing to touch **all but** a handful of familiar foods].: [ ]는 부대상황을 나타내는 분사구문, 'all but ...' 「… 외에 모두, 거의」

(15행) In some cases, however, it becomes a serious problem [that they must deal with for the rest of their life].: [ ]는 a serious problem을 선행사로 하는 목적격 관계대명사절

문제해설

⑤ 뒤의 문장은 앞 문장과 'however(그러나)'로 연결되어 신기혐오증이 남은 일생 동안 커다란 문제가 될 수 있다는 내용을 다루고 있으므로, 이와 반대되는 내용을 다루고 있는 주어진 문장이 ⑤에 오는 것이 적절하다.

39 ② 주어진 문장의 위치

엘도라도의 전설은 1500년대 언젠가에 생겨났다. 그것은 남아메리카의 유럽 탐험가들에 의해 기록된 황금으로 가득 찬 도시에 대한 이야기에서 시작되었다. 남아메리카의 북쪽에 위치한 것처럼 보였던 그 신비로운 도시는 보석과 보물들로 넘쳐난다고 전해졌다. 그러한 묘사에 이끌려, 수천 명의 탐험가들이 엘도라도의 위치를 밝혀내고 그곳의 부를 자신이 차지하려고 애썼지만 실패했다. 이러한 탐험가들 중에서 가장 잘 알려진 사람들 중의 하나는 퍼시 해리슨 포셋이라는 이름의 영국인이었다. 그의 1925년의 탐험대는 아마존 정글의 오지를 헤매었고, 다시 발견되지 못

했다. 엘도라도의 위치를 밝히려 했던 다른 모든 사람들은 죽거나 낙심한 채로 돌아왔다. 사실, 오늘날 보물을 찾는 사람들은 목숨을 바쳐 그 전설의 도시를 찾으려고 애쓰기보다 복권을 사는 것이 더 나을지도 모른다.

어휘

entice 꾀다, 유혹하다   description 기술, 서술; 묘사   locate (위치 등을) 알아내다, 밝혀내다   apparently 보기에, 외관상으로는   mythical 신화의; 상상의   expedition 탐험 여행; *탐험대   wander 돌아다니다, 헤매다   discouraged 낙담한   lottery 복권   risk 위태롭게 하다, (목숨 따위를) 걸다

구문해설

(14행) Everyone else [who has attempted ... El Dorado] has **either** died **or** returned discouraged.: [ ]는 Everyone else를 선행사로 하는 주격 관계대명사절, 'either A or B' 「A와 B 둘 중 하나」

(17행) ... may **be better off buying** a lottery ticket than **risking** their lives [trying to find the legendary city].: 'be better off v-ing'는 「…하는 것이 더 낫다」라는 의미로 동명사 buying과 risking 이하를 비교, [ ]는 동시동작을 나타내는 분사구문

문제해설

주어진 문장의 such descriptions는 ②의 앞 문장 전체를 가리키고, ② 다음 문장의 these adventurers는 주어진 문장의 thousands of explorers를 가리키므로 주어진 문장의 위치는 ②가 가장 적절하다.

40 ③ 요약문 완성

달리기는 정말 건강에 좋을까? 최근에 마라톤 선수들을 대상으로 실시한 의학적 연구는 그렇지 않을 수도 있다는 가능성을 내비쳤다. 그 연구 결과에 따르면 달리기 선수들은 격렬한 훈련 기간 동안, 그리고 마라톤을 뛴 직후에 감기나 독감 같은 전염성 질병에 걸릴 확률이 더 높은 것으로 나타났다. 더욱이, 일주일에 60마일 이상 달린 장거리 주자들은 일주일에 뛴 거리가 20마일 미만인 사람들보다 두 배 더 많은 병에 걸린 것으로 보고되었다. 그리고 경주 전에 몸에 이상이 없었던 마라톤 선수들 중 12.9퍼센트가 경주 후 1주일 동안 몸에 이상이 생겼다. 이는 그 특정한 경주에 참가하지 않은 2.2퍼센트밖에 안 되는 비슷한 상태에 있는 선수들에 대비된다.

어휘

infectious 전염되는   conditioned 조건부의; *(어떤) 상태에 있는   take part in …에 참가하다   [문제] significantly 상당히   immunity 면역(력)   occasional 가끔의   moderate 보통의, 적당한   excessive 과도한   insufficient 불충분한   diminish 감소하다   impair 손상시키다

구문해설

(1행) A recent medical study [done on marathon runners] suggests [that it may not be (good for your health)].: 첫 번째 [ ]는 A recent medical study를 수식하는 과거분사구, 두 번째 [ ]는 suggests의 목적절

(6행) **What's more**, long-distance runners [who ran more than 60 miles a week] reported *twice as* many illnesses *as* those [who ran less ... per week].: 'what's more' 「더구나, 더욱이」, 두 개의 [ ]는 각각 long-distance runners와 those를 선행사로 하는 주격 관계대명사절, '배수사 +as ... as' 「~배만큼 …한」

문제해설

③ 과도한 달리기는 전염성 질환에 대한 사람의 면역력을 크게 감퇴시킬 수 있다.

41 ④   42 ① 장문

사람들은 항상 현실 생활의 스트레스에서 벗어날 방법을 찾고 있다.

소설을 읽거나 연극을 관람하거나 영화를 보면서, 사람들은 가상의 세계로 도피하고 자신이 공감하는 실제의(→ 허구의) 이야기 속에서 사는 것을 상상한다. 가상 현실 기술이 최근 또 하나의 도피 수단으로 추가되었다. 그러나 가상 현실은 많은 점에 있어서 다른 도피 수단과는 다르다.

소설 속에서 우리는 상상을 하고 감정이입을 하는 반면, 사이버 공간에서 우리는 실제로 다른 세계에 발을 들여놓는다. 연극, 소설, 영화와 같은 다른 도피 수단에서 우리는 작가가 미리 정해놓은 이야기를 수동적으로 따라갈 뿐이다. 그러나 가상 현실에서는 이야기에 능동적으로 참여해 우리가 직접 이야기를 만들어 나간다.

가상 현실에서 우리는 자신이 바라는 자아를 선택할 수도 있고, 일어나는 일들을 통제할 수도 있다. 그러나 그러한 가상 현실이 현실 세계보다 더 낫다면 어떻게 될까? 사람들은 가상 현실 기술에 중독되어 그것을 이용하며 대부분의 시간을 보낼 수도 있을 것이다. 심지어 현실 세계에서 자신의 책임에 소홀해지기 시작할지도 모른다.

바로 텔레비전이 수십 년 동안 그래왔듯이, 가상 현실은 우리가 깨닫기도 전에 우리 일상에서 큰 비중을 차지하게 될 수도 있다. 사람들은 매혹적인 장소로 들어가는 통로를 열고 그곳에서 시간을 보낼 것이다. 실제로 우리들 중 일부는 현실 세계의 일상의 혼돈으로 다시는 돌아오지 않기를 바랄지도 모른다. 어쩌면 언젠가는 가상 현실이 마약처럼 불법이 될지도 모른다.

구문해설
2행 **By reading** novels, **attending** plays, or **watching** movies, people escape ... and *picture* themselves *living* in fictional stories [that they identify with].: 'by v-ing'는 「…함으로써」의 의미로, reading, attending, watching이 병렬 연결, 'picture+O+v-ing' 「…가 ～하다고 상상하다」, [ ]는 fictional stories를 선행사로 하는 목적격 관계대명사절
17행 ..., we are able to choose a desired identity and (are able to) control [what happens].: [ ]는 control의 목적어로 쓰인 관계대명사절

문제해설
41 현실 세계의 또 다른 도피 수단으로 떠오른 사이버 공간 속의 가상 현실에 대해 설명하며 많은 사람들이 이에 빠져들 수도 있다는 내용의 글이므로, ④ '가상 현실: 다른 세계에서 길을 잃다'가 가장 적절한 제목이다.
42 사람들이 소설, 연극, 영화 등을 통해 가상의 세계로 도피한다는 내용으로 보아 자신이 '허구의' 이야기 속에서 사는 것을 상상한다고 하는 것이 자연스러우므로, ① real(실제의)은 fictional(허구의) 등으로 바꿔야 한다.

43 ② 44 ⑤ 45 ⑤ 장문

(A) 찰스 다윈의 진화론을 상세히 기술한 1859년 출판작인 '종의 기원에 관하여'는 과학계를 뒤흔들었다. 과학자들은 즉시 멸종된 인류의 조상들에 대한 여러 종류의 화석 증거를 찾기 시작했다. 그들은 인류가 지난 수천 년간 어떻게 진화해 왔는지를 정확히 알고자 했다. 1910년에 찰스 도슨이라는 한 연구원은 그가 그러한 '잃어버린 고리'를 나타낸다고 믿었던 어떤 것을 발견했다.

(B) 그가 발견한 것은 필트다운인(人)으로 불리게 되었고, 인간의 두개골과 치아로 보이는 것들의 조각들이 포함되어 있었다. 그는 그것들을 영국 서섹스 주(州)의 필트다운이라는 지역에서 발굴했다. 흥분한 그는 그 뼈와 치아들을 유명한 과학자인 아서 스미스 우드워드에게 가져갔고, 그는 그 조각들이 정말로 초기 인류의 것들이라고 발표했다. 필트다운인에 관한 뉴스는 전 세계로 퍼져나갔지만, 차츰 진실이 드러났다.

(D) 우선, 그 지역의 추가적인 발견들로 필트다운인의 진위에 대해 의혹이 제기되기 시작했고, 그 존재가 인류의 진화에 관한 이야기와 일치하지 않는다는 것을 보여주었다. 그리고 다음으로 1950년대에, 새로운 연구로 필트다운인의 두개골이 겨우 600년 가량 되었고 치아들은 유인원의 것임이 증명되었다. 누군가가 마치 그것들이 고대 인류의 것인 것처럼 보이도록 만들기 위해 그 뼈들을 배열하고 이들을 채색한 것이었다. 전 세계의 과학자들이 속았던 것이다.

(C) 이 사실이 알려지자, 한 가지 의문이 제기되었다. 이 사기 행위의 배후는 누구인가 하는 것이었다. 오늘날까지도 우리는 확신하지 못하지만, 현재의 의견은 (필트다운인의) 발견 당시 한 자연사 박물관에서 자원봉사를 하고 있었던 마틴 힌튼이라는 이름의 남자를 지목하고 있다. (자원봉사자라는) 그의 지위는 그가 그러한 속임수를 만들 수 있는 도구와 지식을 제공했다. 게다가, 필트다운 화석들의 뼈들과 유사한 뼈들이 그의 소지품들 사이에서 발견되었다. 소식통들은 힌튼이 그의 상사를 난처하게 만들려고 했던 것인지도 모른다고 전하는데, 그는 그 당시에 그의 상사와 돈과 관련해서 논쟁을 하고 있었다고 한다.

구문해설
6행 They wanted to learn exactly [how human beings **had evolved** over the previous thousands of years].: [ ]는 learn의 목적어로 쓰인 의문사절, had evolved는 계속을 나타내는 과거완료
11행 His discovery came to be called the Piltdown man and included pieces of [what appeared to be a human skull and teeth].: [ ]는 of의 목적어로 쓰인 관계대명사절
29행 Sources say Hinton **may have been trying** to embarrass his boss, [whom he was having a dispute about money with around that time].: 'may have been v-ing' 「…하고 있었을지도 모른다」(과거에 대한 불확실한 추측), [ ]는 his boss를 선행사로 하는 계속적 용법의 목적격 관계대명사절
33행 ..., further discoveries in the field began to cast doubt on the authenticity of the Piltdown man, [showing {that its existence didn't fit the story of human evolution}].: [ ]는 부대상황을 나타내는 분사구문, { }는 showing의 목적절
40행 ... to **make** them **appear** *as if* they *belonged to* an ancient human.: 'make+O+동사원형' 「…을 ～하게 만들다」, 'as if …' 「마치 …인 것처럼」 (이 문장에서는 현재 사실과 반대되는 내용을 가정하는 가정법 과거와 함께 쓰임)

문제해설
43 ② (A)에서 언급된 찰스 도슨의 발견에 관한 구체적인 내용이 (B)에서 필트다운인 화석의 내용으로 서술되고, (B)의 마지막에서 언급된 '진실이 차츰 밝혀졌다'는 내용은 (D)의 필트다운인 화석이 인류 조상의 것이 아닌 조작된 것임이 밝혀졌다는 내용으로 이어진다. 마지막으로 이러한 사기의 배후에 관한 추가적인 의문에 대한 내용을 다루는 (C)로 이어지는 것이 적절하다.
44 ⑤ (e)는 마틴 힌튼을 가리키고, 나머지는 모두 찰스 도슨을 가리킨다.
45 ① 진화론을 기술한 '종의 기원에 관하여'는 1859년에 발표되었다. ② 필트다운에서 화석을 발견한 것은 찰스 도슨이었다. ③ 찰스 도슨이 발견한 필트다운인은 거짓으로 판명되었다. ④ 마틴 힌튼은 자연사 박물관의 자원봉사자였다.

12 영어독해 모의고사

본문 ▲ p.116

18 ③	19 ④	20 ④	21 ②	22 ⑤	23 ④
24 ②	25 ①	26 ②	27 ③	28 ④	29 ③
30 ⑤	31 ④	32 ④	33 ③	34 ①	35 ④
36 ④	37 ⑤	38 ②	39 ⑤	40 ②	41 ⑤
42 ②	43 ④	44 ③	45 ②		

18 ③ 글의 목적

존슨 교장 선생님께,

레이크사이드 고등학교에 다니는 두 학생의 학부모로서, 귀교의 보안 상태와 관련한 제안을 드리고자 합니다. 감시 카메라를 설치함으로써 선생님들에게 유용한 도구를 제공할 수 있을 것입니다. 가장 먼저, 카메라는 잘못된 행동에 대해 훌륭한 억제제의 역할을 해줍니다. 이는 학생들이 규칙을 위반할 가능성이 더 적어질 것임을 의미합니다. 그리고 만일 학생들이 실제로 학교 규칙을 위반했다면, 선생님들이 그 행동을 볼 수 있게 해주는 영상 기록이 남게 될 것입니다. 또한, 카메라는 학교에서의 범죄율을 실제로 낮춰주기 때문에 학부모들은 안전에 대해 걱정할 필요가 없을 것입니다. 이러한 이유들로, 귀하께서 저의 제안을 고려해 주셨으면 합니다.

진심을 담아서,
샬롯 밴더빌트 드림

어휘
surveillance 감시   serve as …로써 역할을 하다   deterrent 억제하는 것, 제지물   wrongdoing 범법 행위, 비행   take ... into consideration …을 고려하다

구문해설
[9행] And if students **did** break school rules, there would be a video history of it [that would *allow* teachers *to see* the act].: did 는 동사 break를 강조하는 조동사, [ ]는 a video history of it을 선행사로 하는 주격 관계대명사절, 'allow+O+to-v'「…가 ~하게 하다」

문제해설
③ 학교에 감시 카메라를 설치하면 얻을 수 있는 긍정적인 효과를 언급하며 설치를 제안하는 학부모의 편지글이다.

19 ④ 분위기

내가 잠이 깨서 아기가 우는 소리를 들은 것은 새벽 2시를 막 지난 늦은 시간이었다. 나는 아기방으로 가서 요람에서 아기를 들어 올려, 따뜻한 우유 한 병을 준비하기 위해 아기를 주방으로 데리고 갔다. 갑자기 한기가 나를 둘러쌌고, 나는 방 안에 섬뜩한 무언가가 있음을 느꼈다. 미친 듯이 주위를 둘러보았지만, 별다르게 보이는 것은 아무것도 없었다. 그때, 올 때와 마찬가지로 순식간에 한기가 사라졌다. 나는 잠시 꼼짝 않고 서 있다가 내가 상상을 했던 것이라고 스스로를 납득시켰다. 나는 위층으로 가서 이제 곤히 자고 있는 아기를 요람에 다시 눕혔다. 하지만 불을 끄러 주방에 돌아왔을 때, 나는 뒤쪽의 베란다 문이 활짝 열려 있는 것을 보았다.

어휘
lift 들어 올리다   crib 유아용 침대   draft 외풍   surround 둘러싸다

presence 영혼, 존재   wildly 거칠게, 미친 듯이   out of the ordinary 보통과 다른   still 정지한, 움직이지 않는   convince 납득시키다, 확신시키다   soundly (잠든 모양이) 곤히   back porch 뒤쪽의 베란다   [문제] vigorous 활기 있는   frightening 무서운   irritating 짜증 나는

구문해설
[1행] It was late, just after 2 a.m., when I woke up [to **hear** the baby **crying**].: [ ]는 결과를 나타내는 부사적 용법의 to부정사구, 지각동사 hear 의 목적격보어로 현재분사 crying 사용
[10행] I went upstairs and put the baby, [now sleeping soundly], back into his crib.: [ ]는 삽입구로 the baby를 수식하는 현재분사구

문제해설
필자가 한밤중에 집 안에서 한기와 함께 섬뜩함을 느꼈고, 뒤쪽의 베란다 문 또한 열려 있었다는 내용으로 보아 ④ '겁나고 무서운' 분위기임을 알 수 있다.

20 ④ 글의 요지

최근, 활생균에 관하여 많은 주장들이 제기되어 왔다. 활생균을 포함한 음료들은 아픈 아이가 울지 않게 할 수 있다고 한다. 임신 기간 동안 활생균을 먹는 것은 또한 신생아들에게 천식이 생기는 것을 예방할 수 있다고 보고되었다. 이에 대응하여, 미국 소아과학회는 활생균에 관해서 무엇이 사실이고 무엇이 허구인지를 명확하게 하려는 보고서를 발표했다. 도달된 결론은 활생균이 아직 기적의 치료제로서의 자격을 얻지 못한다는 것이다. 비록 그것이 해로운 것으로 여겨지지는 않지만, 요거트와 그래놀라와 같은 식품의 보충물로서 활생균을 활용하는 것의 효과성에 대해서 시행된 연구는 거의 없다. 그리고 활생균이 임신 중이거나 아이에게 수유하는 엄마들에 의해 섭취되었을 때 아기들의 천식이나 습진의 위험을 줄이는 데 효과적이라는 근거는 훨씬 더 적다.

어휘
claim 주장   regarding …에 관하여   probiotics 활생균   consume 소비하다; *먹다   pregnancy 임신 (기간)   asthma 천식   release 발표하다   clarify 명확하게 하다   fiction 허구   when it comes to …에 관한 한   qualify …할 자격을 얻다   supplement 보충물, 추가물   nurse 간호하다; *젖 먹이다

구문해설
[2행] **It** has been said [that drinks {containing probiotics} can *stop* a sick baby *from crying*].: It은 가주어이고 [ ]가 진주어, { }는 drinks를 수식하는 현재분사구, 'stop+O+from v-ing'「…가 ~하는 것을 막다」
[15행] ... probiotics are effective in reducing the risk of asthma or eczema in babies [when (they are) taken by mothers {who are pregnant or(who are) nursing a child}].: [ ]는 때를 나타내는 부사절('주어+be동사'가 생략된 형태), { }는 mothers를 선행사로 하는 주격 관계대명사절

문제해설
④ 활생균의 효과와 관련해 많은 주장들이 제기되고 있으나 그 효과에 대한 연구는 거의 없으며, 활생균을 기적의 치료제로 보기에는 그 근거가 부족하다고 이야기하고 있다.

21 ② 함축 의미 추론

어떤 사람들은 스스로 성형수술을 받는다. 그러나 다른 사람들은 그들 개의 귀나 꼬리의 일부가 잘리는 데 돈을 지불하면서 성형수술을 받게 한다. 이 잔인한 관행은 고대 로마로 거슬러 올라가는데, 그곳 사람들은 그것이 광견병을 예방한다고 믿었다. 그것은 또한 부상을 예방하기 위해서 사냥이나 싸움에 이용된 개들에게 행해졌다. 그것이 세금을 피하는 방법인 곳들도 있었는데, 제거된 꼬리는 개가 일에 이용되어서 애완동물로 과세되지 않는다는 것을 나타냈다. 그러나 요즘에는 단순히 특정 품

종에 더 호감 가는 외모를 부여하기 위해 그것이 시행된다. 다시 말해서, 개들은 어떤 사람들이 그들을 패션 액세서리로 간주하기 때문에 불필요하고 고통스러운 수술을 받고 있다. 개의 꼬리를 제거하는 것은 특히 잔인한데, 개의 꼬리는 개들이 서로 의사소통하는 방식의 필수적인 부분이기 때문이다. 꼬리가 없는 개는 다른 개들에게 오해받아, 아마 <u>사회적 추방자</u>가 되게 할 것이다.

어휘
cosmetic surgery 성형수술   brutal 잔혹한   practice 관행, 관례   injury 부상, 상처   tax 세금(taxable 과세되는)   breed 품종   desirable 바람직한, 호감 가는   appearance (겉)모습, 외모   undergo 겪다   surgical 외과의, 수술의   procedure 절차, 방법   accessory 액세서리   cruel 잔인한   outcast 따돌림[버림]받는 사람   [문제] unusually 대단히; *특이하게   aggressive 공격적인

구문해설
(2행) Others, however, **have** it **done** to their dogs, [paying to **have** part of their ears or tail **cut off**].: 'have+O+p.p.' 「…가 ~되게 하다」, [ ]는 부대상황을 나타내는 분사구문
(7행) There were even places [where it was a way of avoiding taxes]—a removed tail showed [that a dog was used for work and therefore not taxable as a pet].: 첫 번째 [ ]는 places를 선행사로 하는 관계부사절, 두 번째 [ ]는 showed의 목적어로 쓰인 명사절
(17행) A tailless dog will likely be misunderstood by other dogs, [possibly causing it to become a social outcast].: [ ]는 결과를 나타내는 분사구문

문제해설
개의 꼬리는 다른 개들과 서로 의사소통하는 데 중요한 부분이며 꼬리가 없으면 다른 개들에게 오해를 받는다고 했으므로, 밑줄 친 '사회적 추방자'가 의미하는 바로 가장 적절한 것은 ② '다른 개들에게 받아들여지지 않는 개'이다.

22 ⑤ 필자의 주장

최선을 다하는데도 성적이 나아지질 않는가? 무엇이 이런 소득 없는 결과를 초래하는지 아는가? 두뇌는 시간당 최소한 10분간의 휴식이 필요하다는 것을 아는 사람은 거의 없다. 따라서 학생들이 쉬지 않고 몇 시간 동안 공부를 하면, 실제로 기억력 감퇴를 초래하게 된다. 쉴 틈이 없으면 두뇌는 정보를 중간 기억으로 저장하게 되는데, 그 기억은 일시적으로만 지속된다. 결과적으로 학생들은 공부하는 동안에는 정보를 기억하지만 장기 기억으로 저장하지는 못한다. 다음 날 시험 치는 동안 학생들이 기억할 수 있는 것이라고는 어제는 답을 알았지만 오늘은 모른다는 것뿐이다! 그러니 매 시간마다 적어도 10분간의 휴식을 취하면 기억력과 회상력이 크게 향상될 것이라는 점을 기억하라.

어휘
fruitless 열매를 맺지 못한; *보람 없는   loss 상실; *쇠퇴   store 저장하다   intermediate 중간의   temporarily 일시적으로   recall 상기하다; *회상(력), 상기   dramatically 극적으로

구문해설
(2행) Do you know [what causes this fruitless result]?: [ ]는 know의 목적어로 쓰인 의문사절
(11행) …, all [that students remember] is [that yesterday they knew the answer and today they don't (know the answer)]!: 첫 번째 [ ]는 all을 선행사로 하는 목적격 관계대명사절, 두 번째 [ ]는 주격보어로 쓰인 명사절

문제해설
⑤ 매 시간마다 10분씩 휴식을 취하면서 공부하는 것이 쉬지 않고 공부하는 것보다 학습한 내용을 기억하고 회상하는 데 더 효과적이라는 내용이다.

23 ④ 글의 주제

얼핏 보면 마이애미에 있는 침례교 병원의 응급 센터는 병원이라기보다는 고급 호텔처럼 보인다. 아름답게 꾸며진 정원에서부터 멋지게 장식된 로비까지, 그곳에 고통이나 피의 흔적은 전혀 없다. 수 세기 동안 병원이라는 말은 고통과 죽음의 이미지를 떠올리게 했다. 그러나 침례교 병원 응급 센터와 미국에 있는 여러 다른 새 병원 시설들이 증명하듯, 이러한 이미지는 빠르게 변하고 있다. 1980년대에 새로운 도구와 사고방식, 그리고 생명을 연장하는 치료법에 의해 이루어진 보건 분야의 혁명은 건축에서의 비슷한 혁명과 일치한다. 밋밋한 흰색의 병원 인테리어는 이제 파스텔톤의 벽과 우아하게 설계된 병실들로 교체되고 있다.

어휘
at first glance 얼핏 보기에   emergency 응급   fancy 고급의   landscape 풍경; *미화하다, 꾸미다   decorate 장식하다   facility 시설   revolution 혁명   prolong 연장하다, 늘이다   architecture 건축   plain 밋밋한, 장식 없는   replace 대체하다   pastel-colored 파스텔톤의   elegantly 우아하게   [문제] innovation 혁신   appearance (겉)모습, 외양

구문해설
(9행) The 1980s revolution in health care, [driven by new tools, attitudes, and cures {that prolong life}], is matched by a similar revolution in architecture.: [ ]는 The 1980s … health care를 수식하는 과거분사구, { }는 cures를 선행사로 하는 주격 관계대명사절

문제해설
의학·보건 분야의 혁명과 함께 병원의 내외부적 건축 양식에도 혁명이 일어났다는 내용이므로, ④ '병원 외양의 변화'가 주제로 가장 적절하다.

24 ② 글의 제목

1970년대 중반에 랩 음악이 처음 나왔을 때, 그것이 계속되리라 생각한 사람은 거의 없었다. 음악 평론가들은 그것이 진정한 음악이 아니라고 말했으며, 음반 회사들은 그것이 너무 흑인 중심적이라 백인 청중들이 받아들이기 어렵다고 느꼈고, 부모들은 최신의 일시적 유행으로 여겨 그것을 무시했다. 1992년 1월경, 래퍼들은 공식적으로 발표되는 200개의 최고 인기 앨범 목록에서 3위만큼 높이 올랐다. 다음 10년 동안, 랩 음악은 미국 대중문화에서 강력하고도 논쟁을 불러일으키는 세력이 되었다. 할렘과 남브롱크스의 거리에서부터 초라하게 시작해서, 랩 음악은 라디오, 뮤직비디오, 토크쇼, 콘서트, 배우인 래퍼, 영화음악과 광고뿐만 아니라 음악 CD를 통해 주류 대중매체로 진출했다.

어휘
critic 평론가   cross over 넘다, 건너다   dismiss 해산시키다; *(생각 등을) 묵살하다   fad 변덕; *일시적 유행   controversial 논쟁의 여지가 있는   force 힘, 세력   humble 겸손한; *초라한   mainstream 주류의   soundtrack (판매용의) 영화음악   advertising 광고   [문제] origin 기원

구문해설
(4행) … it was **too** black-oriented **to cross over** to a white audience, …: 'too … to-v' 「너무 …해서 ~할 수 없다」
(6행) …, rappers had reached **as** high **as** number three on the official top 200 album list.: 'as … as ~' 「~만큼 …한」
(12행) … through CDs, **as well as** radio, music videos, …, and advertising.: 'A as well as B' 「B뿐만 아니라 A도」

문제해설
② 랩 음악이 처음 나왔을 때 다들 회의적이었지만, 지금은 대중음악의 주류가 될 정도로 성장했다는 내용이다.

25 ① 도표 내용 불일치

위 그래프는 사람들이 하루에 앉아서 보내는 시간과 그들의 전반적인 수면의 질 사이의 관련성을 보여준다. (하루에 6~8시간을 앉아서 보낸 사람들은 자신의 전반적인 수면의 질을 '아주 좋음'이라고 보고할 가능성이 가장 높았는데, 해당 그룹의 4분의 3이 그렇게 했다.) 하지만, '꽤 좋은' 수면을 보고한 응답자의 비율은 하루에 8~10시간 동안 앉아 있었던 그룹에서 가장 높았다. 그에 반해서, 하루에 10시간 또는 그 이상 앉아 있었던 사람들은 '몹시 나쁜' 또는 '꽤 나쁜' 수면의 질을 보고할 가능성이 가장 높았다. 하루에 가장 적은 시간 동안 앉아 있었던 그룹과 가장 많은 시간 동안 앉아 있었던 그룹은 '몹시 나쁜' 수면을 보고한 사람들의 비율이 같았다. 하지만, 가장 짧게 앉아 있었던 사람들은 가장 오래 앉아 있었던 사람들의 2배만큼 '아주 좋은' 수면의 질을 보고할 가능성이 있었다.

어휘
connection 관련성 quality 질(質) fairly 상당히, 꽤 overall 종합적인 be likely to-v …할 가능성이 있다 report 보고하다 quarter 4분의 1 respondent 응답자 in contrast 그에 반해서

구문해설
3행 People [who **spent** six to eight hours **sitting** each day] were most likely to report the overall quality of their sleep as "very good," *with* three quarters of the group *doing so*.: [ ]는 People을 선행사로 하는 주격 관계대명사절, 'spend+시간+v-ing' 「…하는 데 시간을 보내다」, 'with+O+현재분사' 「…가 ~하면서, ~한 채」, doing so는 report the overall quality of their sleep as "very good"을 대신함

15행 However, the people [who sat the least] were **twice as** likely to report "very good" overall sleep quality **as** those [who sat the most] were.: 첫 번째 [ ]는 the people을 선행사로 하는 주격 관계대명사절, '배수사+as … as' 「~배만큼 …한」, 두 번째 [ ]는 those를 선행사로 하는 주격 관계대명사절

문제해설
① 도표에서 하루에 6~8시간 앉아 있었던 사람들의 25퍼센트(4분의 1)가 '아주 좋은' 수면의 질을 보고했다.

26 ② 내용 불일치

트리스탄 다 쿠냐를 방문하는 것은 마치 다른 세계, 다른 삶, 그리고 다른 시대를 방문하는 것과 같다. 인구는 고작 300명 미만으로 섬 주민들 사이에는 헤이건, 로저스, 글라스, 라바렐로, 스웨인, 그린, 그리고 리페토라는 7개의 성씨만이 존재한다. 많은 사람들이 수도인 에든버러에 사는데, 그곳은 모든 현대적 편의 시설을 갖췄음에도 불구하고 몇 세기나 뒤진 것처럼 느껴진다. 비록 모국어가 영어이긴 하지만, 특이한 옛날식 영어이다. 트리스탄 다 쿠냐는 튼튼한 경제와 낮은 소득세로 자급자족을 한다. 실업은 거의 없으며 흉악한 범죄도 없다. 어업 이외에 섬의 주요 수입원은 우표 판매인데, 이 우표들은 전 세계 수집가들에 의해 높이 평가된다.

어휘
population 인구 surname 성(姓) convenience (*pl.*) 편리한 설비 old-fashioned 구식의, 유행에 뒤떨어진 self-sufficient 자급자족할 수 있는 income 수입 tax 세금 unemployment 실직, 실업률 crime 범죄 postage stamp 우표 prize 높이 평가하다, 소중히 하다

구문해설
5행 Many live in **the capital city, Edinburgh,** [which feels centuries old … conveniences].: the capital city와 Edinburgh는 동격, [ ]는 Edinburgh를 선행사로 하는 계속적 용법의 주격 관계대명사절

12행 **In addition to** fishing, a main source … postage stamps, [which are prized … world].: 'in addition to' 「… 외에」(= besides), [ ]는 postage stamps를 선행사로 하는 계속적 용법의 주격 관계대명사절

문제해설
② 수도인 에든버러는 몇 세기나 뒤진 것처럼 낡아 보이지만 현대적 편의 시설을 모두 갖추고 있다.

27 ③ 내용 일치

금성과 지구는 몇 가지 유사한 점을 공유하고 있기에 두 행성은 종종 '쌍둥이 행성'이라고 불려왔다. 이 둘은 크기와 색상에서 비슷하다. 두 행성의 직경은 대략 650킬로미터 정도밖에 차이가 나지 않는데, 지구가 금성보다 약간 크다. 또한 이 둘은 모두 파란색으로 보이는데, 물이 지구를 푸르게 보이게 하는 반면, 금성의 대기의 상층 구름들이 금성을 희고 푸른 행성으로 보이게 한다. 이 둘은 모두 육지를 가진 행성이며 이는 그것들이 '단단하다'는 것을 의미하지만, 그것들의 대기는 매우 다르다. 금성의 대기는 지구의 대기보다 밀도가 90배 높은데, 이는 금성이 태양계의 육지 행성 중에 가장 밀도가 높은 대기를 가지고 있음을 의미한다. 언뜻 보기에는 이 두 행성이 매우 비슷하게 보이지만 더 자세히 들여다보면 비슷한 점보다 차이점이 더 많다.

어휘
similarity 유사점 diameter 직경 roughly 대략 terrestrial 육지의 solid 단단한 dense 밀집한, 농후한 at first sight 언뜻 보기에 in detail 상세하게, 자세하게

구문해설
5행 …, **with** Earth **being** a little larger than *the other*.: 'with+O+현재분사' 「…가 ~하면서, ~한 채」, the other는 특정한 둘(금성과 지구) 중 나머지 하나인 금성을 가리키는 부정대명사

6행 They both also **appear to be** blue in color; water *makes* Earth *appear* blue, …: 'appear to-v' 「…처럼 보이다, …인 것 같다」, 'make+O+동사원형' 「…을 ~하게 하다」

11행 The atmosphere of Venus is **90 times denser than** *that* of Earth, …: '배수사+비교급+than …' 「…보다 몇 배 더 ~한」, that은 The atmosphere를 지칭

문제해설
① 두 행성 모두 파란색으로 보인다. ② 지구가 금성보다 약간 크다고 했으므로 지구의 직경이 금성의 직경보다 길다. ④ 두 행성 모두 육지를 가지고 있다. ⑤ 태양계의 육지 행성 중 가장 밀도가 높은 대기를 가지고 있는 행성은 금성이다.

28 ④ 내용 불일치

스프링빌 여름 미술 캠프
스프링빌 시민 문화 회관은 이제 초등학생들을 위한 미술 캠프를 제공할 예정입니다.
요금 및 시간
종일반: 9:00 ~ 15:00, 200달러
반일반: 9:00 ~ 12:00, 100달러
수업료에는 수업 시간, 미술 용품, 앞치마 및 점심이 포함됩니다.
환불 정책
캠프 첫날 전에 취소하면 전액 환불을 받을 수 있습니다. 첫날 이후에 취소하면 50퍼센트를 환불받을 수 있습니다.
등록 현황 및 등록 서류
6월 18일 ~ 22일 남은 자리: 종일반 0, 반일반 7

6월 25일~29일 남은 자리: 종일반 0, 반일반 19
학생의 이름 및 나이와 함께 아래 양식을 작성하십시오. 자세한 내용은 (415) 773-9244번으로 문의하십시오.

어휘
rate 속도; *요금 cover 덮다; *포함하다 refund 환불 policy 정책 cancellation 취소 be eligible for …에 대한 자격이 있다 availability 유효성; *이용할 수 있는 것 registration 등록 (서류) fill out (양식을) 작성하다

문제해설
④ 캠프 시작 전에는 전액 환불을 받을 수 있다고 나와 있다.

29 ③ 어법

독립 선언문은 미국 역사상 가장 영향력 있는 문서 중의 하나이다. 영국의 왕 조지 3세의 통치하에 있던 미국 식민지 개척자들은 그들의 권리를 위해 투쟁했다. 그들은 부당한 과세, 영국 군인들의 미국 영토 주둔, 그리고 하원의 지방 자치권 결여에 대해 이의를 제기했으나, 결국 혁명에 착수하게 되었다. 토머스 제퍼슨에 의해 초안이 쓰여진 그 선언문은 그들의 독립 주장을 왕에게뿐만 아니라 전 세계에 공표했다. 1776년 7월 4일에 선언문을 채택함으로써 대영제국으로부터의 공식적인 독립이 완성되었다. 그 날은 현재 미국의 독립 기념일로서 기념된다.

어휘
declaration 선언; *선언문 independence 독립 influential 영향을 미치는, 유력한 document 문서 colonist 식민지 개척자 objection 반대 taxation 과세 presence (군대 등의) 주둔 soil 흙, 땅; *국토 authority 권위, 권한 draft 초안하다 separation 분리, 독립 adoption 채택 celebrate 기념하다, 축하하다

구문해설
(10행) ... their claim of independence to the world **as well as** to the king.: 'A as well as B' 「B뿐만 아니라 A도」

문제해설
③ 문장의 주어는 The declaration이며 which ... Jefferson은 이를 선행사로 하는 계속적 용법의 주격 관계대명사절이므로 문장의 동사가 필요하다. 따라서 announcing은 announced가 되어야 한다.

30 ⑤ 어휘

뱅크런은 수많은 은행 고객들이 공황 상태에 빠져 동시에 은행에서 자신의 돈을 인출하는 상황이다. 대개 그러한 사태의 원인이 되는 일련의 점진적인 사건들이 있는데, 그 사건들은 사람들이 그들의 돈의 안전에 대해 걱정하게 하는 경기 침체에서 시작된다. 그들은 자신의 거래 은행이 파산할 위험에 처했다고 여기면, 더 안전하다고 여기는 또 다른 은행으로 돈을 옮기기 시작한다. 다른 은행 고객들은 일어나고 있는 상황을 지켜보고, 그들 역시 자신의 돈을 되돌려줄 것을 요구하기 시작한다. 하지만 은행들은 예금주들이 예금한 돈을 투자하기 때문에, 만약 모든 사람이 동시에 돈을 보류하면(→ 인출하면) 충분한 현금을 수중에 보유하지 못하게 되고, 이는 은행이 지불 불능 상태가 되게 할 수도 있다.

어휘
panic 공황 상태에 빠지다 withdraw 인출하다 institution (은행 등의) 기관, 단체 gradual 점차적인 lead up to …의 원인이 되다 occurrence 사건, 일어난 일 downturn 침체 transfer 옮기다 deposit 예금하다; 예금(액) account 계좌 holder 보유자 on hand 수중에 withhold 억누르다; 보류하다 at once 즉시; *한꺼번에, 동시에 insolvent 지불 불능의, 파산한

구문해설
(4행) There is generally a series of gradual events [that lead up to such an occurrence], [beginning with an economic downturn {that makes people worry about the safety of their money}].: 첫 번째 [ ]는 gradual events를 선행사로 하는 주격 관계대명사절, 두 번째 [ ]는 부대상황을 나타내는 분사구문, { }는 an economic downturn을 선행사로 하는 주격 관계대명사절

(12행) However, **as** banks invest the money [deposited by account holders], they do not have enough cash on hand if everyone withdraws their money at once, [which can *cause* the bank *to become* insolvent].: as는 이유를 나타내는 접속사, 첫 번째 [ ]는 the money를 수식하는 과거분사구, 두 번째 [ ]는 they do not ... at once를 선행사로 하는 계속적 용법의 주격 관계대명사절, 'cause+O+to-v' 「…가 ~하게 하다」

문제해설
⑤ 은행 고객이 모두 한꺼번에 돈을 인출하면 은행이 지불 불능 상태가 된다는 흐름이 적절하므로 withholds(보류하다)는 withdraws(인출하다) 등이 되어야 한다.

31 ④ 빈칸 추론

특정 채소를 먹는 것을 완강히 거부하는 어린아이들은 정서적 혐오 반응을 자주 보인다. 이러한 혐오는 자식들에게 건강한 음식을 주고 싶어 하는 부모에게는 도무지 이해할 수 없는 것으로 보일 수도 있지만, 청결에 대한 태도에 관심이 있는 과학자들은 이를 논리적으로 설명한다. 그들의 주장은 사람들이 낯설고 해로울 수 있는 대상에 대한 보호하는 수단으로서 혐오감을 키워왔다는 것이다. 최근의 연구는 혐오감이 사람들로 하여금 위험한 물질을 먹는 것뿐만 아니라 위험 가능성이 있는 상황에 들어서는 것도 막아준다는 것을 보여주었다. 예를 들어, 그 연구의 참가자들은 붐비는 열차가 비어 있는 열차보다 더 혐오스러우며 이가 벼룩보다 더 혐오스럽다고 했다. 따라서 부모들은 자녀들이 모르는 음식을 먹거나 낯선 곳에 들어가는 것에 대해 방어적인 자세를 보일 때 놀랄 필요가 없다.

어휘
stubbornly 고집스레, 완고하게 refuse 거부하다 reaction 반응 disgust 혐오(disgusting 혐오스러운) rational 합리적인, 논리적인 explanation 설명 measure 수단 object 대상; 물체 demonstrate 논증하다, 증명하다 substance 물질 potentially 잠재적으로 participant 참가자 railcar 철도 차량 defensive 방어적인 [문제] reactive 민감한 detective 탐정(의) protective 보호하는

구문해설
(3행) Though this disgust may seem crazy to parents [who want to ... food], scientists [interested ... cleanliness] have a rational explanation.: 첫 번째 [ ]는 parents를 선행사로 하는 주격 관계대명사절, 두 번째 [ ]는 scientists를 수식하는 과거분사구

(6행) Their argument is [that people have developed disgust as a protective measure against objects {that are ... possibly harmful}].: [ ]는 주격보어로 쓰인 명사절, { }는 objects를 선행사로 하는 주격 관계대명사절

(9행) A recent study has demonstrated [that disgust **prevents** people *not only* **from eating** dangerous substances *but also* **from entering** potentially dangerous situations].: [ ]는 has demonstrated의 목적절, 'prevent+O+from v-ing' 「…가 ~하지 못하게 하다」, 'not only A but also B' 「A뿐만 아니라 B도」

문제해설
최근 연구에 따르면 혐오감이 위험한 음식을 먹거나 위험한 상황에 처하게 되는 것을 막아준다고 했으므로 빈칸에는 '보호하는'이라는 뜻의 ④ protective가 적절하다.

32 ④ 빈칸 추론

사람이 나이가 들수록 잠을 더 적게 자는 것은 잘 알려진 사실이다. 이제 연구는 이러한 수면 양상의 변화가 실제로 진화적 적응일 수도 있음을 보여준다. 먼 과거에 자고 있는 인간들은 밤에 사냥하는 포식자에게 취약해서, 한 사람이 항상 깨어 있으면 무리 전체에게 도움이 되었다. '수면 질 저하 조부모 가설'에 따르면, 나이가 많은 사람들이 결국 이 역할을 하기 시작했다. 이것은 왜 초기 인류는 연령대가 섞인 무리에서 잠을 자는 경향이 있었는가를 설명할 수도 있다. 연구원들은 탄자니아에 있는 한 무리의 수렵 채집인들을 대상으로 그들의 가설을 시험했다. 220시간이 넘는 시간 중에, 그들은 총 18분 동안만 모든 성인들이 깊이 잠들었음을 관찰했다. 나머지 시간 동안에, 그 무리의 약 3분의 1은 깨어 있거나 선잠을 잤다.

어휘
suggest 제의[제안]하다   distant 먼   vulnerable 취약한, 연약한   predator 포식자   entire 전체의   benefit 유익하다; 득을 보다   hypothesis 가설   eventually 결국   observe 관찰하다   sound asleep 깊이 잠이 든   [문제] evolutionary 진화의   adaptation 적응   temporary 일시적인   transformation 변화, 변형

구문해설
1행 **It** is a well-known fact [that people sleep less *as* they get older].: It은 가주어이고 [ ]가 진주어, as는 「…함에 따라」라는 의미의 접속사

4행 In the distant past, **sleeping** humans were vulnerable to predators [that hunted at night], ...: sleeping은 humans를 수식하는 현재분사. [ ]는 predators를 선행사로 하는 주격 관계대명사절

13행 ..., they observed a total of only 18 minutes [during which all of the adults were sound asleep].: [ ]는 a total of only 18 minutes를 선행사로 하는 목적격 관계대명사절

문제해설
④ 연구에서 초기 인류는 밤에 사냥하는 포식자로부터 무리를 보호하기 위해 나이가 많은 사람들이 깨어 있는 역할을 했다고 했으므로, 사람이 나이가 들수록 잠을 더 적게 자는 수면 양상은 '진화적 적응'임을 추론할 수 있다.

33 ③ 빈칸 추론

이상하게 들릴지 모르지만, 과학적 가설의 대다수는 <u>옳다고 증명될 수 없다</u>! 이 간단한 가설을 예로 들어 보자. "같은 높이에서 떨어진 모든 물체는 동시에 땅에 부딪힐 것이다." 만약 이것이 틀린 가설이라면, 그것이 옳지 않다는 것을 보여주는 것은 꽤 쉬울 것이다. 그런데 만약 그것이 사실이라면, 당신은 어떻게 이것을 확실히 알 수 있겠는가? 그것이 '모든 두 물체들'의 움직임을 설명하기 때문에, 당신은 존재하는 모든 물체들의 조합을 실험해야 할 텐데, 이는 확실히 불가능한 일이다. 광범위한 실험을 통하여, 당신은 그 가설에 굉장한 자신감을 얻을 수 있겠지만, 그것이 확실한 사실이라고는 결코 확신할 수 없을 것이다. 당신이 실험한 그 다음 한 쌍의 물체들은 그 가설과는 일치하지 않는 방식으로 움직일 가능성이 항상 있을 것이다.

어휘
majority of 다수의   hypothesis 가설(*pl.* hypotheses)   object 물건, 물체   false 틀린, 사실이 아닌   behavior 움직임   combination 조합[결합](물)   in existence 현존하는   extensive 광범위한   absolute 완전한, 완벽한; *확실한   manner 방식   inconsistent 내용이 다른, 모순되는   [문제] involve 수반하다, 포함하다   completely 완전히, 전적으로   supernatural 초자연적인   phenomenon 현상(*pl.* phenomena)

구문해설
1행 **As strange as it might sound**, the majority of scientific hypotheses cannot be proven correct!: 'as+)형용사+as+S+V' 「…일지라도」(양보의 의미)

5행 If this **were** a false hypothesis, *it* **would be** quite easy [to show {that it was incorrect}].: 'If+S+동사의 과거형 .... S+조동사의 과거형+동사원형 ~'은 현재 사실과 반대되는 일을 가정하는 가정법 과거. it은 가주어이고 [ ]가 진주어, { }는 show의 목적절

14행 **There** would always **be a chance that** the next pair of objects [that you tested] would behave in a manner [inconsistent with the hypothesis].: 'there is a chance that ...'은 「…할 가능성이 있다」의 의미로, that은 a chance의 동격절을 이끄는 접속사. 첫 번째 [ ]는 the next pair of objects를 선행사로 하는 목적격 관계대명사절, 두 번째 [ ]는 a manner를 수식하는 형용사구

문제해설
빈칸 뒤에서 과학적 가설의 사실 여부 확인이 현실적으로 불가능한 예시가 제시되었으므로 빈칸에는 ③ '옳다고 증명될 수 없다'가 가장 적절하다.

34 ① 빈칸 추론

서양의 의사들은 전통적인 치료사들이 항상 숙지하고 있었던 사실을 마침내 배우고 있는데, 그것은 바로 <u>몸과 마음은 분리될 수 없다</u>는 것이다. 서구에서는 최근까지, 몸을 치료하기 위해 (내과) 의사를, 마음을 치료하기 위해 정신과 의사를, 그리고 영혼을 치유하기 위해 성직자를 찾아갔다. 그러나 이제 서양의 의학계는 전인적 의학에 더 많은 관심을 기울이는데, 이는 인간의 마음 상태가 신체 건강에 영향을 미칠 수 있고, 그 반대도 가능하다고 믿는다. 전인적 의학에 대한 인식이 매우 널리 퍼져서 세계 보건 기구는 심지어 그들의 권고사항을 변경했다. 세계 보건 기구는 현재 어떤 경우에는 의사들이 처방약과 함께 전통적인 치료법을 사용하는 것을 고려한다면 더 큰 성공을 거둘지도 모른다고 말하고 있다.

어휘
healer 치료자, 의사(heal 치료하다)   physician (내과) 의사   consult (의사에게) 진찰받다   psychiatrist 정신과 의사   priest 성직자   wellness 건강   vice versa 반대의 경우도 마찬가지   recognition 인식   World Health Organization (유엔) 세계 보건 기구   state 진술하다. (분명히) 말하다   therapy 요법, 치료   alongside …와 함께   prescription 처방전   [문제] inseparable 분리할 수 없는

구문해설
4행 ..., physicians **have been consulted to heal** the body, psychiatrists (have been consulted to heal) the mind, and priests (have been consulted to heal) the soul.: 두 개의 ( )는 모두 앞에 언급된 have been consulted to heal과 공통된 어구이기 때문에 생략되어 있음

10행 ... is spreading **so** much **that** the World Health Organization has even changed ...: 'so ... that ~ 「너무 …해서 ~하다」

문제해설
서양 의사들이 주목하고 있는 전인적 의학의 핵심은 신체 건강과 마음 상태의 상호 관계성이므로 빈칸에는 ① '몸과 마음은 분리될 수 없다'가 적절하다.

35 ④ 흐름과 무관한 문장

한 사람의 쓰레기가 다른 사람의 보물이라고 종종 이야기된다. 이것은 Robert Bezeau라는 이름의 한 남성의 프로젝트를 서술하는 적절한 방법이다. 그것은 2012년에 시작되었는데, 그가 파나마에서 재활용 프로그램을 담당했던 때였다. 수천 개의 플라스틱병을 모은 후, 그는 그것들로 유용한 어떤 일을 하기로 결심했다. 한 팀의 지역 주민들과 함께, 그는 '벽

돌'을 만들기 위해 병을 철사로 감았다. 이 벽돌들은 그러고 나서 건물을 만드는 데 사용되었다. 사실, 그들에게 너무 많은 벽돌이 있어서 사람들이 하룻밤 보낼 수 있는 4층짜리 성을 포함하여 마을 전체를 만들었다. (결과적으로, 사람들은 그들의 생존 기술 덕분에 플라스틱 건물의 환경에 적응했다.) Bezeau는 그의 마을이 사람들에게 얼마나 많은 플라스틱 쓰레기가 존재하는지 깨닫게 하고 그것을 사용하는 다른 혁신적인 방법을 생각하게 만들기를 바란다.

어휘
apt 적절한　be in charge of ~을 담당하다　wire 철사　brick 벽돌 story 이야기; *(건물의) 층　consequently 그 결과, 따라서　adapt 적응하다 exist 존재하다　innovative 혁신적인

구문해설
(2행) This is an apt way [to describe the project of a man {named Robert Bezeau}].: [ ]는 an apt way를 수식하는 형용사적 용법의 to부정사구, { }는 a man을 수식하는 과거분사구

(10행) In fact, they had **so** many bricks **that** they made a whole village, [**including** a four-story castle {that people could spend the night in}].: 'so ... that ~' 「너무 …해서 ~하다」, [ ]는 including(…을 포함하여)이 이끄는 전치사구, { }는 a four-story castle을 선행사로 하는 목적격 관계대명사절

(15행) Bezeau hopes [(that) his village will **make** people **realize** {how much plastic waste exists} and **think** of other innovative ways *to use it*].: [ ]는 hopes의 목적어로 쓰인 명사절, 'make+O+동사원형' 「…가 ~하게 하다」의 의미이며 realize와 think는 등위 접속사 and로 병렬 연결, { }는 realize의 목적어로 쓰인 의문사절, to use it은 other innovative ways를 수식하는 형용사적 용법의 to부정사구

문제해설
Bezeau가 추진한 프로젝트를 통해 사람들이 플라스틱 쓰레기가 얼마나 많은지 깨닫고 그것을 사용하는 혁신적인 방법을 생각하기를 바란다는 내용으로, 사람들이 생존 기술 덕분에 플라스틱 건물의 환경에 적응했다는 내용인 ④는 전체 흐름과 무관하다.

36 ④ 글의 순서

　인간은 어떤 선천적인 맛의 선호를 갖고 태어난다. 예를 들어, 우리는 달콤한 맛이 나는 것들을 좋아하지만, 쓴 맛이 나는 음식을 싫어한다. (C) 이것은 달콤함이란 음식에 우리에게 유익한 열량을 주는 설탕이 함유되어 있다는 표시이기 때문이다. 반면에, 쓴 맛은 독성 물질이 있음을 나타낸다. 이러한 선호는 우리가 나이 들어감에 따라 변하며, 경험에 의해서도 영향 받을 수 있다. (A) 예를 들어, 아이들은 흔히 쓴 맛 때문에 특정 채소들을 기피한다. 하지만 그들이 이 채소들을 주기적으로 먹으면, 그 맛에 익숙해질 것이고 심지어 그 채소들을 좋아하기 시작할지도 모른다. 하지만 풍미의 선호는 다르다. (B) 맛은 미뢰로 감지되는 반면, 풍미는 주로 후각에 의해 감지된다. 우리가 가장 좋아하는 풍미는 우리가 어린 시절에 경험하는 것에 영향을 받는다. 이것은 우리가 아직 태아일 때 임신 상태의 어머니가 먹는 음식을 기반으로 시작된다.

어휘
natural 자연의; *타고난, 선천적인　preference 선호(도)　bitter (맛이) 쓴 avoid 피하다　detect 발견하다[감지하다]　influence 영향을 주다 pregnant 임신한　contain …이 들어[함유되어] 있다　beneficial 유익한, 이로운　indicate 나타내다　toxic 유독성의　compound 화합물

구문해설
(2행) For example, we enjoy things [that taste sweet], but we

dislike foods [that taste bitter].: 두 개의 [ ]는 각각 things와 foods를 선행사로 하는 주격 관계대명사절

(12행) The flavors [(that) we enjoy most] are influenced by [what we experience at an early age].: 첫 번째 [ ]는 The flavors를 선행사로 하는 목적격 관계대명사절, 두 번째 [ ]는 by의 목적어로 쓰인 관계대명사절

(17행) This is because sweetness is a sign [that a food contains sugars, {which give us beneficial calories}].: a sign과 [ ]는 동격, { }는 sugars를 선행사로 하는 계속적 용법의 주격 관계대명사절

문제해설
④ 특정한 맛(taste)에 대한 선호를 가지고 태어나는 인간은 달콤한 것을 좋아하고 쓴 것을 싫어한다는 주어진 글에 이어, 달콤한 맛과 쓴 맛의 선호도 차이에 대한 이유와 이러한 선호가 나이와 경험에 따라 변할 수 있다는 (C)가 온 뒤, 특정 채소를 싫어하던 아이가 꾸준히 먹는 경험을 통해 그 채소를 좋아하게 될 수 있다는 예시인 (A)가 오고, 맛(taste)과 달리 풍미(flavor)는 어린 시절 경험의 영향을 받는다는 내용의 (B)로 이어지는 것이 자연스럽다.

37 ⑤ 글의 순서

　집을 환하게 하고 산소를 생성하며, 우리가 숨쉬는 공기를 정화해주는 등 실내 화초는 우리를 위해 많은 좋은 역할을 한다. 그러나 이 모든 것에도 불구하고, 우리는 규칙적으로 물을 주어 그것들을 돌볼 것을 종종 잊어버린다. (C) 고맙게도 이제는 (물 주는 것을) 잘 잊어버리는 화초 주인들을 위한 해결책이 있다. 자주 물 주는 것을 필요로 하는 실내 화초들의 흙 속에 넣을 수 있는 감지 장치이다. (B) 이 감지 장치는 휴대전화나 인터넷으로 메시지를 보냄으로써 식물의 현재 상태에 관한 정보를 전달한다. 그것은 (물 주는 것을) 상기시키는 신호와 식물로부터 고맙다는 내용의 메시지, 그리고 심지어 물을 과하게 주었거나 덜 준 것에 대한 경고(의 메시지)를 보낼 수 있다. (A) 그러한 메시지들은 이 장치들이 전자파를 내보내 수분의 정도에 대한 데이터를 수집하고, 그것들을 최적의 수준과 비교하기 때문에 (전송) 가능하다. 그리고 나서 이 정보는 지역 네트워크로 보내지고, 메시지가 전송된다.

어휘
purify 정화하다　houseplant 실내 화분용 화초　water 물을 주다　emit 방사하다, 내뿜다　moisture 습기, 수분　optimal 최선의, 최적의　transmit 전달하다; *(전파를) 보내다, 전송하다　convey 전달하다　reminder 상기시키는 조언, 암시, 신호　in need of …을 필요로 하는

구문해설
(4행) ..., we often **forget to take** care of them by watering them regularly.: 'forget to-v' 「…할 것을 잊어버리다」(cf. 'forget v-ing' 「…했던 것을 잊어버리다」)

문제해설
⑤ 주어진 글에서 제시된, 사람들이 화초에 물 주는 것을 종종 잊어버리는 문제점에 대한 해결책이 (C)에서 제시되고 있다. (C)의 a sensor를 (B)의 This sensing device로 받아 설명하고, (B)에서 설명되고 있는 메시지들을 (A)의 첫 부분의 Such messages로 받아 이 메시지들이 어떤 과정을 통해 사람들에게 전달되는지를 설명하는 것이 자연스럽다.

38 ② 주어진 문장의 위치

　러시아의 심리학자이자 의사인 이반 파블로프는 아마도 개가 종소리를 듣고 침을 흘리도록 훈련시킨 실험으로 가장 잘 알려져 있을 것이다. 초기 연구에서 파블로프는 타액 분비가 먼저 일어나지 않는다면 위는 소

화 작용을 시작하지 않을 것이라는 점에 주목했다. 다시 말해, 그는 그 두 가지 과정들이 비록 신체의 다른 부분에서 일어날지라도 어떻게 해서든지 신경계에서는 연결되어 있다는 것을 인지했다. 실험에서, 그는 실험용 개들에게 먹이를 줄 때, 울리는 종과 같은 자극에 개들을 반복해서 노출시켰다. 이것은 결국 그 개들이 먹이가 없을 때조차도 종소리에 의해 자극을 받으면 침을 흘리게 만들었다. 그는 또한 그 자극이 너무 자주 '잘못된' 것으로 밝혀진다면 이러한 종류의 조건 반사는 사라진다는 것을 보여주었다. 예를 들어, 만약에 계속해서 먹이는 나타나지 않은 채 종이 울린다면, 개들은 그 소리에 침을 흘리는 것을 멈출 것이다.

구문해설
13행) This eventually **caused** them **to salivate** [when (they were) stimulated by the bell], *even if* there was no food **present**.: 'cause+O+to-v' 「…가 ~하게 하다」, [ ]는 때를 나타내는 부사절(주어+be동사가 생략된 형태). 'even if' 「비록 …할지라도」, present는 food를 뒤에서 수식하는 형용사

17행) For instance, *if*, over and over, the bell **rang** without *food appearing*, the dogs **would** *stop* salivating at the sound.: 'If+S+동사의 과거형 …. S+조동사의 과거형+동사원형 ~'은 현재 사실과 반대되는 일을 가정하는 가정법 과거. appearing은 without의 목적어로 쓰인 동명사이며 food는 동명사의 의미상 주어. 'stop v-ing' 「…하는 것을 그만두다」

문제해설
주어진 문장에서 언급된 신체의 다른 부분에서 일어나는 the two processes는 ② 앞에 나온 타액 분비와 소화 작용을 일컫는 말이므로 ②에 들어가는 것이 적절하다.

39 ⑤ 주어진 문장의 위치

한때 석탄 산업이 번창했던 지역인 홋카이도의 유바리는, 이제 그 도시가 기능을 수행하기 위해 필요한 자금이 부족해진 것을 알게 되었다. 여러 해에 걸쳐 그 도시의 부채는 연간 예산의 13배에 이를 정도로 엄청나게 늘어났다. 그러나, 그 기간 동안 유바리는 대출을 받아 도시의 부채를 조용히 은폐했는데, 이는 그 도시의 재정적인 문제를 악화시켰다. 더 심각한 것은 생활비용이 너무 높이 올라서 주민들은 결코 그곳에서 살 수가 없다는 것이었다. 인구는 결국 1960년의 12만 명에서 단 1만 명으로 감소하였다. 더 많은 시민들이 떠나는 것을 막으려는 절박한 시도로, 그 도시는 관광 수입을 벌어들이기를 바라며 호텔과 스키 휴양지와 같은 다양한 인기시설에 투자했다. 그러나, 그러한 시도들은 도시의 안 좋은 이미지에 의해 성공하지 못했고, 시 정부가 그것의 재정상의 실패로부터 회생할 수 있을지 의심스러워 보인다.

구문해설
5행) Yubari, Hokkaido, [once the site … industry], now **finds** itself **lacking** the money [[(that) it needs *to function*].: 첫 번째 [ ]는 Yubari와 동격. find의 목적격보어로 현재분사 lacking가 쓰임. 두 번째 [ ]는 the money를 선행사로 하는 목적격 관계대명사절. to function은 목적을 나타내는 부사적 용법의 to부정사

12행) **Worse**, the cost of everyday expenses rose *so high that* residents simply could not afford to live there.: worse는 「더욱 심하게, 더 나쁘게」라는 의미의 부사. 'so … that ~' 「너무 …해서 ~하다」

문제해설
재정 악화에 따른 급격한 인구 감소에 대한 내용 다음인 ⑤에 이러한 인구 감소를 막기 위해 유바리 시가 새로운 시도를 했다는 내용의 주어진 문장이 오는 것이 자연스럽다.

40 ② 요약문 완성

아메리카 대륙의 초기 문명에 대한 신뢰할 만한 지식은 고고학적인 기록에 한정되어 있다. 그 이유는 원래의 유물들 대부분이 유럽의 정복자들에 의해 파괴되었기 때문이다. 그럼에도 불구하고 우리는 건축, 의술, 천문학, 수학, 공학 분야의 인상적인 업적들에 대한 증거를 가지고 있다. 그러한 업적들은 그들의 지식을 상실한 것에 대한 안타까움뿐만 아니라 이 문명들에 대한 경외감 또한 불러일으킨다. 농업 분야에서, 이들 문명은 감자, 옥수수, 콩, 토마토, 초콜릿 등을 포함시켜 오늘날 지구의 식량을 대단히 풍족하게 했다. 그러나 우리는 많은 의약적인 경험뿐만 아니라 마야의 천문학자들과 잉카의 건축가들의 비법까지도 잃어버렸다. 아마도 가장 큰 손실은 인생과 우주에 대한 아메리카 원주민들의 사고방식이었을 것이다. 왜냐하면 이들은 좀처럼 자연에 맞서 싸우지 않고, 그 대신 자연에 순응하는 것을 선택했기 때문이다.

구문해설
17행) … seldom warred with nature, [**choosing** instead **to adapt** to it].: [ ]는 연속동작을 나타내는 분사구문. 'choose to-v' 「…하는 쪽을 택하다, …하기로 결정하다」

문제해설
② 아메리카 원주민 문명의 풍부한 문화유산이 파괴된 것은 무척 유감스러운 일이다.

41 ⑤   42 ② 장문

로버트 카파는 젊은 시절을 파리에서 주로 지역 신문의 사진 기사를 작성하며 보냈다. 그의 상사가 스페인 내전의 사진을 찍으라고 그를 파견한 1936년이 되어서야 그의 작품이 유럽 전역의 일류 잡지와 신문에 실렸다. 그에게 광범위한 국제적 명성을 가져다준 사진은 죽어가고 있는 어느 반(反) 프랑코 장군파 병사의 사진이었다. 그 사진은 언론에서 널리 사용되는 전쟁의 강렬한 상징이 되었다. 1939년, 스페인 내전이 끝난 직후, 카파는 뉴욕에서 잠시 일했다. 그러나 그는 제2차 세계대전이 발발하자 재빨리 유럽으로 돌아가 그곳에서 사진을 찍으며 6년을 머물렀다. 노르망디에 상륙하고 있는 영국 병사들을 찍은 그의 사진들은 역사상 가장 기억에 남을 전쟁 사진 중 일부가 되었다. 카파가 자유공로훈장을 받은 것이 바로 이 사진들 덕분이었다.

전쟁 사진작가로서의 카파의 일은 매우 위험한 경우가 많았지만, 위험에도 불구하고 그는 항상 "당신의 사진이 만족스럽지 않다면, 당신은 충분히 가까이 다가가지 않은 것이다"라고 말했다. 그러나 1954년 5월 25일, 아시아에서 임무를 수행하던 도중, 카파는 지뢰를 밟아 즉사했다. 오

늘날 로버트 카파는 사상 최고의 전쟁 사진작가 중 한 명으로 간주된다. 그는 카메라를 이용해 전쟁의 참상을 기록한 뛰어난 사진기자였다. 놀라운 일도 아니지만 카파는 전쟁을 증오했고, 그것을 바꿀 수 없음을 증오했다. 한 인터뷰에서 그는, 타인의 고통을 기록하는 것 외에 아무것도 할 수 없으며, 단지 한쪽으로 비켜 서 있는 것이 얼마나 힘들었는지를 이야기했다.

43 ④ 44 ③ 45 ② 장문

(A) 1820년에, 페루의 리마에 사는 사람들이 그들의 스페인 지배자들에 대항하여 반란을 일으키려고 준비하고 있는 것처럼 보였다. 그 도시의 엄청난 재산을 보호하기 위해, 도시를 책임지고 있던 스페인 대표자는 그 재산을 멕시코에 있는 스페인의 식민지로 옮기기로 결정했다. 약 6천만 달러 상당의 보석과 황금상, 그리고 기타 보물들이 11척의 배에 실려 보내졌다.

(D) 불행하게도, 리마의 재물들을 수송하는 책임을 맡고 있던 그 함대의 지휘관은 잘못 선택되었다. 메리 디어 호의 윌리엄 톰슨 선장은 사실 무자비한 해적이었고, 그는 이같은 기회를 허비하지 않으려 했다. 배들이 바다로 나가자마자, 그는 메리 디어 호에 타고 있던 페루인 병사들을 죽이고, 그들의 시체를 바다에 던져버렸다.

(B) 배의 통제권을 얻자, 톰슨과 그의 선원들은 즉시 인도양에 위치한 코코스 섬으로 항해했다. 이곳에서 그와 그의 선원들은 보물을 나누어 땅에 묻었다고 여겨졌다. 그들의 계획은 스페인인들이 그들을 찾기를 포기할 때까지 기다렸다가 그 보물을 되찾으러 코코스 섬으로 돌아오는 것

이었다. 그러나, 그런 일은 결코 일어나지 않았는데, 메리 디어 호가 곧바로 붙잡혀 톰슨의 선원들 중 대부분이 해적 행위에 대한 혐의로 재판에 회부되어 교수형에 처해졌기 때문이다.

(C) 톰슨과 그의 일등 항해사는 비슷한 운명에 처해졌고, 목숨을 구하기 위해 그들은 스페인인들에게 훔친 보물의 위치를 알려주기로 동의했다. 그들은 당국 관계자들(스페인인들)과 함께 코코스 섬으로 돌아갔지만, 가까스로 정글로 달아났다. 톰슨도 그의 동료 선원도, 그리고 보물들도 다시는 볼 수 없었고, 리마의 보물을 찾으려던 300팀 이상의 원정대들이 실패했다. 지금은 톰슨이 실제로는 그것을 중앙아메리카 근처의 어느 알려지지 않은 섬에 묻었다고 여겨지고 있다.

18 ⑤	19 ②	20 ③	21 ⑤	22 ⑤	23 ①
24 ③	25 ③	26 ①	27 ⑤	28 ⑤	29 ③
30 ③	31 ①	32 ③	33 ③	34 ①	35 ④
36 ⑤	37 ②	38 ⑤	39 ②	40 ②	41 ②
42 ④	43 ④	44 ①	45 ③		

18 ⑤ 글의 목적

친애하는 이웃 여러분께,
    요즘같은 경제 위기의 시대에, 많은 사람은 재정적으로 안정적이 될 방법을 찾고 있습니다. 따라서, 지역 사회를 위한 서비스의 하나로, 우리 대학은 우리의 모든 이웃에게 무료 투자 세미나에 참석할 좋은 기회를 제공하려 합니다. 세미나는 11월 12일 목요일 저녁 7시에 엘드리지 홀 강당에서 개최될 것입니다. 개인 투자에 있어서 유명한 전문가인 폴 웨슬리 교수가 이 행사를 주최할 것이며, 이 행사는 기본 투자 원칙부터 여러분의 현재 투자를 최대한 활용하는 것에 이르기까지 모든 것을 포함할 것입니다. 우리와 함께할 계획이시라면, 적어도 24시간 전에 812-0921로 본관에 전화하여 알려주십시오.
진심을 담아,
마샤 디아즈
MSU 경제학부

어휘
economic 경제의 crisis 위기 financially 재정적으로 stable 안정된, 안정적인 local community 지역 사회 auditorium 강당 renowned 유명한, 명성 있는 on the subject of …에 관하여 host (행사를) 주최하다 fundamental (*pl.*) 기초, 원칙 make the most of …을 최대한 활용하다 current 현재의 in advance 미리, 이전에

구문해설
(5행) ..., the university is **providing** a great opportunity **to** all of our neighbors [to attend a free investing seminar].: 'provide A to B' 「A를 B에게 제공하다」, [ ]는 a great opportunity를 수식하는 형용사적 용법의 to부정사구
(10행) Professor Paul Wesley, [a renowned expert on the subject of personal investing], will be hosting the event, [which will include everything **from** basic investing fundamentals **to** making the most of your current investments].: 첫 번째 [ ]는 Professor Paul Wesley와 동격, 두 번째 [ ]는 the event를 선행사로 하는 계속적 용법의 주격 관계대명사절, 'from A to B' 「A에서부터 B까지」

문제해설
대학에서 주최하는 무료 투자 세미나에 지역 주민들이 참석할 기회를 제공한다고 했으므로, ⑤가 글의 목적으로 가장 적절하다.

19 ② 심경

    부엌에 들어갔을 때, 타라는 담배 연기 냄새를 맡고 깜짝 놀랐다. 그녀는 즉시 건물 관리인에게 전화를 했는데, 그는 그 연기가 아마도 아파트 아래층에서 나오고 있는 것 같다고 설명했다. 막 이사 온 남자는 흡연자였다. 그 관리인은 그녀에게 냄새를 없애기 위해 공기 정화 필터를 살 것을 제안했다. 타라는 그의 조언을 따랐지만, 그 필터는 통풍구를 통해 들어오는 강한 담배 연기 냄새를 없애지 못했다. 그 상황에 진절머리가 나서, 타라는 아래층으로 내려가 이웃의 현관문을 두드렸다. 그가 문을 열자마자 거대한 연기구름이 복도로 떠밀려와 타라가 걷잡을 수 없이 기침을 하게 했다. "그만 좀 하세요."라고 그 남자가 말했다. "당신이 나를 피곤하게 할 것 같네요." 타라는 그녀가 들은 것을 믿을 수가 없었다. "사실 당신이야말로 나를 피곤하게 만드는 사람이에요!"라고 그녀가 대답했다.

어휘
cigarette 담배 immediately 즉시 explain 설명하다 suggest 제안하다; 추천하다 get rid of …을 제거하다 advice 조언, 충고 vent 통풍구, 환기구 drift 떠가다, 표류하다 cough 기침하다 uncontrollably 제어하기 힘들게, 감당하기 어렵게 reply 대답하다 [문제] irritated 짜증이 난 accepting 흔쾌히 받아들이는 amused 즐거워하는

구문해설
(1행) [Walking into her kitchen], Tara was surprised [to smell cigarette smoke].: 첫 번째 [ ]는 때를 나타내는 분사구문, 두 번째 [ ]는 감정의 원인을 나타내는 부사적 용법의 to부정사구
(6행) The manager **suggested** (that) she (should) **buy** an air filter [to get rid of the smell].: suggest가 제안이나 주장의 의미일 때 목적어인 that절의 동사는 '(should+)동사원형'의 형태, [ ]는 목적을 나타내는 부사적 용법의 to부정사구
(9행) [(Being) Tired of the situation], Tara **went** downstairs and **knocked** on her neighbor's door.: [ ]는 이유를 나타내는 분사구문, went와 knocked가 등위 접속사 and로 병렬 연결

문제해설
타라가 아래층에서 올라오는 담배 연기 냄새로 계속 불편을 겪다가 이웃을 찾아갔더니 오히려 그 이웃이 불만을 표하는 상황이므로, 타라의 심경으로는 ② '짜증이 나고 화난'이 적절하다.

20 ③ 필자의 주장

    왜 일부 여성들은 신체적으로 학대를 받는 관계를 그토록 오랫동안 유지하는 것일까? 간단히 대답하자면, 그들은 대개 갈 곳이 없으며 자신의 아이들을 지키려 애쓰고 있기 때문이다. 미국에는 학대받은 여성들을 위한 1,200개의 보호소가 있지만, 이들 시설 중 단 5퍼센트만이 아이가 있는 여성들을 받아준다. 보통 피해자들은 폭력적인 배우자로부터 도망치려고 노력한다. 그러나 돈의 부족, 갈 곳의 부재, 자신을 부양할 능력이 없음으로 인해 대부분은 집으로 돌아갈 수밖에 없으며, 으레 사과하는 배우자들에게 용서를 베풀도록 사회화된다. 가정 폭력은 심각한 폭력 범죄이며 다른 범죄들과 다르게 취급되어서는 안 된다. 우리는 범법자들을 사법처리해야 하며 피해자들에게 지원 서비스를 제공해야 한다.

어휘
physically 신체적으로 abusive 학대하는 shelter 거처; *피난처, 보호소 batter 때리다, …에게 폭력을 가하다 facility (*pl.*) 설비, 시설 victim 피해자, 희생자 make an effort 노력을 기울이다 get away from …(으)로부터 도망치다 violent 난폭한, 폭력적인 inability 무능, …할 수 없음 socialize 사회화하다 extend (은혜 등을) 베풀다, 제공하다 apologetic 미안해하는, 사과하는 domestic 국내의; *가정의 prosecute 사법처리하다, 법으로 처단하다 offender 범법자

구문해설
(8행) But, [with a lack of money, no place to go, and the inability to support themselves], most **are forced to return** and *are socialized to extend* ...: [ ]는 most의 상태를 설명하는 전치사구, 'be forced to-v' 「…하라고 강요받다」, 'be socialized to-v' 「…하도록 사회화되다」, are forced와 are socialized가 and에 의해 병렬 연결

③ 가정 폭력이 심각한 범죄임에도 불구하고 가해자 처벌과 피해자 지원이 제대로 이루어지고 있지 않음을 지적하며, 가정 폭력 피해 여성들을 위한 대책 마련을 촉구하고 있다.

21 ⑤ 글의 요지

사람들은 다양한 질병에 대처하기 위해 처방 약과 처방전 없이 살 수 있는 약물을 복용한다. 이런 물질들이 매우 도움이 될 수 있는 반면, 그것들은 종종 '드럭 머깅'이라 알려진 상황을 야기한다. 이것은 약이나 약물이 의도된 효과를 제공하지만 결국 신체로부터 필수적인 영양소를 빼앗아 가 버릴 때를 말한다. 예를 들어, 산 차단제는 흔히 고통스러운 속 쓰림을 줄이기 위해 복용된다. 그것은 고통을 완화해 줄 수 있지만, 동시에 칼슘, 철분, 비타민 D, 그리고 비타민 B12를 포함한 많은 영양분의 체내 수치를 낮출 수 있다. 결과적으로, 당신의 면역 체계가 약해질 수 있고 기운이 떨어질지도 모른다. 드럭 머깅은 분자 수준에서 약, 약물, 그리고 음식 간의 상호 작용에 의해 야기된다고 여겨지므로, 확인하거나 예측하기 어렵다. 이런 상황을 피하는 최적의 방법은 당신의 의사나 약사가 당신이 어떤 약과 다른 약물을 복용하고 있으며 그것들을 얼마나 자주 복용하고 있는지 정확하게 알게 하는 것이다.

어휘
prescription 처방, 처방전 over-the-counter 처방전 없이 살 수 있는 medication 약[약물] medical condition 질병 substance 물질 mug 강도짓을 하다 intended 목표로 하는, 의도하는 end up 결국 …가 되다 vital 필수적인 nutrient 영양소, 영양분 heartburn 속 쓰림 relief 안도; 경감, 완화 iron 철; 철분 immune system 면역 체계 weaken 약화시키다 interaction 상호 작용 molecular 분자의 identify 확인하다; 찾다, 발견하다 pharmacist 약사

구문해설
16행 ... on a molecular level, so it is difficult [to identify or predict].: [ ]는 형용사인 difficult를 수식하는 부사적 용법의 to부정사구
17행 The best way [to avoid this situation] is **by** *letting* your doctor or pharmacist *know* exactly [what drugs and other medications you are taking] and [how often you are taking them].: 첫 번째 [ ]는 The best way를 수식하는 형용사적 용법의 to부정사구, 'by v-ing'「…함으로써」, 'let+O+동사원형'「…가 ~하게 하다」, 두 번째 [ ]는 know의 목적어로 쓰인 의문사절로, 등위 접속사 and로 병렬 연결

문제해설
⑤ 약을 복용할 경우 약효가 있지만 분자 수준에서의 여러 상호 작용에 의해 몸 안의 영양소 수치를 낮출 수 있다는 드럭 머깅에 대한 글이다.

22 ⑤ 글의 제목

자각몽을 꾸는 것은 학습된 기술이다. 잠들어 있는 동안 자신이 꿈을 꾸고 있다는 것을 자각하고 꿈에서 벌어지는 일을 통제할 수 있다면 자각몽을 꾸고 있는 것이다. MILD(자각몽의 기억 유도)는 자각몽을 꾸는 하나의 성공적인 기술이다. MILD는 잠자리에 들 때 자신이 꿈꾸고 있다는 것을 기억하겠다고 자신에게 말하는 것에서 시작한다. "다음에 꿈을 꿀 때는 내가 꿈을 꾸고 있다는 것을 기억하겠다"라고 자신에게 되풀이해서 말하라. 그다음에는 최근에 꾼 꿈을 기억하려 노력하고 자신이 꿈을 꾸고 있다는 것을 스스로에게 말해야 한다. 그러고는 다음번 꿈에서 무엇을 하고 싶은지 생각한다. 예를 들어, 다음번 꿈에서 하늘을 날고 싶다면, 자신이 날고 있는 것을 상상하라. 이러한 과정들을 잠들 때까지 반복하라.

어휘
lucid dream 자각몽(수면자 스스로 꿈을 꾸고 있다는 것을 지각하면서 꾸는 꿈); 자각몽을 꾸다 induction 유도, 유발 repeatedly 반복해서 [문제] attempt 시도 analyze 분석하다 interpretation 해석, 설명 soundly 깊이, 곤히

구문해설
1행 You are lucid dreaming when you realize [that you are dreaming] and can control {what happens in your dream} while you are still asleep.: [ ]는 realize의 목적절, { }는 control의 목적어로 쓰인 관계대명사절

문제해설
자각몽의 정의 및 자각몽을 꾸는 방법을 설명한 글이므로 제목은 ⑤ '자각몽 꾸기: 꿈을 제어하는 방법'이 가장 적절하다.

23 ① 글의 주제

불꽃놀이는 축제 분위기를 고조시키기 위해 전 세계 문화에 의해 수백 년간 사용되어 오고 있다. 그러나 형형색색의 폭발을 보는 것이 재미있을지는 모르지만, 그 과정은 이후에 관중들과 접촉할 수도 있는 여러 가지의 유독 물질들을 방출한다. 예를 들어, 당신이 불꽃놀이에서 보는 초록색은 바륨에 의해 만들어지는데 이것은 독성이 있고 방사능이 있는 것으로 알려져 있으며, 암을 유발하는 물질인 다이옥신을 함유하고 있는 구리 화합물은 파란색을 만든다. 리튬, 카드뮴, 그리고 납과 같은 다른 유독 물질들도 불꽃놀이에 흔히 사용된다. 인간의 건강에 미치는 그것들의 부정적인 영향 외에도 이 물질들은 산성비의 생성을 초래하는데, 이것은 환경에 해를 입힌다. 이 문제에 대한 인식이 증가함에 따라, 일부 전문가들은 불꽃놀이를 레이저 빛 쇼로 대체할 것을 도시에 촉구하고 있다.

어휘
enhance 높이다, 향상시키다 festive 축제의 explosion 폭발 process 과정 release 방출하다 a variety of 다양한 toxic 유독성의 come into contact with …와 접촉하다 spectator 관중 radioactive 방사능이 있는 copper 구리 compound 화합물 agent 대리인; *물질 acid 산성의 awareness 의식 replace A with B A를 B로 대체하다 [문제] alternative 대안 principle 원리

구문해설
4행 ..., the process releases a variety of toxic materials [that can then come into contact with spectators].: [ ]는 a variety of toxic materials를 선행사로 하는 주격 관계대명사절
6행 For instance, the green colors [(which/that) you see in fireworks displays] are produced by barium, [which is known to be poisonous and radioactive], while copper compounds [containing the cancer-causing agent dioxin] create blue colors.: 첫 번째 [ ]는 the green colors를 선행사로 하는 목적격 관계대명사절, 두 번째 [ ]는 barium을 선행사로 하는 계속적 용법의 주격 관계대명사절, 세 번째 [ ]는 copper compounds를 수식하는 현재분사구
16행 ..., some experts are **urging** cities **to replace** their fireworks displays with laser light shows.: 'urge+O+to-v'「…에게 ~하도록 촉구하다」

문제해설
① 불꽃놀이의 색을 내는 데 사용되는 유독 물질들이 건강과 환경에 미치는 해로운 영향에 대해 설명하고 있다.

24 ③ 글의 주제

난독증은 사람들이 단어들을 구성 요소들로 쉽게 나누지 못하게 하는 학습 장애로, 그들이 읽고 쓰고 철자를 제대로 쓰는 것을 더 어렵게

한다. 정확한 증상은 연령에 따라 다르다. 어린아이들에게, 증상으로는 발화 지연, 단어의 철자를 기억하지 못하는 것, 그리고 지시를 따르는 것의 어려움이 있다. 이런 증상들은 좌절감과 자신감 부족으로 이어질 수 있다. 결과적으로, 난독증이 있는 아이들은 보통 수업에 지장을 주고 전반적으로 학교에 반감을 나타낸다. 그들이 우둔하거나 게으르다는 꼬리표가 달릴 수도 있지만, 이 아이들은 사실 뇌가 그들이 받아들인 정보를 해석하는 방식에 단순한 문제가 있는 것이다. 난독증에 대한 치료법은 없지만, 그것이 학습에 끼치는 영향을 최소화할 수 있는 처치는 있다.

어휘
dyslexia 난독증 break down 나누다, 분류하다 component (구성) 요소 spell (단어의) 철자를 말하다[쓰다] symptom 증상 delay 지연, 지체 frustration 불만, 좌절감 self-confidence 자신감 disruptive 지장을 주는 dislike 반감, 싫음 label (부당하게) 딱지[꼬리표]를 붙이다 unintelligent 우둔한, 영리하지 못한 translate 번역하다; 해석하다 treatment 처치 minimize 최소화하다 [문제] identify 확인하다 condition 상태; 질환

구문해설
(1행) Dyslexia is a learning difficulty [that **prevents** people **from** easily **breaking down** words into their components], [which makes *it* more difficult **for them** {to read, write, and spell properly}].: 첫 번째 [ ]는 a learning difficulty를 선행사로 하는 주격 관계대명사절, 'prevent+O+from v-ing' 「~가 ~하지 못하게 하다」, 두 번째 [ ]는 앞 절 전체를 선행사로 하는 계속적 용법의 주격 관계대명사절, it은 가목적어이고 { }가 진목적어이며, them이 { }의 의미상 주어
(13행) ..., these children actually have a simple problem with the way [their brains translate the information {they receive}].: [ ]는 the way를 선행사로 하는 관계부사절(선행사 the way와 관계부사 how는 둘 중 하나를 생략), { }는 the information을 선행사로 하는 목적격 관계대명사절
(15행) There is no cure for dyslexia, but there are treatments [that can minimize the impact {it has on learning}].: [ ]는 treatments를 선행사로 하는 주격 관계대명사절, { }는 the impact를 선행사로 하는 목적격 관계대명사절, it은 앞의 dyslexia를 지칭하는 대명사

문제해설
③ 난독증의 증상과 학습 활동에 끼칠 수 있는 부정적인 영향에 대해 설명하는 글이다.

25 ③ 도표 내용 불일치

위의 도표는 선택된 7개의 국가에서 사용자 100명당 휴대전화와 유선전화의 수를 보여주고 있다. 스웨덴에는 유선전화보다 휴대전화가 더 많은데, 덴마크에서는 유선전화가 휴대전화보다 더 많다. 휴대전화는 이탈리아에서 가장 인기 있는데, 여기서는 휴대전화가 유선전화를 2대 1 이상의 비율로 앞선다. (그러나 미국에서는 휴대전화와 비교하여 유선전화를 두 배만큼의 사람들이 사용하며 유선전화의 수가 휴대전화의 수를 초과한다.) 캐나다도 비슷한 상황인데, 이 국가에서는 100명당 휴대전화가 40개 미만이다. 유선전화는 덴마크에서 가장 보편화되어 있으며, 덴마크에서는 100명 중에서 거의 90개의 휴대전화가 사용된다.

어휘
landline (전신의) 지상통신선; *유선전화 outnumber …보다 수적으로 우세하다 exceed 초과하다

구문해설
(5행) Cell phones are most popular in Italy, [where they outnumber landlines by more than two to one].: [ ]는 Italy를 선행사로 하는 계속적 용법의 관계부사절

문제해설
③ 도표를 살펴보면, 미국의 경우 100명당 휴대전화 수는 50대 미만이고 유선전화의 수는 70대 미만이므로, 유선전화의 수가 휴대전화 수의 두 배에 미치지 못한다.

26 ① 내용 불일치

앨커트래즈는 샌프란시스코 만에 있는 바위섬으로 그래서 '더 록'이라고 불린다. 그 섬의 대부분의 공간은 한때 군사 요새였던 것이 차지하고 있다. 1934년에 그것은 흉악범들을 위한 연방 정부 교도소로 전용(轉用)되었다. 앨커트래즈의 각 감방은 가로 폭 2미터, 세로 폭 3미터, 높이 1.8미터가 채 되지 않았다. 죄수들은 낮인지 밤인지도 모른 채 철저한 어둠 속에서 살았다. 그들이 가끔 탈옥을 시도하였으나 어느 누구도 성공한 적이 없다. 몇몇 죄수들이 물가에 간신히 다다르기는 했으나, 아무도 해안까지 1킬로미터에 이르는 거리를 헤엄치는 중에 살아남지 못했다. 그 교도소는 경제적인 이유로 1963년에 폐쇄되었지만, 이제는 관광객들이 그 옛 교도소 감방을 방문할 수 있다.

어휘
take up (공간을) 차지하다, 쓰다 military 군의, 군사의 fortress 요새 federal 연방 정부의 criminal 범죄자 cell 감방 escape 탈출하다 shore 해안 jail 교도소

구문해설
(2행) Most of the space on the island is taken up by [what was once a military fortress].: [ ]는 by의 목적어로 쓰인 관계대명사절
(7행) Prisoners lived in complete darkness, [**not knowing** {whether it was night or day}].: [ ]는 부대상황을 나타내는 분사구문으로, 분사구문의 부정형은 분사 앞에 not을 붙임, { }는 knowing의 목적절

문제해설
① 앨커트래즈는 한때 군사 요새였으나 1934년부터 교도소로 이용되었으며, 1963년에 경제적인 이유로 폐쇄되어 현재는 관광 명소가 되었다.

27 ⑤ 내용 일치

세계 천문학 기구들에 의해 발사된 모든 우주 탐사선들 중, 보이저 프로그램이 가장 긴 업적 목록을 기록했을지도 모른다. 이 프로그램은 1977년에 NASA에 의해 따로따로 발사된 두 탐사선인 보이저 1호와 보이저 2호로 구성되어 있다. 이 탐사선들의 첫 번째이자 유일한 공식적인 임무는 목성과 토성으로의 접근 비행을 수행하는 것이었다. 그것들은 1980년에 이 임무를 완수하여 중요한 자료와 놀랄 만한 사진들을 지구로 보냈다. 탐사선들이 그것들의 임무를 마친 후 보이저 2호는 계속해서 천왕성과 해왕성에 관한 자료를 모았고 한편 보이저 1호는 지구와 지구를 둘러싸고 있는 행성들의 원거리 사진을 찍기 위해 태양계 가장자리를 향해 계속 속도를 냈다. 현재, 보이저 1호는 태양으로부터 약 110억 마일 떨어져 있다고 믿어지며 현재 지구에서 가장 멀리 있는 인간이 만든 물체인데, 이것은 조만간에는 깨질 것 같지 않은 기록이다.

어휘
probe 탐사선 launch (우주선 등을) 발사하다 astronomical 천문학의 consist of …으로 구성되다 official 공식적인 flyby 접근 비행 Jupiter 목성 Saturn 토성 stunning 놀랄 만한 Uranus 천왕성 Neptune 해왕성 solar system 태양계

구문해설
(1행) Of all the space probes [launched by the world's astronomical organizations], the Voyager program **may have recorded** the longest list of achievements.: [ ]는 all the space probes를 수식하는 과거분사구, 'may have p.p.' 「…했을지도 모른다」(과거에 대한 불확실한 추측)
(10행) ..., Voyager 2 **went on to gather** data on Uranus and

Neptune, while Voyager 1 kept speeding toward the edge of the solar system [to take a long-distance photo of Earth and the planets {that surround it}].: 'go on to-v' 「계속해서 …을 하다」, [ ]는 목적을 나타내는 부사적 용법의 to부정사구, { }는 the planets를 선행사로 하는 주격 관계 대명사절

(16행) ... is currently the farthest manmade object from Earth, [a record {that is not likely to be broken anytime soon}].: [ ]는 the farthest manmade object from Earth와 동격, { }는 a record를 선행사로 하는 주격 관계대명사절

문제해설
① 보이저 1, 2호는 1977년에 각각 따로 발사되었다. ② 두 탐사선은 발사 3년 후인 1980년에 임무를 완수했다. ③ 두 탐사선 모두 목성과 토성으로의 접근 비행에 성공하여 지구로 자료를 보내는 임무를 완수했다. ④ 보이저 2호가 천왕성과 해왕성에 관한 자료를 모았다.

28 ⑤ 내용 불일치

오후 파리 투어
  시간 여유가 없는 손님들을 위한, 하루 만에 도시에서 가장 유명한 명소를 볼 수 있는 옵션입니다.
명소: 에펠 탑, 노트르담 대성당, 루브르 박물관 (야외에서만)
시간: 매주 화요일과 목요일 14:30. 가끔 다른 요일도 가능하지만, 각각의 가격은 다를 수 있습니다.
소요 시간: 약 4시간 30분
취소: 투어 시작 72시간 전에는 전액 환불 가능
추가 정보:
→ 각 그룹에 최대 8명이 있습니다.
→ 이것은 도보 투어입니다. 따라서 참가자들은 대중교통 요금을 지불할 필요가 없습니다.

어휘
attraction 명소, 명물 cathedral 대성당 available 이용할 수 있는 on occasion 가끔 individual 각각의 vary 달라지다, 다르다 duration 지속 (기간) approximately 대략 cancellation 취소 full refund 전액 환불 prior to …에 앞서 additional 추가의 maximum 최고, 최대 participant 참가자 transportation 운송

구문해설
(2행) An option for guests with little time [to view the most famous attractions in the city in one day].: [ ]는 An option을 수식하는 형용사적 용법의 to부정사구

문제해설
⑤ 도보 투어이므로 참가자들은 대중교통 요금을 지불할 필요가 없다고 나와 있다.

29 ③ 어법

  연구에 따르면 공기역학, 즉 물체가 공기를 가르며 움직일 때 관여되는 힘에 대한 연구 분야에 관심 있는 과학자들은 꿀벌과 호박벌에게서 상당한 지식을 배울 수 있다. 이 곤충들이 날 때 사용하는 독특한 날갯짓은 공기역학을 새롭고 종전과 다른 영역으로 인도한다. 이 두 종류의 벌들은 대부분의 다른 작은 날벌레들의 비행방식과는 전혀 다른 비행방식을 사용한다. 다른 곤충들은 일반적으로 큰 원호를 그리며 날개를 움직이는 반면에, 꿀벌과 호박벌은 날개를 더 빨리 퍼덕거리면서 훨씬 더 짧은 원호를 그리며 날개를 움직인다. 이러한 특별한 움직임이 벌이 다른 곤충들보다 훨씬 더 넓은 동력 범위를 갖게 한다.

어휘
a thing or two *상당한 지식; 솔직한 충고 honeybee 꿀벌 bumblebee 호박벌 flap (날개 등을) 퍼덕거리다 motion 움직임 flight 비행 unconventional 인습에 얽매이지 않는; *색다른 employ 고용하다; *사용하다 arc 원호 range 범위

구문해설
(5행) The unique flapping motion [that these insects use {when they are in flight}] carries ...: [ ]는 The unique flapping motion을 선행사로 하는 목적격 관계대명사절, { }는 때를 나타내는 부사절
(11행) ..., honeybees and bumblebees move theirs in much shorter arcs [while flapping them more rapidly].: [ ]는 동시동작을 나타내는 분사구문(접속사 while은 뜻을 분명히 하기 위해 생략되지 않음)
(13행) This special motion gives the bees a **by far** wider power range than other insects.: by far는 「훨씬」의 의미로 비교급을 강조하는 부사

문제해설
③ a flight system을 가리키는 지시대명사를 사용해야 하므로, 복수형 those가 아닌 단수형 that을 써야 한다.

30 ③ 어휘

  세계에서 가장 오래된 쇼핑몰이라고 여겨지는 트라야누스 시장은 서기 98년에서 117년까지 통치했던 로마 황제에 의해 지어졌고 그의 이름을 따서 이름 지어졌다. 트라야누스는 로마 제국을 확장하는 데 기여했고, 현재 고대 건축의 인상적인 예로 여겨지는 그 시장을 비롯해 많은 건축물들이 도시 곳곳에 지어지게 했다. 콘크리트와 벽돌로 만들어져 있으며, 그것은 아치형 천장, 아치 모양의 복도, 그리고 계단으로 단절된(→ 연결된) 3층 구조를 갖는다. 그 시장 내부의 가게들은 그 광대한 제국 전역에서 온 식품들을 팔았으나, 이후 중세 시대 동안 그 건축물은 요새로 개조되었다. 그때, 토레 델레 밀리치아라고 불리는 커다란 탑도 추가되었다. 오늘날, 그 시장의 대부분이 여전히 그대로 남아 있으며, 그곳은 관광객들에게 인기 있는 행선지가 되었다.

어휘
name after …의 이름을 따서 명명하다 emperor 황제 expand 확대[확장]하다 structure 구조; *구조물, 건축물 consider 고려하다; *여기다 impressive 인상적인 architecture 건축(술), 건축학 vaulted 아치형의 arched 아치 모양의 level 수준; *(건물의) 층 vast 어마어마한, 광대한 convert 전환시키다[개조하다] fortress 요새 destination 목적지, 행선지

구문해설
(1행) Trajan's Market, [(which is) believed to be the world's oldest shopping mall], **was built** by and **named** after the Roman emperor [who ruled from 98 AD until 117 AD].: 첫 번째 [ ]는 Trajan's Market을 선행사로 하는 계속 용법의 주격 관계대명사절로, '관계대명사+be동사'가 생략됨, 문장의 동사로 was built와 (was) named가 등위 접속사 and에 의해 병렬 연결, 두 번째 [ ]는 the Roman emperor를 선행사로 하는 주격 관계대명사절
(4행) Trajan *helped expand* the Roman Empire and **had** many structures **built** throughout the city, including the market, [which is now considered an impressive example of ancient architecture].: helped와 had가 등위 접속사 and로 병렬 연결, 'help+(to-)v'「…하는 것을 돕다」, 'have+O+p.p.'「…가 ~되게 하다」, [ ]는 the market을 선행사로 하는 계속 용법의 주격 관계대명사절
(7행) [(Being) Made of concrete and brick], it has vaulted ceilings, arched hallways, and three levels [that are connected by stairs].: 첫 번째 [ ]는 부대상황을 나타내는 분사구문, 두 번째 [ ]는 three levels를 선행사로 하는 주격 관계대명사절

문제해설

트라야누스 시장은 3층으로 되어 있고 이는 계단으로 연결되었다고 하는 것이 자연스러우므로, ③ disconnected(단절된)를 connected(연결된) 등으로 고쳐야 한다.

31 ① 빈칸 추론

대부분의 사람들에게 놀라운 일이지만, 전 세계에는 500개 이상의 활화산이 있으며, 그 중 10개 이상이 매일 폭발하고 있다. 화산 폭발은 대기 오염을 상당히 가중시킨다. 하지만, 화산에 의한 오염은 자연이 지구의 유기체와, 땅과 물 같은 지구의 구성 요소들 사이의 균형을 가져오는 한 방법의 일부다. 가장 놀라운 화산 폭발은 1991년 6월에 필리핀의 피나투보 산에서 발생했다. 엄청난 양의 황산 가스가 대기 중으로 분출되었다. 그 직접적인 영향으로 지구가 상당히 냉각되었는데, 그 영향이 너무 커서 온실 효과로 인한 지구 온난화가 실제로 둔화되었다.

어휘

volcano 화산   erupt (화산이) 폭발하다(eruption 폭발, 분출) substantially 두드러지게   organism 유기체, 생물   element 요소, 구성 요소   measurable 측정할 수 있는; *상당히 중요한   [문제] misfortune 불운, 불행   breakdown 실패; 결렬, 와해   disharmony 부조화

구문해설

[5행] However, pollution [caused by volcanoes] is part of nature's way ...: [ ]는 pollution을 수식하는 과거분사구

[11행] The immediate effect was a measurable cooling of the earth [(which was) **so** great **that** the warming of the earth ... down].: [ ]는 a measurable cooling of the earth를 선행사로 하는 주격 관계대명사절 ('관계대명사+be동사'가 생략됨), 'so ... that ~'「너무 …해서 ~하다」

문제해설

① 빈칸 뒤에서 화산 폭발로 인해 지구 온난화가 둔화되었다고 언급된 것으로 보아, 화산에 의한 오염이 지구의 유기체와 구성 요소들 사이에 '균형'을 이루는 데 도움이 되었다는 것을 추론할 수 있다.

32 ⑤ 빈칸 추론

다양한 이유로, 사람들은 종종 자신의 진실된 감정을 말하지 못하거나 말하기를 꺼려한다. 사람들은 종종 누군가의 행동에 화가 났을 때 자신의 실제 감정을 표현하는 것을 피하기 위해 유쾌한 이야기를 한다. 어떤 경우에는 자신이 무엇을 느끼고 있는지 실제로 알지 못할 수도 있다. 예컨대 어떤 아들은 실제로는 아버지를 두려워하면서도 자신이 아버지를 사랑한다고 주장할 수 있다. 우리는 자신의 감정을 알고 있을 때조차 때로는 수위를 낮추어 표현하는데 사실은 어떤 것에 잔뜩 겁을 먹었으면서도 무언가에 '조금 긴장된다'고 말한다. 또는 그 감정이 부정적인 것이라면 그것을 완전히 부정할 수도 있다. 그러므로 사람들이 하는 말은 종종 그들이 느끼고 있는 것을 반영하지 않는다.

어휘

relate 말하다, 진술하다   avoid 피하다, 삼가다   figure out …을 알아내다, 이해하다   claim 주장하다   underplay 덜 심각해 보이게 만들다   terrified 겁에 질린   deny 부인하다, 부정하다   [문제] concern 영향을 미치다   reflect 반사하다; *반영하다   mirror 비추다, 반영하다

구문해설

[5행] ..., individuals cannot really figure out [what they are feeling].: [ ]는 figure out의 목적어로 쓰인 의문사절

[9행] ..., we sometimes underplay them, [saying we are "a little nervous" about something ... it].: [ ]는 동시동작을 나타내는 분사구문

[12행] So, often [what people say] does not mirror [what they are feeling].: 두 개의 [ ]는 각각 문장의 주어와 목적어로 쓰인 관계대명사절

문제해설

⑤ 사람들이 자신의 감정을 솔직하게 얘기하지 않는다는 첫 문장의 내용과 이어진 예시들을 통해 종종 사람들이 말하는 것이 그들의 감정을 있는 그대로 반영하지 않는다는 것을 추론할 수 있다.

33 ③ 빈칸 추론

한 실험에서, 연구원 한 명이 대학 캠퍼스에서 길을 잃어버린 학생인 척했다. 그녀는 어느 교수에게 다가가서 그에게 특정 건물로 가는 법을 물었다. 교수가 길을 알려주는 동안, 커다란 문을 들고 가던 두 명의 다른 연구원들이 그들 사이로 걸어갔다. 그들이 그렇게 할 때, 원래의 '길 잃은 학생'이 다른 비슷한 또래의 여성으로 교체되었다. 이런데도 불구하고, 그 교수는 마치 아무 일이 없었던 것처럼 계속해서 길을 알려주었다. 연구원들에 따르면, 이것은 '변화 맹시'라고 불리는 것의 한 예시였다. 본래의 사람과 교체된 사람 둘 다 동일한 기본 범주에 맞는 한, 교수는 아마 변화를 알아채지 못했을 것이다. 이는 그가 길을 알려주는 것에 집중하고 있었기 때문이다. 사람이 한 가지 일에 집중하고 있으면, 그 혹은 그녀의 뇌는 들어오는 다른 정보를 무시할 가능성이 있다.

어휘

experiment 실험   get lost 길을 잃다   approach 다가가다   give directions 알려주다, 길을 가르쳐주다   original 원래의, 본래의   replace 대신하다, 대체하다(replacement 대체, 교체)   blindness 맹목; *무분별, 무지   chances are ... 아마 …일 것이다   concentrate 집중하다   ignore 무시하다   incoming 들어오는   [문제] fit 맞다, 적합하다   category 범주

구문해설

[1행] ..., a researcher pretended to be a student [who had gotten lost on a college campus].: [ ]는 a student를 선행사로 하는 주격 관계대명사절

[5행] ..., two other researchers [carrying a large door] walked between the pair.: [ ]는 two other researchers를 수식하는 현재분사구

[8행] ..., the professor continued to give directions **as if** nothing **had happened**.: as if는 「마치 …인 것처럼」이라는 뜻으로 이 문장에서는 과거 사실에 반대되는 가정법 과거완료 시제와 함께 쓰임

문제해설

③ 원래 있던 사람과 교체된 사람이 길을 묻는 또래의 여학생이라는 동일한 기본 범주에 들었기 때문에, 길을 가르쳐 주는 것에만 집중하고 있던 교수는 변화를 알아채지 못한 것이다.

34 ① 빈칸 추론

어떤 사람들은 이동을 주로 조류와 연관시킨다. 분명 조류는 먼 거리를 이동하지만 포유류 역시 이동을 한다. 예를 들어, 삼림순록은 따뜻한 계절을 캐나다 북부의 푸른 산비탈에서 풀을 뜯어먹으며 보내지만, 날씨가 추워지면 봄이 될 때까지 남쪽으로 이동한다. 그들이 지나간 자취는 길이 매우 잘 다져져서 그 자취가 공중에서도 명확하게 보일 정도이다. 또 다른 예는 알래스카 물개이다. 이 물개들은 베링해의 프리빌로프 제도에서만 번식을 한다. 새끼들은 6월에 태어나서 9월이면 어미와 함께 남쪽으로 3천 마일이 넘는 여행을 가기에 충분할 만큼 튼튼해진다. 그들은 함께 북아메리카의 태평양 해안을 헤엄쳐 남캘리포니아의 따뜻한 바다까지 내려간다.

어휘

associate 관련시켜 생각하다   migration 이주, 이동(migrate 이주하다)   vast 광대한   graze 풀을 뜯어먹다   grassy 풀이 우거진   slope 비탈   track 지나간 자취   well-trodden (길이) 잘 다져진   fur seal 물개   breed (동물이) 새끼를 낳다, 번식하다   [문제] mammal 포유류   settle down 정착하다

구문해설

[2행] Birds **do** travel vast distances, but mammals also migrate.: do는 동사 travel을 강조하는 조동사

[6행] Their tracks are **so** well-trodden **that** they are clearly visible from the air.: 'so ... that ~' 「너무 …해서 ~하다」

[11행] ... and by September are strong **enough to go** south ... over 3,000 miles.: 'enough to-v' 「…할 만큼 충분히 ~한」

문제해설

① 빈칸 뒤에 언급된 삼림순록과 알래스카 물개는 포유류도 조류처럼 철 따라 이동한다는 것을 뒷받침하는 예시이다.

35 ④ 흐름과 무관한 문장

요리는 아이들이 배워야 하는 중요한 기술인데 왜냐하면 요리는 그들에게 많은 것을 가르쳐 주기 때문이다. 대부분의 사람은 음식을 요리하는 데 어떤 것들이 포함되는지 실제로 생각해보지 않지만, 많은 것이 있다. 그리고 아이들이 요리에 관심을 갖게 한다면 그들은 이런 것들을 쉽게 이해하게 된다. 아이들이 요리로부터 배울 수 있는 가장 중요한 것 중 하나는 조직화 기술이다. 아이들이 음식을 요리하려고 할 때, 심지어 간단한 요리라도 그들은 그 활동을 계획해야 하고 재료가 모두 있는지 확인해야 하며, 요리법을 이해하고 그런 다음 실행에 옮겨야 한다. 게다가, 아이들이 자신의 음식을 만들면 마지막에 그들은 성취감을 얻게 되는데, 이것이 자부심을 심어준다. (너무 높은 자부심은 낮은 자부심만큼 문제가 될 수 있다.) 또한, 어린 나이에 요리를 배우는 것은 그들이 요리에 무엇이 들어갈지 관리할 수 있기 때문에 아이들에게 독립적인 의사결정을 가르쳐줄 것이다.

어휘

a great deal 많은 것   pick up on …을 이해하다, 알아차리다   organizational 조직의, 조직하는   make sure 확인하다   ingredient 재료   recipe 요리법   execute 실행하다   a feeling of accomplishment 성취감   at the end 결국에는, 마지막에   instill 심어주다   self-esteem 자부심   problematic 문제가 있는

구문해설

[6행] One of the most important things [(that) children can learn from cooking] is organizational skills.: [ ]는 One of the most important things를 선행사로 하는 목적격 관계대명사절

[16행] Plus, [learning to cook at a young age] will teach children independent decision-making since they can control [what is going into their food].: 첫 번째 [ ]는 문장의 주어로 쓰인 동명사구, 두 번째 [ ]는 control의 목적어로 쓰인 의문사절

문제해설

④ 요리를 통해 아이들이 배울 수 있는 것들을 설명한 글로, 너무 높은 자부심이 문제가 될 수 있다는 내용은 글의 흐름에 맞지 않는다.

36 ⑤ 글의 순서

흔히 무언가에 대하여 열정과 능력을 둘 다 가지는 것은 행복의 열쇠라고 말해진다. 그러므로 많은 사람들이 그들이 좋아하는 일을 해서 돈을 버는 소박한 꿈을 공유한다는 것은 놀랍지가 않다.

(C) 이러한 꿈을 이루는 것은 거의 불가능하다고 흔히 여겨지지만, 이는 사실이 아니다. 이익을 가져다주는 직업으로 바뀔 수 있는 좋아하는 일들이 사실 많이 있다.

(B) 예를 들어, 건강에 대한 열정이 있는 사람들은 근력 운동, 요가, 산악자전거 수업을 해 줌으로써 자신의 능력을 다른 사람들과 나누는 직업을

가질 수 있다. 또는 그들이 원한다면, 운동팀을 지도할 수도 있다.

(A) 최신 패션 경향에 주목하는 것을 좋아하는 사람들도 또한 그들이 좋아하는 일을 생계 수단으로 활용할 수 있다. 몇몇은 패션 선택에 대해 조언을 원하는 고객들을 위한 개인 스타일리스트가 될 수 있는 반면 또 몇몇은 디자이너가 되기를 선택할 수 있다.

어휘

passionate 열정적인(passion 열정; 열정적으로 하는 활동)   get paid 돈을 벌다   pay attention to …에 주목하다   latest 최근의, 최신의   living 생계 수단   fitness 신체 단련, 건강   weight lifting 근력 운동   prefer 선호하다   profitable 이익이 되는

구문해설

[3행] **It is** therefore **no surprise that** many people share the simple dream of getting paid to do [what they love].: 'it is no surprise that ...' 「…은 놀라운 일이 아니다(당연한 일이다)」, [ ]는 do의 목적어로 쓰인 관계대명사절

[8행] Some may become personal stylists for clients [who want advice on fashion choices], ...: [ ]는 clients를 선행사로 하는 주격 관계대명사절

문제해설

⑤ (C)의 such a dream은 주어진 글의 the simple dream을 받는 말이며 좋아하는 일을 직업으로 삼을 수 있는 사례는 많다는 내용으로 이야기를 시작하고 있으므로 주어진 글 바로 뒤에 와야 하고, 이어서 그 구체적인 예시를 들고 있는 (B)가 온 후에, also라는 말로 또 다른 예시를 소개하고 있는 (A)가 오는 것이 적절하다.

37 ② 글의 순서

1697년, 한 프랑스 변호사가 친척의 사망 증명서를 요청하는 편지를 썼다. 편지는 기밀이었기 때문에 변호사는 '편지지 잠금방식'으로 그것을 잠갔다. 이것은 봉투가 존재하기 전 편지에 보안 장치를 하는 데 사용된 고대의 접기 기술이다.

(B) 그 편지는 목적지에 도달하지 못했다. 대신, 그것은 결국 우체국장의 트렁크에 있었는데, 현대 연구원들이 그것을 발견할 때까지 남아 있던 곳이다. 그들은 그 300년 된 편지를 읽고 싶었지만, 열기를 원하지 않았다.

(A) 이는 편지가 너무 손상되기 쉬워 펼 수 없었기 때문이다. 그것에 손상을 주는 것을 피하기 위해, 연구원들은 엑스레이 기계로 그것을 조사했다. 이는 내부 글의 상세한 이미지를 드러나 보이게 했지만, 단어들이 같이 접혀 있어서 읽을 수 없었다.

(C) 이 문제를 해결하기 위해, 그들은 접힌 단어들을 해독할 수 있는 알고리즘을 만들었다. 그것은 거의 5년이 걸렸으며, 그들은 그것을 여러 번 시험해야 했다. 그러나 마침내 그들은 '잠긴' 편지의 내용을 가까스로 읽어 냈다.

어휘

relative 친척   death certificate 사망 증명서   confidential 비밀[기밀]의   ancient 고대의   fold 접다   secure 획득[확보]하다; *단단히 보안 장치를 하다   envelope 봉투   fragile 부서지기[손상되기] 쉬운   examine 조사[검토]하다   reveal 드러내다   detailed 상세한   destination 목적지   postmaster 우체국장   algorithm 알고리즘   decode 해독하다   content 내용

구문해설

[4행] This is an ancient folding technique [that **was used to secure** letters before there were envelopes].: [ ]는 an ancient folding technique을 선행사로 하는 주격 관계대명사절, 'be used to-v' 「…하는 데 사용되다」

[6행] This was because the letter was **too** fragile **to unfold**.: 'too ... to-v' 「너무 …해서 ~할 수 없다」

12행 Instead, it ended up in a postmaster's trunk, [where it stayed until modern researchers discovered it].: [ ]는 a postmaster's trunk를 선행사로 하는 계속적 용법의 관계부사절

문제해설
② 1697년에 한 변호사가 고대의 접기 기술로 기밀 편지를 잠갔다는 주어진 글 다음에, 현대 연구원들이 이 편지를 발견했으나 열고 싶지 않았다는 (B)가 오고, 이는 편지가 손상되기 쉽기 때문이며 편지 내부의 단어들이 접혀 있어 읽을 수 없었다는 (A)가 이어진 후, 이 문제를 해결하기 위해 알고리즘을 만들어 결국 그 편지를 읽어냈다는 (C)의 순서로 이어지는 것이 자연스럽다.

38 ⑤ 주어진 문장의 위치

스트레스는 종종 우리 삶의 주요한 변화에서 기인하는데, 심리학자들은 이 변화들을 인생의 사건이라고 일컫는다. 이것들은 실직이나 사랑하는 사람의 죽음과 같은 부정적인 사건일 수도 있다. 또한 그것들은 결혼하는 것, 승진하는 것, 아이를 갖는 것과 같은 긍정적인 사건일 수도 있다. 다시 말해서, 좋은 쪽으로 또는 나쁜 쪽으로의 변화는 우리에게 스트레스가 되는 부담을 안겨줄 수 있다. 우리가 인생의 사건을 평가하는 방식 또한 그것이 우리에게 얼마나 스트레스가 되느냐와 많은 관계가 있다. 임신 같은 인생의 사건은 아이를 갖기를 갈망하는 사람에게는 스트레스가 덜 된다. 마찬가지로, 당신이 일이 스트레스를 준다고 느끼느냐 그렇지 않느냐는 일단 당신이 그 일을 좋아하느냐 그렇지 않느냐에 많이 좌우된다.

어휘
pregnancy 임신 long 갈망하다, 열망하다 promotion 승진 impose 부과하다 burden 부담, 짐 evaluate 평가하다 in the first place 일단, 우선

구문해설
3행 Stress often **results from** major changes in our lives, [which psychologists call life events].: 'result from ...' 「…에서 비롯되다」, [ ]는 major changes in our lives를 선행사로 하는 계속적 용법의 목적격 관계대명사절
10행 The way [we evaluate a life event] also **has** much **to do with** [how stressful it becomes for us].: 첫 번째 [ ]는 The way를 선행사로 하는 관계부사절(선행사 the way와 관계부사 how는 둘 중 하나를 생략), 'have to do with ...' 「…와 관계가 있다」, 두 번째 [ ]는 with의 목적어로 쓰인 의문사절
12행 Similarly, [whether or not you find your work stressful] depends a lot on [whether or not you like ... place].: 첫 번째 [ ]는 문장의 주어로 쓰인 명사절, 두 번째 [ ]는 on의 목적어로 쓰인 명사절

문제해설
주어진 문장의 내용은 우리가 인생의 사건을 평가하는 방식의 한 예시이므로, 우리가 평가하는 방식에 따라 인생의 사건이 스트레스를 얼마나 가져오는지가 달라진다는 설명의 뒤인 ⑤에 오는 것이 가장 적절하다.

39 ② 주어진 문장의 위치

음원 파일을 공유하는 것은 모든 인터넷상의 웹사이트와 커뮤니티에서 발생한다. 저작권자의 허가 없이 파일을 공유하는 것이 불법이라는 것을 알고 있었는가? 음악 스트리밍 서비스에 돈을 지불하면 당신은 집에서 컴퓨터로 듣거나 밖에서 휴대전화로 그것을 들을 권리 또한 구매하는 것이다. 그러나 다른 사람이 그 음악을 복제하도록 한다면, 당신은 엄밀히 말하면 저작권법을 어기고 있는 것이다. 물론 많은 사람들이 음악 트랙을 교환하기 위해 파일 공유 프로그램을 이용한다. 그러나 이러한 행동은 법적인 관점에서는 대부분 항상 불법이다. 예술가가 실제로 이러한 과정을

허락하지 않았다면 음악을 공유하는 것은 불법이다. 이는 비디오, 텔레비전 쇼, 영화도 마찬가지이다.

어휘
technically 기술적으로; *엄밀히 말하면 break 깨다; *(법·약속을) 어기다 copyright 저작권 share 공유하다 illegal 불법의 holder 소유자 permission 허락, 허가 swap 교환하다 in the eyes of …이 보는 바로는 approve 허락하다 the same goes for …도 마찬가지이다

구문해설
12행 **Unless** the artist has actually approved this process, ...: unless는 「…하지 않는 한, …한 경우 외에는」라는 의미(= if ... not ~)

문제해설
스트리밍 서비스를 이용하는 것은 본인이 그 노래를 들을 권리를 사게 되는 것이라는 내용 다음에 이와는 반대로 그 노래를 다른 사람이 복제하도록 하는 것은 법을 위반하는 것이라는 내용이 오는 것이 자연스러우므로, 주어진 문장은 ②에 와야 한다.

40 ② 요약문 완성

유명한 이솝 우화에서, 배고픈 여우 한 마리가 포도나무에 걸려 있는 익은 포도를 잡아채려고 하며 공중으로 뛰어오른다. 몇 번을 시도하고 실패한 후, 그는 포도가 아마 신맛이 날 거라고 단언하고 떠나버린다. 다시 말해, 그 여우는 맨 처음에 꼭 성공하길 원한건 아니었던 척 함으로써 실패를 감추려고 하는 것이다. 이것은 '합리화'로 알려져 있다. 합리화는 우리가 잘못되거나 용납되지 않아 보이는 것을 설명하기 위한 이유를 지어낼 때 발생한다. 그것들은 우리 신념의 갈등에 의해 일어나는 인지적 불일치로부터 우리를 무의식적 수준에서 보호한다. 여우처럼, 우리는 우리가 가질 수 없는 어떤 것이 어차피 가질 가치가 없다고 합리화하는지도 모른다. 또는 우리가 부정적인 결과를 갖는 결정을 내릴 때, 우리는 일이 보기보다 실제로 나쁘지 않다는 합리화 뒤에 숨을지도 모른다.

어휘
fable 우화 leap 뛰다, 뛰어오르다 ripe 익은 vine 포도나무 sour 신, 시큼한 pretend …인 척하다 rationalization 합리화(rationalize 합리화하다) make up 만들어 내다, 지어내다 unacceptable 받아들일 수 없는, 용납할 수 없는 unconscious 무의식적인 cognitive 인지의, 인식의 disagreement 불일치, 차이 conflict 갈등 consequence 결과 [문제] explanation 이유; 설명 hardship 어려움, 곤란 pleasantness 유쾌함

구문해설
1행 In a famous fable by Aesop, a hungry fox leaps in the air, [trying to grab some ripe grapes {hanging from a vine}].: [ ]는 동시동작을 나타내는 분사구문, { }는 some ripe grapes를 수식하는 현재분사구
3행 [**After** trying and failing several times], he *announces* [that the grapes probably taste sour] and *walks* away.: 첫 번째 [ ]는 시간을 나타내는 분사구문으로, 의미를 정확히 전달하기 위해 접속사 After를 생략하지 않음, 두 번째 [ ]는 announces의 목적어로 쓰인 명사절, 문장의 동사 announces와 walks가 등위 접속사 and로 병렬 연결
13행 Like the fox, we may rationalize [that something {we can't get} isn't worth having anyway].: [ ]는 rationalize의 목적어로 쓰인 명사절, { }는 something을 선행사로 하는 목적격 관계대명사절
15행 Or when we make decisions [that have negative consequences], we might hide behind the rationalization [that things aren't really as bad as they seem].: 첫 번째 [ ]는 decisions를 선행사로 하는 주격 관계대명사절, 두 번째 the rationalization과 [ ]는 동격

문제해설
② 사람들은 불만족스러운 상황을 덜 부정적으로 보이게 만드는 잘못된 이유를 만들어 냄으로써 불만족스러운 상황의 불편함에 대처하기 위해 합리화를 사용한다.

41 ② 42 ④ 장문

시카고 대학의 교수인 엔리코 페르미는 자신의 학생들에게 답하기 불가능한 것 같은 질문들을 하는 것으로 유명했다. 그들이 이의를 제기하면, 그는 그들이 해답을 찾는 데 필요한 지식과 도구를 이미 가지고 있다는 것을 그들에게 증명하곤 했다. 이러한 종류의 질의는 마침내 '페르미의 추정'으로 알려지게 되었다.

페르미의 추정은 일반적으로 답을 하는 사람에게 직접적인 물리적 수단을 통하여 측정하기 불가능할 대략의 수량을 빨리 산출하도록 요구한다. 특정 호수에는 몇 방울의 물이 들어 있는가라고 질문하는 것이 한 예가 될 수 있다. 그 질문에 답하려면 당신은 우선 한 방울의 평균 크기를 추정하고 나서 그 호수의 크기와 깊이를 바탕으로 하여 호수의 부피를 결정해야 할 것이다. 물론 정확한 수치를 내는 것이 목적은 아니다. 페르미의 추정은 정확한 답을 산출하기보다는 오히려 <u>타당한 가설을 세우는 것</u>에 의해 해결된다.

이 때문에, 페르미의 추정에 관한 한, 답을 찾기 위해 사용되는 과정이 실제 해답보다 더 중요하다. 정확한 답은 없고, 오직 허용 가능한 범위만이 있을 뿐이다. 이러한 질문들의 목적은 정답을 암기하는 습관으로부터 학생들을 멀리 떨어뜨려 놓아 그들이 논리적인 사고 과정을 발달시키도록 장려하는 것이다. 이는 과학에 관심이 있는 누구에게나 매우 유용한 기술이다. 그러나 대부분의 학생들에 관한 한, 페르미의 추정에 관한 가장 좋은 점은 그 문제들이 해결하기에 무척 재미있을 수 있다는 것이다.

어휘

protest 항의하다, 이의를 제기하다 **possess** 소유하다 **solution** 해결책; *해답 **query** 문의, 의문, 질의 **come up with** 찾아내다, 내놓다 **rough estimate** 대충의 어림(셈) **direct** 직접적인 **mean** (*pl*.) 수단, 방법 **contain** 들어[함유되어] 있다 **determine** 결정하다; *알아내다 **specific** 구체적인, 명확한 **when it comes to** …에 관해서라면[관한 한] **actual** 실제의, 사실상의 **acceptable** 허용할 수 있는 **range** 범위, 정도 **logical** 논리적인 **invaluable** 매우 유용한, 귀중한 **as[so] far as … be concerned** …에 관한 한 [문제] **key** 가장 중요한, 핵심적인 **formula** 공식 **assumption** 추정, 가정 **reasonable** 타당한, 사리에 맞는

구문해설

[4행] …, he **would** then prove to them [that they already possessed the knowledge and tools {needed to find the solution}].: would는 「…하곤 했다」라는 의미의 조동사, [ ]는 prove의 목적절, { }는 the knowledge and tools를 수식하는 과거분사구

[9행] Fermi questions generally **require** answerers **to** quickly **come up with** a rough estimate of a quantity [that would be impossible *to measure* … physical means].: 'require+O+to-v' 「…에게 ~하기를 요구하다」, [ ]는 a quantity를 선행사로 하는 주격 관계대명사절, to measure는 impossible을 수식하는 부사적 용법의 to부정사

[23행] …, the process [used to find the solution] is more important than the actual answer.: [ ]는 the process를 수식하는 과거분사구

[31행] …, the best thing about Fermi questions is [that they can be enjoyable **to solve**].: [ ]는 주격보어로 쓰인 명사절, to solve는 enjoyable을 수식하는 부사적 용법의 to부정사

문제해설

41 ② 이 글은 (알기) 불가능해 보이는 것에 대한 질문에 논리적인 사고를 통해 답을 하게 하는 페르미의 추정에 대하여 이야기하고 있다.

42 페르미의 추정은 정확한 답을 찾는 것이 아니라, 허용 가능한 범위 안에서 논리적인 사고를 하는 것이라고 했으므로, 빈칸에는 ④ '타당한 가설을 세우는 것'이 가장 알맞다.

---

43 ④ 44 ① 45 ③ 장문

(A) 유럽의 정복자들이 들어오기 전에, 오늘날 콜롬비아로 알려진 곳에 살고 있던 토착민들은 금에 대해 높은 존경심을 갖고 있었다. 우리 고유의 문화와 비슷하게도, 그들은 지도자들의 사회정치적이고 이념적인 권력을 나타내고자 금을 사용하였다. 그러나, 고대 콜롬비아에서의 금의 역할은 사회의 또 다른 영역에까지 확대되었다. 바로 영적 세계였다.

(D) 이러한 영역에서 금은 올바르게 사용된다면 어떤 사물을 다른 사물로 전환시키거나, 태양의 힘을 이용하고, 심지어 그 자체로 생명체를 만들어내는 것과 같은 일들을 실현시킬 수 있는 어떤 신비로운 특성들을 가진 것으로 여겨졌다. 인간 세계와 영적인 세계에 동시에 존재한다고 여겨졌던 종교 지도자인 샤먼들은, 신성한 금을 돌보고 사용하는 일을 책임졌다. 죽은 자들과의 대화를 시도하는 의식을 치르는 동안 샤먼들은 일반적으로 금으로 만든 가면과 다른 장식품들을 걸치곤 했다.

(B) 게다가, 금의 영적인 특성은 고대 콜롬비아인들에 의해 거행된 장례 의식에서 금이 특별한 위치를 차지하게 했다. 이 문화의 종교적인 관점에서, 죽음의 실재는 새로운 생명이 태어나기 위해 필요한 것이었고, 금은 죽음과 삶 사이의 전환에 필수적인 요소였다. 샤먼들은 이러한 의식들 또한 통솔했고, 만약 죽은 자들이 중요한 인물이었다면 그들은 귀고리, 코걸이, 그리고 가면과 흉갑으로 꾸며졌는데, 이 모든 것이 금장식을 특징으로 했다.

(C) 불행히도 콜롬비아인들이 금에 두었던 영적인 중요성은, 1500년대에 들어와 이 문명과 다른 많은 문명을 정복했던 스페인 사람들에게는 존중받지 못했다. 그들은 금을 단지 그것이 주는 금전적인 가치와 사회적 지위 때문에 얻으려 했다. 그래서 그들은 샤먼과 금을 기반으로 한 콜롬비아의 의식들을 금지하였고, 배에 실어 스페인으로 보낼 그들이 찾을 수 있는 가능한 한 많은 양의 금을 훔쳤다. 그러나 그들이 그 모든 금을 찾을 수는 없었으며, 현대의 고고학자들에 의해 발견된 고대 콜롬비아의 금 공예품의 예시들은 보고타의 황금 박물관(Museo del Oro)에 전시되어 있다.

어휘

indigenous 토착의, 지역 고유의 **hold … in high esteem** …을 매우 존경하다 **sociopolitical** 사회정치적인 **ideological** 이념적인 **spill over** 넘치다, 넘쳐흐르다 **realm** 범위, 영역 **spiritual** 영적인; *종교적인 일 **ritual** 종교적인 의식 **observe** (의식·제례 등을) 거행하다, 집행하다 **preside** 통솔하다 **breastplate** (갑옷의) 가슴받이, 흉갑 **Spaniard** 스페인 사람 **outlaw** 추방하다; *금지하다 **artifact** 공예품 **on display** 전시된, 진열된 **harness** 이용하다 **simultaneously** 동시에 **ornament** 장식품, 장신구 [문제] **mining** 채광, 채굴

구문해설

[25행] …, so they outlawed shamans and gold-based rituals in Colombia and stole **as much** gold **as they could** find [to ship back to Spain].: 'as+형용사(+명사)+as+S+can[could]' 「…가 할 수 있는 한 ~한」, [ ]는 much gold를 수식하는 형용사적 용법의 to부정사구

[36행] Shamans, [spiritual leaders {who were thought to exist in both human and spirit worlds simultaneously}], **were responsible for** caring for and using the sacred gold.: [ ]는 Shamans와 동격, { }는 spiritual leaders를 선행사로 하는 주격 관계대명사절, 'be responsible for …' 「…에 책임이 있다」

문제해설

43 ④ 고대 콜롬비아에서 금의 역할이 영적 세계에까지 미쳤다는 내용의 (A) 다음에, 이를 구체적으로 설명한 (D)가 이어지고, 금의 이러한 영적 역할이 장례 문화에 영향을 미쳤음을 추가적으로 언급한 (B)가 온 후, 스페인의 정복으로 인하여 고대 콜롬비아인들의 금의 영적 중요성은 무시되었고 남은 유물들이 현재 박물관에 보존되

어 있다는 내용의 (C)가 오는 것이 자연스럽다.

44 고대 콜롬비아인들에게 금은 금전적 가치 이상의 의미를 가지고 있었음을 보여주고 있으므로, 제목으로는 ① '금의 더 심오한 가치'가 적절하다.

45 ③ (B)에서 죽은 사람이 생전에 중요한 인물이었을 때 금으로 치장했다고 언급되어 있다.

---

14 영어독해 모의고사

본문 ▶ p.136

18 ④	19 ②	20 ⑤	21 ③	22 ②	23 ③
24 ⑤	25 ②	26 ②	27 ②	28 ⑤	29 ④
30 ⑤	31 ③	32 ①	33 ①	34 ⑤	35 ②
36 ④	37 ③	38 ③	39 ②	40 ①	41 ④
42 ④	43 ③	44 ④	45 ①		

18 ④ 글의 목적

다음 주 월요일인 6월 4일을 시작으로 하여, 콜드웰 다리가 일시적으로 폐쇄될 예정입니다. 지난 몇 년 동안 증가하는 교통량으로 인해, 스타크 카운티 도로 부서는 다리가 중대한 보수를 받을 필요가 있다고 결정했습니다. 작업은 두 개의 추가 차선들을 포함시키기 위해 다리를 가로지르는 기존의 도로를 넓히는 것을 수반할 것입니다. 추가 차선들은 장기적으로 교통량과 다리를 건너는 이동 시간을 크게 줄일 것입니다. 건설팀이 작업을 마치는 데는 6주가 걸릴 것으로 예상됩니다. 작업이 다리에서 진행되는 동안, 운전자들은 콜드웰 항구를 왕복하는 데에 그것을 이용할 수 없을 것입니다. 대신에, 바턴 고속도로를 따라서 우회해야 할 것입니다. 스타크 카운티 도로부는 이로 인해 발생할 수 있는 모든 불편에 대해 사과드립니다.

어휘
temporarily 일시적으로   department 부서   undergo 겪다, 받다
significant 중요한, 중대한   renovation 수리, 보수   widen 넓히다
existing 기존의   lane 차선   additional 추가적인   in the long term 장기적으로   construction 건설, 공사   carry out 수행하다, 실행하다
motorist 운전자   take a detour 우회하다   inconvenience 불편

구문해설
11행 It is expected to **take** the construction team six weeks **to complete** the work.: 'take+사람+시간+to-v' 「…가 ~하는 데 시간이 걸리다」

문제해설
④ 증가하는 교통량으로 인해 다리의 차선을 추가하기 위한 보수 공사가 시작될 것이며, 공사가 진행되는 동안 다리를 이용할 수 없음을 운전자들에게 공지하는 글이다.

19 ② 심경

미첼 씨는 골동품을 수집했다. 그에게 그것은 취미 이상의 것이었다. 친구들이 정성 들여 장식된 그의 집에 감탄할 때마다 그는 자신감에 가득 찼다. 어느 화창한 오후에 그는 한 노부부를 따라 이삿짐으로 가득한 집으로 들어가던 중이었다. 보통 이러한 이사 세일은 값싸고 현대적인 쓸모없는 물건밖에 없었지만, 미첼 씨가 운이 좋을 때도 가끔 있었다. 그는 구식의 주방을 둘러보았으나, 그 안에 있는 어느 것도 진짜로 30년 이상 된 것이 없었다. 거실도 별로 나을 게 없었다. 그러다가 그는 서재에서 멈췄다. 그의 눈이 커졌고 심장이 두근거리기 시작했다. 잠시 동안 그는 자신이 꿈을 꾸고 있을지도 모른다고 생각했다. 그의 입술은 미소가 지어지기 시작했다. 그가 사진에서 보고 그의 수집품에 추가하고 싶었던 바로 그 스타일의, 골동품 장인이 만든 오크 나무 책장이 그의 앞에 있었다!

어휘
antique 골동품   admire 감탄하다, 칭찬하다   decorated 훌륭하게 꾸민, 장식된   glow with pride 자신감에 차 있다   junk 쓸모없는 물건   every

once in a while 가끔　study 공부; *서재　widen 넓어지다, 커지다
pound 세게 치다; *(심장이) 두근거리다　curve 곡선을 그리다　craftsman 장
인　collection 수집품　[문제] hurt 다친; *기분이 상한　grateful 고마워하는

구문해설

4행 One sunny afternoon, he was following an old couple
through a house [full of moving boxes].: [ ]는 a house를 수식하는 형
용사구

10행 The living room was **no better**.: 'no better (than)' 「(…보다) 별로
나을 게 없는」

14행 Standing in front of him **was an antique craftsman oak
bookcase**, [the very style he *had seen* in pictures and (had)
wished to add to his collection]!: 보어인 Standing in front of
him이 문두로 나와 주어와 동사가 도치, [ ]는 an antique craftsman oak
bookcase와 동격, 주절의 시제(was)보다 앞선 시점을 나타내는 과거완료 had
seen과 (had) wished가 등위 접속사 and로 병렬 연결

문제해설

소장하길 소망하던 가구를 우연히 발견한 상황이므로 ② '(너무 좋아서) 흥분하고 기쁜'
심경일 것이다.

20　⑤　글의 요지

안타깝게도 오늘날의 사회에서 많은 사람들은 낯선 사람을 두려워해
야 한다는 견해를 갖고 있다. 이러한 생각은 유감스러울 뿐만 아니라 잘
못된 것이기도 하다. 그 생각은 언론 보도에서 비롯되는데, 언론은 종종
정신적으로 문제가 있는 살인자나 납치범, 어린이 유괴범 그리고 다른 범
죄자들의 범죄 행위를 상세히 보도하는 경우가 많다. 하지만 사실은 낯선
사람에 의해서 보다는 아는 사람들에 의해 피해를 입는 희생자들이 더
많다. 여성들은 낯선 사람들보다는 자신의 남편이나 남자친구에게 폭행
을 당하기가 더 쉽다. 사회복지사나 의사들은 노인들이 방치되고 학대받
을 때, 그 가해자는 고용된 간병인이 아니라 친척들이라는 사실을 자주
발견한다. 그리고 아이들이 학대당할 때, 학대자는 부모나 양부모, 혹은
친척인 경우가 더 많다.

어휘

notion 견해　regrettable 유감스러운　stem from …에서 유래하다
document 상세히 보도하다　psychopathic 정신병(성)의　kidnapper 납치
범　snatcher 유괴범　criminal 범죄자　victim 희생자　neglect 방치하다
abuse 학대하다　perpetrator 가해자, 범인　relative 친척　paid 유급의; *
고용된　mistreat …을 학대하다　step-parent 양부모

구문해설

6행 But the truth is [that more victims are hurt by people {(that)
they know} than by strangers].: [ ]는 주격보어로 쓰인 명사절, { }는 people
을 선행사로 하는 목적격 관계대명사절

10행 Social workers and doctors frequently find [that {when the
elderly … abused}, the perpetrators … care-workers].: [ ]는 find의
목적절, { }는 that절 안에 삽입된 때를 나타내는 부사절

문제해설

⑤ 낯선 사람들이 위험하다는 통념과는 달리, 원래 아는 사람에 의해 폭력 피해를 입
는 경우가 더 많다는 내용이다.

21　③　함축 의미 추론

꿀빨이새는 개체 수가 고작 몇백 마리로 감소한 희귀한 호주의 명금
이다. 그것은 보통 다른 새들의 노래를 흉내 내지만, 과학자들은 왜 그런
지 전혀 확신하지 못했다. 일부는 흉내 내는 것이 짝짓기 철 동안 암컷에

게 깊은 인상을 주기 위해 수컷이 사용한 기술이라고 믿었지만, 새로운
이론은 더 우려스럽다. 한 연구는 그들의 흉내 내기가 '노래 문화의 상실'
때문일 수도 있다는 것을 보여주었다. 그것의 개체 수가 너무 적어져서,
어린 수컷 새들은 적절한 짝짓기 울음소리를 배우지 못하고 있을 것이다.
새끼가 처음에 부화할 때, 그것의 아비는 둥지에 관심을 끄는 것을 피하
기 위해 조용히 있는다. 그래서 나중에야 비로소 어린 수컷이 다 자란 수
컷으로부터 짝짓기 노래를 배운다. 그러나 남아있는 수컷 꿀빨이새가 거
의 없기 때문에, 그들은 대신 다른 종들의 노래를 배우고 있는 것일지 모
른다. 이것은 암컷 꿀빨이새들이 이런 노래에 응답하지 않아, 어린 수컷
들이 짝을 찾을 가능성을 더 적게 만들기 때문에 문제이다.

어휘

rare 드문, 희귀한　songbird 명금(고운 소리로 우는 새)　shrink 줄어들다
imitate 모방하다, 흉내내다　mimicry 흉내　male 남자; 수컷(↔ female 여
자; 암컷)　mating 짝짓기, 교미　hatch 부화하다　draw attention 관심을
끌다　species 종(種)　[문제] pass on to …로 전하다　mimic 흉내를 내다

구문해설

4행 Some believed [that mimicry was a skill {(which/that) males
used **to impress** females during mating season}], but a new
theory is more troubling.: [ ]는 believed의 목적어로 쓰인 명사절, { }는 a
skill을 선행사로 하는 목적격 관계대명사절, to impress는 목적을 나타내는 부사
적 용법의 to부정사

11행 When the young first hatch, their fathers remain silent [to
avoid drawing attention to the nest].: [ ]는 목적을 나타내는 부사적 용법의
to부정사구

16행 This is a problem because female regent honeyeaters won't
respond to these songs, [making **it** less likely {that the young
males will find a partner}].: [ ]는 결과를 나타내는 분사구문, it은 가목적어이
고 { }가 진목적어

문제해설

꿀빨이새의 개체 수가 감소하여 어린 수컷들이 다 자란 수컷으로부터 적절한 짝짓기 울
음소리를 배울 수 없는 대신 다른 종의 노래를 흉내 내고 있다는 내용이므로, 밑줄 친
'노래 문화의 상실'이 의미하는 바로 가장 적절한 것은 ③ '어린 수컷들에게 전수되고 있
지 않은 짝짓기 노래'이다.

22　②　필자의 주장

여러모로 인터넷은 쇼핑을 더 용이하고 편리하게 만들었다. 하지만,
그것은 또한 무엇을 구매할지 선택하는 것을 더 어렵게 만들었다. 이것은
골라야 할 선택 항목들이 너무 많기 때문이다. 가능한 것들을 좁혀 나가
기 위해, 사람들은 종종 다른 소비자들에 의해 게시된 온라인 리뷰와 평
가에 의지한다. 하지만 이 정보는 특히 믿을 만하지 않다. 연구들은 상품
들이 온라인에서 받는 평가는 그것들의 객관적 품질과 대략적으로만 관
련되어 있다는 점을 보여주었다. 이것은 거짓 리뷰의 존재와 사람들이 상
품에 대해 긍정적이든 부정적이든 강한 감정을 가질 때만 리뷰를 쓰는
경향이 있다는 사실을 포함하여 몇 가지 요인들에 기인한다. 구매자들이
신경써야 하는 것은 그들이 온라인에서 찾은 다른 사람들의 의견보다도
상품들 그 자체이다.

어휘

convenient 편리한, 간편한　purchase 구입[구매]하다　option 선택(할 수
있는 것)　narrow down 좁히다　possibility 가능성, 가능한 일　turn to …
에 의지하다　consumer 소비자　particularly 특히, 특별히　reliable 믿을
[신뢰할] 수 있는　loosely 느슨하게; *막연히, 대략　objective 객관적인
quality 질　presence 있음, 존재(함)　attention 주의, 주목

2행 However, it has also made **it** harder [to choose {what to purchase}].: it은 가목적어이고 [ ]가 진목적어, { }는 choose의 목적어로 쓰인 의문사구

5행 [To narrow down the possibilities], people often turn to online reviews and ratings [posted by other consumers].: 첫 번째 [ ]는 목적을 나타내는 부사적 용법의 to부정사구, 두 번째 [ ]는 online reviews and ratings를 수식하는 과거분사구

8행 Studies have shown [that the ratings {(which/that) products receive online} are only loosely connected to their objective quality].: [ ]는 have shown의 목적절, { }는 the ratings를 선행사로 하는 목적격 관계대명사절로 목적격 관계대명사가 생략된 형태

② 타인에 의해 게시된 온라인 리뷰나 평가는 거짓으로 작성되거나 상품에 대해 강한 감정을 느끼는 경우에만 쓰여질 가능성이 있기 때문에, 상품을 구매할 때 온라인 후기에만 의존하기보다는 상품 자체에 집중해야 한다는 내용의 글이다.

23 ③ 글의 제목

한때 많은 서양 의료 전문가들은 침술이 효과가 없다고 생각했지만, 침술이 여러 과학적인 근거를 가진 것으로 최근 밝혀졌다. 침술은 중국 사람들이 기(氣)라고 부르는 에너지가 신체를 따라 순환한다는 믿음에 바탕을 두고 있다. 기(氣)의 흐름이 막히면 불균형이 생기고 고통이나 질병을 초래하게 된다는 것이다. 침술사들은 신체의 특정 지점을 자극해 기(氣)의 적절한 균형과 흐름을 회복시켜 준다. 연구 결과에 따르면 침술은 엔도르핀이라 불리는, 자연적으로 생성된 모르핀 같은 물질을 방출하는 데 영향을 줄 수 있다고 한다. 침술은 또한 신경을 통해 통증 자극이 전달되는 것을 막음으로써 적어도 일시적으로 고통을 완화시켜 줄 수 있다. 침술 치료를 받는 환자들은 그들이 더 진정되는 것 같다고 말한다.

health professional (의사·간호사 등의) 의료 종사자   acupuncture 침술; 침을 놓다(acupuncturist 침술사)   ineffective 비효율적인; *쓸모없는   be based on …에 근거하다   circulate 순환시키다   block 막다   imbalance 불균형, 불안정   restore 복구하다   proper 적절한   substance 물질   endorphin 엔도르핀(진통작용을 하는 호르몬)   hold back 제지하다   transmission 전달, 이송   impulse 충동; *자극   nerve 신경   [문제] alternative 대신의, 대안의, 양자택일의   approval 동의; *인정   conventional 관습적인; *전통적인   skeptical 회의적인, 의심 많은

4행 Acupuncture is based on the belief [that energy, {which the Chinese call Qi}, circulates along the body].: [ ]는 the belief와 동격, { }는 energy를 선행사로 하는 계속적 용법의 목적격 관계대명사절

6행 …, an imbalance is created, [resulting in pain or disease].: [ ]는 결과를 나타내는 분사구문

7행 Acupuncturists **stimulate** specific points in the body **to restore** the proper balance and flow of Qi.: 'stimulate+O+to-v' 「…을 자극하여 ~하게 하다」

15행 Patients [who receive acupuncture treatment] say [(that) they feel calmer].: 첫 번째 [ ]는 Patients를 선행사로 하는 주격 관계대명사절, 두 번째 [ ]는 say의 목적절

③ 최근 연구를 통해 침술이 실제 효능이 있음이 과학적으로 증명되고 있다는 내용이다.

24 ⑤ 글의 주제

유럽인들이 17세기와 18세기 동안 카리브해 지역을 식민지로 만들었을 때, 그들은 수십만 명의 아프리카인들을 노예 노동자로 섬에 데려왔다. 오늘날의 아이티인 프랑스의 생도맹그는 이 노예 무역 식민지들 중에서 단연코 가장 많은 이득을 보았다. 그것의 거대한 커피와 설탕 농장들은 막대한 양의 부를 창출했다. 그러나, 이 모든 부는 프랑스 농장주들의 수중에 남아있었다. 한편, 10대 1의 비율로 그들보다 수가 더 많았던 흑인 노예들은 비참한 삶을 살았다. 그들은 고된 노동에 대한 어떠한 보수도 받지 못했고 명령에 불복종한다는 이유로 잔인하게 맞았다. 이 부당한 대우에 대한 그들의 커져가는 분노는 1791년에 아이티 혁명을 초래했다. 15년간의 반란은 이전 노예 계급에 의해 주도된 자유롭고 독립적인 아이티 선언으로 끝이 났다. 이것은 아이티를 식민지 건설의 시작 이래로 유럽으로부터 독립을 쟁취한 최초의 라틴 아메리카 국가이자 세계 최초로 흑인이 이끄는 국가가 되도록 만들었다.

colonize 식민지로 만들다(colonization 식민지화, 식민지 건설)   laborer 노동자   by far 훨씬; *단연코   profitable 수익성이 있는   massive 거대한   plantation 농장   generate 발생시키다   meanwhile 한편   outnumber …보다 수가 더 많다   miserable 비참한   cruelly 잔인하게   beat 때리다   disobey 불복종하다   treatment 대우   result in (결과적으로) …을 야기하다   revolution 혁명   uprising 반란   declaration 선언   independent 독립된, 독립적인(independence 독립, 독립심)   former 이전의   [문제] compensation 보상

9행 Meanwhile, the black slaves, [who outnumbered them ten to one], lived miserable lives.: [ ]는 the black slaves를 선행사로 하는 계속적 용법의 주격 관계대명사절

15행 The 15-year uprising ended with the declaration of a free and independent Haiti [led by the former slave class].: [ ]는 the declaration of a free and independent Haiti를 수식하는 과거분사구

프랑스의 식민지였던 아이티가 혁명을 통해 최초의 라틴 아메리카 독립국이자 세계 최초로 흑인이 이끄는 국가라는 독특한 지위를 얻게 된 과정을 설명하고 있는 글이므로, 글의 주제로 가장 적절한 것은 ⑤ '아이티는 어떻게 프랑스 식민지에서 독립국이 되었나'이다.

25 ② 도표 내용 불일치

위의 그래프는 대형견과 소형견을 소유한 사람들이 자신의 반려 동물에게 매년 얼마나 많이 지출하는지를 카테고리별로 나누어 보여준다. 전반적으로, 대형견을 소유한 사람들은 소형견을 소유한 사람들보다 반려 동물에게 평균 연간 295달러를 더 쓴다. (소형견 주인들은 예산의 10퍼센트를 먹이에 쓰는 반면에, 대형견 주인들은 예산의 3분의 1 이상을 그것에 지출한다.) 소형견 주인들에게 보험은 가장 큰 비용이 드는 일로, 예산의 40퍼센트 가량을 차지하는 반면에, 배변용 깔개는 가장 적은 비용이 드는 일이다. 배변용 깔개는 대형견 주인들에게도 가장 적은 비용이 드는 일이지만, 그들에게 가장 많은 비용이 드는 일은 의료 비용이다. 두 가지 유형의 개를 소유한 사람들 모두에게, 장난감과 특별 간식은 두 번째로 적은 비용이 드는 일이며, 대형견 주인들은 소형견 주인들보다 이것에 2퍼센트포인트를 더 쓴다.

annual 매년의(annually 매년)   expense 비용; 비용이 드는 일   litter 쓰레기; *(배변용) 깔개   treat 대접; *간식   insurance 보험   break down (분석할

수 있도록) 나누다 budget 예산 take up 차지하다, 쓰다

(1행) The above graphs show [how much owners of large and small dogs spend on their pets annually], **with** the spending **broken down** by category.: [ ]는 show의 목적어로 쓰인 의문사절, 'with+O+과거분사' 「…이 ~된 채로」(부대상황을 나타내는 분사구문)

(4행) Overall, owners of large dogs spend an average of $295 per year more on their pets than the owners of small dogs **do**.: do는 spend on their pets를 대신하는 대동사

② 대형견 주인들이 먹이에 쓰는 비용은 예산의 3분의 1 미만(27퍼센트)이다.

26 ② 내용 불일치

로랑 클럭은 1785년 프랑스 리옹 근처의 작은 마을에서 태어났다. 그는 한 살 때 화재를 당해 청각과 후각을 모두 잃었다. 열두 살 때, 로랑은 파리에 있는 왕립 농아학교에 입학했고, 뛰어난 학업 성적을 거두었다. 그가 졸업한 후, 학교에서는 그에게 보조교사가 되어 달라고 요청했다. 그는 그렇게 했고, 헌신적인 교사가 되었다. 한편 미국의 토마스 홉킨스 갈로데는 미국에 농아학교가 없다는 것을 알고 근심스러워했다. 어느 날, 토마스는 파리의 왕립 농아학교를 방문해서 로랑을 만났고, 그에게 미국에서 학생들을 가르쳐 줄 것을 요청했다. 로랑은 동의했고, 그들은 함께 미국 최초의 농아학교를 설립했다.

royal 왕의, 여왕의 institution (학교 · 병원 등의) 공공 시설 excel 빼어나다, 탁월하다 assistant 보조(의) dedicated 헌신적인 found 설립하다

(3행) ... he fell into a fire, [losing both his hearing and his sense of smell].: [ ]는 결과를 나타내는 분사구문

(9행) ..., Thomas Hopkins Gallaudet was upset [to learn {that there were ... in America}].: [ ]는 감정의 원인을 나타내는 부사적 용법의 to부정사구, { }는 learn의 목적절

(11행) ..., Thomas visited the Royal Institution for the Deaf in Paris, [where he met Laurent], ...: [ ]는 the Royal ... Paris를 선행사로 하는 계속적 용법의 관계부사절

② 로랑의 청각 장애는 선천적인 것이 아니라 한 살 때 겪은 화재 때문이다.

27 ② 내용 일치

역사가 기록되기 이전 시대부터, 인간은 인형을 만들어왔고 그것을 다양한 용도로 사용해왔다. 가장 초기의 인형들은 아마도 점토나 나무 같은 단순한 재료로 만들어졌을 것이며, 종교적 물건이나 아이들을 위한 장난감으로 쓰였을 가능성이 높다. 비록 이 시대의 인형은 오늘날 전혀 존재하지 않지만, 고고학자들은 고대 바빌론 시대에서 비롯된 것으로 추정되는 인형 파편을 찾아냈다. 또한 수천 년 된 이집트 무덤에서 출토된 인형들도 있었다. 평평한 목재 조각으로 만들어진 그것들은 그 위에 문양이 그려져 있었고, 머리카락을 나타내는 구슬 꿰미들을 특징으로 했다. 역사학자들은 또한 고대 그리스와 로마의 어린 소녀들이 인형을 가지고 놀았으며, 성인기로 접어들면 여신에게 그것을 제물로 바쳤다는 것을 알게 되었다.

material 재질, 재료 clay 점토 religious 종교의 plaything 장난감 era 시대, 시기 archaeologist 고고학자 recover 회복되다; *되찾다, 찾아내

다 fragment 조각, 파편 assume 가정하다 originate 비롯하다, 유래하다 extract 뽑다, 추출하다 grave 무덤 flat 평평한 pattern 무늬 feature …을 특징으로 하다 string 줄, 꿰미 bead 구슬 represent 대표하다; *나타내다 historian 역사학자 sacrifice 희생하다; *제물로 바치다 goddess 여신 adulthood 성인기

(7행) ..., archaeologists have recovered a doll fragment [which is assumed **to have originated** from the ancient Babylonian period].: [ ]는 a doll fragment를 선행사로 하는 주격 관계대명사절, to have originated는 술어동사(is)의 시제보다 이전의 때를 나타내는 완료부정사

(11행) [(Being) Made of flat pieces of wood], they had patterns [painted on them] and featured strings of beads to represent hair.: 첫 번째 [ ]는 부대상황을 나타내는 분사구문, 두 번째 [ ]는 patterns를 수식하는 과거분사구

① 역사 기록 이전부터 인형이 다양한 목적으로 사용되었다. ③ 초기의 인형들은 남아 있지 않으나, 바빌론 시대 인형의 파편이 고고학자들에 의해 발견되었다. ④ 고대 이집트 인형들의 머리카락은 구슬 꿰미로 만들어졌다. ⑤ 고대 그리스와 로마에서는 여신에게 제물로 인형을 바쳤으며, 신의 형상을 본떠 만들었다는 내용은 없다.

28 ⑤ 내용 불일치

노스빌 십 대 청소년 패션쇼

노스빌 청소년 센터에서 사상 최초의 십 대 청소년 패션쇼를 선보입니다. 이 행사는 지역 내 의류 가게 주인인 애슐리 찰스가 주최하며 세 명의 젊은 패션 디자이너들의 작품을 선보일 예정입니다.

일시: 5월 11일 토요일 오후 6시부터 8시까지

장소: 주얼 호텔, 3층 연회장

티켓 가격: 1인당 35달러

티켓 포함 사항: 패션쇼 입장 및 쇼 이후의 뷔페

구매 가능한 티켓은 100장뿐입니다. 쇼 일주일 전부터 판매될 예정이며 청소년 센터의 웹사이트인 www.northvilleyouth.org에서 구매하실 수 있습니다.

first-ever 사상 최초의 host (행사를) 주최하다 feature 특별히 포함하다 work 작품 banquet hall 연회장 admission 입장; 입장료 available 구할[이용할] 수 있는 on sale 판매되는, 구매할 수 있는 purchase 구매하다

(12행) There are only 100 tickets **available**.: available은 tickets를 수식하는 형용사(-ible, -able로 끝나는 일부 형용사는 명사를 뒤에서 꾸며줄 수 있음)

⑤ 입장권은 쇼 일주일 전에 판매가 시작될 것이라고 나와 있으므로, 5월 4일부터 판매되는 것을 알 수 있다.

29 ④ 어법

신체는 당분을 두 가지 방법으로 사용한다. 세포 내에서 당분은 활동에 필요한 에너지를 공급하는 데 사용되거나 지방으로 저장된다. 지방은 이후에 운동과 같은 활동들을 위해서 신체가 에너지를 만들 필요가 있을 때 분해된다. 당분은 에너지원으로 쓰일 뿐만 아니라 뇌를 자극해서 '행복 호르몬'을 만들어 내는데, 이는 당신이 더 쾌활하다고 느끼게 한다. 이것이 과자나 사탕과 같은 단 음식이 그렇게 인기 있는 간식인 이유 중 하나이다. 그러나 당분이 든 음식은 주의해서 취급되어야 한다는 것을 기억하라. 지나친 당분은 치아를 썩게 하고 심장병을 일으킬 위험을 증가시킬

수 있다. 그러므로 섭취하는 당분의 양을 최소로 유지하려고 노력해야 한다.

어휘
cell 세포   fuel 연료를 공급하다; 연료; 에너지원   stimulate 자극하다   hormone 호르몬   sugary 당분이 든   caution 주의   decay 부패; *충치   consume 소비하다; *먹다   minimum 최소(한도), 최저치

구문해설
[1행] In cells, sugar is **either** used to fuel activity **or** stored as fat.: 'either A or B' 「A 또는 B」
[5행] ..., sugar stimulates the brain to produce "happy hormones," [which **make** you **feel** more cheerful].: [ ]는 happy hormones를 선행사로 하는 계속적 용법의 주격 관계대명사절, 'make+O+동사원형' 「…을 ~하게 하다」

문제해설
조동사 can에 동사원형인 lead와 병렬 연결된 것이므로 ④ increasing은 동사원형인 increase로 고쳐야 한다.

30 ⑤ 어휘

루이 파스퇴르는 음식의 부패를 연구했던 19세기의 프랑스 화학자였다. 다른 학자들이 음식의 부패가 자연적인 화학 변화에서 기인한다고 주장했던 반면, 파스퇴르는 공기 중에 있는 미생물이 음식을 상하게 한다고 믿었다. 그는 수프를 가열하여 그 안의 미생물을 죽인 후 밀폐함으로써 자신의 이론을 증명했다. 수프는 밀폐되어 있는 동안에는 부패하지 않았지만, 다시 개봉되어 공기에 노출되자 부패했다. 파스퇴르는 와인, 식초, 맥주가 부패하지 않게 하는 데 같은 원리를 적용했다. 그의 방법은 아주 효과적이어서 영국은 아프리카와 인도의 식민지로 맥주를 수송하기 시작했다. 후에 그는 같은 기술을 이용해 우유를 저장했다. 오늘날 많은 유제품들이 음식의 부패를 막는 방법을 수정한(→ 고안한) 그 사람을 기리기 위하여 '파스퇴르화된(저온 살균된)'이라는 라벨을 달고 있다.

어휘
chemist 화학자   spoilage 부패(spoil 상하다, 부패하다)   organism 유기체, 미생물   broth 국물, 묽은 수프   seal 봉하다, 밀봉하다   expose 내놓다, 노출시키다   apply 적용하다   principle 원리   vinegar 식초   preserve (썩지 않게) 저장하다   label 라벨을 붙이다   pasteurize 저온 살균법을 행하다   in honor of …에게 경의를 표하여   revise 수정하다

구문해설
[4행] ..., Pasteur believed that tiny organisms in the air **caused** food **to spoil**.: 'cause+O+to-v' 「…가 ~하도록 하다」
[7행] The broth did **not** spoil [while (it was) sealed], **but** it spoiled when ... to the air.: 'not A but B' 「A가 아니라 B」, [ ]는 때를 나타내는 부사절 ('주어+be동사'가 생략된 형태)
[10행] ... to **prevent** wine, vinegar, and beer **from spoiling**.: 'prevent+O+from v-ing' 「…가 ~하는 것을 막다」

문제해설
음식의 부패를 연구한 파스퇴르가 부패를 막는 방법을 '고안했다'고 하는 것이 자연스러우므로 ⑤ revised(수정했다)를 devised(고안했다) 등으로 고쳐야 한다.

31 ③ 빈칸 추론

모든 거미들은 실을 만들어 내지만, 그들은 각각 다른 이유로 그것을 생산한다. 사람들은 우선 거미줄을 치고 사냥을 하기 위해 자신의 실을 사용하는 거미들을 생각하겠지만, 인간이 다양한 방법으로 건축 재료들을 사용하는 것과 같이 거미들은 그것에 대한 많은 다양한 응용을 한다.

수많은 거미들은 자신이 위험으로부터 빠져나오게 하기 위해 실을 이용한다. 이리저리 움직이면서 그들은 그들 뒤에 한 줄의 실을 남기는데, 이것은 안전줄이 산악 등반가를 위해 하는 것과 동일한 기능을 수행할 수 있다. 위험에 처한 거미는 이 가닥을 따라 쉽게 탈출할 수 있다. 다른 많은 거미들은 새끼를 위한 보호막을 짓기 위해 자신의 실을 이용한다. 이 두꺼운 구조들은 거미의 알들을 위한 아기방의 역할을 한다. 물론 많은 거미들이 거미줄을 만들기 위해 자신의 실을 사용하지만, 각각의 거미는 그것을 다르게 짓는다. 거미집은 체계성이 없는 망처럼 엮인 것에서부터 기다란 실관, 거대한 실판에 이르기까지 다양하다.

어휘
spin a web 거미줄을 치다   material 재료   thread 실, 가닥   function 기능   escape 달아나다, 탈출하다   cocoon (곤충의) 고치; *보호막   structure 구조; 구조물   cobweb (망처럼 엮어 놓은) 거미줄   organization 조직; 구조; *체계성   massive 거대한   [문제] method 방법   application 응용, 적용   explanation 설명

구문해설
[2행] Although people first think of spiders [using their silk {to spin webs and hunt}], spiders have a number of different applications for it, ...: [ ]는 spiders를 수식하는 현재분사구, { }는 목적을 나타내는 부사적 용법의 to부정사구
[8행] ..., they leave a line of silk thread behind them, [which can serve **the same** function **as** a safety line does for a mountain climber].: [ ]는 a line of silk thread를 선행사로 하는 계속적 용법의 주격 관계대명사절, 'the same ... as ~' 「~와 같은 …」

문제해설
빈칸 이후의 내용에서 거미들은 위험에서 빠져 나오기 위해, 그리고 새끼를 위한 보호막을 짓기 위해 등등 거미줄을 다양한 용도로 사용한다고 했으므로, 이는 실의 다양한 ③ '응용, 적용'이라고 할 수 있다.

32 ① 빈칸 추론

세계의 주요 종교들은 사람들의 시간에 대한 태도에 영향을 끼쳐왔다. 힌두교에서는 사람이 결국 시간으로부터 자유로워질 때까지 계속 다시 태어난다고 가르친다. 힌두교도들은 시간이 주기적으로 순환한다고 믿는다. 그들에게는, 시간의 수레바퀴 속에 절박감은 없다. 불교에도 이와 비슷한 믿음이 있다. 불교는 인생의 일시성을 강조한다. 불교도들에게는 현생 이후에 또 다른 삶이 있다. 그러나 시간이 일직선으로 흘러간다고 생각하는 경향이 있는 다른 종교들도 있다. 기독교에 따르면 신이 태초에 시간을 창조했고 미래에 끝이 있을 것이라고 한다. 마찬가지로, 이슬람교도들은 시간이 유한하다고 믿는다. 그들은 우리가 만약 제 위치를 너무 많이 벗어나면, 다시 돌아올 수 없을지도 모른다고 생각한다.

어휘
Hinduism 힌두교(Hindu 힌두 사람, 힌두교 신자)   reborn 다시 태어난   release 풀어주다, 해방시키다   cyclical 주기적인   urgency 긴급, 절박   wheel 수레바퀴   Buddhism 불교(Buddhist 불교신자)   impermanence 일시성   beyond (특정한 시간을) 지나, 그 이후로   Christianity 기독교 (정신)   Muslim 이슬람교도   limited (시간·수 등이) 한정된   stray 제 위치[길]를 벗어나다   make back 돌아가다

구문해설
[2행] Hinduism teaches [that people will be reborn again and again {until they finally **are released** from time}].: [ ]는 teaches의 목적절, { }는 때를 나타내는 부사절이므로 미래의 일을 나타낼 때 현재시제 사용

문제해설
① 힌두교와 불교의 윤회론적 시간 관념과 기독교와 이슬람교의 직선적 시간 관념을 대

조하면서 주요 종교들이 시간에 대한 사람들의 태도에 영향을 주었다는 것을 설명하는 글이다.

33 ① 빈칸 추론

최근의 한 연구는 개인의 일기에 고생과 역경에 대해 기록하는 것이 실제로 신체 건강에 긍정적인 영향을 미칠 수 있다는 것을 보여주었다. 연구원들은 병원 환자들을 두 집단으로 나누었다. 첫 번째 집단에는 그들이 매일 겪고 있는 모든 불쾌한 경험들의 세부 내용들을 기록하라고 지시했고, 반면 두 번째 집단에는 단순히 일상의 사건들을 기록하도록 요청했다. 이 행동을 몇 달간 지속적으로 유지한 후, 첫 번째 집단의 피실험자들은 그들의 전반적인 건강 면에서 두 번째 집단의 피실험자들보다 두드러진 향상을 보였다. 연구자들에 의해 내려진 결론은 정신적인 충격에 대해 기록하는 것이 우리가 이러한 괴로운 사건들을 더 잘 받아들일 수 있게 해주고, 그로 인해 스트레스의 수위를 낮추며 건강을 향상시킨다는 것이다.

어휘
adversity 역경   instruct 지시하다   request 요청하다   subject 피실험자   significantly 상당히, 두드러지게   draw (결론 등을) 내다   trauma 정신적 외상[충격](traumatic 정신적 충격이 큰)   disturbing 불안한, 불편한, 괴로운   thereby 그것에 의하여   [문제] impact 영향, 효과   treatment 치료

구문해설
(12행) The conclusion [drawn by the researchers] is that writing about trauma **allows** us **to** better **accept** these disturbing events, [thereby lowering our stress levels and improving our health].: 첫 번째 [ ]는 The conclusion을 수식하는 과거분사구, 'allow+O+to-v'「…가 ~하게 하다」, 두 번째 [ ]는 결과를 나타내는 분사구문

문제해설
빈칸은 연구의 결과에 해당하는 부분으로, 일상생활의 불쾌한 경험들을 구체적으로 기록한 집단이 그렇지 않은 집단보다 신체 건강이 좋아졌다는 내용으로 보아, ① '신체 건강에 긍정적인 영향을 미친다'가 적절하다.

34 ⑤ 빈칸 추론

때때로 발명가들은 그들이 실제로 얻고자 했던 것이 아닌, 유익한 무언가를 우연히 발견할 수도 있다. 이런 종류의 발견은 '세렌디피티'로 알려져 있다. 이런 식으로 발견을 하는 발명가들 일부는 그 결과가 우연한 것이었다고 인정하지만, 어떤 사람들은 그것을 은폐하려고 한다. 하지만 사실 세렌디피티는 과학적인 발견과 발명품의 주요한 구성요소이다. 예를 들어, 전자레인지는 한 과학자가 자신이 연구 중이던 전파가 주머니에 들어있던 막대사탕을 녹게 했다는 것을 발견했을 때 발명되었다. 이와 같은 일들 때문에, 과학자들은 우연한 사건들에 대해 열린 마음을 갖는 경향이 있다. 따라서 우연한 발견들은 대개 과학자가 선택한 전공 분야 내에서 일어난다.

어휘
stumble upon …을 우연히 발견하다   beneficial 유익한, 이로운   occurrence 발생, 사건   serendipity 우연히 발견하는 능력; *운수 좋은 뜻밖의 발견(물)(serendipitous 우연히 발견하는)   admit 인정[시인]하다   accidental 우연한   cover up 숨기다, 은폐하다   radar wave 전파   specialization 전문 과목[분야]   [문제] component 구성 요소, 성분

구문해설
(1행) ..., inventors may accidentally stumble upon something **beneficial** [that they hadn't actually been seeking].: 형용사 beneficial이 something을 뒤에서 수식. [ ]는 something을 선행사로 하는

목적격 관계대명사절
(4행) Some inventors [who make discoveries in this manner] admit [(that) the results were accidental]; ...: 첫 번째 [ ]는 Some inventors를 선행사로 하는 주격 관계대명사절, 두 번째 [ ]는 admit의 목적절
(9행) ... discovered [that the radar waves {(which) he was working with} **had melted** a candy bar in his pocket].: [ ]는 discovered의 목적절, { }는 the radar waves를 선행사로 하는 목적격 관계대명사절, had melted는 술어동사(discovered)의 시제보다 더 이전의 때를 나타내는 과거완료

문제해설
세렌디피티가 과학 분야에서 종종 일어나며 상당한 기여를 한다는 것이 글의 요지이므로, 빈칸에는 ⑤가 가장 적절하다.

35 ② 흐름과 무관한 문장

만일 당신이 잠시 동안 누운 후에 침대에서 벌떡 뛰어 오르면, 당신은 아마도 가벼운 어지러움을 경험할 것이다. 이것은 중력이 산소가 풍부한 혈액을 당신의 머리에서부터 몸의 나머지 부분으로까지 빠져나가게 한 결과이다. 어떤 경우에는, 그 결과로 나타나는 어지러움이 너무 심해서 당신은 의식을 잃을지도 모른다. 그러나 모든 동물이 이 현상을 겪는 것은 아니다. 예를 들어, 기린은 7피트만큼이나 긴 목을 가진 종이다. (놀랍게도 기린은 인간과 같은 개수의 목뼈를 가지고 있다.) 먹이를 먹는 동안 그것은 나뭇잎에 다다르기 위해 땅 위에 있는 풀에서부터 17피트만큼이나 높은 곳까지 일상적으로 머리를 움직인다. 하지만 이러한 머리 높이의 극적인 변화에도 불구하고 기린은 어지러움을 느끼지 않는다. 기린은 중력에 대응하고 높이의 변화에 관계없이 머리로 계속 피를 퍼 올리는 고성능의 순환 체계를 발달시켰다.

어휘
leap up 뛰어 오르다   light-headedness 약간의 어지러움(light-headed 약간 어지러운)   consequence 결과   gravity 중력   drain 빼내다; 빠지다   dizziness 현기증   consciousness 의식   routinely 일상적으로   shift 옮기다, 이동하다   high-powered 고성능의   circulation 순환   counteract 대응하다   pump 퍼 올리다, 퍼내다   regardless of …에 관계없이

구문해설
(1행) If you **leaped** up from bed after lying down for a while, you **would** probably **experience** light-headedness.: 'If+S+동사의 과거형 ..., S+조동사의 과거형+동사원형 ~'으로 현재 사실과 반대되는 일을 가정하는 가정법 과거 구문
(3행) This is a consequence of *gravity* **draining** oxygen-rich blood from your head down to the rest of your body.: draining 이하는 전치사 of의 목적어로 쓰인 동명사구이고 gravity는 동명사의 의미상 주어
(15행) It has evolved a high-powered circulation system [that counteracts gravity and **keeps** blood **pumping** ... in elevation].: [ ]는 a high-powered circulation system을 선행사로 하는 주격 관계대명사절, 'keep+O+v-ing'「…을 계속 ~하다」

문제해설
② 고성능의 순환 체계가 발달되어 머리 높이의 변화에도 어지러움을 느끼지 않는 기린에 대해 설명하는 글로, 기린의 목뼈 개수에 관한 내용은 글의 흐름에 맞지 않는다.

36 ④ 글의 순서

윌리엄 펜의 저주는 필라델피아의 프로 스포츠팀들 중 아무도 1987년부터 2008년까지 선수권 대회에서 우승 해내지 못한 이유를 설명하기 위해 사용되었다.
(C) 저주의 근원으로 역할을 한 것은 바로 1894년 시청 꼭대기에 놓였던 윌리엄 펜의 동상이었다. 그 동상은 필라델피아에서 가장 높은 지점을 상

징했고, 아무도 더 높은 무엇인가를 건립하지 않겠다는 전반적인 합의가 있었다. 이 합의는 1987년까지 계속되었다.
(A) 그해 그 동상보다 훨씬 더 높은 탑이 건립되었는데, 그 도시의 팀들은 갑자기 우승을 멈추었다. 사람들은 그 동상을 스포츠 셔츠와 모자로 장식함으로써 저주를 끝내려고 노력했지만, 아무것도 효과가 없었다.
(B) 그러나 몇 년 후 누군가가 기막힌 아이디어를 생각해 냈다. 도시 내에서는 훨씬 더 높은 건물이 건설 중이었다. 그것이 끝났을 때, 아주 작은 윌리엄 펜 동상이 그 꼭대기에 놓였다. 그해 필라델피아는 저주를 끝내며 월드 시리즈 우승을 차지했다.

어휘
curse 저주   erect 똑바로 세우다; 건립하다   put an end to …을 끝내다. 그만두게 하다   adorn 꾸미다. 장식하다   jersey (운동 경기용) 셔츠   come up with …을 생각해 내다   atop 꼭대기에, 맨 위에   basis 근거, 기반   represent 대표하다; *나타내다. 상징하다

구문해설
1행 The curse of William Penn was used [to explain (the reason) {why none of Philadelphia's professional sports teams managed to win a championship from 1987 to 2008}].: [ ]는 목적을 나타내는 부사적 용법의 to부정사구, { }는 이유를 나타내는 관계부사절, 선행사 the reason이 생략된 형태
16행 It was a statue of William Penn [that had been placed atop City Hall in 1894] that served as the basis of the curse.: 'it is[was] … that ~' 「~하는 것은 바로 …이다[였다]」(강조구문), [ ]는 a statue of William Penn을 선행사로 하는 주격 관계대명사절
19행 …, and there was a general agreement [that no one would build anything taller].: a general agreement와 [ ]는 동격, -thing으로 끝나는 부정대명사는 형용사가 뒤에서 수식함

문제해설
④ 필라델피아의 프로 스포츠 팀들이 1987년부터 2008년까지 선수권 대회에서 우승을 하지 못한 이유가 윌리엄 펜의 저주 때문이라는 주어진 글 뒤에, 저주의 근원인 윌리엄 펜의 동상에 대해 기술하는 (C)가 오고, 그 동상보다 훨씬 더 높은 탑이 건립되자 프로 팀들이 우승하지 못하게 되었다는 (A)가 온 후, 마지막으로 그 저주를 끝내기 위한 기발한 아이디어에 대해 언급하는 (B)가 오는 것이 자연스럽다.

37 ③ 글의 순서
1914년 제1차 세계대전 중, 군인들은 면 붕대가 필요했으나 미국에 면이 충분하지 않았다. 킴벌리 클라크 사는 면의 대용품으로 셀루코튼을 만들었는데, 이는 매우 성공적이었다.
(B) 1918년에 전쟁이 끝났을 때, 회사에는 그 신소재의 재고가 많이 남았다. 그래서 킴벌리 클라크 사의 개발자들은 제품의 새로운 용도를 생각해 냈다. 그것이 클리넥스 커치프였다.
(A) 그들은 여성들이 화장을 지울 때 그 제품을 사용하도록 권장하는 광고를 했다. 그러나 킴벌리 클라크 사 직원들은 그들의 신제품의 또 다른 용도에 대한 편지를 받고는 놀랐다.
(C) 많은 여성들이 그들의 남편들이 그 티슈에 코를 풀고 있다고 편지에 썼다. 남성들은 그 티슈를 손수건보다 선호했다. 손수건과 달리 그것들은 한 번 쓰고 버릴 수 있어서 남성들이 좋아했던 것이다.

어휘
cotton 면   bandage 붕대   substitute 대용품   remove 제거하다   material 재료   leftover 남은 것. 나머지   come up with …을 생각해 내다   kerchief 스카프; *손수건   blow one's nose 코를 풀다   disposable 일회용의, 한 번 쓰고 버리는

구문해설
3행 Kimberly-Clark created cellucotton, [a substitute for cotton], [which was very successful].: 첫 번째 [ ]는 cellucotton과 동격, 두 번째 [ ]는 cellucotton을 선행사로 하는 계속적 용법의 주격 관계대명사절
5행 They made advertisements [that encouraged women to use the product {when removing their makeup}].: [ ]는 advertisements를 선행사로 하는 주격 관계대명사절, 'encourage+O+to-v' 「…가 ~하도록 장려하다」, { }는 때를 나타내는 분사구문

문제해설
③ 제1차 세계대전 때 면 붕대의 대용품으로 셀루코튼이 만들어졌다는 주어진 글 다음에, 전쟁 후 셀루코튼의 재고를 처리하기 위해 신제품을 개발했다는 (B)가 오고, 그 신제품의 여성을 대상으로 한 용도뿐만 아니라 또 다른 용도에 대해 쓴 소비자들의 편지를 받았다는 내용의 (A)로 이어진 후, 구체적으로 그 용도(남편들이 그것을 코를 푸는 데 사용한다는 것)를 서술한 (C)가 오는 것이 자연스럽다.

38 ③ 주어진 문장의 위치
최근 출판사들 사이에서 걱정스러운 관행이 생겨났다. 그들은 요즘의 작가들을 고용하여 오래전에 사망한 작가들의 소설의 속편을 쓰게 하고 있다. 속편은 원작과 원작의 등장인물을 토대로 쓰여지기 때문에, 독자가 원작과 같은 높은 질과 재미를 기대하게 만든다. 안타깝게도 실상은 그렇지가 않았다. 예를 들어, 어느 작가는 마가렛 미첼의 '바람과 함께 사라지다'의 속편을 썼는데, 이는 조금도 원작만큼 훌륭하다고 여겨지지 않았다. 이러한 속편들은 단지 작가의 팬이나 작품의 팬들이 돈을 쓰게 하기 위해 쓰여진 것이 분명하다. 그러나 이 모방작들은 결코 원작에 미칠 수 없기 때문에 독자들은 실망할 수밖에 없다.

어휘
disturbing 어지럽히는, 불안하게 하는   contemporary 동시대의; *현대의   long-dead 죽은 지 오래된   original 원작(의)   solely 오직, 단지   imitation 모방; 모조품   equal …와 동등하다, …와 맞먹다

구문해설
11행 It's clear [that these sequels are written solely {to get an author's or a literary work's fans to spend money}].: It은 가주어이고 [ ]가 진주어, { }는 목적을 나타내는 부사적 용법의 to부정사구, 'get+O+to-v' 「…가 ~하게 하다」
15행 …, readers cannot help but be disappointed.: 'cannot help but+동사원형' 「…하지 않을 수 없다」(= cannot help v-ing, cannot but+동사원형)

문제해설
요즘 작가들이 오래된 유명 작품들의 속편을 출판하는 것에 대해 반대하는 내용의 글로서, 주어진 문장에서 언급한 '실상 그렇지 않은 예'가 ③ 바로 뒤 문장에 나오므로 주어진 문장은 ③에 들어가는 것이 자연스럽다.

39 ② 주어진 문장의 위치
미국에서 소규모 기업들의 창업과 성공을 막는 몇 가지 현재의 경제적 환경들이 있다. 한 가지는 예비 기업가들이 자금을 확보하려 할 때 겪는 어려움이다. 은행들은 그들 자신의 이익을 보호하기 때문에 그들(예비 기업가들)에게 대출을 해주기를 꺼린다. 그들이(은행들이) 사업 아이디어를 자금원으로 바꿀 수 있는 능력을 아직 입증하지 못한 누군가에게 대출을 해줄 때, 대출금이 상환되지 않을 가능성이 있다. 게다가, 연방 세법은 소규모 기업들에게 제공하는 것보다 대기업들에게 훨씬 더 큰 세금 혜택을 제공한다. 최근 경기 침체의 결과로 줄어든 소비자 지출은 소규모 기업들이 직면하는 또 다른 장애물이다. 그러나 미국 노동 인구의 대다수

가 소규모 기업들에 의해 고용된다는 것이 간과되어서는 안 된다. 미국이 세계에서 경제적 우위를 유지하기를 원한다면, 경제의 이러한 부문이 번창하는 것을 더 수월하게 해야만 한다.

어휘
reluctant to …을 주저하는 loan 대출(금) economic 경제의 discourage 막다, 방해하다 prospective 장래의, 미래의 entrepreneur 기업가 secure funds 자금을 확보하다 demonstrate 입증하다 capital 자본 repay 갚다, 상환하다 tax code 세법 corporation 기업 recession 경기 침체 obstacle 장애물 ignore 무시하다 workforce 노동 인구 dominance 우세 sector 부문, 분야 thrive 번창하다

구문해설
5행 One is the difficulties [(which/that) prospective entrepreneurs face {when trying to secure funds}].: [ ]는 the difficulties를 선행사로 하는 목적격 관계대명사절, { }는 때를 나타내는 분사구문

10행 In addition, the federal tax code provides **far** greater tax benefits to large corporations than it *does* to small businesses.: far는 「훨씬」의 의미로 비교급을 강조하는 부사, does는 provides tax benefits를 대신하는 대동사

13행 Reduced consumer spending [as a result of the recent recession] is another obstacle [(which/that) small businesses face].: 첫 번째 [ ]는 Reduced consumer spending을 수식하는 전치사구, 두 번째 [ ]는 another obstacle을 선행사로 하는 목적격 관계대명사절

18행 ..., it must make **it** easier *for this sector of the economy* [to thrive].: it은 가목적어이고 [ ]가 진목적어, this sector of the economy는 [ ]의 의미상 주어

문제해설
주어진 문장의 them은 예비 기업가들(prospective entrepreneurs)을 가리키며, 주어진 문장은 은행이 그들에게 대출을 해주는 것을 꺼린다는 내용으로 ② 앞에 있는 첫 번째 어려움으로 제시된 자금 확보에 대한 구체적인 설명이므로, ②에 오는 것이 적절하다.

40 ① 요약문 완성

사람들은 종종 특허 제도가 경쟁을 막아 과학 발전을 방해한다고 주장한다. 그러나 지적재산권법은 독점권 없이는 누구도 연구와 개발에 시간과 돈을 투자하려 들지 않을 것이라는 전제를 깔고 있다. 특허 제도는 발명가들이 그들의 지적 재산을 숨기지 않고서도 보호할 수 있게 해 준다. 특허는 다른 사람들이 특허 보유자의 허락 없이 발명품을 만들거나 사용하거나 판매하는 것을 금지할 권리를 부여한다. 특허를 얻기 위해서 발명가는 자신의 발명을 완전히 공개해야 한다. 특허 제도는, 숨기는 것이 경쟁자들을 배제하는 유일한 방법일 때 공개되는 것보다 더 많은 공개를 장려한다. 특허는 또한 혁신적인 발명가들의 이익 장려금을 보호함으로써 기술 공유를 촉진한다.

어휘
patent 특허; 특허를 얻다[주다] hinder 방해하다 advancement 발전, 진보 prohibit 금지하다, 막다 intellectual property 지적재산권 rest on …에 근거하다 assumption 전제, 가정 exclusive 독점적인, 배타적인(exclude 제외하다, 배제하다) secrecy 비밀 엄수, 비밀주의 grant 부여하다, 수여하다 ban 금지하다 permission 허락, 허가 disclose 공개하다(disclosure 공개) promote 장려하다, 촉진하다 incentive 격려; *장려금 innovative 혁신적인 [문제] secure 확보하다; 보호하다 acknowledge 인정하다 standardize 표준화하다 secrete 비밀로 하다

구문해설
4행 ... rests on the assumption [that, without exclusive rights, no one ... in research and development].: [ ]는 the assumption과

동격
8행 A patent grants the right [to **ban** others **from making, using, or selling** the invention ... holder's permission].: [ ]는 the right을 수식하는 형용사적 용법의 to부정사구, 'ban+O+from v-ing'「…가 ~하는 것을 금지하다」 making, using, selling이 병렬 연결

12행 The patent system promotes more disclosure **than** *would* occur *if* secrecy *was* the only way to exclude competitors.: than은 disclosure를 선행사로 하는 유사관계대명사로 주격 관계대명사 역할을 함, than 이하는 현재 사실의 반대를 가정하는 가정법 과거 구문(if절의 주어가 단수이면 be동사로 were 대신 was도 쓰임)

문제해설
① 특허 제도는 우리가 지식을 공유할 수 있게 하는 동시에 개인의 지적 재산을 보호한다.

41 ④ 42 ④ 장문

경찰이 범죄를 저지른 혐의를 받는 사람을 붙잡을 때, 그 사람은 보통 수사관에게 심문을 받는다. 그동안 다른 경찰관들은 옆방에 조용히 앉아, 한쪽 방향에서만 보이는 거울로 모든 것을 자세히 듣고 보고 있다. 당신은 이런 거울이 단순히 한쪽은 반사되고 나머지 한쪽은 투명하다고 생각하겠지만, 사실은 그보다 더 복잡하다.

한쪽 방향만 보이는 거울은 사실 한쪽 면에 매우 얇은 층의 반사 물질이 있는 유리 조각이다. 이것은 '반도금 거울'로 알려져 있는데, 그 층에 보통 거울에서 발견되는 반사 분자 수의 절반만이 들어 있기 때문이다. 이는 그것이 거울에 닿은 빛의 절반은 반사하고 나머지 절반은 통과하게 한다는 것을 의미한다. 결과적으로 한쪽 방향만 보이는 거울은 부분적으로 투명하고 부분적으로 반사한다.

그런데 이것이 사실이라면, 용의자는 왜 '부분적으로' 경찰관들이 다른 방에서 지켜보는 것을 보지 못할까? 이 질문에 대한 답은 꽤 간단하다. 용의자는 밝게 불이 켜진 방에 있는 반면, 경찰관들은 어두운 방에 있다. 이것의 결과는 밤에 어두운(→ 밝은) 방에 있는 것과 비슷하다. 길에 있는 사람들은 방 안에서 일어나고 있는 일을 창문을 통해 쉽게 볼 수 있지만, 당신이 밖에서 일어나고 있는 것을 보기는 어렵다.

어휘
capture 붙잡다, 포획하다 suspect 의심하다, 혐의를 두다; 혐의자, 용의자 commit a crime 죄를 범하다 detective 형사, 수사관 meanwhile 그동안에 reflective 반사하는(reflect 반사하다) complicated 복잡한 layer 막, 층 contain …을 포함하다, …이 들어 있다 molecule 분자 pass through …을 빠져 나가다[관통하다] transparent 투명한, 속이 들여다보이는

구문해설
3행 Meanwhile, other police officers sit quietly in the next room, [listening carefully and watching everything through a one-way mirror].: [ ]는 동시동작을 나타내는 분사구문

15행 This means [(that) it **reflects** half of the light {that hits it} and **allows** the other half *to pass through*].: [ ]는 means의 목적어로 쓰인 명사절, that절의 동사인 reflects와 allows가 and에 의해 병렬 연결, { }는 the light를 선행사로 하는 주격 관계대명사절, 'allow+O+to-v'「…가 ~하도록 허용하다」

20행 But if this is the case, why doesn't the suspect "partly" **see** the police officers **watching** from the other room?: 지각동사 see의 목적격보어로 현재분사가 쓰임

26행 People [who are on the street] can easily see [what's going on inside the room] through the windows, but **it** is difficult *for you* [to see anything {that is happening outside}].: 첫 번째 [ ]는 People을 선행사로 하는 주격 관계대명사절, 두 번째 [ ]는 see의 목적어로 쓰인 관

계대명사절, it은 가주어이고 세 번째 [ ]가 진주어, you는 세 번째 [ ]의 의미상 주어, { }는 anything을 선행사로 하는 주격 관계대명사절

문제해설

41 한쪽 방향에서만 투명하게 보이는 거울의 원리를 사례와 비유를 통해 자세히 설명한 내용이므로, 제목으로 가장 적절한 것은 ④ '한쪽 방향만 보이는 거울: 그것이 어떻게 작용하나'이다.

42 밝게 불이 켜진 방에 있는 용의자가 어두운 방에 있는 경찰관을 보지 못하고, 어두운 방에 있는 경찰관들은 밝은 방에 있는 용의자를 잘 볼 수 있는 상황을 밖에 있는 사람들이 불이 켜진 방 안이 잘 보이는 반면, 밝은 방 안에서는 어두운 밖이 잘 안 보이는 상황에 비유하는 것이 자연스럽다. 따라서, ④ dark(어두운)를 bright(밝은) 등으로 고쳐야 한다.

43 ③ 44 ④ 45 ① 장문

(A) 1990년 이전에 인간이 우주에 대해 포착했던 거의 모든 사진들은 지상에 있는 망원경으로 촬영되었다. 그리고 그러한 망원경들이 아무리 발달되었다 하더라도, 그것들은 항상 같은 문제에 의해 방해를 받았다. 그것은 바로 지구의 대기였다. 우리의 대기권에 존재하는 모든 먼지 입자와 물 분자, 그리고 가스는 멀리 떨어진 우주에 있는 물체에 의해 방출되는 빛을 왜곡시켜, 그 물체를 보는 우리의 시야도 왜곡되게 만든다.

(C) 수십 년 동안 천문학자들은 머리 속에 해결책을 가지고 있었다. 방해받지 않은 우주의 모습을 얻기 위해, 그들은 그저 망원경을 대기권 밖의 지구 궤도상에 두는 것이었다. 이것이 바로 천문학자인 에드윈 허블의 이름을 딴 허블 우주 망원경이었는데, 먼 거리의 별들이 방출하는 빛에 대한 허블의 이론은 망원경이 발사되면 마침내 실험이 가능해질 것이었다. 그 프로젝트에 대한 작업은 1975년에 시작되어, 과학자들이 그 장치에 들어가는 40만 개의 부품들을 하나하나를 조심스럽게 조립하면서 15년간 계속되었다.

(D) 1990년, NASA는 허블 망원경을 지구의 궤도에 성공적으로 진입시켰다. 곧 천문학자들은 세밀함과 거리감의 정확성에 있어서 그들이 이전에 결코 가지지 못했던 우주의 사진들을 받기 시작했다. 허블 망원경은 또한 우주에 대한 대중들의 이해가 새로운 경지에 달할 것임을 의미했는데, 그것은 그 망원경(허블 망원경)이 이전의 다른 어떤 망원경보다도 훨씬 더 나은 해상도와 감광도를 보유하고 있다는 사실 이상의 이유들 덕분이었다. 또한 매우 다른 기술이 이 시기에 발달하기 시작하고 있었는데, 그것은 누구나 상상할 수 있는 것보다도 더욱 쉽게 허블 망원경의 사진들에 접근할 수 있게 하는 것이었다.

(B) 이 기술이 바로 인터넷이었고, 허블 망원경이 찍은 사진들은 월드와이드웹(WWW)을 통해 전 세계의 열성적인 관찰자들에게 전해졌다. 역사상 처음으로 사람들은 집안에 편안히 앉아서 우주의 심연을 전보다 훨씬 깊이 들여다 볼 수 있게 되었다. 비록 허블 망원경이 이미 구식으로 여겨지고 있고 차세대 우주 망원경에 대한 작업이 진행 중이지만, 그것(허블 망원경)은 우주에 대한 관심과 알려지지 않은 세계에 대한 탐험의 새로운 시대로 (우리를) 인도한 것으로서 언제나 기억될 것이다.

어휘

telescope 망원경(telescopic 망원경의) plague 괴롭히다. 귀찮게 하다 atmosphere 대기 particle 극소량; *입자 molecule 분자, 미립자 distort (사실 등을) 왜곡하다 give off 발하다; 방출하다 snap (사진을) 찍다, 순간 촬영을 하다 transmit 전송하다 peer 자세히 들여다보다 recess 깊은 속; 심연 outdated 구식의, 시대에 뒤진 underway 진행중인 usher 안내하다, 인도하다 output 생산, 산출 launch 시작하다; *발사하다 assemble 조립하다 insertion 삽입(물), 끼워 넣음; *(우주선을) 어떤 궤도에 올려놓기 in terms of …의 면에서 clarity 명쾌함; 명료 resolution 해상도 sensitivity 민감도; *감광도 predecessor 전임자; *이전에 사용되었던 물건

[문제] unhindered 방해받지 않은 inadvisable 권할 수 없는 unmatched 균형 잡히지 않는, 부조화의 inadequate 부적당한 improbable 있음직하지 않은

구문해설

6행 All of the dust particles, water molecules, and gases [present in our atmosphere] distort the light [given off by objects far away in space], …: 첫 번째 [ ]는 All of … gases를 수식하는 형용사구, 두 번째 [ ]는 the light를 수식하는 과거분사구

25행 This was the Hubble Space Telescope, [named after the astronomer Edwin Hubble], [whose theories about the light output of distant stars would finally be able to be tested once the telescope was launched].: 첫 번째 [ ]는 the Hubble Space Telescope를 수식하는 과거분사구, 두 번째 [ ]는 Edwin Hubble을 선행사로 하는 계속적 용법의 소유격 관계대명사절

40행 …, for reasons beyond the fact [that the telescope … its predecessors].: [ ]는 the fact와 동격

42행 A very different technology was also taking off at this time, **one** [that *made* access to Hubble's images *easier* than anyone could have imagined].: one은 a technology를 지칭. [ ]는 one을 선행사로 하는 주격 관계대명사절, 'make+O+형용사' 「…을 ~하게 만들다」

문제해설

43 ③ 1990년 이전에 망원경으로 찍은 우주 사진의 문제점을 지적하는 (A) 다음에, 이 문제점을 해결하기 위한 새로운 망원경인 허블 망원경의 등장에 대한 (C)가 이어지고, 허블 망원경의 장점을 설명하는 (D)가 온 후, 오늘날 인터넷과 연동하여 허블 망원경이 사람들에게 우주에 대한 새로운 이해를 가능하게 했다는 내용의 (B)로 이어지는 것이 자연스럽다.

44 망원경 기술에서 새로운 시대를 연 허블 망원경에 대한 내용의 글이므로 제목으로는 ④ '망원경 기술의 혁신'이 적절하다.

45 빈칸의 앞부분인 (A)에서 망원경으로 우주를 볼 때 대기권의 여러 방해 물질들에 의해 우주에서 들어오는 빛이 왜곡되었다는 내용이 언급되었고, 뒷부분에서는 그 문제점을 해결할 수 있는 방법을 이야기하고 있으므로, 빈칸에는 ① '(다른 요인에 의해) 방해받지 않은'이 적절하다.

15 영어독해 모의고사

본문 ◆ p.146

18 ④	19 ⑤	20 ⑤	21 ⑤	22 ⑤	23 ②
24 ④	25 ②	26 ③	27 ⑤	28 ④	29 ②
30 ③	31 ⑤	32 ②	33 ①	34 ②	35 ①
36 ②	37 ③	38 ②	39 ④	40 ④	41 ③
42 ②	43 ④	44 ⑤	45 ③		

18 ④ 글의 목적

시의회 의원님들께,

저번 주 제 딸과 함께 갈랜드 가(街)의 놀이터에 갔습니다. 어린이들의 부모들이 조용히 벤치에 앉아서 바라보고 있는 동안 어린이들은 무리 지어 시끄럽게 놀고 있었습니다. 바로 그때, 종이 울리기 시작했고 아이스크림을 파는 한 남자가 놀이터 안으로 수레를 밀고 들어왔습니다. 저희가 길을 걸을 때마다 무언가를 파는 광고에 둘러싸여 있다는 것만으로도 충분하지 않을까요? 놀이터는 행상인과 판매원들이 없는 안전한 안식처여야 하지 않습니까? 저는 이에 대해 예전에도 여러 번 항의했지만, 아직 어떤 종류의 회답도 받지 못했습니다. 제 생각에는, 우리의 놀이터에 이런 류의 성가신 일이 없도록 즉각적인 조치가 필요합니다.

진심을 담아,
대런 존스 드림

어휘
surround 둘러싸다 haven 안식처, 피신처 vendor 행상인 nuisance 성가심, 방해

구문해설
(8행) Isn't **it** enough [that we're surrounded by advertisements {selling things} whenever we walk down the street]?: it은 가주어이고 [ ]가 진주어, { }는 advertisements를 수식하는 현재분사구

문제해설
④ 놀이터에서 잡상인을 마주한 불쾌한 경험을 이야기하며, 놀이터가 안전한 안식처가 되도록 잡상인의 놀이터 출입을 금지해달라고 시의회에 촉구하는 편지글이다.

19 ⑤ 필자의 주장

젊은이들의 섭식 장애에 대처하는 최선의 방법은 애초에 섭식 장애가 발생하지 않도록 예방하는 것이라는 데 영양 전문가들은 동의한다. 다시 말해서 문제가 아예 발생하기도 전에 잡으라는 것이다. 부모들은 흔히 언론 매체에 의해 조장되는 몸매에 대한 비현실적인 메시지를 차단하면서, 아이의 자아상을 고양하는 건전한 가정환경을 만듦으로써 이를 해낼 수 있다. 부모들은 아이들이 자신의 몸에 대해 만족하도록 가르쳐야 한다. 부모들은 다른 사람들의 외모에 대해 비판적이어서는 안 되고, 아이들이 외모를 가지고 누군가를 놀리도록 두어서도 안 된다. 오히려, 부모들은 아이들 자신들이 대우받고자 하는 바대로 다른 사람들을 대하도록 장려해야 한다.

어휘
nutritional 영양의 deal with …에 대처하다 disorder 장애 in the first place 우선, 처음부터 foster 기르다; *조장하다, 촉진하다 self-image 자아상 discourage 막다, 말리다 unrealistic 비현실적인 promote 조장하다, 조성하다 critical 비판적인 tease 괴롭히다, 놀리다 treat 다루다, 대우하다

구문해설
(1행) … the best way [to deal with … in young people] is [to **prevent** them **from happening** … place].: 첫 번째 [ ]는 the best way를 수식하는 형용사적 용법의 to부정사구, 두 번째 [ ]는 주격보어로 쓰인 명사적 용법의 to부정사구, 'prevent+O+from v-ing' 「…가 ～하는 것을 막다[예방하다]」

(5행) … a healthy home environment [that fosters … a self-image], [while discouraging unrealistic messages about the body {that are … by the media}].: 첫 번째 [ ]는 a healthy home environment를 선행사로 하는 주격 관계대명사절, 두 번째 [ ]는 부대상황을 나타내는 분사구문, { }는 unrealistic messages about the body를 선행사로 하는 주격 관계대명사절

문제해설
⑤ 자녀의 섭식 장애를 예방하기 위해 부모가 해야 할 일에 관해 쓴 글이다.

20 ⑤ 함축 의미 추론

한 그룹의 연구원들은 보츠와나 농장주들에게 특이한 조언을 했다. 그들은 사자, 표범, 그리고 치타와 같은 대형 고양잇과 동물들에 의한 공격을 방지하기 위해 소의 엉덩이에 가짜 눈을 그릴 것을 권장한다. 연구원들은 눈을 닮은 자연적인 무늬인 '눈꼴 무늬'를 진화시켜온 곤충과 새에서 아이디어를 얻었다. 이 눈꼴 무늬는 다가오는 포식자들에게 자신이 감시당하고 있다고 생각하게 만들어서 겁을 주어 쫓아버린다. 과학자들은 과거에 대형 고양잇과 동물들에게 공격을 받은 적이 있는 14 무리의 소떼에게 그들의 이론을 시험했다. 소들은 세 개의 그룹으로 나뉘었다. 첫 번째는 몸에 눈이 그려졌고, 두 번째는 몸에 간단한 X표를 그렸으며, 세 번째 그룹은 내버려 두었다. 4년의 기간 동안, 두 번째 그룹에서 4마리, 표시가 없는 소 중에서 15마리에 비해, 첫 번째 그룹의 소는 아무도 죽임을 당하지 않았다. 보아하니, 인위적인 눈꼴 무늬는 대자연에 의해 만들어진 것만큼이나 효과적인 것 같다.

어휘
offer 제안하다, 권하다 fake 가짜의 rear end 후미; *엉덩이 cattle 소 big cat 대형 고양잇과 동물 evolve 진화하다 eyespot (공작의 꼬리에 있는) 눈꼴 무늬 resemble 닮다, 비슷하다 scare off 겁을 주어 …을 쫓아 버리다 approach 다가오다 predator 포식자 herd (짐승의) 떼 cross 십자가 기호; *X표 unmarked 표시가 없는 apparently 분명히; *보기에 (…인 듯하다) Mother Nature (만물의 어머니 같은) 대자연 [문제] prey 먹이, 사냥감 fool 속이다, 기만하다

구문해설
(5행) The researchers got their idea from insects and birds [that have evolved "eyespots," {natural patterns **that resemble eyes**}].: [ ]는 insects and birds를 선행사로 하는 주격 관계대명사절, "eyespots"와 { }는 동격, that resemble eyes는 natural patterns를 선행사로 하는 주격 관계대명사절

(8행) These eyespots scare off approaching predators by [**making** them **think** {(that) they are being watched}].: [ ]는 전치사 by의 목적어로 쓰인 동명사구, 사역동사 make의 목적격보어로 동사원형(think)이 쓰임, { }는 think의 목적어로 쓰인 명사절

(9행) The scientists tested their theory on 14 cattle herds [that **had been attacked** by big cats in the past].: [ ]는 14 cattle herds를 선행사로 하는 주격 관계대명사절, had been attacked는 주절의 시제(tested)보다 더 이전에 일어난 일을 나타내는 과거완료

(18행) Apparently, manmade eyespots are just **as effective as** the ones [created by Mother Nature].: 'as+원급+as …' 「…만큼 ～한[하게]」, ones는 앞의 eyespots를 지칭, [ ]는 ones를 수식하는 과거분사구

문제해설

자연적인 눈꼴 무늬로 포식자들에게 겁을 주는 곤충과 새에게서 아이디어를 얻어 농장의 소를 보호하기 위해 소의 엉덩이에 눈을 그렸고, 이로 인해 소들이 포식자들로부터 살아남았다는 내용이다. 따라서 '인위적인 눈꼴 무늬는 대자연에 의해 만들어진 것만큼이나 효과적이다'가 의미하는 바로 가장 적절한 것은 ⑤ '그려진 눈은 자연적인 눈꼴 무늬와 동일한 방식으로 포식자들을 속인다'이다.

21 ⑤ 글의 요지

신문사들은 자신들이 독자들에게 오직 사실만을 제공하면서 객관적인 진실을 게재한다고 믿는다. 그러나, 상황이 항상 그렇게 간단한 것은 아니다. 기자가 사실들을 모으기는 하지만 공간은 어쩔 수 없이 제한되어 있기 때문에, 기자는 무엇이 중요하고 무엇이 그렇지 않은지를 선택해야 한다. 그다음에 기자나 편집자는 이 사실들 중 어떤 것이 기사의 도입부 역할을 하여 다른 것들보다 더 큰 중요성을 가질 것인지 결정해야 한다. 다음으로, 또 다른 편집자는 그 기사가 주목을 많이 받는 1면에 나올 것인지, 아니면 관심을 거의 받지 못하는 20면에 숨겨져야 할지에 대해 이야기해야만 한다. 따라서, 순수한 사실들은 해석에 관여되는 일련의 판단에 의해 영향을 받을 수 있다. 그렇다면, 신문은 단순히 소식을 전하는 것이 아니라 그것을 해석한다고 말하는 것이 타당하다.

어휘

objective 객관적인 necessarily 어쩔 수 없이 restrict 제한하다 editor 편집자 take on (성질·태도를) 취하다 significance 중요성 be subject to …의 영향을 받다[받기 쉽다] interpretation 설명, 해석(interpret 설명하다, 해석하다)

구문해설

1행 Newspapers believe [(that) they publish objective truth], [providing readers with nothing but the facts].: 첫 번째 [ ]는 believe의 목적절, 두 번째 [ ]는 부대상황을 나타내는 분사구문

4행 ..., [space being necessarily restricted], he or she has to select [what's important and what isn't].: 첫 번째 [ ]는 이유를 나타내는 분사구문(주절의 주어(he or she)와 일치하지 않아 주어 space를 생략하지 않음), 두 번째 [ ]는 select의 목적어로 쓰인 의문사절

문제해설

⑤ 신문의 객관성은 기사를 편집하는 과정에서 기자나 편집자의 결정과 일련의 판단에 의해 영향을 받을 수 있다고 이야기하고 있다.

22 ⑤ 글의 주제

동물들이 일상적인 식생활의 일부로 진흙을 핥아먹는 모습이 관찰되어 왔다. 말, 소, 코끼리와 같은 큰 동물들은 외상과 상처의 고통을 덜기 위해 진흙 속에서 뒹군다. 아마존 앵무새들은 그들이 먹는 씨앗에서 발견되는 독에 대한 방어 수단으로서 진흙을 먹기 위해 강둑을 따라 모여든다. 그리고 수의사들은 다양한 부상과 감염을 치료하기 위해 반려동물들에게 진흙을 사용한다. 진흙이 설사를 진정시키고 소화 능력을 향상시킨다고 강력히 믿기 때문에 심지어 몇몇 사람들은 몸이 아플 때 진흙을 먹고 싶은 욕구를 발현시키기도 한다. 게다가 특수하게 배합된 진흙 목욕은 마치 자석처럼 사람의 몸에서 오염 물질들을 완전히 끄집어내어, 단 한 번의 목욕으로 수년 간의 독성 축적물을 제거하는 것으로 나타났다.

어휘

lick 핥다 clay 진흙 diet 식사, 음식 obtain 획득하다 relief 안도; *(고통을) 덜어 줌 wound 상처, 부상 sore 상처, 종기 defense 방어 veterinarian 수의사 injury 부상 infection 감염 longing 갈망, 열망 alleviate (고통 등을) 줄여주다 diarrhea 설사 digestion 소화 formulate 계획을 짜다; *성분을 적절히 배합하다 literally 말 그대로; *정말로,

완전히 pollutant 오염물질 magnet 자석 eliminate 제거하다 toxic 독성이 있는 accumulation 축적, 쌓임 [문제] pros and cons 장단점; 찬반

구문해설

11행 Moreover, specially formulated clay baths have **been shown to** literally **draw** pollutants out of people's bodies like a magnet, [eliminating ... one bath].: 'be shown to-v' 「…하는 것이 입증되다」, [ ]는 부대상황을 나타내는 분사구문

문제해설

⑤ 진흙이 동물과 사람의 건강 회복과 일상적인 건강 관리에 유용하게 쓰인다는 것을 서술한 글이다.

23 ② 글의 제목

미국 내에 비만이 증가하고 있다. 실제로, 통계 자료에 의하면 현재 전체 미국인의 60퍼센트 이상이 과체중이다. 비만이 건강 문제라는 데 동의하지 않는 사람은 거의 없지만, '몸집 용인'이라고 알려지게 된 것에 대한 뚜렷한 증거가 존재한다. 많은 영화관들이 더 넓은 좌석을 설치하기 시작했고, 항공사들은 과체중인 사람들이 추가 요금을 내지 않고 두 자리를 차지하는 것을 허용하라는 압박에 직면해 있다. 큰 사이즈만 판매하는 전문 의류점을 사실상 모든 쇼핑몰에서 찾아 볼 수 있다. '몸집이 큰 사람들에게 우호적인' 휴양지와 호텔들은 심지어 플라스틱으로 된 해변용 의자를 보다 튼튼한 나무 의자로 교체하고 있다. 이러한 시설들이 뚱뚱해도 괜찮다는 메시지를 전달한다고 생각하여, 일부 건강 전문가들은 이러한 경향을 걱정스럽다고 여긴다.

어휘

obesity 비만(obese 뚱뚱한, 살찐) statistics 통계 자료, 통계 indicate …을 나타내다 overweight 과체중의, 비만의 acceptance 인정, 용인 install …을 설치하다 pressure 압력 occupy 차지하다 extra 추가로 specialty 특수성; *전문 practically 사실상 replace 대체하다 accommodation 숙박[수용] 설비; (열차 등의) 자리, 좌석 convey …을 나르다; *(뜻·사상 등을) 전달하다 worrisome 걱정스러운 [문제] gene 유전자 discrimination 차별 대우

구문해설

3행 Although few disagree [that obesity is a health concern], there is clear evidence of [what has become known as "size acceptance."]: 첫 번째 [ ]는 disagree의 목적절, 두 번째 [ ]는 of의 목적어로 쓰인 관계대명사절

7행 ..., and airlines are facing pressure [to allow overweight people to occupy two seats without having to pay extra].: [ ]는 pressure를 수식하는 형용사적 용법의 to부정사구

13행 [Considering that such accommodations convey the message {that being obese is okay}], some health experts ...: [ ]는 이유를 나타내는 분사구문, { }는 the message와 동격

문제해설

미국에서 비만을 사회적으로 용인하는 경향이 나타나고 있음을 몇 가지 예를 들어 설명하고 있으므로, 글의 제목으로는 ② '미국의 경향: 비만을 용인하는 것'이 적절하다.

24 ④ 글의 제목

제2차 세계대전 중에, 미국은 태평양 지역에서 일본과 싸우고 있었다. 미국인들은 일본군의 기밀 메시지를 읽고 있었지만 그들은 그것을 완전히 이해할 수 없었다. 그 메시지에는 'AF'라고 알려진 위치가 언급되어 있었는데, 그곳은 미군이 미드웨이섬일 것으로 짐작한 곳이었다. 하지만, 그들은 확실하지 않아서 기발한 생각을 고안해 냈다. 그들은 미드웨이가

물 부족을 겪고 있다고 주장하는 거짓 메세지를 보냈다. 잠시 후, 일본군은 'AF에 물이 부족하다'라고 적힌 메시지를 보냈다. 이 전략적인 거짓말은 미국인들이 일본군의 메시지를 더 잘 이해할 수 있게 했고 결국 그들이 전쟁에서 이기도록 도왔다. 사람들은 일반적으로 부정직함이 나쁘다는 것에 동의하지만, 그것은 때때로 이로운 방식으로 사용될 수 있다.

구문해설
[4행] The messages mentioned a location [known as "AF," {which the American military forces suspected might be Midway Island}].: [ ]는 a location을 수식하는 과거분사구, { }는 "AF"를 선행사로 하는 계속적 용법의 주격 관계대명사절, the American military forces suspected는 삽입절

[8행] They sent a fake message [that claimed {(that) Midway was suffering from a water shortage}].: [ ]는 a fake message를 선행사로 하는 주격 관계대명사절, { }는 claimed의 목적절

[12행] This strategic lie *allowed* the Americans *to* better *understand* Japanese military messages and eventually **helped** them **win** the war.: 문장의 동사 allowed와 helped가 등위 접속사 and로 병렬 연결, 'allow+O+to-v' 「…가 ~하도록 하다」, 'help+O+(to-)v' 「…가 ~하도록 돕다」

문제해설
제2차 세계대전 당시 미군이 일본군의 기밀 메시지를 해독하는 과정에서 거짓 메시지를 보내어 정확한 정보를 얻음으로써 전쟁에서 승리할 수 있었다는 내용의 글이므로, 제목으로는 ④ '거짓말: 전쟁에서의 유용한 무기'가 적절하다.

25 ② 도표 내용 불일치

전 세계적으로 해마다 많은 양의 석탄이 사용된다. 남아프리카는 조사된 어느 나라보다도 1인당 가장 많은 석탄을 소모하는데, 중국의 두 배 이상이다. (미국에서 일반인에 의해 사용되는 석탄의 양은 세계에서 두 번째로 많으며, 그것은 한국과 캐나다에서 1인당 사용된 석탄의 양을 합친 것보다 더 많다.) 독일의 일반인은 중국의 일반인보다는 더 많지만 보통의 캐나다 사람보다는 더 적은 석탄을 소모한다. 반면에, 중국과 일본은 1인당 동일한 양의 석탄을 소모한다. 인도를 제외하고 이 국가들 모두 1인당 0.5톤 이상의 석탄을 소모한다.

구문해설
[3행] ..., more than **twice as** much **as** China.: '배수사+as ... as' 「~배만큼 …한[하게]」

문제해설
② 미국의 1인당 석탄 사용량(1.8)은 한국(1.2)과 캐나다(1.1)의 1인당 석탄 사용량의 합(2.3)보다 크지 않다.

26 ③ 내용 불일치

잉카인들은 한때 남아메리카의 넓은 영역을 포괄하는 거대한 제국을 통치하였다. 그 제국은 16세기에 스페인 탐험가들이 도착했을 때 5백 년

이상의 역사를 가지고 있었다. 잉카인들은 진보한 민족이었다. 그들은 도로를 포장하고 튼튼한 다리를 지은 숙련된 기술자들이었다. 바퀴에 대해 몰랐음에도 불구하고, 잉카인들은 장벽을 건설하기 위해 몇몇은 10톤만큼이나 무거운 거대한 석재들을 산비탈을 타고 위로 옮길 수 있었다. 이 장벽은 많은 현대식 건물들을 파괴한 큰 규모의 폭풍과 지진에도 굳건히 버텨 왔다. 잉카인들은 또한 훌륭한 예술가였다. 오늘날 잉카의 도자기는 훌륭한 디자인으로 인해 높이 평가된다. 그리고 금과 은 모두의 공급량이 많았기에 잉카인들은 이들 귀금속으로 훌륭한 작품들을 만들어 냈다.

구문해설
[5행] They were skillful engineers [who paved their roads and built strong bridges].: [ ]는 skillful engineers를 선행사로 하는 주격 관계대명사절

문제해설
③ 잉카인들이 세운 장벽은 폭풍과 지진에도 굳건히 버티고 있다고 했다.

27 ⑤ 내용 일치

1938년 필라델피아에서 태어난 맥코이 타이너는 재즈 피아니스트로서 길고 성공적인 경력을 쌓아왔다. 13세에 피아노를 공부하기 시작한 후, 음악을 연주하는 것이 그가 자신의 삶에서 하고 싶은 일이라는 것을 결정하는 데에는 오래 걸리지 않았다. 그의 첫 번째 커다란 기회는 그가 밴드 리더 베니 골슨의 그룹인 재즈텟에 그 그룹 최초의 피아니스트로 합류했을 때 찾아왔다. 그러나 채 1년도 안 되어, 타이너는 유명한 색소폰 연주자인 존 콜트레인이 이끌었던 그룹과 함께 연주할 기회를 갖게 되었다. 콜트레인은 타이너가 이전에 썼던 곡들에 익숙했고 그 진가를 인정했기 때문에 그를 고용했다. 이러한 관계는 1965년까지 지속되었는데, 이때 콜트레인의 스타일이 변하기 시작했고 타이너는 따라가기를 거부했다. 대신에 그는 자신의 그룹을 시작했고 나중에 재즈에서 가장 유명한 솔로 피아니스트들 중의 하나로 명성을 확고히 했다.

구문해설
[10행] Coltrane hired him because he was familiar with and appreciated the compositions [(which/that) Tyner had previously written].: [ ]는 the compositions를 선행사로 하는 목적격 관계대명사절

문제해설
① 재즈 피아니스트로서 오랜 경력을 쌓아왔다. ② 13세에 피아노를 배우기 시작했다. ③ 재즈텟에서는 1년이 채 되지 않는 기간 동안 활동한 후 콜트레인이 이끄는 그룹에 합류했다. ④ 직접 작곡한 곡들이 콜트레인에게 인정받았다.

28 ④ 내용 불일치

2021 아마추어 사진작가들을 위한 아름다운 전 세계 사진 대회

최고의 작품을 제출하고 푸짐한 상을 탈 기회를 잡으세요 — 신형 카메라도요! 우리는 전 세계의 특별한 자연 사진을 기대하고 있습니다. 모든 사진은 2021년 11월 1일까지 제출되어야 합니다.

출품 부문
세 가지 부문 중 한 곳에 당신의 사진을 출품하세요: 동물, 풍경, 또는 해저

심사
- 한 명의 대상 수상자는 세계적으로 유명한 세 명의 사진작가에 의해 선정됩니다.
- 특별상 수상자는 각 부문별로 선정됩니다. 이 수상자들은 11월 2일부터 16일까지 진행될 사람들의 온라인 투표로 선정됩니다.

상품
- 대상 수상자는 5,000달러와 후원사가 제공하는 신형 카메라를 받습니다.
- 특별상 수상자는 2,500달러를 받습니다.

어휘
amateur 아마추어, 비전문가 submit 제출하다 brand-new 아주 새로운, 신품인 look for …을 바라다[기대하다] unique 독특한, 특별한 enter 출품하다 landscape 풍경 vote 투표 sponsor 광고주, 후원 업체

구문해설
(6행) All photos **must be submitted** *by* November 1, 2021.: must be submitted는 조동사가 쓰인 수동태, by는 「…까지」라는 완료의 의미의 전치사
(19행) The grand-prize winner will receive $5,000 and a brand-new camera [provided by our sponsors].: [ ]는 a brand-new camera를 수식하는 과거분사구

문제 해설
④ 특별상 수상자는 온라인 투표로 뽑힌다고 했다.

29 ② 어법

루브르 박물관에 들어서면 당신은 모든 방문객들에게 뛰어다니거나, 휴대전화를 사용하거나, 큰 소리를 내거나, 플래시를 터뜨려 사진을 찍는 것들이 모두 엄격히 금지되어 있다는 것을 알리는 다양한 언어로 쓰여진 커다란 표지판을 보게 될 것이다. 나는 공식적으로 보이는 이 표지판으로 인해 고무되었지만, 이러한 규칙들이 지켜지지도 않을뿐더러 강제되지도 않는다는 것을 발견하고는, 유명한 박물관으로 간 최근 여행에서 몹시 실망했다. 나는 다빈치의 걸작인 모나리자를 자세히 보고 싶었지만, 불행하게도 그것은 위대한 작품에 대한 예의를 전혀 보여주지 않는 시끄러운 군중들에게 둘러싸여 있었다. 휴대전화 울리는 소리가 내 귀를 가득 채웠고, 카메라의 플래시들로 인해 잠시 눈이 안 보였다. 그러는 동안 박물관 경비원들은 마치 아무것도 잘못된 게 없다는 듯이 멍하니 옆에 서 있었다.

어휘
strictly 엄하게, 엄격하게 prohibit 금지하다 sorely 심하게, 몹시 enforce 시행하다; *강요하다 get a good look at …을 자세히 보다 absolutely 《부정문에서》 전혀 … 않다 temporarily 일시적으로, 임시로 all the while 그동안 내내 idly 하는 일 없이, 멍하니

구문해설
(1행) [Entering the Louvre museum], you will encounter a large sign **written in a variety of languages** [that informs all visitors {that *running, using a cell phone, making loud noises, and taking photographs with a flash* are all strictly prohibited}].: 첫 번째 [ ]는 때를 나타내는 분사구문, written in a variety of languages는 a large sign을 수식하는 과거분사구, 두 번째 [ ]는 a large sign을 선행사로 하는 주격 관계대명사절, { }는 informs의 직접목적어로 쓰인 명사절, running … a flash는 that절의 주어로 쓰인 동명사구
(6행) **As encouraged as I was** by this official-looking sign, I

was sorely disappointed ... [to find that these rules are *neither* followed *nor* enforced].: 'as+형용사[부사]+as+S+V' 「비록 …일지라도」, [ ]는 감정의 원인을 나타내는 부사적 용법의 to부정사구, 'neither A nor B' 「A도 B도 아닌」
(16행) ..., **as if** nothing **were** wrong.: 'as if …' 「마치 …인 것처럼」(이 문장에서는 현재 사실과 반대되는 내용을 가정하는 가정법 과거와 함께 쓰임)

문제해설
② 단수명사인 a large sign을 선행사로 하는 주격 관계대명사절의 동사이므로 inform은 단수형인 informs로 고쳐야 한다.

30 ③ 어휘

체벌의 역사적 기원은 분명하지 않지만, 그것은 많은 고대 문명에서 사용되었다고 알려져 있다. 그 당시에, 그것은 종종 매우 잔혹한 방법으로 일반 대중들이 다 보는 데서 행해졌다. 이것은 다른 사람들이 같은 범죄를 저지르는 것을 그만두게 하기 위함이었다. 18세기에, 철학자들과 법률 개혁가들은 응징보다는 교화가 형사 사법제도의 목적이 되어야 한다고 주장하며, 체벌의 사용에 대해 이의를 제기하기 시작했다. 이 때문에, 19세기까지, 유럽과 북미에서의 체벌의 사용은 급격히 감소했다. 영국에서는, 사형당한 일부 범죄자들이 겪은 끔찍한 죽음이 여론을 체벌에 반대하도록 바꾸었다. 결국 이것은 많은 나라에서 체벌의 사용을 규제하는 엄격한 법률의 도입으로 이어졌다.

어휘
corporal punishment 체벌, 신체적 형벌 exceedingly 극도로, 대단히 cruel 잔혹한, 잔인한 manner 방법 in full view 다 보는 데서 deter 그만두게 하다 defer 연기하다, 미루다 commit 저지르다, 범하다 legal 법률의 reformer 개혁가 question 이의를 제기하다 reformation 교화, 개선 retribution 응징, 징벌 criminal justice system 형사 사법제도 sharply 급격히 decline 감소하다 descend 내려가다, 내려오다 execute 처형하다 reduction 축소, 삭감 strict 엄격한 regulate 규제하다

구문해설
(8행) ... began to question the use of corporal punishment, [arguing that reformation, rather than retribution, should be the goal of the criminal justice system].: [ ]는 부대상황을 나타내는 분사구문
(14행) ..., the horrible deaths [suffered by some criminals {who were executed}] turned public opinion against corporal punishment.: [ ]는 the horrible deaths를 수식하는 과거분사구, { }는 some criminals를 선행사로 하는 주격 관계대명사절

문제해설
③ (A) 다른 사람들이 같은 범죄를 저지르는 것을 '그만두게 하기(deter)' 위해 잔혹하고 공개적으로 처벌한 것이다. (B) 18세기에 체벌의 사용에 대해 이의가 제기되기 시작하여 19세기에 급격히 '감소했다(declined)'고 하는 것이 적절하다. (C) 체벌의 사용을 규제하는 법률이 '도입(introduction)'된 것이다.

31 ⑤ 빈칸 추론

뛰어난 학업 능력으로 인해 중학교와 고등학교를 건너뛰고 초등학교에서 곧바로 대학으로 진학한 어느 젊은 여성이 있었다. 15세가 되었을 때 그녀는 이미 일류 대학을 졸업했고, 18세에 박사학위를 받았다. 이러한 성과들은 인상적이고 흥미롭다. 정확히 무엇이 그녀를 그렇게 영리하게 만들었을까? 그녀가 타고난 천재인지 아닌지를 알아내기는 불가능하지만, 우리는 그녀의 아버지가 엄격하게 그녀로 하여금 아이들의 놀이를 하지 못하게 했다는 것을 알고 있다. 대신에, 그는 열심히 지적 추구가 그녀의 인생에서 주된 초점임을 확실하게 했다. 그녀가 게임을 하고 싶다고 하면 그는 그것이 체스와 같이 지적으로 자극을 주는 것인지를 확인했

다. 사실, 그녀의 상황이 특이한 것도 아니다. 역사는 우리에게 아인슈타인이나 피카소를 포함하여, <u>의욕적인</u> 부모에 의해 조성된 고무적인 환경 속에 놓여졌던 많은 천재들에 대해 알려 준다.

[어휘]
prowess 용기, 용맹; *능력, 재능 bypass 뛰어넘다 prestigious 일류의, 훌륭한 doctorate degree 박사 학위 intriguing 흥미를 자아내는 sternly 엄격히, 단호하게 discourage 말리다, 단념시키다 pursuit 추구 mentally 지적으로 immerse …에 빠지다 stimulating 자극적인 [문제]affluent 부유한 ambitious 야심이 있는, 의욕적인

[구문해설]
(9행) It is impossible [to determine {whether she was born a genius or not}]; ...: It은 가주어이고 [ ]가 진주어, { }는 determine의 목적절, 'whether ... or not'「…인지 아닌지」

[문제해설]
⑤ 글에서 제시된 여성의 사례처럼 많은 천재들이 뛰어난 학업 능력을 보일 수 있었던 것은 그들의 부모가 의욕적으로 교육 환경을 조성하였기 때문이다.

32 ② 빈칸 추론

세계의 많은 고대 종교들이 서로 수천 마일 떨어진 곳에서 발달했다는 사실에도 불구하고, 그 종교들은 동일한 <u>기본 요소</u>를 공유하는 창조 신화를 발전시켰다. 예를 들어, 기독교인들과 중국인들, 그리고 바빌로니아인들은 모두 최초의 인간이 신에 의해 흙에서 비롯된 물질로부터 창조되었다고 믿는다. 성경의 창세기는 신이 흙먼지로부터 아담을 빚으며 그를 창조한 순간을 묘사한다. 중국 신화에서는, 한 신이 진흙 덩어리로 최초의 인간을 빚어냈다. 비슷한 시기에, 바빌로니아인들 또한 신이 흙으로부터 인간을 창조했다고 믿었다. 이들 문화를 떨어뜨려 놓은 지리적 차단에도 불구하고 어떻게 이런 비슷한 이야기들이 생겨날 수 있었는지를 생각해 보는 것은 흥미롭다.

[어휘]
ancient 고대의, 먼 옛날의 creation myth 창조 신화 earthy 흙의 substance 물질 mythology 신화 (체계) lump 덩어리 fascinating 매혹적인 geographical 지리상의, 지리적인 obstruction 방해; *차단 separate …을 분리하다, 떼어놓다 [문제]multiple 다수의 element 구성 요소

[구문해설]
(1행) Despite the fact [that many of the world's ancient religions developed thousands of miles away from one another], they developed creation myths [that share the same basic elements].: 첫 번째 [ ]는 the fact와 동격, 두 번째 [ ]는 creation myths를 선행사로 하는 주격 관계대명사절
(8행) ... describes the moment [when God created Adam, {forming him from the dust of the ground}].: [ ]는 the moment를 선행사로 하는 관계부사절, { }는 부대상황을 나타내는 분사구문
(13행) It is fascinating [to wonder {how such similar stories ... despite the geographical obstructions separating these cultures}].: It은 가주어이고 [ ]가 진주어, { }는 wonder의 목적어로 쓰인 의문사절, separating 이하는 the geographical obstructions를 수식하는 현재분사구

[문제해설]
② 기독교와 중국, 바빌로니아의 창조 신화를 예로 들어, 지리적으로 멀리 떨어진 곳에서 발달한 여러 고대의 창조 신화가 서로 유사한 공통 요소를 가졌음을 설명하고 있다.

33 ① 빈칸 추론

초기 인류는 먹을 것을 찾는 동안 그들의 일을 성별로 나누었다고 오랫동안 여겨져 왔는데, 남자는 사냥을 하고 여자는 채집을 하는 것이었다. 그러나 남아메리카의 9,000년 된 여성 사냥꾼의 발견은 이것이 항상 사실은 아니었다는 것을 보여준다. 고고학자들은 큰 동물을 죽이고 잘게 자르기 위한 도구와 함께 묻힌 시신을 발견했는데, 그것이 사냥꾼의 무덤임을 시사했다. 뼈의 분석 결과 그 사냥꾼이 여자였을 가능성이 있다는 것이 밝혀졌다. 이것은 그 주제에 대한 추가 연구로 이어졌고, 사냥 도구와 함께 묻힌 많은 고대의 시신이 여성임을 알아냈다. 이 정보는 연구원들이 초기 인류의 성역할에 대한 우리의 추정이 현대의 사고방식에 잘못 근거했다고 결론 내리도록 이끌었다. 사실 여성은 선사 시대에 <u>큰 동물의 사냥</u>에 중요한 역할을 했던 것 같다.

[어휘]
divide 나누다 gender 성별 female 여성인 archaeologist 고고학자 bury (시신을) 묻다, 매장하다 analysis 분석 reveal 드러내다, 밝히다 subject 주제 conclude 결론을 내리다 assumption 추정 gender role 성역할 attitude 태도 significant 중요한 prehistoric 선사 시대의 [문제]renowned 유명한 distribution 분배 manufacture 제조, 생산

[구문해설]
(1행) It has long been believed [that early humans divided their tasks by gender {while (they were) searching for food} — men hunted and women gathered].: It은 가주어이고 [ ]가 진주어, { }는 '주어+be동사'가 생략된 형태의 부사절
(6행) Archaeologists found the body [buried with tools for killing and cutting up large animals], [suggesting it was the grave of a hunter].: 첫 번째 [ ]는 the body를 수식하는 과거분사구, 두 번째 [ ]는 부대상황을 나타내는 분사구문
(10행) This led to further research on the subject, [which found that many ancient bodies {buried with hunting tools} were female].: [ ]는 further research on the subject를 선행사로 하는 계속적 용법의 주격 관계대명사절, { }는 many ancient bodies를 수식하는 과거분사구

[문제해설]
초기 인류의 역할이 성별로 구분되어 남자는 사냥을 하고 여자는 채집을 했을 것으로 여겨졌으나, 사냥 도구와 함께 묻힌 선사 시대의 시신이 여자임이 밝혀지면서 성역할에 대한 우리의 추정이 잘못된 것임을 알았다는 내용이다. 따라서 선사 시대에 여성이 중요한 역할을 했던 영역은 ① '큰 동물의 사냥'이라고 하는 것이 적절하다.

34 ② 빈칸 추론

수감 제도가 어떻게 사람들의 행동에 영향을 주는지 알아내기 위해, 심리학자 몇 명이 실험을 했다. 그들은 피실험자로 24명의 남자 대학생들을 신중히 뽑았고, 임의로 가짜 감옥에서 그들 중 절반에게는 교도관 역할을, (나머지) 절반에게는 수감자 역할을 하게 했다. 그 실험은 2주 동안 지속될 예정이었다. 그러나 단 이틀 만에 그 역할들이 학생들의 행동을 지배하기 시작했다. 일주일도 채 지나기 전에 수감자들 중 절반이 극도의 불안감과 우울증 때문에 일찍 석방되어야 했다. 교도관들은 수감자들을 학대하기 시작했고 실험은 단 6일 후에 중단되었다. 이 실험은 <u>우리의 행동</u>이 사회적 역할에 의해 얼마나 쉽게 변할 수 있는지 보여 준다.

[어휘]
psychologist 심리학자 conduct 시행하다 subject 대상, 피실험자 randomly 무작위로 assign 할당하다; *임명하다, 명하다 fake 가짜 be supposed to-v …하기로 되어 있다 release 석방하다 due to … 때문에 extreme 과도한 depression 우울, 우울증 abuse 학대하다 [문제]contribute 기여하다 achievement 성취

4행 ... **assigned** half of them **to play** the role of guards and half **to play** prisoners ...: 'assign+O+to-v' 「…에게 ~하라고 임명하다」

문제해설

임의로 주어진 교도관과 수감자라는 역할에 따라 학생들의 행동이 쉽게 변했다는 실험에 대한 글이므로, 빈칸에는 ② '우리의 행동이 사회적 역할에 의해 얼마나 쉽게 변할 수 있는지'가 가장 적절하다.

35 ① 흐름과 무관한 문장

미술 프로그램은 학교 주요 교과 과정의 일부는 아닐지라도 학생들에게 많은 혜택을 제공한다. 미국예술연합(AFA)의 연구에 따르면, 미술 프로그램은 여러 영역에서 학습 능력 향상에 도움을 줄 수 있다. 이 연구는 미술이 언어, 의사결정, 비판적 사고 능력을 발달시키는 데 도움이 된다는 것을 보여주었다. (많은 예술가들이 광고나 제품 포장을 위한 상업 미술품 제작으로 큰 돈을 번다.) 같은 연구에 의하면 미술을 하는 어린 학생들은 또한 팀에서 더 잘 활동하는 방법을 배우고 다른 문화의 새로운 사고방식을 이해할 수 있다고 한다. 더욱이 이 학생들이 자유롭게 사고하고 자신을 표현하도록 격려를 받을 때 그들은 자신감을 발전시키게 된다. 아마도 미술 수업의 가장 큰 혜택은 학생들이 창의력을 향상시킨다는 점일 것이다. 이러한 창의력은 학생들이 자신을 다양한 방식으로 표현하게 해줄 뿐 아니라 창의적으로 사고하며 살아갈 수 있게 해주고, 일반적인 문제에 대한 새로운 해결책을 찾을 수 있게 해준다.

어휘

curriculum 교과 과정 decision making 의사결정 critical thinking 비판적 사고 engage in …에 관여하다 appreciate 이해하다 furthermore 더욱이 self-confidence 자신(감) creativity 창의력

구문해설

9행 The same study found [that young students {who engage in art} also learn how to work better in teams ... cultures].: [ ]는 found의 목적절, { }는 young students를 선행사로 하는 주격 관계대명사절

17행 This sense of creativity **allows** students *not only* **to express** themselves in various ways, *but* **to think** and **live** creatively and **find** new solutions to common problems.: 'allow+O+to-v' 「…가 ~하게 하다」, 'not only A but (also) B' 「A뿐만 아니라 B도」

문제해설

미술이 여러 방면에서 학습 능력 향상에 도움을 준다는 글이므로, 상업 미술품을 통해 많은 돈을 버는 예술가들에 관한 내용인 ①은 글의 흐름에 맞지 않는다.

36 ② 글의 순서

관광업의 안타까운 모순은 그곳을 감상하기 위해 한 장소를 방문하는 바로 그 행위가 그곳의 지속적인 존재를 위태롭게 한다는 것이다.
(B) 남극은 이러한 모순된 일이 벌어지고 있는 완벽한 예이다. 이곳은 극한의 추위와 거대한 대륙 빙하들과 우뚝 솟은 산들의 땅이다. 그러나 이 얼어붙은 대륙은 또한 세계에서 가장 민감한 생태계 중 하나의 근거지로, 그 생태계는 인간의 존재의 압박을 견뎌낼 필요가 전혀 없었던 자연스러운 균형 상태였다. 지금까지는 말이다.
(A) 지난 20년간 남극의 관광객 수는 급등해왔고, 여름철마다 50,000명에 다다른다. 이러한 호기심 많은 모험가들과 함께, 유람선에 의해 생기는 더 많은 오염과, 더 많은 쓰레기 및 기타 폐기물, 그리고 이 손상되기 쉬운 얼음 지형에 더 파괴적인 발자국들이 따라온다.
(C) 더 큰 문제는, 다른 인기 있는 관광지들과 달리 남극에는 방문을 규제할 힘을 가진 단 하나의 관리 기관도 없다는 것이다. 그 결과는 해를 입

지 않은 독특한 자연환경으로서의 남극의 미래가 불확실하다는 것이다.

어휘

paradox 모순된 일 admire 존경하다; *감상하다 existence 존재 Antarctica 남극 대륙 skyrocket 급등하다 litter 쓰레기 destructive 파괴적인 fragile 손상되기 쉬운 landscape 풍경; *지형 massive 거대한 ice sheet 대륙 빙하 towering 높이 치솟은 delicate 민감한, 섬세한 withstand 견뎌내다 presence 존재 destination 목적지 visitation 방문권 unspoiled 해를 입지 않은

구문해설

6행 With these curious adventurers **come** [more pollution {produced by cruise ships}, more litter and other waste, and more destructive footsteps on the fragile frozen landscape].: [ ]는 문장의 주어(부사구 With these curious adventurers가 문두에 오면서 동사 come과 주어가 도치), { }는 more pollution을 수식하는 과거분사구

19행 ..., there is no single governing body in Antarctica [with the power {to regulate visitation}].: [ ]는 single governing body를 수식하는 전치사구, { }는 the power를 수식하는 형용사적 용법의 to부정사구

문제해설

② (B)의 this paradox는 주어진 글의 The unfortunate paradox를 가리키는 말이며, (B)에서 그 역설의 예시로 남극의 상황을 설명하기 위한 도입이 제시되므로 가장 먼저 와야 한다. 이어서 남극의 관광객 수 급등에 따른 위험이 소개되는 (A)가 오고, 앞에 나온 문제보다 더 심각한 문제가 서술되는 (C)가 가장 마지막에 오는 것이 자연스럽다.

37 ③ 글의 순서

고대부터 사람들은 곱슬머리를 원했다. 단순한 시작에서부터 지속적인 혁신이 마침내 현대의 파마에 이르게 했다.
(B) 파마는 고대 이집트로 거슬러 올라갈 수 있는데, 그 시대에 여성들은 그들의 머리카락에 진흙을 바르고 나무 막대기들에 감았다. 이후에 헤어드라이어의 발명으로 사람들은 곱슬머리를 더 쉽게 만들게 되었다. 그러나 그들의 머리카락이 일단 젖게 되면, 그 곱슬머리는 사라지곤 했다.
(C) 칼 네슬러는 더 오래 지속되는 곱슬머리를 만들기 위한 발명품을 고안해낸 최초의 사람이었다. 1906년에 그는 파마 막대기를 전기로 데우는 기구를 만들었다. 그리고 나서 물과 젖소 오줌의 혼합물이 곱슬머리를 고정시키는 데 사용되었다. 그러나 그 기구는 인기를 얻지는 못했다.
(A) 아놀드 윌럿이라는 이름의 사람에 의해 현대의 파마 과정이 만들어지기까지 다른 혁신들이 뒤따랐다. 그는 1920년대에 영구적인 웨이브를 만드는 기계를 만들기 시작하여, 마침내 1930년대에는 그 과정을 완성하였다.

어휘

ancient 고대의 curly 곱슬곱슬한(curl 곱슬곱슬한 머리카락) continuous 계속되는, 지속적인 innovation 혁신, 쇄신 invention 발명(품) process 과정, 절차 permanent 영구적인 wave (머리카락의) 웨이브 trace back to 기원이[유래가] …까지 거슬러 올라가다 blow dryer 헤어 드라이어 come up with 찾아내다. 내놓다 long-lasting 오래 지속되는 device 장치, 기구 rod 막대 urine 소변, 오줌 hold ... in place …을 고정시키다

구문해설

6행 He began constructing permanent wave machines in the 1920s, [finally perfecting the process in the 1930s].: [ ]는 결과를 나타내는 분사구문

9행 Perms can be traced back to ancient Egypt, [when women would put mud in their hair ... sticks].: [ ]는 ancient Egypt를 선행사로 하는 계속적 용법의 관계부사절

(17행) ..., he constructed a device [that heated perm rods with electricity].: [ ]는 a device를 선행사로 하는 주격 관계대명사절

문제해설
③ 고대의 단순한 시작에서부터 현대의 파마로 이어졌다는 주어진 글 다음에, 고대의 파마에 대해 설명하고 있는 (B)가 오고, 그 다음 현대의 파마 기술과 관련된 내용이 시대순인 (C)에서 (A)로 이어지는 것이 가장 자연스럽다.

38 ② 주어진 문장의 위치

생수가 요즘 대유행이다. 당신은 그것을 사무실과 비행기, 그리고 모든 곳의 상점에서 볼 수 있다. 병에 붙여진 라벨들은 종종 산 속의 개울을 보여주며, 소비자들에게 그 물의 깨끗함을 확신시킨다. 이것 때문에, 사람들은 그것을 수돗물에 대한 더 건강한 대안으로 여긴다. 그러나, 생수가 수돗물보다 더 잘 관리된다거나 더 안전하다고 믿는 것은 잘못된 것이다. 한 비영리 단체가 최근에 100개 이상의 생수 브랜드를 검사했다. 그것들 중 3분의 1이 주(州)(의 기준)나 산업 표준을 초과하는 수준의 세균이나 화학적 오염물질을 포함하고 있다는 것을 발견했다. 게다가, 생수 브랜드의 4분의 1이 실제로 그 물을 산 속의 개울에서보다는 오히려 공공 자원에서 얻는다. 그들은 단순히 그것을 정화하고 병에 담아서 터무니없이 높은 가격으로 판매한다.

어휘
bottled water 생수 regulate 규제하다, 조절하다 tap water 수돗물 all the rage 매우 인기 있는, 유행하는 convince 납득시키다, 확신시키다 purity 깨끗함, 순결(purify 정화하다) alternative 대안 nonprofit 비영리의 contain 함유하다, 포함하다 contaminant 오염물질 bottle 병에 담다 ridiculously 터무니없이

구문해설
(1행) However, **it** is wrong [to believe {that bottled water is *either* better regulated *or* safer than tap water}].: it은 가주어이고 [ ]가 진주어, { }는 believe의 목적절, 'either A or B' 「A와 B 둘 중 하나」

문제해설
However로 시작하는 주어진 문장은 생수가 수돗물보다 더 안전하다는 생각이 잘못되었다는 내용이므로, 앞에는 이와 대조되는 내용으로 사람들이 생수를 선호한다는 문장이 오고, 뒤에는 생수의 위험성에 관련된 내용이 있는 ②에 오는 것이 적절하다.

39 ③ 주어진 문장의 위치

최근 몇 년 동안 대학들은 특별한 컴퓨터 프로그램을 사용하여 학생들의 심각한 표절 문제에 대처하기 시작했다. 이 소프트웨어는 학생들에게 그들이 자신들의 것으로 제출한 보고서에서 직접 뽑아낸 문장들을 보여준다. 그러나 이 문장들의 매 다섯 번째 단어는 지워지고 빈칸으로 대체된다. 그리고 나서 학생들은 그들이 썼던 것을 떠올려서 빠진 단어들을 채우도록 요구받는다. 시험이 치러지고 나면 그 프로그램은 결과를 분석하는데, 학생들이 그들 자신이 썼던 문장들을 정확하게 완성할 수 있어야 한다고 가정한다. 그리고 나서 시험에서의 오류의 수와 그것을 완성하는 데 걸린 시간의 양이 그 학생이 실제로 그 보고서를 썼는지 아닌지를 결정하는 데 사용된다. 소프트웨어 회사에 따르면 그 프로그램은 거의 100퍼센트 정확하고 아직까지 어떤 잘못된 표절 혐의도 제기하지 않았다고 한다.

어휘
recall 기억해 내다, 상기하다 address 연설하다; *대처하다, 착수하다 submit 제출하다 remove 제거하다 assume 가정하다 accurately 정확하게 require (시간·돈이) 들다, 걸리다 have yet to-v 아직 …하고 있지 않다 accusation 혐의

구문해설
(5행) This software presents students with sentences [taken directly from the papers {(which/that) they have submitted as their own}].: [ ]는 sentences를 수식하는 과거분사구, { }는 the papers를 선행사로 하는 목적격 관계대명사절
(13행) The number of errors in the test and the amount of time [required to complete it] **are** then **used to determine** if the student actually wrote the paper *or not.*: [ ]는 the amount of time을 수식하는 과거분사구, 'be used to-v' 「…하는 데 사용되다」(cf. 'be used to v-ing' 「…하는 데 익숙하다」, 'used to-v' 「…하곤 했다」), 'if[whether] ... or not' 「…인지 아닌지」

문제해설
학생들의 표절 여부를 알아내기 위한 시험에서 학생들이 썼던 문장들의 매 다섯 번째 단어를 지우고 빈칸으로 만들었다는 내용 다음에 학생들에게 그 빈칸을 채우도록 했다는 내용으로 이어지는 것이 자연스러우므로, 주어진 문장은 ③에 와야 한다.

40 ④ 요약문 완성

민간 항공기에 탑승하여 승객들이 건강상의 응급 상황을 겪을 때, 종종 그들은 공항에 도착할 때까지 그들이 필요로 하는 의료처치를 받을 수 없다. 이러한 문제를 해결하기 위해, 영국의 한 회사는 기내에 설치될 수 있는 특수 원격 진단 시스템을 개발했다. 승객들이 질병을 호소하면 모니터가 그들의 몸 위에 놓여지고, 이 시스템이 (환자의) 생명에 관한 정보를 병원에 있는 의사에게 전송하도록 한다. 이러한 정보를 바탕으로 의학 전문의들은 진단을 내리고 나서 승객의 건강을 보장하기 위해 어떤 조치가 취해져야 하는지를 승무원들에게 알려줄 수 있다. 만약 그 상태가 생명을 위협하는 것으로 판명되면, 그 승객을 가장 가까운 병원으로 이송하기 위하여 구급차가 활주로에 대기한 채 비상 착륙이 이뤄질 수 있다.

어휘
emergency 비상 (사태) address (문제를) 다루다, 처리하다 remote 먼, 원격의 diagnostic 진단의(diagnosis 진단) install 설치하다 complain (병·고통을) 호소하다 transmit 전달하다 vital 생명의, 생명에 관한; 극히 중대한 inform 알리다 landing 착륙 runway 활주로 rush 급히 보내다

구문해설
(8행) ..., monitors are placed on their bodies, [**allowing** the system **to transmit** vital data to doctors at a hospital].: [ ]는 부대상황을 나타내는 분사구문, 'allow+O+to-v' 「…가 ~하도록 하다」
(12행) ... inform flight attendants [what steps need to be taken to ensure the passenger's well-being].: [ ]는 inform의 직접목적어로 쓰인 의문사절
(15행) ..., **with** ambulances **waiting** by the runway [to rush the passenger to the nearest hospital].: 'with+O+현재분사' 「…을 ~한 채로, …을 ~하며」, [ ]는 목적을 나타내는 부사적 용법의 to부정사구

문제해설
④ 원격 진단 기술은 지상에 있는 의사들이 비행기에 탑승한 아픈 승객들을 도울 수 있게 해준다.

41 ③ 42 ② 장문

카일은 팔꿈치까지 밖에 없는 팔을 가지고, 다리가 없이 태어났다. 그의 부모는 카일 같은 아이를 본 적이 없었기 때문에 어떻게 해야 할지 몰라서, 상황을 하나씩 받아들이기로 결심했다. 그리고 카일은 여기저기 기어다니고 장난감을 갖고 놀며 여느 아기가 할만한 모든 일을 했기 때문에 그들은 곧 그를 장애가 있는 아이로 여기지 않게 되었다.

카일의 부모는 이어서 세 명의 아이들을 더 낳았는데, 모두 딸이었다. 카일은 여느 큰오빠처럼 그들과 같이 놀았다. 카일이 학교에 들어갔을 때, 그는 새로운 것들을 배우고 친구들을 사귀며 (학교생활을) 아주 잘했다. 그는 운동을 시작하여 팔과 상체의 힘을 키우는 데 실패했고(→ 성공했고), 학교 레슬링팀에 들어갔다. 그는 심지어 고등학교를 졸업할 때 레슬링팀의 우수 선수로 주목을 받기도 했다.

자신의 장애에 대해 좌절한 적이 있는지 질문을 받으면 카일은 "누구에게나 어려움은 있죠. 제 어려움이 좀 더 드러나 보일 뿐입니다."라고 대답한다. 그러한 태도는 사람들이 자신도 카일이 한 것처럼 할 수 있을 것이라고 믿게 만든다. 비록 그의 업적이 독특해 보일지라도, 그가 그저 보통의 남자라는 바로 그 이유로 훨씬 더 인상적이다. 사람들이 카일이 해낸 일을 보면, 이는 우리 모두가 우리 내면에 이와 같은 잠재력이 있다는 것을 깨닫게 한다. 우리는 그저 이따금 카일의 경우와 같은 본보기를 통해 일깨워질 필요가 있을 뿐이다.

어휘

elbow 팔꿈치 a[one] day at a time 하나씩, 한 걸음씩 think of A as B A를 B로 여기다 disabled 장애를 가진(disability 불구, 장애) crawl 기다 torso 흉부 standout 뛰어난 사람 struggle 분투 apparent 명백한; *또렷이 보이는 achievement 업적 unique 독특한 precisely 정확히; 바로 potential 잠재력 remind 상기시키다 every once in a while 이따금씩 [문제] refuse 거부하다

구문해설

13행 He began working out, [**succeeding** ... and **joining** ... team].: [ ]는 결과를 나타내는 분사구문, succeeding과 joining은 and로 병렬 연결

18행 When Kyle is asked **if** he's ever frustrated about ...: if는 「…인지」라는 의미의 명사절을 이끄는 접속사

21행 Such an attitude **makes** people **believe** that they can do exactly [what Kyle's done].: 'make+O+동사원형' 「…을 ~하게 하다」, [ ]는 do의 목적어로 쓰인 관계대명사절

문제해설

41 카일이 선천적인 장애에도 좌절하지 않고 여러 업적을 성취했다는 이야기이므로 글의 제목으로는 ③ '장애를 가진 것이 사람에게 차이를 가져오지는 않는다'가 가장 적절하다.

42 카일이 학교에 입학한 후 새로운 것들을 배우고 운동을 시작하여 학교 레슬링팀에도 들어갔다는 내용을 통해 팔과 상체의 힘을 키우는 데 '성공했다'라고 하는 것이 자연스러우므로, ② failing(실패하다)은 succeeding(성공하다) 등으로 고쳐야 한다.

43 ④ 44 ⑤ 45 ③ 장문

(A) 90년대 중반을 뒤돌아보면, 월스트리트의 주식 중개인으로서 캐서린의 경력은 급상승하고 있었다. 여섯 자릿수(수십만 달러)의 수입으로 그녀는 호화롭게 살았고, 도시로부터 벗어나고 싶다고 느낄 때마다 피지나 그라나다와 같은 이국적인 곳으로 여행을 다녔다. 열심히 일한 대가로 그녀는 보상과, 동료들 및 상사 올리비아로부터 인정을 받았으며, 그녀의 분야에서 최고의 자리에 있었기 때문에 그녀는 정기적으로 전국 방송의 뉴스 프로그램에 출연하여 투자에 대한 조언을 했다.

(D) 모든 것이 완벽하게 진행되고 있었던 그때는 앞으로 그녀의 미래에 놓인 것을 알 리가 없었다. 그녀의 몰락은 뉴욕 시의 한 사업상의 만찬에서 버나뎃을 만났을 때 시작되었다. 그녀는 언제나 완벽하게 손질되어 보이는 흰 머리카락에 마르고 여윈 몸매의 나이가 지긋한 여성이었다. 그들은 만찬에서 그녀의 금융옵션에 대해 논의했고, 그리고 나서 그 다음 주에 그녀는 예금액의 거의 전부를 캐서린과 함께 개설한 계좌로 옮겼다.

(B) 그 후, 버나뎃과 캐서린은 그녀의 요구에 맞는 포트폴리오를 만들기 위해 열심히 일했고, 얼마 동안 모든 일이 잘 돌아가는 듯했다. 그러나, 1995년에 (주식) 시장이 급락했고, 이는 버나뎃과 같은 투자자들을 공황상태로 만들었다. 캐서린은 시장의 일시적 하락은 자연스러운 것이니 그저 인내심을 가져야 한다고 설명하려 노력했지만, 그녀가 (그렇게) 안심시키는 것은 소용이 없었다. 주식 시장의 하락으로 거의 모든 예금을 잃어서 버나뎃은 분개했고, 캐서린의 고용주에게 그녀를 해고하라고 설득했다.

(C) 공식적인 통보를 받기 전에 캐서린은 소문을 들었고, 곧 일어날 일을 믿을 수가 없어 멍한 상태로 돌아다녔다. 마침내, 그녀는 올리비아의 사무실로 불려갔다. 그녀는 "캐서린, 당신의 운명은 주식 중개인이 되는 것이 아닌가 보네요."라고 말했다. 그녀는 캐서린에게 상황이 어쩔 수 없었더라도 그녀가 버나뎃의 모든 자금을 그렇게 좁은 범위의 주식에 투자해서는 안 됐었다고 설명했다. 캐서린은 주식 중개인으로서 그녀의 화려한 삶은 끝이 났음을 알았지만, 그녀는 미래에 도움을 줄 만한 값진 교훈도 얻었음을 깨달았다.

어휘

stockbroker 주식 중개인 soaring 날아오르는; *급상승하는 figure (숫자와 함께) …자리의 exotic 이국적인 national 국가의; *국가 전체의 portfolio 【금융】 투자 자산 구성, 포트폴리오 suit (…에) 알맞다, 적합하다 dip 살짝 담금; *일시적 하락 reassurance 안심시킴 daze 멍한 상태 fabulous 기막히게 멋진 downfall 몰락, 실패 bony 여윈, 뼈만 앙상한 account (예금) 계좌

구문해설

5행 ... whenever she **felt like getting** away from the city.: 'feel like v-ing' 「…하고 싶다」

11행 ... worked hard [to build a portfolio {to suit her needs}], ...: [ ]는 목적을 나타내는 부사적 용법의 to부정사구, { }는 a portfolio를 수식하는 형용사적 용법의 to부정사구

18행 [**Having lost** nearly all of her savings in the stock market drop], Bernadette was upset ...: [ ]는 이유를 나타내는 분사구문(주절의 시제(was)보다 더 이전의 시제를 나타내기 위해 완료형 분사가 쓰임)

23행 ..., and she walked around in a daze, [(being) unable to believe {what **was about to happen**}].: [ ]는 이유를 나타내는 분사구문, { }는 believe의 목적어로 쓰인 관계대명사절, 'be about to-v' 「막 …하려는 참이다」

28행 ..., she **should**n't **have invested** all of Bernadette's money into such a narrow range of stocks.: 'should have p.p.' 「…해야만 했는데 (하지 않았다)」

문제해설

43 ④ 주식 중개인으로서 최고의 위치에 올라 있던 때를 이야기하고 있는 (A) 다음에, 만찬에서 만난 버나뎃과 투자를 구상하는 내용의 (D)가 이어지고, 주식 시장의 하락으로 버나뎃이 투자한 금액을 거의 모두 잃고 화가 났다는 내용의 (B)가 온 후, 결국 회사에서 쫓겨났다는 내용의 (C)로 연결되는 것이 자연스럽다.

44 ⑤ (e)는 버나뎃을 지칭하고 나머지는 모두 캐서린을 지칭한다.

45 ③ 버나뎃에게 빚을 진 것이 아니라, 캐서린의 조언대로 투자를 한 버나뎃이 큰 손실을 보게 되었다.

18 ④	19 ④	20 ③	21 ②	22 ①	23 ④
24 ②	25 ②	26 ③	27 ③	28 ②	29 ②
30 ④	31 ⑤	32 ④	33 ⑤	34 ③	35 ④
36 ②	37 ③	38 ④	39 ③	40 ②	41 ②
42 ④	43 ③	44 ①	45 ⑤		

18 ④ 글의 목적

권 선생님께,

저희 기록에 따르면, '월간 육아'의 6월호는 고객님의 12개월 구독의 마지막 호입니다. 지난해 동안 고객님께서 저희 잡지를 읽는 것을 즐기셨기를 진심으로 바랍니다. 보다 중요한 것은, 고객님께서 앞으로도 계속 그러시기를 바랍니다. 따라서, 고객님께서 계속 '월간 육아'를 읽으시도록 장려하기 위해, 현재 고객 신분으로서 다음 12개월간의 구독에 대해 15퍼센트 할인을 고객님께 제공해 드리고 싶습니다. 이 후한 제의는 현 계약의 마지막 날까지만 이용 가능하므로 조속히 행동해 주십시오. 이 기회를 이용하기 위해서는 저희의 친절한 고객 지원 직원 중 한 명에게 555-090-780으로 전화해 주십시오.

진심을 담아,
웬디 존슨 드림

어휘
edition (시리즈 간행물의) 호　issue 쟁점; *(출판물의) 제 …쇄[호]　subscription 구독　generous 후한, 넉넉한　agreement 동의; *계약, 협정　take advantage of …을 이용하다　assistance 도움, 지원

구문해설
7행 So, **in order to** encourage you to continue [to read Parenting Monthly], ...: 'in order to' 「…하기 위해서」, 'encourage+O+to-v' 「…가 ~하도록 장려하다」, [ ]는 continue의 목적어로 쓰인 명사적 용법의 to부정사구

문제해설
정기 구독 만료를 앞둔 고객에게 구독 비용을 할인해주겠다고 제안하며 구독 연장을 권유하는 내용이므로 ④가 글의 목적으로 가장 적절하다.

19 ④ 필자의 주장

리버사이드 공원에는 장애인들이 모든 높이의 구역에 갈 수 있도록 설치된 콘크리트 경사로가 있다. 그러나 최근 이 경사로가 스케이트보드를 타는 사람들에게 침범당하고 있다. 빠르게 움직이는 스케이트보드를 타는 사람들과 휠체어에 탄 더 느린 사람들의 조합은 위험한 상황을 조성한다. 분명히, 이 두 사용자들은 같은 공간에 있어서는 안 되고, 분리될 필요가 있다. 하지만 이(분리될 필요성)는 보행자나 유모차를 밀고 가는 사람들과 같은 다른 공원 사용자들의 안전 역시 위협받고 있다는 점에서 단지 그들만을 위한 것이 아니다. 스케이트보드를 타는 사람들뿐만 아니라 모든 공원 사용자들을 보호하기 위해서, 별도의 공간이 스케이트보드 전용으로 마련되어야 한다. 거기서 스케이트보드를 타는 사람들은 그들을 위해 특별히 설계된 더 고난도의 경사면을 이용할 수 있을 것이다.

어휘
concrete 콘크리트로 된　ramp 비탈, 경사로　install 설치하다　the disabled 장애인　access 접근, 출입　terrace (경사지를 층층이 깎은) 계단

모양의 구역　level 높이　invade …에 침입하다　combination 조합, 연합　make for …을 조장하다　separate 분리하다　baby carriage 유모차　challenging 도전적인, 힘든

구문해설
9행 ... **in that** the safety of other park users, ..., *is* also threatened.: 'in that ...' 「…이므로, …라는 점에서」, 주어가 단수명사인 the safety이므로 단수동사인 is가 쓰임

문제해설
④ 안전을 위해 스케이트보드를 타는 사람들을 위한 별도의 전용 공간이 마련되어야 한다고 주장하고 있다.

20 ③ 글의 요지

오늘날 현대 사회의 많은 이들이 노화와의 전쟁을 치르고 있다. 그들은 아주 가느다란 주름 하나 생기는 것조차 두려워하며, 이 자연스러운 과정에 맞서기 위해 비싼 크림과 화장품을 사고 심지어 성형 수술까지 한다. 불행히도 젊은 외모를 유지하기 위한 열망 속에서 사람들은 정말 중요한 것, 즉 노인들의 깊은 주름 속에 진정한 아름다움이 있다는 것을 잊어버린 것 같아 보인다. 할머니의 얼굴에 있는 주름들은 아주 오랫동안 그녀의 일부였던 선뜻 짓는 미소를 증명한다. 그녀의 빛나는 눈, 상냥한 표정, 삶에 대한 이해는 어떤 성형 수술, 주름 (방지) 크림, 혹은 다른 화장품이 줄 수 있는 것보다 훨씬 더 큰 아름다움을 발한다.

어휘
contemporary 현대의, 당대의　at war 전쟁 중인　aging 노화　slight 가느다란　wrinkle 주름　counter 대항하다, 거스르다　pricy 비싼　cosmetic 《보통 pl.》 화장품　undergo 겪다　plastic surgery 성형 수술　quest 탐색, 추구　maintain 유지하다　attest to …을 증언[증명]하다　expression 표현; *표정　appreciation 감사; 감상; *이해　reveal 드러내다

구문해설
6행 ..., people **seem to have forgotten** *something* really important — [that there is true beauty ... aged].: 'seem to have p.p.' 「…했던 것 같다」, 형용사 important가 something을 뒤에서 수식, [ ]는 something really important를 부연 설명
10행 ... attest to the ready smile [that has been so much a part of her for so long].: [ ]는 the ready smile을 선행사로 하는 주격 관계대명사절

문제해설
③ 현대인의 젊음에 대한 지나친 집착을 비판하며 나이 드는 것의 아름다움을 설명하는 글이다.

21 ② 함축 의미 추론

노인 차별은 사람들이 그들의 나이 때문에 차별받을 때 발생하는 심각한 사회 문제이다. 이것은 노인들에게 큰 문제가 될 수 있으며, 그들은 그들이 어떻게 행동해야 하는지에 대한 부정적인 고정 관념에 대처해야 한다. 예를 들어, 고령인들은 때때로 그들의 일이나 다른 혜택을 더 젊은 사람들에게 넘겨줄 것으로 기대된다. 이것은 노인들은 인생에서 필요한 모든 것을 다 가졌고 다음 세대를 위해 기꺼이 물러나야 한다는 고정 관념 때문이다. 그러나 사실은 우리 모두 인종, 성별, 또는 나이에 상관 없이 우리가 원하는 것을 마음대로 해야 한다. 노인들은 그들이 이미 '자기 순서를 맞이한 것'처럼 대우받지 않아야 한다. 그들은 다른 모든 사람들처럼 유일무이한 개인으로 대우받아야 한다.

어휘
ageism 노인 차별　discriminate against …을 차별하다　stereotype 고정 관념　individual 개인　expect 기대하다　content to-v 기꺼이 …하려

하는 step aside 비켜나다 generation 세대 regardless of …에 상관하지 않고 race 인종 have one's turn 자기 순서를 맞다 [문제] defined 정의된

3행 This can be a big problem for the elderly, [who must deal with negative stereotypes about {how they're supposed to act}].: [ ]는 the elderly를 선행사로 하는 계속적 용법의 주격 관계대명사절, { }는 about의 목적어로 쓰인 의문사절

8행 This is due to the stereotype [that the elderly have gotten everything {(that) they need out of life} and should be content to step aside for the next generation].: the stereotype과 [ ]는 동격, { }는 everything을 선행사로 하는 목적격 관계대명사절

12행 The elderly should not be treated **as if** they have already "had their turn.": 'as if ...' 「마치 …인 것처럼」

노인 차별 문제는 고령인들이 인생에서 필요한 모든 것을 다 가졌기 때문에 개인으로서 자유롭게 누려야 할 권리나 혜택을 젊은 사람들에게 기꺼이 내주어야 한다는 고정 관념에서 비롯되었다는 내용이므로, 밑줄 친 '그들이 이미 '자기 순서를 맞이했다''의 의미로 가장 적절한 것은 ② '그들은 적극적인 삶을 사는 것을 그만둘 준비가 되어 있다'이다.

22 ① 글의 제목

최근 몇 년간 대량으로 제품을 판매하는 상점들이 인기를 끌게 되었다. 예를 들어, 당신은 대량 제품을 취급하는 상점에서 상자당 30센트가 할인된 가격으로 시리얼 20상자가 들어 있는 상자를 구매할 수 있을지도 모른다. 구매자들은 대량으로 사는 것이 돈을 절약하는 방법이라고 믿기 때문에 때때로 일 년에 100달러에 달하는 상점 회비를 낸다. 그러나 정말 그럴까? 당신은 시리얼 20상자에 대해 상자당 30센트를 절약할지는 모르지만 스스로에게 물어봐야 한다. 만약 그것이 대량으로 제공되지 않는다면 그 모든 시리얼을 사고 싶을까? 그리고 그것이 상하기 전에 그것을 모두 먹을 수 있을까? 많은 경우에 이 질문들에 대한 대답은 '아니요'이다. 이것은 대량 구매가 실제로는 돈이 더 많이 든다는 것을 의미하는데 당신이 그렇지 않았다면 구매했을 상품들보다 더 많은 상품들을 구매하는 것이기 때문이다.

bulk 큰 규모(양); 대량으로 판매되는 case 경우; *상자 membership fee 회비 consume 소비하다; *먹다, 마시다 go bad (음식이) 상하다, 썩다 in effect 사실상 [문제] illusion 오해[착각], 환상 bargain 싼 물건 deceive 속이다 reasonable 합리적인

9행 **Would you want** to buy all that cereal **if it were not offered** in bulk?: 'If+S+동사의 과거형 ..., S+조동사의 과거형+동사원형 ~'으로 현재 사실과 반대되는 일을 가정하는 가정법 과거 구문

14행 ..., since you are buying more goods than you **otherwise** would.: otherwise는 「(만약) 그렇지 않으면」이라는 의미의 부사(여기서는 '대량 구매를 하지 않았다면'이라는 뜻)

대량으로 싸게 판매되는 상품들이 실제로는 과소비를 조장하여 더 많은 돈을 쓰게 한다는 내용의 글이므로 제목으로는 ① '대량으로 싸게 판매되는 물건에 대한 착각'이 적절하다.

23 ④ 글의 주제

대부분의 여성에게 임신은 기대에 찬 기쁨의 시간인 것 같아 보이지만, 적지 않은 수가 보통 수준에서부터 심각한 수준의 우울증을 겪는다.

이런 여성들은 출산 전의 건강 관리를 더 소홀히 하는 경향이 있다. 그들은 검진 예약을 놓치거나, 일부는 우울증에서 벗어나고자 술이나 담배에 의존하기도 하는데, 이런 것들은 태아에게 손상을 입힐 수 있다. 임신 중에 치료되지 않은 우울증은 더 높은 비율의 유산, 사산, 조산, 저체중아와 관련지어져 왔다. 건강하지 못한 임신으로 인해 작게 태어난 아기들은 성인이 되어서 고혈압과 심장병에 걸릴 위험이 더 크다. 마지막으로 출산 후의 우울증은 여성에게서 아이가 새로 태어난 기쁨을 앗아가며 아기를 키우고 돌보는 능력을 심하게 손상시킬 수 있다.

pregnancy 임신, 임신 기간 expectant 기대하는 significant 중대한; *상당한 minority 소수 moderate 보통의 severe 심한 overlook 간과하다 turn to …에 의존하다 tackle (문제 등을) 다루다 untreated 치료를 받고 있지 않은 miscarriage 유산 stillbirth 사산 premature delivery 조산 high blood pressure 고혈압 rob A of B A에게서 B를 빼앗다 impair (건강 등을) 해치다 nurse 양육하다 infant (7세 미만의) 유아 [문제] post-delivery care 산후 조리 threaten 위협하다

11행 Babies [born smaller ... pregnancy] face a bigger risk of ... as (they become) adults.: [ ]는 Babies를 수식하는 과거분사구

14행 ... robs a woman of the joy **of** having a new baby and can seriously impair her ability [to nurse and care for the infant].: of는 동격의 의미를 나타내는 전치사로, the joy와 having a new baby는 동격. [ ]는 her ability를 수식하는 형용사적 용법의 to부정사구

④ 임신 중이나 출산 후의 우울증을 제대로 치료하지 않을 경우 초래될 수 있는 위험성에 관한 글이다.

24 ② 글의 주제

우리 발의 근육은 우리가 걸을 때 끊임없이 땅을 대고 밀도록 설계되어 있다. 그러나 신발을 신는 것은 울퉁불퉁한 땅을 평평하고 단단하며 편안한 표면으로 대체하는 것인데, 이는 우리의 발 근육이 그렇게 열심히 일할 필요가 없다는 뜻이다. 이것은 완벽한 상황처럼 들릴지 모르지만, 결국 우리의 발을 더 약하고 부상 당하기 쉽게 만든다. 이것을 방지하기 위해 어떤 사람들은 얇고, 신축성 있는 바닥이 있는 신발을 선호한다. 연구는 그것을 신는 것은 그 사람들이 마치 맨발로 걷는 것처럼 그들의 발을 움직이게 한다는 것을 보여준다. 결과적으로, 그들의 발은 더 강하고 건강하다. 이런 이유로, 당신이 맨발로 걷는 것이 용인되는 상황에 있는 것이 아니라면 이런 신발이 가장 좋은 선택이다.

muscle 근육 constantly 끊임없이 replace 대신하다 uneven 평평하지 않은, 울퉁불퉁한 firm 단단한, 딱딱한 prone to …하기 쉬운 flexible 신축성 있는 barefoot 맨발로(bare 벌거벗은) acceptable 용인되는, 받아들여지는

2행 **Wearing shoes**, however, replaces the uneven ground with a flat, firm, comfortable surface, [meaning our foot muscles don't have to work nearly as hard].: Wearing shoes는 문장의 주어로 쓰인 동명사구, [ ]는 부대상황을 나타내는 분사구문

9행 Research shows [that wearing them **allows** people's feet **to move** as if they were walking barefoot].: [ ]는 shows의 목적어 역할을 하는 명사절. 'allow+O+to-v' 「…가 ~하게 하다」. 'as if ...' 「마치 …인 것처럼」(이 문장에서는 현재 사실과 반대되는 내용을 나타내는 가정법 과거와 함께 쓰임)

12행 ..., these shoes are the best option **unless** you're in a situation [where *walking in bare feet* is acceptable].: unless는 「…하지 않는 한」이라는 의미(= If ... not ~), [ ]는 a situation을 선행사로 하는 관계부사절. walking in bare feet은 관계부사절의 주어로 쓰인 동명사구

문제해설
② 신발을 신으면 평평하고 단단한 상태의 바닥으로만 걸어서 발 근육이 약해져 발이 다치기 쉬우므로, 이를 방지하기 위해 바닥이 얇고 신축성 있는 신발을 신는 것이 건강에 가장 좋다는 내용이다.

25 ② 도표 내용 불일치

위 도표는 일과 삶의 균형이 사무실에서 일할 때 더 좋은지 또는 집에서 일할 때 더 좋은지 질문을 받은 대략 4,000명의 사람들의 응답을 보여 준다. 가장 많은 비율의 사람들이 집에서 일할 때 균형이 훨씬 더 좋다고 말했다. (이 비율은 다음으로 가장 많은 응답이었던 집에서 일할 때 균형이 조금 더 좋다는 응답 비율의 두 배 이상이었다.) 단 13퍼센트의 사람들만이 사무실에서 일할 때 일과 삶의 균형이 훨씬 더 잘 맞는다고 응답했다. 그들의 답변은 사무실에서 일하든 집에서 일하든 그 균형이 같다고 말한 사람들의 그것과 공동으로 가장 흔하지 않은 응답에 올랐다. 사무실에서 일할 때 그 균형이 조금 더 낮다고 말한 사람들의 비율은 두 가지 가장 낮은 항목의 비율보다 단 1퍼센트포인트 더 높았다.

어휘
balance 균형 remotely 원격으로 response 대답, 응답(respond 대답[응답]하다) nearly 거의, 대략 report 보고하다; *말하다 double 두 배의 common 흔한 tie 묶다; *동점을 이루다, 비기다 single 단 하나의

구문해설
(1행) The above chart shows the responses of nearly 4,000 people [who were asked {**whether** their work-life balance was better when they worked in the office **or** when they worked from home}].: [ ]는 nearly 4,000 people을 선행사로 하는 주격 관계대명사절, { }는 were asked의 목적절, 'whether A or B' 「A인지 B인지」
(7행) This percentage was more than double that of the next most common response, [which was {that the balance was a little better when they worked from home}].: [ ]는 the next most common response를 선행사로 하는 계속적 용법의 주격 관계대명사절, { }는 관계대명사절의 주격보어로 쓰인 명사절
(12행) Their answer was tied for the least common response with **that** of people [who said {(that) the balance was the same *whether* they worked in the office *or* from home}].: that은 answer를 지칭하는 대명사, [ ]는 people을 선행사로 하는 주격 관계대명사절, { }는 said의 목적절, 'whether A or B' 「A이든 B이든」

문제해설
② 집에서 일할 때 일과 삶의 균형이 훨씬 더 잘 맞는다는 응답의 비율(39%)은 집에서 일할 때 조금 더 낮다는 응답의 비율(20%)의 두 배에는 미치지 않는다.

26 ④ 내용 불일치

대부분의 사람들은 신선도를 유지하기 위해 음식을 냉장고에 보관한다. 그러나 너무 많은 사람들이 뜨거운 음식을 냉장고에 넣기 전에 너무 오래 기다린다. 음식이 식을 때까지 기다림으로써 전기를 절약할 수는 있지만, 이는 박테리아가 더 쉽게 번식하게 만들 수 있다. 음식물 내의 박테리아는 사람이 다양한 질병에 걸리게 할 수 있다. 박테리아는 일반적으로 섭씨 35도의 온도에서 가장 쉽게 번식하며, 섭씨 10도 미만의 온도에서는 보다 느리게 번식한다. 냉장고가 보통 섭씨 4도에 맞추어져 있기 때문에, 냉장고에 보관된 음식은 실온에 둔 음식보다 박테리아가 덜 자랄

가능성이 높다. 그러므로 뜨거운 상태에서 음식을 냉장고에 넣는 것이 최선이다.

어휘
store 저장하다, 보관하다 refrigerator 냉장고 electricity 전기 breed 번식하다 develop (병을) 발병시키다, 일으키다 reproduce 재생하다; *번식하다 Celsius 섭씨 room temperature 실온

구문해설
(1행) Most people store food in the refrigerator [to maintain its freshness].: [ ]는 목적을 나타내는 부사적 용법의 to부정사구
(11행) ..., food [stored in refrigerators] is likely to grow **fewer** bacteria **than** food [left at room temperature].: 두 개의 [ ]는 각각 바로 앞의 food를 수식하는 과거분사구, 'fewer ... than ~' 「~보다 적은 …」
(13행) Thus, **it** is best [to put food in the refrigerator while it is still hot].: it은 가주어이고 [ ]가 진주어

문제해설
④ 박테리아는 섭씨 35도에서 가장 쉽게 번식한다고 했다.

27 ③ 내용 일치

남반구는 남반구 극진동(SAM)이라고 불리는 기후의 주기적이고 자연적인 변동을 겪는다. 수 세기까지는 아니라 하더라도 수십 년간 지속될 수 있는 강력한 SAM 활동 기간 동안 남극 대륙을 둘러싸고 있는 지역은 비교적 낮은 기압을 경험한다. 이것은 결국 남반구에서의 더 온난하고 더 건조한 기후 양상의 원인이 된다. 파타고니아라고 알려진 남아메리카의 남부 지역은 특히 이것에 의해 영향을 받는다. 그런 기후 변화의 한 가지 극적인 결과는 증가된 산불의 확산이다. 이것은 파타고니아 숲의 (나무) 나이테 분석에 의해 확인되어 왔다. 현재 대기 과학자들은 파타고니아가 강력한 SAM 활동의 새로운 국면에 접어들고 있으며, 이것은 인간이 유발한 지구 온난화의 영향으로 인해 심화될 것이라고 예측하고 있다. 그 결과 파타고니아에는 적어도 향후 수십 년간 엄청난 손상을 입힐 산불이 점점 더 발생하기 쉬울 것이다.

어휘
the Southern Hemisphere 남반구 undergo 겪다 periodic 주기적인 incident 일, 사건 relatively 비교적 atmospheric 대기의 in turn 차례차례; *결국 contribute 기여하다; *(…의) 한 원인이 되다 dramatic 극적인 shift 변화 prevalence 널리 퍼짐 confirm 확인하다 phase 국면 predict 예측하다 intensify 심화시키다 induce 초래하다, 유발하다 increasingly 점점 더 be prone to …하기 쉽다 devastating 엄청난 손상을 입히는

구문해설
(3행) During incidents of strong SAM activity, [which can last decades], **if not** centuries, areas [surrounding Antarctica] experience relatively low atmospheric pressure.: 첫 번째 [ ]는 incidents of strong SAM activity를 선행사로 하는 계속적 용법의 주격 관계대명사절, 'if not ...' 「…까지는 아니라 하더라도」, 두 번째 [ ]는 areas를 수식하는 현재분사구
(13행) ... Patagonia is entering a new phase of strong SAM activity, [which {they predict} will be intensified by the effects of human-induced global warming].: [ ]는 a new phase of strong SAM activity를 선행사로 하는 계속적 용법의 주격 관계대명사절, { }는 삽입절
(17행) ... a Patagonia [that will be increasingly prone to {devastating wildfires for at least the next few decades}].: [ ]는 a Patagonia를 선행사로 하는 주격 관계대명사절, { }는 전치사 to의 목적어로 쓰인 동명사구

① 주기적으로 발생하나 수 세기까지 지속되지는 않는다. ② SAM 현상으로 대기압이 낮아져 온난하고 건조한 기후로 바뀌게 된다. ④ 지구 온난화의 영향을 받아 심해지는 것이지, 그 자체가 지구 온난화의 결과는 아니다. ⑤ 새로운 국면에 접어들고 있고 더 심화될 것으로 예측된다.

28 ② 내용 불일치

교내 포스터 대회

연례 교내 포스터 대회가 이번 달에 개최될 것입니다. 올해의 주제는 '에너지 보존'입니다.

가이드라인

- 작품의 원본만 받습니다. 사진이나 인쇄본은 안 됩니다.
- 각 포스터는 28 × 43cm 크기의 종이에 그려져야 합니다.
- 포스터는 가로 또는 세로로 배치될 수 있습니다.

제출

- 모든 포스터는 5월 25일까지 제출되어야 합니다.
- 다수 작의 출품은 가능하지만, 김 선생님에게 승인을 받아야 합니다.

상품

- 5개의 가장 우수한 출품작이 대회 심사위원들에 의해 선정될 것입니다.
- 각 수상자는 100달러 상당의 맥 미술 용품점 상품권을 받을 것입니다.

어휘
annual 연례의 **take place** 개최되다 **theme** 주제 **conservation** 보존 **original** 원본의 **arrange** 배열하다 **horizontally** 수평으로, 가로로 **vertically** 수직으로, 세로로 **multiple** 다수의 **entry** 출품작 **permission** 허락

구문해설
10행 The poster may be arranged **either** horizontally **or** vertically.: 'either A or B' 「A와 B 둘 중 하나」
13행 All posters must be received **by** the end of the day on May 25.: by는 「…까지」라는 의미로 동작·상태의 완료 기한을 나타내는 전치사

문제해설
② 가로 및 세로 형태 모두로 배치 가능하다고 했다.

29 ② 어법

콜레라는 장에 있는 박테리아에 의해 발생되는 질병이다. 그것에 걸리는 사람들의 약 5퍼센트는 구토, 설사, 탈수와 가끔은 쇼크를 포함하는 심각한 반응을 일으킨다. 오염된 물이 그것이 확산되는 주된 매개체로, 이는 1800년대의 콜레라 대유행 동안 가장 만연해 있던 상황이었다. 그 당시의 의사들은 그 연관 관계를 의심하여 더 위생적인 하수도 체계의 건설을 촉구하였다. 그것은 콜레라 발병의 급격한 감소를 가져왔고, 수십 년 동안 그 병은 사라진 듯했다. 그런데, 1961년 인도네시아에서 그것은 새로운 변종으로 다시 등장했고 세계의 많은 곳으로 퍼졌다. 그것은 아직 멈춰지지 않았으며, 매년 수천 명의 사람들을 죽게 하고 이보다 더 많은 사람들을 병들게 하고 있다.

어휘
bacterium 박테리아(*pl.* bacteria) **intestine** 장(腸) **contract** 계약하다; *(병에) 걸리다 **vomit** 토하다 **diarrhea** 설사 **dehydration** 탈수 **contaminated** 오염된 **primary** 주요한, 주된 **prevalent** 널리 퍼진 **epidemic** 유행병, 전염병; (흔히 나쁜 것의) 급속한 유행 **sanitary** 위생적인 **sewer** 하수(도) **incident** 일어난 일, 사건 **vanish** 사라지다 **strain** 종족; *변종 **sicken** 구역질 나게 하다; *병나게 하다

구문해설
14행 ..., [killing thousands of people every year] and [sickening many more].: 두 개의 [ ]는 모두 부대상황을 나타내는 분사구문

문제해설
② 관계대명사 which 뒤에 완전한 문장이 오고, 선행사 the primary means가 방법·수단을 나타내므로, 「전치사＋관계대명사」인 by which가 되어야 한다.

30 ④ 어휘

오프브로드웨이 연극은 브로드웨이의 상황에 대한 불만의 결과로 1950년대 뉴욕시에서 생겨났다. 그것의 설립자들은 브로드웨이가 예술성이 있는 연극보다는 위험성이 없고 상업적으로 성공적인 히트 연극을 제작하는 데 지나치게 관심을 갖고 있다고 생각했다. 오프브로드웨이 제작자들은 일거리를 찾지 못했던 극작가, 연출가, 그리고 배우들을 지원했다. 그들의 공연은 독창적이고 참신했으며, 표의 가격도 저렴했다. 관객들은 예술 공연에 대한 알맞은 가격의 티켓에 기뻐했고, 오프브로드웨이 연극은 쇠퇴했다(→ 번창했다). 그러나 1960년대에 이르러서는 비용이 오르기 시작했으며 1970년대에 오프브로드웨이 연극은 브로드웨이와 동일한 많은 어려움들에 직면하게 되었다. 오프브로드웨이 연극의 쇠퇴와 함께, 오프오프브로드웨이 연극이라고 불리는 실험적인 움직임이 전개되었다.

어휘
theater 극장; *연극 **dissatisfaction** 불만, 불평 **founder** 창설자, 설립자 **overly** 지나치게, 몹시 **commercially** 상업적으로, 영리적으로 **artistic** 예술의, 예술적인 **assist** 거들다, 원조하다 **playwright** 극작가 **performer** 배우 **audience** 청중, 관중 **affordable** (가격이) 알맞은 **decline** 쇠퇴하다 **encounter** 직면하다 **experimental** 실험적인

구문해설
7행 ... playwrights, directors, and performers [who could not find work].: [ ]는 playwrights, directors, and performers를 선행사로 하는 주격 관계대명사절
16행 ..., an experimental movement [called Off-Off-Broadway theater] developed.: [ ]는 an experimental movement를 수식하는 과거분사구

문제해설
알맞은 티켓 가격에 관객들이 기뻐했다는 내용이 앞에 있으므로 ④ declined(쇠퇴했다)는 prospered(번창했다) 등으로 고쳐야 한다.

31 ⑤ 빈칸 추론

가난은 현재 상태를 유지하는 특별한 정치적 압력의 기능으로 사회에 존재한다. 특권층의 기득권은 사회 전반에 걸쳐 부를 재분배하기 위한 어떤 시도든지 장애에 직면할 것임을 의미한다. 개인은 오직 다른 사람들이 상대적으로 가난해야만 상대적으로 부유할 수 있으며, 돈을 가진 사람들이 권력도 갖고 있기 때문에, 그들의 이익은 항상 가난한 사람들의 이익보다 우선시된다. 중산층은 가난한 사람들이 저축하고 열심히 일하는 기질이 부족하기 때문에 고통을 받고 있다고 인식하지만, 변화의 비용을 부담하는 건 가난한 사람들이다. 가난한 사람들을 계속 빈곤하게 하는 사전 모의된 전략은 없을지 모르지만, 현대 경제체제의 현실은 사람들이 자신의 환경을 바꿀 만한 권력을 갖지 못하게 한 채로 내버려둔다.

어휘
status quo 그대로의 상태, 현상 유지 **vested interest** 기득권 **privileged** 특권이 있는 **obstacle** 장애(물) **take precedence over** …보다 우위에 서다, …에 우선하다 **absorb** 흡수하다; *(비용을) 부담하다 **premeditated** 미리

계획된, 사전 모의한 [문제] surrender 굴복하다; 포기하다 accumulate 축적하다 redistribute 재분배하다

구문해설
3행 The vested interests of the privileged classes mean [that any attempts {to redistribute wealth throughout society} will face obstacles].: [ ]는 mean의 목적절, { }는 any attempts를 수식하는 형용사적 용법의 to부정사구

11행 ..., but **it's** *the poor* **who** absorb the cost of change.: 'it is ... who[that] ~' 「~하는 사람[것]은 바로 …이다」(강조구문), 'the+형용사' 「…한 사람들」(복수보통명사)

문제해설
⑤ 빈칸 이후의 내용에서 부와 권력을 가진 사람의 이익이 가난한 사람들의 이익보다 우선시되고 가난한 사람들은 자신의 이러한 환경을 바꿀 만한 권력을 갖기 힘들다고 했으므로, 부를 '재분배하는' 것이 어려울 것이라는 내용이 적절하다.

32 ④ 빈칸 추론

1982년에, 로스앤젤레스 시장이었던 톰 브래들리라는 이름의 미국 흑인 남성이 캘리포니아 주지사에 출마했다. 선거 전날 밤, 그는 조지 듀크미지언이라는 이름의 백인 남성인 경쟁 상대보다 7퍼센트포인트 앞섰다. 이 큰 우세에도 불구하고, 브래들리는 선거에서 패했다. 전문가들은 그 이유가 인종이라고 생각하는데, 많은 백인 유권자들이 브래들리에게 투표할 것이라고 말했지만, 막상 그들은 기표소에 혼자 있을 때 그렇게 하지 않았다. 이러한 현상은 사람들이 소수파의 후보자를 지지한다고 거짓으로 주장하는 것으로, 오늘날 브래들리 효과로 알려져 있다. 이것은 정치적으로 옳게 보이고 인종 차별주의적인 행동으로 비난받는 것을 피하려는 바람에서 일어날 가능성이 있다. 결과적으로, 상당수의 유권자들이 여론 조사를 하는 사람들에게 거짓말을 한다.

어휘
mayor 시장 run for 출마하다 governor 통치자; *주지사 election 선거 rival 경쟁자, 경쟁 상대 lead 선두[우세] race 인종, 종족 vote 투표하다 (voter 투표자, 유권자) falsely 거짓으로, 속여서 claim 주장하다; 의견을 말하다 support 지지하다 correct 적절한, 옳은 accuse 고발하다; *비난하다 racist 인종 차별주의자(의) significant 중요한; *상당한, 아주 큰 poll 여론 조사 [문제] restriction 제한, 제약 minority 소수; 소수의, 소수파[당]의 candidate 입후보자[출마자]

구문해설
1행 In 1982, an African-American man [named Tom Bradley], [who was the mayor of Los Angeles], was running for governor of California.: 첫 번째 [ ]는 an African-American man을 수식하는 과거분사구, 두 번째 [ ]는 an African-American man named Tom Bradley를 선행사로 하는 계속적 용법의 주격 관계대명사절

10행 This phenomenon, [in which people falsely claim to support a minority candidate], **is** now **known as** the Bradley effect.: [ ]는 This phenomenon을 선행사로 하는 계속적 용법의 목적격 관계대명사절, 'be known as ...' 「…으로 알려져 있다」

12행 It is likely caused by a desire [**to appear** politically correct and **to avoid** {being accused of racist behavior}].: [ ]는 a desire를 수식하는 형용사적 용법의 to부정사구로 to appear와 to avoid가 등위 접속사 and로 병렬 연결, { }는 avoid의 목적어로 쓰인 동명사구

문제해설
④ 여론 조사에서 지지율이 우세했던 흑인 후보가 실제 선거에서 백인 후보에게 패한 사건은 브래들리 효과라고 일컬어지며, 사람들이 인종 차별주의적인 행동으로 비난 받는 것을 피하려고 여론 조사에서 흑인과 같은 '소수파의 후보자'를 지지한다고 거짓말을 한다는 내용이다.

33 ⑤ 빈칸 추론

사람들은 종종 신체적인 매력은 다른 사람들이 우리에 대해 형성하는 초기 인상에 크게 영향을 미친다고 생각한다. 예를 들어, 신체적으로 매력적인 사람들은 덜 매력적인 사람들보다 더 긍정적으로 보인다. 심리학자들은 이 현상을 후광 효과라고 일컫는다. 버세이드와 월스터가 실시한 연구에서, 실험 대상자들에게 다양한 정도의 신체적 매력을 지닌 남녀의 사진을 보여주었다. 그들의 성격 특징을 추측해 보라고 요청받았을 때, 실험 대상자들은 신체적으로 매력적인 사람들이 덜 매력적인 사람들보다 더 섬세하고, 친절하고, 재미있고, 강인하고, 겸손하고, 사교성 있고, 지적이고, 재치있고, 정직하고, 행복하고, 성공적이라고 평가했다. 이 연구의 결과로, 사람들이 흔히 외모에만 근거하여 다른 사람들에 대한 다양한 첫인상을 형성한다는 것이 나타났다.

어휘
attractiveness 매력(attractive 매력적인) influence …에 영향을 주다 psychologist 심리학자 phenomenon 현상 subject 실험 대상자 varying 다양한 trait 특징 rate …의 등급을 매기다; *평가하다 sensitive 예민한; *섬세한 modest 겸손한 sociable 사교성 있는 indicate 가리키다, 나타내다 impression 인상 appearance 외모 [문제] academic 학교의; *학문적인

구문해설
5행 Psychologists **refer to** this phenomenon **as** the halo effect.: 'refer to A as B' 「A를 B라고 일컫다」

9행 [When (they were) asked to guess their personality traits], subjects rated ...: [ ]는 때를 나타내는 부사절('주어+be동사'가 생략된 형태)

문제해설
⑤ 예시로 든 실험에서 신체적으로 매력적인 사람들이 타인으로부터 첫인상에 대한 긍정적인 평가를 받았으므로, 신체적 매력은 '다른 사람들이 우리에 대해 형성하는 초기 인상'에 큰 영향을 미친다는 내용이 되는 것이 적절하다.

34 ③ 빈칸 추론

대체 역사는 역사가 다른 방향으로 진행된 세계를 묘사한다. 다시 말하자면 대체 역사는 역사 소설과 유사한 일종의 공상 과학 소설이다. 그 소설은 어떤 허구의 역사적 사건이 발생할 때까지 우리의 세계와 동일한 세계를 묘사한다. 이 시점에서, 세계는 대체 역사를 가진 상상의 세계가 된다. 대체 역사는 로마 제국이 결코 몰락하지 않은 세계를 묘사할 수 있다. 그것들은 몇몇 기술이 실제로 일어난 것보다 역사상 훨씬 더 일찍 도입된 것에 대해서 쓸 수도 있다. 예를 들어, 컴퓨터가 빅토리아 시대에 발명되었다면 어떻게 되었을까? 많은 독자들은 이러한 이야기가 상상력을 자극하고 역사에 있어서의 원인과 결과라는 현상을 고찰하기 때문에 흥미롭다고 생각한다.

어휘
alternative 대신의, 대체의 resemble …을 닮다 identical 동일한, 똑같은 fantasy 상상, 공상 empire 제국 stimulate 자극하다 examine 검사하다; *고찰하다 cause and effect 원인과 결과

구문해설
2행 In other words, alternative history is a type of science fiction [which resembles historical fiction].: [ ]는 a type of science fiction을 선행사로 하는 주격 관계대명사절

9행 They may write about **some technology** [being introduced *much* earlier ... actually happened].: [ ]는 about의 목적어로 쓰인 동명사구이며 some technology는 동명사구의 의미상 주어, much는 「훨씬」이라는 의미로 비교급을 강조하는 부사

(11행) ...: **What if** computers *had been invented* in Victorian times?: 'what if ...' 「…하면 어떻게 될까, …하면 어땠을까」, if 뒤에는 과거 사실과 반대되는 일을 가정하는 가정법 과거완료가 쓰임

문제해설
③ 대체 역사는 역사의 어느 시점을 실제 역사와 다르게 상상하여 이야기를 풀어나가는 일종의 공상 과학 소설이므로, 빈칸에는 '역사가 (실제와) 다른 방향으로 진행된' 세계를 묘사한다는 내용이 적절하다.

35 ④ 흐름과 무관한 문장

당신이 백화점에서 쇼핑을 하다가 50달러인 향수 한 병을 발견한다고 가정해 보라. 당신의 처음 생각은 백화점이 아주 적은 양의 물과 섞인 알코올과 기름에 대해 너무 많이 (값을) 청구하고 있다는 것일지도 모른다. 그러나 당신은 이 가격이 원자재의 비용뿐만 아니라 다양한 추가 비용도 반영한다는 것을 고려해야 한다. 우선 첫째로, 백화점은 판매대 뒤에 있는 판매원의 급여를 지불하고 있다. 그리고 향수 제조업자는 향기 자체보다 그것의 화려한 병에 더 많은 비용을 들였을지도 모른다. (따라서, 정부는 여론을 반영하여 사치품들에 더 많은 세금을 부과하는 것을 고려 중에 있다.) 또한, 그 회사가 그 제품을 광고하고 운송하는 데 얼마나 많이 돈을 쓰는지에 대해 생각해보라.

어휘
perfume 향수   initial 처음의   charge (대금·요금을) 청구하다   raw material 원자재   manufacturer 제조업자   fancy 화려한   fragrance 향기   impose (의무·세금 등을) 부과하다   transport 운송하다

구문해설
(5행) However, you should consider [that this price reflects **not only** the cost of the raw materials, **but also** a wide variety of additional expenses].: [ ]는 consider의 목적절, 'not only A but also B' 「A뿐만 아니라 B도」
(10행) And the manufacturer **may have spent** more on the fancy bottle ...: 'may have p.p.' 「…했을지도 모른다」(과거에 대한 불확실한 추측)
(15행) Also, think about [how much the company spends on advertising and transporting the product].: [ ]는 about의 목적어로 쓰인 의문사절

문제해설
원자재 외에 추가로 들어가는 비용들에 대해 언급하면서 상품의 소비자 가격이 높게 책정되는 여러 가지 요인들을 설명하고 있는 글이므로, 정부가 사치품에 세금을 더 부과하는 것을 고려하고 있다는 ④의 내용은 흐름에 맞지 않다.

36 ② 글의 순서

서로 데이트하는 것을 부모들이 금지하는 십 대의 소년과 소녀를 상상해 보라. 그 소년과 소녀는 그들 부모의 지시를 따를 것인가?
(A) 한 심리학적 관점에 따르면, 그들은 십중팔구 그렇게 하지 않을 것이다. 오히려 그러한 금지는 함께 있고자 하는 그 커플의 욕망을 증가시킬 뿐일 것이다. 이것은 금지된 사랑에 관한 셰익스피어의 비극적인 이야기에서 이름을 따온 로미오와 줄리엣 효과로 알려져 있다.
(C) 이 효과의 이름이 문학 작품의 가장 유명한 연인 둘의 이름에서 차용되었다는 사실에도 불구하고, 이것은 이성 관계에만 국한되지 않는다. 실제로 우리는 사회의 많은 다른 분야에서 작용하는 로미오와 줄리엣 효과를 볼 수 있다.
(B) 예를 들어, 특정 유형의 정치적 연설을 금지하는 법은 종종 더 많은 사람들이 불법으로 정해진 것에 참여하도록 만든다. 따라서 이 이론에 따르면, 권위자가 개인의 자유에 제한을 둘 때마다 그러한 제한에 도전하

려는 강력한 충동이 있을 것이다.

어휘
forbid 금지하다   obey 따르다, 순종하다   psychological 심리학적인   perspective 관점   prohibition 금지(prohibit 금지하다)   tragic 비극의, 비극적인   authority 권위; *권위자   limitation 제한   urge 충동   confine 제한하다   observe 보다, 관찰하다   at work 작용하여

구문해설
(1행) Imagine a teenage boy and girl [whose parents **forbid** them **to date** each other].: [ ]는 a teenage boy and girl을 선행사로 하는 소유격 관계대명사절, 'forbid+O+to-v' 「…가 ~하는 것을 금지하다」
(7행) This **is known as** the Romeo and Juliet effect, [named after ... illicit love].: 'be known as ...' 「…으로 알려져 있다」, [ ]는 the Romeo and Juliet effect를 부연 설명하는 과거분사구
(10행) ..., laws [that prohibit certain types of political speech] often **drive** more people **to participate in** [what has been made illegal].: 첫 번째 [ ]는 laws를 선행사로 하는 주격 관계대명사절, 'drive+O+to-v' 「…가 ~하도록 만든다」, 두 번째 [ ]는 participate in의 목적어로 쓰인 관계대명사절

문제해설
② 연애를 반대하는 부모를 둔 소년과 소녀가 부모의 말을 따를 것인지 질문을 던지는 주어진 글 다음에, 이 질문에 대한 답을 하며 로미오와 줄리엣 효과를 소개하는 (A)가 오고, 그 이름의 유래와 다르게 이 효과가 이성 관계 외에도 작용한다는 설명의 (C)가 이어진 후, 이러한 상황에 대한 예시를 제시하는 (B)가 오는 것이 자연스럽다.

37 ③ 글의 순서

요즘 경제 위기로 인해 직업을 잃은 많은 사람들이 취업시장을 떠나 학교로 돌아가고 있다.
(B) 이러한 새로운 학생들의 요구를 충족시키기 위해, 일부 대학교들은 전문화된 강좌를 제공하고 있다. 이러한 강좌를 제공하는 학교들과 그 강좌에 등록하는 학생들 모두를 지원하기 위해 많은 정부 프로그램들이 설계되었다.
(A) 그러나 단순히 학교로 돌아가 새로운 학위를 취득하는 것이 이 사람들이 그 후에 직업을 구할 수 있다는 것을 보장하지는 않는다. 학교로 돌아가는 것은 모험이며, 막대한 시간, 돈, 그리고 노력의 투자를 수반한다.
(C) 그러므로 공부할 과목을 선택하기 전에, 어느 정도 심도 있는 조사를 하는 것이 중요하다. 학교로 돌아갈 가능성이 있는 학생들은 그들이 종사하고 싶은 업계와 그 업계의 미래 고용 전망에 대해 그들이 알아낼 수 있는 모든 것을 알아 두어야 한다.

어휘
financial 경제적인   crisis 위기   ensure 보장하다   risk 위험, 모험   significant 중요한; *막대한   meet 충족시키다   enroll 등록하다   potential 가능성 있는, 잠재적인   prospect 전망

구문해설
(1행) These days, many people [who have lost their jobs due to the financial crisis] **are leaving** the job market and **(are) returning** to school.: [ ]는 many people을 선행사로 하는 주격 관계대명사절, are leaving과 (are) returning은 문장의 동사로 등위 접속사 and로 병렬 연결
(11행) A number of government programs have been designed [to support **both** the schools {offering these courses} **and** the students {enrolling in them}].: [ ]는 목적을 나타내는 부사적 용법의 to부정사구, 'both A and B' 「A와 B 둘 다」, 두 개의 { }는 각각 the schools와 the students를 수식하는 현재분사구

문제해설

③ 경제 위기로 인해 직업을 잃은 사람들이 취업 대신 학교로 돌아간다는 내용의 주어진 글 다음에, 이에 부응하기 위한 대학교와 정부의 노력에 대해 서술한 (B)가 오고, 학교로 돌아가는 것이 재취업을 보장하는 것은 아님을 지적한 (A)가 온 뒤, 이에 대비하기 위한 조언인 (C)의 순서로 이어지는 것이 흐름상 자연스럽다.

38 ④ 주어진 문장의 위치

하나의 종(種)이 별개의 두 종으로 점차 발달할 때, 이것은 분지진화라고 알려져 있다. 이는 일반적으로 특정 개체군이 그 종의 나머지와는 다른 환경에서 서식할 때 일어나는데, 시간이 갈수록 그것은 그 서식지의 독특한 요구를 충족시키도록 변화한다. 분지진화가 일어나는 방법의 한 예로, 원숭이와 인간의 발의 극명한 차이점들을 생각해 보라. 인간과 원숭이가 한때는 단일 종이었지만, 원숭이들은 계속 나무에서 움직이는 데 그들의 시간의 대부분을 보낸 반면에, 인간은 땅 위에서 살기 시작했다. 이 새로운 환경에 적응하기 위해 인간은 직립 보행을 시작했다. 시간이 흘러, 인간의 발은 걷거나 뛸 때 더 나은 속도와 균형을 감안하여 변화했다. 원숭이와 공통의 조상을 공유함에도 불구하고, 인간들이 살던 서식지는 그들이 다른 신체적 특징을 발달시키도록 요구했다.

어휘

adapt to …에 적응하다 walk upright 직립 보행하다 gradually 점차적으로 distinct 뚜렷이 다른, 별개의 population 인구; *개체군 inhabit 살다, 서식하다 meet 만나다; *충족시키다 unique 유일무이한, 독특한 demand *요구; 수요 habitat 서식지 swing 흔들다; *휙 움직이다 allow for …을 감안하다 common 흔한; *공통의 ancestor 조상 trait 특성

구문해설

9행 For an example of [how divergent evolution works], consider the stark differences ...: [ ]는 방법을 나타내는 관계부사절(선행사 the way와 관계부사 how는 둘 중 하나를 생략)

13행 ... while monkeys continued to **spend** most of their time **swinging** from trees.: 'spend+시간+v-ing' 「…하는 데 시간을 보내다」

18행 ..., the habitat [in which humans lived] required them to develop different physical traits.: [ ]는 the habitat을 선행사로 하는 목적격 관계대명사절(in which는 관계부사 where로 바꿔 쓸 수 있음)

문제해설

주어진 문장은 새로운 환경에 적응하기 위한 인간의 변화를 나타내므로 인간이 원숭이들과 달리 땅 위라는 새로운 곳에서 살기 시작했음을 이야기하는 문장 뒤인 ④에 오는 것이 적절하다.

39 ③ 주어진 문장의 위치

수천 년간 사람들은 올빼미가 동물이라기보다는 신에 가깝다고 믿었다. 심지어 오늘날에도 올빼미는 지혜, 마법, 힘을 나타내는 데 사용되고 있지만, 사실 올빼미는 다른 새들보다 더 신적이지는 않다. 비범한 지능을 나타내는 것으로 여겨지는 커다랗고 둥근 머리와 정면을 향한 큰 눈은 단순히 그들이 작은 동물들을 사냥하는 것을 돕도록 발달된 자연적인 적응에 불과하다. 비록 신비한 힘은 없을지라도 올빼미는 다른 맹금들을 능가하는 기술을 가진 강력한 사냥꾼이다. 올빼미들의 날카로운 감각은 그들이 잠재적 먹잇감을 포착하지 못하는 일이 좀처럼 없도록 한다. 게다가 소리 없이 날 수 있는 능력은 이미 늦었을 때에서야 비로소 먹잇감이 자신이 공격당하리라는 것을 눈치챘다는 것을 의미한다.

어휘

owl 올빼미 lack …이 없다, 결핍되다 mystical 신비한, 초자연적인 surpass 능가하다 bird of prey (독수리나 매 등의) 맹금 signify 나타내다

divine 신의, 신성의; 비범한 adaptation 적응 acute 예리한, 날카로운 ensure 보장하다 rarely 거의 …않다 potential 잠재적인

구문해설

1행 ..., they are powerful hunters [whose skill surpasses **that** of other birds of prey].: [ ]는 powerful hunters를 선행사로 하는 소유격 관계대명사절, that은 skill을 지칭

8행 The large ... eyes [that were ... intelligence] **are** simply natural adaptations [developed to *help* them *catch* small animals].: 첫 번째 [ ]는 문장의 주어인 The large ... eyes를 선행사로 하는 주격 관계대명사절, 주어가 복수명사이므로 복수동사인 are가 쓰임, 두 번째 [ ]는 natural adaptations를 수식하는 과거분사구, 'help+O+(to-)v' 「…가 ~하도록 돕다」

14행 Moreover, their ability to fly silently means [that their prey **never** realizes they *are to be attacked* **until** it's too late].: [ ]는 means의 목적절, 'never[not] ... until ~' 「~할 때까지 …하지 않다, ~해서야 비로소 …하다」, are to be attacked는 예정을 나타내는 'be동사+to-v' 용법의 to부정사구

문제해설

주어진 문장은 올빼미가 신비한 힘은 없지만 뛰어난 사냥꾼임을 나타내는데, ③ 뒤에서 올빼미가 가지고 있는 사냥 능력을 서술하고 있으므로 주어진 문장은 ③에 오는 것이 적절하다.

40 ② 요약문 완성

탐정소설은 19세기 중반에 처음 인기를 얻기 시작했는데, 이때는 과학이 크게 진보한 시기였다. 가장 인기 있는 탐정소설 작가들 중에 아서 코난 도일 경이 있었다. 그는 과학자들이 실험에서 사용하는 논리적 접근법에 매료되었다. 예를 들어 셜록 홈즈라는 등장인물은 과학적 정신에 대한 코난 도일의 흠모를 보여준다. 홈즈가 수사하는 각 사건에서, 그는 매우 적은 증거를 이용하여 상대방을 추적한다. 홈즈는 놀라운 관찰력과 독창적인 추리력으로, 범죄현장에 남겨진 담뱃재의 종류나 손으로 쓴 편지에 사용된 잉크의 종류와 같은 쉽게 눈에 띄지 않는 세세한 것들로부터 범인의 신원을 밝혀낸다.

어휘

detective 탐정, 형사 fascination 매혹, 매료됨 logical 논리적인 illustrate 설명하다, 예증하다; 분명히 보여주다 admiration 존경, 선망 investigate 조사하다 insubstantial 내용이 없는, 박약한; *적은, 미량의 track down …을 추적하다 opponent 적, 상대방 observation 관찰 ingenious 재치 있는, 창의력이 있는 reasoning 추리, 추론 figure out 알아내다 identity 신원, 신분 unremarkable 눈에 띄지 않는 ash (보통 *pl.*) 재 [문제] capture 포착하다 equip A with B A에게 B를 갖추게 하다 outstanding 탁월한 adventurous 모험적인 pragmatic 실용적인 theoretical 이론적인 experiential 경험적인

구문해설

3행 Among the most popular detective storywriters **was Sir Arthur Conan Doyle**.: 부사구인 Among ... storywriters가 문두에 나오면서 주어와 동사가 도치

13행 ..., Holmes figures out the criminal's identity from **such** unremarkable details **as** the type of cigar ashes [left ... scene] or the kind of ink [used ... letter].: 'such A as B' 「B와 같은 A」, 두 개의 [ ]는 각각 cigar ashes와 ink를 수식하는 과거분사구

문제해설

② 작가 코난 도일은 탐정 영웅인 셜록 홈즈에게 뛰어난 논리적 추리력을 부여함으로써 그 당시의 과학적 정신을 포착했다.

41 ② 42 ④ 장문

자메이카는 오직 그 섬나라에서 그리고 세계 곳곳에 살고 있는 자메이카인들에 의해서만 사용되는 독특한 언어를 가지고 있다. 이 섬나라에서 사용되는 영어의 방언 형태인 자메이카 영어와는 달리, 이 언어는 유럽 침략자들의 출현으로 시작된 그 섬(자메이카)의 특별한 역사적 배경에서 생겨났다.

그 기간 동안, 자메이카의 원주민들에게는 완전히 생소했던 언어인 영어가, 자메이카인들과 유럽인들 사이의 의사소통을 용이하게 하고자 정복자들에 의해 사용되고 있었다. 효과적으로 의사소통해야 할 필요가 영어와 다른 유럽 언어들, 그리고 카리브어들의 요소를 결합한 한 언어의 형성을 부채질했다. 마침내, 그것은 언어학자들에 의해 자메이카 크리올이라고 알려진 것을 탄생시켰다. '크리올'이라는 용어는 둘 혹은 그 이상의 언어들의 혼합에서 생겨난 언어를 일컫지만, 자메이카에서 구어체의 크리올은 프랑스어에서 유래된 단어인 'patois'라는 비슷한 의미의 지역 용어로 알려져 있다.

시간이 흘러 자메이카의 독립과 함께 자메이카 크리올은 국가 정체성을 대표하게 되었고 높은 위상을 얻었다. 영어가 자메이카의 공용어이자 공식 언어로 남아있기 때문에 때때로 엉터리 영어의 한 형태로 오해를 받기도 하지만, 자메이카 크리올은 영어의 파생어 그 이상이다. 오히려 그것은 하나의 독립된 언어이며, 그것을 사용하는 고유의 작가, 가수, 연설가, 그리고 시인을 가진 하나의 언어이다.

어휘
dialect 방언, 사투리 emerge from …에서 나타나다 context 문맥; *배경, 환경 invader 침략자 facilitate 용이하게 하다. 쉽게 하다 fuel 연료를 채우다; *불러일으키다, 자극하다 derive from (단어·관습 등이) …에서 비롯되다 fusion 융합, 통합 decolonization 자치 (독립), 비식민지화 prominence 두드러짐, 탁월 divergent 갈라지는; 다른 branch (나무)가지; 파생물, 분파; *어파(語派) [문제] alteration 변경, 개조 formation 형성, 구성 resentment 분노

구문해설
3행 [(Being) Different from Jamaican English, {a dialect of English spoken on the island}], this language emerged ...: [ ]는 부대상황을 나타내는 분사구문. { }는 Jamaican English와 동격
25행 [Though (it is) at times misunderstood as ... Jamaica —] Jamaican Creole is ...: [ ]는 양보를 나타내는 부사절('주어+be동사'가 생략된 형태)

문제해설
41 자메이카인들과 유럽인들의 원활한 의사소통을 위해 당시에 사용되고 있던 여러 종류의 언어들을 결합시킨 자메이카 크리올이라는 언어가 만들어졌다는 내용이므로, 빈칸에는 ② '한 언어의 형성'이 적절하다.
42 ① 자메이카는 유럽국가들의 침략을 받았다. ② 크리올은 새로 생겨난 언어이다. ③ 영어는 유럽의 침략으로 인해 자메이카에 들어오게 되었다. ⑤ 현재 영어가 자메이카의 공용어로 사용되고 있다고 했다.

43 ③ 44 ① 45 ⑤ 장문

(A) 어느 날 유명한 작곡가인 모차르트는 대문을 두드리는 소리를 들었다. 어느 주요 인사가 모차르트와 상의하라고 보냈다는 잘 차려 입은 낯선 사람이었다. 모차르트는 그 주요 인사가 누구인지 물었지만, 그 남자는 대답하기를 거부했다. 그가 말한 전부는 그분은 사랑하는 사람을 잃었고, 모차르트가 고인에게 경의를 표하는 레퀴엠을 작곡해 주기를 원한다는 것이었다. 알 수 없는 요청에 호기심이 생긴 모차르트는 가격을 협상했고, 한 달 후에 완성된 곡을 전달하기로 했다.

(C) 그 이방인이 떠난 후 얼마 되지 않아, 모차르트는 갑자기 창작의 열망에 휩싸였다. 펜과 종이를 붙잡고서 그는 열광적으로 작곡을 하기 시작했고, 여러 날에 걸쳐 밤낮으로 작곡을 계속했다. 불행히도 그의 건강은 좋지 않았고, 그는 곧 과로로 쓰러졌다. 일을 그만두고 충분한 휴식을 취해야 했던 그는 그가 쓰고 있는 레퀴엠이 결국 자신의 장례식에서 연주될까 두렵다고 아내에게 말했다.

(B) 그의 건강은 나아지지 않았지만, 모차르트는 속히 자신의 작업으로 돌아갔다. 한 달이 지나자 약속대로 그 알 수 없는 이방인이 대문에 다시 나타났다. 부끄럽게도 모차르트는 곡을 완성하지 못했다는 것을 인정해야만 했다. 그는 작곡을 향한 그의 열정이 곡을 기대 이상으로 더 복잡하게 만들었다고 설명하면서, 한 달의 시간을 더 줄 것을 요청했다. 모차르트에게는 매우 놀랍게도, 그 이방인은 불평하기는커녕, 오히려 (기간의) 연장을 허락했고, 레퀴엠의 가격을 두 배로 올려주겠다고 말했다.

(D) 건강이 악화되면서 모차르트는 그 남자가 천사나 악마 둘 중의 하나이며, 그의 존재가 자신의 죽음이 임박했음을 나타낸다고 의심하기 시작했다. 그는 전보다 더 큰 열정을 가지고 작곡을 계속했고, 이것이 그의 마지막이자 가장 위대한 작곡이 될 것이라고 확신했다. 한 달 후 그 이방인이 모차르트의 대문을 두드렸을 때, 그는 위대한 작곡가가 사망했다는 소식을 들었다. 미완성으로 남은 그 레퀴엠은 음악에 대한 애정을 갖고 있던 지방의 어느 백작에 의해 의뢰되었던 것으로 밝혀졌다.

어휘
in honor of …에 경의를 표하여 the deceased 고인 intrigued 호기심이 동한, 흥미로워 하는 astonishment 놀람, 경악 grant 주다; *허가하다 extension 연장, 연기 be thrust into 갑자기 …해지다 rage 격노; *열망; 열의 feverishly 열광적으로 collapse 무너지다; *쓰러지다 exhaustion 소모, 고갈; *피로 remark …에 주목하다; *말하다 funeral 장례식 failing 약해 가는, 쇠한 presence 있음, 존재 impending 임박한, 절박한 resume 다시 시작하다, 다시 계속하다 commission 위임하다; *의뢰하다, 주문하다 count 백작

구문해설
2행 ... a well-dressed stranger [who said he **had been sent** ... with Mozart].: [ ]는 a well-dressed stranger를 선행사로 하는 주격 관계대명사절. had been sent는 과거시제(said)보다 앞선 시점을 나타내는 대과거
9행 [(Being) Intrigued by the mysterious request], Mozart ... in one month.: [ ]는 이유를 나타내는 분사구문
19행 **Much to Mozart's astonishment**, ... he would double the price [paid for the requiem].: 'much to one's+명사 「…가 ~하게도」, [ ]는 the price를 수식하는 과거분사구
29행 ..., he remarked to his wife [that he feared the requiem {(which/that) he was writing} would **end up being** played ... funeral].: [ ]는 remarked의 목적절. { }는 the requiem을 선행사로 하는 목적격 관계대명사절. 'end up v-ing 「결국 …이 되다」
36행 ... with even greater passion, [(being) convinced that this **was to be** his final ... composition].: [ ]는 부대상황을 나타내는 분사구문. was to be는 운명을 나타내는 'be동사+to-v' 용법의 to부정사

문제해설
43 ③ 어느 날 모차르트를 찾아온 이방인이 레퀴엠을 의뢰했다는 내용의 (A) 다음에, 모차르트가 약속한 한 달 동안 레퀴엠을 작곡하는 과정을 이야기하고 있는 (C)가 이어지고, 약속한 기간을 지키지 못한 모차르트가 한 달 더 기간을 연장해 줄 것을 요청하는 내용의 (B)가 온 다음, 연장 기간이 지난 후 이방인이 찾아왔을 때 모차르트가 이미 사망했다는 내용의 (D)가 이어지는 것이 자연스럽다.
44 모차르트가 생애 마지막으로 레퀴엠을 작곡하게 된 사연에 관한 글이므로 제목으로는 ① '한 작곡가의 마지막 레퀴엠'이 적절하다.
45 ⑤ (e)는 이방인을 가리키는 반면, 나머지는 모두 모차르트를 가리킨다.

18 ②	19 ①	20 ③	21 ④	22 ④	23 ⑤
24 ②	25 ②	26 ②	27 ③	28 ⑤	29 ③
30 ⑤	31 ⑤	32 ⑤	33 ⑤	34 ②	35 ④
36 ②	37 ②	38 ③	39 ③	40 ③	41 ①
42 ⑤	43 ⑤	44 ②	45 ③		

18 ② 글의 목적

관계자분께,

저는 미셸 윌리엄스의 요청으로 이 편지를 보냅니다. 미셸은 말리부 고등학교에서 제가 가르치는 과학 수업 중 몇 개를 들은 학생이었습니다. 그녀는 수업 시간에는 성실한 학생이었고 수업이 끝난 후에는 이야기 나누기에 유쾌한 사람이었습니다. 제 수업에서 그녀의 학업 수준은 보통 수준보다 훨씬 높았고, 그녀는 학급 친구들에게 모범이 되었으며, 그들은 종종 그녀에게 의지하며 도움을 받았습니다. 따라서 저는 귀교의 입학에 그녀를 추천하게 되어 기쁩니다. 저는 미셸이 장래에 추구하려고 선택하는 어느 학업 과정에서든 성공할 것이라고 확신합니다. 질문이 있으시거나 더 많은 세부적인 내용이 필요하시다면, 221-8824로 제게 얼마든지 전화 주세요.

진심을 담아,

조나단 이토 드림

어휘

at the request of …의 요청에 의하여   average 평균, 보통 수준   turn to …에 의지하다   assistance 도움   recommend 추천하다   admission 입학   academic 학문의   pursue 추구하다   require 필요로 하다   detail 세부 사항

구문해설

(5행) She was a hard worker in the classroom and a pleasure [to speak with after class].: [ ]는 a pleasure를 수식하는 형용사적 용법의 to부정사구

(8행) ..., and she was a role model for her classmates, [who often turned to her for assistance].: [ ]는 her classmates를 선행사로 하는 계속적 용법의 주격 관계대명사절

(11행) I am sure Michelle will succeed in [whatever academic path she chooses to pursue in the future].: [ ]는 전치사 in의 목적어로 쓰인 복합관계형용사절

문제해설

② 고등학교 교사가 자신의 수업을 들었던 학생의 장점을 설명하며 대학교에 학생을 추천하는 글이다.

19 ① 글의 요지

창의력은 거의 예외 없이 긍정적이라고 여겨지는 특성이다. 동시에, 업무 현장에서 제안되는 창의적인 아이디어들 중 단지 극소수만이 실제로 실행에 옮겨진다. 왜 이러한가? 정의에 의하면, 창의적인 아이디어는 새로운 것이다. 그것은 일반적인 것을 넘어서는 관점을 나타내며 이전에 결코 생각되거나 시도된 적이 없는 행동 방침을 제안할 수도 있다. 그리고 대부분의 사업가들은 새롭고 검증되지 않은 행동 방침에 직면할 때 불안해하게 되는데, 왜냐하면 그들은 후회하는 것보다 차라리 안전한 것을 선호하기 때문이다. 그래서 그들은 창의적인 아이디어들을 터무니없고 고려의 가치가 없는 것으로 취급하는 경향이 있다. 이것은 극히 유감스러운 일인데, 왜냐하면 그렇게 함으로써 그들은 그들의 사업을 개선하고 그들의 고객들에 이익을 줄 수 있는 명백한 기회들을 놓치게 되기 때문이다. 창의력은 진보를 향한 진정한 길이다. 우리가 이것을 빨리 인지하면 할수록 우리의 사정은 더 나아질 것이다.

어휘

trait 특성   universally 보편적으로; 예외 없이   slim 날씬한; *아주 적은, 얼마 안 되는   put into action 실행에 옮기다   the case 사실, 실정   novel 새로운, 신기한   represent 나타내다   perspective 관점   norm 표준, 일반적인 것   conceive 생각하다, 품다   be confronted with …에 직면하다   absurd 터무니없는   unfortunate 불운한; *유감스러운   pass up 거절하다; *(기회를) 놓치다   progress 진보   well off 부유한, 잘 사는; *사정[형편]이 좋은

구문해설

(9행) And most businesspeople become anxious [when (they are) confronted with new and untested courses of action], as they **would rather** be safe **than** sorry.: [ ]는 때를 나타내는 부사절('주어+be동사'가 생략된 형태), 'would rather A than B' 「B하느니 차라리 A하겠다」

(17행) ... **the sooner** we recognize this, **the better off** we will be.: 'the+비교급, the+비교급' 「…하면 할수록 더 ~하다」

문제해설

창의력은 대개 긍정적인 것으로 여겨지지만 실제 업무 현장에서는 오히려 창의적인 생각들이 무시되는 경향이 있음을 비판하는 글이므로 ①이 요지로 가장 적절하다.

20 ③ 필자의 주장

어떤 사람들은 삶이 힘든 여정이라고 생각하고 그저 빨리 지나가기만을 바란다. 나는 어떤 점에서는 그들을 이해하지만, 그들이 깨닫지 못하는 것은 우리가 겪는 어려운 순간들이 바로 이 여행을 할 가치가 있게 만드는 것이라는 사실이다. 또한 우리의 길에 나타나는 모든 시련들이 우리를 더 나은 사람으로 만드는 데 도움을 준다. 다시 말해, 자신의 문제들에 대처함으로써 우리는 다른 사람들을 더 잘 이해하게 되고 우리 스스로에 대해서 더 자신감을 갖게 된다. 따라서 우리는 시련을 넘어서 나중에 올 수 있는 많은 이익을 바라보아야 한다. 삶은 우리가 직면하고 있는 문제들에서 의미를 찾을 때 훨씬 더 값지다.

어휘

pass by 지나가다   go through …을 겪다   trial 시련, 고난   understanding of …에 대해 이해심이 있는   confident 확신하는, 자신을 가진   precious 귀중한, 값진

구문해설

(3행) ... [what they don't realize] is [that the difficult moments {(that) we go through} are exactly {what make the journey **worth taking**}].: 첫 번째 [ ]는 주어로 쓰인 관계대명사절, 두 번째 [ ]는 주격보어로 쓰인 명사절, 첫 번째 { }는 the difficult moments를 선행사로 하는 목적격 관계대명사절, 두 번째 { }는 that절의 주격보어로 쓰인 관계대명사절, 'worth v-ing' 「…할 가치가 있는」

(10행) Therefore, we should **look beyond** our difficulties **to** the many benefits [that may come later].: 'look beyond A to B' 「A를 넘어서 B를 바라보다」, [ ]는 the many benefits를 선행사로 하는 주격 관계대명사절

문제해설

③ 필자는 우리가 직면한 문제에서 삶의 의미를 찾을 수 있으며 문제 해결 과정에서 성숙해질 수 있다고 주장하고 있다.

21 ④ 글의 주제

미국에서 9·11 테러 공격에 뒤이어, 미국 항공 여행의 안전을 보장하기 위해 교통 안전청(TSA)이 설립되었다. TSA는 어떤 위험한 인물이나 물건을 확인하기 위해 탑승 전에 승객들과 그들의 짐을 수색하는 임무를 맡고 있다. 그러나 최근 몇 년간 TSA 자체가 미국으로 여행하는 사람들에게 커다란 문제들을 제기한다는 것이 분명해졌다. 승객들에게 신발을 벗으라고 요구하고 휴대 가능한 가방 내의 액체를 허가하지 않는 것과 같은 이 안전국의 복잡한 수색 규칙들 중 일부가 여행객들을 불편하고 짜증나게 한다. 게다가, 더 최근의 정책들은 훨씬 더 심각한 우려를 일으킨다. 우선 첫째로, 위험한 수준의 방사선을 방출하는 전신 보안 스캐너의 사용은 사람들의 건강을 위험에 처하게 한다. 한편, '강화된 보안 몸수색'은 개인의 사생활을 침해하고 인권 문제를 일으킨다. TSA는 단지 더 엄격한 보안보다는 그 이상까지 고려하기 시작해야 한다.

어휘

transportation 운송, 교통 기관　security 보안　screen 차단하다; *심사하다, 가려내다　board 탑승하다　identify (신분을) 확인하다　pose (문제 등을) 제기하다　complicated 복잡한　disallow 허가하지 않다　carry-on (비행기 안에) 휴대할 수 있는　inconvenience 불편하게 하다　concern 우려　emit 방출하다　radiation 방사선　put ... at risk …을 위험에 빠뜨리다　enhanced 강화한　pat-down 몸수색　infringe 침해하다　[문제] strict 엄격한

구문해설

[4행] The TSA is tasked with screening passengers and their luggage **prior to** boarding *in order to identify* any dangerous persons or objects.: 'prior to' 「…에 앞서」, 'in order to-v' 「…하기 위해」

[7행] ..., it has become obvious [that the TSA *itself* poses big problems to people {traveling to the U.S.}]: it은 가주어이고 [ ]가 진주어, itself는 the TSA를 강조하는 재귀대명사, { }는 people을 수식하는 현재분사구

문제해설

미국 교통 안전청(TSA)의 엄격한 보안 정책이 오히려 여행객들의 건강, 사생활 및 인권을 침해한다는 내용이므로 ④ 'TSA의 강경 보안 정책의 부정적인 영향'이 글의 주제로 가장 적절하다.

22 ④ 글의 제목

교배된 개들, 일명 '디자이너 개'가 미국에서 빠르게 새로운 유행이 되고 있다. 사람들이 가장 기르고 싶어하는 디자이너 개는 래브라두들인데, 이것은 래브라도와 푸들의 잡종이다. 이러한 교배로 인해 푸들의 지능과 섬세한 골격이 래브라도의 귀여움 및 충성심과 결합된다. 많은 전문가들은 교배된 개들이 순종보다 더 다양한 유전적 배경을 가지고 있기 때문에 더 건강하다고 믿는다. 반려동물 주인들은 퍼그의 다정함과 비글의 충성심과 같은 두 종의 최고의 특성을 겸비한 동물들을 찾는다. 따라서 이런 디자이너 개들이 반려동물 애호가와 비평가들 모두의 마음을 사로잡은 것은 놀라운 일이 아니다.

어휘

crossbred 잡종(의), 교배종(의)　trend 경향, 추세　breed 기르다; 품종　cross 잡종　combine 결합하다; 겸비하다　delicate 섬세한　frame 골격, 뼈대　lovability 귀여움, 매력　loyalty 충성심　varied 여러 가지의　genetic 유전의　purebred 순종　win the hearts of …의 마음을 사로잡다　critic 비평가

구문해설

[2행] The designer dog [that people most want to breed] is the Labradoodle, [which is ... poodle].: 첫 번째 [ ]는 The designer dog를 선행사로 하는 목적격 관계대명사절, 두 번째 [ ]는 the Labradoodle을 선행사로 하는 계속적 용법의 주격 관계대명사절

[12행] **It** is no surprise then [that ... alike].: It은 가주어이고 [ ]가 진주어

문제해설

④ 다른 종 간의 교배로 탄생한 디자이너 개들이 인기를 끌고 있는 이유에 대해 서술한 글이다.

23 ⑤ 글의 제목

2016년에, 아주 작은 우주 쓰레기 한 조각이 국제 우주 정거장(ISS)을 들이받았다. 그것은 고작 직경 1밀리미터의 천분의 몇에 불과했지만, 창문에 심각한 손상을 초래했다. 만약 더 큰 우주 쓰레기 조각이 언제 국제 우주 정거장을 들이받는다면, 그것은 정거장 전체를 파괴해서 탑승한 전원을 죽게 할 수도 있다. 유감스럽게도, 지구 궤도에 1억 개 이상의 우주 쓰레기 조각들이 있으며, 이들 중 약 34,000개는 10센티미터보다 더 크다. 만약 이 숫자가 계속 증가한다면, 머지않아 우주 비행사가 지구 궤도를 돌거나 우주를 여행하는 것이 너무 위험할 수 있다. 그렇기 때문에 우리는 현재 우주 쓰레기 문제에 대한 해결책을 찾아야 하며, 그렇게 하는 것이 우리가 장차 우주를 계속 탐험할 수 있게 해줄 것이다.

어휘

tiny 아주 작은　international 국제적인　diameter 지름, 직경　entire 전체의　aboard 탑승[승선]한　orbit 궤도; 궤도를 돌다　astronaut 우주 비행사　solution 해결책　explore 답사[탐사/탐험]하다　[문제] threat 위협, 위험

구문해설

[5행] ..., it could destroy the entire station, [killing everyone aboard].: [ ]는 결과를 나타내는 분사구문, aboard는 everyone을 수식하는 형용사

[10행] If this number continues to grow, **it** could soon be too dangerous *for astronauts* [to orbit Earth or travel into space].: it은 가주어이고 [ ]가 진주어, astronauts는 [ ]의 의미상 주어

[12행] **That is why** we need to find a solution to the space junk problem today—*doing so* will **allow** us **to continue** exploring the universe tomorrow.: 'that is why ...' 「그것이 …한 이유이다」, doing so는 주어로 쓰인 동명사구로 find a solution to the space junk problem today를 대신함. 'allow+O+to-v' 「…가 ~하도록 허용하다」

문제해설

아주 작은 우주 쓰레기 조각이라도 국제 우주 정거장에 큰 손상을 초래할 수 있으며, 지구 궤도에 있는 우주 쓰레기양이 상당하기 때문에 우주 탐험을 계속하기 위해서는 이에 대한 해결책이 필요하다는 내용이므로, 글의 제목으로는 ⑤ '우주 쓰레기: 우주 탐험에 있어 커지는 위협'이 가장 적절하다.

24 ② 도표 내용 불일치

이 그래프는 여러 다른 운동 수업 활동들에 대한 다양한 연령대의 참여율을 보여준다. 18세에서 34세에 이르는 가장 어린 연령대는 도표에 포함된 모든 활동에 가장 높은 참여율을 보였다. (55세 이상 연령대는 모든 활동에서 20퍼센트보다 적은 참여율을 보였는데, 근력 운동이 가장 흔한 활동이었고 권투가 가장 흔하지 않았다.) 35세에서 54세 사람들의 30퍼센트 이상이 근력 운동 수업에 참여했는데, 이는 댄스 수업에 참여한 비율의 약 2배였다. 권투는 모든 세 연령대에서 가장 흔하지 않은 활동이었지만, 18세에서 34세 사람들의 참여 비율은 35세에서 54세 사람들의 비율의 2배만큼 높았다. 마지막으로, 가장 어린 연령대의 4분의 1이 요가 수업에 참여했는데, 근력 운동 수업에 참여한 비율보다 14퍼센트포인트 적었다.

의 감자 작물에 영향을 미치기 시작했고 나라 전역으로 빠르게 퍼졌다. 그다음 해까지 아일랜드 감자 농작물의 75퍼센트가 손실되었고 사람들이 굶주림으로 죽기 시작했다. 그 후 6년간, 100만 명의 사람들이 죽었고 또 다른 100만 명은 이주했다. 이러한 피난민들 중 많은 이들이 미국 동부 해안 도시에 정착하여 아일랜드 지역사회를 만들었다. 그곳에서 그들은 다수의 산업 분야에 걸쳐 값싼 잉여 노동력을 제공했고, 이후 수십 년간 미국의 경제 성장을 극적으로 촉진시켰다. 따라서, 아일랜드의 감자 기근은 19세기 미국 역사에 간접적으로 의미 있는 영향을 미쳤다.

어휘
starvation 기아, 굶주림 perish 죽다 emigrate 이주하다, 이민을 가다 refugee 피난민 settle 정착하다 surplus 잉여 multiple 다수의 dramatically 극적으로 boost 신장시키다 famine 기근 have an impact on …에 영향을 주다

구문해설
[1행] Sometimes, natural disasters can greatly affect the history of places [far away from (the place) {where they occur}].: [ ]는 places를 수식하는 형용사구, { }는 from의 목적어로 쓰인 관계부사절(선행사 the place가 생략된 형태)
[8행] ..., 75% of Ireland's potato crop **had been lost**, and people began *dying of* starvation.: had been lost는 과거완료와 수동태가 결합된 형태. 'die of' 「…(주로 병, 굶주림)으로 죽다」
[14행] There, they provided a surplus of cheap labor across multiple industries, [dramatically boosting American economic growth for the next several decades].: [ ]는 결과를 나타내는 분사구문

문제해설
① 1845년 당시 인구는 800만에서 1,000만 명 사이였다. ③ 질병으로 인한 감자 농작물 피해 때문에 기근이 발생했다. ④ 1840년대 많은 사람이 사망한 것은 극심한 기근 때문이었다. ⑤ 기근으로 인해 발생한 피난민들이 미국으로 이주한 것이다.

27 ③ 내용 불일치

피자를 즐기고, 굶주린 이들에게 음식을 주세요
지노 피자 전문점은 링컨 카운티의 푸드 뱅크를 돕기 위해 이번 주말 모금 행사를 개최할 것입니다!
일시: 9월 22일 금요일부터 9월 24일 일요일까지
장소: 버몬트주, 뉴턴시, 워터가 247번지, 지노 피자 전문점
참여 방법:
1) 저희 웹사이트 www.ginospzz.net에서 모금 행사 특별 쿠폰을 다운받으세요.
2) 식당에 오시거나 배달시켜서 피자를 주문하세요.
3) 값을 지불할 때 쿠폰을 제시하세요. 여러분은 10퍼센트 할인을 받고 저희는 5달러를 푸드 뱅크에 기부할 것입니다.
참고: 테이블이나 가구당 한 개의 쿠폰만 사용 가능합니다. 최소 15달러의 주문 금액이 요구됩니다.

어휘
feed 음식을 주다 pizzeria 피자 전문점 fundraiser 모금 행사 order 주문하다 deliver 배달하다 present 주다, 제시하다 donate 기부하다 household 가정, 가구 minimum 최소한의 require 필요하다, 요구하다

구문해설
[2행] Gino's Pizzeria will be holding a fundraiser this weekend [to support the Lincoln County Food Bank]!: [ ]는 목적을 나타내는 부사적 용법의 to부정사구
[12행] Order any pizza, **either** in the restaurant **or** to be delivered.: 'either A or B' 「A와 B 둘 중 하나」

어휘
weight training 근력 운동 participation 참여 rate 비율 range from A to B 범위가 A에서 B에 이르다 common 흔한 take part in …에 참여하다 approximately 약, 거의 quarter 4분의 1

구문해설
[3행] The youngest age group, [ranging from 18 to 34 years of age], had the highest participation rate in all the activities [included on the chart].: 첫 번째 [ ]는 The youngest age group을 수식하는 현재분사구, 두 번째 [ ]는 all the activities를 수식하는 과거분사구
[13행] ..., but the percentage of 18- to 34-year-olds participating was **twice as** high **as** the percentage of 35- to 54-year-olds.: '배수사+as ... as' 「~배만큼 …한[하게]」
[16행] Finally, a quarter of the youngest age group took part in yoga classes, 14 percentage points fewer **than** took part in weight training.: than은 유사관계대명사로 took part in의 주어 역할

문제해설
55세 이상 연령대의 24퍼센트가 근력 운동 수업에 참여했으므로, 해당 연령대의 모든 활동 참여율이 20퍼센트 이하라는 ②는 도표의 내용과 일치하지 않는다.

25 ② 내용 불일치

이곳 지구의 사진사들과 달리, 우주 비행사들은 누구도 경험한 적 없는 지점에서 사진을 찍을 수 있다. 그러나 지구에서는 상당히 간단한 일인 사진 촬영이 우주에서는 훨씬 더 번거롭다. 무중력 상태가 무거운 카메라 장비를 다루는 것을 쉽게 해주는 것은 사실이지만, 또한 가만히 서 있기 힘들게 만들기도 한다. 더 기본적인 차원에서, 우주 비행사들이 착용하는 우주복과 그 외의 부속 장치는 사진을 찍기 위해 막상 버튼을 누르려고 할 때 매우 불편하다. 다른 기술적 문제들 또한 우주 촬영을 까다롭게 만든다. 예를 들어 창 위의 먼지로 인해 사진이 흐려질 수도 있고, 아주 적은 양의 방사선에 노출되어도 필름이 손상될 가능성이 있다.

어휘
viewpoint 견해; *관찰하는 위치 fairly 꽤, 상당히 gravity 중력 equipment 장비 spacesuit 우주복 accessory 부속 장치; 액세서리 awkward 어색한; *불편한 click 딸깍 소리 나게 누르다 tricky 까다로운 blur 번지게 하다, 흐리게 하다 exposure 노출

구문해설
[1행] ..., astronauts can take photographs from viewpoints [never experienced by anyone else].: [ ]는 viewpoints를 수식하는 과거분사구
[5행] Lack of gravity does make **it** easy [to deal with heavy camera equipment], but *it* also makes **it** difficult [to stand still].: 두 개의 [ ] 앞의 it은 가목적어이고 두 개의 [ ]가 각각의 진목적어, but 바로 뒤의 it은 앞 절의 Lack of gravity를 지칭
[8행] ..., the spacesuits and other accessories [worn by astronauts] are very awkward [when trying to ... picture].: 첫 번째 [ ]는 the spacesuits and other accessories를 수식하는 과거분사구, 두 번째 [ ]는 때를 나타내는 분사구문

문제해설
② 우주에서는 중력이 없어서 무거운 카메라 장비를 다루기가 쉽다고 했다.

26 ② 내용 일치

때때로 자연재해는 그것이 발생한 곳에서 멀리 떨어진 장소들의 역사에 크게 영향을 미칠 수 있다. 예를 들어, 1845년에 아일랜드에는 800만에서 1,000만 명 사이의 사람들이 살고 있었다. 그들 중 거의 절반이 단하나의 농작물인 감자에 의존했다. 그해 여름 동안, 어떤 질병이 이 나라

문제해설

③ 쿠폰을 제시하면 10퍼센트 할인을 받는다고 했다.

28 ⑤ 어법

　멸종 동물의 화석 뼈로부터 그들의 골격을 재구성하는 것은 어렵고도 까다로운 과학이다. 화석 뼈는 부서지지 않은 채 남아 있는 경우가 거의 없다. 발견될 당시에 단일 동물의 뼈가 널리 흩어져 있을 수도 있다. 더구나, 여러 동물들의 뼈 조각들이 같은 강바닥이나 모래톱 속에 함께 있을 수도 있어서, 그것들을 잘못 맞추지 않도록 세심한 노력을 기울여야 한다. 그러므로, 고생물학자는 박물관 전시물을 조립하려고 시도하기 전에 현재 살아있는 동물들의 골격을 연구하고, 그들의 형태와 기능을 기록하며, 관련 있는 동물들의 구조적인 세부사항을 비교하는 데 수 년을 보내야 한다. 화석 수집물은 아무리 매혹적이라 하더라도 헌신적인 전문가에 의해 조립되었을 때에만 진정한 가치를 드러낸다.

어휘

reconstruct 재구성하다　skeleton 골격, 뼈대　extinct 멸종된　fossil 화석　challenging 도전적인, 힘이 드는　exacting 힘든, 까다로운　scatter 흩뿌리다　far and wide 널리, 도처에　fragment 파편, 조각　riverbed 강바닥　sandbar 모래톱　mismatch 짝을 잘못 맞추다　document …을 문서에 기록하다　structural 구조상의　assemble 조립하다　fascinating 매혹적인　reveal 드러내다　dedicated 헌신적인, 전념하는　expert 전문가

구문해설

(8행) Accordingly, paleontologists must **spend** years **studying** the skeletons ..., **documenting** ..., and **comparing** ...: 'spend+시간+v-ing'는 '…하는 데 시간을 보내다'라는 의미로 studying, documenting, comparing이 and로 병렬 연결

(13행) A collection of fossils, **however** fascinating (it is), reveals its true worth only [when (it is) assembled by a dedicated expert].: however는 '아무리 … 하더라도'라는 의미의 복합관계부사('주어+동사'는 문맥상 분명한 것일 경우 종종 생략), [ ]는 때를 나타내는 부사절('주어+be동사'가 생략된 형태)

문제해설

⑤ 문장의 주어는 A collection of fossils이고 however fascinating은 삽입구인데, 문장의 동사가 없으므로 revealing은 reveals로 고쳐야 한다.

29 ③ 어휘

　국제 관계에 대해 이야기할 때, 우리는 하드 파워와 소프트 파워를 구별해야 한다. 하드 파워는 다른 국가들을 특정한 방식으로 행동하도록 강요하기 위해 군사력이나 경제력을 사용하는 것을 지칭한다. 대조적으로, 소프트 파워는 강한 국가가 바라는 행동을 먼저 취해서 다른 국가들이 따를 수 있는 본보기로 행동하는 것을 요구한다. 따라서, 소프트 파워에는 당신의 바람에 따르도록 다른 이들의 선호도를 바꿀 수 있는 능력이 있다. 이것과 동일한 원리가 재계에서도 유효하다. 예를 들어, 가장 유능한 경영진들은 직원들이 특정 방식으로 행동하도록 강요하는 자들이 아니다. 오히려, 솔선수범이 가장 큰 성공을 가져온다. 소프트 파워의 사용을 통해, 경영진들은 직원들이 회사의 목표를 그들 자신의 것으로 만들도록 장려하고, 그 과정에서 그들이 행해져야 하는 일을 자발적으로 하도록 설득한다.

어휘

international 국제적인　relation 관계　distinguish 구별하다　alternate 번갈아 나오게 하다　military 군사의　adopt (태도를) 취하다　preference 선호(도)　prevalence 널리 퍼짐, 유행　conform 따르다, 순응하다　hold true 진실이다; *딱 들어맞다, 유효하다　business world 재계　executive 경영진　dissuade 만류하다　leading by example 솔선수범

convince 납득시키다; *설득하다　voluntarily 자발적으로

구문해설

(3행) Hard power refers to the use of military or economic strength [to **force** other nations **to behave** a certain way].: [ ]는 목적을 나타내는 부사적 용법의 to부정사구, 'force+O+to-v' '…가 ~하게 하다'

(16행) ..., executives **encourage** employees **to make** the company's goals *their own* (goals), and in the process convince them to do [what needs to be done] voluntarily.: 'encourage+O+to-v' '…가 ~하도록 장려하다', 'make+O+OC(명사)' '…을 ~로 만들다', [ ]는 do의 목적어로 쓰인 관계대명사절

문제해설

③ (A) 하드 파워와 소프트 파워의 차이점에 관한 내용이 이어지므로 '구별하다(distinguish)'가 적절하다. (B) 소프트 파워는 강한 국가가 먼저 본보기를 보여 다른 국가가 따르도록 만든다는 내용으로 보아, 다른 이들의 '선호도(preferences)'를 바꾸는 것으로 볼 수 있다. (C) 직원들이 해야 할 일을 자발적으로 하도록 만든다는 내용으로 보아, 직원들이 회사의 목표를 자신의 것으로 만들도록 '장려하다(encourage)'라고 하는 것이 적절하다.

30 ⑤ 빈칸 추론

　흔히 과학이라 일컬어지는 점성술을 진짜 과학인 천문학과 혼동해서는 안 된다. 사실 점성술은 여러 세대 동안 과학적 사고에 있어서 골칫거리였다. 학문적으로 보이는 책 더미와 행성의 위치에 관한 복잡한 도표들을 가지고 진정한 과학으로 위장한 채, 점성술은 개인의 성격을 설명할 수 있다고 주장한다. 점성술은 그의 주장을 고수해 왔지만 어떠한 과학적 연구도 이러한 주장을 증명할 수는 없었다. 실제로 그렇게 하려는 시도는 그 주장이 얼마나 공허한지를 증명했을 뿐이다. 특정한 별자리에 태어나는 것이 누군가를 '창의적'이거나 '목표 지향적'으로 만든다는 주장은 실제로 검증될 수가 없는데, 이는 그러한 성향의 존재가 주로 해석의 문제이기 때문이다.

어휘

confuse 혼동하다　so-called 소위, 이른바; 흔히 …라고 일컬어지는　astrology 점성술　authentic 진정한, 믿을 만한　astronomy 천문학　a thorn in the[one's] side 걱정[고통]의 원인, 골칫거리　disguise 변장시키다, 위장시키다　planetary 행성의　insistence 고집, 주장　assertion 단언, 주장　sign 신호; *(천문) 황도 12종의 하나, …좌(座) (= star sign)　goal-oriented 목표 지향적인　[문제] persistence 고집　faithfulness 충실함　responsibility 책임감　interpretation 해석

구문해설

(5행) [Disguised as true science], with ... positions, astrology claims [(that) it can explain individual personality].: 첫 번째 [ ]는 부대상황을 나타내는 분사구문, 두 번째 [ ]는 claims의 목적절

(11행) The claim [that being born under a particular sign **makes** somebody "**creative**" or "**goal-oriented**"] can't really be tested, ...: [ ]는 The claim과 동격, 'make+O+OC(형용사)' '…을 ~하게 만들다'

문제해설

⑤ 점성술이 성격을 설명할 수 있다는 것은 증명될 수 없는데, 이는 과학적 연구로 증명될 수 있는 사실이 아니라 '해석'의 문제라고 하는 것이 적절하다.

31 ⑤ 빈칸 추론

　사전을 집필하고 편집하는 사전 편찬자들의 일이 단순하게 들릴지 모르지만, 보기보다 더 복잡하다. 이는 사전을 만드는 것이 공동의 과업이기 때문이다. 그 과정은 정의를 작성하는 정의하는 자로 알려진 사람에서 시작한다. 다음으로, 편집자가 모든 관련된 항목들이 제대로 참조 표시가

되어 있는지 확인한 뒤, 발음 전문가가 단어의 표음식 철자를 확인한다. 그 후, 어떤 사람은 단어의 어원을 찾아내고, 다른 어떤 사람은 모든 것을 시스템에 입력한다. 마지막으로, 교열 담당자와 교정자가 입력된 것에 어떤 오류도 남아있지 않은지 확실하게 하기 위해 검토한다. 사전에는 수십 만 개의 단어가 들어 있기 때문에, 그것들을 모으는 데는 많은 시간과 노력이 필요하다.

어휘
lexicographer 사전 편찬자 **edit** 편집하다 **complicated** 복잡한 **definition** (특히 사전에 나오는 단어나 구의) 정의 **ensure** 반드시 …하게 하다 **related** 관련된 **entry** 들어감; 항목; 입력 **properly** 적절히, 올바로 **reference** 참고[참조] 표시를 하다; 참조 문헌(목록)을 달다 **pronunciation** 발음 **phonetic** 음성[발음]을 나타내는; 표음식의 **trace** 추적하다, 찾아내다 **proofreader** (책의) 교정자 **contain** 담고 있다, 포함하다 [문제] **high-tech** 첨단 기술의 **outdated** 구식인 **collaborative** 공동의, 협력적인

구문해설
(1행) The job of lexicographers, [which is {to write and edit dictionaries}], may sound simple, …: [ ]는 The job of lexicographers를 선행사로 하는 계속적 용법의 주격 관계대명사절, { }는 주격보어로 쓰인 명사적 용법의 to부정사구

(4행) The process starts with a person [known as a definer, {who writes the definition}].: [ ]는 a person을 수식하는 과거분사구, { }는 a definer를 선행사로 하는 계속적 용법의 주격 관계대명사절

(14행) …, **it** requires a great deal of time and effort [to put them together].: it은 가주어이고 [ ]가 진주어

문제해설
빈칸 뒤에서 사전을 만들기 위해 여러 사람들이 각자 맡은 과업을 순서대로 처리하는 과정을 보여주고 있으므로, 사전을 만드는 것이 복잡한 이유는 그것이 ⑤ '공동의 과업' 이기 때문임을 추론할 수 있다.

32 ⑤ 빈칸 추론

이름이 영어의 동사가 된 역사상 몇 안 되는 사람들 중 하나인 토마스 바우들러는 많은 셰익스피어 작품들을 바우들러화(bowdlerize)한 사람으로 알려져 있다. '바우들러화한다'는 것은 작품 중 부적절하다고 여겨지는 부분을 삭제하는 것을 뜻한다. 바우들러는 영국의 의사였으나 여동생인 해리엇과의 공동 작업으로 '가정용 셰익스피어'를 만든 것으로 유명하다. 1807년 이 남매는 여성들과 아이들 앞에서 낭독되기에 부적절하다고 여겨지는 단어들과 표현들을 삭제하여 10권짜리 셰익스피어 편집본을 발행했다. 비록 몇몇 사람들은 그가 셰익스피어의 작품을 오염시켰다고 비판했지만 다른 사람들은 그가 셰익스피어의 독자층을 넓히는 데 기여했다는 것을 인정했다. 그리고 결국 1936년에 바우들러의 작업은 '바우들러화하다'라는 용어를 만들어 냈다.

어휘
verb 동사 **collaboration** 합작 **sibling** 형제자매 **edit** 편집(발행)하다 **delete** 삭제하다 **unsuitable** 부적절한 **contaminate** 오염시키다 **contribution** 기여 **creation** 창조, 창작 [문제] **devote** 바치다, 헌신하다 **determined** 단호한; 굳게 결심한 **translate** 해석하다, 번역하다 **enthusiastic** 열광적인, 열심인 **inappropriate** 부적합한

구문해설
(2행) …, Thomas Bowdler has **become known as** the man [who bowdlerized … works].: 'become known as …' 「…로 알려지다」, [ ]는 the man을 선행사로 하는 주격 관계대명사절

(4행) To bowdlerize means to delete sections of work [considered inappropriate].: [ ]는 sections of work를 수식하는 과거분사구

(9행) … by **deleting** words and expressions [that were considered unsuitable {to be read aloud in front of women and children}].: deleting은 전치사 by의 목적어로 쓰인 동명사, [ ]는 words and expressions를 선행사로 하는 주격 관계대명사절, { }는 형용사 unsuitable을 한정하는 부사적 용법의 to부정사구

문제해설
⑤ Bowdler라는 사람은 셰익스피어의 작품에서 낭독되기에 부적절하다고 여겨지는 부분을 삭제하고 편집했는데, 그의 이름을 따서 이와 같은 일을 하는 것을 의미하는 동사(bowdlerize)가 만들어졌다.

33 ⑤ 빈칸 추론

진심 어린 바람과 단순한 예의를 구별하는 것은 때때로 어렵다. 새로 알게 된 사람이 "만나서 반가웠습니다. 계속 연락하고 지내죠."라고 말할 때, 당신이 그 사람에게 다시 연락한다면 그 사람은 놀라거나 언짢아할까? 사회적 관계에서는 실제 겉으로 보이는 의미를 뜻하지 않는 예의상의 말을 주고 받을 때가 많다. 예를 들어, '안녕하세요?'라는 말이 누군가의 건강에 대한 질문인 경우는 거의 없다. 하지만 이와 같은 많은 사회적 신호는 오해를 불러 일으킬 수 있다. 어떤 사람의 (성이 아닌) 이름을 부르거나 헤어지면서 따뜻한 포옹을 해 주는 것은 진심 어린 표현이라기보다는 그저 사회적인 관습의 표현일 수 있다. 이러한 신호를 오해하는 것은 양측 모두에게 종종 실망이나 당황스러움으로 이어질 수 있다.

어휘
acquaintance (친하지는 않고) 아는 사람 **stay in touch** 계속 연락하고 지내다 **contact** …에게 연락하다; 접촉, 관계 **ritual** 의례적인; 의례, 예의 **exchange** 교환; 회화, 대화 **rarely** 거의 …않다 **signal** 신호, 기호 **misleading** 오해를 일으키는 **hug** 포옹 **expression** 표현 **embarrassment** 당황 [문제] **keep in contact with** …와 연락하고 지내다 **distinguish between A and B** A와 B를 구별하다 **sincere** 참된, 진실의 **mere** 단순한

구문해설
(3행) … **would** that person **be** surprised or annoyed **if you contacted** him or her again?: 'If+S+동사의 과거형, S+조동사 과거형+동사원형' 형태의 가정법 과거 구문(현재의 사실과 반대되는 일을 가정하거나 가능성이 낮은 상상을 나타냄)

(5행) There are a lot of ritual exchanges in social contacts [that don't mean {what they actually appear to mean}].: [ ]는 ritual exchanges in social contacts를 선행사로 하는 주격 관계대명사절, { }는 mean의 목적어로 쓰인 관계대명사절

문제해설
빈칸 이후의 내용에서 사회적 관습상 겉으로 하는 말과 실제 뜻이 다른 경우가 많다고 했으므로 빈칸의 문장은 ⑤ '진심 어린 바람과 단순한 예의를 구별하는 것'은 어렵다는 내용이 적절하다.

34 ② 빈칸 추론

무심코 말을 할 때, 사람들은 종종 '북쪽'을 의미하기 위해 '위'라는 표현을, '남쪽'을 의미하기 위해 '아래'라는 표현을 사용한다. 하지만 지리학적으로 말해 '위'는 지구의 중심으로부터 우주로 향하는 것을, '아래'는 우주로부터 지구의 중심 쪽으로 떨어져 있는 것을 아는 것은 중요하다. 또한 강의 흐름에 관해서도 '위'와 '아래'를 정확히 이해하는 것이 중요하다. 강물은 높은 수원지에서 낮은 강어귀로 흘러 내려가서, 결국 바다로 흘러 들어간다. 문제는 몇몇 사람들이 '위'와 '북쪽'을 부정확하게 동일시해서 모든 강물은 북쪽에서 시작하여 지도상 남쪽으로 흘러 내려간

다고 생각하는 것이다. 예를 들어, 그들은 나일 강이 북쪽에 있는 지중해에서 남쪽에 있는 아프리카로 흘러 들어간다고 생각할지도 모른다. 물론, 그 반대가 맞다.

어휘
casually 우연히, 무심코   geographically 지리학적으로   in reference to …와 관련하여   downhill 내리받이로, 기슭 쪽으로   elevated 높여진, 높은   mouth 입구, 강어귀   equate 동등하다고 생각하다, 동일시하다   originate 시작되다   Mediterranean Sea 지중해

구문해설
2행 However, **it** is important [to know that geographically speaking, ... earth].: it은 가주어이고 [ ]가 진주어
8행 ... lower mouths, [where they eventually enter the sea].: [ ]는 lower mouths를 선행사로 하는 계속적 용법의 관계부사절

문제해설
② 빈칸 앞부분에서 '위·아래' 개념을 강의 흐름에 있어 '북·남'으로 연결시키는 오류를 언급하고 있으며 나일 강은 그 예시에 해당하므로, 앞 문장에서 언급한 방향의 반대가 맞다는 것을 유추할 수 있다.

35 ④ 흐름과 무관한 문장

'mid-century modern'이라는 용어는 1930년대 중반과 1960년대 중반 사이에 서양에서 대중화된 디자인 양식을 말한다. 그것은 주로 건축 양식과 가구와 같은 실내 제품에서 보여졌다. 스칸디나비아의 디자인이 주된 영향을 미쳤고 통일적인 특징들은 단순함과 흐르는 듯한 자연스러운 선들에 대한 강조를 포함했다. mid-century modern 건축 양식은 커다란 창문들과 탁 트인 평면도가 가장 두드러지는 특징인 프랭크 로이드 라이트의 시각의 연속으로 여겨질 수 있다. 이것은 옥외의 세상이 실내에 포함되고 있는 듯한 환상을 만들도록 도왔다. (이후에 라이트는 사무실, 학교, 호텔, 박물관 등을 포함하여 많은 다른 건물 형태들의 혁신적인 본보기들을 디자인하였다.) 가구 디자인은 또한 기능뿐만 아니라 형태의 단순함을 중심으로 했다. 예를 들어, 전형적인 mid-century modern 의자는 단순한 틀과 쿠션만을 특징으로 했다.

어휘
popularize 대중화하다   primarily 주로   architecture 건축 양식   interior 내부(의)   unify 통일하다   emphasis 강조   simplicity 간단, 단순   organic 유기농의; *자연스러운   continuation 계속, 연속   floor plan 평면도   dominate …의 가장 두드러진 특징이 되다   incorporate (법인을) 설립하다; *포함하다

구문해설
1행 The term "mid-century modern" refers to a design style [that was popularized ... the mid-1960s].: [ ]는 a design style을 선행사로 하는 주격 관계대명사절
11행 This **helped create** the illusion [that the outdoor world *was being incorporated* with the indoor].: 'help+(to-)v' 「…하는 것을 돕다」, [ ]는 the illusion과 동격, was being incorporated는 과거진행형 수동태로 「…되고 있었다」의 의미

문제해설
④ 1930년대 중반과 1960년대 중반 사이에 서양의 건축 양식 및 실내 제품에서 유행하던 mid-century modern 디자인의 특징들에 대해 설명하는 글로, 훗날 라이트의 다양한 건축 활동에 관한 내용은 전체적인 흐름에 맞지 않는다.

36 ② 글의 순서

많은 사람들은 일부 빙하가 몇 년 안에 완전히 녹을지도 모른다고 믿

지만, 한 과학 보도에 따르면, 실제로는 상황이 그렇게 나쁘지 않을 수 있다.
(A) 비록 히말라야 산맥을 덮고 있는 빙하들이 녹고 있기는 하지만, 그 속도는 과학자들이 원래 생각했던 것보다 더 느리다. 빙하들이 얼마나 빨리 녹고 있는지를 알아내기 위해, 한 연구팀은 일정 기간 동안 100평방킬로미터보다 더 큰 모든 빙하들의 크기를 비교했다.
(C) 이 과정을 통하여 그들은 히말라야 산맥과 카라코람 산맥에서 (연구원들이) 이전에 예상했던 것보다 훨씬 더 적은 얼음이 유실되고 있다는 것을 발견했다. 놀랍게도, 그 빙하들은 매년 40억 톤을 유실하고 있었는데, 이는 그것들이 유실한 것으로 예측되었던 500억 톤보다 훨씬 양이 적다.
(B) 그 추정치와 실제 수치 간에 차이가 발생한 가능성이 있는 이유는 추정치가 낮은 해발 고도에 있는 몇 백 개의 빙하를 관측한 것만을 바탕으로 했기 때문이라는 것이다. 그런데, 지구 전체의 사진을 찍은 NASA 인공위성들의 새로운 측정은 2035년에도 여전히 히말라야 산맥에 얼음이 있으리라는 것을 보여준다.

어휘
glacier 빙하   melt 녹다   completely 완전히, 전적으로   pace 속도   likely 아마도; *가능성이 있는   projection 예상; *추정(치)   observation 관찰, 관측   altitude (해발) 고도   measurement 측정, 측량   entire 전체의   process 과정   mountain range 산맥

구문해설
15행 However, the new measurements from NASA satellites, [which photographed the entire earth], show [that the Himalayas will still have ice in 2035].: 첫 번째 [ ]는 NASA satellites를 선행사로 하는 계속적 용법의 주격 관계대명사절, 두 번째 [ ]는 show의 목적절
19행 ..., they found [that the Himalayan and Karakoram mountain ranges are losing **much** less ice ... thought].: [ ]는 found의 목적절, much는 「훨씬」이라는 의미로 비교급을 강조하는 부사
22행 Surprisingly, the glaciers are only losing 4 billion tons each year, [which is much less than the 50 billion tons {(which/that) **they** were expected to lose}].: [ ]는 4 billion tons를 선행사로 하는 계속적 용법의 주격 관계대명사절, { }는 the 50 billion tons를 선행사로 하는 목적격 관계대명사절, they는 the glaciers를 지칭

문제해설
② 많은 사람들이 빙하가 몇 년 안에 완전히 녹아버릴 것이라고 믿지만, 이것이 현실과는 다를 수 있다는 주어진 글 뒤에, 실제 빙하가 녹는 속도를 측정하기 위해 과학자들이 빙하의 크기를 측정했다는 내용의 (A)가 온 후, 이 과정을 통해 한 해에 예측보다 훨씬 적은 양의 빙하가 유실된다는 것을 알게 되었다는 (C)가 오고, 마지막으로 추정치와 실제 유실된 빙하의 양이 차이가 났던 이유를 언급하는 (B)가 오는 것이 자연스럽다.

37 ② 글의 순서

최근의 연구에 따르면, 매년 의료용 영상진단은 적어도 400만 명의 65세 미만 미국인들을 높은 수치의 방사선에 노출시킨다.
(A) 이 연구는 계속해서, 이런 노출이 수천 명의 사람들에게 암의 원인이 될 수 있음을 제시한다. 그 연구에 따르면, 의료용 영상진단으로 인한 낮은 수준의 방사선조차도 한 사람이 암에 걸릴 위험을 증가시킨다.
(C) 이 문제의 한 부분은 많은 의사들이 CT나 PET 촬영기를 그들의 진료실에 설치하고, 이윤을 증대시키기 위해 그것들을 빈번히 사용한다는 것이다. 하지만 돈이 의료용 영상진단 검사의 증가에 대한 유일한 원인은 아니다.
(B) 주된 이유는 의료 문화의 변화이다. 환자들을 진찰하기보다는, 의사들은 대신 습관적으로 영상진단을 사용한다. 현명한 환자들은 각각의 의

료용 영상진단 검사가 정말로 필요한 것인지를 의사에게 물어볼 필요가 있다.

medical imaging 의학 화상(畵像) (초음파 단층 장치 등의 기계를 이용하여 체내의 상태를 화상화하는 방법)   expose 드러내다, 노출시키다(exposure 노출)   radiation 방사선   primary 첫째의; *주된   shift 변화   examine 검사하다, 진찰하다   informed 견문이 넓은, 학식 있는   install 설치하다

11행 Informed patients need to ask their doctors [if each medical imaging test is truly necessary].: [ ]는 ask의 직접목적어로 쓰인 명사절, if는 「…인지 아닌지」라는 의미의 명사절을 이끄는 접속사

14행 ... many doctors **have had** CT and PET scanners **installed** in their offices, [using them frequently to increase their profits].: 사역동사 had(have의 과거분사)의 목적어와 목적격보어의 관계가 수동이므로 과거분사 installed가 쓰임, [ ]는 부대상황을 나타내는 분사구문

② (A)의 this exposure는 주어진 글에서 언급된 방사선 노출을 받고 있으므로 주어진 글 다음에는 (A)가 와야 하고, 방사선 노출의 위험성을 제기한 (A) 뒤에는 의사들의 영상진단 기술 남용이 수익성 때문이라고 설명하는 (C)가 온 뒤, 수익성 이외의 또 다른 주요 원인을 설명하는 (B)가 오는 것이 가장 적절하다.

38 ③ 주어진 문장의 위치

1년은 365일로 이루어져 있고 하루는 24시간으로 이루어져 있다는 것은 상식이다. 그러나 실제로 이 수치들은 둘 다 근사치이다. 해와 날의 정확한 길이를 결정하는 요소는 지구가 태양의 궤도를 돌 때의 지구의 움직임, 즉 궤도를 한 번 도는 데 얼마나 오래 걸리는지 그리고 자신의 축을 중심으로 회전하는 데 얼마나 오래 걸리는지와 관련이 있다. 이 결과들 중 어느 것도 충분히 대략 맞는 수치가 아니다. 자연은 그야말로 그것보다 더 복잡하다. 그러나 시간 기록원들은 우리의 시간 체계가 해와 날의 진짜 길이와 계속 비슷한 상태로 있도록 조정하는 독창적인 방법들을 제안했다. 그것이 매번 네 번째 해가 '윤년'인 이유인데, 이 해에는 추가 하루가 더해진다. 유사하게, 시간 수정의 훨씬 더 미세한 수단을 대비할 필요가 있을 때 '윤초'가 더해진다.

round 둥근; *어림수의, 대략의   measurement 치수; 측정, 측량   approximation 근사치   factor 요인   orbit …의 궤도를 돌다; 궤도   rotate on …을 중심으로 회전하다   axis 축   come up with …을 제시[제안]하다   ingenious 독창적인   in line with …와 비슷한   provide for …을 대비하다   fine 미세한   temporal 일시적인; *시간의

4행 It is common knowledge [that a year *is composed of* 365 days and a day *is made up of* 24 hours].: It은 가주어이고 [ ]가 진주어, 'be composed of' 「…로 이루어져 있다(= be made up of)

14행 **That is why** every fourth year is a "leap year," [to which an extra day is added].: 'that is why …' 「그것이 …한 이유이다」, [ ]는 a "leap year"를 선행사로 하는 계속적 용법의 목적격 관계대명사절

16행 Similarly, "leap seconds" are added [when (they are) needed to provide for an **even** finer means of temporal correction].: [ ]는 때를 나타내는 부사절('주어+be동사'가 생략된 형태), even은 「훨씬」이라는 의미로 비교급을 강조하는 부사

주어진 문장의 these results는 ③의 앞 문장에 설명된 해와 날의 길이를 계산하는 방법들을 일컬으므로, 주어진 문장은 ③에 오는 것이 적절하다.

39 ③ 주어진 문장의 위치

많은 사람들에게 음식은 최악의 적이다. 그들은 살찌는 것에 대해 너무 걱정해서 먹는 것에 심하게 제한을 두거나, 마음껏 먹고 나서 즉시 토해 낸다. 그런 사람들을 치료하는 의사들은 그들이 섭식 장애를 가지고 있다고 말한다. 섭식 장애는 비만만큼 흔하지는 않다. 하지만 섭식 장애가 건강에 미치는 좋지 않은 영향도 그만큼 심각할 수 있다. 예를 들어, 충분히 먹지 않는 것은 졸도, 장기 손상, 뼈 약화, 심지어는 심장마비까지 초래할 수 있다. 그리고 반복적으로 토하는 것은 위에 심한 손상을 주고 체내의 화학적 불균형을 가져오며, 치아를 부식시킬 수 있다. 당신이 섭식 장애를 가지고 있을지도 모른다고 생각한다면, 즉시 상담을 받아야 한다.

consequence 결과; *영향   disorder 장애   severe 심한(severely 심하게)   immediately 즉시   throw up 토하다   treat 치료하다   obesity 비만   organ (생물의) 기관; 장기   damage 손상, …에 손상을 입히다   heart attack 심장마비   chemical 화학적인   imbalance 불균형   corrode 부식시키다   counseling 상담

4행 They worry **so** much about getting fat **that** ...: 'so … that ~' 「너무 …해서 ~하다」

주어진 문장의 just as severe를 통해 섭식 장애를 어떤 것과 비교하고 있음을 알 수 있는데, ③ 앞에 비만과 섭식 장애를 비교하는 문장이 나오고 ③ 뒤에 섭식 장애가 건강에 미치는 여러 부정적인 영향들이 나열되어 있으므로, 주어진 문장은 ③에 오는 것이 적절하다.

40 ③ 요약문 완성

확실히 관광산업은 개발도상국들에게는 매력적이라고 말할 수 있다. 그것은 절실하게 필요한 돈을 끌어들이며, 귀중한 일자리를 제공한다. 그러나 그것은 어떤 면에서 위험도 수반한다. 아름답고 고요한 해변이 있는 태국과 같은 나라를 예로 들어 보자. 해안 휴양지를 개발하려는 결정은 근처에 대규모 호텔들을 건설한다는 것을 포함한다. 머지않아, 낭만적이고 인적이 드물던 그 해변들은 시끄러운 관광객들로 가득 찬 거대한 높은 빌딩들에 가려진다. 결과적으로, 더 부유한 관광객들은 더 조용한 장소로 옮겨가고, (그 지역의) 관광업은 대체로 저렴한 음식과 시끄러운 음악을 원하는 덜 부유한 관광객들에게 봉사해야 한다. 따라서 역설적이게도, 관광객들은 그들이 보러 온 바로 그 환경을 해칠 수 있다.

tourism 관광산업   desperately 필사적으로, 몹시   resort 휴양지   deserted 인적이 끊긴, 사람이 살지 않는   overlook 못 보고 지나치다; 내려다보다   skyscraper 초고층 빌딩   provide for …을 원조하다; 부양하다   ironically 역설적으로   spoil 망치다, 못쓰게 만들다   [문제] enormous 거대한   prosperity 번영, 번창   revenue 수익, 수입   costly 많은 비용이 드는   threat 위협   mean (pl.) 수단, 방법   selective 선택적인

14행 So ironically, tourists can spoil **the very** environment [that they've come to discover].: 'the very+명사'에서 the very는 강조어로 「바로 그 …」라는 뜻, [ ]는 the very environment를 선행사로 하는 목적격 관계대명사절('the very+명사'가 선행사일 때 관계대명사는 주로 that을 사용)

③ 관광산업은 개발도상국에게 막대한 이익을 가져다 줄 수 있지만, 또한 심각한 위협이 될 수도 있다.

41 ① 42 ⑤ 장문

과거에는 아이들에게 애정을 주는 것이 실제 발달의 목적에 기여하지 않는다고 생각되었다. 대신 그것은 어떠한 심각한 결과도 없이 무시될 수 있는 감정적인 행위로 여겨졌다. 그런데 1960년대에 해리 할로우라는 미국의 심리학자가 이것이 틀렸음을 입증하는 일련의 실험을 했다. 애정의 부족이 어린 붉은털원숭이에게 미칠 수 있는 강력한 영향을 입증함으로써, 그는 사랑과 보살핌이 아동 발달에 미치는 중요한 역할을 보여주었다.

이 실험 중에서 가장 유명한 것은 아기 원숭이들을 그들의 친어미의 보살핌으로부터 떼어놓은 후에 (아기 원숭이들에게) 두 개의 가짜 어미에 대한 선택권을 주는 것을 포함했다. 첫 번째 것은 부드러운 형겊으로 만들어졌는데, 그것은 아기들에게 어떠한 음식도 제공하지 않았다. 두 번째 가짜 어미는 철사로 만들어졌지만, 우유를 제공하는 젖병이 그것에 달려 있었다. 관찰 결과 아기 원숭이들이 그들의 시간의 대부분을 철사로 만들어진 어미보다는 오히려 형겊 어미들과 함께 보내기로 선택했다는 것을 보여주었다. 할로우는 이것이 애정이 담긴 신체적 접촉이 아기들에게는 음식을 제공받는 것보다 더 중요하다는 것을 의미한다고 결론 내렸다.

할로우의 연구 덕분에 심리학자들은 이제 애정이 건강한 아동기 발달의 필수 요소라는 것을 인지한다. 추가 실험들에서 그는 애정의 충분함(→ 결핍)이 심각한 심리적·감정적 트라우마를 일으킬 수 있다는 것을 계속해서 보여주었다. 이 연구는 고아원과 학교, 그리고 보육 서비스 제공자들이 어린아이들을 다루는 방법에 있어서 중요한 역할을 했다.

어휘
affection 애정(affectionate 다정한, 애정 어린) serve 제공하다; *도움이 되다, 기여하다 sentimental 정서적인, 감정적인 neglect 방치하다 consequence 결과 disprove 틀렸음을 입증하다 deprivation 박탈, 부족 infant 유아, 아기 artificial 인공의, 인조의 baby bottle 젖병 attach 붙이다 observation 관찰, 관측 conclude 결론을 내리다 contact 연락; *닿음, 접촉 recognize 알아보다; *인정하다, 인지하다 component (구성) 요소, 부품 additional 추가의 trauma 정신적 외상, 트라우마 orphanage 고아원 [문제] rearing 양육 beneficial 유익한, 이로운 similarity 유사성

구문해설
(9행) By demonstrating the powerful effect [that a deprivation of affection could have on young rhesus monkeys], he showed the important role [that love and caring have on child development].: 첫 번째 [ ]는 the powerful effect를 선행사로 하는 목적격 관계대명사절, 두 번째 [ ]는 the important role을 선행사로 하는 목적격 관계대명사절

(18행) The second artificial mother was made of wire, but had a baby bottle [attached to it] [which provided milk].: 첫 번째 [ ]는 a baby bottle을 수식하는 과거분사구, 두 번째 [ ]는 a baby bottle을 선행사로 하는 주격 관계대명사절

(30행) ..., he went on to show [that a lack of affection could cause severe psychological and emotional trauma].: 'go on to-v' 「계속해서 …하다」, [ ]는 show의 목적절

(32행) This work has played an important role in [how orphanages, schools, and child care providers deal with young children].: 'play a role in ...' 「…에서 역할을 하다」, [ ]는 in의 목적어로 쓰인 관계부사절(선행사 the way와 관계부사 how는 둘 중 하나를 생략)

문제해설
41 해리 할로우의 실험을 통하여, 먹이를 주는 것보다는 애정이 담긴 신체 접촉을 하는 것이 유아에게 더 중요하다는 것을 관찰했다는 내용의 글이므로, 글의 제목으로는
① '애정이 큰 차이를 만든다'가 가장 적절하다.
42 애정이 아이들의 발달에 큰 영향을 끼친다는 할로우의 실험을 바탕으로 한 추가 실

험에서 애정이 결핍된 것이 심리적·감정적 트라우마를 일으킬 수 있다고 하는 것이 자연스러우므로, ⑤ sufficiency(충분함)는 lack(결핍) 등이 되어야 한다.

43 ⑤ 44 ② 45 ③ 장문

(A) 일반적으로, 박물관 소장품으로 전시되는 유물들은 정부나 연구 기관에 의해 후원을 받은 고고학적 발굴물들에서 비롯된 것이다. 그러나 어떤 경우에는 박물관이 고대의 물건들을 개인 수집가들로부터 선물로 받거나, 심지어 예술품 판매상으로부터 구입하기도 한다. 비록 박물관이 그 사실을 알지 못한다 하더라도, 때로는 이러한 방식으로 얻어진 유물들은 원래 있던 장소에서 밀수되어 가장 높은 가격에 입찰한 사람에게 판매된 도난품이기도 하다.

(D) 이러한 일이 발생하지 않도록 하기 위해, 많은 박물관들은 새로운 유물의 획득을 관리하는 데 엄격한 정책을 가지고 있다. 그러나 모든 큐레이터들이 그러한 정책에 동의하는 것은 아니다. 물론 어떤 큐레이터도 도난당한 물품들을 박물관의 소유물에 추가하고 싶어하지는 않는다. 하지만 때때로 유물의 출처에 대한 증거물은 얻을 수 없는 경우가 있는데, 이는 단순히 유물이 많은 사람들의 손을 거치면서 오랜 시간이 흐르는 동안 (증거물이) 분실되었기 때문이다. 다시 말해, 수백 년 된 문서의 흔적을 찾을 수 없다는 사실이 반드시 그 물건이 불법으로 획득된 것임을 의미하지는 않는다는 것이다.

(C) 만약 박물관의 큐레이터가 그들의 전시품을 문서화된 기원이 있는 물품들로 제한한다면, 그들의 역사 설명은 불완전할 것이다. 예를 들어, 뉴욕의 메트로폴리탄 미술관은 최근에 출처를 알 수 없는 많은 물품들을 오늘날 아프가니스탄 지역인 박트리아의 고대 문화에 관한 전시회에 포함시켰다. 특히 전 세계의 이러한 곳과 같은 지역, 즉 격정의 역사를 지녔으며 현재도 전쟁이 진행 중인 지역에서는 유물의 출처에 대한 증거물을 얻는 것이 항상 가능한 것은 아니다.

(B) 분명히, 인류의 역사를 공유하고 보존하는 그들의 임무를 수행하기 위해서, 메트로폴리탄 미술관의 전시회의 경우에서처럼 박물관은 완전한 시간의 흐름을 보여주도록 어떤 경우에는 출처가 알려지지 않은 유물들을 전시해야만 한다. 게다가, 만일 그들이 그러한 물품들을 기피한다면, 중요한 역사적인 유물들이 개인의 수중에 남겨져서 학자도 일반 대중도 그것들(유물들)이 담고 있는 비밀에 접근할 수 없게 될 위험이 있다.

어휘
artifact 공예품; *유물 archaeological 고고학상의 excavation 발굴 smuggle 밀수하다 bidder (경매에서의) 입찰자 fulfill 이행하다 humanity 인류, 인간 timeline 연대표, 시각표 curator (박물관의) 큐레이터, 전시 책임자 documented 문서[기록]에 의해 입증된(↔ undocumented 증거 자료가 없는) representation 표현, 묘사; *설명 turbulent 사나운; 격한 proof 증명, 증거; *증거물 govern 지배하다; *관리하다 acquisition 취득물; 획득, 습득 relic 유물, 유적 trail 자국, 흔적 [문제] traffic 교통(량); *밀거래

구문해설
(8행) ..., artifacts [acquired in this way] are stolen goods [that have been smuggled out of their place of origin {to be sold to the highest bidder}].: 첫 번째 [ ]는 artifacts를 수식하는 과거분사구, 두 번째 [ ]는 stolen goods를 선행사로 하는 주격 관계대명사절, { }는 결과를 나타내는 부사적 용법의 to부정사구

(13행) ..., museums must in some cases display artifacts with unknown origins so as to present a complete timeline, as was the case in the Metropolitan Museum of Art exhibition.: 'so as to-v' 「…하도록」, was 앞의 as는 앞 절 전체를 선행사로 하는 유사관계대명사

(18행) ... will remain in private hands, [where neither scholars nor the general public has access to the secrets they contain].: [ ]는

---

private hands를 선행사로 하는 계속적 용법의 관계부사절, 'neither A nor B' 「A도 B도 아닌」, 'have access to …' 「…에 접근할 수 있다」

(40행) …, the fact [that a centuries-old paper trail cannot be found] does **not necessarily** mean [(that) an object was acquired illegally].: 첫 번째 [ ]는 the fact와 동격, 'not necessarily' 「반드시[꼭] …는 아닌」(부분부정), 두 번째 [ ]는 mean의 목적절

문제해설

43 ⑤ 박물관이 소유한 유물들 중에는 출처를 알 수 없는 밀수품들이 있다는 내용의 (A) 다음에, 이러한 밀수품이 반입되지 않도록 하려는 박물관의 정책과, 모든 유물이 불법으로 들어온 것은 아니라는 내용의 (D)가 이어진 다음, 출처를 알 수 없는 유물을 전시한 사례를 언급한 (C)가 오며, 마지막으로 그러한 유물들을 전시해야 하는 박물관의 책임에 대한 내용인 (B)가 오는 것이 자연스럽다.

44 비록 출처가 분명하지 않은 유물이라 하더라도, 역사의 전체적인 흐름을 보여주기 위해 그것이 전시되어 대중에게 공개되어야 한다는 내용의 글이므로, ② '증거 자료가 없는 물품들에 대한 박물관의 필요'가 제목으로 가장 적절하다.

45 ③ 출처를 알 수 없는 유물들이 전시되는 경우도 있다고 했다.

---

18 ④	19 ④	20 ④	21 ②	22 ④	23 ③
24 ③	25 ③	26 ④	27 ④	28 ④	29 ⑤
30 ③	31 ②	32 ④	33 ③	34 ④	35 ③
36 ④	37 ④	38 ④	39 ②	40 ①	41 ④
42 ⑤	43 ③	44 ④	45 ③		

18 ④ 글의 목적

친애하는 마샤 룬드 부인께,

어린이 암 자선단체와 제휴해 주셔서 감사드립니다. 지난 5년 동안 보내주신 귀하의 지원에 감사드립니다. 어린이 암 자선단체는 전 세계 어린이들에게 치료를 제공하기 위해 노력하고 있습니다. 목표를 달성하기 위해, 저희는 세계 각 지역의 후원자분들께서 보내주시는 너그러움에 의지하고 있습니다. 귀하의 이타적인 지원이 없다면, 저희는 귀하의 지역 사회에 사는 아이들을 효과적으로 지원할 수 없을 것입니다. 저희는 귀하가 올해 '우리 아이들을 위한 희망' 연례 기금 모금 행사에 참여하시길 바랍니다. 귀하의 지역에 대한 저희의 목표는 10,000달러이며, 언제나처럼 귀하가 기꺼이 기부하고자 하시는 어떤 금액이든 감사드립니다.

귀하의 지원에 미리 감사드립니다.

디에나 엘머,

지사장 드림

어휘

partner 파트너가 되다 cancer 암 charity 자선단체 appreciate 진가를 알아보다; *고마워하다 support 지지, 지원 treatment 치료 meet (필요·요구 등을) 충족시키다 rely on …에 의지[의존]하다 generosity 너그러움 region 지역, 지방 globe 세계 selfless 이타적인, 사심 없는 serve 제공하다; *도움이 되다, 기여하다 effectively 효과적으로 take part in …에 참여하다 fundraiser 기금 모금 행사 contribute 기부하다; 기여하다 regional director 지사장

구문해설

(4행) The Children's Cancer Charity is working [to **provide** treatment **to** children around the world].: [ ]는 목적을 나타내는 부사적 용법의 to부정사구, 'provide A to B' 「A를 B에게 제공하다」

(9행) **Without** your selfless support, we **would not be** able to serve children in your community effectively.: without을 사용한 가정법 과거 구문으로 현재 사실과 반대되는 일을 가정

(14행) …, and as always we appreciate any amount [(which/that) you **are willing to contribute**].: [ ]는 any amount를 선행사로 하는 목적격 관계대명사절, 'be willing to-v' 「기꺼이 …하다」

문제해설

올해의 연례 기금 모금 행사에 참여하길 바란다는 내용이므로, ④가 글의 목적으로 가장 적절하다.

19 ④ 심경

린지는 그날 아침 한 마리의 물고기도 잡지 못했다. 사실 그는 두어 번 이상의 입질도 느끼지 못했다. 그는 배에서 그렇게 비생산적인 아침을 보냈던 것을 기억조차 할 수 없었다. 짜증이 나서, 그는 한 번 더 낚싯줄을 던져 보려고 애썼다. 그는 낚싯대를 뒤로 뻗었다가 거칠게 휘둘렀다. 그러

나 그가 그렇게 했을 때, 낚싯바늘이 그의 티셔츠의 접힌 부분에 걸렸다. 그것은 천을 뚫고 들어갔고 그의 티셔츠를 완전히 벗겨 그것을 물속에 **빠뜨렸다**. 린지는 너무 놀라 낚싯대가 그의 손에서 미끄러졌고 배 밖으로 날아가 버렸다. 그는 그것이 어둡고 컴컴한 물속으로 가라앉을 때 그저 바라보고 있을 수밖에 없었다. 린지는 이제 물고기도 낚싯대도 그리고 티셔츠 또한 없이 항구로 돌아가야 할 것이다.

[어휘]
bite 물기; *입질   unproductive 비생산적인   cast 던지다   fishing pole 낚싯대   swing 휙 움직이다   hook 고리; *낚싯바늘   fold (천 등의) 주름, 접힌 부분   slash 베다   fabric 천   rip off 뜯어내다   clean 완전히   slip (손에서) 미끄러지다, 빠져 나가다   overboard 배 밖으로   murky 어두컴컴한   harbor 항구

[구문해설]
[3행] He couldn't **remember having** *such an unproductive morning* on the boat.: 'remember v-ing' 「…했던 것을 기억하다」, 'such a[an]+형용사+명사 「그렇게 …한 ~」
[8행] ... and ripped his shirt clean off, [hurling it into the water].: [ ]는 부대상황을 나타내는 분사구문
[10행] Lindsay was **so** surprised **that** the pole slipped out of his hands and flew overboard.: 'so ... that ~' 「너무 …해서 ~하다」

[문제해설]
낚시를 하러 갔으나 물고기를 한 마리도 잡지 못했을 뿐만 아니라 낚싯대와 티셔츠도 없이 돌아가야 하는 상황에 처했으므로 심경은 ④ '속상하고 좌절스러운'이 가장 적절하다.

20 ④ 필자의 주장

회사들은 종종 직원들을 다양한 자기 계발 활동에 참여하도록 독려하지만, 보통의 근로자는 그러기 위해 하루에 10분도 시간을 내는 것이 힘들다고 느낀다. 최근의 한 조사는 대부분의 한국인들이 자기 계발이 매우 중요하다고 생각하지만, 단 5퍼센트만이 하루에 10분 이상을 새로운 기술을 배우는 데 할애한다는 것을 보여준다. 이런 상황에 대처하기 위해, 고용주들은 (직원들이) 그렇게 하는 데(자기 계발을 하는 데) 필요한 시간을 가질 수 있도록 직원들을 도와주기 위해 노력할 필요가 있다. 직원들이 자기 계발 수업에 참여할 수 있도록 보장하는 것은 직원들의 사기를 진작시킬 뿐만 아니라, 잠재적으로는 회사의 미래 인력의 기술과 능력을 증대시켜, 회사의 미래를 위한 투자로서도 역할을 한다.

[어휘]
push 밀다; *몰아붙이다, 독려하다   self-improvement 자기 계발   put aside …을 따로 남기다   pursuit 추구; 수행   dedicate 바치다, 전념하다   assure 보장하다   morale 사기, 의욕   workforce 전 종업원, 노동력

[구문해설]
[3행] ..., the average worker finds **it** difficult [to put aside even 10 minutes a day for such pursuits].: it은 가목적어이고 [ ]가 진목적어
[11행] Assuring [that workers ... classes] **not only** raises employee morale, **but** serves as an investment in the company's future **as well**, [potentially increasing the skills and abilities of its future workforce].: 첫 번째 [ ]는 Assuring의 목적절, 'not only A but (also) B' 「A뿐만 아니라 B도」(also 대신 같은 의미의 as well 사용), 두 번째 [ ]는 부대상황을 나타내는 분사구문

[문제해설]
④ 직원들이 자기 계발을 위한 시간을 할애하지 못하고 있는 현실을 지적하며, 회사는 직원들과 회사 모두를 위해서 직원들이 자기 계발에 시간을 투자할 수 있도록 보장해 주어야 한다는 내용의 글이다.

21 ② 함축 의미 추론

한 무리의 연구원들은 우리의 행성이 파괴될 경우에 대비하여 인류가 '달의 방주'를 지어야 한다고 제안했다. 방주는 우주선이 아니고, 대신에 달 표면 아래 깊숙이 지어진 구조물일 것이다. 연구원들은 그것이 우리 행성에 있는 모든 살아있는 종에서 얻은 냉동 유전자 물질로 가득 차야 된다고 생각한다. 그들은 지구가 현재 핵무기, 소행성, 감염병 대유행, 그리고 기후 관련 위험을 포함한 다수의 원인으로부터의 심각한 위협에 직면하고 있는 것이 두려워서 이러한 제안을 했다. 세계의 생물 다양성을 손상될 수 없는 곳에서 보호함으로써, 우리는 끔찍한 재난으로부터 우리 자신을 안전하게 지킬 것이다. 만약 지구가 파괴된다면, 생존한 사람들은 어쩌면 미래에 우리 행성을 재시동하기 위해 그 방주의 내용물을 이용할 방법을 찾을 수 있을 것이다.

[어휘]
propose 제안하다   lunar 달의   ark 노아의 방주   spacecraft 우주선   beneath … 아래에   be filled with …로 가득 차다   genetic 유전자의, 유전학적인   material 물질   currently 현재, 지금   threat 위협   source 근본, 원인   nuclear weapon 핵무기   pandemic 감염병 대유형   biodiversity 생물 다양성   insure (위험 등에서) 지키다, 안전하게 하다   disaster 재난, 재해   potentially 잠재적으로; 어쩌면   content 내용물   reboot 재시동하다

[구문해설]
[11행] **By protecting** the world's biodiversity in a place [where it cannot be harmed], we would be insuring ourselves against a terrible disaster.: 'by v-ing' 「…함으로써」, [ ]는 a place를 선행사로 하는 관계부사절
[14행] **If** the earth **were to be** destroyed, the surviving humans could potentially find a way [to use the contents of the ark] [to reboot our planet in the future].: 'If+S+were to-v'의 형태로 실현 가능성이 전혀 없는 미래의 일을 가정. 첫 번째 [ ]는 a way를 수식하는 형용사적 용법의 to부정사구, 두 번째 [ ]는 목적을 나타내는 부사적 용법의 to부정사구

[문제해설]
지구가 파괴될 것을 대비하여 지구상의 모든 종의 냉동 유전자를 '방주'에 넣어 저장해 놓으면, 재난으로부터 생존한 사람들이 지구를 다시 살리기 위해 방주 안의 내용물을 사용할 수 있을 것이라는 내용이다. 따라서 밑줄 친 '우리 행성을 재시동하다'의 의미로 가장 적절한 것은 ② '지구의 종을 되살리다'이다.

22 ④ 글의 요지

우리는 재난으로 인해 긍정적으로 변화된 사람들의 이야기를 듣는 것을 매우 좋아한다. 그 사람이 비행기 추락에서든 허리케인에서든 또는 암에서 살아남았든지 간에 그들의 이야기는 '인간은 가장 어려운 상황에서조차도 번성할 수 있다'는 입증된 심리학적 진실을 증명하는 것으로 보인다. 위기 상황의 인생을 바꾸는 효과는 현재 재난과 관련된 심리학의 영역이다. 그 분야의 연구는 고난과 싸웠던 사람들 중 대략 절반 정도가 자신의 삶이 몇 가지 점에서 더 나아졌다고 말한다는 것을 밝혀냈다. 재난과 관련된 스트레스가 그 사고 직후에는 보편적이지만, 오직 적은 비율의 성인들만이 장기간에 걸쳐 어려움을 겪는 것으로 보인다. 결국 대부분의 사람들은 그들의 삶이 향상되었다고 전한다.

[어휘]
positively 명확하게; *긍정적으로   transform 변형시키다   disaster 재난   plane crash 비행기 추락   testify to …을 입증하다   flourish 번창하다   circumstance 환경   crisis 위기(pl. crises)   province 지방; *영역   adversity 역경, 고난   proportion 비율   chronically 장기간에 걸쳐, 만성적으로   enhance 향상시키다

[2행] **Whether** the person has survived a plane crash, a hurricane, **or** cancer ...: 'whether ... or ~'는 「…이든 ~이든」의 의미로 양보의 부사절을 이끄는 접속사

[8행] Research in the field has found [that roughly half the people {who have struggled with adversity} say that their lives ... way].: [ ]는 has found의 목적절, { }는 the people을 선행사로 하는 주격 관계대명사절

문제해설

④ 재난이 오히려 사람들이 발전하는 계기가 될 수 있다는 내용의 글이다.

23 ③ 글의 주제

경제학자들은 종종 자유 무역의 혜택을 옹호하지만, 안타깝게도 이 체제는 그 내부의 노동자들의 복지를 보장하는 데는 거의 도움이 되지 않는다. 이것은 특히 빈곤 국가에서 사실인데, 그곳에서 국제 기업들은 더 높은 이익을 내기 위해 부당하게 낮은 임금을 이용한다. 공정 거래의 개념은 이것에 대한 반향으로서 발달되었다. 공정 거래는 개발 도상국의 공급자와 선진국의 소매업자 사이의 동업자 관계를 통해 실현된다. 소매업자들은 고용인들에게 건강한 근무 환경도 보장하는 동시에 고품질의 제품을 생산하겠다는 공급자들의 약속에 대한 대가로 상품에 대한 공정하고 일관된 가격을 지불할 것에 동의한다. 이런 방식으로, 공정 거래 동업자 관계는 소규모 기업들에게 그들이 국제 시장에서 대기업들과 경쟁할 수 있기 위해 필요로 하는 안정감을 준다.

어휘

economist 경제학자   advocate 옹호하다   guarantee 보장하다; 보장, 약속   welfare 복지   take advantage of …을 이용하다   reaction 반응, 반작용   partnership 동업자 관계   supplier 공급자   retailer 소매업자   in return for …에 대한 대가로   generate 만들어 내다   ensure 보장하다   operation 수술; *기업   security 안심, 마음 든든함   compete 경쟁하다   marketplace 시장

구문해설

[4행] This is especially true in poor countries, [where international corporations take advantage of ... higher profits].: [ ]는 poor countries를 선행사로 하는 계속적 용법의 관계부사절

[11행] ... in return for suppliers' guarantees [that they will generate high-quality products, {while also ensuring healthy working conditions for their employees}].: [ ]는 suppliers' guarantees와 동격, { }는 부대상황을 나타내는 분사구문(의미를 정확히 전달하기 위해 접속사 while을 생략하지 않음)

[15행] ... the sense of security [(that/which) they need {to be able to compete with large corporations in the global marketplace}].: [ ]는 the sense of security를 선행사로 하는 목적격 관계대명사절, { }는 목적을 나타내는 부사적 용법의 to부정사구

문제해설

자유 무역의 부정적인 효과에 대한 반향으로 공정 거래가 발달하게 된 과정과 그것이 어떻게 실현되고 있는지를 구체적으로 서술하고 있으므로 글의 주제는 ③ '공정 거래는 무엇이며 어떻게 발달했나'이다.

24 ③ 글의 제목

롤러코스터는 얼핏 보면 여객 열차와 꽤 유사해 보인다. 그것은 선로를 따라 이동하는 일련의 연결된 차량들로 구성된다. 그러나 여객 열차와 달리, 롤러코스터에는 엔진이나 자체 동력원이 없다. 출발하기 위해 롤러코스터는 첫 번째 고개로 끌어 올려진다. 이렇게 처음에 위로 올려지면 위치 에너지를 비축하게 된다. 더 높이 올라갈수록 중력이 그것을 끌어 내릴 수 있는 거리는 더 길어진다. 당신이 자전거를 타고 높은 언덕 꼭대기에 올라갈 때 이와 같은 현상을 경험하게 된다. 언덕을 올라가면서 쌓는 위치 에너지는 당신이 언덕을 내려가도록 하는 운동의 동적 에너지로 방출된다.

어휘

at first glance 얼핏 보면   consist of …로 구성되다   a series of 일련의   track 선로, 궤도   power source 동력원   initial 처음의, 시작의   build up 축적하다, 쌓다   reserve 비축   gravity 중력   phenomenon 현상(*pl.* phenomena)   release 방출하다   motion 운동

구문해설

[7행] ...; **the higher up** it goes, **the greater** the distance gravity can pull it down.: 'the+비교급, the+비교급' 「…하면 할수록 더 ~하다」

[10행] The potential energy [(which/that) you build {going up the hill}] is released as the dynamic energy of motion [that takes you down the hill].: 첫 번째 [ ]는 The potential energy를 선행사로 하는 목적격 관계대명사절, { }는 부대상황을 나타내는 분사구문, 두 번째 [ ]는 the dynamic energy of motion을 선행사로 하는 주격 관계대명사절

문제해설

③ 엔진이나 자체 동력원이 없는 롤러코스터가 에너지를 발생시키는 원리에 관한 내용이다.

25 ③ 도표 내용 불일치

위 도표에서, 네 개의 서로 다른 연령대가 스코틀랜드의 전체 인구 비율로 나타나 있다. 17세 이하의 사람들의 비율은 2000년에서 2015년 사이에 약간 감소했다. 또한 같은 시기 동안 26세에서 50세 사이의 연령대에서 감소가 나타났다. (하지만 가장 큰 변화는 50세 이상의 사람들에게서 일어났는데, 15년 동안 5퍼센트포인트 이상 감소했다.) 인구의 가장 변동이 없는 부문은 18세에서 25세 사이의 사람들로, 그들은 2000년과 2010년 사이에서 아주 적은 증가를 보였다. 그러나, 2010년에 최고점에 도달한 후에, 2015년에는 이 연령대의 비율이 약간 감소했다.

어휘

population 인구   proportion 비율   overall 전체의   stable 안정적인; *변동이 없는   segment 부분, 구분

구문해설

[8행] The most stable segment of the population was people between the ages of 18 and 25, [which experienced only a very small rise ... 2010].: [ ]는 people between the ages of 18 and 25를 선행사로 하는 계속적 용법의 주격 관계대명사절

문제해설

③ 50세 이상의 인구 비율은 15년간 5퍼센트포인트 이상 감소한 것이 아니라 증가했다.

26 ④ 내용 불일치

적황색에 검은색 잎맥 같은 무늬가 있는 제왕나비는 몇 세대가 지난 후에도 서식지로 돌아올 수 있는 능력으로 유명하다. 매년 봄, 제왕나비의 한 세대가 태어나서 그들의 겨울 서식지였던 멕시코에서 캐나다로, 북쪽으로의 여정을 시작한다. 이 나비들은 겨우 5주 만을 사는데 여행을 끝마치지 못한다. 사실, 이 곤충의 여름 서식지인 캐나다에 이르는 데는 3세대가 걸린다. 그리고는 가을에 제왕나비의 특별한 세대가 태어난다. 그들은 8주 동안을 살아남을 수 있는데, 이것은 멕시코로 다시 돌아갈 수 있을 만큼 충분히 길다. 과학자들은 이 나비들이 태양의 위치에 반응함으로써 이 위대한 세대 간의 이주를 완수할 수 있다고 생각한다.

어휘
vein 정맥; *잎맥   marking 무늬   northward 북쪽으로   inter-generational 세대 간의   migration 이주, 이동   react to …에 반응하다

구문해설
6행 These butterflies, [which live for only five weeks], do not complete the trip.: [ ]는 These butterflies를 선행사로 하는 계속적 용법의 주격 관계대명사절
12행 Scientists believe [(that) the butterflies are able to … by {reacting to the position of the sun}].: [ ]는 believe의 목적절, { }는 by의 목적어로 쓰인 동명사구

문제해설
④ 가을에 태어나는 세대는 8주 동안 생존할 수 있고, 그 기간 동안 멕시코로 충분히 다시 돌아갈 수 있다고 했다.

27 ④ 내용 일치

아메리카는 사상 최고의 사기꾼들 중 하나인 아메리고 베스푸치의 이름을 따서 명명되었다. 실제로 일어나지도 않은 일이었음에도, 그는 1497년에 그가 이끌었다는 항해에 관한 이야기를 출판했다. 베스푸치의 글을 읽은 후, 포르투갈의 왕은 그에게 포르투갈의 탐험가 코엘료가 이끄는 두 차례의 항해에 함께 가서 그 항해에 대해 기록해 줄 것을 요청했다. 베스푸치는 그의 글에서, 자신이 두 차례의 항해를 이끌었다고 적었으며 코엘료에 대해서는 언급조차 하지 않았다. 1507년에 프랑스의 한 젊은 지리학 교수가 신세계를 아메리고의 변형인 '아메리카'라고 명명했다. 사람들이 콜럼버스가 신세계를 발견한 사람이라고 의견을 모았을 때에는 너무 늦어버렸다. 신세계는 이미 아메리카라 이름 붙여져 있었던 것이다.

어휘
fraud 사기; *사기꾼   publish 출판하다   account 설명, 이야기   voyage 항해   take place 일어나다   explorer 탐험가   mention 언급하다   geography 지리학   variation 변화; *변형물

구문해설
2행 He published an account of a voyage [(which/that) he **had led** in 1497], …: [ ]는 a voyage를 선행사로 하는 목적격 관계대명사절, 항해를 이끌었던 시점이 항해기를 출간한 시점(published)보다 앞서므로 대과거가 쓰임
5행 …, the King of Portugal **asked** him **to go** on two voyages [led by the Portuguese explorer Coelho] and (**to**) **write** about the voyages.: asked의 목적격보어 역할을 하는 to go와 (to) write가 and로 병렬 연결, [ ]는 two voyages를 수식하는 과거분사구
9행 …, a young French professor of geography **named the New World "America,"** [a variation of Amerigo].: 'name A B' 「A를 B라고 이름짓다」, [ ]는 America와 동격

문제해설
① 베스푸치는 1497년에 실제로 항해를 하지 않았다. ② 포르투갈 왕은 베스푸치에게 항해에 대한 기록을 할 것을 부탁했다. ③ 베스푸치가 코엘료가 이끄는 항해에 참여한 것이다. ⑤ 사람들은 콜럼버스가 아메리카를 발견했다는 것에 동의한다고 했다.

28 ④ 내용 불일치

코나 어린이 도서 축제
일시: 7월 23일 토요일, 오전 11시에서 오후 7시
장소: 성 세바스찬 교회의 주차장

코나 예술 위원회는 연례 코나 아동 도서 축제를 선보이게 되어 자랑스럽게 생각합니다. 이 행사는 하루 동안 진행되며 전국 도서상 수상자인 에리카 강을 비롯한 많은 지역 및 국내 저자들이 참여합니다. 또한 모든 연령의 어린이들을 위한 도서 판매 및 재미있는 활동이 있을 것입니다.

티켓:
• 티켓은 사전 예매 시 5달러, 현장 구매 시 10달러입니다.
• 티켓은 신간 및 중고 서적(구매)을 위한 5달러 쿠폰을 포함합니다.
• 5세 미만의 어린이는 무료로 입장합니다.
참고: 무료 티켓을 가진 분들은 쿠폰을 사용하실 수 없습니다.

어휘
council 위원회   annual 연례의   last (특정한 시간 동안) 계속되다   feature 특별히 포함하다, 특징으로 삼다   in advance 사전에, 미리   available 이용할 수 있는, 얻을 수 있는

구문해설
4행 The Kona Arts Council is proud [to present the annual Kona Children's Book Festival].: [ ]는 감정의 원인을 나타내는 부사적 용법의 to부정사구
5행 The event **lasts** for one day and **features** many local and national authors, including National Book Prize winner Erica Kang.: 동사 lasts와 features가 등위 접속사 and로 병렬 연결

문제해설
④ 신간 및 중고 서적 구매 시 5달러 쿠폰을 사용할 수 있다고 나와 있다.

29 ⑤ 어법

당신의 코어 근육은 당신의 상체와 하체를 연결하는 사슬의 중앙에 있는 강력한 연결 고리와 같다. 당신이 공을 차든 설거지를 하든, 요구되는 움직임은 당신의 코어에서 시작되거나 그것을 거쳐간다. 움직임이 어디에서 시작되건, 그것은 그 비유적인 사슬의 부착된 연결 고리를 통해 파동을 보낸다. 이는 당신의 코어 근육의 힘과 유연성이 팔과 다리가 얼마나 잘 움직이는가에 영향을 미친다는 것을 의미한다. 당신의 코어가 강할수록, 당신은 더 나은 균형과 안정성을 갖출 것이며, 이는 당신이 하는 거의 모든 것에 영향을 미친다. 떨어진 연필을 줍는 것, 옷을 입는 것, 또는 전화를 받는 것조차도 코어 근육에 의지하여 당신이 매일 하는 많은 일상적인 행동 중 일부일 뿐이다.

어휘
core 중심부, 핵심   link (쇠사슬의) 고리; 연결하는 것   chain 사슬; 띠   pass through …을 거쳐가다, 지나가다   attached 부착된, 붙어 있는   metaphorical 은유(비유)적인   flexibility 유연성   stability 안정, 안정감   typical 전형적인; *일상적인

구문해설
5행 **No matter where** the movement begins, it sends waves through the attached links of that metaphorical chain.: 'no matter where+S+V' 「어디서 …가 ~하더라도」
10행 **The stronger** your core is, **the more** balance and stability you will have, [which affects almost everything you do].: 'the+비교급, the+비교급' 「…하면 할수록 더 ~하다」, [ ]는 앞 내용 전체를 선행사로 하는 계속적 용법의 주격 관계대명사절
12행 **Picking up** a dropped pencil, **getting** dressed, or even **answering** your phone are just a few of the many typical actions [you do each day] …: Picking up, getting, answering이 등위 접속사 or로 병렬 연결, [ ]는 the many typical actions를 선행사로 하는 목적격 관계대명사절

문제해설
⑤ 선행사인 the many typical actions를 수식하는 주격 관계대명사가 필요하므로 what을 which나 that으로 고쳐야 한다. what은 선행사를 포함한 관계대명사이다.

30 ③ 어휘

사람들의 손과 손가락은 그들의 신원을 확인하는 데 종종 사용된다. 특히 높은 수준의 보안을 필요로 하지 않는 사업체에서는 사용자들의 신원을 파악하기 위해 손 모양 인식 장치를 사용한다. 예를 들어 디즈니 테마 공원은 입장권 소유자가 공원의 여러 곳으로 들어가도록 허용하는 데 손 모양 인식 장치를 이용한다. 몇몇 사업체들은 출퇴근 기록 카드 대신 손 모양 인식 장치를 이용한다. 손 모양 인식 장치를 이용하려면, 정확한 판독을 방해하기(→ 보장하기) 위해 몇 개의 표시 지점에 손가락을 위치시키면서 인식 장치에 손을 올려놓으면 된다. 인식 장치에 설치된 디지털 카메라가 손의 사진을 찍고 나면, 인식 장치는 이 정보를 손이나 손가락의 길이, 너비, 두께, 모양 등을 탐지하는 데 사용한다. 그리고 나서 그 인식 장치는 당신의 신원을 확인하기 위해 그 정보를 숫자 형태로 바꾼다.

어휘
verify 증명하다; *확인하다 identity 신원(identify …임을 확인하다) hand geometry reader 손 모양 인식 장치 timecard 타임카드(종업원들의 출퇴근 시간을 기록하는 카드) mark 표시, 흔적, 자국 accurate 정확한 install 설치하다 detect …을 탐지하다 thickness 두께 translate 번역하다; *바꾸다, 변형하다 numerical 수의, 수에 관한

구문해설
[2행] ..., businesses [that don't require high security] use hand geometry readers [to identify users].: 첫 번째 [ ]는 businesses를 선행사로 하는 주격 관계대명사절, 두 번째 [ ]는 목적을 나타내는 부사적 용법의 to부정사구
[8행] ..., you place your hand on the reader, [putting your fingers against several marks {to ensure an accurate reading}].: [ ]는 동시동작을 나타내는 분사구문, { }는 목적을 나타내는 부사적 용법의 to부정사구
[11행] After the digital camera [installed in the reader] takes pictures ...: [ ]는 the digital camera를 수식하는 과거분사구

문제해설
손 모양 인식 장치의 표시 지점에 손을 올려놓는 것은 정확한 판독을 '보장하기' 위한 것이므로 ③ hinder(방해하다)는 ensure(보장하다) 등이 되어야 한다.

31 ② 빈칸 추론

진정한 행복이란 무엇일까? 시카고 대학의 한 심리학자에 따르면, 행복은 '몰입'의 상태에서 살아갈 때 성취된다고 한다. 몰입 상태란 일할 때든 놀 때든 그 사람이 어떤 행위에 완전히 열중한 상태이다. 그는 화가들을 연구하면서 몰입이라는 개념을 생각해 냈다. 그는 화가들이 종종 자신의 작업에 너무나도 몰두하여 주변 상황을 의식하지 못하는 정도, 즉 심지어 완성된 그림을 보는 것보다 더 만족스러운 기분에 이른다는 점에 주목했다. 심층적인 연구를 통해 그는 몰입은 당신의 역량의 전부 혹은 대부분을 사용하는 것을 필요로 한다고 결론지었다. "너무 적은 역량을 발휘하면 권태와 불안이 생겨나고, 그것은 행복에 가장 큰 위험이 될지도 모릅니다."라고 그는 말했다.

어휘
state 상태 flow 흐름; *몰입 involved 열중한 unaware 눈치 못 채는, 모르는 further 그 이상의 conclude 결론짓다 skill 능력, 역량 generate 가져오다, 발생시키다 boredom 권태, 지루함 anxiety 불안 threat 위협 [문제] absorbed 열중한, 몰두한 detached 사심 없는; 독립된

구문해설
[4행] A flow state is one [in which the person is totally absorbed in an activity, whether at work or play].: one은 a state를 가리키는 대명사, [ ]는 one을 선행사로 하는 목적격 관계대명사절

[13행] ..., "generates boredom and anxiety, [which may be the biggest threats to happiness].": [ ]는 boredom and anxiety를 선행사로 하는 계속적 용법의 주격 관계대명사절

문제해설
예시로 든 화가의 경우에서 a flow state란 주변 상황을 의식하지 못할 정도로 완전히 '몰두한' 상태라는 것을 알 수 있으므로 ②가 적절하다.

32 ④ 빈칸 추론

현대 경제가 점점 더 자본 집약적 산업으로 이동하고 있다. 그러나, 지역 문화와 정체성뿐만 아니라 약화된 지방의 농업 역시 보호되어야 한다. 이러한 경제 이동이 일어날 때조차도, 사회는 지방의 농업 생산을 통해서만 얻을 수 있는 기본적 수요를 계속 가지고 있을 것이다. 우리는 소규모 농업 프로그램, 그리고 그것을 지탱하는 사람과 환경에 재정적인 지원을 해야 한다. 동시에, 소규모 생산 및 처리 과업에 대한 의료 및 가축 복지 혜택 역시 개발되어야 한다. 이것은 오직 이익과 저비용의 국외 노동력을 고용하는 것에만 근거하는 대규모 집약 농업과 다양화 방안보다 훨씬 더 나은 접근법이다.

어휘
capital-intensive 자본 집약적인 shift 이동 welfare 복지 diversification 다양화 scheme 계획, 방안 solely 단지, 오로지 [문제] redefine 재정립하다 suppress 진압하다, 억제하다

구문해설
[2행] However, the weakend rural agricultural industry, **as well as** local culture and sense of identity, ...: 'A as well as B' 「B뿐만 아니라 A도」
[8행] We need to provide financial support to smaller agricultural programs and the people and environments [that support **them**].: [ ]는 the people and environments를 선행사로 하는 주격 관계대명사절, them은 smaller agricultural programs를 지칭

문제해설
④ 빈칸 이후의 내용에서 농업 프로그램이나 다양한 의료 및 가축 복지 혜택을 개발해야 한다고 했으므로 빈칸에는 지방의 농업이 '보호되어야' 한다는 내용이 적절하다.

33 ③ 빈칸 추론

채식주의자들은 그들의 음식 섭취의 제한에 따라 분류될 수 있다. 엄격한 채식주의자들, 혹은 완전 채식주의자들은 유제품과 달걀을 포함한 모든 동물성 음식을 피한다. 이러한 범주 안에 속하는 소수의 사람들은 그들의 신체에 필요한 모든 필수 영양소를 확실히 섭취하기 위해 열심히 노력해야 한다. 락토 채식주의자는 훨씬 더 흔한 경우로, 그들은 유제품은 먹지만 육류는 먹지 않는다. 그들의 식단에는 지방과 콜레스테롤이 적을 수 있으나, 그것은 탈지 우유나 다른 저지방 혹은 무지방 제품을 섭취하는 경우에만이다. 오보 채식주의자들은 그들의 식단에 달걀만 추가하는 반면에, 락토 오보 채식주의자들은 유제품과 달걀을 둘 다 먹는다. 페스코 채식주의자들은 생선과 유제품, 그리고 달걀을 먹는 반면, 세미 채식주의자들은 닭고기, 생선, 유제품과 달걀을 먹는다.

어휘
vegetarian 채식주의자 classify 분류하다 vegan 완전 채식주의자 dairy 우유의, 유제품의 fall into …에 빠지다; *…으로 분류되다 ensure …을 확실하게 하다 nutrient 영양분, 영양소 skim milk 탈지 우유 nonfat 무지방의 [문제] intake 섭취 dietary 음식물의 restriction 제한, 한정 preference 선호(도)

[4행] The few people [who fall into this category] must work ...: [ ]는 The few people을 선행사로 하는 주격 관계대명사절
[7행] Far more common **are lacto-vegetarians**, [who eat dairy products but avoid meat].: 보어인 Far more common이 문두로 나오면서 주어 lacto-vegetarians와 동사 are가 도치, [ ]는 lacto-vegetarians를 선행사로 하는 계속적 용법의 주격 관계대명사절

문제해설
어떤 음식을 먹고 어떤 음식을 먹지 않느냐, 즉 음식 섭취 제한에 따라 채식주의자도 여러 유형으로 나뉜다는 내용이므로, 빈칸에는 ③ '그들의 음식 섭취의 제한'이 들어가는 것이 가장 적절하다.

34 ④ 빈칸 추론

고대 로마의 전성기에, 로마 제국의 엄청난 부유함에도 불구하고 로마 시민들의 절반은 실직 상태였다. 노예들이 너무 많은 일을 하고 있었기 때문에, 상대적으로 일자리가 거의 없었다. 실제로 '빵' 계급이라고 알려진, 순전히 국가에서 배급하는 식량에만 의존해서 살았던 하층 계급의 사람들이 있었다. 국가는 또한 서커스라고 알려진 무료 검투사 시합을 제공했다. 이러한 구경거리들은 빵 계급이 자신들의 가난한 경제 상황으로부터 주의를 다른 데로 돌리게 하려는 의도였다. 로마의 작가 유베날리스가 진술했듯이, 실직 상태에 있는 군중의 반란을 막는 유일한 것은 '빵과 서커스'뿐이었다. 이제 '빵과 서커스'는 대중의 불안에 대한 단기적인 해결책을 추구하는 정부 정책을 일컫는 편리한 일반 용어가 되었다.

어휘
height 높이; *절정, 한창때   empire 제국   unemployed 실직한, 직업이 없는   relatively 상대적으로   underclass 하층 계급   live on …을 먹고 살다   purely 완전히, 순전히   handout (정부의) 보조금   gladiator 검투사   distract 주의를 딴 데로 돌리다   observe 진술하다, …이라고 말하다   revolt 반란을 일으키다   term 용어   [문제] reform 개혁   lack …이 없다[부족하다]   substance 내용, 알맹이   public 대중의   unrest (사회적인) 불안

구문해설
[11행] ..., the only thing [**keeping** the unemployed masses **from revolting**] was ...: [ ]는 the only thing을 수식하는 현재분사구. 'keep+O+from v-ing' 「…가 ~하지 못하게 하다」

문제해설
④ '빵과 서커스'라는 용어는 고대 로마 제국이 빈곤층의 관심을 어려운 경제 상황으로부터 다른 데로 돌리고 그들의 반란을 막기 위해 식량과 서커스를 제공했던 것에서 비롯되었으므로 '대중의 불안에 대한 단기적인 해결책을 추구하는' 정부 정책을 일컫는다는 것을 알 수 있다.

35 ③ 빈칸 추론

교양 과목 교육의 개념은 고대 그리스와 로마까지 거슬러 올라간다. 'Liberal'은 라틴어 *liberalis*에서 왔는데, '자유민에게 적합한'이라는 뜻이다. 이 고대 문명에서는 모든 시민에게 교육이 필요하다고 여겨졌다. 그러나 그들은 직업적이고 기술적인 학문을 노예와 시민으로 여겨지지 않았던 사회의 가장 낮은 계층의 사람들에게 더 적합한 것으로 여겼다. 교양 과목 교육만이 시민에게 적합했는데, 이것은 그들에게 시민 의무의 원칙과 인간으로서 잠재력을 최대한 발휘하는 방법을 가르쳤기 때문이다. 그것은 문법, 수사학, 그리고 논리학의 연구를 강조했는데, 이것들이 훌륭한 시민이 되는 데 가장 필수적이었기 때문이다. 이후 중세 시대에 이 과목들은 산수, 기하학, 음악, 그리고 천문학을 포함하는 것으로 확장되었는데, 이것들은 모두 훗날 철학과 신학 연구에 필수적으로 여겨졌다.

오늘날, 교양 과목 교육의 주된 목적은 여전히 많은 과목에 대한 일반적인 지식을 지닌 전인격을 갖춘 학생을 만드는 것이다.

어휘
liberal arts 교양 과목   date back to …까지 거슬러 올라가다   appropriate 적절한   civilization 문명   require 요구하다, 필요로 하다   vocational 직업과 관련된   slave 노예   class 학급; *(사회의) 계층   principle 원칙, 원리   duty 의무   reach one's full potential …의 잠재력을 최대한 발휘하다   emphasize 강조하다   rhetoric 수사학   logic 논리; 논리학   medieval 중세의   expand 확대하다, 확장하다   geometry 기하학   astronomy 천문학   philosophy 철학   well-rounded 균형이 잡힌, 전인격을 갖춘   [문제] scholar 학자

구문해설
[5행] However, they **viewed** vocational and technical studies **as** *being* more appropriate for slaves and people from the lowest classes of society [who were not considered citizens].: 'view A as B' 「A를 B로 보다[여기다]」, being은 전치사 as의 목적어로 쓰인 동명사, [ ]는 people from the lowest classes of society를 선행사로 하는 주격 관계대명사절
[14행] Later, during medieval times, these subjects were expanded to include arithmetic, geometry, music, and astronomy, [all of which **were seen as** necessary for the later study of philosophy and theology].: [ ]는 arithmetic, ..., and astronomy를 선행사로 하는 계속적 용법의 목적격 관계대명사절, 'see A as B' 「A를 B로 간주하다」의 수동태 구문

문제해설
③ 고대 그리스 로마 시대부터 교양 과목 교육을 통해 시민 의무의 원칙과 인간으로서 잠재력을 최대한 발휘하는 방법을 가르쳤다는 내용이므로 문법, 수사학, 논리학을 강조한 것은 이러한 과목들이 '훌륭한 시민이 되는 데 가장 필수적'이기 때문이라고 하는 것이 가장 적절하다.

36 ④ 흐름과 무관한 문장

모든 규모의 인구에서, 폭력적이고 공격적인 행동은 외부 기온과 관련하여 증가한다. 환경 심리학자 크레이그 앤더슨이 2001년에 이 이론을 제안했고 그때 이후로 그는 여러 도시에서 일어난 폭력 범죄의 비율을 비교함으로써 증거를 모을 수 있었다. 그는 기온이 한 인구가 또 다른 인구보다 더 폭력적인 행동을 보일지 아닐지에 대한 가장 믿을 만한 지표임을 발견했다. 그의 연구에 따르면, 높은 기온은 개인의 불편한 감정, 적개심, 그리고 타인을 향한 공격성을 증가시키고 이것은 결국 더 많은 폭력을 일으킨다. 앤더슨의 연구는 전문가들 사이에서 지구 온난화가 이러한 가장 기본적인 수준에서 사회에 어떻게 영향을 미칠 수 있는지에 대한 우려를 고조시켰다. (지구 온난화를 일으키는 요인들 중 하나는 이산화탄소 생성의 증가이다.) 식량과 물 부족, 해안 지역 홍수, 그리고 격렬한 폭풍의 활성화 외에도, 더 더워진 행성 또한 폭력 범죄의 더 높은 평균 발생률을 의미할지도 모른다.

어휘
aggressive 공격적인(aggression 공격성)   correlation 연관성, 상관관계   reliable 믿을 만한   indicator 지표   discomfort 불편   hostility 적개심   in turn 차례차례; *결국   contribute 기부하다; *…의 한 원인이 되다   coastal 해안의   intense 극심한, 강렬한   incidence 발생 정도, 발생률

구문해설
[7행] ... temperature is the most reliable indicator of [whether one population will exhibit more violent behavior than another].: [ ]는 of의 목적절
[10행] ..., high temperatures increase individuals' feelings of

discomfort, hostility, and aggression towards others, [which in turn leads to more violence].: [ ]는 앞 절 전체를 선행사로 하는 계속적 용법의 주격 관계대명사절

문제해설
기온과 폭력의 연관성에 관한 글이므로, 이산화탄소 생성의 증가가 지구 온난화의 원인이라는 내용의 ④는 글 전체의 흐름과 무관하다.

37 ④ 글의 순서

여러 해 동안 의학계에 종사하는 사람들은 빨간 머리카락을 가진 사람들이 다른 색의 머리카락을 가진 사람들보다 수술을 위해 마취하는 것이 더 어렵다고 생각해 왔다. 그것은 근거 없는 이야기 같았지만, 새로운 연구가 이 놀라운 사실 뒤에 숨어 있는 과학에 빛을 밝혔다. (C) 정의에 따르면, 빨간 머리카락을 가진 사람들은 색소를 만드는 몸 안의 유전자들 중의 하나에 돌연변이를 가지고 있는데, 이는 그들이 다른 사람들보다 더 많은 빨간 색소와 더 적은 어두운 색소를 생성하게 한다. (A) 바로 이 유전자가 고통과 어떤 관련이 있는지는 알려져 있지 않지만, 어쨌든 빨간 머리카락을 가진 사람들에게만 유일한 그 돌연변이는 고통에 대한 증가된 민감도와 관련이 있다. (B) 결과적으로, 금발, 검은색, 또는 갈색 머리카락을 가진 사람들과 비교해 보면, 빨간 머리카락을 가진 사람들에게는 수술을 받는 동안 고통을 느끼지 않도록 하기 위해 더 많은 양의 (마취)약이 필요하다.

어휘
put ... to sleep ···을 마취시키다   surgery 수술   shed 발하다, 발산하다   mutation 변화; *돌연변이   unique 독특한; *유일무이한   dose 복용량   definition 정의   pigment 안료; *색소

구문해설
2행 ... redheads are more difficult [to put to sleep for surgery] ...: [ ]는 형용사 difficult를 한정하는 부사적 용법의 to부정사구
11행 ..., [(being) compared to people with blond, black, or brown hair], redheads need larger doses of medicine to **prevent** them **from feeling** pain during surgery.: [ ]는 조건을 나타내는 분사구문. 'prevent+O+from v-ing' 「···가 ~하지 못하게 하다」

문제해설
④ 빨간 머리카락을 가진 사람이 다른 색의 머리카락을 가진 사람보다 마취가 어렵다는 사실이 밝혀졌다는 주어진 글 다음에, 빨간 머리카락을 가진 사람들에게 색소 유전자 돌연변이가 있다는 내용의 (C)가 이어지고, 이 돌연변이가 그 사람들을 고통에 더 민감하게 만든다는 내용의 (A)가 온 후, 결론적으로 빨간 머리카락을 가진 사람들이 더 많은 양의 마취제를 필요로 한다는 내용의 (B)가 오는 것이 자연스럽다.

38 ④ 주어진 문장의 위치

직장을 자주 옮기는 것은 피고용인으로서 당신을 나쁘게 비출 수 있다. 채용 담당자들이 당신을 자기 동기 부여가 부족한 사람, 또는 쉽게 불만을 갖는 사람으로 여길지도 모른다. 게다가, 그들은 당신이 어떤 직장에서도 오래 머문 적이 없기 때문에 경력이 부족하다고 생각할지도 모른다. 그들은 또한 당신이 너무 금방 그만둘 가능성이 높다고 우려할지도 모른다. 어떤 근로자들은 잦은 이직이 다양한 업무 환경을 널리 접해 볼 수 있게 해 준다고 생각할지도 모른다. 게다가, 직장을 옮기는 것이 그들이 급여를 인상받는 보다 빠른 방법처럼 보일 수 있다. 그러나, 이러한 사람들은 그러한 이점들을 미래의 고용인들이 그들의 계속되는 이직 습관에 대해 가질지도 모르는 부정적인 인식과 저울질해 보아야 한다.

어휘
job-hopping 직업을 이리저리 자주 옮기기   exposure 노출   frequently

자주, 빈번히   employee 피고용인   recruiter 채용자, 모집자   self-motivation 자기 동기 부여   dissatisfied 불만스러운   switch ···을 옮기다, 전환하다   raise 올리기; *(물가·급료의) 인상, 승급   weigh 심사숙고하다, 비교 검토하다   negative 부정적인   perception 지각; *인식   potential 잠재적인, 가능한   constant 지속적인, 끊임없는

구문해설
5행 Recruiters may see you as someone [who lacks self-motivation] or [who becomes easily dissatisfied].: 두 개의 [ ]는 someone을 선행사로 하는 주격 관계대명사절이며 or로 병렬 연결
7행 ..., they may think [that you lack experience] since you have not stayed long at any job.: [ ]는 think의 목적절
13행 ... against the negative perception [that potential employers may have ... habits].: [ ]는 the negative perception을 선행사로 하는 목적격 관계대명사절

문제해설
주어진 문장에서는 근로자 입장에서 보는 이직의 한 장점을 이야기하고 있는데, ④의 앞부분에서는 고용주 입장에서 보는 잦은 이직의 단점을 서술하다가 뒤에서는 직장을 바꾸는 것에 대한 또 다른 장점을 이야기하므로 ④에 들어가는 것이 적절하다.

39 ② 주어진 문장의 위치

독립을 얻은 뒤, 많은 라틴 아메리카 국가들은 독자적인 통화 체계를 구축한 것에 큰 자부심을 느꼈다. 그 행위는 이전의 식민통치자들로부터의 독립을 가시적으로 표현한 것이었다. 그럼에도 불구하고, 이 나라들 중 일부는 최근에 미 달러화를 채택했다. 자국 통화의 중지는 그들의 경제를 부흥시키는 수단으로서 행해졌다. 예를 들어 에콰도르는 인플레이션을 중단시키려는 노력으로서 수크레화를 (미화로) 대체했고, 반면, 엘살바도르는 미국과의 상거래를 더 효율적으로 하기 위하여 콜론화를 포기했다. 국가들이 더 큰 안정을 얻고자 자국 통화를 포기한 이러한 경제적 모험이 보편적으로 인기를 얻은 것은 아니다. 자국의 통화를 국가의 상징으로서 자랑스럽게 여기는 사람들 사이에서는, 달러화 채택이 과거 식민지 시절로의 후퇴를 의미한다.

어휘
adopt 채택하다   independence 독립   take pride in ···을 자랑스러워하다   establish 수립하다, 확립하다   currency 통화, 화폐   visible 눈에 보이는   colonial 식민지의   discontinuation 중지, 단절   halt 중지시키다   inflation 인플레이션   commercial 상업의   transaction 거래   gamble 도박; *모험   stability 안정성   universally 널리, 보편적으로   represent 나타내다, 의미하다

구문해설
10행 ..., while El Salvador gave up the colón **in order to make** its commercial transactions ...: 'in order to-v' 「···하기 위해서」
13행 This economic gamble, [in which countries have given up ... stability], has not been universally popular.: [ ]는 This economic gamble을 선행사로 하는 계속적 용법의 목적격 관계대명사절

문제해설
주어진 문장에 Despite가 있으므로 글의 흐름이 전환되는 곳에 들어가야 하는데 남미 국가들의 독자적인 통화 체계 확립을 언급한 다음 ②의 뒤에서 그와 반대되는 상황(경제 부흥을 위한 자국 통화의 중지)을 서술했으므로, 주어진 문장이 ②에 들어가는 것이 자연스럽다.

40 ① 요약문 완성

한 실험에서, 하버드 대학의 한 사회 심리학자가 복사기를 이용하려고 기다리는 사람들에게 반복해서 다가갔다. 실험의 전반부에서 그녀는 다

음 질문을 했다. "실례합니다, 제가 다섯 페이지가 있는데요. 복사기를 써도 될까요?" 이 질문에 대한 응답으로, 그 사람들의 약 60퍼센트는 그녀가 복사기를 이용하게 하는 것에 동의하였다. 실험의 후반부에서는, 그녀는 질문을 약간 바꿔서, "실례합니다, 제가 다섯 페이지가 있는데요. 제가 복사를 해야 하기 때문에 복사기를 사용해도 될까요?"라고 말했다. 놀랍게도, 이것은 그 당시에 93퍼센트의 긍정적인 반응을 가져왔다. 그러면 무엇이 이러한 변화를 일으켰을까? 요컨대 사람들은 그들이 하는 결정을 정당화할 이유가 있는 것을 좋아한다. 비록 '제가 복사를 좀 해야 하기 때문에'가 실제로 어떤 새로운 정보를 제공하는 것은 아니지만, 그것은 실험 대상자들의 대다수에게서 긍정적인 반응을 일으키기에 충분했다.

어휘
repeatedly 되풀이하여; *여러 차례   following 다음의, 다음에 계속되는   response 대답, 응답; 반응   request 요청, 요구   approximately 거의   affirmative 긍정의, 긍정하는   justify 정당화하다(justification 정당한 이유)   initiate 시작하다, 일으키다   positive 긍정적인   reaction 반응   majority 다수   subject 주제; *실험 대상   [문제] proposal 제안, 제의   consultation 협의, 상의   assertion 주장   alternative 대안

구문해설
(2행) ... repeatedly approached people [waiting {to use a copy machine}].: [ ]는 people을 수식하는 현재분사구, { }는 목적을 나타내는 부사적 용법의 to부정사구
(14행) **The bottom line is that** people like to have a reason [to justify the decisions {(which/that) they make}].: 'the bottom line is that ...'「요컨대 ···이다」, [ ]는 a reason을 수식하는 형용사적 용법의 to부정사구, { }는 the decisions를 선행사로 하는 목적격 관계대명사절

문제해설
① 만약 사람들이 자신의 결정에 대한 이유를 제공받았다고 느끼면, 그들은 요청에 동의 가능성이 더 높다.

41 ④ 42 ⑤ 장문

'각테일 파티 효과'는 주의력이 우리가 지각 자극을 처리하는 방식에 어떻게 영향을 미치는지에 대해 많은 것을 말해주는 흥미로운 현상이다. 시끄러운 음악이 있고 다른 많은 대화들이 오가는 붐비는 파티에서 대화를 하는 동안, 우리는 어쨌든 그럭저럭 우리가 얘기하고 있는 한 사람(상대방)의 목소리에 귀를 기울인다. 방 안의 다른 모든 소리는 걸러지고 무시된다. 이는 일반적으로 모든 지각에서 일어난다. 어떤 자극은 의식적 분석을 위해 여과된다. 이것이 우리가 파티에서의 다른 대화를 무시하고 단 한 사람의 목소리에만 집중할 수 있게 해 준다. 이렇게 할 수 있는 능력은 화자의 성별, 목소리의 강도, 화자의 위치 등을 포함하여 우리가 집중하고 있는 담화의 특성에 의존한다. 그것은 또한 화자의 목소리와 존재하는 다른 소리들 간의 차이에 의존한다.

각테일 파티 효과는 '전경(前景)-배경' 현상이라고 불리는 것을 필요로 한다. 이것은 청각 정보를 '전경 요소(목표가 되는 목소리)'와 '배경 요소(주변에 있는 다른 모든 것)'로 분리하는 뇌의 능력을 말한다. 하지만 흥미로운 점은 방 반대편에 있는 누군가가 갑자기 우리 이름을 부른다면, 우리는 대개 즉시 무시한다(→ 알아차린다)는 것이다. 이는 다른 정보에 대한 모종의 처리가 분명히 일어난다는 것을 암시하는데, 특히 친숙한 목소리나 우리의 이름인 경우와 같은 특정 상황에서 우리가 그것을 알아차릴 수 있게 할 만큼 (그 처리는) 충분히 일어난다.

어휘
process 처리하다   perceptual 지각의(perception 지각)   stimulus 자극(pl. stimuli)   crowded 붐비는   take place (일이) 일어나다   tune into ···에 귀 기울이다   filter out ···을 거르다, 여과하다   ignore 무시하다

---

conscious 의식적인   analysis 분석   concentrate 집중하다   gender 성별   intensity 세기, 강도   present 존재하는   rely on ···에 의지[의존]하다; *···을 필요로 하다   figure (윤곽이 뚜렷한) 형상, 형태   ground 배경   separate 나누다, 분리하다   auditory 귀의, 청각의   input 정보, 입력   component 구성 요소, 성분   call out (큰소리로) 외치다   neglect 무시하다   [문제] disorder 장애   evolution 발달, 진화   selective 선택적인

구문해설
(1행) ... is an interesting phenomenon [that tells us a lot about {how attention affects the way **we process perceptual stimuli**}].: [ ]는 an interesting phenomenon을 선행사로 하는 주격 관계대명사절, { }는 about의 목적어로 쓰인 의문사절, we process perceptual stimuli는 the way를 선행사로 하는 관계부사절
(4행) During a conversation at a crowded party, [where there is ... place], we somehow **manage to tune** into the voice of the one person [(who(m)/that) we are talking to].: 첫 번째 [ ]는 a crowded party를 선행사로 하는 계속적 용법의 관계부사절, 'manage to-v'「간신히 ···하다」, 두 번째 [ ]는 the one person을 선행사로 하는 목적격 관계대명사절
(11행) This **enables** us **to ignore** the rest of the conversations at a party ...: 'enable+O+to-v'「···가 ~할 수 있게 하다」

문제해설
41 ④ 청각을 통해 들어오는 여러 정보를 선별해서 필요한 소리를 들을 수 있다는 내용이므로, 제목으로는 '청각 체계의 선택적 주의력'이 가장 적절하다.
42 글 후반부에서 특정 상황에서 친숙한 목소리나 우리 이름은 정보에 대한 어떤 처리에 의해 바로 알아차릴 수 있다고 했으므로, 방 반대편에서 누군가 우리의 이름을 갑자기 부르면 즉시 알아차린다고 하는 것이 자연스럽다. 따라서 ⑤ neglect(무시하다)는 notice(알다, 알아차리다) 등이 되어야 한다.

43 ③ 44 ④ 45 ③ 장문

(A) 마야 문명은 그것이 가장 번성했던 시기에 북부 중앙 아메리카와 현재의 멕시코의 남부 지방의 많은 지역에 걸쳐 전파되었다. 그것의 역사는 세 개의 주요 기간으로 나뉘는데, 기원전 300년에서 서기 250년까지 지속된 고전기 이전 시기와 서기 250년에서 900년 이후까지의 고전기, 그리고 서기 900년 이후부터의 시간을 포함하는 고전기 이후의 시기다. 그런데 서기 750년경, 강력한 마야 문명이 서서히 붕괴되기 시작했다. 많은 이론들이 있었지만, 역사가들은 무엇이 이 몰락을 가져왔는지 정확히 알지 못한다.

(C) 이제 대부분의 전문가들은 소작농의 반란이 마야 문명의 쇠퇴로 이어졌다고 믿고 있다. 수는 적지만 강력한 귀족층과 사제층이 도시들을 먹여 살리는 농장에서 일하는 노역에 의존하면서, 마야인들 사이에는 뚜렷한 계층이 있었다. 이 노동자들은 그 상황에 질려 정글로 도망쳐 살았다는 것이 이론화되었다. 들판에서 일할 노동 인구가 없었다면, 사제들과 귀족들은 그들의 문명을 함께 지탱할 수가 없었을 것이다.

(D) 그러나, 그 몰락이 형편없는 농업 기술에 의해 일어났다고 믿는 또 다른 역사가들이 있다. 그들 모두를 먹이기 위한 충분한 식량을 생산하려는 시도에서, 마야인들은 땅을 남용했을지도 모른다. 이것이 토양 내의 영양분의 결핍, 물 부족, 그리고 침식으로 이어졌을 것이다. 또 다른 문제는 그들의 '화전' 관습이었을 수도 있는데, 이것은 정글을 없애버리고 그것을 작물 재배를 위한 농경지로 전환하는 데 사용되었다. 이는 마야인들이 사냥했던 현지 야생동물을 위한 먹이의 부족으로 이어져, 그 동물들이 다른 지역으로 이주하게 했을지도 모른다.

(B) 게다가, 기후 변화, 내전, 인구과잉, 그리고 질병을 포함해 제시되었던 많은 다른 이론들이 있다. 이들 중 어느 것도 처음에 언급된 두 개의 이론만큼 고고학자들로부터 많은 지지를 받지는 못 하지만, 그것들 또한

배제될 수 없다. 결국, 마야 문명의 붕괴는 수수께끼로 남아 있다. 만약 앞으로 고고학자들에 의해 새로운 증거가 드러나지 않는다면, 그것은 영원히 풀리지 않은 채로 남아 있을지도 모른다.

어휘

peak 절정, 최고조 civilization 문명 spread 펼치다; *전파[확산]되다 portion 부분, 일부 last 계속되다 collapse 붕괴되다, 무너지다; 붕괴 downfall 몰락 civil war 내전 overpopulation 인구과잉 archaeologist 고고학자 mention 말하다, 언급하다 rule out …을 배제하다[제외시키다] peasant 소작농 revolt 반란, 봉기 distinct 뚜렷한, 분명한 hierarchy 계급, 계층 priest 사제, 성직자 theorize 이론화하다 workforce 노동자; *노동 인구, 노동력 abuse 남용하다, 오용하다 nutrient 영양분 shortage 부족 erosion 부식; *침식 slash and burn 화전을 일구다 convert A into B A를 B로 바꾸다[전환하다] migrate 이주하다, 이동하다 [문제] found 기초를 세우다; *설립하다 similarity 유사성

구문해설

(20행) Unless new evidence is uncovered ...: unless는 「…하지 않는 한, …한 경우 외에는」이라는 의미(= if ... not ~)

(25행) ..., with a small but powerful class of nobles and priests depending on slave labor [to work on the farms {that fed the cities}].: 'with+O+현재분사' 「…가 ~하면서[~한 채]」, [ ]는 slave labor를 수식하는 형용사적 용법의 to부정사구, { }는 the farms를 선행사로 하는 주격 관계대명사절

(30행) Without a workforce [to work their fields], the priests and nobles would have been unable to hold their civilization together.: if 대신 without이 쓰인 가정법 과거완료 구문으로 과거 상황과 반대되는 일을 가정. [ ]는 a workforce를 수식하는 형용사적 용법의 to부정사구

(41행) This might have led to a lack of food for local wildlife [that the Maya hunted], [causing the animals to migrate to different areas].: 첫 번째 [ ]는 local wildlife를 선행사로 하는 목적격 관계대명사절, 두 번째 [ ]는 결과를 나타내는 분사구문

문제해설

43 ③ 마야 문명의 몰락 원인을 정확히 알 수 없다는 내용의 (A) 다음에, 대부분의 학자들이 믿는 이론을 설명하는 (C)가 오고, 그 외의 또 다른 이론에 관하여 설명하고 있는 (D)가 온 후에, 마지막으로 앞서 언급된 두 개의 이론과는 다른 새로운 이론에 대해 언급한 (B)가 오는 것이 순서상 자연스럽다.

44 ④ 이 글은 원인이 밝혀지지 않은 마야 문명의 붕괴에 대한 여러 가지 이론을 설명하고 있다.

45 ③ 마야 문명의 멸망과 관련된 가장 지배적인 이론은 기후 변화가 아닌 (C)에서 언급된 소작농의 반란이다.

---

19 영어독해 모의고사

본문 ▲ p.186

18 ①	19 ②	20 ⑤	21 ④	22 ③	23 ⑤
24 ⑤	25 ②	26 ④	27 ④	28 ①	29 ②
30 ②	31 ③	32 ④	33 ④	34 ④	35 ②
36 ③	37 ⑤	38 ④	39 ⑤	40 ①	41 ⑤
42 ③	43 ④	44 ②	45 ③		

18 ① 글의 목적

랜달 마르쿠스 부스토에게,

저는 학과장 헤더 시몬스로 미네소타 주립 대학을 대표하여 편지를 드립니다. 우리는 당신이 제출한 문서를 받았습니다. 그것들을 검토한 후에, 당신이 2018년 가을 학기에 우리 학교 학생으로 한 자리를 확보했다는 것을 당신에게 알려드리게 되어 기쁩니다. 미네소타 주립 대학은 150년 동안 학생들에게 최고의 교육을 제공해 왔기 때문에 당신은 이 성취를 자랑스럽게 여기셔도 됩니다. 이 편지와 함께 이 제의를 수락하는 방법에 대한 정보를 담은 입학 패키지를 살펴보십시오. 우리가 대기자 명단에 있는 장래의 학생들에게 어떠한 결원된 자리라도 지체없이 제공할 수 있도록 당신이 이 편지를 받고 28일 내에 답장을 보내줄 것을 요청드립니다.

가을에 뵙기를 바라며,
헤더 시몬스 드림

어휘

dean 학과장 on behalf of …을 대신[대표]하여 inform 알리다, 통지하다 secure 획득하다, 확보하다 student body 학생 총수 accomplishment 성취 admission 입학 respond 대답하다, 답장을 보내다 promptly 지체없이 prospective 장래의, 유망한

구문해설

(5행) After reviewing them, we are pleased [to inform you {that you have secured a spot in our student body for the fall of 2018}].: [ ]는 감정의 원인을 나타내는 부사적 용법의 to부정사구, { }는 inform의 직접목적어로 쓰인 명사절

(7행) You can be proud of this accomplishment, as Minnesota State University has been providing students with the highest quality education for 150 years.: as는 이유를 나타내는 접속사, has been providing은 계속을 나타내는 현재완료 진행형

(13행) We ask that you respond within 28 days of receiving this letter so that we can promptly offer any unaccepted spots to prospective students on our waiting list.: 'so that+S+can ...' 「~가 …할 수 있도록」

문제해설

학과장이 지원자에게 대학 합격을 알리는 내용이므로 글의 목적으로는 ①이 가장 적절하다.

19 ② 심경 변화

헬레나의 아들에게는 그가 고형의 음식을 먹기 힘들게 만드는 질병이 있다. 이전에 그녀는 그에게 비타민과 영양분을 제공하기 위해 특별한 스무디를 만들고는 했지만, 그가 먹는 음식이라고는 계피와 메이플 시럽으로 만들어진 특정 브랜드의 냉동 와플뿐이었다. 하지만 어느 날 그녀는

이 와플을 동네 슈퍼마켓에서 찾을 수 없었는데, 그 회사가 와플 생산을 멈춘 것으로 밝혀졌다. 그녀는 다른 와플 브랜드들을 시도했지만, 그는 그것들을 먹지 않았다. 아들을 간절히 돕고 싶어, 그녀는 그 회사와 연락을 했다. 그들은 그들의 연구 개발팀에게 집에서 와플을 만들기 위한 조리법을 제작하게 하여, 그것을 그녀에게 보냈다. 회사의 친절한 조치 덕분에, 이제 그녀의 아들은 그녀가 집에서 만든 와플을 먹는다.

어휘

medical condition 질병　solid 단단한; 고체의, 고형의　nutrient 영양분, 영양소　desperate to-v 간절히 …하고 싶은　get in contact with …와 연락하다　put together 만들다, 합하다　[문제] anxious 불안해하는　frustrated 좌절감을 느끼는　ashamed 부끄러운

구문해설

①행 Helena's son has a medical condition [that makes it difficult *for him* {to eat solid food}].: [ ]는 a medical condition을 선행사로 하는 주격 관계대명사절, it은 가목적어이고 { }가 진목적어, him은 { }의 의미상 주어

③행 ... special smoothies [to provide him with vitamins and nutrients], but the only food [(that) he would eat] was a specific brand of frozen waffles [made with cinnamon and maple syrup].: 첫 번째 [ ]는 목적을 나타내는 부사적 용법의 to부정사구, 두 번째 [ ]는 the only food를 선행사로 하는 목적격 관계대명사절, 세 번째 [ ]는 a specific brand of frozen waffles를 수식하는 과거분사구

⑧행 ... it turned out that the company **had stopped** producing them.: had stopped는 주절의 과거시제(turned out)보다 앞선 시점을 나타내는 대과거

⑪행 They **had** their research-and-development team **put** together ... and *sent* it to ...: 사역동사 had의 목적격보어로 동사원형(put)이 쓰임, 문장의 동사 had와 sent가 등위 접속사 and로 병렬 연결

문제해설

질병이 있는 아들이 유일하게 먹는 특정 브랜드의 냉동 와플이 생산 중단되어 걱정했지만 그 와플 회사의 도움으로 집에서 와플을 만들 수 있게 되었으므로, 헬레나의 심경 변화로 가장 적절한 것은 ② '걱정하는 → 감사하는'이다.

20 ⑤ 글의 요지

많은 사람들에게 직업은 그들의 정체성의 중요한 일부이다. 하지만 일과 그토록 긴밀한 일체감을 갖는 것은 문제를 일으킬 수 있다. 일자리를 잃는 것은 끔찍한 일이지만, 당신이 막 잃은 그 직업이 당신의 자아상의 일부라면, 당신은 자신이 누구인지에 대한 판단력 또한 잃을 수 있다. 그와 마찬가지로, 만약 당신의 자아상이 업무 성과와 연결되어 있다면, 사무실에서 별로였던 날은 당신이 보잘것없다고 느끼게 만들지도 모른다. 자신의 일과 지나치게 일체감을 갖는 사람들에게 해줄 조언이 있다. 당신의 일은 당신이 하는 일일 뿐, 당신 자신은 아니라는 것이다. 내가 친구들이나 가족과 휴식을 취하고 있을 때, 나는 의사가 아니라 그저 평범한 한 사람일 뿐이다. 그리고 내가 다른 무언가를 하기 위해 의사이기를 포기한다 해도, 여전히 나는 평범한 한 사람일 것이다.

어휘

individual 개인, 개체　identity 동일함; *정체성　identification 동일시, 일체감　self-image 자아상　performance 성과, 성취　worthless 가치 없는, 하찮은

구문해설

②행 But [having such a close identification with your work] can cause problems.: [ ]는 문장의 주어로 쓰인 동명사구

⑫행 And **if** I **gave up** being a doctor to do something else, **I'd still be** a normal guy.: 'if+S+동사의 과거형 ...., S+조동사의 과거형+동사원형 ~'

「만약 …라면, ~할 텐데」(현재 사실과 반대되는 상황을 가정하는 가정법 과거)

문제해설

⑤ 일과 지나친 일체감을 갖는 것을 경계하며, 자신의 일과 인격체로서의 자신을 구분할 것을 조언하고 있는 글이다.

21 ④ 필자의 주장

나의 환자들이 내가 의사로서 모든 답을 갖고 있다고 여길 때, 그들은 때때로 과도하게 의존적이고 소극적인 인상을 주는데, 이것은 내가 그들에게 가능한 한 최상의 치료를 제공하려 할 때 전혀 도움이 되지 않는다. 그 대신 나는 이러한 환자들이 그들의 건강에 대한 책임을 지고, 수동적으로 받아들이는 사람이 되기보다는 그들의 치료에 적극적인 파트너로서 나와 함께 하기를 바란다. 자신을 향해 (자신이) 더 긍정적이고 열정적인 사람이라는 견해로의 변화는 건강한 생활 방식의 일부분으로서 도움이 된다. 환자들에 대한 나의 조언은 다음과 같다. 건강하기를 선택하고, 일상 생활 속의 작은 기적들에 기뻐하며, 잘 먹음으로써 당신의 신체를 존중하라. 다른 사람들과 깊은 우정을 나누고, 자주 운동을 하며, 창조성을 찾아 나서라. 당신이 믿든 그렇지 않든, 생활 속에서 이 유익한 습관들을 따르는 것이 당신의 건강을 유지하는 데 도움이 될 것이다.

어휘

come across as …라는 인상을 주다　passive 수동적인, 소극적인　take charge of …을 맡다, 담당하다　recipient 수령인, 받는 사람　outlook 예측; *견해, 관점　passionate 열정적인　beneficial 유익한

구문해설

⑤행 Instead, **I wish** patients like these **would take charge of** their health and join me as active partners in their care, *rather than* passive recipients.: 'I wish+가정법 과거' 「…가 ~하면 좋을 텐데」(현재 사실에 반대되는 일을 가정), 'A rather than B' 「B라기보다는 오히려 A」

⑧행 ... to one [that is more positive and passionate toward oneself] **goes a long way** as part of a healthy lifestyle.: [ ]는 one을 선행사로 하는 주격 관계대명사절, 'go a long way' 「유용하다」

문제해설

④ 환자가 스스로 가꾸는 긍정적이고 적극적인 생활 방식과 태도가 건강을 유지하는 데 무엇보다 중요하다는 내용의 글이다.

22 ③ 함축 의미 추론

오늘날의 소비자들은 신속한 결정을 내리고 즉각적인 만족감을 요구한다. 이는 주로 그들이 눈 깜빡할 사이에 정보를 찾고 과업을 완수하기 위해 스마트폰을 사용한다는 사실로 인한 것이다. 즉각적인 만족감을 위해 그들의 기기에 의지하는 이러한 사례들은 마이크로 모먼트로 알려져 있다. 통상적으로, 제품을 구매하는 사람들은 인식, 숙고, 그리고 결정이라는 뚜렷이 구별되는 세 단계를 거쳤다. 그러나, 마이크로 모먼트 덕분에 이 행동은 공룡의 길을 가고 있다. 대신에, 대부분의 소비자들은 수십 번의 짧고 개별적인 온라인 사용 시간에 정보를 수집하고 결정을 내린다. 이것 때문에, 현대 브랜드들은 확고한 인터넷 존재감을 확립하는 데 집중함으로써 그들의 마케팅 접근법을 바꿔야 한다. 이런 방식으로, 소비자들은 마이크로 모먼트 동안 그들의 제품에 대한 정보를 우연히 마주칠 가능성이 더 커질 것이다.

어휘

consumer 소비자　gratification 만족감　accomplish 완수하다, 성취하다　in the blink of an eye 눈 깜빡할 사이에　instance 사례, 실례　turn to …에 의지하다　device 장치, 기기　immediate 즉각적인　satisfaction 만족(감)　purchase 구매하다　distinct 뚜렷한; 뚜렷이 구별되는　awareness 인식, 자

각 consideration 사려, 숙고 go the way of …와 같은 길을 가다, …의 전철을 밟다 unconnected 관련이 없는 session 시간, 기간 approach 접근법 establish 확립하다 presence 존재, 있음 [문제] abandon 버리다, 버리고 떠나다 predictable 예측할 수 있는 instinct 본능

구문해설

[2행] This is mainly due to the fact [that they use their smartphones {to **find** information and (to) **accomplish** tasks in the blink of an eye}].: the fact와 [ ]는 동격, { }는 목적을 나타내는 부사적 용법의 to부정사구, find와 accomplish가 등위 접속사 and로 병렬 연결

[13행] Because of this, modern brands need to change their marketing approach **by focusing** on *establishing* a strong internet presence.: 'by v-ing' 「…함으로써」, establishing은 on의 목적어로 쓰인 동명사

문제해설

밑줄 친 '이 행동은 공룡의 길을 가고 있다'에서 '이 행동'은 이전 소비자들이 제품 구매 시 거쳤던 세 단계를 가리키며 이러한 행동들이 '공룡의 길을 가고 있다' 또는 '공룡의 전철을 밟고 있다'는 것은 사라진다는 것을 의미한다. 지금의 소비자들은 마이크로 모먼트 덕분에 소비 양상이 이전과 달라졌다고 했으므로, 밑줄 친 부분이 의미하는 바로 가장 적절한 것은 ③ '쇼핑객들은 더 이상 예측 가능한 단계를 따르고 있지 않다'이다.

23 ⑤ 글의 제목

나는 매우 의욕이 넘치는 성격을 지녔다. 한번 운동에 몰두하기로 결심을 했으면, 나는 그것에 최대한의 노력을 쏟아붓고 그 결과를 보기를 원했다! 그렇지만 결국 일주일에 7일 운동하는 것이 일주일에 4일 운동하는 것보다 효과가 적다는 것을 깨달았다. 때로 휴식은 운동의 나머지 절반이라고 일컬어진다. 당신의 몸이 그간 받았던 스트레스에 반응함에 따라, 휴식하고 회복하는 동안에 실제로 그 모든 운동의 성과를 얻게 된다. 만약 당신이 가만히 앉아 있을 수 없다면, 걷기 같은 '활동적인 휴식'을 취해 보라. 이것은 당신을 계속 움직이게 하되 정기적인 운동처럼 몸에 무리를 주지는 않는다.

어휘

driven 의욕이 넘치는 commit oneself to …에 헌신[전념]하다 maximum 최대한(의) refer to A as B A를 B라고 부르다 workout 운동 recovery 회복 [문제] combat 싸우다, 투쟁하다 efficient 효율적인

구문해설

[8행] ... **as** your body responds to *the stress* [that it's been put under].: as는 「…함에 따라」라는 의미의 접속사, [ ]는 the stress를 수식하는 목적격 관계대명사절

[10행] ..., try "active rest," like walking, [which **keeps** you **moving** but isn't *as* hard on your body *as* a regular workout].: [ ]는 "active rest"를 선행사로 하는 계속적 용법의 주격 관계대명사절, 'keep+O+v-ing' 「…을 계속 ~하게 하다」, 'as ... as ~' 「~만큼 …한[하게]」(동등비교구문)

문제해설

일주일 내내 운동을 하는 것보다 적당한 휴식을 취하는 것이 운동 효과를 더 높인다는 내용이므로, ⑤ '효율적인 운동을 위한 휴식의 필요성'이 글의 제목으로 가장 적절하다.

24 ⑤ 글의 주제

나는 광고주들이 아이들에게 물건을 판매하는 방식에 더 주의를 기울여야 한다고 생각한다. 아이들을 대상으로 하는 마케팅은 너무 문제가 되어 일부 국가에서는 편성된 프로그램 한 시간 동안 아동용 제품 광고에 할당될 수 있는 시간 분량을 제한하는 법을 도입했다. 예를 들어, 캐릭터 상품을 아이들에게 파는 것은 그들이 실제로 필요하지 않은 것에 돈을 낭비하게 한다. 마케터들은 대부분의 아이들이 만화 캐릭터와 같이 새롭고 흥미로운 것에 이끌린다는 사실을 활용한다. 식품을 마케팅하는 것 또한 아이들 사이에서 증가하고 있는 체중 문제의 일부로 여겨진다. 많은 식품 회사들은 선진국 아이들을 과체중으로 만드는 것에 대해 어떠한 책임도 부인한다. 그러나 그들의 광고 속에서, 그들은 아이들을 겨냥해 고안된 방법들로 분명히 패스트푸드나 당분이 함유된 음료를 매력적으로 보이게 만든다. 그러므로, 나는 그 제품을 실제로 구매하는 아이의 부모들과 더불어 광고주도 분명 책임이 일부 있다고 생각한다.

어휘

advertiser 광고주 market 상품을 내놓다 introduce 도입하다 allot 할당하다 commercial 광고 deny 부인하다 overweight 과체중의 appealing 매력적인 share the blame 공동으로 책임지다, 비난을 함께 받다 along with …와 함께 purchase 구입하다 [문제] consumption 소비 strategy 전략 when it comes to …에 관한 한

구문해설

[1행] I think advertisers have to be more careful about the way [they market things to children].: [ ]는 the way를 선행사로 하는 관계부사절

[2행] Marketing to children has become **such** a problem **that** some countries have introduced laws [limiting the amount of time {that can be allotted to commercials ... programming}].: 'such ... that ~' 「너무 …해서 ~하다」, [ ]는 laws를 수식하는 현재분사구, { }는 the amount of time을 선행사로 하는 주격 관계대명사절

[18행] Therefore, I think advertisers **do** share part of the blame, along with the children's parents [who actually purchase the items].: do는 동사 share를 강조하는 조동사, [ ]는 the children's parents를 선행사로 하는 주격 관계대명사절

문제해설

⑤ 아이들을 대상으로 한 마케팅이 아이들에게 미치는 안 좋은 영향을 언급하면서 광고주들이 그에 대해 책임이 있다는 내용의 글이다.

25 ② 도표 내용 불일치

위의 도표는 9개의 선택된 국가들의 비만 인구 비율을 보여주며, 성별에 따라 나뉘어 있다. 프랑스와 네덜란드는 비슷하게 낮은 비만율을 보이고 있는데, 각국 인구의 10퍼센트 미만이 비만이라고 여겨진다. (반면에 체코 공화국은 전체적으로 가장 높은 비만율을 보이고 있는데, 남성과 여성 모두 25퍼센트 이상이 비만으로 간주된다.) 그러나, 약 27퍼센트의 가장 높은 비만율을 보이는 것은 바로 러시아 여성으로, 이는 (비만율이) 단 10퍼센트뿐인 러시아 남성과 대조적이다. 선택된 국가들 중 4개국인 러시아, 영국, 독일, 그리고 체코 공화국에서는 여성이 남성보다 더 높은 비만율을 보이는 반면에 다른 국가들 중 4개국에서는 남성이 더 비만이다. 한편, 캐나다에서는 남성과 여성의 비만율이 동일하다.

어휘

obesity 비만(obese 비만인) percentage 비율 population 인구 selected 선택된, 선발된 break down 나누다 gender 성, 성별 overall 전반적인, 전체의 equal 동일한, 같은

구문해설

[1행] The above graph shows the percentage of the population of nine selected countries [that is obese], (being) broken down by gender.: [ ]는 the percentage ... countries를 선행사로 하는 주격 관계대명사절

[5행] ..., **with** less than 10% of each country's population **considered** obese.: 'with+O+과거분사' 「…가 ~된 채로」

However, **it is** Russian women **who** have the highest obesity rate of about 27%, ...: 'it is ... who[that] ~'「~한 사람[것]은 바로 …이다」(강조구문)

문제해설
② 체코 공화국 남성들의 비만율은 25퍼센트가 채 되지 않는다.

26 ④ 내용 불일치

　많은 사람들이 크리스토퍼 콜럼버스가 북미대륙으로 나아간 최초의 유럽인이라고 믿지만, 스칸디나비아인, 즉 바이킹들이 그곳에 처음 도착했다는 것을 증명하는 충분한 증거가 있다. 1961년, 고고학자들은 캐나다의 뉴펀들랜드의 북단에서 약 천 년 전에 세워졌다고 믿어지는 스칸디나비아인의 정착지를 발견했다. 그 정착지에 있는 건물들은 주택과 금속 작업장 그리고 보트 수리점 등을 포함한다. 이에 덧붙여, 고대 스칸디나비아의 전설은 그린란드 출신의 스칸디나비아인들이 그린란드 서부까지 땅을 탐사하러 갔을 때 겪었던 경험에 대해 이야기하고 있다. 그 이야기는 스칸디나비아 탐험대가 어떻게 신대륙에 정착지를 세웠는지 말해주고 있는데, 연구자들은 그 정착지가 캐나다에서 발견된 그것이라고 믿고 있다. 고대 이야기에는 심지어 초기 스칸디나비아 정착민들이 많은 학자들이 아메리카 원주민이라고 믿고 있는 신대륙의 부족을 어떻게 만나게 되었는지에 대한 정보도 있다.

어휘
make one's way to …로 나아가다　continent 대륙　archaeologist 고고학자　settlement 정착(지)　set up 세우다　workshop 작업장　tradition 전통; *전설　explore 탐험하다　encounter 만나다, 마주치다　scholar 학자

구문해설
（2행）... the first European [to make his way to the North American continent], there is enough evidence [that proves {that the Norse, or Vikings, reached there first}].: 첫 번째 [ ]는 the first European을 수식하는 형용사적 용법의 to부정사구, 두 번째 [ ]는 evidence를 선행사로 하는 주격 관계대명사절, { }는 proves의 목적절
（7행）... that was believed **to have been set up** about 1,000 years ago.: to have been set up은 술어동사(was believed)의 시제보다 이전에 일어난 일을 나타내는 완료부정사
（13행）The stories talk about [how Norse explorers made a settlement in the new land], [which researchers believe to be the **one** {found in Canada}].: 첫 번째 [ ]는 about의 목적어로 쓰인 의문사절, 두 번째 [ ]는 a settlement를 선행사로 하는 계속적 용법의 목적격 관계대명사절, one은 settlement를 가리키는 대명사, { }는 the one을 수식하는 과거분사구

문제해설
④ 그린란드 서부를 탐사하던 스칸디나비아인들이 캐나다에 정착지를 건설했다.

27 ③ 내용 일치

　영국을 침략했을 때 백파이프를 들여온 것은 로마인들이었다. 백파이프가 스코틀랜드인의 생활의 일부가 되기 수 세기 전에, 백파이프는 영국(잉글랜드)의 악기였으며, 에드워드 1세의 군대가 13세기 말경 스코틀랜드인들과 대면했을 때 이것을 불었다. 백파이프는 한때 유럽 전역에서 인기가 있었으나, 그 관심이 여전히 남은 곳은 스코틀랜드였다. 일본과 같이 전혀 그럴 것 같지 않은 세계의 몇몇 지역에서까지 백파이프가 인기를 얻게 된 오늘날에도, 스코틀랜드와의 관련성은 여느 때만큼이나 강력하다. 얼마나 많은 세계의 다른 지역들이 백파이프를 가지고 있다 하더라도, 그것은 스코틀랜드의 악기로서 독특한 정체성을 계속 간직하고 있다.

어휘
invade 침략하다　instrument 악기　confront 맞서다　unlikely 있음직하지 않은　association 연합; *관련　distinct 별개의, 다른; *독특한　identity 정체성

구문해설
（1행）**It was** the Romans **who** brought bagpipes with them when they invaded Britain.: 'it is[was] ... who[that] ~'「~한 사람[것]은 바로 …이다[였다]」(강조구문)
（11행）**No matter how** many other places in the world have pipes, they continue ...: 'no matter+의문사'「…하더라도」

문제해설
① 스코틀랜드에 들어오기 전 영국에서 먼저 사용되었다. ② 에드워드 1세가 거느린 군대가 연주한 적이 있다. ④ 현재 스코틀랜드를 제외한 유럽 국가에서는 인기가 사라졌다. ⑤ 아시아 지역 중 일본에서 인기를 얻고 있다.

28 ① 내용 불일치

자원봉사자를 찾습니다: 뉴 시티 영화제
　뉴 시티 영화제는 축제가 순조롭게 진행되도록 유지하는 데 도움을 줄 수 있는 열정적인 자원봉사자들을 찾고 있습니다. 우리의 축제는 8년 동안 매년 열려 왔으며 현지 감독들의 매우 다양한 영화를 특징으로 합니다.
일시: 12월 11일부터 17일까지
장소: 뉴 시티 아트 시네마
필요조건
• 자원봉사자는 적어도 18세여야 합니다.
• 자원봉사자는 축제 전에 두 차례의 교육에 참석할 수 있어야 합니다.
업무
자원봉사자는 마케팅 활동을 돕고, 사무를 보조하며, 매표소에서 일해야 합니다.
　축제 웹사이트인 www.ncffart.org를 방문하여 자원봉사자로 지원하십시오.

어휘
volunteer 자원봉사자　enthusiastic 열정적인　run 달리다; *운영하다　smoothly 부드럽게; *순조롭게　feature 특별히 포함하다, 특징으로 삼다　a wide variety of 매우 다양한　director 감독　requirement 필요; *필요조건, 요건　duty (pl.) 업무　assistance 도움, 지원　ticket booth 매표소　apply to …에 지원하다

구문해설
（3행）The New City Film Festival is looking for enthusiastic volunteers [who can **help** *keep* the festival *running* smoothly].: [ ]는 enthusiastic volunteers를 선행사로 하는 주격 관계대명사절, 'help (to-)v'「…하는 것을 돕다」, 'keep+O+v-ing'「…가 ~하도록 계속 (특정한 상태에) 있게 하다」
（5행）Our festival, [which **has been held** annually for eight years], features a wide variety of films by local directors.: [ ]는 Our festival을 선행사로 하는 계속적 용법의 주격 관계대명사절, has been held는 계속을 나타내는 현재완료의 수동태

문제해설
① 영화제는 12월 11일부터 17일까지 총 7간 열린다.

29 ② 어법

　키위는 달걀 크기 정도로, 작은 검정색 씨들이 여러 줄 있는 밝은 녹색이나 금빛 과육을 지닌다. 키위는, 비타민 C가 풍부한 것으로 알려져

있는데, 중국 남동부가 원산지인 중국 다래가 개량된 것이다. 20세기 초반에 중국 다래 나무들은 개인 정원을 장식할 목적으로 뉴질랜드로 수입되었다. 그것들은 그 나무의 맛 좋은 열매 때문이 아니라 보기 좋은 외양 때문에 선택되었다. 훗날, 뉴질랜드의 과일 재배자들에 의해 그 과일은 크기와 맛, 내한(耐寒)성이 개량되었다. 털로 덮인 키위의 갈색 껍질이 날지 못하는 키위 새의 몸통을 닮았기 때문에, 새로운 이름이 그 '새로운' 과일에 붙여졌다.

어휘
flesh 과육 abundance 풍부 modify 변경하다, 개조하다 beautify 아름답게 하다 alter 바꾸다 furry 털로 덮인 resemble 닮다 flightless 날지 못하는 adopt 채택하다

구문해설
3행 The kiwi, [which is known for ... vitamin C], is a modified version of the Chinese gooseberry, [native to Sotheastern China].: 첫 번째 [ ]는 The kiwi를 선행사로 하는 계속적 용법의 주격 관계대명사절, 두 번째 [ ]는 the Chinese gooseberry를 부연 설명하는 형용사구

문제해설
② 키위가 '개량하는' 것이 아니라 '개량된' 것이므로 능동의 의미를 나타내는 현재분사 modifying을 수동의 의미를 나타내는 과거분사 modified로 고쳐야 한다.

30 ② 어휘

대학 입학 원서를 작성하는 것은 특히 학습 장애를 겪고 있는 학생들에게 있어서 까다로운 일일 수 있다. 어떤 면에서는, 장애가 지원자의 강점으로 작용할 수도 있다. 대학 입학 사정팀들은 개인적인 어려움들을 극복해서 동료 학생들과 학문적으로 경쟁할 수 있게 된 학생들에게 끌리기 때문이다. 그러나 동시에 그들은 낮은 성적이나 형편없는 시험 점수에 대한 변명으로 장애를 이용하는 것처럼 보이는 학생들에 대해 (입학을) 불허하는 경향도 있다. 이러한 이유로 인해 학생들은 이러한 종류의 장애를 대학 입학 원서에 어떻게 나타내야 하는지에 관해 매우 신중해야 한다. 만약 학생이 자신의 장애와 그것이 어떻게 극복되어 왔는지를 조리 있게 설명하지 못한다면, (장애 학생의) 평균 이하의 성적은 대학 수준에서 저조한 성적을 예고하는 것으로 비춰질 수 있다.

어휘
application 신청, 지원 tricky business 까다로운 일 disability 무능, 장애 admission 승인; *입학 draw 당기다; *(사람의 마음을) 끌다 academically 학문적으로 competitive 경쟁적인; *경쟁할 수 있는 repetitive 되풀이하는 disapprove 찬성하지 않다 as to …에 대하여 spectacle 광경 obstacle 장애, 장애물 skillfully 솜씨 있게 predator 포식동물 predictor 전조가 되는 것

구문해설
5행 ... students [who have overcome personal difficulties {to become academically ... their peers}].: [ ]는 students를 선행사로 하는 주격 관계대명사절, { }는 결과를 나타내는 부사적 용법의 to부정사구
14행 If the student **fails to** skillfully **explain** his or her disability ...: 'fail to-v' 「…하지 못하다」

문제해설
② (A) 장애를 극복하고 동료 학생들과 '경쟁할 수 있는(competitive)' 학생이 되었다는 내용이 적절하다. (B) 대학 입학 원서에 지원자가 자신이 가진 '장애(obstacle)'에 대해 어떻게 나타낼 것인지에 대해 신중해야 한다는 내용이 되어야 한다. (C) 문맥상 저조한 성적을 '예고하는 것(predictors)'으로 여겨질 것이라는 내용이 적절하다.

31 ③ 빈칸 추론

예절과 도덕은 흔히 때로는 혼란스럽게 중복되어 쓰이는 단어이지만, 여기서는 두 단어가 구별하기 더 쉬운 방식으로 사용된다. 예절은 한 집단 안에서 보편화되어 있는 행위의 기준으로 간주될 수 있고, 따라서 집단에 따라 그리고 시간에 따라 변한다. 반면에, 도덕은 자신의 양심과 어떤 사람 간의 관계뿐만 아니라 자식과 부모, 남편과 아내의 관계와 같이한 개인과 다른 개인 간의 일대일 관계를 결정짓는 기준으로 여겨질 수 있다. 그것들은 믿음, 희망, 자비, 사랑, 예술, 의무 등과 같은 오래된 문제들에 대한 해결책이며 따라서 상대적으로 변함없다.

어휘
manner (pl.) 예의범절 moral (pl.) 도덕 overlap 겹쳐지다, 중복되다 confusingly 혼란스럽게 distinguish 구별하다 conduct 행위, 행실 prevail 유행하다, 보급되다 one on one 일대일 conscience 양심 age-old 옛날부터의 charity 자비(심), 자선 relatively 상대적으로 [문제] flexible 융통성 있는 constant 끊임없는; *변함없는

구문해설
7행 ... the standards [that determine the relations of individuals ... — *as well as* the relations of any person with his or her conscience].: [ ]는 the standards를 선행사로 하는 주격 관계대명사절, 'A as well as B' 「B뿐만 아니라 A도」

문제해설
③ 집단과 시간에 따라 변하는 예절과는 대조적으로 도덕은 사람들 간의 관계 및 믿음, 희망 등과 같이 오래된 문제들을 다루므로 상대적으로 '변함없는' 것이라고 하는 것이 적절하다.

32 ④ 빈칸 추론

해수면 아래에서 고래 노래는 엄청난 거리를 넘어 들릴 수 있다. 사실, 이 노래 중 일부는 너무 소리가 커서 해저 밑 암석을 관통한다. 훨씬 더 흥미롭게도, 이 고래 노래가 암석에 튕길 때 만들어지는 메아리는 지각의 지질학적인 구조를 더 잘 이해하기 위해 과학자들에 의해 사용되고 있다. 과학자들은 태평양 바닥에 위치한 특수 감지기를 활용하고 있다. 그것들은 주로 지진으로 유발된 지진파를 감지하는 데 사용된다. 그러나 고래 노래의 음파가 해저에 닿을 때, 그 에너지의 일부는 지진파로 유사하게 전환될 수 있다. 이 지진파가 암석층에 튕겨 나가는 길을 추적함으로써, 과학자들은 암석의 유형과 두께를 알아낼 수 있다.

어휘
beneath … 아래[밑]에 vast 어마어마한, 방대한 penetrate 뚫고 들어가다, 관통하다 echo 울림, 메아리 bounce 튀다, (빛·소리가) 산란하다 utilize 활용하다 detect 발견하다, 감지하다 earthquake 지진 convert 전환시키다 determine 알아내다, 밝히다 [문제] geological 지질학의; 지질학적인

구문해설
2행 In fact, some of these songs are **so** loud **that** they penetrate the rock beneath the ocean's floor.: 'so ... that ~' 「너무 …해서 ~하다」
4행 Even more interestingly, the echoes [that are created {when these whale songs bounce off the rock}] are being used by scientists [to better understand the geological structure of the earth's crust].: 첫 번째 [ ]는 the echoes를 선행사로 하는 주격 관계대명사절, { }는 때를 나타내는 부사절. 두 번째 [ ]는 목적을 나타내는 부사적 용법의 to부정사구

문제해설
④ 빈칸 뒤에서 고래 노래의 음파가 해저에 닿을 때 지진파로 일부 전환될 수 있고, 과학자들은 이 지진파가 튕겨나가는 길을 추적해서 암석의 유형과 두께를 알아낸다고 했으므로, 고래 노래가 암석에 튕길 때 만들어지는 메아리는 지각의 '지질학적인 구조'를

이해하는 데 사용된다는 것을 추론할 수 있다.

33 ④ 빈칸 추론

　인간은 '스스로 규제하는' 능력을 가지고 있다. 우리는 목이 마르면 마실 것을 찾는다. 위협을 당하면 우리는 싸우거나 혹은 도망을 가기로 결정한다. 이러한 종류의 반응들은 우리가 문제를 처리하고 적절한 해결책을 찾게 해준다. 그런데, 몇몇 아이들에게서는 이 스스로 규제하는 능력이 올바르게 발달하지 않는다. 이것은 잦은 짜증과 충동적인 행동, 그리고 불규칙한 수면과 식사 습관을 포함하여 많은 문제들로 이어질 수 있다. 이러한 종류의 어려움을 피하고 아이들이 스트레스가 되는 상황을 대처할 수 있게 하기 위해서는, 그들이 통제 가능한 도전적인 일들에 반복적으로 노출되어야 한다. 아이들은 그들이 새로운 무언가를 접할 때 활성화되는 타고난 경보 체계를 가지고 있다. 그런데 시간이 흐를수록, 반복은 잠재적인 위협을 편안하고 친숙한 것으로 전환시킨다. 아이들이 안전하고 보호받는다고 느끼는 환경에 있는 한, 낮은 수준의 예측 가능한 스트레스는 유익한 회복력을 만들어낼 수 있다.

어휘
self-regulate 자중하다, 자주규제하다　threaten 협박하다, 위협하다　flee 달아나다, 도망하다　reaction 반응　suitable 적합한, 적절한　frequent 잦은, 빈번한　impulsive 충동적인　assure 장담하다; 확실하게 하다　repeatedly 되풀이해서　expose 드러내다; *노출시키다　natural 자연의, 타고난　activate 작동시키다; *활성화시키다　convert A into B A를 B로 전환시키다　predictable 예측[예견]할 수 있는　beneficial 유익한, 이로운　resilience 회복력　[문제] strict 엄격한, 엄한　regulation 규정, 규칙　controllable 통제 가능한　challenge 도전, 어려운 일

구문해설
(3행) ..., we make the decision [to **either** fight **or** flee].: [ ]는 the decision을 수식하는 형용사적 용법의 to부정사구, 'either A or B' 「A와 B 둘 중 하나」
(10행) [To avoid these kinds of difficulties and assure {that children can deal with stressful situations}], ...: [ ]는 목적을 나타내는 부사적 용법의 to부정사구, { }는 assure의 목적절
(17행) **As long as** children are in an environment [in which they feel safe and protected], low levels of predictable stress can create beneficial resilience.: 'as long as' 「…하는 한」, [ ]는 an environment를 선행사로 하는 목적격 관계대명사절(in which는 관계부사 where로 바꿔 쓸 수 있음)

문제해설
④ 통제 가능한 힘든 일들을 되풀이해서 겪음으로써 위협을 편안하고 친숙하게 받아들이며, 아이들의 스스로 규제하는 능력을 길러준다는 내용을 담고 있다.

34 ④ 빈칸 추론

　중립적인 단어와 감정적인 단어 사이에는 근본적인 차이가 존재한다. 중립적인 단어들은 '기차가 10분 후에 출발합니다.'라는 문장에서와 같이 단순히 정보를 전달할 뿐이다. 이런 단어들은 감정을 불러일으키지 않는다. 하지만 '신', '사랑', '자유'와 같은 단어들은 삶에 대한 우리의 태도와 너무나도 밀접하게 연관되어 있어서 감정적인 반응을 불러 일으키기 쉽다. 그러나 이렇게 단어를 중립적 혹은 감정적으로 분류하는 것은 우리의 개인적인 경험에 따라 상대적이다. 만일 어떤 단어가 당신에게 정보밖에 제공하지 않는다면, 그것은 당신에게 중립적이다. 그러나 만일 그것이 당신의 감정을 불러일으킨다면 그것은 당신에게 감정적이다. '빵'이라는 단어가 당신에게는 중립적일지도 모르지만, 무엇이든 먹지 않고는 못 배기는 사람이나 굶주리고 있는 사람에게는 그것이 감정으로 가득 찼을지

도 모른다.

어휘
fundamental 근본적인　distinction 차이　neutral 중립적인　emotive 감정의, 감정에 관한　merely 그저, 단지　convey 전달하다　arouse 깨우다; 자극하다, 환기하다　categorization 분류　compulsive 강박관념에 사로잡힌　starve 굶주리다　[문제] relative 상대적인

구문해설
(6행) ... and "freedom" are **so** closely connected with our attitudes to life **that** they *are likely to arouse* emotional reactions.: 'so ... that ~' 「너무 …해서 ~하다」, 'be likely to-v' 「…하기 쉽다」
(10행) If a word gives you **nothing but** information, ...: 'nothing but ...' 「오직, 그저 …일 뿐인」(= only)

문제해설
④ 빈칸 뒤에 제시된 예를 통해 중립적인 단어와 감정적인 단어의 분류가 개인의 경험에 따라서 상대적임을 알 수 있다.

35 ② 빈칸 추론

　글과 말을 통한 의사소통에 대한 전통적인 접근은 우리가 절대적인 일련의 규칙들을 따라야 한다고 요구한다. 다시 말해, 우리는 모든 주어와 동사는 일치해야 하고, 문장의 요소들은 그들의 올바른 용법이라는 측면에서 정확하게 배치되어야 한다는 것을 명심해야 한다. 물론 앞서 언급한 규칙들과 더불어 모든 단어는 철자가 정확해야 하고 항상 적절한 구두법이 사용되어야 한다. 나는 이 모든 규칙들을 배우고 사용하는 것이 처음에는 힘든 일처럼 보일지도 모른다는 것을 이해하지만, 자신을 정확히 표현하는 능력은 효과적인 의사소통의 핵심이다. 매우 지적이고 고등 교육을 받은 사람이더라도 올바른 문법을 사용하지 않으면 우둔하다고 여겨진다.

어휘
oral 입의; *말로 하는　keep in mind 마음에 담아 두다, 잊지 않고 있다　element 요소, 성분　usage (단어의) 용법　punctuation 구두법, 구두점　educated 많이 배운, 학식이 있는　come across as …인 것처럼 보이다, …인 것으로 여겨지다　simple-minded 우둔한, 똑똑하지 못한　[문제] absolute 완전한; *절대적인　fluently 유창하게　strengthen 강화하다　bond 유대

구문해설
(2행) ... requires [that we (should) follow an absolute set of rules].: [ ]는 requires의 목적절로, require, suggest 등과 같이 요구·제안 등을 나타내는 동사에 연결되는 that절의 동사는 '(should+)동사원형'의 형태로 쓰임
(13행) Even the most intelligent, most highly educated individual [who does not use proper grammar] ...: [ ]는 the most ... individual을 선행사로 하는 주격 관계대명사절

문제해설
② 사람들이 지켜야 할 문법 규칙들을 열거하며 이를 지키지 못하는 사람들은 우둔한 인상을 준다고 하였으므로, 문어 또는 구어 의사소통에서 요구되는 것은 절대적인 언어 규칙들을 따르는 것이다.

36 ③ 흐름과 무관한 문장

　천문학자들에 따르면, 별의 질량은 그것이 그 수명을 다하는 방식에 있어 결정적인 요인이다. 매우 거대한 별들은 결국 블랙홀이나 중성자성이 되는 경향이 있다. 보통의 질량을 가진 별들에 관해 말하자면, 그것들은 대부분 초신성으로 알려진 거대한 폭발 후에 중성자성으로 줄어드는 경향을 보인다. 그리고 마지막으로 적은 질량을 가진 별들은 일반적으로 백색왜성으로 불리는 것으로 그들의 삶을 마감한다. (어떤 백색왜성은 그

대기 아래 약 50킬로미터 두께의 딱딱한 층을 가지고 있다고 여겨진다.) 백색왜성은 태양의 질량과 유사한 질량을 가진 별이지만, 지구보다 아주 조금 더 크다. 이것이 그것들을 우주에서 발견되는 가장 밀도가 높은 물질의 형태 중 하나가 되게 한다.

어휘
astronomer 천문학자 mass 질량 deciding 결정적인 lifespan 수명 massive 거대한 end up as 결국 …이 되다 as for …에 관해 말하자면 shrink 줄어들다 gigantic 거대한 explosion 폭발 crust 껍질; *딱딱한 표면, 층 dense 빽빽한; *밀도가 높은

구문해설
1행 According to astronomers, a star's mass is the deciding factor in the way [it will end its lifespan].: [ ]는 the way를 선행사로 하는 관계부사절
9행 It is believed [that some white dwarfs have a crust {that is about 50 kilometers thick beneath their atmosphere}].: It은 가주어이고 [ ]가 진주어, { }는 a crust를 선행사로 하는 주격 관계대명사절

문제해설
별이 그 질량에 따라 다른 방식으로 수명을 다한다는 글이므로, 백색왜성이 대기 아래에 딱딱한 층을 가지고 있다는 내용의 ③은 글의 흐름에 맞지 않는다.

37 ⑤ 글의 순서

스페인의 건축가 가우디는 바르셀로나의 가장 유명한 대성당들 중 하나인 사그라다 파밀리아에 대해 구상해냈다. 그는 1882년부터 그가 사망한 해인 1926년까지 그것의 건축을 지휘하였다.
(C) 당시 그 성당은 단 15퍼센트만이 완성되어 있었고, 그때 이후로 그것은 아직도 완공되지 않았다. 사실 (건설) 작업은 오늘날까지 계속되고 있고, 가우디의 미완성 성당은 전 세계로부터 관광객들을 끌어들이고 있다.
(B) 그러나 어떤 사람들은 진행 중인 그 작업에 반대하는데, 왜냐하면 가우디의 원래 설계도들은 사라져 버렸고, 재구성된 디자인은 1926년에 그 건축가(가우디)가 생각했던 것을 거의 반영하지 않기 때문이다. 가우디의 창의적인 비전은 어쩌면 관광산업을 위해 희생되었는지도 모른다.
(A) 그럼에도 불구하고, 관광산업이 중요한 수입원이기 때문에, 관광산업의 중요성은 그 프로젝트의 책임을 맡고 있는 사람들에 의해 간과될 수 없다. 적어도 지금은 그 성당에 대한 작업을 멈출 계획이 없다.

어휘
architect 건축가 come up with …을 고안하다 concept 개념; *구상, 발상 cathedral 성당 significant 중요한, 중대한 revenue 세입, 수입 overlook 간과하다 halt 중지시키다 ongoing 진행 중의 plan 계획; 설계도, 도면 reconstructed 재건된, 개조된 sacrifice 희생하다 for the sake of …을 위하여 incomplete 미완성의

구문해설
2행 ... the concept of the Sagrada Familia, [one of Barcelona's most famous cathedrals].: [ ]는 the Sagrada Familia와 동격
11행 ... the reconstructed designs hardly reflect [what the architect had in mind in 1926].: [ ]는 reflect의 목적어로 쓰인 관계대명사절

문제해설
⑤ 가우디가 사망 시점까지 지휘한 성당 건축에 대한 설명인 주어진 글 다음에, 그때(at that time)에는 완성도가 15퍼센트였으나 현재 건축과 관광업을 지속하고 있다는 내용의 (C)가 오고, 일부 사람들이 이러한 건축에 반대하는 이유인 (B)가 온 뒤에, 그럼에도 불구하고 관광업이 주요 수입원이기 때문에 건축을 중단할 예정이 없다고 마무리하는 (A)가 오는 것이 자연스럽다.

38 ③ 주어진 문장의 위치

참다운 진실은 "무엇이 배우기 가장 어려운 언어이고 가장 쉬운 언어인가?"라는 질문에 대한 확정적인 답이 없다는 것이다. 그것은 순전히 그 사람의 모국어에 달려 있다. 예를 들어, 스페인어, 프랑스어 그리고 이탈리아어는 밀접하게 관련된 로맨스어이다. 그러므로, 프랑스어는 한국어처럼 완전히 관련 없는 언어를 말하는 사람보다 스페인어를 모국어로 하는 사람이 훨씬 더 배우기 쉬울 것이다. 개인의 적성 또한 중요한데, 특히 표준 중국어나 태국어 같은 성조 언어를 배우려고 할 때 그렇다. 유년기 이후에는 이런 언어들의 특정 성조들을 구별해내는 능력이 사람마다 크게 다르다. 어떤 영어 사용자는 태국어를 빨리 습득할 수 있는 반면에, 또 다른 이(영어 사용자)는 그것을 결코 완전히 익히지 못할 수도 있다. 다른 말로 하면, 외국어 학습에 관한 한 난이도는 상대적이라는 것이다.

어휘
aptitude 적성 definitive 최종적인, 확정적인 depend on …에 달려 있다 completely 완전히 distinguish 구별하다 tone 말투; *성조 vary 서로 다르다 pick up (습관 등을) 익히게 되다 master …을 완전히 익히다 when it comes to …에 관한 한

구문해설
9행 Therefore, French will be much easier **for a native Spanish speaker** [to learn] than for someone [who speaks a completely unrelated language, such as Korean].: 첫 번째 [ ]는 형용사 easier를 한정하는 부사적 용법의 to부정사구, a native Spanish speaker는 첫 번째 [ ]의 의미상 주어, 두 번째 [ ]는 someone을 선행사로 하는 주격 관계대명사절
13행 ..., **the ability** [to distinguish the specific tones of these languages] **varies** greatly from person to person.: 주어가 단수명사 the ability이므로 단수동사 varies가 쓰임. [ ]는 the ability를 수식하는 형용사적 용법의 to부정사구

문제해설
③ 다음 문장의 these languages가 가리키는 것은 주어진 문장의 tonal language, like Mandarin or Thai이므로, 주어진 문장은 ③에 들어가는 것이 적절하다.

39 ⑤ 주어진 문장의 위치

미국의 한 저소득층 아파트 거주자들은 보수를 해 주기를 거부한 무관심한 집주인 때문에 비위생적이고 끔찍한 상태에서 살면서 수년을 보냈다. 세입자들이 그에게 물이 새는 파이프를 수리해 달라고 하고, 쥐를 없애기 위해 처리하는 사람을 고용해 달라고 했음에도 불구하고, 그는 그들의 호소를 무시했다. 결국 거주자들은 인내심의 한계에 도달하여 그 집주인을 법원에 고소했다. 증거 자료를 검토하고 난 후 판사는 거주자들의 손을 들어 판결했고, 주인에게 흥미로운 선택사항을 제시했다. 처벌로써 판사는 그에게 감옥에 가거나 또는 그의 황폐한 건물의 아파트 중 하나로 이사하라는 선택권을 주었다. 당연히 그는 두 번째 선택지를 골랐다. 거주자들은 그들과 똑같은 환경에서 사는 것이 집주인의 태도를 변하게 할 것이라는 것을 알고 판사의 현명한 판결에 기뻐했다.

어휘
resident 거주자 unsanitary 비위생적인 neglectful 무관심한 landlord 집주인, 임대주 tenant 세입자 leak 새다 exterminator 박멸하는 사람 reach the end of one's rope 인내심의 한계에 도달하다 take ... to court …을 법원에 고소하다 in favor of …을 지지하여 present 주다; *제시하다 run-down 황폐한 thrilled 흥분한, 감격한

구문해설
16행 ..., [knowing that {living in the same conditions as them}

would **force** the landlord **to change** his ways].: [ ]는 이유를 나타내는 분사구문, { }는 that절의 주어로 쓰인 동명사구, 'force+O+to-v' 「…가 ~하도록 강요하다」

주어진 문장에서 the second option이라는 말이 나오므로 두 가지 선택사항이 제시된 다음인 ⑤에 들어가는 것이 적절하다.

40 ① 요약문 완성

요즘에는 매니큐어를 바르는 것이 자신을 유행에 따르는 것처럼 보이게 하는 흔한 방법이지만, 과거의 다른 시기에는 더 깊은 의미를 지니곤 했다. 고대 바빌로니아에서 전사들은 전투 전에 손톱을 칠했는데, 상류층의 사람들은 검은색으로 칠한 반면, 하층 계급의 사람들은 초록색으로 칠했다. 고대 이집트에서는 여성들이 손톱을 칠하기 위해 헤나를 이용했다. 그들은 권력이 높을수록, 더 짙은 색을 사용했다. 고대에는 중국인들도 자신들의 사회적 신분을 보여주기 위해 매니큐어를 사용했는데, 상류층의 사람들은 붉은색과 같이 강렬한 색을 발랐다. 하층 계급의 사람들은 연한 색을 발랐으며, 종종 매니큐어 칠하는 것이 아예 금지되기도 했다. 만일 그들이 왕족과 동일한 색조를 발랐다면, 그 벌은 사형이었다.

어휘
nail polish 매니큐어 fashionable 유행하는, 유행을 따른 ancient 고대의 warrior 전사 battle 전투 class 학급; *계층 henna 헤나(적갈색 염료) powerful 강력한; *권력 있는 status 신분, 지위 vibrant 활기찬; *강렬한, 선명한 pale 창백한; *(색깔이) 엷은[연한] forbid 금지하다 shade 그늘; *색조 royal 왕족 punishment 벌, 형벌 [문제] belong to …에 속하다 ethnic 민족의

구문해설
1행 These days, [wearing nail polish] is a common way of [**making** yourself **look** fashionable], ...: 첫 번째 [ ]는 문장의 주어로 쓰인 동명사구, 두 번째 [ ]는 전치사 of의 목적어로 쓰인 동명사구, 'make+O+동사원형' 「…가 ~하게 하다」
9행 **The more** powerful they were, **the deeper** the color they used.: 'the+비교급, the+비교급' 「…하면 할수록 더 ~하다」
10행 The Chinese also used nail polish [to show their social status in ancient times], **with** people from the upper classes **wearing** vibrant colors, such as red.: [ ]는 목적을 나타내는 부사적 용법의 to부정사구, 'with+O+현재분사' 「…가 ~하면서[~한 채로]」

문제해설
① 과거에는 사람들이 손톱에 사용한 <u>색</u>이 때때로 그들이 속한 <u>사회적 계층</u>을 보여주는 역할을 했다.

41 ⑤ 42 ③ 장문

맬 행콕의 전도유망한 운동선수로서의 이력은 그를 하반신 마비로 만든 추락 사고를 겪었던 고등학교 때 갑자기 끝이 났다. 그것은 맬이 육체적, 정신적으로 적응하려고 노력했던, 인생에서 어렵고 가슴 아픈 시기였다.

병원에 있는 동안 맬은 매일의 병원 생활에서 본 것들에 대해 예리한 유머감각을 발휘했다. 그는 만화를 이용해 그가 관찰한 것을 기록하기 시작했다. 머지않아, 병원 직원들이 맬이 그린 것을 보기 위해 들르곤 했으며, 아마도 그들은 그때쯤 관심의 중심이 되고 있었던 그 만화의 일부가 되기를 몰래 바라고 있었을 것이다.

마침내 맬은 그의 만화 중 한 편을 잡지사에 팔게 되었는데, 그것은 훗날 그가 만화가로서의 경력을 <u>포기하는(→ 개발하는)</u> 데 도움이 되었다.

그의 이름은 자신의 책인 '병원 유머'의 표지뿐만 아니라 '새터데이 이브닝 포스트'와 'TV 가이드'의 만화에 실리게 된다.

맬 행콕은 인생에서 일어나는 일들을 통제할 수는 없지만 그 사건들에 대한 자신의 반응은 통제할 수 있다는 사실을 배웠다. 그는 인생을 바꿔놓은 불행을, 자기 주변의 세상에 관한 유머를 표현하는 기회로 변화시켰다. 인생에서 '마비시키는' 사건의 결과를 결정하는 강력한 힘으로 작용하는 것은 바로 태도이다.

어휘
promising 장래성 있는, 전도유망한 cut short …을 줄이다; *…을 갑자기 끝나게 하다 paralyze 마비시키다 heartbreaking 가슴 아프게 하는 adjust 적응하다 keen 예리한 cartoon 만화(cartoonist 만화가) observation 관찰 stop by 들르다 transform A into B A를 B로 변모[변화]시키다 attitude 태도 outcome 결과

구문해설
1행 Mal Hancock's promising athletic career was cut short in high school [when he had a fall {that **left** him **paralyzed** from the waist down}].: [ ]는 high school을 선행사로 하는 관계부사절, { }는 a fall을 선행사로 하는 주격 관계대명사절, 'leave+O+과거분사' 「…이 ~되게 두다」
6행 [While (he was) staying in the hospital], Mal developed a keen sense of humor about the things [(that) he saw in everyday hospital life].: 첫 번째 [ ]는 때를 나타내는 부사절('주어+be동사'가 생략된 형태), 두 번째 [ ]는 the things를 선행사로 하는 목적격 관계대명사절
9행 Soon after, the hospital employees **would** stop by to see [what Mal *had drawn*], ...: would는 「…하곤 했다」라는 의미의 조동사, [ ]는 see의 목적어로 쓰인 관계대명사절, had drawn은 대과거를 나타내는 과거완료형
25행 **It is** an attitude **that** acts as a powerful force [determining the outcome of life's "paralyzing" events].: 'it is ... that ~' 「~한 것은 바로 …이다」(강조구문), [ ]는 a powerful force를 수식하는 현재분사구

문제해설
41 한 남자가 하반신 마비로 운동선수로서의 이력이 끝나는 비극을 겪었지만 그 비극을 딛고 만화가로서 성공을 거둔 내용이므로 ⑤ '한 남자의 비극을 거친 성공'이 제목으로 가장 적절하다.
42 뒤에서 맬의 이름이 책 표지와 만화에 실리게 되었다는 내용으로 보아 맬이 자신의 만화를 잡지사에 판 일은 만화가로서의 경력을 '개발하는' 데 도움이 되었다고 하는 것이 자연스러우므로, ③ abandon(버리다, 포기하다)은 develop(개발하다) 등으로 고쳐야 한다.

43 ④ 44 ② 45 ③ 장문

(A) 1955년 12월 1일, 일터에서 집으로 돌아가기 위해 로자 파크스가 몽고메리 시의 버스에 탔을 때 그녀는 다섯 번째 줄에 앉았는데, 당시 그 자리는 미국 흑인들이 앉을 수 있는 가장 앞줄이었다. 버스가 승객들로 가득 차면서 사람들이 통로 쪽에 서기 시작했고, 결국 버스기사는 서 있는 백인 승객에게 자리를 양보하라고 파크스에게 말했다. 하지만 그녀는 그렇게 하려 하지 않았다.

(D) 버스기사가 요청한 대로 하기를 거절한 것은 파크스를 커다란 곤경에 처하게 하였다. 실제로 그것은 그녀의 체포와 감옥으로 보내지는 것으로 이어졌다. 파크스의 체포는 다른 훌륭한 지역 지도자들, 그리고 시민권 행동주의자들뿐만 아니라 젊은 목사인 마틴 루터 킹 2세를 포함하여 흑인 사회의 많은 이들을 분노하게 만들었다. 그 결과, 몽고메리 버스 체제에 대한 불매운동이 조직되었고, 소문은 도시 전역에 퍼져 나갔다. 파크스와 킹 목사의 운동을 지지했던 모든 이들은 한 해 동안 몽고메리 버스를 타는 것을 거부하기로 했다.

(B) 불매운동을 이끄는 추진력은 매우 강력했다. 흑인 택시기사들은

버스 요금과 동일하게 (택시) 요금을 낮추는 것으로 이 운동에 대한 그들의 지지를 나타내었다. 교회는 버스를 타는 대신 어디든 걸어 다니느라 신발이 닳아버린 몽고메리의 시민들을 위해 새 신발을 구매하기 위한 기금을 모았다. 이에 대응하여, 불매운동을 반대하던 백인들은 요금을 인하한 택시 기사들에게 벌금을 부과하였고, 킹 목사와 같은 시민권 운동가들을 체포한 것은 한두 번이 아니었다.

(C) 그러나 이러한 전략들은 실패했고, 마침내 백인 극단주의자들은 폭력적으로 바뀌었다. 흑인들의 교회는 폭파되었고, 사람들이 총에 맞았다. 그러나 이러한 행동들은 기대에 어긋난 결과를 가져왔고, 불매운동을 멈추게 하는 대신에 몽고메리에서 일어난 사건에 대해 전국적인 주목을 받게 했다. 마침내, 1956년 11월, 연방 대법원은 완전한 인종 통합에 유리한 판결을 내렸고 그다음 달에 불매운동이 끝났다. 그것은 자유와 시민권을 향한 전국적인 투쟁이 일어나게 하였고, 마틴 루터 킹 2세를 그 운동의 지도자로 만들었다.

어휘
aisle 통로, 복도   momentum 운동량; *추진력   boycott 불매운동   equivalent 동등한, 대응하는   oppose 반대하다   fine 벌금을 부과하다   arrest 체포하다; 체포   tactic (*pl.*) 전술, 작전   extremist 극단주의자   backfire 기대에 어긋난 결과가 초래되다, 실패하다   Supreme Court 연방 대법원   rule in favor of …에 유리하게 판결하다   full 완전한   racial 인종의, 인종간의   integration 통합   minister 성직자, 목사   respected 훌륭한   activist 행동주의자   cause 주의, 주장; *운동   [문제] trial 재판   interracial 다른 인종간의

구문해설
(3행) …, she sat in the fifth row, [which at that time was the closest to the front of a bus {that black Americans could sit}].: [ ]는 the fifth row를 선행사로 하는 계속적 용법의 주격 관계대명사절. { }는 the front of a bus를 선행사로 하는 목적격 관계대명사절

(16행) …, whites [who opposed the boycott] fined cab drivers [who lowered their fares] and arrested …: 첫 번째 [ ]는 whites를 선행사로 하는 주격 관계대명사절. 두 번째 [ ]는 cab drivers를 선행사로 하는 주격 관계대명사절

(32행) [Refusing to do {what the bus driver asked}] got Parks into a great deal of trouble; …: [ ]는 문장의 주어로 쓰인 동명사구, { }는 do의 목적어로 쓰인 관계대명사절

문제해설
43 ④ 백인에게 자리를 양보하라는 말을 들었지만 거절한 로자 파크스의 이야기인 (A) 다음에, 파크스가 이를 거절하여 체포됨으로써 발단이 된 버스 불매운동에 대한 내용의 (D)가 이어지고, 그다음으로 불매운동에 대한 흑인들의 구체적인 행동과 이에 대응하는 백인들의 행위에 대한 내용인 (B)가 오며, 마지막으로 이에 대한 법원의 판결과 이 사건이 미친 영향에 대해 언급한 (C)가 오는 것이 자연스럽다.

44 몽고메리에서 일어난 버스 승차 거부 운동의 발생 배경과 과정 및 영향에 대한 내용이므로, 글의 제목으로는 ② '몽고메리 버스 체제에 대한 불매운동'이 가장 적절하다.

45 ③ (C)에서 1956년 11월 대법원 판결 후 다음 달에 불매운동이 끝났다고 했다.

18 ①	19 ⑤	20 ⑤	21 ①	22 ①	23 ②
24 ③	25 ④	26 ③	27 ①	28 ⑤	29 ②
30 ④	31 ④	32 ④	33 ③	34 ②	35 ④
36 ③	37 ④	38 ⑤	39 ②	40 ④	41 ②
42 ③	43 ④	44 ②	45 ④		

18 ① 글의 목적

유나이티드 택배사 직원들에게 알림
셀프서비스 주유소의 인기로, 우리 기사들 중 많은 이들이 주유소 직원들이 그들에게 해 주던 정기적인 자동차 점검을 하지 않고 있습니다. 그러나 모두가 이러한 간단한 안전 점검을 정기적으로 해야 합니다. 먼저, 측정 막대로 (엔진) 오일의 양을 점검해야 하는데, 충분한 (엔진) 오일 없이 차를 모는 것은 엔진을 망가뜨릴 수 있기 때문입니다. 그다음 화상을 입는 것을 피하기 위해서 엔진이 충분히 식어 있는지를 확인한 후에, 냉각장치에 냉각제가 더 필요한지 점검하십시오. 마지막으로, 타이어의 기압을 점검하십시오. 너무 높거나 너무 낮은 압력은 타이어가 더 빨리 닳게 할 수 있습니다. 이러한 정기 점검은 차의 손상을 예방할 수 있으며 심지어 도로에서의 위험한 경험을 막아 줄 수도 있습니다.
경영진 알림

어휘
fail to-v …하지 못하다[않다]   routine 정기적인   attendant 시중드는 사람, 종업원   conduct 실행하다   on a regular basis 정기적으로   sufficient 충분한   ruin 망치다   radiator 방열기; *(엔진) 냉각장치   get burned 화상을 입다   pressure 압력   wear 닳게 하다; *닳아 떨어지다   management 경영; *경영진

구문해설
(4행) …, many of our drivers are failing to do the routine car checks [that gas station attendants **used to do** for them].: [ ]는 the routine car checks를 선행사로 하는 목적격 관계대명사절. 'used to-v' 「…하곤 했다」(과거의 반복적인 습관)

(12행) …, after **making sure** (that) the engine is cool enough *so as to avoid* getting burned.: 'make sure …' 「반드시 …하도록 하다, …하는지 확인하다」, 'so as to-v' 「…하기 위해서」(= in order to-v)

문제해설
① 택배사 직원들에게 자동차 점검 시 확인할 내용을 열거하며, 자동차 정기 점검을 촉구하는 글이다.

19 ⑤ 필자의 주장

한국의 대학들이 외국인 학생들에게 적용할 수 있는 장학금 제도를 마련하는 데 긍정적인 행보를 시작했다 하더라도, 이러한 장학금 제도에 관한 거의 모든 정보는 계속해서 오직 한국어로만 이용 가능하다. 이러한 대학들은 다른 문화권에서 한국으로 온 학생들의 요구를 충족시키기 위해 특별한 조치를 취해야 한다는 사실을 받아들여야 한다. 한국어를 배우는 것은 필수 단계이지만, (한국에) 도착하기도 전에 모두가 한국어에 유창할 것이라고 기대하는 것은 부당하다. 한국에서 공부하려는 많은 젊은이들의 결정의 이면에 있는 원동력 중의 하나는 그들의 나라에서 한국어를 배울 기회가 별로 없다는 것이다. 지원서 형식과 기타 서류들을 다

른 언어들로도 이용 가능하게 만드는 것이 이러한 학생들에게 있어서 어려운 과정을 더 쉽게 만들어주는 하나의 방법이다.

어휘
take a step forward 한 걸음 앞으로 나아가다   scholarship 장학금   measure (*pl.*) 수단, 대책, 조치   accommodate 편의를 도모하다; *(요구 등에) 부응하다   fluent 유창하게 말하는   application 신청, 지원; *지원서

구문해설
(6행) ... the fact [that they have to take special measures **to accommodate** the needs of students {who have come ... culture}].: 첫 번째 [ ]는 the fact와 동격, to accommodate는 목적을 나타내는 부사적 용법의 to부정사, { }는 students를 선행사로 하는 주격 관계대명사절
(9행) ..., but **it** would be unreasonable [to *expect* everyone *to be* fluent ... arriving].: it은 가주어이고 [ ]가 진주어, 'expect+O+to-v' 「…가 ~할 것을 기대하다」
(14행) [**Making** application forms and other documents **available** in other languages] is one way [to **make** a difficult process **easier** for these students].: 첫 번째 [ ]는 문장의 주어로 쓰인 동명사구, 'make+O+OC(형용사)' 「…을 ~하게 만들다」, 두 번째 [ ]는 one way를 수식하는 형용사적 용법의 to부정사구

문제해설
⑤ 한국의 대학들이 외국인 학생들의 편의를 도모하려면 장학금 제도에 관한 정보나 지원서 등 관련 서류를 그들의 자국어로 제공해야 한다는 내용의 글이다.

20 ⑤ 글의 요지

공자의 유명한 인용문으로 '승리는 천 명의 아버지를 가지고 있지만 패배는 고아다'라는 말이 있는데, 이는 사람들이 항상 성공한 것에 대해서는 그 공로를 인정받기를 간절히 원하지만, 무언가 잘못되었을 때는 비난을 좀처럼 받아들이려 하지 않는다는 사실을 나타낸다. 이러한 행동은 당신과 당신 동료의 업적을 왜곡하기 때문에 불명예스러울 뿐 아니라, 살아가는 동안 나중에 당신에게 되돌아와서 상처가 될 수도 있다. 만약 당신이 성공적인 업적에서 실제로 당신이 받을 만한 것보다 더 많은 칭찬을 원한다면, 당신이 미래에 그 결과를 재현하리라는 기대는 높아질 것이다. 당신은 그것을 할 수 없을지도 모르는데 말이다. 마찬가지로, 당신이 실패한 것에 대해 당신의 역할을 축소해 버린다면, 당신은 자신의 실수로부터 배우지 못하고 당신의 역량을 향상시키지 못할 것이다.

어휘
quote 인용문   take credit for …의 공로를 인정받다   dishonorable 불명예스러운, 비열한   misrepresent 잘못 전하다   credit 명성, 공; 칭찬   deserve …할[받을] 만하다   recreate 다시 만들다; *재현하다   outcome 결과; 성과   downplay 경시하다, 과소평가하다

구문해설
(6행) This behavior is **not only** dishonorable, [misrepresenting your own work and that of your partners], **but** it can **also** come back ...: 'not only A but also B' 「A뿐만 아니라 B도」, [ ]는 이유를 나타내는 분사구문

문제해설
⑤ 성공과 실패에 미친 자신의 영향과 역할을 과대평가나 과소평가하지 말고 있는 그대로 정확히 받아들여야 한다는 내용의 글이다.

21 ① 글의 주제

개나 고양이를 키우는 것과 마찬가지로, 컴퓨터를 갖는다는 것은 당신의 의무를 소홀히 할 경우 재앙으로 끝날 수도 있는, 쉽지 않은 책무이

다. 방치된 휴대용 컴퓨터는 바이러스에 쉽게 감염될 수 있고, 이는 하드웨어의 손상이나 전체 시스템의 파괴로 이어지게 되는데, 이는 그 다음으로 당신으로 하여금 소중한 데이터를 잃게 할 것이다. 그러나 당신이 당신의 기계(컴퓨터)를 잘 다룬다 하더라도, 여전히 예상치 못한 문제점들이 발생할 수 있다. 따라서 컴퓨터상의 문서, 사진과 음악 파일 등을 포함하여 중요한 모든 것들의 백업(예비) 사본을 만들어두는 것이 중요하다. 일주일에 한 번 몇 분간 시간을 할애함으로써, 당신은 커다란 슬픔을 면할 뿐 아니라, 어쩌면 또한 많은 돈을 절약하게 될 것이다. 전문가들이 컴퓨터 파괴로 인해 잃어버린 데이터를 복구하는 것은 가능하겠지만, 그들은 당신에게 그 서비스에 대하여 많은 금액을 요구할 것이다.

어휘
serious 중대한; *용이치 않은   neglected 무시된; *방치된   infect 감염시키다   crash 파괴, 붕괴   charge (대가·요금을) 청구하다   [문제] evolution 진화   budget 예산

구문해설
(12행) ... you'll be saving yourself **not only** a lot of grief, **but** possibly a large sum of money **as well** ...: 'not only A but (also) B' 「A뿐만 아니라 B도」(이 문장에서는 also 대신 as well이 쓰임)

문제해설
① 컴퓨터에 있는 소중한 자료들을 보호하기 위해 정기적으로 데이터의 백업 사본을 만드는 것이 좋다는 내용의 글이다.

22 ① 글의 주제

페루의 과학자들이 언덕 비탈에 새겨진 2천 년 된 35미터 길이의 고양이 그림을 최근에 발견했다. 이 커다란 그림은 기원전 200년에서 서기 600년 사이 나스카 문명에 의해 사막 지역에 만들어진 거대한 그림 모음인 나스카 라인의 일부로 여겨진다. 땅의 밑면이 드러나도록 바위와 모래를 옮김으로써 만들어진 이 수백 개의 그림들은 원숭이, 벌새, 그리고 거미의 그림을 포함하여 발견되었으나, 과학자들은 여전히 그것들의 용도를 확실히 알지 못한다. 과거에 일부 전문가들은 그것들이 별의 움직임을 기반으로 한 천문학용 달력이라고 생각했지만, 이 이론은 더 이상 일반적이지 않다. 우리는 그것들이 왜 만들어졌는지 결코 알 수 없을 가능성이 있다.

어휘
uncover 덮개를 벗기다; *발견하다   etch (동판 등에) 식각(에칭)하다, …을 새기다   enormous 막대한, 거대한   civilization 문명   shift 옮기다   expose 드러내다   underneath 아래에, 하부에   purpose 목적, 용도   astronomical 천문학의, 천문학적인   theory 이론, 학설   [문제] mysterious 기이한, 불가사의한   ancient 고대의, 아주 오래된   worship 예배하다, 숭배하다

구문해설
(3행) The enormous image is believed to be part of the Nazca Lines, [a collection of giant drawings {that were created in desert areas by the Nazca civilization between 200 BC and 600 AD}].: the Nazca Lines와 [ ]는 동격, { }는 giant drawings를 선행사로 하는 주격 관계대명사절
(7행) Hundreds of these drawings, [which were made **by shifting** rocks and sand {to expose the soil underneath}], have been found, ...: [ ]는 Hundreds of these drawings를 선행사로 하는 계속적 용법의 주격 관계대명사절, 'by v-ing' 「…함으로써」, { }는 목적을 나타내는 부사적 용법의 to부정사구
(15행) **It** is possible [that we will never know {why they were created}].: It은 가주어이고 [ ]가 진주어, { }는 know의 목적어로 쓰인 의문사절

문제해설

페루의 나스카 라인에 대해 설명하며 그것이 만들어진 이유를 알 수 없다고 했으므로, 글의 주제로는 ① '페루에서 발견된 불가사의한 고대 예술 작품'이 가장 적절하다.

23 ② 글의 제목

한 국가의 진정한 위대함은 광대한 영토나 많은 인구, 또는 많은 양의 수입과 수출에 의해서가 아니라, 세계의 삶과 사상, 그리고 진보에 기여한 정도에 의해 평가된다. 마찬가지로, 한 사람의 위대함은 그의 몸집이나 재산, 그리고 가족 관계나 사회적 지위에 의해 평가되는 것이 아니다. 한 사람의 위대함은 변하기 쉽고 스쳐 지나가는 군중들의 표와 공허한 환호에 대한 영향력이 아니라, 그들의 생각과 사고 방식, 그리고 결과적으로는 행동 방식에 미치는 그 사람의 지속적이고 고무적인 영향력에 의해 평가된다.

어휘

measure 측정하다; *평가하다   vastness 광활, 광대함   territory 영토   multitude 다수   extent 범위, 정도   contribute 기여하다   progress 진보, 발전   likewise 마찬가지로, 유사하게   estimate 추정하다, 평가하다   abiding 지속적인   inspiring 고무하는, 영감을 주는   consequently 결국, 결과적으로   [문제] boost 밀어 올리다, (경기를) 부양하다   enhance 높이다, 강화하다   reputation 평판   interpersonal 대인 관계의

구문해설

[1행] The true greatness of a nation is measured **not** by the vastness of its territory, ..., **but** by the extent [to which it has contributed to the life, ... the world].: 'not A but B' 「A가 아니라 B이다」, [ ]는 the extent를 선행사로 하는 목적격 관계대명사절

문제해설

국가의 위대함을 평가하는 척도에 대해 비유를 들어 설명하며 뒤이어 사람의 위대함 역시 비슷한 척도로 평가된다고 했으므로, ② '무엇이 사람을 위대하게 만드는가'가 가장 적절한 제목이다.

24 ③ 도표 내용 불일치

위 도표는 미국 성인이 하루에 디지털 미디어에 접근하는 데 사용한 시간의 양을 보여주는데, 연도와 사용된 기기의 유형별로 나누어져 있다. 도표에 제시된 기간에 걸쳐, 무선 단말기로 디지털 미디어에 접근하는 데 사용된 일일 시간은 2.5시간 증가한 반면, 컴퓨터로 디지털 미디어에 접근하는 데 사용된 시간은 겨우 0.1시간 증가했다. 전체적인 가장 큰 증가는 2011년과 2013년 사이에 발생한 반면, 전체적인 가장 작은 증가는 2013년과 2015년 사이에 발생했다. (컴퓨터로 디지털 미디어에 접근하는 데 사용된 하루 평균 시간의 양은 실제로 2011년에서 2013년 사이에 0.3시간 증가했다.) 2009년에 컴퓨터로 디지털 미디어에 접근하는 데 사용된 평균 시간은 무선 단말기로 그것에 접근하는 데 사용된 시간을 하루에 2시간만큼 초과했다. 하지만, 무선 단말기로 디지털 미디어에 접근하는 데 사용된 시간은 꾸준히 증가했는데, 실제로 2015년에는 컴퓨터로 디지털 미디어에 접근하는 데 사용된 시간을 뛰어넘는다.

어휘

mobile device 무선 단말기   adult 성인   access 접근하다   break down 나누어지다   via (특정한 사람·시스템 등을) 통하여   overall 전반적인, 전체의   take place 일어나다   average 평균의   exceed 넘다, 초과하다   steadily 꾸준히, 끊임없이   surpass 능가하다, 뛰어넘다

구문해설

[1행] The above chart shows the amount of time [(which/that) adults in the U.S. spent accessing digital media per day],

[4행] Over the years shown on the chart, daily time [spent accessing digital media via mobile devices] increased by 2.5 hours, **while** time spent accessing ...: [ ]는 daily time을 수식하는 과거분사구, while은 「…인 데 반하여」라는 의미의 접속사

[16행] However, the time spent accessing digital media via mobile devices increased steadily, [actually surpassing the time {spent accessing it via computers} in 2015].: [ ]는 부대상황을 나타내는 분사구문, { }는 the time을 수식하는 과거분사구

문제 해설

③ 도표에서 컴퓨터로 디지털 미디어에 접근하는 데 사용된 하루 평균 시간은 2011년에 2.6시간, 2013년에 2.3시간으로 0.3시간 감소했다.

25 ④ 내용 불일치

포장 음식은 현대 생활의 필수적인 부분이 되었으며, 사람들에게 자신의 집에서 편히 먹을 수 있는 전문적으로 준비된 음식을 제공한다. 놀랍게도, 포장 음식은 새로운 발명이 아니다. 그 개념은 사실 수천 년 전의 고대 로마까지 거슬러 올라간다. 많은 로마 도시들에는 *테르모폴리아*라 불리는 장소가 있었는데, 이것은 기본적으로 자기 집에 부엌이 없는 사람들을 위한 길거리 부엌이었다. 거기엔 앞쪽에 커다란 개수대와 뒤쪽엔 사람들이 음식을 먹는 테이블이 둘 다 있었다. 그러나 대부분의 사람들은 포장 음식을 사기 위해 *테르모폴리아*에 갔고, 생선, 고기, 치즈, 그리고 말린 과일을 포함한 메뉴에서 골랐다. 고고학자들은 *테르모폴리아*를 여러 로마 도시의 유적에서 발견했고, 그것들이 고대 제국 전역에서 인기가 있었음을 시사한다. 베수비오산 폭발로 인해 그것이 파괴되기 전, 폼페이에는 약 150개의 *테르모폴리아*가 있었다고 여겨진다.

어휘

takeout food (사서 식당에서 먹지 않고) 가지고 가는 음식, 포장 음식   invention 발명, 발명품   date back to …으로 거슬러 올라가다   purchase 구입하다   archaeologist 고고학자   ruin 붕괴; *유적, 진해   indicate 보여주다, 시사하다   destroy 파괴하다   eruption 폭발, 분화

구문해설

[1행] Takeout food has become an essential part of modern life, [**providing** people **with** professionally prepared food {that can be eaten in the comfort of their own homes}].: [ ]는 부대상황을 나타내는 분사구문, 'provide A with B' 「A에게 B를 제공하다」, { }는 professionally prepared food를 선행사로 하는 주격 관계대명사절

[6행] Many Roman cities had places [called *thermopolia*], [which were basically street kitchens for people {who didn't have kitchens in their own homes}].: 첫 번째 [ ]는 places를 수식하는 과거분사구, 두 번째 [ ]는 *thermopolia*를 선행사로 하는 계속적 용법의 주격 관계대명사절, { }는 people을 선행사로 하는 주격 관계대명사절

[11행] However, most people went to *thermopolia* to purchase takeout food, [choosing from a menu {that included fish, meat, cheese, and dried fruit}].: [ ]는 연속동작을 나타내는 분사구문, { }는 a menu를 선행사로 하는 주격 관계대명사절

문제해설

④ 테르모폴리아는 고대 로마 제국 전역에서 인기가 있었다고 했다.

26 ③ 내용 일치

대부분의 나선 은하들은 평평한 원반, 볼록한 부분, 그리고 헤일로로

구성된다. 원반은 대다수 은하계의 별뿐만 아니라 많은 양의 성간 가스와 먼지를 발견할 수 있는 곳이다. 원반 안에서 발견되는 모든 물질들은 초당 수백 킬로미터의 속도에 이르면서 한 방향으로 은하의 중심 주위를 회전한다. 이것은 가끔씩 형성되는 인상적인 나선형의 모양을 설명해준다. 원반의 중심에는 불룩한 부분이 있는데 이것은 성간 물질이 거의 없는 몇몇 더 오래된 별들의 집이다. 한편, 헤일로는 원반을 둘러싸고 있는데 암흑 물질이라고 불리는 엄청난 양의 무엇인가를 포함하고 있다고 믿어진다. 비록 암흑 물질이 어떤 면에서는 보통의 물질과 같은 반응을 보이지만, 그것은 눈에 보이지 않는다. 천문학자들은 성간 가스와 별들의 움직임을 토대로 그 존재를 추측할 수 있을 뿐이다.

어휘
spiral galaxy 나선 은하 be made up of …로 구성되다 bulge 불룩한 부분 quantity 양, 분량 interstellar 항성 간의, 성간의 rotate 회전하다 account for …의 이유가 되다; *…을 설명하다 vast 거대한 matter 문제; *물질 presence 존재

구문해설
[2행] The disk is (the place) [where you'd find large quantities of interstellar gas and dust, **as well as** the majority of the galaxy's stars].: [ ]는 관계부사절로 선행사 the place가 생략된 형태. 'A as well as B' 「B뿐만 아니라 A도」
[9행] At the center of the disk **is the bulge**, [home to some older stars with little interstellar matter].: 부사구인 At the center of the disk가 문두에 나오면서 주어 the bulge와 동사 is가 도치, [ ]는 the bulge와 동격

문제해설
① 원반은 다수의 은하계 별과 성간 가스, 먼지를 포함한다. ② 원반 안의 물질들은 한 방향으로 회전한다. ④ 헤일로는 원반을 둘러싸고 있다. ⑤ 암흑 물질은 눈에 보이지 않는다.

27 ③ 내용 불일치

호화 커피 관광

우리 지역은 커피 재배에 완벽한 장소입니다. 이 관광에는 지역 커피 농장 방문이 포함되는데, 그곳에서 여러분은 커피콩이 어떻게 볶아지고 전 세계로 배송되기 위해 준비되는지 보실 수 있습니다.

■ **시간**
하루에 세 번의 예정된 관광이 있습니다: 오전 9시, 오후 1시, 오후 5시
■ **가격**: 일 인당 25달러
■ **세부 사항**
• 각 관광은 전문 가이드에 의해 안내됩니다.
• 단체와 개인 여행자 모두 환영합니다.
• 관광은 다섯 가지 다른 종류의 커피 시음이 포함되는데, 그것들 모두는 관광 마지막에 구입하실 수 있습니다.
참고: 마지막 관광 시간대는 5월부터 9월까지만 이용 가능합니다.

어휘
region 지방, 지역 local 지역의 plantation 농장 roast 굽다, 볶다 ship 실어 나르다, 수송[운송]하다 scheduled 예정된 detail 세부 사항 taste 맛보다 available 구입[이용]할 수 있는 purchase 구입

구문해설
[3행] This tour includes a visit to a local coffee plantation, [where you can see {how coffee beans are roasted and prepared to be shipped all around the world}].: [ ]는 a local coffee plantation을 선행사로 하는 계속적 용법의 관계부사절, { }는 see의 목적어로 쓰인 의문사절
[15행] The tour includes tasting five different types of coffee, [all

of which are available for purchase at the end of the tour].: [ ]는 five different types of coffee를 선행사로 하는 계속적 용법의 목적격 관계대명사절

문제 해설
③ 단체와 개인 여행자 모두 환영한다고 했다.

28 ⑤ 어법

일반적으로, 세상을 극적으로 바꾸는 사상가들은 그들 시대의 지배적인 견해들을 거스를 용기가 있는 사람들이다. 천문학자 니콜라스 코페르니쿠스가 반대로(태양이 지구의 궤도를 도는 것으로)가 아니라 지구가 태양의 궤도를 돈다는 그의 우주 이론을 처음 발표했을 때 그는 동시대인들에 의해 멸시를 당했다. 현재 우리는 그가 우주 연구에서 새로운 시대를 연 것으로 인정한다. 마찬가지로, 에이브러햄 링컨이 미국에서 노예제도를 폐지했을 때 그는 나라의 전례를 깬 것이었다. 그는 남북전쟁 도중에 이것을 해냈는데, 이것은 주(州)들의 노예제도를 허가할 권리를 두고 싸운 것이었다. 우리는 이제 노예 해방 선언을 링컨의 가장 위대한 업적으로 기억한다. 1세기가 넘게 지난 후, 미하일 고르바초프는 소련의 지도자로서 러시아의 70년간의 공산주의 실험을 끝내고 구 소비에트 연방의 도처에 민주주의의 확산을 고취했을 때, 이 정신을 이었다.

어휘
thinker 사상가 dramatically 극적으로 dare …할 용기가 있다, 감히 …하다 counter 대항하다, 거스르다 prevailing 지배적인 astronomer 천문학자 orbit …의 궤도를 돌다 the other way around 반대로, 거꾸로 scorn 멸시하다 contemporary 동시대인 era 시대 cosmos 우주 precedent 선례, 전례 abolish 폐지하다 slavery 노예제도 achievement 업적 channel 나르다, 전하다 experiment 실험 communism 공산주의 promote 홍보하다; *고취하다 democracy 민주주의 former 예전의

구문해설
[1행] Typically, the thinkers [that change the world dramatically] are those [who dare to counter the prevailing views of their times].: 첫 번째 [ ]는 the thinkers를 선행사로 하는 주격 관계대명사절, 두 번째 [ ]는 those를 선행사로 하는 주격 관계대명사절
[4행] ... presented his theory of a universe [in which the Earth orbits the Sun ... around], he was ...: [ ]는 his theory of a universe를 선행사로 하는 목적격 관계대명사절
[7행] Now, we recognize him **to have started** a new era in the study of the cosmos.: to have started는 술어동사(recognize)의 시제보다 이전의 때를 나타내는 완료부정사

문제해설
⑤ 앞뒤의 절을 이어주는 접속사가 없으므로 관계대명사 what 대신 부사절을 이끄는 접속사 when이 오는 것이 적절하다.

29 ② 어휘

벌꿀오소리들은 쉽게 겁을 먹지 않는다. 그들의 두껍고 거친 가죽은 쉽게 뚫리지 않기 때문에 그들은 전통적인 무기를 두려워할 필요가 없다. 게다가, 벌꿀오소리의 느슨한 가죽은 포식 동물이 공격하는 동안에도 벌꿀오소리가 가죽 안에서 움직이는 것을 비교적 쉽게 해준다. 벌꿀오소리는 종종 기다란 발톱과 날카로운 이빨로 포식 동물을 해치기에 충분할 만큼 움직일 수 있다. 따라서, 포식자가 벌꿀오소리를 즉시 죽이지 않고 붙잡고 있는 것은 꽤 위험하다. 벌꿀오소리의 턱은 상당히 튼튼해서 먹이를 먹는 데 매우 유용한데, 이는 그들이 뼈나 거북의 껍질을 포함하여 동물을 통째로 쉽게 먹을 수 있기 때문이다. 벌꿀오소리가 사용하는 또 다

른 무기는 등에 있는 주머니다. 연구원들은 가장 큰 포식 동물조차도 도망가게 만들 수 있는 강력한 냄새를 내뿜으면서 벌꿀오소리들이 이 주머니를 뒤집는 것을 관찰했다. 전체적으로 이러한 능력들이 벌꿀오소리가 포식자들을 두려워할 이유가 거의 없게 만든다.

어휘

scared 무서워하는, 겁먹은   pierce 뚫다, 찌르다   relatively 비교적
predator 포식자, 포식 동물   claw 발톱   instantly 즉각, 즉시   prey 먹이,
사냥감   pouch 주머니   turn ... inside out …을 뒤집다   release 풀어 주다;
*발산하다   odor 냄새   fear 두려워하다

구문해설

[4행] Furthermore, the loose skin of honey badgers **makes** *it*
relatively **easy for a badger** [to move within its skin ... attacking].:
'make+O+OC(형용사)' 「…을 ~하게 만들다」, it은 가목적어이고 [ ]가 진목적어, a
badger는 [ ]의 의미상 주어
[11행] The jaws of honey badgers are quite strong, [which is very
useful when honey badgers eat their prey], ...: [ ]는 앞 절 전체를 선행
사로 하는 계속적 용법의 주격 관계대명사절
[17행] ..., [releasing a strong odor {which can **cause** even the
largest predators **to run away**}].: [ ]는 연속동작을 나타내는 분사구문, { }
는 a strong odor를 선행사로 하는 주격 관계대명사절. 'cause+O+to-v' 「…가
~하게 하다」

문제해설

② (A) 가죽 안에서 움직이기 쉽게 해주는 피부 조직은 '느슨한(loose)' 것이라고 하는
것이 적절하다. (B) 앞에 벌꿀오소리는 발톱과 이빨로 포식 동물을 해치기에 충분할 만
큼 움직일 수 있다고 나와있으므로, 포식 동물이 벌꿀오소리를 즉시 죽이지 않고 붙잡
고 있는 것은 '안전하지 않은, 위험한(unsafe)' 것이다. (C) 뒤 문장에 이러한 능력들이
벌꿀오소리가 포식 동물을 두려워하지 않게 만드는 이유라고 나와있으므로, 강한 냄새
를 일으키는 것이 포식 동물을 '도망가게(run away)' 만든다고 하는 것이 자연스럽다.

30 ④ 어휘

북극을 포함한 북극 지방의 많은 부분이 수십 년간 두꺼운 해빙층에
덮여 있었다. 이러한 이유로, 아무도 누가 그것을 소유했는지에 대해 크
게 관심 갖지 않았다. 그러나 최근에 기후 변화가 그 얼음을 녹이고 배에
새로운 길을 열어주기 시작했다. 캐나다는 현재 수중 영토 중 거의 50만
평방 마일이 자국에 속한다고 주장하고 있고, 러시아와 덴마크를 북극
지방 통제권에 대한 다툼에 합류시켰다. 북극 지방을 소유하는 어떤 국
가든 그것의 해저 천연자원에 대한 통제권 또한 갖게 될 것이다. 약 900
억 배럴의 석유와 수조 입방피트의 천연가스가 그 지역에 있다고 추정된
다. 캐나다는 국제 연합에 그들의 주장을 서술하는 보고서를 제출했다.
그것은 많은 과학 탐험에 의해 감춰진(→ 밝혀진) 대로, 캐나다 북쪽 해안
지대를 따라 있는 대륙붕의 크기와 모양에 대한 자세한 정보를 포함한다.
이 상황이 어떻게 해결될 것인지는 지켜볼 일이다.

어휘

layer 층   be concerned about …에 관심을 가지다, 걱정하다   possess
소유하다   melt 녹이다   passage 통로, 길   claim 주장하다   square mile
제곱 마일   territory 영토, 영역   belong to …에 속하다, … 소유이다   barrel
배럴(석유 단위로 120~159리터)   trillion cubic feet(tcf) 조 입방피트
submit 제출하다   outline 개요를 서술하다   case 경우; *주장   coastline
해안 지대   expedition 탐험(대)   resolve 해결하다

구문해설

[6행] Canada is now claiming [that nearly half a million square
miles of underwater territory belongs to them], [joining Russia
and Denmark in the fight for control of the Arctic].: 첫 번째 [ ]는

---

claiming의 목적어로 쓰인 명사절, 두 번째 [ ]는 부대상황을 나타내는 분사구문
[10행] [**Whichever** country owns the Arctic] will also have control
of its undersea natural resources.: '…하는 어느 쪽이든지'의 의미로 쓰인 복
합관계대명사로, whichever는 명사절을 이끌어 [ ]가 문장의 주어 역할을 함
[17행] ... **as** (it is) determined by a number of scientific
expeditions.: as는 '…대로, …와 같이'의 의미로 쓰인 접속사이며, 뒤에 it is가 생
략됨

문제해설

기후 변화로 북극의 얼음이 녹으면서 드러난 새로운 영토와 항로, 해저 천연자원에 대
한 여러 국가 간의 소유권 분쟁이 일어나는 상황을 설명하며 캐나다가 과학 탐사에 의
해 밝혀진 대로 북극의 대륙붕 일부가 자국 영토임을 주장하는 것이 자연스럽다. 따라
서 ④ concealed(감추었다)는 determined(밝혔다) 등으로 고쳐야 한다.

31 ④ 빈칸 추론

개미들은 항상 자기 자신의 이익보다 공동체를 우선시한다는 사회
적 통념이 잎 자르는 개미를 대상으로 행해진 연구에 의해 최근에 사실
이 아닌 것으로 증명되었다. DNA 지문 감식 기술을 이용하여, 연구자들
은 특정한 개미의 자손들이 여왕개미가 될 가능성을 높이는 유전적인 이
점을 갖고 있다는 사실을 입증했다. 이 '왕족의' 유전자를 지닌 수컷 개미
들은 그 사실을 비밀로 하기 위해 주의를 기울인다. 만약 너무 많은 여왕
개미가 같은 수컷에게서 나온다면, 다른 개미들은 이런 여왕들 중 일부
를 죽일지도 모른다. 따라서 이 수컷들은 다수의 집단에 골고루 자신의
자손들을 퍼뜨릴 만큼 주도면밀하다. 이들 '왕족' 개미들이 의심과 보복
을 피하기 위해 동료 개미들을 속이고 있기 때문에, 어떤 집단도 같은 수
컷에게서 나온 여왕을 지나치게 많이 보유하고 있지 않다.

어휘

myth 신화; *사회적 통념   colony 식민지; *(개미·꿀벌 등의) 집단, 군생
disprove …의 반증을 들다, 그릇됨을 증명하다   fingerprinting 지문 감식법
offspring 자식, 자손   genetic 유전학적인, 유전자의(gene 유전자)   destroy
파괴하다; *(동물을) 죽이다   prudent 신중한, 조심성 있는   suspicion 혐의, 의
심   retaliation 보복   [문제] breed 번식시키다

구문해설

[1행] The myth [that ants always put the colony before their own
interests] was recently disproven by research [conducted on
leaf-cutting ants].: 첫 번째 [ ]는 The myth와 동격, 두 번째 [ ]는 research
를 수식하는 과거분사구
[3행] [Using DNA fingerprinting techniques], researchers proved
[that the offspring of certain ants have a genetic advantage
{that makes them more likely to become queens}].: 첫 번째 [ ]는 동
시동작을 나타내는 분사구문, 두 번째 [ ]는 proved의 목적절, { }는 a genetic
advantage를 선행사로 하는 주격 관계대명사절
[8행] **If** too many queens **were** coming from the same male, the
other ants **might destroy** some ...: 'If+S+were ...., S+조동사의 과거
형+동사원형 ~'은 현재 사실과 반대되는 일을 가정하는 가정법 과거

문제해설

왕족의 유전자를 가진 수컷 개미가 자신의 자손을 퍼뜨리기 위해서 동료 개미들을 속인
다는 내용의 글이므로 빈칸에는 '속이다'라는 의미의 ④ cheating이 적절하다.

32 ④ 빈칸 추론

과학이 마침내 장수의 비밀을 발견한 것일지도 모른다. 새의 유전 물
질을 조사하는 연구원들이 최근에 DNA의 특정 부분의 길이와 새가 얼
마나 오래 살 것인지 간의 상관관계를 문서로 입증할 수 있었다. 우리의
DNA는 똑같은 부분을 가지고 있는데, 그것은 말단소립이라고 알려진

것으로 우리의 염색체 말단에 위치해 있다. 시간이 지남에 따라 우리의 세포들은 분열하고, 세포가 분열함에 따라 이 말단소립들은 점점 더 짧아진다. 어느 시점에 말단소립들은 너무 짧아져서 세포들은 분열을 멈추게 되는데, 분열하지 못하고 결국에 소실되는 세포의 무력함에 의해 우리는 나이를 먹으며 쇠하기 시작한다. 과학자들은 이제 말단소립을 늘림으로써 우리의 수명을 연장시키는 것이 가능한지를 판단하려고 서두르고 있다.

document …을 증거 서류로 입증하다 correlation 상관관계(correlate 연관성을 보여주다) section 부분, 구역 decline 거절하다; *쇠하다 extend 연장하다 lifespan 수명 [문제] eliminate 제거하다 lengthen 길게 하다, 늘리다

구문해설
2행 Researchers [studying the genetic ... birds] were recently able to document a correlation **between** the length ... **and** how long that bird would likely live.: [ ]는 Researchers를 수식하는 현재분사구, 'between A and B' 「A와 B 사이」
8행 **As** time passes, our cells divide, and **as** our cells divide, these telomeres grow *shorter and shorter*.: 두 개의 as는 모두 「…함에 따라」라는 의미의 접속사, '비교급 and 비교급' 「점점 더 …한[하게]」
11행 ..., our telomeres get **so** short **that** our cells cease to divide, ...: 'so ... that ~' 「너무 …해서 ~하다」

문제해설
④ 빈칸 앞의 내용에서 DNA의 말단소립이 짧아질수록 결과적으로 사람은 나이를 먹고 쇠한다고 했으므로 과학자들이 말단소립의 길이를 '늘림'으로써 수명을 연장시키는 것이 가능한지 판단하려고 한다는 것이 자연스럽다.

33 ③ 빈칸 추론

'광택제 바르기'는 유성 물감이나 아크릴 물감으로 작업하는 대부분의 미술가들에게는 아마 친숙할 용어이다. 그것은 광택제라 불리는 투명한 물질의 도포를 지칭한다. 광택제는 그림이 일단 마르면 그 위에 직접 발리는데, 보호층 역할을 한다. 그것은 햇빛으로부터 자외선을 차단함으로써 그림의 색이 바래는 것을 방지한다. 그러나 그것은 광택제가 하는 것의 전부가 아니다. 그것은 연기와 먼지 같은 공기 중의 오염 물질이 그림에 닿는 것도 막아준다. 대신 그것(= 오염 물질)은 광택제 막에 내려앉아, 시간이 지날수록 그것을 천천히 노르스름하거나 탁하게 한다. 이런 일이 생기면, 광택제는 제거되고 다시 도포될 수 있다. 제대로 된다면, 이는 미술 작품을 몇백 년 동안 생생하고 선명해 보이게 유지할 수 있다.

varnish 광택제; 광택제를 바르다 oil paint 유성 물감 acrylic paint 아크릴 물감 refer to 언급하다, 지칭하다 application 바르기, 도포(apply 바르다) transparent 투명한 substance 물질 fade (색이) 바래다, 희미해지다 ultraviolet ray 자외선 pollutant 오염 물질 make contact with …와 닿다 vibrant 선명한, 활기가 넘치는 [문제] wipe away 제거하다, 없애다

구문해설
1행 "Varnishing" is a term [that most artists {who work with oil or acrylic paints} are probably familiar with].: [ ]는 a term을 선행사로 하는 목적격 관계대명사절, { }는 most artists를 선행사로 하는 주격 관계대명사절
4행 The varnish, [which goes directly onto the paint {once it has dried}], acts as a protective layer.: [ ]는 The varnish를 선행사로 하는 계속적 용법의 주격 관계대명사절, { }는 때를 나타내는 부사절
14행 [If (this is) done properly], this can keep works of art **looking** fresh and vibrant for hundreds of years.: [ ]는 조건을 나타내는 부사절로,

'주어+be동사'가 생략된 형태, 'keep+O+v-ing' 「…가 계속 ~하게 하다」

문제해설
③ 그림을 말린 후 광택제를 바르면 자외선이 차단되고 오염 물질이 그림에 닿는 것을 막아준다는 내용을 통해 광택제가 그림의 '보호층 역할을 한다'는 것을 추론할 수 있다.

34 ② 빈칸 추론

에드거 앨런 포는 그의 동시대 작가들 중 오늘날 가장 널리 읽히는 작가이며, 이는 우연이 아니다. 왜냐하면 이 지나치게 근심 많고 불만이 많았던 예술가는 기묘하게도 우리가 사는 오늘날과 매우 유사하게 현대적이었기 때문이다. 그는 프로이트가 자살 충동의 의미를 정의하기 훨씬 전에 그것이 무엇인지 알고 있었다. 그는 헤밍웨이가 태어나기 50년 전에 폭력에 탐닉했고, 심리 스릴러가 태동하기 오래 전에 (작품의) 긴장감을 키우는 방법을 알고 있었다. 또한 그는 내적 갈등에 끊임없이 관심을 가졌는데, 이는 공교롭게도 현대 문학의 주요 주제이다. 그러나 그로서는 불행하게도, 그는 미국의 문화 발전이 막 시작되고 있던 때에 태어났다. 그의 생각은 시대를 너무 앞섰던 것이다.

accident 사고; *우연 overly 지나치게, 과도하게 death wish 【심리】 자살 충동 define …의 뜻을 규정하다, 정의하다 suspense 긴장 conceive (새로운 것을) 생각해 내다; *시작하다, 일으키다 continually 계속, 끊임없이 concerned 관심이 있는 inner 내면적인 conflict 갈등, 충돌 theme 주제 [문제] passion 열정 in advance of …에 앞서서 age 나이, 수명; *(역사적으로 특정한) 시대 outdated 진부한, 구식의

구문해설
7행 ..., and he knew [how to develop suspense] [long before the psycho-thriller was conceived].: 첫 번째 [ ]는 knew의 목적어로 쓰인 의문사구, 두 번째 [ ]는 때를 나타내는 부사절
9행 Also, he was continually concerned with inner conflict, [which **happens to be** a major theme of present day literature].: [ ]는 inner conflict를 선행사로 하는 계속적 용법의 주격 관계대명사절, 'happen to-v' 「우연히[공교롭게] …하다」
12행 ..., he was born at a time [when American cultural development was just beginning].: [ ]는 a time을 선행사로 하는 관계부사절

문제해설
에드거 앨런 포가 다루거나 관심을 표했던 것들이 후대에 와서야 정의되고 사람들의 관심사가 되었던 예시들이 주어졌으므로 빈칸에는 ② '시대를 너무 앞섰던' 것이었다는 내용이 적절하다.

35 ④ 빈칸 추론

자세히 관찰하면, 얼굴이 붉어지는 현상은 상당히 이상해 보인다. 왜 인간은 우리가 당황하고 있다는 것을 사람들에게 보여주는 과정을 발달시켰을까? 일부 심리학자들은 얼굴 붉힘이 사회가 원활하게 기능하기 위해 필요한 다양한 사회적 행동들을 시행하는 한 방법으로서 진화했다고 주장한다. 얼굴 붉힘은 우리가 실수한 것을 알고 그것 때문에 괴로워한다는 것을 다른 사람들에게 나타내 준다. 게다가, 그것은 어떤 어려운 상황에 처한 사람들과 공감하는 방식을 우리가 감정적으로 이해한다는 것을 보여주는데, 이것은 인간이 학교 교육을 시작하고 사회에서 동료를 만나는 시기 즈음에 발달시키는 특징이다. 심리학자들은 당혹감에서 오는 얼굴 붉힘이 타인에 대한 의식과 함께 진화한다는 것을 이 공감 지능으로부터 추론하였고, 따라서 얼굴 붉힘이 순전히 사회적 기반을 가진다는 개념을 뒷받침한다.

어휘

phenomenon 현상   blush 얼굴을 붉히다   contend 주장하다   evolve 진화하다   enforce 실시하다   smoothly 매끄럽게, 원활하게   indicate 나타내다, 가리키다   empathize 감정이입하다, 공감하다(empathy 감정이입, 공감)   encounter 만나다, 마주치다   consciousness 의식, 자각   [문제] purely 순전히, 완전히   have nothing to do with …와 관계가 없다

구문해설

[4행] Some psychologists contend [that blushing evolved as a method to enforce the various social behaviors {that are needed *for society* **to function smoothly**}].: [ ]는 contend의 목적절, { }는 the various social behaviors를 선행사로 하는 주격 관계대명사절, to function smoothly는 목적을 나타내는 부사적 용법의 to부정사구이고 society는 to부정사의 의미상 주어

[17행] …, [thus supporting the concept {that blushing has a purely social basis}].: [ ]는 결과를 나타내는 분사구문, { }는 the concept와 동격

문제해설

얼굴 붉힘은 다양한 사회적 행동을 시행하는 한 방법으로서 타인에 대한 의식과 함께 진화했다는 심리학자들의 주장을 설명하고 있으므로, 빈칸에는 ④ '얼굴 붉힘이 순전히 사회적 기반을 가진다'가 가장 적절하다.

36 ③ 흐름과 무관한 문장

식물은 토양과 더불어 지구상의 탄소 대부분을 저장하는데, 대기 중의 이산화탄소에서 탄소를 추출한다. 이것은 그것들이 햇빛을 에너지로 전환하는 때인 광합성 동안에 일어난다. 그것들은 나중에 호흡 작용이라고 알려진 과정에서 이산화탄소를 대기 중으로 돌려보낸다. 나무는 이산화탄소를 흡수하는 데 특히 효과적인데, 이는 그것들이 보태는 것보다 더 많은 탄소를 대기에서 없앤다는 것을 의미한다. (최근에 한 연구는 실내용 화초가 집안 공기에서 일부 유독가스를 어떻게 없앨 수 있는지를 보여주었다.) 숲에서처럼 많은 나무들이 한 장소에서 함께 자랄 때, 이러한 효율성은 증가한다. 지구에 있는 숲이 지상에 존재하는 탄소의 75퍼센트 이상을 저장하고 있는 것으로 추정된다.

어휘

along with …와 더불어   soil 토양   store 저장하다   carbon 탄소   extract 추출하다   carbon dioxide 이산화탄소   atmosphere 대기   convert 전환하다   respiration 호흡 (작용)   take in 흡수하다   remove 제거하다   houseplant 실내용 화초   toxic 유독성의   efficiency 효율(성)   aboveground 지상에

구문해설

[1행] Plants, [which {along with soil} store most of the Earth's carbon], …: [ ]는 Plants를 선행사로 하는 계속적 용법의 주격 관계대명사절, { }는 삽입구로 [ ] 전체를 수식

[13행] It is estimated [that the planet's forests hold more than 75% of the carbon {that exists aboveground}].: It은 가주어이고 [ ]가 진주어, { }는 the carbon을 선행사로 하는 주격 관계대명사절

문제해설

대기 중의 탄소를 흡수하는 식물의 역할에 관한 글이므로 유독가스를 제거하는 실내용 화초에 대한 내용인 ③은 글의 흐름에 맞지 않는다.

37 ④ 글의 순서

갓난아기 주변에 있어 본 적이 있다면, 당신은 아기가 대부분의 시간을 자는 데 보낸다는 것을 안다. 사실 아기들은 하루에 18시간까지 잘 수 있다. 그런데 전문가들에 따르면 이것은 시간 낭비가 아니다.
(C) 한 대학의 과학자팀이 신생아의 뇌는 끊임없이 정보를 처리한다는 것

을 발견했다. 이것은 아기들이 잠들어 있을 때조차도 배우고 있다는 것을 의미한다.
(A) 그들의 실험에서, 잠자는 아기들은 그들의 머리에 연결된 전극이 생체전기 활동을 기록하는 동안 비디오로 녹화되었다. 이 시간 동안 녹화된 뇌파들의 일부는 변화를 겪었다. 이것은 그들이 자면서도 학습을 하고 있다는 것의 증거라고 여겨진다.
(B) 이 정보는 유아의 습득 과정을 전문으로 하는 과학자들을 도울 수 있다. 그들은 그들의 시간의 매우 많은 부분을 잠들어 있는 채로 보내기 때문에, 이것은 신생아들이 어떻게 자신의 새로운 환경에 그렇게 빨리 적응할 수 있는가를 설명하는 데 도움을 줄 수 있다.

어휘

newborn 갓 태어난   up to …까지   electrode 전극   attach 붙이다, 첨부하다   bioelectrical 생체전기의   brainwave 뇌파   undergo 겪다   specialize in …을 전문으로 하다   process 과정, 절차; 처리하다   adapt to …에 적응하다   continuously 계속해서, 끊임없이

구문해설

[2행] …, you know [that they **spend** most of their time **sleeping**].: [ ]는 know의 목적절, 'spend+시간+v-ing' 「…하는 데 시간을 보내다」

[6행] …, sleeping infants were videotaped [while electrodes {attached to their head} recorded bioelectrical activity].: [ ]는 때를 나타내는 부사절, { }는 electrodes를 수식하는 과거분사구

[10행] **It** is believed [that this is proof {that they were learning as they slept}].: It은 가주어이고 [ ]가 진주어, { }는 proof와 동격

[15행] …, it could **help explain** [how the infants are able to adapt to their new environment so quickly].: 'help (to-)v' 「…하는 것을 돕다」, [ ]는 explain의 목적어로 쓰인 의문사절

문제해설

④ 아기들이 대부분의 시간을 자면서 보내는 것이 시간 낭비가 아니라는 주어진 글 뒤에, 과학자들이 신생아의 뇌가 끊임없이 정보 처리를 한다는 것을 발견했다는 내용의 (C)가 오고, 이들의 구체적인 실험 과정을 설명하는 (A)가 온 후에, 이 실험의 시사점에 대한 내용인 (B)의 순서로 이어지는 것이 가장 자연스럽다.

38 ⑤ 주어진 문장의 위치

사람을 식별하기 위해 필체를 이용하는 것은 그다지 믿을 만해 보이지 않을 수도 있다. 무엇보다 약간의 연습만으로도 거의 대부분의 사람들이 다른 사람의 필체를 모사하는 것을 배울 수 있다. 그러나 생체 인식 시스템은 단순히 당신이 각 글자를 어떤 모양으로 쓰는지 살펴보는 것이 아니다. 대신에 그것은 글씨를 쓰는 행위를 분석한다. 그것은 당신이 글을 쓰는 동안 펜을 누르는 압력을 조사한다. 그것은 또한 당신이 글자를 쓰면서 i에 점을 찍고 t에 횡선을 긋는지, 아니면 각 단어를 다 쓴 후에 그렇게 하는지와 같은, 글자를 쓰는 순서를 기록한다. 글자의 단순한 모양과는 달리, 이러한 특성들은 모방하기가 매우 어렵다. 비록 당신이 다른 사람의 서명을 베낀다고 하더라도 그 시스템은 그것이 가짜임을 탐지할 것이다.

어휘

trait 특성, 특색   extremely 극히, 극도로   imitate 모방하다; 모사하다   handwriting 필적, 서체   identify 식별하다   reliable 믿을 수 있는   shape 형성하다, …의 형체로 만들다   analyze 분석하다   sequence 연속; *순서   dot 점을 찍다   cross 횡선을 긋다   trace 베끼다   detect 발견하다; *탐지하다   fake 위조품, 가짜

구문해설

[8행] They examine the pressure [with which you press down on your pen {while (you are) writing}].: [ ]는 the pressure를 선행사로 하

는 목적격 관계대명사절, { }는 때를 나타내는 부사절('주어+be동사'가 생략된 형태)
[10행] They also record the sequence [in which you write letters], such as **whether** you dot your i's and cross your t's as you write them **or** after you finish each word.: [ ]는 the sequence를 선행사로 하는 목적격 관계대명사절, 'whether A or B' 「A인지 B인지」
[13행] Even **if** you **were to trace** ..., the system would detect ...: 'If+S+were to-v'의 형태로 실현 가능성이 없는 미래의 일을 가정

주어진 문장의 모방하기 매우 어려운 특성들(these traits)은 글을 쓸 때 펜을 누르는 압력과 글자를 쓰는 순서를 가리키므로, 이들을 언급한 뒷 부분인 ⑤에 오는 것이 적절하다.

39 ② 주어진 문장의 위치

우리 중 많은 이들이 대중 연설, 고통, 뱀 같은 것들을 공통적으로 두려워한다. 그러나 보편적인 두려움과 같은 것이 존재할 수 있을까? 연구에 따르면 인간은 유전적으로 뱀이나 쥐처럼 독이나 질병을 통해 한때 인간에게 실질적인 위험이 되었던 특정 동물들을 두려워하는 경향이 있다고 한다. 이는 예전에 뱀을 본 적조차 없지만 뱀을 두려워하는 사람들의 경우에서 관찰될 수 있다. 그들의 두려움은 실제로 진화론적 본능이라고 여겨진다. 그것이 실제로 본능적이라는 견해는 과학적 연구에 의해 뒷받침된다. 한 실험에서 심리학자 마틴 셀리그먼은 사람들에게 특정 대상에 대한 두려움을 심으려고 했다. 그는 사람들이 뱀과 거미 같은 것들을 꽃처럼 무해한 것들보다 훨씬 더 쉽게 두려워하기 시작한다는 사실을 발견했다.

universal 보편적인 be inclined to-v …하는 경향이 있다 genetically 유전(학)적으로 pose 자세를 취하게 하다; *(위협·문제 등을) 제기하다 poison 독 evolutionary 진화(론)적인 instinct 본능(instinctual 본능적인, 직관적인) psychologist 심리학자 object 물체, 대상

[1행] ... people [who have never even seen a snake before], but have been found to fear them.: [ ]는 people을 선행사로 하는 주격 관계대명사절
[8행] ... certain animals [that once posed real danger ... and rats].: [ ]는 certain animals를 선행사로 하는 주격 관계대명사절
[11행] The idea [that it is indeed instinctual] is ...: [ ]는 The idea와 동격

주어진 문장의 This는 ② 앞 문장의 위협이 되는 특정 동물에 대해 인간이 유전적으로 두려워하는 경향이 있다는 것을 가리키며, ② 다음 문장의 their fear는 주어진 문장에서 제시한 뱀을 본 적도 없는 사람들이 뱀에 대해 느끼는 두려움을 가리키므로, 주어진 문장은 ②에 들어가는 것이 적절하다.

40 ④ 요약문 완성

세계에서 가장 추운 대륙인 남극은 연 평균 기온이 화씨 영하 70도이다. 얼음과 눈에 뒤덮인 남극은 또한 세계에서 가장 바람이 많이 부는 대륙이기도 하다. 가장 거센 돌풍은 거의 시속 200마일이나 된다. 그곳의 환경은 인간이 거주하기에는 매우 부적당하며, 어떤 형태의 야생 생물이든 생존한다는 것을 상상하기가 어렵다. 그러나 이상하게도, 남극은 실제로 세계 어느 곳보다도 더 많은 야생 생물 개체수를 보유하고 있다. 극히 작은 해양 식물에서부터 펭귄, 고래, 물개와 같은 커다란 새와 포유동물에 이르기까지, 남극은 생물학자의 연구를 위해 제공할 많은 것을 보유하

고 있다. 이들 생물 종들이 그토록 험한 환경에서 어떻게 생존하는지는 자연의 신비이다.

continent 대륙 the Antarctic 남극 mean 평균의 Fahrenheit 화씨 fierce 사나운; *거센 gust 돌풍 condition (*pl.*) 환경, 날씨 hostile 적대적인; *적당하지 못한 inhabitation 거주, 서식 wildlife 야생 생물 microscopic 극히 작은 vegetation 식물, 초목 mammal 포유동물 seal 물개 species (생물의) 종(種) [문제] harsh 가혹한; 혹독한 unpredictable 예측할 수 없는 deficient 부족한, 결핍된 abundant 풍부한 plentiful 풍부한, 많은

[1행] [The world's coldest continent], the Antarctic, has ...: [ ]는 the Antarctic과 동격
[7행] ..., and **it** is hard [to imagine *any form of wildlife* surviving].: it은 가주어이고 [ ]가 진주어, any form of wildlife는 동명사 surviving의 의미상 주어
[14행] [How these species survive in such tough conditions] is a wonder of nature.: [ ]는 문장의 주어로 쓰인 의문사절

④ 가혹한 기상 조건에도 불구하고, 남극에는 다양한 야생 생물이 풍부하다.

41 ② 42 ③ 장문

모든 망원경은 별과 같이 먼 곳에 있는 물체로부터 나오는 빛을 모으기 위해 굴곡 렌즈를 사용한다. 일반적으로 망원경의 크기가 크면 클수록 확대력도 더 크다. 두 개의 서로 다른 종류의 렌즈가 사용될 수 있다. 16세기에 만들어진 최초의 망원경은 굴절경이었다. 이 망원경의 문제점은 완벽한 구형의 렌즈가 빛을 초점에 정확히 모으지 못한다는 것이었다. 한 조각의 유리로 만들어진 렌즈는 또한 여러 색깔의 빛을 서로 다른 방향으로 굴절시켜 색깔의 왜곡을 초래했다.

굴절경의 문제점은 일부 망원경 제작자들이 반사경을 실험해 보게 했다. 그들은 완벽한 구형이 아닌 거울을 사용하며 그 결과 빛이 정확히 초점에 맞지 않았다(→ 초점이 모였다). 게다가 거울은 색깔의 왜곡을 일으키지 않았다. 그러나 이 초기 반사경에는 다른 문제점들이 있었다. 그것들은 연마한 금속으로 만들어진 것이라 빛을 잘 반사시키지 못했다. 또, 금속 거울은 주조된 후 식는 과정에서 종종 금이 갔다.

2세기 동안 광학 기계 제작자들은 이 두 종류의 망원경을 개선하기 위해 노력했다. 드디어 1851년에 두 명의 영국인 바니쉬와 멜리쉬가 아주 얇은 은박으로 유리를 덮는 새로운 방법을 발견했다. 이로 인해 은을 입힌 유리로 만든 커다란 굴곡 거울을 사용한 반사경을 만들 수 있게 되었다. 이 망원경은 이전의 반사경보다 훨씬 더 많은 빛을 반사시켰고 그렇게 쉽게 금이 가지도 않았다. 오늘날의 거의 모든 대형 망원경은 바니쉬와 멜리쉬가 고안한 기본 디자인을 토대로 만들어진다.

curved 구부러진, 곡선 모양의 focus (빛 등을) 초점에 모으다 magnify 확대하다 bend 구부리다 distortion 왜곡 reflector 반사경(reflect 반사시키다) polish 윤을 내다; *연마하다 crack 금이 가다 cast 던지다; *주조하다 strive to-v …하려고 노력하다 perfect 완전하게 하다; *개선[개량]하다 sheet 얇은 판 conceive 고안하다 [문제] refraction 굴절 high-tech 첨단 기술의

[8행] Lenses [made of a single piece of glass] also bent ... ways, [producing color distortions].: 첫 번째 [ ]는 Lenses를 수식하는 과거분사구, 두 번째 [ ]는 부대상황을 나타내는 분사구문

(13행) They used mirrors [that were not perfectly round], **so that** light was …: [ ]는 mirrors를 선행사로 하는 주격 관계대명사절, so that은 결과를 나타내는 접속사

(25행) This made **it** possible [to build reflecting telescopes using a large curved mirror {made of silver-covered glass}].: it은 가목적어이고 [ ]가 진목적어, { }는 a large curved mirror를 수식하는 과거분사구

문제해설

41 역대 망원경 중 굴절 망원경과 반사 망원경이 발명된 계기와 이 두 방식의 문제점을 설명하고, 이를 개선시키기 위해 바니쉬와 멜리쉬가 발견한 방법을 적용한 망원경을 소개하고 있으므로 ② '망원경의 역사'가 글의 주제라고 할 수 있다.

42 완벽한 구형의 렌즈가 빛을 초점에 정확히 모으지 못한다는 문제점을 알고서 완벽한 구형이 아닌 거울로 반사경을 실험했다는 내용이므로, ③ unfocused(초점이 맞지 않는)는 focused(초점이 모이는) 등이 되어야 한다.

43 ④ 44 ② 45 ④ 장문

(A) 요하네스 베르메르는 1600년대에 활동한 유명한 네덜란드 화가였다. 그러나 그의 죽음 이후 거의 300년이 지나도록 비평가들은 여전히 그의 작품의 범위에 대해 논쟁을 벌이고 있었는데, 말하자면 베르메르가 일련의 성서의 장면들을 그렸는지 아닌지에 대한 것이었다. 현대의 비평가들이 자신을 제대로 평가하지 않는다고 생각했던 20세기 네덜란드 화가인 한 판 메헤렌은 이러한 논쟁을 자신의 재능을 증명할 수 있는 기회로 여겼다. 그는 성서를 묘사한 베르메르의 작품이 어떠할지를 상상하여 위작을 만들기 시작했고, 그 위작을 (베르메르의) 원작으로 가장할 작정이었다.

(D) 그는 그의 작품을 '엠마오의 제자들'이라고 이름 붙였으며, 베르메르의 화풍을 모방하고 300년 된 그림에서 사람들이 볼 수 있으리라 예측할만한 갈라진 금과 흠을 흉내 내는 데 수많은 시간을 보낸 후에, 그의 힘겨운 작업은 성과를 보였다. 미술 전문가들은 판 메헤렌의 작품을 (베르메르의) 진품으로 인정했다. 본래의 계획을 고수하고 그의 천재성을 보여주는 데 위작을 이용하는 대신에, 그는 계속해서 위작을 만들기로 하고, 그것들을 수집가들에게 높은 가격에 팔았다.

(B) 판 메헤렌에게는 불행하게도, 그의 그림을 수집하는 사람들 중 한 명이 독일 나치당의 주요 인물로 밝혀졌다. 제2차 세계대전이 종결된 후, 네덜란드 정부는 '국보'로 여겼던 가짜인 베르메르의 작품을 적에게 판매한 혐의로 판 메헤렌을 구속했다. 다른 대안이 없었기 때문에 판 메헤렌은 그가 판매했던 모든 그림들이 그 유명 화가(= 베르메르)의 진품들이 아니라 그가 직접 만든 위작이라는 것을 인정할 수밖에 없었다.

(C) 그의 이야기가 사실이며 그가 나치에게 판매했던 그 그림은 진품이 아니라고 당국을 납득시키기 위해, 판 메헤렌은 그가 위작을 만드는 과정을 한 무리의 관료들 앞에서 보여주게 되었다. 그는 그가 받은 혐의에 대한 결백을 증명할 수 있었고, 그의 위작 행위에 대해 단지 징역 1년에 처해졌다. 그러나, 재판이 끝난 지 겨우 두 달 만에 그는 심장마비로 사망했다.

어휘

celebrated 유명한, 저명한 breadth 폭, 넓이 biblical 성서의, 성서와 관련된 appreciate 진가를 인정하다; *(제대로) 인식하다 set about …에 착수하다, …을 시작하다 forgery 위조; *모조 작품 convince 확신시키다, 납득시키다 genuine 진짜의, 진품의 demonstrate 논증[증명]하다; 설명하다 innocence 결백, 무죄 charge 요금; *혐의 sentence 형에 처하다; 선고하다 disciple 사도, 제자 mimic 흉내 내다 stick to …을 고수하다

구문해설

(9행) He set about creating a forgery of [what he imagined a Vermeer biblical painting would look like], [intending to **pass** it

off as an original].: 첫 번째 [ ]는 of의 목적어로 쓰인 의문사절, 두 번째 [ ]는 부대상황을 나타내는 분사구문, 'pass … off as ~' 「…을 ~인 체하다」

(19행) [(Being) Faced with no other alternative], van Meegeren was forced to admit [that all the paintings {(that) he had sold} were **not** works of the famous painter **but** rather his own forgeries].: 첫 번째 [ ]는 이유를 나타내는 분사구문, 두 번째 [ ]는 admit의 목적절, { }는 all the paintings를 선행사로 하는 목적격 관계대명사절, 'not A but B' 「A가 아니라 B」

(34행) … and simulating the cracks and flaws [(that) one would expect to see in a 300-year-old painting], …: [ ]는 the cracks and flaws를 선행사로 하는 목적격 관계대명사절

문제해설

43 ④ 판 메헤렌이 베르메르의 작품의 위작을 만들어 자신의 재능을 입증하려고 했다는 내용의 (A) 뒤에 베르메르의 화풍을 모방하여 판 메헤렌이 위작을 만드는 과정을 설명하고 있는 (D)가 오고, 판 메헤렌이 베르메르의 위작을 나치에게 판매했다는 이유로 구속되었다는 내용의 (B) 다음에, 자신의 혐의에서 벗어나기 위해 위작 과정을 관료들 앞에서 보여주었다는 (C)로 이어지는 것이 자연스럽다.

44 ② (b)는 판 메헤렌이 위작한 유명 작가인 요하네스 베르메르를 가리키고, 나머지는 모두 판 메헤렌을 가리킨다.

45 ④ (C)에서 판 메헤렌은 자신의 결백을 증명하고 위작 행위에 대해 징역 1년 형을 선고받은 지 두 달 만에 사망하였다고 언급되었다.

MEMO

만만한 수능영어

수능
만만

영어독해
20회

1. 최신 수능 및 평가원 모의고사를 철저히 분석하여 반영

2. 수능에 대비할 수 있는 충분한 양의 실전 모의고사 제공

3. 실전 난이도와 유사한 독해 지문 및 문항 유형들로 구성

4. 학습 지원 자료인 어휘리스트 파일 무료 제공